THE CAMBRIDGE

History of the Book in Britain

*

VOLUME VI
1830–1914

The years 1830–1914 witnessed a revolution in the manufacture and use of books as great as that in the fifteenth century. Using new technology in printing, paper-making and binding, publishers worked with authors and illustrators to meet ever-growing and more varied demands from a population seeking books at all price levels. The essays by leading book historians in this volume show how books became cheap, how publishers used the magazine and newspaper markets to extend their influence, and how book ownership became universal for the first time. The fullest account ever published of the nineteenth-century revolution in printing, publishing and book-selling, this volume brings the *Cambridge History of the Book* up to a point when the world of books took on a recognisably modern form.

DAVID MCKITTERICK, FBA is Fellow and Librarian of Trinity College, Cambridge, and Honorary Professor of Historical Bibliography in the University of Cambridge. His many publications include *A History of Cambridge University Press* (three volumes, Cambridge, 1992–2004) and *Print, Manuscript and the Search for Order 1450–1830* (Cambridge, 2003). He is a past President of the Bibliographical Society and recipient of its Gold Medal.

History of the Book in Britain

The history of the book offers a distinctive form of access to the ways in which human beings have sought to give meaning to their own and others' lives. Our knowledge of the past derives mainly from texts. Landscape, architecture, sculpture, painting and the decorative arts have their stories to tell and may themselves be construed as texts; but oral tradition, manuscripts, printed books, and those other forms of inscription and incision such as maps, music and graphic images, have a power to report even more directly on human experience and the events and thoughts which shaped it.

In principle, any history of the book should help to explain how these particular texts were created, why they took the form they did, their relations with other media, especially in the twentieth century, and what influence they had on the minds and actions of those who heard, read or viewed them. Its range, too – in time, place and the great diversity of the conditions of text production, including reception – challenges any attempt to define its limits and give an account adequate to its complexity. It addresses, whether by period, country, genre or technology, widely disparate fields of enquiry, each of which demands and attracts its own forms of scholarship.

The Cambridge History of the Book in Britain, planned in seven volumes, seeks to represent much of that variety, and to encourage new work, based on knowledge of the creation, material production, dissemination and reception of texts. Inevitably its emphases will differ from volume to volume, partly because the definitions of Britain vary significantly over the centuries, partly because of the varieties of evidence extant for each period, and partly because of the present uneven state of knowledge. Tentative in so many ways as the project necessarily is, it offers the first comprehensive account of the book in Britain over one and a half millennia.

JOHN BARNARD · DAVID MCKITTERICK · I. R. WILLISON
General Editors

THE CAMBRIDGE

History of the Book in Britain

*

VOLUME VI
1830–1914

*

Edited by

DAVID MCKITTERICK

Fellow and Librarian, Trinity College, Cambridge

CAMBRIDGE
UNIVERSITY PRESS

CAMBRIDGE UNIVERSITY PRESS
Cambridge, New York, Melbourne, Madrid, Cape Town, Singapore, São Paulo, Delhi

Cambridge University Press
The Edinburgh Building, Cambridge CB2 8RU, UK

Published in the United States of America by Cambridge University Press, New York

www.cambridge.org
Information on this title: www.cambridge.org/9780521866248

First published 2009

Printed in the United Kingdom at the University Press, Cambridge

A catalogue record for this publication is available from the British Library

ISBN 978-0-521-86624-8 hardback

Contents

Contents

Illustrations

Tables

Contributors

BRIAN ALDERSON has been involved with children's books for most of his working life, among other things as critic, translator and collector. Much of his recent published work has been devoted to the history and bibliography of the genre.

JOHN BARNES is Emeritus Professor of English at La Trobe University and Senior Honorary Research Associate in the Centre for the Book at Monash University. His books include *The Penguin Henry Lawson: short stories* (1986), *The order of things: a life of Joseph Furphy* (1990) and *Socialist champion: portrait of the gentleman as crusader* (2006). He is currently writing a study of Charles Joseph La Trobe.

BILL BELL is Director of the Centre for the History of the Book at the University of Edinburgh. He is General Editor of the *Edinburgh history of the book in Scotland* and has held visiting posts at the Australian National University, the University of Ottawa and St John's College, Oxford.

RIMI B. CHATTERJEE is a novelist and academic, at present teaching English at Jadavpur University, Calcutta. Her recent work includes *Empires of the mind: a history of Oxford University Press in India under the Raj* (2006) and a novel, *The city of love* (2007).

STEPHEN COLCLOUGH is Lecturer in nineteenth- and twentieth-century literature in the School of English, Bangor University. He has written extensively on text distribution and the history of reading and is the author of *Consuming texts: readers and reading communities, 1695–1870* (2007). He is also a contributor to the third volume of the *Edinburgh history of the book in Scotland* (2007).

VICTORIA COOPER is Senior Commissioning Editor at Cambridge University Press for the music and theatre lists. Her publications include *The house of Novello: practice and policy of a Victorian music publisher, 1829–1866* (2003).

SIMON ELIOT is Professor of the History of the Book at the Institute of English Studies, University of London, and Deputy Director of its Centre for

Manuscript and Print Studies. He is the General Editor of the multi-volume *History of Oxford University Press* and is editor of the journal *Publishing History*. He has recently edited (with Jonathan Rose) *The Blackwell companion to the history of the book* (2007) and (with Andrew Nash and Ian Willison) *Literary cultures and the material book* (2007).

RICHARD FREEBURY is Head of Hansard Printed Indexes in the House of Commons Library. He is currently using *The Bookseller* as a source for research into the book trade, underselling and copyright in the second half of the nineteenth century.

AILEEN FYFE lectures in the History Department at the National University of Ireland, Galway. She is the author of *Science and salvation* (2004) and co-editor of *Science in the marketplace* (2007), and is completing a project about the impact of technological changes on the nineteenth-century book trade.

ANDREA IMMEL is Curator of the Cotsen Children's Library, Princeton University Library. She is co-editor of *Childhood and children's books in early modern Europe 1550–1800* (2006), *Under fire: childhood in the shadow of war* (2008) and the forthcoming *Cambridge companion to children's literature*.

WALLACE KIRSOP is an Honorary Professor and Director of the Centre for the Book in the School of English, Communications and Performance Studies at Monash University. He is General Editor of *A history of the book in Australia* and has worked extensively on the French book trade in the seventeenth, eighteenth and early nineteenth centuries.

GRAHAM LAW is Professor in Media Studies, Waseda University. His books include *Serializing fiction in the Victorian press* (2000), and he is preparing *Wilkie Collins: a literary life*, written with Andrew Maunder.

PATRICK LEARY is in the History Department of Northwestern University, and is a co-founder of the Society for the History of Authorship, Reading and Publishing (SHARP). He is completing a book about the *Punch* circle.

MICHAEL LEDGER-LOMAS is a Fellow and Director of Studies at Selwyn College, Cambridge and a research associate of the Cambridge Victorian Studies Group. He is writing a book entitled *Selective affinities: England and Protestant Germany, c.1825–1870*.

DAVID McKITTERICK is Librarian and Fellow of Trinity College, Cambridge, and a Vice-President of the British Academy. His books include *Print, manuscript and the search for order* (2003) and the *History of Cambridge University Press* (3 vols., 1992–2004).

ANDREW NASH is Lecturer in English Literature at the University of Reading. He has published essays on various aspects of nineteenth- and twentieth-century literature and publishing history. He is the author of *Kailyard and*

Scottish literature (2007), editor of *The culture of collected editions* (2003) and co-editor of *Literary cultures and the material book* (2007).

ROBERT L. PATTEN is Lynette S. Autrey Professor in Humanities, Rice University. His publications include *Literature in the marketplace: nineteenth-century British publishing and reading practices*, written with John O. Jordan (2003), and many studies of Charles Dickens.

DAVE RUSSELL is Professor of History and Northern Studies in the Institute of Northern Studies, Leeds Metropolitan University. His most recent work is *Looking north: northern England and the national imagination* (2004) and he has published extensively on the history of English popular culture, especially sport and music.

WILLIAM ST CLAIR, formerly Senior Research Fellow of Trinity College, Cambridge, is author most recently of *The reading nation in the romantic period* (2004) and *The grand slave emporium* (2006).

JAMES A. SECORD is Professor of History and Philosophy of Science at the University of Cambridge and director of the Correspondence of Charles Darwin. The author of *Victorian sensation: the extraordinary publication, reception, and secret authorship of* Vestiges of the natural history of creation (2000), he is currently completing a book on science in newspapers in nineteenth-century London, Paris and New York.

CATHERINE SEVILLE is Vice-Principal and Director of Studies in Law at Newnham College, Cambridge. She is the author of *Literary copyright reform in early Victorian England* (1999) and *The internationalisation of copyright law: books, buccaneers and the black flag in the nineteenth century* (2006).

CHRISTOPHER STRAY is Honorary Research Fellow in the Department of Classics, Swansea University. His recent work includes studies of the history of examinations, textbooks and classical scholarship. He edited and contributed to *Classical books: scholarship and publishing in Britain since 1800* (2007).

GILLIAN SUTHERLAND is a Fellow of Newnham College, Cambridge and has written extensively on the social history of education in the nineteenth and twentieth centuries. Her most recent book is *Faith, duty and the power of mind: the Cloughs and their circle 1820–1960* (2006).

MICHAEL TWYMAN is Emeritus Professor of Typography and Graphic Communication at the University of Reading, and is presently Director of the Centre for Ephemera Studies there. His most recent book is *Images en couleur*, a study of early chromolithography (2007).

DAVID VINCENT is Professor of Social History and Pro Vice-Chancellor of the Open University. He is the author or editor of fifteen books on British and European social history including *Literacy and popular culture* (1989) and *The rise of mass literacy: reading and writing in modern Europe* (2000).

MICHAEL WINSHIP is the Iris Howard Regents Professor of English II at the University of Texas at Austin. He is a co-editor of and contributor to *The industrial book, 1840–1880* (2007: volume 3 of *A history of the book in America*), and the author of *American literary publishing in the mid-nineteenth century: the business of Ticknor and Fields* (1995).

Preface

This volume of the *Cambridge history of the book in Britain* both complements and is complemented by other projects, most notably those dealing with Ireland, Scotland and Wales. Of these, only the last has been published in its entirety, as a collection of essays *A nation and its books: a history of the book in Wales*.[1] The first volume of the *Oxford history of the Irish book*, dealing with the Irish book in English, 1550–1800, appeared in 2006.[2] The third and fourth volumes (and first to appear) of the *Edinburgh history of the book in Scotland*, covering the nineteenth and twentieth centuries, were published in 2007, shortly before these words went to the publisher.[3] The existence of these projects has influenced the structure and approach of the present volume, and they should be read alongside it. Nonetheless, though all these enterprises are loosely connected both by their subject matter and by personal ties, they are emphatically independent. They share common methodologies only incidentally; they share common viewpoints still less. More importantly, they do not seek, as a group, to be comprehensive. To do so would be impractical, even overweening. In each of them, and not least in the present volume, not only have large areas of activity been ignored; it will also be plain how much is still tentative, and how much more work needs to be done even at quite fundamental levels. Given the size of the book trade in the nineteenth century, and the immense volume of evidence in the shape of printed material and manuscript documentation that has survived, readers may perhaps find occasion for some relief. Besides these other national projects, the more general *Cambridge history of libraries in Britain and Ireland*[4] is an essential companion to the following pages.

1 Ed. Philip Henry Jones and Eiluned Rees (Aberystwyth, 1998).
2 Ed. Raymond Gillespie and Andrew Hadfield (Oxford, 2006). A further four volumes are planned.
3 Bill Bell (ed.), *Ambition and industry, 1800–1880*; David Finkelstein and Alistair McCleery (eds.), *Professionalism and diversity, 1880–2000* (Edinburgh, 2007). A further two volumes are planned for previous periods.
4 Giles Mandelbrote and K. A. Manley (eds.), *The Cambridge history of libraries in Britain and Ireland. 2. 1640–1850* (Cambridge, 2006); Alistair Black and Peter Hoare (eds.), *The Cambridge history of libraries in Britain and Ireland. 3. 1850–2000* (Cambridge, 2006).

This volume is tentative in other respects as well. As an activity, the history of the book is still finding its feet: that is plain from the debates and position papers that appear in abundance each year.[5] Under its generous umbrella shelter dozens of claims and approaches, some based more than others on the evidential, artefactual and archival value of books themselves. Contributors to this volume have been encouraged to found their work on the physical archival record, whether books, periodicals and newspapers, or other written, printed and visual related documentation. The wealth of surviving evidence, on a scale many times greater than for any previous period and perhaps greater than for any other country at this time, is both a strength and a difficulty. It is impossible to attain the relative coverage of earlier volumes in the *Cambridge history of the book in Britain*.

Where so much has survived, conclusions must frequently imply further questions even more than usual. Some are raised explicitly in the following pages; others by implication or even by their absence. In important and quite fundamental respects, this volume is tentative. At the most basic level, there is still no adequate bibliographical record of the output of the press in the British Isles after 1800, the closing date of the *English short title catalogue*. The *Nineteenth century short title catalogue*, which in any case covers only part of the period with which this volume is concerned, is avowedly selective, based on a small and, in important respects, unrepresentative selection of libraries. We still have no idea of the real scale of the pamphlet literature that was such a feature of nineteenth-century publishing. Excellent though it is, the *Waterloo directory* of Victorian periodicals is by no means complete. Moreover, while retrospective bibliographies are adept at describing titles and editions, they are not designed to provide details of how many copies of an edition were printed, or (often) how frequently reprints were called for, or over how long a period. For this, we rely on the business archives of printers and publishers. Not only have these survived very incompletely. Even for those that have survived, there has thus far been no concerted and systematic attempt to recover from them the quantities of books or periodicals that were manufactured. Understandably, all forays that have been made into archives for statistical purposes have been selective and unrepresentative in various ways. As a result of these two shortcomings, one concerning print and one mostly concerning manuscript, not only are we still very far off from knowing how far and in what ways society was saturated with

---

5 See among recent examples, with copious reference to previous literature, Michael Suarez, 'Histo-riographical problems and possibilities in book history and national histories of the book', *Studies in Bibliography* 56 (2003-4; published 2007), pp. 147-70; David L. Vander Meulen, 'How to read book history', *ibid.*, pp. 171-93.

print even of a permanent or semi-permanent kind, let alone more ephemeral materials. There is, at present, not even an agenda that elaborates the limitations and potential benefits of such archives as have survived, or how they relate to wider contexts of authorship, use and reading.

The chapter by William St Clair, that serves as an endpiece, is deliberately personal in its approach and tentative in its theme. In part, it continues discussions about his book *The reading nation in the romantic period* (2004), which has refashioned questions on periods far beyond that suggested in his title. It also calls for the collecting of a broader statistical basis, and analysis of better figures than are currently available. It implies the need for a fuller understanding of contexts and their relationships – bibliographical, topical, geographical, financial and human – than has so far been developed. It is to be hoped that this volume as a whole will contribute to that debate, and to others.

In preparing this volume, I am firstly grateful for their support, advice, encouragement and criticism to the other general editors of the *Cambridge history of the book in Britain*, John Barnard and Ian Willison. Simon Eliot brought crucial advice in shaping the volume and in the early stages of recruiting authors, and was to have been joint editor until other demands on his time made that impossible. Bill Bell generously shared with me the nineteenth-century volume of the *Edinburgh history of the book in Scotland*, while it was still in proof. This volume was given its preliminary form at a seminar held at Trinity College, Cambridge. The Leverhulme Trust provided a grant to support Alexis Weedon in a project on statistics, and some of the fruit of that work can be seen in her guides to archives and in her *Victorian publishing* (2003), referred to at many points in this volume. I have unashamedly drawn on the experiences and lessons not just of editors and contributors in other volumes in this series, but also of those involved in similar projects in other parts of the world, especially Australia, Canada, France, Germany, the Netherlands, New Zealand and the United States. At the University Press, Linda Bree, Maartje Scheltens and their colleagues have brought to this volume, as they have to others in the series, a degree of friendly patience as well as skilled interest for which every contributor is grateful and for which I am profoundly so. As always, however, my wife Rosamond is the person who has lived with this volume as long as anyone. For her willingness to listen, offer suggestions and read drafts with a judicious eye, and for her continuing support of all kinds, I am more thankful by the year.

David McKitterick

Introduction

DAVID MCKITTERICK

Dates

Unlike the date that marks the beginning of the previous volume in the *Cambridge history of the book in Britain*, the year 1830 has no exceptional significance for the trades of printing and publishing. In 1695, the last of the Licensing Acts was allowed to lapse, and with it the legislation that had (amongst other matters) prevented the expansion of printing in England outside London and the university towns of Cambridge and Oxford. The year thus marked an end to ways of thinking about the book trade that could be traced back at least to the founding of the Stationers' Company in 1557; and it proved to be the beginning of a long period in which the eventual abolition of perpetual copyright signalled the end of control of publishing and the book trade by a cartel whose interest lay in dominating, and often restricting, growth and, frequently, in maintaining high prices.

If there is no equivalent dominating and determining event in 1830, there are nonetheless strong reasons for dividing the sequence of the history of the book in Britain at about this date. They have nothing to do with the preoccupations of historians who have seen in the passing of the 1832 Reform Bill a severance with a conservative past in favour of a period of reform under the Whigs. More general historians have justifiably moved away from insisting on the 1830s as so straightforward a watershed; and in seeking the roots of the nineteenth century in the last two decades of the eighteenth, they have also pruned – or, rather, lopped – the long eighteenth century.[1] Others have identified a watershed with the Regency and the reign of George IV. Certainly in one critical area of publishing, the caricature, by about 1830 there was a new sense of restraint that drove bawdiness underground. Where self-importance had once been pricked, self-improvement took its place. The conversion of the caricaturist

---

1 Hilton, *A mad, bad, and dangerous people?*, pp. 664–71. Cf. Asa Briggs's apologia for what he termed an 'unconventional' period, in his *The age of improvement*, p. 1.

George Cruikshank from a drunken sot to a campaigning teetotaller seemed to epitomise a period of extraordinarily rapid change in social outlooks.[2]

On the other hand, historical bibliographers, writing about the relationship of printed text to its manufacture, have habitually divided their tale between the so-called hand-press period and the machine-press period, the date falling conventionally at 1800. But even Philip Gaskell, who thirty-odd years ago constructed his standard *New introduction to bibliography* round this date, wrote also of two periods in the history of printing technology being 'separated by developments that took place soon after the beginning of the nineteenth century'.[3] In other words, the year 1800 was not entirely sacrosanct. Indeed, there is no reason why it should be, save in the most approximate of terms. The first machine press was not introduced until 1812. No less importantly, this was but one aspect of book production. The first paper-making machine in Britain was installed in 1803. Though David Bruce patented his typefounding machine in America in 1838, and it found favour with German manufacturers, it was not used by a British founder until Miller & Richard installed his equipment in 1853. Typesetting machines could be dated from the invention of William Church, in London, in 1822; but it was almost twenty years before such equipment was installed for regular use.[4]

Clowes, subsequently printer of the *Penny Magazine*, installed steam machinery in 1823, and had eighteen steam-driven presses by 1832, each printing between 700 and 1,000 impressions per hour.[5] For most book printers, the cost of machinery, the need to overcome employees' resistance and to retrain them, the physical confines of the printing house, and the slow return on outlay, meant that investment in new equipment was always cautious, even slow. Partly because of the extra care required by them in make-ready, the new machine presses tended also to be more suited to long runs. It was partly for this reason that expensive new machinery tended to be introduced first in the newspaper trade. In 1828 *The Times* installed the first cylinder press, capable of delivering 4,200 impressions an hour – far more than required by most book printers. In its turn, this was replaced by successively faster machines. But it was the slower Napier platen press, first marketed in the mid-1830s, that attracted the interest of book printers and that held their support until it

---

2 Gattrell, *City of laughter*, ch. 17. For the watershed see also Patten, *George Cruikshank's life, times, and art* 1, pp. 390–402.
3 Gaskell, *A new introduction to bibliography*, p. 2. For the principal dates, see Berry and Poole, *Annals of printing*.
4 See further below, chapter 1.   5 Timperley, *Encyclopaedia*, p. 920.

was displaced after 1858 by David Payne's Wharfedale. In its turn, this stop-cylinder machine and its derivatives remained in use in many printing houses even in the second half of the twentieth century.

For decades after 1800, books, periodicals, newspapers and all kinds of minor work continued to be set by hand, with type cast by hand, and printed by means of hand-presses (admittedly increasingly often of iron, rather than wood) on paper made by hand. Books were bound by hand. In their turn, publishers changed their practices at different paces again.[6] This confused and often tardy process of change, piecemeal and at varying speeds according to needs, opportunities or resources, was not unique to the book, magazine and newspaper industries. The same can be seen in the introduction of mechanisation and new labour practices to most other industries. But, nevertheless, by about 1830 some of the major changes in manufacture, materials, market demands and economic possibilities had become sufficiently widespread for it to be possible to claim that a revolution of some kind had been effected.

If conclusions are as important as innovations in identifying moments of change, then death must also be a measure. Within the space of six years around 1830, there died several leading members of a generation of printers who had both established the term 'fine printing' and begun to address the implications of mechanisation. Miller Ritchie, of Edinburgh, and Luke Hansard, printer to the House of Commons, both died in 1828; William Bulmer died in 1830; Andrew Strahan and Thomas Davison in 1831; John M'Creery in 1832; John Ballantyne of Edinburgh in 1833; and Thomas Bensley in 1835. Among the newcomers, the printer Charles Whittingham had established himself in Took's Court, off Chancery Lane, in 1828. He succeeded his uncle as proprietor of the Chiswick Press in 1840, and by then his relationship with the publisher William Pickering had for several years commanded notice in their attention to typography, presswork and binding.[7]

National politics had their own indirect reflections on the book trades. The death on 15 September 1830 of William Huskisson, when he was struck by a train drawn by Stephenson's steam locomotive *Rocket* at the opening of the Liverpool and Manchester railway, was one of the defining episodes in the development of a means of communication that was to transform the country intellectually as much as socially or economically. At the Board of Trade, Huskisson had worked vigorously to extend Britain's trading interests as an imperial power, and thus contributed substantially to the shaping of political thought

---

6 St Clair, *The reading nation*, ch. 11.   7 Keynes, *William Pickering*.

as well as to subsequent commercial evolution.[8] Wellington's government did not last long after the death of George IV. The confused politics of autumn 1830, culminating in defeat on the civil list, finally saw Lord Grey take his place, and a coalition government on a route that was to lead to electoral reform. The running sore of Ireland and Catholic emancipation had been partially and temporarily resolved with the Catholic Relief Act in 1829, leaving a substantial body of conservative opinion discontented, but isolated. The July revolution in France, which placed Louis-Philippe on the throne, brought to Britain an influx of Bourbon refugees including Charles X. Elsewhere in Europe, revolt at Brussels in August led to independence for Belgium from the Netherlands; and in November Poles revolted against Russian rule in Warsaw. Fears of major social unrest in England eventually proved unfounded. It was an uncomfortable year, but not, in the British Isles, one of political revolution. The years covered by this volume witnessed changes in the political, social and financial structures of Britain that are not least remarkable for being achieved without violent upheaval.

The closing year of this volume, 1914, provides its own political frame. In some ways, and despite the watershed that is so often, understandably, perceived in this year, for much of the world of books and publishing it marks not so much an end as an interruption of developments that can be seen in embryo during the last few years before the outbreak of war.

1830: the book trades in a new mood

For the publishing trade in 1830, the dominant recent event in popular memory was the disastrous year of 1826–7, following a bank crisis in December 1825 that left the country short of cash, troubled and apprehensive. Notoriously, the firm of Archibald Constable had been made bankrupt thanks to overexposure to its London agents Hurst & Robinson. Even Murray had been forced to retrench. The memory lingered for years, kept green by chroniclers of the trade such as Charles Knight, who had been severely affected, and by the exaggerations of Thomas Frognall Dibdin's *Bibliophobia* published in 1832. The Constable disaster left Sir Walter Scott liable for debts that chained him to his pen for the rest of his life.[9] The events of the mid-1820s were a reminder of the risks of working on credit in a tightly interdependent industry, and of the endemic shortage of capital in the book trade as a whole. The problem was not

---

8 Hilton, *Corn, cash and commerce*.
9 Sutherland, 'The British book trade and the crash of 1826'. See also Hilton, *A mad, bad, and dangerous people?*, pp. 398–401. For Knight, see Gray, *Charles Knight*.

unique to Britain.[10] Much of the success of the expansion of the British book trade in the following decades was the result of spreading risks, and extending the sources of profit.

For the literary world, the publishing event of the year was a two-volume work from Murray, the *Letters and journals of Byron*, with a life by Thomas Moore. As a piece of book design, it was generous, a reflection of the esteem in which Murray held its subject. It provoked editions in France and America. John Murray claimed to have lost at least £300 in the publication by May 1831, but this did no harm to his reputation as he assembled the copyrights to enable him to publish, at last, a properly collected edition of Byron's works.[11] The year also witnessed the appearance of the first part of Lyell's *Principles of geology*, of *Rural rides* and *Advice to young men* by William Cobbett, and of the first of Thomas Hood's *Comic annuals*. Tennyson's first solo volume of poems, *Poems, chiefly lyrical*, was widely and on the whole favourably welcomed: his career spans almost the whole of the present volume, until his death in 1892. The first parts of the seventh edition of the *Encyclopaedia Britannica* appeared from the firm of Adam Black, who had acquired the title following the collapse of Constable in 1827. Coming hard on the heels of the *Encyclopaedia metropolitana* (1828–) and a reissue of Chambers's *Cyclopaedia*, it was completed only in 1842.[12]

Publishers were seeking fresh ways of presenting their work to broadly middle-class audiences. The launch of the weekly *Spectator* and *Athenaeum* in 1828 had been followed in 1829 by two publishers' series of books at prices designed to appeal to a middling market. Some of this was simply a dress for cheap editions of older work, but many other books were specially written for these series. The new projects were not entirely innovative. In the mid-1820s, J. F. Dove and the proprietors of a publishers' library of British classics had offered dozens of books at prices mostly between four and six shillings a volume. The list included Byron and Paley, but most of the titles were out of copyright. Bound first in paper boards, and later in cloth, the duodecimo volumes were advertised as being set in type 'more than usually distinct and clear', with emphasis on the first three words. The new ventures moved away from established literature, to more recent work. Murray launched his five-shilling Family Library, with lives of Napoleon and Alexander the Great. Charles Knight produced the first volumes of his Library of Entertaining Knowledge, at 4s 6d

---

10 For the French crises of 1826, 1846 and 1890, the latter partly the result of over-expansion, see for example Parinet, *Une histoire de l'édition à l'époque contemporaine*, pp. 160–5.

11 Smiles, *A publisher and his friends* 2, pp. 305–28.   12 [North] *Adam and Charles Black*.

a volume and with books on menageries, vegetable substances and insects. G. L. Craik's *Pursuit of knowledge under difficulties* was an early inclusion, followed immediately by a study of New Zealanders that was inspired by the prospects (and profits) offered by the introduction there of western civilisation. In 1830, *Fraser's Magazine* was launched under the editorship of the independently minded William Maginn, a refugee from *Blackwood's Magazine*.[13] In the same year, Longman launched both Dionysius Lardner's *Cabinet cyclopaedia* and his Cabinet Library: the *Cabinet cyclopaedia*, at six shillings a volume, was eventually to run to 133 volumes, contributors including Scott, Thomas Moore, Southey, Mary Shelley and Herschel. Undercutting all of these, volumes in Constable's Miscellany, published by Whittaker, cost just 3s 6d each. In Edinburgh, *Chambers's Edinburgh Journal* and *Tait's Edinburgh Magazine* were both launched in 1832, the latter posing a direct challenge to *Blackwood's*.

Novels are discussed in more detail in chapters 3 and 11, below. The first edition of *Pride and prejudice*, in three volumes, had cost eighteen shillings in 1813. The three volumes of Scott's *Waverley* (1814) cost a guinea, or twenty-one shillings. In December 1815, *Emma* (dated 1816) was published, also in three volumes, at a guinea. But *Kenilworth* (1821), *The pirate* (1822 [1821]) and *The fortunes of Nigel* (1822), each likewise in three volumes, all cost 31s 6d, a guinea and a half, and this was to remain an industry standard.[14] The three-volume format, with its set price, dominated the market in new fiction, and hence much of publishing, for the next seventy-odd years. Its high price often supported other kinds of publishing, but it was too much for casual buying by most individuals. After Robert Cadell launched the 'Author's edition' of the Waverley novels at five shillings a volume, public appetite was whetted for different price structures. Cadell's venture proved an immense success.[15] In his pioneering series of Standard Novels, launched in February 1831, the publisher Richard Bentley offered a six-shilling series as means of republishing all kinds of recent novels at lower prices. Imitators followed, notably Colburn's Modern Novelists in 1835. Roscoe's Novelists Library, launched in 1831, was deliberately of older titles, the publisher Cochrane & Co. 'disclaim[ing] any intention of trespassing on the ground occupied by other publishers'.[16] But none of Bentley's competitors proved as successful as Bentley himself.[17] The

13 Thrall, *Rebellious Fraser's*; *Wellesley index* 2, pp. 302–521.
14 For Jane Austen, see Gilson, *A bibliography of Jane Austen*; for Scott, see Todd and Bowden, *Sir Walter Scott*.
15 Millgate, *Scott's last edition*; Todd and Bowden, *Sir Walter Scott*, pp. 885–931. For trends in novel prices, 1800–40, see St Clair, *The reading nation*, p. 203.
16 Advertisement in *Tom Jones* (1831).   17 Sadleir, *XIX century fiction* 2, pp. 91–122.

emphasis was constantly on reduced prices, though publishers were not always candid. Dove's British Classics, taken over by Scott & Webster and reset in slightly larger type, were advertised as having been reduced by a third, a claim that was only partially true.

As a genre, the new novel offers a uniquely long-term measure against which to set other retail prices, its price and format depending not so much on the number of words as on packaging for a market to whom familiarity was crucial. Its artificially high price, supported by a market dominated by circulating libraries for whom three volumes meant thrice the income that could be obtained from just one, remained a retail benchmark long after it could no longer be justified by the ordinary costs of production. Copyright books were usually liable to higher costs for publishers than those that were out of copyright, but books of all kinds tended to rise in price in the years after 1815. In the various activities of the late twenties designed to marry the economics of printing and publishing to growing markets anxious for self-improvement (a more complex desire than simply the accumulation of knowledge), and with the money to afford entertainment, are to be seen some of the preoccupations, practices and debates of the rest of the century.

The first meeting of the British Association in 1831, and the enthusiastic audiences that crowded into lectures and demonstrations at the Royal Institution, were but two measures of public thirst for knowledge.[18] For the artisan, the new mechanics' institutes and their several imitators, in town and country alike, were intended to provide for similar needs.[19] When in 1833 the disgraced but now contrite former Scottish minister Thomas Dick followed a series of books on Christian philosophy with a more general consideration *On the improvement of society by the diffusion of knowledge*, he gave much of his space to arguing for both social and theological links between scientific (for him that meant largely astronomical) knowledge, mechanical knowledge and divine revelation.[20] Like others, he had a strong sense of change, the scientific advances of the previous half-century presaging a period, now imminent, for a 'general diffusion of knowledge'. In a passage that followed, he summarised the signs and means of this expansion:

> from the numerous publications on all subjects daily issuing from the press; from the rapid increase of theological, literary and scientific journals, and the extensive patronage they enjoy; from the numerous lectures on chemistry,

18 Berman, *Social change and scientific organization*; Caroe, *The Royal Institution*.
19 Traice, *Handbook of mechanics' institutions*; Tylecote, *The mechanics' institutes of Lancashire and Yorkshire*.
20 For Dick (1774–1857), see Astore, *Observing God*.

astronomy, experimental philosophy, political economy, and general science, now delivered in the principal cities and towns of Europe; from the adoption of new and improved plans of public instruction, and the erection of new seminaries of education in almost every quarter of the civilized world; from the extensive circulation of books among all classes of the community; from the rapid formation of Bible and Missionary societies; from the increase of literary and philosophical associations; from the establishment of mechanics' institutions in our principal towns, and of libraries and reading societies in almost every village; from the eager desire now excited, even among the lower orders of society, of becoming acquainted with subjects hitherto known and cultivated only by persons of the learned professions . . . [21]

Dick's book, repeatedly republished, and widely read in America, caught a public mood, if not always in the particularities of his religious and philosophical claims. His alert topical sense of possibilities offered confidence; and even if reality sometimes proved different, he touched on issues that persisted, in one form or another, long into the future.

The same sense of engagement, fertilised and trained by the weekly and daily newspapers, was to be seen in later theological and scientific controversies.[22] Novels, poems and theatre responded to, and developed, the terminology and expectations of theology and the natural sciences. Inevitably amongst all this, pseudo-science and scientific and religious quackery flourished, whether in the study of phrenology or in Mme Blavatsky's later theosophy.[23] True or false, established wisdom or passing fads, all depended on printing for their success. In a different way, it is also to be seen in an insatiable demand for biographies and memoirs. The possibilities of illustration in all kinds of publications, from the most expensive folios to penny newspapers, further extended public knowledge, enjoyment and debate. But, though efforts were made to reduce the prices of some categories of books, prices for many new publications remained high; and at the other extreme there were few substantial titles costing less than two shillings save for children's books and some schoolbooks.

The radical literature of the 1820s and earlier, fuelled by the phenomenal public interest in 1820–1 concerning the trial of Queen Caroline and the confusions of the coronation of George IV, had provoked over-enthusiasm in some parts of the printing trade. When excitement died down, the demand for work diminished accordingly. William Hone, whose many radical pamphlets on the trial and on contemporary politics had enjoyed best-seller status in 1820–1,

---

21 Dick, *On the improvement of society by the diffusion of knowledge* (1833), pp. 15–16.
22 Secord, *Victorian sensation*. See chapter 12, below.
23 For Blavatsky, see Richard Davenport-Hines in *ODNB*.

was bankrupt in 1828. But the energies of the 1820s re-emerged in 1831–2 as activists worked with printers to ignore stamp duty, and thus publish at the lowest possible price, often as low as one penny: since stamp duty on newspapers in 1830 was fourpence a copy, the difference was considerable. For many people, newspapers took the place of pamphlets as the preferred means of exhortation. Political and ecclesiastical scandal peppered the pages of hundreds of titles published between the early 1830s and 1836, when the genre was brought effectively to an end with the reduction of duty to one penny.[24] Few of the unstamped papers had lasted more than a few months, or even weeks, but they outnumbered the regular press. While many of them were deliberately offensive to church and state, others pursued a milder course. For their circulation, they depended chiefly on agencies and itinerant salesmen and women: few were stocked by regular booksellers, and even then there was disagreement as to what was a risk. Though they were generally published in London, their circulation was national: Henry Hetherington, one of the most active of their promoters, had agencies in Glasgow and Edinburgh as well as Darlington and Newcastle, and as far west as Falmouth (an important port) and even Land's End. In South Wales, he had agencies in Carmarthen, Swansea and Newport: the nearest to North Wales was in Liverpool.[25] In part, the so-called war of the unstamped was about the price of knowledge. In part, it was born out of working-class and middle-class radicalism. Apart from objections to the tax, there was no single motive. As a consequence, politicians at Westminster and many of the clergy were often not merely sympathetic, but vociferous in their support. While the demand for cheap news was frequently linked to working-class radicalism, it was not exclusive to it. And, just as in eighteenth-century France,[26] the necessarily clandestine nature of much of this market, combined with the need to make money in difficult circumstances, provided natural allies to the trade in pornography.[27]

With irregular patterns of population went irregular patterns of book owner-ship and of reading. Put at its simplest, it was usually (if by no means universally) easier to buy a book in a town than it was in villages or hamlets; and the choice was greater in the middling or larger-sized towns with their own clienteles than in those whose weeks were more shaped by the influxes of money and

24 Wiener, *The war of the unstamped*; Hollis, *The pauper press*; Wiener, *A descriptive finding list*; Haywood, *The revolution in popular literature*.
25 An advertisement of 1834 listing Hetherington's stock is reproduced in Haywood, *The revolution in popular literature*, p. 115.
26 Darnton, *The literary underground of the old régime*; Darnton, *The forbidden best-sellers of pre-Revolutionary France*.
27 McCalman, *Radical underworld*.

people on market days. The dearth of booksellers in thinly populated Wales north of Aberystwyth was reflected in *Hodson's booksellers, publishers and stationers directory*, published in 1855, though Ireland and Scotland were hardly better served in a list that was defined by the needs of the London trade. Much of the country, and by no means only the countryside, continued to depend on itinerant salesmen and, for newspapers or more substantial books, on businesses such as grocers or on general stores whose primary concern was not the sale of print.

Defining Britain: politics

By 1830, for many purposes the British Isles were under a single jurisdiction. The Scottish Act of Union (1707) and that for Ireland (1800) left many rights in the controls of the respective countries, but the fortunes of the book trades in each were to prove very different during the period covered by the present volume. The Dublin trade was in decline in the 1790s, and once the 1710 Copyright Act was applied to Ireland from 1801 it was no longer possible to enjoy a profitable reprint business for the English market.[28] In both Ireland and Scotland, as in Wales, language issues played a large part in the shaping of publishing, bookselling and reading; but only Scotland found a way of profiting from the city that continued to dominate the book industry: London.

While the principal constitutional structures within the British Isles were set out in 1707 and 1800, many long-standing issues about different parts of those islands remained confused.[29] On the one hand Tennyson included two overtly English patriotic poems in his 1830 volume, neither of which he retained in later collections.[30] On the other, there was real confusion over

---

28 Cole, *Irish booksellers and English writers*, pp. 152–3; Pollard, *Dublin's trade in books*.

29 Cf. Edward Wells, *A treatise of ancient and present geography* (1701): 'In the Northern Ocean over against France and Germany lies a body of Islands, which, as they were anciently call'd *Insulae Britannicae*, so still go under the common name of the British Isles' (p. 43). Modern studies of searches for definitions are legion. For the concept of England, see for example Kumar, *The making of English national identity*; for early sixteenth- and early seventeenth-century tensions between English and Welsh, see Schwyzer, *Literature, nationalism and memory*; for the 'three kingdoms', and the 'Atlantic archipelago', see Pocock, *The discovery of islands*. See also Grant and Stringer (eds.), *Uniting the kingdom?*, especially Eric Evans, 'Englishness and Britishness: national identities, c.1790–c.1870', pp. 223–43. Parry, in *The politics of patriotism*, believes that Peter Mandler underestimates the ability of many writers at the time to think about the English as a nation: see Mandler, '"Race" and "nation" in Victorian thought', pp. 224–44. Withers, in *Geography, science and national identity: Scotland since 1520*, builds on ideas advanced by Patrick Geddes in the early twentieth century, and for further related contexts may be read alongside Nora (ed.), *Les lieux de mémoire*. Lord, in *The visual culture of Wales*, extends the creation of national identity to the visual and industrial record.

30 'English warsong'; 'National song'. Tennyson, *Poems, chiefly lyrical* (1830): *Poems* ed. Ricks, 1, pp. 274–6.

the meaning of nationhood. Thomas Moore's Ireland, and Galt's, Scott's and Allan Cunningham's Scotland asserted separate identities and even polities. Concepts of Britain and Britannia that had served a period from Addison to Pitt to the Napoleonic wars, and that had their roots partly in the sixteenth century and partly in the revolution of 1688–9, did not survive the close of the long eighteenth century in the late 1820s. One recent historian of England has sought to explain ideas of nation by distinguishing 'three contemporary versions of the national past – Gothic, Whig, and Catholic – the first two of which offered competing national stories, while the last denied the concept of a national story altogether'.[31] And yet, for its gothic (or gothick) past, England was content, when it suited, to use the Scotland created in the Waverley novels.

In Scotland, there was a world of difference between Edinburgh and the Lowlands, and parts more remote from English influence. In Ireland, Ulster and Belfast prospered, encouraged by thriving linen and ship-building industries, while Dublin and the south enjoyed no such industrial prosperity: the population of Belfast rose almost tenfold between 1821 and 1901, and that of Dublin increased by one-third during the same period. Ireland's status had been formalised with the Act of Union, but it was still very far from clear, to politicians as to other people, whether it was a colony, a part of England or a foreign country. The Irishman (and woman) was caricatured in racist terms, in Protestant Dublin and in England alike.[32] In Wales, where nonconformity and chapel-going thrived in the face of English-speaking land-owners, factory-owners and bishops, the Welsh Church was finally disestablished by Act of Parliament in 1914.[33] Religion and nationality were handmaids as much in the minds of those who, thinking of Ireland, fought over Roman Catholic emancipation at the end of the 1820s, as they were in the mind of Gladstone many years later.

Amidst these broad loyalties, in all parts of the kingdom there were regional divisions and variations in language, customs, beliefs and social structures: between town and country; between highland and lowland Scotland; between the area round Dublin and the west and north of Ireland; between increasingly industrialised South Wales, the thinly populated centre, and North Wales with its developing connections into Liverpool and Cheshire; between Wales

---

31 Hilton, *A mad, bad, and dangerous people?*, pp. 483–4. See also Kearney, *The British Isles*, which discusses some of the literature.

32 Curtis, *Apes and angels*. But see also Parry, *The politics of patriotism*, pp. 26–30, with more recent references. Ireland and ideas of colonisation are further explored in Kinealy, 'At home with the Empire'.

33 Cragoe, *Culture, politics and national identity in Wales*.

and the marches; between the different parts of England from Berwick-on-Tweed to Penzance.[34] Thanks partly to the uneven reach of booksellers, partly to economic disparities and partly to habits formed by buying other kinds of printed literature, religious or secular, books were not even necessarily sold in the same way in different regions. In Wales there were complaints throughout the Victorian and Edwardian periods concerning the difficulty of obtaining Welsh-language books.[35] Mass migrations of Welsh, Scottish and Irish labourers to build the railways added further to complexities, distinctions and self-awareness. Canals, improved roads and then the railways drew much of the population together in some ways, and dispersed it in others, yet regional distinctiveness remained powerful; and in the hands of local printers, publishers and newspapers it was not just encouraged, but often enhanced.

These confusions were only partly settled when the Great Exhibition of 1851 served as a focus of achievement that could be readily compared with other countries and, in the social mixture of those attending, also demonstrated to the often bewildered inhabitants of London something of the range of Britain's wider population.[36] Events in mainland Europe served to remind the British peoples of their sea-girt unity, but uncertainties persisted that no proffered religious, scientific or political verities could settle. The several different issues that were summed up in the shorthand of the Irish question, already a dominant matter in British politics in 1830, remained a shoal on which governments foundered. Home rule may have been the prevailing theme for many, whether protagonists or antagonists, especially from the 1880s onwards; but subsumed in this political discussion were questions as much social and religious, literary and linguistic, artistic and historical. The Irish question was so far from resolution in 1914 that two years later it erupted in rebellion. If Britain could watch aloof the nationalist movements in Belgium, Poland, Italy and Germany, and (much to public relief) she was immediately affected only to a limited extent by the revolutions of 1848,[37] the central questions of national identity remained even in home affairs.

In politics, economic prosperity, religion, employment and education, this was more than a question of geography. The legislation of 1707 and 1800 was but background. The issue was not unique to Britain and Ireland. In 1862, the young Acton took the constitutional changes of the French Revolution as his

---

34 See also the Introduction to Bell (ed.), *The Edinburgh history of the book in Scotland* 3.
35 Jones, 'A golden age reappraised'.
36 In an immense literature, see for example Auerbach, *The Great Exhibition of 1851* and (especially for some of the aftermath) Hobhouse, *The Crystal Palace and the Great Exhibition*. For international exhibitions more generally, see for example Greenhalgh, *Ephemeral vistas*.
37 Saville, in *1848*, offers a detailed chronology of events during the year.

starting point in an attempt to determine the distinguishing features of nationality and nationhood across Europe.[38] 'Qu'est-ce qu'une nation?' asked Ernest Renan at Paris in 1882, searching into the ancient world for a clue. To him, neither language, ethnographical background, geographical features, religion, nor common interests expressed (for example) in commercial treaties provided an adequate definition. To J. G. Fichte at the beginning of the century, lecturing in French-occupied Berlin, language and nationality had seemed indissoluble: if his emphases were born out of current politics, they are nonetheless curious in that he was thinking of German, a language spoken in many forms across several boundaries.[39] In the 1880s, Seeley spoke in comparable terms of 'the modern nation, of which the peculiar badge is language', thus also ignoring for a moment the realities of the contemporary political system at both national and international levels.[40] In Wales, Welsh was still spoken by about 70 per cent of the population, and in both Scotland and Ireland a language other than English was an essential part of national identity.[41] 'Ein gwlad, ein hiaith, ein cenedl' (one land, one language, one nation): what had become a familiar concept was carved amateurishly on a country bridge over a narrow-gauge slate railway in Wales.[42] Like many others, Renan found his most satisfactory answer in reflecting on common memory, experience and purpose, 'une conscience morale qui s'appelle une nation'.[43] He did not reflect at any length on modern ideas of empire, though for the European colonial powers – and not least for Britain and Germany as they tussled in Africa and South America[44] – the two issues, nation and empire, were intimately linked. Franco-British economic, territorial and artistic rivalry was a constant theme in international exhibitions in several different countries, and in steps taken consequently in Britain to attempt to catch up.[45] French colonies had been regarded as part of

---

38 Acton, 'Nationality'.

39 Fichte, *Reden an die deutsche Nation*, trans. as *Addresses to the German nation* (1808). Fichte's words (lecture 12) were 'Wie es ohne Zweifel wahr ist, daß allenthalben, wo eine besondere Sprache angetroffen wird, auch eine besondere Nation vorhanden ist, die das Rechte hat, selbständig ihre Angelegenheiten zu besorgen, und sich selber zu regieren'; 'Just as it is true beyond doubt that, wherever a separate language is found, there a separate nation exists, which has the right to take independent charge of its affairs and to govern itself' (*Addresses to the German nation*, ed. G. A. Kelly (New York, 1968).

40 Seeley, *Introduction to political science*, p. 374. His remarks were delivered during a lecture to students at Cambridge, first in 1886. On language, see further below, pp. 25–31.

41 Searle, *A new England?*, pp. 8–9.   42 J. I. C. Boyd, *The Tal-y-llyn railway* (Didcot, 1988), p. 98.

43 Renan, *Qu'est-ce qu'une nation?*

44 Kirchberger, *Aspekte deutsch-britischer Expansion*. But for transitions in thinking in some colonial societies, see for example Eddy and Schreuder (eds.), *The rise of colonial nationalism*, and for Asia see Bayly, 'The evolution of colonial cultures'.

45 Crouzet, *De la supériorité de l'Angleterre sur la France*; Greenhalgh, *Ephemeral vistas*; Porter, *The absent-minded imperialists*.

France since 1790. For Britain, issues of citizenship were much less clear-cut. Industrial development, with its consequent changes in patterns of living, the headings in the new census returns that imposed their own kinds of definitions, the gradual extension of the electoral franchise, the strong family ties marked in letters home that featured in migration whether within the British Isles or to other parts of the world: all spoke of clans, alliances and associations that had in themselves little to do with larger questions of nationhood, but much to do with the way that the nation operated. Palmerston's celebrated quotation from Cicero in 1850, when speaking in Parliament on compensation for damage to the property of a Jew in Athens who was also a British subject, was much closer to economic and social, as well as political, *Realpolitik*: a British subject, anywhere, should always be able to say in self-defence, 'Civis Romanus sum.'[46] In itself, this particular episode was allowed to grow far beyond what ordinary diplomacy should have allowed. But the sentiment was real enough. Great Britain was a nation both seeking its definition in traditional terms and also challenging the meaning of international.[47] It was doing so in the contexts of several political spheres whose overlapping interests obliged the more thoughtful to search for reconciliations of opinion and practice that were in fact ever elusive. Domestically, it was what has been called 'the Britannic melting pot'.[48] On the other hand, interests of empire competed with interests in Europe in political and economic activity, thought and spheres of influence.

All these issues, and not merely the much-contemplated questions of nationhood, state and nationalism as formed by so many political, social and religious thinkers and historians in the nineteenth century, both affected and were shaped by the possibilities and limitations of the trades in printing and publishing. While there were many exceptions, both in Britain and (for example) in the clashes between American and British copyright laws,[49] and in publishing interests in India and Australia, it was nonetheless usually easy for publishers to work in a world of well-defined boundaries. For authors and for many readers, these spheres were often interdependent: in the book trades as in most other kinds of manufacturing, customers did not expect to need to understand all the technical and commercial issues that determined what they could buy. In this as in so many other matters, the history of the book in Britain implies

---

46 Hansard 25 June 1850, col. 444. Cf. Cicero, *In Verrem* v.lvii.147. For British policy more generally on this and related issues, see for example Parry, *The politics of patriotism*, pp. 199–201.

47 For further reflections on this complicated network of questions, see the references in Hilton, *A mad, bad and dangerous people?*, pp. 711–16.

48 Kearney, *The British Isles*, ch. 9. For contemporary debate after 1832 on what has been termed the English national character, see for example Mandler, *The English national character*, pp. 39–58.

49 Seville, *The internationalization of copyright law*. See also chapter 5, below.

both domestic and international themes: not just in defining Britain, or the British, but also in the interplay of foreign and home production. Thanks to commercial and linguistic pre-eminence, her publishers became publishers to much of the world.

Geography: memory, orality and print

Printing, the ability to share, disperse and preserve ideas, propaganda, information and record, is but one mechanism, but a crucial one. At different periods and in different degrees it was the mechanism of moulding and imposing all the major western European languages.[50] Yet, while the increase in printed matter in the sixteenth century was influential, even instrumental, it was not by itself formative of the early modern nation-state. Oral literature, speeches religious (as in sermons) and secular, popular memory and legend, songs and music, and the continuing traditions of writing both as communication in correspondence and more formally in the copying of literary, religious and legal texts and documents: all these supported memory and practice to different degrees.[51] The brothers Grimm in Germany, Sir Walter Scott in Scotland, Thomas Crofton Croker in Ireland, Thomas Wright in England and J. F. Willems in Flanders were but some who, in a mingling of philology and the study of folklore, translated and transposed oral traditions into print. In Wales, an example had been set in 1764 by Evan Evans, in *Some specimens of the poetry of the ancient Welsh bards*. The partners of these antiquarians, linguists and anthologisers were the later philologists, such as F. J. Furnivall, W. W. Skeat and James Murray. In their work, and in their several different ways, they created their own versions of local – and ultimately national – memory.[52] Pictorial traditions added their further support and comment.

Modern countries are print-dependent for such basic matters as their laws and administration. On the other hand, in early nineteenth-century Germany, written correspondence and comment was a significant means by which individuals engaged with government and the political sphere.[53] In Ireland,

50 Anderson, *Imagined communities*, pp. 37–9, 42–4. For further reflections from other perspectives, see Berger and others (eds.), *Writing national histories*.
51 For correspondence, see for example Brant, *Eighteenth-century letters and British culture*; for some foreign examples, see Dauphin, 'Letter-writing manuals in the nineteenth century'. For American experiences of letter-writing and receiving, see Henkin, *The postal age*, and Gerber, *Authors of their lives*. There is so far no adequate study of handwriting styles in nineteenth-century Britain.
52 Bluhm, *Die Brüder Grimm*; Leerssen, *De bronnen van het vaderland*; Dorson, *The British folklorists*; Hüther, 'A transnational nation-building process'. For the work of Ferdinand Brunot and his *Histoire de la langue française* (1905–), see for example the account by Jean-Claude Chevalier in *Les lieux de mémoire* 3, pp. 3385–3418.
53 McNeely, *The emancipation of writing*.

a continuing manuscript tradition provided the environment within which much of Irish history was circulated and recorded even in the nineteenth century.[54] While the use of print is widely assumed as underpinning political, religious, economic and social activity, the use of books in the community as a whole remained (and to a large extent remains) an activity associated with elites in many different kinds of social groups. Education was defined by the book. Middle-class values respected book ownership. Yet full literacy – defined as the ability to read, understand and write fluently – has never become universal. On the other hand, by 1914 almost everyone of school age and above had a working knowledge.[55] There remains a largely uncharted mass of cheap literature, printed on low-grade brownish wood-pulp paper from worn stereos and often reusing materials that had begun their existence somewhat further up the economic scale. Much of this kind of mass-produced literature, for which no-one expected a long life, has disappeared completely. Much of it has no doubt been pulped. Much of it has simply disintegrated. Even when it was new, little found its way into the contemporary surveys of press output. It is difficult now to recover much of its manufacture, circulation and use.[56]

No less importantly in this respect, oral traditions have enjoyed their own trajectories only partly dependent on print and manuscript. The extent to which popular memory for song and story-telling was recorded in print is not clear: figures of 90 per cent and more overlap have been suggested for song. Conversely, much of the inspiration for such song came from print. The Percy Society was founded in 1840 to collect and print some of this oral heritage, and the Ballad Society followed in 1868. These were self-funding publishing societies; and though one of the leading pioneers, William Chappell, was primarily interested in ballads old or recent, Thomas Wright was more attracted to medieval traditions. They and others did not just search out manuscript or early printed sources. Considerable efforts were made to collect locally, such as by J. O. Halliwell in Yorkshire and in Norfolk, John Harland in Lancashire, John Stokoe in Northumbria, William Motherwell, Charles Mackay and many others in Scotland, and Croker and others in Ireland.[57] These and enterprises like them were inspired by antiquarian and musical enquiry. More than many other literary activities, they were closely related in concept and in practice to

---

54 See for example de Brún and Herbert, *Catalogue of Irish manuscripts*.
55 See below, chapter 7.   56 See below, chapter 20.
57 Thomson, 'The development of the broadside ballad trade'; Gregory, *Victorian songhunters*.

the exploration of foreign traditions being made available in English translation.[58] On the other hand, there is considerable evidence that many people in
the nineteenth century who were persuaded to buy the cheap street ballads
produced by printers across the country were unable to read their purchases.
In such oral traditions of song and story-telling were often embodied the social
assumptions about morality and communal structures that were also recorded
more formally in print.[59] Oral traditions apart, with the advent of recorded
sound, the relationship between print, performance and hearing was still further complicated. The cadences of the spoken voice, and the tempi and style
of musical interpretation, did not challenge the supposed authority of print
for the first time: such issues had been aired ever since sermons and musical
compositions had first seen print. But mass-produced recordings now meant
that, as with print, it was possible to test and compare reactions and understanding. In such now-celebrated recordings as Tennyson reading 'The charge
of the Light Brigade', or Yeats reading 'The lake isle of Innisfree', typography's
relationship to meaning was given a further dimension. The recordings made
by the Gramophone Company from 1914 onwards, of Elgar conducting his
own works, offer similar interplay between score, instruments, players and
composer, summed up in performances whose authority was defined not least
through the technical limitations of acoustic recording, including the need to
assemble players as closely as possible round the collecting horn: the effect was
inevitably different from that in a concert hall. Places and circumstances of
performance, like those for reading, directly affected understanding and interpretation of printed texts – be they books, magazines, newspapers, handbills,
notices or musical scores – whose appearance was otherwise uniform.

Geography: beyond Britain

This volume is concerned primarily with books published in Britain. But the
title implies more.[60] British publishers were active across the world, and by the

---

58 Kenneth Haynes, 'Oral literature', in France and Haynes (eds.), *The Oxford history of English literature
in translation* 4, pp. 430–40.
59 Bushaway, ' "Things said or sung a thousand times" ', with further references. See also Fielding,
Writing and orality and Finnegan, *Literacy and orality*.
60 For some international contexts, see the standard histories for countries close to the British
book trade, including Kapp and Goldfriedrich, *Geschichte des deutschen Buchhandels: Geschichte des
deutschen Buchhandels im 19. und 20 Jahrhundert*; Martin, Chartier and others (eds.), *Histoire de
l'édition française. 3. Le temps des éditeurs*; Casper and others (eds.), *A history of the book in America.
3. The industrial book*; Fleming, Gallichan and Lamonde (eds.), *History of the book in Canada*; Lyons
and Arnold (eds.), *A history of the book in Australia* 2, and vol. 1, *Establishing a colonial print culture*,
ed. Wallace Kirsop and Elizabeth Webby (in preparation).

early twentieth century were dominant. It was a position they enjoyed only for a few years, as American interests drove into the English-speaking world after 1918. Conversely, much of what was read in Britain was imported. In 1843, the novelist G. P. R. James lamented the poor state of English publishing when compared with that in France.[61] He claimed that English books cost 10 per cent more than French ones; that authors were several times better remunerated there; that the mass of newspapers and journals available in England took away time that might be spent reading books; that British authors were unprotected against foreign 'pirates'; that the British book trade in general was depressed; and that the government showed a 'total want of encouragement to literature'. His position, based on a mixture of private morality and public policy, was not wholly tenable, though he was on firmer ground when he discussed the illegal import of foreign-printed copyright books into Britain. Yet, while it was impractical to search all baggage for copies of novels published by Galignani or Baudry at Paris, or any of the several other continental English-language publishers, the scale of the imports meant that more than casual baggage escaped the attention of the customs officers at the Channel ports. According to James, there was an organised illicit trade, making use of returning tourists as mules – to adopt the terminology of another illegal trade today. In this way, the circulating libraries of the south coast were supplied with books from cheap sources overseas, at the expense of British publishers and their authors.

If this particular trade was notorious, there were many other kinds of books whose import caused no such offence. Allusion is further made below to the foreign-language booksellers in London in the early part of the nineteenth century. At the end of the century, and at the beginning of the twentieth, the trade in foreign-language imports expanded again. The specialist oriental booksellers Luzac & Co. were established in Great Russell Street, near the British Museum, in 1890. Probsthain opened a few doors along the road in 1902. Quaritch dealt largely in oriental languages, and in 1910 was offering several books imported from Tokyo on Japanese art. In European languages, Asher, of Berlin, were established in London in 1864. In the West End, French fashion journals were to be had from Langlois in South Audley Street, and in Berners Street Rolandi's foreign subscription library, founded in 1820, offered 'a choice of upward of six hundred thousand volumes' of French, German, Spanish and Italian literature.

---

61 James, 'Some observations on the book trade'.

It is not simply that the practices of reading and the use of books, direct or indirect, transcend geographical and political boundaries; or that the conventions of book design and manufacture were both nationally distinctive and yet often dependent on foreign suppliers; or that Britain possessed a world-wide empire in which English was the main language of government and law; or that much of this linguistic dominance (by no means confined to the British Empire) was created by mass emigration. The present volume deals with a period that trumpeted its achievements in education, literacy, cheap print that was universally available, and the world-wide presence of what Dilke, Seeley and others called Greater Britain.[62] Not all such claims can be unequivocally upheld, and the history of the book in this period offers one way of testing them.

Prosaically and fundamentally, national histories of the book, like other national histories, are interdependent at the most practical levels. In 1854, when Britain was in the midst of one of her periodic crises in paper supply, Charles Knight allowed himself to reflect on the rag trade of Europe, and in his imaginative wanderings among far-flung parts of the continent he reminded his readers of the country's dependence on imports in the printing trades as in other industries:

> The material of which this book is formed existed a few months ago, perhaps, in the shape of a tattered frock, whose shreds, exposed for years to the sun and wind, covered the sturdy loins of the shepherd watching his sheep on the plains of Hungary; – or it might have formed part of the coarse blue shirt of the Italian sailor, on board some little trading-vessel of the Mediterranean; – or it might have pertained to the once tidy *camicia* of the neat straw-plaiter of Tuscany, who, on the eve of some festival, when her head was intent upon gay things, condemned the garment to the *stracci-vendolo* (rag-merchant) of Leghorn; – or it might have constituted the coarse covering of the flock-bed of the farmer of Saxony, or once looked bright in the damask table-cloth of the burgher of Hamburgh; – or, lastly, it might have been swept, new and unworn, out of the vast collection of the shreds and patches, the fustian and buckram, of a London tailor; or might have accompanied every revolution of a fashionable coat in the shape of lining – having travelled from St. James's to St. Giles's, from Bond Street to Monmouth Street, from Rag Fair to the Dublin Liberty, till man disowned the vesture, and the kennel-sweeper claimed its miserable remains. In each of these forms, and in a hundred more which it would be useless to describe, this sheet of paper a short time since might have existed.[63]

---

62 Dilke, *Greater Britain*; Seeley, *The expansion of England*. For the wider political implications of this term, see Bell, *The idea of Greater Britain*.

63 Knight, *The old printer and the modern press*, pp. 256–7.

The international search for the raw materials of paper-making; the international sourcing of printing (by the late nineteenth century much printing for British publishers was executed in Germany, for example); the international bases of publishers such as Trübner, Putnam, Lippincott, Appleton or Scribner in America, Asher or Brockhaus in Germany,[64] or Thacker in Calcutta; the branch system of firms such as Nelson (Paris), Macmillan (New York, India, etc.), Oxford University Press (New York, etc.), Longman (by 1910 in New York, Boston, Chicago, Bombay and Calcutta) or Angus & Robertson (Sydney): these were some of the more obvious aspects of international or multi-national outlooks, arrangements and collaborations. Long established in the London retail trade, Hachette were also publishers of books originating in both England and France. Other firms formalised agency arrangements. By 1912, Oxford University Press were agents for Yale, Harvard, Princeton and Columbia University Presses.[65] Of the ten books on mining and manufacturing listed in their 1916 catalogue, three each were from Harvard, Yale and Angus & Robertson, and one was from Columbia. Of the dozen on transport and communications, just three were from the Clarendon Press. The same catalogue listed hundreds of such imports.[66] Whether having their origins in London or Edinburgh, or as foreign firms with settled bases in Britain, these international organisations and others like them provided economic foundations that created a readership for whom national boundaries meant little.

Booksellers and publishers built their careers on negotiating and trading across boundaries of language and government, creed and currency. By the early nineteenth century, in the aftermath of the Napoleonic wars, European trade was redefined yet again, and it now had a global reach. By the beginning of the twentieth century, internationalism was the dominant defining characteristic of the book trade – at least in Britain, the United States, France, Germany and their respective global offshoots. London and American east coast publishing were intertwined.[67] The American firm of Wiley & Putnam had a London office by the end of the 1830s. Harper were represented by Sampson Low from 1847 onwards. *Harper's Magazine*, founded in New York in 1850, was by the 1880s published in two editions, in Britain and America. By 1900, the British edition, edited by Andrew Lang, was more successful

---

64 For Germany, see Jäger and others (eds.), *Geschichte des deutschen Buchhandels im 19. und 20. Jahrhunderts. 1. Das Kaiserreich 1870–1918*, with further references.
65 Sutcliffe, *The Oxford University Press*, p. 168.
66 Oxford University Press, *General catalogue* (November 1916).
67 See for example Gohdes, *American literature in nineteenth century England*; Weintraub, *The London Yankees*.

than its American counterpart, and enjoyed a circulation of 100,000 copies.[68] Its main rivals, *Scribner's* and the *Century*, were likewise published in both countries. The New York magazine for children, *St. Nicholas* (1872–), found an appreciative audience in Britain. Much of the appeal in these magazines and others like them lay in the exceptional quality of their illustrations, and especially the wood-engravings; those in *Harper's* were outstandingly good and well printed. Ginn & Co., in Boston, enjoyed strong links to American higher education and to British school publishing. *Cosmopolis*, a monthly journal founded in 1896 and including articles in English, French and German, was published in London by Fisher Unwin, and copyrighted in the United States through Stone & Kimball. John Lane worked with Copeland & Day of Boston and Stone & Kimball of Chicago, the two firms sharing his interest in contemporary book design.[69] British firms opened offices in New York: by the mid-1890s Cassell, Longman, Macmillan, Nelson, Oxford, Routledge, Ward Lock and Frederick Warne all had addresses in America, and were embedded in the American trade. For authors, matters were more complicated, by copyright and royalty agreements, but the principle of international dependence remained.

In some senses much of this was perforce a modest trade. In 1852, Sampson Low issued their first catalogue of American imports, and four years later this had grown to a list of over 5,000 titles, arranged by subject. Many of these books were also published in England, but conversely the catalogue for 1856 pointed out that during the previous year there had been 1,092 new books and new editions published in America, of which 250 were reprints of English books.[70] If parity in the published output of Britain and America was still some way off, the trend was clear enough. In the British domestic trade as a whole, by the early twentieth century the power of a small number of wholesalers was ever more noticeable. Simpkin Marshall, whose links to small local publishers all over Britain enabled them to act both as wholesale booksellers and as publishers, were based firmly in London; yet they also had a substantial overseas business, and claimed in the 1870s to be able to supply any American law book not in stock within five weeks of an order being received.[71] William Dawson, their main rival, and with a history dating from 1809, had branches in six towns in southern England, as well as Dublin, and abroad at Cape Town, Johannesburg

---

68 Exman, *The house of Harper*, pp. 250–1.
69 Kraus, *Messrs Copeland & Day*; Kramer, *A history of Stone & Kimball*. See also Nelson, *The early nineties*, esp. appendixes D and E.
70 *The American catalogue of books: or, English guide to American literature* (1856).
71 *Inns of Court Calendar 1877*, advertisement.

and Toronto. In Edinburgh, the main wholesaler was John Menzies. But one of the greatest differences in the trade by 1914 was the large number of firms a substantial part of whose business consisted in export. In London alone there were almost two hundred firms of this kind, and there were others in Birmingham, Manchester and Glasgow. At one level there were major firms like Gordon & Gotch, whose principal connections lay in Australia and New Zealand but who also had interests in Canada and South Africa, or Stechert, exporters to America and the Far East and with offices at New York, Paris and Leipzig. At a much lower level were those like H. I. Jones & Son, exporters to Wanganui in New Zealand, or Beirne & Co., with links to Brisbane. Mitsui & Co. specialised in exports to Japan.

For many more general historians today, this insistence on what has been termed the 'need to transcend the boundaries of states' has become received opinion and practice.[72] But it needs to be emphasised in a volume such as the present, bearing a title that seems to insist on the defining weight of national circumscription. Perhaps it is all the more necessary in a volume that covers a period so aware of the passing of old political orders and the struggles to create fresh identities, whether in Europe or further afield. In 1903, John Morley recalled events of the 1850s in Greece, the Neapolitan kingdom and the Balkan peninsula, and wrote of 'the vague, indefinable, shifting, but most potent and inspiring doctrine of Nationality'.[73] When he wrote, England and Germany were competing head to head; and (though it must be doubtful that Morley had this also in mind) in the less violent world of books England and the United States were still at loggerheads over copyright. We are concerned here not only with the making of books in Britain, and the use of books there whether they have been produced domestically or abroad: the book in Britain rather than the British book. Economic, religious, linguistic, demographic and ethnic issues all, to differing degrees and in different ways, require a global perspective that has its roots in the beginnings of the trade in printed books and in European expansion since the fifteenth century. The period of this volume was not just one of change; it was also one of absorption and development on unprecedented scales.

A divergent population

Whatever some of the claims in the last years of the reign of Queen Victoria, as journalists, politicians and literary figures looked back over fifty and then sixty

---

72 Bayly, *The birth of the modern world*, p. 2.   73 Morley, *The life of William Ewart Gladstone* 2, p. 2.

and more years, the nation was certainly not defined by any kind of uniform technological or social advance. A. R. Wallace gave his widely read *The wonderful century* (1898; fourth edn 1901) a sub-title: *Its successes and its failures*. At the head of the scientific failures was the obligation for vaccination against smallpox, a precaution that he thought unproven.[74] His dismay at the neglect of phrenology after its fashionable heyday, and at opposition to psychical research, was of less interest. But he was also alert to social issues, the health of London, the 'curse' of militarism, the demon of greed, the 'unblushing selfishness of the greatest civilized nations' that allowed the murder and starvation of thousands of Armenians, and, in conclusion, the plunder of the earth. If he saw hope in what he termed the 'movement towards socialism', it was also a hope based on education, which would provide the power and knowledge required to initiate reforms. Much of this would depend on writers, and therefore (though he did not develop this) on print.[75] The sombre second half of Wallace's book was at odds with the more common – and entirely justifiable – celebrations of achievement. The ends of centuries, like the ends of reigns, breed nostalgia, and Wallace was as nostalgic as anyone. If his was a qualified nostalgia, it was also a reminder that social, political, economic and industrial progress proceeded irregularly, and not necessarily to universal benefit.

In 1831, the population of Great Britain – that is, of England, Scotland and Wales – was 16.3 million. By 1851 it had risen to 20.8 million. In 1901 it was 37 million, and in 1911 it was 40.8 million. The raw figures, recording a growth of two and a half times in eighty years, conceal much more complicated changes. Two in particular need to be stressed here. In the first two decades of the nineteenth century the population was growing younger as fertility increased; and by roughly the last quarter of the century contraceptives and better sexual education were two factors contributing to a declining fertility rate, while at the same time life expectancy was increasing. Hence, the population was ageing again.[76] Second, while all towns grew, some grew proportionately faster than others. By this measure, London, already large, grew more slowly in the first half of the century than did (for example) Manchester, Liverpool or Bradford.[77]

Disraeli, famously, wrote of two nations, the privileged and the labouring classes, the wealthy and the exploited.[78] He had ample support in the findings

---

74 See also Durbach, *Bodily matters*.   75 Wallace, *The wonderful century* 4th edn (1901), pp. 376–9.
76 Woods, 'The population of Britain in the nineteenth century', fig. 2. But see also Szreter, *Fertility, class and gender in Britain*.
77 Hilton, *A mad, bad, and dangerous people?*, pp. 5–6.
78 Benjamin Disraeli, *Sybil, or the two nations* (1845).

of Royal Commissions that examined industrial conditions. The fascination with poverty evinced in the work of observers like Henry Mayhew, Friedrich Engels or Arthur Munby, and reformers such as General Booth, emphasised similar distinctions. But disparities of wealth, occupation and privilege provided only one way of defining the population in a century marked, inter alia, by successive legislation for electoral reform.[79] Even leaving aside the political divisions of the British Isles, boundaries of interest, of knowledge, of belief and religious practice, of national and international awareness, and of practical and imaginative creativity all provided their own definitions and cross-currents. George Cruikshank's celebrated etching of 'London going out of town – or the march of bricks and mortar'[80] to take over the countryside had its human counterpart, since first-generation migration from country to town helped temporarily to ensure an outlook possessing some residual comparative knowledge in memories of the former. Distinctions were often blurred, and the apparent ordered tidiness of records such as census returns or local directories concealed multitudes of overlapping boundaries between social groups.

The 1881 census showed that more than twice as many people lived in towns as in the country.[81] Only thirty years previously, town-dwellers in England had but slightly outnumbered those in the country. During Queen Victoria's reign, the populations of some of the mainly industrial counties – Lancashire, Yorkshire, Durham and Glamorganshire – had increased at rates far above the national average, while those of Radnor and Montgomery, and of the Scottish Highlands, had declined. Ireland's population had declined by 3 million. These shifts in an increasingly mobile population entailed changes in standards of living, changes in religious belief and observance, changes in life expectancy, changes in entertainment and changes in ways of learning. They were also instrumental in advancing distinctions between the industrialised north and the less industrialised south of England – the industrial west midlands were included in the north. Authors such as Mrs Gaskell, Disraeli and Dickens were quick to respond to the change.

The so-called industrial revolution was not only piecemeal and spread over a long period (it was still in progress in 1914); it also affected different parts of the population in different ways at different times and at different paces. Arguably it is still in progress, revolution having evolved into a way of life, a habit of change. On the one hand it could be measured mechanistically by (for example) applications for patents, or by the output of steel, or by the

---

79 For the mid-century, see for example Hall, McClelland and Rendall, *Defining the Victorian nation*.
80 Reproduced for example in George, *Hogarth to Cruikshank*, p. 180.
81 See also Lampard, 'The urbanizing world'.

application of steam power. But it was also dependent on attitudes of mind, and the willingness or opportunities to apply new knowledge. Nor was its fractured nature simply a difference between town and country, non-agricultural and agricultural. One consequence of this unevenness was ever more complicated social and economic patterns, of wealth, of education, of material expectations, of political aspirations.

Partly for this reason it is impossible to talk of different classes without very considerable qualification. It is doubtful, in the context of printing and writing, if there was such a thing as a distinctively working-class culture, even regionally or locally.[82] It is equally impossible to talk consistently of middle or upper classes as common entities in respect of their reading tastes and buying habits. Instead, and as the new public libraries found sometimes to their consternation, there were many inter-mingled cultures. High-minded reformers worried at the amount of fiction being borrowed from public libraries, but this term encompassed not just the high to the low, but also much other literature besides, sometimes even poetry. In 1833 Sir John Herschel fretted about provision of novels for what he called the 'humbler classes': 'not the foolish romances which used to be the terror of our maiden aunts; not the insolent productions which the press has lately teemed with, under the title of fashionable novels – nor the desperate attempts to novelize history, which the herd of Scott's imitators have put forth'. If Cervantes, Richardson, Goldsmith and Scott represented the higher and better class, then many of his contemporaries failed the test.[83] In the early twentieth century, Florence Bell recorded not only that working-class men in Middlesbrough read more than their wives, who preferred penny stories, but also that Mrs Henry Wood's *East Lynne* headed the list of the most popular novels.[84] All socio-economic boundaries within the population of Britain were fluid, indeterminate and disputed; the boundaries between different parts of the market for print, whether expressed as reading preferences or as economic activity, were still less defined.

Language

While government, clergy, writers and artists alike worked to assert a spirit of nationalism, the old ties to regionalism and to language remained, to work both

---

82 Cf. Joyce, *Visions of the people*. This question has been usefully explored for the first half of the twentieth century in Hilliard, 'Modernism and the common writer', which takes issue with some aspects of Rose, *The intellectual life of the British working classes*. For an older, and highly influential, view see Williams, *Culture and society*, pp. 307–18.

83 Herschel, 'Address delivered to the subscribers to the Windsor and Eton Public Library', p. 44.

84 Bell, *At the works*, p. 236.

with and against concepts of nationhood whose modern history was founded in the sixteenth and early seventeenth centuries. In the minds of many educated people, British identity, with all its internal contradictions, was defined as what it was not: it was distinct from what were thought to be French or (later, and more complicated) German interests and manners. Concepts, rather than definitions, were arrived at by external comparisons, a process encouraged by figures such as Matthew Arnold in England, Hippolyte Taine in France, and the increasing numbers who started their European journeys from the United States.[85] For the whole of this period, Britain was involved in no major European war. Despite scares of invasion by France, the arms race with Germany that dominated foreign policy from the 1880s onwards, the huge expenses consequent on the Naval Defence Act of 1889, and the bruising experiences of the Boer war, questions of national identity were thus often phrased in social, commercial and intellectual environments rather than in the crude distinctions of the battlefield or sea-fight.[86] Religion, the ambivalent reconnoitring between Protestantism and Roman Catholicism – cautious, pitifully slow, and riddled with suspicions that have never been entirely discarded – remained a principal cause of Anglo-Irish tension long after the French threat of papacy had been demolished. Nonconformity took a financial as well as social toll of the established church, but refused to fit into any single political, financial or social category other than by what it was not. Globally, national identities were defined in emigration and, more confusedly, in the multiple distinctivenesses of the British Empire. Simply in numerical terms, the 1911 census figures identified in the empire a white population of about 60 million (of whom 36 million were in the United Kingdom), about 315 million native to India and Ceylon, 6 million Arabs and a million Chinese. The largest religious beliefs distinguished about 210 million Hindus, 100 million Muslims, 63 million Protestants, 12 million Buddhists and 7 million Catholics.[87]

On the other hand, language and dialect defined different parts of these islands, just as they defined different social strata. Scottish Gaelic was the first language for people in the Highlands and the west of Scotland, and was spoken by over 250,000 people in 1891. But it was also spoken in the Lowlands, and remained especially in use amongst migrants from the Highlands to the cities:

---

85 Lockwood, *Passionate pilgrims*, provides a portrait of Americans who came to Britain often seeking to understand their own histories and identities; for views in each direction, see Mulvey, *Anglo-American landscapes*.

86 In this, the pre-Victorian century arguably differed, where anti-French belligerence, including several wars, has been identified as a principal feature of Britishness: Colley, *Britons*.

87 All population figures here are from *Whitaker's almanack*, 1914.

linguistic and physical boundaries never coincided.[88] Welsh dominated parts of Wales, socially, politically and religiously, though English was dominant in parts including south Pembrokeshire, the marches, and – under the influence of tourism – the north coast;[89] and in the Isle of Man there were still about 5,000 Manx speakers in the early twentieth century, but the market was never strong enough to support more than a small industry. In Ireland, efforts to impose English as the language of Protestantism met only mixed success, and Gaelic persisted in the rural west. The divide there was never a wholly religious one, between Catholic and Protestant.[90] Census returns suggest that between 1851 and 1891 the percentage of those speaking Irish declined from 23.3 to 14.5 per cent; but this national figure disguised many difference among regions and between age-groups, and it was in any case almost certainly affected by the famine that contributed to the decline in population from 8.2 million in 1841 to 6.6 million in 1851: the population continued to decline, to 4.7 million in 1891, and then lower again. In 1881 the percentage of those aged between 20 and 29 speaking the language was just 16.44 per cent, well under half the percentage in the 60–69 age-group, and a little over one-third of the 45.87 per cent of those in their eighties.[91] In the Channel Islands, French and English existed side by side. In 1830, the Cornish language was reported (prematurely) to be 'utterly extirpated'.[92] On the mainland, habits were changed with the development of the railways as, for example, the line from Shrewsbury and Welshpool was driven through to Aberystwyth and north up the coast of Merioneth in the early 1860s. Bilingualism accompanied the steam engine.

In none of these larger regions was there a clear distinction in linguistic habits between one social activity and another, between home and school, between religious occasions and secular ones. Linguistically, such distinctions were, cumulatively, tendencies rather than absolutes. Social class was liable (there were always exceptions) to be much more influential. The significance of dialects became better understood thanks to authors who had a national following, whether in the Dorset of William Barnes and Thomas Hardy, the midlands of George Eliot, or to those who remained primarily local, such as in the publications of the Heywoods of Manchester. John Jamieson's

88 Withers, *Gaelic Scotland 1698–1981*; Withers, *Gaelic Scotland: the transformation of a culture region*; Withers, *Urban highlanders*; Bell (ed.), *The Edinburgh history of the book in Scotland 3*.
89 Jenkins (ed.), *Language and community in the nineteenth century*; Jenkins, *The Welsh language and its social domains*.
90 Crowley, *Wars of words*.   91 Ó Murchú, 'Language and society in nineteenth-century Ireland'.
92 *Pigot & Co.'s National commercial directory* (1830), 'Cornwall', p. 1.

Etymological dictionary of the Scottish language, originally published by subscription at Edinburgh in 1808, and abridged and revised in 1846 and 1867, remained standard for generations. Joseph Wright's *English dialect dictionary* (1898–1905) was the work of a dedicated and, to some, eccentric scholar; but in reflecting the self-evident search for a national language in James Murray's English dictionary, Wright's work was a powerful reminder of structures within the linguistic polity, where there were always distinctions to be made between those who used dialect for literary effect, and those for whom it was everyday speech.[93]

These and other enterprises set a scholarly seal on some of Britain's linguistic traditions and practices, but in some respects they represented a tradition wholly unknown in other parts of the community. There were worlds of difference between schooled and unschooled English.[94] The inspectors sent out by Parliament only a few decades earlier to report on mines or on factory conditions or on education found themselves confronted with vocabulary and forms of speech that required interpreters.[95] When education in Wales was under investigation in the 1840s, language became a bone of contention. Quite apart from the dozens of local history, natural history and antiquarian societies that were established in the nineteenth century, ideas of difference were further maintained in such phenomena as a fashion for regional settings of novels in the mid-century and, towards the end of our period, the popular successes of Thomas Hardy (Wessex), R. D. Blackmore (Devon), Arnold Bennett (the Potteries), Beatrix Potter (the Lake District), John Buchan (Scotland) or S. R. Crockett (Galloway). Ireland was given a different aspect thanks to Samuel Lover, Charles Lever and Somerville and Ross, all of whom found enormous followings in England and with English publishers. William Carleton, who depended much more on Dublin publishers, became a favourite of Routledge and of the publishers of yellowbacks.[96] Yeats and Synge were part of an Irish political revival, as well as a literary one. If there was much that was self-conscious in some of these writers and others like them, this in turn was a reflection of the decline in regional differences in the face of population shifts. Robert Forby (d.1825), rector of a Norfolk village, had

93 Wright, *The life of Joseph Wright*; for problems of literary and everyday speech, see Skeat and Nodal (eds.), *A bibliographical list*.
94 Fairman, 'Words in English record office documents'.
95 *Reports of the Commissioners of Inquiry into the State of Education in Wales* 3 parts. *Parliamentary papers* 1847.xxvii; Frankel, *States of inquiry*, p. 196.
96 Leclaire, *A general analytical bibliography of the regional novelists of the British Isles*; Leclaire, *Le roman régionaliste*; Loeber, *A guide to Irish fiction*.

believed that 'upon the whole, we may rest satisfied that the provincial dialects are in very safe keeping, and very likely so to remain'.[97] His confidence was misplaced.

For England at least, immigrant languages were of much more importance to the book trade. French-language booksellers and publishers had been familiar in London since the late seventeenth century. By 1820 they included A. Dulau in Soho Square, Bossange in Great Marlborough Street, Bohn in Frith Street and Treuttel & Würtz in Soho Square.[98] By the 1860s the largest general foreign booksellers included Baillière in Regent Street, Barthès & Lowell in nearby Great Marlborough Street, and Dulau. Hachette opened a branch in King William Street, the Strand.[99] From 1826 onwards, when the *Act for establishing regulations for aliens arriving in this kingdom* (passed in 1793 in response to the French Revolution) was repealed, Britain followed an open-doors policy on immigration.[100] It was only modified with the Aliens Act in 1905, in the face of increasing numbers of Jewish refugees from eastern Europe. This liberal attitude ensured an ever more cosmopolitan populace – particularly in London but also in Manchester,[101] Liverpool, Leeds, Edinburgh and some other large centres – not just as a consequence of trade (this had been true for centuries) but as the country extended hospitality as a place of refuge, and absorbed skills into the general economy. The result was a first-generation immigrant population both increasingly diverse and markedly varied in needs, social structures and character. Revolutionaries from Italy found a haven in the 1820s and 1830s, their number including not only Antonio Panizzi, who created in the British Museum the greatest library in the world, but also Giuseppe Mazzini and Gabriele Rossetti, who became the first Professor of Italian at King's College, London.[102] In 1847, Salvatore Ferretti (1817–74), a former Catholic priest, founded *L'Eco di Savonarola*, a monthly newspaper for Protestant émigrés that lasted until 1860.[103] The revolutions of 1848 brought an influx of Germans and, more numerously, of French.

Britain had already absorbed previous generations of French refugees, after 1789 and after 1830. In London, Louis-Philippe's interests were supported

---

97 Forby, *The vocabulary of East Anglia* 1, p. 74.
98 Samuel Leigh, *Leigh's new picture of London* (1819); Shaw, 'French-language publishing in London to 1900'; Shaw, 'French émigrés in the London book trade'.
99 Mollier, *Louis Hachette*.
100 Porter, *The refugee question in mid-Victorian politics*, p. 3. Legislation introduced briefly in 1848 was never implemented.
101 Williams, *The making of Manchester Jewry*.
102 Vincent, *Gabriele Rossetti in England*; Wicks, *The Italian exiles in London*; Sponza, *Italian immigrants in nineteenth-century Britain*.
103 Vinay, *Evangelici italiani esuli a Londra durante il Risorgimento*.

by the *Courrier de l'Europe*, founded in 1840 and comparable for the émigré community with *Galignani's Messenger* for English speakers in Paris and other parts of Europe. The *Observateur Français*, also strictly royalist, and supporting free trade, provided its readers with selections from Sue, Thiers and others, and recommended itself particularly to families wishing to learn or practise their French – an incidental reminder that publications in foreign languages were not necessarily only for expatriates. The revolution in 1848 brought an influx of *Orléanistes* led by Louis-Philippe. Others fled persecution later in the century, including Emile Zola following his publication of *J'accuse!* and his open advocacy of Dreyfus.[104]

Most famously, Karl Marx arrived to settle in 1849, and was to die in London in 1883. Nikolaus Trübner settled in London in 1843, and founded a publishing and bookselling partnership that specialised in European books, extended later to the United States and to oriental works.[105] The mid-century German-language newspapers published in London were short-lived, including the sixpenny weekly *Deutsche Londoner Zeitung*, founded in 1845, which mixed politics and literature and lasted until 1851, *Das Volk* (1859), *Germania* (1859), the threepenny weekly *Londoner Deutsches Journal* (1855–8) and Gottfried Kinkel's radical *Hermann* (1859). Poles, most of them much poorer than the Italians, began to arrive after the failed revolution in 1830–1, and their numbers increased after 1848. Zeno Swietosławski established a Polish printing press in Jersey in 1852, and then moved it to London in 1865,[106] and Alexander Herzen created a Russian press to smuggle materials back to Russia.[107]

Thousands of Jews fled from discrimination and pogroms in eastern Europe. It has been estimated that between 1880 and 1914 some 120,000 Jews from eastern Europe settled in Britain, about half of them in London's East End.[108] For many east European Jews, the printed book was a rarity; but they were latecomers. In the older Jewish communities, many of whose members strove to integrate into British society, education and religion, needs for reading matter were more complicated. Among Jewish newspapers in London (there was little publishing outside the capital), the *Voice of Jacob* and the *Jewish Chronicle* were both founded in 1841, the latter first as a fortnightly but soon as

---

104 Vizetelly, *With Zola in England*.
105 Kirchberger, *Aspekte deutsch-britischer Expansion*, pp. 217–20. For more general issues, see Ashton, *Little Germany*.
106 Brock, 'A Polish "proscrit" in Jersey'.   107 Raahman, 'Russian revolutionaries in London'.
108 Feldman, 'The importance of being English', p. 56. For background to this complicated subject, see for example Williams, *The making of Manchester Jewry* and Feldman, *Englishmen and Jews*.

a weekly. No copy seems to be known of the short-lived *Hebrew Intelligencer*, published as early as 1823. The first Yiddish paper, the *London Jews' Weekly Times*, appeared in 1867.[109] At the end of the century, specialist printing houses in the East End of London produced not only the liturgical, biblical and legal essentials of religious practice. Israel Narodiczsky, who arrived in London in 1896 and established himself as a printer in Whitechapel, had close contacts with left-wing politics, but printed whatever would make a living, including even lives of Jesus and St Paul.[110]

With the exception of Jews in the last decades of the century, the long-term numbers of these refugees were not especially large. Many returned home when amnesties allowed. Others, by no means all political refugees, were simply passing through, en route from the European mainland to Liverpool and America.

Topographies of the book trades

In all this, London publishing, printing and bookselling dominated as it had always done. Edinburgh was of declining importance, to its chagrin: in 1897 the loss of the *Encyclopaedia Britannica* to two American entrepreneurs, after the ninth edition had been published by A. & C. Black, was felt almost as a personal affront. National pride was damaged. Of firms founded in Edinburgh, John Murray had moved south in the eighteenth century. William Blackwood remained staunchly, and successfully, in Edinburgh, the firm's prosperity built partly on its magazine and partly on the novels of George Eliot. William and Robert Chambers founded *Chambers's Edinburgh Journal* in 1832, only a few weeks before Charles Knight published the first *Penny Magazine*, the brothers thus having a fair claim to be the pioneers in cheap journal publishing. They moved part of their operation to London in 1853, and in 1859–68 published *Chambers's encyclopaedia* in penny-halfpenny weekly parts for a total of just £4 10s. Thomas Nelson, with a large printing business on the outskirts of Holyrood Park as well as a long list of publications in which cheap colour printing was a major selling point, remained based in Edinburgh and opened offices in London, New York and Paris. Among the smaller firms, William Nimmo had at the front of its list the works of the best-selling geologist and evangelist Hugh Miller: the firm had offices in both Edinburgh and London. Alexander Strahan opened his business in Edinburgh in 1858, but quickly

---

109 Fraenkel, *The Jewish press in Great Britain*.   110 Sanders, *Jewish books in Whitechapel*.

realised that his popular religious magazine *Good Words* required closer collaboration with English booksellers, authors and readers: he moved to London in 1862.

Though some other cities and towns provided the resources for working within the book trades on a national scale, in practice they were few. In Glasgow, the firm of William Collins had been founded in 1819, and had a strong educational list. As a Scottish printer it was also able to challenge the English privileged presses in printing the Bible, to the dismay of Oxford, Cambridge and Eyre & Spottiswoode: with close links to the stationery trade, it reached parts of the market where the other presses were at a disadvantage. Some of the largest cities, such as Manchester, Glasgow, Liverpool and Birmingham, provided environments in which new publishers could make their way, but in order to expand it was necessary to be in London, or at least to have a London agent.

In England, one of the largest publishers measured according to numbers of books produced was William Nicholson in Halifax, who printed books on the cheapest paper and cased them in cloth. As most of their list was out of copyright, there was usually no need to pay royalties or fees. In the 1870s, the Cottager's Library offered collected editions of Burns, Byron and Longfellow alongside *Maria Monk*, *Uncle Tom's cabin* and *The Scottish chiefs*, besides an assortment of more recent fiction, at just a shilling a volume in cloth, including a coloured plate printed by Kronheim. William Walker, in Otley, made a point of advertising that they published copyright works, and their 32mo Cottar's Library, with volumes containing up to 448 pages at just a shilling apiece, often with frontispieces engraved on steel, was an obvious competitor in this field that depended so much on bulk for any profits; they also worked hard at the popular religious market, and much of their list was priced at sixpence or less. The third of these cheap Yorkshire publishers was also by far the largest. Milner & Co. made their name in Halifax, before moving to London and the centre of the book trade in Paternoster Row. For a while they had links with two other cheap publishers, George Clark in Aberdeen and J. M. Burton in Ipswich. By 1895 it was claimed that the firm had sold 183,000 copies of Burns and 127,000 of Byron. Keats, published by the firm in the late 1860s, had sold only 3,500 copies in about thirty years.[111] More like most publishers, Jarrold in Norwich built a list partly on religion and partly on children's books and novels. *Black Beauty*, now the firm's most famous book, was only cautiously received by London booksellers in 1877. The firm

---

111 Details from Wroot, 'A pioneer of cheap literature'. See also *William Milner of Halifax*.

traced its history to 1770, and in 1847 established its publishing business mainly in London, whilst retaining its printing in Norwich. In Newcastle, the Walter Scott Publishing Company was founded in 1882. First there, and later in London, it built up a list not just of cheap reprints, but also including translations of Ibsen and the early work of George Bernard Shaw.[112] In Bristol, J. W. Arrowsmith became celebrated as publishers of Jerome K. Jerome's *Three men in a boat* (1889), the Grossmiths' *Diary of a nobody* (1892) and the novels of Anthony Hope. Macmillan was founded in Cambridge in 1843, but following the death of Daniel Macmillan in 1857 the publishing side was moved to London under the guidance of Alexander Macmillan, whilst the Cambridge bookselling business was left in the hands of his nephew Robert Bowes.

The book trades did not necessarily follow the most profitable manufacturing industries and the largest shifts in population. The percentage in England and Wales of Londoners employed in printing dropped from 46 per cent in 1861 to 40 per cent in 1891, partly reflecting the growth in provincial newspaper and magazine printing during this period.[113] On the other hand, the percentage of bookbinders in the capital remained more or less steady, at 62–65 per cent. Manufacturers of book cloth had a natural affinity with Lancashire.[114] Among the new manufacturers of composing machines, the Linotype Company (fig. intro.1) built a factory at Altrincham, in Cheshire, in 1897, and the Lanston Monotype Corporation built its factory near Redhill, in Surrey, in 1899–1900. In 1841, just under half of those employed in typefounding in Great Britain were in London. In 1891, on the eve of Linotype and Monotype expansion, 67 per cent of those in England and Wales alone were in London. By the end of the nineteenth century, no fewer than seven different firms in Otley, north of Leeds, were manufacturing Wharfedale printing machines, and supplying the world (fig. intro.2).[115] Seventy years earlier, Otley had been a small market town in the Yorkshire countryside. Geographically, manufacturing and printing followed different routes. That of publishing was different again, though changes in the census occupational groupings do not permit long-term comparisons. Without the railway network these various developments would have been impossible. While London stood at the centre, its position maintained by the spokes of the national railway map just as it had been by the same features of the main road system, the provincial trade grew. Vitally, it did not do so entirely at the expense of the capital.

112 Turner, *The Walter Scott Publishing Company*.
113 Details of this and of typefounders (below) from the census returns on employment.
114 Tomlinson and Masters, *Bookcloth 1823–1980*.
115 Wood, 'Otley and the Wharefedale printing machine'.

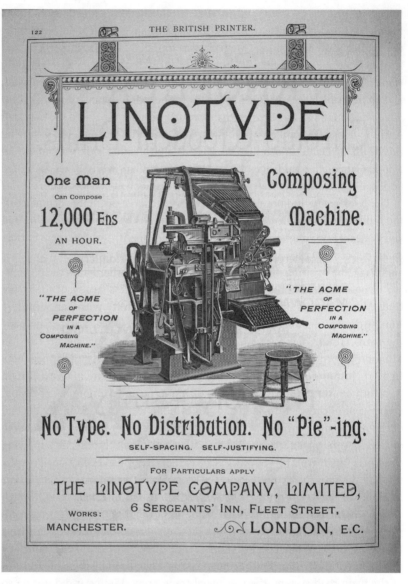

Intro.1 Advertising for the Linotype composing machine. *The British Printer* July–August 1891. (Private collection)

Intro.2 Advertising for the 'latest improved' Wharfedale press, using a typeface derived from one introduced by Caxton. *The British Printer* September–October 1891. (Private collection)

The decennial census returns amalgamate paper, printing, books, stationery and yet more in the descriptors for employment; but under this broad range of activities the increasing presence of women is clear to see. In 1841, about 6,000 women came under these heads, a figure that almost trebled to 16,000 in 1851, and more than trebled again, to 53,000, by 1881. In bookbinding, female labour dominated in the second half of the century, and in London by 1891 it represented 60 per cent of the workforce. While the largest numbers were employed in bookbinding and bookselling, the lower cost of employing women encouraged their use in printing. The masthead of the *Family Herald* newspaper in 1842 showed two women engaged at the new machinery for typesetting – an obvious challenge to the high wages traditionally paid to compositors. The 1841 census had recorded 183 women employed in printing in Great Britain, forty-three of them under the age of 20. Emily Faithfull, founder in 1860 of the Victoria Press whose purpose was to employ women for all but the heaviest work, quoted Gladstone: 'The printer's monopoly is a powerful combination, which has for its first principle that no woman shall be employed – for reasons obvious enough – viz., that women are admirably suited for that trade, having a niceness of touch which would enable them to handle type better than men.'[116] But the largest increases in female employment occurred in the 1890s, when numbers grew 42 per cent in a decade, before easing to a 30 per cent increase between 1901 and 1911. In the 1890s, male employment in these industries grew more slowly, by only 19 per cent. Whereas in 1851 women constituted a little under a quarter of the relevant workforce, by 1911 they were well over half.

By no means all the extra women were employed as binders or (in early twentieth-century Scotland) as compositors.[117] Publishers' offices, stationery manufacture and bookshops all absorbed large amounts of female labour. In the first decade of the new century the number of women in domestic and personal service grew even faster than it did in the book, stationery and related trades. Growth did not reflect outright numbers in the national workforce as a whole, and child labour was a constant presence in the world of printing where boys had by long tradition been employed from a young age. Domestic service and the textile, clothing and food trades all employed more women than did the book and stationery trades. But, for women, these latter trades provided increasing employment. In 1851, about 0.6 per cent of employed women were

---

116 Faithfull, *Three visits to America*, p. 24; see also Fredeman, 'Emily Faithfull and the Victoria Press'.
117 For Scotland, see Reynolds, *Britannica's typesetters*. More generally, see MacDonald, *Women in the printing trades*.

in these trades. In 1911 the figure was about 2.7 per cent. The comparable figures for men were 0.9 per cent and 1.9 per cent.[118]

British books in a wider world

In common with other volumes in this series, this one is concerned with the book in Britain. Immigrant communities, with their own linguistic, religious and historical demands, contributed to the shaping both of imports and of British printing and publishing. But their demands, and their contributions, were small compared with the consequences of emigration and of Britain's global expansion.[119]

The Treaty of Paris in 1815 left Britain in possession of a greater portion of the known world than any previous European power: by 1911, the estimated population of the British Empire had grown from 355.5 million in the mid-1880s to 434.3 million. Thanks to its overseas possessions, thanks also to a merchant navy that dominated international trade, and thanks to the linguistic policies and assumptions of the United States of America in assimilating immigrants from Europe, West Africa, the Caribbean and China, English was a world language by the end of the century. Quite apart from ordinary trade in printed matter, and quite apart from pockets of English-language publishing by local entrepreneurs, English-language newspapers were published not just in countries of the Empire, but also in the Argentine Republic, Brazil and Colombia (Panama); in China (Hong Kong, Shanghai, Tientsin), Siam and Japan (Kobe, Nagasaki, Tokyo and Yokohama); in Egypt, Sudan and Morocco; and in the older markets of Belgium, Denmark, France, Germany and Italy. Migration, both from the shores of Britain and Ireland and re-migration between colonies, further shaped shifting demands. Between 1853 and 1915, about 4.7 million people left England and Wales, and 0.9 million left Scotland, for places beyond Europe.[120] Some returned, but migrants always took with them languages and assumptions that bound them in some degree to their home countries. Colonies, wrote General Booth in 1890, 'are simply pieces of Britain distributed about the world, enabling the Britisher to have access to the richest parts of the earth'.[121] Partly for this reason, overseas developments, and overseas communications, had as great an effect on the structures and practices of authorship and publication as did any change within what geographers,

---

118 Mitchell, *British historical statistics*, p. 104. 119 See also below, chapter 17.
120 Woods, 'The population of Britain in the nineteenth century', p. 309. See also below, p. 39.
121 Booth, *In darkest England and the way out*, p. 144.

publishers and traditional parlance reaching back to classical times referred to as the British Isles.[122]

But this did not happen all of a sudden, in 1815 any more than in the early or mid eighteenth century. Imperial consciousness dawned only gradually, and in some respects it was as remarkable for what it did not pursue as what it did.[123] The slave trade had been officially abolished by Act of Parliament in 1807, but that did not mean the end of slavery, or of ways of thought. It was formative in shaping public morality, both directly as the social, religious and commercial implications of the slow process of emancipation were worked out in the colonies, and indirectly as missionaries pursued their callings in Africa where slavery and the slave trade remained widespread. Nor was the world of British books – authorship, publishing and reading – synonymous with the British Empire, for it extended (to take just two, very large, examples) to the United States and to South America.[124] Quite apart from the Irish exodus, over half of all emigrants from England, Wales and Scotland in the second half of the century went to the United States, where a competitive and increasingly profitable domestic market clashed with British publishing.

The rise to dominance of English as a world language came about thanks both to the United States of America and to Britain. By 1913 it was estimated that about 160 million people spoke English, out of a world population of 1,623 million – about 10 per cent of the whole. German was next, at 130 million, and French was known to 70 million.[125] Such figures were little more than approximate estimates, and they are open to various interpretations; but they do demonstrate relativities in the major European languages. The effect of this dominance on British publishing was complicated. As American domestic publishing developed a home market in a society made up of a mixture of self-confident city cultures and of pioneering exploration and settlement, so dependence on British books diminished. Colonial patterns of publishing, led by London, had survived the revolution, but by the 1820s they were being replaced. Publishers in Boston, New York and Philadelphia competed to issue American editions of British authors. Later on they were joined in competition by Chicago and Cincinnati. In the absence of any copyright protection for non-American authors until the Chace Act in 1891, there was no need to heed any

---

122 See above, p. 10.   123 For some aspects of this, see Porter, *The absent-minded imperialists*.
124 For the United States, see Michael Winship, below, pp. 608–13. For South America, see for example Davies, 'The Welsh book in Patagonia'; Roldán Vera, *The British book trade and Spanish American independence*.
125 *Whitaker's almanack* 1914, p. 853.

original British arrangements for publication: a very few did so out of courtesy. British publishers complained at this freedom, and they were powerless.[126]

Whatever the large number of British authors involved, the American market was of mixed direct profit to London and Edinburgh. The position elsewhere was yet more complicated. Though constitutionally attached to Britain, the relatively small population of Canada (even in 1911 the total, other than chiefly French-speaking Quebec, was only 5.2 million, compared with a total of about 92 million in the United States) was the cause of frequent trade skirmishes between American and British interests fighting for the same market. Other areas were much more important to the book trades. Between 1851 and 1860 alone, almost 500,000 people emigrated from Britain to Australia, many of them in search of gold in Victoria and New South Wales.[127] In 1901, the year of federation, the population was about 4.1 million (aborigines were not counted until 1911). As in the United States, by no means all immigrants spoke English as their first language, but it was easily the dominant one. In India, the market was very much larger thanks to the demands of education, a heavy military presence and a civil service made up largely of expatriates; in the 1890s there were about 20,000 white men employed in the Indian Civil Service and in the Colonial Service, as well as about 146,000 in the army.[128] New Zealand, first colonised by British settlers when Church Missionary Society evangelists arrived in 1814, had by 1911 a population of only just over one million, slightly smaller than the European population of South Africa. English-language books, in demand from the Mediterranean to the Cape of Good Hope, in the West Indies, in South America and in the Far East, all drew on the British book trade, and their readers contributed to it. For this was not just an export market from which profits could be extracted partly by careful manipulation of copyrights. Authors in all parts of the world depended on British publishers to see their work into print and brought before more than the most local of audiences.[129]

It is easy to assume in all this a high level of demand for reading matter. In practice it was irregular, and reflected the needs and expectations of migrants and others from widely differing social and educational backgrounds. Those fleeing from the Irish famine, those chasing gold in California or in Australia, those persuaded to help build the Canadian agriculture and forestry industries in the later part of the century, those sent overseas on military or government service, those transported for crime, those called to missionary endeavour,

126 Seville, *The internationalisation of copyright law*. See also below, chapters 5 and 17.
127 Jupp (ed.), *The Australian people*, p. 35.
128 Searle, *A new England?*, p. 23. But cf. the rather lower figures given in *Whitaker's almanack*.
129 See below, chapter 17. See also Eggert and Webby (eds.), *Books & empire*.

those seeking better opportunities of all kinds in Australia, New Zealand or South Africa: many had little or no direct need for printed books, though many others again depended on them.

By the late 1840s, London was well supplied with specialist newspapers providing intelligence from distant parts of the empire. Some were critical of government. Advertising for the *Colonial Gazette* spoke of 'the least responsible department of Government, the Colonial-office', while at the same time drawing attention to the new opportunities for investment whether in railways or in land once the post-emancipation disturbances had run their course.[130] The *New Zealand Journal* likewise alluded to recent disturbances, adding more hopefully that the number of immigrants must mean that there was considerable interest in Britain.[131] W. H. Allen & Co.'s *Indian Mail* ('published on the arrival of the Marseilles portion of the *Indian Mail*') and the *Indian Post* sought to present condensed accounts selected from a number of Indian newspapers. Rather than purchase such summaries, another course was to buy the original newspapers published overseas. Simmonds & Ward's Foreign Newspaper Office, in the City, existed to provide for just such requests. They claimed to hold files of the leading newspapers from all over the world, and they offered titles for sale from the West Indies, the Cape of Good Hope, Australasia, South America, the main east coast cities of America, and Canada, as well as from the East Indies and China. Conversely, they took in advertisements for many countries.[132]

News was not only imported. In 1843 the Liverpool booksellers Willmer & Smith launched the *Liverpool European Times*, a project whose connections reached far beyond Europe. Apart from claiming a wide circulation in British and Irish newsrooms, it was aimed mainly at the American and West Indies markets. Publication dates were arranged to coincide with steamer sailings to Boston, and to catch the *Great Britain* and the *Great Western* when they were departing. In London, the *Home News* offices at Westminster founded separate series of *Home News* for export to India and China in 1847 (sent via Brindisi), and for Australia and New Zealand in 1852. With the opening of South Africa, the *Empire* (founded in 1870), the *South African Mail* (1876) and the *South African* (1880s) all sought out new export markets. Most ambitious of all was the *European Mail*, also established in 1843 and by the 1880s divided amongst eight different editions for different parts of the world, with sections also in Spanish and French. It depended heavily on advertising, and was

---

130 Charles Mitchell, *The newspaper press directory* 1846, p. 368.   131 *Ibid.*, p. 78.
132 Advertisement in *ibid.*, p. 423.

perhaps the first newspaper that could be said to be published globally. The monthly edition prepared for the east claimed to reach India, Burma, Egypt, China, Japan, Ceylon, Penang, Singapore, Siam, Sumatra, Java, Borneo, the Philippines, Mauritius and other places besides. West Africa likewise had a monthly edition, while the edition for South Africa, St Helena and Ascension was published every Thursday.[133]

In the 1840s, newspapers could be sent free of charge to all the British dominions, and could be received likewise from all except Canada. But in most people's experience, the Empire was knit together not so much by newspapers or books as by correspondence and by stale news, the thousands of letters that made their ways along the shipping lanes, and the weeks-old newspapers that were received on opposite sides of the world.[134] As telegraphic links were built up into a global network, a new world-wide rapidity of communication complemented, and eventually replaced, centuries-old familiarities of time and distance. With the telegraph cable successfully installed between Dover and Calais in 1851, Britain was no longer literally cut off from mainland Europe. The first successful Atlantic cable, completed in 1866, eight years after the first attempt had failed after working for only just over two months, was a modern marvel.[135] Overland communication with India, and then (again under the ocean) with Australia in 1872 transformed ways of thinking as well as business, government and social practices. Radio signals improved speed further, and Marconi's first commercial transatlantic service opened in 1907. Such developments supplemented, and even interpreted, existing media. But they could not by themselves replace the written and printed word. It was not just that these new media were expensive to use. In the early1870s the American Associated Press paid £100 to transmit the Queen's speech at the opening of Parliament across the Atlantic, and it commonly paid half that and more to transmit an ordinary day's news. Between 1872 and 1891 the Australia rate was ten shillings a word.[136] More importantly, the formalities of print, embodied in statutes and government documents, defined communities and countries in their own ways, and gave credence to administration. For many, the Bible was the unifying medium. But the real strengths of print lay in its variety, in its durability combined with flexibility, and in its relation to the written and spoken word.

---

133 Advertisement in *May's British & Irish press guide* 1883, p. 187.
134 See for example Laidlaw, *Colonial connections*; Bowen, *The business of empire*, ch. 6. Though concerned primarily with northern India, and usually with more local phenomena, Bayly, *Empire and information*, raises similar issues.
135 Bright, *The story of the Atlantic cable*; Headrick, *The invisible weapon*.
136 Headrick, *The invisible weapon*, p. 40; Grant, *The newspaper press* 2, pp. 346–9.

In 1887, Walter Besant was just one amongst many who realised that the pattern of European colonisation meant that any future war would be fought on a world scale.[137] That was also just one of the differences to be seen as he looked back over fifty years, to the accession of Queen Victoria. Mass tourism can in some respects be traced to the reopening of most of Europe following the end of the French revolutionary wars, and the downfall of Napoleon. Paris was quickly crowded with visiting English, and Galignani's English and foreign-language bookshop, founded in 1801, thrived in the rue Vivienne. By 1827, Edward Planta's *New picture of Paris*, a popular guidebook, was in its fifteenth edition. Greater change came with the railways, as the middle classes made their way south to the cities and sights previously the privilege of those able to afford the time and the money to travel more slowly. Murray's *Handbook for travellers on the continent*, of which the first edition appeared in 1836, became essential luggage for generations of British tourists.[138] The market for English-language books that followed 1815 was of a kind and on a scale far different from that seen in the eighteenth century. Across most of Europe, reading rooms with English-language books and newspapers became expected features of at least the larger towns.[139] With this market came, increasingly persistent and challenging, questions of European copyright. Galignani and Baudry in Paris, Tauchnitz and Fleischer in Leipzig, and Louis Hauman, Adolph Wahlen and others in Belgium were well known not only to travellers, but also to people in Britain as their books were gradually brought back and smuggled past the customs at the Channel and North Sea ports.[140] The tacit and illicit trade in Tauchnitz editions survived, and thrived, until the Second World War.

The poor man's library

While the ability to appreciate – at least in part – the importance or significance of a book does not necessarily depend on an ability to read it, questions of literacy underlie most of this volume. Just as the term literacy itself denotes a range of skills and values, so also the functions and meanings of books vary

137 See also Burroughs, 'Defence and imperial disunity', with further references.
138 Lister, *A bibliography of Murray's handbooks for travellers*. English versions of the guides published by Baedeker in Coblenz and later Leipzig first appeared in the mid-1860s: see Hinrichsen, *Baedeker's Reisehandbücher*. See further below, chapter 13.
139 See for example Desideri (ed.), *Il Vieusseux*; Parent-Lardeur, *Les cabinets de lecture*; Parent-Lardeur, *Lire à Paris*.
140 Barber, 'Galignani and the publication of English books'; Barnes, 'Galignani and the publication of English books in France; a postscript'; Cooper-Richet and Borgeaud, *Galignani*; Todd and Bowden, *Tauchnitz international editions in English*; Godfroid, *Aspects inconnus et méconnus de la contrefaçon en Belgique*.

among their users. For individuals, the meaning of literacy ranges from the most basic ability to spell out a word, through functional ability, to comfortable understanding for enjoyment. At one of the most basic levels of competence, in 1830, about 50 per cent of brides getting married in England were able to sign their names, and both partners were able to sign in about 43 per cent of cases. By 1901 the figures had risen respectively to about 98 per cent and 95 per cent.[141] Variations in ability in different parts of the country depended not just on town and country distinctions (in a population that was migrating so much from country to town this is not surprising), but also on local traditions. The new industrial cities did not guarantee literacy: indeed, the long hours required of children as factory workers allowed scant opportunity to learn. In Wales in 1861, bridal ability to sign was low in almost all areas.[142] Change did not come uniformly, or rapidly, after the 1870 Education Act, and the succeeding legislation, like the value of what was taught in school, continued to elude many.

For most books and for most people, price is the main determinant in decisions about purchase as distinct from borrowing or ignoring. The eighteenth-century circulating libraries, with their stocks of novels, travel literature and essays, offered one way of overcoming price, a subscription giving access to much more than could be bought, or housed at home.

The popular educator and literary scholar George Lillie Craik made an economic point when he wrote in the early 1830s – the beginning of our period – that

> the habit of reading is extending itself rapidly, even among the humblest ranks. A book is emphatically the poor man's luxury: for it is of all luxuries that which can be obtained at the least cost. By means of itinerating libraries for the country, and stationary collections for each of our larger towns, almost every individual of the population might be enabled to secure access for himself to an inexhaustible store of intellectual amusement and instruction, at an expense which even the poorest can scarcely feel.[143]

'So far as the humbler orders were concerned', wrote William Chambers sixty years later, 'it almost appeared as if the art of printing, through certain mechanical appliances – particularly the paper-making machine and the printing-machine – was only now effectually discovered.'[144] Chambers was in

---

141 Woods, *The demography of Victorian England and Wales*, pp. 147–8. For fuller remarks on literacy, see below, chapter 7.
142 Woods, *The demography of Victorian England and Wales*, fig. 4.14 (colour section, p. d).
143 [Craik] *The pursuit of knowledge under difficulties* 2, pp. 2–3.
144 Chambers, *Memoirs of William and Robert Chambers*, p. 230.

the van of cheap printing, but Charles Knight was close behind. By means of the *Penny Magazine* (1832–), the *Penny cyclopaedia* (1833–58) and other innovations, all designed to reduce and then keep down the cost of reading, Knight laboured to extend reading to ownership. The *Penny Magazine* was by no means the only periodical marketed at this price, but it had the advantage of being copiously illustrated. At its zenith, it was claimed to have a circulation of 200,000 copies per month.[145] Whether in his enthusiastic embracing of stereotype printing, which allowed him to reuse woodcuts many times over again in picture books (so, incidentally, spreading costs and increasing profits), or in his experiments with cheap colour printing, or in his innovative maps, Knight set an example that others were quick to exploit. Cheap books became a reality. Knight died in 1873. By then, the Society for the Diffusion of Useful Knowledge, in which he and Lord Brougham were leading figures,[146] had slipped into a much reduced afterlife. This apart, Knight left a legacy not only of cheap literature but also of changes in public attitude. While some parts of the market enjoyed the advantages of technology that produced ever more elaborate publications, the price of older titles had by the 1880s dropped unrecognisably. For new titles, prices remained high – thanks not just to copyright protection, but also (in the view of Matthew Arnold) because of commercial lending libraries 'eccentric, artificial and unsatisfactory to the highest degree'.[147]

Always, price was critical. Expensive books were beyond the reach of most people, and publishers structured their programmes so as to reap as much benefit from each part of the market in turn, from highly priced first editions through smaller formats, smaller type and cheaper paper and bindings, to, eventually, for some books, prices at sixpence and below. For this, copyrights might be retained, or they might be licensed to specialist cheap houses. For authors, the benefits were not always financially obvious. For self-publishers, and not least for social reformers, the ability to control one's own literary destiny was an advantage.

It seems that literacy and the wider ability to read had its effect on the size of the population. While publications on contraception were more widely available (and generally more authoritative than the traditional *Aristotle's masterpiece*) after the 1870s, population historians are uncertain as to their effectiveness in themselves. Schoolchildren were examined in their knowledge of human reproduction well before the question became a *cause célèbre* with the

---

145 Timperley, *Encyclopaedia of literary and typographical anecdote*, p. 920; Altick, *The English common reader*, p. 335.
146 Gray, *Charles Knight*, pp. 43–80.
147 Arnold, 'Copyright'; see also Altick, *The English common reader*, p. 310.

unsuccessful prosecution in 1877 of Charles Bradlaugh and Annie Besant for publication of Charles Knowlton's *Fruits of philosophy*, a book first published at New York in 1832. The case prompted huge popular interest and demand: annual sales, formerly of about 700, were now increased both by the legal publishers and by pirated copies: 125,000 copies of the authorised edition were sold in the three months preceding the trial.[148] Annie Besant's own sixpenny *Law of population* (1879) sold about 170,000 copies within about thirteen years, and H. A. Allbutt's usefully detailed sixpenny pamphlet *The wife's handbook* (1884 or 1885) sold many more again: when he was struck off the Medical Register, sales simply increased.[149] Conscious social and economic decisions about family size, whether informed or not by so-called 'Malthusian' pamphlets, books or newspaper debate, were instrumental in the late nineteenth-century decline in the birth rate. But, as always, printed instruction was more easily available to some parts of the population than others. Part of Annie Besant's defence for publishing *Fruits of philosophy* rested on the fact that she was making available for sixpence what richer people could buy at W. H. Smith's bookstalls (she claimed) for 2s 6d, 5s. or 6s.[150]

But cheapness was not, in everybody's mind, good in itself. In 1833, the novelist and politician Edward Bulwer-Lytton reflected on the rage for cheap publications, and sought to demonstrate a danger in diluting the press's output:

> Cheap publications of themselves are sufficient for the *diffusion* of knowledge, but not for its *advancement*. The schoolmaster equalizes information, by giving that which he possesses to others, and for that very reason can devote but little time to increasing his own stock.[151]

Comprehension and reading ability, as distinct from the most fundamental competencies, were linked to educational attainment. Insofar as reading depends on practice and developing experience, they were also linked to expectations. Charlotte Mary Yonge, influential alike as a successful novelist and as a promoter of Sunday schools and of parish visiting, assumed that girls and women would incline to stories and to fiction.

---

148 *In the High Court of Justice, Queen's Bench Division, June 18th, 1877; The Queen v. Charles Bradlaugh and Annie Besant* [1877], pp. 30–1, 125–7, 149. For Knowlton, who developed a respected reputation, see Horowitz, *Rereading sex*. For Britain, see also Porter and Hall, *The facts of life*.
149 Teitelbaum, *The British fertility decline*, pp. 200–10; Woods, *The demography of Victorian England and Wales*, pp. 144–50.
150 *In the High Court of Justice, Queen's Bench Division, June 18th, 1877; The Queen v. Charles Bradlaugh and Annie Besant* [1877], pp. 30, 139.
151 Edward Bulwer-Lytton, *England and the English*, book 4, ch. 3.

Though men either read with strong appetites or not at all, their wives, in these days of education, generally love fiction. They do not want to be improved, but they like to lose their cares for a little while in some tale that excites either tears or laughter. It is all very well to say that they ought to have no time for reading. An ingenious or thrifty woman has little or none, but the cottager's wife who does as little needlework, washing or tidying as possible, has a good many hours to spend in gossip or reading.[152]

In such a world-picture, the need was at least as much to avoid reading the wrong kind of book – sensational novels, or (for boys) tales of Jack Sheppard and other criminals or undesirables – as to develop knowledge or skills. Children needed to be kept off the streets after dark, and directed reading would achieve it. If children could not attend school during the working week, Sunday schools provided one means to learning – and to reward. Though Yonge wrote in the 1880s, the underlying social challenge was little different from that which had faced Brougham and the founders of mechanics' institutes half a century earlier. And, still, the hoped-for middle-class panacea proved as elusive. Printed books were more numerous than ever before. They were better printed than ever before. They were better and more attractively illustrated than ever before. They were cheaper than ever before. But, as even Harmsworth found with his unprecedentedly successful mass-market magazines, they did not suit everyone. As the owners of the new cinemas were quickly to discover in the new century, there could be stronger attractions than the book or magazine.

It was easy to forget that this search for knowledge and improvement did not have a monopoly of cheap print. For those who had no such thirst, there was a wealth of sensational reading matter priced at a penny or two (fig. intro.3). The catalogue of street ballads and song sheets issued by James Catnach of Seven Dials in London in 1832 listed about a thousand titles, including a number of small books priced at just a farthing.[153] Biographies of criminals, tales of adventure and low life, and lurid accounts of tragedies real or imaginary, had been mainstays of street literature since the early eighteenth century and earlier. Sheet ballads had been printed since the sixteenth century. Their printing, however poor in execution, was well organised; and channels of distribution in the hands of pedlars and hawkers, in markets and fairs, were easily adapted to shifts in population. Such material was familiar in villages and country towns as well as in the cities. The well-meaning efforts of Knight and Brougham, of the Religious Tract Society, of the Bible Society and of other groups had

152 Yonge, *What books to lend and what to give*, p. 7.
153 Reproduced in Shepard, *The history of street literature*, pp. 216–23. See also below, pp. 68, 296.

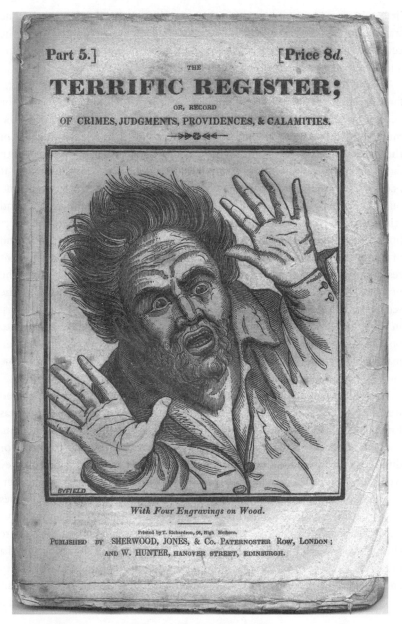

Intro.3 *The Terrific Register*. Published in London and Edinburgh in the 1820s by two of the most prolific publishers. Like many of its kind it was issued in undated parts, each part simply taking up the tale – often mid-sentence – where the previous one had ended. (Private collection)

little relevance to this market other than in seeking to match it in price.[154] The trade continued. Sensational ballads were still widely available at the end of the century, and cheap journals and pamphlets undercut attempts by publishers and reformers to raise moral or literary standards.

The disadvantages as well as the advantages of print were old subjects, familiar since the fifteenth century. The origin of such anxieties lay in the ancient world. Further developed, they expressed fears of there being too much, of there being no means of arranging and selecting the outpourings of the press. But if the seventeenth century found much to alarm, the nineteenth faced problems on a vastly greater scale. By the late eighteenth century it became almost fashionable in some circles to decry sensational novels, and many other people held deeper moral anxieties. The nineteenth century had still greater cause for concern. The battle against immorality began with street literature, the Religious Tract Society expressing in its very title both the kind of enemy and the kind of armoury with which to repel it. But the fear of print reached much further up the social and educational scale. It reached into the private circulating libraries. It reached into the new public libraries of the second half of the century. It reached to Thackeray's portrayal of Becky Sharp in *Vanity Fair*, and to the best-selling *Jane Eyre*. And, of course, it reached into politics and religion. Print, like literacy, was indifferent. In turn, its control, management and direction set values on it that could be assessed by economic and by social criteria.[155]

With the rise of public examinations, for the Civil Service and the army and reaching downwards through school ages, measurement of competency was formalised.[156] The practice of prize-giving was deeply embedded in education, and spread readily. Sunday-school prizes – for attendance, for reading, for different subjects and skills – were sometimes medals, but far more often they were books. Reward cards, printed in colour, offered another, and cheaper, alternative: the high-church National Society published cards depicting scenes from the life of Christ painted by old masters. Publishers found a lucrative and eager market for books that could be printed at little cost and where cheaply made cloth bindings decorated in gilt or printed in colour provided a judicious measure of attraction. Thomas Nelson, the Religious Tract Society and the Society for Promoting Christian Knowledge (SPCK) all expanded their businesses, and became omnipresent. The Sunday School Union published a

---

154 See also chapter 8.
155 For aspects of this, see for example Brantlinger, *The reading lesson*; Hiley, ' "Can you find me something nasty?" '
156 Roach, *Public examinations in England*. See further below, chapter 14.

series of 'reward books' in the 1880s, which were praised for their cheapness (prices began at ninepence) as much as for their excellence.

In the mid-nineteenth century, in the wake of the Public Libraries Act of 1850, public libraries began to offer books on a larger and wider scale, for no direct cost.[157] By no means all local authorities leapt to embrace the new possibilities of raising money from the rates to pay for such facilities. Even in 1896, towns as significant as Bath, Bury, Dover, Durham, Huddersfield, Huntingdon and Wakefield had still not adopted the legislation. If there were special reasons in Glasgow, thanks to the Mitchell Library, other towns in Scotland were no more forward than in England: Stirling, Motherwell and Dumfries figured in the same list.[158] The use of public money for mere entertainment, such as reading novels, exercised supervising committees and ratepayers alike, whereas it was just this kind of literature that was most profitable in the old commercial circulating libraries: the warring demands of fiction versus non-fiction remained a characteristic of public library funding and administration. Many of these issues had been rehearsed already in the changing priorities of book collections in the older mechanics' institutes, as earnestness fought a losing battle with frivolity. More immediately for many people, the continuing success of the commercial circulating libraries such as Mudie's and W. H. Smith, and a host of smaller ones across the country, both offered the gratification of not having to wait while others read new books, and (for the more sensitive among their customers) avoided the need to share books with the general – and dirty – public. Grimy hands and the fear of contagious disease were not the only problems. Such an attitude grew from the complexities of social structures and awareness, where money was but one distinguishing mark.

The meanings of print

In the present volume as in others in this series, the term 'book' bears more than its most obvious meaning. To some people brought up in the late nineteenth century, and indeed the twentieth, the word signified what to others was a magazine. Print came fresh from the press in many forms, from bulky encyclopaedias to scraps of proprietary wrapping paper. Some was intended to have a long life. Much more was ephemeral. The study of ephemera, closely related to the history of the book, has attracted its own investigators over the last forty

157 See below, chapter 15.   158 *Greenwood's library year book* (1897), pp. 10–11.

or so years, in the wake of John Johnson, the University Printer at Oxford.[159] But amongst all this variety of printed matter, and even within the restricted realms of printed books, pamphlets and periodicals, there are no statistics that provide an adequate guide to overall output. While the trade literature and other sources can be made to reveal something of trends in the numbers of titles published, they do not tell us how many copies were printed, or even how often books or pamphlets were reprinted.[160] For this, we depend on a far from representative surviving group of publishers' and printers' archives, most of which have still to be analysed.[161] Richard Altick's classic study of *The English common reader* (1957) assembled an invaluable survey of sales figures for best-sellers (albeit many of them based on publishers' claims) and of periodical and newspaper circulation.[162] It was self-evidently a partial view, and much has been learned even of these titles since. For journal publishing, on which publishers and authors alike increasingly relied for their profits and their livelihoods, figures are perhaps especially elusive. In the world of reading, newspapers were at least as important to many people as were books. Until the abolition of stamp duty there are figures that are at least partially reliable for some kinds of newspapers. Besides these forms of output, the reading environment also encompassed (among others) advertisements, children's games and labels on packaging. As usual, it is a world for which the term 'print culture' is inadequate, since these words fail to convey the contexts of reading, composition and communication that also include the written word, pictures, theatrical spectacle, lettering in public spaces, and speech. By the end of the century they included film and recorded sound.

The book was but one form in all this. Moreover, it could itself metamorphose. Most obviously, pictures could be cut out of books, magazines or other periodicals and pasted or hung on walls. In 1881, a notice appeared in the *British Workman*, a missionary penny four-page newspaper published by S. W. Partridge. Each month, the front page was entirely taken up with a wood-engraving measuring about 15 × 11 inches with an accompanying moral tale on

159 Lewis, *Printed ephemera*; *The John Johnson collection*; James, *Print and the people*; Rickards, *The encyclopedia of ephemera*. For a study of one historical phenomenon in America, that draws substantially on both ephemeral and more permanent kinds of printed matter, see Morgan, *Protestants & pictures*.

160 Eliot, in *Some patterns and trends in British publishing*, is concerned mainly with output of titles.

161 The most convenient guide to British book trade archives, Weedon and Bott, *British book trade archives, 1830–1939*, is primarily concerned with financial records. For production figures of editions of romantic authors in Victorian times, see St Clair, *The reading nation*, appendix 13. St Clair provides a further selection of archive locations on pp. 724–6. See also below, chapter 20.

162 Altick, *The English common reader*, pp. 381–96. See also his 'Nineteenth-century English bestsellers: a further list'.

the page overleaf. When to their dismay the publishers discovered that readers were in the habit of cutting out the picture and pasting it up, they responded by advertising that the same picture could be had with the text printed alongside. Thus, image and text would accompany each other, rather than one suppress the other; and with these 'illustrated wall-papers' readers unable to visit the Royal Academy would have their own Home Academy.[163] In this way informal reuse was formalised. In thousands of other instances the original intentions of publishers were forgotten as printed matter was reused and rearranged in scrapbooks, as extra-illustration in other books, as lining paper, as wallpaper, as paper patterns for dressmaking, or simply as wrapping.[164]

One, albeit strictly limited, way of arriving at some determination of how far different kinds of books and other reading matter were shared across the population is to examine retail prices. A great deal more work remains to be done on this subject, and on the contexts of choices among luxuries and necessities of life. Like most manufacturers, publishers could only survive if they both possessed a clear sense of their market, or markets, and also understood how this knowledge could be exploited by price differentials. Publishers have always tended to concentrate on chosen parts of the market, defining their clientele according to their interests or their buying powers. But since printed books are also traded across economic, educational or other boundaries, and since evidence of ownership can be difficult to unearth, some further criteria are desirable in unravelling readerships. With the explosion of advertising in the nineteenth century we have one such extra potential. By no means all books were widely advertised; but the places chosen by publishers, whether in magazines, in newspapers, in other books or in public spaces, and the contexts in which these advertisements appeared, help to locate reading socially as well as geographically. In the threepenny volumes of Cassell's National Library, a collection of reprints in small format of out-of-copyright works, there were advertisements in the 1880s for Hudson's soap, hair renewer, toothpaste, gripe water and black lead (for fireplaces) – all basic, and cheap, household necessities that many readers could be expected not just to need, but to be responsible for buying either as householder or servant. By contrast, contemporary readers of the *Quarterly Review* were waylaid with advertisements not only for books but also for pianofortes (price ten guineas and upwards), organs, educational and seaside establishments, life insurance and the ubiquitous patent medicines and

---

163 *The British Workman* May 1881, p. 66.
164 For some American practices, see Garvey, 'Scissorizing and scrapbooks'.

invalid foods. At the end of the century, the *Windsor Magazine*, an undemanding sixpenny monthly modelled on the *Strand Magazine*, and where several novels ran in parallel in each issue, depended very considerably – like its many competitors – on advertising content in order to keep the price low. Here the emphasis was, as so often in the late Victorian press, on advertisements for medicines, diet, aids to better posture, and tonics. The new fashion for amateur photography proved a fruitful source of revenue, and there was always space for advertisements for special furniture such as roll-top desks, billiard tables or patent seats. Unlike the catch-all street and railway hoardings, advertising in books and magazines could be focussed on the most likely markets, whether in the established confidence of the *Quarterly* or in the aspirations of readers of the *Windsor Magazine*.

Over all this stood questions of what was meant, or implied, by print and by the ways in which it supported, permitted or interpreted further aural or visual creativity.[165]

The transformations in illustration techniques, and the unending search for methods that combined cheapness, speed of production, and suitable quality, are explored by Michael Twyman in chapter 2. With photography and its applications, the making and reading of books underwent the greatest revolution since the fifteenth century. The earliest applications of photography to books were the work of amateurs, in the albums of cyanotypes made up by Anna Atkins from 1843 onwards to illustrate British algae, and in Henry Fox Talbot's calotype *Pencil of nature* (1844–6). With remarkable rapidity, commercial publishers moved into this new field. Some of what were to become the largest firms – Francis Frith, Joseph Cundall, James Valentine (Dundee) and George Washington Wilson (Aberdeen) – were established in the 1850s.[166] Trade editions, from firms such as Alfred W. Bennett and from general publishers such as Bell & Daldy, Murray and Nelson, replaced private publications. By the 1870s, the firm of W. A. Mansell in London's Oxford Street claimed to have a stock of over a million photographs. They were agents for Alinari in Florence, Naya in Venice, Charnaux in Geneva and Stillfried & Anderson in Japan; they had photographs of over two hundred paintings in the National Gallery and were agents for the British Museum; they were publishers of Frank Mason Good's pictures of the Middle East and stocked the work of Mrs Cameron. Defective photographs were available from them at suitably low prices, and cheap lots of scraps could be had for as little as 2s 6d.

165 Curtis, *Visual words*.   166 Gernsheim, *The rise of photography*, p. 121.

Customers could select what they wanted, and buy albums in which to mount them.

The activities of such a firm, placed in the centre of the West End amidst shops catering to a leisured market, indicated one course whereby books themselves were being redefined. The arrival of photography did not just herald new ways of making separate pictures, any more than cheaper reproduction methods led only to the illustrated book. As with the engravings and scraps of print or manuscript that were assembled by amateurs and by specialist dealers into hundreds of extra-illustrated, 'grangerised' books between the late eighteenth century and the twentieth, so photographs made every customer a potential creator of books. Mansell had its lesser equivalents in most of the major towns and centres of tourism. The publishers Ward Lock, founded in 1854 in Fleet Street,[167] who built up their business largely with remainders and by buying most of the stock of Moxon and of S. O. Beeton when these firms closed, also offered photographic albums to hold fifty or one hundred photographs, besides ones in larger format designed to hold cabinet portraits.

The discovery of ways to photograph down onto lithographic zinc plates, or onto woodblocks that could then be engraved by hand, generated excitement for artists, printers, publishers and readers alike. But it was the discovery of a way of making what became known as half-tone plates, and thus of reproducing continuous tone photography mechanically for printing on an ordinary letterpress machine at the same time as type, that brought costs dramatically down. Henry Talbot had sought such a method, but it was not until the 1880s that it was introduced into ordinary book printing. In 1896 the Harmsworth brothers launched the broadsheet *Daily Mail* priced at a halfpenny ('a penny newspaper for one halfpenny', in the words of its advertising), and later on made its reputation with its photographs, the costs supported by heavy advertising content. The widespread availability of cheap likenesses of well-known people, and the opportunities to print photographs of events, places and activities, wrought changes not just of knowledge, but of attitudes. Where a century earlier only the copper-plate and the wood-engraving had been available to disperse images and, for example, through the work of Gillray and his contemporaries to make the features of William Pitt the younger or of Charles James Fox more widely familiar than any previous member of any government, photographs and line-blocks of the aged Queen Victoria were used by newspapers and magazines covering the golden and then diamond jubilee celebrations of

---

167 Living, *Adventure in publishing*.

1887 and 1897.[168] Nonetheless, amidst a culture that was increasingly familiar with cheaply printed photographs in some parts of the press, newspapers did not adopt half-tones immediately. For all the later reputation of the *Daily Mail*, the first number contained no pictures outside the advertisements apart from two somewhat elementary line drawings for the fashion page. The first number of the *Daily Mirror*, seven years later (1903), another Harmsworth venture and aimed specifically at the women's market, likewise at first had only line blocks, and no news pictures. When Queen Victoria died, the Liberal *Daily News*, in common with other newspapers, went into mourning, with thick black rules surrounding every column of its twelve pages. But the pictures, again, were all in line, with no half-tones, and none added significantly to the news content. Six decades after the foundation of the *Illustrated London News*, the London daily press had still to learn how to use pictures. Though the first half-tone illustration in a newspaper seems to have been included in a New York paper, the *Daily Graphic* in 1880, it was not until the London *Daily Graphic* ran a special feature in 1891 that Britain saw the technology applied in a newspaper context. And it was not until 25 January 1904, when the *Daily Mirror* was transformed a few weeks after its founding into a heavily illustrated daily, that photographs were regularly printed in a British national newspaper.[169]

The latter part of the period 1830 to 1914 is remarkable for the development of recorded sound; for the development of cinema – first silent and then with sound, first in black and white and then in colour; for the development of the telegraph and of the telephone: by 1891 there were almost 100,000 telephones installed in Britain, though this figure was small compared with the enthusiasm with which the device had been adopted in the United States.[170] In their different ways, these innovations not only offered alternatives to, and developments of, what was feasible or expected with the medium of print. They also affected notions of geographical and temporal distance, and they affected the structures of social relationships. They did not require literacy.

But other extensions of ways to communicate were in existence long before the telegraph and the telephone.[171] If, as it must, the history of the book has

---

168 See for example Richards, *The commodity culture of Victorian England*, pp. 73–118.
169 Hutt, *The changing newspaper*, pp. 83–7.   170 *Whitaker's almanack* 1891, p. 632.
171 For histories of communication, see for example Briggs and Burke, *A social history of the media*; Barbier and Bertho-Lavenir, *Histoire des medias*. Gitelman and Pingree (eds.), *New media* focuses on America. For some aspects of relationships between some of the media in nineteenth-century America, see for example Gustafson, *Eloquence is power*, and her Wiggins lecture at the American Antiquarian Society, 2005, 'The emerging media of early America'.

to engage also with the history of preaching, of speech (formal and infor-mal), of oratory and with the history of the stage, it is also related, for exam-ple, to the history of music in performance. The fortunes of Novello, the music publishers, were made by the publishing demands of large-scale orato-rios and other choral works, while on a more modest scale, and in a market that was much less musically educated, John Curwen launched his printing and publishing firm with printed lesson-books for tonic sol-fa.[172] Through the music hall, so clearly and explicitly based on what was spoken or sung, further avenues of publication were explored, while domestic music-making underwent its own revolution (and with it a revolution in the scale of music publishing) accelerating rapidly thanks not least to sales of moderately priced German-made pianos that appeared in large quantities in the British mar-ket during the 1880s.[173] By no means all these various activities were uni-versally welcomed. The pipe-organ was given new life, not just in church music but also in municipal town halls. Every nuance had its effect on music publishing. In both private and public performance, from solo song to ora-torios and opera, long-standing disputes of boundaries and interpretations concerning sacred and secular proprieties dogged composers and perform-ers alike. But once arrived, the success of many modern inventions meant that they would only be abandoned when, as for example the piano roll and the recording cylinder were replaced by the gramophone record, they were superseded.

Reading[174]

For some people, the act of reading was almost a definition of the age and of nineteenth-century civilisation. In 1872, Walter Bagehot sought to explain this 'new world of inventions – of railways and of telegraphs': 'a new world of ideas is in the air and affects us, though we do not see it'. In his view, these new ideas modified 'two old sciences – politics and political economy'.[175] In reflecting on nation-making and race-making, he moved to the Australian aborigine, and sought to define why a village of English colonists was superior to a tribe of Australian indigenous people. His interest was not primarily in the different forms of social organisation, but in more mundane matters. In war, the former was obviously superior. More immediately for our present purpose, Bagehot

---

172 Cooper, *The house of Novello*; Simon, *Song and words*.
173 Ehrlich, *The piano*; for a wider European view see Simpson (ed.), *The Cambridge history of nineteenth-century music*. See also below, chapter 13.
174 See also below, chapter 7.   175 Bagehot, *Physics and politics* 1887 edition, p. 1.

then moved on to his next criterion, the means to happiness and what he called the accumulation of the instruments of enjoyment. 'The English have all manner of books, utensils, and machines which the others do not use, value or understand.'[176] Books were not only a means of memory and of education. They were themselves an indicator of racial and national superiority. They were never more so than in the hands of missionaries whose calling was to translate the gospels, and have them printed, in the tongues of parts of the world for whom written language was a novelty.

Quite apart from the ubiquity of print and manuscript, in daily newspapers, in books of all qualities and all prices, in the exploitation of the penny post (and, later, in the halfpenny post for postcards, which led to an astonishing growth where in 1890–1 no fewer than 229.7 million postcards were sent[177]), literacy in daily life became assumed. In London, efforts were made from the 1760s onwards to remove the old shop signs, hanging out over the streets and obstructing the thoroughfares, and to replace them with numbering systems for addresses.[178] Names of proprietors were instead painted on fascia boards. Public lettering, familiar in classical times and a constant presence since the renaissance, became omnipresent, labelling everything from buildings to drain covers.[179] The billsticker was a public nuisance, as he sought any possible surface for his sheets. But for at least one observer he was also 'a literary man', who 'caters for the major part of the population almost the only literature that they ever peruse'.[180] Billstickers' activities were curtailed with the advent of advertisement contractors, but the insistent presence of print and lettering remained.[181] On the railways, stations proclaimed the names of towns and villages, and the high walls that protected platforms and train sheds provided ideal sites for hoardings designed to beguile and entice captive audiences. In 1835 the amateur artist John Orlando Parry exhibited a painting of a wall in London almost entirely composed of reproductions of printed bills for theatre productions, rewards, sales, concerts and other entertainments of all kinds.[182] Omnibuses and, later, trams were mobile billboards. Printed advertisements, used since the fifteenth century for books as well as public entertainments,

---

176 *Ibid.*, p. 208.   177 *Whitaker's almanack* 1892, p. 382.
178 Larwood and Hotten, *The history of signboards*.
179 Changing tastes in such lettering have been much studied. See for example Gray, *Lettering on buildings*; Bartram, *Lettering in architecture*; Bartram, *Street name lettering in the British Isles*. For a longer perspective, see Petrucci, *Public lettering*.
180 Smith, *Curiosities*, 'The billsticker', p. 117.
181 Sampson, *A history of advertising from the earliest times*, pp. 24–7. Among the several general histories of the poster, Barnicoat, *A concise history of posters*, includes photographs of displays in London streets in the late nineteenth century.
182 Now in the possession of Alfred Dunhill Ltd. See also Curtis, *Visual words*, pp. 63–7.

pressed their messages with ever bolder typography, not just on hoardings but on any surface that would take paste. Walls were painted with further advertisements. In the more populous towns, hardly a surface was safe, and everywhere notices sought to warn, advise, inform and control a public often unfamiliar with new environments.

> Advertisements now overflow into our omnibusses, our cabs, our railway carriages, and our steamboats. Madame Tussaud pays 90l. monthly to the Atlas Omnibus Company alone for the privilege of posting her bills in their vehicles. They are inked upon the pavement, painted in large letters under the arches of the bridges and on every dead wall. Lloyd's weekly newspaper is stamped on the 'full Guelph cheek' of the plebeian penny; the emissaries of Moses shower perfect libraries through the windows of the carriages which ply from the railway stations; and, as a crowning fact, Thackeray, in his Journey from Cornhill to Cairo, tells us that Warren's blacking is painted up over an obliterated inscription to Psammetichus on Pompey's Pillar![183]

In 1907, Parliament sought to regulate the larger and more intrusive hoardings, but the principle of the ubiquity of print and lettering had long been established. The new cinema posters, gaudy and objectionable to the more sensitive, simply added to the indiscipline. Reading was a habit, even if such reading in public places was very different from the concentration required for the paragraphs and pages of books and of newspapers.[184]

Publicity

Books were used to advertise their authors' wares and skills in the seventeenth and eighteenth centuries, whether to promote medical cures or sell mathematical and scientific instruments. The link between the book trade and the trade in so-called patent medicines was well established by the mid-eighteenth century. But the second half of the nineteenth century saw the possibilities of print explored with an energy that made all previous expeditions into these realms seem hesitant, even half-hearted. As has been frequently remarked, there was a potentially valuable correlation between the avenues required to advertise and distribute books and magazines throughout the country, and the needs

---

183 [Andrew Wynter] Review of the *Scottish newspaper directory* and Hunt, *The fourth estate*, *Quarterly Review* 97 (1855), pp. 183–225, at p. 212.

184 For comparison, see for example Henkin, *City reading*; Henkin, 'City streets and the urban world of print', in Casper and others (eds.), *A history of the book in America* 3, pp. 331–45; and Fritzsche, *Reading Berlin, 1900*. For the general history of advertising, see for example Sampson, *History of advertising*; Turner, *The shocking history of advertising*.

of manufacturers in a national consumer market. The railways made distribution easier; bulk printing for customers spread from Cornwall to the north of
Scotland offered a wider and deeper penetration of the country than was to be
found even in the supposedly national newspapers.

Books became not just the medium for advertising. They were themselves
the advertising. From this it was an easy step to publishing. Pears' Soap, which
already advertised extensively, published the first edition of its eponymous
Cyclopaedia in 1897. Like *Pears' Annual* (1891–), it was the brainchild of an
advertising genius, Thomas J. Barratt. Both were regularly illustrated with
well-printed colour, depicting soap in use. In successive revisions this handy
Cyclopaedia, printed in tens of thousands of copies originally on cheap paper
and at first heavily subsidised by the company, has lasted into the present
century. Lever Brothers sought a similar market with the *Sunlight Year-Book*
in the 1890s though this never achieved the same renown. Manufacturers of
foodstuffs lent their names to cookery books and to less obvious publications
such as the *Bovril musical album*, produced for the Christmas trade in 1890.

Behind such advertising ploys lay a greater change in the book trades. The
extent to which it has ever been accurate to speak of book printing, publishing
and sale as a distinct commercial activity is by no means clear. Inventories and
other documents from the sixteenth and seventeenth centuries reveal many
businesses that depended on more than bookselling. Links between the book
trade and that in patent medicines in the eighteenth century have already been
mentioned. Many firms combined bookselling with publishing and printing,
a structure that remained common even in the late twentieth century. In the
1860s, the Manchester wholesale booksellers Harrison & Co. also advertised
themselves as stationers, die-sinkers, perfumers and general dealers in pearl,
tortoise-shell, ivory, bone, hardwood, Scotch tartan, cabinet, leather and other
fancy goods and photographic materials.[185] But to some members of the book
trade the great increase in the numbers of new publications seemed to carry
with it an assumption that booksellers could enjoy an independent existence.
This was far from universally possible. The late nineteenth century witnessed
widespread anxiety at the ways that booksellers were compromised by the
need to sell stationery and fancy goods as well as what had become regarded as
the staple stock, of books. It was generally forgotten just how recent was the
trend to specialisation, and how widespread was the continuing need to find
profits wherever possible. Few shops could afford to stock books only. In 1906,
a manual offering advice on successful bookselling included recommendations

---

185 *Business directory of London* 1869, classified directory, p. 303.

not just on newspapers but also on stocking purses and wallets, pens and writing cases, glove and handkerchief sets, typewriter supplies and clocks, cutlery and stationery. Other services might include not just circulating libraries, but also afternoon teas and an agency for domestic service.[186] Manufacturing fancy stationers such as Myers, in the City of London, provided for many such needs, besides suitably attractive presentation bindings on books of devotion, books for birthdays, and school prizes.

These were but the public manifestations of what was happening less obviously. By broadening trading bases, whether in manufacturing, publishing, distribution or retail sales, not only were risks spread and profits made complementary; more importantly, turnover was increased. By mixing sales of novelties and time-sensitive goods with the traditional sales of books that had always depended on back-lists, part of the difficulty of shortage of capital could be overcome. The principle of mixing short- and long-term goods was centuries old, and underlay the business model that mixed book and periodical publishing. But it was Harmsworth who took it to its logical next stage with a mixture of mass-market journals such as *Answers* and *Home Chat* with part publication of topical books.[187]

Newspapers, magazines and books were seen as, and became, natural mutual supports. Periodicals such as *Blackwood's Edinburgh Magazine* (1817–1980), *Bentley's Miscellany* (1837–68), *Macmillan's Magazine* (1859–1907), *Tinsley's Magazine* (1867–92) and *Longman's Magazine* (1882–1905) proclaimed even in their titles their relationships to their parent book publishers. They served both as nurseries and complements to book-publishing programmes. Not all succeeded. *Murray's Magazine* lasted from just 1887 to 1891. Thanks to their subscription-based sales the more successful titles helped to ensure a regular income. On their covers, and in their end-pages (both have usually been discarded by librarians and binders, and few sets survive in the form they were published), they provided space for advertisements, and thus for further income. Publishers, insurance companies, musical instrument makers and private educational establishments occupied most of the advertisement space available. The ideas and experience in the use of covers, endpapers and inserts was easily extended. Novels issued in monthly parts by Dickens and others were treated like magazines in this respect as well as in much of their marketing.[188] The same was true in the millions of cheaply printed novels published

---

186 *The successful bookseller.*   187 *The romance of the Amalgamated Press.*
188 See for example Patten, *Charles Dickens and his publishers.* For serial publication, see chapter 3 below.

between paper covers for less wealthy markets by Macmillan, Ward Lock, A. & C. Black, Cassell and others between the 1850s and the First World War.[189] Prices for this kind of literature were kept down not just by careful husbanding of copyright costs, by the cheapest possible materials, and by the application of newspaper-printing methods to books, but also by advertising revenues from manufacturers of proprietary medicines, brand-name foods and household goods. And, just as the publication of the novel contained between the two covers depended on the accompanying advertising, so the act of reading shifted between one part of the book and another, from the paratextual pictorial wrappers and advertisements to the central body of text and illustration.

While there could be much advantage for book publishers in also publishing fortnightly, monthly or quarterly magazines, there was a further and no less profitable motive. In the magazines of the mid-century, serialised novels moved easily from magazine to volume. *Oliver Twist* first appeared in *Bentley's Magazine* in 1837–9, before its début as a three-volume novel in 1838. *Romola* first appeared in the *Cornhill Magazine* in 1862–3, before it was published by Smith, Elder in 1863. The eighteenth century had discovered not just a market for fiction, but also that there were many people, especially women, eager to write: the magazine provided a route to publication where other routes did not.[190] By the last third or so of the nineteenth century, the demand for fiction, whether of whole novels or of short stories, provided an environment in which magazines could flourish. The fact that the magazine did not dictate length, as was to some extent true of the three-decker, made it a more flexible vehicle. *Belgravia* (1866–99), edited by M. E. Braddon, the *Pall Mall Magazine* (1893–1914), the *Strand Magazine* (1891–1950)[191] and the *Windsor Magazine* (1895–1939) were but part of this market. Though some of the best-known work of Conan Doyle (Sherlock Holmes in the *Strand*) and of Kipling (*Just So Stories*; *Stalky & Co.* in the *Windsor Magazine*) appeared in the pages of such periodicals, many of the contributors were women. These magazines encouraged and extended authorship. Most importantly for authors, publishers of magazines paid for contributions not in some perhaps far-distant royalty, but as fees.

The increasingly influential and moneyed market for women's reading depended fundamentally on fiction, but not exclusively so. It was a market heavily populated with magazines (fig. intro.4). Beeton's *Englishwoman's Domestic Magazine* (1852–) was a pioneer in some of the subjects that it discussed,

189 Topp, *Victorian yellowbacks & paperbacks.*   190 Brake, *Subjugated knowledges.*
191 Pound, *The Strand Magazine*; Jackson, *George Newnes and the new journalism in Britain*, pp. 87–117.

Intro.4 Cheap magazines. *The Ludgate Monthly*, May 1891, one of several titles launched in imitation of the *Strand Magazine* and challenging it at half the price (threepence, monthly). The *Idler*, February 1892 (sixpence, monthly) opened with Mark Twain's *The American claimant*. The *Ladies' Gazette*, 16 February 1895 (one penny, weekly) included a coloured fashion plate and several other pictures of the latest clothes, besides advice on health and on decorating the home, and a short romance about a second-hand bookseller. The *Home Circle*, 29 April 1901, '*the new ladies' paper*' (one penny, every Friday), a 24-page magazine that included two complete stories and a children's section: the half-tone illustration on the cover was unusual at this time. (Private collection)

to the point where it touched pornography.[192] *The Queen*, founded by Beeton in 1861 as a sixpenny weekly, and its various subsequent imitators of which *The Lady* (1885) was the most enduring, offered a mixture of light news, court gossip and occasional scandal, together with discussion of fashion. They aimed at the comfortable middle class, and propagated domestic values. As a broadsheet, *The Queen* broke with many of the traditions of the women's press. The changes, sometimes summarised as the 'woman question', in higher education for girls epitomised in the foundation of Girton and Newnham colleges in 1870–1, in suffrage disputes, and in the place of women in society, found their expression in the weekly and monthly press. With the foundation in 1880 of the *Girl's Own Paper*, published weekly at a penny by the Religious Tract Society and read by many adults as well, women's magazines took a new turn. It was a profitable market, and by the 1890s the range of choice had developed considerably, with several magazines priced at a penny. The short-lived weekly *Women's Penny Paper* (1888–90), campaigning for women's rights, was succeeded by the *Women's Herald* (1891–3). *Woman*, founded in 1890 as a penny weekly for 'women who do not fight for rights but are womanly without being dolls', lasted longer, until 1912. These magazines, and others like them, depended on advertising – no longer on the generic fashion plates that had decorated earlier magazines for the women's market, but on advertising from the new London department stores and on specialist suppliers of other needs.

In 1839, the publishers Saunders & Otley issued an anonymous octavo of about sixty pages, *The author's printing and publishing assistant*. It was the first of its kind, acknowledgement of a long-standing need. But though it had much of potential use, its real purpose was to offer the services of the publishers as midwives to what in its fully developed state became known after the First World War as vanity publishing. The army (it is impossible not to use the term much used at the time) of aspiring authors could not all be satisfied. Many years later, Arnold Bennett, who was employed as editor of *Woman*, knew himself to be a rare success when he had his first novel accepted by an established publisher.[193] The new breed of authors depended mostly on self-help. Partly for this, partly for self-defence, and partly for encouragement, authorship became more organised. The Society of Authors was founded in 1884 thanks to the campaigning enthusiasm of Walter Besant, expressly to represent the interests of authors in the face of publishers. Its sole predecessor, the Society of British Authors, founded in 1843, had been remarkable for its mildness even

---

192 Hughes, *The short life & long times of Mrs Beeton*, pp. 348–52. For some of these magazines, see Beetham, *A magazine of her own?*
193 Bennett, *The truth about an author.*

in its principal purpose, to seek changes in international copyright law: though it had attracted the support of many well-known authors it had failed within a few months. The circumstances of the 1880s, in a vastly larger publishing industry, demanded stronger measures: the collapse of the older society in a cocoon of amiability was not lost on Besant.[194] Others saw the needs of authors in different ways. The London Literary Society survived only briefly, but published Percy Russell's *Literary manual: a complete guide to authorship* (1886) as well as a number of authors who could find no success in the ordinary trade. For the thousands who made up what Besant firmly called the profession of letters – that is, those who made at least a substantial part of their living from their pen – some knowledge of publishing practice, of contracts and of the mechanics of printing was essential. Besant's own manual, *The pen and the book* (1899), was, like much of this advice literature, partly autobiographical.

Quite apart from Besant's distrust of the new breed of literary agents, there was a more general danger in all this literature. The more prescriptive such guides became, as they sought to give both comfort and guidance by providing apparently sure paths to successful writing, so they threatened the imagination that they sought ostensibly to foster. Authorship might, with luck, be a profession, but for every successful piece of writing that lasted more than a few months, there were tens of thousands more, whether printed in the journals available only to the comfortably off or in the hundreds of cheap periodicals costing only a penny or two. Most writing, by most authors, was forgotten after a few days. It involved a cash transaction only a little less ephemeral than most of those in everyday life. In a world where authors depended for a living on selling their stories, reviews and sketches to newspapers and magazines, there was frequently little difference between authorship and journalism, and each often depended on the other. Thousands more authors were forgotten than were remembered, or even recognised. 'Cheap books there are in plenty', wrote Besant in 1889. 'But it has now been found that the mass of the people will not buy books in order to improve themselves. They read, but they read the papers only.'[195] As usual, he was willing to subsume complicated issues to vindicate his own special pleading. Popular magazines easily outsold newspapers, and it was for such magazines that many authors wrote, not for newspapers. Authorship had changed; but so too had readers. Most of the paper used in Britain was not used for printing. Of what was printed, most was thrown away.

194 Besant, 'The first Society of British Authors'; Bonham-Carter, *Authors by profession*.
195 Besant, 'The first Society of British Authors'.

Newspapers

The present volume is necessarily concerned with many kinds of printed matter besides books, including magazines, periodicals, pamphlets and newspapers. Of these, the last requires particular attention. Newspapers are addressed and referred to frequently in the following pages, but this is not a history of the newspaper in Britain, or of journalism. Both subjects deserve treatment at more length than is appropriate or possible here.[196]

By the mid-nineteenth century the concept of newspapers as the fourth estate was well established. One writer summed it up in 1839: 'The Press, unquestionably constitutes the Fourth of the Great National Estates. The Lords, Commons, and Body Politic, that is to say, the Peoplearchy and People, comprising ... the First, Second, and Third of the Four Estates, and of the comprehensive and Constitutional whole.'[197] 'All men, now-a-days, who read at all, read Newspapers', wrote F. Knight Hunt, author of the first substantial history of the subject to appear, in 1850.[198] As founder of the *Medical Times* in 1839, and one involved in the founding of the *Illustrated London News* in 1842, as well as having experience in more ordinary newspapers, most recently in the new *Daily News* in 1846, he well understood the changes in the climate of newspapers and journalism in the 1840s. Socially, politically and financially, in many ways – but not wholly – it was many steps away from the unstamped press of the previous decade, but the theme persisted of the press as the champion of liberty and liberal thought.[199] Alexander Andrews, another journalist, offered a history of British journalism in 1859, that is, a few years after the all but total repeal of stamp duty in 1855.[200] Like Hunt, whom he nonetheless criticised, he was driven not so much by the history of his subject as by its recent progress. In 1871, James Grant, editor of the *Morning Advertiser* since 1851, divided his history of the newspaper press in such a way as to devote all the second volume to the modern press; and then he followed this in 1872 with a concluding volume on the metropolitan, weekly and provincial press.[201] He drew attention to the explosion in the number of titles that had been published since 1855, and in particular to the number of provincial papers that had been founded

---

196 Among many calls for a fuller history, see for example Lee, *The origins of the popular press in England*; Boyce and others (eds.), *Newspaper history from the seventeenth century to the present day*; Koss, *The rise and fall of the political press in Britain*. For various aspects of the nineteenth-century press, see for example Lucy Brown, *Victorian news and newspapers*; Harris and Lee (eds.), *The press in English society*; and Legg, *Newspapers and nationalism*.
197 *The fourth estate: or the moral influence of the press* By a student at law (1839), p. 1.
198 Hunt, *The fourth estate* 1, p. 1. For Hunt, see the *ODNB*.   199 See also pp. 9, 300.
200 Andrews, *The history of British journalism*.
201 Grant, *The newspaper press*; Grant, *The metropolitan weekly and provincial press*.

subsequently. Then in 1887 H. R. Fox Bourne, civil servant, human rights campaigner and editor of the radical working-class *Weekly Dispatch* from 1876 until 1887, drew on his own experiences as a journalist there and elsewhere to bring the tale up to date, drawing attention to changes in attitudes and expectations of editors, contributors and readers, and lauding the triumph of a free press in Britain if not in Ireland.[202]

All of these various histories could be criticised, sometimes for their inaccuracies and sometimes because they smacked too much of journalists' anecdotes. But they all bore witness to what was further clear in contributions to periodicals of all prices and kinds: an acute public awareness of the power of newspapers in modern times, greater even than the cheap press itself.

Histories of printing and publishing in the nineteenth century tend to quote the history of *The Times* as an example of the mechanisation of printing, and of the powers of the press. And quite rightly so. Between 1837 and 1850, the circulation of *The Times*, helped by favourable advertising rates, rose from 9,800 to 38,000 while the *Morning Chronicle* declined from 6,200 to 2,900.[203] The career of the downmarket *Daily Telegraph* was at first disastrous, until its printer acquired it from its founder as a contribution to paying off the paper's debts. Established in 1855 to take advantage of the abolition of stamp duty, it was priced first at twopence and then a penny: the appalling quality of the paper used meant that it was barely legible. But by 1870 it was claiming average daily sales of 190,885, a figure that had risen to over 240,000 by 1883. Grant compared its rise with that of James Gordon Bennett's *New York Herald*, which was said to have a circulation of about 100,000 copies in the early 1870s.[204]

While *The Times* dominated circulation and technological progress, it was but one London daily amongst many by the mid-century. Until the mid-century it was, however, the only London paper that could claim to have truly a national circulation. Just as some locally published papers at the beginning of the century – perhaps especially the radical ones – claimed circulation hundreds of miles away, many local papers in cities and larger towns outside London, Edinburgh and Dublin, morning, evening and weekly, possessed considerable influence and importance for much more than local matters. While the several hundred papers up and down the country enjoyed very much smaller circulations than the main London dailies, all these publications had their

---

202 Fox Bourne, *English newspapers*. For Fox Bourne, see *ODNB*.
203 Howe, *Newspaper printing in the nineteenth century*, p. 13.
204 Grant, *The newspaper press* 2, pp. 92–100.

own adherents, advocates and policies. Whether in mainland Britain or in Ireland, they did not simply contribute to national debate; they were part of it.[205]

Thanks to the railways and the telegraph, the national circulation of news was ever more rapid. In 1871 James Grant devoted a chapter to the electric telegraph, and particularly to the networks established by Julius Reuter.[206] Some of the mechanics of news publication remained noticeably fragmented. In other respects newspapers were drawn together, whether in common ownership or in the increasing availability and attraction of shared matter for news and entertainment. Nationally and internationally, the new industry structure was reflected in the increasingly well-organised syndication of copy and of advertising.[207] William Saunders, operating in the 1870s from 112 Strand, provided stereotype plates for the newspapers he owned throughout the country, to the point where it was said that about half of each issue consisted of copy set in London.[208] By the early 1880s, the London advertising agency Brown, Gould & Co. claimed to be able to place advertisements almost simultaneously in 250 weekly newspapers nationwide. It was by no means the only such agency. Advertising, on which most newspapers relied for their survival,[209] became a more effective tool than the printed circular that had been so widespread after the introduction of the penny post in 1840. Just as books had long since found a commonly shared reading nation, so by these several means, of common stocks, the locally based and structured newspapers acquired a mixture of shared and independent quality. Just as with books, so in newspapers, readers at opposite ends of the country could find themselves reading exactly the same matter.

A mass reading public?

From the above, it will be easily seen that though literacy and the assumption of literacy were widespread, and even embedded in the social fabric, it is difficult to define the reading public. That there were many reading publics was obvious. For the editor of Harriet Martineau's autobiography, writing in the 1870s, the 'reading public' was our 'millions', readers who would one day become leaders

---

205 Legg, *Newspapers and nationalism*, p. 174.   206 Read, *The power of news*.

207 Singleton, *Tillotsons, 1850–1950*; Turner, 'Tillotson's fiction bureau'. Comparisons with American practices are appropriate: see Johanningsmeier, *Fiction and the American literary marketplace*. For Saunders, see *ODNB*.

208 Grant, *The newspaper press* 2, pp. 349–51.

209 Brown, *Victorian news and newspapers*, pp. 15–24.

in national and local politics. For her, the term denoted a social distinction between the governing and the governed.[210]

But if *Blackwood's* and the novels and tales of Harriet Martineau represented the interests of a large and educated audience, what of the much larger part of the public who had no interest in such work? Though the phenomena were familiar by 1914, notions of a mass market and of mass media were given expression only in the 1920s and 1930s.[211] The idea of the best-seller, whatever the market, seems to have found expression only in the 1890s. Yet, while these terms made their ways into the language at these dates, the concepts were forming long before.[212] The notion of a political mass was well established, and became much associated with radicalism. The French Revolution and its aftermath had given all too recent demonstrations of the power of the crowd. But this was not the same as a mass public, still less a mass reading public. In practice, mass markets evolved constantly, and need to be defined not so much in terms of numbers, as in terms of what was being offered, or sold. The mass market that Charles Knight addressed was very different from that which bought penny stories in the early twentieth century, or supported Harmsworth's newspaper industry. It differed again from the mass market for leisure, whether Sunday excursions on the railways, the music hall or, later, football or the cinema.[213] It was different again from the market for mass-produced cheap furniture and china.

How far is it therefore possible to speak of a mass reading public for particular kinds of literature in the second quarter of the century? Charles Knight, ever to the fore in promoting the largest possible reading public, wrote of 'what the Printing-Press did for the instruction of the masses in the fifteenth century, the printing machine is doing in the nineteenth'.[214] His journal the *Printing Machine* was certainly not intended for a mass circulation: during its short-lived

---

210 Martineau, *Autobiography* 3, p. 99 (treating of North America). This example is derived from the *Oxford English Dictionary*.

211 Fraser, in *The coming of the mass market*, avoids a concise definition. Walton regards 'the coming of a genuine "mass market" for most consumer goods' as being 'an urban phenomenon of the late nineteenth and early twentieth centuries': Walton, 'Towns and consumerism', in Martin Daunton (ed.), *The Cambridge urban history of Britain*. 3. *1840–1950* (Cambridge, 2000), pp. 715–44, at p. 727. For several of the issues involved in 'mass' society in the late nineteenth and early twentieth centuries, see Searle, *A new England?*, pp. 82–115.

212 Jeremy Bentham, *An essay on political tactics* (1816), *Works*, ed. John Bowring, 11 vols. (Edinburgh, 1843) 2, pp. 301–73; Franta, *Romanticism and the rise of the mass public*. Altick, in *The English common reader*, offers on pp. 379–80 a 'chronology of the mass reading public, 1774–1900', that is, spanning the period between the copyright case of *Donaldson v. Becket* and the founding of the *Daily Mail* in 1896.

213 For some of this, see Searle, *A new England?*, pp. 538–53.

214 Quotation from the *Penny Magazine* at the head of the first number of another of Knight's periodicals, *The Printing Machine: a Review for the Many* (1834).

existence its reviews included long notices of Bentley's six-shilling editions of Jane Austen's novels, of the first edition of Manzoni's *I promessi sposi*, of Burnes's *Travels into Bokhara* and of the first collected edition of Coleridge's poetry (1834). In seeking an educated or aspirant middle-class readership, with articles on mechanics' institutes, on the new colonies and on political economy, Knight was extending and developing arguments begun in the much more successful and much more widely read *Penny Magazine*. But though in its prime the latter achieved huge circulations – its readers presumably several times the number printed – and in price competed with the very cheapest of street literature, it did not flourish at this level for more than a few years. The numbers printed of tales of popular or notorious figures such as Dick Turpin, Jack Sheppard or Blueskin were (to the dismay of social reformers) very much greater, though their manufacture and sale were spread over many years rather than the short life-span of a periodical part.[215] G. W. M. Reynolds's *Mysteries of the court of London* sold 40,000 copies a week, the same number to which the monthly *Pickwick papers* had settled down in 1836–7, only a few years earlier. In the 1840s, penny-issue novels enjoyed vast sales, most notably perhaps *Sweeney Todd* and *Varney the vampire*. Sales of street ballads from the major London specialist printers such as James Catnach or John Pitts, or P. Brereton in Dublin, were greater still. In the short term, all were outsold by *Uncle Tom's cabin*, which sold 1.5 million copies with English publishers alone in its first year.[216]

The changes in the reading public came not just with popular fiction, lurid or otherwise. It came rather with the possibilities in the 1840s of linking cheap steam printing to a cheap periodical press, and in particular cheap weekly newspapers. The new mass readerships were at first most evident, and most regular, in the newspaper and periodical trades. The first adequate national newspaper press directory for Britain and Ireland was published in 1846, and was intended primarily as an aid to advertisers.[217] It showed clearly that the number of new titles established was growing as never before: for 1845 it listed forty-six new titles, and for the first three months alone of 1846 it identified twenty-two. The number of new titles in the 1840s already outnumbered the total for the whole of the 1830s. The Liberal *News of the World*, established in 1843, cost fivepence weekly, and was printed in several editions over Friday evening and Saturday

215 [Burn] *The language of the walls*.
216 Hindley, *The life and times of James Catnach*; Summers, *A gothic bibliography*; Webb, *The British working class reader*; James, *Fiction for the working man*, with further lists of penny-issue novels; Altick, *The English common reader*; James and Smith, *Penny dreadfuls and boys' adventures*.
217 Mitchell, *Newspaper press directory* 1846.

morning, so as to ensure that as batches were sent out over the country the news should be as current as possible. Prices for newspapers outside London were generally lower, Newcastle upon Tyne, for example, having four weekly papers priced at $4\frac{1}{2}$ pence, and one at threepence, and Glasgow having a dozen published at various intervals at $4\frac{1}{2}$ pence. But even in this expanding market there were no daily papers outside London: for elsewhere, the railways were becoming of critical importance in supplying national, international and up-to-date news.

By the end of the century, with the *Daily Mail* priced at a halfpenny, and enjoying a circulation of almost a million copies as the public thirsted for news of the war in South Africa, it was at last possible to speak unequivocally of mass media. *Tit-Bits*, founded in Manchester by George Newnes, further identified this market as one possessing curiosity but short attention spans. In content and to a greater degree in expectations of their readers, the two papers were very different, but both sought support from newly literate parts of the population. By Easter 1897 the circulation of *Tit-Bits* reached 671,000. A year later, the *Harmsworth Magazine* and the *Royal Magazine* achieved circulations of a million.[218] At Middlesbrough in the first years of the new century, comic papers and sporting papers such as the *Winning Post* were bought widely. Sunday papers, a recent phenomenon, were especially popular amongst the working classes since this was the only day on which there was any real leisure to read. Local halfpenny evening papers met needs during the week.[219] Nationally, and by contrast, the circulation of *The Times*, which had dominated the Crimean war half a century earlier, was about 68,000 in the late 1870s, but had collapsed to about 38,000 in 1908, and even by 1912 under Northcliffe had only recovered to 47,500.[220] There were gulfs between the several markets in more than price; but as the new *Daily Express*, founded in 1900 by C. A. Pearson, gained ground against the *Daily Mail*, so also *The Times* fought for survival against its upmarket rivals and against upstart possible owners.

Of thirty-nine essays in one of Andrew Wynter's series of popular essays gathered from the magazines, more than a quarter were on matters having to do with communication, including advertising, photography, the telegraph in town and under the Atlantic, Mudie's circulating library, the early history of *The Times*, and railways. In an earlier collection he had also written about

---

218 Altick, *The English common reader*, p. 396; Friederichs, *The life of Sir George Newnes*; Jackson, *George Newnes and the new journalism in Britain*.
219 Bell, *At the works*, pp. 206–8.
220 *The history of The Times: the twentieth century test, 1884–1912*, pp. 118, 768, 770.

W. H. Smith, Reuters, shop windows, map printing and the Post Office. Modern wonders of communication and shopping were an integral part of a world view, albeit one that was predominantly metropolitan.[221]

Towards 1914

The Victorian age was identified and named several years before it was completed. Jubilee celebrations in 1887 and 1897 ensured that was so. With the Queen's death on 22 January 1901 there was further opportunity. The urge to identify and compartmentalise periods was perfected in a mixture of historical awareness and celebration of national achievement. Within a few years, works such as Oliver Elton's *Survey of English literature, 1780–1830* (1912), Quiller-Couch's *Oxford book of Victorian verse* (1919) and Holbrook Jackson's *The eighteen nineties* (1913) framed the century in explicitly chronological ways. For an earlier period, G. M. Trevelyan's *England under the Stuarts* (1904) demonstrated a similar need. 'Where is he to begin? – Where to end?' asked Quiller-Couch, as anthologist, in the preface to his *Oxford book of Victorian verse*. He answered his own rhetorical question by reminding his readers that Wordsworth was Poet Laureate in the 1840s; and he found space for James Joyce (from *Chamber music*, 1907) and Pound (an American) before ending with Lascelles Abercrombie. Despite appearances, periods were not to be defined according just to dates. On a much larger scale, the *Cambridge modern history*, of which the first volume appeared in 1902, was both a tardy catching-up with publishing ideas taken from Germany and France and also a further clarification of historical identity – this time of Britain within the world at large.[222]

Some issues remained the same in 1914 as they had been eighty years earlier. Various publishers' series offered reasonable production quality at the lowest possible cost to buyers. As in 1830, the trade was deeply concerned with cheapness; and as in 1830 many of the arguments and claims focussed on the price of new, or at least recent, novels. Since the 1890s, the customary price for a new novel had been six shillings; but there was plenty of room for sales in less affluent parts of the market.[223] Macmillan's new Shilling Library offered both fiction and non-fiction, but this was a high price compared with much else that was available. The same firm's own sevenpenny series of novels offered work by such popular authors as Rhoda Broughton, F. Marion Crawford, Maurice Hewlett and A. E. W. Mason, though it did not offer Thomas Hardy, who had

---

221 Wynter, *Our social bees*; Wynter, *Subtle brains and lissom fingers*.
222 McKitterick, *Cambridge University Press* 3, pp. 154–8.   223 See also chapter 11.

been published by Macmillan since 1886.[224] Methuen ran with very similar principles: a shilling series of fiction and general literature, and a sevenpenny series of novels. For other tastes, including that for tales of crime, the firm of C. Arthur Pearson offered shilling novels, and a sixpenny series, likewise including copyright works: by 1914 the latter stretched to over two hundred titles. John Long offered novels either in cloth (sevenpence) or paper (sixpence). Hurst & Blackett and Hutchinson similarly offered novels at both prices, the closeness in the pricing reflecting the desperate need for all these publishers to make the best of the large print-runs that alone could permit such low retail prices. Sales could be prodigious in a world where cheap books and magazines were offered side by side in stationers' shops: Hutchinson claimed to have sold over 2 million sixpenny novels by 1914.[225] Chatto & Windus offered a sixpenny series of copyright novels, of which over 150 had been published by March 1914, including Hardy, Arnold Bennett, Conan Doyle and Hall Caine. Moving slightly up the price scale, Constable offered a New Shilling Library, of reprints bound in cloth, gilt, and in spring 1914 J. M. Dent announced a new Wayfarer's Library, 'the best books in the lighter field of modern literature', at one shilling each, the series explicitly designed to complement the success of Everyman's Library, which had been running since 1906.[226] A. E. W. Mason, H. G. Wells, H. de Vere Stacpoole and Arnold Bennett were among the first to appear in the venture. The mid-nineteenth-century battle for cheap literature, which had been won by publishers such as Dicks, who issued non-copyright work for as little as a penny for a Shakespeare play, and a shilling for Shakespeare's complete works, had been replaced by a world in which the eyes of readers were on copyright books, by modern and well-established authors.

As always, some parts of the market for books could almost look after themselves. But many people – perhaps most of the population – were not in the habit of book-buying, or of newspaper-buying. For all but a few thousand, it scarcely mattered that under Lord Northcliffe the price of *The Times* was dropped from threepence to twopence in 1913 and to a penny in 1914. As always, people had to be persuaded to buy books, whether by whetting their curiosity, emphasising educational or religious values, or appealing to peer comparisons. For these reasons and others, part-publication of large-scale, ambitiously cast works remained a mainstay of the book trade and for many readers. In the 1890s, led by Harmsworth, publishers launched subscription-based books such as Sir Herbert Maxwell's *Sixty years a queen* (ten sixpenny

---

224 Millgate, 'Thomas Hardy and the house of Macmillan'.
225 *Publishers' Circular* 10 January 1914, advertisement.
226 Dent, *Memoirs*, pp. 123–9; Rhys, *Everyman remembers*, pp. 237–49.

parts, 1897), *With the flag to Pretoria* (thirty sixpenny parts, 1900), and the *Harmsworth encyclopaedia* (forty sevenpenny parts, 1905–6, and later reissued with extra colour plates). Arthur Mee's *Children's encyclopaedia* began to appear in 1908, planned for fifty parts. Because one of the main proponents of the method, Horace Everett Hooper, was from the United States, it was tarred as American. In fact it was of much greater age, and had never really dropped out of use in Britain since the seventeenth century. The difference was that, instead of seeking a socially select market, the purpose now was to engage as many people as possible, and to persuade sometimes entirely new markets that book-buying bought social status. In 1904, Edward Marston, a publisher of long experience, thought that the public were 'tired of being dosed in this way'.[227] He spoke too soon, for some of the largest schemes were yet to come. *The historian's history of the world* appeared in 1908, and in 1909 Funk & Wagnall published the *Jewish encyclopaedia* in parts.[228] Hutchinson launched a *History of the nations* in 1914, planned in up to fifty fortnightly parts at sevenpence a part. Like others of its kind, it was advertised in phrasing that sought to combine reassurance with the widest possible appeal: 'a popular, concise, pictorial, and authoritative account'. Purchasers needed to have no fear of its bulk, or that it would be overloaded with words, or that it would be too abstruse; and yet, it would also be 'authoritative'. But, unlike the subscription works that had caused such belligerent anguish among booksellers only a few years earlier, most notoriously and noisily the eleventh edition of the *Encyclopaedia Britannica*,[229] this was to be sold through ordinary retail outlets with the help of advertisement sheets and show-cards.

Behind these and other ventures lurked changes that were still less understood. The first motion pictures were of little consequence to the book trade. They were novelties, and they were short – too short for a book, or even much more than a sketch. But by 1914 the cinema was established, technical challenges were being steadily overcome, and many sections of the public were relishing it. Periodicals such as *Cinema News*, *Bioscope* and the *Kinematograph Weekly*, all launched within the previous two years, served the trade and public interests, while the launch of *Film Censor* in June 1912 was a reminder of the need for vigilance in this new medium.

The annual report for Cardiff Public Libraries in 1913 recorded a drop in borrowing of most kinds of books – not just fiction – and proposed that one reason might be the cinema: with nearly twenty local performances daily it was

227 Marston, *After work*, p. 305.   228 Arbour, *Canvassing books*.
229 McKitterick, *A history of Cambridge University Press* 3, ch. 8.

a powerful, and successful, counter-attraction.[230] Where some commentators saw difficulties, others saw opportunities. The success of the London Film Company, with studios at St Margaret's, near Richmond, suggested ways in which publishers and booksellers might profit. Early productions included *The house of Temperley* (based on Doyle's *Rodney Stone*), stories of Sherlock Holmes, and adaptations of work by W. W. Jacobs. *Trilby* starred Sir Herbert Tree, and a start had been made on Dickens. Further plans included *Rupert of Hentzau*, *The prisoner of Zenda*, *Dracula* and *Bootle's baby*, the last a perennial stage and book favourite based on Henrietta Stannard's best-selling novel. Films of Jack London's novels were being made in America, and could be expected in Britain. For this market, newspaper serialisations, screen advertisements for local bookstalls and bookshops, and further exploitation of sevenpenny novels all beckoned.

The legacy

Many of the commercial and technological achievements in printing and publishing between 1830 and 1914 were underpinned by imperial confidence and expansion, and by the challenges, possibilities and anxieties that these brought. Beside these sat the growth of the English-speaking world more generally, not just in the United States but also as English increasingly became the preferred second language in all continents. While the First World War heralded the end of imperial dominance that had been so notably and noisily celebrated in Victoria's diamond jubilee, structures had been put in place for the national and international book trades for much of the twentieth century. Within the space of a lifetime, changes in the manufacture, publication, selling and reading of books and kindred literature had been established that were to prove remarkably resilient until the late twentieth century. Some of these changes have become permanent; others have been displaced by developments in the past fifty years. For much of the nineteenth century, the most vociferous commentators and campaigners insisted on the need for and importance of cheap books: as we have seen, this was as strong a theme in the early 1830s as it was at the end of the century. By the 1890s, cheap books were no longer matters for special publishers, or special interests. They were no longer a sub-class. They figured prominently in the lists of some of the largest and most respected publishers of all. The establishment of the Net Book Agreement in 1899 helped to stabilise publishing and bookselling, but it also demonstrated the very limited

---

230 *Publishers' Circular* 28 February 1914, p. 208.

extent to which competition would be tolerated.[231] The book trades remained intensely protectionist. Books had become cheaper, but underlying attitudes had not changed. In an industry where few people made the kinds of profits achieved by the wealthiest of industrialists, margins remained comparatively tight. Newspaper empires could make money. Book publishing was in this respect a comparatively poor relation.

Pricing apart, the most obvious changes were visual. George Cruikshank's change in career, from a successful caricaturist in the traditions of Gillray to one of the most prolific of book illustrators, epitomised not just a change in taste, but also a revolution in book design. 'Boz is the Cruikshank of writers' trilled a reviewer of Dickens's *Sketches by Boz* at Christmas 1836, a reminder not just of the collaborative association of author and illustrator, text and image, but also of the importance of publisher and printer in bringing about such matrimony.[232] Between the 1830s and the First World War the illustrated book came of age. Lithography, photography and a host of new techniques for printing pictures, allied to a new command of colour printing and new inventions of inks, created their own revolution in the presentation of fiction and non-fiction alike. These developments in turn dominated subsequent book design, and the later and much wider application of litho printing. Illustration became assumed, on both the insides and the covers of books, as well as in newspapers and magazines. The assumptions concerning reading involved in this consumer revolution were in turn absorbed into the experiences of film. The changes in the materials and appearance of books, and the accompanying consequences for expectations among authors and readers, form the subjects of the next two chapters.

231 Macmillan, *The net book agreement.*   232 *The Spectator* 26 December 1836, p. 1234.

1

Changes in the look of the book

DAVID MCKITTERICK

Queen Victoria has been described as the 'first media monarch'.[1] It is a term that demands some explanation, for it depends on understanding how print and visual culture changed during her reign, and how the cheap illustrated pamphlets, journals and newspapers, the invention of photography and its application in large-scale markets, faster means of communication like the telegraph, and new, faster and more convenient means of travel, all contributed to the creation and manipulation of images of the monarch, her consort and her family.[2] In simple terms, she was by no means the first media monarch. Since ancient times, rulers have depended on whatever media are available to them. 'Whose is this image and superscription?' asked Jesus, knowing that the coin shown to him by the Pharisees depicted Caesar.[3] Thanks to the printing press and to the programmes of painters such as Holbein and Isaac Oliver and their copyists, representations of Henry VIII and Elizabeth I linked royal power with personal likenesses of a detail and on a scale unavailable previously. George III became more familiar to his subjects than any of his predecessors thanks to the hand-coloured etchings of James Gillray, sold for the high price of half a crown each and displayed for public amusement in shop windows. The matrimonial and other adventures of the Prince of Wales, later George IV, were depicted with yet more freedom.[4] Gillray showed how it was possible to intrude into royalty, and thus began a debate that continues today: it concerned not just appearance and representation, but also a myth that

---

1 Plunkett, *Queen Victoria, first media monarch*. For further aspects, see Richards, *The commodity culture of Victorian England*, ch. 2, 'The image of Victoria in the year of jubilee'.
2 Tritton, *The lost voice of Queen Victoria*.   3 Mark 12.16; Luke 20.24.
4 In a substantial literature, see more generally the recent collection Gaehtgens and Hochner (eds.), *L'image du roi*; Strong, *The cult of Elizabeth*; for Britain, see for example Lloyd and Thurley, *Henry VIII*; for Gillray and Carlton House, see Hill, *Mr. Gillray the caricaturist*, pp. 118–23. But see Anglo, *Images of Tudor kingship* for important distinctions between public and private circulation and sharing of images.

depended on a carefully modulated sense of distance, a topic that is not part of this book. In more limited terms, while (to repeat) Victoria was certainly not the first media monarch, she was nonetheless in her turn exploited and presented to her subjects and other audiences with the latest available technology. Just as earlier generations had used woodcuts, new artistic techniques, engravings and lithographs, so photography and new printing opportunities were used for Victoria. In this way she stands centre-stage in the history of the book.

To compare a book published in 1830 with one published in 1914 is not just to place an article that was largely hand-made next to one that was almost completely the product of a machine. Just as in 1830 there were many books printed on machine-made paper, and printed by steam presses, so in 1914 there were still a few that were printed by hand, on hand-made paper. Some of the most important changes in the means of manufacturing books had been invented long before 1830. The first paper-making machine in England was installed at Frogmore, Hertfordshire, in 1803, and the first book to be printed on machine-made paper was published in 1804. The first Stanhope iron printing press was introduced to the world in probably 1800, and within five years printers were installing the latest models. The introduction of stereotyped plates in place of loose type for some printing made possible the success of the British and Foreign Bible Society's programme for mass circulation of the scriptures.[5] In 1814 *The Times* installed its first steam-driven press. These various building-blocks of printing technology did not in themselves amount to an industrial revolution. As in other industries, there was a world of difference between invention and development, and widespread acceptance and application. None of the changes was accomplished without disappointments and setbacks. Labour skills and practices, decisions on capital investment, equipment manufacture and customer acceptance all contributed to a process that was drawn-out, where some developments were accepted more quickly than others.

Most printers did not need steam presses in 1830: the print-runs for most books did not justify the expenditure.[6] Newspapers were another matter, though the dozens of titles whose circulations were counted in little more than hundreds continued to be printed on large iron hand-presses. In the mid-1830s *The Times* had a circulation of about 9,800 copies, a figure that was to triple in the next ten years. Its competitors were the *Morning Chronicle* and the

5 Hart, *Charles Earl Stanhope and the Oxford University Press*; Howsam, *Cheap Bibles*; McKitterick, *A History of Cambridge University Press. 2. Scholarship and commerce, 1698–1872*, ch. 13.
6 Weedon, *Victorian publishing*, pp. 70–1.

Morning Herald, each with about 6,200. It was not surprising that metropolitan newspapers led the way in innovation. Though the technology existed, and was developed in America, rotary printing was introduced tardily in Britain. For many years, the rolls of paper produced by the new paper-making machines had all to be cut into sheets for printing.[7] *The Times*, which had replaced the old Koenig steam press of 1814 with Applegath & Cowper presses in 1828, and then installed Applegath's rotary machinery in 1848, before turning to a mixture of Applegath vertical machines and Hoe's horizontal presses in 1858, installed a web-fed machine only in 1868. This technology remained in use until 1895. From 1909, the press-room was equipped with electrical Goss rotary presses, which not only were easier to operate, but also had much faster folding machines at the delivery end. By itself, speed of printing was not necessarily a help if other activities could not keep up.[8]

Typesetting and type design

In two areas of book manufacture, typesetting and bookbinding, hand methods remained for much longer. In typesetting, the first attempts at meeting demands for faster work had been made in the 1780s, when John Walter introduced a process that he called logography. This was not a mechanical development, but one in typefounding, where dozens of common letter-sequences were cast as single sorts. It was cumbersome, and was never significantly faster than a good trained compositor using the old methods. It was adopted by the *Daily Universal Register* (later *The Times*) in 1785, but was abandoned in February 1792.[9] William Church, an American from Vermont who also worked in London and Birmingham, seems to have been the first to realise that for machine-setting to be possible it would be more efficient to cast type new each time.[10] But it was only in 1840 that a patent was taken out by James Young and Adrien Delcambre for a machine that was commercially adopted. With the help of Henry Bessemer (better known for his invention of the Bessemer steel converter) they developed the 'Pianotyp'. Though used to set the *Family*

7 Moran, *Printing presses*, chs. 12–13; Silver, 'Efficiency improved'. For further details of machines, see Wilson and Grey, *A practical treatise upon modern printing machinery*. For taxes, see Dagnall, *The taxation of paper in Great Britain, 1643–1861*, and for the wider background see Daunton, *Trusting Leviathan*.

8 *The Times printing number* (1912), p. 130. The *Daily Mirror* was the first newspaper in Britain to be printed on Goss machines, in 1905.

9 Johnson, *An introduction to logography*; Feather, 'John Walter and the Logographic Press'; [Morison] *Printing The Times since 1785*, pp. 17, 20.

10 For the manufacture of printing type, see James Mosley in the *Cambridge history of the book in Britain 5*.

Herald in 1842 it enjoyed little success; and only with an invention by Robert Hattersley, an engineer in Manchester, were real advances made. Hattersley's machine, patented in 1857, was (unlike the Pianotyp) operated by one man, who pressed a key to obtain a particular sort. It was primitive, simple, and required no power. His work featured in the Great Exhibition in 1862. But it was said that a fast compositor could work as well; and some printers found the machine itself was unreliable. The two examples installed in the *Eastern Morning News* in Hull in 1866, for example, were sold off to a London book printer – for whom, presumably, time was of less essence.[11] The Kastenbein machine, patented in 1869, was quicker, and was installed in *The Times* in 1870, where it remained in use until Monotype keyboards and casters were installed in 1908-9. There were dozens of other ideas and machines, all searching for faster setting. The problem was obvious enough, and inventors were not wanting. But, so far as the printing industry was concerned, until its final decade the nineteenth century was a century of experiment rather than achievement in typesetting.[12]

Most machines, both those that found some success and those that quickly sank forgotten, depended on a supply of already cast type, delivered by gravity. It was the realisation that type could be cast anew each time, from matrices supplied with the machine, that eventually led to the revolution that had been so long sought. The first Linotype machine, invented by Ottmar Mergenthaler, was used to set part of the *New York Tribune* in 1886. His machine produced slugs, cast lines of type. Having undergone several modifications (the problem of spacing and justification proved particularly difficult), by 1892 the first machines for British customers were delivered by the English Linotype Company to the *Leeds Mercury*, the *Sheffield Telegraph* and the *Newcastle Evening Chronicle* – all outside London. The company was heavily advertised, partly with full-pages on the back of the *Financial Times* and partly with carefully placed stories. By 1901 Linotype setting was in use in a dozen London newspapers and well over two hundred in the suburbs and provinces.[13]

Mergenthaler was the first person to create a machine that proved a complete success, demonstrated in its use over most of the following century. The

---

11 Hunt, *Then and now*, pp. 175-6.
12 Moran, *The composition of reading matter*; Huss, *The development of printers' mechanical typesetting methods*; Legros and Grant, *Typographical printing surfaces*. On Legros and Grant, see L. W. Wallis, 'Legros and Grant: the typographical connection'.
13 *List of some newspapers and other publications in Great Britain set by the Linotype Company machine* (1901); Kahan, *Ottmar Mergenthaler*. The exact dates of the introduction of Linotype setting to individual newspapers have apparently still to be established.

Monotype machine, likewise developed in America, was based on a quite different principle. Where the Linotype depended on matrices that, once used, were returned to their place to be used again, each character thus requiring several duplicate matrices, the Monotype contained just a single matrix case. Instead of slugs of type, each sort was cast individually, a principle that made correction much easier since it could be done by hand. Most obviously, the Monotype was made up of two distinct parts, a keyboard, on which the operator produced a punched paper tape, and a caster, driven by this paper tape. The first patent for what developed into the equipment that was to dominate book composition in Britain was granted in 1887; but it was only in 1898 that the first model was put on the market, in America. The first machine to be installed in a British printing house was bought by Wyman in 1898, and was a primitive affair; in 1900 the much superior model, redesigned in 1899, was installed by Cassells.[14]

These machines were not always immediately and unreservedly welcomed by either compositors or the reading public. At first, John Southward, one of the most respected of trade printers and a supporter of the older Thorne typesetter, wrote of the Linotype as a machine 'of the past'.[15] But the writer in the *Daily Mail* in 1897 surely had his tongue partly in his cheek when he wrote of having seen a demonstration of the Monotype keyboard and caster, the latter 'the most appalling machine in the whole range of demonology'. What had been described to him as a kind of Linotype, whose drowsy hum he could hear overhead in his office, proved to be quite different:

> a thing having all the outward seeming of a machine. It was mounted on a pedestal, an awe-inspiring complication of wheels and levers and cogs and cranks and belts and springs and ratchets and plungers and legs and teeth and taps and handles and grippers and pins, with an uncanny looking chimney rising out of the middle of it like a ventilating shaft from the brimstone furnace.[16]

Nothing was said of the most noticeable feature of all when the caster was at work, its deafening noise. Readers of the *Daily Mail* had nothing to fear other than a machine that set type 'without any show of human assistance' – an achievement, as the report said, 'quite outside human imagining'. To a generation whose fathers had become attuned to the noise and dirt of the steam engine, and that was now witnessing the daily effects of electricity and the internal combustion engine, the Monotype machine was, in truth, little

---

14 *One hundred years of type making, 1897–1997.*   15 Kahan, *Ottmar Mergenthaler*, p. 170.
16 *Daily Mail* 2 August 1897.

more than yet another modern novelty. For the *Daily Mail*'s million and more readers it made good copy. For the printing and publishing industries it was the answer that dozens of inventors had sought. But in hundreds of smaller printing houses hand-setting remained dominant for several years more. In 1900 there were just twenty-two Monotype machines in Britain. They not only required capital investment, and further running costs. They also needed operators of greater skill than many compositors. Training costs always had to be added as well.[17]

On the one hand, printing became ever more industrialised. On the other, it moved out of the printing house and into the non-specialist world of the office and the study. The first typewriter, termed a typographer, was patented in the United States in 1829 by William Austen Burt, in the back-woods of Michigan. His invention was followed by those of many others, all seeking to improve methods of mechanical reproduction, but it was not until 1873 that the firm of Remington began to market commercially produced machines. The first models produced only capitals. 'I think you will be surprised by the manner of this letter', wrote a correspondent in Utica to a colleague in Cambridge, England. 'It is put in print by one of the latest inventions of some Yankee, who writing, I suppose, an illegible hand, or at least knowing that some of his countrymen did, concluded to put an end to that difficulty for ever.'[18] Manufacture was dominated by American firms until the twentieth century, and when in 1908 the Imperial Typewriter Company was established in Leicester, it was by an American named Hildago Moya. In Dresden, the engineering firm of Seidel & Naumann manufactured bicycles before they turned their attention in 1892 to typewriters. Their first machines appeared in 1900, and by 1910 the first portable 'Erika' machines were on the market. By then, the typewriter had long ceased to be solely a machine designed for the office. Professional authors on both sides of the Atlantic were being encouraged to use them. In 1896, contributors to the new journal *The Savoy*, published by Leonard Smithers, were instructed only to submit their work in typescript.[19]

Writing had become mechanised, and with it came advantages in reproducing copies in office or amateur environments. The copying book, with its accompanying damping equipment and iron copying press, was familiar. Where multiple copies were needed there were table-top lithographic presses,

17 Duffy, *The skilled compositor*.
18 Alexander S. Johnson to C. W. King, 8 January 1875: Trinity College, Cambridge MS King D3. 69(1). Of the several histories of typewriters, see for example Adler, *The writing machine* and Beeching, *Century of the typewriter*.
19 *The Savoy* 1 (January 1896), facing title-page.

and an abundance of patent systems designed for, in effect, short-run printing. Waterlow & Sons, among the largest of the manufacturing stationers, claimed in 1882 to have sold 2,000 table-top lithographic presses ('every person may become his own printer'), to government offices, railway companies, banks, missionary societies and a prison. Prices started at seven guineas, compared with the same firm's Multiplex Copying Portfolio, which by means of a special transfer paper could produce forty or fifty copies, with the price of the basic equipment starting at 15s 6d and with the assurance 'the process being so simple that it may be done by a boy'.[20]

In reading, as in many human occupations, the most successful innovations are those which are least noticed. For printers, and hence for their customers, the advent of machinery that could, by proper management, keep costs down and drive production up was in principle much to be welcomed. But it depended on reader, or customer, acceptance. Few inventions in the printing and related industries have been immediately taken up and applied by numerous manufacturers. This was not simply a result of patent limitations. Nor was it wholly a result of capital costs, though this was certainly a major consideration in the replacement of machinery by its next generation. Book typography, with its demands quite unlike the attention-grabbing needs of publicity-printing, had most often to assume deeply conservative expectations and requirements. As a consequence, the revolutionary mechanical innovations of the Linotype and the Monotype were not matched at first by any change in type design other than what was required of the machine's mechanisms – changes too subtle to be noticed by most readers.

Type design looks constantly over its shoulder. At one level this was, and is, a straightforward characteristic of the necessary conventions of the alphabet. At another, it invited comparison and competition. Most obviously, a zest in the nineteenth century for decorative type led to what were, in the eyes of some of the more critical observers, weaknesses. 'Herod is out-heroded every week in some new fancy which calls itself a letter, and which, in response to a voracious demand, pours into our market, either from native foundries or from the more versatile and supple contortionists of America and Germany.' The typefounder and historian of his trade Talbot Baines Reed, who addressed these words to the Society of Arts in 1890, took as his theme the relationship of new to old fashions in typography, from the fifteenth century onwards. He made plain his admiration for Caslon's work in the eighteenth century; and though he did not

---

20 Waterlow & Sons Limited, catalogue, February 1882. More generally, see Rhodes and Streeter, *Before photocopying*.

name his competitors in typefounding (most obviously Miller & Richard, whose reintroduction in 1860 of old-style type based on Caslon's models proved to be a turning-point), he clearly regarded the renaissance as welcome. 'The typography of the last half century owes a great deal to this opportune return to the past; and the continued favour of the old styles, I venture to think, is a hopeful sign for the future.' He also singled out for approval what he identified as a 'Basle' style, characterised partly by the thicker sides of the letter 'o' being set at an angle rather than vertically. The styles developed from Bodoni and Didot, with their sharp contrasts between thick and thin lines, and the tendency to carry these to extremes was to him much less welcome. As a typefounder, he remarked on the harder metal introduced for typefounding in order to meet the demands of machine presses. This also made ever finer lines possible. In his view, Scottish founders in particular had pursued this particular course, following Didot rather than the rounder forms of the English tradition. Not least importantly, the narrowness of letter possible with modern faces had more than visual implications. Since compositors were paid by the en, that is, the length of text that they set, their tariff exercised its own influence on type design. In a part of book production where costs were otherwise difficult to control, there was a direct correlation between type design and labour costs in setting.[21]

In two areas, Reed looked forward. First, he was one of the earliest people in England to pay serious public attention to the work done by the French ophthalmologist Emile Javal, who in 1881 had published a pioneering paper on legibility.[22] Some of Javal's observations and theories were later to be widely challenged, but they were the real beginning of a new field of study that was to influence all aspects of type design. In Britain, they were introduced to a much wider audience through a textbook by Edmund Burke Huey, of Pittsburgh, *The psychology and pedagogy of reading*. First published in 1908, by 1910 this was in its fourth printing. Of especial concern was the market for schools, and the sizes and designs of type appropriate for readers in their first years; Huey's was just one voice calling for government intervention. By 1910, publishers neglected the subject and its implications at their peril, as local education authorities began to take account of regulations issued by the Board of Education calling attention to the need for suitable-sized type in textbooks. As was quickly realised, it was a question not only of type size, but also of its character, of paper, of the weight of illustration, of the presentation

21 Reed, 'Old and new fashions in typography'.
22 Javal, 'L'évolution de la typographie considérée dans ses rapports avec l'hygiène de la vue'; see also his *Physiologie de la lecture et de l'écriture*.

of cartographic information in atlases, of the printing of music – all related to such questions as lighting, myopia and changes in children's eyesight as they grew up. In 1912 the British Association received a report from a committee which had taken evidence from J. H. Mason, one of the most respected printers of his generation and a keen advocate of old-face type with its less sharp contrasts between thick and thin lines that most readily characterised modern faces. The committee not only recommended greater attention to design in the selection of textbooks, but even observed that a standard should be introduced – such a standard rendering unprofitable any books which did not reach it.[23]

More obvious to most people, since it affected the look of books much more dramatically, were the implications of Reed's closing words of his paper:

> I take it as a hopeful sign that the aesthetics of typography are at present being studied by men of artistic taste and authority. The result cannot fail to be of benefit. For printing, in all its career, has followed close in the wake of its sister arts.

The reference to William Morris, and others like C. R. Ashbee and Charles Ricketts, could hardly have been clearer. The foundation of the Arts and Crafts Exhibition Society in 1887 brought together a group including Morris, Walter Crane, Emery Walker, Selwyn Image and Reginald Blomfield (fig. 1.1). Only Morris could exhibit the range of experience in design in such a range of media – stained glass, wallpaper, tapestry and furniture, quite apart from calligraphy and printing types. He established the Kelmscott Press in 1891, after several experiments in the publication of his work, some involving the publishers Reeves & Turner and, as printers, the Chiswick Press. In the course of these, he had acquired a taste for a revival of the sixteenth-century Basle type, cut by William Howard in the 1850s. Reed knew the photographic enlargements of early type that had been prepared by Emery Walker in 1888 for what proved to be a seminal lecture to the Arts and Crafts Exhibition Society, one of the formative moments leading to Morris's decision to establish his own press; and he knew also of Walker's work with Morris in the preparation of his own type designs.[24]

Morris's chosen medium, possible because he was master of his own press, was deliberately anomalous. By using iron hand-presses rather than machine presses he demonstrated the importance of the skilled workman having as

23 'School-books and eyesight; report of the committee'.
24 Dreyfus, 'Emery Walker's 1888 lecture on "letterpress printing": a reconstruction and a reconsideration'. Walker's copies of slides of early books made to help Morris, and given to Reed, are now in the St Bride Printing Library, and others are in the Emery Walker collection at Cheltenham Art Gallery. See also Peterson, *A bibliography of the Kelmscott Press* and Morris, *The ideal book*.

OF THE DECORATIVE ILLUSTRATION OF BOOKS OLD AND NEW BY WALTER CRANE

New Volume of the Ex-Libris Series. Price 10s. 6d. net. Also a Large Paper Edition, 25s. net.

THIS book had its origin in the course of three (Cantor) Lectures given before the Society of Arts in 1889; they have been amplified and added to, and further chapters have been written, treating of the very active period in printing and decorative book-illustration we have seen since that

Extract from the author's preface.

Figure 1.1 Prospectus for Walter Crane, *Of the decorative illustration of books old and new* (George Bell & Sons, 1896). The book was published in two forms: ordinary copies at 10s 6d and a hundred copies on tall Japanese vellum at 25s, twenty-five of the latter being reserved for America. (Private collection)

complete control as possible over his task. He worked with paper-makers to obtain hand-made paper of the highest quality appropriate to take type and blocks printed by letterpress, and with ink-makers to obtain ink of the blackest and of sufficient stiffness. But, while this was of the essence in the arts and crafts movement, there was also a practicality about all that Morris strove for in the Kelmscott Press. When appropriate, he was perfectly content to use modern methods involving photography. Some of its books were expensive: the Kelmscott Chaucer, published in 1896, cost £20. Most were more modestly priced: *Maud*, printed for Macmillan, cost two guineas and the three-volume *Golden legend* (1892) was underpriced at five guineas. Morris had been interested in the appearance and design of books long before he founded the Kelmscott Press, and in the 1860s had thought with Burne-Jones of producing an edition of his *Earthly paradise* in which text and illustration would be integrated. In his own press, he was able to demonstrate principles to the printing and publishing trades, as well as to readers. His insistence on the importance of materials – paper and ink – was a lesson of which much of the trade stood in need. In rejecting the commercially available types, he demonstrated in his own way an important principle: how older typefaces could be adapted to modern needs. With the help of photographic enlargements, and encouraged and guided by Emery Walker, Morris turned to fifteenth-century Venice.[25] The results, perhaps inevitably, were archaic – distractingly so for many people who looked at his books and could see no further than their appeal to medievalism. Inspired by a mixture of fifteenth-century printing and medieval illuminated manuscripts, his page designs were as perplexing to some people as they were attractive to others. In his disciplined insistence on the importance of not mixing different families of typefaces within a volume, in his return to what he considered the best of the older traditions, in his attention to his materials, especially paper and ink, and in ensuring a visual balance between illustrations and areas of text, Morris set out a manifesto that challenged widely held assumptions and practices in book design and production.

The line of descent that can be traced from Morris and his advisers to dominating tastes in much twentieth-century typography is a strong one. When T. J. Cobden-Sanderson, in partnership with Walker, established the Doves Press in 1901, the two men took a different typographical route.[26] They chose as their models the roman types of Nicolas Jenson and Jacobus Rubeus in fifteenth-century Venice. Walker's analysis of early types underpinned the designs used for both presses, and the results could hardly have been more different visually; but the historical principles were the same.

There were others at work as well. The *Printer's International Specimen Exchange*, founded by the antiquarian Andrew Tuer in 1880 and then gradually

25 Peterson, 'The type designs of William Morris'.   26 Tidcombe, *The Doves Press*.

displaced by the *British Printer* founded in 1888, demonstrated some of the ferment among printers who took the design of their work seriously, who were anxious to experiment but who were also anxious for the judgements of their peers.[27] In books such as Hardy's *Tess of the D'Urbervilles* (R. & R. Clark for Osgood McIlvaine, 1889, designed by Charles Ricketts), Whistler's *The gentle art of making enemies* (1890: the Ballantyne Press for Heinemann) and Oliver Wendell Holmes's *The autocrat of the breakfast table* (Walter Scott, c.1897), printers and publishers attempted with more or less success to break away from some of the conventions of centred typography. Though the fluid lines of art nouveau never quite achieved the same widespread presence in book design in Britain as they did in Belgium or the Netherlands, some of the same ideas were to be seen in so-called artistic printing. Seeming to defy requirements to use types in harmony with each other, and to defy the ordinary standards of letter design, and setting colours in unexpected contrasts, the roots of this were to be found in the early years of the nineteenth century. In hindsight, it was looked on by some as deliberate indiscipline. And so it was, in many hands. In the work of Charles Ricketts, Aubrey Beardsley, Jessie M. King and their imitators and contemporaries, Britain found its own versions of art nouveau, a tradition made demotic in the designs for the title-pages and endpapers of the volumes in Dent's Everyman's Library.[28]

Stereotyping

Stereotyping, where metal plates were cast from set pages of type, proved itself within less than a decade after its introduction at the university presses in both Oxford and Cambridge, and at the press of Andrew Wilson in London. But it was better suited to some books than others, depending on patterns of market demand, and its efficiency was still a matter of intense debate among printers and publishers in the 1820s.[29]

The process not only brought economic benefits to reprints, and to the possibilities it offered for simultaneous printing of the same setting of type on different machines. It also made possible new structures in printing and publishing. Sets of plates for a book that were worn, and of editions in which printer or publisher had no further interest, could be auctioned off to others who were less concerned about the sharpness of the plates, and who would

---

27 Hudson, 'Artistic printing: a re-evaluation'.
28 *The turn of the century, 1885–1910*; Taylor, *The art nouveau book in Britain*, interprets the term more widely.
29 Hansard, *Typographia*.

print them for lower-priced editions.[30] Plates could also be sold overseas, on the same principle, or could be made and sold new. Charles Knight claimed to have sold stereotype casts of his best woodcuts originally prepared for the *Penny Magazine* to Germany, Holland, France, Livonia (Russian and German), Bohemia, Italy, the Ionian islands, Sweden, Norway and Spanish America. The whole journal was reprinted in the United States from plates sent over from Britain.[31] Using the same methods, the first years of *Punch* were reprinted to meet later demand. It was the same, and on a far greater extent, for reprints of works on smaller scales, the hundreds of novels, books of poetry, domestic manuals and schoolbooks that made up the bulk of the book trade. At the beginning of the century the early exponents of stereotyping had discovered that it was economical to print comparatively small numbers of copies, and often – thereby lessening the risk of over-exposure to a sometimes fickle trade. While it was much used for large editions, it was also of value in printing books that had a steady sale. A few hundred copies could be printed as needed, and the market fed without the need for surges in investment in paper, or for large quantities of books to be warehoused. This remained true; but the real power and value of stereotyping, which had been widely regarded with such suspicion in the 1810s and 1820s, was proved when stereotypes and the harder electrotypes were worked to their limits in order to meet demands from a reading public used to the idea of cheap books.

Illustration

The illustration of books is studied further in chapter 2 below. To the casual observer, no aspects of printing were more obvious than the change from line to half-tone, and the change from monochrome to colour. Early aniline inks tended to be too fugitive for ordinary printing, but there were plenty of other experiments to improve and develop printing ink. Prior to 1850 there had been only four patents for inks for printing and other miscellaneous purposes. Between 1850 and 1880 there were almost a hundred, and in the next thirty years the number was greater still.[32] Methods of block-making and of printing attracted even more experiment. By 1830, lithography was well established. As a means of scientific illustration its flexibility and cheapness in showing shading or colour made it attractive until well into the twentieth century: in 1913 Cambridge University Press took over a local business that specialised in

30 See below, chapter 20.
31 Knight, *Passages of a working life* 2, pp. 223–4; Knight, *The old printer and the modern press*, pp. 258–9.
32 Mitchell, *Inks*, pp. 370–80.

this form of work, and only closed the department in the 1920s. Lithography proved also to be ideally suited to the increasingly flexible page-design of children's books. But it was never ubiquitous. The coloured illustrations of the Kate Greenaway picture books, printed by Edmund Evans in the 1880s and 1890s, were printed from woodcuts, in three or four colours using cross-hatching as a further aid to achieving different shades.[33] The watercolours in Beatrix Potter's Peter Rabbit books, published by Warne, were printed in three colours from letterpress half-tones.[34]

In the 1830s, most illustrations for ordinary trade books depended on wood- or steel-engraving, two very different processes despite the similarity in the terminology. One was letterpress, having its origins in the fifteenth century and brought to a pitch of achievement in the work of Thomas Bewick in Newcastle upon Tyne at the end of the eighteenth century. Unlike the older woodcuts, which were cut with a knife on the side of the plank, wood-engraving was cus-tomarily executed with a graver on the end of specially prepared box-wood, a hard surface whose close grain made it ideally suited to detailed work. Either the artist drew directly onto the block, or the engraver copied a drawing. The demand not just for more, or better, illustrations was felt throughout the printing trade. The 1846 Post Office Directory recorded Jabez Hare, a commercial wood-engraver, as 'engineering & perspective draftsman & wood engraver, &c.' – a reminder of how much was commonly left to the engraver. Collaborations between wood-engravers and named artists were rare before the mid-century, and much more work was required for everyday advertising, guidebooks, catalogues of machinery and similar commercial purposes than was needed for literature. Increasing emphasis on this collaboration, and the improved status of the artist as illustrator, brought new tensions. The transla-tion from drawing to cut lines in wood demanded considerable interpretation by the engraver, and some authors or artists could be particularly demanding at this stage: Lewis Carroll (C. L. Dodgson) and Dante Gabriel Rossetti are celebrated examples.[35]

> O woodman, spare that block,
> O gash not anyhow;
> It took ten days by clock,
> I'd fain protect it now.
>> Chorus, wild laughter from Dalziel's workshop.

33 Kiger (ed.), *Kate Greenaway*.
34 Linder, *A history of the writings of Beatrix Potter*. See further below, pp. 407, 409, 413.
35 Cohen and Gandolfo (eds.), *Lewis Carroll and the house of Macmillan*; Cohen and Wakeling (eds.), *Lewis Carroll & his illustrators*; for Rossetti, see Munro and Goddard (eds.), *Literary circles*, pp. 38–41.

Because (thanks to the diameter of the trunk of most box trees) only quite small blocks of wood were possible, larger pictures had to be made by tongue and groove joints setting blocks together. By the 1840s this was done on sometimes a substantial scale. A further development was the multiple-part block that was bolted together, invented by the firm of Charles Wells in Bouverie Street – its address at the centre of the London newspaper and magazine trade is a reminder of the most considerable and most important customers. This development made possible the practice of sharing out parts of large illustrations among several engravers.[36] The large news illustrations in the *Illustrated London News* (founded 1842), sometimes spread over two folio pages, required teams of engravers who worked separately on different parts of the pictures, and whose work was only brought together at a late stage: the merging of their different contributions, where time was of the essence, required separate and special skill. In all but the very finest work it is easy to see where the parts of blocks are joined, while variations in the natural shrinkage of the wood mean that the density and impression of the printed image can vary across the block.

With a few notable exceptions, the generation immediately after Bewick and his circle showed little sign of having learned from him. The best of the wood-engravings, but in a very different style that emphasised line, came from a handful of people including Mary Byfield (whose prayer book of 1569 was printed by Charles Whittingham in 1853, and published by Pickering) and the antiquary Orlando Jewitt, who specialised in architectural work.[37] The wood-engravers of the mid-century have long been celebrated, since Gleeson White published an appreciative and still valuable monograph in 1897. He was followed by Forrest Reid in 1928.[38] Both approached their subject as artists, more alert to aesthetic and technically skilled aspects than to functional issues and possibilities. But artists such as the prolific J. E. Millais, or Arthur Boyd Houghton, or D. G. Rossetti, working for magazines such as the *Cornhill* or *Good Words*, depended as much on commercial wood-engravers as did the more workaday artists employed by the *Illustrated London News* or *Punch*.[39] Artist and engraver were almost invariably separate. One trade classified directory for London in the late 1860s listed over eighty wood-engravers. As some (such as Jewitt or William Linton) worked independently, and some of the entries such

36 *The brothers Dalziel*; Lindley, *The woodblock engravers*.
37 Carter, *Orlando Jewitt*; Broomhead, *The book illustrations of Orlando Jewitt*.
38 White, *English illustration: 'the sixties': 1855–70*; Reid, *Illustrators of the eighteen sixties*. See further below, p. 125.
39 Goldman, *Victorian illustrated books, 1850–1870*; Goldman, *Victorian illustration* rev. edn; Goldman, *John Everett Millais, illustrator and narrator*; Goldman, *Beyond decoration: the illustrations of John Everett Millais*.

as that for Dorrington of Chancery Lane, or Straker, with three City addresses, represented large firms, the number of individuals was very much larger. While a few engravers (or rather, engraving firms) such as the brothers Dalziel or Swain gained fame and reputation, even being credited on the title-pages of books, very many more worked anonymously and obscurely. At its best, the printing of wood-engraved illustrations was a highly skilled operation; but as with many manufacturing processes it was also easy to produce work that was merely adequate or even slapdash. The fact that pictures could be printed at the same time as type did not guarantee any level of quality.

The introduction during the 1870s of the line-block, or zinco as it became known after the usual metal from which it was made, and its alliance to photography, eventually offered a cheaper alternative to wood, and one that was much easier to print. The earliest attempts were crude, and the lines were thick. But as skills and methods developed, so the process became capable of considerable delicacy. The principles of the half-tone block were originally explored by Fox Talbot, but it was only in the mid-1880s that the first successful patents were taken out.[40] By the 1890s, half-tone illustrations were commonplace. For the first time photographs could be reproduced quickly and cheaply, at the same time as the rest of a book, newspaper or magazine. While photographs can always be edited, cut down or altered either on the negative or (generally more obviously) on the print, the advent of relief-printed half-tones was one of the greatest revolutions of all. They provided, for the first time, pictures that had every appearance of verisimilitude. The peculiar authority attached to photographs reached to the humblest of printed matter and, with it, to all classes of society. Those who wished to see photographs no longer had to peer in the windows of specialist shops. The pictures – portraits, events, places and objects – were in the weekly and monthly magazines and, later, the newspapers.

Though the half-tone block proved to be the cheapest and most widely used means of reproducing continuous tone, it was far from being the only process. Collotype, invented in the mid-1850s but only applied in Britain after patents had been taken out in 1869, was a planographic process that was capable of enormous fidelity. When used ambitiously, for example by the Chiswick Press in the early years of the twentieth century, it was supplemented by hand-touching of individual copies. More cheaply, photogravure was introduced into Britain in the early 1880s, and reel-fed rotogravure in the 1890s. New

---

40 See further below, pp. 130–1.

methods contributed in fundamental ways to the development of richly illustrated magazines including the *Studio* (1893-)[41] and the *Burlington Magazine*
(1903-), but they were not confined to the more expensive end of the market. Cassell, who possessed a large stable of popular magazines, launched the
monthly shilling *Magazine of Art* in 1888, with pictures printed as half-tones,
zinc line-blocks, wood-engravings, photogravure, heliogravure and etching. It
was a period of great resources in methods, and great experiment.

Intaglio illustration was based on traditional principles, requiring different
skills in its preparation as well as a rolling-press in its printing. The first steel-
engravings (in practice they were often a mixture of engraving and etching)
were produced in 1820-1, and were used for an edition of Thomas Campbell's
Pleasures of hope published by Longman.[42] Most obviously, the use of steel
overcame one of the problems of printing with copper-engravings, where
the image deteriorated after only a few hundred copies: in the eighteenth
century, to meet the large circulations of magazines, plates had sometimes
been engraved in duplicate.[43] The same procedure was possible with steel-
engravings, and enabled similar savings in time. But steel also lasted longer, and
its hard surface meant that finer detail was possible. It lent itself especially well
to reproductions of paintings, whether of Turner's landscapes or of portraits in
dozens of annuals and albums of pictures. Steel-engraved pictures were usually
printed on a smoother paper than that used for letterpress, and the separate
printing process meant that they were inserted as independent leaves in books.

For publishers, the ability to choose among different kinds of manufacture,
and different qualities of material, had always meant that costs could be flexible. Some costs, and in particular the costs of literary property, left little room
for manoeuvre. By contrast, printing and binding costs offered opportunities
in which various parts of the market could be explored, either on initial publication or, for example, in successive releases of editions of modern authors, in
different formats.[44] Books of topography and natural history lent themselves
especially to copies on both large and ordinary paper, plain or coloured. Some
atlases were likewise offered plain, or coloured by hand, until colour printing
made this no longer necessary. In 1830, Whittaker, Treacher & Co., publishers
in London, were offering a translation of Cuvier's *Animal kingdom* in parts,
either demy octavo or royal octavo, plain or coloured, or demy quarto on India

---

41 Holmes, *Self & partners (mostly self)*; *The Studio: a bibliography*.
42 Hunnisett, *Steel-engraved book illustration in England*, p. 15; Hunnisett, *Engraved on steel*, pp. 112–13.
   See also below, p. 125.
43 See Timothy Clayton in the *Cambridge history of the book in Britain* 5.
44 For Byron in the hands of Murray and others, and for further examples, see St Clair, *The reading
   nation*, especially appendix 9.

paper, at prices ranging from twelve to twenty-four shillings a part. For so long as illustrations had to be hand-coloured, books might be offered with or without colouring, especially in the field of natural history. There were still markets just before the First World War for special copies of books on large paper or on thin paper, meeting the demands sometimes of bibliophiles but also, in the case of the latter, for practicalities such as portability.

Paper

Most paper had always been made from rag – linen, cotton, or mixtures of the two. The extent to which second-hand rags could be used was very greatly extended by the discovery of chlorine bleaching in the eighteenth century. But by the beginning of the nineteenth century there had been many experiments in making paper from vegetable substances. In Germany, a collection of specimens of papers made from different vegetables was published at Regensburg in 1765.[45] If Matthias Koops's straw was the most notorious (partly because he published a book on the subject in 1800), others had attempted with more or less success to make it from materials as improbable as potatoes or beetroot. In 1801, Koops published a second edition of his book, this time on recycled paper.[46] Underlying these experiments was a triple problem. First, there was an obvious economic need to discover a new cheap source of supply for the raw materials, in order to meet a rapidly growing demand especially for cheaper papers; second, only matter with a reasonably long fibre provided a finished product that was not brittle; and third was the problem of supply of raw materials. Any new material would have to be cheap, plentiful and readily available. There were, to be sure, those who were optimistic, such as the author of a book on vegetables and manufactures, who remarked in 1833 of cotton rags that 'the vast quantity of these rags of all descriptions which are now available to the purpose, renders the adoption of any other material of little moment'.[47] In his view, the abundance of possible vegetable alternatives provided excellent further grounds for optimism. Nonetheless, by the mid-century the problem was acute. Although the Lancashire cotton mills were producing very large quantities of waste, it was nowhere near adequate to keep up with demand. The trade in second-hand rags, vital to the paper industry,

45 J. C. Schäffer, *Versuche und Muster ohne alle Lumpen oder doch mit einem geringen zu Satze derselben Papier zu machen*, 6 vols. (Ratisbon [Regensburg], 1765–71).

46 Koops, *Historical account of the substances which have been used to describe events . . . from the earliest date to the invention of paper*.

47 *Vegetable substances: materials of manufactures* (1833), pp. 152–3.

was insufficient, and demand for them was growing, especially in the United States. The trade in rags was an international one, and countries competed for materials from Hamburg to Italy: France, the Low Countries and the Iberian peninsula were for this purpose virtually closed to international trade. In 1830, duty was charged in England, Scotland and Wales on 28,000 tons of paper. In 1861 (the year duty was abolished) the figure was 98,000 tons: it had grown by about 50 per cent just in the past ten years.[48] In the printing industry, the greatest shortages were felt for the cheapest papers, while the single largest factor in demand was the expansion of the newspaper press. Quite apart from widespread demands for reductions in the duty on paper, one estimate suggested that just between the years 1852 and 1855 the cost of raw materials alone, for the equivalent of 1852 needs, rose by £1 million. Between 1852 and 1854, the price of imported rags rose by about 25 per cent. But, thanks not least to export demand, the amount manufactured was rising as well, with all its attendant demands on raw materials.

In 1830, about two-thirds of all paper made in Britain was made by machine, and by 1850 hand-made paper accounted for just 8.6 per cent of total output.[49] Total production more than doubled between 1830 and 1850, and almost doubled again by 1870; by 1880 it had doubled yet again. Only a very small proportion of this was used for books: newspapers, magazines, wallpapers, industrial papers, wrapping papers and materials for children's games all contributed to these figures to different extents. But the need for raw materials was increasing for each.

Nevertheless, between 1810 and 1850 the price of paper dropped almost every year, before rising gradually in the 1850s. The selective reduction in tax in 1836 brought a sharp drop, but the price continued to fall afterwards as well. The trend was mainly the result of increasing machine production, which overtook hand-made paper in the mid-1820s, but it was also attributed to falls in the prices of machinery, buildings, coal, salts and other additives.[50] British production and demand could not be interpreted in isolation. No part of international trade affected the printing industries as much as the demand for paper. After generations of protectionist policies, lower duties made it realistic to import finished paper (rather than just the raw materials) from the 1850s onwards. But other kinds, particularly printing and writing qualities, were exported – mainly to the English-speaking markets.

48 Mitchell, *British historical statistics*, pp. 413–14.   49 Spicer, *The paper trade*, appendix 9.
50 Coleman, *The British paper industry*, pp. 203, 206, 215–17; see also Dagnall, *The taxation of paper in Great Britain, 1643–1861* and Dagnall, 'The taxes on knowledge: excise duty on paper'.

By the mid-1850s, much attention was focussed on further alternatives: plantains from India and the West Indies, straw and flax from nearer home, and even horse dung.[51] After the reduction in the tariffs on paper in 1853, imports of foreign-manufactured paper grew rapidly, meeting about 20 per cent of the country's needs. When the tariffs were repealed in 1860 they grew again, from 1.47 million lb in 1859–60 to 4.74 million lb in 1860–1.[52] Following experiments, it was still thought that the difficulties of reducing wood to pulp were too costly.[53] The mid-century crisis was answered with the discovery of esparto ('Spanish grass') as a suitable vegetable substitute. It grew plentifully in southern Spain and north Africa, and was thus easy to obtain. The first experiments with it in Britain were made in the late 1850s by a civil engineer named Thomas Routledge. Although there were others who thought it was too expensive, in Hertfordshire John Dickinson began production.[54] Imports escalated, and by 1865 about 25,000 tons out of a total of 113,000 tons of paper made in the United Kingdom were made from esparto.[55] By the late 1880s the country imported over 200,000 tons of the grass annually.[56] By itself, the plant produces a somewhat light and bulky paper, of a kind that was much used later for novels. It was better mixed with other ingredients, rag or (later) wood.

The development in the 1880s of chemical wood-pulp, where the pulp was broken down either by an alkaline (soda) process or by an acid (sulphite), brought some of the greatest changes of all in the better book-printing papers. Mechanical wood-pulp became widely used for cheaper work. Imports of wood-pulp (both mechanical and chemical) climbed rapidly between the late 1880s and the end of the century, rising from 122,000 tons in 1889 to 415,000 tons ten years later: by 1905 the figure was about 20 per cent higher again.[57] By 1907, the country was importing annually about 203,000 tons of esparto and other vegetable fibres, about 282,000 tons of chemical wood-pulp, and about 193,000 tons of mechanical wood-pulp. This further affected the qualities and prices of paper. Quite apart from successive reductions in tax, and its final repeal

---

51 J. Forbes Royle, *The fibrous plants of India fitted for cordage, clothing, and paper* (1855), p. 87; *The Times* 27 February 1855.

52 *Report from the Select Committee on paper (export duty on rags)* (1861), p. iv: Parliamentary papers 1861.xi.

53 For various contributions and suggestions concerning materials for paper manufacture, see for example *Journal of the Society of Arts* 2 (1853–4), pp. 403, 486, 554, 756. The whole question was summarised by Charles Tomlinson in the *Quarterly Review* 97 (1855), pp. 225–45.

54 Tillmanns, *Bridge Hall Mills*; Carter, 'Thomas Routledge and the introduction of esparto in paper-making'; Evans, *The endless web*, pp. 111–12.

55 Spicer, *The paper trade*, pp. 34, 100.

56 Spicer, *The paper trade*, appendix 1. See also Magee, *Productivity and performance in the paper industry*.

57 Spicer, *The paper trade*, appendix 1.

in 1861, the average price of comparable qualities of paper fell from about tenpence a pound in 1836 to twopence a pound in 1902.[58] This was partly the result of new methods and materials of production, but it was also the result of improved labour productivity even as wages crept upwards. Between 1860 and 1900 the price of esparto more than halved, and by mixing it with wood-pulp manufacturers were able to produce paper of acceptable quality at ever less cost. By the early twentieth century the rate of paper consumption, especially of newsprint, was once again causing concern. Once again new sources were sought out, this time in the spruce and balsa forests of Canada.

There had always been plenty of critics ready to find fault with machine-made paper, with more or less justice in their accusations. One of the most forward was John Murray, who in the 1820s echoed Hansard in his anxiety about the short life of modern paper.[59] In 1898 a committee of the Society of Arts reported on deterioration in paper.[60] But the point was not whether or not it was machine-made. As the summary of recent chemical literature, conveniently reproduced in the Society of Arts's report, made clear, the problems lay principally in the materials, including salts or other chemicals used in the course of production. In the same year the librarian J. Y. W. MacAlister proposed to publishers that they should print some copies of their books on better paper, for the use of libraries.[61] He met a predictably mixed response, of sympathy mingled with commercial hard-headedness concerning who should pay: the idea was left to lie dormant until similar concerns about so-called permanent paper were raised, again from libraries, after the Second World War. The evidence of the deteriorating quality of paper, which so alarmed publishers, librarians and the public in the last decades of the nineteenth century, was in some measure contained and understood by about 1910.[62] But this new understanding of the chemistry and structure of paper did not imply all-round improvements. Instead, it made possible better-informed decisions about when to use cheap paper – a world to which publishers and government adapted themselves with relish.

With the need for ever smoother surfaces to take illustrations, so-called art papers were developed. The first clay-loaded papers had been made at the

---

58 *Ibid.*, pp. 89–90.
59 Murray, *Practical remarks on modern paper*: this followed his earlier contribution to the *Gentleman's Magazine* in 1823. Cf. Hansard, *Typographia*, p. 231.
60 *Report of the committee on the deterioration of paper* (Society for the Encouragement of Arts, Manufactures, & Commerce, 1898); see also the summary 'Report of the committee on the deterioration of paper', *Journal of the Society of Arts* 46 (1897–8), pp. 597–601.
61 MacAlister, 'The durability of modern book papers'.
62 Chivers, *The paper of lending library books*.

beginning of the century, but the new generation of art papers was quite different from the hot-pressed papers that had been in use since the eighteenth century, and different again from super-calendered papers made by passing the web of paper through a tower of rollers and thus subjecting it to friction under very great pressure. The best of the art papers manufactured in the second half of the nineteenth century, which could be made of any of the ordinary basic ingredients, or a mixture of them, were coated mechanically with a mixture of water, china clay and glue. Imitation art papers, which were much used in magazines by the end of the century, differed from true art papers by the clay's being mixed in the pulp, a process that was cheaper but that resulted in a weaker paper: after leaving the paper-making machine it was super-calendered so as to impart a surface that the earlier stages of manufacture could not provide. Of the other specialist papers used in the book trades, the most familiar was Oxford India paper. A parcel of exceptionally thin, opaque paper was brought back from India in 1841 and was used at Oxford to print a small number of Bibles in the following year. It took thirty years to discover how to make it, until in 1875 the Press published a Bible made on a similar paper at its paper-mill at Wolvercote.[63] Demand was immediate, and heavy; and the Press introduced it for some of its other books. The secrets of the process were jealously protected, but several derivatives and imitations of different qualities were made by other manufacturers who realised that the main ingredient was rag, and that the method of beating was critical to success. A version of this paper, with its characteristic hard surface, became still more widely familiar when it was used for the thin-paper edition of the eleventh edition of the *Encyclopaedia Britannica* (1910).[64]

Bookbinding

To the passing observer of a shop window, nothing changed more obviously between 1830 and 1914 than the outward appearance of books. In 1830, most books were still published in plain wrappers or drab paper-covered boards, usually grey, brown, or dull pink, and quickly stitched together. Title, name of author and (importantly) often the price were printed on labels pasted to the spine: the presence of the price was a reminder that there was no longer necessarily a distinction between retail prices in town and country. Many books never received more than this as a covering. For most books, it was assumed

---

63 Carter, *Wolvercote Mill*, pp. 44–5.
64 Fisher, 'Paper: India paper', *Encyclopaedia Britannica* 11th edn (1910).

that a new, stronger binding would be supplied subsequently, for the better books in calf or, more ornamentally (and it was believed more durably), in russia leather. There were trade binders in even quite small towns, while at the top end of the market were binders such as Charles Lewis or Charles Hering in London or, elsewhere in the country, like John Shalders in Great Yarmouth, or Carss in Glasgow. The choice of a more permanent covering was made either by the bookseller or by the final purchaser: decoration, gilt or blind, was likewise according to taste and purse. A few books were issued in printed paper-covered boards, sometimes with a decorative element as well. Though printed paper-covered stiff bindings had been known in Italy since the fifteenth century, and were common in late eighteenth- and early nineteenth-century Germany, they never became as widely used in Britain even in the midst of crises in leather supply due to wartime demands for equipment. Plain brown canvas had been used to cover some kinds of books, notably schoolbooks and practical manuals, since the second half of the eighteenth century, and lighter calicoes were employed on a wider range of new books in the mid-1820s.[65] For schoolbooks, publishers continued to use sheep, a cheap leather, even when other kinds of books were increasingly being issued in cloth. The half-dozen editions of Goldsmith's history of England in the 1830s priced between 3s 6d and 6s were all covered in leather. William Pinnock's many books addressed to children from their first reading lessons onwards were almost all sold likewise at this time.

Most publishers were hesitant to adopt the notion of using cloth as an ordinary covering for new publications.[66] The first examples seem to date from 1823, and the publisher William Pickering was prominent in its use: by the early 1830s he was using it regularly, and suppliers were producing cloth for other publishers as well. At first, smooth highly glazed cloth was much used, until means were found of embossing patterns. Some of the more innovative publishers and manufacturers used watered silk for the annuals that enjoyed a reign of popularity especially between the mid-1820s and the mid-1840s: with their steel-engravings, and usually slight literary contents, these were books for the adornment of drawing rooms rather than use in the study or library.[67] In 1836, some copies of Samuel Rogers's popular poem *Italy*, with vignettes by

65 Leighton, 'Canvas and bookcloth'; see also Nicholas Pickwoad in the *Cambridge history of the book in Britain* 5.
66 Sadleir, *The evolution of publishers' binding styles*. Further general surveys of the period include Potter, 'The development of publishers' bookbinding in the nineteenth century'.
67 Faxon, *Literary annuals and gift books*.

Turner and others, were bound in red watered silk: the intended market was the same as for the annuals.

During the 1830s cloth became more common in several ways – not only for books case-bound in full cloth, but also as a means of providing strengthening for spines, so that many books were now published in quarter cloth, still with paper labels providing title, author and price on the spines. Case-bindings could be made cheaply and quickly, and required less skill than binding in leather. Cloth was also usually cheap, and readily available. These bindings, more durable than those composed of paper over boards, made customer's binding no longer such a necessity, and increasingly leather was used more for ornate or special bindings. Gilt lettering was successfully applied to cloth on the second volume (early copies of the first simply have a paper label) of a collected edition of Byron in 1832–3. It proved to be the start of a revolution in the appearance of books which has remained innovative into our own times. Printed cloths were familiar in dress and furnishings, but means were soon also found of printing words and decorations onto starch-loaded cloth, and of blocking solid colour. In the mid-1820s the introduction of embossing machines, and with them the metal dies and counter-dies bearing decorations, added further ornamental elements and also introduced new standardisation into what had hitherto been a hand process.[68] This was not, however, the same as edition binding as it came to be understood only a few years later.[69] Quite apart from the endless varieties of finish offered in the Bible and prayer book trade, which made heavy use of the cheap but decorative possibilities of embossed leather and cloth, other kinds of books were also offered in different garbs. In 1838, for example, the English Classic Library was advertised 'handsomely bound in embossed leather, with gilt edges, at *only one shilling extra*', and also in the best Turkey morocco, at three shillings extra.

Unlike the printing and paper-making trades, mechanisation was slow in bookbinding.[70] But mechanisation was not all. Binders had always sought out ways of saving time, effort or materials.[71] The introduction of case-binding, which saved time and made uniform decoration of multiple copies much easier,

---

68 Jamieson, *English embossed bindings*.
69 For some of the similarities and differences compared with the French trade, and particularly differences in the use of materials, see Malavieille, *Reliures et cartonnages d'éditeur en France au XIXe siècle*.
70 Comparato, in *Books for the millions*, is primarily concerned with the United States, but offers much on British practices: see also Rogers, 'The rise of American edition binding'. For Britain, see Stephen, *Commercial bookbinding* and his enlarged *Die moderne Grossbuchbinderei* adapted for the German-speaking market by Hermann Scheibe. Biesalski, *Die Mechanisierung der deutschen Buchbinderei, 1850–1900*, deals to some extent with the first half of the century as well.
71 Pickwoad, 'Onward and downward'.

had both economic and aesthetic effects. It made possible the rapid preparation of identical covers, which were then glued rather than sewn to the text-block, usually with hollow backs. It was not universally welcomed. The writer of publicity for one firm of craftsmen observed in the mid-1850s that the new practice of passing freshly printed sheets straight to the binder meant that they were sometimes pressed when the ink was still wet, and thus were spoiled with off-set. Moreover, opportunities for choice were taken away.

> The whole edition being once bound with the same ornaments and in the same colour, the purchaser has no choice left to him; whatever his taste may be, he must take the work as he finds it, or go to the expense of having it bound anew; in addition to which, such bindings are for the most part rickety, and fall to pieces when they come to be much handled.[72]

Cloth itself presented a multiplicity of qualities. The discovery that it could be gold-blocked led to some of the greatest changes in the appearance of bindings – and, hence, in the ways that books could be publicised and presented to potential readers. It transformed the relationship between publisher, bookseller, customer and reader. Books could be sold almost as much by their outside as by their contents. In a world obsessed with decoration and pattern, gold-blocking on cloth provided the book trade with a language also for self-advertisement. From its first use, it offered a new world of decoration (fig. 1.2). But most processes in bookbinding remained stubbornly resistant to mechanisation. The introduction of the rolling machine from 1827 onwards did away with the laborious process of beating the folded and sewn sheets with heavy hammers, in order to drive out pockets of air and to shape the spines of sewn blocks into the rounded shape that would take the covering of a book. Such books did not meet with universal approbation amongst journeymen, who in 1830 called for them to be abolished. As so often, the fear was not of the machinery, but of its possible implications: that it would increase unemployment in the trade. Nonetheless, according to one calculation the number of people engaged in bookbinding just in London rose sixfold, to over 3,600, between 1830 and 1861.[73] Demand for books ensured demand for skills. In a trade where so much depended on hand labour, not everyone was well paid. The women employed to bind the thousands of Bibles and New Testaments printed for the British and Foreign Bible Society were shamelessly exploited until the scandal broke in 1849–50.[74]

72 [Soane] *A hand-book of taste in book-binding.*   73 Knight, *Passages of a working life* 2, p. 162.
74 Howsam, *Cheap Bibles*, pp. 138–46; Potter, 'The London bookbinding trade: from craft to industry'.

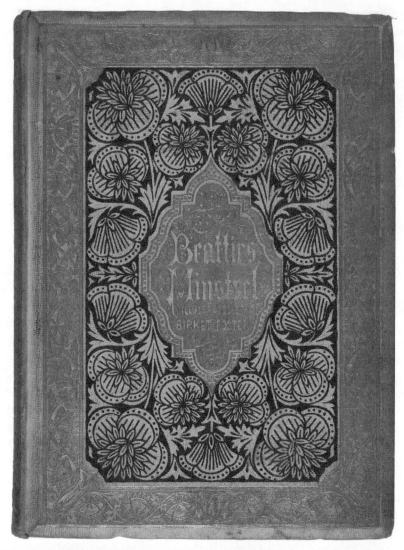

Figure 1.2 James Beattie, *The minstrel*, illustrated by Birket Foster (George Routledge & Co., 1858). Binding blocked in gold and black ink, designed by Albert Warren. (Private collection)

One of the most labour-intensive parts of bookbinding was in sewing the sheets together. Costs were kept down by employing female labour, but other means of manufacture became increasingly necessary as the numbers of books grew. In 1843 Walter Hancock, a pioneer of steam carriages on roads, took out a patent for the manufacture of caoutchouc, a thin India rubber, for a method of binding whereby the folds of the sheets in the spine were cut off, and the exposed edges painted with thin coatings of latex that were then in turn covered with a thin cloth. The result, which worked best on thicker paper, was to provide a flexible spine that gradually stiffened, as the rubber hardened, until within a few years it was all but impossible to open a book bound thus without its disintegrating. Nevertheless, the material enjoyed a considerable vogue especially for the more lavish illustrated books printed by chromolithography; by 1843 the London binders Westley & Clark had a busy 'caoutchouc' department.

The largest bookbinding establishments were specially designed. In 1842, Westley & Clark occupied a six-storey building in the City of London, each floor allocated to particular tasks. On the first floor was the 'Pinnock room' so named after the constant work to meet demand for the ninepenny *Pinnock's Catechism*. Further up the building were special rooms for the binding of annuals, for the making of cloth cases, for gilding and for the 'caoutchouc' bindings. There was no mechanisation. Sheets of paper received from the printer were folded by hand, usually by women; and after folding they were passed to other women who sewed them ready for binding. During busy seasons, the firm employed about two hundred women, paid between ten and eighteen shillings a week, and it was observed that bookbinding was one of the few occupations open to women for regular paid employment. Only after sewing was the process taken over by men, for the backs of the new volumes to be rounded, a heavier process that involved much hammering. Any edge-decoration, such as colouring, marbling or gilding, was done before the covers were added. For books that were case-bound, embossed decoration to the covers either could be added to the cases while they were still flat, or could be done once the book was bound. Imitation morocco and roan, two cheap kinds of sheepskin, were widely used for the covers of prayer books and Bibles, as well as for some schoolbooks: binders were adept at making them appear suitably attractive. Skiver, split sheepskin, was cheaper still. In Bermondsey in the 1840s, the centre of leather manufacture, there were between twenty and thirty fellmongers working with sheepskins for various finished goods.[75]

The cloth bindings used by publishers such as Pickering in the 1820s and early 1830s were usually of undecorated cotton loaded with dyed starch and then calendered.[76] With the invention of a means of producing rolls of cloth embossed

---

75 'A day at a leather-factory'; 'A day at a bookbinder's'.   76 Leighton, 'Canvas and bookcloth'.

with patterns, publishers were presented with a vastly increased choice. Pebble, ribbed, bead-grained, diapered and even morocco leather-grained cloths were widely used, and the increasing use of colour in book cloths added further to variety.[77] In the large gift-book market that developed in the mid-century as costs went down and cash for recreation increased, thicker boards were used, bevelled edges became commonplace, and leather or paper overlays added their further eclectic effects to ever more ornate gold- and colour-blocking. Gilt edges added further to the gaudiness. Firms such as Routledge made their reputations and fortunes by feeding and encouraging a taste for gift-books that flaunted their decoration. Bookbinders such as Edmonds & Remnant, Leighton and Bone & Son met challenges in materials that had scarcely been imagined a generation earlier. The gift-book market was not alone. Although other kinds of books tended to comparative restraint, the last third of the century was noticeable for the ways in which decorative conventions were applied increasingly to other kinds of books, by publishers striving for attention in an over-decorated world. Books of travel and natural history, having claim to a general sale, tended also to be published in decorated cloth. Some bindings were signed by their designers, and others were distinctive enough for the name of the designer to be clear to an informed eye. W. Harry Rogers, John Leighton, Owen Jones, Walter Crane, D. G. Rossetti and William Nicholson were, at different periods, among the better-known. Hand-in-hand with new ideas in the late nineteenth and early twentieth centuries for the display of books (it is usually difficult to be certain about which led the other) went an increasing dependence on decorative cloth covers for novels clamouring for space and attention.

The advent of glazed printed paper bindings transformed the much larger reading environment in the mid-nineteenth century.[78] As has already been mentioned, the first paper bindings had been introduced centuries earlier. In the 1820s, publishers such as Longman, Thomas Tegg and J. F. Dove employed buff paper boards, printed letterpress and decorated with some typographic ornament. The contrast with the more elaborate paper bindings of Christmas and New Year gift-books published by Ackermann and others at the same period was all the more striking. By 1850, glazed paper boards were commonplace, printed either letterpress or by lithography, and with decorations either

77 Ibid.; Darley, Bookbinding then and now; Tanselle, 'The bibliographical description of patterns'; McLean, Victorian publishers' book-bindings in cloth and leather; Ball, Victorian publishers' bindings; Tomlinson and Masters, Bookcloth, 1823–1980. For an international context, see Morris and Levin, The art of publishers' bookbindings, 1815–1915 and Krupp 'Bookcloth in England and America, 1823–50'.

78 McLean, Victorian publishers' book-bindings in paper.

drawn (for lithography) or engraved in wood (for letterpress). Colour was normal. The shiny hard surface, which repelled minor dirt, was perfectly suited to more prolonged use, and it was the basis for the decorated paper-covered boards of the Railway Library and its many rivals in a market where uniform low prices and distinctiveness in display were paramount. Paper also lent itself easily to stamping or embossing, while elaborate black papier mâché bindings, sometimes looking at first glance more like carved wood, became fashionable for the gift market in religious literature. Card covered in coloured paper and printed in further colours proved ideal for children's books, though in this as with so many publications of the century customers might be offered a choice: *The pet lamb*, published by Darton & Hodge in the 1860s, and with illustrations printed in colour from woodblocks, was available at sixpence, one shilling ('indestructible') or 1s 6d ('washable indestructible'). Paper was cheap, and it was easily decorated; its adoption for the covers of new novels, with pictures suggesting something of the contents, was formative in the new ideas in design and presentation in the 1890s and early years of the twentieth century.

The immense increase in the numbers of books printed in the last two decades of the century and in the early twentieth century forced publishers and book-binders to find ever cheaper and faster methods and materials. Stitched wire bindings, and wires stabbed through the text-block, made their appearance in the 1870s. They were certainly cheap; but they had several disadvantages. Wire-stabbed bindings on thick books made volumes rigid, and difficult to open. And wire was itself liable to rust. Sewing with ordinary thread was finally mechanised with the invention of the Smyth sewer in America, patented in 1868. It was introduced into Britain in the early 1880s, and the first machines in Britain seem to have been installed by Frederic R. Daldy, in London.[79] A dozen machines were in use at James Burn & Son by 1885.[80] By the early twentieth century, other manufacturers were in play, of which the most important were Martini and Brehmer. Gradually, binding had been all but completely mechanised.

Leather bindings were not necessarily durable. They remained popular especially for show, in private collections, even when cloth would last longer. The introduction of hollow backs in the early 1820s brought a structure that placed the greatest strain on just the part of a leather binding that was the weakest, where the leather had been pared away at the joints.[81] Heavy, or even just moderate, use led to the parting of the spine from the boards. By 1900, half a

79 Comparato, *Books for the millions*, p. 177.   80 Darley, *Bookbinding then and now*.
81 Middleton, *A history of English craft bookbinding technique*, pp. 111–14.

century of heavy use of books in public libraries had tested the physical properties of books on a scale that had never before been even approached. The results were not encouraging. While it was commonly thought that leather was best, it was plain that different tanning practices, the use of poor imported leathers, the practice of splitting skins for even thickness, the unnecessary use of acids for improving colour, and some of the embossing processes in common use all contributed to a measurable decline in longevity, and to the disastrous appearance of books bound only quite recently. The Royal Society of Arts followed its report of 1898 on paper deterioration[82] with another on leathers in 1905. Bindings were inadequate, and when repairs were called for it was clear that librarians had inadequate knowledge of what to order. Leather itself was prepared in ways that provided superficial short-term attractions but led to quick deterioration, and by 1901 Douglas Cockerell, one of the most respected bookbinders and repairers of his generation, wrote confidently that 'it is no exaggeration to say that ninety per cent. of the books bound in leather during the last thirty years will need rebinding during the next thirty'.[83] Materials and methods apart, he also blamed the conditions under which books were kept: gas light was among the most damaging factors of all. It was all too obvious to others as well that the papers selected by some publishers had little life or strength in them. For papers, some authorities blamed the processes of manufacture, and other blamed the ingredients: the bulky and widely popular featherweight, or antique paper, much used in novels, children's books and general literature, was a mixture of esparto and wood-pulp that was easily marked and was next to impossible to repair satisfactorily.[84]

The decorative dust-jacket, with pictures replacing plain typography, seems an obvious piece of advertising artillery, but it developed slowly. The paucity of surviving specimens before about 1900 makes generalisation difficult, and it is still more difficult to assess how far these often stray examples are representative of their publishers, or their generation. But protective card coverings and slip-cases for books had been used at the end of the eighteenth century, and by the 1830s they were frequently employed for children's books, almanacs and annual keepsakes. A little later, other coverings of paper, rather than card, were folded over the entire book, like wrapping paper. The jacket in its modern sense was developed in the 1860s, and in 1889 examples are recorded from the

---

82 See above, p. 95.
83 Cockerell, *Bookbinding, and the care of books*, p. 18. See also below, p. 667.
84 Chivers, *The paper of lending library books* (dealing also with American books); Coutts and Stephen, *Manual of library bookbinding*. See also pp. 16, 95.

Clarendon Press, Griffin, Longman, Sampson Low, Routledge and Frederick Warne. The list is but a shadow of what has now been lost or discarded. In the first decade of the twentieth century the jacket became an essential marketing tool, and much more than a protective cover.[85] Colour pictures on the fronts and spines provided devices for bookshop displays especially of fiction, while the value of wrappings with plain typography was recognised even for the most recondite of other books. Plain glassine or ordinary paper was employed where no extra expense was wished.

In all this, the publisher was paramount, arranging for design and printing as well as for binding. Though a few publishers still released stocks of new-printed books only in sheets, the notion of a publisher's binding was still not the same as a binding uniform in all copies of an impression. Books were bound (or, more strictly, cased[86]) as required by the market, and unbound stocks of paper might be held for decades: inevitably the result was variation. Even books released at the same time might be in different colours or patterns of cloth, depending on what the binder had in stock that most nearly matched the publisher's specification. So-called 'remainder' bindings, usually cheaper than those originally employed, were put on slow-selling stock that it was wished to clear at lower prices. Colonial editions[87] usually had their own bindings, sometimes to fit in with publishers' series: such books might be available either in cloth or in paper wrappers. The publishers' aim in this market, for cheapness and for profit, was not universally appreciated among customers.

The trade with Australia was important, but it was not always understood. In manufactured goods, by the late nineteenth century Britain was competing with continental Europe and with America for a demanding market. In printed matter, language generally gave Britain an advantage over Germany or France, but not over America. When in summer 1914 a correspondent of the *Author* reported on his impressions from a visit there, he was immediately taken up by the *Publishers' Circular*. The core of his complaint was a visual one: that British publishers were being endangered by the greater attention being paid by American publishers to the outward decoration of their books, and that window-dressing was being ignored. 'Australian booksellers prefer gaily coloured picture covers, highly glazed paper, plentiful decoration and illustrations, and, it may be, gilt tops. The American publisher provides all this, whilst the English publisher in very many cases prefers to supply in his

---

85 Tanselle, in 'Dust-jackets, dealers, and documentation', provides a list of almost four hundred British and American examples down to 1890, with an emphasis firmly on America.
86 Cockerell, *Bookbinding, and the care of books*, pp. 19–20.   87 See further below, pp. 200–1, 600–1.

"Colonial edition" – Australians detest that phrase – a format somewhat more drab and unexciting than he uses for his English editions.'[88] The comparison was not unfair, but the question was a larger one, touching not just on area rights, but also on publishing as a world activity. In Sydney, the Australian edition of *Scribner's Magazine* was a reminder of the attention being paid to a significant market by New York publishers. With trade boundaries difficult to police even where it was desired, publishers were competing both amongst themselves, title against title, and with foreign rights holders as well. As always, price and presentation both affected choice. In a market where monopolies could be controlled that hardly mattered. In an international environment it was critical. Debate was shifted from copyright to competing production values, and thus placed the customer, not the author, to the fore.

Price and appearance

The concern for prices that had preoccupied publishers, authors and readers in 1830 remained very similar in the different environment of the early twentieth century. It has already been emphasised how important price structures were to the market in the early 1830s, not least in the sale of fiction and in the efforts of Charles Knight, Robert Chambers and others to produce cheap informative literature.[89] As was repeatedly demonstrated by publishers who first issued new books at a high price and then gradually produced editions in smaller formats, in smaller type and on cheaper paper, each gradation of edition exploiting another sector of the market, book-buying was always highly price-sensitive. Though the real price of new books had dropped markedly by the end of the century, the same structures were still key to successful publication of many kinds of literature. This had been true of Bible and prayer book publishing since the sixteenth century. For the most popular authors, publishers strove to provide a choice to suit every taste and pocket. In the 1870s, copyright in Scott's Waverley novels belonged to A. & C. Black, in Edinburgh. They offered a sixpenny edition (four volumes, in decorated cloth or half-French morocco at a guinea, or £1 7s in half calf), a shilling edition (twelve volumes, at £1 11s 6d in cloth, £2 in half leather, or £2 12s in half calf), a centenary edition (four guineas in cloth for twenty-five volumes, or half-bound in calf

---

88 A. J. Dawson, quoted from the *Author* July 1914, in the *Publishers' Circular* 11 July 1914, p. 27. For further remarks, especially on increasing sales of American magazines in Australia, see the *Publishers' Circular* 15 August 1914.
89 See above, Introduction, pp. 43–4.

or morocco), a pocket edition (£1 17s for twenty-five volumes in cloth, or £3 5s in limp Cape morocco, and also available at 1s 6d a volume), an 'author's favourite' (£7 4s, forty-eight volumes in cloth, and kept in print for decades), a Roxburghe edition (£11 5s a set, in half leather, in forty-eight volumes, or in cloth for ten guineas) and a library edition (8s 6d a volume, published monthly). Specially designed bookcases were available for each. The sixpenny edition was further available in individual volumes, with paper covers. Printed in small type in double columns, it was obviously inferior to the shilling edition, which was printed in single columns and in larger type. For those who could not accommodate a bookcase, there was also a boxed set, crammed into a space of $12 \times 9 \times 9^{1}/_{4}$ inches. The poetical works were offered on the same principle of maximum choice. All these were from Black, but other publishers also offered Scott, including a 'best library edition' from Henry Sotheran in London, with illustrations by Stanfield, Leslie and others, for prices between nine guineas and £21 ('a choice set for presentation' in morocco super extra, with borders of gold and gilt edges). Much was made in publishers' advertising of convenience; but from much of this advertising it is evident that appearance was at least as important. The cheap leathers and imitations whose descriptions can only have been partly understood by shopkeepers, let alone customers, made it clear that these were books for furnishing.

Tennyson, eventually, became available in comparable variety, in different formats, different bindings, different type sizes, on different qualities of paper and at accordingly different prices. Copyrights in his work were divided between several publishers for much of his career, and it was not until 1884 that Alexander Macmillan was finally able to achieve his long-sought ambition of obtaining most of them.[90] At the most expensive end of the market, the four Arthurian poems *Elaine, Guinevere, Enid* and *Vivienne*, each with illustratons by Gustave Doré, were available in the mid-1870s on separate sheets, in four portfolios for £21, from Henry Sotheran (who also offered them bound up into a half-morocco scrapbook for £30), or could be had separately bound in decorated cloth from Ward Lock, who had taken over the stock from Moxon, at a guinea each. Most of Tennyson's work at this time was controlled by Henry S. King, who offered four main collected editions, from the 'Imperial Library' to the 'Miniature', variously bound in cloth, Roxburghe-style leather or imitation vellum. *Idylls of the king and other poems*, illustrated with Julia Margaret Cameron's photographs, cost six guineas for each of the two volumes, but the *Idylls* were also available at five or six shillings. The small green

90 Hagen, *Tennyson and his publishers*, p. 158.

cloth volumes that became almost ubiquitous presences in private libraries cost between three and six shillings, and this was the form most familiar to those who possessed Tennyson. King retired in 1877, and for a few years Charles Kegan Paul was Tennyson's main publisher until his copyrights passed to Macmillan. Thereupon, Macmillan immediately issued a new one-volume edition for 7s 6d and another in seven volumes, available also on hand-made paper. A school edition appeared in the same year in four parts at half a crown apiece. Macmillan continued the tradition of green cloth octavos for individual titles, but he also needed to recoup his investment, and in 1885 extended the market further with a new edition of the *Tennyson birthday book*, whilst a selection by Francis Palgrave and a new edition of *In memoriam* were published in the Golden Treasury series, both available also on large paper. In the following year a new miniature edition was published, the plays and the poems in two separate series.

From this kind of market analysis it was a simple step to selling all kinds of books by price. Ward Lock's catalogue in the 1870s was organised both by title and in gradations of price, from the penny books taken over from Beeton, and a penny Shakespeare, to five guineas for a large folio collection of heliotypes of Windsor Castle taken by the Queen's Librarian, Bernard Bolingbroke Woodward. Most of their books were between sixpence and five shillings. By the early twentieth century, the practice of arranging lists of books by price had become widespread. Though there were a few specialist publishers who did so, such as Pitman (shorthand), and the religious publishers Skeffington, most were notable for being generalists. Cassell, Constable, Grant Richards, Hurst & Blackett, Hutchinson, John Murray, W. P. Nimmo, Thomas Nelson and Smith, Elder all did so in their catalogues. All were major publishers of new novels. Berenson's *Florentine painters* topped Murray's list, at £21; but for all these publishers the more important parts, both for investment and for income, were at the middle and the bottom, in the novels priced at 4s 6d to 6s, and in the shilling, sixpenny and threepenny libraries that were such a feature of the pre-war trade.

From mid-Victorian to Georgian

Between about 1860 and the mid-1880s the outlook for the printing trades was transformed. New materials on a large scale had been introduced for the first time since the middle ages. New issues arose concerning the longevity of books and other paper-based products. The appearance of books was fundamentally changed, though the change was not always obvious in books freshly published. It changed again, almost as dramatically, during the last thirty years or so of this volume. Visually in its covers, its typography and its illustration, the British printed book of 1914 was far removed from its ancestor of 1830. Manufactured almost entirely by machine, mostly printed on paper manufactured with materials unthinkable in 1830, and dependent for its publicity and mobility on the modern electrically driven presses of newspapers and on steam trains that only just existed in 1830, its differences were obvious even to the uninformed.

John Southward's *Practical printing* was first published in 1882. It became the principal handbook until the First World War, republished in successively revised and enlarged editions. By the sixth, of 1911, methods and practices had changed substantially. Composing machines, innovations in three-colour printing, labour-saving devices for make-ready on the presses, and the definition of an agreed point system (accepted in Britain in 1898) for measuring type all had their effect not just on working practices, but also on the appearance of books. When Southward's book was originally published,

> composing by machinery was but tentative, on lines now superseded, and was confined to a few enthusiastic pioneers; a uniform standard for type-bodies was wished for, but seemed hopeless to attain; display composition was but a rudimentary art; half-tone blocks were unknown; printing on damped paper with soft packing was usual, and the use of the hand-press for working off was far from uncommon; while fast-running machines with solid beds and geared inking arrangements were reserved for the future.[91]

Nonetheless, and in quite basic ways, the printed book looked backwards. The tradition of the codex had not been replaced, or even threatened; and the fundamentally conservative essentials of reading remained, adjusted and sometimes even challenged, but not superseded.

As demand grew alongside some publishers' determination to find as large a market as possible, so there was a transfer of technology. The application of newspaper and magazine printing methods and machinery to book production had become commonplace by the 1890s, and thanks to the use of cheap newsprint enabled publishers such as A. & C. Black, Macmillan and Cassell to publish full-length novels at sixpence apiece. In Manchester, W. H. White's Manchester Library included *Oliver Twist*, *Ivanhoe* and Darwin's *Journal of a voyage round the world* at threepence each in paper covers, or sixpence in cloth. *Vanity Fair*, in two volumes, and with Thackeray's illustrations, was crammed

---

91 Southward, *Practical printing* 6th edn, Preface, p. iii.

into just under three hundred two-column pages. Edited by the radical journalist W. T. Stead, the *Review of Reviews* provided substantial selections from poets, and abridged versions of full-length novels, in the 1890s for one penny each: *Mary Barton*, for example, was reduced (with some difficulty according to the anonymous woman who did this) to just sixty-eight pages. Clowes was the leading printer for this series. The type was reasonably large, unlike that in most of the small volumes from Milner of Halifax, which had been selling by the tens of thousands since the mid-1830s. Prices were kept down not just by stereotyping and cheap paper, but also by advertising revenue: Fry's cocoa, Beecham's pills, Pears' soap and Hovis bread all featured regularly in the endpapers and on the cover-sheets of these paper-backs, and the Victorian obsession with medical ailments was further reflected in advertisements – some from quacks – promising remedies for tooth-ache, deafness, ruptures and corpulence. Both old, non-copyright, authors and contemporary writers were printed with the new, cheap, technologies and materials, and in the same contexts of heavy advertising.

From another point of view, the year 1914 presented a dichotomy. In June that year Wyndham Lewis launched his new periodical *Blast!* and thus forced into the world of the British printed book issues of recent design that were to be seen at art galleries in the work of painters and sculptors such as Kandinsky, Gaudier-Brzeska, Edward Wadsworth and William Roberts. With its heavy sans-serif title set at a defiant angle, its pink-violet wrappers and its text printed on thick brown paper it challenged convention and taste.

In cubism, vorticism, futurism and other movements, the world of print, and of the printed book, was being examined anew. Most of this activity was overseas. At the beginning of the new century, Ambroise Vollard's publication of Verlaine's *Parallèlement* (1900) and Longus's *Daphnis et Chloé* (1902), both with lithographs by Bonnard, had set their roots in older exploitations of lithography applied to book design; but they introduced the *livre d'artiste* to fresh markets and were a timely challenge to the widespread undervaluing of lithographs and to the traditionally based assumptions of art nouveau. In 1913, Blaise Cendrars's *La prose du Transsibérien et de la petite Jehanne de France* printed in two columns on four long sheets of paper, the text justified variously against the left and right margins brightly overlaid with washes of colour, broke with the codex tradition. Mallarmé's poem *Un coup de dés*, first published in 1897 and then again in 1914, exploited typographic drama to achieve emphasis and relationships and, like the work of Cendrars and of Apollinaire a little later, sought to overcome the sequential insistence of conventional typesetting. But the 1914 setting was quite different from the earlier one.[92] Aggressively, typography created meaning, and thus could also change it. More explicitly, in Italy, Marinetti's *Zang Tumb Tumb* (1914) offered a manifesto against 'the so-called typographical harmony of the page, which is contrary to the ebb and flow, the jolts and explosions of the style which moves over the page itself'.[93] In Russia, Aleksey Kruchenykh used lithography, and the cheapest of papers, to explore overlapping relationships between text and print in books that were deliberately made to appear crude.

Though they achieved varying degrees of post-war influence, none of these experiments could be considered in the mainstream of book design and production. Instead, they had a common desire to re-examine old assumptions. With *Blast!*, published by John Lane, the boundaries between the world of ordinary commercial book publishing and that of artists seemed to be partly overcome. Lane's other authors, especially in the 1890s, included several who were considered advanced, and his artists had included Aubrey Beardsley, Walter Crane and Charles Ricketts, all innovative. He had published the *Yellow Book*, equally advanced for its time. For his printing, he relied chiefly on C. T. Jacobi of the Chiswick Press and Walter Biggar Blaikie of T. & A. Constable: given guidance, ordinary commercial printers were as capable of producing original work as well as were others who were noisier. The trial in 1895 of Oscar Wilde, one of Lane's authors, proved a turning-point. By 1914 his firm issued A. C. Benson, G. K. Chesterton and H. G. Wells. Conventionality and adventurism became bedfellows.[94] In *Blast!* ideas from one world were selected and absorbed into the other; conventionality was challenged, and perceptions of the book (more than just book design) were required to be re-examined just as they had been in the sixteenth, seventeenth and eighteenth centuries with the separate, related and finally partly integrated trade in copper-engravings and etchings. The contrast between the typography of the main part of *Blast!* and the conventional setting employed at the end of the volume for Lane's advertisements for his other publications (complete sets of the *Yellow Book* were still to be had new for £3 5s) made the point all the more forcefully.

Visitors to the great international exhibition of the book that opened at Leipzig in May 1914, the largest of its kind ever to be undertaken, found a very different and cautious approach on the part of British publishers and printers

---

92 Both the 1897 and the 1914 versions are reproduced in Bartram, *Futurist typography and the liberated text*, pp. 10–11. These themes are further explored in Bury (ed.), *Breaking the rules*.

93 F. T. Marinetti, *Zang Tumb Tumb* (Milan, 1914); English translation in Franco Riva, 'Book printing in Italy from 1800 to the present day', in Day (ed.), *Book typography, 1815–1965*, pp. 177–223, at p. 206.

94 May, *John Lane and the nineties*; Nelson, *The early nineties*; Stetz and Lasner, *England in the 1890s*.

if they compared it with many continental counterparts. The British pavilion was determinedly rearward-looking, a stone Tudor-style mansion with mullioned windows, a cobbled courtyard and timber mock-Tudor ceilings. Outside was a sunken Tudor garden. An exhibition of Shakespeare was laid out on old oak tables.[95] This was composed of facsimiles and photographs, but in special sections of travel and discovery and of illustrated books there were several works of considerable value, including a vellum copy of the Kelmscott Chaucer and some rare eighteenth-century children's books borrowed from the St Bride Printing Library and from F. J. H. Darton. The exhibits, old or recent, were suitably conventional, and achieved the desired result of bringing to a largely German-speaking audience some of the British developments in manufacturing, typography, illustration and bookbindings, within a reassuring historical context of literary accomplishment. There was a heavy emphasis on arts and crafts, and as contributors to the catalogue Emery Walker and B. H. Newdigate ensured that the work of the major private presses was adequately covered. The lack of any mention of Linotype or Monotype machine typesetting was a glaring omission, and served to emphasise the regressive mood. A special section concentrated on the work of women artists, and another, housed in the separate Kultur-Halle, was devoted to graphic art. Publishers made little attempt to present themselves as forward-looking: the emphasis was on past achievement, which could almost speak for itself. No British typefounder exhibited, perhaps because there was no chance of any serious export business: books and pictures are more readily transportable and saleable. By contrast, German exhibitors included the great typefounding houses of Bauer, Flinsch and Stempel, all of Frankfurt-am-Main, besides several smaller ones. There were representatives from Berlin of Mergenthaler (Linotype), of Monotype and of Typograph GmbH, and dozens of German press-manufacturers, printers' suppliers, paper-makers and industrial bookbinders. In the event, the exhibition proved not a beginning, but a terminus. With the outbreak of war in August, before the planned end of the display, there was considerable anxiety in Britain for the well-being of the more valuable books and for the hundreds of other exhibits that could not be rescued in time and had to remain in Germany.

One effect of this retrospection was to isolate the period leading up to the First World War, years that were on the one hand determinedly different ('Edwardian England', 'Georgian') and on the other self-consciously modern. The term 'Georgian poetry' won widespread acceptance thanks to Edward

95 *Publishers' Circular* 11 April 1914, p. 431.

Marsh's anthologies of that title in 1912–22. The new publishers of the last years of the nineteenth century, such as William Heinemann, John Lane and the Bodley Head, T. Fisher Unwin, Edward Arnold and J. M. Dent, were absorbed into the mainstream. The ferment of book design that marked the 1890s, in work by Aubrey Beardsley, Walter Crane, Charles Ricketts, William Morris and others was only partly carried forward. Some of the initiatives in pocket libraries survived and prospered, such as Dent's Temple Classics (1896–) and Everyman's Library (1906–), and Grant Richards's World's Classics (1901–; later taken over by Henry Frowde and then by Oxford University Press). Others, not seeking canons of literature or knowledge, enjoyed briefer careers, such as Fisher Unwin's pioneering Pseudonym Library. Not only did experiments not always develop; in many respects there was a reaction against innovation. Both Everyman's Library and the World's Classics survived and prospered because their lists were, for the most part, built on authors whose reputations were already established, and they provided convenient editions at low prices. Just as in the late 1820s and the 1830s publishers such as Bentley or Colburn had sought to consolidate and extend their markets with series, so the final decades of the nineteenth century witnessed a resurgence of interest in such methods, with both general series and more focussed ones like Longman's Badminton Library (for sport) or Fisher Unwin's Mermaid dramatists, mainly of the seventeenth century.

Most book typography of the first two decades of the twentieth century remained tenaciously conservative. Nowhere was this more obvious than in the strictly commercial decisions of manufacturers of the new typesetting equipment to concentrate on old and familiar typefaces. In printing for the sciences, where major advances in engineering, physics, medicine and the infant field of electronics all required to be set in print, in journals, monographs, textbooks or more general works, willingness to explore printing technology lagged behind advances in knowledge. As we have seen, the means to print colour photographs had been available to the book trade since the 1890s, and had been used by A. & C. Black for their series of Colour Plate Books. It was not suited to all books: Gray's *Anatomy*, for example, was still – and effectively – illustrated with drawings and line diagrams, with colour superimposed to draw attention to particular features. Furthermore, in hundreds of books the use of black and white half-tone printing of photographs was unimaginative and technically poor, when compared with many popular illustrated publications about places associated with leisure. Typefaces whose thinness was ill-suited to the shiny surface of art paper were nevertheless used, so that half-tone pictures could be printed on the same page in one operation: this resulted in useful savings in costs, often at the expense of clarity. In new novels, publishers frequently succumbed to the temptation to offer bulk in return for price, with too much white space on the pages and paper in which the high esparto content provided both thick leaves and a surface that required little make-ready by the printer – thus, again, giving a saving in cost.

Amidst these contradictions, celebrations and anxieties, the Janus-like qualities of the Leipzig exhibition, both historic and of the present, were to some extent captured by the publisher John Murray, whose introduction on the history of British publishing began in 1403 and ended with reflections that had an applicability far beyond the English Channel and the North Sea.

> Perhaps the dominant influence in the trade of to-day is the enormous number of books published yearly, monthly, almost daily . . .
>
> The consequence is that the stock of a publisher and of a bookseller is always tending to become dead sooner and sooner. Remainders and second-hand copies are thrown on the market at ruinously reduced prices, almost before a book has passed its infancy, a glut sets in, and booksellers complain that they can scarcely earn a living by selling books alone. This seems to me the great drawback and danger which now besets the book trade.[96]

The need for publicity was paramount. It was disingenuous of Murray to repeat booksellers' complaints about the urgency to diversify. They had diversified ever since the sixteenth century. At different times, and in different combinations, beer and wine, patent medicines, stationery, office equipment, refreshments and newspapers had all supplemented businesses and livelihoods. Diversity was a fact of bookselling, not a consequence of modern publishing practices. But the pace of publishing and bookselling had indeed changed. In 1913, the last full year unaffected by war, the fullest and most readily available figures reported that some 12,379 titles were published, quite apart from newspapers, magazines and other periodicals. Of these, 9,451 were new works. These figures excluded most pamphlets, most government printing, and a mass of locally published materials: the actual figures may have been twice these. Nevertheless, numbers had grown by almost a half since 1904, in a period of just ten years.[97]

As numbers increased, so inescapably did the pace of new arrivals. For booksellers and for the reading public, needing to choose, prompt help was essential. Publishers had to advertise, more frequently and more ostentatiously.

---

96 Murray, 'History of British publishing', p. xxvi.   97 *Publishers' Circular* 3 January 1914, p. 7.

Figure 1.3 'Yellowbacks' all published at a shilling, from the 1850s to 1870s. Fenimore Cooper's *The pilot* was available at various prices, not only (as here) as a paperback but also in limp cloth gilt, in picture boards, or in cloth gilt, with a frontispiece. Ward Lock's Lily Series was designed to counter the many books issuing from the press 'low in tone and lax in character': its authors included Louisa M. Alcott and Susan Coolidge, and it was claimed that over 1.6 million volumes had been sold by the time that this volume was published. (Private collection)

The brightly coloured paper bindings on the novels and other undemanding literature that had quickly come to characterise railway bookstalls in the mid-century were designed for one purpose: to catch attention. Their glazed yellow, green or blue paper shone out distinctively among more obviously worthy publications (fig.1.3). The dust-jackets that became increasingly frequent in the last years of the nineteenth century provided not just protection against accidental dirt, but also ready-made vehicles for information and publicity. Though they were employed on all kinds of books, they were most effective on novels. In shop-windows, in table displays and on shelves, new books jostled for attention by their designs and by their prices. Ranked on the shelves, spines showed prices in type often more prominent than that used for authors' names or titles of books. Set in piles on tables (a method of book display to which the picture cover, either on the dustwrapper or printed direct on the cloth cover, was ideally suited) multiple copies could be offered in bulk, with the hint that in stocking so many copies the shopkeeper was helping his customers keep abreast of general taste. Publishers provided special show cards, and shops were encouraged to devote entire window displays to individual new publications.

Nevertheless, if by 1914 books and magazines were strikingly diverse in their outward appearance and in their inward design, they all depended on the same kinds of technology. Changes in methods and fashions for illustration are examined in more detail in the following chapter, for the changes here were not only among the most obvious; they also enabled new ways of presenting content and new ways of guiding the experience of reading. This volume then turns to different kinds of books, and the ways in which authors, publishers and booksellers created books that fuelled revolutions in demand for reading matter.

2

The illustration revolution

MICHAEL TWYMAN

The nineteenth century brought illustrated books and periodicals to large sectors of the British population for the first time.[1] The task fell jointly on the printing, publishing and allied trades, which responded organisationally, technologically and creatively to the demands made on them. In doing so they contributed substantially to the impact pictures in general had on society. Initially, Britain was at the forefront of the many advances in printing and publishing that brought this about, but as the century progressed its influence waned. On technical matters, for example, the initiative passed to Germany and the United States in the second half of the century, particularly in photo-mechanical reproduction and chromolithography.

The first serious efforts to bring large numbers of illustrated publications within the pockets of ordinary readers were made in Britain in the 1830s with the rise of pictorial journals, particularly the *Penny Magazine* (founded 1832). From then on the story is one of wider dissemination across an increasingly broad range of books and journals, greater and faster production, and a steady improvement in the technical quality of pictorial reproduction. The range embraced publications for enjoyment, including children's books, books relating to travel and natural history, popular literature and leisure magazines, in addition to others intended for information and elucidation, such as technical manuals, guidebooks, schoolbooks on certain subjects, catalogues, scientific monographs and journals, and encyclopaedias.

Three points of reference provide some measure of the increasing importance of pictorial images in Britain. The artist and engraver Thomas Bewick, who

---

1 In addition to the publications cited below in relation to specific points see Bland, *A history of book illustration*; Buchanan-Brown, *Early Victorian illustrated books*; Chick, *Towards today's book*; Hardie, *English coloured books*; Knight, *Natural science books in English*; Muir, *Victorian illustrated books*; Ray, *Illustrators and the book in England*; Thorpe, *English illustration: the nineties*.

died in 1828, recorded in his memoirs that when he was a child in Northumbria, which would have been around 1760, his only sources of pictorial images were inn signs and the local church. 'But of patterns or drawings', he wrote, 'I had none . . .'.[2] This paucity of visual imagery in the lifetime of an illustrator who provided one of the main stimuli for the growth of illustration in Britain can be compared with claims made by George Baxter in the *Art-Journal Advertiser* less than a hundred years later. Though probably exaggerating, he stated that more than 500,000 copies had been sold of his colour prints of Queen Victoria and Prince Albert, and – even more astonishingly – 20 million copies of his miniature album illustrations and 100 million of his album series.[3] A further fifty years on and newspapers were being printed on a daily basis in hundreds of thousands of copies with countless photographic illustrations, in some cases with a turn-around of no more than half an hour from the receipt of photographs.[4]

Another measure of the progress of illustration in nineteenth-century Britain is provided by the use made of pictures in popular periodicals. One of the earliest of these illustrated journals, the *Mirror of Literature, Amusement, and Instruction* (founded 1822), was published for some years with a single wood-engraving on the first of its sixteen pages. Ten years later, the *Penny Magazine* of the Society for the Diffusion of Useful Knowledge and the *Saturday Magazine* of the Society for Promoting Christian Knowledge, both founded in 1832, scattered instructive and elevating images throughout the eight pages of each issue, the format being twice as large as that of the *Mirror*. A further ten years on, Herbert Ingrams's *Illustrated London News* (founded 1842) bombarded its readers with wood-engravings of various shapes and sizes on its sixteen pages, which were twice the size of those of the *Penny Magazine* and *Saturday Magazine*. By the end of the nineteenth century both the *Illustrated London News* and it younger competitor the *Graphic* (founded 1869) were publishing double-spread and even fold-out pages of large illustrations. Right at the close of our period the impact of photographic methods led the *Illustrated London News* to experiment with photogravure reproduction, which it turned to for its entire publication shortly after World War I.

This astonishing growth of illustration in nineteenth-century periodicals was echoed in some categories of book publishing, though less dramatically. These changes can be traced back to shifts in attitude to pictures triggered by the enlightenment and exemplified by Diderot and D'Alembert's *Encyclopédie*

2 Bewick, *My life*, p. 29.
3 January 1852. These figures were challenged by Seeley, *The production of a Baxter colour print*.
4 Twyman, *Printing 1770–1970*.

(Paris, 1751–72) with its hundreds of superbly conceived and executed intaglio plates, which demonstrated convincingly the value of illustrations as carriers of information. The idea of educating through the eye was provided with additional, though somewhat controversial, support from Rousseau's *Emile, ou de l'éducation*, which was first published in several European centres outside France in 1762, and appeared in an English translation in the following year. The influence of such publications on the practice of illustration is hard to pin down, but there is an echo of both the *Encyclopédie* and Rousseau in the thinking of Charles Knight, one of the pioneering publishers of popular illustration in Britain. He published the *Penny Magazine* and countless other popular illustrated works, and in later years referred to his early plans for 'rendering wood-cuts real illustrations of the text, instead of fanciful devices – true eye-knowledge, sometimes more instructive than words'.[5]

The practical consequences of these new attitudes to pictorial language took many forms in Britain. In the hard-nosed world of the army, partly as a consequence of failures identified during the Napoleonic wars, engineers began to receive serious training in drawing; on the domestic front, drawing became a more widespread polite accomplishment, particularly among women; and in the professional world of design the poor performance of British work at the French national exhibitions of the early nineteenth century drew attention to the need for schools of art and design, which were established from 1836. Alongside these developments, the opening up of continental Europe following the peace of 1815 led to a period of travel and the pictorial recording of things seen. The coming of the railways extended this activity, stimulating the guidebook market and also generating its own illustrated publicity. Expeditions to far-off lands, usually with a draughtsman on hand, called for pictorial records of fauna, flora and anthropological discoveries, which were then published in various forms. Discovery at home and the founding of scientific, archaeological and antiquarian societies also fuelled the need for illustrations, as did the growth of trade and commerce and the need to sell increasingly large quantities of manufactured goods beyond the local marketplace, often internationally.

All such demands for illustration, particularly when associated with the need for affordable publications, would not have been possible but for several technical advances made before our period begins. In the late eighteenth century two developments paved the way for the rapid increase in illustrative material: Thomas Bewick's refinements to the process of producing relief prints from

---

5 Knight, *Passages of a working life* 2, p. 262.

wood in the 1780s and 1790s, and Alois Senefelder's invention of the plano-graphic process of lithography in Germany in 1798/9. Another early technical advance in the reproduction of illustrations was made possible by the introduction from America of steel-engraving, which was protected in Britain on behalf of its inventor Joseph Perkins in 1810. To these new or improved methods of printing we have to add the mechanisation of the means of taking impressions, which effectively began in 1814 with the successful application of steam power to the production of *The Times*. It took time for books with quality illustrations to be printed on powered machines, and the lithographic printing trade did not become mechanised in a serious way until half a century later, but the idea of harnessing printing presses to steam power was already seen as the way forward. By the beginning of our period all these technical innovations had gained a foothold in the printing trade, and in their different ways had begun to prepare the ground for a revolution in illustration later in the century.

Before this, the growing use of pictures in books had begun to raise editorial and technical questions about the relationship between text and illustration. At one extreme, picture or plate books continued to be issued (often in large formats) with sets of pictures bound up in volume form, with or without explanatory text, the one physically separate from the other. At the other extreme, books began to appear in which pictures and text were fully integrated, both physically and in terms of their content, so that a picture and its related text fall together on the same page.

In the first case, the book simply provided a convenient receptacle for what might otherwise be seen as prints. This approach suited the publisher, who could bring out a work in parts over a period of time and, on completion, provide buyers with a version in bound form. John Doyle's political caricatures provide a good example of this approach to publishing prints. His caricatures were issued under the pseudonym 'HB' by Thomas McLean in batches of four or five between 1829 and 1851 while Parliament was in session.[6] Those issued in the first decade or so were also offered by McLean, mounted in folio volumes, with a separate letterpress key, under the title *Political sketches &c. by HB* (1831–43).

Sets of landscape and topographical views were commonly published this way, particularly before around 1860.[7] Pictures were the *raison d'être* for publication, and usually any accompanying text was minimal. The model had already been established before our period, but the Victorian era produced many grand

---

6 G. M. Trevelyan, *The seven years of William IV: a reign cartooned by John Doyle* (1952).
7 See in particular Abbey, *Scenery* and *travel*.

and ambitious publications of this kind, and they preserve the pictorial images of some of the most esteemed artists of the day. Themes ranged from stately mansions, picturesque views, scenes of London and other European cities, to records of travel to the Middle East and beyond.

The favoured process for producing the plates of such picture books was initially aquatint, but by the 1830s this had begun to give way to lithography, which dominated the scene thereafter. Sets of prints were normally issued loose or lightly sewn in wrappers, and were frequently offered in alternative forms, plain or coloured by hand and sometimes on India paper, to cater for different pockets. When coloured, the plates served as substitutes for the watercolour paintings on which they were usually based, though it was important that uncoloured versions worked satisfactorily too. This accounts for the success of the tinted lithograph from the mid-1830s, since it could stand on its own but did not interfere with hand-colouring in skies and similar subtle areas.[8] In the more valued publications of the period artists often undertook their own drawing on stone, especially when the task was not too onerous. On the other hand, many capable amateur artists were only too happy to have their drawings worked up for publication by professional lithographic draughtsmen.

The finest of these landscape and topographical publications date from the mid-nineteenth century. Among them are Thomas Shotter Boys's *London as it is* (T. Boys, 1842), James Duffield Harding's *The park and the forest* (Thomas McLean, 1841) and David Roberts's *The Holy Land, Syria, Idumea, Arabia, Egypt & Nubia* (F. G. Moon, 1842–9). Boys's publication was issued with minimal descriptive text, and Harding's had no more than a list of plates, but Roberts's plates were accompanied by extensive commentaries by George Croly and William Brockedon. All these publications, and many others, are picture based, and anyone who tries to read the text of the large folio volumes of *The Holy Land* soon realises that the format was chosen for viewing rather than reading. Boys and Harding made their own drawings on stone for the single-tint lithographs of the two publications referred to above, but the enormous task of putting the 248 tinted lithographs of *The Holy Land* on stone was undertaken by Louis Haghe and his assistants at Day & Son's establishment. In this case, as in many others, an artist of some distinction was prepared to put his skills at the disposal of another.

A more modest example of this type of publication is provided by Robert O'Callaghan Newenham's *Picturesque views of the antiquities of Ireland*, which

8 Twyman, 'The tinted lithograph'.

came out in parts with plates drawn on stone by Harding after Newenham's sketches. It demonstrates as well as any other the thin line that separates sets of prints from books of plates, and the oddity of some publishing operations. Initially its parts, each consisting of eight lithographs in royal quarto format, were issued to subscribers in loosely sewn decorated wrappers without any text. They were jointly published in this form by Ackermann in London and Hodges & McArthur in Dublin, beginning in 1826 with just over three hundred subscribers. The parts were to come out every six weeks, some copies of the second and following parts being printed on India paper. The complete set of plates was then published in volume form by Thomas and William Boone of the Strand in 1830, with an augmented list of subscribers and twenty-five pages of letterpress text describing the plates.

Many other books of our period, including sumptuous ones on natural history, among them Edward Lear's *Illustrations of the family of Psittacidae, or parrots* (E. Lear, 1830–2) and the bird books of John Gould, fall into much the same category, as do numerous chromolithographed works on decoration, such as Owen Jones's *Grammar of ornament* (Day & Son, 1856), the books of Christopher Dresser, and various pictorial publications arising from the exhibitions of 1851 and 1862. Though some of these books have significant texts, they are essentially picture books: the plates provided the driving force and determined their physical form.

What all these books have in common is that their plates and texts were printed separately, using a different printing process and often a different paper. This approach to book design arose partly from the importance of the pictorial component, and partly because text and pictures required different technologies. Type remained the norm for text matter, but the relief-printing processes used for pictures (wood-engraving and woodcutting) offered only very limited graphic possibilities. Wood-engraving catered for small images reasonably well, but in the first half of the nineteenth century not large ones; woodcuts, though capable of being produced in large sizes, were relatively crude. It was because these two relief methods failed to meet all the needs of artists that intaglio processes (particularly aquatint, etching and line engraving) and lithography became the favoured means of producing illustrations in picture books and that, almost without exception, plates produced by these means were printed separately from text.[9]

9 See Holloway, *Steel engravings*; Hunnisett, *Steel-engraved book illustration in England*, and *Engraved on steel*; Tooley, *English books with coloured plates*; Twyman, *Lithography 1800–1850*.

Books in which text and pictures were fully integrated with one another normally relied on blocks with their image standing in relief, initially wood-engravings, but towards the end of the century blocks made by photomechanical means. Bewick had used wood-engraving successfully in this way at the close of the eighteenth century, and the periodical press followed his example, as did serious works of reference, such as Charles Tomlinson's *Cyclopaedia of useful arts & manufactures* (London and New York: George Virtue, 1854). The contribution of illustrated journals was crucial in promoting wood-engraving.[10] Not only did they help turn a craft into an industrial trade by providing a critical mass as far as demand was concerned, but they offered an informal training ground for prospective illustrators and wood-engravers. The *Illustrated London News* and *Punch* were at the forefront in this respect from the 1840s. Later in the century the *Graphic*, which had a high ratio of pictures to text, even founded its own schools for illustrators and wood-engravers.

Such was the demand for books with illustrations and text printed together that wood-engraving dominated most areas of illustrated publishing throughout our period. Some quality publications, among them the series of handbooks to the cathedrals of England published by John Murray in the 1860s, printed full-page wood-engravings with the other side of the leaf left blank so as to ensure good presswork. But generally wood-engraved illustrations were integrated with the text, sometimes to the extent of having it run around them, as was often the case with ornamented letters at the beginning of chapters. The major category of illustrated book that did not normally make use of wood-engravings was the plate or picture book of the kind discussed above. Some publications included both plates and wood-engravings, as did the *Art-Journal* (founded 1839 as the *Art-Union*), which continued to have its full-page illustrations of works of art engraved on metal and printed intaglio on a robust paper well into the second half of the century, even though its text pages regularly included wood-engravings.

Towards the end of our period wood-engraving began to be ousted by photomechanically produced line and half-tone blocks. Such blocks could be integrated with type in much the same way as wood-engravings, but they were quicker and cheaper to produce and began to find their way into publications from the 1880s, particularly in periodicals. Line-blocks were no real substitute for fully tonal wood-engravings, which had their photomechanical equivalent in half-tone blocks. Coarse blocks of this kind could be used in newspapers,

---

10 See in particular Anderson, *The printed image and the transformation of popular culture*, and Fox, *Graphic journalism in England*.

but more refined illustrations for quality books required fine-screen blocks, and had to be printed on calendered (smooth) or, preferably, coated paper to pick up the details of an image. These limitations dictated some aspects of book production: if text and high-quality pictures were needed either the whole book had to be printed on coated paper, possibly at the expense of ease of reading the text, or the illustrations had to be printed separately on it and included as individual sections or leaves (tipped or guarded in). Both approaches were adopted, particularly for art books. Popular periodicals began to turn to half-tone blocks from the 1890s, the *Strand Magazine* (founded 1891) doing so from its inception. But for many years thereafter, the integration of letterpress text with high-quality pictures was achieved at the cost of the illustration determining the stock on which a book was to be printed.

Integration of text and illustration was sporadically achieved in the nineteenth century by the use of lithography, which was equally suited to the reproduction of handwriting, lettering and pictures.[11] In the middle of the century several small monochrome books in strip-cartoon style, probably influenced by the comic books of Rodolphe Töpffer in Switzerland, were produced by John Leighton, using his pseudonym Luke Limner, one of them being *London out of town or the adventures of the Browns at the seaside* (David Bogue, c.1847). The first two editions of Edward Lear's *Book of nonsense* (Thomas McLean, 1846; 2nd edn c.1855) were also produced entirely by lithography, with Lear's limericks written by hand or transferred from type beneath his illustrations. Late in the century, when chromolithography was at its peak commercially, numerous small books of sentimental verse, with their pictures and words integrated, were published by Castell Brothers, Griffith, Farran & Co., Ernest Nister and Raphael Tuck.

The need to find satisfactory ways of combining text and illustrations has to be considered alongside efforts to make printed images more refined. What might have been seen as detailed when Bewick and his school of wood-engravers were working failed to meet the more exacting requirements of later decades. Attitudes had shifted as a result of the influence of steel-engraving (strictly speaking steel-etching with, perhaps, some engraving), which began to be taken up as a book illustration process in the 1820s, and the impact of photography a couple of decades later. Pressure for greater refinement in illustrations came particularly from their use as carriers of information for scientific and cultural purposes, and especially from the need to reproduce works of art.

11 Twyman, *Early lithographed books.*

The challenge presented to the existing printing processes by steel-engraving affected wood-engraving and copper-engraving most of all. Not only could steel-engraving produce two or three times the number of lines to the centimetre as a typical Bewick wood-engraving, but it withstood edition printing far better than copper-engraving (fig. 2.1). For these reasons it was a real threat to existing processes even though, when competing with wood-engraving, it meant printing illustrations separately from the text pages. Fine examples of its use can be seen in the vignettes engraved after Thomas Stothard and J. M. W. Turner for an edition of Samuel Rogers's *Poems* (Edward Moxon, 1838) and after Turner for *The rivers of France* (H. G. Bohn, 1853).

The response of the wood-engravers to this threat was to become much more refined in their mark-making. Samuel Williams was one of the wood-engravers who tried to match the precision of steel-engraving, as he did in the delicate vignettes he engraved in the 1840s for E. Jesse, *Favorite and rural studies* (John Murray, 1847) and P. J. Selby, *A history of British forest-trees* (John Van Voorst, 1842). Orlando Jewitt's wood-engravings for books on architecture, among them M. H. Bloxam's *The principles of Gothic ecclesiastical architecture*, which came out in many editions in the 1840s, show a similar development in the recording of information pictorially.[12] Over the following decades hundreds of publications, many of them books of verse, were issued with illustrations drawn by leading artists of the day and engraved on wood by, among others, the firms of Edmund Evans and the Dalziel Brothers. William Falconer's *The shipwreck* (A. & C. Black, 1858), William Cowper's *The task* (James Nisbit and Co., 1855) and Charles Mackay (ed.), *The home affections pourtrayed by the poets* (Routledge, 1858) provide fine examples of precision wood-engraving in such literary works.[13]

All such wood-engravings would have been impossible to print effectively without the use of calendered paper and careful presswork, and the need for quality sometimes overrode the advantages of printing text and pictures together on the page. On occasions publishers decided to print some wood-engravings with the text, but to treat more important ones as though they were traditional plates, printing on one side of the sheet only and tipping or guarding the leaves into appropriate points in the text block. This was the approach adopted by John Murray and David Bogue for the publications with wood-engravings by Orlando Jewitt referred to above. Decisions of this kind, taken in the interests of greater refinement, continued into the era of

---

12 Carter, *Orlando Jewitt*.
13 For others, see Reid, *Illustrators of the eighteen sixties*, and White, *English illustrators: 'The sixties'*.

Figure 2.1 From Samuel Rogers, *Italy, a poem* (1830). Steel-engraving by Edward Goodall after J. M. W. Turner. (Private collection)

photomechanical reproduction, when it was common for high-resolution half-tone blocks to be printed on art paper and inserted into the book as separate sections or individual leaves. In both cases, quality must have been considered more important than any economies that could have been made by printing relief blocks along with type matter. Practices of this kind remind us that though words carry their meaning almost regardless of the quality of printing, this is not so with pictures; they also provide further evidence of the growing respect for pictures and what they convey.

Throughout our period, or at least until near its close, representation of the visible or imagined world governed picture-making in all its forms. This applied as much to the scientist recording natural objects and the illustrator of literary works and popular magazines as it did to painters. Inevitably, therefore, verisimilitude – the quality of appearing true or real – became a significant goal for those who developed illustration processes. The long history of efforts to capture 'sun images' on paper, which eventually led to photography, provided a backdrop for this search for verisimilitude, as did the greater refinement of picture-making technologies and a growing interest in colour theory and colour printing.

By the middle of the century photography provided the impetus for most technological developments in printing that related to picture-making, but it was not the only route to verisimilitude. Even before J.-L.-M. Daguerre and Henry Fox Talbot announced their different photographic processes to the world in 1839, John Bate in England and Achille Collas in France had come up with methods by which relief sculpture, medals and similar three-dimensional items could be reduced to a series of scanned lines on an intaglio plate that simulated the effect of a relief surface. The process was variously called medal engraving and anaglyptography.[14] Bate patented his process in 1832, but the most ambitious application of the method came from the hands of Collas, who produced the plates for a grandiose French publication, *Trésor de numismatique et de glyptique* (Paris, 1834–58). In Britain, Collas produced a series of portrait plates for H. F. Chorley, *The authors of England: a series of medallion portraits of modern literary characters* (Charles Tilt, 1838), some copies of which include an extensive note about the history of 'medallic engraving'. A further attempt at verisimilitude came twenty years later with a process called nature printing, which was developed by Alois Auer in Vienna in the 1850s and imported into England by Henry Bradbury in 1853.[15] It involved pressing natural objects,

---

14 Harris, 'Experimental graphic processes in England 1800–1859' (1968).
15 Harris, 'Experimental graphic processes in England 1800–1859' (1970).

usually plants (but even a squashed bat), into soft pewter to obtain a sunken die, from which copies could be made in a harder metal for intaglio printing. The firm of Bradbury & Evans explored the possibilities of the process in Britain, notably for Thomas Moore's *The ferns of Great Britain and Ireland* (London, 1855) and W. G. Johnstone and A. Croall, *The nature-printed British sea-weeds* (Bradbury & Evans, 1859–60). Neither of these processes was widely used in Britain, but together they emphasised the need for methods that offered the elusive quality of verisimilitude, which was to be achieved – or at least approached – only with the industrial application of photography to printing at the close of our period.

For more than half a century this goal occupied hundreds of inventors in many parts of Europe and the United States. In France, Daguerre's form of photography was so closely associated with the making of prints that Daguerre-otypes were soon used as the starting point for printing plates, and in the middle of the century some convincing photographic images were also produced there for lithographic printing. A Dorset photographer, John Pouncy, made experiments along similar lines, which led to a set of plates for his *Dorset-shire photographically illustrated* (London: Bland & Long, 1856–7). These and other examples of the combination of the two technologies of photography and printing are beguilingly convincing, though close inspection often shows that they involved retouching or reworking by hand, in Pouncy's case a considerable amount. Photography was first applied to intaglio and lithographic printing, but the real challenge was to find methods of producing photographic images that could be printed with type matter, preferably at one pass through the press.

Four main approaches were adopted for the production of photographic illustrations in books before the development of photomechanical relief blocks in the closing decades of the century. The first and most obvious was for illustrators to copy photographs by hand. This was mostly done, with or without acknowledgement, where illustrations were meant to carry information, and has never really stopped. What is probably the first example of this in a British publication was a wood-engraved illustration for the *Mechanic and Chemist*, 13 April 1839, which was followed soon afterwards by a wood-engraving of ferns, described as a 'Fac-simile of a photogenic drawing' on the first page of the *Mirror of Literature, Amusement, and Instruction* of 20 April 1839.[16]

The second, and in many ways the simplest approach, was to paste photographic prints onto the pages of books. And since the branch of photography

16 Bodleian Library, *Photography & the printed page*, pp. 4–5.

that Talbot invented relied on the production of negatives from which multiple copies could be made, which he called calotypes, it could even be regarded as a form of printing. Talbot's *Pencil of nature* (Longman, 1844), in which twenty-four of his finest calotypes were pasted onto the leaves of a book, was the first of its kind.[17] It came out in six parts between 1844 and 1846, the calotypes being produced at his Reading establishment in at least 274 copies. Other pasted-down photographs, described as Talbotypes, appeared in the *Art-Union* in 1846. Though not an immediate success, this approach to using photographic images was adopted for some trade books, particularly in the 1860s.[18] However, it was no long-term solution as it was so labour intensive. In one case, F. W. Maynard's *Descriptive notice of the drawings and publications of the Arundel Society* (J. B. Nichols, 1869, 1873), hundreds of small photographic prints had to be pasted down individually, often five or more to a page.

The third approach was to use photography as an aid to the engraver by applying a photosensitive coating to a printing surface and exposing this to light through a negative. In effect, the resulting image was a photograph on a block or plate. Though not the first process to employ photography in this way, wood-engraving benefited most, and continued to do so for some kinds of work into the middle of the twentieth century. The idea had been proposed in 1839, in an article in the issue of the *Mirror* referred to above, but the first such wood-engraved illustrations appeared twenty years later in a collection of translations of German hymns, *Lyra Germanica* (Longman, 1859). For two of the book's illustrations the engraver, Thomas Bolton, worked over the varied tones of photographic images of relief sculpture by John Flaxman, producing a series of parallel lines of different thickness in an almost mechanical way. The photographing of images onto wood changed the nature of the craft of wood-engraving, primarily when the subjects of illustrations were scientific, technical or commercial. It also liberated illustrators. Instead of having to draw on the surface of the block, it was now possible for them to draw on paper and have their work transferred photographically to the wood.[19]

The fourth way of relating photography to printing before the photomechanical revolution was to explore further the possibility of producing printing blocks, plates and stones directly from photographic images that had been exposed on their surface. There were scores of such processes, many of them

17 *Ibid.*, p. 3. See also the introduction by Larry J. Schaaf to the facsimile edition of Talbot's *The pencil of nature*.
18 For books illustrated with photographs, see Gernsheim, *Incunabula of British photographic literature*, and the chapter 'Books illustrated with pasted-in photographs' in Wilson, *The literature of photography* 2, nos. 745–965, 1234–58.
19 Fildes, 'Phototransfer of drawings in wood-block engraving'.

very similar to one another but going under different names. What most of them had in common was that they involved a great deal of handwork, were slow and expensive to produce, and could not be printed with type at one pass through the press. The ones that made an impact in our period were collotype, which was invented (in one form) by Louis-Adolphe Poitevin in Paris in 1855 and improved by Josef Albert in Germany in 1868; Woodburytype, a form of permanent photography that was patented by its eponymous inventor in 1865; and photogravure (of the kind that did not involve the use of screens), which came on the scene commercially in a variety of forms from the 1880s. All had limited applications, and in book illustration were used mainly for the reproduction of works of art and similar demanding jobs.

The technical breakthrough to the production of illustrations that could replace wood-engravings in bread-and-butter publications came with the production of photomechanically produced relief blocks: the line-block and half-tone block.[20] The first emerged after almost a century of experimentation with etching in relief drawings that had been made on metal blocks, stretching from William Blake in eighteenth-century Britain to Firmin Gillot in mid-nineteenth-century France. Gillot explored the idea commercially, patenting his process of Paneiconography (later called Gillotage) in 1850. His son Charles took the idea further by replacing the drawn marks of an artist on metal with line images that had been photographically produced. A drawing made in undiluted black ink on white paper or board was photographed, and its image exposed through a negative onto the photosensitized surface of a metal block (normally zinc, but copper for more refined work). The resulting image was then etched, using various preparations to protect it, so that the drawn lines stood in relief. The idea was slow to take root in Britain, but by the mid-1880s line-blocks produced by similar methods were finding their way into publications, particularly journals.

Half-tone blocks came later and were dependent on the manufacture of precision photographic screens. They were made in much the same way as line-blocks, but simulated the continuous tones of photographs or wash drawings by converting them into arrays of dots of varying size, using cross-lined screens to break up the light. The lighter the tone of the original, the smaller the dot. The screens that determined the breakdown of tones came in various resolutions to suit different papers and other requirements. The pioneering

---

20 For the photomechanical production of illustrations in general see especially Gamble, *Modern illustration processes*; Hackleman, *Commercial engraving and printing*; Harper, *A practical handbook of drawing*; Kainen, 'The development of the halftone screen'; Wakeman, *Victorian book illustration*; Wilkinson, *Photo-engraving, photo-litho, collotype and photogravure*.

work in screen manufacture was done in America and Germany in the early 1880s, and soon afterwards one of these inventors, Georg Meisenbach, set up a company to exploit his process in Britain. In the following decade half-tone letterpress blocks began to appear regularly in journals and were beginning to oust wood-engravings from some books too. In 1901 George and Edward Dalziel, partners in one of the major wood-engraving houses in London, admitted that the standard of commercial block-making was so high that the days of the professional wood-engraver were effectively over.[21] This proved not to be the case in all fields, but it was certainly the beginnings of the demise of the trade and some unemployed wood-engravers began to find work with the process engravers, often touching up blocks with the burin to give half-tone images composed of dots some of the graphic sparkle they lacked.

Letterpress printing, which already had several advantages over its competitors, was given an additional boost with the introduction of photomechanical blocks. Not only were they cheaper and quicker to produce than wood-engravings,[22] but they could reproduce images that were more in tune with the age. They also opened up new opportunities by offering a speedy turnaround of printing blocks to meet the pressing deadlines of illustrated journals. Not to be outdone, however, the lithographic and intaglio printing trades found their own ways of producing photographic illustrations, though in our period they offered no serious threat to the traditional letterpress-printed book.

The most influential of these methods was described in its day as 'photozincography'. It was a means of providing predominantly line copies of documents by photolithography, using zinc plates as a substitute for lithographic stone.[23] The process was invented independently by Sir Henry James and his staff at the Ordnance Survey Office, Southampton, and J. W. Osborne at the Survey Department in Melbourne at more or less the same time in 1859. It involved exposing an image onto photosensitised paper through a negative, and then coating the paper all over with lithographic ink. On immersion in water, the ink was coaxed away from the paper, except where the image had been exposed to light through the negative. All that remained to be done was to transfer the image to a zinc plate or stone for lithographic printing. Like many innovations, it began on a grand scale with a project to reproduce in line, but in two colours, the whole of Domesday Book in thirty-five volumes (Southampton, 1861–3). This opened the way for facsimiles of all sorts of

21 [Dalziel] *The brothers Dalziel*, p. vii.   22 Harper, *A practical handbook of drawing*, pp. 12, 74, 76–7.
23 Twyman, *Early lithographed books*, pp. 243–58. James, *Photozincography*.

documents, though mainly manuscripts, in the final decades of the century. Very soon other methods of photolithography were used to provide facsimiles of autographs for the *Autographic mirror* (London, 1864–6) and, more ambitiously, a facsimile edition of Shakespeare's first folio, which was edited by Howard Staunton and printed and published by Day & Son in 1866.

A further challenge to the printing and allied trades came with the need for illustrations in colour.[24] From the beginnings of printing it had been common for colour to be added to illustrations by hand, and this custom continued throughout our period. In some cases it was found preferable to colour printing, particularly when it was cheaper, or where quality was paramount, as with upmarket natural history books. But the spirit of the age and the greater demand for illustrated books called for effective methods of printing pictures in colour. In the eighteenth century some convincing colour prints had been made in Britain and France using intaglio processes and, ten years before our period opens, William Savage had produced some ambitious specimens of colour printing from numerous woodblocks for his *Practical hints on decorative printing* (London, 1822). But with the greater demand for printing and the introduction of steam-driven printing machines, pressure was put on the printing and allied trades to come up with more efficient and economical methods of producing pictures in colour.

The quest began on a broad front both geographically and technically, and seems to have been prompted, at least in part, by the writings on colour of Goethe, J.-F.-L. Mérimée and M.-E. Chevreul abroad, and George Field at home.[25] The 1830s were the crucial years. In Britain, Thomas de la Rue took out a patent in 1832 for a method of printing playing cards in colour, either in relief or by lithography, and in 1836 George Baxter patented a process that now bears his name, which involved printing a succession of relief blocks in colour onto an intaglio foundation print. Two years later Charles Knight patented a process he called 'Illuminated printing', whereby images could be printed from relief blocks in a limited number of colours on a specially adapted handpress. Meanwhile, the leading lithographic printer in Britain produced his first major work in colour lithography, four double-page plates for G. A. Hoskins, *Travels in Ethiopia* (Longman, 1835).[26] A few years later, inspired by Godefroy Engelmann, who had patented his own version of colour printing in France in 1837 called 'chromo-lithographie', Hullmandel produced his landmark set of

---

24 For colour printing see especially Burch, *Colour printing*; Gascoigne, *Milestones in colour printing*; McLean, *Victorian book design and colour printing*; Wakeman and Bridson, *A guide to nineteenth century colour printers*.
25 Gage, *Colour and culture*. 26 See Gascoigne, 'The earliest English chromolithographs'.

plates for Thomas Shotter Boys, *Picturesque architecture in Paris, Ghent, Antwerp, Rouen etc* (T. Boys, 1839), using the word 'chroma-lithography' to describe his process.

Whereas it took a long while for photography to be applied to printing, for several reasons the impact of colour printing was almost immediate. It met an evident need for verisimilitude in illustration, particularly in books on the decorative arts and popular science; it also led to greater precision and reliability in cartography, and made possible the publication of popular atlases. In addition, it was seen to have an educational value, demonstrably so with Oliver Byrne's *The first six books of the elements of Euclid* (Pickering, 1847), where diagrams, printed in four colours from relief blocks, were used throughout to explain Euclidian principles to the privileged young.

Both Charles Knight and George Baxter brought colour-printed images to a wide public within a few years of announcing their processes. Knight's *Old England* (Charles Knight, 1845–6) was probably the first publication with colour plates to have a massive circulation, and this was followed soon afterwards by his *Old England's worthies* (Charles Cox, 1847). In both cases the colour plates were printed by William Clowes to accompany text pages bearing monochrome wood-engraved vignettes. *Old England* appears to have been a great success and ran to further, but inferior, editions. Baxter's process was used mainly for the reproduction of popular paintings and sets of small prints, and only to a lesser degree for the illustration of books. But in 1849 he licensed the process to other printers and some of them, notably J. M. Kronheim, used it for books, particularly for the religious market.

Chromolithography, a process that was never patented in Britain, came to public notice here with the publication of Boys's *Picturesque architecture* in 1839, which revealed for the first time the possibilities of the process when in the hands of a capable artist. But it was the enthusiasm for illuminated manuscripts that provided the stimulus for the take-up of chromolithography on a broader front. They were the inspiration for the small, jewel-like gift-books of Henry Noel Humphreys, which he designed and lithographed with the help of his family, among the earlier ones being *Parables of our Lord* (Longman, 1846) and *Miracles of our Lord* (Longman, 1847).[27] These publications, some of which were printed in France, set a pattern for countless gift-books later in the century, which were nearly always chromolithographed. More ambitiously, Humphreys worked with Jones on a folio work, *Illuminated manuscripts of the middle ages*

---

27 Leathlean, 'H.N.H.: The work of Henry Noel Humphreys'.

(Longman, 1844–9), which reproduced pages from a range of sources with a self-confidence and degree of validity that had never been seen before.

Chromolithography had to fight its corner for most of the second half of the nineteenth century with colour-printed wood-engravings. The Baxter process was hampered by its use of an intaglio foundation plate, which would have been slow to print, and the next step was for colour printers to abandon this part of his process in the interest of economy and print from woodblocks alone. This was the method adopted by the Leighton Brothers, who used their 'chromatic process' for illustrations in countless books and journals of the 1850s and 1860s, including supplements for the *Illustrated London News*. It was also adopted by Edmund Evans for the best part of half a century, notably for James Doyle's *A chronicle of England* (Longman, 1846), with its eighty illustrations engraved on wood in around eight colours and printed on the text pages using a hand-press. In the long run, however, chromolithography emerged as the major colour-printing process of the nineteenth century. At one end of the market it satisfied the need for exceptionally high-quality reproductions of works of art and craft, such as the series of facsimiles of bindings at Windsor and the British Museum reproduced in the 1890s by William Griggs, and at the other robust plates for the *Boy's Own Paper* and similar popular magazines of the final decades of our period.

The complexity of all these colour-printing methods, which involved the allocation of different colours to sets of blocks or stones (over thirty in the case of some chromolithographs) inevitably led to a separation of the artist from the manufacture of the printing surface. Though skilled artisans undertook the translation of original images (or copies made from them), they simply acted as intermediaries. It is hardly surprising, therefore, that they were to be replaced by the camera, though this happened only at the very end of our period, and was by no means complete even then. The path was prepared for this development by James Clerk Maxwell, who demonstrated in 1860 that colour filters could be used to capture photographically the colour components of a subject, and that they could be combined to produce a fully coloured image.

In printing, filters were used in conjunction with the process engraver's half-tone screen to break down the hues and tones of coloured images. In letterpress printing this meant making separate half-tone blocks, each with an array of dots of varying size for cyan, yellow and magenta workings (with black as an optional extra to give greater richness). From the early 1890s such relief blocks were being made more or less experimentally, and then gradually found their way into books. Before World War I nearly all such printing was done from three blocks for reasons of economy and, as with fine-screen half-tone illustrations printed in a single working, art paper was essential. Among books of the early twentieth century that made good use of three-colour process blocks are those of Beatrix Potter, published by Frederick Warne, beginning with *The tale of Peter Rabbit* in 1900, and some of Arthur Rackham's early illustrated works. An extravagant application of the four-colour process (in modified form) is found in Elizabeth Stanhope Forbes's *King Arthur's wood: a fairy story* (Simpkin, Marshall, Hamilton, Kent & Co., [1904]), which was published in a large landscape-format reminiscent of plate books of half a century before. Generally, however, the three- and four-colour processes were too expensive for widespread use in this period, and in trade books they were normally limited to frontispieces and the occasional tipped-in plate, as was the case with the travel books published by A. & C. Black from the beginning of the new century.

The impact that photography and colour printing made on illustrated publications was visible, whereas other significant technical developments in printing would probably not even have been noticed. But without the steam-powered press it is unlikely that the *Penny Magazine* and other illustrated journals of the period could have been produced at affordable prices, which is an argument made in the magazine itself.[28] How widely steam-driven presses were used for the printing of quality illustrated books in the following decades is difficult to establish, though book printers would have used flatbed cylinder machines rather than the high-speed rotary ones that were introduced for newspaper printing.

Even illustrations in text came at a cost, and in the 1830s an additional charge per sheet was made for work containing delicate wood-engravings that required overlays,[29] which printers on hand-presses applied to the tympan to make subtle adjustments of pressure. The introduction of powered printing machines even began to affect the practice of wood-engraving, as the expense of applying overlays to the impression cylinders of machines forced wood-engravers to compensate for the lack of overlays by lowering those parts of a block's surface that needed to be printed lightly.[30] The limitations of machine printing help to account for the fact that books containing quality wood-engravings continued to be printed on hand-presses for some time to come, and in the case of colour wood-engravings into the second half of the century. An indication of changing production methods is provided by Chatto and

---

28 *Penny Magazine* (monthly supplement) 112, 30 November to 31 December 1833, pp. 508–10.
29 [Chatto and] Jackson, *A treatise on wood engraving*, p. 705.
30 *Ibid.*, pp. 696, 701, 705–11, 724, 729–30.

Jackson's *A treatise on wood engraving*, the first edition of which was printed on the hand-press in 1839, the second by machine in 1861.

The increased output of wood-engraved illustration, coupled with the introduction of powered machines, led to the need for replicas of actual blocks. The technology of stereotyping, by which casts could be made from relief surfaces, already existed and was commonly used for duplicating formes of type, but in the early 1830s it was extended to copying wood-engraved blocks. The process offered the possibility of printing the same illustration on several presses or many times on the same press; it also preserved the block from potential damage. Initially, two methods were used to make moulds from which casts could be taken in type metal: in one the wood-engraved block was coated with plaster of Paris, in the other the face of the block was struck into a mass of molten metal (slightly harder than type metal) just at the point that it was solidifying.[31] From the 1840s the process of electrotyping began to replace both these methods when high-quality duplicates of wood-engraved blocks were needed. Using the newly invented process of electrolysis, a thin deposit of copper was made on a woodblock that had been coated with graphite or, more usually, on a graphite-coated cast made from the original block in wax or similar material. This film of copper was then filled with type metal to make it rigid. Prints from such electrotype blocks are virtually identical to those taken from the original woodblock.

In practice, what are called wood-engraved illustrations were nearly always printed from stereotype or electrotype copies, for one or more of the reasons given above. *Punch* was exceptional in taking the risk of printing its continental edition of 70,000–80,000 copies directly from the wood.[32] And when a selection of a hundred illustrations from the *Cornhill Magazine* was published as the *Cornhill gallery* (Smith, Elder, 1864), the publishers were at pains to point out in their preface that 'The Wood-blocks themselves have now been printed from for the first time.'

The principle of replicating images to increase output was also applied to intaglio and lithographic printing, though the evidence for such practices in books is largely circumstantial. Early in the century, the process of siderography was developed specifically to multiply steel-engraved images for security printing,[33] and it would be surprising if it had not also been used occasionally for similar purposes in popular publications with steel-engraved illustrations, such as the annuals of the 1830s and 1840s. In lithography, images could be

31 *Ibid.*, pp. 721–3.   32 Spielmann, *The history of 'Punch'*, pp. 250–1.
33 Harris, 'Experimental graphic processes in England 1800–1859' (1968).

transferred from a master stone as many times as necessary to a fresh stone. The method was as old as lithography itself, but with the widespread take-up of powered machines by the trade from the 1870s onwards, lithographic stones began to be marketed in such large sizes that it was often a commercial necessity for them to bear multiple images. This became a regular practice in chromolithography and was adopted for the production of plates for some large circulation publications.[34]

Several other technical developments in our period affected the manufacture and use of illustrations. The steel-facing of etched or engraved copper plates from the 1860s made them virtually indestructible, particularly as the process could be reversed and the plates faced with steel again. At much the same time a method was introduced for assembling large woodblocks in parts by bolting them together. This had important implications for illustrated journalism as it meant that the laborious work of engraving a large block could be divided among a team of craftsmen when deadlines were tight. It also became possible to enlarge and reduce images without much human intervention. Before photographic methods were widely used for this purpose a trampoline-like apparatus was invented that made use of the elasticity of a sheet of India rubber. In the case of enlargement, an image was transferred to the rubber in its relaxed state, after which both the rubber and the image on it were stretched; for reduction, the rubber was stretched before receiving the image and relaxed afterwards.

In the first few decades of our period, when landscape and topographical plates featured strongly in illustrated books, artists often used the print-making processes themselves, as was the case with Boys, Harding and Haghe in lithography, though all three were also prepared to put the works of other artists onto stone. By this time, however, the separation of artist from making the printing surface was well established in other processes. In wood-engraving, for example, the usual practice was for an artist to provide a drawing on the woodblock for the engraver to work on. The artist would usually draw on a whitened surface of the block, either in line using pencil or undiluted black ink, or in tone using ink washes. In the first case, the engraver removed those parts of the block around the drawn lines in a more or less mechanical way. In the second, the tones had to be interpreted by an appropriate set of linear marks. In both cases there was plenty of room for misinterpretation, and this division of labour often led to tensions between artist and wood-engraver. The same

---

34 See examples in Alf Cooke, *Album of colour printing* (Leeds, 1890, and c.1896), St Bride Library, 3358, 14982, and Yale Center for British Art, CP 340.

also applied when there was a division of labour in the making of plates for intaglio printing, as was nearly always the case; and even the photomechanical processes led to unanticipated variations from the original.

Many illustrators who worked for journals and technical publications remain anonymous, but artists who illustrated literary works were nearly always acknowledged. There were hundreds of such artists, including some primarily noted for their paintings, among them Myles Birket Foster, John Everett Millais, William Mulready and Dante Gabriel Rossetti. John Gilbert was among the most efficient and prolific illustrators, turning work around overnight when required. He provided drawings for *Punch* and many thousands for the *Illustrated London News*, in addition to others for numerous publications, including eight hundred rather routine illustrations for an edition of *Shakespeare's works* (Routledge 1856–8), and a very successful edition of *Longfellow's poems* (Routledge, 1856).

The mid-1850s to around 1870 is generally seen as the finest period of the book illustrated with wood-engravings. From the numerous works published by Routledge, Moxon and others, the following provide a broadly representative selection: William Allingham's *The music master* (Routledge, 1855), illustrated by Hughes, Millais and Rossetti; *Tennyson's poems* (Moxon, 1857), with Hunt, Millais and Rossetti as the main illustrators; Birket Foster's *Pictures of English landscape* (Routledge, 1863); Millais's *Parables of Our Lord* (Routledge, 1864); and *The Arabian nights* (Warne, 1865), with illustrations by A. B. Houghton and T. Dalziel.[35] Generally described as books of the 'sixties', they had their precursors a decade or so earlier in, for example, Mulready's illustrations for Goldsmith's *The vicar of Wakefield* (John Van Voort, 1843).

Some illustrators so captured the spirit of an author's work that the two are inextricably linked in the public imagination. Most obviously this applies to the etched illustrations to Dickens's works of George Cruikshank and Hablôt K. Browne (under the pseudonym 'Phiz'),[36] and to John Tenniel's interpretations of the sketches of Lewis Carroll, which were engraved on wood for *Alice's adventures in wonderland* (Macmillan, 1865) and *Through the looking glass* (Macmillan, 1871).

The extraordinary range of subject matter in nineteenth-century illustration led to the emergence of specialists in various fields, since draughtsmen needed to understand what they were illustrating, especially when working for scientific and technical publications. In an increasingly demanding world,

35 For others see Reid, *Illustrators of the eighteen sixties.*   36 Kitton, *Dickens and his illustrators.*

it was no longer acceptable for authors with a talent for drawing to illustrate their own publications; apart from anything else, they usually needed a craftsman to produce the printing surface. As a result, specialists emerged, both original draughtsmen and wood-engravers and lithographers. In ornithology John Gould, John Keulemann, Archibald Thornton, Joseph Wolf and others established reputations as illustrators, some of them working on stone themselves.[37] In botany Walter Fitch and his nephew John Fitch spent their working lives as illustrators of *Curtis's Botanical Magazine*. Between them they produced some 5,000 lithographed illustrations for the journal from the 1830s until the end of our period, the latter mainly after the drawings of others, particularly Matilda Smith.[38] Even wood-engravers developed their specialties. Orlando Jewitt established a reputation as an engraver of architectural illustrations in the middle of the nineteenth century,[39] and the firm of Hare,[40] working first in Ipswich and then in London, specialised in producing wood-engraved illustrations of agricultural machinery, later making good use of the technique of photographing on wood.

The era of the delicately produced, imaginative book illustration came to an end towards the close of the nineteenth century, and the reaction to it took several forms. One was the historicism of William Morris and a return to some of the methods of earlier times in *The works of Geoffrey Chaucer* of 1896, using robust wood-engravings after Burne-Jones for the book's illustrations and also for his own decorative borders. Another was a response to the painter-engraver movement in France in the form of William Nicholson's series of woodcut picture books (also published in popular lithographed editions by William Heinemann): *London types* (1898), *An alphabet* (1899) and *An almanac of twelve sports* (1900). A third, represented principally by Aubrey Beardsley in the the *Yellow Book*, the *Savoy* and Wilde's *Salome* (Elkin Mathews and John Lane, 1894), explored the freedom offered by photomechanical illustration, the only limitation being that a drawing had to appear before the camera in either pure black or pure white. In their various ways, all had a considerable influence in the period leading up to World War I.

Britain's illustrators did not work in isolation. Its wood-engravers regularly worked for French publications in the 1830s and 1840s, and some of its leading lithographers contributed to that monument to France's heritage, the *Voyages pittoresques et romantiques dans l'ancienne France* (Paris, 1820–78). But the traffic was not all in one direction. Tony Johannot's illustrations found

---

37 Jackson, *Bird illustrators*. 38 Blunt, *The art of botanical illustration*.
39 Carter, *Orlando Jewitt*. 40 Andrews, 'Hare & Co.'

their way to Britain in the 1840s and 1850s, and a decade or so later Gustave Doré's melodramatically illustrated books were greeted in Britain with great enthusiasm, several of them being issued in English editions shortly after publication in France. As a promotional exercise a Doré gallery was opened in London to exhibit the artist's paintings, and his stay in London led to what is now regarded as his finest publication, *London, a pilgrimage* (Grant, 1872). German illustrators also made their presence felt, including Friedrich Schenck, who came to Edinburgh in 1840, where he set up a successful lithographic establishment and worked as an illustrator, Adolf Menzel, whose *History of Frederick the Great* was published in an English edition in 1843, and Wilhelm Busch, several of whose illustrated books appeared in English editions. Late in our period Lucien Pissarro (from France) and James McNeill Whistler and Joseph Pennell (both from the United States) all worked in London.

The growing expectation of publishers and readers that certain categories of publication should be illustrated led to difficulties over finding appropriate sources. Photography helped, but was only relevant in certain situations and for a long while was very limited in what it could record. In many cases, therefore, particularly when there was a degree of urgency, illustrators resorted to plagiarism or sheer invention. The temptation offered by a good source of illustrations led the *Saturday Magazine* to run a series of articles on cathedrals in 1834, using as its model a set of monographs on French cathedrals, which had been published a few years before in France.[41] Events presented special difficulties, and there are several documented cases of illustrators making drawings on the basis of descriptions provided in advance of an occasion, only to find that things did not turn out as planned.[42] The rise of the pictorial journalist, often specially trained in memory drawing, made certain kinds of pictorial recording more authentic. Such artists covered court scenes and wars with remarkable skill for the *Illustrated London News* and the *Graphic*. The role of the special war artist dates from the Crimean war, when J. A. Crowe and E. A. Goodall sent back sketches for the *Illustrated London News* which provided a far more convincing record of the horrors of war than the censored lithographs of William Simpson for his *Seat of war in the east* (Colnaghi, 1855–6) and even Roger Fenton's haunting photographs.

---

41 Twyman, *Printing 1770–1970*, pp. 98–9.
42 Jackson, *The pictorial press*, p. 263; Vizetelly, *Glances back through seventy years* 1, pp. 231–2.

A short cut to the provision of illustrations was for a publisher to acquire wood-engraved blocks, or casts made from them. John Jackson, a wood-engraver himself, revealed in 1839 that casts of wood-engravings made for popular periodicals were being sent to seventeen different countries for use in similar publications,[43] and Charles Knight reported a few years earlier that he regularly sold blocks to France and Germany.[44] Though Britain held itself to be the leader in popular illustration, it is unlikely that such a trade was in one direction only. Economy in the use of blocks took other forms, and Knight frequently reused his own blocks, which is evident from the curious shapes of some of the wood-engravings he used in his *Old England*.[45]

Not all illustrations in books and journals were pictorial, and the nineteenth century broadened the idea of illustration in the interests of both decoration and elucidation. The decorative book was a feature of nineteenth-century publishing, and ornamental borders played a particularly important role throughout our period. Though inspired by the unique borders of medieval books, the combination of refined wood-engraving and stereotyping made the repeated border practicable. R. Thomson's *An historical essay on the Magna Charta of King John* (London: J. Major, 1829), with monochrome wood-engraved examples on all its many pages, provides an early example; J. G. Lockhart's *Ancient Spanish ballads* (John Murray, 1841, 2nd edn 1842) introduced colour and more varied designs, all engraved on wood by Henry Vizetelly after designs by Owen Jones. Soon after this, chromolithography became the preferred process for decorative work, particularly in gift-books, and most spectacularly so in Owen Jones's *Victoria Psalter* (Day & Son, 1862). A return to monochrome and technical purity came with William Morris's *The golden legend* (1892) and *The works of Geoffrey Chaucer* (1896), which led to the border finding its way into the books of Dent and other trade publishers in the early twentieth century.

More or less in parallel with the historicism underlying the use of decorated borders we see the promotion of ways of presenting information in graphically new ways.[46] The roots for this go back to Joseph Priestley and William Playfair in the eighteenth century and to the growing interest in education through the eye. Chronological and genealogical charts were among the most common methods used for 'mapping' information visually, and many were published in the nineteenth century, some in book formats. The most ambitious, an

---

43 [Chatto and] Jackson, *A treatise on wood engraving*, p. 722.
44 *Penny Magazine* (monthly supplement) 107, 31 October to 30 November 1833, p. 471.
45 Twyman, 'The emergence of the graphic book in the 19th century', fig. 14.
46 See Tufte, *Envisioning information*; Twyman, 'Articulating graphic language'; Twyman, 'The emergence of the graphic book in the 19th century'.

English edition of C. Adams, *A chronological chart of ancient, modern, and biblical history* (New York: Colby & Co., many editions from c.1871) was published as *Deacon's synchronological chart of universal history* (London: C. W. Deacon) before the close of the century. Though folding into an upright folio book format, this chromolithographed pictorial chart was designed for display in the classroom and, when extended, runs to twenty feet. Statistical and quantitative diagrams found their way into British publications from the mid-nineteenth century, for example in the official catalogue of the Great Exhibition, but they reached a wider readership principally through popular atlases, such as *Bacon's popular atlas of the world* (G. Bacon & Co., 1895) and *The Harmsworth atlas and gazetteer* (London, c.1906). In the latter, a thirty-two-page section is devoted to maps and diagrams of the world's commerce, using pictures of different sizes to compare quantities, an approach that seems to have had its British beginnings some decades earlier in the first volume of *Nature* (Macmillan & Co., 1870).[47]

The nineteenth century produced such a diverse range of illustrated publications that any attempt to characterise them stylistically seems doomed to failure. Illustrators and publishers responded to all the major changes in taste of the period, and at various times embraced romanticism and the love of the pastoral, the gothic revival, Pre-Raphaelitism, the arts and crafts movement and art nouveau. In specialised fields they also responded to the more utilitarian demands of technical drawing, pictorial journalism and information graphics. But if illustrated publications of the period reveal no easily definable stylistic features, some specific qualities can be identified. Among these are visual audacity (sometimes bordering on vulgarity), a love of the grand project, a taste for technological innovation and extraordinary levels of technical skill.

Nevertheless, some kinds of publication can be considered representative of our period, either because they are rarely found outside it or because they were pioneered in it. Most obviously, there are publications that integrate refined illustrations and text, which became practicable for the first time with improvements made to engraving on wood. Associated with this was the pictorial vignette, which emerged from an eighteenth-century decorative tradition to become a distinctive feature of the period. It was almost *de rigueur* in wood-engraving when blocks were integrated with text, but it was also adopted in lithography, steel-engraving and even photomechanical illustration. The Goncourts referred to the eighteenth century as the age of the vignette, but

---

47 No. 14, 3 February 1870, p. 354. The diagram, which is described as displaying results 'in a most forcible manner', appears in a review of Georges Ville, *L'école des engrais chimiques: premières notions de l'emploi des agents de fertilité* (Paris, 1869), where it was originally published in a fuller form. There were earlier uses of the same method in France.

the nineteenth century can lay equal, if not greater, claim to that epithet. The use of a background tint, usually straw in colour, to support a black working was another popular graphic device in our period, most obviously in lithography, but to a lesser degree in wood-engraving and, in the early twentieth century, the reproduction of half-tone blocks. The ambitious, large-format chromolithographed plate book was also a particularly distinctive product of the period, and effectively died with it. Finally, the picture book – as distinct from the illustrated book – evolved in the nineteenth century and took numerous forms, including gift-books, picture story-books, pop-up books, shaped books, panoramas and sets of concertina-folded pictures.

Though most books issued between 1830 and 1914 were not illustrated, it can still be argued that the illustrated book was a major factor in defining publishing in the period, and that it changed the concept of the book for good. The following half-century was one of consolidation and relative stability technologically, but the innovations of the nineteenth-century can now be seen as preparing the way for the almost seamless relationship between text and illustration of the second half of the twentieth century.

3

The serial revolution

GRAHAM LAW AND ROBERT L. PATTEN

This chapter concerns changing patterns of serial publication, a term we use to cover two related practices: the publishing of periodicals with miscellaneous contents, including both magazines and newspapers, and the issuing of unified texts at intervals in independent fascicles or parts. In practice, there is a good deal of overlap between these two modes, as indeed between serial publication in general and book publication itself. Parts are typically issued within paper covers bearing advertising material and are marketed alongside issues of magazines that look much the same. Periodicals commonly give over a significant proportion of their space to the serialisation of lengthy homogeneous works (the aspect we tend to focus on here), while the texts issued in parts can be remarkably heterogeneous ones like encyclopaedias or dictionaries. Both parts and periodicals are generally formatted so that either the purchaser or the vendor can have them bound up into volumes when the sequence is complete. This blurring of boundaries is also apparent in the instability of the terminology used to describe serial publication in the early decades of the Victorian period especially. Judging by the citations in the *OED*, though 'number', 'part' and 'fascicle', 'miscellany', 'journal', 'magazine' and 'periodical' have a rather longer history, the term 'serial' itself – whether as adjective or noun – only comes into common usage around the 1830s. The emergence of this new word helps to justify the use of the concept of 'revolution' to define the changes taking place in instalment publication during the nineteenth century.

After the Napoleonic wars, issuing print materials in instalments at recurring intervals appealed to publishers, printers, booksellers and consumers. Markets were tight and racked by depressions and bank failures; capital was scarce and national banking only in its infancy. Instalment issue enabled publishers to recycle their investment and to gauge the market, and let printers count on regular business, set large jobs without increasing their stock of fonts, and, in the case of artisans such as Samuel Bentley, produce crafted books at affordable prices. Booksellers liked serials because repeat customers might purchase other materials as well; and consumers could obtain expensive publications on an instalment plan. In 1830, one could buy 'piecemeal' books on many subjects: fine arts (often by subscription), geography, history, poetry, fiction, essays, religion and theology, reference works, surgery, botany and other sciences, and reprints of celebrated titles: Edward Gibbon's *History of Rome* in ten two-shilling monthly parts, William Hone's *Every Day Book* in shilling monthly parts. Serial publications appeared in regular cycles of fortnightly, monthly, quarterly and half-yearly issue; but also sometimes more irregularly, whenever they were released by the press or publisher.

Certain kinds of books seemed particularly appropriate for this kind of release and potential customer: reproductions of artworks, accompanied by letterpress; travel guides for continental tourists; collections of sermons; scientific, ornithological and gardening books. Readers brought up on the pamphlets and caricatures of the war years were accustomed to seeing nearly every day new pictures and text addressing hot topics. After the Peterloo uprising (1819) and agitation about Catholic emancipation (1823–9), a principal concern was reconstituting the franchise for the House of Commons. When the Reform Bill passed in 1832, the nation turned away from political activism and towards reassessment of its cultural and educational opportunities. Print caricaturists became illustrators of poetry and fiction. Enterprising publishers such as Henry Colburn and Richard Bentley concocted 'libraries', reprints of British and American titles whose copyrights could be obtained cheaply, and sold these books in uniform bindings as a series. Thus middle-class readers could purchase substantial collections of literature one per month, a marketing ploy that blurred the distinction between instalment publication and series issue. In either case the benefits to all participants in the communications circuit remained the same.

During the early decades of the century, some printers invested substantially in equipment that significantly increased their capacity to run off large numbers of sheets quickly. The Fourdrinier paper-making machines produced larger sheets that could print thirty-two or even sixty-four rather than sixteen pages at once. The cost of paper halved between 1840 and 1910.[1] In November 1814 *The Times* installed a steam-driven press; and by 1834 the printers Bradbury & Evans had installed in Whitefriars a Middleton steam-driven cylinder press that required a steady stream of large jobs to keep the presses running six

---

1 Weedon, *Victorian publishing*, p. 67. For assistance with research and commentary on earlier drafts, the authors would like to thank Richard Altick, David Finkelstein, Linda Kay Hughes, Suzanne Rindell, Peter Ross, Amelia Scholtz, and the staffs of the British Library and the Harry Ransom Humanities Research Center at the University of Texas.

days a week and thereby make the heavy investment worthwhile. Stereotyping and, by the end of the century, electrotyping substantially reduced the costs of reprinting and made possible issuing from the same plates both serial and later bound editions. While composition costs rose throughout the century (with the exception of a dip in the decades on either side of 1900), machining remained relatively stable as a percentage of production cost. As the number of copies of a title increased (1,000 was a standard run, but much larger editions were common by the Edwardian era), and production costs were distributed across more units, books could be sold cheaper while profits increased. Consequently technology itself to some extent drove publishers and writers to devise kinds of publications that would appeal to larger audiences and institute a steady demand for new products. In general, the very economic advantages that encouraged serialised issue when Victoria came to the throne transferred to newspapers, magazines and one-volume formats before the end of her reign.

Moreover, various economic and ideological forces combined to eliminate, by the 1860s, the so-called 'taxes on knowledge'. The tax on houses with more than six windows, a revenue enhancement first levied in 1697 and falling most heavily on the middle classes, was halved in 1823 and abolished in 1851. While a house tax was substituted, at least thereafter homeowners could glaze openings previously bricked up and let daylight into their rooms. Spaces and times for reading were thus increased. Taxes were also imposed on paper: Charles Knight reckoned that he had paid £16,500 in paper duties to publish his *Penny Cyclopaedia* (weekly parts and twenty-seven volumes, 1833–44). Free traders, advocates for literacy and promoters of education combined to force successive governments to reduce the duty on paper, eventually abolished in 1861; import duties on foreign paper and printed materials were also reduced. And the charge for stamps levied on newpapers and pamphlets, which could for cheap publications nearly equal the production cost, was finally abolished in 1855. Postal services improved, making national circulation of print products easier. Since the value per pound of printed products is small, bulk shipping via the rapidly expanding railway system was the economical solution to national distribution. Books and periodicals were stacked not only in boxes in the goods waggons, but also on shelves on the platform: W. H. Smith started his railway stalls in 1848. And steamships sailing on reliable schedules year-round enabled printed serials or stereotype copies to be shipped to India, the US and Canada by the 1840s, and to Australia, New Zealand and other distant English-speaking settlements on a regular basis shortly thereafter.

The emergence in Britain of print-capitalism – in Marxist terminology, the shift from petty-commodity-text production to commodity-text production[2] – is apparent rather earlier in the part and periodical sectors than in that for books themselves,[3] where the first edition tended to remain something of a limited circulation luxury item until relatively late in the century, and even series of cheaper reprint volumes only gradually began to reach a mass audience. Bibliometric studies confirm this point. Simon Eliot's compilation of the government tax returns shows that there was a fivefold increase in the production of stamped periodicals in the first half of the nineteenth century, with the steepest rise occurring after 1836, while the abolition of knowledge taxes in the mid-1850s provoked a further phase of even more rapid growth.[4] By contrast, Alexis Weedon's estimates suggest that, despite a significant increase in overseas sales, total British book production increased only moderately between the 1830s and 1860s, though publication rose steeply from the 1880s.[5]

The principal motivations underlying the success of serial publications were speed and economy. Serial issue itself, and the more dispersed channels through which serials could be distributed, notably colporteurs or canvassers, general stores and the postal service, continued to offer the reader an immediacy of access to written information that traditional booksellers could not hope to match. In the early to mid-Victorian period, as the balance of serialisation shifted from predominantly reprinted to original material commissioned for piecemeal issue, aesthetic considerations took on a much larger role; it became important to recognise not only the mechanisms of serial publishing but also the art of serial composition and the psychology of serial reading. In other words, serial publication facilitated not only the transformation of texts into commodities but also the creation of communities of readers. This aspect of serialisation has been investigated most thoroughly by Linda Hughes and Michael Lund, who conclude that 'something in the culture of the time made it especially receptive to the serial'.[6]

There is a large degree of overlap between apparently discrete classes of serial. For example, news itself is a slippery category to define with legal

2 See, for example, Feltes, *Modes of production*, ch. 1.
3 In the early 1830s, Charles Knight's *Penny Magazine* had achieved regular weekly sales of around 200,000 (Bennett, 'Revolutions in thought', pp. 235–7), while by the end of the decade Dickens's early monthly part-novels from Chapman & Hall were reaching sales of 50,000 (Patten, *Charles Dickens and his publishers*, chs. 3–5); by the mid-century, penny weekly part-novels and miscellanies aimed at a proletarian readership from publishers like Edward Lloyd and G. W. M. Reynolds were achieving sales of well over a quarter of a million (James, *Fiction for the working man*, ch. 3).
4 Eliot, *Some patterns and trends in British publishing*, pp. 78–86, 147–8.
5 Weedon, *Victorian publishing*, pp. 45–58.   6 Hughes and Lund, *The Victorian serial*, p. 4.

precision,[7] and for tax reasons publishers deliberately mixed reports on current events with other kinds of prose. It is hard to specify the differences between newspapers and magazines, especially in the case of news weeklies that often issued supplements, sometimes in the form of fascicles of lengthy works. These might be fictional or non-fictional,[8] though fiction is not always easy to distinguish from other narrative modes such as biography, history or travel-writing.[9] Many Victorian miscellanies appearing weekly were also available to monthly subscribers at a commensurate rate, while quite a few novels appeared concurrently in cheaper weekly and more expensive monthly portions. Some examples: Harrison Ainsworth's *Jack Sheppard* was serialised first in the monthly numbers of *Bentley's Miscellany* (January 1839–February 1840) and later (1840) in fifteen weekly parts by the same publisher. In 1859, Dickens's *A tale of two cities* appeared simultaneously in weekly numbers in his own *All the Year Round* and in monthly parts from Chapman & Hall. Wilkie Collins's *Heart and science* was printed both in Chatto & Windus's monthly *Belgravia* (August 1882–June 1883) and in a syndicate of around a dozen weekly newspapers. In this last case, typical of what has been termed 'belt-and-braces' serialisation,[10] a subscriber to *Belgravia* would have paid eleven shillings (132 pence) to receive the complete text of the novel (among other material), while the typical cost to a reader of one of the weekly papers would have been only 2s 4d (28 pence). Another strategy widely employed by mid-century was to release a collected edition of an author's works in cheap weekly parts: Scott and Dickens reached hundreds of thousands of readers in this form.

Nevertheless, the categories of independent monthly number and miscellaneous weekly or monthly periodical remain useful in sub-dividing the years from 1830 to 1914 into three sub-periods, with the transitions occurring around the late 1850s and the later 1880s. For instance, in the first period monthly serialisation of fiction, magazines and other serial issues represents the dominant though far from exclusive mode for middle-class publications.

---

7 See Collet, *History of the taxes on knowledge* 1, ch. 1.
8 W. E. Norris's *Thirlby Hall*, for example, was issued as a supplement with the weekly *Graphic* from 2 June 1883, though the practice was halted owing to opposition from the postal authorities. The Post Office judged that it fell outside the definition of a newspaper according to the Post Office Act of 1870, which regulated the sending of newspapers through the mail at cheaper rates, and the serial thus returned to the columns of the paper itself. (See 'The Graphic and the Post Office', p. 58.) This practice in fact seems to have been rather more common in the eighteenth century; see Wiles, *Serial publication in England before 1750*, ch. 2.
9 For example, it is difficult to categorise George Gissing's late works *By the Ionian Sea* (1901) and the *Private papers of Henry Ryecroft* (1903) as fiction or travel sketches and autobiographical essays, respectively. Both of these appeared initially as serials in the *Fortnightly Review*, by then a monthly publication.
10 Law, *Serializing fiction in the Victorian press*, pp. 105–7.

For late Victorians and Edwardians, however, the weekly number lost some of its associations with a proletarian readership and became more respectable. By the 1890s morning and evening newspapers selling millions of copies daily incorporated everything from international reporting to puzzles and prizes, while independent original part publication moved from the centre to the margins, having been replaced by inexpensive one-volume books and serialised original or republished stories marketed by authors' agents to newspapers around the world through fiction bureaux. Though serial prices declined considerably overall, the rate of change from decade to decade was far from uniform. And whilst general economic, technological and social transformations may have been determining influences on production, pricing, marketing and consumption throughout this eighty-five-year period, the abating of knowledge taxes seems crucial to the first period of transition, as the formalisation of international conventions protecting literary property is important to the second.

The early years, 1830–1850s

Piecemeal publication blurred generic distinctions between news and fiction, but also between new print, revised print and reprint editions, and between serialisation, book, sequel and series. One of the most influential series, Bentley's Standard Novels (1831–54), boasted that it supplied the authors' revised texts of popular titles; these volumes appearing one per month encouraged a regular diet of reading and the consumption of diversified fiction by English, Scottish, Irish, American, French, German and Danish authors. Parts publication of original works, especially of fiction, grew up alongside serialisation in periodicals. Frederick Marryat is credited with being the first to issue instalment fictions designed for publication in magazines; but his early experiments needed some fine tuning. He stopped his first novel, *Peter Simple* (June 1832–September 1833), midway through its run in his own monthly, the *Metropolitan Magazine*, fearing that if it continued the public would prefer the cheap periodical instalments to the completed volume edition (December 1833).

One mid-1830s innovation had profound effects on mid-Victorian fiction. Robert Seymour, a comic artist who contributed to the humour papers that replaced separate social and political caricatures, shopped around the idea of a series of images depicting the hapless sporting exploits of city-dwellers. A small publishing and bookselling house recently opened by Edward Chapman and William Hall in the Strand considered the idea of issuing these plates and letterpress monthly, an alternative to their projected Library of Fiction, an illustrated monthly collection of short stories. But they had trouble finding any writer willing to compose the narrative that led up to and explained the plates. Eventually, in February 1836, a young reporter making a name for himself as 'Boz' agreed to the collaboration, though from the start he pushed for his 'own way'. The resulting publication, *The posthumous papers of the Pickwick Club*, appeared in twenty monthly numbers at a shilling each over nineteen months, with the last part being a 'double number' (parts xix and xx) at two shillings containing sixty-four pages rather than thirty-two, with four illustrations instead of two, and comprising all the necessary front matter to convert the monthly instalments into a bound volume. Seymour did not live to see the success of his project, which owed only its inception to him in any case. But Chapman, Hall and the author, Charles Dickens, reaped huge rewards from the recycled capital, the expanding sales (reaching 40,000 per month at the end), the repeated notices month after month, the word of mouth circulating among readers, the advertising supplement that became another remunerative feature of serialisation, and the subsequent reissue of bound sheets as a one-volume novel. At a stroke, this serial, comprising over six hundred pages and more than forty illustrations, reduced the cost of *owning* a new novel from $1\frac{1}{2}$ guineas for three volumes paid at once – the standard price and format from 1821 to 1894 – to a pound, *paid out over nineteen months*.[11] Publishers profited enormously; authors learned to lease rather than sell copyrights for serials and benefited by being paid while writing as well as sharing net receipts after publication; and illustrated serial novels released in varying numbers of weekly or monthly instalments rivalled three-deckers for the next thirty years.

Serials were particularly hospitable to weaving multiple plots and classes of characters into a verbal tapestry, and to accompanying the story with illustrations that shifted over time from deploying the style and imagery of caricature (into the 1840s) to utilising theatrical and realistic pictorial conventions (in the 1860s) both to depict and to critique the letterpress.[12] At least sixteen mainline Victorian authors published nearly two hundred novels in some variant of this parts formula, either as separate numbers or in periodicals, and in many cases in both formats concurrently.[13] Thus Dickens, editing the richly illustrated *Master Humphrey's clock*, published *The old curiosity shop* (1840–1) and *Barnaby Rudge* (1841) in the magazine's threepenny weekly instalments (bound up half-yearly as volumes) and also in separate monthly parts; after each novel's completion

11 Patten, *Charles Dickens and his publishers*, ch. 3.   12 Maxwell, *The Victorian illustrated book*.
13 Vann, *Victorian novels*.

unsold sheets or reprints from the original plates were bound for sale as single volumes. Because these serialised fictions were read, discussed, circulated, dramatised and pictorialised in the press, their characters and stories became a part of the nation's regular diet of news. Whether Little Nell died or Becky Sharp lied became nearly as widespread a topic of conversation as Chartism or the Irish famine.

By the 1840s, serial issue was accommodated to various calendrical cycles: not only weekly and monthly parts extending to eighteen, twenty or twenty-four months, but also monthly numbers timed to begin in January and conclude, thirteen as twelve monthly parts, so that a one-volume edition could be issued for the holiday trade which picked up with the renewal of Christmas festivities and gift-giving in the 1840s. Starting in the 1850s, twopenny weekly miscellanies of fiction and essays such as *Household Words* not only issued half-yearly volumes but also printed Christmas numbers selling 40,000 copies or more and containing specially commissioned seasonal tales. An index accompanied each biennial compilation, so that the resulting volume served some of the purposes of a reference work. Since many customers lost some numbers of a serial, publishers anticipated a need for reprints to fill in the run, and secondhand retailers advertised that odd parts could be taken in exchange in order to complete a volume.

Not only were some books neither conceptualised nor experienced as fixed entities, they were also not read at a sitting. Serialisation encouraged regular, periodic revisiting of a story, received either as a silent reading experience or as a public oral one. Our most substantial evidence concerns the reception of novels, with less information about poetry and almost none about other genres. But as novels took a central role in the construction of mid-Victorian culture, their regular appearance as instalments in separate numbers or magazines promoted public airing of the fiction alongside other 'news'.[14] By the heyday of sensation fiction in the 1860s, the overstimulation of fiction's effect came in for extensive discussion. Critics self-appointed as society's guardians instructed the enlarging middle-class reading public in the protocols and practices of reading; they began to inveigh against short attention spans and literary 'snacking'.[15]

14 Serials did not always come out regularly; Dickens missed a month (June 1837) on *Pickwick* and *Oliver Twist* when his sister-in-law died, Thackeray three months (October–December 1849) on *Pendennis* because of illness, and Harrison Ainsworth completed the twelve-as-eleven-part *Mervyn Clitheroe* after a four and a half year hiatus (December 1851–March 1853; December 1857–June 1858).
15 Mays, 'The disease of reading'.

In 1842 Charles Edward Mudie established his 'Select Library' in Bloomsbury to cater to the respectable classes. For a few guineas a year, patrons could check out books on assorted topics, from poetry to science. Mudie insisted that his stock exclude trash and anything that would upset family values. Since his business depended on lending volumes, he did not stock serials. 'Library fiction' could mean anything from improving tracts to discreet romances, and by the 1850s some commercial rivals did also stock serials. Consequently major Victorian serial fictions circulating in large quantities to readers throughout the kingdom evaded both Mudie's censorship and his commercial model of lending; parts publications were more often sold than rented, and sold not only in bookshops and railway stalls but by pedlars tramping the countryside and wholesalers distributing large quantities to warehouses in Britain and abroad. In the 1850s, however, this distinction between middle-class fare circulated through commercial libraries and more demotic parts publications began to break down. William Makepeace Thackeray, until the mid-1840s primarily a journalist selling articles and serials throughout Grub Street, in 1852 wrote *The history of Henry Esmond* for George Smith, who commissioned it as a three-volume novel. Thereafter Thackeray reverted to parts publication, and Dickens never deserted the format, though *Great expectations* appeared post-serial in three volumes for the circulating libraries. By the 1860s if major middle-class novelists did write for serial issue in magazines or parts, the novels were likely to appear after serialisation as three-deckers. The extent to which migrating to the canonical volume format raised the cultural status of serialised fiction has not yet been thoroughly assessed.

Meanwhile, the vast majority of Britain's population was working class, poor, lacking stable housing, much education, places in which to read, and time. For these consumers there were two opposite (though often simultaneously experienced) options: reading improving texts in subscription and other libraries, or picking up whenever possible penny bloods, convoluted and violent stories extended over many months. The largest volume distributors of serials were religious and educational organisations. The Religious Tract Society handed out 23 million books in the 1840s, and the annual production of the Society for Promoting Christian Knowledge increased from 1.5 million in 1827 to 8 million forty years later.[16] Generally the tracts were purchased as charitable benefactions by the middle class and distributed to working-class households by volunteers whose visits were sometimes unwelcome. At a higher level, preachers converted sermons into tracts arguing theological

16 St Clair, *The reading nation*, p. 569.

points; the most famous of these was the series of ninety tracts issued monthly by Oxford theologians between 1833 and 1841, culminating in John Henry Newman's apostasy. Beginning in the 1820s, the Society for the Diffusion of Useful Knowledge established mechanics' institutes, incorporating circulating libraries for literate working men often run and supported by their employers, who saw to it that the shelves held only improving utilitarian texts, no fiction or Byronic poetry.[17]

At the other end of the spectrum in London's Salisbury Square, Edward Lloyd, one of the most prolific publishers of working-class serials, issued plagiarisms of early Dickens and helped to start the vogue for sensational instalments; from the later 1830s onwards he issued around 200 lurid Gothic, historical and romantic tales in penny weekly numbers, including *Varney, the vampyre* (1845-7). Some of these publications, like the *Arabian nights' entertainments* (1847), were lavishly illustrated by wood-engravings surrounding and framing the texts. Lloyd also prospered as the proprietor of cheap weekly newspapers, notably *Lloyd's Weekly London Newspaper* in January 1843 (2½d, later 3d) and various penny magazines. In the 1850s he moved upmarket, abandoning penny dreadfuls for respectability and mass circulation.[18] G. W. M. Reynolds became famous and intermittently solvent through similar expedients – penny knock-offs of Dickens and cheap miscellanies. Then, beginning in 1844, he penned and published the serial that outsold Dickens – *The mysteries of London* (1844-8), with a circulation of 40,000 copies a week and over a million parts before being reissued in volumes.[19]

As in other cases we have adduced, the boundaries separating genre, price, periodicity and audience melded by mid-century: half-crown quarterlies gave way to shilling monthlies, shilling numbers dropped to sixpenny or penny parts, fivepenny newspapers devolved to penny dailies, while blood-and-thunder adventures rose into the respectable ranks. *Lloyd's Weekly* became a leading Liberal organ and achieved a daily sale of one million copies in 1896, while Reynolds's penny *Reynolds's Miscellany*, featuring illustrated serials, achieved a sale of 30,000 copies in its first year, 1846.[20] Although Reynolds offended the middle class, Dickens and Marxist radicals, he brought French notions of class warfare – villainous rich versus deserving poor – into British fiction, to which he added the capitalist calculations (Thomas Carlyle's 'cash nexus') of the rising middle class; these class types influenced more complex

17 *Ibid.*, pp. 260-1.   18 Haywood, *The revolution in popular literature*, pp. 163-9.
19 Maxwell, *The mysteries of Paris and London*, ch. 3.
20 James, *Fiction for the working man* (1963), p. 41.

versions in such monthly number fiction as *Vanity Fair* (1847–8) and *Bleak House* (1852–3).

The middle years, 1850s–1880s

As we have seen, in the second quarter of the nineteenth century those attempting to reach a readership beyond the privileged few who could afford to subscribe to a circulating library, or even purchase the latest literature in editions de luxe, had little choice but to adopt some form of serial publication. Nevertheless, despite some relief from tax reductions in the mid-1830s, fiscal constraints long continued to counteract the benefits from economies of scale enjoyed by the serial publisher. At the time of the Great Exhibition of 1851, journals incorporating information on and discussion of current events – to take the most onerous case – thus still faced excise duty of three halfpence per pound on 'Class One' paper for printing, plus eighteen pence tax on each and every advertisement carried, as well as the newspaper stamp at a penny per issue. For weekly papers striving to reach a popular audience like the *News of the World* (1843–), this amounted to a rate of taxation far greater than 100 per cent of the cost of production, thus pushing up the purchase price to threepence, beyond the reach of much of its intended audience. In theory, the removal after the mid-century of the principal fiscal constraints on the publisher ought to have resulted not only in the cheapening of serials like the *News of the World*, but also in a significant reduction in the cost of a fresh post-octavo volume from the inflationary heights of half a guinea, but this did not in fact happen. Parliament debated and abolished the taxes on knowledge not at a single sitting but gradually through the 1850s, beginning in 1853 with the advertisement tax, and followed in 1855 by the newspaper stamp, that is, the two imposts borne principally by producers of serials. In contrast, the paper duty, which, though a burden to all publishers, weighed most heavily on those producing editions for the libraries,[21] was removed only in 1861 after especially trenchant opposition. Collet Dobson Collet, in his personal record of the twelve-year campaign against the taxes, suggests that this was not only for budgetary reasons – 'the Paper Duty brought to the revenue nearly three times as much as the Advertisement and Stamp Duties put together' – but also because of a residual 'fear of knowledge, in the House, and outside it'.[22] Certainly the prolongation of the debate reinforced the engrained conservatism of the library system, so that

21 See Wiener, *The war of the unstamped*, ch. 1.
22 Collet, *History of the taxes on knowledge* 1, pp. 126, 130.

the ensuing phase of rapid growth occurred first and foremost in the serial market. However, the publishing boom was reflected not only within existing serial formats – by marked reductions in price, accompanied by steep increases in both the number of titles and the volume of sales – but also in the emergence of new serial modes, or new functions for old ones. This suggests not just the releasing of market forces but in addition the impact of changing social structures.

As the medium hitherto most fiscally hampered, though, the newspaper clearly benefited most rapidly from liberation, as demonstrated dramatically in Charles Mitchell's *Newspaper Press Directory*, which itself moved to regular annual publication from 1856 (see table 3.1). Between 1854 and 1856 alone, Mitchell calculates, the number of newspaper titles published in the United Kingdom and the British Isles (Jersey, Guernsey and the Isle of Man) rose from 624 to 801, a nearly 30 per cent increase which occurred predominantly among country journals. By 1866, the total had doubled to 1,257, with a large gain found also in metropolitan newspapers, and it continued to rise, though slightly less steeply, to 1,642 titles during the following decade. Already by 1856 there were penny journals on sale each morning in both the metropolis and the provinces, putting a daily paper within the economic grasp of the lower middle class for the first time. Among the pioneers were the *Daily Telegraph* of Sheffield, one of the first English industrial cities to host two cheap dailies of different political complexions,[23] and the London *Daily Telegraph*, which by the early 1870s was claiming sales of over 200,000, the largest daily circulation in the world.[24] From the late 1860s there was also a new wave of halfpenny daily evening papers, with Tillotson's *Bolton Evening News* (1867) in industrial Lancashire and Cassell's *Echo* in London (1868) among the early instances.

For our purposes, however, the most distinctive development was the emergence of the penny weekly news miscellany, which typically appeared at the weekend and featured not only a summary of the week's intelligence but also a variety of instructive and entertaining matter. The popular news miscellany reached a broad social readership, to begin with based principally in the outlying provinces where metropolitan periodicals had penetrated little – the *Dundee People's Journal* and the *Newcastle Weekly Chronicle* were important pathbreakers. However, the new format gradually reached back towards the

---

23 See Lee, *The origins of the popular press*, tables 1–3, pp. 274–7.
24 See Altick, *The English common reader*, p. 355. From the end of the official stamp returns in 1855 until early in the twentieth century, when advertisers began to demand audited evidence of sales, claimed circulation figures for specific newspapers are sometimes hard to find and often unreliable. For an attempt to estimate circulations over the period 1855 to 1870 using a combination of anecdotal information and statistical method, see Ellegård, *The readership of the periodical press*.

Table 3.1 *UK periodical titles, 1846–1916*

Year	Total	Newspapers	%	Magazines	%
1846	–	550	–	–	–
1847	–	555	–	–	–
1851*	–	563	–	–	–
1854*	–	624	–	–	–
1856*	–	801	–	–	–
1857	–	816	–	–	–
1858	–	866	–	–	–
1859	–	967	–	–	–
1860	1,445	1,039	72	406	28
1861	1,583	1,102	70	481	30
1862	1,680	1,166	69	514	31
1863	1,743	1,206	69	537	31
1864	1,787	1,250	70	537	30
1865	1,825	1,271	70	554	30
1866	1,814	1,257	69	557	31
1867	1,882	1,294	69	588	31
1868	1,945	1,324	68	621	32
1869	2,027	1,372	68	655	32
1870	2,016	1,390	69	626	31
1871	2,088	1,450	69	638	31
1872	2,095	1,456	69	639	31
1873	2,166	1,536	71	630	29
1874	2,224	1,585	71	639	29
1875	2,252	1,609	71	643	29
1876	2,299	1,642	71	657	29
1877	2,500	1,692	68	808	32
1878	2,583	1,744	68	839	32
1879	2,716	1,763	65	953	35
1880	2,868	1,835	64	1,033	36
1881	2,983	1,886	63	1,097	37
1882	2,997	1,817	61	1,180	39
1883	3,273	1,962	60	1,311	40
1884	3,275	2,015	62	1,260	38
1885	3,350	2,052	61	1,298	39
1886	3,461	2,093	60	1,368	40
1887	3,597	2,135	59	1,462	41
1888	3,685	2,177	59	1,508	41
1889	3,779	2,186	58	1,593	42
1890	3,986	2,234	56	1,752	44
1891	4,012	2,234	56	1,778	44
1892	4,156	2,255	54	1,901	46
1893	4,229	2,268	54	1,961	46
1894	4,352	2,291	53	2,061	47

Table 3.1 *(cont.)*

Year	Total	Newspapers	%	Magazines	%
1895	4,385	2,304	53	2,081	47
1896	4,452	2,355	53	2,097	47
1897	4,582	2,396	52	2,186	48
1898	4,621	2,396	52	2,225	48
1899	4,654	2,364	51	2,290	49
1900	4,799	2,471	51	2,328	49
1901	4,914	2,468	50	2,446	50
1902	4,923	2,437	50	2,486	50
1903	4,943	2,412	49	2,531	51
1904	4,948	2,444	49	2,504	51
1905	5,149	2,456	48	2,693	52
1906	5,185	2,440	47	2,745	53
1907	5,207	2,302	44	2,905	56
1908	5,313	2,353	44	2,960	56
1909	5,155	2,322	45	2,833	55
1910	5,104	2,331	46	2,773	54
1911	5,365	2,395	45	2,970	55
1912	5,537	2,390	43	3,147	57
1913	5,664	2,456	43	3,208	57
1914	5,796	2,504	43	3,292	57
1915	5,804	2,413	42	3,391	58
1916	5,903	2,421	41	3,482	59

Sources: Mitchell's *Newspaper Press Directory* (1846–1916) and Eliot, *Some patterns and trends in British publishing*, fig. 39, and table E3, pp. 148 and 83. The data provided here revise and supplement those found in Eliot, *Some patterns and trends in British publishing*, which does not cover the years 1846–63, 1876 and 1904–16. The abrupt rise in the number of recorded magazine titles in 1877 probably reflects less a publishing boom than a change in methods of recording. The NPD 'Publisher's Address' for 1877 (p. [iv]) reports that 'The Directory of Magazines, Reviews, etc has been specially revised and added to.' This suggests that the data for 1860–76 may underestimate the true number of magazine titles.

Notes:
- Data not given in *Newspaper Press Directory* volume
* No *Newspaper Press Directory* volume(s) issued in intervening year(s)

home counties and the metropolis. A good deal, though by no means all, of the material in these journals was supplied through various modes of syndication, initially local and informal, but by the 1870s highly systematic and nationwide in scope. The two most successful agencies here were Cassell's General Press in the metropolis, best known for their partly printed sheets, and Tillotson's Fiction Bureau of Bolton, specialising in material cast into stereotype. Though serial fiction became an increasingly popular ingredient of these miscellanies, the syndicators often began by supplying metropolitan advertising and intelligence, and soon also provided regular features such as poetry and critical essays, or columns aimed at women and children.[25] Throughout the second half of the nineteenth century, these news miscellanies remained the most comprehensive print resource for many of the members of the communities they served, and today they represent one of the most detailed records of developments in local social and regional culture.

A further effect of the news miscellany boom in the second half of the nineteenth century is that it then becomes even more difficult to maintain a clear distinction between newspapers and magazines. Nevertheless, it remains important to recognise that the impact of the abolition of the taxes on knowledge was a good deal less decisive in the magazine market. The classification employed in Mitchell's *Newspaper Press Directory* suggests that, throughout the decade and a half from 1861, newspapers continued to represent rather more than two-thirds of the total of UK periodical titles, with the number of magazines increasing only from 481 to 657 by 1876 (see table 3.1). Yet the later 1850s and 1860s did witness a number of significant transformations, especially in the field of the general miscellany. Changes in the literary monthlies serving the middle classes have been well documented. Best known is the appearance of a new generation of lighter literary miscellanies, now elegantly illustrated and prominently featuring serial works by best-selling novelists, whether Thackeray or Anthony Trollope, Elizabeth Braddon or Ellen Wood, yet priced at only a shilling. The most successful examples, both founded in 1860, were Smith, Elder's *Cornhill Magazine* and John Maxwell's *Temple Bar*, taken over by Richard Bentley in 1866. But there were also original monthlies of a heavier kind, which, while finding room for superior instalment fiction by the likes of George Meredith, sought to take over many of the traditional intellectual functions of the quarterly review – yet at a much reduced cost; here the most distinguished examples are *Macmillan's Magazine* (1859) and Chapman & Hall's *Fortnightly Review* (1865), which quickly shifted to monthly issue. Both varieties were typically published by the established literary houses serving the circulating libraries, and occasionally featured works of non-fiction in instalments, including critical works in the fields of politics and philosophy.

Perhaps less familiar are the simultaneous developments in the weekly miscellany, as prejudice against the weekly number and the common reader simultaneously eroded. In 1861, when Lord Lytton condescendingly allowed his

---

25 See Law, *Serializing fiction in the Victorian press*, chs. 2–4.

latest work to be serialised in Dickens's new humble twopenny weekly, *All the Year Round*, rather than in the venerable *Blackwood's*, the *Publishers' Circular* commented with only a touch of exaggeration:

> Perhaps one of the most striking features of the periodical literature of the day is the general levelling of all distinctions grounded upon mere price. The eminent author may now descend from the six shilling Quarterly even to the penny weekly without the slightest fear of losing caste; and Cobbett's well-known defiance of the prejudice of his time by calling one of his own publications 'Two-penny Trash' would have been unintelligible to the present generation.[26]

With *Household Words* from 1850 Dickens had taken the lead in creating a literary journal in weekly numbers 'designed for the instruction and entertainment of all classes of readers'.[27] In this, he was belatedly followed by a number of literary houses, including Bradbury & Evans in 1859 with their own *Once a Week* after Dickens had abandoned them to start up *All the Year Round*. Yet there were earlier and more significant moves by publishers in other sectors. Instructional papers in the utilitarian and/or evangelical traditions, such as *Chambers's Journal* (1832), the Religious Tract Society's *Leisure Hour* (1852) and *Cassell's Illustrated Family Paper* (1853), sought to reach a less sectarian audience by increasing the leaven of entertainment. The Salisbury Square publishers followed the example of the *Family Herald* in seeking female and juvenile readers, and the penny fiction journals thus became both less bloody and lustful and more instructive. Stimulated by the success of the provincial news miscellanies, the metropolitan press began to issue weekly journals in newspaper format, which included little in the way of public intelligence but a good deal of literary material. Notable examples include cheap popular sheets like the *Weekly Budget* (1860), and more expensive middle-class papers like the illustrated *Graphic* (1869), or the *World* (1874) with its concentration on society gossip. Though all of these weeklies relied a good deal for their appeal on instalment fiction, they also included many other works in serial, notably biographies, histories, travellers' tales and other modes of narrative. The *Cornhill* was famous for attracting over 100,000 subscribers to its early issues,[28] but there is no doubt that the weekly

---

26 *Publishers' Circular*, 31 December 1861, p. 694. By the mid-1860s weeklies reached sales hitherto attained only by penny dreadfuls; the 1866 Christmas number of *All the Year Round* sold 265,000 copies within the first month (Patten, *Charles Dickens and his publishers*, p. 301).

27 See the advertisements for the opening numbers, reproduced in Gasson, *Wilkie Collins*, pp. 49, 53.

28 Sales of the *Cornhill* had fallen to 26,000 by December 1868, though 110,000 copies of the first issue had been distributed in January 1860; see Sutherland, 'Cornhill's sales and payments'.

miscellanies were generally attracting a far larger audience than the monthlies by the late 1860s.

Whether issued in weekly or monthly formats, serialised fictions built in expectations about structure and effect that were articulated by reviewers and perfected by some, but by no means all, of the authors who exploited the format. In the early days, critics scanned for plot and character; by the 1840s, more attention was being paid to motivation and credibility; and by the 1850s and 1860s, the social functions of popular fiction came under increasing scrutiny. Reviewing *David Copperfield* and *Pendennis* in July 1850, the *Prospective Review* grumped that serials afforded 'the greatest excuse for unlimited departures from dignity, propriety, consistency, completeness, and proportion'. Sixteen years later Elizabeth Gaskell was considered inferior to Dickens or Disraeli in invention, vividness and vigour, but she excelled in producing an 'air of perfect reality' (*Saturday Review*, 24 March 1866). Trollope, who released novels in weekly and monthly instalments in magazines and parts, sometimes running two stories in two different formats simultaneously, was repeatedly chastised for composing, 'as usual, no plot'. But by the 1860s critics granted that something other than suspense might make serial instalments attractive: 'A little of it once a month is just what everybody would like' (*Saturday Review*, 19 August 1865).

In this middle period serial authors were not just Grub Street scribblers, some were statesmen or celebrities, another marker of the respectability of the genre. Benjamin Disraeli, who became Prime Minister in 1868, never issued first editions of his novels in parts, but Edward Bulwer-Lytton, eventually Baron Lytton of Knebworth, did, and also served in Parliament for more than seventeen years. Dickens thought of campaigning for a seat in the Commons but didn't; Trollope ran as a Liberal in 1868 but lost. Other prominent serialists included Thomas Carlyle, George Eliot, Thomas Hardy, Cardinal Newman, John Ruskin and Herbert Spencer. James Murray initiated the *New Oxford dictionary on historical principles* in 1884 in the same way reference works had been published for a century, by issuing fascicles in alphabetical sequence; the series was completed in 126 parts in 1928. John Gould, Britain's leading ornithologist, commenced his sumptuous *Birds of Great Britain* in 1862: it ran to twenty-five semi-annual parts and contained 367 hand-coloured lithographs. *Uncle Tom's cabin* was a runaway best-seller in Britain, appearing in a variety of part issues including one from Cassell illustrated by George Cruikshank, and Harriet Beecher Stowe became as famous in Britain as in the United States. Isabella Beeton's *Book of household management*, serialised by her publisher husband from 1859 to 1861, instructed the growing population of householders on everything from cookery to medicine and transformed its author into a trade name. Even poets sometimes resorted to instalment publishing: Robert Browning, during his obscure early years, put out *Bells and pomegranates* in six yearly parts, 1841–6, and Alfred Tennyson, eventual poet laureate and baron, issued various versions and parts of his serial poem *Idylls of the king* in at least twelve trial and first editions and one magazine instalment over more than half a century.

From the later 1870s the periodical boom was sustained more strongly in the magazine than the newspaper or parts sectors. Mitchell's statistics suggest that between 1876 and 1896 the number of British newspaper titles increased by only 43% to 2,355, whereas magazine titles more than tripled to 2,097. Indeed, early in the new century the number of newspapers peaked, so that magazines then began to take a clear lead and accounted for close to 60 per cent of the total by the First World War (see table 3.1). The major increase was in 'class' periodicals, a category that the *Newspaper press directory* began to employ in its statistics from 1879, in contrast to 'mass' periodicals targeting a broad and undifferentiated readership. It referred to the rapidly increasing number of magazines serving specific professional, social and cultural communities. Though the proportion of the total 'of a decidedly religious character', to use Mitchell's categorisation, declined in the last quarter of the century, the absolute number continued to increase until around 1900.[29] Thus, the period from 1875 to 1900 witnessed a dense proliferation of scientific, technical and trade journals, and also of magazines affiliated to political parties, Christian denominations and regional interests, and ones catering to fans of leisure activities, including sport, music and gardening, as well as to demographic groups based on gender, age or ethnicity.

In terms of individual circulation, of course, these segmental periodicals were not in the same league as the latest generation of 'mass' miscellanies, of which the pioneer was George Newnes's *Tit-Bits* (1881), which was selling over 300,000 copies per week within five years.[30] Unlike the first generation, represented by *Chambers's Edinburgh Journal* or Charles Knight's *Penny Magazine*, papers like *Tit-Bits* reflected not so much the common reader's need for useful knowledge as the growth of disposable income and leisure time and the desire to escape from the tedium of repetitive work. The 'class' periodicals tended to remain committed to serialising lengthy works in their pages, including a surprising quantity of instalment fiction tailored to the community

29 Eliot, *Some patterns and trends in British publishing*, table E6, p. 150.
30 See Law, *Serializing fiction in the Victorian press*, table 5.1, pp. 128–9.

in question, while, as the title of *Tit-Bits* suggests, the 'mass' journals generally turned away from texts of any length and complexity. For Newnes, of course, *Tit-Bits* was merely the foundation stone of what was to become Britain's first modern press empire, which would eventually seek to exploit the 'class' and 'mass' markets indifferently.[31] We will return to the implications of these shifts in the final section.

The 'number trade' altered significantly during the high Victorian decades. Publication of original novels in fascicles lost ground in the face of the new wave of literary miscellanies, whether monthly or weekly, which sold at lower prices once knowledge taxes were abolished and mechanical improvements cheapened book production and distribution. Moreover, the economic incentive to purchase new fiction in penny parts or shilling numbers was considerably diminished when, for the same outlay, the reader could choose among a range of magazines, some illustrated, containing only slightly shorter episodes from a couple of original novels, together with a cornucopia of non-fictional features. Indeed, in the 1850s and 1860s Victorian print culture moved towards cultivating a mass audience: for instance, the style and content of penny bloods moved upward into middle-class sensation fiction, while 'higher-brow' works were issued in multiple formats appealing to many different purses. Even three-deckers appeared in one-volume six-shilling editions within a year of original publication. So the familiar pattern of new works reaching the wealthy while labourers read out-of-date material in cheap reprints and excerpts began to change.

So long as Dickens's fictions appeared inside the familiar duck-green wrappers of the monthly part, novelists challenging his celebrity such as Thackeray and Trollope might continue to favour the same format. But after 1857 only one of Dickens's novels was completed in twenty parts (*Our mutual friend*, 1864-5, fig. 3.1); two others appeared in his weekly magazine *All the Year Round*, and his last, twelve monthly part, fiction, *The mystery of Edwin Drood*, which commenced in April 1870, was discontinued when Dickens died in June without finishing it. The boom in monthly part novels for middle-class readers passed its peak in the late 1850s; twenty years later the odd belated example must have appeared almost 'as antediluvian as the powdered wig or the buckled shoe'.[32] And, as the vogue for the proletarian penny blood read by working-class men and boys was displaced by that for the 'penny dreadful', a rousing tale of adventure marketed for a juvenile audience, the preferred mode of initial publication

---

31 See Jackson, *George Newnes and the new journalism*, especially pp. 199-261.
32 Sutherland, *Victorian fiction* 2nd edn, p. 108.

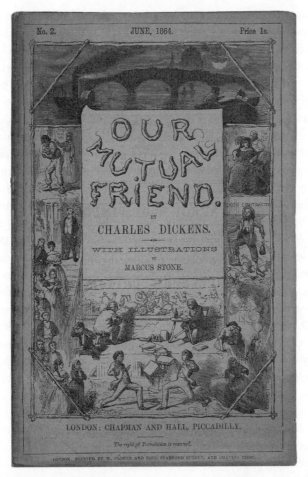

Figure 3.1 Charles Dickens, *Our mutual friend*. Cover for the monthly part for June 1864, illustrated by Marcus Stone. The goods advertised inside included not only household and other daily needs, but also new books from A. & C. Black, Macmillan and Hurst & Blackett, besides Chapman & Hall. Apart from *Our mutual friend*, Chapman & Hall were also publishing Trollope's *Can you forgive her?* and Lever's *Luttrell of Arran* in parts at this time. (Private collection)

shifted noticeably from parts to periodicals, with Edwin J. Brett's *Boys of England* (1866) among the most popular and typical titles. With reprinted fiction, however, part-issue remained an option for rather longer, especially in the case of well-known authors. For example, in 1866 John Blackwood counselled George Eliot to have her back-list novels reissued not as a series of flimsy two-shilling yellowback volumes, but each in seven or eight sixpenny monthly parts on superior paper, to be distributed by 'the "Number Men," i.e. men who sell the weekly and monthly publications in large numbers'.[33] Similarly, from the 1860s John Dicks started reissuing Reynolds's old romances in halfpenny weekly parts, though by the 1880s he had removed the issue numbers from the plates and was selling tales like *Wagner the Wehr-Wolf* in complete paperback volumes at sixpence each in his series of Dicks' English Novels.

In contrast, the part-issue of non-fiction, whether reprinted classics or new works of reference, seems to have continued to enjoy steady growth in the mid-Victorian decades, although production and distribution were increasingly concentrated in the hands of a small number of specialist firms. There were many sides to this serial trade. On the one hand, as publishing firms consolidated capital, new titles might be issued in various formats simultaneously for different classes of customer. Serialised release was no longer an economic necessity for publishers or a growing consumer base. In 1860 Henry Lea provided scientific books 'for working men' in weekly three-halfpence numbers and monthly sixpenny parts; an illustrated edition of Byron in monthly sixpenny parts with numbers 1–14 appearing in February 1860; and sixpenny monthly parts of Shakespeare and a *Topographical dictionary of England and Wales*.[34] Concurrently Edward Moxon offered Wordsworth's complete works, in six foolscap volumes, cloth, for thirty shillings, in six pocket volumes, cloth, for twenty-one shillings, or in one octavo volume for twenty shillings. These same publishing houses might offer a range of other types of publication – magazines, schoolbooks, scholarly histories and even newspapers addressed either to mass or special (secular, religious, gendered) audiences.

Choice of format and potential range of consumers meant that publications issued at predictable punctuated reading times diversified into printed products offering multiple kinds of reading experience: weighty newspapers and monthlies for careful perusal, inexpensive dailies for a quick skim, multi-volume works that improved the mind or professional competence, and miscellaneous magazines picked up and put down as time permitted. The lively new publishing houses known for cheap reprints, like Routledge & Sons (founded in 1836) or Ward & Lock (founded in 1854), issued their fiction titles predominantly in cheap uniform series of yellowbacks or paperback volumes aimed at the railway traveller. Yet they often preferred to employ part publication for works of non-fiction, especially in the case of lengthy and/or heavily illustrated works. Routledge's Railway Library of fiction, beginning in 1848, included

---

33 John Blackwood to George Eliot, 21 December 1866: George Eliot, *Letters* 4, pp. 320–3.
34 *Publishers' Circular*, 1 February 1860, p. 77.

over 1,300 titles before the end of the century, but the parallel Popular Library of non-fiction starting up in 1850 petered out in under four years and fewer than sixty volumes.[35] On the other hand, such projects as J. G. Woods's lavish *Illustrated natural history*, with artwork by Joseph Wolf and others, and first issued in monthly parts over nearly four years from February 1859, became one of George Routledge's long-standing best-sellers.[36]

The most persuasive evidence of the continuing popularity of non-fiction in numbers, however, can be found in the histories of those Victorian publishers committed long-term to fascicle publication, notably Cassell in London and Chambers in Edinburgh. William Chambers complained concerning his house's *Miscellany of useful and entertaining tracts* – 'adapted for parish, school, regimental and similar libraries' and issued in 177 weekly numbers at three-halfpence each from 1844 – that, though the circulation was 'immense', the entire profits had been eaten up in paper duty.[37] In contrast, *Chambers's encyclopaedia: a dictionary of universal knowledge*, appearing in the same format from 1859 to 1868, paid handsome rewards and became their 'crowning effort in cheap and instructive literature'.[38] The house of Cassell enjoyed a season of substantial growth from the 1860s to the 1880s, due not only to their entry into the field of country newspapers, but also to the expansion of their network of 'number men'. Compared to fewer than a dozen back in the 1850s, at the peak more than fifty different number publications were distributed simultaneously by these door-to-door canvassers.[39] The titles included both reprints of works that had stood the test of time such as Cassell's *Illustrated history of England* (first issued 1856–64) and such original publications as Cassell's *Natural history* (1876–82). Like many of the new weekly literary miscellanies, typical instalment works could be purchased indifferently in weekly numbers, monthly parts and annual volumes, priced respectively at three-halfpence, sevenpence and ten shillings.[40] This development is indeed a symptom of a fundamental change in Victorian patterns of serial publication: earlier the distinction between monthly and weekly instalments was constructed overwhelmingly on the basis of the social status of the intended audience, and thus carried with it a weight of ideological baggage; from the mid-Victorian decades, it

35 See Topp, *Victorian yellowbacks and paperbacks*. 1. *George Routledge*.
36 See Mumby, *The house of Routledge*, pp. 78–9.
37 Chambers, *Story of a long and busy life*, pp. 93–4.
38 Chambers, *Memoir of Robert Chambers*, p. 259.
39 See Nowell-Smith, *The house of Cassell*, chs. 5–6.
40 See *ibid.*, p. 36, where it is noted that Cassell's part publications were sometimes 'issued in five forms: *viz.*, weekly *numbers*, monthly *parts*, quarterly *sections*, half-yearly *divisions*, and annual *volumes*'.

increasingly became a question of pragmatic choice, depending not only on the price but also on the genre or length of the work and the location and economic means of the customer.

The late years, 1880s–1914

Primary developments in serialisation at the end of the century included both the expansion of the mass periodical and newspaper market and the segmentation of the market into diversely identified readerships: boys, girls, men, women, sportsmen, the military, homemakers, office workers of both genders, and country, metropolitan, imperial, religious, political and fashion audiences. One of the many signs of the rapid changes occurring in the serial market was the 'twenty years of descent' suffered by Cassell & Co. from around 1888.[41] A major reason was the house's continued dependence on methods of serial publication that had by the 1890s largely exhausted their marketing niche and passed their peak of profitability. Their flagship general miscellanies, the monthly *Cassell's Family Magazine* (1853–1932, the old *Family Paper* in new guise) and the weekly *Quiver* (1861–1926), reflected the utilitarian and evangelical impulses of much earlier decades, while the new *Cassell's Saturday Journal* (1883–1921) could only manage to be a pale and timid imitation of *Tit-Bits*. Deteriorating international situations, first in the Empire and then in Europe, left less space for literary and entertainment material purchased from the syndicators. Yet Cassell's General Press continued to offer a menu of such serial material to provincial journals, which were steadily losing ground to metropolitan newspapers with a nationwide readership. Produced by the new media magnates in rivalry with Newnes, these notably included Alfred Harmsworth's *Daily Mail* (1896) and Cyril Pearson's *Daily Express* (1900), both aggressively populist halfpenny dailies.[42] Above all, Cassell's relied on the 'number trade' for too long – 'half a century and more', in Simon Nowell-Smith's telling phrase[43] – to distribute a by then ageing list of part publications house to house.

Symptomatically, in 1893 the firm was attacked in the correspondence columns of *The Times* by an irate Canon Ainger for originating 'a new custom in the book trade which threatens to add a new terror to life', that is, recruiting the 'fashionably-dressed young lady' to call and tout their wares in the drawing-room, rather than the traditional male hawker (the commercial

41 *Ibid.*, p. 157.
42 On the concentration of circulation according to ownership that had emerged in the metropolitan press by 1910, see Lee, *The origins of the popular press*, table 31, p. 293.
43 Nowell-Smith, *The house of Cassell*, p. 36.

incarnation of the religious tract distributor) whose visits had been 'confined to the kitchen entrance'.[44] Though the firm replied defending the move towards social and sexual equality in modern business,[45] they could not erase the perception that, as trade practices, both colportage and part publication were themselves already outmoded.

The effects of such changes were not limited to Cassell. Chambers recognised rather earlier the signs of general retreat in the number trade, so that new reference projects like *Chambers's biographical dictionary* (1897) were issued from the beginning only in compact volume form. Though Tillotson's Fiction Bureau survived until the eve of the Second World War, 'in both literary and commercial terms, from the first decade of the new century at least the story is one of long and slow decline'.[46] The turn of the twentieth century also witnessed the demise of most of the miscellanies founded by the literary houses in the 1860s, including *Temple Bar* and *Macmillan's* in 1906 and 1907 respectively. Though the *Cornhill* itself somehow survived the death of George Smith in 1901, it was by then no competition for the latest generation of monthly magazines, which were more liberally illustrated yet sold for only sixpence. The longest-surviving miscellany, *Blackwood's*, struggled to sustain its traditions and Scots thrift within a marketplace dominated by more modern periodicals paying higher prices for material.[47] The market leaders came from the new press magnates, with Newnes's *Strand Magazine* (1891) once more in front of *Pearson's Magazine* (1896) and the *Harmsworth Magazine* (1898), though all three could claim a circulation over a quarter of a million before the end of the century.[48]

Like *Tit-Bits* and its imitators, these periodicals featured a greater variety of articles than their predecessors and preferred to avoid lengthy items, including instalments of the traditional Victorian serial novel. Instead, they turned to sequences of short tales by up-and-coming authors like Rudyard Kipling and 'Q' (the Cornishman Arthur Quiller-Couch, sometimes a Cassell's author), though most memorable of all were the illustrated detective stories serialised in the *Strand*, featuring Arthur Morrison's 'Martin Hewitt, investigator' and Arthur Conan Doyle's 'Sherlock Holmes'. There were parallel changes in the newspaper market. From the early 1890s, Tillotson's Fiction Bureau had begun

44 Alfred Ainger to the Editor, 'Messrs. Cassell and the "Number Trade"', *The Times* 23 May 1893, p. 10c.
45 Cassell and Company to the Editor, 'Canon Ainger and Messrs. Cassell', *The Times* 24 May 1893, p. 12d.
46 Law, *Serializing fiction in the Victorian press*, p. 91.
47 Finkelstein (ed.), *Print culture and the Blackwood tradition*.
48 See Altick, *The English common reader*, p. 396.

to promote semi-annual packages of short stories by a team of authors, followed by quarterly bundles of 1,500-word 'storyettes', each designed to occupy only half a column or so in their clients' diminishing feature pages.[49] By the turn of the century even big-selling metropolitan weeklies aimed at a family audience, such as the *Illustrated London News*, had dropped serial novels altogether, instead preferring to run sequences of juvenile tales by the likes of Edith Nesbit. Though narrative fiction thus retained a prominent place in the magazines and, for a time, in the weekly journals, these developments in the character of periodicals finally signalled a decline in the hitherto apparently limitless demand for full-length serial novels.

In uncovering the causes of this transformation in the patterns of serial publication, we must first of all recognise that they coincide with equally crucial changes in the market for books. Elsewhere in this volume will be found detailed discussions of the long-anticipated demise of the multi-volume first edition in the mid-1890s and the regulation of price discounting through the Net Book Agreement established in January 1900, developments which together served significantly to weaken the circulating library system and greatly to encourage the middle-class reading public to buy rather than borrow new books. The consequent reduction of the price of a standard new work to a maximum of six shillings put downward pressure on the pricing of all reprint formats, so that popular works were soon available in paperback volumes at sixpence or less. This effectively ended the purely economic motive for the production and consumption in instalments of all but the lengthiest and/or most lavishly illustrated of publishing projects, such as the substantially rewritten twenty-nine-volume eleventh edition of the *Encyclopaedia Britannica* issued from 1910. Yet among the constraints enforcing a revolution in the book market were those that also had a direct effect on patterns of serial publication.

One pattern which has received rather less than its due attention in several earlier studies of the collapse of the circulating-library system is the growing pressure from external markets on British publishing.[50] Weedon provides detailed quantitative evidence of the steadily increasing commercial importance of exports to foreign and colonial markets in the expansion of the British book industry in the later Victorian decades.[51] The formalisation of international copyright mechanisms previously bilateral and ad hoc, through the

49 Law, *Serializing fiction in the Victorian press*, pp. 87–91.
50 See, in particular, the anecdotal, bibliometric and neo-Marxist approaches of, respectively, Griest, *Mudie's circulating library*, Gettmann, *A Victorian publisher* and Feltes, *Modes of production*.
51 Weedon, *Victorian publishing*, table A3.4, pp. 189–91.

Berne Convention of 1886 and the American Chace Act of 1891, did much to accelerate the process.[52] Publishing formats like the three-decker and the monthly fascicle, with their associated mechanisms of distribution – those networks of circulating libraries and teams of number men which had continued to thrive under what Matthew Arnold famously called Britain's 'highly eccentric, artificial, and unsatisfactory system of book-trade'[53] – were obviously ill-suited for use in overseas societies taking a much more direct route towards the supply of cheap literature, whether in the Americas, Asia or the Antipodes. This then was clearly a major factor in the timing and pace of their decline. Nevertheless, we should not underestimate the importance in this process of the ideological and intellectual reaction at the turn of the century against forms, practices and values perceived as essentially Victorian. This can be illustrated most effectively in the field of literature, where the various literary tendencies representative of early modernism, from naturalism and impressionism to symbolism and expressionism, were united in their resentment against the moral and aesthetic tyranny of the 'select' library and the 'family' magazine.[54]

Thomas Hardy's experience with the manuscript of *Tess of the D'Urbervilles* illustrates the difficulties attendant on his trying to satisfy distinct classes of readers and publishers with a single text. Contracted in 1887 to Tillotson's for a serial for their fiction syndication bureau, Hardy had to postpone delivery of the whole beyond the stipulated date. But he did by September 1889 supply the first half, of which sixteen chapters were typeset before his publisher could read them. Dealing as they did with Tess's rape and illegitimate baby, these episodes shocked the publisher, who thereupon cancelled the contract. Then Hardy agreed to supply the conservative periodical the *Graphic* with a full-length story (not telling them he had already written half of it), while at the same time showing the first part of *Tess* to two other journals, both of which turned him down on account of the immorality of the story. Hardy responded in part by publishing in the January 1890 *New Review* a protest against the censorship of circulating libraries and timid publishers. When Arthur Locker and his *Graphic* staff read the opening chapters of *Tess*, now newly set in type by their staff compositors, they had the same reaction as Tillotson's: these incidents could not appear in their magazine. Hardy returned a heavily blue-pencilled manuscript, excising the rape and baptism scenes, and further bowdlerised *Graphic* proofs forwarded to Harper's in New

---

52 Nowell-Smith, *International copyright law and the publisher.*   53 Arnold, 'Copyright', p. 334.
54 See, for example, Keating, *The haunted study*, ch. 4.

York for serialisation in America. He published the objectionable passages in periodicals 'addressed to adult readers' – the *Fortnightly Review* and the *National Observer* – and more or less reconstituted his uncensored whole for the first three-volume edition of December 1891. But for some years thereafter, although *Tess* went through several editions and into one volume quickly, he was chastised by the 'genteel' reader for immorality, vulgarity and irreverence.

At the turn of the century, alienated from the comfortable expectations of middle-class readers, innovators in verse, short fiction and the novel alike demanded radical change not only in literary form but also in publishing format. George Moore successfully fought the domination of the circulating library and the three-decker, whilst George Gissing submitted to their tyranny out of necessity. Joseph Conrad resorted to serialisation, publishing almost all his fiction first in magazines. Illustrators, too, sometimes felt the reprobation of a bourgeois public – Aubrey Beardsley for instance; but others, such as Randolph Caldecott, Hugh Thomson and Kate Greenaway, turned out series after series of new works and reissues for the genteel. In 1903 the Baroness Orczy, who had been writing a series of detective tales for the *Royal Magazine*, decided to dramatise her novel, *The Scarlet Pimpernel*, which a dozen publishers had rejected over the previous three years. A revamped script featuring Ellen Terry's brother Fred in the title role proved a big hit in London in 1905. Then the author published the novel (the 62nd edition appeared in 1935), extended it in a series of further adventures over the next forty years, sold several of these stories to film makers (the first released in 1928), oversaw many translations as well as publication in Bernhard Tauchnitz's Collection of British Authors (1911), and even promoted unrelated works as belonging to 'The Scarlet Pimpernel Series'.[55] In short, in the early decades of the new century, writers and their agents (Orczy's was A. P. Watt) could choose from a variety of options for first publication, subsequent reissues and dramatisations, and publishers energetically released new editions and collections of back stock in inexpensive reprints for sale in global markets. Modernists such as Virginia Woolf, James Joyce, Ezra Pound and T. S. Eliot often self-published or found backers willing to underwrite the cost of publishing little magazines and short runs of experimental writing. In the pre-war era formats were less instruments of class differentiation than choices made by authors and publishers for reasons of aesthetics, prestige and money.

55 *ODNB*; a somewhat different version, emphasising that the courts held that the play rights were owned by Terry, is told in Waller, *Writers, readers and reputations*, pp. 9–10. Orczy got possession of the dramatic rights after Terry died in 1932.

During the late years of our allotted span Britain thus witnessed widespread changes in publishing mechanisms not excluding the various modes of publication in instalments. The result, it must be stressed, was by no means the superseding of serial issue in itself. Still today newspapers, magazines and book series continue to flourish, so that instalment publication remains a major device for adding surplus value to texts in print, as indeed to those transmitted via more modern communications media, whether film, broadcasting or the Internet. But the long-term effect was a marked decline in precisely those serial modes that had played such a central role during the reign of Queen Victoria in gradually building a mass readership, thus serving in both their form and content to reinforce that era's faith in progress, growth and continuity.

4

Authorship

PATRICK LEARY AND ANDREW NASH

The emergence of the newly professional author, like the perennially 'rising' middle class, has been confidently located in many places and periods. Only in Victorian Britain, however, do we find a significant number of authors themselves claiming the mantle of professional status. Although the secure social and financial standing ideally associated with the traditional professions would remain tantalisingly elusive to all but a few full-time writers, the ubiquity and persistence of these claims reflect significant shifts in authors' roles in the literary marketplace over the course of the nineteenth century. An age that saw the great flowering of the novel from Dickens to Eliot to Hardy, as well as the appearance of such influential figures as Carlyle, Tennyson and Ruskin, also witnessed the emergence of an ideal of respectable authorial status equidistant from both the ignominy of the Grub Street hack and the unworldliness of the writer as romantic seer. 'Literature has become a profession', George Henry Lewes declared in 1847. 'It is a means of subsistence almost as certain as the bar or the church.'[1] While chronic financial uncertainty – the chasm concealed by Lewes's 'almost' – continued to define the lives of most of those who wrote for a living, more and more sons and daughters of the educated classes, particularly, nevertheless came to view writing as an entrepreneurial activity as well as an artistic, political or intellectual one, an activity that held out the promise of mending family fortunes, furnishing a respectable career, and even granting, for the lucky few, untold fame and wealth.

An enormous expansion in the scale and variety of that marketplace, detailed elsewhere in this volume, was the chief engine of this increase in the numbers of men and women pursuing authorship during the period. Between 1846 and 1916, the production of books increased fourfold and the price dropped by half, while the number and circulation of magazines and newspapers grew at an even more astounding rate, dropping in price as taxes on paper and newspapers

---

1 [Lewes] 'The condition of authors', p. 285.

were repealed between the 1830s and the 1860s, and proliferating into literally tens of thousands of titles.[2] Noting 'the great and increasing desire of readers to become authors', a mid-century 'advice to authors' booklet put out by the firm of Saunders & Otley merely registers a commonplace of the period by remarking that 'writers were never so numerous as at the present time; and the profession of an author appears likely to become as general as that of an artist or musical composer'.[3]

The dimensions of that growth remain unclear. In part the difficulty is one of definition. In its broadest sense, authorship is the act of writing for publication, whether or not the author relies mainly on writing for his or her income, or describes his or her occupation as that of author, or is paid at all; by this reckoning there is no question that the age saw an unprecedented growth in the numbers of men and women who contributed in some way to the expanding realm of print culture. Although the identity of the vast majority of these writers will forever be hidden to historians by the long-standing custom of anonymity in the newspaper and periodical press, the most sustained attempt to pierce the veil of that anonymity, the *Wellesley index to Victorian periodicals*, lists the names of some 12,000 writers, a figure that represents the identified contributors to a mere forty-three of the most influential quarterly and monthly periodicals.[4]

We do not know how many among those 12,000 writers were able to make a living solely from their writing (the ordinary meaning of 'author by profession' as most Victorians used the phrase) because sufficient biographical data on even a substantial portion of them, to say nothing of contributors to the vast remainder of the press not included in the *Wellesley*, is simply not available. Nevertheless, although the census data on authorship in England and Wales must be treated with caution, the general trend, at least, is unmistakable. Between 1841 and 1861, for example, the count rises from 626 authors, newspaper editors, proprietors and reporters to 1,673 included under the heading 'author, editor, writer' twenty years later; the later censuses, in which the category has stabilised as 'authors, editors, journalists, publicists', show a steady increase, from 6,111 in 1881 to 13,786 in 1911.[5] Much of this increase may reflect the expansion of staff employment within the newspaper press, and the lumping together of disparate categories muddies the picture, but it is clear that the number of people who identified themselves as employed in some aspect of literary production rose dramatically in the second half of the century.

2 Weedon, *Victorian publishing*, p. 158.   3 *Advice to authors*, p. 1. BL shelfmark 11899.f.12(2).
4 *The Wellesley index* 5, p. vii.   5 Altick, 'The sociology of authorship', p. 336.

The *Oxford dictionary of national biography*, which includes only entries for people who were remarkable in some way and about whom adequate information has survived, features biographies for about 2,000 men and 300 women active between 1830 and 1914 who can be described primarily as authors, and close analysis of this growing database will ultimately tell us more about the shape of the careers of the most prominent writers.[6] Preliminary studies using other sources suggest that writers who depended primarily upon their literary earnings always made up a small proportion of those who were active in the literary world. John Sutherland has estimated that the roughly 50,000 novels that appeared in print during Victoria's reign were the work of some 3,500 novelists, of whom basic biographical data can be assembled for perhaps 1,200. Although steady production of published novels is not a sure test of dependence on income from them, his analysis of the careers of 878 of these revealed that a small percentage of writers accounted for a large proportion of the novels produced.[7] Despite the centrality of the novel to the expansion of both reading and authorship during the period, the chief characteristics shared by most Victorian novelists appear to have been literary failure and obscurity.

As Lewes commented in his 1847 manifesto, any count of the number of authors must recognise that the largest proportion by far will include 'barristers with scarce briefs, physicians with few patients, clergymen on small livings, idle women, rich men, and a large crop of aspiring noodles'.[8] The writer James Grant observed in 1841 that of the 10,000 persons who had attempted to live by their pens over the preceding twenty years, 'it would be hard to name twenty individuals, or one of every five hundred, who have been able to convert their literary talents into the means of procuring for themselves a permanent and ample living'.[9] Comments like these remind us that too narrow a focus on familiar writers, or on the precise sociological reach of 'professionalisation' in defining who is to count as an author, is likely to overlook the sheer variety of experiences involved in nineteenth-century authorship, and the many shapes and vicissitudes of an authorial career. Many writers drifted in and out of full-time literary employment, depending on the opportunities available, others never abandoned other occupations, while still others cobbled together small

---

6 *ODNB*.   7 Sutherland, *Victorian fiction*, pp. 152–3.
8 Lewes, 'The condition of authors', p. 285.
9 [Grant] 'Authorship as a profession'. Some of the remarks in this article later found their way into Grant's autobiographical novel, *Joseph Jenkins: leaves from the life of a literary man* (London: Saunders & Otley, 1843). Grant estimates in the latter book (p. 169) that, in London alone, the number of people who have adopted authorship as their only means of subsistence is between 3,000 and 4,000. This roughly tallies with an 1836 estimate recalled by Walter Besant of 4,000 persons living by literary work in London, of whom 700 were journalists (Besant, *Fifty years ago*, p. 195).

legacies with whatever they could earn at writing to eke out a living. At the same time, increasing numbers of writers came to rely on their pens for a respectable middle-class income, while a handful would become world-wide celebrities. All of them, from hack to literary lion to 'aspiring noodle', form part of the intricate story of nineteenth-century authorship.

1830–1870

At the time of the First Reform Bill in 1832, predictions of a sharp and accelerating increase in literary opportunity would have struck most people in the book trade as mere whistling in the dark. The trade as a whole had only begun to recover from the cascading series of bankruptcies and tight money brought on by the credit crisis of 1825–6, which had claimed Walter Scott's publisher and printers among its victims. That crash had left Scott himself, the most successful and admired author of the age, saddled with the task of paying off a mountain of debt, a heroic struggle that hastened his death in 1832. With the market for new imaginative literature uncertain, most publishers turned to the safer expedient of cheap reprints. Publication of poetry in individual volumes, particularly, reached a new low, as most publishers abandoned the genre, while others turned to the high profit margins associated with the production of sumptuous gift-books, or 'literary annuals', that featured engravings of picturesque scenes accompanied by appropriate verses.[10] Original novels also bore the stamp of luxury commodities for the wealthy, as price and format stabilised at the 31s 6d mark for three volumes, familiar from Scott's novels, that they would retain for most of the century.

Dickens and the rise of the novelists

Yet the 1830s also saw the beginnings of a revolutionary expansion in the market for fiction and the periodical press, as well as the launch of the most successful and influential authorial career in all of the nineteenth century, that of Charles Dickens. There had been other signs of growth in the market for fiction, such as Colburn's 'silver fork' best-sellers of the late 1820s and the appearance of the Bentley's Standard Novels series of six-shilling reprints. But it was the runaway success of *Pickwick papers* in 1836–7 that captured the imagination of authors and publishers alike. By spreading the cost of a new novel across twenty or twenty-one monthly instalments, publication in parts not only put fiction within reach of a vastly wider readership of potentially

10 Erickson, *The economy of literary form*, pp. 29–32.

tens of thousands every month, but also held out the prospect of a kind of steady remuneration for both author and publisher that had proven elusive in the publishing of new works.

By the end of the 1840s, the novel was well on its way to becoming the dominant literary form of the age, a shift that would have important consequences for the status and practice of authorship.[11] In 1859, critic David Masson referred to the 'legion of new recruits' to novel-writing that had sprung up since the death of Scott, while ten years later the *Westminster Review* observed that the novel 'has almost swamped all other literary ventures, and divides with the newspaper press the empire of the popular taste'.[12]

Successful novelists could reap substantial rewards. In this as in so many other ways, Dickens's career came to be seen, then and since, as a kind of epitome of nineteenth-century authorship. The sheer scale of his success – the huge world-wide sales that continued unbroken for year after year, the ubiquity of his novels' characters in the print culture and the theatre of the time, the charismatic celebrity that brought crowds to his readings, the unprecedented (for a literary man) personal fortune – was itself a powerful influence on early Victorian society's attitude towards the literary life. In his own time he became not merely the centre of a devoted group of literary disciples, but a focus of the admiration and envy of countless other writers. Thackeray, his nearest competitor for popular and critical status in the late 1840s and 1850s, in truth never came close to achieving the same degree of success, obsessed as he was with the rivalry.[13] Dickens himself took his responsibilities as the preeminent writer of his time quite seriously, advocating insistently for the new independence and dignity of the literary calling. As he declared in 1853:

> From the shame of the purchased dedication, from the scurrilous and dirty work of Grub Street, from the dependent seat on sufferance at my Lord Duke's table today, and from the sponging-house and Marshalsea tomorrow . . . from all such evils the people have set Literature free.[14]

Certainly Dickens himself came to enjoy a degree of such freedom unmatched by any other Victorian novelist. His fiction appeared in a fabulous array of editions and formats, so that Dickens's career furnishes examples of virtually every kind of publishing practice available to the successful nineteenth-century author, from part-issue (of which he was the undisputed master) to railway

---

11 Tillotson, *Novels of the eighteen-forties*, pp. 13–14.
12 Masson, *British novelists and their styles*, p. 220; quoted in 'The empire of novels', *Spectator* 42 (9 January 1869), p. 43.
13 See Patten, 'The fight at the top of the tree'.   14 Dickens, *Speeches*, p. 157.

editions to magazine serialisation to collective reissues.[15] Despite this varied and aggressive publishing programme, it was not until ten years after the success of *Pickwick* that Dickens was free of debt and financially secure. By the 1850s, however, his profits from one new novel alone, *Little Dorrit*, amounted to some £11,000.[16]

The greatest influence on the income that a writer could earn from a novel was the success or failure of the writer's previous works. Untried novelists, therefore, could have difficulty in finding a publisher at all, or, having done so, in obtaining acceptable terms. Of the three most common kinds of publisher-author contracts during this period – publishing on commission, half-profits and outright sale of copyright – the latter two came into play for most novels. Commission publishing, in which the author bore the costs and paid the publisher a 10% commission, was much more common for poetry and special-interest non-fiction, but in some cases it was applied to fiction. T. C. Newby demanded £50 in advance from Anne and Emily Brontë towards the costs of a combined edition of 350 copies of *Agnes Grey* and *Wuthering Heights*; in the event, he reduced the edition to 250 copies, took six months to publish, and reported no profits to divide from the sale. The same notoriously shady operator published Anthony Trollope's first novel on half-profits, from which, again, the author received nothing.[17] Such experiences led Trollope to prefer the outright sale of copyright, an arrangement that appealed to many young writers both for its straightforwardness and for its provision, however small, of ready cash; £100 seems to have been a common sum for the copyright of first novels – Elizabeth Gaskell, for example, was paid this by Chapman & Hall for *Mary Barton*, while George Smith offered the same to Charlotte Brontë for *Jane Eyre* – although lesser publishers might pay as little as £50, the payment Ouida received from William Tinsley in 1863 for *Held in bondage*.[18]

Once established, a novelist could look for a considerable rise in the value of his or her copyrights. Frederick Marryat's earnings rose from £400 from Colburn in 1829 for *Frank Mildmay* to £1,200 in 1839 for *Mr Midshipman Easy*.[19] Dinah Mulock (later Craik), who received £150 for her first novel in 1849, was getting £2,000 a novel by the late 1850s.[20] At the end of her career, Mrs Gaskell received £1,600 for the serialisation of *Wives and daughters* in the *Cornhill Magazine*. In the midst of the 'sensation novel' craze that she had helped to create, Mary Elizabeth Braddon was receiving £2,000 a novel. By the 1860s,

15 See the classic study by Patten, *Dickens and his publishers*.   16 *Ibid.*, p. 10
17 Sutherland, *Victorian novelists and publishers*, pp. 44–9.   18 Tinsley, *Random recollections* 1, p. 82.
19 Sutherland, *Victorian novelists and publishers*, p. 415.
20 Sutherland, *The Longman (Stanford) companion to Victorian fiction*, p. 152.

George Eliot's earnings were little short of spectacular; with £7,000 from George Smith for *Romola*, she and G. H. Lewes were able to purchase a luxurious home in St John's Wood.[21] After receiving £100 in advance of half-profits for *Barchester Towers* in 1857, Trollope saw his literary earnings steadily rise until he was able to command £2,500 a novel, a level he maintained for ten years.[22]

These, of course, were among the great success stories of Victorian authorship, writers whose novels brought them wealth, and as such their examples came to provide powerful incentives for young writers seeking their fortune in the literary marketplace. Besides gifts and luck, maintaining such earnings also demanded steady production. Trollope's extraordinarily disciplined and methodical writing habits, memorably chronicled in his posthumously published *Autobiography*, enabled him to produce forty-seven novels in the course of his career. G. P. R. James was able to turn out as many as three three-volume novels a year, for which at one time he received £600 apiece from George Smith.[23] G. A. Lawrence's ability to turn out adventure stories on demand drew £1,000 a novel from the cautious William Tinsley.[24] Yet even for successful novelists who could meet these demands, the earnings curve was likely to decline as sharply as it had risen; Harrison Ainsworth, widely considered on a par with Dickens as one of the literary giants of the 1830s and 1840s, saw his earnings drop from a high of £2,000 in his prime to £100 a novel in middle age.[25] Comparatively few writers, even in the heyday of the novel's popularity, were able to sustain a literary career on novel-writing alone, particularly given the effort required to produce a three-volume novel for which the average writer in mid-career might receive a one-time payment of a few hundred pounds. Even the most successful novelists, including Dickens, turned to the expanding periodical press as an outlet, not simply for their fiction, but for stories and non-fiction of various kinds, as well as for the steady income promised by staff and editorial positions. For the vast majority of writers who may have experimented with fiction but for whom novels were simply one among many literary activities, the new opportunities afforded by the press were what made a 'professional' life and income possible.

Writing for the press

The growth of the market for newspapers and magazines remained central to the development of authorship for most of the nineteenth century. At one end

---

21 *Ibid.*, pp. 80, 211.
22 For an overview of Trollope's earnings, see Sutherland, *Victorian novelists and publishers*, pp. 133–151.
23 Sutherland, *Victorian novelists and publishers*, p. 88.   24 Tinsley, *Random recollections* 1, p. 80
25 Sutherland, *Victorian novelists and publishers*, pp. 152–60.

of the scale, the rising tide of cheap periodicals called forth a matching tide of literary adventurers, commonly and derisively known as 'penny-a-liners', many of them young bachelors. Some moved easily between other work in the printing and bookselling trades and writing for the press and the theatre. In the late 1830s, William Dorrington, who would later become proprietor and editor of the printers' trade journal *Press News*, worked as a journeyman compositor in the printing shop of Bradbury & Evans and yet found time in the evenings to dash off pantomimes for the theatres, a sensational romance for a weekly literary paper, and crime reports for various penny weekly broadsides published out of back rooms in Holywell Street. One 'police news' paper paid the author thirty shillings a week to write a story, sketch the design of the illustration for the artist, assist in setting up the story in type and help to proof the result.[26] James Bertrum, who came to this London world of cheap weeklies in the 1840s after working as a shop assistant for bookseller James Tait in Edinburgh, recalled a colleague who earned £1 a week turning out highwaymen novels, each of which appeared in one-penny, eight-page instalments with illustrations, the publisher supplying his writers with sheets ruled like a telegraph form to facilitate the calculation of payment.[27] Such penny-dreadful serials might run for years, and were sold in quantities that dwarfed the sales of even the most successful novels aimed at a middle-class readership.[28]

Morning papers paid freelance reporters as much as £3 a week for coverage of coroners' inquests, fires, public meetings and the like.[29] Specialisation among reporters was common but not universal. Joseph Crowe attended at Bow Street daily in the summer of 1844 to report police cases for the *Morning Chronicle* at two guineas a week before mastering enough shorthand to report trials at the Central Criminal Court; two years later he was engaged by the newly established *Daily News* as what he later called 'a reporter for all work' at four guineas a week.[30] Near the top of this penny-a-liner hierarchy stood the parliamentary reporters, whose energy and skill at shorthand commanded higher pay; the twenty-two-year-old Charles Dickens was engaged as parliamentary reporter for the *Morning Chronicle* at five guineas a week, after stints with the *Mirror of Parliament* and the *True Sun*.[31] Yet from these payments reporters were

26 [William Dorrington], 'Incidents of my life', *London, Provincial, and Colonial Press News* October 1886, p. 18.
27 Bertrum, *Some memories of books*, pp. 154–5.   28 Altick, *The English common reader*, pp. 289–92.
29 Grant, *The newspaper press* 2, pp. 261–2.   30 Crowe, *Reminiscences*, p. 36.
31 Dickens *Dickens's journalism: the amusements of the people and other papers* 2, p. xi.

frequently obliged to lay out sums for such things as appropriate clothing, cab fares, entrance fees, library subscriptions and stationery.[32]

The more respectable segment of the press likewise supplied invaluable outlets and income for such young authors as Carlyle and Thackeray, who were closely associated with James Fraser's magazine and bookselling business in the 1830s and early 1840s. The 'higher journalism' pioneered by the great quarterlies, in which authors sought to shape public opinion on political and literary questions of the day, was increasingly carried on through an expanding range of monthly and weekly periodicals. At the same time, other similarly priced periodicals, less committed to the earnest purposes of the 'essay-like review', carried more fiction, sketches, travel narratives and other entertaining literature.[33] Both kinds of publications paid writers by the 'sheet', which yielded sixteen pages of letterpress. Payment was almost invariably calculated in guineas (21s), a legacy of the eighteenth-century practice enshrined by the great quarterlies of the previous generation and originating from the sense that talk of guineas lent such transactions a more gentlemanly air. The reviews themselves had begun to lower their payments in the 1830s in response to competition from the new monthlies. An observer in 1837 listed a number of payment rates to be expected from different London periodicals: twenty guineas a sheet for the *British and Foreign Review*, ten guineas for the *Westminster Review*, sixteen for *Fraser's*, twenty-four for the *Literary Gazette*, ten to sixteen for the weekly *Athenaeum*.[34]

Yet any author relying on these estimates would have been disappointed more often than not, for rates of pay among periodicals, and even payments by the same periodical to different authors and at different times, could vary enormously. The patterns and causes of the fluctuations in periodical payments to authors await further study, but anecdotal evidence suggests that the amount given for any particular submission could depend upon a number of factors, including the type and profitability of the periodical, the genre of the contribution, the stature or seeming promise of the author, an author's own willingness to accept a particular amount, and the rates of payments current among competing periodicals for similar work. For editors and proprietors, an informal authorial hierarchy governed what must otherwise have appeared to writers as a vexing arbitrariness about how much might be expected. In the early 1830s, for example, James Fraser candidly explained to one aspirant

---

32 Stocqueler, *The memoirs of a journalist*, pp. 196–7.
33 The distinction is Walter Houghton's. See his 'Periodical literature and the articulate classes', pp. 17–19.
34 James Grant, quoted in Erickson, *The economy of literary form*, p. 100.

that only one or two prized contributors to *Fraser's Magazine* could expect to receive more than £7 a sheet; among these was Carlyle, who received fifteen guineas a sheet for his articles and twelve for his translations.[35]

Negotiating for a higher place in that hierarchy was a common practice of more experienced writers. In 1838, on the strength of the popularity of his *Yellowplush papers* series, Thackeray threatened to 'strike for wages' unless Fraser raised his pay from ten guineas a sheet to twelve, with an additional two guineas for each accompanying drawing; in a later negotiation he hinted broadly that 'Blackwood and Bentley are offering big prices.'[36] The *Westminster Review* of the 1840s, by contrast, never managed to offer rates of payment that were competitive with other journals of its class, paying G. H. Lewes ten guineas per article, regardless of length, at a time when he was receiving the same for a sheet from the *Foreign Quarterly*. Instead the magazine was obliged to rely on its reputation as an influential organ of progressive reform to lure authors to fill its pages.[37] Many of the new periodicals of the 1850s and 1860s, which ran shorter articles, calculated payment by the column rather than the page. (*Punch* had adopted this system early on, to keep track of the quantity of each staff member's weekly contributions.) Here, too, variation was the rule rather than the exception. The *Household Words* payment for non-fiction prose, for example, was stated to be a guinea for a two-column page, but sub-editor W. H. Wills exercised wide discretion and almost always pared individual payments to some shillings below the official rate.[38]

With luck, skill and steady application, it was just possible to earn the income of a gentleman from periodical writing on a range of payments like these, a fact noted with satisfaction and occasional surprise by several contemporary observers. In the 1840s and 1850s, Lewes published hundreds of articles, most of them unsigned, on an astounding range of subjects, from current novels and drama to marine biology to German philosophy, for such periodicals as the *Westminster Review*, *Fraser's* and *Blackwood's*. The record of his own earnings for these bears out his contention in the 1847 article for *Fraser's* that professional literary men in England were able to earn an average of £300 a year by writing for reviews, journals and magazines.[39] This figure resonated with the Victorian middle class as the bottom rung of the professional ladder, believed by many to be the smallest annual income on which a man could set up a proper

35 Leary, '*Fraser's Magazine* and the literary life, 1830–1847', p. 109.   36 *Ibid.*, pp. 122–3.
37 '*Westminster Review*: introduction', *Wellesley index* 3, p. 542.
38 Lohrli, *Household Words*, p. 21.
39 See 'Appendix II: GHL's literary receipts', in Eliot, *Letters* 7, pp. 365–83.

household.[40] Less versatile or fortunate writers did not fare so well; despite steady application, E. L. Blanchard's annual earnings after over a dozen years of constant literary labour still hovered between £150 and £200.[41]

The quest for steady income

'Literary labour', observed the *Critic* in 1859, 'is necessarily intermittent'.[42] More troubling to many authors than the variable and sometimes paltry rates of payment to be expected from various periodicals and booksellers was the uncertainty of being able to place a sufficient amount of letterpress with publishers to generate a reliable income from month to month and from year to year, even when payments were high. As was frequently pointed out in print, the literary profession lacked the sorts of prizes that came with livings attached. Charlotte Riddell, the popular novelist to whose subsequent career we will return, spoke for many authors in noting wryly: 'There are no fat bishoprics, no fair deaneries that the lay professors of Great Britain may hope to possess. For them no seat on the bench, whether as magistrate, recorder, or judge; for them no grant from Parliament... Of the literary worker it may truly be said that he is always either fishing or mending his net.'[43] For those not already established in a profession, therefore, the search for steady remuneration could be never-ending.

Salaried positions in the press in the first half of the nineteenth century were few and highly valued. The goal of many of those who wrote regularly for periodicals was to find a salaried position as editor, a post that required a degree of skill and experience not commonly found in a literary marketplace thronged with aspirants. In 1837, William Maginn, who had held several such posts, expressed the opinion that there were no more than a dozen men in London capable of taking on the task of editing a monthly periodical.[44] Maginn's own editorships, however lucrative (he was said to be making £600 a year from *Fraser's* in the 1830s), were not sufficient to keep him out of debt. A magazine editor's responsibilities and remuneration took various forms, but usually entailed a salary combined with additional payment for writing done for the magazine. Yet given the volatility of the publishing world of the 1830s and 1840s, in which magazines failed or changed hands with dizzying rapidity, the hoped-for stability of the editorial chair could prove elusive. Samuel

40 See Hoppen, *The mid-Victorian generation*, pp. 40–8 on the range of professional and other incomes in this period.
41 Scott and Howard, *The life and reminiscences of E. L. Blanchard* 1, pp. 78–9, 89, 102, 127, 150.
42 'Sayings and doings', *Critic* 26 March 1859, p. 293.   43 Riddell, 'Literature as a profession'.
44 *Fraser's Magazine* 15 (January 1837), p. 137.

Carter Hall laboured at a succession of editing and sub-editing positions for some fifteen years before at last being offered the editorship of the new *Art-Union* (later the *Art-Journal*), a post he was to hold until his retirement in 1880.[45]

The publisher Henry Colburn had pioneered the strategy of featuring a celebrity editor on a magazine's title-page when he persuaded poet Thomas Campbell to become editor of the *New Monthly Magazine* in the 1820s, while hiring Cyrus Redding as sub-editor to do much of the actual editorial work. By the 1840s, *Ainsworth's Magazine* and *Hood's Magazine* embodied the same tactic; Bradbury & Evans, proprietors of *Punch*, set up *Douglas Jerrold's Shilling Magazine* in 1845 to capitalise on the success of Jerrold's *Punch* writings.[46] In the following decades, *Household Words* and its successor, *All the Year Round*, were famously 'conducted by Charles Dickens', while George Smith hired Thackeray at the then princely sum of £1,000 a year to edit his new shilling monthly, the *Cornhill Magazine*, in 1860. Popular sensation-novelist M. E. Braddon brought the appeal of her celebrity as well as the promise of her own new novels to *Belgravia*, founded in 1866 by her husband, John Maxwell, and edited by Braddon for ten years. Before a name had even been chosen for *Saint Paul's Magazine*, publisher James Virtue advertised the periodical's imminent appearance in 1867 by reference to its new celebrity novelist-editor, as 'New Monthly Magazine by Anthony Trollope'.[47] Editors commonly wrote for the magazines that they edited, as well, often as part of their contract with the proprietors, and such writing was paid for separately. On the death of Mark Lemon in 1870, Shirley Brooks succeeded to the editorship of *Punch* at an annual salary of £1,000, with an additional six guineas a week for his contributions.[48] For the ordinary editors of more ordinary magazines and newspapers, of course, the rewards remained much more modest, yet even comparatively minor staff positions were eagerly sought after. In 1848, proprietor James Wilson of *The Economist* received seventy applications for the post of sub-editor, a job whose salary came to £100 a year and included lodging above the paper's offices in the Strand.[49]

Authors could achieve something akin to the regularity of an editor's income by becoming a steady contributor to a newspaper or magazine. Most periodicals had a 'staff' of such contributors, although these positions rarely came with a guaranteed salary attached; when they did, it was usually, as with most

---

45 Peter Mandler, 'Hall, Samuel Carter (1800–1889)', *ODNB*.   46 Slater, *Douglas Jerrold*, p. 189.
47 Hall, *Trollope*, p. 309.   48 Layard, *A great 'Punch' editor*, p. 411.
49 He offered the job to the young Herbert Spencer, who accepted. Spencer, *An autobiography*, pp. 383–4.

newspaper reporters, a weekly salary rather than an annual one. *Punch* was unusual in being written almost entirely in-house by a permanent staff, each of whom received a salary, with additional payments for extra contributions. The *Daily Telegraph*'s invitation to E. L. Blanchard in 1863 to join the staff as drama critic marked a turning-point in that writer's fortunes; he would remain in the post for twenty-five years.[50] Some writers who were not formally on staff were nevertheless able to establish themselves as columnists even though the column was unsigned. The popularity of W. J. Thoms's folklore column in the *Athenaeum* led him to found *Notes and Queries* in 1849.[51] In the 1850s and 1860s, Edmund Yates pioneered the breezy gossip column and earned a steady income with 'Lounger at the Clubs' in the *Illustrated Times* and 'The Flâneur' in the *Morning Star*, while Shirley Brooks earned some £160 a year from his weekly 'Nothing in the Papers' column in the *Illustrated London News*.[52] As self-described 'general utility woman' at *Blackwood's*, Margaret Oliphant contributed as much as one-third of the contents of some issues.[53] Beginning in 1869, Frances Power Cobbe wrote three 1,200-word leading articles each week for the halfpenny *Echo*, which together with reviews and news articles earned her almost £300 for each of the six years that she kept up this demanding schedule.[54]

One way to secure a steady paying outlet for such writing was to start or acquire a periodical of one's own, usually with borrowed money. Although most successful periodicals were begun by book publishers, for whom they served various promotional purposes, many young authors in the 1830–70 period tried their hands at organising magazines or newspapers from scratch. Gilbert Abbot à Beckett was an especially prolific founder of short-lived comic or literary miscellanies in the 1830s, enjoying some success only with *Figaro in London*.[55] Nautical novelist Frederick Marryat became editor and proprietor of the *Metropolitan Magazine*, where he pioneered the serialisation of fiction, including his own. The original 1841 agreement for *Punch*, which took *Figaro* as one of its models, attempted what was essentially an authors' collective, appointing Mark Lemon, Henry Mayhew and Stirling Coyne as co-editors, with each to receive a one-third share of the magazine in lieu of payment. On the brink of financial failure, the magazine was sold to its printers, Bradbury & Evans.[56] In 1861 Sheridan Le Fanu acquired the *Dublin University Magazine*,

50 Scott and Howard, *The life and reminiscences of E. L. Blanchard* 1, p. 280 and *passim*.
51 'Mr. W. J. Thoms, F.S.A.', *Athenaeum* 22 August 1885, pp. 239–40.
52 Edwards, *Dickens's young men*, pp. 41, 113–17; Layard, *A great 'Punch' editor*, p. 277.
53 Elisabeth Jay, 'Oliphant, Margaret Oliphant Wilson (1828–1897)', *ODNB*.
54 Mitchell, *Frances Power Cobbe*, p. 187.   55 Spielmann, *The history of 'Punch'*, pp. 272–4.
56 *Ibid.*, pp. 575–80.

and proceeded to serialise several of his own novels in its pages and to use his influence as its owner and editor to place his fiction in the lucrative London market.[57] Dickens became his own publisher with *All the Year Round* in 1859, under an arrangement in which sub-editor W. H. Wills and other members of the Dickens circle also had shares in the periodical; serving as a kind of 'fiction workshop' for several years, *All the Year Round* was the most successful and influential of all author-owned periodicals.[58]

Fame and anonymity

The custom of unsigned contributions in the newspaper and magazine press that prevailed almost universally until the late 1860s and 1870s had important consequences for the practice of authorship. Writers who belonged to the traditional professions were able to contribute to the press without risking their professional respectability. Although this consideration waned in significance as authorship itself became more respectable, the determinedly elitist *Saturday Review*, for instance, staked its case for the practice squarely on the desirability of keeping the 'professional journalist' out of its pages in favour of 'a man who has a public or professional position [whose] writings form only a parenthesis in his avocations, and are not a part of his main business'.[59] Some career writers chose to spend their entire working lives under the cloak of this anonymity, preferring the stability of a staff position or the privilege of speaking through a prestigious newspaper or magazine over the process of attempting to 'make a name' in the literary marketplace. The Rev. Thomas Mozley, who published leading articles in *The Times* almost every day between 1844 and 1886, was by any measure one of the most powerfully influential authors of the Victorian period, yet few readers then or since have known his name; in this way, Mozley's opinions came to represent the position of the paper itself on many of the controversial issues of the day.[60] Indeed, the custom helped to sustain a separate oral culture among those working within or closely involved with the literary world, a culture in which the names of the authors of unsigned works circulated privately while remaining unknown to the general reading public. As the system was beginning to come to an end, John Morley argued that this insider knowledge of the identity of the authors of important articles in various papers and magazines had had a healthy restraining effect on those writers, and that the corresponding absence of such knowledge about those

---

57 W. J. McCormack, 'Le Fanu, (Joseph Thomas) Sheridan (1814–1873)', *ODNB*.
58 Sutherland, *Victorian novelists and publishers*, pp. 166–86.
59 Bevington, *The Saturday Review: 1855–1868*, pp. 40–2.
60 S. A. Skinner, 'Mozley, Thomas (1806–1893)', *ODNB*.

who wrote for the less respectable organs of the press encouraged bad writing and irresponsible behaviour.[61]

The anonymous system was much more important for new writers than for established ones. By lowering the barriers to entry to periodical authorship, anonymity made possible a kind of apprenticeship that did away with considerations of gender, social rank, marketability or recognised expertise in a particular field of study. The all-round, 'miscellaneous writer' who could be counted on to 'work up' a subject with an air of authority was the lifeblood of the general-interest magazine. In a culture in which 'authorship' was defined as a male pursuit, anonymity was particularly crucial in making wider access to the press possible for women writers, whose names alone would otherwise have barred them from appearing in the pages of many periodicals as reviewers or as commentators on political or social subjects. Marian Evans's work for the *Westminster Review* as an anonymous contributor and sub-editor proved an essential stage in her development as an author years before her adoption of the 'George Eliot' pseudonym for her fiction. Elizabeth Gaskell's anonymous contributions to the reformist periodicals of the 1840s allowed her to work out the ideas that would inform her early novels. Margaret Oliphant's long connection with *Blackwood's* was the mainstay of her career as a literary journalist, and as the 1860s saw the appearance of new magazines like *Macmillan's* that insisted on signature, she remained wary. 'Not feeling myself, as myself, to be a person of any great weight or authority', she wrote to Alexander Macmillan, 'I am always glad to take refuge under the mantle of Maga.'[62] The determinedly masculine public image of the staffs of magazines like *Fraser's* and, later, the *Saturday Review* concealed such substantial female contributions as, respectively, Selina Bunbury's Irish stories and Eliza Lynn Linton's sensationally vitriolic articles.[63] Between 1849 and her death in 1880, Geraldine Jewsbury wrote over 2,000 anonymous book reviews for the *Athenaeum*, in addition to her work as a novelist and as a reader for Richard Bentley & Son.[64]

The great disadvantage of unsigned journalism, for authors and their publishers alike, was that it hampered the building of the kind of public recognition that could help to place new articles and books. 'I should have been better known to the public', complained poet and critic J. A. Heraud in his 1847 application for aid, 'had not so large a proportion of my labours been

---

61 [Morley] 'Anonymous journalism'.
62 Worth, *Macmillan's Magazine*, p. 100.   63 See Easley, *First person anonymous*.
64 Joanne Wilkes, 'Jewsbury, Geraldine Endsor (1812–1880)', *ODNB*.

anonymous – having . . . contributed more than two hundred papers' to various periodicals.[65] Many authors published collections of unsigned articles over their names in book form, yet, apart from extraordinary instances like Macaulay's essays, these compilations rarely sold well. Both Harriet Martineau and Frances Power Cobbe published their books and many articles over their signatures, while also steadily writing anonymous leading articles for newspapers, and both were shrewd about choosing which mode of self-presentation would provide the best means of achieving their aims.[66] Later in the century, the increasing centrality of serial fiction to the success of periodicals, as well as growing public interest in authors as celebrities, helped lead to the demise of the anonymous system in most magazines and some newspapers.[67]

Dramatic authorship

The steady economic decline of the theatre from the 1830s through the 1850s, and the dominance of actors and managers in preference to playwrights, made dramatic authorship a particularly perilous trade. The early custom of 'author's nights', on which the playwright received the house's proceeds, was slow to die out, and its replacement by a fee for a certain number of performances together with a smaller sum for the copyright did nothing to improve the author's lot.[68] Douglas Jerrold's experience was typical: although his *Black-eyed Susan* proved a goldmine for theatre managers, who staged hundreds of performances of this perennial Victorian favourite over the years, the £60 paid to Jerrold for the initial run in 1829 (which included £10 for the copyright) was all the income the play would ever bring him.[69] The short runs that were characteristic of the period, and the smaller theatres' consequent reliance on an ever-changing variety of entertainments, made for a market based on quick returns and small margins, in which authors were obliged to take what they could get from hard-pressed theatre managers. Unsurprisingly, most authors who wrote for the theatre combined that work with journalism and other outlets. Many of the same young men who got their start in the cheap comic and literary miscellanies of the 1830s and 1840s, men like Mark Lemon, Albert Smith, Shirley Brooks, E. L. Blanchard and Robert Brough, were at the same time busily turning out farces, burlesques and pantomimes for small sums.

65 *Archives of the Royal Literary Fund: 1790–1918* (London: World Microfilms, 1984), case no. 1167, application dated 18 May 1847.
66 See the discussion of these strategies in Easley, *First person anonymous*.
67 Maurer, 'Anonymity vs. signature in Victorian reviewing', pp. 10–11; see also Liddle, 'Salesmen, sportsmen, mentors'.
68 Stephens, *The profession of the playwright*, pp. 30–2.   69 Slater, *Douglas Jerrold*, pp. 70–2.

At the other end of the scale, Bulwer-Lytton, whose income of £1,800 from three plays staged in 1839–40 made him the best-paid dramatist of that period, abandoned the theatre altogether for novel-writing on the grounds that 'the utmost pay [a play] can receive is not half the profit derived from a fiction'.[70] Two of the longest-running plays of the late 1850s and early 1860s, the comedy *Our American cousin* and the melodrama *The ticket of leave man*, made many thousands for their respective theatre managers but brought author Tom Taylor only £150 each. It is no wonder, then, that Taylor incorporated a consistently prolific play-writing career with such other sources of income as a post with the Board of Health, a long stint as art critic of *The Times*, and a coveted position with *Punch* as staff writer and, later, editor.[71] Although the Dramatic Copyright Act of 1833 and the founding of the Dramatic Authors Society provided some small measure of protection against exploitation and undoubtedly contributed to playwrights' sense of professional respectability, it was left to the entrepreneurial vigour of popular actor and playwright Dion Boucicault in the 1860s to revolutionise the potential financial rewards of dramatic authorship. Boucicault's profit-sharing contract with Benjamin Webster, manager of the Adelphi Theatre, concerning *The Colleen Bawn* netted the author £10,000 during its first year alone and marked the beginning of a decisive shift towards a theatrical marketplace based on shared returns from long-running productions that could offer playwrights substantial earnings and something approaching long-term security.[72]

Authors and publishers

One Victorian memoir tells of a disappointed author who, on having his manuscript returned to him, at once went round to the offending publishers' offices in Conduit Street and declared to the first man he saw, 'You have rejected my book of poems. If you are Saunders, d— Otley; if you are Otley, d— Saunders.'[73] A time when an author could stride into a publisher's bookshop and speak directly to Mr Longman or Mr Blackwood came to many to represent a lost golden age of author–publisher relations. As the scale of publishing grew, some would look back with longing to a more intimate, personal relationship that had been overtaken by cold commercial calculation. As early

---

70 Stephens, *The profession of the playwright*, p. 48.
71 See Tolles, *Tom Taylor and the Victorian drama*.
72 Stephens, *The profession of the playwright*, pp. 54–7; Fawkes, *Dion Boucicault*, pp. 120–4.
73 Lennox, *Celebrities I have known* 2, p. 16. Various versions of this possibly apocryphal anecdote were in circulation in the last decades of the nineteenth century; the author in question has been identified variously as Bulwer-Lytton and Count d'Orsay.

as 1858, writer and editor Cyrus Redding waxed nostalgic for 'the old book-selling firms' of his youth, when 'there was a friendship between the author and his publisher which has disappeared', to be replaced by 'literary bargaining'.[74]

Nostalgia aside, it is clear that the structure and complexity of the publishing business did change markedly over the course of the century, as detailed in the next section. James Raven has argued that the 1840s and 1850s represent a kind of golden age for publishing firms dominated by a single individual.[75] It is not surprising that this dominant figure's personal relationship with an author could have enormous influence on a literary career. Thomas Longman IV's exemplary fairness toward Macaulay over *The lays of ancient Rome* in 1842 paved the way for a relationship that was to prove hugely profitable to both parties.[76] Young George Smith's tact and energy won Charlotte Brontë's unswerving loyalty for the whole of her career after her early, unpleasant experience with T. C. Newby, while the long, cordial relations between George Eliot and John Blackwood took on a nurturing, paternal quality that gave Eliot the support she needed to explore new avenues in her fiction. John Sutherland has memorably documented the 'shaping power' of author–publisher interactions on novels as different as *Westward ho!* and *Henry Esmond*. On a more mundane level, publishers often acted as bankers for their longtime authors, either loaning money directly in the form of advances or co-signing bills of exchange.

Yet much of the longing for an earlier world of less overtly commercial, more gracious and cordial relations between publishers and authors reflected a kind of wistful elitism at odds with most authors' actual experience. Few writers' dealings with publishers in the middle decades of the century resembled the image of author and publisher conducting business over a glass of fine claret in John Murray's parlour in Albemarle Street, and few would enjoy the years of friendship and professional guidance that characterised the relationship of a few successful writers with their career-long publishers. Such ongoing relationships were invariably premised on the continuing success of the author's books, something which no new author could promise and few longtime authors could sustain. A master of the 'literary bargaining' that Redding so deplored, Anthony Trollope preferred to take his work to the highest bidder, a practice that accounts for the sixteen different publishers represented on the title-pages of his numerous books.[77]

The comparatively intimate, personal nature of publishing in this early period could make disputes between author and publisher all the more

74 Redding, *Fifty years' recollections* 3, p. 240.   75 Raven, *The business of books*, p. 349.
76 Mumby, *Publishing and bookselling*, pp. 284–5.
77 Sutherland, *Victorian novelists and publishers*, p. 136.

painfully acrimonious. The long career of Richard Bentley is replete with bitter quarrels, through which he lost many of the authors – Dickens, Wilkie Collins, Charles Reade and others – whose early works he had published. Late in life, he confided defensively to his diary, 'I have facts to prove that they one and all quarreled with me, and compelled me by extortion to yield to them in several instances. With men I loved too, with dear Barham and Haliburton!'[78] The breach between Dickens and Bradbury & Evans in 1858 illustrates how the personal nature of such conflict could be profoundly consequential for the literary marketplace. When the break came, not over a contractual matter but over Bradbury & Evans's failure to insert in *Punch* Dickens's extraordinary announcement about his separation from his wife, it was marked by hurt and bewilderment on the publishers' side and by an unrelenting fury on that of the author, who broke off all personal and business relations. As a result, their joint property, the periodical *Household Words*, was wound up, and author and publisher set up competing magazines: *All the Year Round* and *Once a Week*. In the longer term, the loss of Dickens, followed by the loss of Thackeray to the pecuniary blandishments of George Smith, heralded the collapse of Bradbury & Evans as a major publisher of books.[79]

'It is one of the facts never told in print, but everywhere told in private', one writer asserted in 1845, 'that the literary men residing in the metropolis are generally regarded by their publishers with the utmost degree of distrust.'[80] The distrust was decidedly mutual, and on the authors' side the reasons for it lay primarily in the nature of the profit-sharing contracts that were so common in the mid-Victorian period. Such contracts left it to the publisher to calculate the costs to be deducted before any division of profits could begin, an arcane process that easily led to suspicions that the publisher was inflating costs by charging the author a profit on paper, printing and advertising. The author of *Perils of authorship* hyperbolically warned the novice writer that by this arrangement, 'except in extraordinary circumstances, *he will never receive one penny*'.[81] 'If he seeks explanations', scholar James Spedding would later add, 'he will find that the matter cannot be made intelligible without the knowledge of particulars which the custom of the trade does not permit to be revealed.' In such circumstances, Spedding argued, even perfectly fair transactions between authors and publishers were laid open to suspicion, with the result that 'the

---

78 Entry for 5 January 1859, Richard Bentley diary, papers of Richard Bentley and Son, University of Illinois at Urbana-Champaign.
79 Patten, *Dickens and his publishers*, pp. 260–3; Robert L. Patten and Patrick Leary, 'Evans, Frederick Mullett (1803–1870)', *ODNB*.
80 'The position of literary men', *Chambers's Edinburgh Journal* 79 (July 1845), p. 10.
81 *The perils of authorship*, p. 21.

suspicion is itself a serious objection' to the half-profits mode of publishing.[82]
The elimination of this poisonous element in the author–publisher relationship, through the replacement of such arrangements with royalty agreements
on the American model, would not come until the last quarter of the century,
as a result of organised pressure from authors themselves.

Literary lives

Given the difficulties in the way of making a respectable living entirely from
literary work alone, it is not surprising to find most male writers not born to
wealth following a number of other occupations, professional and otherwise,
over the course of their lives. To mention only a few of the better-known
names gives some idea of how often the practice of authorship depended upon
parallel careers. Finding that one in five of his sample of Victorian novelists
had trained for the law, John Sutherland observed that, ' "Called to the bar,
never practised" is . . . the commonest prelude to a career in writing novels.'[83]
In many instances, the appalling overcrowding of the legal profession – the
interval between entering one of the Inns of Court and being called to the bar
could stretch into years, and Lewes's 'briefless barristers' were commonplace
– was a significant motive for young men to strike out on a literary career in
the meantime. Those writers who actually pursued a legal career for at least
a portion of their lives included Gilbert Abbot à Beckett, Samuel Warren,
John Forster, James Fitzjames Stephen, Frederic Harrison, Thomas Hughes,
Henry Maine and Theodore Martin. Government service attracted Thomas
Babington Macaulay, John Stuart Mill, Charles Wentworth Dilke, Matthew
Arnold, Peter Cunningham, Anthony Trollope and many lesser lights. R. H.
Barham, F. W. Farrar, Edward Bradley ('Cuthbert Bede') and Charles Kingsley were clergymen. Thomas Hughes, Benjamin Disraeli and Grant Duff, to
name but three, made careers in Parliament. Frederick Marryat had a distinguished career as a naval officer. Charles Reade was one of many contributors to
the 'higher journalism' who held a university fellowship. Both the *Athenaeum*
and the *Saturday Review* were begun by men with university connections,
while one observer estimated that at least a quarter of the articles appearing in a twelve-month period in the *Contemporary Review* and the *Fortnightly
Review* were written by fellows or former fellows of Oxford or Cambridge
colleges.[84]

---

82 Spedding, *Publishers and authors*, pp. 10–11.   83 Sutherland, *Victorian fiction*, p. 170.
84 Kent, 'Higher journalism and the mid-Victorian clerisy', p. 189.

Among those who supplemented their earnings with other non-literary employments were Coventry Patmore, who used his literary connections to get appointed to the department of printed books at the British Museum, and Dudley Costello, who was a half-pay army officer when he found work copying illuminated manuscripts. J. Hain Friswell was apprenticed as an engraver and worked for a Bond Street jeweller. In their later years, Charles Lever, G. P. R. James and James Hannay each managed to wangle diplomatic appointments in the consular service. Barred from most occupations and from all traditional professions, women writers without a father's or husband's income to depend upon had much more limited choices. Teaching in schools or private homes, with annual earnings beginning as low as £7 and ranging as high as £80, was the most common extra-literary occupation among women writers who applied for assistance.[85] Charlotte Brontë and Anne Brontë each found work as private governesses, experiences memorably depicted in *Jane Eyre* and *Agnes Grey*. Camilla Toulmin worked successively as a governess and as a maker of jewellery; at the time of her marriage to a wine merchant Newton Crosland in 1848, she was earning about £60 a year from school-teaching and £50 from her writing.[86] Mary Elizabeth Braddon supported her mother and herself as an actress in a touring company before turning to the writing of penny dreadfuls.

Steady income from a profession or other occupation provided no guarantee of financial stability. Despite a Post Office salary of £520, another £500 as editor of *Tinsley's Magazine* and several hundred pounds from his novels and other writings, Edmund Yates was forced to appear before the bankruptcy court in 1868, an appearance that would not prove to be his last.[87] Peter Cunningham, miscellaneous writer and author of the popular *Handbook of London*, received a £600 salary for his work in the Audit Office, in addition to considerable literary earnings, but neither was sufficient to keep his family from want.[88]

Especially vulnerable to crisis and debt, of course, were those 'authors by profession' who were fully exposed to the rigours of a capricious literary marketplace. The old Grub Street image died hard in the nineteenth century, in spite of the expansion of opportunities for writers; financial disaster runs like a recurring motif through many literary lives of the 1830s and 1840s, especially. Maginn and others who made up the original *Fraser's* circle, for example, were

---

85 Mumm, 'Writing for their lives', p. 9.
86 Rosemary Mitchell, 'Crosland, Camilla Dufour (1812–1895)', *ODNB*.
87 Edwards, *Dickens's young men*, pp. 116–17.
88 Bentley diary, entry for 5 January 1859; Cross, *The common writer*, p. 74.

frequently obliged to contribute to the magazine from debtors' prisons, or from the safety of Boulogne.[89] Fear of poverty was never far from the thoughts of even many outwardly successful writers. Douglas Jerrold spoke for a host of lesser authors when he confided to Dickens in 1846, 'I have a feeling of dread – a something almost insane in its abhorrence of the condition of the old, worn-out literary man; the squeezed orange ... flung upon literary funds while alive, with the hat to be sent round for his coffin and his widow.'[90] Single women writers, with fewer alternative means of employment, were the most vulnerable of all; fully 85 per cent of the women who applied to the Royal Literary Fund between 1840 and 1880 were either unmarried, widowed, deserted or separated. Many of them were the sole support of children, parents and other relatives.[91]

The files of the Royal Literary Fund, established in 1790, reveal how common the condition described by Jerrold remained throughout the century. One striking feature of the list of recipients of grants from the Fund is how many of those applicants, particularly in this earlier period, were not unknown minor scribblers but some of the most prominent and successful writers in England, who had nevertheless either fallen on hard times or had died leaving their families in distress.[92] Yet the growth of the RLF itself in the middle decades of the century, and, after 1840, the increased willingness of successful writers themselves to support its activities, testifies to a growing tendency among authors to think of themselves as professionals with responsibilities to the profession as a whole. Dickens's ill-starred Guild of Literature and Art of the 1850s, although unsuccessful in its aims, reflected much the same impulse.[93] Another hopeful sign was the establishment of the Newspaper Press Fund in 1864, which importantly supplemented the efforts of the RLF, particularly as the latter had not until 1858 made writers for periodicals, as distinct from authors of books, eligible for grants, and still declined to consider applicants who worked as newspaper reporters.[94] Following the Civil List Act of 1837, the government increasingly awarded small pensions to literary men and women, as well as to their widows and children, although the selection of recipients was frequently criticised.[95]

In *Pendennis* (1850), Thackeray looked back with mingled fondness and cynical amusement on the world of 1830s journalism and hack-work from which he had emerged, painting a portrait of Captain Shandon, the thriftless,

89 Cross, *The common writer*, pp. 41–3.   90 Slater, *Douglas Jerrold*, p. 199.
91 Mumm, *Writing for their lives*, pp. 4–5, 12.   92 Cross (ed.), *The Royal Literary Fund*, p. 15.
93 See Hack, 'Literary paupers and professional authors'.   94 Cross, *The common writer*, pp. 60–4.
95 *Ibid.*, pp. 81–9.

brilliant writer and editor that was instantly recognisable as William Maginn. The ensuing controversy with Dickens and Forster over 'the dignity of literature' – the latter two feeling that Thackeray had compromised the new-found dignity of the literary profession by dredging up these unwelcome reminders – testifies to an emerging self-confidence among successful writers that their own success reflected a kind of maturity of the occupation as a whole.[96] Certainly, as Richard Altick has argued, the 1850s begins a new phase in the growth of a 'mass reading public', while the beginning of the long domination of Mudie's circulating library exercised a profound influence on authorial prospects, particularly among authors of fiction.[97] In this decade Dickens and Thackeray emerged as the two most acclaimed novelists in Britain, and each, not coincidentally, found at last a comfortable financial stability. In the 1860s, with the abolition of the last duties on paper, and the establishment of shilling monthlies like *Cornhill*, *Temple Bar*, *Macmillan's*, *Belgravia*, *Saint Paul's*, etc., the periodical market, particularly for writers of fiction, seemed for a time less volatile and more remunerative. Literary work remained a slender reed on which to support a family, and the numbers who were able to do so remained small, through growing. Yet while Dickens's death in 1870 seemed to many to have ended one era in the life of the nation's literature, the estate of £93,000 that he left to his children, an estate comparable to that of a successful industrialist, must have seemed to many to have signalled, as well, a kind of coming of age of authorship as a profession.

1870–1914

The expansion of authorship

Looking back in 1934 H. G. Wells wrote: 'The last decade of the nineteenth century was an extraordinarily favourable time for new writers and my individual good luck was set in the luck of a whole generation of aspirants.'[98] There was a growing sense that literature had become a profession. In 1878 Alexander Shand commented:

> in the last twenty years or so there have been changes in the world of literature that almost amount to revolution. Literature has taken its place among the professions; and if its most magnificent pecuniary prizes are not what they once were, at all events the number of those who get a living by it have multiplied almost indefinitely.[99]

96 See the account of this controversy in Lund, *Reading Thackeray*.
97 Altick, 'English publishing in 1852'.   98 Wells, *Experiment in autobiography* 2, p. 506.
99 [Shand] 'Contemporary literature: 1. Journalists', p. 641.

More than anything else, it was the expansion of journalism that was responsible for these changes. Shand considered that 'Novel-writing nowadays may be all very well . . . but those who devote themselves earnestly to the literary profession, whether for the sake of a livelihood or with the idea of influencing opinions, will naturally turn towards the journals or periodicals.'[100] What he did not anticipate was the nature of the explosion in popular journalism that would take place in the 1880s. The number of weekly, monthly and quarterly magazines quadrupled between 1875 and 1903. The appearance in 1881 of George Newnes's penny paper *Tit-Bits*, which had an average weekly circulation of between 400,000 and 600,000 over 1881–1910, marked the beginning of a growth in cheap newspapers and magazines as publishers began to target the new mass market. At the end of the century *Lloyd's Weekly News* and the *Daily Mail* claimed sales of over a million. The New Journalism, as it came to be known, offered an unprecedented demand for miscellaneous articles and reviewing. As a consequence journalism became not just an outlet but, as Walter Besant stated in 1892, 'a means of subsistence – not a mere pittance, but a handsome income – to hundreds of writers'.[101]

Until the late 1870s journalism had few salaried posts for writers, as opposed to editors, sub-editors and other technical staff.[102] The expansion of the market increased the number of stable positions. Leader-writing offered small remuneration. J. M. Barrie earned three guineas a week over 1883–4 as leader-writer on the *Nottingham Journal*. Better paid was the regular columnist. From 1877 G. R. Sims received a stable income from his 'Dagonet' column on the *Sunday Referee* for over forty years, whilst in the new century G. K. Chesterton could rely on a payment of £350 a year for his column in the *Illustrated London News*. Earnings from journalism varied considerably. In the 1891 edition of his *Author's Manual*, Percy Russell recorded that for paragraphs daily newspapers paid $1\frac{1}{2}$d or 2d per line and between 10s 6d and 30s for a column. A general reporter on a provincial or minor London weekly would earn between 25s and 30s a week; a sub-editor's salary ranged from 30s to 60s a week; an editor of a small weekly might have a stipend of only £70 or £80 a year but on 'better papers' that figure might be £200 a year and on a daily paper £250 to £500. Altogether, Russell concluded that 'a working journalist of fair ability and industry should, after the first few years, be in a position to earn from £300 to £400 or even £500 a year'. This figure might rise, with experience, to £1,000.[103]

100 *Ibid.*, p. 644.   101 Besant, 'Literature as a career', p. 702.
102 Cross, *The common writer*, p. 115.
103 Russell, *The author's manual*, pp. 124–8. See also below, chapter 20.

Not surprisingly, journalism was the most common entry route into author-ship in this period. Arnold Bennett wrote in 1903 that 'very many, if not most, authors begin by being journalists'.[104] The climate suited the writer who combined journalism with other types of authorship. In *The truth about an author*, Bennett declared himself 'an author of several sorts' who wrote 'half a million words a year'. That half-million was made up of 'one or two books, one or two plays, and numerous trifles not connected with literary criticism; only about a hundred and fifty thousand words are left for reviewing'.[105] The most striking thing about this estimate is that the 'numerous trifles' must have constituted over a third of his total output.

The spread of journalism provided outlets for various kinds of authorship. Nigel Cross judges that 'by the end of the 1880s the favourite standby of the would-be-writer – book reviewing – had become, for many, a full-time occupation'.[106] Reviewing could be fairly remunerative. George Saintsbury estimated that he could average £3 10s for an evening's reading and a morning's working.[107] George Bernard Shaw, who had earned only £6 by his pen in his first nine years in London, netted £117 from his first year of book reviews in the *Pall Mall Gazette*.[108]

The religious press was a constant source of opportunity throughout the period whilst the increased number of women's magazines at the end of the century provided greater opportunities for the professional female journalist. Catherine Drew observed in 1894 that 'Ladies' papers and the interests they served have become a great social and economic power' for women.[109] The importance of journalism as a potential profession for women is reflected by the publication in 1898 of Arnold Bennett's 'practical guide' *Journalism for women*.

The New Journalism signalled the decline of the periodical essayist. In contrast to the money that could be made through contributions to the popular press, remuneration for scholarly articles in monthly magazines was small. In 1880 John Oldcastle estimated that if a single writer made one monthly appearance in one of the magazines his annual income would be less than £150.[110] As Besant commented in 1899: 'a writer cannot live by contributing to magazines, except in the way of fiction'.[111] In place of the periodical essayist came a new class of author, what John Gross in *The rise and fall of the*

---

104 Bennett, *The truth about an author*, p. 155.   105 *Ibid.*, p. 96.
106 Cross, *The common writer*, p. 210.   107 Gross, *The rise and fall of the man of letters*, p. 154.
108 Saunders, *The profession of English letters*, p. 206.
109 Quoted by Onslow, *Women of the press*, p. 138.
110 Oldcastle, *Journals and journalism*, p. 41.   111 Besant, *The pen and the book*, p. 137.

man of letters (1969) called 'bookmen'. Writers such as Saintsbury, Edmund Gosse and Andrew Lang exploited the widening opportunities provided by the periodical and newspaper market to earn a living through miscellaneous authorship. Lang's work spanned poetry, translation, anthropology, fairy tales and folklore, fiction, biography, historical works and an incalculable amount of criticism and miscellaneous prose in newspapers and periodicals. Lang's critical voice became ubiquitous. In the words of Frank Swinnerton: 'he wrote everywhere... upon almost every subject in the world'.[112]

Lang once remarked: 'if I could have made a living out of it, I might have been a great anthropologist'.[113] It was the need to earn a living that pushed him towards being a miscellaneous author. Grant Allen was in the same predicament. Eager to make a reputation as a scientific writer but also determined to earn his living by authorship, Allen began with books and essays on evolutionary biology which earned him little money. Riding the boom of New Journalism, he turned to writing miscellaneous articles for periodicals before drifting, seemingly accidentally, into fiction, eventually becoming a highly successful novelist renowned for hitting the popular taste. In 1891 he won a fiction prize of £1,000 in a competition run by the magazine *Tit-Bits* and in 1895 achieved a scandalous success with *The woman who did*. But his writing career spanned a whole catalogue of subjects: biography, classical studies, folklore, geology, entomology, interior design and travel. He wrote full-length serials for monthly magazines and newspapers which were republished in volume form by major publishing houses; detective stories for the *Strand*; children's books; and popular novelettes.[114]

Allen's career illustrates the numerous forms that authorship could take in this period. He quickly found that scientific books were unremunerative. He contributed £120 for the publication of his first scientific work which sold fewer than three hundred copies, leaving him with a loss of £30.[115] Earnings from non-fictional books were not generally sufficient to allow authors to devote themselves entirely to that sphere. Margaret Oliphant secured quite large payments for some of her non-fictional books. Macmillan paid her £450 for *The makers of Venice* (1887) with £200 in advance to help with expenses of the visit, but the book took six years to write from the date of the first payment in 1881. During the intervening period Oliphant arranged for Macmillan to pay her £2,000 over a period of two years in exchange for three novels.[116] Clearly,

---

112 Swinnerton, *Background with chorus*, p. 63.   113 Green, *Andrew Lang*, p. 74.
114 See Morton, 'The Busiest Man in England', pp. 2–3.   115 *Ibid.*, p. 47.
116 Worth, 'Margaret Oliphant and *Macmillan's Magazine*', p. 95.

carrying out an expensive trip to Venice to write a historical book could not have been possible for her without writing fiction at the same time.

J. R. Green did manage to make a living out of popular history. He began contributing to the *Saturday Review* in 1867 and became dependent upon reviewing work when he gave up his clerical career. The success of his *Short history of the English people* (1874), which was republished in four volumes over 1877–80, gave him a steady income for many years which was augmented by editorial projects for Macmillan. In 1877 he estimated he could earn £100 a year from royalties.[117]

Though religious publishing diminished in size after 1870 it remained a productive area for authors. So too was the expanding market for school and educational books. Sprigge judged that, on average results, fiction was less valuable a property than theological or educational books.[118] Most authors of religious or educational books combined authorship with professional work, however. The juvenile market, which expanded during the nineteenth century, was especially important to women writers. Payments were generally small, however. Mrs Molesworth (who received advance payments on account of royalties from Macmillan) enjoyed a lengthy and generally prosperous income but most others were confined to the tiny sums paid by specialist firms such as Nisbet and the SPCK (Society for Promoting Christian Knowledge).

Authorship and the literary market

Along with journalism, it was the literary market which provided most opportunities for the writer pursuing authorship as a full-time – or near full-time – occupation. Poetry continued to be a very small market. Sprigge judged in 1890 that '[t]wo or three living poets make large sums of money; two or three more make very small sums. The poetical works of all the rest put together is worth almost nothing at all pecuniarily.'[119] Chapter 11 in this volume shows how Tennyson was able to make substantial sums from his poetry and at the end of the century Henry Newbolt was able to retire from the Bar on the back of the wide sales of his first two volumes. Generally, however, proceeds were negligible and authors commonly paid for publication. W. H. Davies contributed £19 towards the cost of his first poetry volume in 1905. Nevertheless, the number of published poets in Britain was considerable. One bibliographer has identified 2,964 persons who published poetry in the 1880s and 1890s, mainly in newspapers and magazines.[120]

---

117 See Brundage, *The people's historian*. 118 Sprigge, *The methods of publishing*, p. 19.
119 *Ibid.*, p. 23. 120 Reilly, *Late Victorian poetry*.

The great opportunities came in fiction and drama. From the mid-1880s the production of new works of fiction increased dramatically. In 1880 there were 380 new novels published. In 1886 this figure had risen to 896 and in 1895, one year after the circulating libraries had effectively killed off the three-decker, 1,315 new 'adult' novels were published.[121] Such growth in demand provided opportunities for authors but the collapse of the three-volume system threatened the economic security of the average novelist. Because the three-decker constituted almost a guaranteed market, many authors were able to make a solid, if unspectacular, living from writing one or two novels a year. When the system disappeared the easy market disappeared with it. After 1894 many novelists who had enjoyed steady incomes of around £200 or £300 a year found it much harder to compete in the new commercial market. As Nigel Cross notes: 'the patron was no longer Mudie but the fickle reading public'.[122] The spectrum of payments widened. At the top end of the scale a novelist like Mary Ward was able to sell the copyright of one novel, *Sir George Tressady* (1896), for £10,000. At the bottom, a writer like Sarah Tytler (Henrietta Keddie), who had received sums of £200 for three-volume novels in the 1880s, found her payments cut to £30 or £40. By the end of the Edwardian period, the disparity was even greater. In 1912 Gilbert Parker was allegedly earning £20,000 from a novel, of which £5,000 to £10,000 was paid in advance.[123] By contrast, Florence Warden, author of scores of one-volume and three-volume novels before 1900, had by 1911 seen her payments sink to as low as £10.

The serial market continued to be an important source of income for novelists and in the last quarter of the century newspaper syndication displaced monthly magazines as the dominant mode of serialisation of new novels.[124] Tillotson's Fiction Bureau was able to pay larger sums for serial rights than publishers of established monthlies such as the *Cornhill*, *Blackwood's* or *Temple Bar*. Newspaper publication did not match the prestige of the major monthly magazines, however, and the opening up of this market, and that of popular weekly magazines, contributed to the emerging perception of a split between high and low culture. Some authors, such as George Gissing, considered it too ignoble to write a story for a newspaper. Joseph Conrad, who nevertheless believed that serialisation ruined some of his stories, was prepared to exploit the financial riches of the serial market. Conrad saw the version of *Nostromo* (1904) which appeared in *T.P.'s Weekly* as serving the immediate but ephemeral

121 Cross, *The common writer*, p. 206.   122 *Ibid.*, p. 208.
123 Waller, *Writers, readers and reputations*, p. 293.
124 See Law, *Serialising fiction in the Victorian press*.

readership; the book was for posterity.[125] Arnold Bennett developed a clear distinction in his career between the serious novelist, whose first publication *A man from the north* was published by John Lane, and the writer of popular sensation serial fiction. Bennett wrote his first serial of 60,000 words in twenty-four half-days. His second took just fifteen days.

With the expansion of the serial market and the oversaturation of the book market, most novelists found that receipts for serials were greater than for volume publication, more so than had been the case before 1870.[126] There was also a new demand for short stories. Gissing came close to doubling his income from the sale of short stories in the early 1890s. He received twelve guineas each for six stories in the *English Illustrated Magazine* (£75 12s in total) and was paid two guineas per thousand words for stories in the *Illustrated London News* – more than twice what he could earn from novel writing.[127] Magazine payments for stories were proportionately much higher than for collections in volume form. H. G. Wells was paid five guineas for each of his stories in the *Pall Mall Budget* but received only £10 for a selection of them in volume form, *The stolen bacillus* (1895).[128]

By the 1880s, a novelist could exploit a whole host of markets: serial rights, volume rights, continental rights, translation rights, American rights, colonial rights, stage rights. In the new century film rights could be added to the list. It was the diversification of rights that, in part, led to the rise of the literary agent. English-language editions of British authors on the continent were monopolised by Tauchnitz, who generally paid £30 for the right to include a novel in his Collection of British Authors. For a short time Paul Gradener was a rival to Tauchnitz and was offering larger payments in the 1870s but his challenge petered away. The rights to republication on the continent often caused confusion. Henry James was unaware that parting with 'copyright and all interest' in *Confidence* (1881), as his receipt from Chatto & Windus declared, meant that he had ceded all subsidiary rights. James made a deal with Tauchnitz only to find that Chatto had already sold the rights to Gradener.[129]

The colonial market was more remunerative, particularly after 1880 when several publishers established 'colonial library' editions of novels. Because books were sold more cheaply in the colonies the rate of royalty was lower than that paid on home sales. Macmillan's standard royalty was fourpence; in the case of Kipling they stretched to sevenpence but they had to battle

---

125 Watts, *Joseph Conrad*, p. 99.
126 For examples, see Law, *Serialising fiction in the Victorian press*, pp. 161–2.
127 Cross, *The common writer*, p. 209.   128 See Dickson, *H. G. Wells*, pp. 73, 81.
129 See Anesko, 'Friction with the market', pp. 57–9.

with the author's belief that selling the 'English edition' at a higher price – and therefore a higher royalty – would be more profitable for both author and publisher.[130] Colonial rights became more significant in contract negotiations. E. M. Forster's discontent over the royalties offered by Blackwood on colonial editions of *The longest journey* (1907) led him to take his next novel to Edward Arnold.[131]

The American periodical market was increasingly important for British authors in spite of the lack of copyright protection. On the back of the success of *Dr Jekyll and Mr Hyde* (1886), Robert Louis Stevenson was inundated with offers from American publishers, including $10,000 (approximately £2,000) for a series of weekly essays in the New York *World*, which he declined, $8,000 by McClure for the serial right of his next story and $3,500 by Scribner's for twelve monthly essays. In 1894 Rudyard Kipling was paid $135 (about £27) per thousand words by the *Century* for 'A walking delegate', which amounted to around £200 for the whole story, substantially more than the payments made by British magazines to Gissing and Wells mentioned above.

Before 1891 American volume publication was less remunerative because in the absence of copyright protection American publishers were at liberty to issue works by British authors without the authorisation of the copyright holder and without making any payment to the author. Several of the more prestigious firms, such as Harper, often did pay authors a nominal fee (sometimes as little as £10) out of moral duty and British publishers would sometimes make offers of advance sheets to allow such publishers an early start on the market. In the early 1870s Tennyson was paid an annual fee of £500 by James T. Fields for advance copies of his poems.[132] Once a book appeared in print, however, there was nothing to stop American firms issuing an edition. With the passing of the Chace Act, which took effect in 1891, works by British authors were protected in the United States provided they were printed there and copyright registered. The market for British authors increased substantially. Besant marvelled at the prospect: 'Think! One-hundred-and-twenty millions of possible readers at the present day; against 50,000 in the year 1830.'[133] By the new century the American market had become so large that five-sixths of Mary Ward's receipts for *Lady Rose's daughter* (1903) came from American serial and volume rights.[134]

Perhaps the most important subsidiary right from the 1880s onwards, however, was dramatisation, and in this period the theatre itself became an

130 See the correspondence between A. P. Watt and Frederick Macmillan dated 13 May and 14 May 1909, BL MS Add. 54896 and MS Add. 55494.
131 See Finkelstein, *The house of Blackwood*. 132 Waller, *Writers, readers and reputations*, p. 619.
133 Besant, *The pen and the book*, p. 29. 134 Sutherland, *Mrs Humphry Ward*, p. 238.

attractive source of income for the professional writer. Following the Boucicault revolution of the 1860s the theatre was transformed into a lucrative commercial enterprise as the system of profit-sharing became more widely established. G. R. Sims, who sold the rights in his first play for £150, was paid royalties for *The lights o' London* (1881) on a sliding-scale percentage system which soon became a standard feature of contracts. The play's success earned him £150 in the first week and helped him to increase his annual income tenfold.[135]

If a play proved popular the potential earnings from the theatre were huge. Charles Reade, one of the most popular and successful novelists of his age, made £20,000 out of a single play – *Drink* (1879) – five times as much as his most remunerative novel, *Put yourself in his place*.[136] Even a dramatist like Oscar Wilde, whose proceeds were modest compared to some, nevertheless earned far more from the theatre than from sales of his books, receiving somewhere around £10,000 between 1892 and 1895.[137] The American stage became a rapidly expanding market for the British playwright, especially after the improvements in copyright arrangements after 1891. J. M. Barrie's adaptation of his novel *The little minister* broke box office receipts in America in 1897 and earned the author £80,000 in its first ten years on both sides of the Atlantic.

The earning potential of the stage made it attractive for novelists to compose a dramatised version at the same time as they were writing a novel. Hall Caine's stage version of *The Manxman* (1894) was performed barely three weeks after publication of the book. For his later novels Caine always worked on three versions of his stories – serial, book and play – at the same time. More money was to be made by the printed scripts of plays or the novelisations of the dramas. In 1906 the *Daily Mail* published Hall Caine's *The bondman play* at two shillings.

Dramatic adaptations of novels had long been a disputed area of copyright.[138] In the absence of clear legislation, novelists were vulnerable to unauthorised dramatisations of their works. In 1882 the popular novelist 'Ouida' stormed into the press when she discovered that an adaptation of her latest novel *Moths* was about to appear on the London stage. In order to prevent unauthorised adaptation it was necessary to write the novel up as a play and register it at Stationers' Hall. It became standard practice to give a single performance –

---

135 Stephens, *The profession of the playwright*, pp. 65–6.   136 *Ibid.*, p. 52.
137 Guy and Small, *Oscar Wilde's profession*, p. 133.
138 For a full account see Bonham-Carter, *Authors by profession* 1, ch. 5.

the copyright performance – without audience or scenery to secure rights in a play.

Many novelists turned to the stage in an effort to increase their income but not all had the success of a Caine or a Barrie. Mary Ward, whose experiences as a playwright have been described as 'painful, expensive, and ominous', lost £5,000 when the purchaser of a dramatised version of one of her novels went bankrupt.[139] There was greater risk and financial speculation in drama than in book publishing, especially if an author dabbled in production. The poet and novelist Robert Buchanan, who turned to writing and producing plays to help clear his debts, was declared bankrupt in 1894 when he lost £5,000 on two failed dramas he wrote and produced himself.

Nevertheless, the opportunities for theatrical authorship were such that Walter Besant, writing in 1899, anticipated that in the future novelists 'will turn with one accord to the more promising line of theatre'.[140] Arnold Bennett, who began writing plays in the same year, considered dramatic composition for the market 'child's play compared to the writing of decent average fiction'.[141] By 1914 the arrival of cinema provided a further opportunity for the author. Popular novelists such as Rider Haggard and Anthony Hope found that their novels from the 1890s were given a new lease of life in the cinema, bringing them considerable financial windfalls.[142]

The diversification of the market and the increased opportunities for authorship contributed to another important development after 1870: the emergence of literary agents. Several writers had relied on a friend or relative to manage the business side of their affairs – Dickens was managed by John Forster; Eliot by G. H. Lewes; Stevenson by Charles Baxter; and Swinburne by Theodore Watts. The first professional agent of reputation, A. P. Watt, began in this way, managing the affairs of his friend George MacDonald. In the late 1870s Watt began working for a number of other authors, including Wilkie Collins, and he went on to manage the literary affairs of writers such as Besant, Conan Doyle, Kipling, Hardy and Gissing.[143] Watt advised authors on the value of their literary property, negotiated deals with book publishers and newspaper and magazine proprietors, oversaw contracts and collected payments, charging

---

139 Sutherland, *Mrs Humphry Ward*, p. 293. Few women novelists of note turned to the theatre in this period, an exception being Florence Marryat who toured the country in the late 1880s with her own theatrical company.
140 Besant, *The pen and the book*, p. 109.   141 Bennett, *The truth about an author*, p. 129.
142 Waller, *Writers, readers and reputations*, p. 12.
143 On Watt and literary agents in general, see Hepburn, *The author's empty purse*.

a flat 10% commission on authors' proceeds. S. R. Crockett told Fisher Unwin in 1893 that Watt had trebled his income in six months.[144]

Watt also acted for publishers. Firms like F. V. White and Chatto & Windus, who were in the practice of purchasing full copyrights of novels, found his knowledge of the serial and overseas markets invaluable in helping them to find outlets for their titles. Watt soon had successful rivals, including J. B. Pinker, who served Gissing and Bennett among others.[145] By 1914 there were more than thirty advisory agencies and syndicates advertising their services in trade journals.[146]

Writing in 1898, Leopold Wagner judged that the literary agent 'has entirely broken down the friendly relations formerly existing between author and publisher'.[147] This was not universally true but the relationship did become more formal and businesslike as a result of the agent's intervention. Conrad's employment of J. B. Pinker in 1903 severed the close personal relations he had with the house of Blackwood. Most publishers viewed the agent with resentment – William Heinemann saw him as a 'middleman' and a 'parasite'.[148] Publishers complained that agents prevented authors from establishing mutually beneficial relations with one publishing firm. Because agents were always looking for a higher royalty rate or an extra payment, an author's books could easily become spread among many different publishers.

In some instances the author–agent relationship took on a form of financial sponsorship which had earlier been a feature of some long-established author–publisher relationships. Watt acted as a banker to some of his authors, discounting publishers' bills and advancing payments to authors. Conrad's relationship with Pinker was extraordinary. Until the publication of *Chance* in 1914 Conrad's novels did not sell in any great number; yet from 1905 Pinker paid him an annual sum of £600. Within two years Conrad owed Pinker over £1,500.[149]

The rise of the agent shifted the balance of power in the literary market. For an author, the acquisition of an agent became as significant a step as attracting a publisher. Most agents dealt only with established authors, so becoming a client of Watt, for example, meant that an author had taken a big step in establishing a successful literary career. Publishers and editors began turning to agents to provide them with books, articles and writers. In an address to the

144 Collin, 'Edward Garnett, publisher's reader, and Samuel Rutherford Crockett, writer of books', p. 101.
145 On Bennett and Pinker see Bennett, *Letters to J. B. Pinker*.
146 Keating, *The haunted study*, p. 71.   147 Wagner, *How to publish*, p. 69.
148 Heinemann, 'The middleman as viewed by a publisher'.   149 Watts, *Joseph Conrad*, p. 88.

Authors' Club in 1910 William Robertson Nicoll argued that the great change in publishing in the last quarter of a century was that in 1886 the author was still seeking the publisher, whereas now the publisher was seeking the author.[150]

The Society of Authors and its impact

A critical moment in the development of authorship was the founding in 1883 of the Incorporated Society of Authors.[151] The 1880s was a period of growth in trade unionism and authors formed part of a wider impulse among workers to unite in defence of their rights against employers, in this case publishers and editors. The driving force behind the formation of the society was the novelist Walter Besant, who acted as chairman from 1884 to 1893 and became an energetic spokesman for authorship in the period. The Society's member-ship was open to all those 'who have at any time published work that may fairly entitle them to be described as authors, or those who have been or are at present engaged in journalistic work'. A council and management committee was elected in 1884; Tennyson was the first President. In 1884 there were sixty-eight paying members; in 1890, the year the *Author* was launched, there were over 600. By 1914 membership had reached 2,500.[152]

The Society's three main objectives were: the maintenance, definition and defence of literary property; the consolidation and amendment of the laws of domestic copyright; and the promotion of international copyright. The most immediately important of these was the first. The idea that literary prop-erty needed to be defined was an illustration of how arbitrary contractual arrangements between authors and publishers had been in the past. The Soci-ety wanted the relationship between authors and publishers to be put on a more businesslike footing. A Report for 1889 demanded 'for literary property the same jealousy and the same resolution to obtain just treatment as prevails in all other branches of business'.[153]

Besant set out his own ideas on the subject in 'The maintenance of literary property', his contribution to a book based on a public conference which took place in 1887 on the subject of 'The grievances between authors and publish-ers'. By placing emphasis on *maintaining* literary property Besant was drawing attention to the widespread practice of authors selling copyrights to publish-ers. He argued that in recent years 'the profit of trade in the author's produc-tion' had grown to 'enormous dimensions'.[154] Authors were often ignorant of

150 Darlow, *William Robertson Nicoll*, p. 334.
151 The title was expanded to include playwrights and composers in 1913.
152 Findlater (ed.), *Author! Author!*, pp. 19, 22.   153 Quoted in Sprigge, *The methods of publishing*, p. v.
154 *The grievances between authors and publishers*, p. 15.

their rights and sometimes entered into publishing arrangements without any formal, written agreement.

The Society issued numerous publications designed to educate the author about literary property. These included books on the different methods of publishing and the costs of book production. The data produced in these publications were hotly disputed by publishers. In 1890 the Society launched a monthly magazine, the *Author*, which was edited, and largely written by, Besant. In its first decade the *Author* devoted itself to matters concerning the definition and defence of literary property and from 1898 it began publishing draft agreements intended to equip authors for dealing with publishers. The first twelve issues of the *Author* were published by the literary agent A. P. Watt, who managed Besant's own literary affairs. He and the Society saw Watt as the only reputable agent and the *Author* was hostile to professional agents in general, largely because of Besant's aspirations for the Society to act as a form of literary agent itself. The nearest it came to doing so was when it founded the Authors' Syndicate in 1889 which lasted only a few years.

The debates over literary property contributed to the changing contractual arrangements and methods of payment for authors from the 1880s onwards. The campaigning of the Society and the rise of the literary agent led to the gradual introduction of royalties as the standard method of remuneration.[155] Other methods still existed, however. The half-profit or profit-sharing system, where a publisher took on the risk of publication and divided any profits with the author, persisted widely until the very end of the century, especially in the case of non-fictional books; the system was appropriate for medical, legal and other works which required frequent revision. For the Society of Authors, the desirability of the system depended upon the accuracy and honesty of publishers' accounts. In many public statements, Besant challenged the common charges for advertising and office expenses and alleged that some publishers artificially inflated costs by recording 'secret profits' in their accounts.

Commission publishing, where an author paid a proportion, or all, of the production costs, remained common throughout the period, especially in the case of first-time authors. Gissing, Hardy, Besant himself, Barrie and Galsworthy all paid for their first books to be published. Besant estimated

---

155 Simon Eliot's research in the Macmillan archives shows that royalties displaced half-profit arrangements as the most common form of remuneration over the period 1893–9. Eliot, ' "To you in your vast business" ', pp. 45–6.

in 1899 that three-quarters of novels published were issued subject to the author laying down a sum of money for expenses.[156]

Although Besant and the Society counselled authors never to part with their property, many authors still had recourse to outright sale of the copyright of their work. The rights in a book might be sold for a stated length of time, at the expiration of which copyright would revert to the author. Alternatively, a publisher could purchase the copyright entirely, thus gaining control over subsidiary rights and all future proceeds from the book. With the growing market for cheap reprints at the end of the nineteenth century this could often turn out to be a fruitful investment, as it proved for Ward & Lock who purchased the copyright of Conan Doyle's *A study in scarlet* (1888) for just £25. Sale of copyright was almost universal at the lower end of the literary market. In *The literary handmaid of the church* (1890), Besant attacked the SPCK who sometimes paid as little as £10 for the copyright of fictional and non-fictional works.

Ironically, in view of his public statements on the matter, Besant sold most of his own books outright. It is easy to see why sale of copyright was common. Established authors could secure a large payment upfront whilst those in need of money could not afford to retain their copyrights in the hope that they might one day prove assets. Anthony Trollope, who sold most of his novels outright, reaching a peak payment of over £3,000 in the 1860s, told Thomas Hardy in 1877: 'there is no doubt that the royalty system is best, if you can get a publisher to give you a royalty, & you are not in want of immediate money'.[157] Most writers stood in need of immediate money, however. The children's author Mrs Molesworth dropped the royalty system at the end of her career in favour of larger outright payments.[158]

The full royalty system, though common practice in America, was barely known in Britain before the 1880s. Authors gradually came to see the benefits. When Cassell offered Rider Haggard the option of £100 for the copyright of *King Solomon's mines* or a £50 advance on a royalty, the author opted for the £100 until a clerk in Cassell's firm advised him to take the royalty. The book sold 6,000 copies within the first three months and by the following year he had received over £750 in royalties. Haggard concluded that Cassell had tried to cheat him and took his next novel to Longman.[159] Hall Caine tried, unsuccessfully, to get Chatto & Windus to give him a royalty on his third novel, *The deemster* (1887), eventually selling the copyright for £150. The book

156 Besant, *The pen and the book*, p. 22.   157 Trollope, *Letters*, p. 456.
158 See Cooper, *Mrs Molesworth*, p. 365.   159 Nowell-Smith, *The house of Cassell*, pp. 135–6.

was extremely popular and Caine was much aggrieved when Chatto continued to profit from later sales in cheap editions. He tried on several occasions, unsuccessfully, to repurchase the copyright. On his next novel, *The bondman*, Caine turned down Chatto's offer of £350 and took the work to the new firm of Heinemann, who paid him a £150 advance. Both author and publisher prospered when the book became a best-seller.

The Society of Authors advocated the full introduction of the royalty system and advised authors to adopt a sliding scale, whereby royalty rates increased with increasing sales. The Net Book Agreement of 1899 provided a firmer base for royalties by regulating and fixing retail prices but the system of outright sale was not displaced fully or overnight. Lump sum payments were still frequently made to first-time authors or minor fiction writers. Conrad sold the copyright of his first novel *Almayer's folly* (1895) for £20. After 1911 there was even less reason for authors to part with their copyrights, however. The 1911 Copyright Act increased the value of literary property, first by introducing protection for dramatisations and novelisations and new classes of work such as cinematograph productions, and second by extending the duration of post-mortem copyright from seven to fifty years. Had Conrad not sold the copyright of *Almayer's folly* he and his heirs, not Fisher Unwin, would have benefited from any continued sale until 1974.

The impact of the Society of Authors, like the rise of the literary agent, brought a challenge to the comparatively informal personal relationship that had often characterised author–publisher relations in the Victorian period. Besant's public statements and the Society's publications paraded a mistrust of the motives of publishers. In *The methods of publishing* Sprigge advised authors to remember the common maxim 'there is no friendship in business'.[160] Besant advised would-be authors to meet a publisher 'as one business man should meet another, with the wholesome suspicion, based on experience, that he will "best" you if he can'. No doubt this view of publishers was accurate in some cases but such a blanket view was unfair. Many authors continued to benefit from a relationship with publishers that went beyond pure business. Macmillan seemed content to lose money on Mary Ward's early failed projects. In 1883 they paid her an advance of £250 for a book on the Romantic Movement in France which she never completed. The money was only repaid when *Robert Elsmere* (1888) became such a success.[161] Later in the period, David Storrar Meldrum, editor at Blackwood, was a crucial supporter of Joseph Conrad, persuading his firm to pay £300 for the serial rights of *Lord Jim* (1900) and a

160 Sprigge, *The methods of publishing*, p. 30.   161 Sutherland, *Mrs Humphry Ward*, p. 90.

£200 advance on the book rights. After four years the advance had still not been covered.[162]

Besant had a flawed understanding of publishing. He underestimated the risk involved and failed to consider that publishers might have an intellectual as well as capital involvement in books and literature. He told authors that publishers were 'moved by no enthusiasms for literature, but simply by the consideration of what will pay'.[163] His preoccupation with the author's literary property meant that rather than seeing publishers as partners in the process of literary production he considered them merely 'administrators, or distributors' of literary property; 'agents, in short'.[164] His 'dream of the future' where authors dispensed with publishers altogether and published all of their books through the Society was unrealised.[165]

By educating authors about literary property and the methods of publishing, the Society of Authors contributed to the growing sense of authorship as a professional activity, even if it couldn't be seen as a profession in the strict sociological sense of controlling access, training and accreditation. Though opportunities for authorship were greater than ever in the period after 1870, few authors drew their entire income from writing. As Peter Morton comments, even in the last part of the century 'unassisted professional authorship rarely paid a living wage, except for a talented and popular few'.[166] In 1892 Besant judged that the number of authors who were able to live by the production of original work apart from journalism amounted to half a dozen dramatists, about a hundred novelists, a few successful writers of educational books and a few publishers' hacks.[167]

Typically, writers combined authorship with other professions. Matthew Arnold worked as a school inspector for thirty-five years, Conrad remained a merchant seaman until 1898 and Conan Doyle only gave up medicine in 1891, a year when he earned £1,500 from his pen. Richard Altick's analysis of the sociology of authorship over 1800–1935 indicates a sharp decline in the number of clergyman writers after 1870 and a marked rise in the number of teachers turning to authorship. The law, government service and the arts had a steady role in the support of literature throughout the period.[168]

In 1889 Grant Allen wrote: 'no man, probably, ever became by choice a professional writer ... Men are driven into literature, as they are driven into crime, by hunger alone.'[169] An overstatement, of course, but authorship was

---

162 Watts, *Joseph Conrad*, pp. 97–8, 150.   163 Besant, *The pen and the book*, p. 315.
164 *Ibid.*, p. 17.   165 *The grievances between authors and publishers*, p. 43.
166 Morton, 'The busiest man in England', p. 62.   167 Besant, 'Literature as a career', p. 703.
168 Altick, 'The sociology of authorship', p. 106.   169 [Allen] 'The trade of author', pp. 267–8.

always an attractive pursuit for men and women in need of money, partly because it was an entirely open profession. Although some women writers in the period had the luxury of financial stability through marriage or private means, many others turned to authorship to support their families as a result of a husband's death, illness or financial breakdown. The indefatigable Mrs Oliphant is only the most famous example. Others include Annie Hector ('Mrs Alexander'), who had abandoned her writing career in the 1850s, but resumed it in the 1870s when she separated from her husband and was forced to support her four children by the pen. Emma Marshall became the main breadwinner of her family when her husband went into debt following the collapse of the bank where he worked. In addition to historical novels, Marshall wrote for the juvenile market and was published extensively by the SPCK and Nisbet. Her total output approached 200 volumes. A more extreme case was Charlotte Elizabeth Lawson (Mrs J. H. Riddell) who began writing in the 1850s to support her sick mother. She married in 1857 and achieved considerable literary success in the 1860s, receiving £800 for one novel published by Tinsley. Her husband's bankruptcy in 1871 and death in 1880 forced her to write at a terrific pace to clear the family's debts and, with declining proceeds in her closing years, she fell back on the Royal Literary Fund and the Civil List and became the first pensioner of the Society of Authors when she was awarded £60 in 1901, five years before her death. As Nigel Cross observes, the first thoughts of such women novelists was in most cases to earn a living for their families rather than to write a masterpiece.[170]

State support for authors was available from the long-established Royal Literary Fund, the Royal Society of Literature and the Civil List.[171] The Royal Literary Fund, which made small one-off payments to authors who presented cases of hardship, carried the stigma of charity; the Civil List, which awarded life pensions to authors for their services to literature, was criticised by the Society of Authors in one of its publications for the arbitrariness of its awards, in terms of both the choice of authors and the amount awarded, which could range from £25 to £200 or more.[172] In a few cases grants enabled an author to pursue writing as a profession. Walter de la Mare was 35 when he gave up his job as a clerk on being awarded a Royal Bounty grant of £200 in 1908. With the support of influential literary friends, Joseph Conrad was able to secure a clutch of charity and state payments over 1902–10, including sums of £300 and £200 from the Royal Literary Fund, £500 from the Royal Bounty Special Service

170 Cross, *The common writer*, p. 196.　　171 For a full discussion see Cross, *The common writer*, ch. 2.
172 Colles, *Literature and the pension list*.

Fund and in 1910 a Civil List pension of £100. As Cedric Watts comments, this enabled Conrad to 'produce his masterpieces by the taxed labours of many individuals who may never have read them'.[173]

Increasingly in this period successful authorship involved more than just writing books. In the closing decades of the century authors were able to exploit public interest in their work in a variety of ways. Following the example of Dickens and Thackeray, many authors took to the lecture platform. It is significant that when Matthew Arnold needed to pay off his debts he turned not to writing but to capitalising on the fame that his writing had brought him by embarking on a lecture tour of the United States in 1883. Tours of America became an especially profitable sideline for authors. Dickens's last American tour in 1867–8 earned him £19,000 whilst Edwin Arnold was paid £5,000 in 1891 to read his poems fifty times. The American publisher James T. Fields told Tennyson he could make £20,000 simply 'by standing in a room and shaking hands with 20,000 people'.[174] Collins, Jerome and Yeats were among many other authors who undertook lecture tours of America.[175]

In the new century giving lectures became almost standard for best-selling authors such as Hall Caine, Marie Corelli or Florence Barclay, but public speaking was only one way in which writers could reap financial benefit from their status as famous authors. In the closing decades of the century, changes in the way authors were presented to the public, especially through the media, contributed to the cult of celebrity and what Henry James called 'the mania for publicity'.[176] John Gross argues that between 1880 and 1914 'there must have been proportionately more popular interest in authors and the world of authors than at any time before or since'.[177] Magazines capitalised on the American innovation of the personal interview; gossip columns in literary periodicals, such as the *Bookman*, kept readers up to date with the plans, well-being and whereabouts of authors; articles appeared in illustrated magazines with portraits of the author and photographs of their homes, desks, libraries and gardens. The contemporary cultural interest was as much vested in authors' personalities and backgrounds as it was in their books.

As Peter Keating has summarised, this was an era when 'what anyone connected with books did or looked like became newsworthy'.[178] Some novelists, such as James, Conrad and Barrie, looked with scorn upon this intrusive obsession with authors' lives and personalities and refused to be interviewed or

173 Watts, *Joseph Conrad*, pp. 87–8.   174 Waller, *Writers, readers and reputations*, p. 576.
175 For a survey of the lecture tour in America, see *ibid.*, pp. 575–614.
176 Quoted by Keating, *The haunted* study, p. 74.
177 Gross, *The rise and fall of the man of letters*, p. 216.   178 Keating, *The haunted study*, p. 74

photographed. Others milked the opportunities provided by the new media. Marie Corelli carefully contrived a misleading representation of her physical beauty whilst Hall Caine played on his supposed resemblance to Shakespeare. Authors were happy to lend their names to advertisements of commercial products. Baroness Orczy endorsed a drug for the treatment of nervous distress and Caine had a brand of cigarettes named after him.[179] An author's name became a useful marketing tool. The magazine *Woman at Home* was subtitled Annie S. Swan's magazine even though Swan only contributed to the magazine and was not the editor.

What might an individual earn from authorship in this period? At the very top end of the scale the sums were considerable. George Eliot had an income of about £5,000 a year in 1873; Stevenson was earning £4,000 to £5,000 a year after the success of *Dr Jekyll and Mr Hyde*. Between 1888 and 1898 it is estimated Mary Ward earned £45,000 from her fiction, making her 'probably the highest-paid woman in England'.[180] In the new century earnings were again considerable for the select few at the top of the scale. By 1900 Bennett was earning £600 a year but in 1912 he earned £16,000, receiving £5,000 a year for his *Evening Standard* column alone.[181] Kipling's earnings at the start of century were around £15,000 a year.

Slightly lower down the scale, James Payn claimed to have earned an average of £1,500 a year for thirty-five working years, a figure he nevertheless contrasted unfavourably with a judge or bishop who might secure £5,000 a year and a retiring pension.[182] Grant Allen's annual income at the end of the 1870s was around £650 to £700, a comfortable wage that put him in the top 1 per cent in society.[183] At the bottom end, however, George Gissing never earned more than £300 a year whilst Arthur Machen, author of *The great god Pan* (1894), claimed in his autobiography that his life earnings from literature totalled £635.[184]

As mentioned in the introduction to this chapter, it is too easy to write the history of authorship as the history of great and successful men and women. For the vast majority, literary and financial success was fleeting and the practice of authorship one of constant struggle. The fate of one author provides a fitting conclusion to this survey. David Christie Murray began his career as a journalist. His novels dating from 1879 onwards brought him critical acclaim

179 For an account of authorship and advertising in this period, see Waller, *Writers, readers and reputations*, pp. 329–45.
180 Sutherland, *Mrs Humphry Ward*, p. 159.
181 Bonham-Carter, *Authors by profession* 1, p. 181; Morton, 'The busiest man in England', pp. 52–3.
182 Payn, *Gleams of memory*, p. 186.   183 Morton, 'The busiest man in England', pp. 52–3.
184 Cited in *ibid.*, p. 191.

and a reasonable income. But trials and tribulations in his private life meant that he lived much of his life in debt. In 1890 he was injured in a carriage accident which made it impossible for him to write; he could not afford an amanuensis and was fined £300 by Tillotson for failing to deliver the manuscript of a novel, the payment for which had already been advanced. In 1891 he was declared bankrupt with liabilities of over £1,000 and assets of £21. In 1894 he was brought before a court for failing to contribute thirty shillings a week towards the maintenance of his estranged wife, who was an alcoholic. His defence was that he had no money to give her. The proceeds from his writing diminished. By 1904 he received as little as £40 for the copyright of his novels. His publisher frequently answered his requests for small loans or advances against unwritten works when the creditor called in the debts. By the end of his career he arranged with Chatto & Windus to be paid by a single pound note for every thousand words of manuscript he sent to the publisher.[185] He died in 1907 leaving just £50.

185 See Nash, 'Life in Gissing's New Grub Street'.

5

Copyright

CATHERINE SEVILLE

Domestic copyright – Talfourd's struggles and the 1842 Copyright Act

British copyright's[1] major failing during the nineteenth century was the fragmented and complicated state of the law. The Royal Commission of 1878 described it: 'wholly destitute of any sort of arrangement, incomplete, often obscure, and even when it is intelligible upon long study, it is in many parts so ill-expressed that no one who does not give such study can expect to understand it'.[2] Faced with fresh challenges to the prevailing law, whether domestic or international, legislators scarcely knew where to start. Copyright's influence was felt in many fields, which made it extremely troublesome politically. Diverse groups considered themselves to have a stake in copyright law, so attempted to defend and advance their interests, sometimes demanding change and sometimes resisting it. Successive governments found it impossible to be proactive in their strategy, and were reduced to tinkering with the most urgent difficulties, or simply stalling. A patchwork of statutes chronicled the activities of trade and other interest groups, and, regrettably, mirrored their lack of coordination. The need for a coherent approach to copyright, preferably embodied in a single act, was clear for much of the century. The problem lay first in conceiving and then in negotiating a practical solution.

This was a time of great change in the book trade. Technological innovations, such as the steam press and stereotyping, drove prices downwards and engendered new sources of competition for the established publishers. Production increased very considerably during the nineteenth century, with some periods showing dramatic rises. In the eighteenth century, when books

---

1 For further detail on all this material see Seville, *Literary copyright reform*; Seville, *The internationalisation of copyright law*.
2 *Royal Commission on the Laws and Regulations relating to Home, Colonial and Foreign Copyrights; Report, Minutes of Evidence, Appendix* c 2036 (1878) ('*Royal Commission Report (1878)*'), para. 7.

were a hand-crafted luxury, readers had been concentrated in higher social and income groups. In the early part of the nineteenth century, high-priced books continued to form the greatest percentage share of published titles. By 1835, however, medium-priced books were the largest segment, and these too were overtaken by cheap books by 1855.[3] Population growth and rising literacy rates also fuelled demand. The British population in 1801 exceeded 10 million. It had doubled to over 20 million by 1851, and almost doubled again (to 37 million) by the end of the century.[4] Literacy in England (defined roughly as the ability to sign the marriage register) was around 50 per cent at the end of the 1830s, but approached 100 per cent by 1900.[5] Increasing prizes brought increased competition for the established book publishers, both from overseas and domestically. Accustomed as they had been to cosy oligopoly and restrictive practices, they found the new world both challenging and threatening. Anxious themselves to expand into overseas markets, a task facilitated by much improved distribution networks, they met foreign publishers who were equally keen to return the favour by expanding into the traditional British markets. Colonial markets were much contested. For British authors and publishers, international copyright became an increasingly desirable goal. Yet the various interest groups differed significantly as to the terms on which they would accept international copyright. It was not until the 1908 Berlin revision of the Berne Convention generated overwhelming pressure to conform to international standards that the British government was able to drive through the consolidating Act of 1911. Throughout the nineteenth century, effort after effort was expended on copyright reform. But all these hopeful initiatives ended in disappointment and failure.

Serjeant Thomas Noon Talfourd, elected MP for Reading in 1835, was the first to propose uniting the existing collage of copyright acts. By day a lawyer, by night dramatic critic and aspirant author, his tragedy *Ion* was the hit of the 1836 season at Covent Garden (much assisted by the brilliance of William Macready in the lead role). Encouraged by this, and by his friendship with William Wordsworth, Talfourd introduced a copyright bill in May 1837. His plans were grand, particularly for a backbencher: a fully consolidated copyright bill, covering all areas of the subject, including international copyright, and advocating a very significant extension to copyright term. The 1814 Copyright Act gave a term of twenty-eight years from publication, 'and also, if the author shall be living at the end of that period, for the residue of his natural life'.[6]

3 Eliot, 'Some trends in British book production', pp. 19–43.
4 Mitchell, *British historical statistics*, p. 9.   5 Vincent, *Literacy and popular culture*, p. 22.
6 Copyright Act 1814, s.9.

Talfourd instead proposed a term of the author's life plus sixty years. He was tenacious and unapologetic in his championing of the literary cause. The preamble to the 1837 bill explains the need 'to afford greater encouragement' to authors. Talfourd and Wordsworth had engaged in some discreet lobbying, and were confident of success.

However, the death of William IV brought the Parliamentary session to an early end and the bill had to be brought back in 1838. The government had taken over the international copyright aspect. The provisions affecting copyright term remained. Talfourd was determined that the benefit of the proposed extension would reach authors and their families, rather than publishers, and sought to create a reversionary interest in some cases. As originally drafted, the full extension was given to authors and those benefiting after their death. Although this was subject to existing licences and any partial assignment, the aim was to exclude publishers, on the grounds that they had bargained on the basis of a twenty-eight-year term, so that the extension would represent an undeserved windfall. In addition, authors who had assigned their copyrights were to have the benefit of the full extension once the assignment had expired. This would have obliged the assignee to reopen negotiations with the author, or with the successors to the author's estate. The author would have been free to take the best offer available without giving priority to the existing publisher. Particularly in the case of a successful work, the author would have been in a strong bargaining position. The trade was used to a more cosy practice, under which the established publishers did not reprint the works of others, leaving them all in comfortable possession of works well beyond the copyright term. Talfourd, having received 'from the most respectable parties and eminent publishers so many complaints of practical inconveniences' resulting from the so-called 'retrospective clause', gave up the reversionary aspects of his plans.[7] Later versions of the bill continued to give some preference to the author's family, though.

Talfourd faced considerable and diverse opposition both in and out of Parliament. Almost 500 petitions against the copyright bills were presented in the House of Commons between 1838 and 1840, representing over 30,000 petitioners. Early petitions came exclusively from the printing trade, particularly the London printing houses, but by 1840 it was no longer a single-trade dispute. The copyright question was perceived to encompass issues which Talfourd had not contemplated. More than just a threat to the printing trade,

---

7 *Hansard, Parliamentary debates* (3rd series), xliii, 554.

copyright reform was seen to affect the diffusion of knowledge and political freedom. Radical MPs such as Joseph Hume, Henry Warburton and Thomas Wakeley were practised campaigners in the war against what came to be known as 'taxes on knowledge' – primarily the newspaper stamp and paper duties, but also the various libel laws – used by governments to restrict free political expression. Copyright could be seen as part of the same portfolio of oppressive measures, particularly if a lengthy extension to its term was being proposed. The argument was that prices would rise and that books would be withheld from the public. Copyright would target the working man disproportionately, impeding self-education, and denying political freedom. Speaking in the House of Commons, Warburton expressed the case thus:

> Under the bill as it stood a Government adverse to popular rights might prevent the diffusion of political information, and he did not hesitate to say, that if such a measure were to pass into a law, the public would be deprived of many advantages arising from literature and science which they had long enjoyed, and which of late years they had much improved by means of cheap publications, but according to some hon. Members who had taken a part in the present discussion, those cheap publications were a great evil, and nothing was more to be desired than that books should become dearer than they were at present.[8]

By 1840 the debate had expanded significantly, and petitions came from a wide range of trades and specialisms, reaching those who had little or no connection to printing. Many came simply from 'Inhabitants' of a named place. Publishers – the employers in the book trade – were also practised at coordinated action in defence of their interests. They petitioned also, but selectively, supplementing petitions with letters and articles in newspapers and periodicals, with pamphlets, and with carefully targeted private lobbying. Initially their reaction to Talfourd's proposals was hostile, largely because the 'retrospective clause' would have challenged their customary rights in copyright works. Longman & Co. were particularly active in opposition.[9] Once this aspect of the scheme had been dropped, however, the publishers were relatively indifferent. Although happy to take the benefit of any extension to domestic copyright that Parliament cared to grant, they did not see this as a particular priority.

Talfourd had little to set against these long-established and well-organised mechanisms. Attempts to unite authors in a shared profession had repeatedly

---

8 *Hansard, Parliamentary debates* (3rd series), xlv, 939.
9 See their letter to *The Times*, 16 May 1838, detailing difficulties which the retrospective clause would give rise to.

failed.[10] Support had to be mobilised by way of personal appeals to individuals, and the field was not large. In addition, authors were reluctant to be seen to be arguing for their own gain. Opponents were quick to sneer at authors (Sir Walter Scott, in particular) for their fecklessness and inability to support themselves, and denounced the prospect of legislation which would benefit a few authors at the expense of the reading public. Authors who spoke up for the proposals were likely to face public abuse in the press and in Parliament. Because of these factors only thirty-seven petitions expressing support for Talfourd's bills were received; the work of just 341 supplicants.

Wordsworth is the author most closely associated with the campaign. His interest in copyright was a long-standing one. In 1808 he complained of the existing twenty-eight-year maximum term:

> The law as it now stands merely consults the interest of the useful drudges in Literature, or of flimsy and shallow writers, whose works are upon a level with the taste and knowledge of the age; while men of real power, who go before their age, are deprived of all hope of their families being benefited by their exertions ... Suppose that Burns or Cowper had left at their deaths each a child a few months old, a daughter for example, is it reasonable that those children, at the age of 28, should cease to derive benefit from their Father's works, when every Bookseller in the Country is profiting by them?[11]

He was also exasperated by the cheap foreign reprints being smuggled into Britain, undercutting the authorised editions. Wordsworth discussed copyright with leading MPs in the summer of 1836. Although unwilling to petition at first, throughout 1838 he wrote many letters seeking support for the bills. Once the publishers had been appeased by the removal of the retrospective clause, the campaigners were hopeful of success. But at the committee stage they met unexpected opposition from Lord John Russell, leader of the House of Commons, who expressed concern about 'the progress of information and knowledge'.[12] Talfourd was obliged to withdraw the bill to avoid the ignominy of its being voted out.

The bill was reintroduced in 1839. Wordsworth overcame his scruples and drew up a petition, as did a number of other authors, notably Thomas Carlyle. Obstructive tactics from the Radicals in Parliament made progress impossible, and the bill was postponed. It was again defeated in 1840. Thomas Babington Macaulay was responsible for its defeat in 1841. Macaulay's reputation as a

---

10 See Seville, *Literary copyright reform*, pp. 149–53.
11 Wordsworth to Sharp, 27 September 1808: *Letters of William and Dorothy Wordsworth* 1, p. 266.
12 *Hansard, Parliamentary debates* (3rd series), xlviii, 9556–8.

writer and public speaker gave him an entry into politics, where he made his name during the Reform debates. He went to India to join the Supreme Council of British India, the supreme executive authority, and also a law-making body. As the 'law member' he was responsible for drafting a good deal of important legislation, largely single-handedly. In 1841, newly returned from India, Macaulay gave a famous speech on copyright which is still frequently quoted when any extension to copyright term is discussed.[13] Applying the doctrines of political economy, Macaulay characterised copyright as a 'monopoly': a 'tax on readers for the purpose of giving a bounty to writers'. Although he felt it necessary to give a bounty to 'genius and learning', any extension of copyright term could not be justified unless it was shown to 'increase the bounty' proportionately.[14] Macaulay's view was that publishers would pay authors no more for a longer term, thus the public would suffer an extended period of high prices, without a countervailing benefit to authors. He hypothesised an additional 'taxation' on the public of £20,000 for Johnson's *Dictionary* alone, and suggested that important works might become prohibitively expensive. Monopolies of commodities were regarded by the public with great disfavour, and Macaulay confidently predicted a backlash. The damage was irreparable, and the bill was defeated.

Talfourd did not stand in the 1841 election, and Lord Mahon took over management of the matter. A practical politician, in the 1842 bill Mahon sought to propitiate opponents by proposing only a modest increase in term: to twenty-five years from the author's death. He consulted leading publishers, offered further concessions in other areas, and thereby secured their support. Longman and Murray now organised petitions, from publishers, authors, printers and others, this time in favour of the bill. Macaulay again spoke against the proposals, this time arguing that the proposed extension was too short, and gave too great a role to chance. He proposed a life term, with a minimum of forty-two years. The Prime Minister, Sir Robert Peel, suggested that the author's family should always be provided for, by a seven-year post-mortem term. This was

---

13 Notably and recently in the US Supreme Court: *Eric Eldred, et al. v. John D. Ashcroft, Attorney General* 123 S.Ct. 769 (2003), 802.

14 *Hansard, Parliamentary debates* (3rd series), lvi, 350. This continues to be a controversial point, and to some extent a matter of definition and perspective. Those criticising copyright often describe it, pejoratively, as a 'monopoly'. Talfourd and his supporters took care to use the label 'literary property'. Speaking in one of the earlier debates on the bill, Disraeli addressed the issue explicitly: 'there was no evidence to show that authors themselves enjoyed anything like a monopoly. There was, however, a monopoly, not in favour of authors, but a monopoly in favour of the booksellers. It was a monopoly enjoyed by those who did not labour for it, and which has all the odious features of other monopolies. By the old system that monopoly was called into existence, and he asked the House now to convert that monopoly into a property for authors.' *Hansard, Parliamentary debates* (3rd series), xlii, 555.

the compromise effected, with a guaranteed minimum of forty-two years from publication.[15] Wordsworth regarded the extension as beggarly, and Talfourd continued to believe that anything other than a perpetual term was a compromise of principle. On the whole, though, nineteenth-century commentators welcomed the 1842 Copyright Act, which they thought secured clear improvements. Nevertheless, the task of codification and simplification of domestic law remained unaccomplished.

First steps towards the Berne Convention – the problem of foreign reprints

Throughout this period the need for an effective international copyright law became ever more pressing. The issue which most troubled the book trade in the first half of the century was that of foreign reprints of British copyright works, which found their way onto the British market with increasing frequency. During the 1820s travellers to Paris could buy a wide selection of reprints of British publications, from publishers such as Baillère, Baudry, Bossange and Galignani. An attractive, cloth-bound, single-volume edition of a new British novel was usually available in Paris within days of its publication in London, and at a fraction of the price.[16] Belgian, German and American reprints, although generally of a lesser quality, also represented a threat to the British market. By the mid-1830s, publishers were much exercised by the presence of foreign reprints in London bookshops, circulating libraries and the collections of reading societies. Wordsworth asked in a Piccadilly bookshop for Galignani's edition of his poems, and it was proffered immediately. On enquiring whether he could have ten copies, or a hundred, or five hundred, the bookseller replied, 'Give me only time.'[17] Although these imports were prohibited, the powers of customs officers when dealing with them were unclear. Publishers and authors, led by G. P. R. James, mounted a campaign for a stronger response to the reprinters. Reciprocal copyright arrangements would have offered a solution. The 1838 International Copyright Act gave the power to grant (by Order in Council) copyright to foreign authors if their state offered reciprocal protection.[18] Although this opened the door to negotiations with foreign governments, it was poorly drafted, and no Order in Council was

---

15 An act to amend the law of copyright (1842) 5 & 6 Vict. c.47 s.3.
16 For examples, with prices, see St Clair, *The reading nation*, pp. 520–1.
17 Wordsworth to Mahon, 19 April 1842: *Letters of William and Dorothy Wordsworth* 7, p. 327.
18 An act for securing to authors in certain cases the benefit of international copyright (1838) 1 & 2 Vict. c.59.

ever signed under its terms. The 1842 Copyright Act imposed heavy fines for importing foreign reprints for sale or hire (to catch the circulating libraries), but Lord Mahon refused the publishers' request to exclude foreign reprints entirely, so imports for personal use were not prohibited. However, the 1842 Customs Act obliged customs officers to seize titles which had been duly notified to the Commissioners of Customs, the hope being that a selective system would be more effective than a total ban. Although welcomed by British publishers and authors, the measure did not resolve the problems. Officers were reluctant to search the baggage of individual travellers, and the process of matching imported books to the official lists was a laborious one. Furthermore, by an oversight in drafting, the power of seizure did not apply to the colonies. This omission was in theory rectified in 1845, but in practice there was great reluctance to enforce a law which resulted in the destruction of good cheap British works, which were otherwise scarce. The well-intentioned 1847 Foreign Reprints Act was the result, although it proved hopelessly ineffective in practice.[19]

It was difficult to negotiate bilateral treaties, because the practical advantage of such arrangements was likely to lie very much in favour of British authors, whose works were in demand and widely reprinted on the continent. Nor was the United Kingdom's scheme of copyright protection attractive to other countries; before 1842 the copyright term was comparatively short, for example. The 1844 International Copyright Act increased the range of what could be offered, and the first convention under the Act was signed with Prussia in 1846.[20] Other countries followed gradually, but it proved hard to reach agreement with some of the major threats to the home market; a convention with France was not signed until 1851, one with Belgium only in 1854 – and none with America. The 1838 and 1844 Acts expressly excluded translations, a policy which had to be reversed before agreement could be reached with France.[21] Even then, the protection offered to French drama in translation was widely regarded as useless in practice. In non-convention countries 'piratical' editions could be freely printed and imported, in practice circulating without hindrance even in convention states and in the British territories overseas. Although

19 An act for the general regulation of the customs (1842) 5 & 6 Vict. c.47. An act to regulate the trade of British possessions abroad (1845) 8 & 9 Vict., c.93 s.9. An Act to amend the law relating to the protection in the colonies of works entitled to copyright in the United Kingdom (1847) 10 & 11 Vict. c.95.
20 An act to amend the law relating to international copyright (1844) 7 & 8 Vict. c.12.
21 An act to enable Her Majesty to carry into effect a connection with France on the subject of copyright, to extend and explain the International Copyright Acts, and to explain the acts relating to copyright in engravings (1852) 15 & 16 Vict. c.12.

the patchwork of individually negotiated agreements represented a significant improvement over national protection, a truly international arrangement would have to wait until the Berne Convention of 1886. Even then, it would not include any copyright agreement with the United States – something that the British desired fervently.

America – the long road to international copyright

For almost the whole of the nineteenth century America offered only informal protection to foreign copyright works. Literary copyright was established by federal legislation in 1790, and it left Americans entirely free to reprint foreign works. The American publisher Samuel Goodrich estimated that in 1820, 70% of American book manufacture was the work of British authors.[22] Sometimes publishers were willing to pay something to gain the advantage of being first in the market, and in some circles 'courtesy of trade' restrained (although to a somewhat variable extent) American houses from printing each other's titles. In 1817 the New York publisher Thomas Kirk offered John Murray a third of his net profits for early sheets of British works. In the early 1820s Carey & Lea paid John Miller, a British bookseller and publisher who acted as their London agent, to forward Sir Walter Scott's novels on publication. When this route proved too slow to forestall the competition, they paid Scott's publisher to send early sheets from Edinburgh to America as soon as they were printed. With Emerson's encouragement and assistance, early copies of Carlyle's works were also sold to American publishers, although the enterprise ran far from smoothly.[23] Such arrangements worked to the disadvantage of American authors, as Washington Irving noted:

> the public complains of the price of my work – this is the disadvantage of coming in competition with those republished English works for which the

22 Goodrich, *Recollections of a lifetime* 2, pp. 388–91, 552–3. The figures are necessarily very rough. Goodrich put the British share of American productions at around 60% in 1830, 45% in 1840, 30% in 1850 and under 20% by 1856.

23 Smiles, *A publisher and his friends* 1, p. 27. Eaton, 'The American movement for international copyright, 1837–60'. Scott to Cooper [?6] November 1826: Scott, *Letters 1826–1828*, p. 122. Eidson's often-repeated assertion that Ticknor's payment for Tennyson's *Poems* of 1842 is 'possibly the earliest copyright payment by an American publisher to a foreign author' is misleading, since, in the modern sense of the word, Tennyson had no American copyright to sell. However, in the early part of the century, in America, a royalty payment was sometimes referred to as a copyright payment. This was the most common arrangement for American authors. Foreign authors usually received payment for advance sheets, but occasionally a royalty (normally around 10%) was agreed. It was under this latter scheme that Tennyson was paid $150 (10% of the retail price of the first printing) for the first American edition of his poems (1842). American authors rarely sold their copyrights outright, whereas in Britain this was common. Eidson, *Tennyson in America*, p. 37; Winship, *American literary publishing*, pp. 133–7.

Booksellers have not to pay anything to the authors. If the American public wish to have literature of their own they must consent to pay for the support of authors.[24]

Others complained that the habit of reprinting foreign works hampered the spread of American ideas, thus permitting Britain to retain an ideological foothold long after her political dominion had ceased.[25] There was, as a result, a body of American opinion in favour of international copyright law. But the practice was too profitable for American publishers to relinquish freely, and the 1831 Copyright Act unequivocally barred foreign authors from protection.

As a result, few British authors had any hope of payment from American publishers. Even those with sufficient market power to command offers would have much preferred a legal right to the ad hoc bargains which, in the absence of international copyright, they were obliged to conclude. In an effort to secure British interests more directly, in 1836 the London publishers Saunders & Otley attempted to establish a New York branch. The American book trade was actively hostile, even, or so Frederick Saunders believed, buying proof sheets from his own pressmen and issuing them under an American imprint before the British interloper could reach the market. The London firm sought the assistance of its authors, and Harriet Martineau agreed to organise a petition. Fifty-six British authors signed, and copies were presented to both Houses of Congress in 1837. Senator Henry Clay introduced a bill, which would have extended copyright privileges to British and French authors on condition that their works were reprinted and published in the United States within a month of their appearance abroad. Formidable opposition was mobilised by the American publishing trade, and although Clay was persistent, reintroducing his bill several times between 1837 and 1842, it was always defeated. Early in 1842 Charles Dickens arrived in America on a lecture tour. He was an immensely popular author in America, and unauthorised reprints of his works sold in their hundreds of thousands. At a public dinner Dickens spoke appreciatively of his reception in America, but he also expressed confidence that America would grant international copyright before long. Although not in themselves responsible for the failure of Clay's bill, Dickens's remarks provoked a hail of criticism in the newspapers, reinforcing the already negative publicity generated by the subject of international copyright.

24 Irving to Henry Brevoort, 12 August 1819: Irving, *Letters* 1, p. 554.
25 James Fenimore Cooper wrote to his publishers, Carey & Lea (9 November 1826), 'What Publisher will pay a Native writer for ideas that he may import for nothing?': Cooper, *Letters and journals* 1, p. 172.

During the 1840s there were further efforts, driven by American nationals, to persuade Congress of the importance of international copyright, but little of substance resulted. During this period the copyright status of foreign authors in Britain was somewhat unclear, following conflicting decisions in various different courts. Publishers such as Murray and Bentley, who had paid substantial sums to American authors in the belief that first publication in Britain would secure copyright, were left vulnerable to British reprinters, such as Bohn and Routledge. In *Boosey v. Jefferys* (1850), the Court of Exchequer held that a foreigner had no assignable copyright, leaving the British publisher who had paid for it quite unprotected. On appeal Lord Campbell reversed this decision, holding that wherever a foreigner was residing, first publication in the United Kingdom did entitle him to British copyright.[26] His ruling was not absolutely definitive, however, and given the importance of the matter, the case was appealed to the House of Lords. If Lord Campbell's ruling stood, there was little reason for any foreign state to conclude a copyright treaty with Britain, since copyright would already be available to anyone first publishing there. Edward Bulwer-Lytton chaired a public meeting at the Hanover Square rooms, called to discuss the 'equitable adjustment of British and Foreign Copyright'. There he made the staggering claim that international copyright would have brought him an extra £60,000 from the exploitation of his works in America.[27]

Bulwer-Lytton became an important figure in a prolonged and highly secret initiative intended to secure reciprocal copyright with America. His son Robert was in Washington, acting as unpaid attaché in the British Legation. Robert became aware of a lobbying group, known as 'The Organisation', which would manage the passage of measures for a fee. A figure of $60,000 was quoted. Bulwer-Lytton wrote to Dickens, who was extremely dubious about the scheme, but nevertheless agreed to hold a meeting in his house. The timing was particularly bad, as a dispute over the Bookselling Regulations had heightened tensions between authors and publishers. Several of the principal publishers flatly refused to become involved, but £1,000 was collected and sent in the summer of 1852.[28] A draft treaty was eventually negotiated, but although it

---

26 *Boosey v. Jefferys* (1850) 20 Law J., Ch., 165. Appeal to the Court of Exchequer Chamber at 6 Exch. 580.

27 *The question of unreciprocated foreign copyright in Great Britain* (1851), pp. 9–11. Bulwer-Lytton had received less than £2,500 from his American publishers, Harper & Bros. For more detail see Catherine Seville, 'Edward Bulwer Lytton dreams of copyright: "It might make me a rich man" ', in Francis O'Gorman (ed.), *Victorian literature and finance* (Oxford, 2007).

28 Contributors included authors (Archibald Alison, Bulwer-Lytton, Dickens), publishers (John Blackwood, John Murray) and printers (Bradbury & Evans, William Clowes).

was signed it never passed the Senate.[29] More leverage might perhaps have been applied if the House of Lords' judgment in *Jefferys v. Boosey* (1854) – which held that a foreigner was entitled to copyright protection only if resident in Britain at the time of publication – had come a few months earlier.[30] But international copyright was still not a pressing concern for America. This indifference was reinforced in 1868 by the House of Lords' decision in *Routledge v. Low*, another case which turned on whether foreigners were entitled to copyright.[31] Maria Cummins, an American author living in New York, posted the manuscript of her novel *Haunted hearts* to her publishers Sampson Low in London. The copyright was duly assigned to them, and Miss Cummins took the precaution of visiting Canada for a few days at the time of publication. Sampson Low's two-volume edition cost sixteen shillings, and faced unwelcome competition from Routledge's two-shilling edition. The House of Lords held that a foreigner publishing an original work in England was entitled to copyright under the 1842 Act, provided that at time of publication he was residing, however temporarily, in any part of the British dominions. This generous interpretation of British law offered America little incentive to grant copyright to foreigners.

Further attempts towards reform – the Royal Commission of 1878

British copyright law remained in a state of disarray. In 1857 a government bill to consolidate the then fourteen existing Copyright Acts was drawn up and printed, but subsequently abandoned. This very limited initiative was prompted by the difficulties faced by customs officers, who were struggling to enforce conflicting and contradictory rules, and it did not attempt to modify the main provisions of copyright law. One somewhat copyright-related change was put into effect in 1861, when the duty on paper was abolished. Gladstone, as Chancellor of the Exchequer, had been pressing to reduce taxation generally. Radicals had long demanded the repeal of paper duties, characterised as a 'tax on knowledge', but moderates also supported repeal.[32] The book trade was delighted, although there was anxiety at the decision to repeal import duty on books also, since it was feared that there would be no incentive for customs officers to search for foreign reprints. The government remained uninterested in

29 Dickens to Bulwer-Lytton, 5 May 1852: Dickens, *Letters* 6, p. 662. Lytton to Dickens, 7 May 1852: *Lytton papers* (Hertfordshire Archives and Local Studies) D/EK c26/22. Barnes, *Authors, publishers and politicians*, pp. 219–26.
30 *Jefferys v. Boosey* (1854) 10 ER 681.
31 (1868) L.R. 3 H.L. 110; 37 L.J.Ch. 454; 18 L.T. 874; 16 W.R. 1081.
32 For more see Collet, *History of the taxes on knowledge*.

copyright consolidation, so the Edinburgh publisher Adam Black introduced his own bill in 1864. Black held the copyright of the *Encyclopaedia Britannica*, and of Scott's novels, so he had a keen and practical interest in the matter. Nevertheless, he found preparation of the bill 'a much tougher job than I expected'.[33] A Select Committee chaired by Black himself was eventually forced to admit defeat, remarking on the difficulty and complexity of the task. Consolidation having proved too difficult, in 1866 Lord Lyttelton introduced a bill in the House of Lords with the single aim of granting novelists a dramatisation right, but it was opposed by those who considered dramatisations legitimate because they were original in character, and it was firmly defeated.[34]

Perhaps the greatest concern for British publishers at this time was the situation in Canada. Relations with Canada regarding copyright had been poor for decades. The 1842 Copyright Act had sought to discourage the trade in foreign reprints by imposing heavy penalties on their import. The effect on British colonies was significant, since the North American possessions in particular had been used to plentiful supplies of cheap American reprints of British copyright works. British publishers had made some attempt to supply cheaper editions themselves, but their inability or unwillingness to do so effectively left the colonial markets starved of adequate and affordable reading matter.[35] Vociferous complaints from provincial governments led to the passage of the 1847 Foreign Reprints Act. This permitted the importation of foreign reprints on condition that the rights of British copyright proprietors were secured. The legislative vision was of a local duty, but this never became a practical reality. Only minuscule sums were ever collected, and American reprints again flooded unchecked into the colonies, to the detriment of British authors and publishers. The Foreign Reprints Act was also unpopular with the emerging Canadian publishing trade, because although it permitted the importation of foreign editions, it did not permit local reprinting. The Canadian trade was thus left powerless to compete with the American industry which was supplying its potential customers. This led to Canadian proposals, formalised in 1868, for a licensing scheme which would have allowed Canadian publishers to reprint any British copyright work without the proprietor's consent, simply on payment of a royalty. British reactions to the idea were mostly negative, although there was a minority strand of opinion strongly in favour of accepting

---

33 Nicholson, *Memoirs of Adam Black*, p. 221.

34 The Lord Chancellor, Lord Cranworth, was 'quite certain that its provisions would be as impossible to carry into effect as they were contrary to all reason'. *Hansard, Parliamentary debates* (3rd series), clxiv, 360–4.

35 For more on the Canadian book market see Fleming and Lamonde (eds.), *The history of the book in Canada* 1, pp. 348–54.

it, on the grounds that it was better than the farcical collection scheme then in place.

The Canadian question provided one strong impetus for the formation of the Copyright Association in 1872, founded to work for the protection of British copyright interests.[36] In 1872 the Canadian Parliament lost patience entirely, and passed an Act allowing for the reprinting and publishing in Canada of British copyright works on payment of a $12\frac{1}{2}$ per cent duty. Since its terms conflicted with imperial legislation, it would have needed the imperial government's sanction to come into effect, and this was not forthcoming. In 1875 a much more limited and moderate Canadian Act was passed, which gave Canadian copyright to works published or produced in Canada. Although imperial copyright was not affected, British authors could now acquire a separate Canadian copyright if they chose to do so, by publishing in Canada. The 1875 Canadian Copyright Act was only a limited solution, though, because genuine grievances remained unresolved. Ironically, Canada's persistently hostile attitude to the imperial copyright regime made it extremely difficult for the British government to implement changes to it, whether in the international or domestic context. A new domestic interest group, the Association to Protect the Rights of Authors, had been established. In 1875 it issued a long report on the state of the law of copyright.[37] The report was somewhat diffuse in its targets, addressing large issues such as colonial copyright though for the most part ignoring the absence of an Anglo-American agreement, but giving equal prominence to specific issues such as the dramatisation of novels, copyright in newspaper articles, and the difficulties of protecting translations. A delegation from the Association pressed the Prime Minister, Disraeli, for the appointment of a Select Committee or Royal Commission. Later in the year the government announced its intention to appoint a Royal Commission.

The Royal Commission members included many established contributors to previous phases of the copyright debate. The chairman originally nominated was Lord Stanhope – formerly Lord Mahon – though his death necessitated

36 For more detail see *Memoranda on international and colonial copyright* (1872). The Association was driven and run by the publishers Longman and Murray.
37 Charles Reade's thirteen letters on copyright, *The rights and wrongs of authors*, date from this time: *Pall Mall Gazette*, July and September 1875. The Association lacked cohesion, at least by Sala's account: 'I know very little and care much less about the Rights of Authors, and . . . I fancy that the majority of the members of the Association of which I am a member scarcely know what they want themselves. That most of them hate each other cordially I am glad to believe. I only went up with the delegation to Downing St. because Braddon wished to be introduced to Disraeli, and because I wished to have an opportunity of saying something disagreeable about the Country newspapers which steal your articles, while you are blackguarded in the letters of their London Correspondents. For the rest Copyright may go hang.' Sala to Yates, 20 July 1875: *Letters to Edmund Yates*, p. 190.

the appointment of a new chairman, Lord John Manners. The Commission took evidence for an entire year, meeting two afternoons a week. The formulation of the Report took a considerable time, partly owing to (Commissioner) Anthony Trollope's absence in South Africa for six months.[38] Issued in June 1878, the result was an impressive document; the Report and minutes of evidence ran to four hundred closely printed pages. The Report itself was comparatively succinct, though covering domestic, colonial and international copyright, addressing both general issues and points of detail. Predictably, the primary recommendation for domestic copyright was that it should be 'reduced to an intelligible and systematic form'. The Commissioners were in no doubt that the interest of authors and of the public alike required legislative protection for copyright owners, and that copyright should continue to be treated as a proprietary right.[39] A number of specific matters were also addressed. A good deal of evidence had been heard as to the appropriate term for copyright in books. There was for the most part agreement that the term should be extended, particularly if this would help secure international arrangements. The Commission's recommendation was for a term lasting for the author's life plus a fixed number of years (probably thirty), rather than a term counted from publication, or a renewable term. It was also advised that performing right, dramatisation right, and a right to prevent abridgements, should be coterminous with copyright in the book. The existing system of registration was sharply censured. The Stationers' Company had been, from the earliest days of licensing, the body legally responsible for the registration of books. The 1842 Copyright Act had confirmed the system, and Joseph Greenhill was appointed Registrar, effectively for life. There had been ferocious and specific complaints about the inefficiency and expense of the prevailing arrangements, which Greenhill's own evidence did little to rebut.[40] The Report recommended compulsory registration, combining deposit and registration in a single action at the British Museum. This was coupled with a recommendation to confine the deposit obligation to a single copy (of books and newspapers) to the British Museum.

---

38 Following Trollope's return, John Blackwood quoted Lord John Manners as saying that Trollope was likely 'to drive them all mad at the weary Copyright Commission, going over all the ground that has been discussed in his absence': Porter, *Annals of a publishing house*, p. 317.

39 *Report* (1878) para. 13. Only one witness had urged the royalty scheme as a practical proposition for domestic copyright. Robert Macfie, who had written on patent law, argued for a right to republish on payment of a royalty of 5 per cent on the retail price: *Report* (1878) para. 16, *Evidence* (1878) Qus. 2706–77. In relation to Canadian and American copyright, however, proposals for compulsory licences of this nature were more common.

40 For Greenhill's earlier shortcomings, regarding the delivery of deposit copies to the relevant libraries, see McKitterick, *Cambridge University Library*, pp. 566–81.

The remainder of the Report was devoted to international matters. Much thought had been given to colonial copyright. The Commissioners were critical of the long-standing anomaly that publication in a colony did not give copyright throughout the Empire, whereas publication in the United Kingdom did. This had been a great grievance in Canada, in particular. Several witnesses had commented on the link between cheap books and education, and it was thought important that British literature should be readily available to colonial readers. The Commissioners therefore outlined a licensing scheme which would have allowed local reprinting if suitable supplies were not made available there, subject to a royalty. This would not have led to the repeal of the 1847 Foreign Reprints Act. Although a licensing system might have worked well in colonies with printing and publishing firms of their own, it was recognised that smaller colonies were dependent for their literature on a supply of foreign reprints. For these colonies it was recommended that the import of foreign reprints should still be permitted, subject to satisfactory arrangements for collecting duty. The Commission had taken evidence on the American situation, and the absence of any reciprocal arrangement was widely recognised as unsatisfactory. Understanding that American publishers would resist any agreement which did not grant them protection for their local market, the Commission was prepared to contemplate a manufacturing clause if an Anglo-American treaty could be concluded as a result of this concession. It firmly rejected any suggestion that Britain should take equivalent retaliatory steps, on grounds of policy and principle. The Commission was sympathetic to French requests for a reduction in the formalities required for copyright protection of foreign works, and for improved protection of translations.

The Report was signed by all the Commissioners but one, although nine of even these fourteen signatures were qualified by a dissent, note or separate report. The dissents concerned a number of important aspects of copyright law; the recommendation to transfer registration from Stationers' Hall and other aspects of registration; the method of calculating copyright term; abridgements and dramatisation rights. The most fundamental disagreement concerned the recommendation that colonial reprints should be banned from import into Britain – something which British publishers had argued was essential. Sir John Rose (formerly the Canadian Minister of Finance) argued that inequality of conditions between the home and colonial market could not be justified or defended. The committed free traders of the Commission argued that the trade in books should be treated as trade in any other commodity, and fall within the ordinary laws of political economy. Thomas Henry Farrer, Permanent Secretary to the Board of Trade, who had had close official involvement in copyright issues for many years, gave evidence on several occasions, and was permitted great freedom to structure his extensive contribution. He went to considerable lengths in an attempt to establish that British editions, particularly of copyright works, were more expensive than foreign ones. Farrer claimed that the publisher's interest lay in monopoly and net profit, in conflict with the public interest, which required high volume sales at cheap prices. He produced detailed figures intended to show that books were sold at a price which far exceeded the cost of production, with consequent detriment to the wider reading public. Farrer believed that any edition published with the consent of the author in any part of the world should have free access to the United Kingdom market. He envisaged a copyright system co-extensive with the English language, offering the author the advantage of an enormous market, and the reader the advantage of proportionately reduced prices. However, Farrer's views and evidence were fiercely challenged by several Commissioners, particularly Trollope and J. A. Froude.

Froude and Farrer continued this debate outside the confines of the Royal Commission. Farrer published an article in the *Fortnightly Review*, again arguing for free access to all markets, and challenging the policy of excluding foreign reprints. In the *Edinburgh Review*, Froude offered a brilliant and confident response. Farrer regarded books as a commodity, and considered that they should be subject to normal economic processes, particularly since there was a public interest in cheap books. He did not particularly revere the intangible property which authors produced, and in argument tended to assimilate it to the physical property in the books which contained it. Froude, on the other hand, was sharply aware of the difference between intangible and tangible property in this context:

> The paper and print, an author will say, is not my book, but the shell of my book. The book itself is the information in it which I have collected. It is my thought, which I have shaped into form by intellectual effort; it is the creation of my imagination, in which I have embodied the observation and reflection of my entire life.[41]

The conflict between Froude and Farrer mirrors that between Talfourd and the radical opposition to the extension of term in the 1842 Act. Their differing approaches to intangible property lay at the heart of their mutual incomprehension. Matthew Arnold later published an article on copyright, which did attempt to integrate both positions. Arnold agreed that cheap books were a

---

41 Farrer, 'The principle of copyright', *Fortnightly Review* 24 (1878), pp. 836–51. Froude, 'The Copyright Commission', *Edinburgh Review* 148 (1878), pp. 295–343.

necessity for a civilised society, but he refused to treat books as a commodity to be regulated by purely economic forces. Admitting that a great deal of rubbish would be produced and read, Arnold was nevertheless confident 'that the victory will be with good books in the end'. He acknowledged not only a special quality in these intangibles, but also a public interest in them.[42]

In part because of these fundamental disagreements, the Royal Commission's recommendations remained unimplemented. The project of codification was so daunting that no government department would undertake it. The Board of Trade reluctantly agreed to a consolidating bill, but only on condition that it would be in the personal charge of Lord John Manners, the Commission's Chairman, and that they would not be required to answer questions about it. A bill was drafted and its introduction was announced early in 1880, but even the Parliamentary draftsman involved despaired of it. One Treasury official described it as 'a hornet's nest'. It fell with Disraeli's government. A further comprehensive bill was promoted by the Law Amendment Society in 1881, but it did not progress. In 1885 Britain's imminent accession to the Berne Convention appeared to offer a fresh opportunity to execute the Commission's recommendations. The Society of Authors, the Copyright Association and the Musical Copyright Association combined to propose a draft consolidating bill. But the government was again reluctant. International pressures continued to hamper the reform of British copyright law.

The Berne Convention and its aftermath

The Berne Convention's roots can be traced to a number of congresses, the earliest held in Brussels in 1858. Nothing really concrete resulted before 1878, the year of the Paris Universal Exposition. There Victor Hugo presided over an International Literary Congress, at which an International Association, ALAI (Association Littéraire et Artistique Internationale), was created. Its aim was to defend the principles of intellectual property in all countries. As one of its initiatives, a convention for an international copyright union was drafted, discussed at the Berne conference in 1883, held under the auspices of the Swiss government. There were considerable difficulties in reconciling different views, but a compromise draft was hammered out, and submitted at the first formal international conference for the protection of the rights of authors, held in Berne in 1884. The British attitude to the proposals had initially been somewhat cool, but the prospect of an American delegate at the

42 Arnold, 'Copyright', *Fortnightly Review* 49 (1880), pp. 319–34.

1885 Berne conference had persuaded Britain to send British delegates with full authority. There were disagreements between those (such as the French) who on principle sought the strongest possible protection for authors, and those (such as the British) who took a more pragmatic line. The choice was between a convention whose high standards of protection would have precluded the participation of the many countries with weak copyright systems, or a less rigorous convention which would attract a significant number of countries as members. Pragmatism prevailed, though there were costs.

The 1886 Berne Convention created a 'Union for the protection of the rights of authors over their literary and artistic works'. Literary and artistic works were widely defined to include 'every production whatsoever in the literary, scientific, or artistic domain which can be published by any mode of reproduction'. Newspaper or periodical 'articles of political discussion' and 'news of the day' were expressly excluded.[43] The Convention was based on the principle of national treatment (meaning that whatever rights a state grants to its own citizens must be granted to citizens of other signatory states). The exception was for the term of protection, which was subject to a rule of national reciprocity. There was a ten-year minimum term for translation rights. Formalities such as registration and deposit were not prohibited, being very common in national laws at the time. For several countries, including the United Kingdom, accession to the Convention necessitated changes to their domestic laws. The British government cautiously sidestepped the opportunity to revise UK copyright more widely, and so the International and Colonial Copyright Act 1886 made only the minimum changes necessary to permit signature of the Convention. Numa Droz, President of the Berne conferences, considered Britain's adhesion to the Convention 'of paramount importance for the success of the Union', not least because this brought 300 million people within the Union.[44] The Berne Convention represented an enormous achievement, but its scope was seriously limited by the absence of America from the list of signatories.

43 Berne Convention 1886, Arts. I, IV, VII(2). This was a controversial topic, because of the possibility that copyright could be used to stifle freedom of political expression. In Britain, the reprinting of news items from the London dailies was common practice, particularly by provincial newspapers. The 1842 Copyright Act addressed periodicals but ignored newspaper copyright.
44 Droz is reported as saying, 'we had now not only announced the adhesion of Great Britain, but also that of the whole of her Colonies, amounting in all to more than 300,000,000 of souls'. The National Archives of England, Wales and the United Kingdom FO 881/5528, p. 147. This was more than double the combined populations of the other original signatories. The other states signing in September 1886 were Belgium, France, Germany, Haiti, Italy, Liberia, Spain, Switzerland and Tunisia. The Convention came into force on 5 December 1887, all the signatories except Liberia having ratified it.

America's refusal to grant copyright protection to foreigners caused damage to the interests of national copyright proprietors everywhere. Canada's particular situation – geographically adjacent to America, yet subject to British imperial copyright legislation – made her especially vulnerable to American policy on this subject. Canada did benefit from the passing of the 1886 International Copyright Act, which, as a peripheral matter, altered the inequitable rule on publication to provide that colonial publication gave copyright throughout the empire. The rules on deposit copies were also relaxed. There had been considerable political nervousness as to whether Britain could or should sign the Berne Convention on behalf of her colonies and possessions. Unanimity of approach was virtually obligatory, but tensions were such that the British government felt compelled to consult the colonies, assuring them that no action would be taken without their consent. All the colonies did in fact assent, including Canada. However, Canada's physical proximity to America meant that her Berne status was in practice far more beneficial to American authors than to her own, since (following *Routledge v. Low*) publication in Canada offered a straightforward gateway to Berne protection. Since there were comparatively few Canadian authors and publishers in a position to benefit from the increase in protection offered to Canadian works, the benefits of the Berne Convention proved for the most part theoretical.[45] A frustrated Canadian government continued to demand a compulsory licensing scheme.

The British government hoped that an agreement with America might alleviate tensions. The American Copyright Association, founded in 1868 'for the purpose of securing the rights of authors and publishers among the civilised nations of the earth', had supported several attempts to get international copyright bills through Congress. Unfortunately, even those in favour of it could not agree on specific terms, a weakness which economic protectionists were quick to exploit. In 1878 the New York publishers Harper & Bros., seriously pressed by internal competition in the American book trade, promoted an international copyright treaty. The so-called 'Harper Draft' contained a manufacturing clause and various other protective measures. Even so, the British government was prepared to contemplate it. The discussion drifted on without immediate result. In 1883 the American (Authors) Copyright League was founded, and worked hard to promote international copyright, with the willing assistance of Richard Rogers Bowker, editor of the *Publishers' Weekly*. The

---

45 For more on Canadian authorship and publishing see Fleming and Lamonde (eds.), *The history of the book in Canada* 2, pp. 148–60.

League at first pressed for straightforward reciprocal copyright arrangements, but eventually resigned itself to compromise. Given the power of the trade interests involved, no bill without protectionist safeguards seemed to have the slightest chance of passing. In 1887 George Haven Putnam and other leading publishers founded the American Publishers Copyright League. Both Leagues then worked to secure the passage of Senator Chace's bill. This had been drafted by Henry Charles Lea, an eminent historian from Philadelphia, who had run one of the oldest publishing houses in America. Although supportive of authors' rights, Lea was insistent on a manufacturing clause, to protect trade interests. After much lobbying and negotiation, a version of the Chace bill was passed in 1891, establishing international copyright in America, though with a significant qualification which was to endure for almost another hundred years.

America's passage of the 1891 Copyright Act only added to Canadian dissatisfaction, because American copyright was granted to foreigners only if the work was manufactured in the United States. To the British book trade this condition was unwelcome, but on balance more satisfactory than no protection at all. As far as the Canadian book trade was concerned, however, the American Act simply reinforced the imbalance between the American and Canadian industries, by giving British authors and publishers even less reason to use Canadian publishers to issue their works in Canada. The Canadian Parliament therefore asked for notice to be given that it wished to denounce the Berne Convention. The British government stalled. Positions remained entrenched. Only in 1900 was a new Canadian Copyright Act passed, which did something to ameliorate local conditions without presuming to interfere with imperial copyright. Canadian copyright law was amended to make it more attractive to holders of imperial copyright wishing to license publication of their works in Canada. Of course the 1900 Act could not address the greatest challenge to the Canadian publishing industry, which was America's continuing refusal to cede her manufacturing clause, or to join the Berne Union.

Copyright reform and the 1911 Copyright Act

Given the international tensions and the domestic complexities it faced when signing the Berne Convention, the British government's decision to limit the aims of the 1886 International and Colonial Act is easily understood. The Royal Commission's 1878 recommendations remained unimplemented, though not forgotten by all. The Society of Authors continued to press for copyright reform, and in 1890 its amending and consolidating bill was introduced by

Lord Monkswell. It was opposed by the government, which argued that imperial and colonial policy were not matters for a private bill, and it did not progress. Still no government measure was forthcoming. In 1896 the Society of Authors again took the lead, this time drafting a short amending bill, which tackled only a few issues. The Society sought the input and cooperation of the Copyright Association and the newly formed Publishers Association, although the consultation process proved arduous. The resulting bill was introduced in 1897, and again faced government resistance. It was nevertheless referred to a House of Lords Select Committee, but did not pass the House of Commons before the end of the Parliamentary session. By the autumn the Society of Authors and the Copyright Association had fallen out over the Association's proposals for yet another consolidating bill. In 1898 two rival bills were introduced, an amending bill backed by the Society of Authors, and a consolidating bill drafted by the Copyright Association. Both were referred to the same Select Committee, which took a good deal of evidence but did not finish its task. It had become obvious that both bills were seriously flawed. By way of a compromise, the eminent parliamentary counsel and draftsman Lord Thring agreed to draft a bill on behalf of the Lords' Committee, this time dividing the subject-matter thematically. In 1899 two bills were introduced therefore, one dealing with literary, dramatic and musical works, the other with artistic copyright. The same select committee worked on them, but again could not complete the undertaking. Although both bills were reintroduced in 1900, government resistance to their international dimensions effectively ensured that they could not pass. A further Select Committee was entertained by the evidence of Samuel Clemens, or 'Mark Twain', who argued for a form of perpetual copyright, conditional on the issue of a cheap edition.

The government was reluctant to take any action on copyright which would stir up its already troubled relations with Canada. However, in 1908 the Berlin revision of the Berne Convention forced its hand. The enjoyment and exercise of rights under the Convention were no longer to be subject to any formality, and a minimum term of the author's life plus fifty years was agreed in principle.[46] Translation rights and rights to prevent dramatisation and novelisation were also agreed. These matters were not uncontentious in Britain, and, furthermore, if the Berlin revision was to be adopted, significant changes to domestic law would be required. Following discussions with the Board of

---

46 Until all states had adopted this period, however, term was to be regulated by the law of the country where protection was claimed, and could not exceed the term fixed in the country of origin.

Trade, representatives of the Society of Authors, the Musical Publishers' Association, the Publishers Association and the Copyright Association met in an attempt to agree a common policy. Eventually, all were willing to support the terms of the Berlin revision, the music publishers' concerns having been withdrawn for the sake of uniformity.[47] In 1909 Lord Gorell chaired a departmental committee which was appointed to advise on the legislative changes necessary to give effect to the Convention. The Gorell Report urged that British law should be made 'intelligible and systematic', and brought into line with that of other nations as far as was practicable. On almost all issues the committee recommended that the Convention's approach should be adopted, including the life plus fifty years term. The committee made no recommendation on colonial copyright, however, knowing that a conference of colonial representatives was imminent.

An Imperial Copyright Conference was held in 1910, to consider whether or not to ratify the Berlin Act, and, if so, how. The need for action was obvious to all. The South African delegate complained, 'At present, in the Colonies, we do not know what your law is; it is scattered through so many different Statutes.' George Askwith KC, Britain's delegate at the Berlin Conference, replied at once, 'We do not know either.'[48] Although the British government had been tremendously apprehensive, the Conference proved extremely constructive, helping to resolve the impasse which had blocked British legislation for decades, and outlining a new basis for constitutional relations regarding copyright. The shape of the 1911 Copyright Act owed much to the delegates' discussions. The Conference recommended that the Berlin Convention should be ratified by the Imperial government on behalf of the various parts of the Empire; and that reservations should be kept to a minimum. However, no ratification was to be made on behalf of a self-governing dominion until its assent had been received, and provision was to be made for the withdrawal of each dominion. There was thus an urgent need for a new and uniform copyright law throughout the Empire, and the conference recommended that an Imperial Act to provide for this should be passed. Again, the Act was not to extend to a self-governing dominion without a declaration from its legislature, and was to provide for a dominion's subsequent withdrawal.

These resolutions evidenced a strong measure of agreement, and so at last Imperial copyright law could move forward in the international arena. A bill was quickly introduced at the end of the 1910 Parliamentary session, with a

---

47 *Author*, July 1909.
48 The National Archives of England, Wales and the United Kingdom CO 886/4 item 4, p. 10. Askwith was then assistant secretary to the Board of Trade.

view to wide consultation both at home and in the colonies. G. H. Thring, Secretary of the Society of Authors, described it as 'more of a revolution than a codification'.[49] The interest groups set to work, and the Board of Trade dealt patiently with the representations, communications and deputations. When it reappeared in 1911 the bill was significantly redrafted to take account of them. There was nevertheless a good deal of opposition in the House of Commons. Several of those who supported the bill overall objected to the compulsory licence clause. This was the result of the Imperial Conference's desire to protect the public from possible abuses consequent on the fifty-year term. As enacted the clause provided that after twenty-five years (thirty years for subsisting copyright works), if a work was withheld from the public or published at too high a price, or if the reasonable requirements of the public as to supply were not satisfied, a licence might be granted to publish it. In the House of Lords there was real concern over the provision for deposit copies, with publishers complaining that everything would be demanded whether or not it was of any real use to libraries.[50] The bill nonetheless passed relatively unscathed.

The 1911 Copyright Act came into force on 1 July 1912, with ratification of the Berlin revision of the Berne Convention imminent. Although it accomplished the much-needed consolidation and codification of domestic law, there were inevitable limitations and compromises which somewhat qualified its achievements. In particular, the comparative independence given to the colonies would continue to cause problems.[51] Britain had been forced to acknowledge that arenas which she had previously regarded as her own by customary right – both in narrow terms of trade and in wider terms of political influence – were now fiercely contested. The British book trade and British authors had been compelled to adapt to an increasingly international environment. The process of acceptance was long and often difficult. The 1911 Act set Britain firmly within the new international context, but as one of many players, rather than the dominant one.

---

49 G. H. Thring, 'The Copyright Bill 1911', *Fortnightly Review* 89 (1911), pp. 901–10.
50 On deposit copies see the memorandum to the House of Lords from the Publishers Association: *Publishers' Circular* 18 November 1911. For the full story, and the correspondence, see Partridge, *The history of the legal deposit of books*, pp. 107–9.
51 For example, the 1911 Canadian Copyright Act, although conforming as much as possible to the Berlin requirements, incorporated restrictions inconsistent with Berne obligations which were intended to protect Canadian industry from aspects of American competition which Canada considered unfair.

6

Distribution

STEPHEN COLCLOUGH

'The wagon, the canal barge, the merchant vessel, the post office and the railroad may have influenced the history of literature more than one would suspect.'[1] This chapter looks at the ways in which books, newspapers and periodicals reached the reader during the period 1830–1914. As one member of the book trade noted, by 'making communication and carriage far cheaper and more rapid' changes in 'our railway and post-office systems' were having a profound effect upon the ways in which books were published, distributed and sold during the 1850s.[2] The development of the railway system, which was serving most of the great cities by the 1840s, was very important to the enlargement of the market for print and I look in some detail at those major wholesalers such as W. H. Smith & Son and John Menzies who exploited its potential both as a mode of distribution and as a venue for the sale of texts in the form of railway bookstalls. Several of the journalists who visited Smith's warehouse in the Strand during the 1860s and 1870s compared it to a factory. This metaphor seems apt for a period in which texts began to be produced on an industrial scale, but this chapter is also concerned with those other cultural middlemen, such as travelling salesmen, bookstall clerks, booksellers' assistants and newsboys, whose hard labour helped to shape this new phase in the communication circuit just as much as the new technologies of print and communication.

The middlemen of literature: wholesale, retail and rent, 1830–1880

The year 1852 was one of profound significance for British print culture. It was the year in which Charles Mudie's circulating library moved to its new Great Hall on Oxford Street, the publisher Cassell began his *Popular educator*,

---

1 Darnton, 'What is the history of books', p. 19. 2 Chapman, *Cheap books*, p. 52.

and the bookseller John Chapman aired his case in the pages of the *Westminster Review* in favour of wholesalers and retailers being able to determine the price at which they could retail books. Underselling, the retailing of new books below the advertised price, was attacked by many of the leading London publishers and booksellers during the early nineteenth century. In 1829 they 'formally agreed to drive the undersellers out of business by cutting off their supply of books' and the new Booksellers Association, founded in 1848, was dedicated to the same ends.[3] Chapman 'felt called upon to resist and expose' the workings of this 'combination of the London Booksellers and publishers' when they attempted to stop him selling 'American books at about 30 per cent lower than those previously current' early in 1852.[4] The subsequent campaign for a 'free trade in books' found widespread support and the Booksellers Association was dissolved after the arbitration committee headed by Lord Campbell found in favour of the abolitionists. No further steps were taken to regulate prices until the 1890s.

During the period 1830–52, 'underselling' was clearly widespread throughout much of the British Isles. This is suggested by the fact that neither the booksellers' protection associations nor the debate about their legality was confined to London. Before 1852 booksellers' associations operated in a number of large cities including Birmingham, Bristol, Edinburgh, Glasgow, Liverpool and Manchester. Although not all were identical, most adopted the regulation that the maximum discount that could be given to the public was 10 per cent from the announced published retail price. For example, the Glasgow Booksellers' Protection Association, formed in 1834, adopted this rule in 1835. Iain Beavan has demonstrated that during the early 1840s this association monitored local prices, threatened not to supply anyone discovered giving large discounts to the public, and discouraged retailers from giving orders to wholesalers who supplied the undersellers. At least one retailer, Charles Dewar of Falkirk, had his supply of books stopped when it was discovered that he was selling books 'at more than the acceptable level of discount'.[5] The Glasgow Association came to a temporary end in 1845 after a campaign by the Glasgow publisher and wholesaler John Joseph Griffin drew attention to the fact that its methods of coercion were illegal. Shortly before the Association's revival in August 1851 it was discovered that schoolbooks were being sold at a 25 per cent discount in some parts of Glasgow. These books were imported by Mullan, a Belfast-based supplier, who was also said to be having an impact upon the book trade in Greenock,

---

3 Altick, *The English common reader*, p. 304.   4 Chapman, *Cheap books*, p. 51.
5 Beavan, ' "What constitutes the crime which it is your pleasure to punish so mercilessly?" ', p. 74.

rather than any of the former members of the Association. As Beavan notes, this shows a perhaps unexpected insight into the nature of Irish–Scottish book trade relationships before 1852, but it also suggests that sale prices continued to be monitored and controlled even after the official Association had been dissolved.[6]

The various articles generated by the 'free trade in books' debate of 1852 provide perhaps the best insight into how the book trade operated at this time, as well as the ways in which new forms of distribution were helping to bring about the demand for cheaper books. As an article on 'the Makers, Sellers and Buyers of Books' that appeared in June 1852 argued, the public needed to understand 'the *modus operandi* of the book trade' if they were to participate in this debate. It noted that when a book was produced in London the publisher dealt with 'two classes of customer – the wholesale and the retail bookseller'. In order to entice these customers it was common for the publisher to offer his books to be 'subscribed'. This meant that an early copy was taken around to the main booksellers and wholesalers who agreed to take a certain number of copies. To encourage subscriptions the book would be offered at special 'trade' rates: 'some houses' gave '13 books as 12, with an addition of 25 as 24', others 'tempting their purchasers with 7 as $6\frac{1}{2}$ or 6'.[7] Chapman argued that sales of 25 as 24 were common and that this was in effect a '$33\frac{1}{3}$ per cent discount from the advertised price' of a book. Even single copies were often sold at a 25 per cent discount on subscription day.[8]

The trade was also offered cheap books when a publisher issued a sales catalogue. The author of 'Makers, sellers and buyers' used one of these catalogues to demonstrate that a few large wholesalers dominated the London trade. In this instance, the catalogue offering books at trade prices, 25 as 24, was 'sent round to seventy booksellers in London', of which seven were wholesalers and the remaining sixty-three retail booksellers. Only thirteen of the retail booksellers bought anything from this catalogue and, in all, their purchases came to less than £140, whereas the wholesale houses spent between £100 and £800 each because they were in the business of 'selling again to the retail trade'. The abolitionists argued that it was these wholesale houses, the 'middlemen' of literature, that benefited most from this system.[9]

---

6 Letter from David Robertson to Oliver & Boyd, 28 July 1851, quoted in Beavan, ' "What constitutes the crime which it is your pleasure to punish so mercilessly?" ', pp. 75–6; p. 82, note 19.
7 [Parker] 'The makers, sellers, and buyers of books', p. 722.　8 Chapman, *Cheap books*, p. 51.
9 'Makers, sellers, and buyers of books', p. 723.

Chapman argued that those firms that combined publishing with retailing and wholesaling reaped a particularly rich reward from the regulations that allowed no more than a 10 per cent discount to be passed on to the public because their ability to purchase books in vast quantities 'at the most advantageous prices' gave them control of both the country trade and the supply of 'Literary Institutions and Colleges'. Having purchased books at a 'discount... varying from 30 to 45 per cent' the major wholesalers were able to offer them to institutions 'at discounts of 10, 15, and 17$\frac{1}{2}$ per cent from the retail prices' and sometimes more. He gives an example of one unnamed firm belonging to the London Booksellers Association which was able to undercut a rival by offering 'a certain College' a 25 per cent discount and free carriage of the books from the capital.[10] The abolitionists argued that if each bookseller was allowed to give a discount of more than the stipulated 10 per cent, sales would increase and the smaller retailers would benefit from being able to place bigger orders. Those defending the status quo often quoted Samuel Johnson's argument that each of the 'many hands' through which a book passed before it reached the reader needed to 'retain' a part of the profits. The abolitionists countered that in 'these days of cheap carriage, 60 per cent for cost of production and 40 per cent porterage' was an 'anomalous division'.[11] Chapman argued that it was ridiculous to claim that it was 'still needful to allow to agents for the distribution of books the same large discounts which were necessary under conditions so widely different from those which now exist'. It was 'our railway and post-office systems making communication and carriage far cheaper and more rapid, and our improved modes of transacting business' that had brought about this fundamental change.[12]

One of the ways in which the post office system changed methods of distribution was the 'book post' set up in 1848 on the recommendation of Rowland Hill. The initial cost was sixpence per pound and only one unmarked book was allowed in each package, but this was soon relaxed in order to encourage the transmission of second-hand books, and in 1855 the charge was lowered to a penny for four ounces and fourpence for a pound. When it was extended to include circulars and newspapers in the following year the number of items being sent grew rapidly. By 1870 a book packet weighing two ounces could be sent for a halfpenny. In the same year the number of packets sent by the book and patten posts – the latter established in 1863 – was nearly 300 million

---

10 [Chapman] 'The commerce of literature', p. 541.
11 [Herbert Spencer] Letter to *The Times*, 5 April 1852, p. 6, quoted in Barnes, *Free trade in books*, p. 48. On the use of Johnson in this debate, see Barnes, *ibid.*, pp. 52–3.
12 *Cheap books*, p. 52.

per year.[13] L. M. Cullen has noted that the book post (which allowed packets of up to 5 lb to be sent) proved so effective in supplying Irish readers with books ordered direct from the publishers that it retarded the growth of book-selling at Smith's railway bookstalls until the last quarter of the century.[14] Speed was essential to the expansion of the newspaper trade, but publishers and wholesalers quickly adopted this new all-weather transport system. The Scottish publisher and wholesaler Bell & Bradfute, for example, sent orders to booksellers in Glasgow soon after the Edinburgh to Glasgow line opened in 1842. Bulk orders went to London via the various steamship companies that docked in the Leith. In January 1844 alone, Whitaker & Co. ordered 300 books to be sent 'as soon as convenient by steam' and a further 228 were sent to Simpkin presumably via the same route.[15]

Speed of distribution was important if the publisher was to make the most of the advertising campaign that usually accompanied the publication of a book or magazine. Such campaigns were particularly important to the success of any publication. In 1857 Bentley spent £63 7s 6d on advertising Trollope's *The three clerks* (1857), a novel which made £74 9s 7d of profit for its publisher in the first year.[16] Adverts were usually placed in a variety of magazines and newspapers and were often concerned with encouraging subscribers as much to borrow the text from a circulating library as to purchase it. The *Publishers' Circular* launched in 1837 provided an excellent way for the trade to communicate with itself about which texts were available and who was distributing them. In cases where copyright was shared between publishers in geographically distant locations, or in which a regional wholesaler handled the book, the latter placed advertisements in local periodicals. These advertisements usually informed the reader as to where the book could be purchased locally. Publishers and wholesalers also made use of advertising agencies, such as J. K. Johnston & Co. established in Dublin in 1819, who placed adverts in the local newspapers on their behalf. As an advertisement produced by W. H. Smith & Son after they took over Johnston in the 1850s makes clear, the advantage of using an agency was that they allowed the publisher to place adverts 'in all the Dublin and London Newspapers' using a single account.[17]

The transition to 'free trade in books' after the failure of the various booksellers' associations in 1852 appears to have made little impact upon the way

13 Robinson, *Britain's Post Office*, pp. 165, 194.   14 Cullen, *Eason & Son*, p. 83.
15 'Bell & Bradfute Office Correspondence and Accounts', NLS Manuscript Collections, Dep 317.
16 Sutherland, *Victorian novelists and publishers*, p. 14.
17 This advertisement is reproduced on the end pages of Cullen, *Eason & Son*.

in which publishers dealt with the trade. The surviving subscription lists issued by Richard Bentley in the 1860s suggest that in London the same few wholesalers continued to buy the majority of books published. For example, the subscription list for the third edition of Chermside's *Ned Locksley the Etonian* (1864) reveals that only three companies (Simpkin, Marshall; George Robertson; W. H. Smith & Son) bought more than a hundred copies of a text that was offered at a reduced subscription price, '13 as 12'. Bentley's lists show that it was large wholesalers and circulating libraries that benefited most from buying in bulk. Of the 942 copies of the volume of Dean Hook's *Lives of the Archbishops of Canterbury* subscribed for on 6 January 1864 (again '13 as 12'), almost four hundred went to Mudie's Select Library and 52 to W. H. Smith.[18]

In the 1870s Henry Curwen thought that Simpkin, Marshall & Co. typified the role played by the London wholesaler in the distribution of books and periodicals to the country, 'the colonies' and the 'smaller London' trade. According to Curwen, country booksellers were dependent upon one agent whose job it was to gather together 'the books and periodicals of all the London publishers'. Even in the 1870s, many orders from the 'smaller country booksellers' were sent out in a monthly parcel in order 'to save expense of frequent railway carriage' on what was traditionally known as 'magazine day'. Orders for books and magazines arrived at the wholesaler's by post, often only a few hours before they needed to be dispatched. Most periodicals were sent direct from the publisher to the wholesaler's warehouse(s). Simpkin, Marshall kept a large stock of books on the premises, usually bought at the trade price when the 'subscription' list was circulated around Paternoster Row, or for which they were the publishers. However, in order to fulfil some orders 'collectors' were sent out with a list of publications that needed to be bought from other publishers and wholesalers. The 'collector' usually paid for these goods in cash. A typical wholesale price for a 'cheap periodical' in the early 1870s was fourpence for a sixpenny title, the cost to the 'collector' being further reduced by selling thirteen copies to the dozen. Curwen estimated that on an average magazine day Simpkin, Marshall might send out something between six and eight hundred packages for distribution overnight by rail.[19]

Not all texts were distributed in this way. For more distant markets publishers sometimes dealt directly with a large wholesaler who acted as their 'agent' in that region. For example, during the 1830s and 1840s the Edinburgh wholesaler and retailer John Menzies acted as the main agent in Scotland for

18 British Library MS Add. 46672, 'Bentley Trade Subscription Lists, 1862–68', f. 6, ff. 12–13.
19 Curwen, *A history of booksellers*, pp. 412–20.

Chapman & Hall. This agency was clearly very important to Menzies's business and in November 1844 he informed R. Walker of Dundee that another, nameless, wholesaler had been 'trying to nibble at my agencies' by applying to sell *The chimes* to the 'country' trade, and had even gone as far as to add the title of Dickens's forthcoming work to 'their monthly list' without permission. This letter concludes with a statement confirming that this and 'all Chapman and Hall's other works' remained 'solely with me, for town and country' that was clearly intended to be passed on to other potential poachers as a warning.[20]

London was, of course, a particularly important site of text production, but book historians need to be wary about constructing a model in which the English capital produces and distributes while the rest of the nation consumes. During the 1840s and 1850s John Menzies regularly corresponded with the book trade in Manchester. In September 1845 he wrote to James Galt in Manchester asking him to deal with the distribution 'in your neighbourhood' of a periodical that he was 'publishing' with some success in Edinburgh.[21] Texts produced throughout the nation also came into London to be sold and London firms acted as wholesale agents for many different publishers located in the British Isles and abroad. For example, in 1832 the publishers and booksellers Houlston & Son, based in Paternoster Row, became agents for the Religious Tract and Book Society for Ireland. They took these publications at two-thirds of the retail price, eight copies free in every hundred, with a 10 per cent commission on the net amount of half-yearly sales plus another $2\frac{1}{2}$ per cent if they paid their accounts in cash. The stock was delivered 'free of expense' from the Society's London depository in Piccadilly. These texts were printed in Dublin and other agents listed on the imprint of their publications in the 1830s include James Nisbet & Co., London, and George Gallie, Glasgow. This evidence suggests Houlston were just one node in a print network that helped to distribute religious tracts throughout the nation.

Houlston did not only offer these texts for sale in London, however. During the early 1830s the firm's Mr Edwards took samples out to 105 booksellers in Kent and Sussex and it seems likely that he would have included religious tracts alongside Houlston's own mainly religious publications. Houlston's contract with the Religious Tract Society was formalised by their inclusion on the Society's imprints as one of the firms that 'sold' the tracts, but the majority of wholesale arrangements formulated during the period were entered into after publication and therefore do not appear as part of the imprint in this way.

20 John Menzies Archive, Edinburgh (hereafter JMA), Letter Book I, 14 November 1844, p. 15.
21 JMA, Letter Book I, 30 September 1845, p. 71.

Houlston's records also show that they sometimes entered into 'exchange' deals with other publishers of religious works. For example on 20 April 1833 they ordered '4 dozen 2s books' 'on exchange' from C. C. Wetton, a printer-bookseller in Egham, Surrey.[22] Such deals, in which booksellers exchanged printed materials worth the same amount, may well have been used when capital was in short supply or when a customer lacked creditworthiness, but publisher-wholesalers regularly entered into such agreements during the first half of the nineteenth century. The Edinburgh publishers and wholesalers Oliver & Boyd made 'exchange' agreements with a number of similar London firms, including Gale & Fenner, Law & Whittaker and Dean & Munday. These large orders, which were normally delivered by steam packets, show that books could move rapidly between the main metropolitan markets.[23]

The surviving correspondence and accounts of Bell & Bradfute provide a detailed picture of the way in which one city publisher-wholesaler functioned in the early 1840s. As well as dealing with large orders for the London trade they supplied booksellers in Aberdeen, Arbroath, Dumfries, Dundee, Glasgow, Inverness, Linlithgow, Melrose, Montrose and Stewarton via a range of different transport systems including the mail, local carriers and the railway. These were mainly orders for their own publications, but they also received requests for Bentley's Standard Novels at 'the lowest price you can supply' and instructions to 'commission' a copy of the *Athenaeum* to be sent by post to Robert Walker, a bookseller in Dundee.[24]

The workbooks of the Aberdeen publishers and wholesalers Lewis Smith & Son give some sense of how the trade worked during the 1880s and 1890s. For example, a locally produced book such as the Rev. J. Davidson's *The bass of Inverurie* (Aberdeen: Alexander Brown & Co., 1886), which sold for ninepence, was supplied wholesale at the price of 6s 9d per dozen, 13 as 12, with an extra 10 per cent discount being given to retailers who placed large orders. Lewis Smith regularly offered a 30 per cent wholesale discount to those who ordered more than a dozen copies and for their own publications it could be as much as 35 per cent. *The bass of Inverurie* achieved a very limited number of local orders, perhaps because it was only available on 'firm order'. Other books were offered on 'sale or return', which was a clear benefit to the retail trade, although it raises the question of what happened to the books once they were returned to the wholesaler. These terms allowed booksellers in Aberdeen and the surrounding

22 'Houlston and Wright, Booksellers and Publishers: Correspondence, Memoranda etc 1827–61', British Library MS Add. 45413.
23 Beavan, 'Bookselling'.
24 'Bell & Bradfute Office Correspondence and Accounts', January 1844.

areas to offer a discount to the consumer of up to 25 per cent, as long as they were prepared to take a very small profit. Very few of the retailers supplied by Smith were wholly dependent upon books for their income, however, and they tended to distribute small numbers of texts to several different shops located in the same town. With customers in Elgin and Keith to the north-east and Stonehaven in the south, the Lewis Smith workbooks show something of the geographical reach of a single firm at this time. Large orders from Menzies and other important firms in Edinburgh, Glasgow and London were also taken during this period, but are only occasionally noted in the workbooks, and it is likely that these companies placed mainly 'firm' orders rather than acquiring texts on 'sale or return'.[25]

The Lewis Smith workbooks deal mainly with small retailers in north-east Scotland, but it is clear that the majority of the larger publisher-wholesalers in the British Isles divided their business between the large, urban wholesalers and retailers, and a 'country trade' carefully built up over many years, in much this fashion. These companies also often produced texts with these different markets in mind. In his description of Heywood of Manchester as 'the largest newsvendors and booksellers out of London', Curwen noted that as well as being supplied five times a week by a 'special railway truck' from London 'with a freightage of about two tons', the firm produced some texts which were widely distributed whilst others were mainly purchased by a local audience. Heywood's *Railway guide* was available throughout the nation, whilst *Ben Brierley's journal*, which contained a good deal of local dialect writing, sold mainly in Lancashire.[26]

One way in which the wholesalers built up the kind of regional trade suggested by Curwen and revealed by the Lewis Smith workbooks was by sending out travellers. As already noted, Houlston's Mr Edwards had a circuit of some thirty towns during the 1830s. It was one of Oliver & Boyd's travellers who arranged the 'exchange' deals with the London firms, and they employed yet more to journey round Scotland and the north of England obtaining orders from local booksellers and shopkeepers. Although these small traders were sometimes difficult to deal with and often made small orders, they 'represented a large and ever-expanding market, and for those firms who could overcome the difficulties involved in dealing with what often seemed an unpredictable and inconvenient sector the rewards were potentially high'.[27] One of

25 Beavan, 'Working in the margins'.   26 Curwen, *The history of booksellers*, pp. 467–8.
27 Bell, ' "Pioneers of Literature" ', p. 130.

the largest wholesale houses of the 1830s, Whitaker & Co., employed two travellers to visit 'the leading towns in England and Wales, and the great towns in Ireland and Scotland' twice a year. Longman even took their chief traveller into partnership in the 1850s and the activities of Blackwood's Mr Roberts are frequently mentioned in the firm's correspondence during the 1860s.[28]

Developments in the postal system after 1840 encouraged publishers and wholesalers to invest in other methods of making their goods known. As noted in the introduction to the 1872 edition of a Post Office directory to the print trade, unlike 'the old system of appeals by travellers' the circular could be 'addressed promptly and cheaply'.[29] Many publishers and wholesalers included bundles of prospectuses in parcels as they were dispatched, and advertisements, catalogues and samples could also be sent directly to the bookseller to encourage orders. In 1844 John Menzies began to issue a catalogue of all the texts that he supplied, and it is clear from his correspondence that this was a common practice amongst Scottish wholesalers at this time. During the 1850s Hodson's 'Booksellers' Communications Agency' offered to send out regular packages of 'bills, catalogues [and] specimens of new works' from London to the country trade for a fee of ten shillings per year.[30] This attempt to keep booksellers in touch with the London publishers appears to have failed, however, and it is clear that for many publishers and wholesalers the travelling salesman continued to play an important role in securing orders. The traveller was particularly important to firms that dealt in books with fine bindings, such as school reward books, which needed to be seen by the retailer. During the 1870s, James Askew of Preston, whose business dealt mainly in prize books for schools, employed a traveller to journey as far as south Wales.[31] Perhaps more significantly, as a 'handbook of practical hints for the apprentice and bookseller' published in the 1890s makes clear, the publisher's traveller was much more difficult to ignore than a circular or catalogue. This volume warned the retailer to be wary of a figure whose persuasive tongue might lead to the purchase of too much stock.[32]

In 1864 Simpkin, Marshall subscribed for 208 copies of Hook's *Lives* from Bentley, but the large numbers ordered by Smith & Son and Mudie's Select Library say something about the nature of book distribution during the mid-Victorian period. W. H. Smith had taken over the bookstalls on the London and North Western Railway (LNWR) in November 1848 and as

28 *Hodson's Booksellers, publishers and stationers directory* 1855, pp. vii–ix; Finkelstein, *The house of Blackwood*, pp. 45–6.
29 Quoted in *Hodson's*, p. ix.   30 *Hodson's*, p. vii.   31 Turner, 'Books for prizes'.
32 Growoll, *The profession of bookselling*, pp. 41–7.

James Barnes has argued these stalls very quickly 'came to be regarded as alternative and expanding markets for the existing system of retail distribution'. Single-volume reprints became the stock in trade of the bookstalls. Routledge's Railway Library was launched in the same year that W. H. Smith began to rent the bookstalls and Bentley's Standard Novels 'were offered to Smith in 1850 at lower wholesale prices'.[33] One of the first stalls opened by John Menzies at Stirling in 1857 was stocked with 575 books at a total cost of £59 8s. Most were priced between 1s and 1s 6d and they included a selection of volumes from the Railway Library series. In the same year, the *Saturday Review* noted that the stock at the majority of Smith's stalls sold for less than half a crown.[34] Single-volume reprints were clearly well suited to an audience on the move, and the colourful covers of mid-Victorian yellowbacks were designed to catch the eye of the passer-by. An eighteen-penny edition of Scott's *Waverley novels* could sell 'as many' as two hundred copies a month, but the *Saturday Review* was alarmed that texts in which more time seemed to have been spent on the 'external decorations' than the contents could sell as many as '4,000 copies at Smith's stalls alone'. However, railway bookstalls did not only stock 'fast', cheap literature. Other, more expensive books were also usually available. Menzies's Stirling stall included devotional works such as Robert Candlish's *Scripture characters* (1857), and Robert Ballantyne's guide to the New World, *Hudson's Bay* (1848), probably in a new five-shilling edition. The importance to Smith's stalls of these relatively cheap, usually single-volume reprints is confirmed by the fact that from 1862 they used the imprint of Chapman & Hall to publish their own series, the Select Library of Fiction, which included reprints by popular contemporary authors such as Bulwer-Lytton, Charles Lever and Sheridan Le Fanu.[35]

Richard Altick has argued that by placing books 'in the main-travelled roads of Victorian life' railway bookstalls played a very important role in spreading the habit of reading.[36] As a multiple-outlet retail network they were certainly one of the most innovative methods of book distribution to emerge during the nineteenth century. How did the railway bookstall business develop and what was it like before the arrival of W. H. Smith in the late 1840s? As early as 1839 there were two men and four children involved in selling newspapers at Lime Street Station, Liverpool, but 'no space was reserved for them' and they simply

---

33 Barnes, *Free trade in books*, p. 106.
34 JMA, 'Accounts for Stirling, Bridge of Allan and Dundee, 1857–8'; 'Railroad bookselling', *Saturday Review* 31 January 1857, pp. 100–2.
35 Colclough, 'J. Sheridan le Fanu and the "Select Library of Fiction"'.
36 Altick, *The English common reader*, p. 305.

moved up and down the platform.[37] William Marshall's bid to run the stalls at Euston Station records that he had opened a bookstall at the Fenchurch Street station of the London and Blackwall Railway in August 1841, and Bradshaw & Bradlock of Manchester claimed to be 'amongst the first, if not the first, to begin the sale of books &c at the stations'. The form on which this and other bids for bookstall rights were submitted to the LNWR in August 1848 included a list of 'conditions' that give some sense of the way in which the railway business operated both before and after W. H. Smith took over. Each candidate was instructed to contract for twelve months, to pay rent monthly, and to obey the instructions of the stationmaster when working from the platform. Clause four noted that 'books and periodicals' were only to be sold at those stations 'where there are stalls', whilst the 'adequate supply of newspapers' was needed at each location. This suggests that a mixture of permanent stalls and peripatetic newsvendors (similar to those found at Liverpool in 1839) served the LNWR line between London and Manchester.[38]

During the 1850s W. H. Smith held contracts with numerous other railway companies, including the Great Northern, and owned stalls in England, Ireland, Wales and Scotland, although the 'privilege of selling newspapers etc at the Edinburgh station' granted in 1851 came to an end six years later.[39] Exactly how W. H. Smith worked these lines is difficult to reconstruct from the surviving evidence. The letter books of John Menzies, however, reveal a great deal of detail about the way in which the Scottish bookstall system operated during the 1850s and 1860s. Like W. H. Smith, Menzies supplied many of the individual bookstalls before he took over the line, including those at Stirling, Bridge of Allan, Perth, Aberdeen and Inverness managed by James Henderson of Glasgow. On 15 May 1857 Menzies took over Henderson's business on the Scottish Central Railway (SCR) and in the following year erected new stalls on the Edinburgh, Perth and Dundee (EPD) line, including one in the 'Ladies Waiting Room' at Waverley Station in Edinburgh.[40] The contract with the EPD gave Menzies the right to sell books and newspapers at all of the stations on the line, excluding those already covered by the SCR contract, and to erect bookstalls at Kirkcaldy, Thornton, Dunfermline, Ladybank, Leuchars and Scotland Street, Edinburgh. This contract makes clear that during the late 1850s Menzies combined sales on the platform or train by peripatetic newsboys with a limited number of permanent stalls. It included passes which allowed

---

37 Simmons, *The Victorian railway*, p. 245.
38 All of the surviving bids are contained in Rail 410/873, National Archives, Kew (hereafter NA).
39 WHSA, A23: Railway Ledger; WHSA, A222/79.
40 JMA, Letter Book II, p. 214; Letter Book III, p. 656.

two boys the use of the ferries across the Firth of Forth and the Tay and to move freely 'between station and station'.[41] By the early 1860s boys working for Menzies were dressed in a uniform that included a blue cap with a red band in order to distinguish them from unlicensed rivals who tried to poach their trade. The first stalls erected by Menzies tended to be at major junctions, such as Thornton, or in large towns, because it was only in such large or busy locations that they were profitable. He complained bitterly when the terminus at Dunkeld was excluded from his contract with the Scottish North Eastern (SNER) in 1858, but as with W. H. Smith's early contracts, the income generated by the stalls was probably less important than that created by the boys travelling between stations.[42]

As Smith's bookstalls business expanded during the 1850s and 1860s each contract was carefully negotiated. During the 1850s, many of those with smaller companies such as the East Kent and the East Lancashire included 'free carriage of newspapers and books' to the stalls, but by the 1860s an additional fee was usually paid for carriage. For example, in 1860 W. H. Smith agreed to pay the South Eastern Railway £100 for the bookstalls and £300 for carriage. Subsequently this was changed to a fee of two shillings per cwt, paid weekly.[43] The agreement for bookstall privileges drawn up between W. H. Smith, the LNWR and the Great Western in December 1866 is fairly typical of a contract that allowed the distributor 'free transport' of 'any newspapers, books, pamphlets, periodicals, prints, stationery, caps, [and] wrappers' as long as they were 'offered for sale' on the platforms.[44] This list reveals that the mid-Victorian bookstall sold more than books and newspapers and it goes on to include 'advertisements, announcements, handbills, placards, [and] frames'.

Smith's first began advertising at stations in 1851, and the various agreements that they entered into with other companies suggest that the revenue derived from advertising was particularly important to their success as distributors. Their Railway Advertising Department was formed in 1854 to administer nine contracts, and its turnover showed an almost continual increase over the following decades.[45] Throughout the 1870s railway advertising was often the second most valuable account (after 'trade') in the company's lists of 'Assets'. By 1880 fifty-eight contracts accounted for an annual turnover of over £110,000.[46] In Ireland, as the number of bookstalls increased in the 1870s,

41 JMA, 'Minute of a lease between the EPD and John Menzies, 25 May 1858'.
42 JMA, Letter Book III, p. 322; Letter Book II, p. 413.   43 WHSA A23: Railway Ledger.
44 NA, Rail 404/124, 'The London and North Western and Great Western Railway Companies and Messrs W. H. Smith & Son grant of the right to vend books &c . . . 31 December 1866'.
45 WHSA A78/2: Railway advertising receipts 1854–1917.
46 WHSA, X108: Annual accounts, 1867–77.

advertising orders rose from £2,273 in 1869 to £4,538 in 1875.[47] During the 1850s any company that wanted to place a single advertising board at each of the 188 stations of the LNWR, which controlled the major passenger routes to Manchester and Liverpool and through north Wales to Holyhead, was charged between £75 and £125 according to the size of advertisement they required. A single advert at Euston was £5 15s 6d, whereas those at other large stations, such as Liverpool, cost £4 4s.[48] Advertising became an essential part of the experience of travelling by train. Willing's agreement with the Metropolitan gave him the right to put posters on nine particularly prominent railway arches.[49] Most railway advertising was, however, much less spectacular. During the 1850s and 1860s Smith's sold their customers space at a maximum of 33 × 22 inches including the frame.[50]

During the 1860s and 1870s Smith's rapid expansion continued and they increased the number of stalls that they owned from 167 in 1861 to 385 in 1874.[51] Menzies's expansion in Scotland was not as rapid, however. By the early 1860s they held contracts with five railway companies – the EPD, the Dundee and Arbroath, the SNER, the North British Railway (NBR) and the SCR – but controlled only a handful of stalls outside Edinburgh (Aberdeen, Bridge of Allan, Callander, Dundee, Leuchars, Perth, Stirling and Thornton). Menzies's total turnover increased from £25,397 to £42,053 between 1858 and 1862, but that at the stalls was still only worth £3,637. Total profit at the stalls was less than £400 in 1862, although the recently acquired NBR bookstall at Edinburgh Waverley was already showing a healthy return.[52] During the early 1860s most of the Scottish rail companies attempted to replace 'free carriage' with a set fee 'for the conveyance of parcels'. For example, when Menzies renewed the contract with the SCR in 1863 it included a charge of £50 for parcels.[53] After the amalgamated EPD and the NBR rejected Menzies's offer of £60 (including carriage) to continue as holder of the bookstalls north of Edinburgh, a new contract was drawn up with the Edinburgh bookseller David Mather.[54] Mather's stalls were located in Princes Street, Scotland Street, North Leith and Thornton, and he agreed to sell newspapers on trains between Edinburgh and North Leith, Burntisland and Thornton Junction, as well as on the Tay Ferry. Menzies's business subsequently expanded westwards, with

47 Cullen, *Eason & Son*, p. 89.   48 WHSA, 244/1: LNWR railway advertisements.
49 NA, Rail 252/356: GWR tenants agreement No. 67: The Great Western and Metropolitan Railway Companies and Mr James Willing . . . 27 December 1867.
50 WHSA, 244/1–3.   51 WHSA, 248/2; WHSA x108.
52 JMA, 'Memorandum book, accounts 1851–7, 1833–62'.   53 JMA, Letter Book IV, p. 342.
54 NAS, br/nbr/3/2, 'Agreement between NBR and David Mather', 25 May 1864.

a new 'Glasgow branch' opening in 1867, but even in 1878 they only owned twenty-one stalls in all, and although they now stretched from Aberdeen in the north to Carlisle in the south, the majority were close to Glasgow. In 1877–8 they were worth just £21,828 out of a total turnover of £130,429.[55] All of this evidence suggests that profit margins at the bookstalls remained quite low during the mid-Victorian period, but when run by large wholesalers like Menzies and W. H. Smith they became an important node in the text distribution system.

Most libraries founded after Mudie's attempted to replicate his famous subscription rate of one guinea for one volume at a time. As Bentley's subscription lists attest, Mudie's and Smith's purchased books in large numbers. An 1857 advert for the Select Library boasted that 90,000 volumes were being added to the stock each year and between January 1858 and October 1859 a further 391,000 volumes were acquired. To give some idea of the scale of these operations, the total stock of Westerton's Library on Hyde Park Corner in London was 120,000 books.[56] In 1858 Mudie's adverts declared that the library held 3,250 copies of Livingstone's *Travels in Africa*, 2,000 copies of *Tom Brown's schooldays*, and more than 1,000 copies each of twenty-three other new titles, and it was claimed that 'fresh copies' were 'added as frequently as subscribers' required them.[57] Almost all circulating libraries struggled to supply the books most in demand and subscribers were often asked to provide a list of alternative titles in case their first choice was not available. The Select Library's ability to supply customers with copies of the books they most wanted helped it to attract large numbers of subscribers.

Although publishers were beginning to speed up the issue of (relatively) cheap single-volume editions of texts by the early 1860s, these still often took up to a year to appear. The widespread availability of cheap second-hand copies of recently published books was a by-product of the competition for subscribers between the great commercial libraries and must have been a boon to the reader. Because the sale of books was particularly important to W. H. Smith, the bookstall clerks were instructed to display them 'prominently'. After 1865 even those copies that had not yet been in circulation could be bought 'at a discount of *not more* than 25 per cent (3d in the shilling) off the *retail price*'.[58] Perhaps most importantly, these books were available to any member of the

55 JMA, JM22: 'Ledgers, January 1877–October 1881'.
56 Finkelstein, ' "The secret" '; Advertisement in the *Critic* 15 April 1858, p. 170.
57 Advertisement in the *Critic* 1 April 1858, p. 148.   58 WHSA, General Rules: 1868, p. 2.

public visiting the stalls and not just to subscribers. During the period 1860–1914, many readers must have owned books that had once belonged to these famous libraries because, as Simon Eliot has argued, at Smith's Library 'there was never a time' during the twenty-four years between 1876 and 1900 'when bookselling was not bailing out book borrowing'. Smith's and Mudie's are well known for the role they played in killing off the three-volume novel as a commercially viable form in 1894, a year in which Smith's Library entered the red for the first time in a decade.[59] As the head of their library department made clear in an interview given in 1891, the libraries were opposed to the triple-decker because surplus copies were harder and less profitable to resell:

> Books of a more solid character than the average three-volume novel remain in demand for a much longer time; and when the surplus copies are disposed of, they realize a much larger proportion of the original cost. Messrs W. H. Smith & Son issue at regular intervals a catalogue of surplus library books, and there you may see that whilst the ordinary three-volume novel is offered for three shillings, the average charge for other works is about a third instead of a tenth of the published price.[60]

The circulating library remained an important feature of Smith's stalls – and later shops – throughout the period 1860–1914. Given that it usually only contributed a small amount to the company's total profits – and sometimes returned a loss – it is clear that it was seen as a way of attracting more customers to its key retail sites.

How were subscribers to the commercial circulating libraries supplied with their books? Romantic period libraries based in the West End of London often informed their wealthiest customers that they could be sent books even when they were 'domiciled in their country houses'. Henry Colburn, for example, guaranteed to send books '(in Boxes) to all parts of the kingdom' during the 1810s.[61] Mudie expanded this service, taking advantage of advances in the transport system. In the late 1850s members of his London Book Society paid two guineas per annum for '3 vols at one time' to be delivered to their homes 'by Library messengers' who called once a week. 'Country Subscribers' paid two guineas for four volumes and five guineas for fifteen volumes. The opening of 'branch establishments' at Manchester and Birmingham allowed subscribers who called at these branches to pay the usual 'town' subscription rates, rather than the 'country' rate, thus cheapening access for some provincial readers. However, all of Mudie's customers had to defray the 'cost of carriage

59 Eliot, 'Bookselling by the backdoor', p. 160.   60 May, 'W. H. Smith's & Son's', pp. 167–8.
61 Skelton-Foord, 'Economics, expertise, enterprise', p. 138.

to and from the Library ... at the time of each exchange'. By contrast, Smith's 'Country Bookstall' subscribers paid five guineas for twelve books, but their parcels were delivered 'carriage free' to the nearest stall. In other words Smith's country subscribers received fewer books for their money, but as long as they were prepared to pick up their order from the local railway station they did not have to use the book post to receive and return their books. The same 'carriage free' rules applied to subscribers calling for their books at 186 The Strand or the London railway stations.[62] As the author of an article on Smith's that appeared in the 1890s noted, the only real difference between the two great libraries of the Victorian period was the way in which they 'conveyed' books to their subscribers.[63] To echo Chapman, both of these libraries took advantage of the ways in which the 'railway and post-office systems' were 'making communication and carriage far cheaper and more rapid'.

Both Mudie's and Smith's had special rates for the supply of book clubs, reading societies and other libraries. Throughout the nineteenth century many bookshops contained a collection of books for rent. For example, when F. W. G. Russell purchased a joint bookselling and stationery business in Elgin, north-east Scotland, in 1851, he decided to extend its library provision. Opened in 1852, it was run 'in connection with an extensive London library', which was later identified as Mudie's. Russell charged 12s 6d to subscribe to his 'Popular Circulating Library' and thirty shillings to join his 'First Class Library', which probably consisted of books delivered from Mudie's at the end of each month. This link with Mudie was important to the development of Russell's library business and when he took over the original Elgin Circulating Library in 1855 he again offered books from Mudie's. As Jane Thomas has argued, by 1870 'the books received from Mudie's had become the main element of the town's library provision'.[64] Not everyone was reliant upon Smith's and Mudie's, of course. The Reading publisher, printer, bookbinder and bookseller George Lovejoy ran 'The Southern Counties Library' from the same premises on London Street that he used to sell 'old books, foreign books', newspapers, stationery, and 'fire and life insurance'. In 1868 the library boasted 67,000 volumes 'in every department of literature'. A 'first class' subscription of ten guineas for the year entitled customers to borrow fifty volumes ('thirty new and twenty old') and gave them 'the immediate perusal of all new publications'. He particularly encouraged 'book societies and literary institutions' to join this class. All customers were supplied 'by the New Postal Regulations'

62 Colclough, ' "A larger outlay" ', p. 71.
63 Preston, 'Messrs W. H. Smith and Son's bookstalls and library'.
64 Thomas, ' "Forging the literary tastes..." ', pp. 108–11.

which allowed books to be 'sent to all parts of the kingdom at a cost of six-pence'. As with Mudie's, the 'expenses of carriage' were to be 'defrayed by the subscriber'.[65] The large number of books in Lovejoy's collection suggests that it was possible to run a successful circulating library outside London by using the 'New Postal Regulations' to supply customers.

James Barnes has noted that during the nineteenth century it was often argued that price competition, 'free trade' in books, had reduced the number of shops that sold only books because the trade had 'become so profitless'. Writing in 1868, Alexander Macmillan insisted that bookselling was now often the 'appendage' to another business.[66] However, as both recent research on trade directories and the 'free trade' dispute of the 1850s attest, the shop that specialised only in books was a relatively rare phenomenon even before 1852. Lovejoy's business in Reading suggests that it was possible for some towns to support large establishments that sold and rented books, whilst offering other services such as selling insurance as a sideline, but it is probably true that throughout the period 1830–1914 most booksellers continued to deal in a range of other goods, especially stationery and patent medicines. During the early 1830s Houlston & Son sold printing ink produced by Wilkin of Norwich from their shop in Paternoster Row; during the 1860s the pages of the *Publishers' Circular* were filled with advertisements by those wanting to work for or to purchase a 'booksellers & stationers', and the high street shops developed by W. H. Smith in the early years of the twentieth century sold a similar range of goods.[67] However, more research needs to be done on how these businesses operated and what it was like to experience them as a customer.

In the late 1850s William Harper took over the second-hand bookshop established by Andrew Clark in City Road, near London's Old Street, in the 1840s. In 1860 he moved to new premises in nearby Tabernacle Walk. A few surviving catalogues and letters show how a small business of this sort operated. Harper appears to have sent out his catalogue each month to regular customers who sent in their orders by post, paying for the cost of the book and its postage once their order was received. Books were forwarded to 'all parts of the United Kingdom at one penny the quarter pound; two pence the half pound; or four pence the pound; and two pence each extra pound'. Surviving orders show that

65 *Southern Counties Library: an index to the catalogue of George Lovejoy's General Subscription Circulating Library, London Street, Reading*, Reading University Archives.

66 Barnes, *Free trade in books*, pp. 165–6.

67 The British Book Trade Index, which covers the period up to 1850, includes much information on the range of services offered in conjunction with bookselling.

he sent out books to Oxfordshire, Yorkshire and Scotland as well as to other parts of London. Most of these orders were for books costing between one and three shillings each, some antique, others only a few years old. Harper also clearly catered for passing trade. A photograph of his shop taken in the 1880s shows the proprietor standing in front of an impressive window display with hand-written notices advertising copies of 'The Literary Gazette' and 'Songs'. On the window ledge, exposed to the street, are a number of books and a box marked '2d each'.[68]

Some direct evidence of the street trade has survived. The autobiographical writings and account books of the working-class Manchester bookseller James Weatherley show that he learnt his trade on the streets, where his first bookstall (located near to the busy Exchange) sold second-hand books, music sheets and prints. His stock was acquired from private sellers, local auctions and shops as well as from the travellers sent out by London booksellers. Weatherley was successful enough at this business that he went on to rent a cellar as a store, with a bookstall on the pavement, sheltered from the elements by a set of stairs. This allowed him to display between 1,800 and 2,000 volumes on the street. Even when he worked out of a shop during the early 1830s, he spent up to a quarter of the year selling books on the streets of Liverpool. Many of Weatherley's contemporaries left little or no mark on the historical record. Peripatetic stalls were not listed in trade directories and the men and women who worked them rarely became wealthy enough to establish more permanent businesses. Weatherley's memoirs suggest that he supplied a range of customers, including members of the clergy, but the main beneficiaries of these stalls were those working-class readers who found it difficult to afford books from other sources.[69]

Much of the printed material available in the nineteenth century was not distributed through the official channels of wholesale and retail. Other street sellers of literature included hawkers, chapmen and ballad singers, although their importance as distributors was clearly in decline from the 1850s onwards. Henry Mayhew noted that many different 'wandering "paper-workers"' inhabited the streets of London in the early 1850s, including those 'running patterers or flying stationers' who spent their time 'engaged in vending last dying speeches and confessions – in hawking "second editions" of newspapers – or else in "working" . . . what are technically termed "cocks" ', that is salacious accounts of fictional events, which the patterer implied had taken place locally.

---

68 'William Harper, Bookseller, Shoreditch, London: Catalogues, Orders, Photographs and Correspondence', Hackney Archives, GB/NNAF/B21733.
69 Powell and Wyke, 'Penny capitalism in the Manchester book trade'.

These sellers were constantly on the move as they announced their wares, whilst those engaged in 'board work' took up a permanent pitch at street corners 'with a large pictorial placard raised upon a pole' advertising the contents of the pamphlets that they sold. Other street vendors specialised in stationery, 'almanacs, pocket-books, memorandum and account books', race cards, 'odd numbers of periodicals or broadsheets', and postcards. They sold images of the capital itself – a particularly popular tourist destination in the year of the Great Exhibition. London's theatres also provided customers for those selling playbills and programmes.[70] Most major cities would have enjoyed a similar range of street sellers. What is most remarkable about Mayhew's account is the sheer variety of printed objects, both new and second-hand, that were available on the streets. Mayhew also throws some light onto the seedier side of the street trade, which included the sale of pornography or 'secret papers' by women 'busking' in bars and taverns. He also took note of a relatively new site for the sale of newspapers – the railway bookstall – which he noted served mainly wealthy customers who were prepared to pay a premium of an extra penny on the cost of their daily newspaper.[71]

The 'modern Mercury': newspaper distribution, 1830–1914

In the early nineteenth century Britain enjoyed a good postal service and the mail coaches transported huge numbers of newspapers, especially after 1825 when an Act of Parliament made it legal for *all* stamped newspapers to pass through the post without further payment. In London most publishers and wholesale newsagents supplied newspaper subscribers using the night mail coaches, which left London at about 8.00 p.m. This meant that any newspaper printed that morning was already roughly twelve hours old when it left the capital. As *Once a Week* argued in 1861, 'little more than a quarter century ago . . . the "Times" in the north was fresh two days after date'.[72] Several London newsagents, including W. H. Smith and William Lewer, who were both based on the Strand close to the newspaper offices, recognised that the new fast 'day coach' service that had come into operation during the 1820s offered an alternative to the free mail coach. By collecting the newspapers from the printers and driving them rapidly to their warehouses for packing and addressing, W. H. Smith and Lewer could get the newspapers onto the various

---

70 Mayhew, *London labour and the London poor*, ed. Neuberg, pp. 103–6.   71 *Ibid.*, pp. 105, 107.
72 'Our modern Mercury', *Once a Week* 2 February 1861, p. 160.

coaches that left for the provinces from local inns early in the morning. During the 1820s and 1830s Smith made particular use of coaches to Bath, Birmingham, Brighton, Bristol, Carlisle, Dover, Leeds, Newcastle, Portsmouth, Salisbury, Shrewsbury and York, as well as Holyhead in north Wales (with its connection to Ireland), and Aberdeen, Edinburgh and Glasgow in Scotland. In 1832 Lewer advertised his ability to send *The Times* 'by morning coaches' to Birmingham, Manchester and the north, with important political news forwarded by an express service if necessary. From the late 1820s onwards, W. H. Smith I (1792–1865) placed regular advertisements in *The Times* that drew the reader's attention to his firm's use of '*special express*' coaches to supply political news to the provinces.[73] Subscribers were willing to pay a little extra for the earlier arrival of their newspapers and Smith usually charged a quarterly fee that included delivery.

The Coach Book kept by Smith in the early 1840s reveals that he dealt with five main types of customer: private subscribers, newsrooms, reading societies, newsagents and booksellers. That a single page of the section of the Coach Book dealing with orders for the *Advertiser* includes newsrooms in Sheffield, Glasgow, Leeds, Carlisle, Halifax and Greenock shows just how important this sort of customer was to Smith's business in the second quarter of the nineteenth century. In a series of letters sent to his son, W. H. Smith II (1825–91), in the winter of 1841–2 he noted that although there had been 'no increase of Agencies' a new newsroom in Glasgow which took fourteen papers a day had been added to the business.[74] Most reading institutions took a relatively small number of texts. The Commercial News Room in Sheffield, for example, took five copies of *The Times*, seven *Morning Chronicles*, four *Heralds*, two *Morning Posts* and three weekly papers. Many others, including the Mechanics' Institute in Ipswich, took only single copies of one or two titles.[75] Throughout the nineteenth and into the twentieth century texts were often consumed communally, but, as Alan J. Lee has argued, there was something distinctly different about the way in which newspapers were consumed before the arrival of the penny press in the 1840s and 1850s. Private consumption was reserved for the affluent. When delivery was included in the price many daily newspapers were being sold for the equivalent of sevenpence or eightpence per copy in the 1820s and 1830s.[76]

Newsrooms were not necessarily cheap, however. In January 1830 the *Westminster Review* remarked on the fact that 'every large' and 'almost every small

73 Wilson, *First with the news*, pp. 44–5.   74 WHSA, HMs D/12–13.   75 WHSA A.16: Coach Book.
76 Lee, *The origins of the popular press*, pp. 35–7. See also Barker, *Newspapers, politics and English society*, pp. 57–8.

town in England, and several in Ireland' had subscription reading rooms that supplied 'all the leading London papers' to those willing 'to pay a guinea or so annually'. It went on to note that despite the reach of the London papers via this system of distribution – and the *Review* thought the local press disadvantaged by the newspaper stamp – the British Isles had a healthy provincial newspaper press that was typified by papers such as the *Leeds Mercury* and the *Manchester Guardian*.[77] Most of these newspapers were published weekly and employed three main methods of distribution: 'free' via the postal system, 'by agents in neighbouring towns or by newsmen employed directly by the paper', and by sales over the counter at the newspaper office.[78] The *Westminster* argued that the expense of distributing a 'middle-sized country paper once a week' was greater than for a London weekly, 'because newspaper carriers are sent at the charge of the office to the different small towns and villages, to which there is no post provision, or one too tardy for the interests of the employer'.[79] During the 1830s and 1840s about half the total sale of the *Manchester Guardian* was effected using the newspaper's own newsmen and shop, although as circulation figures increased the proportion sold in the shop 'dropped from 10 or 11 per cent of the total circulation in 1830 to about 5 or 6 per cent in 1845'.[80] As Hannah Barker has argued, from the late eighteenth century onwards a good distribution system that encompassed the surrounding area was vital to the survival of any provincial newspaper, and she gives the example of the *Salopian Journal*, which 'employed five newsmen to deliver the paper to towns up to 50 miles away'.[81]

During the early nineteenth century 'the postal service enabled publishers to reach readers in the previously less accessible rural areas, but only in so far as clear and long-term lines of distribution had been established'.[82] In Wales during the 1830s individual agents painstakingly built up distribution networks for local newspapers by creating lists of subscribers. For example, the account book of the distributor of *Y Gwladgarwr* in Trefriw, Robert Evans, included 148 names. Later in the century some newspapers, such as *Y Papur Newydd Cymraeg*, encouraged the creation of these networks by paying agents like Evans threepence for every new subscriber added to the list. Most of these local retailers were not full-time newsvendors, but used newspaper sales to

77 [Merle] 'Provincial newspaper press', pp. 69–70.
78 When the *Manchester Guardian* was launched in 1825, fourpence out of the sevenpence cover price went in stamp duty. Ayerst, *Guardian*, pp. 82–3.
79 [Merle] 'Provincial newspaper press', p. 79.   80 Ayerst, *Guardian*, p. 83.
81 Barker, *Newspapers, politics and English society*, p. 41.
82 Jones, 'Constructing the readership', p. 155.

supplement their income from other retail activities. In the 1870s the *Carmarthen Express* used grocers, chemists, builders and drapers as agents. Other distribution networks were constructed on a voluntary basis. Religious papers were often distributed via chapels. Even as late as 1864, 30 per cent of the Baptist *Seren Gomer* (Star of Gomer) distributors were Baptist ministers, although others included colliers, quarrymen, tailors, chandlers, ironworkers, saddlers, grocers, chemists, booksellers and, more surprisingly, five publicans. Publishers often took advantage of such free distribution systems, but, as Jones argues, they also operated as social networks binding together relatively small groups of like-minded readers. Fourteen railways had been completed in Wales by 1850, including the Chester to Holyhead line, which connected north Wales with the major urban centres in the north-west of England. Further expansion throughout the 1860s helped supplant the more informal networks of distribution that had been built up in the 1830s and 1840s.[83] The *Wrexham Guardian*, which had built up a distribution network that supplied several towns in north-west England and northern Wales, began to use Smith's bookstalls from the 1870s onwards.[84]

W. H. Smith had begun negotiations for the transmission of newspapers by train from Birmingham to Manchester and Liverpool as early as 1838. As the rail network expanded throughout the 1840s, however, the business relied on a mixture of coach and railway transport. An 1842 letter from W. H. Smith II to his father reveals how other firms had also begun to use the rail to deliver newspapers where available. He noted that a bookseller in Bridgwater was advertising that he 'received *The Times* daily at one (or two) o'clock'. These papers were sent from London on the 8.00 a.m. train by F. C. Westley (who advertised this service in *The Times*), in the same package as 'about a dozen papers' destined for 'Mr May of Taunton'. Smith concluded this letter with a reference to the fact that the railway was due to reach Taunton some three months later – 'thus saving another hour' – and that Westley would be foolish not to exploit this new link in the national chain.[85] Unfortunately, there does not appear to be any material in the Smith archive that demonstrates how they actually combined rail and coach distribution during the 1840s, but by the time Smith junior had joined the business in 1845 organising 'Special Express Engines' to Birmingham, Liverpool and Manchester was a regular part of his job.[86]

---

83 *Ibid.*, p. 156.   84 Peters, 'Distributing Wrexham's newspapers, 1850–1900'.
85 WHSA, Hambledon MS D/36.   86 WHSA, Hambledon MS H20.

According to Smith's coach and letter books they were supplying texts to a number of large provincial wholesalers, including Horsfall in Coventry and Wilmer & Smith in Liverpool, during the 1840s and 1850s. The domination of the distribution of London papers by a handful of metropolitan wholesalers was typical of a system in which publishers dealt in bulk only with those firms who could take direct delivery from the publishing house. One of the provincial companies supplied in this way by W. H. Smith was the Dublin-based J. K. Johnston & Co. Smith supplied five other agents in Ireland during the 1840s, including the Belfast bookseller Henderson, but that most of their business went via Johnston is confirmed by the fact that they took over the firm when it went bankrupt in 1850. Indeed, L. M. Cullen has argued that the 'substantial indebtedness of Johnston's to W. H. Smith & Son reflects Smith's success in supplying the Dublin market'. During the 1830s advertisements for Johnston's boasted that they could 'deliver newspapers in Dublin by their own messengers, a full hour at least, EARLIER than the Post Office Delivery'. Many of the 'Principal Towns in Ireland' could be supplied with news fourteen or eighteen hours before the arrival of the mail because they were 'getting their papers daily by Express direct from London'.[87] In a letter sent to the Admiralty in 1852, Smith senior noted that his firm had sent 'parcels of newspapers and dispatches for the press by the Mail Steamers from Holyhead and Liverpool to Dublin' 'for more than thirty years'.[88] Holyhead had become part of the rail network after the completion of the Britannia Bridge across the Menai Straits in 1850 and was served by the City of Dublin Steam Packet Company who sailed into Kingstown (connected to Dublin by rail in 1843), whereas the City of Dublin cargo steamers from Liverpool docked at Dublin Port (North Wall). Johnston and W. H. Smith served much of the Irish trade via these routes in the 1840s and 1850s, although, as Cullen notes, other English wholesalers also supplied Irish retailers.[89]

Perhaps the most detailed description of how daily newspapers and other relatively cheap printed goods published in London were distributed during the 1840s and early 1850s is contained in the minutes of the Select Committee on Newspaper Stamps. Those who gave evidence to the Committee during 1851 included the publisher John Cassell and two major distributors, Abel Heywood of Manchester and W. H. Smith senior. All three confirmed that only a small number of the 60,000 daily newspapers produced in London were sent by post, the 'majority' being delivered 'by railway trains to large towns

87 Cullen, *Eason & Son*, pp. 18–19, 13.   88 WHSA, Letter Book A1, f.53, 3 May 1852.
89 Cullen, *Eason & Son*, pp. 49–50.

in the country'. In 1838 an Act had been passed to provide for the conveyance of the mails by the railways, but, as Cassell informed the Committee, most publishers and distributors did not use the Post Office because it did not transmit newspapers 'by the first train'. Newspapers travelling from London to Manchester 'by railway' were thus on their way to customers at 6.30 a.m., whereas those that went 'through the Post Office' did not leave the capital 'before 10 o'clock'.[90] According to Cassell speed was already of the essence in the newspaper business: 'the public gives a preference to that which brings them the earliest news'.

Smith's evidence confirms that his firm's prosperity was based on running a faster service than was possible via the mail trains. He described how his firm collected the newspapers by carts from the printers at about 5.00 a.m. They were then taken to his warehouse on the Strand where they were made up into 'parcels for the principal towns' and then taken by cart to be dispatched 'by the first trains at six or half-past six'. As Charles Knight had noted in 1843, trains departing London between 6.00 and 7.00 a.m. allowed newspapers to arrive in Bristol by 11.00 a.m. and the Isle of Wight (via steamer) by 11.30 a.m.[91] Smith explained to the Committee that the dailies arrived in Birmingham at 11.00 a.m. and Manchester and Liverpool at 2.00 p.m. After these newspapers had been put on trains for the north, Smith's men made 'a second dispatch . . . by the Post Office' in order to reach 'country villages chiefly in the neighbourhood of large towns' and those 'distant parts' of Scotland not (yet) reached by the train. Once this early morning work was complete single copies of newspapers were distributed to subscribers via the post, but 'the second editions' were also sent via the rail 'in order to save the expense of a halfpenny postage which is charged by the Post Office, and to ensure an earlier delivery'.

The Committee was interested to find out whether newspapers delivered so 'rapidly' by Smith cost more to the reader than those delivered more slowly via the post. Smith informed them that there was 'scarcely any' additional charge because the costs for distribution (which he calculated at 'a farthing a paper') were 'paid by the agent in the country', who was 'glad to make an arrangement for receiving them by train, in order to attract to himself the whole of the business in the district'. Smith denied that an additional penny was charged for 'early delivery of the "Times" or other morning papers as soon as the train arrives' (although his own bookstalls were certainly doing so in 1855), and he noted that regular subscribers in Manchester could expect their newspaper

90 *Report from the Select Committee on Newspaper Stamps* (London, House of Commons, 1851), pp. 420, 228.
91 Knight, *London* 5, pp. 347–8.

to be delivered to their home for £1 13s 6d per quarter, or a 'fraction over 5d per copy'. Smith's suggestion that newsagents were willing to cover the cost of distribution by rail in order to expand their business confirms Cassell's argument that there was a large audience for the 'earliest news' delivered rapidly from the capital.

In Smith's opinion at least, the patterns of communal consumption, which supported the reading room system, had been speeded up, rather than transformed, by the railway system. During his questioning of Cassell, Richard Cobden confirmed that a large number of the London morning papers sent to Liverpool and Manchester were delivered to 'reading rooms' rather than the homes of individual subscribers, but he also noted that a 'considerable proportion' were sold to readers who called at the newsvendors. Cassell confirmed that this was the case although these purchasers still paid a premium of a penny for the delivery of early news, whereas 'the cheap press' (i.e. unstamped penny papers such as his own *Working Man's Friend*) was sold almost exclusively over the counter as 'the public would not pay them for delivery'.

As Smith admitted, his firm was not much concerned with the distribution of weekly newspapers in 1851 and he made no reference to the dissemination of other cheap texts in his evidence. By contrast, Abel Heywood described his role in the distribution of serialised penny novels and unstamped weekly papers to booksellers in Manchester and the surrounding towns in some detail. Heywood received most of these texts from London via the LNWR, which sent them in the evening in order that they would arrive on the afternoon of the following day. None of these texts, which included more than 9,000 copies of the weekly *Family Herald*, passed through the post. The Select Committee was keen to establish that readers were paying the same price for these texts in Manchester as in London. Heywood's answer, which confirmed that all of the goods he sold retailed at the same price as in London, includes a very important summary of the costs of distribution.

> We get the goods down by the London and North Western Railway at 2s a cwt., and the cost, when taken in the gross, is very trifling upon a dozen; the average price the publishers charge them is 8d a dozen, and it will cost half-a-farthing for the carriage; we sell them again at 9d a dozen to the trade; the paper, plain, is almost worth the money.

As the Committee went on to establish, about 1,700 copies of a weekly paper like the *Family Herald* could be 'sent down from London' for about two shillings as long as they travelled by the slow 'luggage' trains. Speed was less important for the unstamped weeklies as they were not allowed to report the kind of news dealt with by the dailies. This meant that the relatively cheap cost of carriage via the slow trains was absorbed into the price that Heywood charged the trade rather than being passed on to the reader. When asked whether the 'reading portion of the community' had 'greatly benefited' by the use of the railway in text distribution, Heywood argued that a saving of 'something like 500 per cent' in the cost of carriage was as much a benefit as the general speeding up of text distribution. His evidence confirms Cassell's assertion that weekly papers, such as the *Working Man's Friend*, did not rely on subscribers (as most traditional dailies did), but were delivered to 'the trade', who sold them to customers. Cassell reported that 'immense bails' of the *Working Man's Friend* were sent out 'late on Saturday nights' for delivery the next day. This suggests that the railway network played a particularly important role in increasing the circulation of unstamped weeklies, such as the *Family Herald*, *London Journal* and *Reynolds's Miscellany*, which had begun publication in the 1840s. Both Wilkie Collins and Charles Knight attest to the widespread availability of 'penny-novel-journals' during the later 1850s and Cassell's and Heywood's evidence suggests that it was cheap distribution by rail that helped make price uniformity possible.[92] Rapid distribution of unstamped texts was still expensive, however, as 'the railway charges' were '2d per pound for all parcels which go by the mail' (i.e. the faster express services).

The 1851 Select Committee was largely concerned with the distribution of texts from London to the north of England. However, a number of letters written by John Menzies in the 1850s confirm that his Edinburgh-based business distributed weekly newspapers and periodicals in almost exactly the same manner as Heywood in Manchester.[93]

Keeping the cost of distribution down was particularly important to the growth of Menzies's business. As an early history of *The Scotsman* noted, the Edinburgh wholesalers distributed mixed bundles of English and Scottish penny papers to 'local booksellers' at the cost of three farthings a copy. This allowed the retailer a small profit if they sold them at the cover price, but more distant sellers were charged an additional fee for carriage that was often passed on to the reader by the retailer who sold the newspaper at an inflated price.[94] By keeping the cost of distribution from London to a minimum, Menzies was able to expand his business and supply booksellers as far away

92 Knight, *The old printer and the modern press*, p. 264; 'The unknown public', *Household Words* 18 (August 1858), pp. 217–22.
93 For Menzies in Scotland, see Colclough, 'The railways', in Bell (ed.), *Edinburgh History of the book in Scotland*, pp. 141–52.
94 *The story of 'The Scotsman'*, pp. 35–6.

as Berwick in the south and Inverness in the north. By the early 1860s open-ended parcels were dispatched to Inverness each morning by the 6.00 a.m. train and a 'considerable number' of newspaper parcels went to Aberdeen and the 'towns North of it' using the North British Railway line through Fife to Dundee.[95]

Menzies's letters demonstrate that his business covered a much wider geographical area than the twenty miles around Manchester supplied by Abel Heywood, but they also show that he was able to take advantage of modes of transport unavailable to Heywood. For example, in 1844 he noted that a text published by Chapman & Hall was delayed because the steamer bringing copies from London had met with an accident.[96] During this same period Menzies supplied many of his customers with packages of periodicals sent each month by coach, for which he expected a 'monthly remittance', and the same sequence of letters shows that he was regularly dealing with publishers in London and Manchester who wanted him to add their periodicals to the list that he sent out to booksellers to encourage orders.[97]

Of course, not every newspaper distributor operated on the scale of a Menzies, Smith or Heywood during the mid-Victorian period. An article published in *Chambers's Edinburgh Journal* in 1853 documents a day in the life of a newsboy who spent the early hours of the morning working for an 'association of newsmen' who worked out of an old tenement building in a small alley off Fleet Street. This building operated as 'a central depot' for the distribution of newspapers to the 'country districts' via the mail. From the early hours of the morning it was filled with men and boys packing and addressing newspapers brought by hand from the nearby presses in order to get them ready 'for the morning mail' that would deliver them to the 'breakfast tables of the comfortable class' in towns as far away as Birmingham and Bristol. The journey from this building to the post office at St Martin's Le Grand took six and a half minutes by foot and packing continued until the last possible moment. This same newsboy spent the next portion of his day collecting newspapers from his master's shop in order to deliver them to subscribers living in central London. After completing his 'round' he returned to the shop to collect newspapers for sale in the streets. Railway stations and steamboats were favourite venues and first-class passengers a particular target.[98]

For the kind of newsman that this boy worked for, the six o'clock deadline for delivery of the mail to the post office was particularly important. Before six

95 JMA, Letter Book III, p. 449; Letter Book II, p. 372.
96 JMA Letter Book I, p. 22.   97 JMA Letter Book I, p. 16.
98 'The newsboy's day', *Chambers's Edinburgh Journal*, 14 May 1853, pp. 305–8.

all those newspapers 'lent by the hour' needed to be collected and packaged in order that they could be posted on to 'country customers' via the evening mail. These customers would also receive unsold copies of newspapers that had been for sale on the street during the morning and afternoon. However, those newspapers returned from renting by the hour or the streets did not always tally with the newsman's order book for distribution to the country and any unwanted texts were sent to the 'Newspaper Exchange'. This was a gathering of newsboys that usually formed in Catherine Street near the Strand or outside the post office in order to swap newspapers so that orders could be completed without the need to buy additional copies. The *Chambers's* account of the newsboy's day is particularly important because it draws attention to the various roles undertaken by those less affluent newsmen who relied on the postal service to deal with their country customers. Very few firms had large enough orders to be able to enter into private contracts with the railway companies.

During the 1850s newspaper distribution became more and more centred in the hands of those few major distributors who were able to deal with bulk orders from the publishers and dispatch them rapidly via the railway. Particularly important in ensuring Smith's domination of this market was the 1854 agreement with *The Times*, which for an annual fee of £4,000 ensured that they got the first copies from the press. In 1856 they announced that they were 'prepared to deliver the Morning Papers to the Trade in London and the suburbs'. Carts running direct from the Strand arrived at Sloane Square, Kensington Turnpike, Notting Hill Turnpike, St John's Wood Church and Camden Town Station at 7.15 a.m. having made deliveries en route. Parcels could also be collected at the major railway stations. Suburban customers could receive their papers via trains from Hampstead Road, Shoreditch, Fenchurch Street, London Bridge and Waterloo, or by collecting them at these stations. However, throughout the 1850s and 1860s W. H. Smith usually made an additional charge to the sub-wholesaler or consumer who bought these papers and until the 1870s (when the publisher began to take back unsold copies) the price of *The Times* fluctuated according to where it was purchased.[99]

By 1860 Smith's 'great room in the Strand' was recognised as 'one of the most remarkable sights in London' and from that time until the First World War journalists regularly entered this space to document the latest innovations in newspaper distribution. During the 1860s writers from the *Leisure Hour*, *Once a Week* and *Chambers's Journal* noted down exactly what was going on in the

99 Wilson, *First with the news*, p. 176; WHSA 245/1.

'packing room' at 186 The Strand between 4.00 and 6.00 a.m.[100] All remarked that the layout of the building was particularly important to the way in which texts were distributed. A 'large square hall open to the roof, and surrounded by two galleries, rising one above the other', the packing hall also included 'a single cluster of gas-lights in the centre of the domed skylight' to give as much light as possible to the packers.

The newspapers were delivered to the hall in Smith's own 'conspicuously painted carts', which arrived at regular intervals from about 4.30 onwards. The first daily papers to arrive were used to make up orders for their own bookstalls and for the agents and newsvendors outside London who were supplied by train. This was a massive operation with at least six tons of *The Times* being packed and dispatched each day. According to the *Leisure Hour* 'above a hundred and sixty men' were involved 'either at the long tables or benches which run along the floor, or darting from post to pillar'. About twenty packers assembled at the tables on the main floor compiled the orders by calling out the number of each title that they needed ('a hundred Times' – 'ten Fields', etc.) 'according to a list'. The remaining men who were positioned all around the floor and galleries supplied these copies. The speed of the operation was remarkable, with newspapers often being thrown from the galleries in order to save time. Once an order was complete it was folded into an oblong and 'wrapped in strong brown covers, ready addressed' before being 'despatched to the outer door, where the light flying carts were waiting'. These carts, sometimes preceded by 'outriders' whose job it was to clear any obstructions, were en route for the 6.00 a.m. train to the west of England at 5.30. Those to Euston and the other northern stations followed soon after.

Sometimes production could not keep up with distribution. The *Leisure Hour* recorded that the packers sometimes called for 'half Times' or 'a third Times' because not enough copies had arrived. Smith's notices to the trade often included a warning that if the publication of the papers was delayed 'extra carts to complete the supplies' would be sent 'in all cases'.[101] During the period before W. H. Smith took charge of the early delivery of *The Times*, its editor wrote to George Lovejoy of Reading informing him that the paper's 'late publication' resulted from a number of factors, including the late running of trains bringing news into London on the evening before publication. He hoped to remedy this in future by using the telegraph rather than the train as a

---

100 'Smiths' Express Newspaper Office', *Leisure Hour* 18 October 1860, pp. 664–7; 'Our modern Mercury', *Once a Week* 2 February 1861, pp. 160–3; 'How we get our newspapers', *Chambers's Edinburgh Journal* 9 December 1865, pp. 669–74.
101 WHSA 245/ 1.

news-gathering tool and by installing more fast presses to increase production 'by at least 2,000 copies per hour', but he still advised Lovejoy to seek redress from the Great Western for running their trains from Paddington before the newspaper had finished production.[102] It is important to note that the technological innovations espoused in this letter did not prevent some agents being sent less than the number of papers that they required even in the 1860s.

By the 1860s W. H. Smith were not just handling the expensive dailies on which the 'coach' business had been based. *Once a Week* recorded the importance of 'the penny morning papers' such as the *Telegraph*, *Star* and *Standard* and evidence from the orders placed at their bookstalls in 1856 shows that they quickly adapted to the supply of the penny papers created by the removal of the newspaper stamp in the previous year.[103] Weekly papers and other periodicals were increasingly important to W. H. Smith in the 1860s and the *Leisure Hour* witnessed an 'immense number of what are called Saturday and Sunday papers' being 'circulated beforehand' by the rail.

When a contributor to *All the Year Round* visited W. H. Smith during the early hours of a Saturday morning in 1875, packing the weeklies began at 2.00 a.m. and needed to be completed by 4.00 in order that the same men could be redeployed to send out the dailies. This account of a day at W. H. Smith attests to the continued speeding up of British print culture. The earliest trains now left at between 5.00 and 5.30 and the great hall on the Strand had been supplemented by additional 'sorting and distributing' rooms at King's Cross and Paddington which were supplied directly from the publishers. The Strand still dealt with everything sent south via 'the Brighton and other lines', but some of the parcels for the more distant stations served by the Midland and LNWR lines were made up en route.[104]

The 'newspaper train' was a Scottish innovation. In order to increase its circulation in the mid-1860s, *The Scotsman* had made an agreement with the various railway companies that allowed the newspaper to be carried throughout the Scottish railway system for a single fee. This meant that agents in different regions received the paper carriage free and could sell it at the published price of a penny. In 1872 a further innovation in the distribution of this newspaper saw the first use of 'newspaper trains' that allowed the paper to be 'published almost simultaneously in Edinburgh and Glasgow'. The train left Edinburgh at 4.20 a.m. with a 'packing carriage' from which parcels were dispatched while

---

102 University of Reading Archive, Mowbray Morris to George Lovejoy, 29 December 1853 in 'George Lovejoy: Scrap Book', f.13.

103 Colclough, ' "Purifying the sources of amusement and information"?', p. 32.

104 'How we get our newspapers', *All the Year Round* 25 December 1875, pp. 305–9, at p. 306.

the train was still in motion. It arrived in Glasgow some seventy minutes later with 400 parcels ready to be distributed throughout the west of Scotland. This 'complete revolution' in newspaper distribution, as the *Graphic* called it, spread to England in 1875 when *The Times* began to use the same principle to deliver newspapers between London and Birmingham. *The Times* express was quickly replaced by a number of early morning services offered by the Midland, Great Northern and LNWR that were open to all the newspapers. This method of distribution was fairly straightforward if the packages consisted of a single title, such as *The Times*, and in order to compete with this new service W. H. Smith transferred some of the packing of mixed parcels for agents to the rail. In 1875 two 'sorting carriages' were in use on the Midland line and all the papers were sorted during the two-hour journey from St Pancras to Leicester.[105] In 1876 the 5.15 LNWR service, which included several of Smith's sorting carriages, dropped packages at six stations before reaching Birmingham at 8.20. Some of these packages were transferred to express trains that sped them to large towns such as Crewe (9.15 a.m.), Chester (10.27), Manchester (10.00) and Liverpool (10.25). Others were in Glasgow and Edinburgh by 6.00 p.m. and in Dublin by 6.20. This innovation meant that the newspapers were arriving some four hours earlier than they had done in 1851. According to the author of a guide to the LNWR, 'all true news was better soon than late'.[106]

Railway bookstalls were very important to the expansion of W. H. Smith during the 1850s and 60s, not only because they acted as retail outlets, but also because they were wholesale depots from which local newsvendors and agents were supplied. William Vincent, who worked as a bookstall clerk for W. H. Smith and a number of other companies during his career, recorded several examples of how distribution via the stalls operated. Amongst the customers who called at the stall in Didcot during the mid-1860s was an 'old drover', who bought newspapers at the cover price when they arrived on the 7.40 a.m. from London. His profits came when he sold them on at inflated prices ('the penny ones at two-pence') after he had trudged some nine miles to the Isley racing stables. The larger retailers were supplied at wholesale rates. When Vincent moved to the Swansea stall a few years later he was in charge of supplying 'over forty agents at wholesale prices'. The distribution of London papers to south Wales was still very slow even in the 1870s. Although they left London at 6.00 a.m. on the Great Western, it was nearly ten hours later when they reached Swansea. As soon as they arrived at the stall, Vincent and the newsboys repacked

105 *Story of 'The Scotsman'*, p. 40; *Graphic* 15 May 1875, p. 471.
106 *The official tourists' picturesque guide to the London and North-Western Railway*, ed. G. Shaw [1876], pp. 75–9.

them so that they could be sent to the local agents via trains departing at 5.00 and 5.30. Vincent records that it was a campaign organised by newsagents and merchants annoyed by the late arrival of the London dailies that led Smith's to transfer their parcels to the LNWR. However, the new route was longer and involved transferring the parcels mid-journey so that they arrived only an hour earlier. Although only 'four or five heavy parcels' (each containing up to 600 copies of a newspaper such as the *Daily Telegraph*) were delivered to Swansea each day, the Great Western missed the income enough to begin running a new service, which arrived at 1.30 p.m., and W. H. Smith moved their trade back to the original carrier. As this example suggests, local wholesalers and retailers were able to apply pressure on major distributors in order to improve their supply of newspapers.[107]

The Swansea stall also handled weekly papers. This involved opening the stall at 6.00 a.m. on Thursdays, Fridays and Saturdays in order to sort the parcels that had arrived by the night mail. Vincent describes handling nearly 5,000 copies of just three titles in a single morning. Given the large numbers of texts passing through this stall it is perhaps surprising to find that a separate wholesale warehouse was not established in Wales until 1896, when the Cardiff House opened. Other major wholesale houses were established at Birmingham (1857), Manchester (1859), Liverpool (1868) and Belfast (1870) during this period, however. Although Menzies's early contracts prevented him from supplying local agents with goods carriage free, the stalls also became major links in the chain of distribution in Scotland. Before the move into railway bookstalls, retail had been a relatively minor concern for Menzies. For example, in 1856 the shop in Hanover Street generated less than £500 out of a total turnover of £19,262, and when a new wholesale house was opened in Edinburgh three years later, the shop was closed. In 1867 John Menzies & Co. (as they became in that year) opened a combined retail and wholesale house in Royal Bank Square, Glasgow. By 1876–7 the Glasgow branch was contributing nearly £24,000 to a total turnover of £122,741, whereas the bookstalls generated only £19,866.[108]

In order for the wholesalers to prosper in this fashion they needed to nego-tiate with the railway companies to provide the lowest rate of carriage possible whilst maintaining a fast and reliable service to their main distribution centres. Smith's negotiation of favourable carriage rates was crucial for the expansion of their business in Ireland during the 1850s and 1860s. Because newspaper

---

107 Vincent, *Seen from the railway platform*, pp. 45, 74.
108 JMA, JM22: Ledgers, January 1877–October 1881.

distribution outside Dublin was relatively limited until the 1870s, this was mainly the cost of transport from England to Ireland, which was controlled by the LNWR (via Holyhead) and the Great Northern (via Liverpool). In January 1863 it was agreed that the LNWR would deliver all periodicals and newspapers overnight at mail rates, while less urgent goods would go via Liverpool. It is likely that the rate of carriage for the express service was $\frac{3}{8}$d per pound or almost 4s per cwt, with a minimum annual payment of £500 on parcels from Euston to Dublin.[109] In order to supply newspapers to new markets outside Dublin, W. H. Smith needed to negotiate new rates of carriage with the Irish railways, which tended to charge a standard parcel rate rather than by the pound, as was the norm in England and Wales. In July 1860 Smith II hoped to negotiate a rate of a farthing per pound with the GSWR, which was the 'charge common in England', but his manager Charles Eason settled for the rate of a halfpenny per pound in 1862. Smith had to agree, however, that this was a great improvement on the charge made per parcel, which he argued was the equivalent of '1d on the *Times* and $^1/_4$d on the other papers'. Other railway companies agreed to the same charges, and later also carried books at the same rate. This improved carriage rate 'was the first crucial step in establishing the country wholesale business' and was achieved in the same year that W. H. Smith became the main agent for the *Irish Times*, 1862. Before these new carriage rates were established much of the newspaper business in Ireland had involved the distribution of stamped copies of English dailies to subscribers via the post. These subscribers remained important even in the 1870s, but the new carriage rates encouraged the circulation of unstamped newspapers to grow and, when combined with Smith's agency for the *Irish Times*, this significantly increased the importance of the Irish dailies printed in Dublin.[110]

In 1861 W. H. Smith II confirmed that in England 'by far the larger portion of the edition of each newspaper' was transported via the railway 'in its unstamped form'.[111] It was not until 1870 that the newspaper stamp was abolished and the retransmission of stamped newspapers via the post came to an end. The arrival of the unstamped penny press in the 1850s helped to shift the consumption of daily newspapers away from communal institutions such as newsrooms, and private subscriptions that arrived at the subscriber's home, to sales via shops (including 'tobacconists, greengrocers, stationers, booksellers and barbers') and newsboys on the street.[112] The arrival of halfpenny evening newspapers, such as the *Echo*, launched in December 1868, certainly brought the purchase of

---

109 Cullen, *Eason & Son*, p. 49. 110 *Ibid.*, pp. 50–1, 57–8. 111 Quoted in *ibid.*, p. 57.
112 Lee, *The origins of the popular press*, p. 65. As already noted, the cheap weekly papers were already available from the back-street trade even before the abolition of the newspaper stamp in 1855.

a daily newspaper within reach of a much larger audience. By 1913 the success of the halfpenny *Daily Mail* had forced a number of morning newspapers to adopt the same price, but during the last quarter of the nineteenth century most daily papers published in the morning cost a penny. In the 1870s a former editor of the *Northern Echo* argued that the price of a halfpenny paper was 'no obstacle' to even the 'poorest person', although they might not buy the paper every day, and that sales on occasions of 'great general interest' were only 'limited by the power of production and supply'.[113] Newsboys were particularly important to the sale of both penny and halfpenny papers. In 1869 the *Echo* employed 500 wearing caps emblazoned with the name of the newspaper and by the mid-1870s newsvendors dressed to advertise what they were selling had become a familiar sight throughout the nation. Many wholesalers held out against the halfpenny papers (which they thought would not allow them enough profit) and this led the publishers of the *Echo* and some other titles to set up their own mechanisms for distribution. Most of the halfpenny papers became part of the distribution system that had developed from the mid-nineteenth century onwards once they began to offer the distributors better terms, but the *News of the World* developed its own network of newsagents.[114] By the late 1890s some of these newspapers were being dispatched at a much earlier time than before. In 1899 the *Daily Mail* commissioned a special train from the Great Central which left Marylebone for the north at 2.30 a.m. This gave Harmsworth's paper a distinct advantage over its rivals that travelled on the 5.15, but the Midland soon offered a rival service departing from St Pancras at the same time. As both called at almost the same towns, they quickly became specialised services, the Great Central serving Sheffield, the Midland Manchester. However, the rail had been unable to match the speed of the telegraph since the 1860s, and news gathering via the wire, and later the telephone, meant that local papers could now contain much the same news as those produced in London. New local distribution systems emerged as a result. The *Daily Mail* overcame some of its distribution problems, for example, by printing a Manchester edition.[115]

In order to survey the various methods of newspaper distribution available in 1913, J. D. Symon took up the now familiar position on the floor of W. H. Smith's packing room in the Strand. He notes a number of major changes that had occurred since the 1870s, including the much earlier printing times – a 'considerable portion of the morning papers' were now printed by midnight – and

113 Brown, *Victorian news and newspapers*, p. 33.   114 Lee, *The origins of the popular press*, pp. 65–6.
115 Simmons, *Victorian railway*, pp. 241–2.

the fact that 'many of the newspapers do a large portion of their own distribution'.[116] Amongst the first bundles to arrive at the Strand on that night in 1913 were the halfpenny papers that were packed by the 'army of operators' located in the basement. These parcels were sent out for distribution via a 'train run exclusively in the interests of the leading halfpenny papers' known as a Syndicate train. It is important to note that even those packages that contained only texts from a single publisher were still made up by the wholesaler rather than being produced in house. Most of the completed orders were taken to the railway station by horse and cart in much the same way as they had been during the previous sixty years, but motor delivery vans 'bearing the name of some newspaper or other' were now used to deliver to the suburbs. Something of the way in which print distribution had speeded up since the mid-nineteenth century is revealed by the times of various trains 'carrying newspapers to the provinces'.

2.40 a.m.:	Great Central (for Sheffield)
2.40 a.m.:	Midland (for Leicester, including Smith's sorting cars)
2.50 a.m.:	Great Western (Syndicate train)
3.00 a.m.:	Great Northern
3.00 a.m.:	LNWR (for the North of England and Scotland, including sorting cars)
3.00 a.m.:	Syndicate train from Waterloo
3.30 a.m.:	Brighton
3.37 a.m.:	South Eastern and Chatham
4.50 a.m.:	Midland (for Scotland)
5.00 a.m.:	Great Northern (for Scotland)
5.00 a.m.:	North Western (for Scotland)
5.00 a.m.:	Great Western (for Reading, Didcot and Oxford)
5.05 a.m.:	Great Eastern (main line)
5.30 a.m.:	Great Eastern (for Cambridge)
5.30 a.m.:	Great Western (for Land's End)
5.50 a.m.:	Waterloo (for the south-west)
6.10 a.m.:	Waterloo

The 3.00 a.m. from Euston for Scotland did much of the same work as the famous 5.15 'newspaper train' which first ran in the 1870s. Whereas formerly the newspapers were delivered to Rugby at just after 7.00 a.m., in 1913 they arrived at 4.30 (p. 49). Indeed, almost all of the newspapers dealt with by the

---

116 Symon, *The press and its story*, p. 37.

Strand had left the premises by the same hour that the first bundles had started their journeys from the London stations in the 1860s. Symon also noted other modifications to the traditional distribution process such as the addition of yet more sorting rooms, which now included those in Kean Street and Drury Lane, and at Liverpool Street and Waterloo stations.

Perhaps more innovative was the combined use of the telephone and the motorcar to respond to the exceptional demand for newspapers in a particular region or town. Each newspaper had a circulation manager who would contact the distributor by telephone to increase the supply to anywhere where 'a huge temporary increase in circulation was expected'. This often meant arranging for the train to be met by vans or motorcars which would then carry the additional papers 'at express speed' to where they were needed (pp. 52–3). Symon thought 'distribution by motor' one of the 'most wonderful developments' of recent years and he noted that the *Daily Mail* had attempted to distribute the news using an 'army of motor cars' on at least two occasions when no trains were available because of holidays or strikes. Despite these innovations in methods of circulating newspapers, in the years before the Great War the newsboy was still one of the most important distributors to be found within the great towns and cities that produced newspapers. As in the 1850s, the distribution network knew how to get the most out of these young boys, but on the eve of war this link in the chain was threatened by new legislation against child labour.

New methods of wholesale and retail: print distribution, 1880–1914

Many of Smith's bookstalls became too small to manage the combination of retailing and wholesaling that they had taken on since the late 1840s. As a result, they created a dozen new wholesale houses, including those in Cardiff (1896), Newcastle (1898) and Leicester (1899), and began to replace – or complement – the bookstalls with high-street shops. The shop established in Reading in 1904, for example, continued to operate as a joint retail and wholesale facility, whilst the other early shops, mainly located in seaside resorts, concentrated on retail. From the late 1890s, W. H. Smith began to organise the wholesale trade on a regional basis. The 'western wholesale organisation' served as a model. Once hived off from the Cardiff bookstall, the wholesale business expanded rapidly, with an increase in turnover of £22,000 per year within five years. This led to the creation of the two new wholesale branches at Swansea and Newport in 1901. These new branches took over the wholesale trade that had previously been dealt with by thirteen bookstalls. The Gloucester Provincial Wholesale House completed the regional chain.[117]

During this period W. H. Smith also began buying up smaller provincial businesses, often splitting them up into separate retail and wholesale functions. At Bristol, they took over Mapstone's (1903) and later added satellite branches at Exeter and Plymouth so that the trade could be organised on a regional basis. These wholesale branches steadily spread through much of England and Wales. Birmingham, Newcastle and Sheffield were at the centre of the most important and profitable regions after 1901. Originally established in 1857, Smith's Birmingham wholesale house acquired satellites at Wolverhampton (1904), Walsall (1909) and Coventry (1920). During the same period, John Menzies expanded their wholesaling interests in Scotland and northern England in a similar fashion. The establishment of new wholesale houses at Dundee, Carlisle and Aberdeen in 1898–9 followed the addition of extra local branches to assist the Glasgow House. Perth was added shortly before the First World War. The wholesale side of Eason & Son (who had taken over from W. H. Smith in Ireland in 1886) also 'grew rapidly during the period 1900–1910'.[118]

The halfpenny and evening newspapers, periodicals, magazines and other goods (especially stationery) were particularly important to the new wholesale houses in their dealings with small newsagents' shops. In the 1890s, a typical order for one of Menzies's customers in south Glasgow consisted of just ten items, including four halfpenny magazines, and two halfpenny and three penny papers. These texts, which included *Comic Cuts*, the *Glasgow Herald* and *The Scotsman*, were gathered by Menzies from London, Glasgow, Edinburgh and Dundee before being redistributed to the streets of Bridgeton Cross.[119]

In order to make a profit from such small orders, the wholesaler needed to make the best deal possible with the publishers. The firm's letter books reveal how a business like Menzies operated in the 1880s and 1890s. In October 1882, for example, they wrote to the publisher of the *Family Reader* to request that they send the magazine direct rather than via a London wholesaler who was currently delivering their order by the expensive 'mail train' which arrived on Wednesday evening. This request was urgent because they were aware that 'an agent in Glasgow' was beating them to the market because he was 'getting his supply' direct from the publishers 'by goods train' at a 'much cheaper rate of carriage'. As part of their argument to persuade the publishers

117 Wilson, *First with the news*, p. 220.
118 *Ibid.*, pp. 218–24; *The Menzies Group*, p. 17; Cullen, *Eason & Son*, p. 161.
119 Gardiner, *The making of John Menzies*, p. 41.

to give them the same deal as this Glasgow agent, Menzies noted that they supplied many of the newsagents in Edinburgh and Glasgow as well as their own bookstalls, which were to be found on 'nearly all the railway lines in Scotland'. This letter shows just how competitive the wholesale business had become by the last quarter of the nineteenth century. Fearful of having their sales undermined by another local wholesaler, who received his orders earlier, they were prepared to end their contract with their current London supplier. Menzies informed the publishers that this indirect supply was something of an anachronism as they already 'dealt direct' with all the other 'leading publishers of periodicals in London'.[120] Other letters are filled with demands for 'better terms' on newspapers and books. In October 1891 they attempted to persuade the publishers of the *Strand* to pay 'the carriage of your magazine to our houses here [in Edinburgh] and in Glasgow'.[121] In this instance the publishers refused to pay for carriage (which Menzies calculated as 59 per cent of the cost), but this correspondence suggests something of the almost constant battle between distributor and publisher to get the best deal.

For most of the nineteenth century, publishers had only supplied newspapers on wholesale terms to those distributors on their doorstep, who then sold them on to sub-wholesalers or retailers. During the late nineteenth and early twentieth centuries, however, increased competition for sales led many publishers to sell direct to provincial wholesalers. As Menzies's letters indicate, this cutting out of the London wholesaler could dramatically improve the provincial wholesaler's margins and speed up the process of distribution. These changes had a particular impact on the Irish trade. In October 1905 Eason & Son were one of a number of wholesalers who requested that the publishers refrain from establishing a 'direct supply' to agents in Ireland. Later that year, however, they chose to establish direct accounts with publishers rather than acquire their supplies through the traditional link with W. H. Smith. This gave them the advantage of 'carriage paid supplies, with the consequent improvement in gross margins'. Cullen has argued that 'as the basis for mass readership [in Ireland] began to emerge in the period between 1895 and 1913 the effect was seen at first in soaring sales at the railway bookstalls'. After 1907, however, the 'dynamic' passed from the bookstalls to 'the wholesaling of newspapers and periodicals to independent retailers'.[122] Dealing directly with the publishers meant that they were able to strike better deals with the retail trade and their sales to newsagents doubled between 1907 and 1913.

---

120 JMA, Letter Book VI, p. 501. Menzies had a weekly order of 8,000 copies of this magazine.
121 JMA, Letter Book VIII, p. 21.   122 Cullen, *Eason & Son*, pp. 162–7.

Many of these shops began to deal in large numbers of weeklies dispatched from London on Friday or Saturday for sale on Saturday or Sunday. Eason's own stalls were not open on Sundays, so many of these papers were not available until Monday. This led to the emergence of several smaller agents in Dublin, such as Farrell and Kirwan, who dealt mainly in Sunday papers. The arrival of the *Daily Mail* in Ireland on the same day as it was published in London from 1905 also helped to encourage the sales of English dailies, although a large readership for daily papers only really developed in the 1910s and 1920s.[123] In May 1911 English weeklies retailing at a penny and a halfpenny were charged at $8\frac{3}{4}$d and $4\frac{1}{2}$d respectively for twelve copies less 2.5 per cent, including carriage, and carriage charges were eliminated on magazines for the first time. These terms encouraged competition. In March 1911 the English firm William Dawson & Sons set up business in Dublin in response to complaints from local retailers that Eason's supplied their own shop before anyone else's. Competition between the two companies was fierce and in order to speed up the delivery of news to the Dublin retailer Eason began to use motor vans rather than horse-drawn carts from the Irish Sea Ferries to collect the papers. In the 1910s, this combination of different wholesalers began to supply a growing number of shops that hoped that the sale of newspapers would encourage regular customers.[124] During the early twentieth century such shops were beginning to proliferate throughout the urban centres of the British Isles.

During this same period the way in which Smith's business operated underwent a fundamental change. Between 18 October 1905 and 1 January 1906 144 new shops were opened as replacements for the 250 railway bookstalls closed when both the GWR and the LNWR decided not to renew Smith's contracts. In 1905 their contract with the GWR had been similar to those drawn up in the 1860s and 70s, with the railway company taking 12.5% of the receipts from Paddington, 65% of advertising income, and a guaranteed minimum rent of £31,000. Both railway companies were keen to increase their income from the stations and eventually appointed Wyman to take over the stalls. As noted above, W. H. Smith had already opened a number of shops and the increased importance of the regional wholesale houses meant that many of the stalls no longer played an integral role in supplying local agents. During the negotiations W. H. Smith argued that 'half' the business of many bookstalls was 'done outside the Station' and could in fact be undertaken more efficiently from urban shops.[125] This statement was clearly meant as a warning that if they lost

---

123 *Ibid.*, p. 165.   124 *Ibid.*, pp. 168–70. Dawson gave up the Irish business in 1922.
125 Wilson, *First with the news*, p. 236.

the railway contracts they would take much of the trade that had supported the stalls with them into the towns, thus depriving new tenants of much of their income, but it also suggests that the business of selling newspapers to commuters was no longer as important to W. H. Smith has it had been fifty years earlier. The new mass readership was not to be found at the railway stations.

In order to establish the new shops in 1905/6 W. H. Smith often took over established businesses in much the same way as they had done when expanding their wholesale concerns. Refitted and repainted 'to a standard pattern: cream lettering on a ground-colouring of green', they gave the high streets of England and Wales a new feature, a multiple outlet retailer of newspapers, periodicals, books and stationery.[126] The new shops allowed W. H. Smith to continue to diversify their business – selling stationery was easier from a high street shop than a railway bookstall – and new techniques were adopted for the promotion of these and other goods. The art of the window display was particularly important. The shop at Reading was given much praise for the way in which its windows promoted books on a war theme during September 1914.[127] By 1914 W. H. Smith were operating a mix of stalls and shops, with the latter divided into 147 'B' and 26 'A' shops. (The 'B' shops were managed in much the same way as the bookstalls, whereas the 'A' shops were similar to the provincial wholesale houses.) New outlets were also established on much of the London Underground system, where they also often controlled advertising. In a period that saw a great increase in turnover at the wholesale houses, Smith's total profits almost doubled between 1907/8 and 1914/15.[128]

All of this evidence suggests that fundamental changes took place in the distribution and retailing of texts during the period 1880–1914. Although more booksellers and newsagents were being supplied directly from the publishers than in the earlier nineteenth century, this period is dominated by the growth of major wholesalers such as Menzies and W. H. Smith, who took over many smaller regional businesses, and the expansion of the number of retail outlets for newspapers, periodicals and cheap books. Even the library business had expanded and become cheaper with the arrival of Boots Booklovers Library in the 1890s, which used cheap subscription rates to attract customers into their shops, where they also sold books. At the outbreak of war Smith's boasted of 'practically 2,000 branches and sub-branches' and a 'wholesale connection'

---

126 *Ibid.*, p. 242.   127 *Newsbasket* October 1914, p. 221.
128 Wilson, *First with the news*, pp. 242–54.

that put them 'in touch with several thousands of newsagents throughout the country'.[129]

The relationship between the back-street newsagents, the booksellers and the street vendors was not always harmonious. One sign of the increased militancy of the small retailer during the 1910s was the growth of retail newsagents' associations, such as the United Kingdom Federation of Newsagents (UKF). Although the UKF was too small actually to represent the whole of the British Isles, it used the *National Newsagent* as a powerful propaganda tool in campaigns for better terms from the publishers and wholesalers. The issue for 4 January 1913 claimed that during the past year the UKF had been particularly influential in attaining good rates from the publishers, such as eightpence for twelve copies of some penny papers, including the *Daily News*, and in establishing a national timetable of publication, which guaranteed that newsagents received periodicals on the day before they were due for sale.[130] At the beginning of the following year they were celebrating new terms with Harmsworth's Amalgamated Press. Every agent within a fifty-mile radius of Manchester now received 'AP publications' at three farthings per copy for the penny papers and 'all the halfpenny pubs at 13 for $4\frac{1}{2}$d'. Another article on the possibility of charging the customer for delivery noted an increasing dissatisfaction with the terms offered by the wholesale trade, who it was claimed 'take their 15 per cent, rob us of the 13th copy, [and] wrong us on the returns'.[131] In February 1914 the new carriage charges imposed on retailers in Lancashire by a combination of 'northern' wholesalers, including Abel & John Heywood, W. H. Smith and Pollard of Oldham, led to a major dispute that remained unresolved even at the outbreak of war. Indeed the 1910s are typified by this fractious relationship between retailers and distributors. Long-established booksellers and newsagents resented the intrusion of new retailers into the trade and often negotiated with the wholesalers to impose 'distance regulations' (or a 'distance limit' policy) that prevented the supply of a new retailer in proximity to an established business.

Conclusion

During the nineteenth century an increasingly fast and efficient national distribution system emerged. It relied heavily, but not exclusively, upon the railway

---

129 WHSA 135/1.   130 *National Newsagent* 4 January 1913, p. 1.
131 *National Newsagent*, 21 February 1914, p. 12; 31 January 1914, p. 4.

system and by the early part of the twentieth century new modes of communication (the telephone, motor vehicles) were already changing the way in which texts were produced and distributed. However, as the Lancashire dispute of early 1914 makes clear, the wholesalers as 'cultural middlemen' still played a particularly important role in text dissemination and, much as in the 1850s, the cost of carriage remained a determining factor in when a text reached the retailer and how much it cost the reader.

7

Reading

STEPHEN COLCLOUGH AND DAVID VINCENT

The meaning of reading

Since the 1980s the idea that readers invest printed objects with their own expectations and actively construct meaning, rather than finding it already inscribed in the text, has transformed the way in which we think about the history of reading. It is no longer enough to document what was being produced in the past; we now also need to discover how these objects were consumed. As Guglielmo Cavallo and Roger Chartier have argued, however, the reader is never entirely free to make meaning. Reading is always constrained by the protocols of reading embedded within texts, as well as by modes of access or communication, such as oral recitation. It is a skill that is taught and during this training the student also learns a set of meanings that it is legitimate to ascribe to certain texts, or to the act of reading itself, within his or her reading community. They conclude that, despite the appearance of an increasingly common culture throughout Europe by the end of the nineteenth century, in part due to the intervention of the nation-state in the teaching process, there was in fact 'an extreme diversity in both reading practices and markets for the book (or newspaper)' throughout this period.[1]

Recent studies of reading have gone some way to unearthing the range of practices used by readers during the nineteenth and twentieth centuries. Much of this work has concentrated upon the discourse of reading that helped to discipline or legitimate what readers did with texts. Kate Flint's *The woman reader 1837–1914*, for example, looks at the 'wide range of contexts in which "the woman reader" was constructed as a discrete topic', including advice manuals, periodicals, 'paintings, photographs and graphic art', in order to suggest that women's reading was often overdetermined by this discourse.[2] Subsequent work on the iconography of the woman reader has teased out

1 Cavallo and Chartier, 'Introduction' in Cavallo and Chartier, *A history of reading*, pp. 33–6.
2 Flint, *The woman reader*, p. 4.

some of its contradictions by showing that reading purely for pleasure was not always represented negatively.[3] Flint's study is particularly important, however, because it draws on a number of sources for the 'evidence of actual reading activity', including autobiographies, which show that women often espoused 'practices or preferences' directly opposed to those offered by the discourse of the 'woman reader'.[4] Many other historians of reading have used similar sources to reconstruct the practices of what are sometimes called 'real' readers. Both David Vincent and Jonathan Rose have explored working-class reading by placing the autobiographies produced by an unusually articulate elite sector of this class in the context of other writings, such as statistical surveys and library records, which present a broader picture of popular reading practices.[5] Similarly, H. J. Jackson's *Marginalia* (2001) looks at marginal comments and other forms of annotation created by real readers between 1700 and the late twentieth century, and James A. Secord has combined the study of manuscript diaries and journals with annotated books and representations of reading in order to reconstruct the reception of one book, *Vestiges of the natural history of creation* (1844), by a diverse group of readers. Secord's study suggests that during the 1840s the same text could be read in diverse ways, from the rapid skimming of fashionable readers familiarising themselves with a book that was already the subject of conversation, through to the detailed making of notes in the margin performed by a professional reader preparing a review.[6]

Many of these studies acknowledge that they may not be dealing with anything more than a 'randomly surviving, and perhaps highly unrepresentative, sample of the far larger total of acts of reception', which were never articulated.[7] This concern with the 'typicality' of the surviving records of individual readers has led some historians to concentrate upon the practices shared by groups of readers within specific reading communities. There are, for example, several recent studies of the correspondence columns and letters pages of popular magazines and newspapers that suggest a uniform set of responses, but, as Lynne Warren has noted, such columns were controlled by the publisher who wished to construct something between an ideal reader and a corporate identity for a product that needed real readers to feel as though they had some

---

3 See many of the essays in Badia and Phegley, *Reading women*, especially Jennifer Phegley, 'Images of women readers in Victorian family literary magazines', pp. 105–28.
4 Flint, *The woman reader*, p.14.
5 Vincent, *Bread, knowledge, and freedom*; Rose, *The intellectual life of the British working classes*.
6 Jackson, *Marginalia*; Secord, *Victorian sensation*.   7 St Clair, *The reading nation*, p. 5.

control over the text.[8] Those readers who wrote in may well have been just as unorthodox as those who produced autobiographies or kept detailed reading diaries. The sheer variety of practices unearthed so far by these studies suggests something of the essential inventiveness of the reader during the period 1830–1914, but some common patterns are discernible, including the widespread continuance of reading aloud as a social practice. Although it is clear that autobiographical materials tend to provide the greatest insight into how texts were actually put to use throughout this period they need to be examined in the context of, and compared with, other sources, including representations of reading.

For the purposes of this chapter we have combined an investigation of the quantitative evidence of reading skills compiled by the state during a period in which mass literacy was encouraged as a sign of social cohesion, with autobiographical sources which give some sense of how these skills were deployed to meet various individual and communal needs. It is, of course, impossible to map all of the various reading communities, from religious groups through to professional reviewers, that existed during this period and we have not attempted to do so. Their histories are no doubt better suited to individual case studies. Although we offer some insights into the methods deployed by professional readers, such as authors and academics, our main concern here is with the so-called 'common reader' of the middle and lower classes. The chapter addresses how readers were made, or made themselves, in the first era of mass literacy. It then examines four ways in which the skills of decoding print were put into practice: in the home, in public places, by listening and by the use of writing to make sense of reading.

Making readers

In 1858 Dickens's protégé Wilkie Collins contributed an article to *Household Words* which claimed the discovery of a new continent which lay beyond the boundaries of the known literary world.

> Do the subscribers to this journal, [he asked] the customers at the eminent publishing-houses, the members of book-clubs and circulating libraries, and the purchasers and borrowers of newspapers and reviews, compose altogether the great bulk of the reading public of England? There was a time when, if anyone had put this question to me, I, for one, should certainly have answered,

8 Warren, ' "Women in conference" '. For a discussion of other sources, see Gerrard, 'New methods in the history of reading'.

Yes. I know better now. I know that the public just now mentioned, viewed as an audience for literature, is nothing more than a minority.[9]

Collins had found his new land by the simple expedient of walking into the communities of the labouring poor and looking at the print that was on sale. He was offered the most basic forms of literature, not books or serials but small quarto publications consisting 'merely of a few unbound pages; each one of them had a picture on the upper half of the front leaf, and a quantity of small print on the under'.[10] What impressed him most was their sheer ubiquity. 'There they were in every town, large or small. I saw them in fruit-shops, in oyster-shops, in lollypop-shops. Villages even – picturesque, strong-smelling villages – were not free from them.'[11] Their existence, Collins reckoned, reflected the presence of a hidden body of readers. The 'enormous outlawed majority . . . the lost literary tribes' constituted 'a reading public of three millions which lies right out of the pale of literary civilisation'.[12]

Collins's enquiry was more thorough than even his great mentor had ever undertaken, but it remained impressionistic. It is possible that his achievement lay in asking the question rather than finding the answer. To establish whether he had indeed exposed a revolution in reading practices it is necessary to turn first of all to the quantitative evidence that the state had for two decades been compiling on the communication skills of the population at large. The Victorians invented literacy as a concept rather than a practice (although the word itself had to wait until 1893 before its first recorded use in England). The capacity to decode texts was separated from other techniques of communication and other skills for living and subjected to enquiry and debate. The marriage registers which were compiled on a more systematic basis from 1837 onwards permitted the calculation of the numbers of brides and grooms completing the form with a signature or a mark. A private attainment became a public fact. The ability to count reflected the increased self-confidence and infrastructural capacity of the Reform Act state. The returns were seen as a measure both of the task it had accepted of creating a reading public, and of the results of its increasing investment in elementary schooling following the first subsidy in 1833.

When the early returns are combined with the reconstitution of data from those pre-1837 registers where the parish had consistently recorded signatures,[13] the language of revolution is called into question. By the early

---

9 Wilkie Collins, 'The unknown public', *Household Words* 18, no. 439 (27 August 1858), p. 217.
10 *Ibid.*, p. 217.   11 *Ibid.*, p. 217   12 *Ibid.*, p. 218.
13 Schofield, 'Dimensions of illiteracy in England 1750–1850', pp. 205, 207.

nineteenth century England and Wales had become societies in which the capacity to decode print was a commonplace. Around 60 per cent of men and 40 per cent of women could sign their names. This achievement was of long standing. The graph had been rising only very slowly since the 1750s. Three centuries after the invention of printing the demand for instruction in reading and writing and the means for supplying it had become widely disseminated. Nominal literacy was virtually universal across the middling and upper reaches of society and throughout the ranks of male artisans. Even amongst the lowest orders there was a solid tradition of attainment. In the first returns of the reformed marriage registers a fifth of miners and over a quarter of unskilled labourers could form a signature.[14] And whilst there were distinct spatial variations across England and Wales, with scores highest below a line from the Wash to the Severn estuary, there were no blank spots on the map.[15] Every village, every urban neighbourhood possessed those who at least knew what writing was and how to imitate it. And through the presence of vernacular religious literature, and the networks of chapmen fanning out from the urban warehouses,[16] everyone had some contact with the written word. If ever they had existed since the Reformation, the wholly oral communities were now merely a fantasy of the emerging folklore movement.

The official returns for the remainder of the period up to the First World War record a renewed climb from the late eighteenth-century plateau. Neither the rapid population growth nor the industrial revolution nor the creation of the world's first urban society could hold back the rise. Unskilled labourers caught up with the skilled, brides with grooms (even outstripping them in many mid-century communities), until by 1914 virtually the whole of the marrying-age population was completing the register with a signature. Britain, in common with its neighbours in north-west Europe, had achieved a nominally literate society.[17] The rapidly ascending graph appeared to reflect the increased intervention by the state in the provision of literacy, from the initial subsidies to the beginning of an inspected curriculum in the 1840s, the introduction of the Revised Code in 1862 with its foregrounding of instruction in the three Rs, the creation of a nationwide system of elementary schooling in 1870 and the imposition of compulsory attendance in 1880. In an era that was still inventing quantitative social analysis the literacy tables were beacons of consistent, objective measurement. Other demographic data were exposed to underrecording; criminal statistics, with which literacy was often linked, were

14 Vincent, *Literacy and popular culture*, p. 97.
15 Stephens, *Education, literacy and society*, pp. 20–4.
16 Spufford, *Small books and pleasant histories*.   17 Vincent, *The rise of mass literacy*, pp. 9–10.

plagued with problems of categorisation and mis-reporting. Yet soon after the first tables were published critics began to point out that it was not clear if they accurately reflected possession of the skills, or the capacity to use them, or, most importantly, their actual application. At best, as W. B. Hodgson argued in 1867, the skills of reading and writing were no more than 'tools for gaining knowledge; they are not crop, but plough and harrow'.[18] The journey from the signature to the active engagement with the written word was neither predictable nor straightforward.

Subsequent analysis of marriage registers and other related data in Britain and elsewhere would suggest that there is some ground beneath our feet. Where it has been possible in the European countries now compiling literacy scores to compare marriage registers with other evidence such as census enquiries and conscript records, a consistent pattern of change emerges.[19] A close examination of the distribution of marks and signatures left in the English registers by the four parties to the marriage ceremony – bride, groom and two often related witnesses – gives little support to the contemporary suspicion that literate brides or grooms were entering marks in order not to embarrass less educated partners.[20] The signatures themselves are for the most part sufficiently fluent to suggest that the writers had held a pen before and were not merely copying a couple of words set out in front of them. Some kind of communication skill was being measured and its possession was undergoing a significant change over time.

The nature of that skill and its connection to the practice of reading was conditioned by the way it was taught. Prior to the arrival of the inspected curriculum, instruction was a striking combination of the informal and the abstract. For most boys and almost all girls such instruction as took place was fitted around the rhythms and requirements of the family economy. A parent or an elder sibling who had made some progress with their letters might pass on their knowledge in the evenings or in the interstices of the working week. If there was any spare cash in the family economy, a widow looking for a source of income or a working man seeking an escape from manual labour might be paid for intermittent instruction. By the eighteenth century the village schoolteacher was already a recognised occupation, but it was rarely better paid than the labouring men whose pence were contributed to teach their children. Even when the local vicar took lessons or employed a master,

18 Hodgson, 'Exaggerated estimates of reading and writing', *Transactions of the National Association for the Promotion of Social Sciences* (1867), p. 398.
19 See in particular Furet and Ozouf, *Reading and writing*, pp. 14–17.
20 Vincent, *Literacy and popular culture*, Appendix B.

attendance was at the discretion of parents who had other and often more pressing priorities.[21] There was no set age of commencement of learning, and well before their teens those children who had been exposed to instruction drifted off into full-time labour or domestic duties. Neither was there a fixed location for the lessons, with those children possessed of determined parents passing through various kinds of domestic and formal instruction, even in relatively small rural communities.[22]

If there was no single structure of teaching, there was an accepted method. Since the invention of printing, all children exposed to formal instruction encountered the printed word in the same manner.[23] They were presented with the alphabet, then a list of disconnected syllables.[24] Once these were mastered the pupil was required to combine them into words of increasing length and complexity. By the eighteenth century a flourishing industry in cheap primers had emerged, with the market leaders claiming several hundred 'editions' over many decades.[25] The variation between them was confined to the elaboration of the lists of words, with the most complex taking the pupils from monosyllables to seven-syllable tongue twisters accompanied by compilations of the most obscure and complex biblical names. Writing, where it was attempted, was essentially a form of imitation, copying letters and complete words set before the learner. In this sense, there was a marked contrast between the skills of oral and written communication. Whereas the child learned to speak as it needed to, without conscious lessons or gradations of achievement, and put its capacity to immediate use, reading and writing began with units of sound that had no meaning in themselves, and the process of combination always appeared a distinct and artificial attainment, with no inherent relevance to sense and expression.

The adoption by the Anglican and Nonconformist churches of the ambition of mass elementary education in the early decades of the nineteenth century, followed by the introduction in 1841 of systematic state inspection of all schools receiving public funding, had the effect of accentuating the abstract at the expense of the informal.[26] In domestic instruction, in the dame and private day schools and in the parish schools, the artifice of the syllabic method had

---

21 On parental attitudes to schooling see Gardner, *The lost elementary schools of Victorian England*, pp. 91–100.
22 Vincent, *Literacy and popular culture*, pp. 66–72.
23 Michael, *The teaching of English*; Graff, *The legacies of literacy*, p. 72.
24 Michael, *Early textbooks of English*, p. 2; Vincent, 'Reading made strange'.
25 For instance, T. Dyche, *Guide to the English tongue* (2nd edn, 1710); W. Markham, *An introduction to spelling and reading English* (5th edn, 1738); T. Dilworth, *A new guide to the English tongue* (1840).
26 On the new system of inspection see Smelser, *Social paralysis and social change*, pp. 91–2.

been softened by the universal practice of individual instruction. Even in a well-attended parish school each pupil would be taught by being called to the master to receive a few minutes of personal attention, spending the rest of the day left to its own devices with a primer or a piece of chalk. Faced with the need to achieve economies of scale and measurable outcomes, and attracted by the experiments in systematic management being pioneered in factories and prisons, an increasingly self-conscious teaching profession began to develop a new pedagogy based on the simultaneous instruction of an entire class.[27] A single master, operating with a team of 'monitors' – older children who had made some progress in the curriculum – might hope to teach classes of sixty or seventy pupils, every one of whom would be fully engaged in the task of learning their letters throughout the fixed hours and days of the school year.

The centuries-old syllabic method was perfectly suited to this ordered universe. It provided the illusion of structure and progress. The pupil could proceed from level to level by moving from alphabet to syllables to escalating combinations.[28] The hierarchy of classes could reflect the complexity of the words that were being learned.[29] More discursive forms of instructional literature, such as anthologies of prose and poetry which had begun to appear in the marketplace in the late eighteenth century,[30] were pushed back to the margins by a new generation of school manuals combining traditional methods with new ambitions. Literacy became, in modern parlance, the first public-sector performance measurement, indicating the effectiveness of the teacher, the output of the school and, when aggregated in the inspectors' reports and marriage register tables, the consequences of state investment. And whilst the churches had seen in the growing level of spending on elementary schooling a powerful means of extending their reach into the lives and communities of the labouring poor, they found themselves under increasing pressure to subordinate their essentially unquantifiable spiritual instruction in favour of capacities which could be counted, culminating in the Revised Code of 1862 which restricted government funding to examined outcomes in reading, writing and arithmetic.[31]

---

27 Jones and Williamson, 'The birth of the schoolroom'.
28 See for instance *Manual for the system of primary instruction, pursued in the model schools of the B.F.S.S.* (1831); W. M'Cleod, *A first reading book for the use of families and schools* (1848); J. M. M'Culloch, *A first reading book for the use of schools* (Edinburgh: Oliver & Boyd, 1837).
29 Matthews, *Teaching to read*, pp. 19–74.   30 Davies, *Teaching reading in early England*, p. 151.
31 Marcham, 'The Revised Code of Education 1862'.

Attainment in literacy was a means of managing the emerging profession of the formally trained elementary school teacher. At the same time, the creation of the normal schools together with the annual school inspectors' reports and the intermittent Parliamentary enquiries into the use of state funding created an arena for innovation in the pedagogy of reading and writing. By the 1850s a reaction was setting in against the increasingly mechanical nature of the class-based syllabic system. The 'Look and Say' method began to be advocated on both sides of the Atlantic.[32] Instead of constructing words and sentences in the orderly fashion of factory production, the pupil was to encounter complete words and meaningful sentences as soon as she had mastered the alphabet. Guesswork was permitted and the learner was encouraged to create links between competence in oral skills and growing confidence in reading. The standards of the Revised Code were modified by use and began to incorporate passages of prose and poetry extracted from works of approved authors. J. S. Laurie's Graduated Series of Reading Lesson Books of 1866 introduced the handful of pupils who reached Standard v to Macaulay, Spenser, Milton and Byron.[33] In a parallel shift, writing ceased merely to be copying. In the new Code of 1871 what was termed 'composition' was introduced for the top Standard vi.[34] In practice this meant little more than producing simple specimen letters but it was at least a token recognition that the pen could be a means of independent self-expression.

It is difficult to determine how far the new thinking displaced the old, particularly for the mass of pupils who never progressed beyond the lower grades. In 1867 W. B. Hodgson discovered that in the official curriculum:

> The letters are taught by their names, not by their sounds, in the arbitrary order of the alphabet, instead of the natural order of the organs by which they were pronounced. Spelling is still taught by means of columns of long, hard, unconnected words, selected for their very difficulty and rarity, to be learned by rote, or, as is said with unconscious irony, 'by heart'.[35]

The changes in the third quarter of the nineteenth century constituted not a gradual evolution away from primitive times but rather the commencement of the wars over method which continue to this day. Syllabic or, in its later manifestation, phonetic instruction has waned and waxed as the required

32 *Minutes of the Committee of Council on Education, 1851–2* (London, 1852) 2, p. 48; Ellis, *History of children's reading and literature*, pp. 51–3.

33 J. S. Laurie, *Laurie's graduated series of reading lesson books* (1866). See also, E. T. Stevens and the Rev. C. Hole, *The grade lesson books in six standards* (1871). The developments are discussed in Ellis, *Books in Victorian elementary schools*, pp. 21–32.

34 Vincent, *Literacy and popular culture*, p. 89.   35 Hodgson, 'Exaggerated estimates', p. 400.

approach of the inspected curriculum and teacher. What has remained constant in the official mind is the assumption that method itself is critical. Despite research that suggests that a range of contextual factors including the availability of reading matter in the home, the scale of parental involvement, the quality of the physical facilities of the school and the enthusiasm of the teacher are integral to the outcome of the early engagement with formal communication skills,[36] the search has continued for the magic methodological bullet that will guarantee that the ever-increasing cost of public investment in schooling will generate a continuing improvement in the graph of literacy. In the era of the invention of the classroom funded and policed by the state, method served as a key signifier of quality. Traditional parish schools, and more so privately run day and dame schools, and yet more so domestic instruction, stood condemned by the absence of a formally embodied system of teaching.

Historians of education have only recently begun to pay attention to the scale and consequence of unofficial instruction in literacy in the nineteenth century.[37] This is in part because the official record, much the most accessible and supposedly reliable evidence about past practice, refers to non-standard provision only to condemn it. The educational reformers of the period were fired by the twin ambitions of getting the rapidly increasing cohorts of young children off the streets and into the classroom, and replacing amateur by professional instruction. Compulsory attendance when it was introduced in 1880 was aimed as much at the unrecognised instructor as it was at the absent pupil. A critical reworking of official statistics together with a search for alternative sources of evidence, particularly working-class autobiography, have helped to place back on the literacy stage the boys and girls teaching themselves from fragments of print found in the house, the street or the church pew, the mothers reading with their children in the evenings, the fathers teaching sons with a book propped on their loom, the older siblings passing on their scant knowledge, the Sunday school teachers taking a day out of their working week to lead classes, the widows eking a pittance by taking a few small children into their homes, the broken-down labourers looking for a less demanding alternative to physical toil, the groups of working men forming mutual improvement societies to translate their limited childhood skills into the capacity to read and take meaning from extended prose. Taken together the labours of these figuratively anonymous instructors and self-instructors were responsible for the attainment of over 60 per cent nominal literacy rates before the state spent

36 Meek, 'Literacy: redescribing reading'.
37 The first attempt to challenge the orthodoxy was Gardner, *Lost elementary schools*.

a penny on teaching reading and writing, and played a significant role in the final drive to mass literacy. Even where the instruction did take place in the inspected classroom, the child's presence was for most of the period of rapid growth dependent on the decision of the parents to meet the cost of clothing and, where charged, school fees, and sacrifice the value of the son in the economy or the daughter as a child minder. If a notional fifteen years is added to cover the period between leaving school and appearing in the marriage registers, only 5 per cent of the task of achieving a nominally literate society remained by the time the state plucked up its courage to start penalising parents who refused to send their children for inspected lessons in reading and writing.[38]

The rediscovery of the unofficial instructor challenges the official statistical record but cannot replace it. Almost all the questions that might legitimately be asked about the range and quality of reading skills at any point in the nineteenth century cannot be answered with any kind of precision. The only direct measures of the use of literacy in the period is for writing in the returns made by the Post Office following the introduction of the Penny Post in 1840,[39] supplemented by the international data generated by the Universal Postal Union after 1875. These suggest that except in times of domestic emergency the mass of the population did not take up their pens to communicate with each other until the introduction of the picture postcard at the end of the nineteenth century.[40] We know that in Britain, unlike France, reading and writing tended to be taught concurrently rather than consecutively, and therefore marriage register signatures may indicate some kind of twin achievement. Half a century ago R. K. Webb made a pioneering calculation that those signing their names probably were able to make some attempt at reading, and between a half and two-thirds of them could actually use a pen for some task other than writing their names.[41] His estimate has remained the best guess, if only because it is impossible to construct a systematic, nationwide quantitative measure to improve it. On this basis, Wilkie Collins's estimate of an English reading public of around 3 million in the middle of the nineteenth century may not be far from the truth.

The task of making readers in the nineteenth century had the most profound impact on the teachers. The transformative innovations were in the structures

38 Digby and Searby, *Children, school and society in nineteenth-century England*, p. 4.
39 Daunton, *Royal Mail*, pp. 8–11.
40 [Hill] 'The Post Office'; *Twenty-seventh annual report of the Postmaster General* (1881), p. 11; *Thirty-seventh annual report of the Postmaster General* (1891), p. 17; *Forty-seventh annual report of the Postmaster General* (1901), p. 25; Robinson, *Britain's Post Office*, p. 221; Staff, *The picture postcard*, pp. 7–91.
41 Webb, 'Working-class readers in early Victorian England', p. 350.

created to sustain a new category of state activity and to train and manage a new type of public employee. Together with prisons and the Poor Law, elementary education was the site of the most radical growth of non-military spending in the nineteenth century, and the most far-reaching experiment in systems for control and monitoring. Compared with the late twentieth and early twenty-first century, where initiatives such as the literacy hour can be conceived and systematically imposed within months, the infrastructural power of the state remained weak. In the first phase of reform it seemed more practical to work through the voluntary church societies than attempt a parallel construction. Compulsory teaching of reading was not introduced until the great majority of parents had accepted the need to educate their children, and even so did not become fully effective, especially for girls, for several decades. Blueprints for mass instruction were drawn up in most western European states during or soon after the French Revolution but took most of the succeeding century to be implemented. In England, the aspiration for a schooled society was comprehensively set out in the failed Brougham Education Bill of 1820.[42] Nonetheless, over time a handful of modernising states accepted and fulfilled a responsibility to introduce all children to the elements of formal communication. And in place of the untrained instructor, engaging in teaching concurrently with other part-time manual occupations, or moving in and out of schooling according to the fluctuating demands of the seasonal economy and the inconsistent capacity of parents to find surplus pence for an optional investment in their children, there emerged the trained career professional, dedicating a working life to the single task of creating a mass reading public.

For the new readers the consequences were less profound. Within the broad curriculum of a child's upbringing, even in the agricultural sector, literacy was at best one of a range of skills for living and working which might be acquired and by no means the most difficult or time-consuming. For a skilled artisan, mastering the alphabet took its place amongst a variety of early childhood tasks undertaken in preparation for the real course of learning, which did not commence until apprenticeship at the age of 14. As Jeffrey Brooks pointed out with respect to Russia, whilst governments attached increasing importance to the issue, 'it was also a skill the children could acquire quickly during a couple of winters of formal or informal schooling'.[43] In Britain, the seasonal interludes were gradually extended to a block of childhood, with entry around 5 or 6 and a leaving age imposed at 10 in 1880, 11 in 1893 and 12 in 1899.[44] Even so, the

---

42 Smelser, *Social paralysis and social change*, pp. 73–4.
43 Brooks, *When Russia learned to read*, p. xiv.
44 Cunningham, *The invention of childhood*, pp. 172–3.

great majority of children came nowhere near the encounters with extended prose at the summit of the inspected curriculum. There were, for instance, just over 3.5 million children at school in the early years of compulsion. Of these, just under half entered and passed one of the first four standards in reading. At the top, only one in fifty achieved the sixth standard where they demonstrated an ability to 'read a passage from one of Shakespeare's historical plays, or from some other standard author, or from a history of England'.[45] When a new seventh standard was introduced in 1885, it was attempted by a tiny elite of one in six hundred pupils.[46]

The one clear change was a decline in absolute illiteracy, and with it an erosion of the differentials which reflected the structural inequalities of society. Occupation remained the most consistent predictor of attainment in the nineteenth century, but its significance declined over time. For grooms who were unskilled labourers at marriage, a rate of 77 per cent illiteracy in 1839 had fallen to 44 per cent by 1874/9, and 14 per cent by 1894/9, and stood at 1 per cent as the First World War broke out.[47] Brides did not generally enter an occupation in the registers, but if their fathers' occupations are taken as a proxy, there is a parallel rate of decline, starting at 71 per cent in 1839 and reaching 3 per cent in 1914.[48] The gap between men and women, a feature of every modernising society, closed with greater speed. In 1750 brides lagged 20 points behind grooms, and were still 16 points back in the first returns of the reformed registration process. Thereafter they steadily caught up with their menfolk in the national aggregate figures. By the beginning of the third quarter of the nineteenth century, they were only one or two points behind the grooms, and both partners in the marriage ceremonies reached nominal universal literacy virtually together. Recent scholarship has stressed that the experience of girls in official schooling was markedly different from that of boys in terms both of the vulnerability of their attendance to the demands of child-minding and of the time spent in the classroom on the practical training necessary for their future role as domestic servants and housewives.[49] Nonetheless, learning to read and write in the elementary classroom was not intrinsically gendered. All pupils used the same textbooks and in terms of the prescribed standards were expected to reach the same level of attainment. In relation to the continuing differentials in every other aspect of their lives from birth to death, the early encounter with the printed word represented some kind of a haven of equal

---

45 *Report of the Committee of Council on Education 1882–3* (1883), pp. 200–2.
46 *Report of the Committee of Council on Education 1883–4* (1884), pp. 205, 214–15.
47 Vincent, *Literacy and popular culture*, p. 97, table 4.1.
48 *Ibid.*, p. 102, table 4.3.   49 Davin, *Growing up poor*, pp. 116–73; Purvis, *Hard lessons*, pp. 80–93.

access. Indeed where circumstances were propitious, particularly in southern rural areas where boys were more often taken from the schoolroom to take part in the agricultural economy, the capacity to sign a marriage register became a rare example of women out-performing men. As early as 1864 brides were ahead of grooms in almost all counties south of a line from the Wash to Dorset. Although the differences were compressed as illiteracy disappeared, there were actually more literate brides than grooms in two out of three English counties in the period between 1900 and the outbreak of war.[50]

Labourers became more like landowners, women more like men, the countryside more like the city, and the north of England more like the south. Total illiteracy ceased to be a divisive factor across most of the basic social and demographic categories. The one area in which it grew was that of age. Although no systematic analysis has been undertaken for the eighteenth century, it is likely that the very slow movement in the literacy rates confined inequalities between the generations. As soon as the final drive towards mass literacy commenced, gaps opened up between parents and their children. Taking the period between 1839 and 1914 as a whole, the most literate cohort, those appearing in the registers between the ages of 25 and 29, was nearly 40 points more literate than the small group of widows and widowers reappearing in the registers in their sixties and beyond. At any point in the period, those in their early twenties were around 20 points more literate than the next generation up in their late forties.[51]

The age differential had two consequences. The first was that in household after household the pupil–teacher role was reversed. Children read to parents rather than the other way about. When the very rare official document was encountered, ironically most frequently in relation to the school bureaucracy, the adults had often to depend on their dependants to decipher it. The situation was analogous to the more compressed and dramatic effect of the contemporary IT revolution where the 15-year-old is the modern master of communication and the 50-year-old a supplicant apprentice. When the first of the new technologies arrived, the silent cinema, 'a muddled Greek chorus of children's voices rose from the benches', recalled Robert Roberts, reading the captions for the parents who had taken them.[52] The second effect was further to qualify the apparent achievement of a literate society by 1914. Men and women exposed to more limited possibilities of formal education that had occurred decades earlier lived on in the company of children and grandchildren with

50 Vincent, *Literacy and popular culture*, p. 25, table 2.1.
51 *Ibid.*, pp. 26–7, figs. 2.2 and 2.3.   52 Roberts, *The classic slum*, p. 176.

increasing opportunities. Because of the nature of the data set, with only small numbers of older brides and grooms appearing in the registers, it is difficult to be precise, but it is likely that in the early years of the twentieth century, the moment at which illiteracy was nominally vanquished, at least one adult in ten still lacked a minimum command over the basic skills of reading and writing. Robert Roberts wrote of Edwardian Salford that 'Among the lower class, a mass of illiterates, solid and sizeable, still remained.'[53] These were the old men and women still confined to oral communication that Richard Hoggart encountered in his childhood in interwar Leeds.[54]

The Victorians counted what they assumed to be reading and writing in order to pattern a society which threatened constantly to escape their comprehension. Their achievement allows us to gain some sense of the landscape of communication but it is important not to lose sight of the intrinsic disorder beneath the graphs of progress. The regime of inspection, examination and compulsion represented a far-sighted attempt to reduce inequalities of provision, but in the period before 1914 it had only a limited effect. From the child's perspective, chance remained the reality. Statistical analysis has failed to find any regularity in whether older or younger children were more likely to be taught to read; so much depended on the unpredictable fluctuations of the family economy and the inconsistent availability of competent teachers. Autobiographical evidence reveals enormous variations in the experience of private day and dame schools, with establishments opening and closing without warning and individual teachers ranging from inspired, life-transforming amateurs to barely literate drunks.[55] Most inspected schools remained deeply dependent on the character of an individual teacher faced for much of the period with impossibly optimistic expectations of how classes of sixty or more could be kept in order, let alone taught anything of lasting value. Method occupied the writers of textbooks and the heads of teacher-training institutions but for the children what mattered more was whether they had adequate clothing for what could be long walks along muddy lanes to the nearest school, whether they had eaten enough to be able concentrate on their lessons, and, above all, whether they had any opportunity to practise their barely grasped skills outside the classroom.

There is a natural temptation to place the acquisition of reading skills chronologically in front of their use, but in the nineteenth century the reality is one of a complex interaction. In his *History of reading*, Alberto Manguel writes that

53 *Ibid.*, p. 177.　　54 Hoggart, *The uses of literacy*.
55 Vincent, *Literacy and popular culture*, pp. 71–2.

'the methods by which we learn to read not only embody the conventions of our particular society regarding literacy – the channelling of information, the hierarchies of knowledge and power – they also determine and limit the ways in which our ability to read is put to use'.[56] In the specific circumstances of the drive to mass literacy in Britain, the reverse was equally true. Function was as much a cause as a consequence of the rising numbers of readers. The growth of official schooling followed the increase in demand from parents, and the outcome of the lessons depended on what their children thought reading meant and how far they could practise their new skills outside the school.

It can, for instance, be argued that by far the most effective primer for learning to read in the critical period when literacy levels began to take off was to be found on the streets rather than in the classroom.[57] If we take a typical product of the great entrepreneur of the penny broadside in the 1830s and 1840s, James Catnach's *Account of a dreadful and horrible murder committed by Mary Bell on the body of her mother*,[58] we find a text perfectly suited not only to the sanguine imagination of the young but also to their wide range of reading abilities. Those who had yet to master the alphabet could get some sense of the point of print by listening to the five four-line verses in the broadside sung by the street vendor to a contemporary popular tune, or repeated by friends and neighbours. They could be led into the story, in which a daughter poisoned her mother's gruel after she had disapproved of her lover, by the graphic woodcut at the head of the document.[59] Only those bereft not only of literacy but also of sight and hearing could fail to engage with the revolution in the production of popular literature which was now generating seven-figure print-runs of successful items. Those who had been encouraged to gain some fluency in reading could practise their skills on the accompanying 250-word narrative, which contained within its compact frame a complete account of action, motive and consequence. In their combination of print and illustration the broadsides followed in the footsteps of the eighteenth-century chapbooks which had always commenced with a pictorial summary of the story,[60] and as the single-side broadsides gave way to the more substantial penny dreadfuls the visual introduction was maintained.[61] This was the world Wilkie Collins had discovered on his literary exploration, available everywhere at less than the cost

56 Manguel, *A history of reading*, p. 67.   57 Vicinus, *The industrial muse*, p. 26.
58 London, n.d. St Bride Printing Library.
59 Hindley, *Curiosities of cheap literature*, p. ii; Smith, 'Press of the Seven Dials', in *The little world of London*, p. 261.
60 Ashton, *Chapbooks of the eighteenth century*, p. vii.
61 Roberts, 'Lloyd's penny bloods', p. 15.

of a pint of beer, demanding few skills but giving every encouragement to the development of those which had been picked up by some form of instruction.

Reading in the home

As fast as the inspected curriculum isolated reading as a distinct practice, so the market for popular leisure integrated the consumption of literature with that of other mass-produced products and entertainments. An early indication of the phenomenon which was to reach its apotheosis with Dickens was the phenomenon of Paul Pry. This started life not as a text but as a play, the popular hit on the London stage of 1825. It was so successful that within a few years it had appeared in a host of forms. Some were further pirated dramas, but others exploited the growing genres of cheap print, with prose versions, juvenile editions and a sequence of periodicals exploiting themes of the play which continued to appear until the 1870s. At the same time the eponymous hero escaped into the aural and visual world. Song books were compiled loosely based on themes and characters from the play. Paul Pry could be found on pub signs in various parts of the country. Ships and horses were named after him. And the figure of Pry, complete with umbrella as portrayed by Lister in the first production, gained an iconic force in much the same way as the visually similar Mr Pickwick a decade later. He quickly became a three-dimensional object, with the Staffordshire, Rockingham, Derby and Worcester factories all producing figures of Pry by 1826.[62] In a fine example of the sheer fluidity of the textual and the visual in this era, George Cruikshank first of all included Pry in his *Six vignettes illustrating phrenological propensities* in 1826,[63] and subsequently placed a porcelain figure of Pry on the mantelshelf of the workhouse parlour in an illustration for *Oliver Twist*.[64]

There was an intrinsically borderless quality to the consumption of print in the middle decades of the century, which reached its apotheosis in Dickens's public readings between 1857 and 1870 where large audiences consumed print without needing to read it at all.[65] It moved between the home and the street and the purpose-built place of entertainment. At the same time a range of

---

62 'Papers and porcelains', paragraphs 13–14.
63 George Cruikshank, *Six vignettes illustrating phrenological propensities: hope, conscientiousness, veneration, cautiousness, benevolence, causality; illustrated by a dog anxious for scraps, a maid attempting a good price for her masters old clothes, an obese gourmand eyeing an enormous side of beef, a prim couple crossing a muddy road, a man being flogged, Liston acting the part of Paul Pry* (1826). On Cruikshank's satire of phrenology, see Patten, *George Cruikshank's life, times, and art* 1, pp. 285–90.
64 Charles Dickens, *Oliver Twist* (London: Penguin, 1985), p. 220. On Cruikshank's placing of Paul Pry in the picture, see Paroissien, *The companion to Oliver Twist*, Appendix 2. See fig. 2.
65 On Dickens and his readers see Vincent, 'Dickens's reading public'. See also above, pp. 150–4.

demographic, commercial and political changes were beginning to disseminate the phenomenon of the domestic reader. During the phase between the Reform Bill crisis of 1830–2 and the presentation of the third Chartist petition in 1848, when the apprehension of revolutionary violence was at its height, a number of enquiries were undertaken to establish just what kind of literature the mass of the population had in their homes. These revealed that at least half and in some cases more than three-quarters of homes, rural as well as urban, had a book in the house, most frequently a Bible or prayer book. In Bristol, where rioters had burned down much of the town in 1831, 57 per cent of families possessed religious books. The figures were 85 per cent in the Black Country town of West Bromwich, 75 per cent in the seaport of Hull, and in the crowded parish of St George's, Hanover Square in London 89 per cent had a Bible, Testament or prayer book. In the Bedfordshire agricultural parish of Eversholt only 12 out of 209 families lacked a religious book of any sort.[66] This literature had been inherited rather than bought, and was more often owned than used. The chapbooks, whose presence was beneath the notice of the cultural inspectors, were read over and again until they disintegrated. The Bibles existed for consultation, but their chief practical use was for maintaining a private record of births and deaths.[67]

The high base-line of reading material in the home reflected the long-standing Protestant tradition of vernacular spiritual literature as well as the efforts of the eighteenth-century chapmen. It also reflected the phenomenon of domestic literacy. The tables of marriage register signatures were a product of the making of new households but presented the communication skills of society in terms of an aggregate of individual attainments. In practice the readers and non-readers lived together. Between the late 1830s and 1914 the overall literacy rate was 75 per cent but the proportion of marriages in which at least one partner could sign was 85 per cent.[68] In the first period of the drive to mass literacy, just over half the population could sign the marriage register but at least one partner could do so in two-thirds of marriages. If the increasingly educated offspring of the union are added, the proportion of homes in which no individual was capable of making some sense of the printed word declines

66 Fripp, 'Report of an inquiry into the condition of the working classes of the City of Bristol'; Manchester Statistical Society, 'Report on the state of education among the working classes in the parish of West Bromwich'; Manchester Statistical Society, 'Report on the condition of the working class in the town of Kingston-upon-Hull'; Weld, 'On the condition of the working classes in the Inner Ward of St. George's Parish, Hanover Square'; Martin, 'Statistics of an agricultural parish in Bedfordshire'.
67 James, *Print and the people*, p. 29.   68 Vincent, 'Literacy literacy'.

still further. Where these existed, neighbours could be called upon to decipher a rare incoming letter, or help compose a response.

By the middle of the nineteenth century, a tidal wave of print was flowing into these homes. Faced with the rapid growth in population, the churches realised they could no longer rely on texts being handed down between the generations. With immense energy they sought to turn the technical and organisational innovations of the secular publishers against the materialism of the age. The Society for Promoting Christian Knowledge set up a General Literature Committee in 1832 and a Tract Committee in 1834, and by mid-century was distributing about 4 million items a year.[69] The rival Religious Tract Society issued over 23 million items in the troubled decade of the 1840s. Bibles were produced at lower and lower costs, and with the aid of middle-class subscribers a determined effort was made to get them into every home.[70] Whether or not this avalanche of free material either slowed or compensated for the fall in church attendance in the expanding towns and cities is impossible to determine. In terms of cheap print, history was on the side of the profane. 'The general results, then, of our enquiry', concluded the *Fortnightly Review* in 1889, 'are first, that there is an enormous demand for works of fiction, to the comparative neglect of other forms of literature, and, secondly, that there is a decided preference for books of a highly sensational character.'[71] With every year that passed, more could be bought with less. A penny would buy a 250-word broadside in the 1840s, a 7,000-word serial by the 1860s, and a 20,000-word novelette by the 1880s.[72]

The investigators who followed in Wilkie Collins's footsteps were frequently dismayed by their discoveries. There appeared an ever-widening gap between the aspirations of the school teachers and the domestic use being made of their labours by the new generations of readers. The title of one enquiry published in the *Nineteenth Century* in 1894 captured the general verdict: 'Elementary Education and the Decay of Literature'.[73] Q. D. Leavis's pioneering study of the reading public, which used Wilkie Collins's enquiry as an epigraph, continued the lament: 'The fiction habit, therefore, had been acquired by the general public long before the Education Act of 1870 the only effect of which on the book market was to swell the ranks of the half-educated half a generation later (until then educated taste had managed to hold its own).'[74] Thereafter,

---

69 Jones, *The jubilee memorial of the Religious Tract Society*, pp. 246–7; Allen and McClure, *Two hundred years*, p. 98; Ludlow and Jones, *The progress of the working class*, p. 184.

70 Howsam, *Cheap Bibles*, pp. 181–202.   71 Gattie, 'What English people read', p. 320.

72 Altick, *The English common reader*, pp. 294–317; 'Penny fiction', *Quarterly Review* 171 (1890), p. 168.

73 Ackland, 'Elementary education and the decay of literature'.

74 Leavis, *Fiction and the reading public*, pp. 162–3.

all was decline: 'As the century grows older the best-seller becomes less a case for the literary critic than for the psychologist.'[75] But even within the frame of her literary hierarchy, all was not lost. Alongside the new fiction of such questionable quality, the cost of what was coming to be termed the classics was falling with similar speed. By 1896 the sum of money which once had bought an execution broadside could now purchase Shakespeare or Milton with the appearance of Newnes's Penny Library of Famous Books.[76]

At the same time, newspaper reading began to move off the streets and into the home. The decisive moment was the War of the Unstamped of the early 1830s.[77] Faced with the most serious constitutional crisis since the Glorious Revolution, the state attempted to exclude the labouring poor from debating politics in print by pricing their journalism out of their pockets through the imposition of a fourpence halfpenny tax. The strategy backfired when artisan printers were able to use the cheap Stanhope iron-frame printing press to produce unstamped papers in defiance of the law. These were distributed, purchased and consumed in a campaign of civil disobedience which threatened to unite physical and intellectual protest on the streets and public meeting places of London and other major cities.[78] As it became clear that persecution was further undermining the legitimacy of the Reform Act state, an alternative strategy emerged. The newspaper tax was reduced to a penny in 1836 in the hope that papers would now be consumed at home and produced by capitalists with a greater investment in the new order. The Chancellor of the Exchequer explained, as he sacrificed a revenue which he was having so much trouble collecting, that 'he would rather that the poor man should have his newspaper in his cottage than he should be sent to a public house to read it'.[79] Despite the abolition of the tax altogether in 1855, it did not prove possible in the nineteenth century for the mass of the population to find the money or the time to purchase a daily paper and read it by their fireside. Instead a number of Sunday papers founded between 1843 and 1850, including *Lloyd's Illustrated London Newspaper*, the *News of the World*, the *Weekly Times* and *Reynolds's Weekly Newspaper*, entered the ranks of the penny publications following the disappearance of the tax in 1855.[80] To the further dismay of middle-class commentators,

---

75 Leavis, *Fiction and the reading public*, p. 164.
76 Altick, *The English common reader*, pp. 294–317; 'Penny fiction', p. 168.
77 Hollis, *The pauper press*, pp. 118–20.
78 The impossibility of preventing the reading of unstamped papers is discussed in Brougham, 'Taxes on knowledge', pp. 130–1.
79 *Hansard*, 3rd series, 24 (1836), col. 625. Also Hollis, *The pauper press*, p. 38.
80 Williams, 'The press and popular culture', p. 48. The *News of the World* initially lost sales by delaying its response to the abolition of the tax.

during the second half of the century the consumption of print on the sabbath increasingly meant an encounter with sentiments and forms of behaviour far removed from the material pumped out by the tract societies.

The greater availability of print increased demand for the skills required to use it and in turn facilitated its consumption in the home. Whereas a broadside could be casually read on the street and the newspaper in a public house, the more extensive penny fiction available from mid-century encouraged a retreat to domestic space and the search for more private time within the bustle of the household. Here it became possible to respond to the new spare-time discipline of reading, not only the Sunday papers in the second half of the century, but also cheap serials. Dickens's triumphant exploitation of a long-standing publishing form remained a luxury item for the newly educated, appearing at a price of a shilling an instalment.[81] Wilkie Collins's readers encountered him either through the host of cheap pirated versions, which cheerfully took the half-finished serial and developed their own endings, or through the other media in which his stories and figures appeared.[82] At his death in 1870, Dickens had become a text amongst texts,[83] but by this time a mass market in sensational fiction had developed, selling as many as 2 million items a week by the late eighties.[84]

The habit of silent reading, which historians of the book can locate in the homes of the upper and middling orders in the seventeenth and eighteenth centuries, took time to find its way into the lives of the labouring poor. They had to learn the skill for themselves. All teaching in the early inspected school-room was conducted through the human voice, with classes repeating words and sentences dictated to them. The requirement to read or write silently was not conceived as an ambition, let alone achieved as a reality, until the last two decades of the nineteenth century. There was only a narrow tradition of intensive domestic reading, and little improvement in the facilities for undertaking it. Whilst the rise of factory production caused a slow, inconsistent move of work out of the home, there was no revolution in living space. Between 1801 and 1901 the proportion of persons to a household fell only slightly, from 5.67 to 5.20. House size increased, but in 1901 one in twelve of the population still lived two or more to a room, with much higher densities in many towns.[85] The quality of candles improved, but reading on winter evenings or in bed was still

81 See particularly Hughes and Lund, *The Victorian serial.*
82 Law, *Serialising fiction in the Victorian press,* pp. 21–3; Patten, *Charles Dickens and his publishers,* pp. 90–1.
83 Vincent, 'Dickens's reading public', pp. 176–97. 84 Johns, 'The literature of the streets', p. 43.
85 Porter, *The progress of the nation,* pp. 91–6.

at best a strain on eyesight and the pocket and at worst a serious fire hazard.[86] It was only after the invention of the penny slot meter in 1892 that gas lighting became feasible in more prosperous artisan houses.[87]

Lineaments of the key transitions identified by Chartier are clearly visible. Reading on a mass scale became more silent, more private and more extensive.[88] But every change was contested and incomplete. Entering into the secret world of print amidst the bustle of the crowded household required immense concentration and a capacity to withstand resentment at the withdrawal from its sociability.[89] If the women in the home now had comparable nominal reading skills, their ability to isolate free time amongst the relentless household labour was much less than that of their menfolk home from work. The variations in command of literacy amongst its members throughout the century meant that there remained an important role either for reading aloud, or for feeding once-read texts into the rich stock of oral story-telling. The increasing volume of readers and reading matter should not be confused with the level of control over access which the category of extensive reading implies. The price of new full-length books came down from the guinea-and-half three-decker but remained out of reach of the products of elementary schools until well into the following century. No reader consumes literature in the order that it is published,[90] but it remained a characteristic of the serious working-class reader that they encountered the best of their era only after it had filtered down into the second-hand market or exhausted copyright.

Readers were drawn into the home to deploy their newly awakened skills, appetites and opportunities, and, as we shall see in the following sections of this chapter, constantly pushed back out into communal buildings or the street as they sought to fulfil them. Reading and privacy reinforced each other and exposed their respective limitations. They were a measure both of the nineteenth-century revolution in production and consumption and of the continuing reality of material deprivation. At a time when most of the labouring poor owned nothing except the necessities of clothing, bedding and cooking, the construction of anything approaching a personal domestic library was a vast luxury. What could be acquired was put together by strategies of appropriation rather than dedicated purchase. As late as the 1930s the publisher Stanley Unwin complained that 'most people have not yet learned to regard books as a necessity. They will beg them, they will borrow them, they will do everything,

---

86 O'Dea, *The social history of lighting*, pp. 40–54.   87 Ellis, *Educating our masters*, p. 16.
88 Chartier, *The order of books*, p. 17.   89 James, *Fiction for the working man*, p. 44.
90 St Clair, 'The political economy of reading'.

in fact, but buy them.'[91] Autodidacts set out on ambitious schemes of self-improvement, conducted in and around the lives of their families and often at the expense of their contribution to its physical and social needs, but were endlessly thrust out of the home to seek the company of the occasional serious readers in their neighbourhoods.[92] In the company of learned neighbours they exchanged books, shared ideas, provided encouragement, and where feasible developed informal contacts into organised mutual improvement societies. From 1851 they used public libraries as a source of new fiction[93] and as a location of quiet, heated, properly lit spaces in which to read it. The free municipal provision of books was a landmark of the late Victorian urban civilisation, but as with so much of the campaign for mass literacy its benefits were only enjoyed by a minority of the working-class population. The common experience was of the interrupted reading of fragments of print in noisy domestic arenas.

Reading outside the home

The public library was only one of a vast array of new spaces designed for reading that opened up during the period. Such spaces could provide a vital alternative to the overcrowded home, but readers also took over many of the other new public spaces that were emerging at this time, such as the railway carriage, and often found themselves surrounded by texts displayed on advertising hoardings, or plastered on walls.

In July 1844 the journalist Angus Reach argued that 'the working man, at least in towns, is becoming more and more a reading man'. This new urban reader had access to 'cheap schools, cheap publications, cheap lectures, and last, but not least, cheap coffee and reading rooms'. Reach provides a particularly detailed description of the layout and contents of the new sort of coffee house aimed at male working-class readers that became a common feature of urban life during the 1820s and 1830s. He claimed that there were 'upwards of two thousand' in London alone by the 1840s and that up to 1,600 people visited that located near to the Haymarket each day. Unlike other institutions of reading such as the circulating library there was no fee for entry, but coffee was charged at between a penny and twopence per cup. According to Reach the majority of these buildings could seat up to a hundred customers and had a similar layout. Most had a distinctive street frontage that consisted of 'an enormously broad window' covered by 'a perfect curtain of play-bills',

91 McAleer, *Popular reading and publishing in Britain 1914–1950*, p. 85.
92 Rose, *Intellectual life*, pp. 57–91; Vincent, *Bread, knowledge and freedom*, pp. 109–32.
93 Kelly, *A history of public libraries in Great Britain*, pp. 85–8, 192–5.

which made them easy to find on a crowded street. Inside, the main room itself was 'partitioned off into little boxes with a table in each', and, like the windows, the walls were used to display more advertisements for the theatre. He describes the clientele politely exchanging newspapers and periodicals between the boxes. Large coffee houses, such as that in the Haymarket, took in a wide range of newspapers each day, as well as monthly magazines, quarterly reviews and weekly periodicals. Some also included a small library 'consisting principally of works of fiction, and of entertaining and useful information'. Reach's account of the working-class coffee house is somewhat idealised and was clearly intended to persuade working men to abandon the delights of the gin-palace, which is depicted throughout as its 'quarrelling... scuffling' alternative.[94] Other commentators mocked this attempt to take over a characteristically bourgeois environment (and drink) by depicting dustmen politely swapping periodicals as they sipped their coffee, but these spaces clearly fulfilled an important function within urban working-class culture.[95] As already noted, it was often difficult for working-class readers to find a space within the home in which reading could take place, and although the coffee house customer needed to pay at least a penny to read, this guaranteed access both to a wide range of texts and to warmth and adequate lighting.[96]

Communal reading outside the home was not restricted to the working classes. By the 1830s 'every large' and 'almost every small town in England' had subscription reading rooms that supplied newspapers to those who could afford 'to pay a guinea or so annually'.[97] The less well off might visit 'smaller scale penny-a-week' subscription rooms, or hire a paper by the hour to read at a news-walk.[98] From about 1840 onwards, the fee to join a mechanics' institute usually gave the male subscriber access to a library, newsroom and reading room. The range of texts taken in by some of these rooms was extensive. The 'News and Reading Room' at the Manchester Mechanics' Institution received ten daily papers, numerous weeklies and American and Australian papers, as well as periodicals and reviews. However, it was not until the 1860s that this and many other institutes allowed female members access to the news and reading rooms, although they had been able to attend lectures and 'avail themselves' of the library since the late 1830s.[99] Many of the key reading spaces that developed during the nineteenth century restricted access along class

---

94 Reach, 'The coffee houses of London'.
95 For a discussion of the images contained in Richard Seymour's *Sketches by Seymour*, 5 vols. (R. Carlile, 1834), see Maidment, *Reading popular prints*, pp. 75–81.
96 Vincent, *Bread, knowledge and freedom*, p. 118.
97 [Merle] 'Provincial newspaper press', *Westminster Review* 12 (1830), pp. 69–103.
98 Barker, *Newspapers, politics and English society*, p. 60.   99 Purvis, *Hard lessons*, pp. 115–20.

and/or gender lines. Most mechanics' institutes were founded and run by men mainly from middle-class backgrounds. During the 1820s and 1830s there was much debate about whether newspapers should be taken at all because it was believed that they might encourage political discussion, and, as June Purvis has argued, the collections of books and newspapers that were assembled tended to reflect the tastes of the middle-class members and their representatives on the governing committees.[100] An article in the *Westminster Review* argued that newspapers should be included in order to attract working-class men who might otherwise go to the tavern to read them. It also suggested that the reading room should be made as comfortable as possible, with good furniture, pictures and sculptures, as well as a supply of coffee and other 'cheap and temperate refreshments'.[101] The image of the Working Men's Newsroom and Reading Room at York, which appeared in the *British Workman* in 1856, shows a well-lit room appointed in exactly the fashion suggested by the *Westminster*. Most reading rooms were probably not as luxurious as this one, but the men standing reading newspapers propped up on boards in this image are an early representation of an activity that took place in public reading rooms and libraries throughout the period 1830–1914.[102]

In order to have more control over the provision of texts, some working men founded their own alternative spaces for reading. These more democratically organised reading rooms frequently included classes that taught reading and writing skills. Often begun in cheap to rent or borrowed premises, some of these organisations became very successful and moved into buildings that resembled those occupied by the mechanics' institutes, while others faded away as basic literacy began to be taught more efficiently in state schools. As Jonathan Rose makes clear, however, for much of the mid-Victorian period they provided a vital alternative educational space for working-class readers.[103] Similarly, both Rose and Chris Baggs have noted the importance of miners' institutes and welfare halls in helping to make the Welsh miner into 'a great reader'.[104] The surviving catalogues of these institutions of reading, which spread across the Welsh coalfields from the late 1860s to the 1930s, show that they supplied a vast range of texts, from popular novels to Marxist pamphlets, the latter

---

100 *Ibid.*, p. 120. She also notes that very few institutes contained periodicals specifically aimed at female readers.

101 'Mechanics Institutes', *Westminster Review* 41 (June 1844), pp. 416–45, reprinted in King and Plunkett (eds.), *Victorian print media*, pp. 240–5 (at 244).

102 *British Workman* August 1856, p. 78. Similar images of newspaper reading in the 1890s are reproduced in Flint, *The woman reader*, pp. 176–7.

103 Rose, *Intellectual life*, pp. 63–7.

104 *Ibid.*, pp. 237–55; Baggs, 'How well read was my valley?', p. 277. The description comes from James Milne's 1915 survey of the book trade, *Book Monthly* 12 (1915), p. 655.

particularly suited to the development of the 'militant trade unionism and revolutionary politics' which emerged in some of these communities during the early twentieth century. As was the case in the working-class reading rooms of the earlier period, members of the mining community, rather than a middle-class ruling body, determined the stock of these institutions. But as Baggs suggests, however, there was nevertheless sometimes a conflict between what the Library Committee thought its members should be reading, and what they actually wanted to read. He argues that the institutes and welfare halls need to be thought of as part of a broader cultural dynamic, often communal in character, which helped to encourage reading. Penny readings, eisteddfodau, ymanfaoedd ganu, and debating and literary societies were widespread from the 1850s onwards.[105] By the twentieth century, however, texts were much more likely to be borrowed and consumed within the home – or bought from the newsagent – and these institutions of reading probably played only a residual role as reading venues.[106]

Kate Flint has argued that reading clubs and circles provided an important framework for middle-class reading practices during the period 1837–1914. 'Reading Societies, Essay societies, and Societies for the encouragement of Home Study' often forced women to adopt strict regimes of reading. Writing in the 1890s, Edna Lyall noted that some groups even fined their members if they failed to read for the amount of time, and from the types of text, stipulated in their rules. Both this private group and the National Home Reading Union (NHRU) suggested reading at home for at least thirty minutes per day.[107] Founded in 1889 and active until 1930, the NHRU had more than 10,000 members in 1900, and in the period up to 1914 many more must have been influenced by its educational programme, which encouraged a mixture of solitary reading and communal discussion. During the 1890s the Union offered courses for 'Young People', 'Artisans' and the 'General Reader'. Members paid a fee, for which they received a monthly magazine that was designed to perform a tutorial role, and they were encouraged to form 'Circles' that would meet regularly to discuss their reading. Felicity Stimpson has demonstrated that the *General Reader's Magazine* contains important evidence about the advice handed out to readers and the way in which the Circles actually operated. While reading Carlyle's *Chartism*, for example, members were advised to mark

---

105 Baggs, 'How well read was my valley?', pp. 279, 281, 286–97.
106 In her survey of working-class Middlesbrough, Lady Bell records that reading at home was the preferred venue, although at least one man read 'a great deal at the workmen's club' but would not 'bring any books home': Bell, *At the works*, p. 214.
107 Flint, *The woman reader*, p. 107; Lyall, 'A quiet half-hour', pp. 45–6, quoted in Flint, p. 107.

their favourite passages in preparation for reading aloud 'in Circle'. Members' letters reveal that these groups often included men and women from different classes and that they met in a variety of different locations, from schoolrooms to farmhouses. One all-female group used 'the subjects given for thought' at the end of the *Magazine* articles to help structure their discussion and each member contributed 'her share'. At another in Cardiff, one or two members presented papers on their reading at each meeting, but the subsequent discussion was sometimes stilted.[108] Although some groups were clearly more successful than others in encouraging lively debate, what is most remarkable about the NHRU is the way in which it encouraged private reading to be converted into public discussion.

The NHRU and private reading societies were founded towards the end of the nineteenth century because many contemporary intellectuals, including J. G. Fitch, feared that new institutions of reading, such as the public or 'free' libraries, allowed readers to access 'whatever books happen to come nearest, whether good or bad'. As Fitch argued in an article that helped promote reading circles, most of these new libraries included 'facilities for quiet reading in the library itself, or for loan and home study'.[109] How were these new spaces for reading organised and what kind of reading went on there? According to an article that appeared in *All the Year Round* in 1892, the public libraries established at this time were a mix of converted suburban houses and purpose-built facilities. The writer's 'own suburban free library' occupied 'three or four rooms' in an ordinary house. Although the library contained only a very limited number of books, the newspaper and periodicals room was busy throughout the day, with young men and women scouring the situations vacant columns early in the morning and working people wading 'patiently through the monthly magazines and illustrated papers' in the evening. By contrast, the purpose-built library in the predominantly working-class Bermondsey included a newsroom and a lending library on the ground floor, and a magazine room, a reference library and 'a "ladies" room' on the floor above.[110]

During the late nineteenth and early twentieth centuries women-only reading rooms, which usually stocked newspapers, periodicals and reference books, became a feature in many public libraries. In 1892 the *Library* listed twenty-two institutions with such rooms, including those at Belfast, Cardiff and Edinburgh. Some others reserved separate tables and it recommended that many more follow the example set in Bradford, where separate counters for women had been introduced in both the lending and reference rooms.[111] Such gendered spaces were designed to separate women from men who had entered the library for physical warmth rather than mental sustenance, but even that centre of London intellectual life the British Museum reading room had two tables put aside for women readers when it opened in May 1857.

Ruth Hoberman has argued that actual women readers often failed to fit into, or subverted, the spaces designed for them. Many female members of the British Museum, for example, chose not to sit in the reserved seats and in the 1907 refit the ' "ladies" section' was removed.[112] Although, according to the *Library*, separate issue desks and even separate entrances encouraged more women to use the Bradford library, other contributors to the debate noted that women as much as men used the free library to check the racing results and discuss form. While *All the Year Round* found the preponderance of 'Silence is Requested' signs part of an 'oppressive', disciplining force, which seemed to have robbed the human race of speech, others complained that the public library was anything other than quiet. As Flint acknowledges, some representations of women gossiping in the library manipulated stereotypical notions of femininity, but many sources, including the minutes of library committee meetings and autobiographical reminiscences, confirm that these new, often mixed-gender reading spaces allowed both sexes to combine reading with conversation and flirtatious behaviour.[113]

Railway reading was one of the most remarked upon phenomena of the Victorian age, encouraged as it was by the proliferation of bookstalls and newsboys on the platforms from the late 1840s onwards. Much of the evidence that we have for this kind of reading is of the negative sort. In August 1851 the author of an article in *The Times* regretted having seen 'two young ladies and a boy . . . amusing themselves and alarming us by a devotion to a trashy French novel' during a three-hour journey in first class. That this article was subsequently expanded into a short sixpenny pamphlet suggests that its author had hit upon a particular cultural anxiety about the kinds of texts available at the railway station and the nature of unsupervised reading outside the home.[114] Augustus Egg's painting *The travelling companions* (1862) also attacks the practice of reading novels while travelling. It shows two identical looking young women in a railway carriage, the one absorbed in a novel while the other

---

111 Wood, 'Three special features of free library work'.
112 Ruth Hoberman, ' "A thought in the huge bald forehead": depictions of women in the British Museum reading room, 1857–1929', in Badia and Phegley (eds.), *Reading women*, pp. 168–91 (at 186).
113 'A day at the London free libraries', p. 284; Flint, *The woman reader*, pp. 175–8.
114 *The literature of the rail*, p. 4.

sleeps, as the magnificent countryside of the Riviera passes their window unobserved.

Both pamphlet and painting suggest that it was possible to read in some comfort while on the move in a first-class carriage, but the author of an article on 'Railway reading' that appeared in 1853 challenged even 'the most constant of all "constant readers" to make either head or tail of even a child's primer while in a travelling railway carriage'. This author suggests that it was not the motion of the train that was difficult to cope with, for that could be overcome by holding a piece of a paper just below the line of text that was being read, but the hum of conversation emanating from his fellow travellers. His imagined reader gets through only a few lines of Sterne's *Tristram Shandy*, purchased from the station's bookstall specifically for the purpose, before returning it to his pocket.[115] Many purchases from bookstalls may have been quickly abandoned in much this manner once the journey began, but large numbers of readers must have learnt to adapt their reading skills to the peculiar requirements of the railway carriage. Until the 1890s, when corridor trains were widely adopted on British railways, there was no getting away from the other people with whom the reader was compartmentalised, at least until the next station. In the 1850s reading was sometimes recommended to 'young ladies' as a way of avoiding 'entering into conversation with strange fellow-travellers'.[116] This tactic of using a book or newspaper to avoid the unwanted attentions of other travellers is one that has since been adopted by millions of commuters. Mary Hammond has argued that throughout the period 1880–1914 the train tended to be associated with light or illegitimate reading. *Tit-Bits* and other new periodicals made up of extracts were ideally suited to reading on the move, and she notes that books banned at some public libraries were available at Smith's bookstalls.[117] But, of course, the bookstall did not dictate what people took with them onto the train. Several of the NHRU's general readers describe studying a biography of Benjamin Franklin whilst travelling to work. For those with limited time for study the daily commute could not be wasted.[118]

In June 1854 the novelist Elizabeth Gaskell wrote a letter to her friend the Christian Socialist John Ludlow in which she noted that she could not 'be quite certain of the times of the trains to Wimbledon' because her 'copy of Bradshaw' was out of date. She concludes by asking Ludlow to supply the information

115 Allen, 'Railway reading'.
116 Hammond, *Reading, publishing and the formation of literary taste in England*, pp. 57–8; Bowman, *The common things of everyday life*, p. 163, quoted in Hammond, p. 58.
117 Hammond, *Reading, publishing and the formation of literary taste in England*, pp. 75–6.
118 Stimpson, 'Reading in circles', p. 40.

from his own copy of the famous guide to railway travel.[119] For much of the period 1830–1914 making sense of a railway timetable would have been one of the commonest forms of reading experience, but historians of reading have had surprisingly little to say about the way in which mass-produced items such as advertising posters, handbills and tickets were consumed. This invisibility is in part due to the fact that book history has tended to concentrate upon books and newspapers as the most important items produced by the book trade, but, as Leah Price has noted, recent histories of reading have also focussed rather narrowly on the consumption of literary texts.[120] This is in part a response to the surviving sources. Readers rarely refer to their consumption of ephemera in diaries, letters and autobiographies, although, as Gaskell's letter to Ludlow suggests, we may need to look again at these materials with the subject of ephemera in mind. Indeed, Jonathan Rose's work on working-class autobiography has discovered that advertising hoardings and shop windows were important resources for readers whose interpretative skills might otherwise have lain dormant during periods in which they were too poor to buy reading materials. The printer Charles Manby Smith (b.1804) argued that 'every shop-front' was 'an open volume'.[121] Other sources such as scrapbooks suggest some of the ways in which ephemeral publications, including concert programmes and advertisements for holiday resorts, could be invested with personal meaning. During the 1870s Emily Tuke collected these and similar pieces in her scrapbook as a celebration of the present, but her annotations suggest that as time went by they became mementoes of a lost past.[122]

Advertising also frequently surrounded readers when they took to the streets. Dickens's essay 'Bill-sticking', which appeared in *Household Words* in March 1851, describes streets filled with advertising vans, 'each proclaiming the same words over and over again', and pavements 'made eloquent by lamp-black lithograph'. He imagines a reader passing dead walls, deserted houses, warehouses, bridges and buses on which the same images appear. There was no escape from advertising in the modern urban landscape and, as Dickens suggests, if any reader paused to look at those displayed on the side of one of these buildings for more than a moment he or she would recognise that they knew them 'intimately' because they were 'ubiquitous'.[123] This is an early

---

119 Gaskell, *Further letters*, pp. 112–13.   120 Price, 'Reading matter'.
121 Rose, *Intellectual life*, pp. 390–2; Smith, *The little world of London*, p. 9.
122 'Scrapbook of Emmie P. Tuke', Tuke Taylor Papers, Borthwick Institute, University of York.
123 Dickens, 'Bill-sticking'.

observation on the way in which slogans and brand names can become assimilated into patterns of everyday thought in a commodity culture. Unfortunately, the 'real' reader rarely records this sort of response, but in *The language of the walls* (1855) James Dawson Burn notes that he enjoyed the strange and amusing conjunctions that often occurred when one poster partially obscured another. As he also acknowledges, the reader on the street was not just exposed to commercial advertising. For much of the period 1830–1914 the walls carried messages about strikes and other political activities, either in printed form or as graffiti.[124]

The other spaces in which readers experienced advertising were much more disciplined than the street. Contracts for advertising at railway stations prevented the display of anything to do with striking workmen and each advert sat within its own frame. The frontispiece to Sampson's *History of advertising* (1875) reveals that at the major London termini the walls of the station resembled the advertising pages of a magazine blown up to an enormous size.[125] Of course, nineteenth-century readers often dealt with advertising in other contexts. The serial reader of *Little Dorrit* (1855–7), for example, had to wade through twelve pages or so of adverts for consumer goods and magazines before reaching the novel itself, but street advertising was more difficult to ignore.[126]

Reading by listening: reading as performance

Reading aloud constituted a bridge between the private and public arenas. Performance was as vital as in earlier eras of restricted literacy,[127] but now it existed in more complex relations with silent reading. Secord has argued that by the 1840s 'reading was typically a silent, solitary act, but the object of reading was social – to maintain relations through civil conversation'. He goes on to demonstrate that *Vestiges of the natural history of creation* became a major talking point amongst wealthy, fashionable readers in the year after it was first published. For these readers at least, private, silent reading could be converted into brilliant public conversation.[128] Visual representations of reading throughout the nineteenth century certainly tend to concentrate on the silent reader engrossed in the text. Robert Martineau's painting *The last chapter* (1863), for example, shows a young woman reading the last few pages of what is presumably a 'sensation' novel by the light of the fire as the dawn breaks at the window behind her. However, as Kate Flint has argued, such

124 [Burn] *The language of the walls*, p. 57.
125 Sampson, *A history of advertising*.   126 Hartley, '*Little Dorrit* in real time'.
127 Fischer, *History of reading*, p. 274.   128 Secord, *Victorian sensation*, p. 161.

images are part of a critical discourse that played on contemporary anxieties about the unsupervised reading of women.[129] During the 1840s Sarah Stickney Ellis warned against the 'unrestrained and private reading' of novels and plays by young women and children and recommended that all mothers should read aloud to their offspring.[130] Advice manuals frequently advocated that family groups should gather together in order to hear one of their members read aloud. Of course, not everyone followed this advice, but a large number of autobiographies attest to the continued importance of reading aloud within middle-class family groups throughout the nineteenth century. As Chartier has noted, throughout history, reading aloud has tended to take two forms – 'communicating that which is written to those who do not know how to decipher it, and binding together . . . forms of sociability' such as 'the intimacy of the family'.[131] Autobiographical reminiscences and surveys of working-class communities reveal that throughout the period 1830–1914 reading aloud often fulfilled both of the functions identified by Chartier, but perhaps more importantly they also give some sense of what reading meant to those who either performed or listened at such events.

Many autobiographical accounts suggest that reading aloud to children played an important role in passing on a taste for books. In the 1880s, the novelist Florence Barclay encouraged her children to stop her reading every time she uttered a word with which they were unfamiliar. Her daughter recalls that this was not 'a tedious interruption to the story; rather the reading became doubly thrilling, because there was the added excitement of the hunt after unknown words'. Barclay's performative reading turned listening to a novel into an interactive game, but, as already suggested, many parents read aloud in order to have control over their children's reading. Anyone following Sarah Stickney Ellis's advice about reading Shakespeare aloud to the family, for example, would have needed to censor the text by chopping it up into acceptable bits before the performance began.[132]

Reading aloud was particularly important to the family and friends of Emily Shore (1819–39), who recorded many instances in the journals that she kept during the 1830s. Her mother, father, aunt and uncle all regularly read to the family and their friends in the drawing room during the evening in much the same way as is described in the advice manuals of the period, and Emily

---

129 Flint, *The woman reader*, p. 4   130 Ellis, *The mothers of England*, pp. 338–9.
131 Chartier, 'Labourers and voyagers'.
132 *The life of Florence L. Barclay*, p. 240; [Sarah Stickney Ellis] *The young ladies' reader* (1845), pp. 289–90.

even visited a working-class family in order to read to them.[133] Shore's journal entries suggest how much she delighted in reading aloud, but she also notes that when she was a member of the audience her appreciation of the text was often significantly affected by the performance of the speaker. In December 1836 she recorded that she had not 'for a long time heard or read anything which has so interested me and seized upon my fancy as this tragedy'. This interest, she thought, owed much 'to the fact of Papa's having read it, for Papa reads beautifully, and I am sure that if I had only read it to myself, I should not have enjoyed or entered into it half so much'. A few months later, whilst writing about her waning interest in fiction, she noted that she had 'listened with greater pleasure to [the play] "Ion" than to "Ivanhoe". But "Ivanhoe" lost much of its beauty by being badly read.'[134] Readers with sophisticated reading skills must often have found listening to a poor reader frustrating and, as Shore's experience suggests, the way in which a text was performed would also have influenced the way in which the listening audience constructed meaning. That Shore also sometimes makes the distinction between having 'heard or read' a text suggests that she thought of listening as a very different sort of experience from 'reading to myself' and in her discussion of fiction she clearly implies that she sometimes thought of the latter as a superior form ('perhaps if I had read them all to myself, they would have interested me more').[135] However, as is clear from her account and others like it, many middle-class readers were accustomed to moving rapidly between different kinds of reading practice. Shore read in silence, listened to texts in a variety of domestic settings (both as an individual and as a member of a group), and was skilled at reading aloud in front of an audience. Her journal entries suggest that reading aloud was deeply embedded within the rhythms of bourgeois domesticity.

The working-class poet John Clare (1793–1864) said of his father that 'he was but a sorry reader of poetry to improve his readers by reciting it'.[136] In the 1810s Clare and his father, who could read but not write, regularly performed texts aloud for a family audience that included his illiterate mother. As Lady Bell's 1907 survey of Middlesbrough factory workers suggests, reading aloud remained particularly important to working-class communities even in the early twentieth century, because they often contained both literate and illiterate members. Indeed, Bell noted that in some families children were responsible for reading aloud to their parents: 'Husband and wife cannot read.

133 Emily Shore, *Journal* 9 August 1835.
134 Emily Shore, *Journal* 31 December 1836; 3 March 1837.
135 Emily Shore, *Journal* 3 March 1837.   136 Clare, *John Clare by himself*, p. 14.

Youngest girl reads the paper to them sometimes, but "she has a tiresome temper and will not always go on".' In others it was sometimes the literate husband or wife that read to his or her illiterate partner.[137] While these examples confirm that it is wrong to think of the working class as divided into distinct literate and illiterate communities, they also indicate that the *way* in which reading aloud was performed must have affected the nature of the experience. Of course, Parker Clare's poor reading style did not stop his son developing a love of poetry, but it must have been difficult to maintain an interest in the consumption of texts when listening to a hesitant reader or temperamental child.

Not every instance of reading aloud took place in the home. In *London labour and the London poor* (1861–2), Henry Mayhew recorded the account of an 'intelligent costermonger' who sometimes read 'cheap periodicals', such as *Reynolds's Miscellany*, 'to ten or twelve men, women, and boys, all costermongers' who gathered outside their homes for the purpose. Reading aloud to such a group was an interactive experience with the audience regularly vocalising their responses to the text. Mayhew's informant told him that passages mentioning the police, or any 'foreign language', were often met with angry shouts that had nothing to do with the context of what was being read, but his audience also liked to comment on the events of the narrative. Such reactions suggest that the audience treated these readings as a public performance and that they shouted out in much the same way as theatre or music hall audiences tended to do. This was a relatively small gathering, however, and the text itself appears to have played a role in the performance. The penny-novel journals of the 1850s and 1860s always included an illustration on their front page, as did many illustrated newspapers, and the costermonger told Mayhew that illiterate members of his audience often demanded information 'about the picture'.[138] This kind of performance meant that those members of the urban community who could not read were not cut off from developments within print culture. The costermonger community, which contained a range of different reading competencies, had rapid access to the latest productions of the London press via the shared experience of the text.

As Mayhew was keen to show, the costermonger audience was excited by the new penny publications. Like many other working-class communities they wanted to hear the latest news and the latest stories. Many middle-class commentators were worried by this love of the new. Martyn Lyons has argued that 'public recitals or "penny readings" ' in which middle-class audiences engaged

---

137 Bell, *At the works*, p. 209.   138 Mayhew, *London labour and the London poor* 1, pp. 25–6.

show a different kind of 'relationship between the reader/listener and the printed word'. At these performances the audience paid to hear the familiar.[139] Undoubtedly the most famous public readings of the Victorian period were those undertaken by Charles Dickens between 1857 and 1870. Dickens's decision to perform excerpts from his texts was taken after the success of a series of readings from *A Christmas carol* organised to raise money for a new Industrial and Literary Institute in Birmingham in December 1853. Dickens was particularly delighted by the responses of 'the working people' in the audience and the later performances were designed to encourage working-class readers to attend, although, as Helen Small has argued, the shilling entrance fee would perhaps have been too high for many.[140] One eyewitness noted that Dickens's audiences were thrilled by the recitation of scenes familiar from the novels:

> the words he was about to speak being so thoroughly remembered ... before
> their utterance that, often, the rippling of a smile over a thousand faces simul-
> taneously anticipated the laughter which an instant afterwards greeted the
> words themselves when they were articulated.[141]

Like the 'penny readings' described by Lyons, these public performances can be categorised as part of a 'traditional or "intensive"' reading practice that was actually disappearing during the nineteenth century, but they are just as much a celebration of the modernity of Victorian print culture and of the celebrity of the author. Even if there were fewer working-class people in these audiences than is sometimes supposed, they were a tribute to the way in which the serialised text and the cheap reprint had created a very large audience who were familiar enough with Dickens's texts sometimes to reach the punch-line before he did.

Reading by writing

We tend to think of the nineteenth century as the age of print, but throughout the period 1830–1914 the art of transcription remained an important skill and many readers continued to compile manuscript commonplace books in which entries were made under miscellaneous headings. The *Common-place book* of Robert Southey (1774–1843), which included some traditional moral headings as well as a section entitled 'ideas and studies for literary composition', was published in 1849–50.[142] Earle Havens has argued that some Victorian manuscript compilations, which used headings such as 'Chastity' and 'Charity',

---

139 Lyons, 'New readers in the nineteenth century', p. 343.   140 Small, 'A pulse of 124'.
141 Kent, *Charles Dickens as a reader*, p. 20.   142 Southey, *Southey's common-place book*.

'resemble quite remarkably the moral commonplace themes recommended by the Renaissance humanists' and used throughout the early modern period.[143]

The majority of manuscript books compiled during the nineteenth century were far more informal. For example, the forty-one-page volume compiled by Anne Lister (1791–1840) in the mid-1830s adopts only part of the scholarly apparatus first outlined in Locke's 'New method of a commonplace book' in the 1680s, and frequently republished in printed commonplace books throughout the nineteenth century. Lister's manuscript book consists almost entirely of 'extracts' from J. T. James's *Journal of a tour in Germany, Sweden, Russia, Poland in 1813–14* (1819) and Michael Quin's *A steam voyage down the Danube* (1835).[144] She recorded that the seventeen pages of notes from James were made at her home on a single day in 1834. Although there are no formal commonplace book-style headings in this volume, each separate entry contains a highlighted key word. Lister was able to retrieve information by rapidly scanning through the pages of extracts, and the detailed references that she made at the end of each entry would also have allowed her to locate the passage in the original, if necessary. That the remaining twenty-four pages from Quinn were added nearly two years later suggests that unlike the many other volumes of extracts that Lister compiled between 1814 and 1838, which included notes from a range of different genres, this volume was reserved for notes on foreign travel. Lister spent much of the 1830s travelling and she may even have made these extracts in anticipation of a forthcoming trip. The volume that she created was certainly much more portable than either of the texts that she was using as a source, which consisted of more than 1,500 pages in total, and she recorded much that was useful to a traveller. This volume is not just Lister's personalised 'rough guide' to Europe, however. Her dating of when and where extracts were made also suggests that it functioned as a sort of reading diary, which could be cross-referenced with her own manuscript journals at a later date.[145]

Many other nineteenth-century readers also produced their own person-alised versions of the texts that they were reading by reproducing large chunks of them in their manuscript books. Martyn Lyons has argued that 'the pri-vate memo-book or notebook' was particularly important to working-class autodidacts as a 'method of appropriating a literary culture and conducting a personal dialogue with the text'. For Samuel Bamford (1788–1872), Thomas Cooper (1805–92) and other working-class radicals, the act of transcription was often part of an intense programme of acculturation that included the

---

143 Havens, *Commonplace books*, p. 90.
144 'Extracts from books read by Anne Lister, 1834–38', Calderdale Archives, Halifax, SH.7/ML/EX/11.
145 For Lister's journals, see Liddington, *Female fortune*.

memorisation of large chunks of the dominant culture, including works by Shakespeare and Milton.[146] Many working-class readers depended upon the new versions of texts that were published when an author's work was no longer in copyright or had fallen out of fashion. As Jonathan Rose notes, the Welsh collier Joseph Keating (b.1871) read widely amongst the works of dead authors, including Pope, Byron and Dickens, but regretted that 'volumes by living authors were too high-priced for me'.[147] Some contemporary works could be borrowed from libraries, employers or wealthier friends, however, and the process of transcription sometimes allowed those who could not afford to buy the latest works the possibility of creating and owning their own version of the text. Writing in the 1870s, Robert White (b.1802) recalled transcribing part of an otherwise unaffordable edition of one of Scott's poems that he had borrowed from his employer.[148] Book historians have long been familiar with the concept that when a text is republished it takes on a new appearance that can often change its meaning, but we also need to take into account the various ways in which the reader as scribe transformed a text's meaning during the process of transcription.

This kind of transcription was not just the preserve of working-class readers. In August 1848, spurred on by the enthusiasm of his friends, Thomas Archer Hirst (b.1830) borrowed a copy of *Vestiges of the natural history of creation* (1844) from the Mutual Improvement Society in Halifax. Although he was the son of a local merchant, Hirst could not afford either to buy the text or to borrow it from a commercial library because he was a poorly paid apprentice. After taking two weeks to read the entire book, often jotting down what he thought about it in his diary, he decided to keep it for a little longer in order to copy out 'huge chunks into his journals'. Secord argues that by transcribing long passages alongside summaries of his own thoughts about the volume, Hirst 'effectively wrote his own *Vestiges*'. This intensive reading practice may well have been 'shaped by traditions of Bible-reading among Congregationalists, Presbyterians, and the other denominations of learned, liberal Dissent', as Secord suggests; but whatever its origins, the practice of creating a manuscript book filled with extracts from books too expensive to buy appears to have been widespread, at least until the coming of cheaper books in the late nineteenth century.[149]

---

146 Lyons, 'New readers in the nineteenth century', p. 342.
147 Rose, *Intellectual life*, p. 121.   148 White, *Autobiographical notes*, p. 5.
149 Secord, *Victorian sensation*, pp. 350, 343.

Particularly popular in the early to mid-Victorian period, the album usually consisted of extracts from contemporary poets, with perhaps a few concise extracts from novels or travel writing, and some short prose aphorisms. Although some albums were produced by individuals as private documents, the majority were group or family productions and they help to give us some sense of the role played by reading as transcription within the practices of everyday life in middle-class households. It was common for visitors and friends to be asked to contribute to an album as part of an evening's entertainment or as a ritual of friendship. In many books, transcripts of literary texts are interrupted by what one contributor refers to as 'enigmas rare / Charades composed with puzzling care / [and] Riddles for those who like them best'.[150] Such evidence suggests that the communities that compiled these volumes were taking part in a social ritual that celebrated reading as a communal, rather than a solitary, activity. The album was a space in which extracts from the most popular and fashionable texts could be displayed as a sign of the individual's or family's good taste. However, as is the case with Lister's reworking of travel books, and Hirst's creation of his 'own' version of *Vestiges*, those compiling albums did not simply reproduce the text, but reworked it for public consumption, sometimes altering a word or name so that it referred to the book's owner, or fitted the specific interests of the group amongst whom it was circulated.[151] All of these transcribing readers had, at the moment of transcription, a particularly intimate relationship with the original text, but once that text was returned to the library or friend from whom it was borrowed, they were in possession of a version of a text that was truly their own.

By the mid-Victorian period compilations that included both manuscript and pasted (or tipped in) extracts from printed texts were increasingly common. These hybrids gave less opportunity for the reader as scribe to transform the printed text, but each volume should still be thought of as a unique object that reveals something of the range of texts consumed by its compiler(s). Havens notes that 'by the nineteenth century, large blank folio volumes appear to have been produced and sold with thick, stiff pages to hold print, sketches, photographs, and so forth'. Usually coloured, these 'special pages' were 'interspersed with normal blank white pages for handwriting'.[152] The resulting compilations often suggest just how eclectic reading had become. For example, the scrapbook compiled by Emily Tuke in the 1870s contains a series

---

150 From the 'album', compiled by 'M.A.B.' in the 1830s, quoted in Colclough, ' A grey goose quill and an album', p. 168.
151 For a discussion see Colclough, 'A grey goose quill and an album', pp. 167–71.
152 Havens, *Commonplace books*, pp. 91–3.

of letters on 'mission work' cut from a newspaper and a programme for the 'Friends' first-day school association' conference held in Dublin in 1870, alongside a good deal of other material relating to her membership of the Society of Friends.[153] There are several pages of illustrations, perhaps cut from periodicals or annuals, which appear to have been brought together because they depict similar themes. For example, two pages are filled with images of religious women including one entitled 'the reading Magdalene'. However, this volume is dominated by the various pieces of ephemera relating to her everyday life and travels that Tuke decided to preserve. The pasting in of a hotel label and a map of the Scottish railways memorialises a trip to Glasgow, and there are programmes for events at the Crystal Palace, as well as tickets from 'weighing chairs' located at various holiday destinations. This compilation of tickets, labels and cuttings from periodicals and newspapers suggests that we can recover at least something of the way in which readers handled the most commonly reproduced objects of a modern industrial society. In this instance these 'ephemeral' texts gained meaning from their association with events experienced by the compiler.

Tuke's book shows her skill with scissors and paste rather than the pen. It is significant that even though some of the photographs are annotated, there are no handwritten entries in this scrapbook. Other readers chose to use cuttings to create an object that more closely resembled the printed book. For example, a small octavo volume bearing the bookplate of George Ingles Potts consists entirely of reviews of Tennyson's *The Holy Grail and other poems* (1870) cut from a range of newspapers and periodicals published between December 1869 and February 1870. This volume may have been used as an aid to understanding the newly published volume or, because the reviews contained many long extracts, as an alternative, cheaper, version of the text itself.[154] That such self-made books can often be found in collections of nineteenth-century family papers suggests that cutting and pasting remained an important part of the reading experience throughout this period.

The production and sale of blank albums and scrapbooks was an important part of the book trade. Throughout the period 1830–1914 publishers also produced other texts that needed to be completed by the reader. These 'interactive' texts included 'birthday books, autograph albums, decorative commonplace

153 'Scrapbook of Emmie P. Tuke of Saffron Walden', Tuke Taylor Papers, Borthwick Institute, University of York.
154 [George Ingles Potts] 'The Holy Grail and other poems by Alfred Tennyson', University of Wales, Bangor, PR5588.N481859.

books . . . drawing game-books' and confession albums. The autograph confession book was particularly popular with publishers from the 1870s until the 1890s, and experienced a revival during the First World War. These books usually contained a series of questions ('Which are your favourite songs?'; 'Is love at first sight lasting?') followed by a blank space in which a friend of the owner was supposed to write his or her answers in order that their 'character' might be revealed. They tended to elicit a mixture of serious and playful responses and, as Samantha Mathews's study suggests, they provide an intriguing insight into 'popular taste and reader responses'.[155] The manuscript confession book kept by Mary Tuke between 1865 and 1880 provides some information about the dominant attitudes of her reading community.[156] Perhaps not surprisingly, the nature of the interrogation changed during the fifteen-year period in which this book was being compiled, but questions about literature, such as 'who is your favourite poet?' or 'who is your favourite hero or heroine in fiction?' were asked of most contributors. That such questions persisted suggests that Tuke's community assumed that reading tastes provided an accurate guide to character. Whilst some contributors responded faithfully with quotations from Ruskin as their favourite prose writer, and references to 'perusing books relating to the Society of Friends' as their 'favourite study', others chose to subvert the format by recording that their favourite poet was 'NOT Wordsworth' or by choosing 'the inventor of black cloth gloves' as their hero. The former was clearly a reluctant reader, but even he or she was drawn into the social world of the reader via the continuing manuscript book tradition.

Printed confession albums were designed to be annotated, but Victorian and Edwardian readers also delighted in adding to the printed page. According to H. J. Jackson, 'extra-illustration is perhaps best understood as a way of describing a *collection* housed in a book, the book providing both the hard covers and the rationale for the collection'. Such books are also sometimes referred to as 'grangerized'. 'A "grangerized" book is one that has been supplemented with portraits and other images, often cannibalized from other books.'[157] This practice became particularly popular amongst wealthy readers during the last quarter of the eighteenth century and takes its name from James Granger's *Biographical history of England* (1769), which was often used to collect portraits of important historical figures.[158] Although condemned by nineteenth-century book collectors, extra-illustration became a popular pastime amongst

---

155 Matthews, 'Psychological Crystal Palace?', pp. 134, 133.
156 'Mary Maria Tuke: Notebook used for Questionnaires, 1865–80', Borthwick Institute, University of York, Tuke Taylor Papers, TAY/75.
157 Jackson, *Marginalia*, pp. 185, 186.   158 Peltz, 'Facing the text'.

middle-class readers during the Victorian period. Some readers had the book interleaved before the collection was begun, so that the illustrations could be added as soon they came in, whilst others had them mounted and bound once their collection was complete. Some simply pasted additional material into any available space in the book itself. In all cases the extra-illustrating reader was responding directly to the text, but the original did not strictly dictate the kinds of material used. Extra-illustration was a creative act and the surviving books give the historian of reading an important insight into how nineteenth-century readers responded to the texts that they owned.

Jackson describes an edition of Samuel Smiles's *Lives of the engineers* (1861–8) in which the extra-illustrating reader has not only added portraits of the engineers and their inventions, as one might expect, but turned instances of the author's phraseology into an opportunity for illustration: 'for instance the phrase "rude tracks" in 1:160 justifies a pretty picture of a country path'. She also gives several examples of Victorian readers who used an edition of a favourite author's works to store information about the writer's life. An anonymous fan of the Romantic poets added additional plates, autograph letters 'and a flower taken from Wordsworth's garden in 1844' to Sandford's *Thomas Poole and his friends* (1888).[159] Readers prepared to go as far as to collect relics were undoubtedly rather unusual, but something of the popularity of extra-illustration can be seen from the attempts of the publishing industry to supply the market with pre-prepared illustrations cut from magazines and books that were already interleaved.[160] This practice seems to have fallen out of fashion by the end of the nineteenth century, although it did not disappear, and other modes of additional illustration including 'watercolours in the text block and margin' and the pasting in of photographs were popular from the 1890s onwards.[161]

The extra-illustrated book is in many ways a more sophisticated version of the scrapbook. However, extra-illustrating readers rarely stopped at adding portraits, and the margins of such books often contain manuscript notes. Annotated books are a particularly important source for the history of reading. For example, Secord has argued that the surviving books of the Reverend Adam Sedgwick, Woodwardian Professor of Geology, vice-master of Trinity College and canon of Norwich Cathedral, can help us to understand 'a characteristic form of intensive academic reading'. Although now famous for the review of *Vestiges* that appeared in the *Edinburgh Review*, Sedgwick was not a professional

159 Jackson, *Marginalia*, p. 192.   160 Peltz, 'Facing the text', pp. 91–2.
161 Stoddard, *Marks in books*, item 27.

reviewer. He was, however, a professional reader and, as Secord notes, he handled his books roughly, 'marking his name and address in the front matter', and scribbling 'on any available space in the margins'. His copy of the *Vestiges* is marked throughout in pencil, with 'a plus sign against passages he agreed with, a minus sign against those he disliked'. Passages worthy of more extensive commentary in the margin were marked with a double x and listed, often with further comments, at the front and rear of the book. These longer comments, which were often made up of complete sentences, show Sedgwick building up his argument as he read, with the lists acting as a sort of personalised index that allowed him to return to the most controversial passages in the book. In this instance Sedgwick was reading with a review in mind, but Secord argues convincingly that his annotation system was typical of anyone working within an academic context at this time, and he notes that several of Sedgwick's contemporaries used 'similar systems of marking'.[162]

Sedgwick's practices show just how much of the reading experience can be recovered by examining the marks left in books, particularly when they are carefully situated in the context of the life of their creator. Some book historians remain sceptical about using annotations to recover common reading practices but, as Secord's work suggests, when used to gain an insight into a specific reading community they reveal much about the quotidian handling of books that is usually missing from anecdotal accounts of reading in diaries and autobiographies. Of course, it is relatively easy to find evidence of readers like Sedgwick because their libraries have been preserved. We know much about the annotation strategies of other important figures, including Charles Darwin and William Gladstone, because their books have become part of the nation's cultural heritage.[163] The annotated books associated with famous authors are also often intact. Sir Arthur Conan Doyle's collection of books on spiritualism and other pseudo-scientific subjects, for example, shows that he tended to leave a summarising note next to his signature on the title-page in order to remind him whether the book was useful or not, but it is always difficult to determine whether such marks were made for personal or professional reasons in such cases.[164] Large collections from further down the social scale (or from those who were not professional writers) are harder to identify, but the ubiquity of the annotating reader is suggested by the fact that the majority of commercial circulating libraries needed to issue rules forbidding subscribers from adding their own comments to the margins.

162 Secord, *Victorian sensation*, pp. 231, 236, 238.
163 On Darwin's surviving books, see Secord, *Victorian sensation*, pp. 427–8.
164 Jackson, *Marginalia*, p. 27.

Looking back at her childhood from the 1870s, Charlotte M. Yonge (1823–91) recalled that her family were opposed to circulating libraries because they 'consisted generally of third-rate novels, very dirty, very smoky, and with remarks plentifully pencilled on the margins'. They chose instead to become members of a local book club that circulated books amongst a select band of subscribers, and she notes how enjoyable it was to hear her parents reading from these books to the 'assembled family' in the early evening.[165] Yonge's recollection of the polite reading practices of her own family reveals much about contemporary attitudes towards circulating libraries and their clientele, but it is also important because of what it suggests about the variety of different reading practices that were available at this moment in history, from reading in front of the 'assembled family' through to pencilling 'on the margins' of a borrowed book. Indeed, although concerned with defining the differences between the 'family' and 'circulating library' reader, Yonge captures much that united readers in the period 1830–1914, from the use of public spaces or institutions of reading to access literature, to the continuing manuscript tradition that helped make sense of reading through writing. Reading aloud and the consumption of texts amongst family groups within the home remained widespread even in the early twentieth century. However, Yonge's easy access to texts was not shared by all, and throughout this period many readers had to make do with whatever texts came to hand, even if they were 'third-rate novels'. As this chapter has suggested, those readers who were made, or who made themselves, in the first era of mass literacy often did so amongst the dirt, smoke and confusion that Yonge's family were so keen to avoid.

165 Sanders, *Records of girlhood*, p. 216.

8

Mass markets: religion

MICHAEL LEDGER-LOMAS

In 1890, F. W. Farrar, Archdeacon of Westminster and author of *The life of Christ* (1874) and *The life and work of St Paul* (1879), lectured the Church Congress on 'The ethics of commerce'. In his broadside against adulteration, hucksterism and vulgar advertising, Farrar commented sharply on the 'sweating publishers' who passed on to authors only a hundredth of the profits from their works.[1] Surely he was not referring to Cassell, the publisher of his two best-sellers? Feeling their honour slighted, they wrote to *The Times* to defend the generosity of their dealings with him. Farrar had been 'comparatively unknown' when in 1870 they proposed that he write a life of Christ, offering him £500 plus £100 for a research trip to Palestine. After their extensive advertising helped make the book a huge success, they gladly paid out £1,405 in extra-contractual gratuities, making £2,005 for Farrar in all. He was offered £1,000 for *St Paul*, a sum Cassell doubled and added a royalty to when Farrar, having signed a contract, suggested he might make a better deal elsewhere. Together with extra gratuities, he received £4,333 17s 1d for the book.[2] Mortified by this publicity, Farrar sent a grand rebuke to *The Times*, arguing that the 'altogether distasteful' advertising campaign for *Christ* had been nothing to do with him, protesting that Cassell had paraded their generosity while keeping quiet about their profits, and pointedly omitting the firm from the list of his publishers that had his 'gratitude' and 'esteem'.[3] For several days, *The Times* ran numerous letters about the dispute. One letter-writer, 'Commonsense', denounced the 'pharisaism' of the archdeacon, who had profited handsomely from having his books and sermons advertised in just the same way as Beecham's pills. 'Some people, of depraved taste', he added, 'no doubt prefer the pills.'[4]

---

1 Nowell-Smith, *The house of Cassell*, p. 97.   2 *The Times* 8 October 1890, p. 6c.
3 *The Times* 9 October 1890, p. 8c.   4 *The Times* 11 October 1890, p. 7f.

Although nineteenth-century religious publishing had elevated aims, it was hardly exempt, as this quarrel suggests, from the need to make profits, or from tension about their allocation. Since its foundation by a crusading teetotaller, Cassell had been devoted to educating the masses in Christian, improving knowledge. Yet its commitment to low margins had frequently exposed it to charges of 'sweating' its authors – hence its speedy and angry rebuttal of Farrar's allegations.[5] Farrar had played a vital role in moving Victorian evangelicalism away from gloom about human depravity and towards what his most famous sermon called *Eternal Hope*. His post-bag bulged with 'letters from earnest men', crediting his works with setting them on the path to righteousness.[6] Yet he wanted cash as well as gratitude. It was the very scale of the *Life of Christ*'s success – thirty-seven library editions and over 100,000 copies sold – that had provoked his resentment.[7]

This chapter has four main objectives. After sketching the changing position of religious publishing within the growing mass market for books and periodicals, the first is to show that the leading developments in Victorian religious publishing were driven by an evangelical, conversionist imperative, which put a premium on bringing the Bible and a theology of sin and salvation to as many people as possible. The second is to analyse the tension that frequently developed between this imperative and the commercial means adopted to achieve it. The third pursues the theme of tensions between publishing and the conversionist project, showing how mass publishing helped inflame the controversies that bedevilled British Protestants throughout the mid-nineteenth century. Finally, the chapter looks at how publishing opened a space in which to challenge the popular theology of biblicist, supernatural Protestantism.

The changing market

Although religion had been the staple of eighteenth-century publishing, its prominence in the developing nineteenth-century mass market owed much to the evangelical revival. As experienced by members of established churches and dissenters alike, it demanded that believers dedicate themselves to teaching the unregenerate the Bible's message that sinful mankind could only be saved through repentance and faith in Christ's atoning death on the Cross.[8] The Religious Tract Society (RTS, 1799), the Society for Promoting Christian

---

5 Nowell-Smith, *The house of Cassell*, p. 98.
6 Hilton, *The age of atonement*, pp. 274–6; Farrar, *The life of Frederic William Farrar*, pp. 73–82.
7 Pals, *The Victorian 'lives' of Jesus*, p. 79.   8 Bebbington, *Evangelicalism in modern Britain*, ch. 1.

Knowledge (SPCK, 1699) and the British and Foreign Bible Society (BFBS, 1805) were founded or revivified in the belief that the production and distribution of cheap Bibles and tracts could displace an immoral and seditious chapbook literature.[9] They expressed a mood of evangelical entrepreneurship, in which lay and clerical agents tried to save as many souls as possible by adopting the businessman's eye for expanding markets and cutting costs.[10] The SPCK had already circulated 1.5 million items by 1827, providing a model for the avowedly secular Society for the Diffusion of Useful Knowledge (SDUK, 1826).[11] In Ireland, such initiatives were connected with the foundation of societies to educate and ultimately to proselytise Roman Catholics, hopes that had peaked during the 1820s in a crusade for a 'Second Reformation'.[12]

The technological revolution in the production and distribution of print during the 1830s and 1840s raised the stakes for such societies. They felt they must either exploit the new forms of print culture, or be overwhelmed by them. In cutting the price of books by three-quarters, dramatically expanding print-runs and improving distribution, it raised the frightening prospect of a mass readership totally impervious to religious influences and addicted to frivolous, demagogic or pornographic reading. In Wales, these fears took on a nationalist tinge, as the nonconformist ministers who revelled in the 'purity' of Welsh-language publishing anathematised the infidel trash pouring in from England along with the new railways.[13] Yet, just as recent historiography argues that industrialisation and urbanisation were not ineluctably secularising forces but ones which aroused inventive and committed responses from the churches, so the technology of mass publishing could help boost the circulation of the evangelical message.[14] The growing willingness of evangelicals, both established and nonconformist, to cooperate in civilising the British working

9 Pedersen, 'Hannah More meets Simple Simon'; Rivers, 'The first evangelical tract society', draws attention to a neglected eighteenth-century predecessor of these societies.

10 See Richard Helmstadter, 'The Reverend Andrew Reed (1787–1862): evangelical pastor as entrepreneur', in Davis and Helmstadter (eds.), *Religion and irreligion in Victorian society*, pp. 7–28; Hempton, *Methodism: empire of the spirit*, pp. 111–19; David J. Jeremy, 'Important questions about business and religion in modern Britain', in Jeremy (ed.), *Business and religion in modern Britain*, p. 11.

11 Anderson, *The printed image and the transformation of popular culture, 1790–1860*, p. 30.

12 Wolffe, *The Protestant crusade in Great Britain, 1829–1860*, ch. 2.

13 Huw Walters, 'The Welsh language and the periodical press', in Jones (ed.), *The Welsh language and its social domains*, p. 360; Philip Henry Jones, 'Printing and publishing in the Welsh language', in *ibid.*, p. 324.

14 See particularly Smith, *Religion in industrial society*, 'Introduction', ch. 7 and 'Afterword'; Cox, *The English churches in a secular society*; Green, *Religion in the age of decline*, esp. 'Introduction'; Frank M. Turner, 'The religious and the secular in Victorian Britain', in Turner, *Contesting cultural authority*, pp. 3–37.

classes expanded the market and provided distribution networks for the cheap evangelical print thus produced.[15]

Religion therefore initially kept its share of the expanding market. Simon Eliot's analysis has classed around 20 per cent of all British titles published between 1814 and 1846 as religious. This is the biggest single category, though it is outweighed by the portmanteau category 'literature' (poetry, drama, fiction and juvenile literature). Religion's pre-eminence is still more impressive when the colossal print runs of individual religious books (especially Bibles) are taken into account: individual RTS titles could sell well over a million copies.[16] It was still more marked in Scotland and especially in Wales, where the predominance of theology, especially sermons, in Welsh-language lists and the dependence of periodical publishing on Protestant denominations was a matter for pride or lamentation.[17]

In the third quarter of the nineteenth century, hopes that steam-print and railway distribution could conquer new ground for Protestant Christianity began to diminish. The profits that mattered both to the evangelical publishing societies and to general publishers clearly depended on selling books and especially newspapers to existing members of the churches, rather than on reaching out to the indifferent. The literate 'religious world' became a niche market, albeit a vast one, rather than a category potentially synonymous with the whole reading nation. Although provisos about the length of print-runs still apply and the total number of titles had still expanded, religion's share of published titles had fallen to 15.6 per cent by 1870–9. It was clearly overtaken by fiction (23.3 per cent) and even more by 'literature' (29.8 per cent).[18] During what Eliot terms the second technological revolution in nineteenth-century publishing, from 1870 to 1914, religion's share of the market dipped still further. By the beginning of the twentieth century, the proportion of religious titles had fallen to under 9 per cent.[19]

15 Lewis, *Lighten their darkness*; Thorne, *Congregational missions and the making of an imperial culture in nineteenth-century England*; Gunn, 'The ministry, the middle class and the "civilizing mission" in Manchester, 1850–80'.
16 Eliot, *Some patterns and trends in British publishing*, pp. 44–7; Eliot, '*Patterns and trends* and the NSTC: some initial observations', p. 97; Patrick Scott, 'The business of belief: the emergence of "religious" publishing', in Baker (ed.), *Sanctity and secularity*, p. 217; Altick, 'Nineteenth-century English best-sellers: a further list'; Altick, 'Nineteenth-century English best-sellers: a third list'.
17 Jones, 'Welsh language', p. 323.
18 Eliot, *Some patterns and trends in British publishing*, p. 46; Eliot, '*Patterns and trends* and the NSTC', p. 97.
19 Eliot, '*Patterns and trends* and the NSTC', p. 79; Eliot, 'Some trends in British book production', pp. 36–7. Slightly different figures, but the same trajectory, are provided by Scott, 'Business of belief', p. 224.

The increasing dominance of the mass market by fiction and educational publishing for the new schools established by education acts for England, Wales and Scotland was reflected in the decision of major firms, such as Rivingtons, Hodder & Stoughton, or Macmillan & Co. to scale down the proportion of religious titles in their lists.[20] This sometimes reflected a generational shift within firms, as more business-minded sons or nephews replaced their crusading elders.[21] Many Scottish firms, formerly preoccupied by religion, became more intent on tapping the burgeoning market in educational nonfiction based on London.[22] Religion thus became less important even for such a high-minded firm as Thomas Nelson & Sons. In the late 1870s, only 8.29 per cent of its output was straightforwardly religious, producing a meagre 2.13 per cent of total profit. By comparison, its educational output produced a staggering 87.58 per cent of total profits, though it was only 25.03 per cent of total output.[23] Religious publishing became the preserve of specialists catering for religious sub-cultures, such as Morgan & Scott (revivalist evangelicalism), Watts & Co. (free thought) or Burns & Oates (Roman Catholicism).[24] A growing proportion of religious publishing was moreover 'Sunday reading': tit-bits for churchgoers who still felt ashamed of a secular diet on Sunday, rather than the strong meat of theology. In the early twentieth century, though, this market would become increasingly vulnerable, at least in England, as inhibitions against secular diversions on a Sunday dwindled.[25]

Evangelical entrepreneurship

The Bible business

Bible publishing was invariably mass publishing. Because it required a heavy investment of capital and type to produce what was a large book to a high standard of accuracy, it made sense to print it in very large editions. Providing cheap Bibles in their millions was a duty for Protestants and especially evangelicals who wanted every one to know the Word of God.[26] Their enthusiasm

---

20 Rivington, *The publishing family of Rivington*, pp. 151–2, 166; Attenborough, *A living memory*, pp. 25–8, 49–52; Morgan, *The house of Macmillan*, p. 103.
21 Dempster, 'Thomas Nelson and Sons in the late nineteenth century', p. 41.
22 Blackie, *Blackie and Son*, pp. 24, 31–2; Keir, *The house of Collins*, pp. 163–4.
23 Dempster, 'Thomas Nelson', pp. 59–67, 76–7. It should be added that 40 per cent of Nelson's output was quasi-religious moralising fiction, though this too produced only 10.36 per cent of total profit.
24 Scott, 'Richard Cope Morgan, religious periodicals, and the Pontifex factor'.
25 Scott, 'The business of belief', p. 223. On Sunday, see Wigley, *The rise and fall of the Victorian Sunday*.
26 Eliot, '*Patterns and trends* and the NSTC', p. 92, notes that the proportion of religious titles accounted for by Bibles rose markedly in the mid-nineteenth century, a shift in emphasis that would be even greater were length of print-runs taken into account.

corresponded to a genuine popular demand for Bibles.[27] Given that so many Bibles were bought to be given away or placed in institutions, demand was also fairly elastic. Just when demand for the Authorized Version might be thought slaked, the completion of the Biblical Revisers' labours produced a new version to be distributed anew. Oxford University Press sold one million copies of the Revised New Testament in a single day when it was published in May 1881. Observers noted that 'in every omnibus . . . and even while walking along the public thoroughfare, people were to be seen reading the New Testament'.[28] The interest of Victorian Bible publishing lies in the interplay between philanthropic agency and market forces. In England and Wales, the Bible business was long dominated by the privileged printers (the Oxford and Cambridge presses and the Queen's printer) who had the monopoly of printing the Authorized Version, working with their biggest customer, the BFBS. This collaborative relationship had no real parallel in Scotland, where antagonism developed between the Bible societies (separated from and less powerful than the BFBS and keen to obtain cheap English imports) and the privileged printer, ending in the 1839 abolition of the Bible monopoly.[29]

Circulation figures capture the scale of the BFBS's achievement. In 1845–6, it was already circulating 7.6 copies of the Scriptures for every minute of every day in the year, Sundays and Christmas Day naturally excepted. In the half-century from its foundation, it circulated 27,938,631 copies of the Scriptures from London and abroad, a total that rose to 100 million by 1884.[30] Yet the power of the BFBS lay as much in the *way* it circulated Bibles as in their amount. As Leslie Howsam has argued, it wished neither to give Bibles away nor just to sell to the casual purchaser but to circulate them through a 'Bible transaction'. The hope was that Protestants who might be divided by dogmas could come together to support a 'society for furnishing the means of religion', which would exploit, while not being subject to, the power of the market.[31] The constitution of the BFBS was the key to the semi-commercial 'transaction'. Joining one of the BFBS's auxiliary societies entitled the subscriber to obtain Bibles at cost price up to an amount that was half the level of his or her subscription. This was meant as an inducement to support a society whose initial priority

27 Anderson, *The printed image*, pp. 30–1.   28 Sutcliffe, *The Oxford University Press*, p. 51.
29 F. Macdonald, 'The Bible Societies in Scotland', in Wright (ed.), *The Bible in Scottish life and literature*, pp. 24–40. Ireland had the Hibernian Bible Society (1806), affiliated to the BFBS and for a long time very dependent on its financial support.
30 Canton, *A history of the British and Foreign Bible Society* 1, pp. 150, 453; 4, p. 189.
31 Howsam, *Cheap Bibles*, pp. xiii–xv, 2–3, 7; on the ecumenical mood, see Martin, *Evangelicals united*, chs. 3 and 4.

had been to raise funds to send Bibles to the heathen. Yet the eagerness of auxiliary members to obtain Bibles made England and Wales a crucial market for the BFBS, especially after the 'Apocrypha' controversy caused a breach with Scottish and continental societies.[32] In working to sign up new subscribers and giving away the Bibles they obtained, the BFBS's auxiliaries provided it with a distribution network that bypassed conservative booksellers. Because one half of an auxiliary subscription was a 'free' contribution to the BFBS's work and the other half entitled one to cost-price but not free or discounted Bibles, the society paid no financial penalty for increasing its trade.[33] The transaction elevated recipients of cheap Bibles into responsible individuals, rather than depressing them into objects of indiscriminate charity. Members could give away the Bibles they bought, but the BFBS itself held aloof from such practices. Even cholera victims in 1831 received euphemistically stamped 'loan stock'.[34]

The Bible transaction came under increasing strain, particularly because philanthropists or organisations such as Sunday schools constantly begged the BFBS to lower its prices. The only sustainable means of meeting these demands was passing that pressure on to the monopoly printers that produced its Bibles. The BFBS played off one against another, urging them to adopt greater mechanisation, stereotyping and cheaper paper. It was so successful in squeezing printers' margins that its custom was not particularly profitable for them.[35] A different problem, evident from mid-century, was the silting up of distribution networks, as the auxiliary societies stagnated. Many potential Bible purchasers were not subscribing to them, or lived where genteel canvassers feared to tread. One solution was to supplement the subscription system by hiring colporteurs to sell Bibles directly to the people, a policy adopted nationally by the BFBS's 1853 Jubilee meeting.[36] The exploits of colporteurs in selling Bibles on the continent, where they had become a necessary expedient due to the lack of auxiliary societies, had made them romantic figures in Britain.[37] Properly

---

32 Canton, *A history of the British and Foreign Bible Society* 1, pp. 434–5. The issue was whether circulated Bibles should contain the Apocrypha or not. Continental societies insisted they should, Scottish Protestants were just as certain they should not. The BFBS's efforts to seek compromise alienated both.

33 The contrast here was with the SPCK, which exposed itself to losses by allowing its members to buy discounted Bibles: Allen and Maclure, *Two hundred years*, pp. 504–5.

34 Howsam, *Cheap Bibles*, pp. 50, 65–6; cf. the American Bible Society, which likewise realised that covering costs was the key to expanding its operations, but remained more tolerant of simply giving away Bibles: Nord, 'Free grace, free books'.

35 Black, *Cambridge University Press*, p. 141; McKitterick, *A history of Cambridge University Press* 2, pp. 273–80.

36 Howsam, *Cheap Bibles*, pp. 169–78.

37 See e.g. George Borrow, *The Bible in Spain* (1843); Margaret Fison, *Colportage: its history and relation to home and foreign evangelisation* (London, 1859).

supervised at home, they could be popular missionaries, not just salespeople. In London, Ellen Ranyard's Bible women, who lived off the profits of free Bibles they were given to sell, were to coax working-class women back to church simply by getting them to 'purchase' – an act that 'enlists [the purchaser] in the effort to raise herself '.[38] Yet grants of Bibles for Bible women or Sunday schools and salaries for colporteurs all ate into the contributions auxiliary societies sent to the central society.

The society's associational model was threatened from another direction. Its commitment to businesslike philanthropy provoked criticism that it exploited its clout and the Bible monopoly to chase profits. Fuelling these charges was the use of its in-house bindery to produce not just cost-price 'charity' Bibles, but the increasingly ornate editions that wealthy subscribers demanded for their own use. By the later 1850s, anybody could buy these over the counter, from depots opened for this purpose. Given the BFBS's presence in this lucrative market, why did it deserve, along with the privileged printers, to shelter behind an inefficient monopoly?[39] The arrival of cheap Bibles from Scotland after the monopoly was ended there strengthened feeling against its survival in England.[40] Its terms were challenged and circumvented by a whole range of publishers who produced illustrated, annotated and serialised Bibles. The most ambitious was perhaps Cassell's Illustrated Family Bible, issued in penny parts from 1859. It carried 1,000 engravings, cost over £100,000 to produce, and sold 300,000 copies a week.[41] Publishers also competed with the BFBS in selling sumptuously produced and bound Bibles. Establishing a reputation in that market brought spin-off business in biblical commentaries, periodicals and the like.[42] Bound in ever costlier ways – Oxford University Press's bindery used the skins of 100,000 animals a year in 1900 – covered in gold leaf and groaning with plates and annotations, such works challenged the perception that the Bible business was a philanthropic affair in which the BFBS deserved a free hand.[43]

---

38 Lewis, *Lighten their darkness*, pp. 221–3. For Irish examples, see Luddy, *Women and philanthropy in nineteenth-century Ireland*, p. 58, and for a further variation on the Bible woman idea, see Prochaska, 'Body and soul'.

39 Howsam, *Cheap Bibles*, pp. 115–17, 189–90.

40 For the Scottish impact on English monopolists see McKitterick, *A history of Cambridge University Press* 3, pp. 307, 336; Black, *Cambridge University Press*, p. 137; Keir, *The house of Collins*, pp. 166–8.

41 Nowell-Smith, *The house of Cassell*, p. 58. An earlier example was Charles Knight, who produced an illustrated penny-part Bible (1836–9): Knight, *Passages of a working life* 2, pp. 252–3. On family Bibles see generally Carpenter, *Imperial Bibles*, Part One.

42 Thus Cassell not only published Bibles but the *Bible Educator* (1873–5), a serialised New Testament commentary (1873–9) and an Old Testament commentary (1882–4).

43 Sutcliffe, *The Oxford University Press*, pp. 110–11; Leslie Howsam, 'The Bible Society and the book trade', in Batalden, Cann and Dean (eds.), *Sowing the word*, pp. 24–37.

The monopoly was only narrowly renewed by a Select Committee of 1859–60, which heard much evidence, notably from the Scottish Bible publisher William Collins and the useful knowledge publisher Charles Knight, that a totally free market would bring cheaper and better Bibles. When the BFBS tried to produce the price cuts anti-monopolists demanded, it was charged with the kinds of chicanery Christian entrepreneurs were under increasing pressure to disown.[44] Recurrent allegations that 'sweating' practices in its bindery had endangered the morals of female employees were toxic given the suspicion they had been adopted to produce goods for the rich.[45] By 1867, one of its leading officers lamented that the BFBS was now just a '*commercial institution*', facing the keen scrutiny of 'trade jealousy'.[46] Circulation figures admittedly remained healthy enough. In the first fifty years of its history, the BFBS had circulated 27 million Scriptures and Testaments; there were another 72 million in the following thirty years. But the 86 million circulated in the last twenty years of the century outstripped even those gargantuan totals. Further price cuts and new formats helped: a Penny Testament (1884) sold 7,913,191 copies by 1903. Yet by the late nineteenth century, the BFBS was increasingly seen as a fringe evangelical organisation, rather than one central to British culture. Though sales increased, the auxiliaries and their vital free contributions declined, threatening the missionary and philanthropic activities that had sustained the BFBS's claim to be more than just a publisher.[47]

Tract, book and periodical publishing

Tract societies experienced a similar transition from publishing to convert the nation, to publishing for a profitable market. Early nineteenth-century evangelicals believed that mass tract distribution would send out millions of 'silent messengers' to awaken the unregenerate. Tracts were sold to be given away: handed out at public hangings, thrown into railway carriages, even tucked into hedgerows. Cheapness and volume were essential for publications that belong as much to the history of mass leafleting as to the history of the book.[48] The circulation of individual tracts could reach the millions.[49] They not only

---

44 Garnett, 'Evangelicalism and business in mid-Victorian Britain'.
45 Canton, *A history of the British and Foreign Bible Society* 3, p. 63.
46 Quoted in Howsam, *Cheap Bibles*, p. 197.
47 Canton, *A history of the British and Foreign Bible Society* 4, pp. 191, 197, 199–200, 215–16. Although auxiliary contributions did climb modestly by £50,000 from 1884 to 1904, expenditure rose by £566,000 in the same period: *ibid.*, p. 227.
48 Fyfe, 'Commerce and philanthropy', p. 170; Webb, *The British working class reader*, pp. 27–8; Scott, 'The business of belief', p. 218.
49 Eleven tracts by the Rev. Richard Knill had a circulation of 3 million by 1848; three by the Rev. Legh Richmond had 1.5 million: Hewitt, *Let the people read*, p. 41.

saturated mainland Britain but were exported in large numbers, especially to the continent.[50] The Rev. C. Newman Hall, a Congregationalist minister, claimed that his *Come to Jesus!* (1848) had sold over 4 million copies during his lifetime; that 100,000 soldiers had read it during the American Civil War; and that it sold 10,000 copies annually in Catholic Warsaw. On a mountaineering holiday in a remote Swiss valley, Hall was delighted to find peasants reading another of his tracts, *'It is I; be not afraid!'*[51] Ireland was a key destination for tracts, given the Irish Protestant determination to displace what they saw as the ignorant and superstitious literature of hedge Catholicism. The tracts that Irish societies handed out had often been cheaply printed in England.[52] The crusades periodically launched by mainland evangelicals for Ireland's conversion also relied on mass exports of tracts and Bibles. The Society for Irish Church Missions thus commenced operations in 1846 by mailing 90,000 proselytising tracts to 'respectable farmers and traders' across the Irish Sea.[53]

Industrialisation helped publishers to maximise the cheapness, quantity and distribution of their tracts. Peter Drummond, a horticulturalist and obsessive Sabbatarian from Stirling who published his first tract in 1848, thus built up massive circulations for his Stirling Tract Enterprise (60 million items circulated by 1872) by printing tracts on his local newspaper's steam presses and distributing them wholesale via the railways and the Post Office.[54] Yet industrialisation also aroused evangelicals' keen anxiety because it dramatically strengthened the hand of irreligious publishers.[55] Many felt that in addition to circulating tracts, they should diversify into and dominate the mass market for cheap books and periodicals which was being created and which offered access to the minds of the educated and commercial classes, as well as the poor. The history of the RTS clearly shows the tension between simple evangelism and commercial objectives that such a strategic move entailed. The RTS was not the only agency seeking to combine tract distribution with book publishing. Commercial firms such as Morgan & Scott did so too, while the

---

50 The RTS aided their distribution by making grants of tracts to continental societies: Green, *The story of the Religious Tract Society*, pp. 84–105.
51 Hall, *Newman Hall*, pp. 70–1, 117–18.
52 Adams, *The printed word and the common man*, pp. 97–105; O Ciosain, *Print and popular culture in Ireland*, pp. 137–49; Canton, *A history of the British and Foreign Bible Society* 2, pp. 173–5; Hempton and Hill, *Evangelical Protestantism in Ulster Society*, ch. 3.
53 Bowen, *The Protestant crusade in Ireland*, p. 215; Holmes, 'Irish evangelicals and the British evangelical community'.
54 Cormack, *The Stirling Tract Enterprise and the Drummonds*, pp. 12–14. Ironically, many of Drummond's tracts denounced violation of the Sabbath by the same railways and Post Office that carried them around Britain.
55 Fyfe, *Science and salvation*, p. 57 and ch. 2.

SPCK was distributing 2.3 million books (excluding the Bible and the Book of Common Prayer) and 4.8 million tracts yearly by 1877.[56] The RTS, though, is of particular interest. Its constitution pledged all of its publications to a simple statement of the evangelical understanding of sinful humanity's predicament and need for salvation through Christ's atonement. Yet moving into book publishing required that imperative to be squared with energetic efforts to satisfy consumer demand. For unlike the SPCK, its books and periodicals were not subsidised; it did not rely, as the BFBS did, on volunteers for cheap distribution, but dealt directly with the booksellers.[57]

The RTS met the flood of cheap secular print with a deluge of its own. By the mid-1880s, it was circulating 75,721,360 items a year. Such figures represent continued commitment to tracts, supplemented with books, journals and magazines. In 1893, for instance, the RTS issued a total of 50,427,050 items, of which 19,701,300 were tracts.[58] From the 1830s and 1840s, it had exploited the experience it had already gained in high-volume publishing to build up a trade in books and magazines, whose profits would subsidise tract distribution. Like other firms it started by reprinting classics that were out of copyright. It quickly realised the marketing potential of publishing book series, which built up a loyal customer base, allowing a large capital outlay in the expectation of regular returns.[59] The books it commissioned for its successful Monthly Series (1845–55) were shorter and more competitively priced than those in series previously launched by commercial firms. Differential pricing, at sixpence or tenpence, meant they could be marketed both to a popular audience and to a genteel one for whom decent bindings mattered.[60] The RTS was also quick to realise that investing in periodicals, in which books could be advertised or first serialised, was a good way of expanding its trade. Early experiments with periodicals were followed by the highly successful penny weeklies the *Leisure Hour* (1852) and the *Sunday at Home* (1853). Religious fiction, which became the mainstay of RTS and other religious periodicals, was a particular beneficiary.[61] *Jessica's first prayer* (1867), a tear-jerker by 'Hesba Stretton' (Sarah Smith, 1832–1911), sold over 1.5 million copies after it had been serialised in

56 By 1897, 8.6 million books and 3.5 million tracts were being distributed: Allen and Maclure, *Two hundred years*, p. 194.
57 Fyfe, 'Industrialised conversion', pp. 44–58.
58 Green, *The story of the Religious Tract Society*, p. 116.
59 Fyfe, *Science and salvation*, pp. 46–8. On the series, see Howsam, 'Sustained literary ventures'.
60 Fyfe, 'Industrialised conversion', pp. 98–101. Books in series by Bohn, Bogue and Murray sold for around six shillings at this time, those by Knight, Chambers or Collins for around two shillings.
61 Hewitt, *Let the people read*, pp. 50–1; Fyfe, 'Periodicals and book series'. On periodical serialisation, see generally Bennett, 'Revolutions in thought'.

Sunday at Home.[62] Smith's difficult relations with the RTS reveal how low-margin, high-volume publishers could leave their authors feeling exploited, even where both shared ostensibly philanthropic aims. Having received only two bonuses totalling £15 for *Jessica*, followed by a later bonus of £200, Smith hawked *Little Meg*, her next book, around the publishers, before settling with the RTS for £6 5s per thousand, earning her £130 within a year.[63] In 1873, Henry S. King lured her away with an offer of 25 per cent royalties on *Jessica* and subsequent works.[64]

By 1865, the RTS's profits on sales of books and magazines outstripped income from benevolent contributions tenfold.[65] Yet the shift from concentrating on charitable tract distribution to commerce in books had its pitfalls. Tracts addressed the *Anxious enquirer after salvation*, to quote the title of a very successful example published by the RTS: they succinctly taught the doctrines of sin and atonement to the humblest reader.[66] Could the society's 1840s and 1850s reprints of Paley's *Evidences of Christianity* or Joseph Milner's church histories do that?[67] The Monthly Series also softened, while refining, the RTS's mission. Its rationale was that books on history and science written in 'a decidedly Christian tone' could better prevent the secularisation of the public than strictly religious works – an idea taken from Thomas Arnold. Christian tone was all very well, but Monthly Series writers struggled to reconcile descriptions of, say, *Blights of the wheat, and their remedies* (1846) with the clear exposition of evangelical doctrine required by the RTS's constitution. The problem was often solved by adding a few curt or allusive phrases, which chimed with religious readers, but hardly explained what conversion meant to the uninformed.[68] Moreover, even the cheapest RTS books were still too expensive for many readers. They were advertised in periodicals they did not read and sold in bookshops they did not visit. Although the RTS stressed that a profit-making book trade did not detract from, but actually subsidised, tract distribution, anxiety about neglecting popular readers was manifest in its employment of

---

62 Jay, *The religion of the heart*, pp. 200–1.
63 Cutt, *Ministering angels*, p. 142. *Little Meg* was continuously in print until 1921.
64 Howsam, *Kegan Paul*, pp. 35–6. King's reader Charles Kegan Paul thought Stretton's only contemporary equals as stylists were Newman, Walter Pater and Hardy, so this was something of a coup for the firm.
65 Fyfe, 'Commerce and philanthropy', pp. 171–2.
66 Written by John Angell James, 350,000 copies were circulated 1835–49 by the RTS alone: Green, *The story of the Religious Tract Society*, p. 50.
67 See *ibid.*, pp. 52–5, 72–3 for these works.
68 Fyfe, *Science and salvation*, pp. 100–2. The RTS's science writers often produced near-identical books for Chambers or Charles Knight, showing how adventitious 'Christian tone' might be: *ibid.*, pp. 241–62.

hawkers, support for bazaar stalls, and grants of tracts for distribution in such godless resorts as Epsom Races.[69]

The rising proportion of fiction carried in the journals of the RTS and other religious publishers clearly indicated how selling in the open market might verge on selling out to worldliness. One pioneer was the sixpenny monthly *Good Words* (1859), published by Alexander Strahan (1833–1918), a Scot with designs on the English market. Strahan saw *Good Words* writers as '*week-day* preacher[s]', mixing fiction and entertaining information with a Christian tone.[70] He found a fitting editor in the Rev. Norman Macleod (1812–72), a Glasgow minister who had enticed the Free Church Strahan back to the establishment. Macleod was an eloquent representative of the cultured, tolerant wing of the Church of Scotland, and pioneered British evangelicalism's transition from a preoccupation with individual salvation towards a socially aware theology of incarnation.[71] Like Strahan, he wanted *Good Words* to offer an attractive alternative to purely secular reading, dispensing Arnoldian 'Christian tone' while avoiding the alienating cant of tracts whose characters spoke like 'eastern Patriarchs or old apostles'.[72]

Macleod's determination to bring the gospel to 'John Smith and his wife, up one "pair" of stairs, after a tea dinner at six o'clock' soon paid off in monthly circulation figures of 110,000. Entertaining religious readers with primarily secular material, such as Macleod's own fiction, was risky though. The hard-line *Record* newspaper viciously attacked *Good Words* for publishing such dangerous latitudinarians as Charles Kingsley. Lord Shaftesbury's Pure Literature Society – 'pure water, and sometimes pure nonsense', Macleod fumed – refused to endorse reprints of his fiction. Macleod reacted with passionate sarcasm, inviting Scottish Sabbatarians who refused to read *Good Words* on Sunday to turn 'popish' and burn it – provided, for Strahan's profit, they bought a replacement copy on Monday.[73] Yet the *soi-disant* adversary of 'Pharisees and good old women' was too tame for London reviewers of his pious novels, who sneered that they were 'stale pea-slop'.[74] Nerviness about his position led Macleod in 1863 to cancel Trollope's serial *Rachel Ray* in proof, on the grounds that it 'cast a gloom over Dorcas societies, and a glory over balls lasting till four in

69 *Ibid.*, pp. 165–81; Fyfe, 'Commerce and philanthropy', pp. 176–81. Anglicans were also moving into hawking at this time, setting up the Church of England Bookhawking Union, for which see de Bunsen, *The Bookhawker*.
70 See Srebrenik, *Alexander Strahan*.
71 See Macleod, *Memoir of Norman Macleod* 1, p. 306, for a personal confession of faith; Hilton, *Atonement*, ch. 7 for the incarnational shift.
72 Macleod, *Memoir of Norman Macleod* 2, pp. 95–7, 110.
73 *Ibid.* 2, pp. 109, 111, 135–41; Jay, *The religion of the heart*, p. 200.
74 Srebrenik, *Alexander Strahan*, pp. 44–52.

the morning'. Unexceptionable in another context, such satire would 'keep *Good Words* and its editor in boiling water until either or both were boiled to death'.[75]

Macleod's boiling water scalded other editors who attempted to run religious papers that mingled secular fiction and entertainment with religious purpose.[76] By the late nineteenth century, however, fashionable novelists of sensation or adventure were welcome in religious periodicals.[77] *Good Words* turned to the sensational Mrs Henry Wood, while the RTS's *Boy's Own Paper* (1879) featured G. A. Henty, Jules Verne and Conan Doyle. In the 1890s, Cassell's *Quiver* (1861) was publishing Baroness Orczy and Rider Haggard.[78] Stale pea-slop spiced by such writers was very profitable. At the peak of its success, the RTS found that periodicals were its greatest source of profits.[79] By 1881, the nine leading religious weeklies had a combined circulation of 1,250,000 to 1,500,000 a week.[80]

As the *Sunday at Home*'s title suggests, such magazines were mainly in the business of entertaining those who were already committed Christians. Sterner figures grumbled about the ' "new and pleasant" religious journalism'.[81] Like British churches generally, they coped with the proliferating alternatives to a distinctively Christian culture by mimicking them, a tactic that sustained allegiance in the short term, but ultimately worsened the post-Great War slump in church attendance.[82] The enormous best-sellers that Sunday reading magazines continued to generate were sentimental novels for readers who 'like 'em sad' rather than appeals to the wicked. Mrs O. F. Walton's *Christie's old organ* (1873) and *A peep behind the scenes* (1878) each sold over a million copies for the RTS, plus cheap paper-cover reprints, as did Amy Le Feuvre's *Teddy's button* (1896).[83] Yet demand even for this material slackened from the

---

75 Macleod, *Memoir of Norman Macleod* 2, pp. 151–2; Srebrenik, *Alexander Strahan*, p. 60. Macleod had been hurt by Trollope's suggestion that he had sought to serve 'both God and Mammon' and thereby sacrificed him to the *Record*.

76 Thus in the early 1870s, *Cassell's Family Magazine* featured Wilkie Collins, Sheridan Le Fanu and the frank problem fiction of Charles Reade, before protests from readers deflected it back to 'Hesba Stretton': Nowell-Smith, *The house of Cassell*, pp. 120–5.

77 Provided they minded their manners. G. A. Henty commented that 'I never touch on love interest. Once I ventured to make a boy of twelve kiss a little girl of eleven and I received a very indignant message from a dissenting minister': Karr, 'The proud story of Blackie and Son'.

78 Jay, *The religion of the heart*, pp. 200–1; Nowell-Smith, *The house of Cassell*, pp. 60, 128; Hewitt, *Let the people read*, pp. 62–3.

79 Green, *The story of the Religious Tract Society*, p. 116.

80 Altick, *The English common reader*, p. 361.

81 Scott, 'The business of belief', p. 223; Morgan, *A veteran in revival*, pp. 64–5.

82 See Green, *Religion in the age of decline*, pp. 367–90.

83 Hewitt, *Let the people read*, p. 64; Cutt, *Ministering angels*, pp. 155–70. Walton's rewards put Farrar's complaints in context, given that she received only £15 for *Christie's old organ* and a £6 bonus, with gratuities on all her early works amounting to only £492 by 1919.

late 1880s, as the RTS's circulation figures went into a steep decline, albeit from a high level. It was forced to tap capital reserves to sustain the numerous philanthropic and missionary activities that its profits had initially enabled. Circulation figures plunged from over 14 million books and tracts a year to just one million a year over the period 1903–38. 'Christ', complained one 1920s tract writer, 'is no longer popular.'[84]

Sunday school literature

The Sunday school movement thrived on the same evangelical enthusiasm to bring the people the word of God as the BFBS or the RTS. Whether Sunday schools were an instrument of social control, a form of secular working-class education or a purely religious enterprise has been much debated, but the numbers who enrolled in them are indisputable.[85] There were 1.5 million enrolled in English Sunday schools in 1833, 2.6 million in 1851 and 3.5 million in 1870, with numbers rising robustly thereafter. Over 6 million were enrolled in 1903, which was still a respectable 16 per cent of the population.[86] Sunday schools were also very popular in Protestant Ulster, while mid-nineteenth-century Scotland experienced a dramatic growth in Sunday school numbers, which outstripped population growth until the 1890s.[87] All these scholars needed teaching materials and books. Basic teaching materials were from the outset heavily biblical.[88] That bias sharply increased in the late nineteenth century following the creation of board schools, which offered effective instruction in basic secular skills and allowed Sunday schools to concentrate on Bible study as an end in itself, rather than as a path to literacy. Scriptural readers and journals selling in vast numbers systematised such instruction.[89] The demand of Welsh Sunday schools for Bibles and commentaries played an important role in sustaining Welsh-language publishing.[90] In addition to consuming religious literature, Sunday school scholars and teachers were also industrious distributors of it, particularly tracts.[91]

---

84 Hewitt, *Let the people read*, p. 74; Cutt, *Ministering angels*, p. 181.
85 See Laqueur, *Religion and respectability* for a strong statement of the case for working-class control; Snell, 'The Sunday-School movement in England and Wales' pp. 132–3, 148 for a critique.
86 Cliff, *The rise and development of the Sunday school movement in England*, pp. 129, 165.
87 Hempton and Hill, *Evangelical Protestantism*, p. 115; Brown, 'The Sunday School movement in Scotland', p. 15.
88 Laqueur, *Religion and respectability*, pp. 115–16; Brown, 'The Sunday School movement in Scotland', pp. 15–17.
89 Groser, *A hundred years' work for the children*, pp. 80, 133–4; Green, *Religion in the age of decline*, ch. 5.
90 Jones, 'Nonconformity and the Welsh language', pp. 252–3.
91 Smith, *Religion in industrial society*, p. 121 for instance notes that in Oldham a Tract Distribution Agency attached to the Queen Street Independent Sunday School was distributing 38,496 tracts

Publishing for Sunday schools or mediating between publishers and the schools was therefore very profitable. In England, the Sunday School Union (SSU, 1803), a primarily dissenting umbrella body for Sunday schools, did both. Its own publishing activities explain its rise to prominence, with one of its graded religious readers selling 5 million copies from 1830 to 1850. The SSU lobbied religious publishing societies on behalf of Sunday schools, getting the BFBS to supply them with cheap Bibles and cooperating with the RTS to grant cut-price lending libraries to schools.[92] It became a key intermediary between its schools and publishers of 'reward' books given as Sunday school prizes. Readers for firms like Nelson & Sons, which thrived in this market, were already careful to remove passages in manuscripts offensive to ' "good" ladies, accustomed to look to [Nelson] for S.S. rewards or village libraries'.[93] But the Union's imprimatur was also valuable. Its Depository stocked works it had vetted (800 titles a year by 1850) for sale on to schools. Because the Union's vetting staff donated their services, commissions thus earned could be invested directly in the SSU's other activities.[94]

It is difficult to assess how ordinary Victorians read the tens on tens of millions of Bibles, tracts and periodicals sold to them or pressed upon them.[95] Documenting the strategies of evangelical publishing is easier than judging their success. Many were irritated by the more strident tract publishers. *Punch* asked if Stirling had no lunatic asylum in which Drummond could be locked up, while local critics looked askance at his profits.[96] Not many Catholics were converted by print, particularly in Ireland. Protestant volunteer networks were really only dense enough in Ulster to sustain many Sunday schools or circulate tracts effectively. Elsewhere, Protestant literature made little impact on the Catholic Church, which steadily increased its own commitment to propagandist publishing, especially after the Famine.[97] In England, the Catholic Truth Society

---

a year by 1864; on Scottish Sunday schools as tract distributors, see Brown, *Religion and society in Scotland since 1707*, pp. 103-4.

92 Watson, *The history of the Sunday School Union*, pp. 84-5. There were 53,700 such libraries by 1898: Laqueur, *Religion and respectability*, p. 117. Scottish organisations, such as the Glasgow Sunday School Union, played a similar role, as Brown, 'The Sunday School movement in Scotland', p. 16 shows.

93 Nelson's reader Jane Borthwick, quoted in Dempster, 'Thomas Nelson and Sons', p. 8.

94 Watson, *The history of the Sunday School Union*, p. 187; Cliff, *The rise and development of the Sunday school movement in England*, p. 174.

95 On assessing reader-response, see Rose, 'How historians study reader response'; editors' introduction to Raven, Small and Tadmor (eds.), *The practice and representation of reading*, pp. 1-21.

96 Cormack, *The Stirling Tract Enterprise and the Drummonds*, pp. 18-19.

97 Hempton and Hill, *Evangelical Protestantism*, pp. 60-1, 113; O Ciosain, *Print and popular culture in Ireland*, pp. 145-50; Larkin, 'The Devotional Revolution in Ireland, 1850-75', pp. 645, 649, 652.

(1868) was founded to rebut the vulgar Protestant slurs that abounded in evangelical tracts.[98] Indifference rather than hostility may have been the commonest response from the main target of evangelicals, the British working classes. It is too pessimistic to think that most tracts ended up in privies or as pipe lighters, but they were clearly consumed in ways their publishers had not intended.[99] Investigations into popular reading habits suggest that religious texts were accepted as just one element in a bric-a-brac print culture that became ever richer during the nineteenth century. Reward books were thus designed to inculcate middle-class values in the working-class child, but it is not clear whether the preaching was even noticed by the readers, or whether many read the books at all.[100] Even the BFBS, in exposing millions of readers to the unexpurgated Bible for the first time, unwittingly promoted prurience or disgust as well as piety. The rude bits of the Old Testament delighted children, while freethinkers anthologised them in such tracts as *101 Obscenities in the Bible*.[101]

The sheer volume of Bibles and edifying texts circulated did matter. Britain's identity as a Bible-loving people needed a Bible in every home. Bibles became important physical symbols: no royal wedding was complete without the presentation of a deluxe Bible; a BFBS Bible went into the pedestal of Cleopatra's needle.[102] The ubiquity of cheap Bibles meant the cadences and metaphors of the Authorized Version remained the common property of all. Even freethinkers were obsessed with the Bible, assailing its morality or using blasphemous parody to break the spell of its language.[103] These ambiguities physically marked a BFBS Bible left at Coventry railway station in 1878: an irate reader had scribbled 'fierce invective' on the flyleaf and ripped off its covers. But on the last page was written, in another hand: 'God bless the Society for placing this book here!'[104]

98 See Anstruther and Hallet, *The Catholic Truth Society*; Collingwood, *The Catholic Truth Society*.
99 Webb, *The British working class reader*, p. 28; Altick, *The English common reader*, p. 107. 'Everybody knows', wrote a critic of the Stirling Tract Enterprise in 1861, 'the base uses to which as a rule paper so easily come by is put': Cormack, *The Stirling Tract Enterprise*, p. 18.
100 Entwistle, 'Counteracting the street culture'; Entwistle, 'Sunday-school book prizes for children'; Laqueur, *Religion and respectability*, pp. 205–10.
101 Rose, *The intellectual life of the British working classes*, pp. 33–4, 208–29; St Clair, 'Read the world'.
102 Nowell-Smith, *The house of Cassell*, p. 79; Canton, *A history of the British and Foreign Bible Society* 3, pp. 58, 61.
103 Larsen, 'Joseph Barker and popular Biblical criticism in the nineteenth century'; Larsen, *Crisis of doubt*, p. 247; Marsh, *Word crimes*, pp. 170–81, 251–2.
104 Canton, *A history of the British and Foreign Bible Society* 3, p. 18.

Publishing and religious parties

The consensus that British Protestants should cooperate to Christianise and moralise the people was always disrupted by controversy between different factions within established churches and between those churches and dissenters. Recent scholarship on nineteenth-century urban religion downplays the damage denominational and sectarian divisions caused, arguing that quarrels between the church and dissent rarely disrupted collaboration in a 'civilising mission' for long.[105] Notwithstanding these qualifications, the relationship between sectarian controversy and religious publishing was important. The force of religious revival burst the bounds of state churches in the mid-nineteenth century. Tension in Scotland between evangelicals and moderates led in 1843 to the Disruption and the secession of the former into a new Free Church. The Church of England meanwhile was split into feuding parties by the rise of the aggressively anti-Erastian and anti-Protestant Tractarian and later Ritualist movements.[106] These latter inflamed fears about the resurgence of Roman Catholicism that were already running high, owing to heavy Irish immigration.[107] Crises within establishments emboldened dissenters to develop stronger denominational identities and to press harder for the liberation of belief from state control.[108] The new denominations and 'church parties' created in this fissile situation were keen to persuade adherents and enemies alike that their doctrines and ecclesiology made them the representatives of the true church. To do so, they relied heavily on publishers. Publishers in turn stood to benefit from the restless quest for new genres to muster followers and publicise principles.

Books were admittedly less useful than ephemera – newspapers and reviews – in conducting sectarian controversy or defining denominational identities.[109] Hegel's remark that reading a newspaper was the modern equivalent of daily prayer was doubly true for readers of religious papers: 'organs' which taught the phraseology and imparted the news required to participate in the imagined community of 'Evangelicals', say, or 'Congregationalists'. Protestantism's rivals were no less reliant on their press for their coherence. The late

---

105 Smith, *Religion in industrial society*, ch. 6; Gunn, 'The ministry, the middle class and the "civilizing mission" in Manchester'; Green, *Religion in industrial society*, chs. 6–7.

106 Brown, *The national churches*, chs. 4 and 5; Crowther, *Church embattled*.

107 See e.g. Paz, *Popular anti-Catholicism in mid-Victorian England*; Toon, *Evangelical theology, 1833–1856*; Wheeler, *The old enemies*, chs. 1–7.

108 See e.g. Watts, *The dissenters* 2, ch. 4; Larsen, *Friends of religious equality*; Parry, 'Nonconformity, clericalism and "Englishness": the United Kingdom'.

109 Excellent accounts are Billington, 'The religious periodical and newspaper press, 1770–1870', and Altholz, *The religious press in Britain*.

nineteenth-century freethinking movement thus resembled just another dissenting sect in this respect. In the early 1880s, Charles Bradlaugh's weekly twopenny *National Reformer* energised members of the National Secular Society, while G. W. Foote's penny *Freethinker*, selling 10,000 copies weekly, exhilarated them with its daring fun.[110] Scottish and English Catholics used reviews such as the *Dublin Review* (1836–1969) to express a new intellectual confidence and their solidarity with Irish and continental co-religionists. The *Irish Ecclesiastical Record*, founded in 1864 by Cardinal Cullen, and *The Tablet*, after its purchase by Cardinal Vaughan in 1868, voiced the Catholic clergy's professionalised, Ultramontane ambitions.[111] Backing a religious movement could make a fortune for a newspaper publisher. Richard Cope Morgan (1827–1908), the founding partner of Morgan & Scott, prospered after founding the *Revival* to report on the 1859 Ulster revival. Morgan's paper, renamed the *Christian* in 1870, became a clearing house for 'people who sympathise with all good work'.[112] High circulation gave pressmen spiritual clout, particularly in denominations with weak central institutions. The Rev. John Campbell (1795–1867) sold over 100,000 of the journals he published for the Congregational Union, achieving similar figures for his newspapers the *British Banner* (1848–58) and the *British Standard* (1857–66). In the mid-1850s, Campbell bolstered his status by triggering feuds over alleged 'German error' in Congregational pulpits and colleges.[113] Conversely, pressmen in churches with a meddling leadership, such as the Free Church, had a hard time. Although his *Witness* newspaper did much to champion the Disruption, Hugh Miller (1802–56) survived several attempts to replace him with a more compliant editor after it had taken place. In 1856, the Free Church sponsors of the *North British Review* forced out its editor for letting a contributor doubt the genius of the sainted Thomas Chalmers.[114]

The religious newspaper's power was especially noticeable in the last third of the century, when it shared in the general prosperity of newspapers. Anglican factions followed nonconformists in developing penny weeklies:

---

110 Royle, *Radicals, secularists and republicans*, pp. 7, 28–32, 156–64; Marsh, *Word crimes*, pp. 133–40.

111 Edwards and Storey, 'The Irish press in Victorian Britain'; Altholz, *The religious press in Britain*, ch. 11; Comerford, 'Ireland 1850–1870'; O'Neil, *Cardinal Herbert Vaughan*, pp. 178–81.

112 Scott, 'Richard Cope Morgan, religious periodicals, and the Pontifex factor'; Morgan, *A veteran in revival*, ch. 8. By 1908, nearly £500,000 had been donated to philanthropic and mission work through the *Revival* and the *Christian*, with '*The Revival* Homes' and '*The Christian* buildings' being constructed in London to offer shelter and accommodation to women and youths: *ibid.*, pp. 57, 153–4.

113 Altholz, *The religious press in Britain*, pp. 67–70.

114 Shattock, 'The problem of parentage'; Altholz, *The religious press in Britain*, pp. 91–3; Cowan, *The newspaper in Scotland*, pp. 251–3.

high churchmen read the *Church Times*, strict evangelicals the *Rock*.[115] Such papers replaced the graver periodical reviews that had rallied religious parties hitherto and hurt sales of certain religious genres. Hard-up ministers stopped buying 'Sunday' verse or occasional sermons because they could read them in their papers.[116] Yet other kinds of religious books flourished in and through newspapers. The penny *British Weekly*, published by Hodder & Stoughton and selling 100,000 copies weekly by 1902, was an important shop window for nonconformists. Its editor from 1886, the Scottish Free Church minister William Robertson Nicoll (1851–1923) 'acclimatize[d] devout readers in the atmosphere of literature', building up a large audience for novels he had serialised.[117] Among those promoted was the Rev. John Watson (1850–1907), a Presbyterian minister in Liverpool, who as 'Ian Maclaren' wrote nostalgic tales of his native Scotland. *Besides the bonnie briar bush* (1894) – published, like the *British Weekly*, by Hodder & Stoughton – sold 256,000 copies in Britain and another 484,000 in the United States, not to mention a pirated edition.[118] In both Scotland and Wales, newspaper serials – often penned by ministers and recalling tracts or hagiography in their form and tone – made fiction respectable for religious readers.[119] In Ireland, James Duffy's *Irish Catholic Magazine* mixed fiction, history and verse with pervasive Catholic piety and has been credited both with reviving a depressed Dublin publishing trade and with building a post-Famine 'ethno-religious market' that encompassed North America and Australia as well as Ireland.[120]

The close connection between book publishing and the definition of religious parties is well illustrated by the 1830s emergence of Tractarianism, a movement named for its chosen form of publishing. The Tracts for the Times were initially no more than sheets posted from Oxford as letters to country friends for distribution. They were not numbered, nor did they belong to a named series. That changed when responsibility for printing, publishing and marketing the tracts passed to Francis Rivington (1805–85), a discriminating admirer of Newman. He advertised them extensively and backed their republication in volume form, giving them a corporate, saleable identity and

115 See Billington, 'The religious periodical and newspaper press' on this trend.
116 Rivington, *The publishing family of Rivington*, pp. 159, 166; Altholz, *The religious press in Britain*, pp. 12–13.
117 *Ibid.*, pp. 63–64.
118 Nicoll, *'Ian Maclaren'*, pp. 166–74, 213–16; Attenborough, *A living memory: Hodder and Stoughton*, p. 35.
119 Donaldson, *Popular literature in Victorian Scotland*, pp. 82–3; Walters, 'The Welsh language', pp. 360–2; Jones, 'The Welsh language and journalism', pp. 305, 397.
120 Comerford, 'Ireland', pp. 391–2; Kinane, *A brief history of printing and publishing in Ireland*, p. 26.

attracting the notice, often hostile, of reviewers.[121] Thanks to Rivington, other Tractarian publishing initiatives, such as the Library of the Fathers series (1838–85), became successful public instead of semi-private ventures.[122] This kind of serial publishing attracted rivals and analogues. Evangelicals worried by the anti-Protestant message preached by the Tracts and other Rivington publications founded the Parker Society, recruiting 4,000 subscribers through the new penny post to publish a library of Reformation divines (1841–55).[123] In Scotland, Free Church ministers sought to bolster their claim to represent the heritage of the Reformation by projecting a series of Scottish Reformers and Divines of Former Days and a scheme to distribute Merle d'Aubigné's *History of the Reformation* to 100,000 Free Churchmen.[124] From a very different standpoint, the Catholic convert F. W. Faber (1814–63) hoped that the heroic austerities recorded in his forty-two-volume Lives of the Modern Saints (1847–56) would 'do immense things towards the conversion of Protestants and the perfection of Catholics'.[125]

The wages of controversy could be uncertain for publishers who tied themselves too closely to such controversial movements. The notoriety of its Tractarian publications initially benefited Rivingtons: 60,000 copies of the Tracts were sold in 1838–9 alone. Newman's Tract 90 had sold 12,000 copies by the time it went out of print in 1846 – 10,000 of these from February to May 1841 alone.[126] Yet the steady advance of Newman and his followers towards Rome recorded in these publications hurt Rivingtons' lucrative trade with the rest of the church: evangelicals transferred business to Hatchard's, while the SPCK took their publishing in-house. Francis Rivington called a halt to his firm's dangerous partisanship after seeing proofs from Newman's Lives of the Saints series. Their monks and miracles were incompatible with Rivingtons' status as 'Church of England booksellers' and the Lives were turned over to a Catholic publisher.[127] Rivingtons nonetheless forfeited that status, their theological list only recovering in the 1860s. Conversely, when the initial Tractarian threat faded after Newman's 1845 secession to Rome,

121 See Rivington, *The publishing family of Rivington*, pp. 122–30; Crumb, 'Publishing the Oxford Movement'; Turner, *John Henry Newman*, p. 167.

122 Liddon, *Life of Edward Bouverie Pusey* 1, pp. 424–33.

123 Toon, *Evangelical theology*, p. 44; McKitterick, *A history of Cambridge University Press. 2. Scholarship and commerce*, p. 340. Two leading figures in the Society were the evangelical publisher Robert Benton Seeley and the RTS editor George Stokes.

124 Keir, *The house of Collins*, p. 143; Wilson and Rainy, *Memoirs of Robert Smith Candlish*, p. 336.

125 Norman, *The English Catholic Church*, pp. 231–2; Chapman, *Father Faber*, pp. 190–9.

126 Rivington, *The publishing family of Rivington*, p. 131; Altick, 'Nineteenth-century English best-sellers: a third list', p. 237.

127 Rivington, *The publishing family of Rivington*, pp. 133–42; Crumb, 'Publishing the Oxford Movement', pp. 41–2; Turner, *John Henry Newman*, pp. 479–96.

the Parker Society's ponderous tomes became a drug on the market.[128] In Scotland, the Scottish Reformers series proved abortive, while the D'Aubigné scheme collapsed, bringing its financial guarantors heavy losses and causing recrimination between the Free Church and its partner publishers.[129] Faber's Lives were bitterly criticised by some fellow-Catholics and mocked by Punch for their 'more than charnel horrors', making Richardson, his publisher, nervous and moving his bishop to suspend their publication.[130]

Theological controversy undeniably continued to give individual publications a wildfire success, especially when they touched on anti-Catholic nerves. Pamphlets and books responding to the 1850 'Papal Aggression' were thus numerous and popular enough to boost the whole publishing industry. To give a later example, Gladstone's anti-papal broadside on the Vatican decrees rapidly sold 145,000 copies after publication by John Murray in November 1874.[131] Nonetheless, really consistent and long-term rewards for publishers, not to mention success for those wishing to diffuse their religious ideals in Victorian culture, usually came from genres that were devotional or entertaining rather than aridly controversial, which sold to members of the party whose piety they encapsulated, while also drawing an ecumenical public. Tractarianism's distinctive best-seller was thus no rebarbative treatise on baptism or apostolic succession, but John Keble's The Christian year (1827).[132] Keble's poetry flourished in a market for both cheap and deluxe volumes of pious verse that remained buoyant until the 1880s.[133] The Christian year sold an impressive 26,500 copies in its first decades, but more telling was the sheer durability of its appeal. By the time copyright expired in 1873, J. H. Parker had produced 158 editions of the work and sold 379,000 copies.[134] Multiple cheap editions ensured its place thereafter as a 'reward book' until the Great War. The very form of The Christian year diffused Tractarian 'church principles'. Its later editions underwent 'missalisation', acquiring rich illustrations, gilt edges, coloured streamer bookmarks, black and red ruled margins, soft white or red bindings marked with gold crosses, and illustrations indebted to

---

128 Rivington, The publishing family of Rivington, pp. 133–6, 142–3, 149; McKitterick, A history of Cambridge University Press 2, p. 340.
129 Keir, The house of Collins, p. 150.   130 Chapman, Father Faber, pp. 195–7.
131 Eliot, 'Some trends in British book production', p. 28; Altholz, 'The Vatican decrees controversy, 1874–5'.
132 Gilley, 'John Keble and the Victorian churching of romanticism'.
133 Scott, 'Pious verse in the mid-Victorian market place'. A respectable 1.28 per cent of book titles published in 1860 were 'Sunday' verse volumes, but this figure had fallen to 0.46 per cent in 1881.
134 Altick, 'Nineteenth-century English best-sellers: a further list', p. 203; Tennyson, Victorian devotional poetry, pp. 226–7. The canny Parker had offered Keble £1,000 for the copyright in 1846, but he ignored the proposal.

Catholic devotional art. This Tractarian missal was acceptable on evangelical and nonconformist bookcases though, because it made its argument for the apostolic authority of the church not through controversial statements, but structurally, through a romantic exploration of the church's liturgical year.[135]

Novels and religious parties

The religious novel provides an excellent illustration of a genre that enabled feuding church parties with a device for popularising their principles, while also making money for publishers.[136] Despite some suspicion of novels, evangelicals produced the first generation of best-selling religious novelists, notably Mary Martha Sherwood (1775–1851), whose *History of the Fairchild family* went through fourteen editions from 1818 to 1842, and 'Charlotte Elisabeth' Tonna (1790–1846), a ferociously anti-Catholic Irishwoman.[137] Published by evangelical firms like Hatchard & Son, Seeley & Burnside or James Nisbet & Co., and often aimed at children, their books stressed the evil of unregenerate human hearts with macabre flourishes worthy of Roald Dahl: Sherwood's Mr Fairchild shows his children a gibbeted corpse to illustrate the fate of those who quarrel.[138] Sherwood's books became improbable family favourites, because readers could skip their 'pious slaughter' to concentrate on their cosy domestic atmosphere.[139] It also helped that later editions toned down their ageing atonement theology: children were guilty of 'naughtiness' instead of 'general depravity'; Mr Fairchild's gibbet disappeared.[140]

Tractarians seized on the novel as another means of pursuing their crusade against the enemies of the true church, whether defined as 'liberalism', dissent or Mammon-worship. Early novels by the Rev. William Gresley (1801–76) or the Rev. Francis Edward Paget (1806–82) were thus quite crude vehicles for doctrinal or ecclesiological polemic.[141] The hero of *Church restorers* (1841–4) by Frederick Apthorp Paley (1815–88), a Camden Society activist, is actually a church, much mutilated over the ages before recovering its dignity through

---

135 Tennyson, *Victorian devotional poetry*, pp. 89–90. Entering a high church bookshop, Arthur Vincent, the fiery dissenting minister of Salem Chapel feels safe browsing among editions of the *Christian year*: Margaret Oliphant, *Salem Chapel* (1861; London, 1986), p. 62.

136 On religious novels generally, see Jay, *The religion of the heart* and Wolff, *Gains and losses*.

137 Jay, *The religion of the heart*, pp. 8–9; Rosman, *Evangelicals and culture*; Cutt, *Mrs Sherwood and her books for children*. For Tonna's contributions to an evangelical tory, anti-catholic political culture, see Gleadle, 'Charlotte Elizabeth Tonna'; Ryan, 'The siege of O'Connell'.

138 Hilton, *A mad, bad, and dangerous people?*, p. 180, describes the genre as 'psycho-religious terrorism'.

139 Yonge, 'Children's literature of the last century'.

140 Cutt, *Mrs Sherwood and her books for children*, pp. 76–80; Jay, *The religion of the heart*, p. 88.

141 Skinner, *Tractarians and the 'Condition of England'*, ch. 2, argues for Gresley and Paget's neglected importance in formulating and popularising Tractarian principles.

restoration.[142] Newmanite secessions to Rome occasioned equally polemical novels by high churchmen, warning of the risks of going too far.[143] Tractarian novels were so popular, *Fraser's Magazine* noted disapprovingly in 1848, because they gave readers 'the current controversial small talk without the labour of reading grave works of theology'.[144] Many were written by women, such as Elizabeth Sewell (1815–1906) or Charlotte M. Yonge (1823–1901). Often brought up under the overbearing influence of male Tractarians, writing novels gave them (as it had Sherwood or Tonna) a respectable means of voicing their own religious commitment, not to mention an income.[145] Critics of 'Puseyism' looked balefully on 'Tractarian teachings for ladies', written by ladies. They had allegedly turned a serious threat to Protestantism into foolish romance.[146] Such sexist judgements pinpointed how religious novels – 'monsters we do not know how to class', George Eliot called them – could subvert the parameters of debate.[147] Female Tractarians rivalled Keble, whom they often quoted, in recommending a distinctive style of spirituality to a broad readership.[148] This was especially true of Yonge's novels, which preached sacramentalism, reserve, a piety of works, church building and missions, but did so by adeptly appropriating the allure of romanticism and the machinery of the novel of manners.[149] By 1875, Yonge's *The heir of Redclyffe* (1853), whose smouldering hero Guy Morville was loosely based on the Tractarian icon Hurrell Froude, had gone through twenty editions, while Yonge was earning £1,500 a year in royalties from it and other novels.[150]

Anxieties about the popularity of Tractarian and Ritualist principles conversely explain the mid-century revival in popular evangelical fiction led by such writers as Emma Jane Worboise (1825–87), Elizabeth Rundle Charles (1828–96) and the children's writer 'A Lady of England' (Charlotte Maria

---

142 Baker, *The novel and the Oxford movement*, p. 18. Paley later converted to Catholicism.

143 William Sewell's *Hawkstone: a tale of and for England in 184–* (1845), which featured a Jesuit villain eaten alive by rats, was a shrill but very popular example: Maison, *Search your soul, Eustace*, p. 36.

144 'Religious stories', *Fraser's Magazine* 38 (1848), p. 150. They must be mastered, the writer added, by 'the future Church historian . . . describing the workings of the late controversies on the minds of our generation'.

145 See Sewell (ed.), *The autobiography of Elizabeth M. Sewell*, pp. 101–2 for one such relationship.

146 [Hutton], 'Puseyite novels'; 'Tractarian teachings for ladies', *Eclectic Review* n.s. 24 (1848), pp. 294–307; 'Religious stories', p. 154.

147 Maison, *Search your soul, Eustace*, p. 2; Mermin, *Godiva's ride*, ch. 7.

148 On this theme, see Dennis, *Charlotte Yonge*; Engel, 'The heir of the Oxford Movement'.

149 Sanders, '"All sufficient to one another?" Charlotte Yonge and the family chronicle'; Baker, *The novel and the Oxford movement*, ch. 10. There are exceptions to Yonge's emollient mode. For refusing to be confirmed, she has Edgar scalped by Red Indians in *The pillars of the house* (1876).

150 Dennis, *Charlotte Yonge*, p. 57; Dennis, 'Introduction', in Dennis (ed.), *The heir of Redclyffe* (1853; Oxford, 1997 edn), p. vii; Coleridge, *Charlotte Mary Yonge*, p. 183. The transfer of later editions of Yonge's novels from high church publishers James Burns and J. and C. Mozley to Macmillan and Tauchnitz on the continent is evidence of her growing appeal: Sanders, 'Charlotte Yonge', p. 93.

Tucker, 1821–93).[151] Their chief publishers included the crusading nonconformists James Clarke & Co. and Morgan & Scott, whose partners loathed 'Pope and priest'.[152] These writers emulated Sewell or Yonge in appropriating fashionable genres to recommend their vision of the church as the offspring of the Protestant Reformation.[153] They produced sensational domestic dramas, such as Worboise's *Overdale: the story of a pervert* (1869); appeals to social conscience, such as Maria Louisa Charlesworth's *Ministering children* (1854); and historical fiction with Reformation settings, such as Charles's *Chronicles of the Schönberg-Cotta family* (1864).[154] They were joined in the late nineteenth century by nonconformist writers, such as Silas Hocking (1850–1935), a Methodist minister whose 'street Arab' tale *Her Benny* (1879) sold a million copies.[155]

Novels not only defined rival positions within the church or British Protestantism, but dramatised rebellions against both. Female converts to Catholicism – notably Lady Georgiana Fullerton (1812–85), Gertrude Parsons (1812–91) and M. F. Taylor (1832–1900) – were prolific writers of fiction. They aimed to defend and encourage conversion, to raise money for philanthropy, and to edify working- and middle-class Catholic readers, publishing in periodicals dedicated to that purpose, such as the *Lamp* (1860–1905), or series such as Burns & Oates's Tales and Narratives.[156] Doubt too had its best-sellers. The most celebrated was Mrs Humphry Ward's *Robert Elsmere* (1888). Its eponymous hero was a vacillating clergyman who lost his faith in biblical Protestantism, but found peace in slum settlement. *Elsmere* had sold over a million copies in England and America by 1907.[157] *Elsmere* became a genuine best-seller, unlike such notorious predecessors as J. A. Froude's *Nemesis of faith* (1848), because Ward had been careful to couch her exploration of the ethics of belief in a winning, expansive exploration of Victorian domesticity, a trick she had learned from her literary mentor, Charlotte Yonge.[158]

151 Giberne, *A lady of England*; Cutt, *Ministering children*, ch. 6; *Our seven homes: autobiographical reminiscences of Mrs. Rundle Charles* (Cambridge, 1896).
152 On Clarke, see Munson, *The nonconformists*, p. 73; on Morgan and Scott, Morgan, *A veteran in revival*, p. 50 and ch. 18 ('The Pope and the priest').
153 Jay, *The religion of the heart*, pp. 110–13, 129; Maison, *Search your soul, Eustace*, pp. 76–81.
154 Cutt, *Ministering angels*, chs. 5, 8; Wolff, *Gains and losses*, pp. 239–42; Burstein, 'Reviving the reformation'.
155 Munson, *Nonconformists*, p. 71. Hocking received only £20 and no royalties bar a £10 cheque from his publishers Frederick Warne and Co., thereby joining a long list of aggrieved religious authors: Hocking, *My book of memory*, pp. 82–3.
156 Wolff, *Gains and losses*, pp. 27–107; Heimann, *Catholic devotion in Victorian England*, p. 163; Coleridge, *Life of Lady Georgiana Fullerton*; Altholz, *The religious press in Britain*, pp. 104–5.
157 Peterson, *Victorian heretic*, pp. 221–2; Sutherland, *Mrs Humphry Ward*, pp. 128–31.
158 See Ashton, 'Doubting clerics'; Peterson, *Victorian heretic*, pp. 42, 49–50.

Hymn books

Hymn books dwarfed the sales even of popular religious novels and matched them as a means of recommending a religious party's distinctive attitudes to a wide public. Nonconformists and above all Methodists had been keen on hymn-singing since the late eighteenth century. The writing, compilation and publication of hymns really took off when they were joined by the established churches, which rapidly surrendered their prejudices during the mid-nineteenth century against hymn-singing as a dissenting, morbidly emotional pursuit.[159] A hymn book became as essential in defining what a religious group had in common as a newspaper, while a publisher that won approval for a book from denominational or ecclesiastical authorities could sell cheap, multiple copies to congregations whose members needed them to participate fully in worship.[160] There could be a secondary market from purchasers, often outside a target denomination, who wanted the book for domestic devotion.[161] Hymn books essentially designed for that private context also sold well. Catherine Winkworth's *Lyra Germanica* (1855–8), a collection of German translations published by Longman & Co., sold tens of thousands of copies in both cheap and deluxe editions.[162]

Nonconformist denominations were quick to produce official hymn books. The Rev. Josiah Conder's *Congregational hymn book* (1836) thus sold 116,000 copies in eight years. The Congregational Union (1832) published Conder's book and was strengthened financially from its steady sale to member congregations.[163] In 1858, it similarly adopted the Rev. Henry Allon's *The new Congregational hymn book* (1858). Because nonconformist denominations often lacked clear or easily enforced creeds, hymn books had an important part to play in defining what their central doctrines were.[164] 'Let me write the hymns of a church, and I care not who writes the theology', wrote R. W. Dale, an

---

159 John Ellerton noted in 1862 that the hymn 'came to us from an unwelcome source – from the Dissenters, eminently from the Methodists; it was first adopted by those of the clergy who sympathized most with them; for many long years it was that dreaded thing, a "party badge"; but it held its ground until wise men of all parties began to recognise its value': Watson, *The English hymn*, p. 397.

160 Dempster, 'Nelson and Sons . . . part 1', p. 81.

161 Thus a Wesleyan minister wrote of *Hymns ancient and modern* in 1876 that there were 'few Wesleyan homes in this country, with any pretension to the love of sacred song, where there is not at least one copy of "Hymns Ancient and Modern" . . . which in social and domestic life they have learned to love': Drain, *The Anglican church in nineteenth century Britain*, p. 156.

162 Longman were still printing 1,000 copies a year of the first series, priced at five shillings, in 1873, while 9,000 copies of a luxurious edition priced at 1–2 guineas were printed in 1860–7: Scott, 'Pious verse', pp. 38–9.

163 Bradley, *Abide with me*, pp. 55–8.

164 See Brown, 'Martineau's hymn books', on the importance of James Martineau's popular Unitarian hymn books for articulating his changing theological position.

enthusiastic editor of hymns.[165] John Campbell's 1856 newspaper crusade against 'German error' was provoked by publication of the Rev. T. T. Lynch's *The rivulet* (1856), a hymn book whose Wordsworthian enthusiasm for nature over Calvinist dogmas he equated with Unitarianism and Germanism.[166] The feud between Campbell and Lynch's supporters badly shook the Congregational Union – weakened therefore, as it was initially strengthened, by a hymn book.[167] In the long run, Lynch's supporters would be vindicated, as among Congregationalists devotion rather than doctrine became the main purpose of hymns, and 'culture' the main yardstick for inclusion in hymn books.[168] This was another area of publishing, furthermore, that gave women such as Winkworth a say in how British Protestants worshipped.[169]

The Church of England was potentially the biggest, but also a fragmented and overstocked, market for hymnals. There had been individual best-sellers from the 1820s, but no single volume spoke for the whole church. Indeed by 1872, 269 hymnals were in use within it.[170] The Anglican market split along party lines, with 'high' SPCK collections competing with the 'low' volumes of Edward Bickersteth. *Hymns ancient and modern* (1860) did much to prune this wild profusion. Although London's churches still used a total of 294 hymnals in 1894, 97 per cent of them now employed Bickersteth, the SPCK's *Church hymns* or *Ancient and modern*.[171] *Ancient and modern*'s core was made up of translations and compositions by Tractarians or their sympathisers, but its compilers wisely followed Keble's advice to 'make it comprehensive', an aim helped by the decision to print all hymns anonymously in early editions. English hymns could mingle with Latin translations, Isaac Watts with the Catholic Edward Caswall.[172] The book also appeared in a wide range of formats (twenty-two by 1870) the cheapest of which whole congregations could afford. The book's clerical proprietors cannily encouraged this process of mass adoption

165 Bradley, *Abide with me*, p. 81.
166 If the book was ever used in 'British churches', the 'Evangelical glory of England is departed': [John Campbell], 'Nonconformist theology: serious considerations for churches, pastors, and preachers' [11], *British Banner* 3 April 1856, 110 col. a.
167 Campbell's part in this was carried on in *British Banner* articles that were then republished, with financial aid from *Banner* readers, as a pamphlet, a good example of how religious controversies depended on a fluid interplay between book, newspaper and pamphlet: John Campbell, *Negative theology: analysis of the letter of the Rev. Thomas Binney, addressed to the Congregational Union of England and Wales: an exposure of its fallacies, perversions, and misrepresentations* (1856).
168 Binfield, 'Hymns and an orthodox dissenter'; Green, *Religion in the age of decline*, pp. 312–22.
169 Maison, ' "Thine, only thine!" '; Watson, *The English hymn*, ch. 16.
170 Lowther-Clarke, *A hundred years*, p. 58. In 1879, William Alexander, Bishop of Derry, claimed to speak 'for the minority of the clergy – those who have never made, and who never intend to make, a collection of hymns': *ibid.*, p. 31.
171 Bradley, *Abide with me*, pp. 70–1.
172 Lowther-Clarke, *A hundred years*, p. 24; Watson, *The English hymn*, p. 388.

by discounting wholesale orders.[173] The issue of a supplement in 1868 and the 1875 Revised Edition cemented the book's popularity by including many more English hymns, so defusing charges that it was the pawn of a Romanising party in the church. Sales now exceeded one million copies a year.[174]

The book's proprietors displayed not just acumen but ruthlessness in promoting it. Led by their chairman the Rev. Sir Henry Williams Baker (1821–77), a forceful squarson, they exploited ambiguous copyright conventions to stifle competitors.[175] The book's contributors were encouraged to surrender copyrights for the church's benefit. Having done so, they discovered that charity only worked in one direction. Once altered or newly set in what was nicknamed *Hymns altered and mutilated*, hymns were lost to their original writers, who might wish to give them to other editors.[176] Baker and his colleagues did not welcome fellow-labourers in the vineyard. Most churchmen who wanted help in compiling their own hymnals were bluntly told that *Ancient and modern*'s whole object was to reduce the need for more such productions. Offenders against copyright were first privately reprimanded and then threatened by solicitors.[177] The proprietors were more forthcoming with those whose books did not threaten their Anglican preserve. Wesleyans could reprint hymns and tunes, as could the *Irish church hymnal*, until it began to circulate in England.[178] So successful were they in cornering the Anglican market that their large dividends (they had dismissed their first printers, Novello, for making too much money from the book) provoked considerable criticism. They sought to deflect this by sending extra-contractual gratuities to popular contributors.[179] Given the considerable resentment their success provoked, the proprietors were perhaps lucky that proposals to make the book the church's official hymnal were never realised. The risks of even quasi-official status were exposed in 1904, when a diligently revised edition was fiercely attacked for tampering with the church's spiritual inheritance. Though selling over 2 million copies, its comparative failure signalled the end of *Ancient and modern*'s dominance.[180] It provided

---

173 Drain, *The Anglican church in nineteenth century Britain*, pp. 145, 158–9.
174 *Ibid.*, pp. 127–8, 144–6, 151; Watson, *The English hymn*, p. 398.
175 Drain, 'An "incomprehensible innovation" '.
176 Drain, *The Anglican church in nineteenth century Britain*, pp. 176–7; Bradley, *Abide with me*, pp. 66–7.
177 Drain, 'An "incomprehensible innovation" ', pp. 75–8. 'A publisher', Baker thundered to one clerical offender, 'is no judge of what a gentleman should do.'
178 *Ibid.*, p. 85; Bradley, *Abide with me*, p. 75.
179 Lowther-Clarke, *A hundred years*, pp. 50–2; Drain, *The Anglican church in nineteenth century Britain*, pp. 145–6. Such gratuities brought their own problems, as when Edward Caswall, a contributor of some very popular hymns but a Catholic convert, requested £50 to build a Calvary on his estate.
180 Lowther-Clarke, *A hundred years*, pp. 56–76; Drain, *The Anglican church in nineteenth century Britain*, pp. 200–1; Routley, 'That dreadful red book'.

an opening for the *English hymnal* (1906), another high church production but one whose typography and music were meant to signal a departure from high Victorian religious sentimentalism.[181]

What effect did these books have on Victorian spiritual culture? Many best-selling hymnals stand accused of encouraging complacency or elitism, with *Ancient and modern* singled out for encouraging a sterile Anglican triumphalism in composition.[182] Even ostensibly more ecumenical and populist books have been similarly criticised. Ira Sankey's *Sacred songs and solos* (1873) sold a staggering 80 million copies in Britain during the first fifty years after publication by Morgan & Scott. Like Moody and Sankey's 1873–5 revivalist campaign, however, it has been dismissed as an anodyne for a churchy lower middle class, not a real agent of conversion.[183] It is hard, as with tracts or Bibles, to determine influence on readers from circulation figures alone. Yet it is worth remembering that hymnals were bought principally not by readers but by singers, whose fondness for their tunes did not necessarily entail acquiescence in their often conservative words.[184]

Idols of the marketplace: publishing's challenge to orthodoxy

One corner of the library assembled by Roger Wendover, the sceptical squire in *Robert Elsmere*, is devoted to German literature. There are autographed books from Schelling, 'most of the early editions of the *Leben Jesu*, with some corrections from Strauss's hand, and similar records of Baur, Ewald, and other members or opponents of the Tübingen School'. As a visiting Oxford don 'stood peering among the ugly, vilely-printed German volumes, [he] felt suddenly a kind of magnetic influence . . . a harsh commanding presence'. No wonder he was disconcerted: Wendover has used these books to write *The idols of the market place*, an attack on 'the Pentateuch, the Prophets, the Gospels, St Paul, Tradition, the Fathers, Protestantism and Justification by Faith, the Eighteenth Century, the Broad Church Movement, [and] Anglican Theology' – a book whose 'coolness and frankness . . . sent a shock of indignation and horror

---

181 Gray, 'The birth and background of the *English hymnal*'; Bradley, 'Vaughan Williams's "Chamber of horrors"'. The *English hymnal* was not of course without problems of its own, with several bishops refusing to endorse its first edition because some of its hymns seemed to encourage Mariolatry.

182 See e.g. Adey, *Class and idol in the English hymn*; Tamke, *Make a joyful noise unto the Lord*; Watson, *The English hymn*, pp. 393–8.

183 Bradley, *Abide with me*, p. 183; Kent, *Hold the fort*, pp. 67, 160 and Watson, *The English hymn*, pp. 491–5, though cf. Coffey, 'Democracy and popular religion'.

184 Tamke, *Make a joyful noise*, p. 12.

through the religious public'. Robert Elsmere's crisis of faith is partly triggered by his exploration of the library.[185] This final section discusses the role
of publishing in introducing the 'religious public' to challenges to orthodox,
biblical Protestantism, particularly those associated with German scholarship.

Pioneers in selling heterodoxy to the respectable, book-buying section of the
British public found it hard work. John Chapman (1821–94) was the leading
publisher of 'dissolvent literature' for a decade from the mid-1840s to the later
1850s. As his *Analytical catalogue* (1852) proudly demonstrated, he published
English Unitarians and American Transcendentalists, Marian Evans's translations of Strauss and Feuerbach, the 'wicked' *Westminster Review* and books
like Froude's *Nemesis*, F. W. Newman's writings or W. R. Greg's *The creed of
Christendom* (1851).[186] Chapman found running a viable business very difficult,
especially after leading a pyrrhic campaign against price-fixing booksellers.[187]
Only donations from wealthy sympathisers kept the *Westminster* afloat and
provided the subsidies required to publish works such as Evans's translation of
Das Leben Jesu – celebrated now but sluggish sellers at the time.[188] His cavalier
use of these donations caused problems. Edward Lombe, a radical Norfolk
landowner expatriated at Florence, thus reacted furiously when he discovered that Chapman was trying to divert into other projects the money he had
offered for an abridged Strauss translation and Harriet Martineau's translation
of Auguste Comte's *Cours de philosophie positive*. Lombe died in 1852, before
relations could be patched up.[189] Chapman similarly alienated other backers,
a pattern that reflected not only his personal shortcomings, but also the difficulty, especially in the *Westminster*, of defining a position acceptable to what
was a disparate liberal audience. One freethinking reader's exciting radicalism
might appear 'wicked' destructiveness to another.[190]

Despite Chapman's travails, it proved increasingly possible to bring material to a wide readership that the clerical establishment would have preferred
to suppress or ignore. One tactic was to emulate the strategies of evangelical
mass publishers. *Vestiges of the natural history of creation* (1844) thus became a

---

185 Mrs Humphry Ward, *Robert Elsmere* (Oxford, 1987 edn), pp. 195, 274.
186 *An analytical catalogue of Mr Chapman's publications* (1852).
187 Ashton, *142 Strand*, pp. 37–9, ch. 4.
188 Evans's 1846 translation needed £150 from the Birmingham politician Joseph Parkes to get
    published, while six years after publication at least 350 copies of the modest print-run were still
    unsold: Ashton, *George Eliot*, p. 50; Ashton, *142 Strand*, p. 24.
189 *Ibid.*, pp. 141–6. Although Martineau did get £500 from Lombe, sales of the *Positive philosophy*
    (1853) were disappointing. Only in 1856 could Herbert Spencer carry less than £20 to Comte in
    Paris by way of a share in profits.
190 Rosenberg, 'The financing of radical opinion'; Rosenberg, 'The "wicked *Westminster*" '.

'Victorian sensation' even though its daring speculations on natural development were initially ignored or crucified by respectable reviewers. Its anonymous author, Robert Chambers, and his publisher John Churchill, appealed
over their heads by quickly bringing the book into large editions that lower-
middle-class readers could afford, knowing as the RTS did that huge print-runs
and low prices could reinforce one another.[191] Another subversive emulator of
the RTS tradition was Thomas Scott (1808–78), a theist who was passionately
committed to breaking up the orthodox Protestant apologetic of the day. In
the 1860s, his Ramsgate house became a 'theological pamphlet manufactory',
from which he and his wife printed hundreds of 'heretical' tracts, dispatching
them for a nominal price to a select educated readership. The aim was not profit
but 'free inquiry and expression'.[192] Such a cottage industry fulfilled a useful
function, but liberal theology was already beginning to permeate the lists of
major publishers, including J. W. Parker & Son, Macmillan & Co., Longman
& Co. and Williams & Norgate.[193] Unlike in Chapman's case, 'heresy' was usually just part of their thriving general business, not its staple.[194] J. W. Colenso,
the controversial critic of the Pentateuch, thus appeared on Longman's list
alongside his earlier self, the writer of maths textbooks, as well as the explorer
Richard Burton and the cook Eliza Acton.[195] Mudie's circulating library was
also friendly to liberal inquiry – Mudie being a prude, but not a bigot.[196]

Books by Colenso, F. D. Maurice, John Stuart Mill or H. T. Buckle were
bought by an educated public that was increasingly impatient with the imped-
iment posed by their clergy to what Froude called in 1863 the 'free discussion
of theological difficulties'. True Protestants, Froude argued, must study theology like any other progressive science, with 'reverence for truth'.[197] Froude
was meditating on the controversial reception of *Essays and reviews* (1860), a

---

191 Secord, *Victorian sensation*, chs. 1 and 4 and pp. 306–8.
192 Holyoake, *Sixty years of an agitator's life* 2, pp. 83–4; Besant, *Annie Besant: an autobiography*, p. 113;
     for Scott's list of authors, see e.g. the catalogue published in Edward Maitland, *How to complete
     the reformation* (Ramsgate, 1871), which includes F. W. Newman, W. R. Greg, Charles Voysey,
     Moncure Conway and William Jevons.
193 Dean, 'John W. Parker'; on Macmillan's liberal sympathies, see Morgan, *The house of Macmillan*
     and Graves, *The life and letters of Alexander Macmillan*.
194 As a sharp critic of Chapman privately noted, 'there is a vast difference between a slight and late
     infusion of heresy in a large and long-established bookselling and public concern, and an attempt
     to add a general business to an almost exclusively heretical connection . . . Heresy may prevent,
     but cannot easily destroy, [commercial] success': Meiklejohn, *Life and letters of William Ballantyne
     Hodgson*, p. 373.
195 Cox and Chandler, *The house of Longman*, pp. 25–7. Colenso had earned £10,000 by selling his
     mathematics copyrights to Longman, money he used to fund his journey to take up his South
     African bishopric.
196 Griest, *Mudie's circulating library*, pp. 19, 144.
197 [J. A. Froude] 'A plea for the free discussion of theological difficulties', *Fraser's Magazine* 68
     (1863), pp. 278, 282, 291.

collection of seven essays, predominantly by Anglican clergymen and published by J. H. Parker. The essayists blended German criticism with positivist and idealist influences to challenge biblical infallibility and question the Paleyan natural theology that was still dominant in Britain.[198] The book's reception showed that the church was losing the ability to control what its clergy could publish or what its lay members read. When two essayists were prosecuted for heresy, the whole book, along with passages from their essays, was cited in evidence against them. Yet their prosecution and a successful appeal to the Judicial Committee of the Privy Council created a crucial space for free enquiry by establishing that the law could not settle a book's orthodoxy, but only determine its agreement with the 'literal and grammatical' sense of Anglican formularies. Convocation's 1865 synodical condemnation of the *Essays*, designed to do what the law could not, was a futile exercise that stirred up considerable anti-clerical sentiment.[199]

For the *Essays* had reached a large readership. Every clerical anathema against it only boosted its sales: 24,250 copies were sold during the 1860s, first by Parker and then by Longman. This meant profits of around £428 for each author – earnings which intensified orthodox disapproval of the 'seven against Christ'.[200] Price cuts popularised the debate begun by the *Essays*. They had originally cost 10s 8d, but the price had fallen to 5d by the tenth edition. The twelfth of 1865 put in quotation marks the passages cited in the prosecution and appeal, helping readers to follow the controversy. The trial of the *Essays* had meanwhile triggered a second sensation: the terms of the judgment on the essayists emboldened Colenso to publish *The Pentateuch and book of Joshua critically examined* (1862), which sold 8,000 copies in three weeks.[201] Just as striking as the appetite for Colenso or the *Essays* was the size of the public for their opponents. Over 150 pamphlets and books were published to answer the *Essays*, while the RTS and BFBS redoubled their activities in a bid to submerge the doubts they had raised.[202] Indeed, the controversy over the *Essays* revealed the existence of two publics: the liberal readership to which the essayists spoke; and a larger 'religious world', craving reassurance that the Bible was still the Word of God. Speaking from the former, Matthew Arnold attacked Colenso

198 The best study of the work and its background is Ellis, *Seven against Christ*.
199 Shea and Whitla (eds.), *Essays and reviews*, pp. 688, 768–73, 806; Altholz, *Anatomy of a controversy*, ch. 14.
200 Shea and Whitla (eds.), *Essays and reviews*, pp. 22, 26; Altholz, *Anatomy of a controversy*, p. 157.
201 Hinchliff, *John William Colenso*, p. 103.
202 Shea and Whitla (eds.), *Essays and reviews*, pp. 19–20, 22, 26, 44, 134–5, 848; Altholz, *Anatomy of a controversy*, ch. 8, p. 143; Canton, *A history of the British and Foreign Bible Society* 3, p. 181; Green, *The story of the Religious Tract Society*, p. 76.

and the essayists for foolishly confusing the two, publishing books that neither instructed the few nor edified the many. W. R. Greg forcibly defended Colenso in the *Westminster*, suggesting that books like his were the only way to free the laity from the harsh and terrifying doctrines preached by ignorant ministers. 'Truth' should not be severed from 'edification'.[203]

Edification remained a constant for publishers who wished to liberalise religious readers without alienating them. To find a broad audience, freethinking books generally had to be thoroughly respectable and invoke a Protestant rhetoric of 'reformation' rather than 'revolution', thus calming the early Victorian dread of an alliance between plebeian scepticism and social and political radicalism.[204] High church enemies of *Essays and reviews* had sought to revive that spectre, claiming that infidel societies were cutting up copies to lend essays to working men at a penny a time.[205] Late nineteenth-century 'rationalism' and materialism certainly did not want for strident publicists, such as the Rationalist Press Association (1899). This was founded by the publisher Charles Albert Watts (1858–1946) as the mirror-image of the RTS, distributing subsidised tracts and a sixpenny series of Humanist Classics.[206] Yet truly successful works of theological liberalisation, like works of partisanship, tended to be conciliatory, offering readers strategies for how to render what was essential to Christianity compatible with modern thought. *Ecce Homo* (1865), published anonymously by J. R. Seeley, son of a noted evangelical publisher, was the type of such a work. Published by Macmillan, it sold 9,000 copies in its first nine months and went continuously into new editions until 1888, despite orthodox disapproval.[207] *Ecce Homo* skimped on discussions of critical questions about the authenticity of the gospels to concentrate on the moral mission of a human Christ and his Comtean 'enthusiasm for humanity'.[208] Another success on the same lines was Henry Drummond's *Natural law in the spiritual world* (1883), which sold 69,000 copies in its first five years after publication by Hodder & Stoughton. Drummond was a lecturer on natural science at a Glasgow Free Church college and a noted explorer, but also an ally of Moody and Sankey and the nephew of the Stirling Tract Enterprise's founder. That background left him well placed to soothe the many readers

---

203 Matthew Arnold, 'The bishop and the philosopher', *Macmillan's Magazine* 7 (1863), pp. 242–5, 254; William Rathbone Greg, 'Truth versus edification', *Westminster Review* n.s. 23 (1863), 503–16; Shea and Whitla (eds.), *Essays and reviews*, p. 853.

204 Moore, 'The crisis of faith'; Moore, 'Theodicy and society'.

205 Altholz, *Anatomy of a controversy*, p. 169; Shea and Whitla (eds.), *Essays and reviews*, p. 707.

206 Gould, *The pioneers of Johnson's Court*, pp. 2–24. Some of Watts's publications, such as Joseph MacCabe's translation of Ernest Haeckel's *Riddle of the Universe at the close of the nineteenth century* (London, 1900) were bona fide best-sellers.

207 Pals, *Victorian 'lives'*, p. 48.   208 Wormell, *Sir John Seeley*, pp. 26–32.

who were worried about the compatibility of evangelicalism and the science of evolution.[209]

If gentle questioning of evangelical orthodoxy succeeded best, then it was also true that fear of the contents of Wendover's library dissipated relatively quickly. German biblical criticism, for instance, became largely permissible, if not popular, in late nineteenth-century Protestant churches, partly because its British publishers worked hard to make it so.[210] From Edinburgh, T. & T. Clark published 180 predominantly German volumes in their serial Foreign Theological Library.[211] Devout Presbyterians, the Clarks kept obviously rationalistic works off this list. Hodder & Stoughton were also important popularisers of biblical criticism, through their journal the *Expositor* (1875–1925) and their publication of Scottish 'believing critics' such as George Adam Smith or William Ramsay.[212] Such enterprises encouraged readers to believe that scholarship could be trusted to vindicate the historical truth of the Bible – especially that of the New Testament – though not its literal inspiration. The 'life' of Jesus or St Paul was the late nineteenth-century genre that made greatest capital from selective quotation of such scholarship. F. W. Farrar was its most gifted practitioner, marshalling archaeology and topography along with German criticism to produce what were biographies of romantic heroes in pre-Raphaelite landscapes. Farrar had successors, particularly among Scottish divines, who were less flamboyant but enjoyed similarly huge sales.[213] Relatively uncritical works on the Old Testament or scholarly 'Teachers' Bibles', for which there was a late nineteenth-century vogue, also came decked in scientific trappings, informed as they were by optimism that the findings of archaeology and Egyptology had refuted the more negative strains of German higher criticism.[214] Even zoology could be exploited to instruct and entertain

209 Bebbington, 'Henry Drummond'; Attenborough, *A living memory: Hodder and Stoughton*, p. 22. *Natural law* remained in print until 1921, while George Adam Smith's *The life of Henry Drummond* (London, 1899) sold 16,000 copies for Hodder & Stoughton in just a few months: *ibid.*, p. 43.

210 See Glover, *Evangelical Nonconformists*; Gerald Parsons, 'Biblical criticism in Victorian Britain', pp. 247, 250–3; Riesen, *Criticism and faith in late Victorian Scotland*.

211 Dempster, *The T. and T. Clark story*, pp. 62, 75–81.

212 Attenborough, *A living memory: Hodder and Stoughton*, pp. 24–5. Hodder & Stoughton eased out Samuel Cox, the *Expositor*'s first editor, when it became clear he was too advanced for the sensibilities of their readers, replacing him with the much suppler William Robertson Nicoll.

213 Pals, *Victorian 'lives'*, ch. 3; Ellis, 'Dean Farrar and the quest for the historical Jesus'. James Stalker's *The life of Jesus Christ* (1879) sold 100,000 copies.

214 Keir, *The house of Collins*, pp. 202–3; MacHaffie, ' "Monument facts and higher critical fancies" '; Gange, 'Religion and science in late nineteenth-century British Egyptology'. For sincere attempts to expose children to higher criticism see MacHaffie, 'Old Testament criticism and the education of Victorian children'.

the Sunday reader of Scripture.[215] Although all these publications were in a sense conservative, they represented the same kind of accommodation with modern culture as did religious fiction: an implicit acceptance that the Bible should be understood as a record of real human lives and must agree with the historical and material investigations of the modern sciences.

The dominance of the 'lives' and cognate publications could not last. After the turn of the century, New Testament criticism once more undermined hopes that the gospels were a simple window onto the life of Christ.[216] British biblical criticism moved closer to its German model of a discipline based in universities and practised by scholars who addressed one another in specialist journals, rather than a public whose appetite for serious non-fiction was in any case on the wane.[217] The fate of the 'lives' is a fitting close to this chapter. They exemplified how well religious writers and publishers had exploited what might have been thought the inherently secularising power of industrialised, mass-market publishing. However, the drawbacks to selling religion like Beecham's pills – as 'Commonsense', Farrar's accuser, put it – have appeared throughout this chapter. It was most profitable to sell to the broadly middle-class public that formed the mass of book-buyers, or else to supply the polemical or devotional needs of churches and religious organisations which recruited from it. Having to compete with other sectors of the trade for the loyalty of this market changed religious publishing, making it the servant of denominational sub-cultures and the purveyor of fiction, news, history and science that readers preferred in time to get elsewhere. Farrar's descendants would not have his prominence, or his sales figures to grumble about.

215 As witness popular productions by clerical naturalists: H. B. Tristram, *The natural history of the Bible* (1867); J. G. Wood, *Bible animals: being a description of every living creature mentioned in the Scriptures: from the ape to the coral* (1869).

216 Tellingly, the Rationalist Press Association were happy to reprint the *Encyclopaedia Biblica* in sevenpenny parts, although it had been compiled by divines and Oxford professors: Gould, *The pioneers of Johnson's Court*, p. 76.

217 Pals, *Victorian 'lives'*, ch. 5.

9

Mass markets: education

CHRISTOPHER STRAY AND GILLIAN SUTHERLAND

The technology of book production was transformed in the course of the nineteenth century and this is explored in detail elsewhere in this volume. In his ground-breaking work of 1994 Simon Eliot argued that one should look for two interrelated but distinct revolutions in book production, producing two great surges: 1830–55, the 'distribution revolution', underpinned by the impact of the Fourdrinier paper-making machine, steam-driven presses, case binding and the progressive abolition of the taxes on knowledge; and 1875–1914, the 'mass-production revolution', underpinned by rotary printing, hot metal typesetting, advances in the use of lithography and photography, and the replacement of steam by electricity.[1] In symbiosis with these developments, feeding and feeding off them, was a series of transformations of the markets for books. This chapter will focus on one key sector, the markets created by the rise of formal schooling, and its associated phenomenon, the rise of public examinations, although it has to ask at least as many questions as it can attempt to answer.

The idea of a textbook in the modern sense solidified around 1830. The commonest spelling then was 'text-book'; by the end of the century it had become 'textbook', perhaps suggesting a reification or embedding in parlance and usage.[2] The emerging educational market was spotted immediately by the newly organising publishers. Fourteen London publishers began to produce the *Publishers' Circular* in 1837; among them was Louis Fenwick de Porquet, one of the Frenchmen who fled after the Revolution and made a living teaching French in England; de Porquet was in turn teacher, author and publisher. In January 1838 Longman offered an educational list as a supplement to the *Circular*; then in 1840 a special 'Education Issue' appeared, becoming

---

1 Eliot, *Some patterns and trends in British publishing*, p. 107.
2 The overall shift is from a book containing an authoritative text, to a book designed to be used for teaching. The nuances remain to be teased out; it should be noted that catalogue entries for specific books are often inconsistent, and that spine and internal titles often differ.

bi-annual in 1842. By 1859 Matthew Arnold could write, 'There is no sale for a book like a school sale.'[3]

Behind these initiatives so eagerly taken lay a long and complex process of shifts in the attitudes of British society to the socialisation of its young; and one which, through its institutional expressions, would shape a series of markets, overlapping but for much of the century distinct and of different sizes, and with different patterns of book use. In the seventeenth century and the first half of the eighteenth century in Britain, formal schooling had played a relatively limited role in the socialisation of children, even in elite families. In the second half of the eighteenth century, this began to change; and the sons of elite families and those whose parents aspired to gentility for them were increasingly being sent to school, often to boarding school. Some rough gauge of the growing demand can be found in the creation of new endowed grammar schools, the remodelling of the curriculum and structures of existing foundations, and the realisation of trustees that opening a boarding house enabled a school to develop a national rather than simply a local appeal – and to make money accordingly. Even clearer signals of growing demand come from the rise of private or joint-stock – proprietary – boarding schools. Two were founded in England and Wales in each of the four decades 1800–39; but 1840–9 saw thirteen new foundations, there were five more in 1850–9 and another thirteen in 1860–9.[4] Simultaneously Oxford and Cambridge were beginning to emerge from the torpor which had marked their recruitment and practice for much of the preceding century and new University institutions were being founded: in 1828 the 'godless institution in Gower St' – the secular Benthamite University of London – opened its doors. Anglican foundations, King's in London in 1831 and Durham in 1832, promptly and reactively followed. In 1836 the government created by royal charter the University of London, a purely examining and degree-giving body, under whose umbrella these colleges and others which might come into being, both in England and in colonial territories, could operate. Coming under the umbrella, the college in Gower Street became University College London (UCL).[5]

As will already be plain, the response of publishers to this new middle- and upper-class market was immediate and they were possibly over-optimistic about its size and growth rates. Without more detailed work in surviving publishers' archives and much more evidence than is currently available about patterns of the use and abuse of books, it is difficult to judge whether (or

3 Arnold, *Letters* 1, p. 500.
4 For a fuller discussion, with sources, see Sutherland, 'Education', pp. 132–7.
5 *Ibid.*, pp. 137–40; Harte, *The University of London*, pp. 22–4.

when) these two segments of the textbook market became mass markets – and indeed, what price level, print-run and reprint sequence signalled a truly mass market. These are major caveats: even so, there is evidence of much publishing activity.

In these years it was generally agreed that the mechanism of the market was the appropriate one to respond to demand from the moneyed and aspirant both in the provision of institutions and in the provision of books. Potentially, however, much the largest market was represented by the emerging working class, that is, 80 per cent or more of the growing population. However, schemes to develop formal schooling for this group, elementary education as it was defined, proved much more contested and raised altogether more complex issues. There were those who wanted to keep the labouring poor illiterate and ignorant. There were more who recognised that this was already a lost cause: by 1840 two-thirds of the male population and a good half of the female population had some grasp of the basic reading skill.[6] Observing the hunger for print that already existed, these campaigners wanted instead to try to manage it, to ensure the provision of an appropriately non-revolutionary diet. Some of those engaging with the middle- and upper-class market became engaged here too and sometimes attempted to address both audiences simultaneously, not always with success.

The Society for the Diffusion of Useful Knowledge was established by Henry Brougham and his allies in 1826, and developed an ambitious publishing programme.[7] Its major publications included the *Penny Magazine*, the *Penny Cyclopaedia* and the *Quarterly Journal of Education*. The SDUK had close links with the new London University, several of whose early professors wrote and/or edited for it, in particular George Long, editor of both *Cyclopaedia* and *Journal*. UCL also had its own printer and publisher, Richard Taylor and John Taylor (not related).[8] Here at university level is a distinctive mode of educational publishing already familiar at school level – production of books for an institution. John Taylor's books, many written by UCL professors, were derived from their teaching and the needs of their classes, though he also

---

6 By 1910, effectively all the population had such a grasp. For the issues involved in measuring literacy and the two skills, reading and writing, usually yoked together under that label, see Sutherland, 'Education', pp. 122–5; Vincent, *Literacy and popular culture*; Vincent, *The rise of mass literacy*. See also Chapter 7.

7 The basic reference source remains Grobel, *The Society for the Diffusion of Useful Knowledge*. There is no adequate published account of the SDUK, on which research is badly needed.

8 For John Taylor's career, see Chilcott, *A publisher and his circle*; for Richard Taylor see Brock, 'The lamp of learning'; Brock and Meadows, *The lamp of learning*.

published for schools and indeed contributed to some series.[9] The same mode can be seen in relation to some public schools, textbooks being produced specifically for an individual school. In some cases, indeed, the books were only available within the school. Such publishing was in part a matter of status, and the fame of Eton, for example, was reflected in the fact that many other schools used its Latin grammar (originally published in 1758).[10] John Taylor had moved from literary publishing (he published Keats in 1818–20, and then Landor in the *London Magazine*) to educational publishing, in part out of concern for stable profits. The publishing crashes of 1826/7 (e.g. that of Constable) are now claimed to have been exaggerated, but they played a part in prompting some firms to move to safer ground.[11] The same pattern can be seen later with Murray in the 1830s and 1840s, moving into non-fiction and reference publishing (Murray's travel handbooks in the mid-1830s, William Smith's classical and biblical dictionaries from the mid-1840s).[12]

Taylor's 'Locke's System' was typical of the systems and series of the 1830s, when self-styled 'professors' hawked their wares to the emerging working-class reader and other autodidacts. Examples are the Hamiltonian system; the algebra and classical textbooks of T. W. C. Edwards; Jeremiah Joyce's natural science books; and Dionysius Lardner and his *Cabinet cyclopaedia* (1830–46).[13] Some of these books were very effective, others were compromised by looking to multiple markets – thus some offer material for both autodidact and taught learner. This was also the heyday of the scissors-and-paste textbook 'author', who in a period before international copyright agreements imported books, especially from Germany, and translated selections under his own name. A good example is the Rev. Thomas Kerchever Arnold (1800–53), not to be confused, as he often has been, with Thomas Arnold of Rugby, who put out dozens of schoolbooks beween 1834 and his death. He was attacked by the headmaster and textbook writer J. W. Donaldson for plagiarism; but the conclusion of most qualified judges was that both had pillaged the same (German) sources.[14]

---

9 Almost from its inception, the University of London (in 1836 renamed University College London) had a 'junior department', later called University College School; some of the early professors taught there and wrote textbooks for it, and one (Thomas Key) was its headmaster, 1842–75. A similar pattern was observable at King's College London.

10 This can be seen in the entries in Nicholas Carlisle's *Concise description of the endowed schools in England & Wales* (London: Baldwin, Cradock & Joy, 1818, repr. Bristol, 2004).

11 On the crashes, see Sutherland, 'The book trade crash of 1826'.

12 Stray, 'Sir William Smith and his dictionaries: a study in scarlet and black'.

13 Peckham, 'Dr. Lardner's *Cabinet Cyclopaedia*'. The series contained 61 titles in 133 parts.

14 See the articles on both men in Todd (ed.), *Dictionary of British classicists*, which also deals with T. W. C. Edwards.

A prolific author and editor in the half-century after 1840 was William Smith (1813–93), who began with Taylor & Walton and later transferred to Murray. Smith learnt his trade as contributor to the *Penny Cyclopaedia*, and then applied its combination of double-columned format, cheap serial publication and abundant woodcuts to a series of classical dictionaries;[15] he went on to write and edit biblical dictionaries, Latin and Greek courses, and histories of England, Greece and Rome. 'Dr Smith' in effect became a brand name, reinforced by a standardised black cloth binding and red page edging.[16] Smith's correspondence with John Murray III gives considerable insight into the opportunities and problems of the educational market; as when he wrote to Murray about a rival book in 1851, 'it is difficult to displace even a bad school book'.[17]

The spread of these affordable books was made possible by the technological advances mentioned above, all well established by 1830. The technology and the markets coincided. What is less easy to find is the undergrowth of self-publishing by teachers and tutors, exemplified by a few surviving lithographed books. Lithography could cope with 'difficult text' – complicated page layout and non-roman fonts – and was also much cheaper than letterpress for short runs. These advantages made it ideal for the small-scale printing of teaching material.[18]

The two ancient universities both had presses, but neither was active in looking for markets in 1830, nor in doing more than service its own needs and those of the Bible business.[19] McKitterick suggests that Cambridge University Press was acting more as a printer than as a publisher at this point. In the 1830s and 1840s, Oxford University Press brought out two books

---

15 *Dictionary of Greek and Roman antiquities* (1840–2); *Dictionary of Greek and Roman biography and mythology* (1844–9); *Dictionary of Greek and Roman geography* (1852–7). See Stray, 'Sir William Smith and his dictionaries'.
16 One of his readers later recalled that

> The very sight of that series of manuals, with their stiff black buckram covers and red edged leaves, makes me think to this day what a helotism for children is uninspired teaching. Years afterwards, when I met Dr Smith in London, and found him dressed from head to foot in black, with ruddy neck and ears and face and hands, a qualm of antipathy rose in me at the semblance between book and author, and I couldn't even tell him that I had been taught from his grammar-books.
> A. B. Piddington, *Worshipful Masters* (Sydney, 1929), p. 153

17 W. Smith to J. Murray, 15 September 1851: John Murray Archive.
18 For some examples, all around 1830, see Stray, 'Paper wraps stone'. The essential background reference is Twyman, *Early lithographed books*.
19 Sutcliffe, *The Oxford University Press*, pp. 11–12; McKitterick, *A history of Cambridge University Press 2*.

whose sales underpinned its mid-century prosperity: the Greek grammar of Charles Wordsworth, 1839/43 (transferred from Murray, over the latter's bitter protests), and Liddell and Scott's *Greek–English lexicon*, 1843. 'These two books transformed the business of the Learned Press.'[20]

Working-class purchasers and users of the more affordable books were likely to be adult, usually autodidact, setting their own priorities and making their own choices.[21] The serious contests and disagreements arose over the provision of schools and thus by extension schoolbooks for working-class children. The absolute priority for the families of the labouring poor was economic survival; and if their children could find work and contribute a few pennies, this overrode all else. In such a situation a school fee represented luxury and day-school attendance had a further opportunity cost; and the situation led inexorably to arguments for a market regulated and subsidised by the state. This was where problems began. The vast majority agreed that any education worth the name should have a moral core; however, most people were unable to see how this could be provided except through religious teaching. In any state-supported scheme, whose denomination was to supply this? The Anglican Church was the established church and claimed the right; but in practice, British society was pluralist. The principal civil disabilities under which dissenters and Roman Catholics had laboured were abolished at the end of the 1820s; and both groups were deeply hostile to Anglican claims in the field of education in particular.

In Ireland the British government faced all these issues head-on. Anxiety about Irish political unrest and disaffection made them commit to state regulated and funded provision for the mass of the population, run by a Board of School Commissioners, from 1831 onwards. The Board's brief was to encourage religious education of a broadly Christian but undenominational nature; and in order to try to steer a safe course through the sectarian minefield, they compiled and published their own titles. By mid-century they were offering forty-one titles, including ten readers, four anthologies of secular and sacred work, *Lessons on the truth of Christianity*, an agricultural class book, a needlework manual and an accountancy manual. They failed, however, to reach agreement

---

20 Sutcliffe, *The Oxford University Press*, p. 12, where sales figures are also given. For Wordsworth and Murray, see Stray, 'Paradigms of social order'; on Liddell and Scott, A. A. Imholtz Jr., 'Liddell and Scott: the predecessors, the 19th-century editions and the American contributions', in Stray (ed.), *Oxford classics*.

21 Rose, *The intellectual life of the British working classes*, pp. 12–57. For autodidact culture, see also Vincent, *Bread, knowledge and freedom*, and Vincent, *Literacy and popular culture*.

on an Irish history book and the anthologies and readers contained virtually no material on Irish topics.[22]

Such a bold approach, in what was essentially a colonial situation, was not perceived to be politically feasible on the mainland. Two societies had already been formed, the National Society for Promoting the Education of the Poor according to the Principles of the Established Church (usually simply the National Society) in 1811, and the British and Foreign School Society, supported by Protestant dissenters and promoting undenominational religious teaching, in 1814. Their objectives were to encourage and support local efforts to found schools, and both printed their own material for teachers and sold it cheap. Already in 1812 the National Society was producing teaching material, in the form of lithographed handwriting cards.[23] By 1850 it had a depository in London which sourced a wide range of approved books and equipment. The BFSS secretary Henry Dunn produced *Popular education, or, the normal school manual: containing practical suggestions for daily and Sunday school teachers: in a series of letters* (1837: at least seventeen editions); and with J. Crossley, *Daily lesson books.*[24]

In 1833 the Whig government made a first grant to support the building of elementary schools in England and Wales – but dodged the 'religious problem', as it became known, by channelling the money through the two societies. Up to the beginning of the 1860s the range of grants on offer was gradually expanded and from 1848 included a subsidy for the purchase of books; but all efforts to develop a secular or unsectarian mechanism for the distribution of government funding, independent of the two Societies, or the Roman Catholic Poor School Committee which joined them in 1847, and which might engage with areas where there was no local initiative, were blocked by one side or the other. In 1844 the evangelical social reformer Lord Ashley had described a situation of stalemate: 'Dissenters and the Church have each laid down their limits which they will not pass, and there is no power that can either force, persuade or delude them'; this proved enduring.[25]

All these initiatives, halting and uneven though they were in terms of the provision of schools and schooling, made a significant contribution to the

---

22 Goldstrom, *The social content of education*, p. 65. Goldstrom's work on the Irish schoolbooks and their context is indispensable.

23 New Script Cards, as used at the National Society's Central School, Baldwin's Gardens. British Library, 1210.g.49(1).

24 Very little work has been done on the Catholic schools in the period: the history and the historiography are alike ghettoised. For an exception which discusses books, albeit within a narrow time-frame, see McLelland, 'The Protestant Alliance and Roman Catholic schools'.

25 Quoted in Gash, *Reaction and reconstruction in English politics*, p. 88. For a fuller account, see Sutherland, 'Education', pp. 130–1.

market for books, coinciding with and presumably interacting with advances in the technology of production. In the 1830s, as the 'distribution revolution' got under way, the Irish School Commissioners were launching their first titles and the two mainland societies were expanding their operations. The decade 1830–40 was a pivotal moment in the development of working-class formal schooling, as well as for middle- and upper-class formal schooling. And book distribution was given a further push after 1840 by cheap postal rates and the rapid expansion of the railway network. So cheap were the Irish Commissioners' books for elementary schools, the most popular ones costing only a few pennies,[26] that they were attractive also to English elementary schools; and the introduction of the book subsidy for schools in England and Wales in 1848 made them cheaper still. In December 1849 Longman and John Murray combined forces to complain to the government about being undercut. Eventually in 1852 the Irish Commissioners lost their publishing privileges. Henceforth the books they compiled or selected were printed by commercial publishers, who were chosen by open bidding. The Commissioners were able still to offer the books at reduced prices to the Irish schools under their control; but everyone else had to buy the books directly from the commercial publishers at full price.[27]

Schools affiliated to the denominational societies in England and Wales could still apply for the book grant and the first specialised collection of books on education, including textbooks, was formed in the aftermath of the 1851 Exhibition. Books and other exhibited items donated for the Exhibition were transferred to the new South Kensington site in 1853, where they became, officially, the Educational Division of the South Kensington Museum.[28] The published catalogues of the collection (ten editions between 1857 and 1893) offer invaluable snapshots of the range of books available; especially those copies with publishers' catalogues bound in. The fifth edition of 1860, for example, includes the catalogues of sixty-seven publishers and equipment suppliers. The largest advertisers stand out: Longman, Murray, Macmillan, Oliver & Boyd.[29] The incidental charms of the volume include blurbs which give a glimpse of publishers' motivations, rhetoric and pricing policies, and information on series which is unlikely to be available elsewhere. In the Longman catalogue, for example, there is a list (p. 13) of G. R. Gleig's series of elementary schoolbooks (thirty-seven titles).

26 For prices in the mid-1840s, see Akenson, *The Irish education experiment*, p. 229.
27 *Ibid.*, p. 239.
28 See Goldstrom, *The social content of education*, p. 5; Stray, 'A cellarful of ghosts?' Most of this collection was sold into the trade in 1993; cf. note 42 below.
29 The only complete set of the catalogues is held by the Science Museum Library.

As a result of all this publishing activity, the Education Committee of the Privy Council had been able in 1857 to list 1,500 titles, the purchase of which they were prepared to subsidise in England and Wales.[30] The Irish books still dominated the list; and a survey of books ordered for elementary schools in Great Britain between September 1856 and May 1859, compiled by James Tilleard for the National Association for the Promotion of the Social Sciences, showed that they represented over half the copies of reading books ordered (almost 481,000 copies out of a total of almost 903,000) and over a third of the arithmetic books ordered (almost 51,000 copies out of a total of 135,000).[31] Tilleard's survey also shows where the real mass market lay: in supporting the learning of the most basic skills. He grouped books into thirty-six different categories; but only in five of these, reading lesson books, grammar, arithmetic, 'political and historical geography' and British history, were more than 20,000 copies ordered. In another four, poetry, dictionaries, atlases and wall maps, orders fell to between 10,000 and 20,000 copies. By comparison, the other twenty-seven categories represented mere handfuls.

Behind these sharply skewed figures there may also lie more complex patterns of distribution and use. Tilleard claimed to compile his figures from a very detailed government return which appears to have been lost, and it may be that the category 'elementary' is a somewhat elastic one. Certainly some of the categories of books, such as chemistry, natural philosophy, mechanics and mechanism, sound more appropriate for middle-class or 'secondary' schools; and the inclusion of Scotland in his figures may pull in the same direction. The curriculum of the Scottish parish school had pretensions and ambitions unheard of in English elementary schools. A good one could teach mathematics, Latin and even a little Greek; and it was possible for a boy to go direct from a parish school to the junior class of a Scottish university.[32]

Some of the books were likely to have been ordered for use in the 'Normal Schools', run by both National and British and Foreign School Societies. These were proto-teacher training colleges, offering training for a privileged subset of would-be elementary school teachers. Here, however, there would be competition for such purchases from the two Societies' own publications. Both societies produced a wide range of books which they sold from central depositories; they were available to the general public but were

---

30 Goldstrom, *The social content of education*, p. 4. In the fifth edition of the South Kensington catalogue (1860), these books are listed by subject on pp. 243–86.

31 Tilleard, 'On elementary school books'; see also the commentary on these data in Goldstrom, *The social content of education*, pp. 198–9, Appendix III.

32 Anderson, *Education and opportunity in Victorian Scotland*, ch. 1; Anderson, 'Education and the state in nineteenth-century Scotland'.

intended mainly to provide a complete resource which fitted each society's ideological position (this itself being the focus of dispute, especially on the question of the inclusion of scriptural texts and their mixing with secular writing). The series of BFSS books began with its *Manual of the teaching . . . in the elementary schools of the British and Foreign School Society* (1816); they were often produced in association with Simpkin & Marshall, until the Revised Code, discussed below, changed this in the 1860s. By the 1870s the Society was stocking titles by several publishers in its depository, but the transfer of many BFSS schools to the new local boards, also discussed below, undercut its role as a supplier of books, and the depository was closed down in 1884.[33]

Other possible purchasers and users of the range of books being listed by the Education Department at the end of the 1850s were the 'pupil teachers', who had come into being as a result of additional grants offered from 1846. These were teenagers who were in effect apprenticed to existing teachers, giving aid in the class-room, but also being allowed a short period of extra study each day. At the end of their five-year apprenticeship they could be examined by the government's inspectors of schools and certificated, and were also allowed to compete for scholarships to the Normal Schools. In practice relatively few could afford to take this elite route; many more, with or without certificates, simply continued in teaching.[34] Behind such likely uses are yet further questions: did every child, pupil teacher or trainee teacher have a copy of a book, or was sharing the order of the day? Probably most elementary school children had a reading book and an arithmetic book. It was these that the Irish Commissioners estimated wore out after about three years[35] and were thus re-ordered and re-ordered. Books beyond these were much more likely to be shared, and schools and institutions, rather than scholars, had sets.[36]

Despite all these unanswered questions, however, the role of the Irish School Commissioners and the existence of the book subsidy from the Education Committee of the Privy Council enable us to form a rough idea of the size of the expanding market for elementary schoolbooks in the decades from 1830 to 1860. Thereafter, it becomes much more difficult. The Irish Commissioners continued to compile and select books;[37] but from 1863 the structure of government grants to elementary education in England and Wales changed radically. In that year a Revised Code of regulations governing grants to

33 Bartle, 'The teaching manuals and lesson books of the British and Foreign School Society'.
34 For the creation and early years of this scheme, see Tropp, *The school teachers*, pp. 18–25.
35 Goldstrom, *The social content of education*, p. 86.
36 Heathorn, *For home, country and race*, pp. 8, 13.
37 Akenson, *The Irish education experiment*, p. 231, n.24; p. 323.

elementary schools came into force, which attempted to introduce the principle of the free market into the provision of education for the masses. Existing grants, with the exception of the building grants, were replaced by a single annual capitation grant of twelve shillings. Four shillings could be earned by the child's regular attendance, the rest depended on his/her performance in examinations in reading, writing and arithmetic, conducted by government inspectors. Children were to be grouped in Standards by age; and no child was to be allowed to repeat a Standard. It was payment by results. The immediate effect was drastically to reduce central government expenditure on elementary schools. In 1861 it had reached just over £800,000; by 1865 it had fallen to just over £600,000 and the levels of 1861 were not reached again until 1869.[38] We can guess that one of school managers' economies in the lean years of the mid-1860s was likely to be books: to try to get one more year's use out of tattered reading or arithmetic books (primers). Although the commercial publishers hastened to bring out series tailored to the exact requirements of each Standard – to aid the teachers in 'teaching to the test', as it would be labelled in the twentieth century – the take-up rate may have been slower than they hoped. Even so, by 1865 there were already six series of readers on the market; and by 1876 there would be at least fifteen.[39]

From the beginning of the 1860s therefore, we have no central list of approved books; and until much more detailed and fine-grained work is done both on the *Publishers' Circular* and the *Bookseller*, and in surviving publishers' archives, we have only clumps of information about popular books, the total size of orders and thus the market. Stephen Heathorn has made a good beginning, exploring the late nineteenth-century publishing activity of the Anglican National Society, and the archives of Macmillan, Edward Arnold and Longman;[40] but more is needed. During the nineteenth century itself, apart from the burst of activity in the wake of the Great Exhibition, no individual or body took trouble over systematic lists or collections of elementary schoolbooks: some were sent to copyright libraries, others escaped.[41] The last South Kensington catalogue was issued in 1893. The core of this collection was transferred to the Board of Education in 1913 and survived in the library of its successor, the Ministry of Education, until the late 1960s, but was then broken

38 For more detail and background, see Sutherland, *Policy-making in elementary education*, pp. 4–9.
39 Goldstrom, *The social content of education*, p. 167.
40 Heathorn, *Home, country, and race*, pp. 279–80.
41 The brief historical account in chapter 1 of the Report of the Board of Education's Consultative Committee on 'Books in Public Elementary Schools' in 1928 underlines this picture of random survival; as does a preliminary survey of those textbooks included in Cambridge University Library's holdings, classmarks Sc.1–20. The online listing of the Library's 'secondary' holdings (some 200,000 volumes), currently in progress, should provide a basis for research in this area.

up and dispersed.[42] Other twentieth-century collections were the product of serendipity; and the same principle has had, perforce, to govern the collections which university Schools of Education, notably in Leeds, Liverpool and London, and interested individuals continue to try to build and to protect in the twenty-first century.[43]

Yet even if the buying of elementary school books was in the doldrums in the 1860s, other opportunities were there for publishers. The choice of formal examinations as the instrument for measuring the success of elementary schools was by no means an isolated occurrence. Formal examinations, mostly written, were gaining ground at every level of society, both in the developing structures of formal education, schools of all kinds and universities, and elsewhere: in the selection of candidates for the Indian and then the Home Civil Service (1853 and from 1870). They were also used as instruments by groups fighting to establish a monopoly of a particular expertise, would-be 'professionals'.[44] Textbooks to help prospective candidates and their teachers to prepare began to proliferate. The London examinations generated a large subgenre of such books as William Stewart's Educational Series: a representative title is William Dodds's *London University matriculation examination: what to read and how to read it* (1885).[45] The late nineteenth-century backlash against exams included a concern that literary creation was taking second place to cramming and mark-gaining, as in the jingle:

> Last night I dreamt that Shakespeare's ghost
> Sat for a Civil Service post,
> And on the paper for that year
> There were some questions on *King Lear*,
> Which Shakespeare answered very badly
> Because he hadn't studied Bradley.[46]

42 For more detail, see Chancellor, *History for their masters*, p. 14. Some collections (Brooke, Baines, Forster, Grenfell) were rescued and are now in the library of the Institute of Education, University of London.

43 The collection of classical textbooks built up by W. B. Thompson at Leeds is now housed at the Brotherton Library, University of Leeds. For an early attempt at cataloguing, see Thompson and Ridge, *Catalogue of the national collection of Greek and Latin school text-books*.

44 For more detail, see Sutherland, 'Examinations and the construction of professional identity', esp. pp. 52–3.

45 Dodds also produced *Latin grammar and composition for London University matriculation, containing the whole of the questions proposed in these subjects since the foundation of the University* (1882: British Library, 12200.cc.5(22)), whose title splendidly summarises its specificity of orientation, resource and market. See also below, chapter 14.

46 Boas, *Lays of learning*; originating, probably, in one of Boas's columns in *Punch*. 'Bradley' is A. C. Bradley's *Shakespearean tragedy* (1904).

In mid-century, school provision for the middle and upper classes was investigated by a pair of Royal Commissions: the Clarendon, which looked at Eton and eight other schools of similar standing between 1861 and 1864; and the Taunton Commission, which looked at every other school that had pretensions to be more than an elementary school, between 1864 and 1867. The processes of enquiry, and the reports and legislation which followed, were both consequences of and contributors to a larger movement towards consolidation and sharper stratification within the sector.[47] Significant for our discussion are the attempts to standardise textbook provision, notably to ease the transition for pupils who changed schools. The tension between differentiation from 'inferior' schooling and competition within manifested itself in the commissioning of standard Latin and Greek grammars – the mainstay of what was still a classically dominated curriculum. Acting on the recommendations of the Clarendon Commission of 1861, the heads of the nine leading schools commissioned Benjamin Kennedy of Shrewsbury (one of their number) to produce a new standard book, and this was published in 1866 as *The public school Latin primer*. Controversy dogged its commissioning, assembly and reception but it became de facto, in the words of one of its critics, 'the new national grammar'. Ironically, the independent schools, prompted by state intervention, produced an authoritative textbook at a time when centralised rule on the continental model was denounced as un-English.[48]

The expanding market provided by the public schools, and the endowed grammar schools which increasingly imitated them, was further stabilised by the founding in 1873 of the Oxford and Cambridge Schools Examination Board, and their prescriptions created regular demand for books in specific areas. By this time both the ancient university presses were in the field. Alexander Macmillan, as publisher to OUP 1851–63, had pressed for expansion into the school market. In 1863 the Press set up a School Book Committee and the first batch of books was published in 1866. CUP soon followed suit with its Pitt Press imprint in 1870.[49] The competition was fierce, and the universities were criticised for acting at the same time as prescribers of examination content and as publishers of books to provide for that content. These markets also attracted commercial publishers, some of them with links to the schools. George Bell set up series of textbooks in the late 1840s aimed at the proprietary schools,

47 Sutherland, 'Education', pp. 146–9; see also Honey, *Tom Brown's universe*.
48 On the *Primer*, see Stray, *Grinders and grammars*, which reprints the thirty-six letters published in *The Times* after the *Primer* was published in September 1866.
49 Sutcliffe, *The Oxford University Press*, pp. 19–24; McKitterick, *A history of Cambridge University Press*, pp. 357–8.

and even opened a bookshop at one of them, Brighton College. The firm of Rivingtons, a prolific schoolbook publisher which was taken over by Longman in the 1890s, was in close touch with a network of public-school masters.[50] The liberal educationist John Percival (1834–1918), headmaster of Clifton College (1862–79) and later of Rugby (1887–95), was related by marriage to the Rivingtons. The major players in this field built up networks of trusted reviewers who advised on proposals, and inevitably contracts and payments tended to circulate within a fairly small circle.[51] Other links between publishers and schools included John Murray's links with Eton (the firm produced Eton books in the 1880s, when the school, at 1,000 boys, constituted a substantial market by itself); and the friendship between the Macmillan brothers and Edward Thring, the reforming headmaster of Uppingham. At university level, one example is that of the young Oxford graduate Algernon Stedman, who published a guide to Oxford, became a tutor, turned his teaching into books and, after having them distributed by George Bell, set up his own firm, moving into general publishing; he changed his name to Methuen in 1899 and was created Baron Methuen in 1916.[52] The firm of Ginn, similarly, was founded in 1867 specifically for the publication of textbooks,[53] as was W. B. Clive's University Tutorial Press in the late 1880s.

The market for elementary schoolbooks began to revive in the course of the 1870s; and by 1882, fifty publishers were advertising in the January education edition of the *Publishers' Circular*.[54] In 1870, the Gordian knot of 'the religious problem' had been hacked through, albeit rather clumsily, by Gladstone's first government. The Education Act of 1870, often known as Forster's Act, after W. E. Forster who was Vice-President of the Committee of Council on Education, committed governments to the provision of elementary school places for all working-class children. In areas where there was no provision, or insufficient provision by the voluntary societies, or where a majority of ratepayers desired it, a new elected local authority was created, the school board, which had powers to build and run schools, and to issue a precept to the local rating authority for a share of the rates. Managers of schools affiliated to the voluntary societies had no access to rate aid, as they had no formal representative status; but in part

---

50 This might be seen as an extension of the public-school kinship network identified by Bamford, *The rise of the public schools*, pp. 116–63.

51 The role of the publisher's reader in this field is important and under-researched. An established teacher like T. E. Page of Charterhouse, advising on proposals for Macmillan, exerted influence for several decades.

52 [Lucas] *Sir Algernon Methuen, Baronet*, pp. 6–7. Stedman's early career thus recapitulated that of Louis de Porquet, mentioned earlier in this chapter.

53 Lawler, *Seventy years of textbook publishing*.   54 Weedon, *Victorian publishing*, p. 111.

compensation, rates of central government grant, still within a payment-by-results framework, were increased for all schools. School boards might, if they chose, frame byelaws to compel attendance at their schools; voluntary schools had no such powers. It was not until 1880 that all boards, and in areas where there were voluntary schools only, all local sanitary authorities, were required to make byelaws to compel attendance.[55] Eliot has expressed puzzlement that there was not an immediate surge in the market for elementary schoolbooks in the wake of the 1870 Act.[56] In part this is because he mistakenly thinks the Act compelled school attendance; in part it is also a consequence of the time it took both central and local government bodies to make an audit of existing provision, estimate the numbers of children in the relevant age-group, and then start finding or constructing buildings in which to house them. Even the Titan of school boards and the national pace-maker, the London School Board and its architect, E. R. Robson, took several years to get going, for precisely these reasons.[57] It is important to remember too that although the financial regime for both board and voluntary schools improved from the low point of the 1860s, none of the funding was tied specifically to book provision, as the old book subsidy had been. Thus the introduction of state-organised elementary schooling in 1870 brought with it new opportunities for publishers, though it looks as if some overstepped the mark, putting out more books than they could sell and retrenching in the early to mid-1870s. Publication of English grammars reached a peak round 1870, for example.[58] And it is probably significant that the Sampson Low catalogues of educational books began to appear at this point.[59]

Enforcing compulsory attendance proved a much slower and more tortuous process than estimating the need for places and providing them. By 1895 only 82 per cent of children whose names were on the registers were attending regularly, a total of just over 4 million. Modest gains would continue until the labour crisis triggered by the First World War played havoc with the schooling of a whole generation of children. The structures of payment by results likewise cast a long shadow. There was endless tinkering at the edges throughout the

---

55 For a fuller account, see Sutherland, 'Education', pp. 142–6.
56 Eliot, *Some patterns and trends in British publishing*, p. 48.
57 Seaborne, 'E. R. Robson and the board schools of London'.
58 Michael, 'The hyperactive production of English grammars in the nineteenth century'. Michael uses a database which includes 860 new grammars published in the period.
59 Low, *A classified catalogue of school, college, classical, training, and general educational works in use in Great Britain*, etc. (Sampson Low, 1871). This edition collected titles from nearly 150 publishers, and marked those in the South Kensington collection. Further editions were published in 1876 and 1887.

1870s and 1880s; but the basis for grant was only substantially changed in the first half of the 1890s. Some writers have argued that the tinkering of the mid-seventies and early eighties, which was presented as encouraging children to go beyond the rudiments, with some reading in subjects like history and geography, expanded pupils' range and the books to which they had access. But a detailed analysis of the Codes, year by year, does not sustain this.[60] Even when the grant basis was at last changed and something much more like a block grant began to take shape, the habits of teaching and working in the elementary class-room engendered by payment by results took much longer to die; and school managers and teachers clung not only to these but to the schoolbooks they had generated, unless and until these actually fell apart. Heathorn is impressed by the care which the school board for London took, to try to select from the publishers' plethora of offerings; and notes that at the end of the century they sent a questionnaire to thirty-five other school boards to enquire into their practice. From this he concludes that 'typical' school board practice was to have some kind of requisitions committee or panel, to select for their schools.[61] But this is to generalise from a wholly unrepresentative sample. London, as everyone recognised, operated at a level of professionalism which other boards could only dream of. Their thirty-five respondents were all large and well-resourced urban boards. There were over 2,000 other boards up and down the country, the vast majority of the minimum possible size, with just five members.[62] In addition there were over 14,000 individual committees of management of voluntary schools. These tiny local authorities and quasi-local authorities were in general impoverished and books and equipment tended to be worked until they disintegrated.

There is nothing to suggest that at the end of the nineteenth century individual children in elementary schools were more likely than they had been at mid-century to have had access to more than a reading book and an arithmetic primer. A decade later, in 1911 the commitment of the London County Council to ensuring that each class had access to readers in history, geography and literature, while for teachers there was also a central library, was recognised as exceptional. Even in the period up to 1940, respondents to a major oral history survey on the teaching of history, some of whom had begun school before 1914, commented that they had had no textbooks; and those who subsequently went on to become teachers themselves reported that they might

---

60 Both Heathorn and Weedon have argued for such expansion; but see Sutherland, *Policy-making in elementary education*, chs. 7–9.

61 Heathorn, *Home, country, and race*, pp. 14 and 219–23 (Appendix A).

62 Sutherland, *Policy-making in elementary education*, pp. 352–3.

have access to one text, often jealously guarded, from which a lesson could be prepared.[63] It is hard to imagine that the late nineteenth-century classroom was better resourced.

There remain, therefore, many unanswered questions about the markets for, and the impact of, the texts pouring forth from the presses. Heathorn has argued strongly for the development of a discourse of patriotism, powerfully gendered and increasingly tinged with imperialist and racialist overtones, engaging in a substantial and subtle content analysis of manuals for teachers, programmatic statements and textbooks published in the period 1880–1914. However, much of his material comes from London; the majority of the textbooks he uses are history and geography textbooks, rather than the historical and geographical passages included in the elementary school readers; and he is reluctant fully to confront the question of how far sets of books of which there might be one per school, or several per pupil-teacher training centre or Normal School, shaped what actually happened in the elementary class-room. Brief mention of comments in oral histories and autobiographies is not enough;[64] it is difficult to know what sources might provide some of the detail about class-room practice and experience that Patrick Brindle's in-depth interviewing extracted from those actively studying and teaching history in the first half of the twentieth century. Perhaps more attention should be paid, too, to class-room practice and experience in secondary schools. Who bought and who read the bulk of the 500,000 copies of H. O. Arnold-Forster's *Citizen reader*, published by Cassell, of which he was a director, between 1886 and 1910?[65] Were some of them shipped off to the colonies? The colonial market is one about which we know little.[66] A similar puzzle is presented by the success and steady sale of books, especially of verse, advertised by publishers as suitable for school prizes.[67] Whether the awarding of these was primarily a feature of privately funded schools, of Sunday schools run by the churches, or of the elementary schools of the larger and better-funded school boards – or of all three groups – is unclear.

63 Brindle, 'Past histories', pp. 142–51.
64 Heathorn, *Home, country, and race*, p. 214. Schoolbooks are notable by their absence from the discussion in Rose, *Intellectual life of the British working classes*.
65 Heathorn, *Home, country, and race*, p. 36.
66 But it is clear that by 1900 several publishers were well established in the colonies: for OUP, see [Chapman] *Some account of the Oxford University Press*, pp. 63–72, and Sutcliffe, *The Oxford University Press*, pp. 200–2; for Collins, Keir, 'Across the oceans, 1865–77', in his *The house of Collins*, pp. 171–85. For India, see Chatterjee, *Empires of the mind*, which covers the period 1880–1947; also her chapter on Macmillan in India in James (ed.), *Macmillan*.
67 Weedon, *Victorian publishing*, p. 119.

None of the nineteenth-century commentators or memoirists ever waxed lyrical about an arithmetic primer. But the reading books developed in response to the Revised Code, and dominating the elementary school class-room for the second half of the nineteenth century, had their staunch defenders. The Irish reading books had been marked by religious moralising and earnest moral tales, and useful knowledge, including political economy; the endless struggle for political correctness in the sectarian conflicts which beset Irish elementary school provision produced texts of surpassing dullness, as many English commentators complained. Charles Dickens's *Hard times* came out in 1854 and it is tempting to construe the scene in the classroom in chapter 2 as a commentary on the Irish style:

> 'Girl number twenty unable to define a horse!' said Mr. Gradgrind ...
> 'Bitzer,' said Thomas Gradgrind, 'Your definition of a horse.'
> 'Quadruped. Graminivorous. Forty teeth, namely twenty-four grinders, four eye-teeth, and twelve incisive. Sheds coat in spring; in marshy countries, sheds hoofs, too. Hoofs hard but requiring to be shod with iron. Age known by marks in mouth.' Thus (and much more) Bitzer.
> 'Now girl number twenty,' said Mr. Gradgrind, 'You know what a horse is.'[68]

The specificity of the Revised Code's requirements elbowed the Irish style to one side. At Standard I in 1863, the examination test of 7-year-olds entailed reading a 'Narrative in monosyllables'; at Standard II, 'One of the Narratives next in order after monosyllables in an elementary reading book used in the school'; at Standard III, 'A short paragraph from an elementary reading book used in the school'; at Standard IV, 'A short paragraph from a more advanced reading book used in the school'; at Standard V, 'A few lines of poetry from a reading book used in the first class of the school'; and at Standard VI, 'A short ordinary paragraph in a newspaper or other modern narrative'.[69] The vast majority of children were presented for examination in Standards I–III; however, the requirement for Standard V meant that even in the elementary reader there was some poetry. Some of the government inspectors in the third quarter of the century disapproved of the inclusion in Revised Code readers of fairy tales, myths and fables; and one inspector took the view that, 'Extracts from the English classics and specimens of high-class poetry are neither fitted

---

68 One of Dickens's own rejected titles for the book was 'According to Cocker', after a well-known arithmetic textbook.
69 Goldstrom, *The social content of education*, pp. 164–5.

for the age of the scholars nor useful to their present or future career.' Others, most notably Matthew Arnold, applauded.[70]

The relentless informativeness and moral earnestness which had been so marked a feature earlier in the century, particularly in the Irish readers, did not disappear entirely. The Standard v volume of the *National reading books*, produced by the National Society and in use during the 1880s, included a 'Social matters section' and three essays 'Of value', 'Wages' and 'Interference with men's dealings with each other', and observed severely in its preface that 'trivial frivolous subjects, and what has been termed "buffoonery", are purposely excluded'. But there are plenty of tales of action and derring-do, and the poetry includes Southey's 'Death of Nelson' and Wordsworth's 'Lucy Gray'. Thomas Nelson & Sons' extremely successful series the *Royal Readers*, which, for a period from the late 1870s on, provided almost half the firm's profits from its educational publishing,[71] eschewed political economy altogether in its Standard v reader. Some sense of the appeal of the series comes from Flora Thompson's memoir *Lark Rise*, first published in 1939. Flora, writing of herself as 'Laura', at school in rural Oxfordshire in the 1880s, remembered that

There was plenty there to enthral any child: 'The Skater Chased by Wolves'; 'The Siege of Torquilstone' from *Ivanhoe*; Fenimore Cooper's *Prairie on Fire*; and Washington Irving's *Capture of Wild Horses* . . . Interspersed between the prose readings were poems: 'The Slave's Dream'; 'Young Lochinvar'; 'The Parting of Douglas and Marmion'; Tennyson's 'Brook' and 'Ring out, Wild Bells'; Byron's 'Shipwreck'; Hogg's 'Skylark', and many more. 'Lochiel's Warning' was a favourite with Edmund [Laura's brother], who often, in bed at night, might be heard declaiming: 'Lochiel! Lochiel! beware of the day!' while Laura, at any time, with or without encouragement, was ready to 'look back into other years' with Henry Glassford Bell, and recite his scenes from the life of Mary Queen of Scots . . . Long before their schooldays were over they knew every piece in the books by heart and it was one of their greatest pleasures in life to recite them to each other . . . The selection in the *Royal Readers*, then, was an education in itself for those who took to it kindly; but the majority of the children would have none of it; saying that the prose was 'dry old stuff' and that they hated 'portry'.[72]

70 *Ibid.*, p. 168. The selective absorption of English literature into schoolbooks is too large a topic to be dealt with here. For some examples, see D. Daiches, 'Presenting Shakespeare', in Briggs (ed.), *Essays in the history of publishing*, pp. 61–112; Ward, ' "Came from yon fountain" '.
71 Heathorn, *Home, country, and race*, p. 15.
72 Thompson, *Lark Rise to Candleford* (Oxford, 1954), pp. 193–4.

Elementary schools, schools for the working classes, had from the beginning been mixed schools. But the expansion of formal schooling for the affluent and aspirant, those who wanted their children to become 'gentlemen' or 'ladies', had initially been a male phenomenon. That is not to say that there were no girls' schools in the late eighteenth and early nineteenth centuries; but they were regarded very much as second best: the general view was that a lady was best educated at home by her mother; and the schools which offered to provide for middle- and upper-class girls in situations where that was not possible made great play with their domestic nature, emphasising that they were small, informal and family-like. It was only in the third quarter of the nineteenth century that those campaigning to improve the position of women began to make a case for institutional structures for ladies as well as gentlemen. The last quarter of the century saw a considerable growth of these, not only through the remodelling of charitable endowments to make provision for girls, but also through the new foundations of the Girls' Public Day School Company.[73] These schools therefore constituted an additional market for the more advanced, subject-specific school texts. There are no signs that at first publishers made specific provision for them; and given the determination of many of these girls' schools to challenge elite boys' schools on their own ground, symbolised by a long battle to be able to teach Greek as well as Latin, it is more likely that they chose to use the boys' texts. Only in the 1890s and in the early 1900s, as the emphasis on domestic skills and motherhood intensified, part of a larger discourse about national efficiency, did books on the subjects for middle-class girls' schools begin to appear.[74]

There were only about 150 such girls' schools by the end of the century. But as formal provision for boys continued to expand, together they provided a promising market for subject-specific texts. Cyril Ransome, father of Arthur, was Professor of History at the new University College in Leeds, and began writing history textbooks to supplement his salary. They sold well and he published with Macmillan, Rivington and Longman. He was doing sufficiently well to take the risk of resigning from his chair in 1897, when he hoped to embark on a political career. Sadly, illness intervened and he died soon after; but his royalties were his widow's principal source of income and it appears that she too began to write, with a *First history of England* in 1903 and

---

73 For the challenges to the domestic model, see Sutherland, *Faith, duty and the power of mind*, pp. 73–83; for the new foundations, see Sutherland, 'Education', pp. 148–9.
74 Heathorn, *Home, country and race*, pp. 158–9.

a *Primary history of England* in 1905.[75] Mrs Ransome's texts were aimed at the younger child; her husband seems to have written for both older and younger children, with some hope, presumably, that the books for younger children would have some sale beyond private schools; if not to elementary schools, at least to their teachers and teacher-trainers. The Ransomes were in good company: both Mandell Creighton, the ecclesiastical historian and bishop, and his wife Louise had been writing what Louise called 'primers', history textbooks, since the 1870s;[76] and other authors of history textbooks included the academic historians Oscar Browning, E. A. Freeman, S. R. Gardiner, York Powell, J. Holland Rose and T. F. Tout.[77] Also publishing substantially were university teachers of the burgeoning subject of education. J. M. D. Meiklejohn, Professor of the Theory, History and Practice of Education at St Andrews, was something of a phenomenon, prolifically producing history books, geography books, books on the teaching of reading and English grammar. By 1903 he was his own publisher, in partnership with Alfred M. Holden.[78]

A further significant expansion of the market in books for older children came in the years after the 1902 Education Act, when the government at last committed itself to state-supported provision for post-elementary or 'secondary' education, beginning a process whereby elementary would slowly metamorphose into 'primary'; and elementary/primary and then secondary would be considered age-related stages rather than distinct and self-contained provision for different social classes.[79] As after 1870, it took time to put physical provision in place, either taking over buildings which had had other uses or constructing new ones. But by 1913–14 the new grant-aided secondary schools in England and Wales were annually admitting just over 60,000 children, boys and girls. It is possible that publishing figures for subject-specific textbooks, of the kind whose content Heathorn has analysed, need to be broken down further by period. Their impact may have been greater in the class-rooms of the new maintained secondary schools than in elementary schools.

---

75 Ransome, *Autobiography*, pp. 16, 22, 24, 50, 68; Chancellor, *History for their masters*, bibliography, p. 146.

76 Creighton, *Memoir of a Victorian woman*, pp. 54, 73, 83. Mandell Creighton's *History of Rome* was one of Macmillan's Shilling Primers, a series of several dozen titles begun by J. R. Green; first published in 1875, it was still in print in 1963. Creighton himself jokingly attributed its success to its suitability as a missile in classroom battles; 'their consequent speedy destruction served to promote a rapid sale' (Creighton, *Life and letters of Mandell Creighton* 1, p. 146).

77 Heathorn, *Home, country, and race*, pp. 44–5. Freeman assembled a group of women to write history textbooks: see Walton, 'Charlotte M. Yonge'.

78 Graves, *John Meiklejohn*.

79 For a fuller discussion, see Sutherland, 'Education', pp. 146–52, 158–65.

Given this additional expansion, the market for secondary textbooks begins to look like a mass market on a scale similar to the already-existing market for elementary textbooks. It is thus puzzling that there is an apparent decline in the total market share of educational books after 1900.[80] Several factors may be at work here. Absolute numbers of texts published may have held up and even increased; in looking at total market share we need to control for the overall rate of growth of the market, and there is a steepening upward gradient from the 1890s onward. Eliot has suggested that there may be changes in classification; and this takes us back once more to the need for much more fine-grained and detailed work. Among other enquiries this might include considering the possibility that the radical restructuring of the local government of education brought about by the 1902 Act had consequences for patterns of textbook buying. School boards were abolished and voluntary schools were finally given access to rate aid and brought under the control of the new Local Education Authorities, county and country borough councils, only 146 of them, a second tier of government which contrasts sharply with the thousands of tiny bodies which had preceded them. Nobody has yet looked to see what policies they adopted for buying textbooks, either for the secondary schools or for the elementary schools under their control, and what they spent. Was the pattern lumpy? Were purchasing policies streamlined? Did they share information, move to create purchasing consortia? We have no idea.

Finally Eliot has also suggested that changing patterns of teaching may mean that texts used in schools are not so easily identifiable. It would be cheering to think that the habits and props of payment by results were finally being eroded in elementary schools. And perhaps there were, in the new maintained secondary schools, a few more English teachers like Mr Bartlett, who transformed the life of the young Victor Pritchett, in Rosendale Road School in south-east London:

> No text books. Our first lessons were from Ford Madox Ford's *English Review* which was publishing some of the best young writers of the time. We discussed Bridges and Masefield. Children who seemed stupid were suddenly able to detect a fine image or line and disentangle it from the ordinary. A sea poem of Davidson's, a forgotten Georgian, remains in my mind to this day: the evocation of the sea rolling on the shingle on the coast between Romney and Hythe:
>
> > *The beach with all its organ stops*
> > *Pealing again prolongs the roar*

80 Eliot, *Some patterns and trends in British publishing*, p. 58.

Bartlett dug out one of James Russell Lowell's poems, *The Vision of Sir Launfal*, though why he chose that dim poem I do not know; we went on to Tennyson, never learning by heart . . . We had a magazine and a newspaper.

Many of Bartlett's methods are now commonplace in English schools; in 1911 they were revolutionary. For myself, the sugar-bag blue cover of the *English Review* was decisive. One had thought literature was in books written by dead people who had been oppressively over-educated. Here was writing by people who were alive and probably writing at this moment.[81]

81 V. S. Pritchett, *A cab at the door* (1968), p. 105.

10

Mass markets: children's books

BRIAN ALDERSON AND ANDREA IMMEL

Introduction

A 'generational theory', with phases running in fairly well-defined thirty-year cycles, has been applied to the development of the British children's book from the first attempts to write its history. James Pettit Andrews and Sarah Trimmer both designated the 1740s as the foundation period, which saw the start of publishing for young readers as a continuously developing sector of the book trade. They also characterised the years between 1770 and 1800 as notable for the increased diversification, specialisation and proliferation of the children's book.[1] Neither lived long enough to pass judgement on the next phase, 1800–30, regarded as the first flowering of imaginative writing, illustration and book design, dominated by innovative entrepreneurs such as John Harris, Benjamin Tabart and the William Dartons. But by 1820, disenchantment had set in, signalling the coming shift from Enlightenment moral priorities to Victorian religious values. John Scott, editor of the *London Magazine*, observed that while instructional books had improved significantly during previous decades, imaginative literature for children had become unacceptably coarse, worldly and superficial to be worthy of its readers or reflect credit upon the authors.[2] More importantly, he grasped that presentation was now integral to the concept of a children's book. Improving the genre meant taking into consideration the way word, image and binding were packaged for an audience whose senses were remarkably receptive to any surface that could be printed upon, coloured or illustrated. The children's book was no longer synonymous with a text-block adorned with cuts.

Of all the general conditions that played a dominant part in determining the nature of reading-matter during the expansion of children's book publishing 1830–1914, three stand out: the changes in the economics and the

---

1 Immel, 'James Pettit Andrews's "Books"'.   2 Scott, 'The literature of the nursery'.

technology of book design, especially where illustration and trade-binding were concerned; the emergence of publishers as independent entrepreneurs determining stasis and innovation in the creating of printed works; and the increased influence of authors, illustrators and printers from northern Europe. We will suggest ways those technological, commercial and cultural factors were instrumental in transforming the children's book from a specialised commodity into a semi-autonomous subsystem of literature during the next ninety years. While this subsystem mirrored the one for adults, increasingly distinctive genres, graphic styles and personnel gradually evolved.

1830–1860

The early years of Victoria's reign have been viewed on the one hand as a falling-back, and on the other hand as the laying of the foundation upon which the unprecedented growth of the Victorian and Edwardian periods would rest.[3] The leading London Regency bookseller-publishers, such as John Harris, were no longer in the forefront. The younger Harris did not launch an ambitious publishing programme of his own after his father retired, but continued reissuing titles from the 1820s *Cabinet of amusement and instruction*. Likewise many new printers, whether in London or the provinces, did not build a back-list of contemporary authors, but relied upon the major publishers, the popular stage or traditional folklore for their content, recycling nursery rhymes, musical adaptations of fairy tales and classic works by Isaac Watts, Aikin and Barbauld, Maria Edgeworth and the Taylor sisters. On the other hand, the trade was certainly open to employment of new technology, evident in the adoption of white-line wood-engraving, in the use of steel-engraving for books aiming for prestige, in the incorporation of fat or Egyptian ornamental faces by Edmund Fry or Stephenson Blake, and in the decoration of editions bound in the recently introduced treated cloth and calico. Overall, this period remains largely unexplored territory and is overdue for reassessment, especially as this stage in the history of children's books coincides with the transformation of British society in response to industrialisation, the growth of empire, etc.

Evangelical publishers, such as Hatchard in Piccadilly and Houlston in Wellington, Salop, who in the 'teens had begun publishing Mrs Sherwood and her sister Mrs Cameron, continued to be important players during this period.[4] The evangelical best-selling authors for children like Sherwood and Cameron have, with Hannah More, been relegated to the canon's fringes because of conservative politics, the belief that art should be subordinated to religion and

---

3 Butts, 'The beginnings of Victorianism (c. 1820–1850)'.   4 Cutt, *Ministering angels*.

the close association with the tract, a genre placed outside the line of development for the novel and children's fiction, in spite of its influence on both.[5] Nevertheless, Sherwood worked in rather different circumstances than her late eighteenth-century predecessors and her long, well-documented career reveals much about changes in taste, values and author–publisher relations over time.[6]

Much energy between 1830 and 1860 continued to be channelled in the creation of books and periodicals designed for home use (rather than school) to give what Maria Edgeworth called 'a taste for truth and realities'. Late Georgian introductory texts to subjects in the social and physical sciences, such as the dialogues by Jeremiah Joyce or Mrs Marcet, remained steady-sellers.[7] Non-fiction books for children were an integral part of publishers' output. Continued stimulus from the Society for the Diffusion of Useful Knowledge, which led to the publication of Charles Knight's *Penny Magazine* in 1832, also suggested a direction for the Religious Tract Society's non-fiction series. The RTS ventured into periodical publishing during the late 1820s with the *Child's Companion; or Sunday Scholar's Reward*. About half the contents of this long-running illustrated magazine, as well as its Anglican rival the *Children's Friend* edited by W. Carus Wilson, consisted of history and descriptions of natural phenomena from a Christian perspective. The editorial policy was not so much a response to readers' demand for knowledge, as to remain competitive by keeping an eye on rival publishers circulating articles with a secular slant on all subjects.[8] It was harder to break into the market with a quality literary magazine, as the experience of publisher Joseph Cundall suggests. In 1846–7 he produced a sixteen-page monthly paper, *Illustrated Juvenile Miscellany*, which included several poems by Elizabeth Barrett. It ran for another year as the *Playmate*, available weekly for a penny or monthly with a hand-coloured etching by John Absolon for sixpence. Compared to its established rivals such as the sectarian *Leisure Hours*, *Peter Parley's Magazine* or the missionary papers, the *Playmate* attempted a livelier and more varied content. Cundall tried again in 1853 with the *Charm*, which, while superior to the *Playmate* in its formal presentation of text and pictures, never really took off.

The strongly utilitarian bent of early Victorian children's book publishing is most closely associated with the works of 'Peter Parley', a character invented by the American educationist Samuel Griswold Goodrich in *Tales of Peter Parley*

---

5 Carter, 'The golden thread: some early tract writers'.
6 Cutt, *Mrs. Sherwood and her books for children*.
7 Polkinghorn, 'Jane Marcet and Harriet Martineau'.
8 Drotner, *English children and their magazines 1751–1948*, ch. 4 and 'Christian knowledge' in Fyfe, *Science and salvation*.

about America (1827). The formula of the avuncular adult serving up facts to an audience of receptive children was successful in the United States, and its importation to Britain marks one of the first substantial influences travelling from west to east across the Atlantic. British publishers like the Dartons, however, were not content merely to edit Goodrich's texts for a home market but – recognising the implicit appeal of Parley himself – commissioned original texts such as *Peter Parley's wonders of earth, sea and sky* (1837) from Samuel Clarke, or launched the monthly *Peter Parley's Magazine* in 1839, under the editorship of William Martin, who also supervised the conversion of these at year's end into *Peter Parley's annual*. That exercise involved the addition of plates, most often steel engraved, but also colour printed: Griffith's chromographic process appeared in the 1844 volume, and Gregory, Collins & Reynolds's woodblocks were used in the 1845 and 1846 volumes (fig. 10.1).

The popularity of the Peter Parley approach is of additional significance for having prompted a counter-revolution in children's book publishing in the late 1830s and early 1840s. Samuel Johnson had previously spoken up for children's need to have 'curiosity gratified with wonders', as had Edgar Taylor, in the preface to his translation of the Grimms' *German popular stories* (1823). In 1839 Catherine Sinclair also complained in the preface to *Holiday house* of mechanised learning, and her novel, set at the end of the Napoleonic wars, endeavoured instead 'to paint that species of noisy, frolicsome, mischievous children which is now almost extinct' who eventually put themselves on the right Christian path. Even more famous was Henry Cole's concerted campaign against Peter Parleyism conducted under the nom de plume Felix Summerly. Cole conceived of the Home Treasury of Books and Pictures as a way 'to cultivate the affections, fancy, imagination, and taste of children'. The first four volumes of the series advertised in the *Publishers' Circular* of May Day 1843 did not do too much to excite expectations as it consisted of *Little Red Riding-Hood*, *Traditional nursery songs*, *Bible events* and a reprint of Thomas Love Peacock's ballad *Sir Hornbook*, an amusing introduction to the parts of speech. But the series rapidly expanded to a couple of dozen items (including a paint-box and a box of terra-cotta bricks) and was joined by a second series of traditional tales, Gammer Gurton's Story Books edited by W. J. Thoms under the pseudonym of Ambrose Merton.[9]

What was significant about this venture was not simply its scale and its editorial planning but the unprecedented sophistication of its design.[10]

9 Summerfield, 'The making of the Home Treasury'.
10 McLean, *Joseph Cundall, a Victorian publisher*.

Figure 10.1 [William Martin, ed.] *Peter Parley's annual* (London: Darton & Clark, 1844). The title-spread from the fifth volume in a long-running sequence of what at the time was a new kind of children's annual, drawing its material from the weekly numbers of the parent magazine. Although edited entirely in Britain it derives from the popular American 'Peter Parley' books. This title-spread in sepia, with an added tint, was printed by a short-lived method using etched steel plates patented by Henry Griffiths. (Princeton University Library)

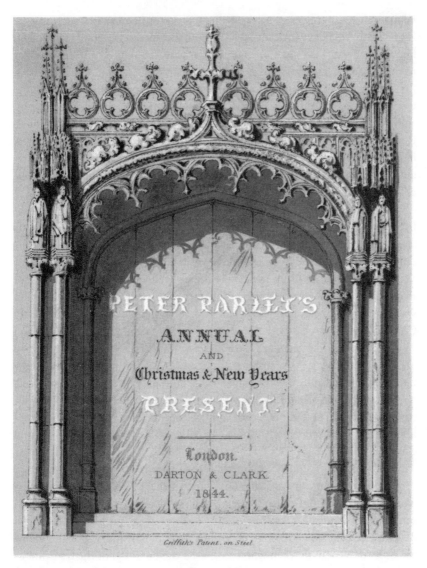

Figure 10.1 (*cont.*).

Evidence in Henry Cole's diary and correspondence makes it clear that he was largely responsible for the books' design treatment – an unusual position for a layman to be in anywhere in the book trade. Through experience and networking he gained technical knowledge and advice from printers such as the

Whittinghams, publishers such as William Pickering, and artists, such as John Linnell and William Mulready, who were concerned with both graphic and fine art. As a result Cole's ambitious plan for a carefully edited series of popular rhymes, ballads and stories was matched by its typography, with Chiswick Press decorated initials and stock-decorations, and by its illustration, where wood-engravings were joined by drawn, and sometimes tinted, lithographs, and by colour printing from woodblocks by the firm of Gregory, Collins & Reynolds. The bindings, gilt on glazed paper wrappers or boards, or full-bound in decorated cloth, praised by Thackeray in *Fraser's Magazine*, were a strong contributory factor to the books' high price at one shilling plain and 2s 6d coloured.

Cole's choice of Joseph Cundall, a 'new man', to administer this new publishing venture, also suggests an awareness of the way in which publishing was separating itself out as a professional activity distinct from bookselling. Certainly Cundall founded his book-producing activities on the tested ground of a retail shop, but as with other 'new men' such as Chapman & Hall and George Routledge, who opened stores in 1830 and 1836 respectively, the intention was to profit by making, not just selling, books. The association with Henry Cole however, coupled with Cundall's own liking for gracious production values, imperilled his slender capital base. Within three years of publication 'The Home Treasury' was sold to Chapman & Hall and its subsequent chequered history usefully illustrates how the Victorian book trade exploited such transfers of literary capital. Economies in production resulted in a lower price (sixpence plain, a shilling coloured) and the sheets from separate titles were also bound up into compendia, some with title-pages for Chapman & Hall and Cundall.

As a bookman, Cundall was unafraid of experimentation and, despite a very modest output, his varied endeavours, such as the series of twenty-one handsomely produced illustrated pamphlets featuring traditional tales and songs, the Pleasure Books for Young Children, were prophetic of fruitful developments in later Victorian children's book publishing. Cundall was not the only 'new man' in town who recognised the potential of the tradition as a foundation for developing a children's list. Almost parallel with his work in the 1840s, and independent rather than imitative, was the more prolific James Burns (1808–71). He likewise published a series of popular tales both as individual titles, with pretty colour-printed wrappers by Gregory, Collins & Reynolds, and as a prestigious three-volume set in 1845 (its preface also included a friendly recommendation of Mr Summerly's more costly Home Library). Those little volumes also were the precursors of several more elaborate collections of stories, nursery rhymes and poetry for children, usually bound in distinctive blind- and gilt-stamped cloth boards and featuring many line illustrations electrotyped or re-engraved from German originals.[11]

The presence of the re-engravings represents a wholesale incursion into the publishing industry of the 1840s and 1850s of influences from Europe, and especially Germany. The works of several major German illustrators, for example, were introduced to English children via translations of German fairy tales and fables. In 1846 Cundall reissued Green's 1839 edition of Grimm, and he was to be closely involved in Addey & Co.'s substantial new translation of no fewer than 190 stories and six 'legends' in 1853–4, illustrated by Edward Wehnert. Cundall also published translations of Musaeus's *Rübezahl*, with lithographed plates after German models, and with Addey co-published Ludwig Bechstein's *The old storyteller* (1854), illustrated with electrotypes of wood-engravings after Ludwig Richter. There was a variable policy among publishers at this time towards the importing of electros or the re-engraving or even reinterpretation of German originals for the English market. Thus the immensely popular *Picture fables* by Wilhelm Hey had Otto Speckter's illustrations first copied by English wood-engravers in a far more refined style than in the German edition for the first translation by Mary Howitt entitled *The child's picture and verse book* (Longman, 1844). When H. W. Dulcken prepared a new text for Routledge in 1858, Speckter's original images were followed more closely, but mostly reversed. His much more finished designs for *Puss in boots*, published in Germany in 1843, were 'drawn [i.e. re-drawn] on stone' by Lewis Haghe in London for Murray's English 1844 edition (fig. 10.2).[12]

The most renowned of the German children's books to arrive in England in the 1840s was Heinrich Hoffmann's picture book *Struwwelpeter*, which was neither printed nor reoriginated in England but imported complete. It had first appeared in 1845 in Frankfurt am Main, where it met with instant success, and by 1848 an anonymous English translation had been made.[13] The work was then printed, hand-coloured and bound in Germany and shipped to London by the publisher's Leipzig agents, Volckmar, who, according to the *English catalogue*, used Williams & Norgate as their wholesale distributors. The impact of *Struwwelpeter* on the English children's book market was of a different order from the ground-breaking but 'polite' works that have so far been considered. The crude energy behind Hoffmann's picture-verses may be seen as a reductionist treatment of the cautionary tale or as a farcical guying

11 Alderson, 'Some notes on James Burns as a publisher of children's books'.
12 Buchanan-Brown, *Early Victorian illustrated books*, pp. 235–44.
13 Sauer, 'A classic is born: the "childhood" of "Struwwelpeter"'.

Figure 10.2 *Puss in boots; and the marquis of Carabas...* (London: John Murray, 1844). Lithographed title-page 'drawn on stone by Lewis Haghe' after designs by Otto Speckter. Although the book was never published in Germany, the title-page, with its decorative trellis-work, and the eleven plates in the text, adhere more closely to a German rather than an English graphic style. (Princeton University Library)

of the same; but part of its historic importance lies in its physical character as the first notable quarto picture book that exhibited the narrative potential of line illustration. Hoffmann was as much amateur draftsman as versifier but the illustrations that accompany his text vary from portraiture to the conventional picturing of events, adding also strip cartoons, drawings which incorporate a sequence of actions within a single design, and pictures including symbolic decorations.

Hoffmann was among the first not only to achieve an international reputation as an author/illustrator of original works for children, but also to achieve cross-over status into the wider literary culture as evidenced by the profusion of Edwardian parodies like Begbie and Carruthers Gould's *The political Struwwelpeter* (1899), *Petrol Peter* (1906) or E. V. Lucas's *Swollen-headed William* (1914).[14] The instant success of *Struwwelpeter* also led to a profusion of German imitations, some of which made their way to England, such as Glassbrenner's *Lachende Kinder* (1850) illustrated by Theodor Hosemann and translated into English by Mme de Chatelain as *A laughter book for little folk* (Cundall & Addey, 1851). But there were also many home-grown versions: publishers such as Dean and Routledge introduced *Struwwelpeter* series which combine pirated versions of Hoffmann with an array of other titles about naughty children either of local origin or adapted from the German.[15]

Struwwelpeter in its varied guises, the Home Treasury series and other early Victorian pamphlets can be seen as forerunners of the immense and rapid expansion of the 'toy book', the first picture book in the modern sense of a signature consisting of a brief heavily illustrated text bound in decorated covers.[16] The series of Large Books issued by James Catnach in the 1830s, for example, included reprints of nursery rhymes with excellent large wood-engravings by George Pickering at the head of each page bound in showy wrappers with elaborate architectural frames or borders composed of fancy type ornaments. By the 1850s the Deans dominated the field with their cheap, miscellaneous series, each with a special cover design and a Parleyesque sponsor such as 'Aunt Affable' or 'Uncle Buncle'. During the fifties, the rear wrappers frequently give the date of printing and size of press run in the lower right-hand corner. The illustrators of Dean toy books rarely signed their work, received credit on title-pages or were identified in advertisements. The example of the Deans was not lost on George Routledge, who in 1852 published thirteen titles in his Aunt Mavor's Picture Books for Little Readers series, many of which attempted to capitalise on public interest in the Great Exhibition of 1851. This series signalled the arrival of a Routledge enterprise that produced over four hundred titles by 1893.[17]

14 Blamires, 'Social satire in English Struwwelpeter parodies'.
15 Rühle, *Böse Kinder: kommentierte Bibliographie von Struwwelpetriaden und Max-und-Moritziaden*.
16 Whalley and Chester, *A history of children's book illustration*, p. 100.
17 Masaki, *A history of Victorian popular picture books*.

In bibliographical terms toy books are important not simply for the evidence they supply of fierce competition for the popular market involving at least a dozen publishers by 1860, but for the quest after new technical processes in the printing of illustrated text, as well as the design challenge to maximise impact of image and text. Initially the toy book publishers printed words and line illustrations together in relief, self-covered or given paper wrappers, and sold plain or hand-coloured and priced accordingly. Efforts were made to extend the presence of colour: Charles Cargill Leighton, the successor to Gregory, Collins & Reynolds, worked out an economical method for printing a complete picture book in colour from relief woodblocks, with the earliest known instance being *Darton's animal alphabet* (1855). Leighton's success led to commissions from other publishers and before long Edmund Evans and J. M. Kronheim were also regularly printing toy books. The economics of toy book printing from this time on dictated that colour-work be printed on one side of the leaf only, although letterpress texts could appear on one or both sides. This allowed for the planographic printing of plates so that the sheets could pass through the press just once.

Alternative procedures were also used to produce complete books with both text and illustration drawn on the stone by a single hand. Lithography (and the very similar anastatic process) was one such alternative (fig. 10.3). The comic *histoires* of the French-Swiss artist Rodolphe Toepffer may have supplied a model for 'Uncle Tom's' anastatic *Giant show* (Ward & Lock, c.1860) with the hand-written text slotting itself in round the caricature drawings, but the most celebrated example was the 1846 two-volume *Book of nonsense* lithographed and printed from stone by Edward Lear and his publisher Thomas McLean. The text was penned out, but in the second printing a clumsy attempt was made to use letterpress transfers. The second experimental process – which was altogether more successful – was an in-house method perfected by the Edinburgh printer and publisher Thomas Nelson. From the 1850s onward, Nelson designed a sequence of luxuriant children's books with gilt-framed letterpress texts (sometimes also printed in gilt), printed on one side only accompanied either by tinted lithograph illustrations or with delicately coloured chromolithographic mounts within gilt frames. The firm also made use of blue or sepia inks in the printing of other children's books, including – sometimes gaudily coloured – toy books.

The overall expansion in the market for children's books contributed to an upsurge and diversification in narrative fiction for children. The later part of this period saw the rise of the adventure novel: Captain Marryat brought forth the three-volume Robinsonnade *Masterman Ready* (Longman,

Figure 10.3 E.V.B [i.e. Eleanor Vere Boyle], *Child's play* (London: Addey & Co., 1851). Printed by Appel's Anastatic Press, this was one of the most popular books to use this form of planographic printing. In 1859, the first of several later editions appeared with the illustrations colour-printed by William Dickes. (Princeton University Library)

1841–2), while in the 1850s Captain Mayne Reid, R. M. Ballantyne and W. H. G. Kingston began producing their own distinctive blends of action, information and colonialism set overseas. These series for boys proved so popular that by the century's end almost every major publisher was producing them.[18] The historical novel also came to prominence with the publication of works such as Marryat's 1836 *The children of the New Forest* (arguably the longest-lived British work of fiction for young readers) and Charlotte M. Yonge's *The heir of Redclyffe* (1853), one of the century's best-sellers. Almost as popular and equally influential was Yonge's family story *The daisy chain* (1856). Finally, the school story came to prominence with the appearance of Thomas Hughes's *Tom Brown's school days* (1856) and F. W. Farrar's *Eric; or little by little* (1858). Many of these novels quickly came to be regarded as classics and offered publishers a respectable, permanent source for the reprint series and school-prize books to be presented to (and perhaps read by) children.

The *Kunstmärchen*, or literary fairy tale, also came into its own as a major genre of children's illustrated fiction in the 1840s.[19] The early examples, like the Rev. Francis Paget's *The hope of the Katzekopfs* (1844), published at Rugely, Staffordshire, with James Burns as associate publisher in London, betrayed a German influence. John Ruskin, a great admirer both of the Grimms' tales and of Cruikshank's etchings for the Taylor translation, composed *The king of the Golden River* in 1841, but published it ten years later with wood-engraved illustrations after drawings by Richard Doyle. The peak of the English *Kunstmärchen* was Thackeray's *The rose and the ring* (1855), whose high spirits were reflected in the author's illustrations, running heads in rhyming couplets and evocation of Twelfth Night celebrations. The *Kunstmärchen* of Ruskin and Thackeray are also important as early examples of major authors crossing over to write for children for fun or a literary challenge.

British publishers were quick to see rich opportunities in the *Kunstmärchen* for their children's lists once they took up Hans Christian Andersen. His first stories (or *eventyr*) had been published in Copenhagen in 1835 and were quickly translated into German. It took eleven years for Andersen's fairy tales to reach Britain, chiefly via the by no means authentic German versions. The 'discovery' of his tales in 1846 resulted in no fewer than five selections being published that year, most of them illustrated. The first, translated from the Danish by Mary Howitt, came from Chapman & Hall, and seems to be illustrated from a steel-engraving overlaid with litho tints and then hand-coloured.

---

18 Briggs and Butts, 'The emergence of form (1850–90)'.
19 Alderson and Oyens, *Be merry and wise*, pp. 248–55.

Cundall published two volumes illustrated with tinted lithographs directly commissioned from the German illustrator Count Pocci, with Charles Boner's wretched translations from the German. The 1846/7 translation for Chapman & Hall (also by Boner) incorporated lithographs by Otto Speckter. The fifth, unillustrated edition translated from the German by Caroline Peachey was issued by Pickering and the Chiswick Press in May 1846, part of a venture into translated *Kunstmärchen*, perhaps for an adult market.[20] Even though Andersen's Victorian translators hardly did justice to an author notoriously difficult to render in another language, his fairy tales were rapidly naturalised into the English tradition of writing for children.[21] A survey of his works in English translation also offers a history in miniature of children's book illustration and design during this period and well into the twentieth century.

1860–1890

By the end of the 1850s all the elements were in place that would characterise children's books as a genre down to the coming of the electronic revolution of the late twentieth century. The interweavings here, nationally between emergent publishers and internationally between authors, translators and illustrators are symbolic of the new forces that would continue to influence the literary and commercial exploitation of children's books during the next thirty years. The history of this next period is a tale of how authors, illustrators and their publishers responded to what they believed to be the constituents of their rapidly growing and increasingly heterogeneous audience at any one time. The critical external influences in these decades that fostered a rapid expansion in the market for print were population growth, urbanisation and the development of communication networks (especially railways). Evidence for this expansion can be seen as early as 1855 in *Hodson's booksellers, publishers and stationers directory* covering London and the provinces, including Wales. Population numbers are given for most towns, along with travelling distances and, where relevant, rail connections to London termini. Expansion was further stimulated by the lowering of capital costs, especially the abolition of the duty on paper, which allowed for the pricing of books and magazines to reach a wider public.

Of critical importance was the Education Act of 1870, which represented the first move towards a formal, national system for teaching the children of

20 Pedersen, *Ugly ducklings?*   21 Briggs, 'A liberating imagination'.

the working and poorer classes, an event not lost on publishers with the energy and foresight to exploit it. One profitable spin-off from the establishment of more 'board schools' throughout the country, as well as the spread of Sunday schools across a wider social constituency, was the adoption of books as suitable rewards for children. Good marks for class-work, behaviour or regular attendance attracted appropriately labelled volumes as prizes, and these generated immense, variably priced series of books from which teachers and superintendents, cognisant that class-room instruction did not go much beyond the three Rs, could choose materials that would be superior to cheap print with respect to the moral values and social aspirations presented (fig. 10.4).[22] Thus, a Cassell 'select catalogue' from the 1880s included over two hundred titles of 'Books for Young People' arranged in twenty-one series, with prices ranging from 6d to 3s 6d and some 'procurable in superior bindings' at five shillings each.

Such factors accelerated the establishment of publishing as an activity wholly distinct from bookselling and increased the likelihood that the making of children's books might occupy its own place within a company's policy. The trend could be observed during the 1840s and 1850s with short-lived firms such as Cundall or Burns, as well as the firms that went on to play a dominant role for decades, such as Routledge, Nelson or Dean. Increasingly their existing competitors – including Bell & Daldy, Cassell, Macmillan and Ward & Lock in London and Black, Blackie and Chambers in Scotland – and new companies such as Frederick Warne or Alexander Strahan recognised that children's books could be a fruitful source of ready sales. The spur to expansion and experiment could not help but encourage new talent at all levels in the creation of children's books and hardly a year would now pass without the publication of at least one title which was to achieve a 'classic' reputation, outlasting the period of its immediate generation.

The rising literary and economic status of children's books is also partly attributable to the vigorous growth of magazines aiming for a popular readership, a process underway well before 1860. Between 1751, the year Newbery's *Lilliputian Magazine* appeared, and 1859, there were approximately seventy efforts to start children's periodicals that were sustained for at least a year. Between 1860 and 1890 there were approximately double that number of attempts.[23] While editorial priorities largely determined the balance and character of a magazine's contents, the options open to editors of any

22 Entwhistle, 'Embossed gilt and moral tales'.
23 Egoff, *Children's periodicals of the nineteenth century*.

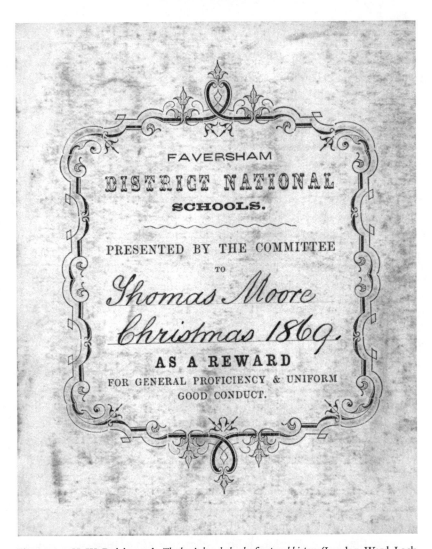

Figure 10.4 H. W. Dulcken, ed., *The boy's handy book of natural history* (London: Ward, Lock & Tyler, not after 1869). The especially handsome example of a reward plate on the front pastedown identifies the granting body, the recipient and the reason for the book's award. (Princeton University Library)

children's periodical were largely confined to predictable features: stories, poems, articles on what were hoped to be subjects of interest or of educational value, features on hobbies, sports and things to do, a 'corner' of jokes, puzzles, riddles, acrostics, and finally regular colloquies between editor and readers, to which might be added a correspondence column. Such contacts between editors and readers – including the announcement of competitions and the awarding of prizes – offer valuable insights into the interests and concerns of Victorian child readers.

The editing and selling of these magazines proved to require different strategies – chiefly the solicitation of copy appropriate to a journal's aims and the need to establish quickly a faithful clientele in order to build and maintain circulation – from those that were developing for book publishing. Nearly all periodicals of any consequence addressed older rather than younger readers, or at least assumed a ready capability in coping with the often solidly printed columns. Boys predominated among the hoped-for customers for many of the magazines for older readers – unsurprising insofar as they had more opportunity to spend money on periodicals. As future movers and shakers, boys could be offered a much wider subject-matter and literary register than their sisters, who had to be satisfied with a higher ratio of religion, conduct and comportment to literature. Only after the publication of the very successful *Little Folks* by Messrs Cassell (1871–1933) were younger readers taken into account, and the Religious Tract Society's pictorial magazine *Our Little Dots* (1887–1938) likewise proved very popular (the 'dots' came from Mrs O. F. Walton's popular 1873 tract *Little Dot*).

Finding a profitable formula regulating the variables of frequency and price with the purchaser's purse was critical. The commonest rate of issue was monthly, although some magazines appeared weekly or fortnightly. The *Girl's Own Paper* (1880–1941), for instance, could be bought weekly for a penny, or monthly, with the weekly parts put up in coloured paper wrappers with twelve pages of advertisements, for sixpence. Lending libraries could obtain half-yearly volumes at four shilling each and – as occurred with many of the more securely based journals – a sumptuous cloth-bound annual, perhaps with extra plates, would come out for Christmas at eight shillings. The prices for other magazines were contingent upon creating demand from their clientele at a price they could afford. E. J. Brett's *Boys of England* (1866–1906), a leading blood and thunder, had many eager purchasers at a penny a week, while Erskine Clarke's *Chatterbox* (1866–1926), which was launched to combat the influence of magazines like *Boys of England*, was priced at a halfpenny a week or fourpence a month to undercut the competition. A superior monthly like *Aunt Judy's Magazine* (1866–85), on the other hand, was sixpence an issue when it started up.

Another challenge was to develop an editorial policy that would facilitate the creation of a distinctive product for its market sector and promote the proprietor's publishing aims. A high proportion of the mid-century titles continued to be devoted to religious matters and were often linked to denominational or missionary concerns (Sunday-school papers, interestingly enough, attempted to be non-denominational to reach the widest possible audience). For example, the *Monthly Packet of Evening Readings for Members of the English Church* (1851–96) owed much to the High Anglican editor Charlotte M. Yonge, many of whose stories aimed at girls in well-off families were serialised in its pages. By tailoring the *Boy's Own Magazine: An Illustrated Journal of Fact, Fiction, History and Adventure* (1855–74) to an audience defined by age, class and gender rather than to a general readership of both sexes, Samuel Orchard Beeton inaugurated a practice other publishers quickly followed. When the chief aim was to turn a profit by providing enjoyable but useful recreational reading for middle-class children, editorial policies differed: conveying information in as palatable a form as possible (e.g. Routledge's *Every Boy's Magazine* (1862–79)); fitting readers for their future role in society (the *Young Ladies' Journal* (1864–1920)); and providing young readers with a regular miscellany of stories, poems, instructive articles and even music, which commanded adherence through what sought to be a lively and friendly editorship.

Pre-eminent among this last type of journal was Strahan's *Good Words for the Young* (1868–72), edited first by Norman Macleod and then by George MacDonald. The magazine's two-column layout was enlivened with numerous wood-engravings in various sizes by leading artists, a title-page with an elaborate wood-engraved border and also an added colour-printed frontispiece and title-page where the names of the editors and most famous illustrators were prominently displayed. The variety of graphic styles was expected to match the variety of content, and designers central to the sixties tradition – F. A. Fraser, A. B. Houghton, Arthur Hughes, J. Mahoney and G. J. Pinwell – supplied images drawing out the fantastic, the comic, the sentimental and the factual aspects of the written contributions (fig. 10.5). Strahan's extravagance in this respect may have caused the journal to founder, while its longer-lived rival, *Aunt Judy's Magazine*, adopted a more frugal policy towards illustration, commissioning fewer prominent names. It was edited first by Mrs Gatty, then by her daughters Juliana Horatia Ewing and H. K. F. Gatty. *Aunt Judy's* correspondence columns, the policy of excluding 'sensational' stories, and editorial matter such as the monthly account of donations to 'Aunt Judy's cots' in the children's hospital at Great Ormond Street, suggest the magazine would have been more widely appreciated by girls than boys. In fact, the Gattys' literary sensibilities drew in readers of both genders into an

AT THE BACK OF THE NORTH WIND.

BY THE AUTHOR OF "DEALINGS WITH THE FAIRIES."

(Continued from p. 443.)

I MUST not go on describing what cannot be described, for nothing is more wearisome.

Before they reached the sea, Diamond felt North Wind's hair beginning to fall about him.

"Is the storm over, North Wind?" he called out.

"No, Diamond. I am only waiting a moment to set you down. You would not like to see the ship sunk, and I am going to give you a place to stop in till I come back for you."

"Oh! thank you," said Diamond. "I shall be sorry to leave you, North Wind, but I would rather not see the ship go down. And I'm afraid the poor people will cry, and I should hear them. Oh, dear!"

"There are a good many passengers on board; and to tell the truth, Diamond, I don't care about your hearing the cry you speak of. I am afraid you would not get it out of your little head again for a long time."

"But how can you bear it then, North Wind? For I am sure you are kind. I shall never doubt that again."

"I will tell you how I am able to bear it, Diamond: I am always hearing, through every noise, through all the noise I am

540

making myself even, the sound of a far-off song. I do not exactly know where it is, or what it means; and I don't hear much of it, only the odour of its music, as it were, flitting across the great billows of the ocean outside this air in which I make such a storm; but what I do hear, is quite enough to make me able to bear the cry from the drowning ship. So it would you if you could hear it."

"No, it wouldn't," returned Diamond, stoutly. "For *they* wouldn't hear the music of the far-away song; and if they did, it wouldn't do them any good. You see you and I are not going to be drowned, and so *we* might enjoy it."

"But you have never heard the psalm, and you don't know what it is like. Somehow, I can't say how, it tells me that all is right; that it is coming to swallow up all cries."

"But that won't do them any good—the people, I mean," persisted Diamond.

"It must. It must," said North Wind, hurriedly. "It wouldn't be the song it seems to be if it did not swallow up all their fear and pain too, and set them singing it themselves with the rest. I am sure it will. And

do you know, ever since I knew I had hair, that is, ever since it began to go out and away, that song has been coming nearer and

Figure 10.5 George MacDonald, 'At the back of the north wind', in *Good Words for the Young*, ed. Norman Macleod (London: Strahan & Co.), no. 1, 1 September 1860, p. 540. Two illustrations within a single two-column page engraved after designs by Arthur Hughes. They received more expansive treatment when the story appeared in book form. (Princeton University Library)

idealised Victorian family circle presided over by an elder sister – modelled on Juliana herself – who could tell stories ranging from domestic tales to the *Kunstmärchen*, as well as devise an endless variety of entertainments educational and recreational.[24]

Serial fiction was the bread and butter of many Victorian magazines, regardless of audience, and it provided another major stimulus to the further development of the literary novel for children. Many categories of fiction may be found: sea stories; Robinsonnades and other tales of adventure; the proto-science-fiction of Jules Verne in translation; historical yarns; high fantasy; and stories of home and school life (Talbot Baines Reed's classic school stories were one of the reasons for the *Boy's Own Paper*'s early success). Another genre which achieved huge sales in the Victorian period was the 'waif' or 'street Arab' story such as *Little Meg's children* by Hesba Stretton, one of the most successful and financially astute of the RTS's authors.[25] The serial had a promotional quality in ensuring (or hoping to ensure) a continuity of subscribing readers, while for contributing authors it offered the potential of a double payment: once for the pro rata columns of the submission, and once more for the book. It proved to be a satisfactory arrangement for both parties, but tracing the history of a text from its periodical to its second, more permanent form as a book is not necessarily a straightforward bibliographic exercise. The commissioning journals were not invariably aimed specifically at children: Charles Kingsley's *The water-babies* – the first notable serialised children's story – appeared in the 'adult' columns of *Macmillan's Magazine*, while Stretton's *Jessica's first prayer* was serialised in the children's section of *Sunday at Home*. Textual changes could occur: Stevenson refined the structure and wording between *Treasure Island*'s weekly appearance in *Young Folks* and the book edition. Illustrations might be reorganised or augmented, as was the case for Arthur Hughes's drawings for George MacDonald's works serialised in *Good Words for the Young*, or added, as were Randolph Caldecott's pictures for the book editions of Mrs Ewing's *Jackanapes* and *Daddy Darwin's dovecot*, whose appearances in *Aunt Judy's* were unillustrated.[26]

Serialisation was by no means de rigueur however, and some best-selling authors, most notably R. M. Ballantyne, G. A. Henty[27] and Mrs Molesworth,

---

24 Knoepflmacher, '*Aunt Judy's Magazine* and the uses of collaboration'.
25 Rickard, ' "A gifted author" '.
26 For Caldecott's correspondence with Mrs Ewing and her sister see Hutchins (ed.), *Yours pictorially*.
27 Newbolt's bibliography of Henty has several detailed appendices on the production, illustration and business arrangements related to his publications.

had much of their work published directly in book form. An exceptional example of those publishing procedures can be found in the history of the period's most famous children's book: *Alice's adventures in Wonderland* by Charles Dodgson writing as 'Lewis Carroll'. *Alice* carries a Macmillan imprint; but because the firm published the books *for* the author the correspondence over the successive stages of the book's production – and the author's close involvement in these stages – provides an unusual insight into the practicalities of publishing during the early 1860s.[28] Not the least of Dodgson's trials occurred in his 'editorial' negotiations with his illustrator. The abortive first printing, withdrawn because of Tenniel's dissatisfaction with the printing of the engraved blocks of his illustrations, was shipped to the United States to be issued by Appleton. But the fact that the relations between author, illustrator and publisher can be documented during *Alice*'s production reflects an important change, underscoring how little is known about the creation of even the most influential steady-selling works from the Georgian period such as Mrs Barbauld's *Lessons for children*.

Alice appeared during the sixties, a boom period in the production of children's books that also coincided with the upswing in illustrated works throughout the book trade due partly to the increased availability of first-class commercial engravers. By 1860 the Dalziels (founded 1840 and setting up their own Camden Press in 1857), Joseph Swain (whose independent activity dates from 1842) and Edmund Evans (setting up the Racquet Court Press in 1851) had built up sufficient experience and resources to confront the increasing demand for black and white wood-engraving and were to undertake much of the industrial-scale commissioning of contemporary artists for the market. (Indeed Evans tended to usurp the publisher Routledge's decision-making as to the printing, pricing and advertising of the children's books of Crane, Caldecott and Greenaway.) Increasingly, major artists like the Pre-Raphaelite John Millais would accept commissions to illustrate important editions of books for young readers.[29] It was also possible to employ a crew of talented designers for elaborate albums from the Camden Press such as *Dalziel's Arabian nights*, made up from part-issue numbers and published by Ward & Lock, or glittering gift-books whose fine attention to the printing of wood-engravings was matched by the decorative cloth gilt of the books' bindings. Thus two almost companion works printed by Richard Clay and bound by Bone & Son are Isaac Watts's *Divine and moral songs for children* (Sampson Low, Son &

28 Cohen and Gandolfo (eds.), *Lewis Carroll and the house of Macmillan*; and vols. 4 and 5 of Dodgson, *Lewis Carroll's diaries*, ed. Wakeling.
29 Goldman, *Victorian illustration*, pp. 1–13.

Marston, 1866) and the anthology edited by John G. Watts *Little lays for little folk* (George Routledge & Sons, 1867), the latter of whose 116 pages have integrated wood-engravings by eleven individual artists – five of the eleven in each book being the same.

Opposed to the miscellany character of such ambitious books were the volumes where author and illustrator worked together to create a unified whole. Tenniel, 'Lewis Carroll' and the *Alice* books are universally recognised as a pre-eminent example of such a collaboration, not least because of the artist's imaginative response to the unprecedented surrealism of his author's texts, but also because the pictures have become inseparable from the text. The *Alice* books should not obscure the presence of an unprecedented number of instances of complete, or near-complete, success in marrying text and illustration during this period: Charles Bennett and his original nursery tales; Arthur Hughes for Christina Rossetti's *Sing-song* (1871); Walter Crane for a sequence of Mrs Molesworth's stories, beginning with *Carrots* (1876), or for his sister's translation of the Grimms' *Household stories* (1882).

If the black and white illustrations of the period, reproduced either from wood-engravings or from photographically originated electrotypes, often demonstrated a high level of skill and artistry, then colour-printed illustrations were witness to a rapidly growing technical accomplishment. Having been used in the 1850s mostly for individual plates, colour printing from the 1860s onward is found in complete suites of pictures recurring alongside letterpress texts (the verso of the plates usually blank) or incorporated on every page-opening throughout. Much of this work was undertaken by specialist printers (most of whom had established themselves in the previous decades) working with either lithographic or letterpress machines: William Dickes, Joseph Kronheim, George Leighton, Edmund Evans in London, and Thomas Nelson in Scotland.[30] Extraordinary effects were achieved in plates whose surface beauty sometimes overshadowed the accompanying texts, as with Allingham's verses for *In Fairy-Land* (1870) illustrated by Evans's majestic printing of the blocks made from Richard Doyle's watercolours – or lent greater distinction to flawed illustrations, as with Eleanor Vere Boyle's set for a folio edition of Andersen, printed in colours from wood and metal relief blocks by George Leighton.

The advances in colour printing likewise had a major impact on the publishing of toy books. Some major artists were given carte blanche: Crane's toy books and Caldecott's picture books – a subtle marketing

---

30 Gascoigne, *Milestones in colour printing 1457–1859*, pp. 54–72.

distinction – appeared as uniform series, but in wholly different graphic styles, and the high esteem in which Caldecott's work in particular is held stems from the fluency he and Evans brought to the narrative illustrations of each separate rhyme or ballad. In the case of Greenaway, however, every book – even the series of almanacs – was individually designed, often drawing upon sophisticated manufacturing techniques.[31] However, most of the thousands of toy books issued by Routledge, Warne, Gall & Inglis, Nelson, Dean and others still gave no title-page credit to the illustrator, even when enough of a name to be touted in the advertisements, as in the case of J. B. Zwecker or Harrison Weir. (The printer's name, on the other hand, always appears on the wrappers, which showcased his skills when producing the colourful extravagances of Victorian advertising typography.) An illustrator's ability to redraw in a fresh way nursery classics like the *House that Jack built* or *Puss in boots*, or to conceive of novel concepts for genres like the alphabet, object lesson or album of animals (all of which depend more upon image than text), was critical because toy book publishers relied so heavily on content in the public domain. New works, such as *Master Mousie's supper party* or *The singing Lancers*, were relatively uncommon. But the scope for the comparative criticism of a frequently reinterpreted rhyme like 'Cock Robin' is immense and would consider contracted and piratical printings found in the United States (many by McLoughlin in New York) and in Sweden,[32] as well as an attempt to identify more of the house artists, whose blocks are usually unsigned.

Another noteworthy development in this very busy field of production was the novelty book.[33] Many toy books were available from Routledge and Warne in 'everlasting' versions, printed or mounted on linen, forerunners of modern untearable texts for the youngest readers. Precursors of the modern activity book appeared in Warne's Picture Puzzle Toy Book series, which featured colour illustrations to be cut out and pasted in their correct places on key plates. At the forefront were the inventive Dean & Son, producing, for the first time, ramifying series of 'movable books'. Utilising the complex design and manufacturing skills now called paper-engineering, the company dominated the genre with over a dozen playful gimmicks ranging from simple pop-ups operated by pulling ribbons to the representation of theatrical performances through a sequence of pages in graduated sizes (fig. 10.6). Nothing of Dean's quite equalled the articulated movables of Lothar Meggendorfer, whose brilliant creations began to appear in English editions in the 1880s; the fertility in

31 Evans, *Reminiscences*, p. 65.
32 Klingberg, *Denna lilla gris går till torget och andra brittiska toy books I Sverige 1869–1879*.
33 Alderson, 'Novelty books and movables'.

Figure 10.6 [William Roger Snow, author and illustrator] *Puss in boots* (London: Dean & Son [1880]). (*Dean's pantomime toy books, with five set scenes and nine trick changes,* 4.) Emrik Binger printed the chromolithograph illustrations in this movable toy book, which is opened at the third set showing the graduated flaps that change the scene to advance the action. (Princeton University Library)

the making of these popular works would not be equalled again until the last decades of the twentieth century.

1890–1914

Population growth and increased life-expectancy continued to enlarge readership during this period, and the level of literacy rose steadily as well. By 1890 some three generations had benefited from the 1870 Education Act and in 1902 a new Act brought a more systematic administrative process to school organisation throughout England and Wales. With national secondary instruction established that much more firmly, the horizon of every book publisher's list was thereby widened. That held good almost instantaneously for educational publishing, but its effect on recreational reading was great but indirect, depending upon demography and social class. Municipal involvement in school administration was joined by the local development of public libraries where, sporadically at first, provision came to be made for child as well as adult readers. (Britain's progress on this front contrasts starkly with events in the United States where, as early as 1900, there was a powerful movement not only to serve children in public libraries but to give specialist training to children's librarians.) The increased scale of book production to meet growing demand led to a far greater stratification in both the range of works provincial booksellers might stock and the strategies of publishers in producing and pricing books for a more fluid market, whether of private buyers or amid the increasingly buoyant institutional sector. Wherever or however the purchasing, the trade as a whole also gained a new stability and a firmer ground for entrepreneurial expansion through the establishment of the Net Book Agreement in 1900.

Evidence for a changed climate in children's book publishing is perhaps most clearly discerned in the renewed energy running through the activities of established firms. The second generation of Warnes showed a new zest when they purchased from the ailing Routledge firm copyrights in the picture books of Caldecott and Greenaway, and husbanded the talents of Leslie Brooke and Beatrix Potter. Humphrey Milford, appointed to the London office of Oxford University Press in 1906, masterminded 'the Joint Venture' with Hodder & Stoughton that same year which would lead to an immensely varied output of children's books by OUP. Smaller firms such as George Bell, A. & C. Black and Wells, Gardner & Darton reconfigured their editorial and production policies to take advantage of changes in the juvenile market.

A new generation of names brought a new approach to the publishing of children's books. In addition to publishing many titles by E. Nesbit, T. Fisher

Unwin edited the elegant Children's Library between 1892 and 1898, an interesting selection of classics, *Kunstmärchen*, folk tales and popular modern fiction from England and the continent, including the first English translation of Collodi's *Pinocchio*.[34] Beginning in the late 1880s, J. M. Dent featured art nouveau design in books illustrated by the 'Birmingham' artists Winifred Green and Georgie Gaskin or in sets like the *Banbury Cross* books illustrated by Anning Bell, Charles Robinson, H. Granville Fell and Alice Woodward The first ten titles of Dent's Everyman's Library, inaugurated in 1906, were notable for the inclusion of five illustrated books for young people. Another champion of art nouveau book design was John Lane, whose edition of Stevenson's *Child's garden of verses*, illustrated by Charles Robinson (1896), became a classic. Algernon Methuen, initially a teacher, was first drawn to publishing in order to bring new life to school textbooks, but his interests shifted to literary works for children, his greatest success being Grahame's *The wind in the willows* (1908). William Heinemann staged the *coup* of William Nicholson's *Alphabet* in 1898 and published many of Arthur Rackham's gift-books. Grant Richards was perhaps the most original of this new group of publishers, before his lack of financial acumen brought the firm down. Richards typically looked for rising talent from whom copyrights could be acquired cheaply (he paid Helen Bannerman just £5 for *Little Black Sambo*), then employed excellent craftsmen to print the texts with colour illustrations on good paper, and bind them uniformly as small pocket-sized volumes for the Dumpy Books series (1897–1908).[35] Although noticeably uneven in quality, the Dumpy Books inaugurated a fashion for 'little books' which Beatrix Potter was to exploit with even greater success.[36]

In addition to the stimulus of an expanding market, enterprising publishers also had the excitement of working in an industry where both technological and aesthetic limitations were diminishing, allowing room for greater flexibility in the creation of a 'house style' both in editorial selection and in physical production. For all the changes of the previous six decades, the children's books of the period retained a certain restraint in their general character. Brilliant though some of the decorative bindings may have been, important for both graphic skill and reproductive techniques the illustrations, the majority of books, from toy books to three-decker novels like Jefferies's *Bevis*, were undistinguished typographically and were often printed on unsatisfactory paper.

34 Jefferson, 'The Children's Library'.   35 Harer, 'Dumpy Books for children'.
36 Stevenson, ' "A vogue for small books" '.

From 1890 onwards Victorian homogeneity was moderated owing to the influence of the English arts and crafts movement and European art nouveau. These powerful trends in design coincided with major technological changes affecting paper-making, the formatting of quires, the range of available typefaces and their setting, and the treatment of binding materials. All these improvements could be employed to reinvigorate the design of children's books, most prominently observable in their illustration. The use of photography in preparing printing-surfaces for graphic work, for example, well antedates the 1890s, and the use of line and half-tone blocks for black and white work through to 1914 could, for those alive to 'the spirit of the age', deploy the camera's immense possibilities for the reproduction of illustrations and decoration within a designed page. The photographically illustrated book for children also came into its own.[37] The jumble of illustrative styles and techniques on offer during this period can be seen most clearly in magazines. On a periodical's pages half-tone photographic or near-photographic illustrations on coated paper mingled with conventional line drawings by illustrators working in the sixties manner (if not recycled from a previous appearance) or with stylish black and white work that owed much to art nouveau. Indeed, regular magazine work could be a financial mainstay for professional illustrators like W. Heath Robinson.[38]

As for illustration in colour, there was considerable diversity partly due to developments in lithographic and relief methods. By the early 1890s the toy books that had so dominated picture-book production had had their day and their printing was more and more undertaken by large chromolithographic firms overseas, such as Van Leer and Emrik & Binger in the Netherlands or Meissner in Germany. The most notable of these firms was Ernest Nister: many hundreds of story and picture books that were conceived, written and illustrated by English writers and artists were submitted to Nister's London office, but printed at his Nuremberg works (German translations were also undertaken there). The operation is significant not simply because of its huge scale and its transatlantic marketing through Dutton in New York, but also because it observed no systematic procedures in the design and formatting of its productions (most notably in its over 125 movables), confirming, if not leading, the trend away from publishing uniformity.[39] Likewise, Raphael Tuck issued attractive colour-printed movable and shape books printed in Germany and marketed in England and America and on the continent. His back-list also

---

37 White, *From the mundane to the magical.*
38 See Beare's bibliography of *The illustrations of W. Heath Robinson.*   39 Hunt, *Peeps into Nisterland.*

featured an astonishing range of novelties on paper, including scrap prints, paper dolls, transfer pictures, peepshows and panoramas, now an integral part of the children's market for print.[40]

The accepted modes of colour printing in the nineteenth century – in relief from wood or electrotype blocks, and planographic from stones or from metal substitutes such as zinc – were overtaken at the end of the 1890s by the three-colour process. One of the earliest examples of this in book-work, as opposed to advertising, was Hentschel's printing of the colour frontispiece for the privately published first edition of Beatrix Potter's *Tale of Peter Rabbit* in 1901. Three-colour or four-colour illustration, which allowed for the photographic separation and printing of the colours in an artist's original, was to become the method of choice for publishers during the first half of the twentieth century and was to be used at all levels of book production from frontispieces for cheap reward books to expensive *éditions de luxe* such as Rackham's *Rip Van Winkle* (1905) or Edmund Dulac's *Arabian nights* (1907). These two artists dominated the fashionable gift-book market, thanks in part to their association with the Leicester Gallery, agent for the limited editions of their books and original artwork. Once the *succès d'estime* of the sumptuous originals had run its course, cheaper editions were published for a younger audience.

The influence of all these technological changes upon children's book production facilitated the refinement of strategies for the appropriation and repackaging of texts that have persisted down to the present. New works of fiction, especially those rapidly installed in the children's literature canon, might be interpreted variously from their original periodical appearances before collection in a bound volume. The young Rudyard Kipling's tales appeared in several journals on both sides of the Atlantic: for example, the *Just so stories* appeared seriatim on fifteen such occasions, illustrated by five different artists, before complete publication in book form illustrated by the author in 1902.[41] This process dovetailed with another much older publishing practice. From the middle of the eighteenth century, publishers of children's books kept a watchful eye on titles that would reward regular reprinting or that could be exploited as safe moneyspinners once out of copyright. What marks this period is the energy and ingenuity with which staple titles were recycled, along with texts from the tradition and the 'classic' titles from near-contemporary writers which arrived in the public domain from the beginning of the century onwards (fig. 10.7).

40 Whitton, *Collector's guide to Raphael Tuck & Sons.*   41 Alderson, 'Just-so pictures'.

Figure 10.7 Mrs Sherwood, *The Fairchild family*, ed. and with an introduction by Mary E. Palgrave, with illustrations by Florence M. Rudland (London: Wells, Gardner, Darton & Co., 1902). The pictorial cloth binding is decorated after designs by the illustrator, whose line drawings throughout the book apply an art nouveau modishness to a classic evangelical story first published in 1818. (Princeton University Library)

An outstanding example of the latter may be seen in the publishing history through the Edwardian period of Charles Kingsley's *The water-babies*, first serialised in *Macmillan's Magazine* 1862–3, and then issued in revised book form in 1863. For more than twenty years Macmillan did little to exploit this regular seller, and its popularity was only made manifest through the publication in 1886 of their refurbished edition illustrated lavishly by Linley Sambourne. That edition became, thanks to multiple reprints in various forms, the most widely encountered version of the story. But when copyright protection lapsed in 1905, British and American publishers fell upon *The water-babies* and they subjected it to a degree of editorial and illustrative reworking beyond anything that would have occurred previously. Between 1905 and 1914 there were over twenty versions of the story put out by as many publishers in Britain – smart full-text illustrated editions, abridgements, annotated school textbooks, etc. – and these versions were themselves subject to variant treatments. Among the first, for instance, was a full-text printing from George Routledge & Sons with black and white plates by May Sandheim which would, in 1915, appear alongside poorly printed stock-blocks in an edition 'retold chiefly in words of one syllable for young children by A. Pitt-Kethley'. Or, in 1908, the octavo edition from Thomas Nelson with four half-tone colour plates by A. E. Jackson was redesigned as a quarto, with the plates enlarged and accompanied by numerous marginal vignettes. Annie B. Wood's 1914 *Story lessons from 'The water babies'* overwhelmed short synopses of the book's chapters with instructions on drawing, clay modelling and paper cutting.

An updated presentation of material from the tradition might attain classic status in its own right, as was the case for the Colour Fairy Book series (1889–1910) edited by the Scottish man of letters Andrew Lang. Lang selected tales chiefly from European languages and his wife Leonora oversaw their translation and revision in a consistent style, doing much of it herself. The Langs' goal was to delight young readers with a form of literature considered timeless and universal that indirectly reaffirmed the common humanity of man, regardless of age or cultural origin. As further volumes appeared, the contents increasingly featured material from around the world, in response to demand for a more international selection as the Empire expanded. The series's immense popularity owed something to Lang's authority as a comparative folklorist, and something to the brilliant packaging with H. J. Ford's line illustrations and the rainbow of cloth bindings with large gilt cover designs by Ford. (Many volumes were also available in a large format limited to seventy-five copies in blue boards and vellum paper.) The series was cleverly promoted to attract sophisticated adults looking for a quality product: a surviving priced list gives the number of copies issued for each title to date, but also has two full-page illustrations, excerpts from reviews, and a poem by St. John Lucas praising the wonders of exploring fairyland with Andrew Lang (fig. 10.8).

A List of Story Books, edited by Mr.
Andrew Lang, illustrated by Mr. H. J. Ford,
Mr. Lancelot Speed, and Mr. G. P. Jacomb-Hood,
and published by Longmans, Green, & Co.

'A continual delight to countless children.'
REVIEW OF REVIEWS.

Figure 10.8 Promotional brochure for Andrew Lang's *Colour Fairy Library* (London: Longman, Green & Co, c.1902). The illustration on the final page suggests that the inhabitants of Fairyland were as charmed by Mr Lang's volumes as the writer from *Review of Reviews* quoted below. (Princeton University Library)

Another long-standing trend, the crossing over of children's classics and nursery characters into other media, became a highly lucrative phenomenon during this period, one that would accelerate considerably in the next century. Frances Hodgson Burnett's best-seller *Little Lord Fauntleroy* is a prime example: serialised in the American children's magazine *St. Nicholas* (1885), it was issued as a book illustrated by Reginald Birch (1886), which sold 43,000 copies in a year, earning Burnett $100,000. Such was the ensuing craze that Burnett adapted the story for the stage, and the play opened in London and New York. Eventually *Fauntleroy* was filmed, the most famous version being the 1921 movie where Mary Pickford played Cedric and his mother. Popular characters from children's books increasingly were exploited for the decoration of merchandise for the nursery.[42] Longman found themselves with a runaway success in Florence Upton's Golliwogg series, which was a staple of Christmas seasons between 1895 and 1909.[43] Subsequently Upton's Golly and the Dutch dolls were spun off as subjects for postcards[44] but also appeared on a wide range of products such as dishes or more famously labels for Robertson's jams. Beatrix Potter, a far sharper businesswoman than Upton, carefully developed and controlled what she called the 'little sideshows' that capitalised on the fame of her Peter Rabbit books: stevengraph bookmarks, a board game, miniature brass figurines, etc.[45]

Such was the wealth of the imaginative literature produced for British children that publishers paid relatively little attention to events abroad in comparison with the previous decades, when there had been considerable importing of American children's fiction, including Elizabeth Wetherell's *The wide, wide world* and Maria Susanna Cummin's *The lamplighter* (sent up by Kingsley in *The water-babies*), Alcott's *Little women* series and Mark Twain's *Tom Sawyer* and *Huckleberry Finn*, almost all of which have remained classics down to the present. (Since the 1852 brouhaha over *Uncle Tom's cabin*, well-known American authors frequently published works first in Britain to ensure copyright protection on both sides of the Atlantic.) Many successful American works such as the Brownie series of Palmer Cox, the picture books of E. Boyd Smith or the Uncle Remus stories by Joel Chandler Harris found an appreciative audience in England, as did books about child life in distant corners of the empire, such as *Jock of the Bushveld* (1907) by Percy Fitzpatrick or *Seven little Australians* (1894) by Ethel Turner. As for translations from Europe, the influential graphic work of Maurice Boutet de Monvel and a scattering of what became classic novels,

---

42 White, *The world of the nursery*.   43 Davis, *A lark ascends*; Beare, 'Florence Upton 1873–1927'.
44 Cope, *Postcards from the nursery*.   45 Durbridge, 'Beatrix Potter's side shows'.

including Joanna Spyri's *Heidi* (1884) and Selma Lagerlöf's *Wonderful adventures of Nils* (1907–8) were introduced to young English readers.

The press monitored the variegated developments in children's book publishing with increasing enthusiasm and discernment. Charlotte Yonge had made a major contribution to the practical criticism of children's books in her three essays for *Macmillan's Magazine* (July–September 1869) on 'Children's literature in the last century' and a manual of advice and criticism for those concerned with parish work, *What books to lend and what to give* (1887). Simultaneously Edward Salmon was publishing essays on current children's books and on their reception by young readers that were eventually gathered into *Juvenile literature as it is* (1888). By the 1890s the reviewing of children's books had became more regular and more extended. While the *Bookseller* had long devoted much space in November or December to publicising new books for the Christmas trade, the popular journals, especially those with a literary turn such as W. Robertson Nicoll's *The Bookman*, added coverage to the subject.

The rapidly growing interest in contemporary graphic arts could not help but extend to children's book illustrators. They were the subject of the 'special winter number' 1897–8 of the *Studio* edited by Gleeson White, and his 1897 study of the 1860s, *English illustration*, had also included material on illustrators of children's books. In her survey of the recent children's book artists, *English book illustration of today*, R. E. D. Sketchley expresses some reservations about what we would call a 'cult of personality' she saw emerging among illustrators, in contrast with the relative anonymity of artists of previous generations. Yet of the over thirty black and white illustrators of children's books enjoying a vogue that Sketchley singled out, most have come to be seen as important figures in the history of illustration, whether representing particular schools, or developing individual talents so diverse in style and technique as those of H. J. Ford, Leslie Brooke, William Heath Robinson or Arthur Rackham.[46]

The criticism of current children's books in the press points to a parallel recognition of children's books as worthy of serious attention by scholars and collectors. Mrs E. M. Field produced the first attempt at a history of the genre in her *The child and his book* (1891), which concentrated on the medieval and early modern periods. Field's monograph stood in marked contrast to the less earnest and more colourful approach to the subject by collectors and the more journalistic antiquarians, such as Andrew Tuer, proprietor of the Leadenhall Press,[47] and E. V. Lucas, man of letters, a children's book author and Lamb scholar who also edited for Methuen and Wells Gardner Darton & Co. Tuer

---

46 Sketchley, *English book illustration of today*.   47 Bury, 'A. W. Tuer and the Leadenhall Press'.

and Lucas set out to celebrate the delights of the Regency's children's books by making examples of those rare books available to a wider public either in semi-facsimile reproductions of excerpts from a wide range of titles, as in Tuer's *Pages and pictures from forgotten children's books* (1898–9), or in actual-size facsimiles as in Methuen's edition of Charles Lamb's *King and Queen of Hearts*, issued with a separate descriptive booklet by Lucas. Perhaps the most important figure in this 'revivalist' movement was Charles Welsh, a director of Griffith, Farran, a publisher descending directly from the house of John Newbery. A precursor of late twentieth-century publishers and scholars on both sides of the Atlantic, Welsh published a major study of the Newbery firms using manuscript sources, *A bookseller of the last century* (1885), and he followed this up by editing facsimiles, as well as involving himself in the exploitation of contemporary children's books (he was acknowledged by Salmon for his help in *Juvenile literature as it is*). On his retirement Welsh moved to the United States where he helped compile the National Library Company's six-volume *Children's own library* that drew together texts and illustrations from Aesop to Victorian children's classics.

By World War I, children, their parents and teachers were taken seriously as an audience for books to a degree that might well have been difficult for a Georgian journalist like John Scott to comprehend. Children's books had come to constitute a market whose commercial potential ensured that the needs of its various overlapping constituencies would and could be addressed. As this market stratified increasingly along class and gender lines so that it could be penetrated and saturated more fully, formats and genres diversified and prolif-erated, and, even more importantly, endured to evolve further during the next century. At one end there was plenty of what Clive James has called 'sludge', the formulaic series fiction to be devoured in spite of explicit prohibitions against the consumption of junk; and at the other were exquisitely crafted vol-umes that would satisfy the most exacting aesthetic and literary standards. An appetising selection of stories, non-fiction and picture books at different prices occupied the middle. Adults increasingly looked back upon their memories of childhood reading as worth setting down in print. It is ironic, nevertheless, to note that now the children's market offered opportunities at every level for authors, artists, members of the book trades, and publishers, when it was rep-resented in contemporary literature, whether for adults or children, it appears more often than not as a destination on New Grub Street where respectable women in straitened circumstances like Dora Milvain or the mother of the Railway Children might earn their bread.

11

Mass markets: literature

SIMON ELIOT AND ANDREW NASH

The materiality of literary publishing

It has often been pointed out that what appears to be a single medieval book is frequently nothing of the sort: commonly between the wooden boards of such a volume will be a range of manuscript texts which may or may not be congruent. Many survivals from our period might suggest that this tradition had not wholly died out. Publishers could often issue between the covers of one volume a collection of literary works that had little or no relation to each other;[1] booksellers could also do the same. Quite apart from what one might call 'accidental anthologies', there were the intended anthologies: collections of selected literary pieces, many specially commissioned, that would appear as expensive gift-books or, from the mid-nineteenth century, as a collection of 'gems' culled from the works of a particular author. In addition there were the serious anthologies such as Palgrave's *Golden treasury* (Macmillan, 1861) and the *Oxford book of English verse* (OUP, 1900). We who are used to having a relatively clear demarcation between complete single literary works and anthologies might find the reading experiences of the past rather odd.

Putting literary texts into different material forms can change the reader's perception of them and, equally importantly, can alter, enrich or diversify the context in which those texts occur. A prose account of a murder or a hanging (frequently 'fictionalised' for sensational effect) in a broadside would usually be accompanied by a dramatic if crude woodcut (which may very well be reused from an earlier broadside), a poem or song, and decorative typographic devices: it was the multimedia experience of its day. Later, cheaper book editions of novels often contained bound-in and cover advertisements. Novels published

---

1 For instance, the second number of Dicks's English Library of Standard Works (thirty-two pages, three columns, weekly) contained Edgar Allan Poe's *The fall of the House of Usher* (incomplete), part of a Paul de Kock novel, part of *The adventures of Joseph Andrews* by Henry Fielding, part of 'Master Timothy's book-case' by G. W. M. Reynolds (an imitation of Dickens's 'Master Humphrey's clock'), part of *The adventures of Gil Blas* by Le Sage, and some 'Tales from Bentley'.

in monthly parts were surrounded by pages of advertisements, and illustrations at the beginning (they would not be properly located unless the parts were finally sent to a bookbinder). Most obviously, a piece of literature published in a periodical would be surrounded, sometimes engulfed, by other texts and images that bore little or no relation to the literary text. Some periodicals would publish three or more serialised novels in the same issue. Breaking literature up into parts, serialising it over many months and sometimes years in parts or periodicals, put a contemporary reader into a position that was at once very powerful (you could choose what serialised literature was read, and in what order) and very vulnerable (you needed to have the money, the organisation and the storage room to collect all the relevant parts, and to read and keep them in the right order).

Printers and publishers had a wide range of forms in which they could issue literature. Some were traditional, such as the chapbook and the broadside. Chapbooks were small pamphlets of usually between eight and thirty-two pages which sold for a penny; they commonly contained traditional stories such as Robin Hood or Dr Faustus, or collections of jokes or recipes. Though declining, they were still evident as late as the 1850s and 1860s and, in their pious form as tracts, they continued to have a presence throughout the period. A broadside was usually a long single sheet of paper printed on one side selling for only a halfpenny or a penny. This might carry a ballad, or prose account – frequently both – commonly of a sensational event. Both chapbooks and broadsides exhibited the characteristics of working-class literature: they cost pennies; text and illustrations were often crudely printed; production continued for many years and could eventually run into the 100,000s or even millions.[2] They were frequently printed by provincial printers or by printers in the less salubrious areas of London such as Seven Dials where both John Pitts and James Catnach operated, or Spitalfields where Neesom produced ballad sheets; they were sold not in bookshops but in streets and markets by pedlars.

Variations on the paper-covered pamphlet were to crop up again and again throughout the period: as weekly or monthly part-works, as single plays, as early paperbacks, as cheap complete novels selling for a penny or twopence. The single-sheet broadside diminished in significance after the 1850s,[3] but we should not forget that advertisers, such as the outfitters E. Moses & Sons, would sometimes use specially commissioned verse to promote their wares.[4] With

---

2 Neuburg, *Popular literature*, p. 143.
3 Although Henry Parker Such continued to produce handbills in the tradition of broadsides until 1917: see Shepard, *The history of street literature*, p. 76.
4 Altick, *The presence of the present*, pp. 237–9.

the development of the penny post and the emergence of printed Valentine and birthday cards, poetry and pictures on a single sheet became very big business indeed.[5] Literature, like stonecrop, could flower in the most unexpected places.

Single sheets, pamphlets and hard-bound books could all be vehicles for literature, but then so could another material form that became progressively more important, both culturally and economically, as the period progressed: the periodical. In 1897 T. S. H. Escott wrote: 'For many Englishmen of all classes, the periodical, daily, weekly, or monthly, is practically an exclusive synonym for literature itself.'[6] Newspapers, journals and magazines could publish belles-lettres, poetry, drama and fiction in the form of short stories and serialised novels. Until 1855, when the Newspaper Stamp Act was finally repealed, any periodical that published news less than twenty-eight days old was subject to tax. For this reason many periodicals aimed at the literate lower classes, such as the *Family Herald* (from 1842) or the *London Journal* (from 1845), did not carry news at all but were almost exclusively devoted to serialising three or four novels in each issue.

The law in the form of copyright (see chapter 5) had its own material impact on literary publishing. The great out-of-copyright canonical authors were published in a variety of forms, many very cheaply (e.g. from the houses of Thomas Tegg or John Dicks) and were also the staple of publishers' series which offered a range of great literature in a uniform package for would-be self-educators. Some contemporary writers, such as those from the USA, were unprotected by copyright until 1891, and *Uncle Tom's cabin*[7] and the poems of Longfellow, among many others, were produced in a host of cheap editions by British publishers. The nature and range of literature that was available cheaply was often determined by copyright and the monopoly control it brought with it.

Two other materially based matters must be kept in mind: the growth of population and the rise in literacy rates over the period. In 1830 the population of the British Isles was nearly 24 million, by 1914 it was over 46 million.[8] In 1841 in England and Wales at least 67 per cent of bridegrooms and 51 per cent of brides were literate; by 1900 the percentage was 97 per cent for both sexes.[9] A higher percentage of a much larger figure meant a remarkable

---

5 In 1871 some 1.5 million Valentines were sent within London alone; see Vincent, *Literacy and popular culture*, p. 44.

6 Escott, *Social transformations of the Victorian age*, p. 375.

7 The publisher Sampson Low estimated that within a year of the novel's first publication in Britain there were 1.5 million copies in circulation within Britain and her colonies; see Winship, 'In the four quarters of the globe', pp. 370–1.

8 Mitchell, *British historical statistics*, pp. 12–13.

9 Cipolla, *Literacy and development in the west*, pp. 121–5.

expansion in the number of readers and thus in the demand for books. This market was further expanded by the growing demand from North America, the British Empire and English readers in Europe. Not all was for literature, of course, but borrowing rates for fiction in the newly founded public libraries of the period suggested that this genre was the most popular choice for many readers. This is confirmed by the statistics: between 1814 and 1846 fiction and juvenile literature accounted for 16.2 per cent of the titles listed in book trade journals (poetry and drama accounted for 7.6 per cent); between 1900 and 1909 it accounted for 30.1 per cent (poetry and drama 5.1 per cent).[10]

The genres

Fiction

In the eighteenth century it had been common to issue novels in multiple volumes. By the early 1820s, shaped by the powerful influence of Sir Walter Scott and his publisher Archibald Constable, the first edition of an upmarket novel would normally be in three volumes (called a 'three-decker') and would be priced at 31s 6d.[11] For most of our period a skilled worker would be lucky to earn 25s–30s a week, so a novel that cost more than an artisan's weekly wage would be beyond the pockets of all but the most affluent. One- and two-volumes novels were also published, but they too would often be sold at outrageously high prices; 31s 6d remained the standard price for a three-volume novel until 1894. This meant that most readers borrowed rather than bought this form of fiction, and did so from that expanding sector of the book trade the circulating libraries, the largest of which were Mudie and W. H. Smith. It has been suggested that the three-decker was sustained for so long by the desire of circulating libraries to monopolise the first edition. This may well have been true in the 1840s and 1850s, but became progressively less so in the late 1860s and 1870s.[12]

Between 1829 and 1833 Scott's then publisher Robert Cadell issued a forty-eight-volume collected edition of the Waverley novels with new introductions and annotations (thus creating a new copyright) in five-shilling monthly volumes.[13] This set a pattern for the reissue of fiction in named series at reduced prices which was a recurring feature throughout the period. Many of the earlier series, such as Murray's Family Library or Lardner's Cabinet Library, published

---

10 Eliot, *Some patterns and trends in British publishing*, pp. 127, 129.
11 The first novel to be priced at this level was Sir Walter Scott's *Kenilworth* in 1821.
12 See Eliot, 'Circulating libraries in the Victorian age and after', pp. 135–6.
13 See Millgate, *Scott's last edition*.

weightier literature than fiction. For fiction, readers might have a long wait. Jane Austen's novels appeared in Bentley's Standard Novels (begun February 1831 under the imprint Colburn & Bentley) at six shillings a volume only in 1833, sixteen years after her death. Richard Bentley & Son (1829–98) was one of the many publishing houses producing three-volume fiction throughout the period whose efforts were amplified by a magazine, *Temple Bar*, in whose pages authors and their fiction could be trialled. This tactic was also used in *Macmillan's Magazine*, *Longman's*, *Tinsley's*, *Blackwood's*, *Cassell's*, *Once a Week* (Bradbury & Evans) and the *Cornhill* (George Smith), among many others.

Some fiction was available cheaply, but it tended to be out-of-copyright material issued in parts through series such Limbird's British Novelist (1823–46) published in twopenny parts.[14] Part-issue, although having a long history, became from the later 1830s a crucial weapon in the battle to make copyright fiction cheaper and thus more accessible. It was the combination of steel-plate illustrations, prose fiction and part-issue (anticipated by Pierce Egan in *Life in London* 1820–1) that inspired the new firm of Chapman & Hall (established 1830) to commission the young Charles Dickens to write *The Pickwick Papers*. This was serialised in twenty monthly parts between April 1836 and November 1837, selling at one shilling a part. Thus if readers were persistent and patient enough they could have a large, unbound novel for £1, the cost being spread hire-purchase-like over nineteen months (19 and 20 were issued as a double-number at two shillings). Alternatively, a bound version would be available at the end of the run for twenty-one shillings. A characteristic feature of such part-issues was that they carried advertisements: the more popular the author and the title, the more numerous the advertisements. Bradbury & Evans (Dickens's publishers 1845–59) produced no fewer than sixteen pages of advertisements wrapped around the first part of *Dombey and Son* published 1 October 1846.[15]

Pickwick established a pattern of production that Dickens followed for most of his novels; the few exceptions were published either in monthly magazines (*Oliver Twist* in *Bentley's Miscellany*) or in weeklies (such as *Great Expectations* in Dickens's own *All the Year Round*). But not only Dickens: Thackeray, Trollope, Ainsworth, Lever and others at one time or another were published in parts issued at different intervals and at different prices. Many variations were played on the part-novel theme: George Eliot's publisher, John Blackwood, issued *Middlemarch* in eight five-shilling 'books' at two-monthly intervals 1871–2;

---

14 Topham, 'John Limbird, Thomas Byerley, and the production of cheap periodicals in the 1820s', p. 95.
15 Patten, *Charles Dickens and his publishers*, pp. 184–5. See also chapter 3, above.

George Smith published Trollope's *Last chronicle of Barset* in 1867 in sixpenny weekly parts over thirty-two weeks.[16]

Who were the major publishers of middle-class fiction? Using an admittedly far-from-random sample of the novels given individual entries in Sutherland's *The Longman companion to Victorian fiction*, the top twelve publishers of first editions were Chapman & Hall (68 titles), Smith, Elder (52), Bentley (44), Blackwood (27), Macmillan (25), Bradbury & Evans (22), Chatto & Windus (22), Longman (18), Sampson Low (17), Colburn (16), Heinemann (16) and Tinsley (15).[17] However, it should be remembered that a list of publishers producing reprinted and cheaper versions of these titles would be unlikely to follow exactly the same order.

Soon after Dickens began his novel-writing career with Chapman & Hall, publishers such as Edward Lloyd and George Vickers – at some time both clustered around Wych and Holywell Streets off the Strand (this area was also a major centre for pornographic publishing)[18] – were producing parodies and plagiarisms such as *The sketch book by Bos* and *The penny Pickwick* issued in weekly parts at a penny each. Popular fiction also paralleled other, earlier, middle-class forms: the gothic novel and the Newgate novel were particularly popular in the 1840s and resulted in long-running novels such as *Varney the Vampyre* (1847) and *Gentleman Jack* (1848–52).[19] These resembled modern soap operas in the sense that they had no predetermined shape or end and would run just as long as there was a demand for their weekly instalments. Book versions that were sometimes issued after the instalments would on occasions run to four or more large volumes. For instance, G. W. M. Reynolds's *The mysteries of the court of London* published by Vickers ran 1849–56 and contained, it has been estimated, no fewer than 4.5 million words.[20] Much of this material was written to order by denizens of Grub Street (such as T. P. Prest and Thomas Rymer) to fill the printed sheet. It thus frequently consisted of dialogue (a new speaker gets a new line so the page fills up more quickly) and was highly repetitious. However, this may frequently have been an advantage for a reader whose grip on literacy was not firm: short lines and lots of repetition would make the prose easier to absorb.

---

16 Sutherland, *Victorian novelists and publishers*, p. 198.
17 Sutherland, *The Longman companion to Victorian fiction*.
18 Given that much pornography was fiction we should not forget that this too was a form of literature, and that some literature (such as *The Arabian nights*) was then regarded by some as pornography. Such publishers as Dugdale, Hotten and Smithers provided expensive titillation, while collections of lewd songs such as *Fanny Hill's new frisky chanter and amorous toast master* were available for a few pennies.
19 James, *Fiction for the working man*, pp. 99–100, 167–8, 185.   20 *Ibid.*, pp. 47, 109.

As with middle-class fiction, magazine serialisation offered an alternative to part-publication. A few social notches up lay such journals as the *Family Herald* and the *London Journal*. Apart from serialised novels these papers often ran some form of correspondence page where readers in need of guidance could ask questions of fact such as 'who was the leading fiction writer of the age?' (in 1863 it was Bulwer-Lytton, apparently), or advertise their marriageable attractions.[21]

The growing demand for downmarket fiction in the period 1850s–1870s illustrates vividly the interpenetration of books, part-issues and periodicals. In 1845 G. W. M. Reynolds set up *Reynolds's Miscellany* which, as the title suggested, published a range of material including serialised novels. These novels might later be accumulated and republished as bound volumes. A feature of many of these popular journals was their claim that back numbers were always available so that missed episodes or answers to earlier correspondence could always be ordered by the reader. Even given stereotyping, if true this does suggest quite remarkable feats of warehousing and information retrieval.[22]

John Dicks became managing clerk and printer and publisher of *Reynolds's Miscellany* in 1847. Dicks had a long and remarkable career in cheap publishing which included, from the late 1860s on, Dicks' English Novels, each a complete novel in paperback selling at sixpence. Dicks finally combined *Reynolds's Miscellany* with his own *Bow Bells* in 1869.

Part-publication was a partial palliative to inflated middle-class novel prices, but the real solution lay elsewhere. As we have seen, by the 1830s Scott and Austen and many other authors were beginning to appear in single-volume reprint editions selling at five or six shillings. By 1842 even cheaper editions could be found abroad under the Collection of British Authors series published by Tauchnitz in Leipzig (although these were forbidden to be reimported, some found their way back); the first two were Lytton's *Pelham* and Dickens's *Pickwick*.[23]

A new and cheaper form emerged in 1849 with the publication by George Routledge of reprints under the Railway Library banner and selling for one or two shillings.[24] As later versions from other publishers were commonly bound in glazed yellow boards, they became known as 'yellowbacks'. They were small – easily slipped inside a greatcoat pocket – and frequently featured on railway bookstalls (progressively more common as W. H. Smith took over

21 *London Journal* 6 February 1864, p. 96, col. 1.
22 See *Family Herald*, 'Contents of the tenth volume' (May 1852–April 1853), p. viii, cols. 3–4.
23 Todd and Bowden, *Tauchnitz international editions in English 1841–1955*, pp. 7–9.
24 Topp, *Victorian yellowbacks & paperbacks 1849–1905. 1. George Routledge*, p. 1.

the supply of books and newspapers on various lines), sometimes with a racy or lurid picture cover. They were the airport lounge novels of their day. By 1866 a new and even cheaper version of the novel was beginning to appear, under the imprints of Routledge, Hotten and others: paperbound books at sixpence offering reprints of novels by Cooper and Scott – and this sixty-nine years before Penguin Books.[25] In 1873 Dicks issued a complete paperback edition of the Waverley novels at just threepence per volume.

By the 1870s a fiction publisher had at his disposal a range of formats which would allow him, in a matter of a few years, to explore a range of readers and markets with the same product: from a three-decker at 31s 6d, to a single-volume cheap reprint (3s 6d–6s), to a yellowback (1s–2s), to a paperback (at sixpence or under). In other words, within a matter of a few years a reader could buy a novel, which had originally appeared at 31s 6d, at 1/63rd or less of its original price – a price flexibility that even computer manufacturers today would find hard to match. Publishers could also sell unbound stock to jobbing printers who would bind and sell the books under their own imprints at even lower prices. The firm of R. E. King flooded the market with cheap fiction in this way in the 1880s and 1890s.

For circulating libraries none of this was important; as long as they could circulate their three-deckers for a year or two without competition they would make a profit on them. However, by the 1860s this safety margin was beginning to narrow. This process can be traced in the publishing history of the most highly successful of the period's female novelists. M. E. Braddon's *Aurora Floyd* published by Tinsley at 31s 6d in January 1863 was available as a six-shilling reprint within seven months. Indeed, of the nineteen novels written by Braddon between 1863 and 1873, thirteen were cheaply reprinted within nine months or fewer. Mrs Henry Wood and Ouida exhibited a similar pattern of shrinking reprint gaps in the 1860s and early 1870s.[26] All this put so much pressure on the libraries that, by the 1880s, most of Mudie's three-deckers were struggling to make a profit.[27] The market had become saturated, and though many new novels continued to be published in three volumes until 1894 the increasing strength of the cheap reprint eventually brought about the collapse of the form. Publishers became more aggressive in marketing their back-lists. In 1880 Chatto & Windus reduced the price of their Piccadilly novels from 6s to 3s 6d. In 1892, in what proved a critical episode for the libraries, Smith, Elder brought out a six-shilling reprint of Mary Ward's *David Grieve*

25 *Ibid.*, p. 175.   26 Eliot, 'The three-decker novel and its first cheap reprint'.
27 Griest, *Mudie's circulating library*, p. 168.

a mere three months after publication in three volumes. Within four months 17,000 copies had been sold.[28] The pressure finally told. In 1894 the libraries revised the terms upon which they were willing to purchase new fiction and by 1897 the three-volume novel had all but disappeared.[29] It was replaced by a single-volume first edition selling at six shillings.

The challenge to the dominance of the three-decker had already gathered pace in the 1880s when several new works of lasting value appeared in the first instance in single-volume editions. Cassell issued six-shilling editions of Robert Louis Stevenson's *Treasure Island* (1883) and Henry Rider Haggard's *King Solomon's mines* (1885) to considerable success. As works of adventure romance these two books were in part a reaction against the procrustean length and domestic subject-matter of the typical three-decker, and with the decline of the three-volume form came the rise of identifiable branches of genre fiction, such as romance, spy fiction, detective fiction and science fiction. In the same decade Arrowsmith began a series of novels at 3s 6d, and two of the titles – Jerome K. Jerome's *Three men in a boat* (1889) and Anthony Hope's *The prisoner of Zenda* (1894) – became best-sellers. At the bottom end of the price scale was the shilling shocker – short, sensational paperback novels priced at one shilling – which became especially successful in the late Victorian period. Robert Louis Stevenson's *The strange case of Dr Jekyll and Mr Hyde* (1886) and Fergus Hume's *The mystery of a hansom cab* (1888) were two of the most famous titles. Such works were one-sixth of the price of the first cheap reprint of a three-volume novel.

After 1894 most new novels were published in one volume and priced at six shillings. The change in format brought about new marketing strategies and the birth of the 'best-seller' as a concept in literary publishing. Authors such as Hall Caine, Marie Corelli and Florence Barclay achieved enormous sales and were marketed as much on account of their popularity as their literary appeal.[30] Yellowbacks continued until the early years of the twentieth century, though according to Michael Sadleir after 1870 quality and character were abandoned in favour of 'trouble-saving uniformity'.[31] In the new century yellowbacks were largely restricted to sensation and sporting novels such as those of Nat Gould. In the late 1890s, however, publishers began to issue more novels in large-format paperbacks at sixpence which began to displace yellowbacks on railway bookstalls. An observer in 1905 noted that 'for railway readers the sixpenny edition has entirely taken the place of the picture-boarded novel

28 Sutherland, *Mrs Humphry Ward*, p. 139.   29 Griest, *Mudie's circulating library*, p. 172.
30 See Waller, *Writers, readers, and reputations*, chs. 18–23.   31 Sadleir, 'Yellow-backs', pp. 144–5.

so popular half a century ago'.[32] These paperbacks were not just reprints of classics but also novels still in copyright which had been on the market in 3s 6d or 2s editions for a decade or more. In 1897, ten years after the book had first been published, Chatto & Windus issued Hall Caine's *The deemster* in a sixpenny edition of 100,000 copies. In 1889, eight years before the work fell out of copyright, Macmillan published Charles Kingsley's *Westward ho!* (1855) in the same format in an edition of 500,000 copies. By the early 1900s these paperbacks were being issued in strikingly designed coloured covers.[33]

These editions had an ephemeral quality and were often thrown away after reading.[34] In the new century, however, came a different cheap reprint enterprise: the sevenpennies. In 1907 both Collins and Nelson began publishing cloth-bound editions of novels still in copyright. These were pocket size, even smaller than yellowbacks, with a colour frontispiece and wrapper. For a time the sevenpennies put pressure on the market strength of the six-shilling novel as more people began purchasing rather than borrowing books. Writing in the *New Age* in 1909, Arnold Bennett considered that 'the tremendous supply of sevenpenny bound volumes of modern fiction [is] making book-buyers where previously there were no book-buyers'.[35] In spite of the competition, the six-shilling novel survived and most new novels were published in the first instance at that price until after the war.

The pattern of decreasing price was matched by developments in the serial market which remained an essential format for the production and consumption of literature. By the time of Dickens's death in 1870, the part-novel was declining in popularity. The last novel to be issued in monthly shilling parts, William Black's *Sunrise* (1880–1), was also serialised in the *Sheffield Weekly Telegraph*, a fact that points to the increasing importance of newspaper serialisation in the period and to the many ways in which a single novel could be packaged and published. By the last quarter of the century, novels could adopt so many forms and appeal to so many markets in the UK, Europe, North America and the Empire that rights associated with them had become difficult to manage. It is mainly for this reason that by the late 1870s the first professional literary agents such as A. P. Watt were beginning to emerge.[36]

In the 1860s and 1870s the standard trajectory for a middle-class novel was serialisation over a year or less in a monthly magazine, with the three-decker

---

32 Shaylor, 'Reprints and their readers', p. 540.   33 See *Sixpenny wonderfuls*.
34 Andrew Chatto told the author William Clark Russell that 'as the books are usually bought for 4½d, we do not think that they [readers] lose much when, having read them, they throw them away'. 21 March 1911. Chatto & Windus Letter Book 75, fol. 272 (Reading University Library).
35 18 February 1909. Reprinted in Bennett, *Books and persons*, p. 107.
36 See Hepburn, *The author's empty purse*, pp. 45–66.

edition being released a few months before the final instalment. Established shilling monthly magazines, such as the *Cornhill*, *Temple Bar* and *Blackwood's*, continued to carry serials, but by the 1880s these were being outmanoeuvred in the market by newer or cheaper publications. Weekly magazines such as *All the Year Round* and *Chambers's Journal* had always been important sites for serialised fiction but in the 1880s it was the sixpenny weeklies such as the *Graphic* and the *Illustrated London News* that began to dominate the market, imposing upon authors a demand for shorter serials and injecting a growing emphasis on illustration in serialised fiction. The major shift, however, came in the development of newspaper syndication, which in the last quarter of the century became the dominant mode of serialisation for new novels.[37] The pioneering firm of Tillotson & Son of Bolton developed the practice of buying up serial rights in novels and leasing them out for simultaneous publication in groups of provincial newspapers, both in Britain and abroad. The size of the potential market was such that newspaper serialisation became more remunerative to authors than magazine publication and it was not just popular novelists such as Collins and Braddon who were published in this way but writers like Trollope, Hardy and Meredith as well.

The magazine market continued to be important, however, and in the period after 1880 there was a growing variety of outlets for serial fiction. The rising number of women's magazines increased the market not just for sentimental and romance fiction targeted at women readers but for all types of litera-ture. Hall Caine's *The eternal city* was the serial in the first number of the *Lady's Magazine* whilst Rider Haggard's swashbuckling romance *Fair Margaret* (1906) appeared in the *Lady's Realm*. The organs of the New Journalism (as it was dubbed by Matthew Arnold) also provided a cheap, and to some authors cheapening, outlet. The pioneering penny weekly 'snippet' magazine *Tit-Bits* began serialising fiction in the late 1880s. In 1902 T. P. O'Connor launched the slightly more pretentious *T.P.'s Weekly* at the same price, prompting George Meredith to remark in the second issue: 'We have entered upon the period of democracy in literature.'[38] Conrad's *Nostromo* was serialised in the paper in 1904.

The fiction magazine which most defines the era after 1880, however, is the *Strand*, which spawned a host of imitations such as the *Windsor*, *Pearson's Magazine* and, in the new century, *Nash's Magazine*.[39] Published by George Newnes, the *Strand* was an illustrated sixpenny monthly around a hundred

---

37 See Law, *Serialising fiction in the Victorian press*.   38 *T.P.'s Weekly*, 21 November 1902, p. 58.
39 See Ashley, *The age of storytellers*.

pages in length. Within a few years of publication it was claiming sales in the region of half a million copies.[40] Serial fiction was published in the magazine after 1896 but its main innovation was the short story series, typified above all by Conan Doyle's Sherlock Holmes stories. This had the advantage over the serial in that it did not matter if a reader missed an episode. The linked series, often centring on an iconic hero or villain, became a feature of late Victorian and Edwardian popular literature, providing a ready market for mystery and detective fiction. Following in the wake of the *Strand*, the *Story-Teller*, which began in 1907, introduced two of the most popular fictional figures of the era: G. K. Chesterton's Father Brown and Sax Rohmer's Fu Manchu.

The Edwardian period saw the introduction of more magazines composed entirely of fiction. Publications such as the *Novel*, the *Grand* and the *Story-Teller*, published by Pearson, Harmsworth and Cassell respectively, were monthlies, priced at $4\frac{1}{2}$d, containing short stories or complete novels in each issue. These magazines were invariably printed on cheap low-grade paper and so had a more downmarket look and feel.

The forms of working-class literature discussed earlier remained in evidence until the end of the period in the form of penny fiction and penny newspapers. In an article of 1890, Francis Hitchman wrote of the 'complete factory of literature of rascaldom' which circulated in a lane not far from Fleet Street. Tales of highwaymen, murderers, burglars, wicked noblemen and persecuted damsels, with titles such as 'Spring-Heeled Jack', 'Sweeny Todd, the Demon Barber of Fleet Street' and 'Turnpike Dick', sold in their 'thousands week by week'.[41] Much of this fiction was targeted at boys and resembled the street literature of a generation before. E. J. Brett and W. L. Emmett, both publishers of penny dreadfuls, turned in the 1860s to issuing penny weekly papers carrying sensational tales with imperialist titles such as *Boys of England*, *Boys of the Empire* and the *Young Briton*. Some of these titles boasted sales of over 300,000 copies a week. Partly in response to the success of such papers the Religious Tract Society launched the *Boy's Own Paper* in 1879 which, along with the *Girl's Own Paper*, published for a penny a large amount of morally improving fiction for children and young adults.

The stories in these papers were often reworkings of earlier literature. In the absence of copyright protection, publishers could draw their material from cheap American literature. Either a story would be reprinted word for word or it would be edited or rewritten by a hack in the publisher's employment. The text would be anglicised, the title changed and the material reorganised.

---

40 *Ibid.*, p. 197.   41 [Hitchman] 'Penny Fiction', p. 154.

Other sources, such as old annuals and magazines, were also used and some publishers solicited 'original, translated or copied' contributions from amateur authors.[42] The Aldine Publishing Company, 'with a profusion of libraries on every subject from highwaymen to horse racing', specialised in reprints of American stories.[43] The company became the most prolific producer of cheap fiction in series. Their numerous libraries included the Aldine Cheerful Library, a penny weekly offering a number of complete stories in each number; the Aldine Detective Tales, with ninety-six pages for twopence, the Aldine O'er Land and Sea Library, also twopence, and the Garfield Library, a three-penny monthly series containing a single story of a hundred or more pages of 'Glorious fun and adventure'. It is in series like these that popular fiction of the period after 1914 has its roots.

In addition to penny papers there were penny novelettes such as the Princess's Novelettes, which ran from the 1880s to 1906. Novelettes were sometimes issued as supplements to newspapers. The *Family Herald Supplement* appeared weekly and had a circulation of over 200,000. The shape and size of novelettes could vary. Each number of the *Bow Bells* series was printed on six-teen large quarto pages in double columns with three illustrations, amounting to about 25,000 words, whilst the *Lady's Own Novelette* offered two complete novels for a penny in thirty-two pages amounting to 40,000 words. As Victor Neuberg observes: 'It is with publications like the penny novels that the divid-ing line between a paper-covered book and a periodical becomes blurred.'[44] Penny novels and novelettes were sold through traditional bookstalls and newsagents as well as by hand outside factory gates and through tobac-conists, sweet vendors and corner-shop grocers. Newsagents surveyed in 1906 reported that their customers bought penny novels more than any other type of book.[45]

Some of these publications were designed as wholesome alternatives to the penny dreadfuls which had become identified as the staple diet of reading for the masses. W. B. Horner & Son issued several series, including Horner's Pocket Library and Horner's Penny Stories for the People. The latter crammed a single complete story into sixteen pages. An advertisement recorded that 19.5 million copies of the first hundred stories had been issued (an average print-run of nearly 200,000 per issue). Reviews (mainly from the religious press) printed inside the front cover of one issue praised the publisher's efforts to 'supplant the bloodthirsty and ultra-sensational stories which flood the market'.[46] Not

---

42 *Ibid.*, p. 159.   43 Turner, *Boys will be boys*, p. 73   44 Neuberg, *Popular literature*, p. 230.
45 *Ibid.*, quoting from Haslam, *The press and the people*, p. 214.
46 No. 81, 'The Mistress of Carleton Towers' by Fannie Eden [1894].

surprisingly, religious publishers were prolific in this area. The SPCK issued the Penny Library of Fiction and the Religious Tract Society published the Leisure Hour series.

Fears about literature, particularly fiction, corrupting vulnerable members of society (usually identified as children, women and the working classes) were commonly expressed by those who liked to see themselves as moral guardians. These concerns were articulated in the Obscene Publications Act of 1857, which was used not only against hard-core pornography but also to attack what was later to become canonical literature. In 1884 the publisher Henry Vizetelly began issuing Zola's novels. The mistake he made was to publish them in English translation and at a low price, thus making them freely available to all and sundry. Vizetelly was prosecuted twice, and on the second occasion, in 1889, the 70-year-old publisher was sentenced to three months' imprisonment, an experience from which he never fully recovered. No-one who published Zola in French, or at a high price, was ever prosecuted.[47]

Drama

On 22 October 1824 *The Times* reported:

> on the room-door being opened, a cloud of smoke issued, and the unfortunate woman was discovered sitting in a chair, her clothes reduced to cinder, and her person burnt in the most horrid manner. The wretched sufferer was conveyed to Guy's Hospital, where she lingers in a hopeless state. A play book lay near her, which it is supposed she was reading, and becoming drowsy, the candle set fire to her head-dress.

Reading by candlelight posed many problems, not the least of which was accidental fires. But what the poor woman was reading might surprise a modern reader. In fact, small (commonly 15.2 × 9.5 cm), paper-covered, single plays usually priced at sixpence or less were produced in considerable numbers in the nineteenth century. Some were canonical works (such as Shakespeare and the eighteenth-century dramatists) but the majority were plays recently performed in the major and minor London theatres. Indeed, many were advertised as 'printed from the acting copy', offering descriptions of the costumes, a cast list and some of the stage business explained. Many would carry an engraving of a scene.[48] Some publishers would reinforce the educational or performative elements of drama by advertising, for instance, a history of male and female

---

47 See Landon, 'A man under fire'.
48 See, for instance, the title-page of George Colman, *The jealous wife* (London: John Cumberland, n.d).

costume in parts,[49] or songs and pianoforte duets for home performance,[50] or portraits of dignitaries.[51] From the 1820s and 1830s onwards many minor or specialist publishers were vying for playreaders' sixpences.[52]

It is clear that these publications were used as acting texts, by either amateurs or professionals, but it is likely that this use alone would not have justified a cheap sixpenny (later a penny) edition that would have had to sell in its tens of thousands in order to make a reasonable profit. In other words, a significant number would have been bought for private or collective reading.[53] Given the short lines, and a new line whenever a new character spoke, the lay-out of a dramatic text was usually much easier (and much shorter) to read than a novel. Add that to the low price and portability, and one begins to understand the form's appeal. Appealing it was. Some publishers issued plays on a weekly basis, creating substantial series such as Cumberland's British Theatre (at least 336 titles by the 1830s), while Duncombe's Acting Editions of the British Theatre was offering at least 418 titles by the 1840s.[54] Plays would be issued weekly, but they would also be repackaged in small collections in boards. Lacy offered fifteen or sixteen plays in volumes for five shillings;[55] by 1850 G. H. Davidson was selling five plays in his Cumberland's Plays series in coloured boards (rather like a yellowback) for one shilling.[56]

The actor-manager Thomas Hailes Lacy established a publishing house in Covent Garden in the mid-1840s and became 'probably the most prominent and catholic of all nineteenth-century publishers of the drama for the masses'.[57] His enterprise expanded by gradually absorbing the lists of Cumberland, Duncombe, Webster and others. Printed in double columns and selling at most for sixpence a copy, Lacy's Acting Editions were offering ninety-nine volumes containing in all 1,485 plays by the time the New Yorker Samuel French took over Lacy's firm in 1872–3.[58]

49 *The wife's secret* carried advertisements for books in parts on male and female costumes.
50 See endpapers of *Davidson's shilling volume of Cumberland's plays* vol. 3 (1850).
51 See advertisements in *Presented at court*, no. 177 in Webster's Acting National Drama (London: Webster & Co., 19 Suffolk Street, Pall Mall East, n.d.).
52 Including Dolby's British Theatre, Webster's Acting National Drama, G. H. Davidson, W. Oxberry, James Pattie, Thomas Richardson and W. Strange. In the early part of our period some established firms such as Longman, Murray and Moxon continued to publish 'serious' plays: see Stephens, *The profession of the playwright*, pp. 116–22.
53 A contrary view is given in Barrett, 'Play publication, readers, and the "decline" of Victorian drama'.
54 See the back cover of Charles Whitehead, *The cavalier* [no. 209] (London: John Duncombe, n.d.).
55 See the inside front cover of *The widow's victim* [no. 153] (London: Thomas Hailes Lacy, n.d.).
56 *Davidson's shilling volume of Cumberland's plays* (London: G. H. Davidson, Peter's Hill, Doctors' Commons, 1850).
57 Stephens, *The profession of the playwright*, p. 130.
58 See the back cover of *The wife's secret* [no. 1216] (London: Thomas Hailes Lacy, c. 1869) and Stephens, *The profession of the playwright*, pp. 130–1.

John Dicks had begun issuing a play a week at a penny in Dicks' Penny Standard Plays (the first being *Othello*) by the early 1860s; by 1882 he was issuing two a week.[59] By 1892 there were 1,074 plays in the series.[60] Most of the Standard Plays consisted of non-copyright texts, especially printed texts of non-copyright dramas acted before 1843.[61] Dicks was also influential in the predictably large field of Shakespeare publishing. In the mid-1860s he was issuing sets of two Shakespeare plays for a penny, and by 1867 was selling the complete works in cloth for two shillings. That edition's sales of 50,000 copies was soon eclipsed by the paperbound shilling edition which sold some 700,000 copies.[62] Shakespeare provided an obvious source of income for publishers, some ambitious to produce newly edited editions, others cheap collections which were sometimes issued in parts (e.g. Charles Knight in fifty-six parts 1838–43 or Routledge in fifty parts from 1856). No fewer than twenty-five editions of the complete works or plays, including type and photolithographic facsimiles (from Lionel Booth 1862–4 and Day & Son 1864–6) and illustrated editions (Routledge 1867), were published between 1830 and 1870.[63]

By the end of the century Shakespeare was being packaged in a variety of different ways. The shilling Shakespeares that appeared in the 1860s – Routledge and Warne had joined Dicks in the market by 1868 – were undercut still further in 1890 by Ward & Lock's sixpenny edition, 'the cheapest Shakespeare edition of the Victorian era.'[64] The spread of school and university education brought even greater demand for cheap editions, typified by the Clarendon Press series, which began in the 1860s, and the Pitt Press Shakespeare issued by Cambridge University Press from 1890. A little higher up the production scale was J. M. Dent's Temple Shakespeare; printed on hand-made paper and issued at a shilling a volume, over 1894–6 this sold 250,000 copies annually.[65] A series of photo-facsimiles of the quartos, priced at six shillings and complete with scholarly introductions, was issued in forty-three volumes over 1880–91, whilst the appearance of the first volumes of the Arden edition published by Methuen in 1899 points towards the emerging industry of scholarly editing that would develop in the twentieth century.

Editions of Shakespeare and of other early dramatists continued to dominate the market of dramatic publishing.[66] So far as contemporary dramatists were concerned, the market continued to be restricted mainly to the production of

59 Dicks, *The John Dicks Press*, p. 28.   60 *Ibid.*, p. 101.
61 Stephens, *The profession of the playwright*, p. 131.
62 See Murphy, *Shakespeare in print*, p. 358; Dicks, *The John Dicks Press*, p. 36.
63 Murphy, *Shakespeare in print*, pp. 353–8.   64 *Ibid.*, p. 178.
65 St Clair, *The reading nation*, p. 714.
66 Dent followed the Temple Shakespeare with the Temple Dramatists.

acting editions. In the period after 1830 it was unusual for dramatists to make a concerted effort to preserve their plays in durable printed form.[67] The point was raised in 1882 by William Archer:

> What three English dramatists have been successful both before the footlights and in Paternoster Row? What three dramatists have even systematically published their plays, except in the quite unreadable form in which Mr French presents them to the 'profession' and amateurs?[68]

Archer found the very form of an acting edition 'a negation at all attempt of literary effect' and 'only a trade publication'. The only playwright who seemed to have explored the possibility of publishing drama as literature was W. S. Gilbert, who published a volume of six *Original plays* in 1876. By the 1890s, however, things had transformed substantially. The dramatist most often credited with effecting the change is Henry Arthur Jones, whose plays were issued by Macmillan in uniform editions in the 1890s. Jones pronounced the benefits of the opportunity to revise dramatic texts and the passing of the American copyright act which protected copyright and performance rights across the Atlantic.[69] Publishers moved quickly to capture the leading playwrights of the day. William Heinemann, whose firm had just been established, revived the tradition of making play texts available in the theatre on the first night when he brought out an edition of Pinero's *The times* (1891). Heinemann issued Pinero's plays in cloth at 2s 6d and paper at 1s 6d. Duckworth, another new firm, began a Modern Plays series in 1898, usually produced shortly after a play's first run in London.

The two leading playwrights of the early part of the twentieth century – George Bernard Shaw and J. M. Barrie – were especially interested in exploring the artistic possibilities of the printed play form. Shaw's declared intention in publishing *Plays pleasant and unpleasant* (1898) was to appeal to an essentially novel-reading public, and both he and Barrie inserted in their texts long passages of narrative and elaborate stage directions which made a direct appeal to the reader's imagination. By 1914, dramatic publishing was securely established as a literary form that circulated in books as well as on the stage.

Poetry

During their working lives the poetry of Scott and Byron had been very successful; after their deaths their work continued to echo commercially: between

---

67 For a consideration of some of the reasons for this, see Barrett, 'Play publication, readers, and the "decline" of Victorian drama', pp. 176–8.

68 Archer, *English dramatists of today*, p. 6   69 Stephens, *The profession of the playwright*, pp. 132–5.

1830 and 1870 there were at least twenty-eight collected editions produced in Britain alone – some reprinted a number of times – of Byron's works, some in parts (1842, 1854-5) and at least one bowdlerised edition (Edinburgh 1857).[70]

However, collected editions are not necessarily the best way of assessing the success of poetry publishing. Unlike fiction or drama, poetry, particularly lyric poetry, is a highly protean form. It can be published or republished in small selections (and thus potentially very cheaply), and it can even occur or reoccur as single poems in anthologies and textbooks – or in newspapers and magazines. A significant amount of the poetry the average reader would have been exposed to during this period would have taken the form of individual poems published in newspapers or gift-books or reproduced by copying into a reader's commonplace or autograph book. Not all of it was of the 'Ode to an expiring frog' variety: the first appearance of Tennyson's 'Charge of the Light Brigade' was in the *Examiner* on 9 December 1854. In 1855 Moxon published 2,000 copies of this printed on slips of paper which were sent, at the request of a chaplain at the military hospital in Scutari, for distribution among the soldiers.[71] Later in the century Rudyard Kipling's series of soldier poems collected in *Barrack-room ballads* (1892) were first published in the *Scots Observer*.

A number of now half-remembered poets flourished in the pages of journals and gift-books in the earlier part of the period. Felicia Hemans published a considerable amount of her work in the pages of *Blackwood's Edinburgh Magazine* (1818-35), the *New Monthly Magazine* (1823-35) and the *Monthly Magazine* (1839-43) among others, as well as appearing frequently in keepsakes of the 1820s and 1830s. Thomas Hood edited and appeared in many such publications and his poetical works were frequently reprinted by, among others, Dicks throughout the later nineteenth century.

Certain poets were able to catch the mood of a period with a particular collection that was then frequently reprinted over a decade or decades. John Keble's *The Christian year*, first published in 1827 by J. H. Parker in Oxford, claimed to be in its 57th edition by 1858 and its 122nd by 1869. However, publishers used 'edition' loosely, and many of these are likely to be no more than new impressions. Reprints were commonly characterised by short print-runs of perhaps something between 1,000 and 3,000 copies. Even so, and allowing for some exaggeration, this is a record of a consistent and high demand over

---

70 Shattock, *The Cambridge bibliography* 4, column 246.
71 Hagen, *Tennyson and his publishers*, pp. 91-2.

forty years and more. This example should remind us that another way in which readers might be exposed to published poetry, at least of a pious sort, was through the hymn books of the period.

A similar though shorter publication burst can be demonstrated by Martin Tupper's *Proverbial philosophy*: first published by Joseph Rickerby in 1838, it was into its 'fifth edition' by 1843. Tupper introduced a second series in 1844, also published by Rickerby. By 1847 J. Hatchard & Son had taken over publication and in 1852 they published a fourteenth edition which claimed '24th thousand' having been published, a figure that would suggest print-runs in the range 1,500–2,000 copies. By 1865 the Tupper literary property had been taken over by Moxon & Co., who in that year announced a '39th edition'. Soon after, Tupper added a third and fourth series, and by 1871 Moxon was selling *Proverbial philosophy* in four series – including the fiftieth edition of the two first series – in Moxon's Popular Poets. Moxon produced further reprints between 1872 and 1874, and one in 1880, and Cassell published a complete set in 1881; but by then, a generation after first publication, the vogue had passed.

As the century progressed it became even harder for publishers or poets to make much money out of poetry. Tennyson, however, was a remarkable exception, though not in his first publications: both *Poems by two brothers* (Jackson, 1827) at five shillings and *Poems, chiefly lyrical* (Effingham Wilson, 1830), also at five shillings, made no money.[72] Encouraged by Arthur Hallam, who was then acting as an unofficial literary agent for his friend, Tennyson switched to Edward Moxon, who had set up his own business in May 1830.[73] At first Moxon had no greater success: Tennyson's *Poems* was published in December 1832 and had sold no more than three hundred copies by 1834.[74] The breakthrough came with a two-volume edition of *Poems* published in 1842 at twelve shillings. Within four months five hundred copies had been sold, out of the eight hundred printed. Moxon responded by printing a new impression of 1,000 in 1843 followed by further reprintings in 1845 (1,500) and 1846 (2,000); Tennyson seems to have been on a generous two-thirds profit arrangement with Moxon (the more usual was a 50:50 split between author and publisher), and this resulted in earnings for the poet in 1843–6 of £720 2s 4d.[75]

Tennyson was a notorious reviser of his texts: he oversaw five different editions of *The princess* between 1847 and 1853. Despite this, his profit on

---

72 *Ibid.*, pp. 7, 15.
73 In his time Moxon was to publish many of the major poets of the day, see *ibid.*, p. 25; see also Merriam, *Edward Moxon*.
74 Hagen, *Tennyson and his publishers*, p. 37.   75 *Ibid.*, p. 66.

the poem over these years was a healthy £624 9s 4d.[76] But it was *In memoriam*, published in May 1850, that secured both Tennyson's reputation and his income from literature. By July 1,500 copies had sold at six shillings a copy and Moxon ordered another 1,500, followed by a third impression of 2,000; Christmas 1850 saw another impression of 3,000 copies. In the first year Tennyson earned £445 from this publication alone.[77] By 1872 *In memoriam* was in its twenty-second impression.[78]

So confident was Moxon in Tennyson's marketability that the print-run for the first edition of *Maud and other poems* (1855) was 10,000 copies. This confidence appeared justified, for a second impression was required before the end of the year. Moxon's confidence extended to the reissuing of the 1842 poems in a lavishly illustrated edition at the high and significant price of 31s 6d with a print-run of 10,000 copies. It was aimed at the Christmas 1856 market but production problems delayed publication until 1857; this almost certainly affected sales but it is unlikely that any such expensive reissue would ever have found a large enough market to justify the ambitious print-run. In 1863, 5,000 copies were remaindered to Routledge.[79] This error may have been due to the fact that Edward Moxon was ailing; in June 1858 he died, leaving an estate of £16,000. Moxon & Co. was from that time on managed by Bradbury & Evans. In July 1859 the new regime published (in a print-run of 40,000) *Idylls of the king* at seven shillings a volume; within six months another impression was being issued. At least six impressions had been published by 1868. During the early 1860s Tennyson appears to have made a yearly average of £2,300 from these poems.[80]

Tennyson's career with Moxon & Co. was capped in August 1864 with the publication of *Enoch Arden* in a print-run of 60,000; by the end of the year the first printing had sold out. In the first year Tennyson made £8,056 1s 10d from the poem. The poet was now such a force in the market that, when he moved from Moxon to his new publisher Alexander Strahan in January 1869, he did so on the basis of being paid £5,000 a year for five years for his existing copyrights.[81] He moved to Macmillan in 1884.

Robert Browning could only have dreamed of such deals. Most of his early publications were published on commission, that is, Browning – or frequently his father – paid the cost of production and distribution. In March 1833 he paid Saunders & Otley £30 to publish *Pauline*;[82] in 1835 his father paid Effingham Wilson to publish *Paracelsus*, and in 1840 Moxon undertook to issue *Sordello* on

76 *Ibid.*, pp. 78–9.   77 *Ibid.*, pp. 84–5.   78 By now it was being published by Strahan & Co.
79 Hagen, *Tennyson and his publishers*, pp. 103–6.   80 *Ibid.*, p. 110.   81 *Ibid.*, p. 117.
82 Irvine and Honan, *The book, the ring, and the poet*, p. 32.

a similar basis. *Sordello* was both a critical and a commercial failure. After this, Moxon proposed an alternative strategy, one that, as we have seen, had just matured in fiction publishing: the cheap pamphlet. Between 1841 and 1846 Browning and Moxon published eight pamphlets of poetry, ranging from lyrics through dramatic monologues to full-blown tragedies under the general (and typically Browning) title of *Bells and pomegranates*. They ranged from sixteen to thirty-two pages in length, with the first (*Pippa passes*) priced at sixpence and the later ones at a shilling, and finally (*Luria*) at 2s 6d. Using poorer-quality paper and double-column printing, production costs were kept low (between £12 and £15). Despite this, none made any money.

Frustrated by Moxon's inability to make money for him, Browning moved to Chapman & Hall in 1848. Between this date and 1868 Chapman & Hall published both Browning's and Elizabeth Barrett Browning's poetry. Despite this, and two remarkable collections (*Men and women* in two volumes 1855, *Dramatis personae* 1864), his poetry still had little impact on the market, though the latter did go into a second edition later in 1864. For *The ring and the book* he moved to Smith, Elder, who tried another novel-imitating publishing form: issuing the poem in four monthly instalments between November 1868 and February 1869.[83] A second four-volume edition was called for in 1872, and the work re-emerged in three volumes as part of the sixteen-volume collected edition issued by Smith in 1888–9. Browning had become canonical without ever being popular or, despite various publishing experiments, creating a significant income for either himself or his publishers.

The publisher John Camden Hotten made the general point in a letter to Gilbert à Beckett in 1870: 'my experience in these matters teaches me *that as a rule poetry does not pay*'.[84] On occasion Hotten would go as far as risking a half-profit arrangement with poets, but most commonly he published poetry 'on commission' – that is, the poet paid all costs, giving the publisher a 10% commission, which allowed the author to pocket any profits. As there were usually losses rather than profits, this suited Hotten and other publishers well. However, on occasions Hotten could make poetry pay. He had the courage to publish Swinburne when Moxon would not risk it, and was rewarded by selling out an edition of 3,000 copies of his *Poems* published in November 1866 (by 1871 he had printed a total of 6,000 copies).[85]

Hotten also risked reprinting Shelley, now out of copyright, at low price. Writing to Horace MacCarthy he observed:

83 *Ibid.*, p. 427. 84 Chatto & Windus Letter Book 5, 352, 2 June 1870.
85 See Chatto & Windus Ledger Book 1, fos. 172, 273.

For some time past there has been a call for a *cheap* (uncastrated) edition of the works of this great poet, and I propose to give 2 vols. of the poetical works and 1 vol. of prose. The books would be got up in the best style, but would be sold at an exceedingly low rate – we thought of 1/8 per volume. In this way we think 10,000 copies of these splendid compositions could be placed in the hands of all who care to read them – rich and poor.[86]

Indeed, reprinting of canonical works that were, or became, out-of-copyright during the period was one of the major sources of income for publishers of poetry. As recent work has pointed out, many of the Romantic poets (such as Wordsworth, Coleridge, Shelley and Keats) became best-sellers only when competition from cheap reprinters – liberated by the expiration of copyright – forced down prices and increased print-runs.[87] This was equally true of Victorian poets: in the first three years after Tennyson's work went out of copyright the average price of his work fell dramatically, with 84 per cent of titles priced at 3s 6d or below.[88]

A poet who had featured strongly in the British poetry market during the period had done so precisely because he was not protected by copyright law: in the 1840s–1860s the American poet Longfellow's works had been produced in large quantities, cheaply, and by no fewer than fifteen different publishers.[89]

The ubiquitous Dicks was also engaged in poetry reprint publishing: by the late 1860s he was offering in his English Classics series the collected works of Byron, Burns, Milton, Cowper, Wordsworth, Moore – and Longfellow – in editions ranging from sixpence to a shilling.[90]

A middle case might be provided by Matthew Arnold. It was only in the later 1860s that Arnold could claim that his poetry, in particular the publication by Macmillan of a two-volume edition of his verse in 1869, was beginning to make a profit (about £500 between 1867 and 1869). By 1876 Macmillan felt able to offer Arnold an additional £250 for five years' rights in the *Poems*.[91] In 1878 Macmillan issued a cheap edition of Arnold's *Selected poems* at 4s 6d; its 3,000 copies sold out within two years. However, for Arnold, as for many others, the real profits lay in editing collections and selections of canonical poets. Arnold's *Poems of Wordsworth* in Macmillan's Golden Treasury series sold no fewer than 17,000 copies between 1879 and 1888.[92]

---

86 Chatto & Windus Letter Book 5, 203, Hotten to MacCarthy, 7 February 1870.
87 St Clair, *The reading nation*, pp. 219, 581, 611–13.   88 Eliot, 'What price poetry?', p. 439.
89 *Ibid.*, p. 436.   90 See the inside cover of Dicks' Standard Plays no. 17 (*Much ado about nothing*).
91 Bell, 'From Parnassus to Grub Street', p. 62.   92 *Ibid.*, pp. 63, 65.

Macmillan's greatest poetry-publishing success followed this pattern. First published in 1861 in a modest edition of 2,000 copies,[93] Palgrave's *The golden treasury* demonstrated the marketability of a broad anthology that could be both a light read and an altar to the canon. The modesty was uncalled for: by December 1861 an impression was carrying the phrase 'ninth thousand'; by 1863 a reprint records 18,000 having been printed.

Many such collections could be viewed and marketed as both recreational and educational. With the rise of English Literature as a formally taught subject in schools – and later universities – a selection of poetry could acquire a new life, and a new commercial value, as a textbook.

Poetic movements have often been mediated through publishing enterprises. In the 1890s Elkin Mathews and John Lane, partners in the Bodley Head, created a vogue for attractively produced volumes which gave impetus to the poets of the *fin de siècle*.[94] Similarly, at the very end of the period, the first volumes of the Georgian Poetry series (1912–22), published by Harold Monro at the Poetry Bookshop, provided a platform for a new generation of poets including Rupert Brooke, John Masefield and D. H. Lawrence.[95] Both of these enterprises had in common the method of bringing together publishing and bookselling. Poetry publishing had such a small market that men like Lane, Mathews and Monro saw it as a specialist activity demanding its own brand of niche bookselling.

Mathews and Lane exploited the demand for limited editions and the late Victorian revival of typography, fine paper and bookbinding. The Bodley Head issued poetry volumes by, among others, Francis Thompson, Oscar Wilde and W. B. Yeats. In the twentieth century Mathews published volumes by Joyce and Pound under his own imprint. One of Mathews's major innovations was publishing poetry in series, in small formats and at cheap prices. The Shilling Garland series was launched in 1896 with Laurence Binyon's *First book of London visions*. Consisting of twelve poems in thirty-two pages with paper wrappers, the volume was notable for its break with the standard price and format of poetry volumes.

Number 8 of the Shilling Garland series was Henry Newbolt's patriotic *Admirals all* (1897). This proved enormously successful. Whereas much of the avant-garde poetry of the 1890s had a limited, coterie market, Newbolt's patriotic volume was reprinted four times in the first fortnight and had sold 30,000 copies by 1910.[96] Along with Newbolt, the most popular poet of the

93 Morgan, *The house of Macmillan*, p. 62.   94 See Nelson, *The early nineties*.
95 See Grant, *Harold Monro & the Poetry Bookshop*.   96 Nelson, *Elkin Mathews*, p. 47.

end of the century was Kipling, whose volume *The seven seas* (1896), priced at five shillings, sold 20,000 copies on publication.[97] That kind of success was exceptional and throughout the period the poetry market remained very small. Much of the poetry of Robert Bridges, who became poet laureate in 1913, was privately printed or issued in very small editions. The increasing number of literary magazines provided an important forum, however. John Masefield's *The everlasting mercy* (1911) appeared in the *English Review* before being published in volume form to considerable notice.

Like fiction, poetry volumes could be published in a variety of formats and prices. A. E. Housman's *A Shropshire lad* was first published in an edition of 500 copies by Kegan Paul in 1896 priced at 2s 6d. It did not sell well but owing to the interest of the publisher Grant Richards, and Housman's peculiar wish not to be paid a royalty, a second edition appeared in 1898, followed by a cheap edition at sixpence in 1900. It continued selling in many editions and in 1914 was published in an expensive *édition de luxe* by the Medici Society as one of the Riccardi Press booklets.[98]

Building a canon: books in series

Richard Altick identifies the appearance of the Aldine Edition of the British Poets in 1830 as 'the beginning of the era when publishers developed cheap classic libraries as an integral – not merely incidental – part of their lists'.[99] As noted above, series publishing was a common way of packaging all types of literature throughout the period. Cheap libraries performed a canonising function through offering readers a package of 'select' or 'classic' works from the past.

After 1842, owing to changes in copyright law (see chapter 5), more standard classics were in the public domain and thus became easier to reprint than new works or works still in copyright. The increased use of stereotyping made reprinting a much cheaper option and stereotype plates could be duplicated, and hired or sold to other publishers. Series often passed from publisher to publisher. Moxon's Library Poets was first sold to Ward & Lock and then passed to Collins, who renamed the series the Grosvenor Poets. Publishers could also purchase unbound printed stock at low rates and dress them up in new editions. The Edinburgh firm of Nimmo seems to have specialised in

97 Mallett, *Rudyard Kipling*, p. 92.
98 Richards, *Author hunting*, pp. 90–1. See also Carter and Sparrow, *A. E. Housman*.
99 Altick, 'From Aldine to Everyman'; repr. in *Writers, readers and occasions*, p. 178.

buying up odds and ends of different publishers' series and repackaging them under new titles.[100]

As the century wore on, series publishing intensified.[101] In the 1850s and 1860s most series had been priced around 3s 6d or 5s but there was a movement towards cheaper prices in the 1870s and 1890s. This was consistent with the reduction in prices of editions of Scott and Shakespeare noted in the sections above and was linked to the increasing purchasing power of the pound in the period. Sampson Low's Choice Editions of Choice Books shrunk both in price (from 5s in the 1850s, to 2s 6d in the 1870s and 1s in the 1890s) and in size (from small quarto to small octavo to royal 16mo).[102] In the 1880s Routledge and Cassell entered into an all-out price war. Routledge had begun their Universal Library in 1883 at a shilling a volume; two years later Cassell started their National Library at threepence in paper and sixpence in cloth; Routledge responded with the World Library at the same price and the rivalry spilled over into a dispute in the pages of *The Times*.[103]

Some of these series sold prodigiously. In 1894 Frederick Warne claimed to have sold 6 million copies of the Chandos Classics, which had begun in 1868, while Cassell's National Library achieved total sales of some 7 million volumes.[104] As new books by contemporary writers were relatively expensive such reprints proved attractive to the book purchaser. Augustine Birrell's 1894 observation, that 'you may buy twenty books by dead men at the price of one work by a living man', was calculated on the difference between the price of a six-shilling new novel and a threepenny classic.[105] As the author Grant Allen commented in 1889: 'who will care to buy a new book by a rising author when he can get the pick of Thackeray, and Dickens, and Carlyle, and Macaulay any day for a shilling?'[106]

Newnes stripped prices still further in 1896 with the Penny Library of Famous Books. Titles by Scott, Dickens and Dumas among others were issued in eighty or more closely printed pages, with longer novels spread over two or three volumes. The first forty-four penny novels sold an average of nearly 100,000 copies.[107] As Richard Altick judges: 'in the last years of the century, a penny bought a great deal more in both quality and quantity'.[108] W. T. Stead's short-lived Penny Novelist series abridged novels into 30,000 or 40,000 words, selling 6.5 million copies in total. Stead also issued the Penny Poets,

100 *Ibid.*, p. 186.   101 For some tables and statistics, see Howsam, 'Sustained literary ventures'.
102 Altick, 'From Aldine to Everyman', p. 178.   103 *Ibid.*, pp. 181–2.
104 *Ibid.*, p. 191; Nowell-Smith, *The house of Cassell*, p. 109.
105 Birrell, *Essays about men, women and books*, cited by Altick, 'From Aldine to Everyman' p. 179.
106 [Allen] 'The trade of author', p. 265.   107 See Parry, 'George Newnes Limited'.
108 Altick, *The English common reader*, p. 315.

selling 200,000 copies of the first number, Macaulay's *Lays of ancient Rome*. With penny editions, readers could purchase an edition of Macaulay, Scott or Byron for less than one-seventieth of the cost of the first edition of Hardy's *Wessex poems* (1898).

The reductions in price were evidence of the gradual cheapening of literature in the period in general, but publishers had always exploited form and price to appeal to different markets. Moxon's Popular Poets, first issued in 1870 at 3s 6d, was then presented in more expensive formats as Moxon's Royal Poets (7s 6d) and Moxon's Library Poets (5s). In 1882 Warne published editions of Longfellow's poems in four separate series whilst an early catalogue of the Walter Scott Publishing Company, which started out in the early 1880s, listed *Ivanhoe* in nine separate series. Joseph Shaylor observed in 1905 that 'within the past few months fourteen different editions of "Bacon" have been published' and some thirty different editions of Austen's novels were available.[109]

It was common for series to offer a range of binding styles – vellum, gilded leather, cloth, buckram, paper – at different prices. There were even editions in 32mo.[110] Warne's Albion Poets was available in four different bindings and prices: 3s 6d through 5s and 7s 6d to 10s 6d. Mass sales and cheapness was not the only option pursued. Kegan Paul, Trench & Co. made quality of design a priority for its Parchment Library. Begun in 1880, these volumes were bound in parchment at 6s or vellum at 7s 6d and printed at the Chiswick Press.

From the 1880s the educational market became increasingly important with the spread of school and university education. Editions of Shakespeare have already been mentioned but school editions of novelists and poets published at a shilling a volume or less were widespread at the end of the century.[111]

Beyond the formal education sector there was a large but ill-defined market for books for self-educators. The creation of a well-defined and very limited canon here was particularly important, because it offered the educationally insecure a clear and affordable path through the jungle of literature. In the 1880s this path was well defined by Sir John Lubbock who, in a speech as the new principal of the Working Men's College, recommended 'a hundred good books'. This generated a debate that was taken up by magazines and newspapers and led to Routledge, from May 1891 on, producing the series 'Sir John Lubbock's 100 Books'. Other authorities came up with their own lists (frequently using the magical 'one hundred') and other publishers repackaged existing series or launched new ones to catch the fashion. Later some of these

109 Shaylor, 'Reprints and their readers', pp. 542–3.
110 Altick, 'From Aldine to Everyman', p. 345 n. 19.
111 For a brief list, see St Clair, *The reading nation*, pp. 722–3.

series would be offered in luxurious uniform bindings or with their own bookcases.[112]

As textbooks and school editions developed, so too did the movement for editorial rigour. In most of the cheap series, editorial policy had been slight or non-existent, and sometimes volumes were abridged or bowdlerised. With the new century came a new commitment to editorial accuracy and authority. The Walter Scott Publishing Company led the way in the 1880s with its Canterbury Poets and Camelot Classics (which consisted of prose and translations), both issued in monthly shilling volumes.

The new century brought further shilling series, including the World's Classics, which was started by Grant Richards in 1901 and transferred to Oxford University Press in 1905, and Collins Illustrated Pocket Classics, dating from 1903, which sold over 400,000 copies in 1906.[113] The most ambitious in scope and production quality, however, was Everyman's Library, commenced in 1906. The series was edited by Ernest Rhys, who had also edited the Camelot series, and various scholars provided introductions to the volumes. Consisting of non-copyright works, the series was dominated by the classics of English literature, but also embraced American and European literature as well as Greek and Latin classics and works of philosophy and history. The publisher J. M. Dent aimed to issue a thousand volumes which would make up a canon of literary and prose works. Issued at a shilling a volume, 152 volumes appeared in the first year, with titles ranging from Aeschylus to Hans Christian Andersen and Charles Reade. In 1907 Dent was advertising that nearly 3 million volumes had been sold.[114]

The outbreak of war stalled the production of these series, as did the 1911 Copyright Act which extended post-mortem copyright to fifty years. This made it harder to reprint more recent texts. Browning's work up to 1869 was published in Everyman's Library by 1911 but the final two volumes could not appear until 1940. Nevertheless, Everyman and its rivals had started a process of canonisation through relatively cheap publication of classics of English literature. Unlike the nineteenth-century editions, Everyman and the World's Classics made claims to durability and a lasting shelf life and early volumes are still to be found in the twenty-first century decorating the shelves of second-hand bookshops.

---

112 See Feltes, *Literary capital*, pp. 41–8.   113 Keir, *The house of Collins*, p. 220.
114 Turner, 'The Camelot series, Everyman's Library, and Ernest Rhys', p. 28.

12

Science, technology and mathematics

JAMES A. SECORD

Hailed as the apotheosis of reason and progress, science became central to defining the meaning of print in the nineteenth and early twentieth centuries. For many readers, cheap periodicals and other products of factory publishing were tangible evidence of spiritual and material progress. Specialist publishing grew rapidly and was often seen as a key sector for innovation. The relation between knowledge and print also changed dramatically, as discovery came to mean previously unknown findings announced in a published journal intended for specialist practitioners. Yet we know surprisingly little about how the press was used after the 1830s to announce novelties and more generally to create images of science and invention.

Since the 1960s, interest in the making of science and technology in the Victorian and Edwardian eras has burgeoned. With a few exceptions, however, the dominant theme of this new literature has been the emergence of the social role of the specialist practitioner. It has been shown how science was transformed through the creation of appropriate institutions, including the British Association for the Advancement of Science and a reformed Royal Society, as well as new educational structures and fresh possibilities for employment in government, industry and the universities. Underlying all these was the emergence of the 'scientist' – a term invented in 1833 but which became widely used only towards the century's end – as gentlemanly, vocational ideals were replaced by the notion that science should be a paid career, independent of church and aristocratic patronage. Although simple teleological models of professionalisation have been rejected, the key questions have continued to involve issues of social organisation and identity.[1]

---

1 The best surveys of this highly sophisticated literature include Barton, '"Men of science"'; Desmond, 'Redefining the X axis'; and White, *Thomas Huxley: making the 'man of science'*. I am grateful to Anne Secord, David McKitterick and Jon Topham for exceptionally helpful comments, and to Chitra Ramalingam for allowing me to refer to her unpublished essay.

443

An approach informed by the history of print shows that this view of the changing structure of science is radically incomplete and sometimes just plain wrong. For it ignores, or at best treats as peripheral, the forms in which knowledge appeared, assuming that publication in specialist periodicals was already established as the only legitimate means for announcing new discoveries, thus downplaying other methods such as conversation, books, letters and museum displays. In this way, it presupposes that specific forums for communicating knowledge were ready to hand, and firmly in the control of a well-defined group of specialists. Except in works devoted to book history, the transmission of knowledge into print is usually treated as relatively transparent. Carrying out procedures in the laboratory, creating scientific organisations and attracting new practitioners: all these are assumed to require work. But the forms of publication, with a few exceptions, have been taken for granted.

What would happen if we considered the story of modern science through the study of printed communication in the widest sense? This chapter will suggest that changes in publishing, printing and readership practices are central to the transformation of science. The debate about the forms knowledge should take was at every point implicated in the making of knowledge. What was the appropriate way for knowledge to appear? Who should be in control of publication? How could technical books and journals – often comprehensible to a tiny minority of not particularly wealthy readers – be financially viable propositions in the volatile publishing market?

To tackle these questions involves considering an extraordinary range of publications, from double-elephant natural history folios to newspapers and 'wee bookies' for children.[2] My focus will be on the sciences, with some attention to the very different circumstances prevailing in mathematical and technological publishing. After surveying controversies about knowledge in relation to the machine in the early industrial era, I will first turn to the periodical, which during the nineteenth century emerged as the form characteristically associated with both specialist publication and accessible science journalism. The second half of the chapter will look at the role of the book: reflective surveys, reference works and introductory manuals intended to entice beginners and educate students. The book, as I hope to show, remained significant for the sciences right through the century, far longer than would be expected given the common (but false) assumption that research articles were all that really mattered. Recent historical studies – which have focussed on children's

---

2 For 'wee booky', see *Literary Gazette* 8 August 1835.

books, accessible primers and the general periodical press – have provided a far broader and richer picture.

One aim of this chapter is to suggest that works aimed at wide readerships played a vital part in the emergence of specialist forms of publication. It is all too easy to see approaches based on publishing and reading as relevant either to so-called 'popular' science, or to the publication of specialist monographs and periodicals, but not as a way of breaking down this easy divide and transforming our vision of the subject as a whole. The forging of the sciences as a distinctive field of enquiry was the product of a much wider contest about access to print and the audiences for knowledge. To set the scene, I want to take us back to 1830 and a virulent debate about the shape of knowledge in print.

The decline of science?

Intellectual debate in the first half of the nineteenth century was dominated by reform agitation and the coming of the machine.[3] Innovations such as the steam press, machine-made paper and distribution by railway were hailed as transforming practices which had changed little since the introduction of printing in the fifteenth century. In previous centuries, the dominance of manual labour in the production of printed works meant, at an extreme, that it was far from certain that two copies of a book were the same. In works such as George Dodd's *Days at the factories* (1843), industrial production was celebrated for its clarity and lack of ambiguity.[4] The power of print, which had depended on an assumption of fixity, appeared to be enhanced. Uniformity extended to the finest details of the printed page: machine-made types made it more likely that every letter was identical; wood- and steel-engravings did not wear out nearly so fast as copper ones had done; the making of stereotype plates in plaster or laminated paper ensured that different printings of a work could be made without the need for resetting type; machine-made paper was uniform and smooth, unlike the hand-made products of the previous centuries.

It is often assumed that mechanised printing made knowledge more secure, but in fact the early industrial era witnessed the most profound debates about science since the seventeenth century. As the revived Baconian slogan put it, 'Knowledge is power', and for many readers that power was epitomised by the manual-operated hand-frame printing press. Relatively inexpensive,

3 Berg, *The machinery question and the making of political economy.*
4 Johns, *The nature of the book.*

such presses produced an outpouring of radical literature in the years around 1830. An unprecedented expansion in literacy created audiences who looked for knowledge relevant to Chartism, socialism and other working-class movements. The freethinker Richard Carlile railed against the failure of scientific men to acknowledge the revolutionary power of their discoveries. From this perspective, an understanding of the facts of nature offered tools for undermining clerical authority and state oppression.[5] Opposing this view, middle-class entrepreneurs such as Charles Knight hoped to subvert the use of knowledge for radical ends by flooding the market with safe, reliable and standardised science produced through the new machine-based printing technologies at prices working-class publishers found hard to beat.[6] As publisher for the Society for the Diffusion of Useful Knowledge (f.1826), Knight had extolled the virtues of the *Penny Magazine* (f.1831), the *Penny Cyclopaedia* (1833–43) and other ventures which brought illustrations of natural history, invention and the fine arts to hundreds of thousands of readers.[7] The aim of creating a rational, educated workforce safe from radical temptation also inspired William and Robert Chambers of Edinburgh, whose firm became the nation's leading publishers of inexpensive part-works and informative tracts.[8] These hopes for the easy diffusion of science as a carrier of moral messages, however, proved a chimera, as readers could not be so easily controlled.

Middle-class publishers and radical agitators alike tended to value science for its propaganda value, using established knowledge to demonstrate the rights or wrongs of the existing order of society. Some working-class readers, in contrast, aimed not so much to find moral messages in science, but rather to participate in its making. Particularly in the north of England, handloom weavers, shoemakers and other artisans became keen observers in esoteric areas of science such as the identification of rare mosses. They demonstrated that labouring people, working in concert, could contribute to the most skilled forms of practice. Their communally held libraries of scientific books, kept in the pubs where they met on Sundays, were potent political symbols of working-class achievement. Works such as the *Penny Magazine* or Carlile's pamphlets had little place on the shelves of these pub libraries, not so much because they were ideologically charged, but because they lacked the detailed information needed for participating in scientific practice. Instead the artisans valued authoritative works of classification and identification,

---

5 Desmond, 'Artisan resistance and evolution in Britain, 1819–1848'; Johnson, '"Really useful knowledge"'.
6 Topham, 'Science and popular education in the 1830s'.   7 Gray, *Charles Knight*.
8 Cooney, 'Publishers for the people'.

such as James Sowerby and James Edward Smith's *English botany* (1790–1824; 3d edn, 12 vols., 1863–86) which gave access to existing networks of elite practitioners.[9]

Different answers to the question of how science was to be used and pursued were thus embodied in different forms of print. Chemistry, for example, was for many educated authors a 'philosophical' subject centred on disputes about the nature of matter. In such cases, publication traditionally took the form of a theoretical treatise, usually an octavo, aimed at an educated genteel readership. Such works belonged on the shelf with systematic theology, Genesis commentaries and abstract metaphysics. But reprinted in radical miscellanies or reinterpreted by the socialist followers of Robert Owen, they also could be associated with freethinking materialism, with the chemist imagined as a potential agent for political liberation. Others saw chemistry as concerned not with philosophies of matter but with hands-on laboratory or factory experience, and published cookbook-like lists and brief notices of new compounds. During the 1840s, the practical aspects of the subject came to the fore, especially in agriculture, so that Justus von Liebig's *Familiar letters on chemistry* (1843) became an international best-seller.[10]

Behind these conflicting views was a fundamental and long-standing question about how knowledge should be related to the act of publication. Across the class spectrum, many settings for science tended to stress the significance of conversation and the delivery of papers at meetings. This was certainly true for many working people, who identified knowledge as embodied skill rather than as words printed on paper.[11] At the other end of the social spectrum, the young naturalist Charles Darwin noted that 'geology is at present very oral' and the only reason for publishing was 'proof of earnestness'.[12] A good example here is the debate about the discovery of the composition of water. In Britain, the natural philosopher Henry Cavendish was often awarded the contested palm of discovery over the inventor James Watt, despite the fact that the latter had published his findings and the former had not.[13] An outstanding collection of books, minerals, fossils or dried plants could place one in the highest rank in certain fields. Those with sufficient wealth could become patrons, encouraging work along certain lines and providing political connections and administrative experience. The botanist Robert Brown and the

9 Secord, 'Science in the pub'.
10 The range of different approaches is apparent in Brock, *The Fontana history of chemistry*.
11 Secord, 'Science in the pub', pp. 291–4.
12 Quoted in Secord, 'How scientific conversation became shop talk', p. 30.
13 Miller, *Discovering water*.

geologist George Bellas Greenough published almost nothing and yet were at the forefront of their respective sciences. The most telling expression of this attitude was in elections to the fellowship of the Royal Society, which until changes were introduced after 1847 depended as much upon social status and a general interest in science as it did upon the number or significance of papers published.[14] In these circumstances, the great experimenter Michael Faraday's celebrated dictum 'work, finish, publish' was not only a personal exhortation but advocacy of a particular way of conducting the scientific enterprise.

Especially in fields relating to practical engineering and technology, the virtues of publishing were far from obvious. Why should commercially valuable information be made available to the casual reading public? Such discoveries were either to be kept secret or to be filed as legally enforceable patent claims. In such cases, publication in any form was seen to be inappropriate. Important initiatives were made in putting the details of new machines into print, especially in technical encyclopaedias and periodicals such as the *Mechanics' Magazine* (f.1825); but, more typically, practical knowledge was passed down through the apprentice system, and new inventions and techniques were kept as valuable trade secrets. The leading London chemist William Hyde Wollaston, discoverer of the element palladium, only gave out the receipt for making it malleable shortly before his death.[15]

The most trenchant critique of this view of science came from Charles Babbage. A leading inventor and man of science, active in reforming mathematics in Cambridge, he was best known for developing a government-funded mechanical calculating engine. Babbage aimed his fire at outmoded publication practices in his *Reflections on the decline of science in England, and on some of its causes* (London, 1830), which argued that science in England was in a bad way, and had been declining since the late seventeenth century. The long-term problems had to do with education and with the lack of any inducement to pursue science as a career. The role of publishing was central. Babbage was especially shocked that out of 714 Fellows of the Royal Society, only seventy-two had contributed two or more papers to the *Philosophical Transactions*; in his view, membership of the Society should require this as a minimum.[16] From this perspective, appearing in print defined what it meant to be a man of science. Babbage's model for the way science should work was taken from the continent, especially France, where men of science were given state support and even occupied high political office. For most British observers and many

---

14 MacLeod, 'Whigs and savants'.   15 Goodman, 'Wollaston, William Hyde'.
16 Babbage, *Reflections*, p. 155. On the declinist debate, see Morrell and Thackray, *Gentlemen of science*, pp. 47–52; Hyman, *Charles Babbage*, pp. 88–102.

on the continent, this suggested that French savants were subject to jobbery and intrigue. 'Wealth and dignities', as one pamphleteer wrote, 'acquired at such a price, cannot be objects of envy in the eyes of a philosopher.'[17] Babbage, however, considered such positions as evidence of independence and state recognition.

Reformers like Babbage were especially appalled that scarce resources for publishing in science were squandered. At least £2,000 of Royal Society funds had been expended on the plates for anatomical papers by one individual, who was on the Council voting for their publication. Five tons of the published data of the Royal Greenwich Observatory were sold as waste suitable for pasteboard, although practising astronomers were not allowed free copies.[18] As Babbage was able to show as a result of his intimate knowledge of the printing trade, the publisher John Murray was paid well over the odds to issue the Royal Society's Presidential Discourses, and yet only a handful were sold. Like many reformers, Babbage felt that the only good thing about the *Philosophical Transactions* was their prompt publication. With their wide margins and hot-pressed paper, they were ponderous and expensive, a waste of precious funds.

At the height of the declinist debate, Babbage confronted the problems created by the public's lack of access to engineering and industrial information, arguing that the apprentice-based oral culture of Britain's workshops and factories led to waste and inefficiency. His *On the economy of machinery and manufactures*, published in 1832, made freely available a wide range of hitherto secret practical knowledge. The book's intended publisher, Benjamin Fellowes, was so outraged by revelations about the costs and techniques of book production that Babbage was forced to look to Charles Knight, who shared many of his attitudes towards the free flow of knowledge.

The comments in Babbage's *Decline of science*, often vituperative and narrowly focussed, sparked a much broader debate about the state of British science in relation to publishing. Perhaps the most serious accusations were summed up by the novelist and social commentator Edward Bulwer-Lytton in *England and the English* (1833), which told the story of a learned man, of great scientific attainments but little worldly wealth, who showed a manuscript treatise to 'a publisher of enterprise and capital'. The publisher explained that since only fifty readers would understand profound research in mechanics, that part of the work was 'mere rubbish' from a commercial point of view. But if the learned doctor could expand the chapter of elementary exposition into a volume, the publisher would pay hundreds of pounds for that. As a result, the book of

17 [Moll] *On the alleged decline of science in England*, p. 21.   18 Babbage, *Reflections*, p. 109.

discoveries remained unpublished, while the familiar principles received yet another retelling. 'The time is come', Bulwer-Lytton concluded, 'when nobody will fit out a ship for the intellectual Columbus to discover new worlds, but when everybody will subscribe for his setting up a steam-boat between Calais and Dover.'[19]

Such stories were not just the fancies of a literary imagination: they expressed actual dilemmas that scientific writers faced every day. Take the case of Mary Somerville, who became an iconic figure of the reformist movement after publication of her *Mechanism of the heavens* (1831) – a densely mathematical redaction of Pierre-Simon Laplace's great work on celestial dynamics. Her next work, however, was the much more accessible *On the connexion of the physical sciences* (1834), which expanded upon the themes dealt with in the 'preliminary discourse'. Somerville then completed the manuscript of a concluding volume of the *Mechanism*, which dealt mathematically with topics such as the tides and the rotation of the planets, but this remained unpublished after being rejected by John Murray. From this point onwards she adopted the role of summarising and linking the results of different sciences.[20] Another example is provided by John Vaughan Thompson's *Zoological researches, and illustrations; or natural history of nondescript or imperfectly known animals*, issued in parts from 1828 to 1834, which had to be stopped for lack of sufficient purchasers.

Yet not all that many great works languished unpublished: more often, they were never begun, or appeared in less imposing forms. Writers were able to take up substantial projects only as time and funds allowed. One of the leading students of optics in the first half of the nineteenth century, the Scottish natural philosopher David Brewster, made a living through editing and scientific journalism. On first hearing of Babbage's book on the decline of British science, Brewster claimed that he would have written on 'the heartbreaking subject' himself, but was prevented from doing so by the press of hand-to-mouth literary labours.[21] His own comments did appear, but as a paying review for the *Quarterly*, which noted with barely concealed irony that many potential discoverers were 'torn from the fascination of original research, and compelled to waste their strength in the composition of treatises for periodical works and popular compilations'.[22]

---

19 Bulwer-Lytton, *England and the English*, p. 294.
20 Secord, 'General introduction', in Somerville, *Collected works* 1, pp. xxvi–xxxi, and Brock, 'The public worth of Mary Somerville'.
21 Brewster to Babbage, 12 February 1830, quoted in Morrell and Thackray, *Gentlemen of science*, p. 47. See also Brock, 'Brewster as scientific journalist'.
22 [Brewster] 'Decline of science in England'.

The term 'popular', as a way of distinguishing forms of knowledge accessible to the people from those that were not, occasionally began to be used in the early nineteenth century as a way of marking readerships without specific forms of expertise.[23] Brewster, like Babbage and their allies in the declinist debate, attempted to set up a contrast between original research and derivative writing for periodicals and elementary readers. This was a polemical divide that went against much of the way that science was still being done, for openness to a range of participants was a prized feature of many areas of natural philosophy and natural history.

The problem, as the declinists saw it, was that the genteel patronage and diverse readerships characteristic of the publishing system in Britain had failed to maintain specialist science at the highest international level. The publishing of 'penny' science was burgeoning, while original research either made tiny sales or languished in manuscript. To a surprising degree, scientific and medical publishing was dominated by a few firms, notably Longman & Co. (who in 1837 controlled nearly a third of the trade), so that decisions by a few entrepreneurs were vital to furthering the scientific enterprise.[24] The Royal Society was filled with genteel fellows who paid their membership fees, but had never published. To end this corruption, the reformers called for state support and educational reform. But the answer they found was a series of commercially engineered transformations in the role of the scientific periodical and the introductory textbook.

The magazine of nature

It is easy to assume that the establishment of the *Philosophical Transactions* of the Royal Society of London in the 1660s marked the point at which all new findings had to be announced in something approaching the form of the modern scientific paper. In fact, what it meant for something to be a scientific periodical, and the role of periodical publication regimes within the sciences, was radically uncertain right through the middle of the nineteenth century. This is evident even in so basic an issue as defining priority, where the conventions dominating the announcement of discoveries were much less secure (especially in Britain) than is usually thought. The contrast with the patenting of inventions – a system which had developed during the early stages of the industrial revolution – was clear. An obsession with priority in

23 Topham, 'Publishing "popular science" in early nineteenth-century Britain'; Cooter and Pumfrey, 'Separate spheres and public places'.
24 Topham, 'Scientific publishing', pp. 584–5.

science was usually identified with France, where publication (usually in the weekly *Comptes rendus* of the Paris Académie des Sciences) became essential for anyone who wished to stake a discovery claim. It was part of the career-oriented, centralised system of science that the reformers such as Babbage wished to emulate. In Britain, priority of discovery in science was traditionally assessed in more flexible ways, involving gentlemanly codes of conduct – the sort of 'delicate arrangement' that led to the announcement of the theory of evolution by natural selection by Charles Darwin and Alfred Russel Wallace in the *Proceedings of the Linnean Society*.[25] In France, individual priority would have been secured through either quick publication (no genteel Darwinian delay) or a sealed note deposited with the Academy.

The second and third quarters of the nineteenth century in Britain were thus a period of unexampled experimentation in periodical publication and its place in the making of knowledge. Just as 'science' and 'scientist' were being defined and debated, so too were the very notions of what a scientific publication might be. For almost all of the new specialist organisations founded during the first half of the century, the issuing of printed volumes, usually quarto transactions modelled on those of the Royal Society, was a significant aim. Such publications offered wide margins, large type, good paper and plenty of illustrations, often hand-coloured. Publication was irregular and schedules often stately. Unsurprisingly, the format was expensive, with a single number sometimes costing a guinea. As a result, print-runs were small by contemporary standards, usually 500 to 750, and sales considerably less than that.[26] Most purchasers tended to have a general interest in the subject rather than a vocation for research. The organisations they joined were thus less professional 'learned societies' in our sense of the term, and more like the Athenaeum and other clubs for those with literary and intellectual interests. In this context, publishing transactions offered a way to associate new and potentially controversial sciences such as geology, zoology, comparative anatomy and stellar astronomy with traditional forms of gentlemanly culture. Luxurious production values made a bound set of transactions a suitable acquisition for a gentleman's library, implying that the knowledge they contained was of permanent value.

Just at the time when the number of transactions began to increase, they were challenged by an alternative format of monthly octavo journals produced by commercial entrepreneurs.[27] These grew out of eighteenth-century periodicals

---

25 Browne, *Charles Darwin: the power of place*, pp. 14–42.
26 These figures are based on the Taylor & Francis account books in the St Bride Printing Library.
27 Brock, 'The development of commercial science journals in Victorian Britain'; also Brock, 'Science periodicals'. The shift from quarto to octavo was first noted in Cannon, *Science in culture*.

such as the *Gentleman's Magazine*, which had encouraged informal communication among the learned. Financial considerations, as much as priority, were significant in encouraging the dominance of such periodicals. From the perspective of a commercial publisher or an independent society, commencing a journal was much less risky than issuing books. If sales proved disappointing and subscribers too few, publication could simply cease, without leaving a warehouse full of expensive unsold stock.

A handful of these commercial periodicals proved exceptionally long-lived, notably the *Philosophical Magazine*, founded in 1798. It did this partly by absorbing the competition but also by becoming more specialised. By the 1830s its scope had already narrowed from the entire circle of the sciences to a primary focus on chemistry and the physical sciences. The *Philosophical Magazine* was published by one of the key firms in the London scientific book trade, run initially by Richard Taylor and then by William Francis. It had originally included natural history, but pressures of space and an increasingly diverse readership led Taylor to establish the *Annals of Natural History* (f.1838, from 1840 known as the *Annals and Magazine of Natural History*). Like the *Philosophical Magazine*, the *Annals* emerged the hardy survivor of a much larger group of natural history monthlies, although sales remained relatively small, with a print-run of only 500 copies.[28]

Despite precarious sales, these commercial monthlies led the way in redefining the meaning of a scientific paper in Britain during the crucial decades of the 1820s and 1830s. By emphasising frequent and regular publication, they stressed timeliness over permanence, practicality over luxurious presentation. They looked and read more like the journals that were appearing across the Channel, such as the *Annales de Chimie* and Poggendorf's *Annalen der Physik*. The papers they published were shorter and focussed on specific new findings: on discovery rather than comprehensive exposition. They were less like monographs, and more like articles in newspapers and weekly periodicals. From the 1820s, the format, frequency and aims of the commercial science journal began to be imitated in scientific clubland, and ultimately at the Royal Society itself. The newer societies, which prided themselves on being progressive and willing to change, were the first to do this; thus the Geological Society began to issue *Proceedings* in 1826 and the Royal Astronomical Society issued its *Monthly Notices* from 1827. Usually appearing in issues of between sixteen and thirty-two pages, these offered an account of the meetings for those who had been

28 Brock and Meadows, *The lamp of learning*, esp. pp. 93–100; Sheets-Pyenson, 'From the North to Red Lion Court'; Sheets-Pyenson, 'A measure of success'.

unable to attend, and a printed record of results for establishing international priority. Because they appeared so quickly, the proceedings of organisations such as the Geological Society and the Royal Astronomical Society became a major outlet for quick announcements: a new comet, a unique fossil, the results of a summer's fieldwork. Only much later did the older societies follow suit: the Linnean Society in 1855, the Royal Society in 1856. Notably, too, when the British Association for the Advancement of Science began to meet in 1831, it offered both opportunities for very quick publication – through newspapers and literary weeklies such as the *Athenaeum* – and the more permanent form of a relatively inexpensive annual report. This was one of the ways that it identified its project with the more general enterprise of reform.

By the mid-1830s, transactions were clearly losing the battle of formats. Only the best-funded elite organisations (the Linnean, the Royal and the Cambridge Philosophical Society) continued with the prestige quartos, albeit in a modified form. Some aspiring new groups, such as the London Electrical Society, made the mistake of issuing a showy volume of transactions that used up all of their resources.[29] In this, they learned the hard way what the leaders of the Geological Society had known for years: it was easy to get fellows to pay the subscription needed to put some letters after their name, but hard to get them to pay for specialist publications. Henry De la Beche drew a caricature of double-entry bookkeeping to make the point (fig. 12.1). On the debit side, an ordinary meeting hears a gloomy report on finances, which are faltering because too few fellows are purchasing the transactions; but on the credit side, they seem eager to applaud the accomplishments made in the science during the year at a costly dinner.

At the same time there were striking changes within the world of commercial science periodicals, challenging the established titles. The 1830s and 1840s witnessed the rise of what was called 'class' journalism, appealing to non-specialist readers with specific interests in (say) law, architecture, gardening, economics or art. The focussed appeal of science and invention meant that these subjects tended to lead the way in the development of this genre. Publishers issued a wide range of titles to test the market. The earliest and most successful dealt with mechanical inventions, with a stress on letters to the editor and informal reviews, as in the weekly *Mechanics' Magazine* (f.1825). Monthlies included the lively *Zoologist* (f.1843) and *Phytologist* (f.1841), both issued by the enterprising

29 As Morus, in 'Currents from the underworld', shows, the Electrical Society went on to issue less expensive proceedings, but it continued to be plagued by a failure to match its publication programme to the potential market.

Figure 12.1 Henry De la Beche complains of those who become members of the Geological Society of London and attend expensive annual dinners, but fail to purchase the published *Transactions*. The lithograph, issued c.1830, had 'Only 15 copies printed – small paper – price 0 – to suit "Illustrious" Fellows as vont buy their own Transactions.' (By permission of the Director, British Geological Survey, GSM 1/558, p. 4)

Quaker naturalist and publisher Edward Newman, who mocked the competing *Annals and Magazine of Natural History* for its 'prescriptive technicalities and chartered obscurities'.[30] In the physical sciences, Sturgeon's *Annals of Electricity* (f.1837) lambasted the formality of the existing periodicals.

The commercial journals were issued by small publishers and printers, most of whom were religious dissenters hoping to encourage contributions from many hands and open debate. By finding the right mix of material and encouraging discussion, it was just about possible to keep a regular monthly journal of this kind afloat. Labours of love, they almost never made money and usually disappeared without a trace after a few issues. Eschewing politics, their general outlook was democratic and egalitarian. Unlike most of the other journals already mentioned, they did not rely on referee reports, taking pride in

30 Brock and Meadows, *The lamp of learning*, p. 126.

printing just about everything they received. Advocating a different ideal of the scientific polity, they set themselves apart from the journals emanating from the scientific societies, viewing those as bastions of privilege. They were, it is important to stress, not just journals of popularised science; rather, they created a forum in which distinctions between 'popular' and 'specialist' were rejected for a more open definition of 'the people'. In contrast, for many within the elite of British science, chatty commercial journals such as the *Zoologist* and *Geologist* were beyond the pale; they did not publish there, unwilling to see their work in such a promiscuous setting. Thus the *Geologist*'s editor was severely reprimanded for reporting in print the discussion after one of the Geological Society's celebrated meetings.[31]

At mid-century, then, different types of periodicals were battling it out for dominance. That these embodied different conceptions of the aim and purpose of science is evident from the fierce debates that occurred whenever one of the scientific societies attempted to change its publication format. The Geological Society adopted a compromise whereby only those papers requiring elaborate illustrations were republished in transactions; otherwise the proceedings were seen as the journal of record. By 1845 even this solution was seen to be unsatisfactory, and a new title, the *Quarterly Journal of the Geological Society of London*, replaced them both in a move widely welcomed by reformers.[32] Change was even more hotly debated at the Royal Society, where (as we have seen) many thought the mode of publication was a waste of money. As a compromise, the *Philosophical Transactions* remained a large quarto, but from the 1840s used a smaller font, smaller margins and narrower line spacing. In these subtle ways did reform insinuate itself even in the standard-bearer of gentlemanly publication. The Royal Society, with its wealthy fellowship and ties to the state, was unusual in having to face the pressures of commerce only indirectly. For most of those involved, from the Royal Astronomical Society's council to individual entrepreneurs, keeping a scientific periodical afloat was a constant challenge.

Specialist journals and professional men

The uneasy alliance between the specialist interests of practitioners and a variety of commercially viable genres and formats lasted from the late 1830s through the 1860s. In the decades that followed, a fundamental transformation

---

31 See the letter printed in Woodward, *The history of the Geological Society of London*, p. 146.
32 On the Geological Society's publications, see Rudwick, 'Historical origins of the Geological Society's *Journal*'.

took place which created, in broad terms, the publishing regime in which British science would operate for the following century.

This change involved three elements. First of these was the impact on the printing and publishing industries of new, science-based technologies, notably photography, machine engineering and scientific management. Photography proved potentially useful in astronomy, physiognomy, physical geography and other fields in which drawings and wood-engravings were generally found to be incapable of producing reliable testimony. By the end of the century, in these fields photographic reproduction by half-tone had largely replaced engraving as the standard method for reproducing illustrations in journals and books. Colour printing, which had emerged in the middle of the century in a few niche markets, was much more common by its end, either in expensive specialist monographs or in works produced for a mass market, such as school atlases and wall charts. Science-based machine engineering made possible new high-speed presses, while chemical technology provided inexpensive paper based on wood-pulp. Typesetting by machine, despite fierce union opposition, replaced hand composition on all but the most technically demanding work. From the 1880s, the American Frederick Winslow Taylor and others concerned with industrial efficiency attempted to apply the lessons of experimental science to the management of production processes. These innovations often involved considerable capital costs and resistance from workers, and were especially important in the production of cheap newspapers and books.

A second change involved the world of specialist science publishing more directly. The older family firms such as Murray and Longman, which had catered for the needs of gentlemanly science, were supplemented by newcomers more in tune with current intellectual trends, such as Routledge, Macmillan and Kegan Paul. Just as the previous generation of publishers had relied on associations with genteel scientific circles, so too did men such as Alexander Macmillan exploit academic connections and other associations with leaders of science.

Third, educational reform led to a rise in demand for scientific textbooks and reference works at all levels. These changes increased the overall significance of scientific and technical works within the publishing industry; and made specialist works depend less upon private patronage and local cultivators, and more upon educational institutions and the state. Forms of publication which had previously depended upon attracting a range of readers could now be undertaken in the expectation (or at least the hope) that they need only appeal to those who defined their interests in the subject as 'professional'.

The transition is clear from the early history of the weekly periodical *Nature* (f.1869). For although *Nature* was supported by the scientific careerists and eventually emerged as the leading international weekly for science in Europe, it initially attempted to appeal to a wider readership. Advertisements stress its attractive illustrations and accessibility, and early issues provided free portraits of famous scientists such as Michael Faraday and Charles Darwin. As Alexander Macmillan explained to William Thomson (Lord Kelvin), the journal was 'meant to be popular in part, but also sound, and part devoted specifically to scientific men and their intercourse with each other'.[33] In format and content, *Nature* thus presented itself as continuing the traditions of the *Athenaeum, Reader, Illustrated London News* and other periodicals intended to encourage topical discussion. Even with this attempt to address a broader public, *Nature* lost money; the publisher kept it going largely because of the access it provided to the best authors in London. It began to break even only when the number of active practitioners in the sciences increased towards the end of the century.

The outstanding trend in periodicals was specialisation. The refocussing of *Nature* illustrates the emergence of the 'scientific periodical' from the more general intellectual weekly, but it was unusual in attempting to reach the full range of scientific disciplines, which it did largely by combining general scientific news and opinion with specialised research reports. The tightening of disciplinary focus is also evident in the continuing evolution of the commercial *Philosophical Magazine*, which by the century's end was a physics journal which published little on what was seen as chemistry, let alone astronomy or geology. It played a dominant role in debates about matter theory during the early twentieth century, with key papers by Niels Bohr, Ernest Rutherford and J. J. Thomson on atomic structure and quantum theory.[34] Across the range of the sciences, founding a journal became a way of furthering new approaches and the work of the academic research schools that were such a characteristic feature of scientific innovation in this period. At Cambridge, the *Journal of Physiology* (f.1878) provided a channel for publication of work in Michael Foster's school of experimental physiology, while the *Journal of Genetics* (f.1910) furthered William Bateson's attempts to create a new science of heredity. Although these periodicals were the products of private enterprise, they were both printed by Cambridge University Press, which also published

33 'Centenary supplement', *Nature* 1 November 1969, pp. 417–76, at p. 438; see also p. 424.
34 See R. MacLeod's contributions to the 'Centenary supplement'; Gooday, '"Nature" in the laboratory'.

Karl Pearson's *Biometrika* (f.1901) and the *British Journal of Psychology* (f.1904).[35]
By the early twentieth century, such journals increasingly featured an international cast of authors and editors, and a correspondingly world-wide range of subscribers in universities, technical institutes and public libraries. They were, in effect, a natural outgrowth of the earlier tradition of commercial science periodicals, attractive to publishers looking for opportunities to expand the realm of profitable science publishing by using improved postal networks and opportunities for rapid communication.

At the core of the new way of pursuing knowledge was the redefinition of key genres for science. In particular, the scientific article achieved something close to its current form – and certainly its dominance within science – during the final decades of the nineteenth century. The number of scientific periodical titles in Europe and America, as Derek J. De Solla Price claimed in the 1960s, increased exponentially during the nineteenth century, from under a hundred to about 10,000 by its end.[36] Although there are obvious problems with Price's analysis (not least, his use of an unchanging definition of a scientific periodical) it does suggest the scale of change in the century's final decades. The work that had to go into redefining the relations between science and publishing in this period is clear from one of its greatest monuments, the Royal Society *Catalogue of Scientific Papers*, which began to be published in 1867. The brief, initially to include only articles on chemistry and physics, was soon broadened to include 'all the branches of Natural Knowledge for the promotion of which the Royal Society was instituted, excluding matter of a purely technical or professional character'.[37] Writings in periodicals such as the *Mechanic's Magazine* and *Scientific American* were definitively excluded, as were reflective essays in the *Edinburgh Review* and the other major quarterly journals. Announcements of new comets and other celestial bodies counted only if they appeared in the Royal Astronomical Society's *Monthly Notices* or the *Astronomische Nachrichten* – not in *The Times* or other newspapers, which had long played a major role in communication among observational astronomers. Anything in the realm of the 'literary' was explicitly excluded. The *Catalogue* was not simply a response to the vast growth in the volume of published science; rather, it retrospectively enforced a rigid and in many ways anachronistic definition of the 'scientific paper' on to the entire nineteenth century.

---

35 McKitterick, *A history of Cambridge University Press* 3, pp. 168–9.
36 Price, *Little science, big science*.
37 Royal Society of London, *Catalogue of scientific papers* 1, p. iv.

Bringing the sciences to book

The increasing dominance of periodicals is often seen as something unique to the sciences, but in fact a glance at statistics shows that it was part of a wider trend. By 1907, only 17.1 per cent of the printing industries' net output involved books, while 28.2 per cent came from periodicals and newspapers.[38] Many of the advantages of periodical publication applied not only to the sciences, but also to other forms of writing. Notably, the serial format made it possible to tailor print-runs more closely to the market than was possible with books. Costs were spread out for booksellers and readers alike; and for those concerned with such matters, publishing in periodicals offered a way to establish priority. In some fields, especially chemistry and experimental physics, these issues dominated to the extent that almost all original research throughout the nineteenth and early twentieth centuries would at first glance appear to have been announced in articles. For all the advantages of this format, however, the book retained specific roles of great significance: as a practical form of reference, as a means for opening out an extended argument, and as a symbol. Periodicals tended to end up in a smaller range of specialist libraries, while books could go on many different shelves and were more often noticed in public debate and discussion.[39]

A broad spectrum of books was issued, the most significant defining entire disciplines and traditions of research. Such 'reflective' works, which considered the aims and purposes of knowledge, were especially characteristic of the decade surrounding the first reform bill in 1832. Works such as Mary Somerville's *On the connexion of the physical sciences* (1834), Charles Lyell's *Principles of geology* (1830–3) and John Herschel's *Preliminary discourse on the study of natural philosophy* (1831) offered reflections on the meaning of particular sciences and their wider goals. They were explicitly not textbooks, although modern readers have sometimes mistaken them as such; rather, they invited a broad reading public to think about the overall shape of disciplines and their underlying principles.[40]

Such works drew on a long-standing British tradition of the philosophical treatise, as exemplified by Adam Smith's *Wealth of nations* (1776) and Isaac Newton's *Principia mathematica* (1687). They borrowed from the French genre of a 'preliminary discourse' preceding an extended treatise or encyclopaedia,

---

38 Eliot, *Some patterns and trends in British publishing*, p. 42.
39 For further reflection on the continuing importance of books, see James, 'Books on the natural sciences in the nineteenth century'.
40 Yeo, *Defining science*; Secord, *Victorian sensation*, pp. 42–76.

as in the case of Samuel Taylor Coleridge's 'Treatise on method' for the *Encyclopaedia metropolitana* in 1818. Not only did such works often sell well, they were also widely read through extracts in reviews. Such works offered opportunities for considering knowledge of nature in relation to issues of the day – questions that might be considered inappropriate for scientific meetings and specialist periodicals, which attempted to keep aloof from political and religious disputes.

The openness of the reflective genre was especially significant in providing a forum for potentially explosive debates about the sciences of mind and the evolution of species. The London publisher John Churchill, best known for medical textbooks and monographs on anatomy and physiology, found in 1844 that he had an unexpected sensation on his hands in the anonymous *Vestiges of the natural history of creation*, which for the first time combined an encyclopaedic range of sciences into an evolutionary story based on a law of development, the 'universal gestation of nature' from gaseous fire-mist to the future elevation of the human race. *Vestiges* brought evolution – a subject that had been canvassed in medical schools and freethought 'Halls of Science' – into middle-class homes and the very heart of public debate. By the time *On the origin of species* appeared in 1859, the reaction to an evolutionary origin of mankind was less violent than is usually assumed, not only because of *Vestiges* but also because it was harder to dismiss a respectable author like Darwin appearing under a respectable imprint like John Murray.[41] The *Origin*, as Darwin had foreseen, would appeal both to 'scientific' and 'semiscientific' readers, and it became the leading example of a series of accessible works on evolutionary topics in the latter half of the nineteenth century. This was a vein quarried with great success not only by Murray, but also by Longman, Williams & Norgate, Macmillan, Kegan Paul and many other firms.[42]

Works in the reflective tradition found an easy place on booksellers' lists alongside titles in philosophy, history, biography and doctrinal theology, fields in which books continued to be a dominant form. John W. Parker, London-based publisher to the University of Cambridge, published many such works, including William Whewell's three-volume *History of the inductive sciences* (1837), two volumes by the same author on the *Philosophy of the inductive sciences* (1840), and John Stuart Mill's competing *System of logic* (1843). In the second half of the century, Macmillan emerged as a key publisher in this field, following out the publisher's personal policy of encouraging a fruitful

41 Dawson, *Darwin, literature and Victorian respectability*; Browne, *Charles Darwin: the power of place*.
42 Secord, *Victorian sensation*; on the later history of the evolutionary epic, see Lightman, *Victorian popularizers of science*, pp. 219–94.

dialogue between science and religion. His firm published many important books on both sides of the Darwinian debate as well as specialised treatises such as William Stanley Jevons's two-volume *Principles of science* (1874).

The tradition of reflective works continued into the early twentieth century, with frequent reprints of works such as Karl Pearson's *Grammar of science* (1892) spurred on by the rise of 'middlebrow' audiences eager to come to terms with exciting new developments in physical theory, scientific psychology and modern biology. The International Scientific Series, an Anglo-American initiative which published ninety-eight books between 1872 and 1911, aimed to prove 'an elegant and valuable library of popular science, fresh in treatment, attractive in form, strong in character, moderate in price, and indispensable to all who care for the acquisition of solid and serviceable knowledge'.[43] A similar readership was targeted with reissued 'classics'. J. M. Dent's Everyman series included books by Faraday, Huxley and Hugh Miller, all of which were highly successful. Meanwhile Alfred Watts's Rationalist Press issued books by Ernst Haeckel, John Tyndall and Richard Carlile. After the copyright on Darwin's *Origin* lapsed in 1909, a wide variety of publishers reprinted it, Murray issuing the work for the first time in paperback. Scientific titles tended to be defined in such lists by the company they kept.

Particularly in more speculative fields, reflective works in science graded into imaginative fiction and poetry.[44] Thomas Carlyle's *Sartor resartus*, first published as a serial in *Fraser's Magazine* in 1833–4 and then as a separate book, was explicitly presented as a natural philosophy of clothes and a contribution to the science of man, as well as being a mock autobiography and an introduction to Teutonic philosophy. Throughout the rest of the century it inspired a range of literary treatments of scientific subjects, including the famous evolutionary dream of Charles Kingsley's fictional working-man's autobiography, *Alton Locke* (1850). As Alfred Tennyson's *In memoriam* (1850) and Elizabeth Barrett Browning's *Aurora Leigh* (1856) suggested, poetry could provide a way of intervening in public scientific debates.

In certain fields books held an overwhelming significance as a way of reporting original results from the laboratory and field. This was not a residual role, but related to the continuing association of science with museums.[45] In a period when much scientific work was dominated by the close analysis of objects

43 Howsam, *Kegan Paul*, p. 33. See also Howsam, 'An experiment with science for the nineteenth-century book trade'; and MacLeod, 'Evolutionary internationalism and commercial enterprise in science'.
44 Beer, *Darwin's plots*, and more generally Beer, *Open fields*.
45 Pickstone, 'Museological science?'

displayed in public and private cabinets, books provided a form of virtual museum. Publication of a substantial treatise on a single subject, often in several volumes, became the touchstone of an author devoted to learning as a vocation. This model of publication, like so much in nineteenth-century British science, derived from continental models from the late eighteenth and early nineteenth centuries, especially great works such as Pierre-Simon Laplace's great *Mécanique céleste* (1798–1827) and Georges Cuvier's *Ossemens fossiles* (1812). In the wider context of the reform debates, maintaining science as a part of polite culture was of considerable political significance. The aristocratic Whigs, notorious in the eighteenth century for dissipation and gambling, were especially anxious to demonstrate moral probity through intellectual leadership. Patronage of fine books and involvement in projects for publishing scientific results were seen as a means towards this end.

Especially in natural history, geology and the study of machines, specialist books of these kinds could be rendered viable by appealing to a constituency wider than that composed of actively researching practitioners. John Phillips's *Illustrations of the geology of Yorkshire* (1829–36) and Roderick Murchison's *Silurian system* (1839), with their wide margins, coloured plates and fine printing, explicitly addressed an audience among the country gentry, whose interest in the subject was motivated by a combination of interests in agriculture and mining.[46] Such works assimilated the new science of geology into older traditions of local antiquarianism. This was not only a way of making science theologically and politically safe; it invited potential purchasers to see such books as belonging on the same shelf as works on classics and theology. A large format and attractive hand-coloured illustrations could attract wealthy collectors and bibliophiles. In this way, relatively esoteric works describing new species could reach a larger readership – and hence the break-even point for publishers – than the tiny handful of expert botanists, geologists or zoologists.[47]

Works describing more specific groups of objects, or requiring substantial illustration, inevitably posed challenges in reaching break-even point, as publication could be expensive and the number of readers using them for research was vanishingly small. Individual entrepreneurs often organised the self-publication of such works, canvassing for subscribers among the aristocracy and gentry and organising production using family members and an inner

46 On the publication of Murchison's books, see Thackray, 'R. I. Murchison's *Silurian system* (1839)'; Thackray, 'R. I. Murchison's *Geology of Russia* (1845)'; and Thackray, 'R. I. Murchison's *Siluria* (1854 and later)'. These short articles remain among the few serious studies of the production of specific scientific works in the period after 1830.

47 Secord, 'Botany on a plate', at pp. 33–5.

circle of collaborators. Subscription publishing remained a significant way of attracting patrons in illustrated natural history works long after it ceased to be commonly used elsewhere in the publishing industry. Outstanding examples include John James Audubon's *Birds of America* (1827–39), James Bateman's outsized book on orchids (1837–43) and Edward Lear's *Illustrations of the family Psittacidae, or parrots* (1832), printed by Charles Hullmandel. Lear had begun as an artist working with John Gould, the artist and publisher of works such as the *Mammals of Australia* (1845–53).[48] Even for the wealthy, such volumes were notable acquisitions. Sir Charles Bunbury, an expert on fossil plants, particularly treasured Joseph Hooker's costly Antarctic flora as a gift from his wife Frances in celebration of their wedding anniversary.[49]

One solution to the problem of cost was to publish in parts, thus assimilating books more closely to a serial format and spreading the costs of production and purchase over a longer period of time.[50] The issues were in many respects similar to those used to market Dickens's novels, as a way of avoiding the excessive costs associated with the three-decker novel. Subscribers were offered not only the opportunity to purchase a substantial work in instalments; each instalment typically offered an inducement to purchase, often a set number of plates. The attractions were not those of narrative suspense (in fact, parts often ended mid-sentence, sometimes mid-word) but rather those of completion and pleasure in fine printing. By the end of the nineteenth century, many of these connoisseurs viewed natural history plate books as the equivalent of imperial trophies, a manifestation of the triumphs of empire that could be shelved in their homes.

Gorgeous illustrations, which make these works so collectible today, thereby broadened the appeal of visually striking natural history subjects such as mammals, birds and flowers. In a few fields – notably botany, zoology and ornithology – the continuing interest of collectors and bibliophiles made it possible to produce monographs that could also be used by specialists. A sudden blossoming of public interest, as in the fern and seaweed crazes around mid-century, similarly encouraged the appearance of detailed and specialised monographs on groups of organisms that might in other circumstances have been deemed unprofitable.[51] Such works were often issued in both coloured and uncoloured versions, the latter targeted at active practitioners unable to afford the extra cost.

---

48 For examples of these books, see Desmond, *Great natural history books and their creators*; Blunt and Stearn, *The art of botanical illustration*; and Knight, *Natural science books in English 1600–1900*.
49 Bunbury, *Memorials of Sir C. J. F. Bunbury. 2. Middle life*, p. 136, journal entry for 3 June 1853.
50 Price, 'Publication in parts'.
51 For these interests, see Allen, *The Victorian fern craze* and Allen, 'Tastes and crazes'.

Many topics that fascinated practising naturalists, however, did not lend themselves to this kind of treatment. The increasing dominance of classifications based on internal anatomy rather than on external characters tended to make gorgeously coloured books of plates less relevant to working taxonomists (except in fields such as ornithology and mammology) than they had been earlier in the century. The production of beautiful natural history books reached a peak of interest around the end of the century, but such works were typically luxury items marketed to wealthy bibliophiles, part of the extraordinary rise of interest in book collecting more generally during this period. Artists such as Archibald Thorburn (known for his bird plates) found themselves in great demand. At the same time, the contemporary expansion in natural history works for the middle classes had little effect on specialist publication, as such readers were unwilling (and usually unable) to pay for the elaborate works demanded by practising specialists.

Zoology and palaeontology were especially affected by this gradual splitting of audiences. As a result, the 1840s witnessed the foundation of publishing societies, in which like-minded purchasers agreed to pay a subscription to receive all of the works issued during a particular year. The first of these was the Ray Society, founded in 1844, which issued both translations and new work in zoology, including Darwin's volumes on barnacle taxonomy. In 1847 a group of fossil experts in London established the Palaeontographical Society, for publishing on subjects such as brachiopod shells and vertebrate fossils. For many fields, the most important patron of scientific works, however, was the state, particularly through reports on mineral, botanical and other resources conducted both at home and in the colonies. Government grants also subsidised the publication of the results of many scientific natural history voyages, most notably the fifty massive volumes of the *Challenger* expedition (1880–95), which became the foundation stone for future work in international oceanography.

Scientific publishing, even on such a grand scale, encouraged a close integration between authors, printers and booksellers. The publication of technical works often made unusual demands not only on authors and readers, but on typesetters, illustrators and printers as well. The production of works in natural history, anatomy and geology was greatly facilitated by lithography, which allowed even a small number of impressions to be produced at a reasonable price. An experienced lithographer such as George Scharf could reproduce delicate variations in shading and nuances of texture. Scientific works were at the forefront of experimental forms of image-making, as in the case of 'nature printing' which involved making plates from direct impressions of natural objects. Only a handful of books were made using this method, notably by

Henry Bradbury in Thomas Moore's *The ferns of Great Britain and Ireland* (1857) and William Grosart Johnstone's *The nature-printed British sea-weeds* (1859–60). From the 1830s scientists were at the forefront of the invention of photography as well as its use for illustration. In 1843 the botanist Anna Atkins produced the first photographically illustrated book, a work on algae.[52] In the end, however, photography proved something of a disappointment in many forms of illustration, as it was seen to bring out the accidental qualities of objects rather than their essential characteristics. Even after the new spectroscopy-based astronomy of the 1860s gave photography a central role, the evidence it provided remained ambiguous.[53]

The greatest challenge for printers was the complex and expensive labour of typesetting works laden with technical terminology, species names and mathematical symbols. Although the major printing firms had capabilities for setting simple geometry and algebra, more advanced mathematical works presented challenges not covered in the standard printers' manuals (fig. 12.2). Much of the work was done at Taylor & Francis and, later, at the University Press in Cambridge, where mathematical typesetting became part of every apprentice's training.[54] The technological demands of science, technology and mathematics made these significant areas for innovation in the printing industry; conversely, the very idea of being a scientist involved skills in negotiating the complex world of printing and publishing.[55]

Gateways to the sciences

The alliance between scientists, engineers, the state and education forged in the final decades of the nineteenth century meant that books on all scientific and technical subjects had a much more secure market niche, relatively independent of other constraints, than they had possessed half a century earlier. This is signalled most tellingly by the ways in which older publishing firms expanded their lists, while several new ones made these areas an important part of their business. Moreover, the proportion of science books was also rising, particularly compared to theology.[56]

52 Armstrong and de Zegher (eds.), *Ocean flowers*. On the role of photography, see Tucker, *Nature exposed*.
53 On photography, see Tucker, *Nature exposed*. Its role in astronomical publication is discussed in Pang, 'Victorian observing practices'; Rothermel, 'Images of the sun'; and Schaffer, 'On astronomical drawing'. For a remarkable discussion of spectroscopy in relation to publishing, see Hentschel, *Mapping the spectrum*, pp. 140–75.
54 McKitterick, *A history of Cambridge University Press* 3, p. 356.
55 I am indebted to the valuable paper by Ramalingam, 'The mathematician and the compositor'.
56 Eliot, '*Patterns and trends* and the NSTC: some initial observations' (1998), at pp. 72, 80.

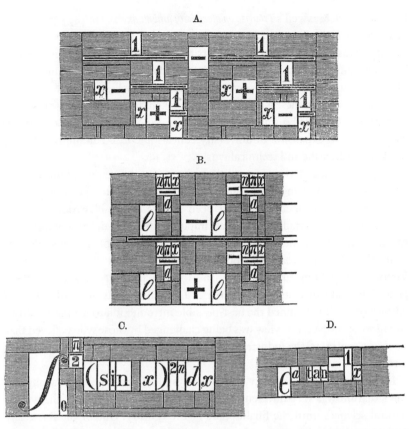

Figure 12.2 Problems in typesetting advanced mathematics, from a report of a committee of the British Association for the Advancement of Science. ('Report of the committee', *Report of the forty-fifth meeting of the British Association . . . held at Bristol in August 1875* (London: John Murray, 1876), pt 1, pp. 337–9, at p. 338)

Books such as Darwin's *Origin* had an obvious symbolic value in this transformation, as well as a practical role in shaping the sciences; but as Thomas Kuhn stressed long ago, the most important genre for doing this job was the textbook.[57] In a period when the very definition of science was controversial, such works were not the routine, mechanical summaries of known facts they are often taken to be, but attempts to define disciplines in particular ways. This is evident in a range of examples, from the translation of Sylvestre François Lacroix's standard treatise on new techniques of French mathematics in 1816

57 Kuhn, *The structure of scientific revolutions.*

to James Clerk Maxwell's *Treatise on electricity and magnetism* in 1873.[58] Michael Foster's *Textbook of physiology* (1870) occupied a key role in creating an evolutionary research tradition at the universities,[59] while Archibald Geikie wrote his thousand-page *Text-book of geology* (1882) to encourage a broad interdisciplinary and international perspective. In terms of publishing, the sciences were key elements in the increasingly active role taken by the university presses at Oxford and (especially) Cambridge from the 1890s onwards.[60] Conversely, the reform and expansion of university education created an unprecedented market for scientific and technical works.

From the point of view of publishers, however, the really significant possibilities were in elementary education. Introductions to the principles of geometry and arithmetic had long been staples of the classroom and the second-hand book trade, playing an important part in debates about education in an era of increasingly widespread literacy. Robert Simson's edition of Euclid's *Elements*, first published in 1756, went through a host of Victorian redactions, abridgements and formats for every imaginable audience. For traditionalists such as Charles Dodgson and Isaac Todhunter, an edition of Euclid remained the best-possible introduction to geometry. From the 1870s, however, this view was being challenged by those who believed that a subject central to the industrial economy was not best taught by an ancient Greek.[61]

In subjects such as chemistry, geology, physiology and experimental physics, the situation was very different, for most schools taught little in the way of natural sciences until the final decade of the century. One of the few really widely used schoolbooks was the *Fifth book of lessons* (1835), which had introduced science as a way of bridging religious divides in Ireland, and which became a standard text in schools elsewhere in the British Isles. Firms such as W. & R. Chambers of Edinburgh had been active in producing textbooks from the 1830s, but much of their output was employed in self-education. The Education Act of 1870, which standardised a national scheme of secular education, inaugurated two decades of transformation and ultimately led to a huge demand for elementary exposition in the sciences.[62] Huxley's *Lessons in elementary physiology* and H. E. Roscoe's *Lessons in elementary chemistry*, both first

58 Warwick, *Masters of theory*; Barrow-Green, ' "The advantage of proceeding from an author of some scientific reputation" '; Topham, 'A textbook revolution'.
59 Geison, *Michael Foster and the Cambridge school of physiology*.
60 McKitterick, *A history of Cambridge University Press* 3.
61 Jenkins, 'Geometry'; Barrow-Green, 'Isaac Todhunter', pp. 193–9.
62 Weedon, *Victorian publishing*, pp. 134–7; Secord, 'Science'; Layton, 'Reading science'.

published in 1866, remained on Macmillan's list for decades, selling 199,845 and 430,000 copies respectively.[63]

The emergence of textbooks targeted at schools and universities was paralleled by the rise of periodicals and books explicitly targeted as 'popular science' for the literate masses. Many of the leading general journals, from the fat quarterlies such as the *Edinburgh* and the *Westminster* to nimble literary journals such as the *Spectator* and *Pall Mall Gazette*, featured topical essays on all aspects of science, from the origins of humanity to the wonders of electricity. A good barometer of this interest is the middle-class comic weekly *Punch*, which mercilessly parodied the British Association for the Advancement of Science and other learned organisations. The *Illustrated London News*, the *Graphic* and other pictorial periodicals regularly carried accounts of technological and scientific marvels.[64]

It is not difficult to perceive, however, an increasing anxiety about the accessibility of science during the course of the century. The term 'popular' became a selling point, leading publishers to issue attractive volumes including the Rev. David Landsborough's *Popular history of British zoophytes* (1852) and Agnes M. Clerke's *Popular history of astronomy* (1885). Their production, especially from the 1860s onwards, often took advantage of the latest printing technologies with machine colour printing of frontispieces, elaborate wood-engravings and splendid cloth casings imprinted in gold. Leading firms involved in reaching this market included Routledge, especially active in reprinting classic works; Cassell, which branched out from temperance and religious publishing to embrace other forms of improving knowledge; Jarrold, which focussed on the lower end of the market; and the Religious Tract Society, which promoted evangelical principles through science imbued with what Thomas Arnold had called 'Christian tone'.[65]

Accessible illustrated weeklies such as *Science Gossip* (f.1865) and *Chemical News* (f.1859) encouraged the development of new roles such as the 'science writer' and the 'science journalist'. Clergymen, Grub Street hacks, science lecturers and many others found they could supplement an income or even make a career out of translating the increasingly inaccessible literature of science for a mass audience. Many of the authors were women. After the death of Lyell, his secretary Arabella Buckley went on to write a sequence of

63 Eliot, '"To You in Your Vast Business"', at p. 24.
64 On science in general periodicals, the best place to start is Cantor *et al.*, *Science in the nineteenth-century periodical*; Cantor and Shuttleworth (eds.), *Science serialised*; and Henson *et al.* (eds.), *Culture and science in nineteenth-century media*.
65 Fyfe, *Science and salvation*.

best-selling books for children and young adults, providing lively introductions to evolutionary natural history and modern physics. Science authorship, however, was rarely a ready route to fortune. Several of the most prolific authors ended up as broken figures, their health ruined by overwork and insecurity.[66]

Books that publishers expected to reach a wide range of readers deployed a rich range of literary and visual resources. Strikingly, some of the same rhetorical techniques can be seen at work in Buckley's writings on scientific 'fairyland' or in the 'Peter Parley' books for children as in Darwin's *Origin* and Maxwell's *Treatise*. Introducing new scientific concepts involved radical changes of perspective, often best explained by analogy, metaphor and anthropomorphism. The Scottish stonemason-turned-newspaperman Hugh Miller was especially effective in employing the language of visual spectacle to recreate ancient landscapes. His books, many of them compiled from newspaper articles, were hugely successful in the half-century after his death in the 1850s.[67] Similarly, astronomical writers such as Thomas Dick, John Pringle Nichol, Agnes Giberne and Robert Ball encouraged readers to imagine the grandeur of the nebular formation of the cosmos.[68] Accessible books by these and dozens of other commercial authors were the mainstays of publishers' lists right through the First World War.

If the scientific populariser was a new figure on the scientific scene in the second half of the nineteenth century, another developing role was that of the scientific 'amateur', a role that grew in relation with the development of the ideal of the scientific professional. There was an unparalleled proliferation of books in natural history for the urban (often suburban) middle classes, with individuals encouraged to form collections and to make observations of their own. The writings of Philip Henry Gosse, Charles Kingsley and George Henry Lewes attracted readers eager to turn a seaside beach holiday into an improving scientific expedition.[69] The size of the audience is indicated by the extraordinary sales of cheap manuals such as the Rev. John George Wood's *Common objects of the sea-shore* (1857), which sold nearly 100,000 copies in just

---

66 Lightman, *Victorian popularizers of science*; Fyfe, 'Conscientious workmen or booksellers' hacks?' On women science authors, see in addition Shteir, *Cultivating women, cultivating science*, and Gates, *Kindred nature*.

67 On Miller, see esp. O'Connor, *The Earth on show*, and Taylor, *Hugh Miller*.

68 Astore, *Observing God*; Schaffer, 'The nebular hypothesis and the science of progress'; Lightman, *Victorian popularizers*.

69 Allen, *The naturalist in Britain*. A list of relevant titles can be found in Freeman, *British natural history books*. The output of one of the most prolific authors is detailed in Freeman and Wertheimer, *Philip Henry Gosse*. Many of these figures, along with significant science publishers, have biographies in Lightman (ed.), *Dictionary of nineteenth-century British scientists*.

four years.[70] This spawned a series of manuals, especially popular at railway bookstalls, each intended to encourage the reader to identify the everyday natural history objects around them. Similar books encouraged experiments in chemistry and physics, or provided detailed instructions on how to build various devices, from telescopes and cameras to air-pumps and salt-water aquaria.

These works marked boundaries around popular science in a new way. Earlier in the century, artisans, women, children and enthusiastic cultivators of science had been seen as potentially serious contributors to science. Typically they had bought and read the same books that had been used by the most accomplished experts. Increasingly, self-taught enthusiasts were placed on the margins of the community of active practitioners, which could only be entered through formal education.[71] Like scientists themselves, divided by their specialities, these groups now needed to be addressed through separate channels for publication. Books like those of Wood were entertaining and packed with facts, but they were divided by an increasingly deep gulf from the kind of works used by specialists in universities and government institutes. When those pursuing knowledge outside these arenas made contributions, it was often within circumscribed limits, as indicated by the title of one local natural history journal from the Welsh Borders, the *Caradoc Record of Bare Facts* (f.1891). They were 'amateurs' pursuing a 'hobby'.

There was, of course, lively controversy about this process of fragmentation. Thus the popular writer Robert Proctor explicitly founded his weekly *Knowledge* in 1881 as a repudiation of the hierarchical, elitist model of science that was being advocated in *Nature* editorials.[72] There was an undercurrent of opposition to scientific exclusionism in many of the other journals, especially those devoted to practical invention and mechanical invention. Mass-market journals such as *Tit-Bits* and *Pearson's Weekly* carried a substantial proportion of technology and science, mostly of a practical progressive kind, but cared little about specialist priorities.[73] In response, men of science continued actively to pursue public education and scientific popularisation. With one hand, authors such as Maxwell, Huxley and E. Ray Lankester wrote works unintelligible to all but the learned; with the other, they contributed prolifically to newspapers, encyclopaedias and textbook series. Rather than retreating from public engagement, as is often assumed, the leaders of science in the early twentieth

70 Lightman, *Victorian popularizers of science*, pp. 173–4.
71 Secord, 'Science in the pub', pp. 297–9.
72 Lightman, *Victorian popularizers of science*, pp. 295–391.
73 Broks, *Media science before the Great War*.

James A. Secord

OUT OF THE STONE AGE INTO THE WONDER AGE

Out of an inaccessible creek in California there rushed, not long ago, a wild man of the Stone Age. Today he is in the University of California. He has walked out of the Stone Age into the Wonder Age; we may imagine him staring amazed at the wonders of civilisation; but no man can say what he thinks of it all, for he speaks a language that nobody knows.

Figure 12.3 'Out of the Stone Age into the Wonder Age', cheaply produced black and white half-tone rotogravure illustration from the *Children's Magazine* (July 1912), facing p. 417. The accompanying narrative (pp. 417–23) tells the story of Ishi, the last survivor of the Yahi tribe, who walked out of the foothills in northern California in the previous year. In the illustration, a Neanderthal-looking primitive bursts into modern civilisation, typified by telegraph wires and the web perfecting press in the lower left corner. (Bodleian Library, 399.d.694, opp. p.417)

century served as intellectual celebrities, fulfilling what they believed to be a responsibility in communicating the findings of science in newspapers, magazines and popular books. Among the most successful of these publications were part-work series issued in the years before the First World War, notably the *Self-educator* (1905–7) and *Popular science* (1911–13), both edited by Arthur Mee and published by Harmsworth. Mee's *Children's encyclopedia* (1908–10) and *Children's Magazine* (1911–14) used rotogravure, cheap paper and an international distribution network to bring fantasies of technological evolution to millions of young people (fig. 12.3).

Highlighting the role of science in empire, these publications allowed a combination of freelance science writers and leading experts to reach the working and middle classes.[74] As specialised scientific research became less obviously tied to other aspects of cultural life among the English elite, other audiences and other means of maintaining a public presence had to be found. In these ways, the Edwardian era witnessed a new alliance between science and mass journalism.

Conclusion

From the moment in 1814 that steam printing was introduced into the press-rooms of *The Times*, nowhere were questions about the relation between print and knowledge asked with more urgency than in the world of science and technology. What was the role of science, mathematics and technical understanding to be in the emerging age of industry? Who was to have control over these forms of knowledge, and towards what ends? What was the role and status of the author? What was the appropriate medium for communicating uncertain or controversial knowledge? The machine belonged to a new set of social relations, which broke down old assumptions about access to knowledge and the means for disseminating it. Controversies about issues ranging from patent law to workshop practice showed that industrialisation was not so much a cause of a transformation as part of the crisis itself.

These debates began to be resolved only in the final decades of the century. It is not so much that controversy ceased – of course, it continues on many of these questions today. But there can also be little doubt that roles and genres became more clearly defined. For example, the relation between 'scientific' and 'literary' writing, which had been so fluid in the mid-Victorian era, became relatively clear to most readers.[75] The 'scientist', 'engineer' and 'man of letters'

---

74 Bowler, 'Experts and publishers'.   75 White, 'Cross-cultural encounters'.

emerged as identifiable characters. Above all, the radical instability of texts, so evident a feature of early modern printing, seems largely to have come to an end.

Scientific and technological publication in the long nineteenth century could well be depicted as the story of the increasing isolation of an intellectual elite. In fact precisely the opposite is true. By the early twentieth century the sciences had become absolutely central to the workings of modern society, as the leading sectors of industrial development drew increasingly on technologies based in science, notably chemistry and electricity. As I have suggested, this transformation forged a new relation between the printing house and the laboratory, signalled by the coming of machine typesetting, rotogravure and the consequent trends towards large-scale capitalisation and monopoly control. The sciences not only provided the impetus for these new technologies, but also served as a touchstone of rational thought, precision measurement and moral probity.[76] From the Cavendish Laboratory in Cambridge to working-men's reading rooms in the industrial north, science became a symbol of regularity, standardisation and progress.

There is an ironic postscript to this story. At the present time, scientific periodicals, textbooks and monographs published after 1860 are, with a few exceptions, Cinderellas of the library world. The same books and papers that contemporaries placed at the heart of a global economic and social transformation are now typically outhoused and poorly catalogued. Science libraries often do not want them because they seem outdated, while humanities collections view them as space-hungry intruders not really belonging under the same roof with philosophy, literature or history. Only a handful of the most prominent titles have been digitised, which for material with many illustrations and poor bibliographical control is by no means a universal panacea. Yet given the persistent belief that science is outside culture, de-accessioning and disposal all too often appear to be attractive options. I remember discovering a full run of the first genetics journal in the world in a skip outside a university science department some years ago; and that is not an isolated incident. More than any other area of human endeavour, science actively consumes its past, and the single-minded belief in progress that motivated the building of great science libraries in the past can today easily become a justification for throwing things away.

---

76 Gooday, *The morals of measurement*; Schaffer, 'Late Victorian metrology and its instrumentation'. On the issue generally, see Collini, *Public moralists*.

13

Publishing for leisure

VICTORIA COOPER AND DAVE RUSSELL

The nineteenth and early twentieth centuries witnessed a transformation in the nature of British leisure habits.[1] Under the impact of decreasing working hours, rising living standards and fundamental changes in technology and communication, all but the poorest sections of society were able to enjoy at least some of the new opportunities so assiduously nurtured by the growing leisure industry. In 1840, a piano was essentially a luxury item: by 1910 there was perhaps one instrument for every ten to twenty of the population. In 1888–9, an estimated 600,000 people watched the matches played by the twelve clubs in the nascent English Football League: by 1905-6, 5 million watched the League's First Division games. In the 1830s, 50,000 people left the Channel ports for Europe each year: by 1913 that figure had risen to 660,000.[2]

Particularly for sections of the middle class, always the major market for the 'leisure book' and thus the main focus of this chapter, the emergence of potential new pleasures was often problematic. While concerned as to how those beneath them in the social scale might use their leisure opportunities, and anxious to provide them with 'rational recreation', many were arguably even more worried about endangering their own morals or social status. Books and magazines were crucial tools in the subsequent process whereby individuals negotiated their way through the problems and possibilities of the new leisure landscape. Provided the subject-matter was suitable, the act of reading was in itself an improving and worthwhile activity, while the knowledge gained from it could lead to the avoidance of all manner of social embarrassments and ease entry to innumerable specialist worlds. More simply, it also gave hours of genuine pleasure. While it will not be possible to cover the full range of hobby and enthusiast publications which occupied and intrigued the Victorians, this

---

1 For guides to the now large literature of leisure, see Bailey, 'The politics and poetics of modern British leisure', Borsay, *A history of leisure*, and Flanders, *Consuming passions*.
2 Ehrlich, *The piano*, p. 97; Mason, *Association Football and English society*, pp. 141-3. There admittedly were twenty clubs in this division; Pemble, *The Mediterranean passion*, p. 1.

475

chapter takes five indicative case studies that can serve as examples of the kind of publishing which was meant to educate and entertain. It begins in the essentially (although never exclusively) 'private' sphere with studies of cookery and gardening books before moving steadily into the more 'public' realm via consideration of works dedicated to music, sport and travel. Although concerned with the book in its own right, with its content, style, publication and consumption, these studies also seek to explore where possible the ways in which books captured and constructed debates and ideologies within the wider society.

Cookery books

Cookery books and instruction manuals for the kitchen had been in circulation for some time, reaching back to the sixteenth century at least, and in the eighteenth century one of the best-known examples was Hannah Glasse, *The art of cookery, made plain and easy* (1747). However, during the Victorian period cookery books gained a wider readership and larger dissemination than ever before. Instructions for cooking and for providing for the kitchen and pantry can be divided somewhat along class lines, with publications designed for the growing middle class as well as for the lower-middle- and working-class households. These titles were often meant as instructions on how the food ought to be prepared and served rather than being a reflection of the reality of many home situations.

There were two extremely successful cookbooks of the period: Eliza Acton, *Modern cookery for private families* (1845; sometimes listed as 1844) and Isabella Beeton, *The book of household management* (1859–61, see below and fig. 13.1). These titles were intended, to some extent, for the middle- and upper-middle-class kitchens.[3] Beeton's book, originally published in twenty-four monthly parts, had its origins as a monthly column in the *Englishwoman's Domestic Magazine*, one of the journals published by her husband, who also published a long list of encyclopaedic reference books on a wide range of topics.[4] Beeton's book was to become a publishing phenomenon and in the first year alone sold 60,000 copies. It is of note that much of the advice, recipes and information in Beeton's *Household management* was taken from other sources and cookery books.[5] In turn, the book became a goldmine of its own, with material

---

3 Briggs, *Victorian things*, p. 215.
4 For a thorough and fascinating examination of Isabella Beeton, her life and work see Hughes *The short life and long times of Mrs Beeton*.
5 Hughes, *Mrs Beeton*, p. 424.

The advertisement reads:

THE CHRISTMAS BOOKSELLER, 1889.

THE BEST OF ALL CHRISTMAS PRESENTS.

Now Ready, strongly bound half roan, price 7s. 6d.; Presentation Editions, Cloth gilt, gilt edges, 8s. 6d.; half calf, 10s. 6d.

ENTIRELY NEW AND REVISED EDITION

(RECOMPOSED THROUGHOUT, GREATLY ENLARGED AND IMPROVED,) OF

THE BEST, MOST USEFUL, AND MOST POPULAR COOKERY BOOK IN THE WORLD,

MRS. BEETON'S BOOK OF

HOUSEHOLD MANAGEMENT

Including 360 Additional Pages of New Recipes and New Engravings.

LUNCHEON-TABLE LAID FOR EIGHT PERSONS.
(Reduced Specimen Illustration from "MRS. BEETON'S HOUSEHOLD MANAGEMENT.")

THE SIZE OF THE PAGES HAS ALSO BEEN INCREASED, SO THAT

The New Edition contains nearly Half as much Matter again as the Old Edition,

IN ALL

1,700 PAGES, THOUSANDS OF RECIPES AND INSTRUCTIONS, HUNDREDS OF ENGRAVINGS AND NEW COLOURED PLATES.

From "THE QUEEN."

"An entirely new edition, revised and corrected up to date, and giving trustworthy information on almost every subject of interest to the much tried person, the mistress of the house. . . . We can imagine no present more useful to a young housekeeper, or, indeed, to any housekeeper, either young or old, lady or gentleman."

London: WARD, LOCK & CO., Salisbury Square, E.C.

154

Figure 13.1 Advertising for Mrs Beeton's *Book of household management* (*The Christmas Bookseller* 1889). In common with many other books, it was available in various binding styles, at different prices. (Private collection)

gathered into smaller editions and collections of material organised by topic, to become an industry in itself with 'Mrs Beeton' becoming a brand name for cookery and household instruction books and later for foodstuffs, throughout the nineteenth and twentieth centuries.[6]

A tradition of such cookery and household advice books had been gaining ground earlier in the century and, in addition to Acton, there had been books intended for the lower-middle and working class, such as Anne Cobbett, *Cottage economy* (1821) and Alexis Soyer's *A shilling cookery for the people: embracing an entirely new system of plain cookery and domestic economy* (1855). Alexis Soyer (1810–58) came to England from France in 1830 and became what is today referred to as a celebrity chef. His cooking for the Reform Club was renowned and he was also known for his advice to the military during the Crimean War on the preparation of food. Soyer's contribution to social welfare can also be seen in his founding of soup kitchens during the 1847 Irish famine.[7] In addition to Soyer, another famous chef and cookery book writer of the period was Charles Elme Francatelli (1805–76): born in London of Italian background, he was educated in France where he studied cookery as a pupil of Carême, and made his career in England, culminating in his position as chief cook to Queen Victoria. Similar to Soyer, Francatelli was part of the elite of British cuisine, and published inspiring books such as *The royal English and foreign confectionery book* (1862) and more down-to-earth titles such as *The modern cook: a practical guide to the culinary art in all its branches* (1845) and *A plain cookery book for the working classes* (1861). Francatelli can also be thanked for being the first English cookery author to publish a recipe featuring the ice cream cornet.

The cookbooks of the period also included innovations in their presentation of information; Acton's books were the first to provide recipes with measurements and to separate instructions from ingredients, a practice which has often been incorrectly ascribed to Beeton. One of the main questions concerning such publications is to determine who would actually use them. In general, this followed class lines: the working and lower-middle class would use the books themselves, while the middle-class housewife might use the book but also pass it to her, somewhat limited, domestic staff if they could manage it, or would instruct from it herself. One clue can be found in the organisation of the book by the journalist and novelist George Augustus Sala (1829–95) *The thorough good cook: a series of chats on the culinary art and nine hundred recipes* (1895); while this is late in the period under investigation it is of note that the

6 See *ibid.* and its bibliography, pp. 489ff, for a list of later editions.
7 Burnett, *Plenty and want*, p. 74.

book contains three prefaces, one to the general reader, one to the lady of the house and one to the household's cook.[8]

The kinds of titles published by Beeton, Acton, Soyer and a large number of other cooks and writers were part of a larger philosophy of the well-managed house and the high moral standards expected within the family circle, and this in turn was a reflection of the Victorian desire for order and civility in society. A number of bibliographies of cookery and household management books have been published and their long lists of titles indicate the wide range of publication in this area.[9]

Gardening

While the philosophy and practice of landscape gardening and garden design had been developed to a sophisticated level in earlier centuries, in particular in the eighteenth century with the innovations of Lancelot 'Capability' Brown, it was during the Victorian period that gardening became a pursuit and hobby for the aspiring middle class. A number of names and fashions from this period still resonate today. The eighteenth-century Romantic philosophy of gardening held that it was the living representation of landscape painting but the Victorians scaled down this ambition to suit the more limited landholdings and means of the upper-middle and middle classes, which often only extended to a few acres or perhaps a small plot in an urban garden. The Victorian interest in gardening was heightened by a number of more general events during the century such as the founding of the Horticultural Society (to become the Royal Horticultural Society in 1861), the opening of Kew Gardens to the public in 1841, and the establishment of what came to be called the garden suburb. It should also be mentioned that 1830 saw a key domestic garden moment with the invention of the lawnmower by Edward Beard Budding (c.1796–1846).

At the end of the eighteenth century a growing number of experts contributed books to the literature, including Humphrey Repton (1752–1818). Repton was a landscape gardener of the highest order, considered the successor to Capability Brown, and part of the group who published on gardening and its philosophy and aesthetic. Repton contributed to the eighteenth- and early nineteenth-century collection of books focussing on gardening aesthetics with works such as *Sketches and hints on landscape gardening* (1795) and *Fragments on the*

---

8 Symons, *A history of cooks and cooking.*
9 See especially: Maclean, *A short-title catalogue of household and cookery books*; Attar, *A bibliography of household books*; Driver, *A bibliography of cookery books*; and, earlier, Oxford, *English cookery books to the year 1850.*

theory and practice of landscape gardening (1816), among others. He was followed later by John Claudius Loudon (1783–1843), landscape gardener, horticultural writer and city planner, best remembered for his development of gardening design he labelled Gardenesque: to place unusual and exotic plants in settings which displayed them, often in lay-outs of geometric shapes – a style which can still be seen in gardening today.[10] His books included the *Encyclopedia of gardening* (1822, and later editions) and, among later publications, *The suburban gardener* (1836–8), *On the laying out, planting and managing of cemeteries* (1843) and, often considered his most influential work, the highly illustrated *Arboretum et fruticetum Britannicum, or, the trees and shrubs of Britain, native and foreign, hardy and half hardy* (1838), initially issued in sixty-three monthly parts, from January 1835 to July 1838, and intended to catalogue all the trees and shrubs in Great Britain. His wife Jane Webb Loudon (1807–58) also contributed to the growing list of publications on gardening with her books of flower prints, such as *The ladies' flower garden of ornamental annuals* (1840), *The ladies' flower garden of ornamental bulbous plants* (1841) and *Mrs Loudon's gardening for ladies* (1844), among others. Mrs Loudon's greatest success was *The ladies' companion to the flower garden* (1841; 9th edn 1879).

In addition to books on gardening, an active publishing industry developed for periodicals and magazines on the topic. From the mid-1820s and well into the 1840s alone, a number of magazines were established, including *Loudon's Gardening Magazine* (1826); the *Floricultural Magazine and Miscellany of Gardening* (1836–42), edited by the influential Scottish garden designer Robert Marnock (1800–89); the *Ladies' Magazine of Gardening* (1842), edited by Mrs Loudon; and the *Magazine of Botany and Gardening* (1833–37), edited by James Rennie and others.

Two additional influential figures in gardening publications must also be mentioned: Joseph Paxton and, at the end of the century, Gertrude Jekyll. Joseph Paxton (1803–65) is now remembered for his famous glasshouse at Chatsworth and the Crystal Palace for the Great Exhibition in 1851. Yet his publications in periodicals and books were some of the most influential of the time, although mostly intended for the professional plantsman and educated enthusiast. Among these were *Paxton's Magazine of Botany and Flowering Plants* (1834–49) and *A pocket botanical dictionary* (1840); and with John Lindley (1799–1865: leading botanist of his time and Professor of Botany at Cambridge) he published *Paxton's flower garden* (three volumes with 108 hand-coloured plates, 1850–3).

10 Fieldhouse and Woudstra, *The regeneration of public parks*.

Although Gertrude Jekyll (1843–1932) published her books at the end of the Victorian period and into the twentieth century, her influence on late Victorian and Edwardian gardening is such that she should be mentioned here. Jekyll is associated with the development of herbaceous borders, arranged and grouped in individual colours (often referred to as 'gold' borders, composed entirely of material in various shades of yellow and orange). Jekyll worked extensively with the architect Edwin Lutyens, collaborating on the creation of house and garden as one unified environment.[11] Jekyll's first book, *Wood and garden*, was published in 1899 and offers information on gardening month by month for every size of garden. The book also described her own garden at Munstead Wood, Surrey. While expounding a sophisticated aesthetic and philosophy for the garden, Jekyll further ensured her material was accessible to the amateur. This combination of sophistication and accessibility carried through in her writing, with her intended readership often invited in, as noted in *Lilies for English gardens* (1901), subtitled 'A guide for amateurs. A short, concise, illustrated handbook on the most stately and beautiful of garden flowers'. By the end of the Victorian period gardening had become a more widespread profession, for men as well as women, and a hobby for enthusiasts at all levels of the social scale. Gardening books, magazines, journals and periodicals counted in the thousands and became one of the major areas of leisure reading and publication.

Music

While cookery and gardening could be seen in the Victorian period as either hobbies or mandatory activities to keep household and property in order, interest in music could be seen as an entirely leisure pursuit. Unlike gardening and cookery, which were domestic and relatively private endeavours, the study and performance of music could move out of the domestic sphere and into the more public realm. The following discussion, however, focusses on books and publications about music, its tuition, history, aesthetic and philosophy, and will not examine printed music itself; for a general coverage of music printing and publishing there are a number of surveys.[12]

Yet it must be acknowledged that the market for books about music had its roots in the growing participation in amateur music performance itself during the Victorian period, made all the more possible through the expanding music

11 Festing, *Gertrude Jekyll*, and Jekyll, *The unknown Gertrude Jekyll*. The latter is a collection of two hundred articles and writings by Jekyll.
12 Krummel and Sadie (eds.), *Music printing and publishing*; Cooper, *The house of Novello*.

printing and publishing trade. Thus, as music literacy grew, so too did an interest in volumes on the history, aesthetics, theory and biography of music. This expansion in music printing and publishing had started in the late eighteenth century and by 1780 a number of music printers and publishers were competing for business. The demand for printed music, for private domestic performance and study, was spurred on by the growing number of public concerts and, nearer London, the presence of the pleasure gardens and their open-air concerts. The middle-class interest in performing and the demand for editions suitable for amateurs was such that by the end of the eighteenth century music printing and publishing was an established and well-developed industry.

Books about music became a sub-category of this flourishing fascination with all things musical and, as well as books, an ever-growing number of music periodicals were published.[13] It is therefore possible that many music enthusiasts and amateur performers came first to writings about music through fine arts and music journals as well as from reviews of concerts in the newspapers. Thus, the road to books about music could have been first through performance and printed music editions, then to articles and reviews and, finally, to the music books themselves.

In that regard it is important to examine the scale of music printing and distribution in England at mid-century and to acknowledge the large number of copies of any one edition of a work which could now, thanks to ever-advancing technology, be printed at any one time. An example can be seen with the printing and distribution figures of Handel's *Messiah*, one of the most popular works of the Victorian period. Following the stockbook of 1858 from the London music publisher Novello, it can be seen that, in May 1859, 6,000 copies of the octavo-size piano–vocal score of *Messiah* and 7,500 copies of the pocket edition were printed.[14] *Messiah* and other Handel works were especially popular at this time, as 1859 saw the Handel Centennial Festival at the Crystal Palace, with Novello appointed by the Crystal Palace Company as publisher of all scores for the Festival, to be used by both performers and audience. Events such as the Handel Festival, and the availability of editions of music for amateurs, inevitably led to a growth in demand for books and periodicals about music.

Among the most popular activities at mid-century were choral groups and musical societies: this growing participation was frequently referred to as

13 For an overview of the development of music journalism and music periodicals see Langley, 'Musical press'; see also Langley, 'A descriptive catalogue'.
14 For further information on the Novello stockbook, additional examples, supply, and demand for choral and popular music, Cooper, *The house of Novello*.

the Choral Movement. In addition to the ever-increasing purchase of music for choral organisations, small or large, there was also the desire for self-improvement, self-tuition and a greater understanding of music history in general. The Choral Movement was marked by the number of large choral festivals – their massive scale, in size of both choir and audience, remains one of the predominant images of Victorian music making. Contemporary accounts of choral festivals suggest the size of these gatherings as well as the social class – both issues which must be addressed when forming a picture of these events. *Aris's Birmingham Gazette* provides an informative observation in the issue of 28 September 1857 of the performance of *The Creation* by the Birmingham Festival Choral Society: 'It was an inspiring sight to mark the eager attention of the crowded auditory, the greatest part of whom were of the working class, while hundreds followed the performance from the cheap editions of Novello and Cocks. This argues strongly for the increasing growth of an elevated musical taste among the masses.'[15] While the tone of the report treads into the realms of hyperbole, such documentation can give a flavour of the numbers attending such festivals and the socio-economic level of both performers and audience.

In addition, the increasing popularity of the piano for amateur and domestic performance was a factor in the wealth of music now available in accessible formats such as piano–vocal scores, sheet music and simplified, edited versions of well-known songs and compositions. Out of this development grew an interest, as well, in the basic elements and the history of music, and books about music were now in demand. The music publisher Vincent Novello, and his son Alfred, responded accordingly and inaugurated their series Novello's Library for the Diffusion of Musical Knowledge, with titles of books such as *Cherubini's treatise on counterpoint* (translated by Vincent Novello's daughter, Mary Cowden Clarke), intended for the more experienced musician; *Dr Marx's general music instruction*; *Kalkbrenner's method for learning the piano-forte, with the aid of the manual guide*; *Rink's practical organ school*; and *Silcher's succinct instructions for the guidance of singing schools and choral societies*.[16] Biographies of composers also became an area of interest and publishers responded with volumes on the main figures such as Mozart, for example with *The life of Mozart* (1845, revised 1878 and 1912) by Edward Holmes (1797–1859), music critic and editor of the *Musical Times*.

The history of music was also of interest to the enthusiast and among the accessible volumes were Thomas Busby, *General history of music* (1819);

---

15 Quoted from Pritchard 'The musical festival and the choral society in England', p. 598.
16 Cooper, *The house of Novello*.

William Stafford, *A history of music*, (1830); and George Hogarth, *Musical history, biography and criticism: being a general survey of music, from the earliest period to the present time* (1835). The histories by John Hullah (1812–83) would, more probably, be too advanced for the general music enthusiast, and intended for scholars, but the experienced amateur would no doubt find them of interest: *The history of modern music, a course of lectures delivered at the Institute of Great Britain* (1862) and *The third or transition period of musical history* (1865).[17] Although earlier than the period under review, the influence of Charles Burney (1727–1814) should be noted, as his monumental *General history of music from the earliest ages to the present period* (1776–89) served as the benchmark for later music histories.

The rise of music education, both in schools and in private, domestic situations also contributed to the growing interest in the fundamentals of the discipline and increased publication of instruction manuals. The first music textbooks for schools were published in the 1830s and included John Turner, *Manual of vocal instruction* (1833).[18] One of the main types of manual was for singing instruction, often published to explain and promote a particular sight-singing system. It was an active and competitive market and at mid-century various systems were in circulation, including those by John Hullah, John Curwen (1816–80), Joseph Mainzer (1801–51) and Sarah Glover (1785–1867). Joseph Mainzer was a music educator and singing teacher and an important influence on the development of the choir movement with his journal the *National Singing Class Circular* (1841), which he expanded in 1842 to become *Mainzer's Musical Times and Singing Class Circular*. Perhaps the most successful sight-singing system of the century was the tonic sol-fa method of teaching vocal music developed by the Congregational minister John Curwen. His system was partly influenced by the method designed by the singing teacher Sarah Glover. Glover's own work with singing instruction had led her to publish a *Scheme to render psalmody congregational* (1835). Curwen developed and enhanced the Glover system and his tonic sol-fa method became an industry in itself with the publication of a number of textbooks and songbooks, including *The standard course of lessons on the tonic sol-fa method of teaching to sing*, first published in 1858; the tonic sol-fa system became the school music teaching method accepted by the English Education Department in 1860.

In addition to the flurry of publications intended for the student and amateur, a large number of music histories and reference books were also published

17 For a discussion of histories of music during this period, see Zon, *Music and metaphor*, pp. 179ff.
18 Rink, 'The profession of music'.

for the music scholar, with topics covered as basic as music history and theory, to more philosophical examinations such as William Gardiner, *The music of nature: or, an attempt to prove that what is passionate and pleasing in the art of singing, speaking, and performing upon musical instruments is derived from the sounds of the animated world, with curious and interesting illustrations* (1832).[19] For the music scholar and informed amateur, in addition to music history there was a growing interest in music theory, with publications such as Alfred Day, *A treatise on harmony*; and later, John Stainer, *A theory of harmony, founded on the tempered scale* (1871) and especially Ebenezer Prout, *Harmony: its theory and practice* (1889; 16th edn 1903). Dictionaries also became fundamental reference works in demand, including the first important English-language biographical dictionary of music: William Bingley, *Musical biography* (1814). This was followed by J. Sainsbury, *A dictionary of musicians* (1824), and later John Stainer and William Barrett, *A dictionary of musical terms* (1876). This area of music literature could be said to culminate with George Grove, *A dictionary of music and musicians (A.D. 1450–1880) by eminent writers, English and foreign, with illustrations and woodcuts* (1879–90), that was to become one of the most important endeavours in music book publishing at the time, with subsequent editions stretching to the end of the twentieth century and having a profound influence on musicology and music research.

Sport

As with all the case studies here, the sports book broadly defined had a lineage that long preceded the nineteenth century. Similarly, that century, and especially the period from about 1870, saw major changes in the scale and nature of sporting book production. One of the most striking features in this field was the sheer range of material on offer.[20] Although few writers of 'canonical' English literature tackled sport – H. G. Wells's cycling novel *Wheels of chance* (1896) is a rare example and anyway came early in his career – there was from about the 1880s a vigorous tradition of popular literature spanning from the public-schoolboy sporting adventure story by writers such as Harold Avery, Walter C. Rhoades and Charles Turley Smith to the horse-racing thrillers of Nat Gould (1857–1919). This prolific author, who often used his ten-year sojourn in Australia as material for plots and settings, made his breakthrough in 1891 with *The double event*, which sold 100,000 copies in its first ten years

19 Temperley (ed.), *The romantic age, 1800–1914*, p. 457.
20 For an excellent overview, albeit of material aimed at the dominant middle-class markets, see Lowerson, *Sport and the English middle class*, pp. 251–7.

and was still in print at his death. Routledge gave him his own two-shilling series, which comprised eleven titles by 1900.[21] Biography and autobiography were similarly popular genres, especially in cricket which was probably the most 'literary' of all sports. John Nyren and Charles Cowden Clarke's *The cricketers of my time* (1832) was an important early contribution, and by 1914 there was a substantial body of 'lives' of varying degrees of quality and seriousness of purpose. W. G. Grace, both the greatest Victorian cricketer and, despite his nominal 'amateur' status, the greatest exploiter of its commercial potential, produced no fewer than three books of reminiscences between 1895 and 1909.[22]

The two types selected for special attention here are the yearbook or, as it was often termed, the 'annual', and a much looser and label-defying genre that might be generally termed the 'sporting guide', a volume that combined in varying degrees historical narrative, contemporary commentary and practical guidance. Although varying somewhat in nature and content according to its specific sport, the yearbook typically listed key events and records from the previous year or season alongside fixtures or events for the next, a digest of current controversies and issues, records over time, sets of rules, and gazetteers giving addresses of a variety of relevant individuals and organisations. To some extent, it had its roots in the *Racing calendar* (1773), effectively the official organ of the Jockey Club, although it probably first became significant within cricket. While *Wisden cricketers' almanack* (1864) is the best known of the Victorian cricket yearbooks it was not the first; there were others of then approximately equal stature that appeared about the same time, most notably the rival products of the cousins Lillywhite, John's *Cricketer's companion* (1865) and James's *Cricketer's annual* (1872).[23] By the 1880s and 1890s, all sports of any consequence were served by a work of this type. Usually fairly modestly priced with some retailing for a shilling or less, they were often the product not of recognised publishing houses but of a variety of companies with commercial interests in sport. John Wisden, for example, was only one of a number of sports outfitters and equipment manufacturers who saw the publicity benefits inherent in yearbook production. The rapidly emerging specialist sports press was another fertile source. Rather like the tourist handbook, the yearbook was the product of a society increasingly demanding immediate, easily digestible and accurate information. At the same time, its tabulation of records, lists

21 P. G. Wodehouse's *Mike* (1909) was a significant and much-loved contribution to the school cricket novel. On Gould, see *Australian dictionary of national biography* and p. 616 in this volume.
22 Padwick, *A bibliography of cricket* 1, p. 646.
23 Vamplew, *The turf*, p. 80; West, *Guide to 'Lillywhite's Cricketers' companion'*, pp. 1–4.

of fixtures, categorisation of events and players part-captured, part-defined the critical period in the modernisation of sport, whereby it passed in Allen Guttman's phrase 'from ritual to record'.[24]

Although blessed with similarly long antecedents, the sporting guide came into its own in the last quarter of the nineteenth century. While, as will be seen, a number of publishers can be regarded as sports specialists, a wide range of houses showed interest in works of this type. A random selection of ten 'boating, sailing and yachting' titles drawn from the sixty listed in the 1911 Mudie's Library catalogue reveals ten different publishers, including Edward Arnold, Blackwood, Chatto & Windus, Methuen and John Murray. There are hints that publishers may have been attracted by sporting works that loosely connected to their established specialist interests – the link between Murray's publication of E. F. Knight's *Small boat sailing* (1901) and the company's wider travel catalogue is, for example, fairly obvious – but, overall, far more research into the exact relationship between sport and individual houses is required before this and many other questions can be properly addressed. Although the sporting guide might best be seen as a tendency rather than a genre, its broad principles can be gauged from a brief description of Prince Kumar Shri Ranjitsinhji's *The jubilee book of English cricket*, published by Blackwood in 1897 in honour of Victoria's Diamond Jubilee. At one level, this lavishly produced twenty-five-shilling purchase – a *de luxe*, signed copy was marketed at £5 – nominally edited and at least partially written by an Indian prince who was one of the finest batsmen of his generation, was about as atypical as could be imagined; this really was the Victorian sports book as status item. Nevertheless, its content was recognisably that of many sporting guides of this period. About half was devoted to what were essentially coaching chapters, illustrated by over one hundred 'staged' photographs showing correct technique, about a third to a survey of recent and contemporary cricket and cricketers, dominated by coverage of public schools and Oxbridge, and the remainder to a survey of cricket across the Victorian era written by 'Ranji' himself. The role of high-profile sportsmen (especially cricketers) such as Ranjitsinhji in sporting publication became increasingly common in this period, with both athlete and publisher anxious to turn sporting celebrity to additional financial advantage. Such ventures raise interesting comparisons with the use of experts in other leisure book genres. The comparison with travel guidebook authors is particularly marked. While the travel book's search for an objective tone encouraged a covert narration that could reduce the author to little more than a name on

24 Guttman, *From ritual to record*, pp. 15–55.

a title-page (and not always that), the kudos given by sportsmen's celebrity status and widely acknowledged expertise allowed, perhaps even demanded, a high level of personal comment and intervention.

While many such books were published as single titles, they often gained higher market visibility and perhaps a certain enhanced authority by being published as part of a 'sportsman's library'. By some way the most prestigious of these was the Badminton Library of Sports and Pastimes, begun by Longman in 1885 as an update of Blaine's 1840 *Encyclopaedia of rural sport*, but eventually running to thirty titles over the next two decades.[25] The series took its name from the country seat of its general editor, the 8th Duke of Beaufort. An exceptionally keen huntsman (hunting was the subject of the launch volume), fisherman and coachman, he was by no means solely a figurehead although much work was delegated to the sporting and theatrical journalist Alfred E. T. Watson. Earning £400 per year in 1879 as the editor of the *Illustrated Sporting and Dramatic News*, Watson was one of a number of writers who were beginning to benefit from the increasingly lucrative specialist world of sports publishing.[26] Many Badminton authors were drawn from the aristocracy or social groups only immediately below – as Asa Briggs has noted, even *Cycling*, its most plebeian title, was co-written by Viscount Bury – and this elite tone was presumably part of its appeal to an audience willing to pay 10s 6d for each elegantly bound volume.[27] The quality of material and writing, however, was often extremely high (the best books can still be used as reference sources) and the illustrations were often lavish. The genuine sports enthusiast as well as the dilettante seeking bookshelf status had much to gain.

A number of other libraries appeared from about 1890, focussed and priced according to perceived market opportunities. Lawrence & Bullen's Angler's Library, which generated at least six individual titles priced at five shillings in 1898–9, exemplifies the specialist single-sport strand although most publishers aimed for wider coverage. Of these, G. F. Bell & Son's All England series, launched in 1890 and eventually running to over twenty titles, matched Badminton most closely in number, although not in its ambition or target audience. Retailing at one shilling and measuring only some fifty pages, they were probably aimed at the lower-middle and possibly the upper working classes. Amongst other series, the Hurst & Blackett Company's short-lived Imperial Athletic Library is one of the most interesting if only because of the later careers of its two editors and ex-Marlborough and Cambridge sporting

25 Briggs, 'The view from Badminton'.   26 Watson, *A sporting and dramatic career*, p. 143.
27 Briggs, 'The view from Badminton', p. 193. This was the standard price by 1900.

friends, E. F. Benson (1867–1940), already a prolific and popular novelist, and Eustace H. Miles (1868–1948), in his turn a major writer on sport and health and a pioneer of the health food shop and vegetarian restaurant.

All sports were embraced by publishers alert to new market opportunities, but it was generally those most enthusiastically pursued by middle- and upper-class males that predominated in the lists. Although exact measurement of titles and sales is not possible from current knowledge, John Lowerson may well be correct when claiming that 'fishing generated the most significant output'. Along with innumerable new titles, Izaak Walton's 1650s classic *The compleat angler* went through thirty-five new editions between 1870 and 1902, with originals (including some rogue German-made facsimiles) selling for £150. Shooting and golf were also exceptionally well served, with 237 and 260 books respectively appearing in the period from 1870 to 1914.[28] The literature of cricket was similarly enriched. Although not a middle-class sport per se, the relatively high cost of most cricket books clearly suggests that its wealthier followers formed the target audience. Interestingly, association football, certainly the national sport in terms of popularity by 1914, was generally poorly served beyond the yearbook. Caxton's elegantly produced and well-illustrated four-volume *Association football and the men who have made it* (1905–6) was its only prestige publication in this period. The Badminton series dealt with the game by compressing both the rugby union and association codes into a volume shared with athletics, with the latter taking up over 60 per cent of the text; association football enjoyed barely 10 per cent.[29] Indeed, it was not until the 1950s that the game began to develop a literature that reached beyond the yearbook and popular fiction. If working-class money and sporting predilections drove much of the commercial expansion of Victorian and Edwardian sport, its literary concomitant was fuelled from within a markedly different social world and by a rather different set of tastes.

The most obvious but most important function of the sporting book was to aid the spread of sport throughout British life. According to its specific function, it gave vital organisational and administrative information as well as often highly sophisticated practical instruction, and spread knowledge of rules when, at least until about 1900, they were very much in a state of flux. Nor was the relationship simply a matter of downward percolation from page to reader. Books were as ever active ingredients in the process of cultural formation, stirring the sporting imagination, helping construct the first real pantheon of modern sporting heroes and engaging in and shaping sporting controversy

28 Lowerson, *Sport and the English middle class*, pp. 254–5.   29 Shearman, *Athletics and football*.

and discourse. In his contribution to the Angler's Library, for example, George Dewar used the opportunity to discuss the growing problems of river pollution by sewage and to criticise southern water companies for lowering spring and river levels. The cricket volume in *Country Life*'s short-lived sport series attacked the vogue for what its author saw as batsman-friendly pitches by referring to them as 'some easy-paced billiard-table wicket, where a blind boy could stay with a toothpick'.[30]

Unsurprisingly, given its utter centrality in contemporary discussion, probably the most frequently debated controversy concerned the role of professionalism, and especially within athletics, rugby and association football.[31] Sports books added significantly to the arguments raging in newspapers and sporting magazines and, while the professional was often watched with a wary eye, different series could take quite notably different views. The football volume in Bell's All England series, for example, contained a damning critique of professionalism within rugby union by Arthur Budd, one of the most virulent and ideological contemporary opponents of the practice. When the Rugby Football Union 'resolved to throttle the hydra of professionalism', he argued, 'they saved the game from a system which would have begun in degradation, and ended in ruin'. Within sport in general, he went on, 'without exception the corrupt element has invariably in time gained the upper hand, and crippled and depraved the sport, or killed it outright'.[32] Interestingly, he used the chapter to criticise Montague Shearman's slightly more sympathetic coverage of the topic in the Badminton series, a contribution in which Shearman claimed that 'we prefer a man who plays for money and says that he does so, to a "gentleman" who receives liberal sums for "expenses"'.[33] That the shilling Bell took a far harder stance than the 10s 6d Badminton volume, written by an Oxford rugby blue later knighted for his services to the legal profession, perhaps demonstrates that professionalism was more readily acceptable to those secure in the upper echelons of society than their counterparts in social positions a little more uncomfortably adjacent to the working classes.[34]

The knowledge that the sporting book disseminated was often of a highly specialist nature that played a crucial role in making the sportsman feel part

30 G. A. B. Dewar, *South country trout streams* (1898), preface and pp. 18–23; H. G. Hutchinson (ed.), *Cricket* (1903), p. 83.
31 The conflict between amateur and professional now has a substantial historiography. The best introduction is still that provided by Holt, *Sport and the British*, pp. 74–134.
32 H. Vassall, *Football: the Rugby game* (1889), pp. 43, 49. On Budd, see Collins, *Rugby's great split*, pp. 57–8, 116–17.
33 Shearman, *Athletics and football*, p. 368.
34 Dunning and Sheard, *Barbarians, gentlemen and players*, pp. 186–7.

of a distinct, often rather closed world. Safe in his understanding of the best place to catch river trout in Scotland, the correct choice of golf clubs or who had headed the batting averages in cricket's County Championship, he could become part of the new sporting communities that were so central to social life in this period. Or, rather, to male social life for the most part. Women's sport might occasionally gain a little attention from publishers. Most cycling guides took women's involvement extremely seriously and the growth of women's golf led to such works as George Duncan's *Golf for women* (1914) which, while arguing that a woman would always be disadvantaged 'by reason of her slight physique', believed that the gender gap could be narrowed and used action shots of leading 'lady' players to encourage that process. Croquet, riding and lawn tennis literature was also capable of paying attention to women readers. Overall, however, the sports book belonged to the study, the 'den', the club house, to those male social republics that sport more widely had so deliberately created and preserved.

Travel

As medieval pilgrims, participants in the continental grand tour and searchers after the picturesque in the eighteenth-century British landscape would attest, travel books long predated the Victorian age.[35] The period from about the later 1830s was, however, to witness major changes in the style, content and sheer range and volume of literature designed to guide those increasingly (and sometimes disparagingly) termed 'tourists' in their journeys amongst the sights of Britain, Europe and often well beyond. 'Travel literature' is a large and inchoate field that crosses over and collapses into many other genres. Rather than attempt to deal with the full range of writing, this section focusses on the structured 'guidebook' or 'handbook' that was both an essentially new product of the Victorian age and probably the dominant type of travel literature within it.

The publication by the house of John Murray in 1836 of *A hand-book for travellers on the continent: being a guide through Holland, Belgium, Prussia and northern Germany and along the Rhine from Holland to Switzerland* is generally taken as the starting point for works of this type.[36] It was written by the young John Murray III who, during his own travels in Europe, found himself disappointed by the lack of accurate, practical information in most contemporary guidebooks. His work, although drawing on existing forms such as the road book,

---

35 Vaughan, *The English guide book*; Ousby, *The Englishman's England*.
36 Lister, *A bibliography of Murray's Handbooks for travellers*; Buzard, *The beaten track*, pp. 64–77.

was immediately recognised by contemporaries as a new phenomenon, with its thoroughness and detail and emphasis on providing current, locally gathered information on the costs and quality of all aspects of foreign travel. The appellation 'hand-book' was both apt and prescient in marketing terms, with the 7 by $4\frac{5}{8}$ inch volumes literally fitting the hand and metaphorically bringing vital information to it. The handbooks rapidly became a central and distinctive feature of the company's list, partly because of Murray's personal interest but also because of the opportunities they offered to reduce the company's reliance on verse and fiction. Before long, the closely clutched Murray became a key signifier of the English (and the British more generally) abroad. 'Into every nook which an Englishman can penetrate he carries his RED HAND-BOOK. He trusts to his MURRAY as he would to his razor, because it is thoroughly English and reliable.'[37] In 1850, a handbook for travellers to Devon and Cornwall commenced a set of guides that, by 1899, covered all English counties.[38]

Others rapidly followed Murray's lead. The company's greatest challenge to their foreign guides always came from the German house of Karl Baedeker, English translations of whose works began to appear from 1861.[39] Both houses were clearly aiming their products at an essentially upper-middle-class market – as late as 1900, Murray's cheapest guides were selling at six shillings and the most expensive (India) for £1 – and much of the imitation came in the form of the production of titles intended for a far less privileged clientele. Edinburgh-based Adam and Charles Black moved into the market from the 1850s with their Black's Guides that ranged from fifty- to sixty-page works on spa towns retailing at a shilling to much more ambitious but not always expensive works on leading European and British destinations. The company was probably the largest single provider of titles aimed at a middle- and lower-middle-class market. By 1900, it was offering about a hundred works, about twenty of them to foreign destinations, ranging in price from 1s to the 10s 6d demanded for a guide to the USA and Canada, but mostly set at 2s 6d.[40] Other significant producers from within the ranks of established book publishers included Dulau, Nelson, Methuen and, from 1896, Ward Lock, whose New Pictorial and Descriptive Guide series became one of the staples of Edwardian domestic tourist literature.

37 *The Times* [n.d.] quoted in Lister, *Bibliography*, p. i. The books were originally in brown covers but quickly adopted the red of rivals Baedeker.
38 The company's guide to London appeared in 1848.
39 Relations between the two companies were initially cordial, but were soured by competition as the century progressed. Gretton, *Baedeker's English guidebooks*.
40 Details from advertisements in *Black's guide to Switzerland*, 1901.

The growing market also drew interest from other sectors of the publishing world and from outside it. Cartographers provided a rich array of material for the tourist guide, from simple sketch railway maps to complex fold-out town plans and topographical surveys, and it is unsurprising that a number 'dabbled in guide-book production as a remunerative sideline'. The cheapness with which lithographic transfers could be taken of portions of their existing maps was a critical factor here.[41] Edward Mogg was one of the first to identify this opportunity in the 1840s, and other leading companies including John Bartholomew and Edward Stanford, whose two-shilling Tourist Guides was a popular series, followed suit. From yet another direction, Thomas Cook & Son added the publication of guidebooks to their most popular destinations to their rich repertoire of tourist aids from the 1870s, and most railway companies produced, or more normally had produced for them, a variety of publications. Some of the earliest and best-known titles were those produced by George Measom between 1862, which saw the appearance of his *Illustrated guide to the Great Western Railway*, and 1867, by which date he had effectively covered the whole of the British network. These books were probably self-published although several bore the imprint of W. H. Smith.[42]

While some of the cheaper titles may well have reached an audience within the upper reaches of the working class, it is significant that some provincial companies thought it commercially viable to produce short guides to British destinations aimed at the emergent 'popular' tourist. Manchester-based Abel Heywood launched a series of penny guides in the 1860s, some of which were still in print in the 1880s, while the York firm of T. A. J. Waddington produced a set of fourteen (mainly) similarly priced Practical Guides to a variety of northern locations in the 1890s. Although accurate data on sales figures are scant, the longevity of certain key titles is suggestive of the scale of the market. Murray's *Switzerland*, for example, went through eighteen editions between 1838 and 1891, with aggregate sales of some 45,000, while Black's *Lake District* managed twenty-four versions between the early 1850s and 1905. Similarly, many of the late Victorian guides to parts of the British Empire were still being published into the 1950s and 1960s.[43]

The hallmark of Murray's and Baedeker's output was a highly rational, codified approach that 'set a style of bureaucratic efficiency that would render individually produced guidebooks idiosyncratic and obsolete'.[44] Most

---

41 Smith, *Victorian maps of the British Isles*, p. 106.   42 See entry by G. H. Martin in *ODNB*.
43 Vaughan, *The English guide book*, p. 47; British Library catalogue; MacKenzie, 'Empires of travel', p. 36.
44 Buzard, *The beaten track*, p. 31.

other guides, irrespective of pricing, happily adopted the same characteristics, although some of the slimmer volumes were less didactic. A classic formula evolved whereby, after a short overview of a country or region's history, geography and crucial administrative peculiarities, readers were provided with detailed itineraries constructed along (closely measured) road or, more normally, railway routes. Advice was given on local idiosyncrasies of habit and character along with practical advice on hotel and restaurant costs and the perennial problems of tipping and other dealings with servants, drivers and guides. Great emphasis was placed on the currency of the information offered, with the best guides especially diligent in keeping their public apprised of changing standards of hotel accommodation. Thus, while the Schwartzer Adler inn at Arth on the Lucerne to Schwytz route was deemed 'tolerably good' in Murray's 1838 *Switzerland*, by 1846 readers were warned that 'care should be taken to guard against *wilful* detention on the part of the landlord'. By 1874 it was simply 'good'.[45]

This rationality, as visible here as it was in Eliza Acton's recipe measurements and every sports writer's interest in records, and so much in keeping with the needs and values of an urban-industrial culture, also impacted upon writing style. Certainly, the earlier titles could include a certain level of individuality and subjectivity. In his 1846 *Switzerland*, for example, Murray witheringly suggested that the recently formed Swiss Confederation of Innkeepers might better be termed '*a combination for extorting the largest possible sums of money from travellers*'.[46] However, although such overt narration might still be encountered in the years ahead, it was generally suppressed by the writers' search for a suitably neutral expert voice that was always economic and directive in style. According to the author of one 1850 guide to Scotland, this process should eschew the more poetic language much loved by many practitioners in favour of 'a plain and intelligible account... much eloquence is often needlessly expended in ambitious eulogiums on the beauty or grandeur of natural scenery, of which no adequate idea can be conveyed to the mind by any written description'.[47] Although some crisp and enjoyable writing could still be found, guidebooks generally became terser and more functional as the century progressed.[48] Indeed, especially in some of the cheaper series, an obvious and uncritical précising of larger works (Murray's were most at risk) could lead to a flat and bland tone. The tendency for authorship to remain anonymous, or at best largely hidden, added considerably to this process.

45 Pp. 40, 43, 40.   46 Original italics, p. xxvi.
47 *Black's picturesque tourist of Scotland*, 8th edn (Edinburgh, 1850), preface.
48 For biographical details of leading writers, see Lister, *Bibliography*, pp. 101–87.

Most fundamentally, the new style of guidebook had a profound impact upon the whole nature of the tourist experience. The 'tourist gaze', the highly directed and systematised habits of vision and ordering of knowledge derived from the writings of the professional experts, was obviously being tutored long before the nineteenth century. However, the sheer scale and downward percolation of travel literature during that century meant that ever greater numbers were encouraged to 'appreciat[e] particular sights from a particular angle' and through a particular narrative.[49] Absolutely crucial to this process was the allotment of both the space given to individual sites within guidebooks and the time recommended for the duration of visits, allocations both made very much in accordance with the dictates of contemporary fashion. This crucial contribution 'to the guidebooks' authority as arbiters of cultural value' was inevitably achieved as much by exclusion as inclusion. Much of northern England, for example, was too 'spoilt from a picturesque point of view by the deleterious character of the commercial pursuits carried on in them' ever to gain significant levels of attention from writers who generally saw the 'true North' as typified by buildings and topography untouched by recent economic change.[50]

In similar fashion, the guidebook became the key mechanism through which the tourist was taught to think of specific sites, cities, regions and nations in terms of highly distinctive signifiers that provided the visitor with an experience 'authentic' to it. Geographies were simplified so that places were reduced to certain buildings, groups of streets or particular districts, with all other elements excluded according to fashion or because they reminded visitors too much of the daily life they had left behind. Claire Hancock, for example, has shown how British guidebooks to Paris in the 1850s and 1860s increasingly identified the boulevards that followed the Haussmannisation of the city as 'revealing the essence of Parisian life and the Parisian character. Tourists were invited to join the crowd of *flâneurs* pacing the *trottoirs* amongst cafés and street entertainments, or to observe the moving panorama from the top of an omnibus.' This was part of a wider discourse in which Paris was cast as the ' "city of pleasure" to be contrasted with the "city of business" across the channel'.[51] There was indeed concern within the city that the imperial government, anxious to attract British tourists, was adopting planning policies that

---

49 Urry, *The tourist gaze*; Ousby, *The Englishman's England*, p. 5.
50 Buzard, *The beaten track*, p. 287; M. J. B. Baddeley, *Yorkshire* (part one) (1902), p. xiii. On tourism and the representation of the north of England more generally, Russell, *Looking north*, pp. 45–78.
51 Hancock, *'Capitale du plaisir'*, p. 70, and generally, pp. 64–76.

encouraged such a version of Parisian life, thus making some inhabitants feel uneasy within their own city.

While the guidebook was increasingly presented as a quasi-scientific text carrying essentially value-free material, it could, therefore, carry all manner of implicit and explicit judgements that helped shape and reinforce contemporary mentalities. Crucially, this function extended well beyond the domain of the tourist location (or non-location): the guidebook was to serve as a powerful vehicle for the discursive construction of a far wider social and cultural landscape. Unsurprisingly for a genre produced within and aimed ultimately at the narrower end of the social pyramid, its dominant narratives reinforced conservative viewpoints. Most guidebooks, for example, were certainly gendered in very distinctive ways. The tourist addressed was invariably masculine, told that 'he' must visit a particular site or place 'himself' in a particular location. Where women were acknowledged they were very much identified as the weaker sex. Murray's 1867 *Handbook* for Yorkshire noted that the climb up Gordale Scar near Malham 'is easy, and is continually made by ladies', while in the next year *Black's spa guide to Buxton*'s entry on the Blue John Mines at Castleton happily reported that 'the exploration can be made easily, even by ladies'.[52] The dominance of male writers was clearly a factor here, with women comprising only about 6 per cent of those writing, editing or updating Murray's handbooks between 1836 and 1914.[53]

Perhaps most importantly, tourist literature played a key role in the maintenance of distinctive racial and national stereotypes, with introductory sections often homing in on the perceived distinctive characteristics of soon to be visited peoples. Explicit comment was perhaps most pronounced earlier in the period as when John Murray III's unflattering comments on Swiss innkeepers were extended to the nation more generally. Some three pages of the 1838 *Handbook* (largely repeated eight years later) were devoted to their failings. He focussed especially on 'that venality of character which has passed into a proverb' and self-interest that sat ill with the country's success in establishing a higher degree of political liberty than its continental European counterparts.

> A spirit of time-serving and a love of money appear the influencing motives in the national character, and the people who have enjoyed freedom longer than any other in Europe, are particularly distinguished for fighting the battles of any master, however tyrannical, who will buy their services; for sending forth

52 Murray, p. 381, Black, p. 36.
53 Derived from Lister, *Bibliography*, pp. 101–87. Women, including groups or individuals 'unprotected' by men, were nevertheless increasingly visible in many countries (especially Italy) as the nineteenth century progressed.

the most obsequious and drudging of varlets; for extortionate innkeepers, and, among the lower classes of Swiss for almost universal mendacity.[54]

These characterisations were certainly not immutably fixed, at least when European peoples were under scrutiny. When T. C. Paris and C. Marrett updated Murray's *Switzerland* for its fifteenth edition in 1874, they drew a slightly more sympathetic picture of the country's population. While the inhabitants of its German parts were depicted as 'often sullen, obstinate and disagreeable', the authors excised many of Murray's earlier observations and gave a more flattering view of Swiss political liberty. They also wondered 'whether an ordinary traveller is competent to form an opinion of the whole nation from those classes with which he is thrown into contact and which have been taught to make him their prey'.[55]

Depictions of the indigenous peoples of Asia, Africa and the Middle East that the more adventurous tourists were increasingly encountering were rather more settled. As with the examples above, attitudes were often laid bare through explicit comment. Readers of Murray's *Handbook for travellers in Syria and Palestine* (1903), written by pioneering Egyptologist Dr Mary Brodrick, were informed that 'The main characteristics of the Syrian, whether he be a townsman, a *fellâh*, or a Bedouin Arab, are ease and courtesy, lighthearted-ness, hospitality, childishness, indolence and deceit... Under the exterior air of politeness and candour, there lurks in every Syrian an ingrained spirit of deceit.'[56] However, contemporary perceptions were more likely to be articu-lated and reinforced by more covert methods. John Mackenzie has noted how guidebook depictions of relationships between Britain and its Indian empire were constructed around a set of distinctive site selections, historical narratives and overall structures that created 'a relentless textualisation of dominion and control'. He notes, amongst other things, a stress on the role of British engi-neering feats in the modernisation of India, a consistent attempt to legitimise British rule through stories of the martyrdom of its subjects during the1857 'mutiny' and even an editorial policy change that reflected contemporary impe-rial propaganda. Four separate volumes on Madras, Bombay, Bengal and the Punjab and North West had appeared between 1879 and 1883 but, from 1891, these were combined into a single volume in an act that echoed the common claim that Britain was creating an empire from a loose assemblage of states.[57] While travel writing could be used to point up shortcomings in the English or British national character – literature on Italy and the Mediterranean more generally often set the lack of impudence and, above all, drunkenness amongst

54 Pp. xxx–xxxiii.   55 P. xlv.   56 P. xxxviii.   57 MacKenzie, 'Empires of travel', pp. 23–6.

the lower orders against their counterparts at home – the overall superiority of British cultures and habits was clearly signalled in a variety of ways.[58]

For all their importance beyond the specific domain of tourism, it would nevertheless be unfortunate if guidebooks were seen here merely as indicators and indices of wider mores within Victorian and Edwardian society. Full acknowledgement must be given to their sheer practical value. The explosion of such writing obviously reflected the growth of tourism but it surely also helped stimulate that growth 'by coaxing timid potential tourists on to the field and easing their way across it'.[59] Armed with local knowledge and many thousands of words of clear direction and guidance that guaranteed a full schedule and the impossibility of missing the key sites, the thought of travelling the world (and not just its foreign parts) became less daunting, more manageable. For those prepared to rise to the challenge, the new literature offered to make travel a true rational recreation for the upper and middle classes, with the best works offering an informal curriculum of great richness, both within their own pages and in terms of the extensive stimulus for further study they encouraged. Murray's 1873 *Rome*, for example, listed some forty titles in its bibliography, many of them in languages other than English.[60] While the Murray, Black or Stanford guide might appear to have been an intellectual straitjacket for the easily satirised Briton in Florence, Cairo or York Minster assiduously working through its pages, it was a helpful and necessary one for many and a starting place and source of freedom for many others.

By about 1900, most major Victorian guidebook series had largely completed their coverage of current and likely destinations and, although new opportunities were constantly afforded to publishers by new social habits such as cycling, golfing and motoring, it is hard to avoid the sense of a genre, if not in decline, then certainly no longer dynamic. In 1901, John Murray IV sold most of the *Handbook* titles to Edward Stanford, the series's flagship status no longer able to offset its limited profitability to a company seeking to be less reliant on non-fiction. Stanford, in turn, was not unhappy to sell it on to Findlay and James Muirhead, editors of the English-language Baedekers, in 1915.[61] The First World War obviously disrupted the tourist trade dramatically and added to publishers' concerns, although the classic Victorian guidebook did not die with the war: 1918 saw the launch by the Muirheads of the *Blue Guide*, and many existing titles remained in publication and in use. Indeed, although their tone may be very different, such distinctive later twentieth-century products as

58 Pemble, *Mediterranean passion*, pp. 128–42.   59 Buzard, *The beaten track*, p. 76.
60 Pemble, *Mediterranean passion*, pp. 68–9.   61 Lister, *Bibliography*, p. xxi.

the Rough Guide and the Lonely Planet series adopt many of their trademark devices.

'Leisure' books were never concerned solely with leisure. In the case of cookery and gardening, they could also serve as manuals for those earning their living in these trades. Moreover, many books, rigorously instructional in intent, demanded much hard work from their readers at the point of consumption and later in the kitchen, music room, foreign museum or wherever. They could also be status symbols, an elegantly bound collection of the Badminton Library or a full set of Grove's *Dictionary of Music* serving as a badge of taste, connoisseurship or a certain standard of living. Whatever their function, they were read in ever greater numbers and helped stimulate a remarkable number of leisure pursuits and to articulate and shape debates and issues within them. They are a rich source for historians of the book and of a great deal else, and if this chapter has encouraged their further exploration it will have succeeded in at least one important regard.

14

Publishing for trades and professions

DAVID MCKITTERICK

When publication of the *Oxford English dictionary* reached the entry for 'profession', readers were reminded of Addison writing in the *Spectator* in 1711: that the word had referred specifically to 'the three learned professions of divinity, law, and medicine'. As three central subjects of the early sixteenth-century curriculum at the ancient universities they were manifestly inadequate as an aid to definitions even in the eighteenth century. The concept of the professional not simply as distinct from the amateur, but, more importantly, as pertaining to those who lived by their professional skills, implied certain kinds of education. In 1828, John Leslie, Professor of Natural Philosophy at Edinburgh, published a slim handbook *Rudiments of plane geometry*, 'designed chiefly for professional men'. Anxious to 'connect the ancient with the modern discoveries', and fearful of the inadequacies of the fifth book of Euclid as it was usually taught, he further included a summary of some of the principles of plane trigonometry for the use of surveyors. This profession was certainly not new. Much more important – for many others quite apart from Leslie – was the contemporary need for mathematical competence among those brought up on a diet of ancient languages. Leslie spoke from the academy, and from Edinburgh rather than Oxford or Cambridge. At Trinity College Dublin, professional students were defined in the late 1860s as those studying medicine, divinity, law and – a mid-century reform – engineering.[1] Other commentators spoke from the street. Charles Knight, with his tongue partly in his cheek, wrote of thieving as a profession.[2] As Walter Besant pointed out in 1888, while new professions had come into existence, public esteem had increased for the three older ones.[3] In a world where the social difference between trade and profession was ever

---

1 *Dublin University Calendar, passim*. For engineering at Trinity College, see McDowell, *Trinity College Dublin*, pp.180–5.
2 Knight, *Once upon a time*, p. 426.
3 Besant, *Fifty years ago*, Conclusion. The fullest general study of the debates over professions, and the definition of new ones, remains Reader, *Professional men*.

more important, and as the latter term was extended by those who had most to gain from the status this implied, writers as different as F. D. Maurice, Matthew Arnold and M. E. Braddon sought to define the term by contrasting it with other orders, whether trade or minor gentry.[4]

As social changes dragged the word into new realms, in 1852 the Commission on the University of Oxford reflected that, if structures and methods of teaching were transformed, then a professorship would itself become a recognised profession.

> If the Professoriate could be placed in a proper condition, those Fellows of Colleges whose services the University would wish to retain, would be less tempted and would never be compelled to leave it for positions and duties for which their academical labours had in no way prepared them, but would look forward to some sphere of usefulness within the University ... A Professorship would then, in fact, become a recognised Profession.[5]

Professions were to be distinguished from business or commerce. Oxford and Cambridge prepared people for professions, but not necessarily for the latter. Elizabeth Gaskell summed up one point of view. 'Where was the necessary income for a marriage to come from? Roger had his fellowship ... but the income for that would be lost if he married; he had no profession.'[6] From the 1860s Oxford and Cambridge increasingly focussed their attention on the sons of professional men. The terminology was slippery, and was understood differently according to place or to individual. But as the old universities accommodated themselves to modern demands, so their curricula were modified, or even in some areas transformed, as their structures of teaching and employment were also gradually changed. A new emphasis on publication, both with trade publishers and with new programmes in the university presses, followed.[7]

Writing, publication and the book trades were intimately connected with identities in professional life. Thus, the failure of senior members of Oxford to produce major published work was a part of their insufficiency as a profession. 'The fact that so few books of profound research emanate from the University of Oxford materially impairs its character as a seat of learning, and consequently its hold on the respect of the nation.'[8] If the immediate context of this discussion

4 For Arnold's evidence to the Taunton Commission on Endowed Schools (1869) see Perkin, *The rise of professional society*, pp. 118–19.
5 Oxford University Commission, *Report and evidence. Parliamentary papers* 1852.xxii, p. 94.
6 Elizabeth Gaskell, *Wives and daughters* (1866).
7 Rothblatt, *The revolution of the dons*; for Oxford see for example Engel, *From clergyman to don*; Curthoys, 'The careers of Oxford men', in Brock and Curthoys (eds.), *The history of the University of Oxford. 6. Nineteenth-century Oxford*, part 1, pp. 477–510.
8 Oxford University Commission, *Report and evidence. Parliamentary papers* 1852.xxii, pp. 93–4.

was specifically of the nineteenth century and of Oxford, there was also a more general point to be made in the failure of the seventeenth-century Laudian statutes to ensure a continuing professoriate. 'It is generally acknowledged that both Oxford and the country at large, suffer greatly from the absence of a body of learned men, devoting their lives to the cultivation of Science, and to the direction of Academical Education.' More comprehensively, the relationship of publishing to professional life was by no means limited to the universities. At a much more profound level, professional life of all kinds was in part actually defined by the book trades. The demands made on publishers were part of the nineteenth-century reforms and extensions of professional practice, not only as new groups of activities were identified but also as they were developed and characterised by the use of print. In turn, the evolution and immense growth of the professional classes both inspired new publishers and provided fresh opportunities for those that were long established.

Although there were earlier attempts, the census of England and Wales for 1861 provided a much-developed and revised study of the numbers employed in clearly identified professions.[9] This divided them into three primary groups: those concerned in national or local government; those in the armed services; and those in other civilian professions. The third group included clergy and other church officers (a group that included 3,053 women, and that ranged from bishops to choristers and sextons), those in law, those in medicine, authors and other literary people, artists, musicians, actors and actresses, teachers and 'scientific persons'. As a whole, teachers were by far the most numerous, with 110,364 employed in this way. Medicine and the churches (established, nonconformist and Roman Catholic) were next, with about 38,500 in each of the two groups. There were only slightly more scientific persons (4,095, with just 42 women) than there were actors and actresses (4,068); and at the bottom came authors, a total of 3,580 including 185 women. The categories naturally overlapped in several ways, in that (for example) a Fellow of an Oxford or Cambridge college might count himself as a clergyman, a man of science or a teacher: there were many who filled all three capacities. There was also a world of difference in the attainments lumped under religion, just as there was between those who made their living on the stage and those who did so at the bar. Nor is it clear how far the authors were living entirely by their pens, or were supported by other means: it may be that there was a difference especially in the ways that women saw themselves at this point. The definition of professions

---

9 Corfield, in *Power and the professions in Britain*, pp. 31–6, provides a snapshot of professional occupations in 1851, but the changes in ordering the data at each census make precise comparisons hazardous.

was by occupational group, not by paper qualifications. They were not in the industrial, commercial, domestic or mechanical classes. Law stationers were entered under law, while booksellers were part of the book trades, with publishers and in a group encompassing art and mechanic productions. Bankers and actuaries were counted as mercantile.

Nonetheless, for all the anomalies, the figures do provide a mid-century background against which to match the development of publishing for the professions. They are also of limited use when comparing groups decade by decade, as definitions changed or were modified, emphases on individuals' multiple occupations varied, and concepts of occupations fluctuated even amongst those making the returns. Within these provisos, however, it is useful to note that between 1861 and 1891, a period of great change in publishing and professional education and practice, the numbers of those employed under the heading of law rose by about 36 per cent; those in medicine more than doubled. The population of England and Wales as a whole rose in the same period from about 20 million to about 29 million. While women were gradually accepted into more professions during the late nineteenth century, most remained predominantly male. In only one major category, teachers, did women outnumber men in the 1861 census, but they did so by a proportion of about 8:3. In medicine, they were in a majority among nurses, but persistent misogyny among doctors prevented the advance of all but a very few women until the end of the century.[10]

The three traditional learned professions had in a manner been augmented generations earlier. The skills of architects, of surveyors, of engineers, of military and naval officers and of accountants were not new to the nineteenth century. The *Assurance Magazine* (1850–), under the auspices of the Institute of Actuaries (founded 1849), is still published. The *Civil Engineer and Architect's Journal* appeared in 1837. In the sense that it was possible to live by one's pen, writing had been a profession in Britain since at least the late seventeenth century, and for some people much earlier. Public service, whether in Whitehall, in Parliament or in the diplomatic or colonial services, could readily be counted as a profession. In the 1870s, librarians organised themselves into a professional association, largely for the management of the new public libraries. Entry to the professions was increasingly often, but by no means universally, by means of written examination. It often, but by no means invariably, implied the possession of a diploma or other certificate. While it was (as James Murray and his assistants found in compiling their dictionary) not easy to define what was

---

10 Bartrip, *Mirror of medicine*, pp. 170–4, with further references.

meant by the word, there was a strong sense of what it was not. Hence, and quite apart from the census headings, while some professions could be defined by their self-imposed standards, often involving examinations and qualifications, others depended on different demonstrations of merit. Some of the changes in attitudes and values as well as practice were a central theme of *Middlemarch* at the beginning of the 1870s. Continuing debates as to the value of experience rather than paper qualifications characterised not just the nineteenth century, but most of the twentieth as well.

Among dozens of titles in the trades, where many of the same commercial principles about publishing held as with those in the professions, a few examples must suffice. For the retail trades the *Draper and Clothier* lasted from 1859 to 1862. More long-lived, the *Grocer* (1862–) soon spawned supplements, the *Oil Trade Review* and the *Wine Trade Review*; the *Brewer's Journal* followed in 1865. Hairdressers, curriers, pawnbrokers and saddlers all had their specialist periodicals. In 1883, one guide to the press listed about 130 journals and newspapers it described as trade organs, from *Adams' National Mineral Water Trades Recorder* to *Wool and Textile Fabrics*.[11] In such publishing, the divide between trade and profession, felt so acutely in social life, was very far from clear. Groombridge, publishers whose strong professional list included the pioneering *Solicitor's Diary* (1848), had a list of journals including the *Banker's Magazine*, the *Civil Engineer and Architect's Journal*, the *Florist's Journal and Gardener's Record*, the *Farmer's Herald*, the *Water Cure Journal and Hygienic Herald*, various religious magazines, and the *Railway almanac*. Money had to be made where it could, and there were very few publishers who could afford to specialise more than to a certain extent. Much of the success of such journals was thanks to manufacturers' need to advertise. The book trade itself had long recognised the possibilities of national collaboration for its daily management and development; and in this new world of journals those listing new publications vied with each other, claiming the widest coverage as well as the greatest reliability.[12]

Just as groups of tradesmen or of skilled manual workers, in industry, manufacture, commerce or agriculture, were linked by publications, so were the professions. At one extreme was the observation, again from the Oxford University Commission, respecting the relationship of speech to print in the specific context of learning:

> It has sometimes been argued that the invention of printing has superseded the use of public Lectures, and that Books now convey the knowledge formerly

11 *May's British & Irish Press Guide* 1883.   12 See below, pp. 561–2.

communicated by Professors. It may be remarked however that, if in former days Professorial Lectures were made necessary by the want of books, at the present day an able Teacher is rendered no less indispensable by their abundance. Such a Teacher furnishes the Student with a chart to guide him through the labyrinth of knowledge that surrounds him.[13]

Whatever the skills – manual, commercial or professional – the printed word sat alongside oral transmission of knowledge, and experience. It was a complement to apprenticeship, not just at Oxford but also in the reformed and examination-dependent Civil Service and, increasingly, in professions of all kinds. Specialised textbooks, handbooks, magazines and newspapers provided news, information, training and entertainment; and in their titles they targeted audiences with growing precision. While the book trade did not create professions, any more than it created trades, it did promote the practices and conventions that strengthened social groups – here as in other parts of the population. As always, by defining activities it also fostered them.

Periodicals and magazines were more important than books in much of this market. The number of such publications grew substantially in the 1840s. By the mid-century there was scarcely an interest group other than the smallest that did not have its own journal or newsletter, and they became even more numerous after the abolition of taxes on paper. Jobbing printing was cheap, and many local publications of this kind have disappeared completely: very few parts of the country had a library able or willing to gather and preserve such transitory material, and the British Museum had neither the wish nor the resources to expend energy on collecting it under the Copyright Act. By contrast, at a national level, publishers paid increasing attention to group interests, particularly in markets where large manufacturers or named brands dominated.

While social judgements sought to distinguish professions from trades or other activities, for publishers seeking to identify potential markets there was often little structural difference. The crucial point was that editorial matter, advertising (on which most journals and magazines depended) and sales efforts could be focussed on particular groups of earners. 'As this work will be constantly referred to by parties interested in Railways during the entire year', remarked Groombridge, for example, in promoting their *Railway almanac* in 1848, 'it will be found a very useful medium for all advertisements addressed to a wealthy class of readers.'

13 Oxford University Commission, *Report and evidence. Parliamentary papers* 1852.xxii, p. 96.

Titles were not everything, even when they seemed at their most explicit. The monthly *Professional World*, launched in 1892, had nothing at all to do with any of the professions conventionally recognised by the more serious-minded. It was 'published in the interests of the musical, dramatic, and artistic professions, and of all artistes who appear before the public'. The need, or at least demand, for such a vehicle was quickly demonstrated, as circulation reached 10,000, but it proved unsustainable, and the journal ceased three years later having made its point: 'Of late years the numbers of lecturers, reciters, entertainers, vocalists, instrumentalists, and representatives of every branch of art, have increased a hundredfold. And yet this immense ... body of artistes has had until now no organ devoted to their interests.'[14] As usual, changes in convention were working at different paces in different parts of society. In 1892, also, the *Professional annual register* made its one and only appearance, as a list of lecturers, musicians and dramatic recitalists. Published in Birmingham rather than London, it was little more than an advertising medium, but it sought to serve these groups as much as *Crockford's clerical directory* had by then been serving Church of England clergymen for decades.

Of all the professions, medicine was more prolifically served with print than any other, as the publication industry throve on professional disagreements and demands for reform. The press also offered a much-needed vehicle to report fresh discoveries[15] Easily the noisiest voice was that of Thomas H. Wakley, a qualified surgeon, who launched *The Lancet* in 1823. Encouraged by the success of the *New England Journal of Medicine*, published at Boston, he set a different course, using his own weekly journal for a series of vigorously outspoken campaigns, notably against the Royal College of Surgeons and against surgical malpractice: some of his most celebrated accusations went to court.[16] Not for nothing was the title chosen on account of its double meaning, as a window by which to admit light, and as an instrument, in his words, to 'cut out the dross'. He had the pugilist instincts of an investigative journalist, with a style to match, and by the late 1820s there were 8,000 subscribers. By the 1860s the journal claimed to have a circulation greater than any other scientific or medical periodical – a claim that the *British Medical Journal* was to make in turn in the 1870s. With no formal list of qualified doctors available until 1858, there was ample room for fraud and incompetence. In 1835 Wakley became MP for the new seat of Finsbury, and took his campaigns to the House of Commons, where he remained until 1852. *The Lancet* became required reading not just

---

14 'To the public', *Professional World* (1892), p. 3.
15 LeFanu, *British periodicals of medicine, 1640–1899*.
16 Bostetter, 'The journalism of Thomas Wakley'. See also Sprigge, *The life and times of Thomas Wakley*.

for general practitioners, but also for anyone interested in the reform of the medical profession.[17] *Punch* paraded him in 1841, and Tom Hood satirised him in his *Whimsicalities* in 1844. In 1855 the price was dropped from eightpence to sevenpence, part of a general trend in prices of periodicals. Wakley remained editor until his death in 1862, when publication passed to his son.

The *London Medical Gazette*, published by Longman and also a weekly, first appeared in 1827; it was to last until 1851. It was generally considered to be less concerned with news than with reflections on current developments – an impression conveyed not least by the format it shared with the serious quarterly journals. In words that were reminders of the connections between oral and printed communication, it also took exception to the way in which unnamed others (Wakley cannot have been far from the editor's mind) had disturbed the tranquil existence of the medical profession:

> A few years ago a set of literary plunderers broke in on the peace and quiet of our profession. Lecturers who had spent their lives in collecting knowledge, arranging for communication, and acquiring the difficult art of oral instruction, saw the produce of their lives suddenly snatched from them, and published for the profit of others, with the additional mortification of finding what they had taken so much pains with, disfigured by bad English and ridiculous or mischievous blunders. Whoever attempted to arrest these piracies became the object of furious and unrelenting abuse.[18]

In this spirit, the new journal sought respectability for the profession. Rather a wider cross-section of the profession – and not a few interested people outside it – relied on the weekly *Medical Gazette*, which was compared to *The Times* itself for its authority and range.

Outside London, the medical profession existed in a confused mixture of traditional city environments such as Edinburgh, Glasgow and the university towns, and various smaller market or cathedral towns. It was a profession that depended on consultation and on sociability, and the level of expertise varied accordingly.[19] There had been local groups in at least Colchester, Gloucestershire, Huntingdonshire and Plymouth since the late eighteenth century, and by 1832 their number had risen to over forty.[20] The *Edinburgh Journal of Medical Science* had lasted only a few months, in 1826–7. Neither the *Liverpool Medical Gazette* (1833) nor the *Liverpool Medical Journal* (1834) managed to establish itself, and both died shortly after birth. The sixpenny weekly

17 See for example Loudon, *Medical care and the general practitioner*, chs. 12 and 13.
18 *London Medical Gazette* 1 (1827), p. 2.   19 Corfield, *Power and the professions*, ch. 6.
20 *Ibid.*, p. 160.

Dublin Medical Press (1839) acquired a following on the other side of the Irish Sea. The quarterly *British and Foreign Medical Review* began in 1836. Much more important, the *British Medical Journal* began its complicated gestation in 1840 at Worcester as the *Provincial Medical and Surgical Journal*, a sevenpenny weekly that was the brainchild of P. Hennis Green, a paediatrician at the Hunterian School of Medicine. He was joined by Dr Robert Streeten, of Worcester, a member of the Council of the Provincial Medical and Surgical Association, a group founded by a local doctor in 1832. The journal was soon adopted by the Provincial Medical and Surgical Association, whose purpose was to bring together the often opposing worlds of hospital consultants and general practitioners, and it quickly established a national circulation.[21] As its influence spread, in 1852 it absorbed the *London Journal of Medicine* whose editor, J. R. Cormack, was also part-editor of the Worcester publication. The title was changed in the following year to the *Association Medical Journal*, and the modern name was adopted in 1857. Cormack had trained in medicine at Edinburgh, where he was founder-editor of the *Edinburgh Monthly Journal of Medical Science* in 1841–6. His move to London and to general practice at Putney in 1845 changed his home city but not his appetite for journalism. This amalgamation of the provincial and London titles met with resentment, and he resigned the editorship of the *Association Medical Journal* in 1855, the year in which the Provincial Medical and Surgical Association became the British Medical Association. His career and influence as an editor were more successful than his several professional disappointments: despite a distinguished early career at Edinburgh, he was refused permission to lecture there; he failed in his attempt to become secretary of the new General Medical Council; he achieved only limited success as a GP; and he sought unsuccessfully to be medical officer for Holborn. After the mid-1850s his career moved away from journalism, but for fifteen years he had been at the centre of the reorganisation of general practice, as provincial medicine was brought into London's orbit and some of the most enduring organs of central administration and professional organisation were established.[22]

The 1840s and 1850s were characterised by further calls for reform in the Colleges of Physicians and of Surgeons. By the 1860s, medical periodical publishing was dominated by the publishers J. & A. Churchill. Their highly regarded sixpenny weekly *Medical Times and Gazette*, which they took over in 1851, was valued especially for the series of lectures it printed, on matters as varied as

---

21 Mitchell, *Newspaper press directory* (1846), pp. 204–5; Bartrip, *Mirror of medicine*.
22 For Cormack's career, see P. W. J. Bartrip in the *ODNB*. See also Bartrip, *Mirror of medicine*.

tuberculosis, ophthalmology and medical jurisprudence. Jenner was among its contributors, and it paid particular attention to developments overseas. The more specialised *British Journal of Dental Science* and *Pharmaceutical Journal* appeared monthly. Their *Asylum Journal of Mental Science* and *British and Foreign Medico-Chirurgical Review* were quarterlies. Besides these, they also published a half-yearly digest of the progress of medical science and the annual medical directories for the separate parts of the British Isles. The three other principal London weeklies were all in private hands: *The Lancet*, the *Medical Circular* and the *British Medical Journal*. The monthly *Edinburgh Medical and Surgical Journal* was handled by Simpkin Marshall; Longman published the *Dublin Quarterly Journal of Medical Science* (1864–, published in Dublin by Fann & Co.); and the quarterly *Glasgow Medical Journal* (1828–) was handled in London by Mackenzie, in Paternoster Row.

The Medical Act (1858) signalled not so much a change of direction or of organisation in the fractured medical profession, as consolidation and definition. It was a professional compromise. For the book trades it made little difference, and it was not until 1868 that Macmillan launched the *Practitioner*, 'a monthly journal of therapeutics and public health'. In 1866–8 the firm had published J. R. Reynolds's standard two-volume *System of medicine*, and in 1867 Henry Maudsley's *Physiology and pathology of the mind*. The more general *Nature* was to follow in 1869, as the late 1860s witnessed a broadening of interests in the company's list, including *Brain*, on neurology, in 1878.

In other areas of medicine, the *Pharmaceutical Journal*, organ of the Pharmaceutical Society, was founded like its parent body in 1841. Together with the School of Pharmacy established in the following year, it formalised what had hitherto been matter for dispute in the medical profession, and made clear the separate status and responsibilities of pharmacists for their own training. The sixpenny *British Journal of Dental Science* was founded in 1856, and the *Dental Review* lasted from 1859 to 1867. With the founding of schools of dentistry, separate from the ordinary medical schools (the London School of Dental Surgery was opened in 1859), and the placing of dental education on a firmly separate footing, there was a natural need for periodical and monograph support. The *Monthly Review of Dental Surgery* (1872–) became also the *Journal* of the British Dental Association in 1880. Following the Dentists Act (1878) and the ensuing register for dentists, the British Dental Association was founded in 1879 and dentistry was gradually brought under professional control. The sixpenny monthly *Dental Record* followed in 1881, and the threepenny *Dental Weekly* in 1895: the second, published by Billings & Co. in Poland Street, Soho, lasted only five months despite (or perhaps because of) its pioneering efforts as a weekly and its wish to be 'free and independent, untrammelled by the selfish desires of small sections'. The *British Dental Journal*, published by the General Council of Medical Education from 1898, was intended to break some of these divisions, and introduce some discipline in a profession that developed more slowly than other branches of medicine. The monthly *Ophthalmic Review*, published by Churchill, was founded in 1881, but it was a decade before opticians had their own journal. Both owed their existence to Jacob Bell, a chemist in Oxford Street.

Large general publishers such as Longman or Macmillan grew their own professional lists as part of much wider concerns, where professional development followed naturally after their educational lists at school, university and training levels. Meanwhile the period between the 1830s and 1914 was especially remarkable for the development and increase in numbers of substantial businesses devoted almost solely to meeting the needs of trades and professions. In some fields, and particularly law and medicine, the old tradition of the bookseller-publisher survived and prospered. Some were carefully placed as to their address. The scientific and medical bookseller H. K. Lewis, in Gower Street, for example, was founded in 1844, eighteen years after University College, its neighbour. University College Hospital was a few steps away. For some years, when many shops did not expect account customers to pay more often than annually, it offered a discount of 20 per cent for cash on new books. It both ran a specialist circulating library, at a guinea per annum, and published books dealing mainly with disease, hygiene, surgery, physiology and gynaecology. As London agent for Cambridge University Press, it published the Cambridge series in biology (edited by A. E. Shipley of Christ's College), physics (edited by R. T. Glazebrook of the Cavendish Laboratory) and geology.

Lewis's geographical position lent it special prominence. As a publisher it was but one amongst several. John Churchill, in New Burlington Street (off Regent Street), has already been mentioned as the most important of the medical publishers in mid-Victorian Britain. In 1863 alone, this firm published forty-seven new books or new editions, mostly by members of the staffs of London hospitals. One of the secrets of its success was a series of manuals on medical and kindred subjects, which by 1864 were said to have sold 128,500 copies.[23] By then, Erasmus Wilson on *Anatomy* was in its eighth edition, and Alfred Taylor on *Medical jurisprudence* was in its seventh. The latter had been first published in 1844, and was to reach its eleventh edition in 1886: perhaps sales were helped by Taylor's involvement with the Palmer poisoning case of 1856. Such firms

---

23 *The London and provincial medical directory* 1864.

had a large market share, but there were many pockets of strength elsewhere. William Osler's *Principles and practice of medicine*, published by Appleton in New York in 1892, was an immediate success on both sides of the Atlantic, and reached its eighth edition in 1912: in Britain it was at first published by Young J. Pentland, a specialist medical firm in Edinburgh. Gray's *Anatomy*, first published by the educational and theological firm J. W. Parker in 1858, was taken over by Longman when they bought Parker's business a few years later.[24] The eighteenth edition was issued in 1913, in a strong medical list that by then also included Quain's *Elements of anatomy* (11th edn 1908–15). Beside such organisations sat the smaller specialist firms, from the most professional to a demi-monde on the edge of respectability. In Shaftesbury Avenue on the edge of Soho, in the years before the First World War, the firm of Rebman offered a list of 'medical, surgical and hygienic books', much of it to do with venereal disease and incidentally heavily populated by authors from overseas, especially America. The firm guarded against prurience by asking for professional identity before selling some of its books: Krafft-Ebing's *Psychopathia sexualis* was to be sold only to members of the 'medical, legal and clerical professions' and Forel's *The sexual question* was sold only to 'members of the medical, legal, clerical, and teaching professions, and to such responsible adult persons who have a genuine interest in social science, eugenics and education'. Almost as reassurance to the public, the same firm offered a half-crown book on jam-making. While it must remain doubtful whether it was able to control its customers as much as it appeared to wish, the advertising for some of its books is a reminder of the difficulties of publishing in a society where interest, legitimate or prurient, was policed. More explicitly than most firms, but as aware as every other publisher of the physical characteristics of its books, it also made sure that potential customers appreciated the scale of what was being offered to them. Gould and Pyle's *Cyclopaedia of practical medicine and surgery* (1900), a book of almost 1,000 pages, was described as being 'about the size of Webster's Unabridged Dictionary' and bound in half-Persia leather. Jacobi's *Portfolio of dermochromes* was illustrated in colour by 'the new Four-Colour Process'. Other books offered virtue in their weight, some weighing as much as ten pounds. The art paper necessary for illustration did not help.

In a world of rapid development in medical techniques and understanding, where there were innumerable private and discreet facilities for the care of the insane or merely disturbed, where the care of women was increasingly specialised, where lawyers were ready to help in cases of disagreement, and

24 Wallis, *At the sign of the Ship*, pp. 22, 68.

perhaps above all where heavily advertised patent medicines could be bought in profusion, medical publishing both met widespread needs and offered a sure road to profit. It was not just for specialists. Hardwicke & Bogue, in Piccadilly, were nowhere near any of the London teaching hospitals, but at a fashionable address in the West End. Their list in 1877 showed a firm focussed on amateur interests in natural history and, as publishers of Walford's guides to gentry families, with an eye to the carriage trade. But they were also the publishers of Edwin Lankester and I. Baker Brown, besides the Royal College of Surgeons. Smith, Elder, under George Smith, publisher of Thackeray, Anthony Trollope, the Brownings, Matthew Arnold and many other of the leading literary figures,[25] established a medical list in the early 1870s with the help of Ernest Hart, editor of the *British Medical Journal*. Fortified initially by the acquisition of unsold stocks of several major works including Quain and Wilson's hand-coloured *Series of anatomical plates, in lithography* (five parts, originally published by Taylor & Walton in 1836–42) and George Viner Ellis's chromolithographed life-size *Illustrations of dissections* (published by Walton in 1867), by the 1890s Smith, Elder were not only in the midst of publishing the *Dictionary of national biography*; they could also be counted as a major medical publisher. Amongst the firm's stalwarts, with continuing healthy sales, was W. S. Playfair on midwifery, first published in 1876 and in its ninth edition by 1910. By then, the presence of Conan Doyle, J. M. Barrie and Robert Louis Stevenson in the firm's list contributed to a profile mingling subjects that other firms sought as well, in the belief that diversity was economically prudent.

Medical publishing was financially attractive, but one of the most successful sallies was made as a result of collaboration, and led directly to the strong list in the subject that became a feature of Oxford University Press. Hodder & Stoughton were best known in the first years of the twentieth century for their theological list and their novels. Following a successful experiment with children's books published in conjunction with Henry Frowde,[26] the two parties launched a very different project, and collaborated in the Oxford Medical Publications under the guidance mainly of Osler: the number rapidly grew to about 130 titles by the publication of Oxford's general catalogue in 1916.

The collaboration with Oxford made serious investment possible for a company that had too little capital. As with other minority interests in learned

25 Glynn, *Prince of publishers*.
26 Oxford University Press bought the juvenile stock in 1916, and thus founded what became a thriving children's department. In 1923 the Press bought Hodder's stock and interest in the medical books. See Sutcliffe, *The Oxford University Press*, pp. 147–8.

topics, so with the professions, societies offered a means of publishing books without undue overheads. The Sydenham Society was founded in 1843. Its earliest projects included a collected edition of Thomas Sydenham, and later ones included Hippocrates, Aretaeus and William Harvey. But its main achievement in its first years was to publish translations of modern German work. The society was dissolved in 1858 and reformed as the New Sydenham Society. By the mid-1860s it claimed a membership of 3,250 subscribers. By the early years of the twentieth century this had declined to about 900. By then, the Society's efforts were almost wholly devoted to publishing in fascicles an *Atlas of clinical medicine*, in which photographs played an increasingly important part, replacing the older tradition of lithographic illustration. The Society was brought to a close in 1911 with funds no longer adequate to pursue the atlas further and with enthusiasm exhausted.[27] It had survived longer than many such bodies, whatever the subject, but in the course of its life it had demonstrated the same as others: that trade publishers were not necessarily organised for niche interests.

No part of the publishing and bookselling trade was better or more tightly organised than that in law. Clustered round the Strand, the Inns of Court and Chancery Lane, some of the firms could trace long pedigrees. Stevens & Son, in Chancery Lane, had been founded in 1810. There had been members of the Butterworth family in legal publishing since the late eighteenth century, and they were proud of their tradition: their advertising in the 1870s boasted of their being at the address occupied by Richard Tottel in the sixteenth century, and from which he had published books on common law.[28] In 1830, legal periodicals were still unusual. The *Law Magazine*, founded in 1828, was primarily a vehicle for conservative reform. The number of titles was few enough for the *Legal Examiner*, launched in 1831 by Maxwell in London and Milliken in Dublin, to remark the lack of periodicals for the profession, compared with the abundance available in medicine. One of the greatest needs was for faster reporting of cases, and it was to address this that the sixteen-page weekly *Legal Observer, or Journal of Jurisprudence* was launched in 1830. The monthly *Legal Record* (1844–5) had a similar purpose. The *Justice of the Peace* (1837–) and the *Magistrate* (1848–) addressed their particular audiences. The quarterly *Law Review* was, as its title suggests, more concerned with new literature than with recent cases. But the most successful of all was the *Law Times* founded in 1843 by Edward William Cox, who was called to the bar

27 Meynell, *The two Sydenham Societies.*   28 Jones, *Butterworths: history of a publishing house.*

in the same year and to whom we shall return.[29] He came from Taunton, and in his mid-thirties joined the western circuit. It was perhaps this non-metropolitan background that provided the inspiration for his journal, which achieved nationwide influence in promoting the cause of legal reform, and reducing the dominance of London in the profession.

Apart from standard manuals, where publishers needed to keep abreast of new legislation, entrants into the profession were also provided with aids. The *Law Students' Magazine* (1844–) opened its first issue with a conventional survey of the main literature, including details of examinations. Similarly, the *Law Examination Journal* (1869–) provided summary articles to simplify the process of learning. Both the *Bar Examination Journal* (1871–) and the *Preliminary Examination Journal* gave specimen questions and answers. Few lasted many years, but the *Law Students' Journal* survived from 1879 to 1917.

In Edinburgh, William Green & Sons' list was built on Scottish law, including the quarterly *Juridical Review* and the weekly *Scottish Law Times*, besides various series of reports and statutes. In the early years of the new century they also published the reissue of the English reports down to 1866, under the auspices of a committee headed by Lord Halsbury. Green did not restrict themselves to law. They also had a powerful, if shorter, medical list, as well as a handful of books on accounting. For generations, law publishing in Britain had been dominated by a few firms. As we have seen, some publishers made a point of advertising their books by weight. Some made a virtue of compactness, such as the original edition of Stone's *Justice's manual* (1842), published by Shaw & Sons in Fetter Lane, which sought within a small octavo of under 300 pages to digest almost everything that would be needed by magistrates. By 1895 the twenty-eighth edition was over 1,300 pages. By its ninth edition (1909), Key and Elphinstone on conveyancing weighed 9 lb 12 oz for the two volumes – a matter of some pride for the publishers, whatever the reaction of those who had to use it. Its publishers, Sweet & Maxwell in Chancery Lane, were of a new generation, founded in 1888; the same firm also published the *Law Journal*, grafting onto it the reports from the higher courts, which could be had, with the statutes, for an annual subscription of £3 4s in 1910.

Law publishing was a distinct and usually well-defined field, reflected partly in the small number of publishers who could be said to be deeply committed to it, and partly in its geography. But the contacts that it brought, the

---

29 For Cox, see R. C. J. Cocks, 'Cox, Edward William (1809–1879)', in *ODNB*, with further references. More generally, see Cosgrove, 'Victorian legal periodicals'.

readerships on which it depended and whose interests spread far beyond a daytime profession, and the possibilities for cross-fertilisation, all offered the tantalising possibility of further profits. The *Law Times* (which was bought by Butterworths in 1947, and closed only in 1965) was read by many other people than lawyers, and became an influential voice in linking social issues with the practice of the law. Cox, as owner, gradually extended his stable of periodicals for the legal profession, including the *County Courts Chronicle* (1847–1920) and the *Law Reporter*, precursor of the *Times Law Reports*. From law, he moved into other markets, always with an eye to projects that would have a national application. From specialising in legal publishing, he broadened his list into the ecclesiastical and the social markets. The *Critic*, a fivepenny weekly founded also in 1843, was aimed mainly at the Anglican clergy market. It lasted only briefly, and later in turn spawned the *Clerical Journal* in 1853, which sought the same mixture of literature and matters of ecclesiastical interest. This too found a wide circulation in the established church, and it became indispensable when it began to publish, haphazardly at first, a directory of clergy. Details were much fuller than in the existing *Clergy list*. By the time Cox published the first edition of John Crockford's *Clerical directory* he had bought the *Field*, 'the country gentleman's newspaper' (in the words of its banner headline) founded as a sixpenny weekly in 1853 and soon concentrating on sporting events.[30] The new magazine was floundering after only a few months, notwithstanding a change of proprietor. In Cox's hands it became highly profitable. In 1862 he acquired the *Queen*, and then in 1868 he launched his most influential and widely read journal of all, *Exchange and Mart*. By 1890s, when the *Queen* and the *Field* moved from their prominent offices in the Strand into a specially constructed building in Chancery Lane where the printing premises were shared with C. Arthur Pearson Ltd, the business founded by Cox had yet further increased, with a portfolio of titles that mingled the leisure market with the professional.

There had been training schemes for school teachers since the first decade of the century, even if the outcome was not always happy in a world where religious divisions were so much to the fore. With the closer involvement of government in the payment of teachers after 1846, and increasing numbers wishing to take certificates, the profession moved (to some people's dismay) closer to the idea of a civil service. For teachers, however, the sense of mutual identity was strengthened: by 1855 there were reported to be fifty-one local associations of schoolmasters in England and Wales, meeting for discussion and

30 Rose, *The Field*.

the exchange of books that had been obtained at favourable rates.[31] The slow process of seeking more self-government among elementary teachers was by no means a steady one. The National Union of Elementary Teachers, founded in 1870 (it was largely motivated by the 1870 Education Act), did not achieve one of its earliest aims, the control of entry into the profession. In that certification depended on either government or, later, teacher training colleges, teaching remained different from professions governed by associations whose authority lay in their charters. But whatever the structural differences, and whatever the religious, gender or social fragmentations, the great increase in numbers of school teachers and their awareness of common interests made them a natural focus for publishers. In the 1830s the principal organ of the profession was the *Education Magazine*, founded in 1835. The critical years 1847–8 saw the foundation of two longer-lived journals, the *Educational Times* (1847–1951) and the *Educational Record* (1848–1929). The *Journal of Education* was founded in 1867 and, following the 1870 Act, the *Schoolmaster* was founded in 1872. By the 1880s there were about two dozen national periodicals having education as their primary interest. Quite apart from the more general ones, girls' education, legal students, Irish teachers, governesses and ragged schools all had their niche titles. The *Times Educational Supplement* was founded in 1910.

As the second half of the nineteenth century developed into an age of examinations, the printing and publishing trades were essential accomplices.[32] Examination papers had to be printed, whether for school or university or for entry into the Civil Service, the Army or the Navy. The Society of Apothecaries instituted written examinations in 1839–40 – well ahead of the celebrated reforms for entry into the Civil Service.[33] Paper qualifications of all kinds were the route to personal advancement. In subject after subject, for the examiners and the examined, textbooks provided the syllabus, while magazines offered incentives and then provided support to the successful candidates for the rest of their careers. When, following the introduction of open examinations for entry into the Indian Civil Service in 1853, examinations were introduced for the lower grades in the home Civil Service in 1855, the book and stationery trades were ready. The first number of the sixpenny *Civil Service Gazette* had appeared in January 1853. Published by Woodfall & Kinder, it was designed to advocate and protect the interests of civil servants. Thanks partly to its providing convenient lists of job openings currently available in government offices,

---

31 Tropp, *The school teachers*, p. 46.
32 Latham, *On the action of examinations*; Roach, *Public examinations in England, 1850–1900*.
33 For the use of examinations in parts of the Civil Service before the reforms of the 1850s, see Carr-Saunders and Wilson, *The professions*, pp. 312–13.

it attracted a loyal readership, and it proved to be long-lived, closing only in 1926. When the examination system was extended to most appointments in 1870 (exceptions included some posts in the Foreign Office and Diplomatic Service), the numbers and calibre of those affected increased substantially. By 1875, there were over 15,000 candidates before the Civil Service Commission, including applicants for military service and the Indian Civil Service. The Civil Service Commissioners published lists of set texts in law, geography, political economy and language for those seeking entry to the Indian Civil Service.[34] But even in this tight-knit world not all journals thrived. The *Civil Service Review* survived from 1873 to 1877; the *Civil Service Candidate*, launched in 1883, was a weekly circular issued by the Civil Service Department at King's College London, and thus enjoyed a more than usually well-guaranteed, if limited, market; the *Civil Service Competitor* (1884) described itself as 'the accredited journal respecting civil service competition and examination'; and the *Civil Service Times*, founded in 1886, lasted less than six years. The *Civil Service Chronicle* lasted seven months in 1892. At the bottom of the heap was the *Civil Service Correspondent*, costing just a penny a month and which lasted from 1894 to 1896.

The brief careers of many journals are reminders that some fields were in danger of overcrowding. For some activities this did not matter: local agricultural magazines were valuable in their own right, for example. On the other hand, by the 1880s there were two dozen educational periodicals – excluding school magazines and those for the universities. There were also ten different lists of bankrupts, including those for Scotland and Ireland. Specialist magazines and periodicals were as likely to fail as were speculations for more general audiences. In common with the pattern of the rest of the periodical trade, many new titles lasted no more than six months.

The inclination to form societies and clubs was established long before 1830. The Society of Antiquaries had been founded in 1707, and had received its royal charter in 1751, and traced its ancestry back to the sixteenth century. Its publication programme dated from 1770.[35] Locally and nationally, societies' influence was felt on all manner of activities, from religion to antiquarianism, from charitable work to recreation. The last thirty years of the eighteenth century witnessed a surge in the number of such groups, some professional and many amateur.[36] In their sociability, professional bodies fulfilled some

---

34 See for example the 23rd *Report of Her Majesty's Civil Service Commissioners* (1879), *Parliamentary papers* 1878–9.xxii, pp. 316–26.

35 For the Society in the nineteenth century, see Pearce (ed.), *Visions of antiquity*.

36 Clark, *British clubs and societies*.

of the same functions as less regulated gatherings. More formally, they were recognition of competence, the means to salaries, fees and, not least, status. The Inns of Court, the Royal College of Surgeons and the Royal College of Physicians could all point to considerable prehistories of professional responsibility. In the middle ground stood the Royal Society, founded in 1660 and for many years open to amateurs in subjects other than natural philosophy, medicine and mathematics. The *Philosophical Transactions* were a defining part of its activities, the sharing of experimental and other knowledge. In 1830 its fellowship included seventy-four clergymen, sixty-three legal men, ten bishops and sixty-six officers from the armed forces. While precise definitions are difficult, one analysis claims that scientific men were in a minority until the late 1850s – two hundred years after the foundation.[37]

These older bodies were quite distinct from the new generation. The professions identified in the reign of Victoria tended to define themselves by their own bodies, some of these also having power to provide certificates of qualification. The Institution of Civil Engineers dated from 1818, and its first president had been Thomas Telford. The Law Society dated from 1825, though it had been known first under other names: it received its royal charter in 1831. It was required not only to promote professional improvement, but also to facilitate the acquisition of professional knowledge, activities in which the publishing trade was of material importance. The British Medical Association, primarily for general practitioners, had originated, also under another name, in Worcester in 1832. The Institute of British Architects was founded in 1834, and received its first royal charter in 1837. The Institution of Mechanical Engineers was founded in 1847, and for its first years was primarily concerned with railways. The Institute of Actuaries was founded in 1848, the Institute of Naval Architects in 1860, the Institution of Surveyors (later the Royal Institution of Chartered Surveyors) in 1868, the Library Association in 1877, the Institute of Bankers in 1879 and the Institute of Chartered Accountants (an amalgamation of several local bodies) in 1880.

One key to all this was the professional directory. Directories of towns were familiar, if not especially widespread, in the eighteenth century. In the nineteenth century they became common, in the hands of publishers such as Pigot and Kelly. Just as these defined localities by their descriptions and accounts of local businesses and residents, so the increasing numbers of nationwide specialist directories of people defined selected parts of the population in other ways. The *Law list* had appeared since 1740, and the *Army*

---

37 Lyons, *The Royal Society*, p. 233; Hall, *All scientists now*.

list since 1798; but other professions managed without their equivalents for many years. The late appearance of so useful a book as the *Parliamentary pocket companion* (1832–) – almost thirty years after the founding of Hansard – coincided with the reformed House of Commons. The first Church of England *Clergy list* was published in 1841. It lasted until 1917, by then overtaken by Crockford's *Clerical directory* founded in 1857 and already mentioned. The first *Medical directory* was published in 1845, a pocket-sized volume of 670 pages at a time when there were thought to be about 30,000 people involved in the medical profession in Great Britain and Ireland. The first *Dentist's register* was published in 1879.

Apart from awarding – directly or indirectly through the agency of others – professional recognition, it was assumed that professional bodies would publish either their proceedings, or research papers and other matters of shared interest. By no means all institutions published a regular journal, either themselves or through a commercial publisher. Among those that did were the British Dental Association, the British Medical Association, the Institute of Actuaries and the Institution of Civil Engineers. For learned societies, the printed journal was an essential means of promoting their interests: the Chemical Society, the Linnean Society, the Zoological Society of London, the Royal Horticultural Society and, at the end of the century, the British Economic Association (later the Royal Economic Society) and the Bibliographical Society were but a few among many. The distinction between a learned society and a professional institution was not universally clear or well defined, and it posed questions. By no means all of these bodies were founded to provide diplomas, or even to permit members to add letters after their names. 'Should its general lines be those of an English "learned" society', asked Alfred Marshall when planning the British Economic Association in 1890, 'or of the American Economic Association . . . the membership of which does not profess to confer any sort of diploma?' Five months later, with membership open to 'all schools and parties', the first issue of the society's *Economic Journal* appeared.[38] In economics, as in some other subjects, publication proved much more influential than certification.

As we have seen, some professions developed close relationships with particular publishers. In the years before 1914, the needs of accountants were met mostly by Gee & Co., who worked with the Institute of Chartered Accountants. Besides a series of manuals devoted to auditing, banking and accountancy in different environments (the list included separate titles devoted to accounting

38 Keynes, 'The society's jubilee, 1890–1940'.

for the theatre, tramways, Australian mining, publishers, the gas trade and many others), the firm also published both the weekly *Accountant* (1874–) and (primarily for students) the monthly *Accountants' Journal* (1883–). Longman's medical reputation was consolidated by their publishing the monthly *Proceedings* of the Royal Society of Medicine, which was formed in 1907 by the amalgamation of fifteen London medical societies. As publishers not only of the *Economic Journal* but also of Alfred Marshall and of Palgrave's *Dictionary of political economy*, Macmillan were in a position with respect to economics that other publishers found difficult to assail.

All these professional areas witnessed growth and development recognisable in the rest of the publishing world. In practice, the boundary between the professional, the skilled and the amateur was sometimes not so much unimportant, as best set aside. Publishers sought out all these parts of the market simultaneously. The weekly *Builder*, founded in 1842 and designed (to quote its own advertising) for the architect, engineer, archaeologist and sanitary reformer, described itself as 'indispensable to all owners of house property, the guardians of public edifices, friends of sanitary improvement, artists, and antiquaries', claiming to be found as much in the hands of clergy and landowners as in 'the more humble dwelling of the operative'. The fourpenny weekly *Agricultural Gazette* pointed out the advantage of its veterinary, poultry and vegetable garden sections being 'under separate professional direction'. In seeking the largest possible circulations, there was virtue in crossing boundaries whether at professional levels or at social ones. While in some activities there were necessarily extremes of competence and interest, in most there was also a profitable middle ground. Trades and manufactures were at least as well supplied as the professions. For both groups of people, many of these journals were published by small concerns, even by individuals. Others were in the hands of large or specialist companies. The importance of focussed advertising has already been stressed. It provided income, content and purpose. For publishers who worked both with periodicals and with books, the commercial and editorial concerns were very similar as markets were identified, shaped and developed.

Not only did the definition of profession become wider, no longer associated solely with the three traditional ones of which Addison had written. At the same time the organisation of opinion and knowledge, formed round the professions or sometimes in opposition to them, brought its own demands to the printing and publishing trades. In a world where the ideas and values of professions and of the professional had come to mean so much, many social activities were defined in tandem. And they were most effectively defined in print. So, too, and to move for a moment beyond the professions, the assumptions and expectations of periodical publication provided influence and self-awareness to pressure groups such as the British Temperance League, the Anti-Compulsory Vaccination League, the Anglo-Oriental Society for the Suppression of the Opium Trade, or the Working Men's National League for the Repeal of Contagious Diseases Act. Print was the one medium that allowed cheap communication among large numbers of people, that provided the means both of record and of debate, and that enabled proselytisation among the wider and unknown public.

But many of the real innovations were in technical publishing. Engineering, mining, the railways, manufacturing processes and marine engineering were but some of the most obvious. Agriculture, building and service engineering developed their own literatures; and, from the late nineteenth century, there appeared manuals and journals on electrical engineering, on telegraphy and, a little later, on automobile engineering, radio and the cinema.

Charles Griffin, whose firm became one of the most successful specialist publishers in some of these fields, came from Glasgow. After attending Anderson's University he trained with his uncle, the local bookseller John Joseph Griffin: the firm later dated its foundation to 1820, the year in which the latter's elder brother Richard had entered into partnership with Thomas Tegg, in London.[39] Charles moved south to London in 1842 or 1843. As the author of several handbooks of chemistry, his uncle also had a business in chemicals and chemical apparatus, and he traded in them alongside publishing until the early 1860s, some of the practical equipment being designed to be used alongside the texts published by the firm. In the mid-1840s, the Griffins purchased the *Encyclopaedia metropolitana* for £5,000, a price that compared very favourably with the reported £26,000 for authorship of the original edition, quite apart from printing, binding and publication costs:[40] a new octavo edition appeared from 1848–9 onwards. For the last few months before he died in 1862, Charles Griffin was in partnership with Henry Bohn. But it was the company that bore his name at 10 Stationers' Hall Court that developed into a primarily technical publisher. In an early list that included religion and medicine, there were signs of how the scientific and technical side was beginning to grow beyond its early commitment to chemistry. The firm was also quick to seize possibilities in the new mood for examinations: apart from series published to meet the revised education code, one of its most successful steady sellers was Craik's *Manual of English literature*, first published by Griffin, Bohn

39 For many details, see Brian Gee, 'Griffin, John Joseph (1802–1877)', in *ODNB*. For the firm more generally, see *The centenary volume of Charles Griffin and Company*.
40 Details of original costs from the prospectus for the Cabinet Edition (1849).

& Co. in 1862 and by 1883 in its ninth edition. This was still listed in the catalogue of 1910; but by this time, now in Exeter Street, the Strand, the company was firmly established in its core interests, with overwhelming emphasis on technology, engineering and handbooks of medicine. Herbert Chatley's *The problem of flight*, with chapters on the aeroplane and aviplane besides dirigible balloons and airships, was in its second edition. The mining list included works on prospecting, gold extraction and assaying as well as on the management of mines.

The firm of Chapman & Hall changed its character even more between the mid-nineteenth century, when it had been notable chiefly as the publisher of Dickens, of George Meredith and of the *Fortnightly Review*, and the early twentieth century. By then, thanks to its agency from 1895 onwards for the long and highly focussed list of John Wiley in New York, it was a specialist in technical books and scientific textbooks.[41] The catalogue of hundreds of titles imported under the Wiley banner was as long as that of its older strengths, in literature. It introduced to the British market American authors, and German authors in English translation. Dickens made the firm money, and made much possible that would otherwise have had to be set aside. But the building up of the technical list, especially in response to the First World War, gave it a new vigour. By the last years just before the war, these and other London firms such as Crosby Lockwood (Ludgate Hill and Victoria Street, Westminster), Greenwood & Son (Ludgate Hill) and Spon (in Haymarket) offered specialist lists, while general publishers such as Longman also sought to profit from a demand generated by international competition, new technologies, military requirements and the needs of students and apprentices.

We have seen how the growth of learned and professional societies met many needs. For some people, however, their existence was a reminder of the urgent need for change in universities. Though both medicine and law had been studied at the ancient universities in the middle ages, with a view to professional careers, they had fallen into neglect. While the University of London, with its medical schools, sought from the first to prepare students for professions other than the church,[42] Oxford and Cambridge were persuaded to do so only gradually. For law, the presiding bodies remained in London, especially at the Inns of Court, in Edinburgh and in Dublin. Henry VIII had founded a chair in Civil Law at Cambridge in 1540. For those reading this subject, there had been a tripos examination since 1816, and in 1824–5 it had

41 Waugh, *A hundred years of publishing*, pp. 251–3; *The first hundred and fifty years of John Wiley and Sons*, p. 221.
42 L. P. Le Quesne, 'Medicine', in Thompson (ed.), *The University of London*, pp. 125–45.

produced Lord Cockburn, future Lord Chief Justice. But, in law as in some other subjects, the existence of chairs at the old universities did not mean that the subject was taught adequately, or that it was examined. The same was true of the Inns of Court and of law at University College London. In 1846, a House of Commons committee discovered scarcely any teaching in the subject, anywhere.[43] In 1858 the Cambridge tripos was reformed, and it was reformed again in 1875 and 1882. But though the tripos system produced an appreciable number who rose high in their profession, and who held prominent positions in the legal world of the colonies, it was not designed to produce only practising lawyers: two years after Cockburn, F. D. Maurice took a first-class degree in law, and among the following year's candidates was a future bishop of Madras. At the end of the 1860s the bishops of both Auckland and Dunedin had read law at Cambridge. Useful as legal knowledge was, it could hardly be claimed that the Cambridge law tripos was more than indicative of legal training. In Oxford, where there had also been a Regius Professor of Civil Law since the sixteenth century, and there had been a Professor of Common Law since 1755, an examination linking jurisprudence with modern history was established in 1853, provision being made for separate examination only in 1872. Frederick Pollock, who graduated from Trinity College, Cambridge in 1867, and was called to the bar at Lincoln's Inn in 1871, reviewed from the vantage point of half a century later the inadequacies of what had been available to him:

> There was very little serious criticism; it was a mere chance where important books received any fitting notice; there was no real editing of the professional journals and no security against the admission not only of poor work but of mere nonsense.[44]

Seeking to improve his case, he exaggerated to some extent. Henry Wheaton's *Elements of international law*, originally published by the small legal bookselling firm of Fellowes in 1836 and later taken up by Stevens, was the customary text set on the subject at Cambridge in the 1860s.[45] It was a valuable enough property to be the subject of dispute over the copyright in the mid-1870s, and it was republished, by then in its seventh English edition, in 1944. Pollock himself contributed the introduction to the fifth edition in 1916.

In 1830, the Scottish universities were publicly criticised for their inadequate teaching in medicine.[46] One of the most serious charges levelled against

---

43 W. L. Twining, 'Laws', in Thompson (ed.), *The University of London*, pp. 81–114, at p. 83.
44 Pollock, 'Our jubilee', at pp. 5–6.
45 *The student's guide to the University of Cambridge* (Cambridge, 1862), p. 174.
46 *General report of the Commissioners appointed to visit the universities and colleges of Scotland* (1830). *Parliamentary papers* 1831.xii, pp. 66–83.

the universities of Oxford and Cambridge in the mid-century was their failure to address the country's professional requirements other than – often inadequately – in the training of clergy for the established church. Others such as Mark Pattison and J. H. Newman maintained a more traditional view, arguing that a liberal education was the soundest foundation for a future career. It was not a view in keeping with public needs or opinion, whether expressed domestically or by international comparisons. The apparent collapse of British manufacturing skills between the triumphs of the 1851 exhibition and the humiliation at the 1867 exhibition at Paris was sufficient reminder of the gulf between complacency and reality: it was not to be dispelled by any amount of allowance for patriotic bias in the awarding of medals and prizes. In the ancient universities the traditional strengths in law and medicine had fallen away, for some people almost to invisibility. The Oxford commissioners in 1852 noted 'the extent to which all separate branches of learning, both professional and preparatory to professions, have been suffered to decay'. At Cambridge, the Commissioners (chaired by John Graham, bishop of Chester) pointed to the urgency for teaching in civil engineering, the need to extend teaching in chemistry so as to meet contemporary demand and international manufacturing competition, and the need to extend the study of law so as to embrace questions of general jurisprudence. 'It is desirable, in all cases where a Student is designed for a learned profession, that the foundations of his professional education should be laid at the University.'[47] In 1870, professional training in engineering was offered in London (including King's College and University College, the Royal School of Mines and the Royal School of Naval Architecture), Edinburgh, Glasgow, Owens College in Manchester, Trinity College Dublin, and Cork. So far as the Institution of Civil Engineers was concerned, the old English universities were still conspicuously absent. Change was slow in some quarters, though Robert Willis had been an assiduous teacher of some aspects of the subject at Cambridge since the 1830s. By 1874, Horace Lamb was lecturing at Trinity College, Cambridge, on the motion of fluids, at a time, he wrote, 'when the need for a treatise on the subject was strongly impressed on my mind'.[48] Five years later, and now Professor of Mathematics in Adelaide, he published one. And yet in 1885 Paul Vinogradoff, trained in Moscow and Berlin, and arrived in England only two years since, could still say that 'a young man goes to Oxford not to learn anything definitely bound

47 Carr-Saunders and Wilson, *The professions*, pp. 314–15; Cambridge University Commission, *Report of Her Majesty's Commissioners appointed to inquire into the state, discipline, studies, and revenues of the University and colleges of Cambridge* (1852), *Parliamentary papers* 1852–3.xliv, pp. 91, 97, 102.
48 Horace Lamb, *A treatise on the mathematical theory of the motion of fluids* (Cambridge, 1879), preface.

up with his future line of work, but to get up a certain amount of general knowledge'.[49] His claim contained sufficient truth to be thought worth publishing: a defensible position, and reflecting that of many going up to Oxford or Cambridge. But if, too, it was no longer wholly applicable, numbers were still alarmingly low. In Oxford that year just twenty-two candidates were classed in the natural sciences examinations, and fifty in law.[50] Classics, modern history and theology dominated.

To an outsider, the changes to the old English universities came most obviously with the establishment of new professorships. In the wake of the Commission of 1850–2, new chairs were established at Oxford in international law, modern history, moral and metaphysical philosophy, chemistry and comparative anatomy. At Cambridge, the foundation of the Cavendish Laboratory in 1873, thanks to the Duke of Devonshire, provided a stimulus wanting elsewhere. The first three Cavendish Professors of Experimental Physics were James Clerk Maxwell, Lord Rayleigh and J. J. Thomson. The first Professor of Mechanism and Applied Mechanics, in 1875, was James Stuart, who was instrumental in founding university extension teaching; he was followed in 1890 by J. C. Ewing, whose textbooks won wide circulation. Chairs in physiology, surgery and pathology followed in 1883, in agriculture in 1899 and in agricultural botany in 1908. A natural sciences tripos existed from 1851, the examiners including the professors of physics, chemistry, anatomy, geology, botany and mineralogy. Among the six candidates in its first year was F. J. A. Hort, famous in his later career not as a scientist but as a theologian and biblical scholar. By 1881 there were two dozen candidates. The subject grew rapidly, especially after the introduction of a tripos examination at the end of the second year. In 1900 there were 136 successful candidates for part I, including fourteen women, and twenty-five, including two women, for part II. The first candidates sat the new mechanical sciences tripos in 1894.

All these changes brought needs for books, whether course textbooks or more general introductions. With new appointments, and new provision for teaching, came new publishing needs and opportunities. The *Journal of Physiology* was founded at Cambridge in 1878 by Michael Foster, who engaged American colleagues as well, in order to extend the venture. Published at first by Macmillan (who had launched *Nature* in 1869), and then from 1880 by Cambridge University Press, it offered a means of disseminating some of the

49 Vinogradoff, 'Oxford and Cambridge through foreign spectacles', p. 864. Quoted in Reader, *Professional men*, p. 197.
50 *The historical register of the University of Oxford* (Oxford, 1900).

research that was being carried out both there and elsewhere. The *Law Quarterly Review* was launched in 1885, likewise for a primarily academic readership. Under the editorship of Frederick Pollock, who later recorded the importance of the Judicature Act (1873) in marking a change in mood and in direction, it brought a new professionalism to the criticism especially of common and of comparative law, and drew its contributors both from the judicature and from the universities.[51]

By the end of the century, the old universities were taking a leading part in training for some professions. They were doing so in three ways: in teaching, in examining candidates and in preparing books for publication. At Cambridge, provision for the training of teachers dated from 1879, when the Teachers' Training Syndicate was established. Its secretary was Oscar Browning, historian and fellow of King's College. Browning was not afraid of making a fool of himself, and he was much mocked. But as an advocate of the need for professional teachers he was powerful, and effective.[52] In 1883 the University further extended its interests, with the establishment of a Board of Indian Civil Service Studies whose purpose was to prepare Cambridge students for the relevant examinations. It proved short-lived, but it was a further expression of the ways in which university and professional life were converging. Most of all, and with far greater consequences, in the sciences Cambridge was to the fore in its teaching, in its research and in its publications.

The foundation of the nineteenth-century universities did not of itself compensate for the inadequacies of the older ones. On the one hand by the 1890s almost half of new Manchester graduates in chemistry and physics went into industry, and in the first years of the twentieth century the total among all graduates from Newcastle doing so was almost 60 per cent. On the other there was anxiety about over-specialisation, especially in the northern universities. The mixed success of the University of London, where individual colleges tended to play to their strengths, developed in the last twenty years of the century, and in the years to 1914, into increasing success especially in electrical sciences and other aspects of engineering, while at University College Sir William Ramsay transformed the chemistry department, built closer relationships with industry, and won a Nobel Prize for his work on 'inert' gases.[53] Ramsay's own *Experimental proofs of chemical theory for beginners* (1884) was published by Macmillan, while he was still Principal of University College, Bristol. Then in 1891 Churchill, the more specialist publisher, issued his *System of*

51 Pollock, 'Our jubilee'.   52 Anstruther, *Oscar Browning*.
53 Sanderson, *The universities and British industry*, pp. 101, 103–4, 106–18.

inorganic chemistry and his *Elementary systematic chemistry*, before Ramsay reverted to Macmillan for his *Gases of the atmosphere* in 1896, a book that reached its fourth edition in 1915.

In much of all this, two publishers assumed a central position thanks to their personal links with the academic world: Macmillan and Cambridge University Press. Though Alexander Macmillan removed the publishing side of his business to London in 1863, leaving the retail part in Cambridge, the connections with the University and its needs remained strong. They coloured much of the firm's activities until 1914 and beyond. Alfred Marshall's *Principles of economics*, published by Macmillan in 1890, was followed by John Maynard Keynes's decision to turn to the firm for the publication of his *Indian currency and finance* (1913) after he had run into difficulties with the University Press. Keynes remained a Macmillan author.[54] Macmillan's evolution as a publisher whose list included much of use to the professions was a gradual one. For many years it was concerned mostly with theology and with literature. Medicine was increasingly present in the 1860s. In 1866, the same year in which it published *Ecce Homo*, and Kingsley's *Hereward the Wake*, and a year after it had published *Alice in Wonderland*, it launched the *Journal of Anatomy and Physiology*. It launched the *Practitioner* two years later, and then *Nature* in 1869. Twenty years later, its publications in 1889 included not only the first one-volume edition of Rolf Boldrewood's *Robbery under arms*, and the completion of Grove's *Dictionary of music*, but also works on hydrodynamics, thermodynamics, meteorology, district nursing, pathology, therapeutics, cholera, the design of steam engines, diseases of timber, and education.[55] Energetic, imaginative, and as a general publisher blessed with several highly popular authors including Charlotte M. Yonge, Charles Kingsley and C. L. Dodgson, Macmillan had an international lead which for many years the University Press was content merely to service, as one of the firm's most frequent printers.

By the early twentieth century Cambridge University Press had a strong list in the practice and history of education.[56] In law it published the first edition of Kenny on criminal law in 1902: in successive editions, the book remained a feature of the Cambridge law list until the 1960s. The Press's considerable engineering list was led by the works of J. A. Ewing, who had been professor of engineering at Tokyo in 1878–83 before returning first to Dundee and then, in 1890, to the chair of mechanics at Cambridge: in 1903 he left to become

54 Skidelsky, *John Maynard Keynes* 1, pp. 273–4.
55 [Foster], *A bibliographical catalogue of Macmillan and Co.'s publications*.
56 McKitterick, *A history of Cambridge University Press* 3.

Director of Naval Education. For justification of the place of mechanical sciences (he much preferred to speak of engineering) in the university, Ewing looked for his inspiration partly to William Rankine, of Glasgow. In 1891 he devoted his inaugural lecture to the place of the university in the teaching of the subject. 'I have to plead for nothing less than the inclusion of a complete School of Engineering in that new Cambridge which is fast springing up within the old.' For this, the prelude to students' first professional appointments, both theory and practice were necessary, lectures combined with reading and with laboratory work. 'Study her [Nature] in books we must, but if our knowledge is to be real it must be of the kind that a face-to-face acquaintance brings.'[57] There were echoes here of remarks on Oxford in 1852. Even though books could only achieve so much, Ewing proved an enthusiastic author. His books on the steam engine (1894; 4th edn 1926) and on strength of materials (1899) became classics in their field. Others' books in the University Press list in the early twentieth century, often drawing on the Cavendish Laboratory, dealt with electricity, hydrodynamics and gases. In medicine, the list was also growing. In numerical terms, and particularly in the sciences, the catalogue was far short of some of the specialist publishers in London, but it signalled a change in direction, as Cambridge and the other universities assumed an active part in training for the professions. By 1905, when the Press launched the *Journal of Agricultural Science*, it was also publishing the *British Journal of Psychology* (1904-) with the British Psychological Society, the *Journal of Physiology* (founded by Michael Foster in 1878, and taken over by the Press from Macmillan), the *Journal of Hygiene* (1901-) and *Biometrika* ('A journal for the statistical study of biological problems', 1901-). Some were titles owned outright by the Press; others were published on behalf of separate bodies; but all found a wide circulation in the relevant professions.

Macmillan were not only active in Cambridge, where they drew on friendships and developed networks of collaboration. In 1863 they also became publishers to the University of Oxford. This was a straightforwardly commercial relationship, but it placed Oxford in a situation that gave the University little incentive to develop its own list, since Macmillan were entitled to a very large share of any profits. The arrangement ended in 1880. Like Cambridge, Oxford developed a strong list for schools, but its principal contribution to professional literature was in medicine. The alliance between Henry Frowde

---

57 J. A. Ewing, *The university training of engineers: an introductory lecture, delivered January 20, 1891* (Cambridge, 1891), p. 15.

and Hodder & Stoughton enabled the development of a series of Oxford Medical Publications, the joint imprint emphasising not only the alliance but also that the list was regarded in Oxford as of more general than purely academic interest. The Clarendon Press imprint was used much more liberally for subjects such as geography, history and the classics, and was a constant reminder of the Press's divided loyalties.

Few publishers, whether of books or journals, or of both, could afford to specialise even in groups of professional subjects. Edward Cox published the *Law Times* and Crockford, besides the *Queen* and the *Field*, and used this diversity to lay the foundations of a press empire a generation before the late nineteenth-century giants Newnes and Harmsworth. Macmillan and Longman both profited from the possession of steady-selling textbooks, but their reputations, and much of their profits, were made as more general publishers. The firms of Churchill and of Lewis were among the handful in the sciences, technology and medicine who built major businesses just out of specialist lists. Small, highly focussed firms could prosper with specialist lists. It was much more difficult for the larger ones: for them, risk was best reduced by diversity. The major exception to this was in law. Publishers such as Butterworth, Maxwell and Stevens were able to supply not only a world that was print-dependent to a greater degree than most other professional activities, but one that was also tightly organised – geographically within London in and near Chancery Lane, the Inns of Court and the Law Courts, and socially in its regional distribution, its network of local specialist libraries and its constant need for consultation in legal practice.[58] Law publishing was helped greatly by the fact that so much of it was based on two kinds of publication: the textbook, which needed to be regularly updated, and the subscription publication not just of journals (in this it was the same as many other professions) but also, indispensably, of law reports.

By 1914 Addison's traditional 'learned' professions had been joined by dozens of others. The previous eighty years had witnessed the identification of new skills, and diversification and reclassification of existing ones. Skills were formalised, and recreated as professions, with all the supervisory organisation that this implied. It was a gradual development, and its integration into social organisation was not one that could be defined by any single event. For some disciplines, the process was in train well before 1860, though later dates have

58 K. A. Manley, 'Engines of literature: libraries in an era of expansion and transition', in Mandelbrote and Manley (eds.), *The Cambridge history of libraries in Britain and Ireland* 2, pp. 509–28, at pp. 526–7.

529

been suggested for more general acceptance.[59] But the process of classification by social organisation and control was only a part of one that had its parallels in the responses of the book trade to demands as they evolved, and often before they were formalised or defined by the creation of professional bodies. Beyond this, specialisation implied denomination; and denomination required further justification. This was straightforward: the new boundaries and relationships were largely worked out in printed books, periodicals and newspapers, and in the curricula and textbooks of education and examination.

There was a more general conundrum, potentially more divisive. Within new apportionments and classifications of knowledge many of the old anxieties persisted. Status was jealously defended: this was the essence of the professional bodies. Additionally, the fact that so much knowledge was available in print was only a partial rejoinder to the traditions exemplified in apprenticeships and the passing on of skills as a mystery. The appropriateness or otherwise of publishing patents, and indeed the wisdom of the entire patents system, alluded to elsewhere in this volume, was a further manifestation of continuing dissent on this matter in the world of invention and manufacturing.[60] For professional bodies representing particular skills and interests, a closely related question was phrased differently: whether, or to what extent, membership of them should be open to all who expressed curiosity, or whether they should be restricted to those already possessing some proven aptitude. The debates concerning whether or not limitations should be placed on membership of learned societies had their origins in the seventeenth century and earlier. They dominated the early life of even as forward-looking a body as the British Economic Association, which in 1890 deliberately broke with the past in preferring the term 'economics' to the traditional 'political economy'. Amidst all this, and whatever the subject, publication did more than advance knowledge. It helped define proficiency. More radically, the publishing trade confirmed a hierarchical democracy of shared experience and comprehension. In an environment of cheap postage costs and efficient rail communication it became easy for the professions to think and operate nationally. Not only by means of books, but also with a new multiplicity of periodicals that defined subject areas in their titles, created new clans of shared concerns, reshaped old loyalties and gave new impetus to publication by weekly, monthly or quarterly appearance, the book trades both forced a break with past attitudes and defined the boundaries of knowledge itself.

59 MacLeod (ed.), *Government and expertise*; Perkin, *The rise of professional society*; Goldman, *Science, reform, and politics in Victorian Britain*, pp. 12–13, 259–61.
60 See pp. 537–9.

15

Organising knowledge in print

DAVID MCKITTERICK

Knowledge is power. 'Knowledge of the electric telegraph saves time; knowledge of writing saves human speech and locomotion; knowledge of domestic economy saves income; knowledge of sanitary laws saves health and life; knowledge of the laws of the intellect saves wear and tear of brain; and knowledge of the laws of the Spirit – what does it not save?'

Sir John Lubbock, who repeated a much misquoted and misunderstood aphorism before quoting Charles Kingsley's particularisation of it, was among the most widely read pundits of the late nineteenth century. Trained as a banker, with informed interests in medical sciences, an active and reforming Member of Parliament, Fellow of the Royal Society, Principal of the London Working-Men's College, President of the London Chamber of Commerce and with dozens of other appointments besides, he became perhaps most widely celebrated for his choice of a hundred best books in 1887.[1] By then he had become a public sage. The book in which this paragraph appears was published by Macmillan in 1894. By 1899 it had been reprinted seven times, and was past its forty-eight thousandth copy. For another pundit, Herbert Spencer (also quoted by Lubbock), the all-important knowledge was science – the means to self-preservation, the maintenance of life and health, and the gaining of a livelihood. Amidst much else besides, science was also the means to the interpretation of national life and to the enjoyment of art.[2] For both men, as for most people in Britain, knowledge was embedded in print, and preserved by its use.

This chapter is designed to be read alongside the following, by Aileen Fyfe. Some of the overlaps are deliberate, for it is impossible to compartmentalise

---

1 Lubbock, *The pleasures of life*. For various assessments of Lubbock following his death, see Duff (ed.), *The life-work of Lord Avebury*.
2 Lubbock, *The use of life*, pp. 111–12. Many aspects of the subject are discussed in an American context in Brown, *Knowledge is power*.

the creation and management of knowledge, or of the kindred, if very different, information. Knowledge not only meant different things to different people. As always, it was acquired in different ways, sometimes by personal experience, sometimes from other people, and sometimes by reading. Francis Bacon, to whom the aphorism was attributed, had originally cast his words in a religious context, 'ipsa scientia potestas est',[3] translated as 'knowledge itself is power'; but by the 1890s his words had long since been adapted and applied to contexts having nothing at all to do with religion. In 1852 James Murray used the flyleaf of Cassell's *Popular educator* to declare, 'knowledge is power'. Charles Knight had used it for the motto of the *Penny Magazine*, and chose it for the title of a book in 1855.[4] In the same year, William Parr Henning used it for 'secret correspondence on scientific principles', published at Wimborne in Dorset. More scrupulously, Samuel Johnson had identified in his dictionary six different kinds of knowledge, quoting in his support Shakespeare, the Bible, Sidney, Jonson and Locke. To Lord Brougham and Charles Knight, instrumental in the Society for the Diffusion of Useful Knowledge, it was most applicable to skills, to acquaintance with facts: 'the Power of Science applied to the Arts, or, in other words, Knowledge', in Knight's words of several years later.[5] Its value was as much social as mechanical. It was not necessarily the same as information, a word that Johnson had also associated with instruction.

The nineteenth century witnessed an information revolution that was directly linked to revolutions in knowledge. The means by which these revolutions were accomplished can be measured and described. But they were accompanied by modifications in attitudes and social practices that themselves contributed to these mutations. Widespread literacy was one factor. More importantly, the habit of letter-writing, especially following the introduction of the penny post, extended even to the very poor the habit of using letters to exchange knowledge of all kinds, personal, social and practical. 'With the exception of the alphabet and the printing press, no human achievement has done more to benefit mankind morally, intellectually and materially than cheap, frequent and efficient postal communication', wrote Henry Pitman some years later.[6] In 1854, 443 million letters were delivered in Britain, the equivalent of about sixteen for each person. By 1898–9, the figure was 2,187

---

3 Bacon, *Meditationes sacrae* (1597), 'De haeresibus'.   4 Knight, *Knowledge is power*.

5 Knight *Knowledge is power*, new edn (1866), preface, p. 9. For Knight, see Gray, *Charles Knight*. For a wider view of some of the issues discussed in the following, see Daunton (ed.), *The organisation of knowledge in Victorian Britain*.

6 Pitman, *Hints on teaching and lecturing on phonography*, p. 156.

million, an average per person of 54.3, quite apart from a further 382 million postcards.[7] In emphasising (as did Knight, tirelessly) the importance of print – in books, periodicals, newspapers and assorted notices – for the dissemination of knowledge, it has also to be emphasised that printing was accompanied by a scribal culture on a scale never previously witnessed in history.

Knowledge was also promulgated and shared pictorially, in engravings, lithographs, paintings and drawings and, not least, with the development of photography. It was shared in formal lectures, a mode of communication much loved and developed by the Victorians, whether in the programmes of the Royal Institution (founded 1799),[8] in mechanics' institutes, in public libraries, or in chapels, churches and meeting-houses. The exhibition as a means of organising and sharing knowledge came into its own, increasingly on the international stage. The present chapter is concerned mostly with print. Newspapers play little part in this and the following chapter, yet they were instrumental not just in the dispersal of knowledge and information, but also in changes of attitude that came with it, in all sections of society. In the felicitous phrase of a report on library provision in the United States in the 1890s, readers of modern newspapers developed 'a sort of epic consciousness' far above the mere gossip that had prevailed hitherto. That was far from the whole truth. Nor was it true, as the same writer claimed, that hostility towards foreign countries was replaced by 'feelings of humane personal interest'.[9] Nonetheless, it was certainly the case that more knowledge and information were circulated by newspapers than by any other means.

Knowledge is not education; but the desire to use both for social management and improvement hinged on the power of print. In 1835, G. R. Porter, head of the statistical office in the Board of Trade and an active member of the young Statistical Society, sent a series of questions to L.-A.-J. Quetelet, a sympathetic colleague in Belgium. Foremost of his seven questions were the following:

> What has been the effect of the extension of education on the habits of the People? Have they become more orderly, abstemious, contented, or the reverse?
> What is the proportion of crimes to education? Are the educated found to be more exempt than the uneducated, or the reverse?
> What description of crime prevails most in the educated provinces, crimes against property or against the person?

---

7 First report of the Postmaster General (1855): Parliamentary papers 1854–5.xx; 45th report of the Postmaster General (1899): Parliamentary papers 1899.xix.
8 Berman, Social change and scientific organisation.
9 Flint, Statistics of public libraries in the United States and Canada, preface by W. T. Harris.

What proportion of criminals, especially in the grosser part of crimes, could read and write, in the returns of 1833, or 1834?

What is the political effect of the diffusion of education, as evinced by the increase of newspapers, pamphlets, etc. etc. etc.?

What is the number of Books published during the last year and how classified?[10]

These questions remained as difficult and controversial eighty years later. Education and politics had their natural extensions concerning political activity as expressed in an educated electorate.[11] In 1914, notwithstanding the book trade's *English catalogue*, there was still no comprehensive national bibliography. There was still no comprehensive list of government publications.[12] There was still no list of the increasing quantities of documents and other publications emanating from local authorities. Despite various commercial guides, there was still no properly comprehensive list of currently published periodicals. There were no fully comprehensive guides to available maps, and there were no summaries of what music was in print. Britain sat at the centre of an empire, and yet there was no guide to what was being published in her possessions. Such legislation as there was to procure the output of the book trade was piecemeal. The 1911 Copyright Act required the deposit in the British Museum of all new publications in the United Kingdom, but this was impractical even for many substantial books. In India, legislation in 1867 required the registration of books published in British India; there was no such legislation in Britain. Even where there might have been advantages, the book trade did not encourage over-organisation or supervision. For some of these categories of publication there were partial guides and even several in competition. For others there was very little.

If some of Porter's enquiries seem over-simplified, they also sought answers that would perforce have to be framed within experiences of education and of print. The final question made Porter's line of reasoning quite clear. In the official mind of Whitehall, books and education in its widest sense were inseparable. But if printing, and publishing, held such a central part in official thinking, how were they to be best promoted? Here successive governments followed in the first instance a laissez-faire policy, allowing markets to develop on their own, according to patterns that had been established in

---

10 Porter to Quetelet, 28 May 1835, Brussels, Bibliothèque Royale, Quetelet papers cahier 2041. Quoted in Porter, *The rise of statistical thinking*, pp. 33–4.

11 For American viewpoints, see Brown, *The strength of a people*.

12 For one call for this, see F. B. F. Campbell, 'A plea for annual lists of state-papers and annual reviews of state-papers, as being essential preliminaries to state-paper catalogues', *The Library* 4 (1893), pp. 175–83.

the past. Publishing and printing did not just remain unsubsidised. They were actually heavily taxed for so long as newspapers, advertisements, and paper itself, were subject to duty.

But besides this were other, newer, enterprises, encouraged or fully funded under various government auspices. Most directly and most obviously was parliamentary printing, notably the blue books, reports of committees and royal commissions on all manner of public issues that often underpinned subsequent legislation. The folio blue books, named after their blue paper wrappers, epitomised a particular kind of knowledge celebrated by Dickens in *Hard times* in 1854.

> Although Mr. Gradgrind did not take after Blue Beard, his room was quite a blue chamber in its abundance of blue books. Whatever they could prove (which is usually anything you like), they proved there, in an army constantly strengthening by the arrival of new recruits. In that charmed apartment, the most complicated social questions were cast up, got into exact totals, and finally settled.[13]

Though they were often mocked, the reports of royal commissions and other documents enshrined in the blue books were the mainstays of public legislation and policy, at local as well as national levels. They were easy to caricature for their mixture of calculated solemnity and artificial thoroughness. Some of the evidence gathered in them was more opinion than fact. In the context of parliamentary printing, they represented a new drain on the public purse. Following reports assembled by the radical MP Joseph Hume, in 1835 the Commons accepted that parliamentary papers in general should be made available to the public to buy at the lowest possible cost. Sales were placed in the hands of Hansard, as printers to the House.[14]

This marked a signal departure, not just in permitting easier access to the deliberations involved in legislation, but also in public education and knowledge. It was not until 1908 that the first government sales office opened, in Edinburgh, and a London equivalent opened only in 1917. The growth in publicly funded printing in the intervening seventy-odd years was unaffected by the absence of obvious mechanisms to sell publications in the book trade at large. Many publications were kept in print in quantities far larger than realistic market projections could justify, and any price adjustments were extremely conservative. Government publishing was by no means alone in this: commercial publishers, and the big university presses, often behaved very similarly. But government publishing, largest of all, was also the most obvious. In this way,

13 Charles Dickens, *Hard times* (1854), ch. xv.   14 Barty-King, *Her Majesty's Stationery Office*, p. 22.

much of publishing in Britain was subsidised not just for the first customers, but also for generations to come.

Overprinting and then hoping for a market was one foible, but only for some kinds of publications. For much other government work, overprinting meant immediate and obvious waste – literally so in the tons of waste paper gathered in each year as forms or instructions went out of date or never even reached those for whom they had been once intended. In a society that depended ever more on printed forms, and with an army spread across the world that had its own mechanisms of communication, demand for paper was immense, with print-runs in the tens of thousands. During the Crimean War, the overall government estimates for printing and paper roughly doubled, thanks merely to the need for paper in which to wrap ammunition.[15] War Office expenditure of this kind was unavoidable. Too liberal use of the printing press might be controlled, and in the 1850s paper represented about one-third of the cost of most printing. The House of Commons repeatedly examined the costs of government printing, seeking ways to reduce them. Various printers were summoned, and the wages paid to their workmen compared. At this time there were five main printers for government work in England, a small number in Edinburgh, and Thom in Dublin. In the 1850s, many hours were spent examining an improbable scheme invented by Bartholomew Beniowski for reducing the costs of type composition, only for his invention to be shown to be a false hope. Among his witnesses was a female compositor, Helen Harris: women commanded lower wages than men.[16] In the 1860s, the usual edition size for a government paper was between 1,500 and 2,000 copies, but some subjects such as sanitation, public health and the poor law regularly required extra: reports of the Poor Law Commissioners were printed in editions usually of 4,000. Exceptionally, the Treasury ordered 12,750 copies of the Revised Code for education in 1862.[17] There was a world of difference between this short document and the much larger reports sometimes engendered by committees. In 1853 the Committee of the Council on Education ordered 10,000 copies of a report that seemed to J. R. McCulloch, Comptroller of the Stationery Office, to be unnecessarily long: 'what would seem to me, if it did not emanate from such a respectable body, to be in great part mere useless rubbish, and they distribute those copies all over the kingdom, gratuitously'.[18] McCulloch was

---

15 House of Commons Select Committee on Printing, *Report. Parliamentary papers* 1854–5.xi.
16 *Ibid.*, Evidence, p. 93.
17 House of Commons. *Printed papers. Return, 1860–64. Parliamentary papers* 1865.xliv. For background, see for example Bishop, *The rise of a central authority for English education.*
18 House of Commons Select Committee on Printing, *Report. Parliamentary papers* 1854–5.xi. Evidence, p. 4.

characteristically outspoken, and his remarks caused offence – as, no doubt, he intended, for it was later explained that 'rubbish' did not refer to the contents. By the late 1880s, the programme for collecting and recycling waste paper that he had instigated was making a useful profit, and prison labour was being used to tear up confidential documents.[19]

In piecemeal fashion, the government moved into much of its publishing almost by accident. But in the prices charged for most of its books it retained the policy that had been proposed for parliamentary papers in the 1830s by Hume: that they should be sold at the lowest possible figure. While much government publishing was priced at little more than cost – and rather less than cost had more stringent calculations been made – not everything was cheap. The four-volume edition of Domesday book, published in 1783, remained in print at ten guineas, and the facsimile of the Codex Alexandrinus (1816–28) was priced at £18 for the three volumes. Sir Francis Palgrave's edition of parliamentary writs (1827–34) cost four guineas. Government departments enjoyed considerable autonomy. Reports of the Public Records Commissioners, of the Patent Office and of other departments were printed by the royal printers of the day, for most of this period Eyre & Spottiswoode, but they were published by the departments concerned.

The new Patent Office was opened in 1852. It was designed to bring an end to centuries of confusion, a world where the publication of patents, and even their need, were matters for debate; no less an engineer than I. K. Brunel was eloquently opposed to the patent system when he appeared before a House of Lords committee in 1851.[20] The vast growth in the number of patents meant that the conventional method of publishing them, selectively and unofficially in journals such as the *Mechanics' Magazine* or *Repertory of Arts*, were no longer adequate: by no means all were published. The new office provoked a torrent of applications. Under Bennet Woodcroft, the Superintendent of Specifications, a programme was devised for the retrospective as well as current publication of patents for inventions granted since the sixteenth century. At the head of his programme of public instruction was an octavo series of abridgements, each volume bound in blue boards reminiscent of the blue books familiar from parliamentary printing, and each devoted to a particular subject. The abridgements of specifications for printing, for example, appeared in 1859,

19 *2nd and 3rd reports of the Controller of Her Majesty's Stationery Office* (1887, 1890): *Parliamentary papers* 1887.xxvii and *Parliamentary papers* 1890.xxvi.
20 Select Committee of the House of Lords appointed to consider the Bill. *Report and minutes* 1851, *Parliamentary papers* 1851.xviii, questions 1767–1837: 'I believe them to be productive of almost unmixed evil with respect to every party connected with them, whether those for the benefit of whom they are apparently made, or the public' (para. 1773).

631 pages long and price seven shillings. Like other volumes in this series, and like the files of patents themselves, it was in chronological order, in this case beginning with legislation of 1483 concerning foreigners in the English book trade. Modern patents could be bought for threepence upwards, the price depending partly on whether drawings were attached and partly on length. By 1866, the number of specifications recorded since the beginning had reached 59,222, and the programme of printing abridgements was still far from finished. But some of the volumes, much referred to in searches in preference to the full documents, continued to carry long historical prefaces: that covering artists' instruments and materials (1872), for example, noted that engraving was written of in Exodus 28, and that Homer did not mention painting as an imitative art.[21]

Fears of publication, and therefore of losing secrecy and leaving the way open to theft by unscrupulous competitors, had been largely forgotten. Even in 1859 the patents lawyer Thomas Webster had remarked the 'copious stream' of patents publications, 'drawn off in a multitude of channels, penetrating the country in all directions and irrigating it with fertilizing information'.[22] In terms of numbers, the patents commissioners perhaps produced more publications than other government departments. By the 1880s, some 17,000 applications a year were being examined. In 1859, Webster was referring not least to the practice of giving sets to the new public libraries established after 1850. The libraries became the recipients of government blue books, of reports of the public records, of printed state papers and of an assortment of other official or semi-official documents. By 1880, sets of patents were being sent out free to over 130 libraries (including a dozen in the United States), and over 300 were receiving sets of the abridgements. Among overseas recipients, three sets of the full patents went to Melbourne alone. Three went to India, and none to South Africa. Two went to Paris but none to Lyons; one to Rome but none to northern Italy; one to Haarlem but none to other Dutch cities. Sets went also to cities including Berlin, Buenos Aires, Dresden, Madrid, Riga, St Petersburg and Stockholm. Surplus sets were sent for pulping, but there were still ample supplies.[23] If the overseas distribution of the full patents exhibits somewhat varied support for, and curiosity in, British interests and enterprise on the part of the recipients in arranging for copies, the distribution of the abridgements was almost more erratic. For these, the main benefactors were at home: mechanics' institutes and 'scientific institutes'. But Norwich was

21 For one comment on all this, see Axon, 'The largest book in the world'.
22 [Thomas Webster] Review of patents, *Quarterly Review* 105 (1859), pp. 136–55, at p. 136.
23 Hewish, *Rooms near Chancery Lane*.

without either the full specifications or the abridgements, while the literary society at Holt, near the north coast of Norfolk, received a free set of abridgements. So did many other small institutions, such as the reading room at Hadleigh in Suffolk, the literary institute at Egham and the nearby Literary and Scientific Institution at Chertsey in Surrrey, and the Institution at St Just and the reading room at Helston in Cornwall. There was a set of the full patents at Crewe railway station, and a set of abridgements at the North Eastern Railway Library at York.[24] It is difficult to perceive a coherent policy in much of the list of recipients. Instead of such a policy, and analysis of where these documents would be most used, it seems that distribution depended on requests from any institution that wished. National distribution of information, however well intentioned in the large numbers of patents printed and in the amount of government money made freely available, was piecemeal and erratic.

The Trustees of the British Museum had been publishing on their own account since the beginning of the century, and had used a parliamentary grant to produce the facsimile of the Codex Alexandrinus. Catalogues of printed books, manuscripts, ancient marbles, drawings and other parts of the collections followed. By the mid-century their publications were handled by Longman. Pricing was conservative, reflecting original costs of production rather than current values: the early descriptions of the ancient marbles were still to be had for two guineas or less for generations after they had been printed. But the Museum's principal purpose was to collect. It bought government publications extensively from some European countries: others were less well represented. For many years after the mid-century, the Museum acquired American federal and state publications through the bookseller Henry Stevens, while others came as gifts through the Smithsonian Institution. As a result, the Museum obtained an exceptionally deep coverage of American materials. When the Smithsonian proposed a wider exchange agreement between Britain and America, it was resisted by the Treasury even to the point where the supplies to the Museum were threatened. But Washington's approach heralded new ways of sharing government publications, and by the late 1880s exchange agreements were in place with France, Italy, the United States and several British colonies.[25]

Among all the national collections, the Museum was exceptional for its international contacts. Most needed to focus principally on Britain and on

24 Details from the catalogue of Patent Office publications, August 1880.
25 Harris, *A history of the British Museum Library*, pp. 349–50.

visiting tourists. The National Gallery, founded in 1824, and the new museums of South Kensington required catalogues, and popular guides. Catalogues of some of the collections in the Victoria and Albert Museum (not so named until 1899) were published by commercial firms, like Samuel Redgrave's catalogue of the watercolours published by Chapman & Hall in 1877: the same firm was responsible for publishing most of the Museum's catalogues in the 1870s and 1880s, other than those issued by HMSO. The many educational materials produced in large numbers by the Science and Art Department in the Museum also came out under the auspices of Chapman & Hall. Printing was almost invariably in the hands of Eyre & Spottiswoode, who thereby, in this as in much other government printing, enjoyed a comfortable monopoly.[26] Because costs were to be kept to a minimum, illustration was generally used very sparingly, though there were many exceptions in the case of special exhibitions. The Great Exhibition of 1851, singular in this as in so much else, was supported by everything from penny guides to the series of four substantial volumes of *Reports by the Juries* magnificently illustrated with photographs.[27] For the national exhibitions of portraits in 1866–8 the Arundel Society made photographs of hundreds of images available for purchase. But most catalogues were unillustrated, whether of permanent collections or of temporary exhibitions, whether in London or elsewhere. Much of the credit for the progressive cheapening of photographs of works of art belongs to the Arundel Society (founded 1848), which developed a programme of reproductions that was closely allied to the South Kensington Museum. In 1859, the Society had its own public sales office within the Museum, and sold reproductions for a shilling upwards. The Society lasted until 1897, its demise coinciding with the rapid changes in reproductive processes at the end of the century.[28] Meanwhile, reproductions of works of art in magazines were usually in wood-engravings, until the new illustrated magazines of the 1890s brought successively closer copies with new photographic processes.

Though to a lesser extent, museums offered the same opportunities as libraries for the organised distribution of government-sponsored knowledge. There were obvious parallels between the distribution of blue books amongst public libraries and the distribution of specimen collections. In 1866, Forbes Watson, head of the India Museum, gathered together twenty sets of 700 specimens of Indian cotton. Each set was bound up into eighteen volumes, and sets were distributed to museums and chambers of commerce in the main

---

26 James, *The Victoria & Albert Museum: a bibliography.*   27 Hamber, 'A higher branch of the art'.
28 *Ibid.*, pp. 303–14; Maynard, *Descriptive notice of the drawings and publications of the Arundel Society.*

textile-producing towns of Britain. Further sets were sent out to India itself. The object was trade as much as emulation or inspiration. An accompanying book, printed in a much larger edition, described the costumes of the peoples of India, and was illustrated with photographs. The decision to use photographs instead of wood-engravings, as had been first planned, allowed the production of a hundred special copies in which the illustrations were hand-tinted. A second series of specimens was published in 1873–80, but the response was less enthusiastic when it was determined that these were to be sold rather than given away: sets were eventually sold off at half price, though only after Sotheran's, the West End booksellers, had offered a sum that was considered ridiculously low. Forbes Watson did not cease with conventional volumes of specimens. He also prepared a display stand that could hold 240 examples set on leaves hinged to a tall central column.[29]

Specialist catalogues of collections provided another route for public education. In the eighteenth century, few museums in Britain bothered to distribute copies of their catalogues even when such catalogues existed. In the nineteenth century, not only did production of printed catalogues become normal practice; their free distribution to other museums, to libraries and to other interested establishments was widely expected. Nonetheless, even where detailed catalogues and other publications were put on sale at the lowest possible prices, room was still found for complaint. In 1888 Thomas Greenwood, champion of free public libraries, complained that the British Museum's catalogues were not sufficiently distributed free of charge, and remarked that 'as the institution is maintained out of the general taxes this claim is both honorable and just'.[30]

They were not free, but they were not necessarily expensive. The Museum's three-volume catalogue of English books down to 1640, compiled by George Bullen (1884), cost thirty shillings. This proved eventually to be the foundation of national retrospective bibliography, and it provoked a series of catalogues of similar books from other libraries: Cambridge University Library followed in 1900–7.[31] In the 1880s Edward Gordon Duff embarked on a survey of books printed in England before 1501, as what became part of an international effort to discover and record all the earliest printing, throughout Europe. Meanwhile, there was no complete list of British books or of British authors. In 1877 Cornelius Walford, a senior member of the insurance industry, and brother of a London bookseller, proposed a project that would list all books printed in English, including those printed in America, and drew especial

29 Desmond, *The India Museum*, pp. 94–100.   30 Greenwood, *Museums and art galleries*, p. 229.
31 Ferguson, 'English books before 1640'.

attention to the importance of private collections.[32] His remarks provoked little immediate interest, and it seemed to many that the only realistic method was to print the catalogue of books in the British Museum. For several generations the Museum's own general catalogue was dogged by personal, political, literary and financial disputes. The first published attempt at such a catalogue foundered in 1841 at the end of the first volume, having covered letter A in about 18,200 entries. It was incomplete, and progress was much slower than anticipated. It satisfied no-one, least of all the person charged with its completion, Anthony Panizzi. No further parts of a printed general catalogue appeared until 1881, when the first entries were published for a catalogue that was completed in 1900. Complaints were naturally voiced that the delay of twenty years between the first and last volumes meant that many recently published books had been omitted. More importantly, it was not just a catalogue of what had by then become the greatest library in the world. Thanks to copyright deposit, immeasurably improved under Panizzi, and a buying policy that (among other things) paid especial attention to early English printing, it was also de facto the nearest that Britain had to a national retrospective bibliography.[33]

At the Ordnance Survey office, a publication programme was established only gradually. Much was learned – of organisation, mapping, engraving and distribution – during the 1830s and 1840s from the widely admired six-inch series for Ireland, which was distributed free of charge to libraries in both Ireland and the mainland.[34] In the 1830s, as the Ordnance Map Office, the British office was based at the Tower of London (it moved to Southampton in 1842). On the engraved maps, named individuals were credited with different aspects of the plates: this was a tradition carried over from the commercial engraving trade, where it was not unusual to see separate credit given to the individuals responsible for the figures, or for the etching that preceded the long task of engraving, as well as the principal engraver. For the one-inch map of central west Wales published in 1837, for example, the names of those separately responsible for the outline, the writing, the hills and the water were all named, and the whole was published by the Director, Thomas Colby. At the beginning of the twentieth century, the publisher was still named as the Director General (now D. A. Johnston) rather than the department. Personal and departmental prides mingled. More significantly, and unlike some other

32 Walford, 'A new general catalogue of English literature'.
33 McCrimmon, Power, politics, and print; Chaplin, GK: 150 years of the general catalogue of printed books in the British Museum; Harris, A history of the British Museum library.
34 Andrews, A paper landscape; Doherty, The Irish Ordnance Survey.

government departments, personal responsibility was thereby acknowledged and accepted.

Until 1866, sales of Ordnance Survey maps were through agents, who were entitled to a discount of 25 per cent. In that year, this system was abolished and just six agents were named instead – four in London, one in Edinburgh (W. & A. K. Johnston) and one in Dublin (Hodges & Smith). Each agent, who was allowed 33 per cent, was supposed to keep sufficient stock for sale, rather than draw it frequently from the Ordnance Survey (or, in London, the War Office) as necessary. It was too restrictive a system, and by the end of the following decade there were once again agents throughout the country, while the number in London had climbed to ten.[35] In 1885 the system was changed yet again. For the first time, the Stationery Office was placed in charge of sales, and Edward Stanford, of Long Acre, was appointed the sole agent for England and Wales. Arrangements in Scotland and Ireland were left unaltered until in 1886 Johnston lost the contract in Scotland to A. & C. Black.[36]

The one-inch engraved series for England and Wales was completed in 1870, and for the whole of the United Kingdom only in 1901. At the end of the century, a concerted effort was made to begin to produce maps with printed colour. Strict insistence was placed on copyright, in a market where commercial publishers were anxious to provide for leisure and business demand and where changing railway networks made up-to-date information essential. Unlike most other government publishing, maps were not an automatic monopoly. The Ordnance Survey could claim unsurpassed accuracy. It could not eliminate competition, and it was not designed as a commercial publisher. In its tardy introduction of colour, it lagged far behind public taste: Charles Knight had produced cheap colour-printed maps in the mid-century, and chromolithography had been developed in the late 1830s.[37] It was slow, too, to enter the ordinary commercial market. In 1860, Stanford published a map of twelve miles round London, at a scale of an inch to a mile. By the late 1880s this had run to at least eight editions.[38] In about 1869, G. W. Bacon issued a rival, on the same scale. Cruchley offered another, based on the Ordnance Survey and priced between a shilling (plain) and five shillings (coloured, mounted on cloth, and varnished). The firms remained in fierce competition, Bacon's revision of about twenty years later claiming to be 'from the new Ordnance Survey'. Larger-scale street plans presented another market again, frequently

35 Seymour (ed.), A history of the Ordnance Survey, pp. 160–1.   36 Ibid., pp. 183–4.
37 Jackson and Chatto, A treatise on wood engraving, 2nd edn, pp. 630–1; Twyman, Lithography, 1800–1850, pp. 160–3.
38 Hyde, Printed maps of Victorian London, p. 102.

using the data from the Ordnance Survey if these were available. Public occasions saw surges in map production for the use of visitors, notably in 1851, when James Wyld published a map with titles in English, French and German.

Cruchley's maps, taken over by Gall & Inglis, included half-inch maps based on the Ordnance Survey, and towns were catered for with visitors' maps on the same scale. As so often, the advertising revealed most of the audience:

> Towns, villages, hamlets, and gentlemen's seats, farm-houses, and adjacent localities, the courses of rivers and canals, the sites of Roman roads and stations, and every object of local or general interest, are also faithfully described, no pains having been spared to render it a complete guide to the student of history, the lover of antiquarian research, the pedestrian, or the commercial man.

The Ordnance Survey had not yet discovered the possibilities of the leisure market, and it was not to do so until the end of the century. Though all map publishers came to depend directly or indirectly on the Ordnance Survey, its business was small in the context of domestic map publishing as a whole. The firm of Bartholomew traced its history to the 1820s, and it remained a family firm until the late twentieth century. Under John (1831–93) and his son John George Bartholomew (1860–1920) the firm both printed maps for others (including that in Stevenson's *Treasure Island* as well as the more ordinary trade) and, increasingly, built up its own list of publications. Its survey atlas of Scotland (1895) was followed by a similar one for England and Wales in 1903: the latter was issued in monthly parts, at half a crown a part, or £2 12s 6d for the whole. In these two projects, based on the Ordnance Survey, Admiralty charts and other sources, and under the patronage of the Royal Geographical Society, the whole of Britain was covered at half an inch to a mile. Contours were marked in colour, an innovation introduced by the firm in Baddeley's guide to the Lake District in 1880. The public quickly appreciated the clarity brought by orographical tinting, and the sheets of the Bartholomew half-inch series became the largest selling of all the popular maps.[39]

By the 1870s, the situation had changed radically from the 1830s. The landscape had been transformed with the development of railway and other transport networks and with the growth and replanning of towns and cities. Specialist maps were needed for mining, tunnelling, ethnology, statistics of health and disease, and social understanding and management. Emigration and casual tourism alike required not only general knowledge at home, and the ability to follow the adventures of loved ones overseas, but also detailed information

39 Gardner, *Bartholomew*.

for people arriving at their destinations. For sea navigation, Admiralty charts stood in a similar relation to commercial needs as did the Ordnance Survey to life on land. Like land maps, they were in competition with those of private publishers, and the agency system for sales did not always encourage preference for the Admiralty's sheets. After a long-standing reluctance to publish them, by 1864 there were 2,500 charts for sale, a figure that had grown rapidly in the previous few years. For much of the second half of the nineteenth century the contract for sales was held by Malby & Sons.[40] In 1914, just before the war, they were available from the bookshops of J. D. Potter in London: one was in the Minories, convenient for the Port of London. As if to emphasise the determined autonomy of the various government departments, maps of the Geological Survey and those of the India Office were both to be had from Stanford, while T. Fisher Unwin noised their appointment as agent for the Ordnance Survey.

There were many people who never learned how to read a map. There were many more who did. Educational policies helped to ensure that; and publishers were eager to supply needs. Whether in flat sheets or in a flourishing atlas trade, the public was offered choice and generally increasing accuracy. In a celebrated phrase, Mary Kingsley described African forest life as 'like being shut up in a library whose books you cannot read'.[41] Atlases helped to explain this and other unknown worlds. Maps followed the flag, and were noticeably more up to date for some parts of the world than for others. The development of Australia, the complications of South Africa, and commercial exploration in South America all brought immediate demands on the map trade. On the other hand, in 1910 Stanford was still offering Sir Robert Schomburgk's map of Barbados, published in 1846, and a map of Mexico on four sheets published in 1845. Progress was far from uniform. If there was a single dominant theme, it was communication. The world was gradually turned to paper, measured not only according to projections but also according to the points reached by explorers, whose achievements were recorded on maps whether in the centre of Australia or in the quest to reach the north pole.

Atlases and maps were available at all prices. In the 1870s, at one end, Collins offered penny maps of different countries, measuring 13 × 11 inches, 'the cheapest and most complete system issued'. They also offered school wall maps, of countries and of individual counties: as a Scottish publisher they paid especial attention to north of the border, offering Edinburgh on the same size sheet as Yorkshire. Library atlases were available from several publishers. Again

40 Ritchie, *The Admiralty chart*. 41 Kingsley, *Travels in West Africa*, p. 102.

in the 1870s, W. & A. K. Johnston offered a new edition of the imperial folio *Royal atlas of modern geography* at six or ten guineas, depending on the style of binding. In the same price-bracket, the Society for the Diffusion of Useful Knowledge, renamed the Useful Knowledge Society, offered its *Complete atlas of ancient and modern geography*: the part dealing just with modern geography was available at five guineas – less than ninepence per map. Blackie offered an *Imperial atlas of modern geography* at £5 10s, its title part of a suite that included an imperial *Gazetteer*, a *Dictionary* and a *Bible-dictionary*. George Philip listed an *Imperial library atlas* at five guineas, engraved after drawings by John Bartholomew, and like all these publishers offered a range of atlases shorter and in smaller formats down to those suitable for the classroom. More modestly and more briefly (it contained just fifty-six maps), Black offered a *General atlas of the world* at three guineas. Here, too, the cheaper end was not neglected. Johnston was thought to have been the first to recognise the 'needs of the million' with a sixpenny atlas of the world in just eleven maps, including one for Palestine.

Publication and appropriate sales arrangements were only two aspects of the organisation of knowledge, often of new kinds and in new ways. For increasing numbers of people the road to knowledge was through the public library, which existed in many forms.[42]

The earliest mechanics' institutes were designed to provide education for working men. George Birkbeck, his followers and imitators could be easily criticised for their assumptions of middle-class values, and for the threat that their creations, which assumed free time, appeared to present to the running of factories. At the core of the new institutes were a lecture hall and a library, not always in separate rooms. Newport in the Isle of Wight was reported in 1826 to possess 5,000 volumes – a thousand more volumes than there were inhabitants. Libraries assumed an ever-increasing importance in the affairs of almost all mechanics' institutes, regardless of whether they were influenced more by one class of people than another. At Leeds, the chief attraction was said by 1846 to be not its classes, nor its lectures, but its newspaper room, which attracted over a hundred people at a time.[43] By 1850, the year of the Public Libraries Act, the library at Manchester contained 12,000 volumes.[44] The foundation of free public libraries was one direct cause of the long-term decline of mechanics' institutes, and of their repositioning primarily as social centres. But though

42 For much more on libraries, see *The Cambridge history of libraries in Britain and Ireland* 2 and 3. For libraries and the organisation of knowledge, see further McKitterick, 'Libraries, knowledge and public identity'.
43 Tylecote, *The mechanics' institutes of Lancashire and Yorkshire*, p. 73. 44 *Ibid.*, p. 70.

the emphases often changed, as resources were invested in leisure from tennis to the ubiquitous billiards, many institutes retained both libraries and lecture rooms. Often the libraries were small, such as that at Felling on Tyne, with a library of just 2,000 volumes, or Louth with 3,000, in 1914. Others, such as that at Burnley, were thriving: with a stock of 22,000 volumes, and open from 10 a.m. to 8.30 p.m. every weekday, Burnley was able to spend £150 a year on books. At Jarrow, the Mechanics' Institute was established comparatively late in the movement, in 1863. The library was still modest, but it spent £50 p.a. on books. One of the largest was at Nottingham: founded in 1837 and with a lending stock alone of almost 25,000 volumes, it spent £60 a year on the purchase of books, was open twelve hours a day, and had a membership of 5,000. Others were very late foundations, such as the Railway Mechanics' Institute at Horley, founded in 1888 and with a technical school attached, or the Midland Railway Institute at Derby, opened in 1894. Three other great railway towns, Swindon, Crewe and York, had possessed similar institutions since 1843, 1846 and 1849 respectively.[45] Jealousies between the older mechanics' institutes and the newer public libraries were rife as most of the former limped into desuetude. The success of Burnley was partly attributable to there being no public library in the town. Yet at Nottingham the public library dated from 1867 and in 1914 had a lending stock of 42,000 volumes besides thirty branch libraries.

Although mechanics' institutes and their libraries were still numerous in 1914, they were by then but one kind of public institution for knowledge among many. During the nineteenth century, libraries multiplied in their kind in far more than just the new public libraries to which we shall turn presently. The old proprietary subscription libraries such as those at Leeds (founded 1768), Hull (1775), Birmingham (1779), Newcastle-upon-Tyne (1793) or Plymouth (1810); a mixture of lyceums and athenaeums (Liverpool Lyceum 1758; Oldham 1839); and literary institutes such as those at Bedford (1832): all provided alternatives or supplements to the new public libraries.[46] Society libraries like those of the Royal Geological Society of Cornwall or the York- shire Geological Society, the specialist medical libraries to be found in most large cities, or the military libraries at Aldershot, Chatham and Portsmouth, provided for their own particular readers. In Leeds, the Yorkshire Village Library, founded in 1852, provided for almost three hundred villages and about 200,000 readers, mostly of what it called the operative classes. Other

---

45 Details from Clegg (ed.), *The international directory of booksellers.*
46 Beckwith, *The Leeds Library*; Parish, *History of the Birmingham Library*; Watson, *The history of the Literary and Philosophical Society of Newcastle-upon-Tyne.*

towns such as Doncaster, Harwich and Huddersfield had cooperative society libraries.

The Public Libraries Act of 1850 was a watershed; but it was a watershed that needs careful examination. Under its terms, local authorities were permitted to make a charge on the rates for the support of free public libraries. The Ewart report of 1849–50 demonstrated clearly the national, not simply the local, need for such provision, in its impressive array of evidence both from overseas and from Britain.[47] But neither the committee nor Parliament could force everyone to accept the extra cost, or to recognise that reading for the masses would be other than inflammatory, a potential threat to political and ecclesiastical stability. Nor could Westminster decide what was to be bought and read. Residual concerns persisted about the possible dangers of education and of reading in mechanics' institutes. It was easy, and inaccurate, to criticise the mechanics' institutes in general for the limitations of their stock, where the need to retain members forced the purchase of what seemed to others undesirable quantities of novels.[48] But, rather like weapons or tools in the wrong hands, libraries posed dangers.

The take-up by local authorities of the powers allowed in 1850 was slow. In 1870 there were still sixteen counties in which there was no free public library under the 1850 Act. In London, West Ham, Stoke Newington, Chiswick and Poplar adopted the Act only in 1890. Opinion in the country was equally hesitant: Salisbury, Carlisle, Workington and Rugby adopted it in the same year. By the end of the century the country was still not agreed.[49] Public leadership was often lacking, and many libraries owed their existence not so much to public opinion as to private philanthropy by men such Andrew Carnegie (whose gifts were shared by 295 libraries between 1897 and 1913), John Passmore Edwards, and others who provided for their home towns.[50]

The new public libraries were different in many ways from already existing libraries, and not just in their funding. They also raised questions concerning what was meant by a library. The Liverpool Athenaeum, founded in 1798, had continued an eighteenth-century tradition in providing coffee with its books and newspapers.[51] In the 1840s, the Russell Institution (just off Tavistock Square in London, on the Bedford estate) was one of several large libraries of

---

47 *Report from the select committee on public libraries* 2 vols. (1849–50).   48 *Ibid.*, paras. 1202–3.
49 Ogle, *The free library*, pp. 40, 64.
50 Paul Sturges, 'Public library people, 1850–1919', in Black and Hoare (eds.), *The Cambridge history of libraries in Britain and Ireland* 3, pp. 110–19, at pp. 117–18.
51 Shaw, *History of the Athenaeum, Liverpool*, p. 14.

its kind open to select groups of people: it had been founded in 1808, using buildings partly converted from assembly rooms. One legacy from this was an elaborate suite of public baths adjoining the library. More pertinently, there was a newsroom, and a lecture room. By 1849, the sixth edition of the printed catalogue listed upwards of 16,000 volumes.[52] This was small beer compared with the lending libraries already existing in Manchester, Leeds or Birmingham, and the founders of the London Library in 1841 were determined that their new foundation should be greater. By 1847 the London Library had already grown to almost 15,000 works, in many more volumes. Unlike many subscription libraries, and in keeping with the needs of its users, it concentrated its money on books and periodicals.[53] Up and down the country, mechanics' institutes strove to provide both books and lectures and, increasingly, recreations. But, by law, the new public libraries founded after 1850 were funded at first for books and periodicals. Librarians frequently found the newspaper room a nuisance, attracting people whose sole purpose seemed to be either to keep warm or, worse, to examine the sports pages as an aid to betting. If early photographs are to be relied on, the newsroom tended to be a male preserve. In some towns, this room opened very early, so as to help people looking for work. But in these same newsrooms many librarians busied themselves either blacking out or excising details of the sports pages. Women were provided with their own reading room in some places, but this was not universally favoured. At Bradford in 1892, the women's reading room took the main London daily papers as well as several provincial ones, and its three dozen other periodicals included extra copies of popular magazines such as the *Graphic*, the *Illustrated London News*, *Punch* and the *Century Magazine*, besides two copies of the *Girl's Own Paper*.[54]

The public library represented an unprecedented extension of knowledge and entertainment, both to those who had previously had access to shared collections and to the many more who had not. The stocks were often vastly bigger than the old private subscription libraries. By 1900, Wigan public library, with a special endowment, an energetic librarian and a chairman who was the greatest bibliophile of his generation, could boast a stock of 53,300 volumes, of which no fewer than 38,000 were classed as reference works.[55] There were more library books per head of population than in perhaps any other non-university town in Britain. Birmingham, Manchester and the other large cities vied with each other and, especially, with London. But, as the many arguments

52 Brayley, *Catalogue of the library of the Russell Institution* (1849).
53 Cochrane, *Catalogue of the London Library* (1847).   54 Wood, 'Three special features'.
55 Folkard, *Wigan Free Public Library*.

and discussions at the annual meetings of the Library Association (founded 1877) demonstrated all too clearly, benevolent liberalism carried with it more than a little social control. When Cambridge Public Library led a revolution and opened its stacks to readers, where formerly staff had (as in other libraries) fetched each book required, there was widespread anxiety that books would be stolen, or be too much handled.[56]

By the end of the century, the public library had become not only familiar. Even more than half a century earlier, it was a main prop of society. The larger authorities organised lecture programmes; Liverpool, Manchester, Nottingham, Norwich and smaller places provided mixtures of general knowledge and lectures addressed more particularly to ways by which libraries could be better used. Links were forged with the Oxford and Cambridge extension lectures, and travelling libraries were sent out to support the lectures. In Cambridge Public Library the books connected with a course on the social history of England were kept reserved in the reading room. Knowledge, a watchword of the 1830s, had evolved into education, aided and sometimes led by government and by new professionalism in the management of libraries.[57]

In the 1890s, Sir John Lubbock, pursuing commonplaces, began an essay on libraries with the fourteenth century and Richard de Bury, and then moved rapidly via Schopenhauer, Herschel and other more obvious people to the fact that more was spent on alcohol than on books. 'It is rather sad', he concluded, 'to think that when we speak of a public-house, we think of a place for the sale of drink. I am glad, however, to know that on all sides public-houses are now rising for the supply not of beer but of books.'[58] Lame though this was as a conclusion, and tardy as he was in his observation, he was reminding his readers of values not dissimilar to those which had preoccupied social reformers of the 1830s and 1840s.

Since not all reading was good, public libraries had a duty to their constituents. Ever since soon after the invention of printing in the West, and in some circles long before then, each generation had complained at the increasing numbers of books, and the confusions consequent upon them. Some spoke of indigestion. Others spoke of the immorality consequent upon too ready access to knowledge for which readers were unsuited, of the dangers to religion, of the lack of control that went with mass markets of cheap literature. 'There are books which are no books, and to read which is mere waste of time; while there are others so bad, that we cannot read them without pollution;

56 Wood, 'Three special features'.
57 For public libraries in the late nineteenth century, see particularly Greenwood, *Public libraries*.
58 Lubbock, *The use of life*, p. 132.

if they were men we should kick them into the street.'[59] Lubbock, artist of the truism, sought to make his point by revealing his own inhumanity. More temperately, he wrote on the same page that 'light and entertaining books are valuable, just as sugar is an important article of food, especially for children, but we cannot live upon it'. Much of his choice of a hundred best books embodied his own, almost desperate, seriousness. *Adam Bede* was in, but there were no Brontës; Green's history of England was preferred to Macaulay; the poets were all safely dead; Scott's novels were included, counting as one entry; Matthew Arnold, Coleridge and Ruskin were all absent.[60] If there was much in this of late nineteenth-century fashion, there was also much that was omitted. Such lists were nevertheless much valued. In 1891, Routledge enterprisingly set about publishing all the hundred books in uniform bindings, pricing most of them between 1s 6d and 3s 6d each.

Lubbock, who introduced into Parliament the new Public Libraries Bill in 1892, shared many concerns with those who oversaw and managed public libraries, and not least in questions of propriety in the selection and management of books. Just as the first mechanics' institutes eschewed light reading, and especially novels, so the committees charged with the new public libraries were much exercised as to how much should be spent on recreation, and how much on more serious matters. Equally, just as the institutes gradually bowed to demand, so public libraries increased their stocks of fiction, until it easily dominated. Unlike the commercial and privately owned circulating libraries such as the giant Mudie's and its offshoots, public libraries owed their existence to public funds, with all the tergiversations involved in local politics and opinion. But, publicly at least, their justification lay less in entertainment than in the sharing and dissemination of knowledge. Pride in the bookstocks lay not in the fiction departments, but in the reference rooms, in the collections of local literature, and, in many towns, in the examples of early printing.[61] Some collections of local literature, often founded by private enthusiasts and benefactors, were by the early twentieth century closer to definitive in their scope and in their detail than were those of the national collections. Money was set aside by public library managements to buy local literature. Piecemeal developments were occasionally brought together, and especially after the founding of the Library Association in 1877. At the first annual meeting of the Association in 1878, W. H. Allnutt of the Bodleian Library drew attention to some recent work on provincial printing, by S. F. Cresswell on Nottinghamshire,

59 *Ibid.*, p. 139.   60 Lubbock, *The pleasures of life*.
61 Madan, 'What to aim at in local bibliography'. See also McKitterick, 'Libraries, knowledge and public identity'.

J. H. Hinde on Newcastle and, above all, Robert Davies on York.[62] The collecting of local printing by the new library authorities was a natural development that enabled much research subsequently, though it always relied on the generosity and interest of private individuals. When, for example, Henry Bradshaw died in 1886 he left his unequalled collection of Irish printing and books on Ireland to Cambridge University Library, and at Carlisle the collection of books on Cumberland and Westmorland was founded on that assembled by William Jackson of St Bees and left to the library in 1890.[63]

The larger public libraries, and even some other local libraries, challenged the university libraries. By 1914 there were ten universities in England and Wales, four in Scotland and two in Ireland. At that date, the Royal Institution at Hull was spending £500 per annum on books out of an annual income of £900. Trinity College Dublin was spending £400 p.a. on books, the University of Liverpool £900, and Birmingham – with a smaller library than that at Hull – about £600, the same as the University of London Library. Manchester Public Library spent more on books, newspapers and bindings (£8,273) than the entire annual income of Cambridge University Library.

The emphasis in the last few paragraphs has been on libraries outside London, which generated its own demand for libraries on a scale all its own, and where national, professional and local interests often overlapped. The stocks of books were often very heavily used, with the annual number of borrowings several times the number of books in stock overall. How far the national picture amounted to organised knowledge is unclear. The range of libraries was greater than ever before; public funds were used for the national collections, for universities and for local public libraries. A library was an attribute of a learned populace, and clerical and cathedral libraries offered resources for lay as well as ecclesiastical readerships. To the extent that many libraries received government publications by gift, there was a clear measure of paternalism in the organised dispersal of information. But the increasing numbers of libraries, and the need to staff and manage them, bred its own independent literature. Melvil Dewey's decimal classification was just one import from America, where the *Library Journal* (1886–) became for a while the organ of the British profession as well.

Book selection, a challenge often daunting to librarians and readers alike, was met with select lists of suitable books, organised by subject, a feature unavailable in the ordinary trade lists of new books. William Swan Sonnenschein's *The*

62 Allnutt, 'Printers and printing in the provincial towns of England and Wales'.
63 *A catalogue of the Bradshaw collection*; Hinds, *Bibliotheca Jacksoniana: catalogue*.

best books, first published in 1887, grew by the 1930s to six volumes. It became a vade mecum for booksellers and librarians, as well as a boon to readers more generally. As the supplements multiplied, and the labour of selection gradually overwhelmed Sonnenschein, so the exercise became more arbitrary. Less ambitiously, because more selectively, E. B. Sargant and Bernhard Whishaw's *Guide book to books* (1891) was the work of a team of over 150 contributors, including university professors, librarians, deans of cathedrals and literary figures – among them William Morris and J. Addington Symonds. The idea of book selection guides according to subject was an old one, with its roots in the sixteenth century. But much of the modern concern was shared with America. In 1893 the American Library Association organised an exhibition of 5,000 books for a 'model' library at the World's Columbian Exhibition in Chicago. All the main British publishers, and many minor ones, collaborated, and found themselves among publishers from North America. The books were listed in the printed catalogue according to both Dewey's classification and the more recent 'expansive' scheme, as well as in a dictionary catalogue. As usual, prices and other publication details were provided. The American Bureau of Education ensured that British libraries received copies of the catalogue as gifts, a further reminder of the common goals perceived in libraries in both countries.

Books were only one form of printed publication. Periodical literature presented its own challenges. Notwithstanding commercial directories such as the *Newspaper press directory*,[64] *May's British and Irish press guide*, and *Willing's press guide*, there was no comprehensive list of titles. The management of contents posed further questions, and here they were met by private enterprise. In 1848, W. F. Poole, a graduate of Yale University, published the first of what proved to be a much revised and extended project to index journal articles. He covered titles in both Britain and the United States, and in 1853 issued a much enlarged edition. Supplements followed to 1906, and *Poole's index* reigned unchallenged until long into the twentieth century.[65] These guides to periodicals, including Palmer's quarterly index to *The Times*, were, like those to books, designed primarily to provide reference to literature by subject. Inevitably they also had a chronological dimension, and never more so than in the rhythm of publication of Palmer's slim volumes insisting on the passage of time and the unfolding relationship of subject-matter day by day. Like periodicals, and

---

64 The Jubilee issue of the *Newspaper press directory* (1895) includes a history of the annual, and a detailed survey of the history of the newspaper press throughout the English-speaking world.
65 Williamson, *William Frederick Poole*.

like the proceedings of learned societies, they placed a new emphasis on the developing and changing nature of knowledge, not its immutable stability.

Some of the distinctiveness of mid-nineteenth-century periodical publishing can be perceived in the fates of two journals launched in the eighteenth century, one private and one institutional. The *Gentleman's Magazine* had been founded by Edward Cave in 1731. It was always a private enterprise, and from 1780 it was edited by successive members of the Nichols family until it was sold in 1856. It went into genteel decline. By contrast, *Archaeologia*, founded in 1770, was the journal of the Society of Antiquaries. The first of these journals died, and the second flourished; yet both were challenged by the same developments in local history and archaeology, as new local societies were formed and launched their own journals. There were several reasons for this. The *Gentleman's Magazine* had always encouraged a clubbable tone, in its correspondence with the editor ('Mr Urban') where letters were often articles in their own right. But when (for example) Dawson Turner, banker in Great Yarmouth, left its pages and preferred to publish his antiquarian pieces with the more local Norfolk Archaeological Society he was merely doing the same as others in different parts of the country, looking for a journal that provided a comparable sodality, yet of a more local and perhaps more immediate nature. There was a further and more serious problem for the *Gentleman's Magazine*. Its interests were general, a mixture of current affairs, literature, antiquarianism and obituaries. By the 1840s the market was full of general periodicals, often noticeably more up to date if not so noticeably hospitable to all comers in editorial policy. The kind of miscellaneous information for which it had been most valued in the past was available in other ways. Where it had once been the main vehicle for parliamentary reporting, it had lost this purpose. John Henry Barrow's *Mirror of Parliament* had been established in 1828 and Hansard began a new series in 1820 with the accession of George IV. The daily newspapers distributed summaries of debates more quickly. Deaths were more fully – and more promptly – reported in *The Times*. An increasing range of reviewing journals was readily available. There was ever less place for the old kind of *omnium gatherum*, while the foundation of *Notes & Queries* in 1849 by William John Thoms, as an extension of the *Athenaeum*, provided a more focussed outlet for amateur and professional sharing of historical and literary knowledge.[66]

The Victorian preoccupation with time, whether geological time in the work of Sidgwick, or evolutionary time in the work of Chambers and Darwin, or archaeological discoveries in Egypt and Asia Minor, or the historicism of the

66 Francis, *Notes by the way*.

New Testament, or the white rabbit in the first chapter of *Alice in Wonderland*, was as clearly displayed in the regular and announced sequences of periodical publications and their indexes as in the pages of Bradshaw's railway timetables. The antiquary Sir Nicolas Harris Nicolas sought to present an accurate account of the world's major chronological systems in a small handbook first published as *Notitia historica* in 1824 and then expanded in 1833 and 1838 as *The chronology of history*. Haydn's *Dictionary of dates*, published in 1841, took such concerns with historical time further, by translating modern terminology of knowledge from alphabetical subject sequences into chronological ones. The dictionary was adapted for America, and published there. In Britain, by 1910 it had become a steady seller and reached its twenty-fifth edition.

In their several ways, the indexes, chronologies and similar enterprises provided a national framework for organised knowledge. Equally importantly, it was possible to see how such knowledge could be strengthened, extended and improved. To this end, and as we have seen, government publications could be readily disseminated to identified locations, for public education. The reference rooms of libraries across the country filled up with complimentary copies of printed calendars of state papers from the Public Record Office, with editions of historical texts from the English middle ages, and with Blue Books from Parliament.

Much of the impetus for the publication of the public records and state papers as the programme developed in the second half of the century was due originally to Henry Cole. In 1842 he advanced proposals for a national record society, that would take up where older projects had ended. He pointed out the lack of such a society as compared with the several devoted to natural history, and he emphasised not just the historical interest of the records, but also their topicality. 'There is hardly a question of moment which may not receive considerable light from the public documents.' But Cole failed to move those whose support he most needed. Sir Francis Palgrave, in the Record Office, was sympathetic, but it seems that others charged with the care of the records were not.[67] It was not until the State Paper Office was absorbed into the Public Record Office in 1855 that any progress was possible. The Calendar of State Papers, recommended to the House of Commons in 1855, was put in hand with remarkable speed, the first volume (beginning in 1547) appearing in 1856. By 1880, about a hundred volumes had appeared. Record publications were put on sale through selected publishers in London, Edinburgh and Dublin. Alongside them were published a series of *Chronicles and memorials of Great*

---

67 Cantwell, *The Public Record Office*, pp. 73–4. See also Bonython and Burton, *The great exhibitor*.

Britain and Ireland during the middle ages, familiarly known as the Rolls Series.[68] It began with an edition of Capgrave's chronicle in 1858. Not all the editions were equally thorough, and much of the calendaring of the state papers was below the standard later expected. A fast pace was set, and some editors proved extraordinarily productive: H. R. Luard, of Trinity College, Cambridge, edited the French and Latin lives of Edward the Confessor, the *Historia anglicana* of Bartholomacus de Cotton, Grosseteste's letters, and five volumes of *Annales monastici*, all for the Rolls Series, and he was not alone in his industry. The sense of urgency was palpable. These series signalled not just government acceptance of the need to publish the records in its care. Unlike the state papers, the manuscripts on which the volumes of the Rolls Series were based were scattered in libraries across the country: this was not simply the government publishing its own. In all of these endeavours, national interest drove historical and commercial ideals. The various series sat in the context of other similar series and enterprises overseas. Bouquet's *Recueil* had been published in 1737–86. The first volume of the *Monumenta Germaniae historiae* had appeared in 1826. In Britain, the state became not just publisher of contemporary administration. In the absence of private enterprise, it also became subsidiser of the nation's history. Custom, not simply Gladstone's enthusiasm, dictated that the state should publish the new edition of Domesday book; and thus the new facilities for photozincography at the Ordnance Survey were used for the first modern facsimile, published in 1861–3. Scientific knowledge needed support as well. The long series of large and illustrated volumes of the reports of the voyage of *HMS Challenger* was thought to have cost the government more than anything else it had ever published. By 1887, twenty-seven volumes had been issued, and the Commission charged with publication of the voyage's discoveries was estimated to have cost so far about £40,000. Direct publishing and printing costs amounted to almost £25,000. As only about £12,000 had been recouped in sales, the public cost thus far (and the project was by no means completed) stood at about £53,000.[69]

Commercial publishing depends on risk-taking, and on profits. As is stressed repeatedly in this volume, books were frequently expensive. The reasons for this were complex, and were not attributable to any single feature of manufacture or publishing. Paper costs were often invoked, but these were by no means the only costs. One difficulty lay in sometimes poor understanding of how to recover the high costs of colour printing, or of stereotyping. Another lay in

---

68 Knowles, *Great historical enterprises*, pp. 101–34. For details of these series, see Mullins, *Texts and calendars*.

69 *2nd report of the Controller of Her Majesty's Stationery Office* (1887): *Parliamentary papers* 1887.xxvii.

how to estimate demand. There was a tendency in some parts of the market to overprint, and in few places more so than in publishing on the fine arts. The result was a large trade in remainders not just at the cheap end of the market, as it had been developed by James Lackington at the beginning of the century, but also by West End booksellers such as Bohn and, later, Sotheran and Quaritch. In the late 1870s, Sotheran was also offering the residue of complete sets of Hansard for £130, and of the *Annual Register* since its beginning in 1758 for £32 10s – less than the price of two sets of Domesday book.

Information was not always new. It also went out of date, and the paper on which it was printed became a drug on the market. By the 1880s there was a Stationery Office committee to consider how best to dispose of unsold stocks of Record Office publications: even the reference rooms of public libraries could not absorb the quantities that had been produced. No-one wanted hundreds of thousands of unsold government publications.[70] But, equally, publishers could be hesitant. Hence, for many subjects, there was considerable attraction in the notion of subsidised publishing. For this, the learned society with a programme of publishing provided an ideal solution.[71] Such a society removed from publishers anxieties about finding suitable authors or editors; it generated its own list; it provided its own scholarly or other suitable guarantees; it provided its own capital, based on members' subscriptions and, to some extent, on private funds; it met minority interests and thus disburdened the ordinary publishing trade; it ensured sales that could be easily quantified. By means of extensive exchange agreements at home and overseas, work was circulated at minimal cost. Above all, publication by societies removed much – but not all – risk. Naturally, the societies saw themselves in different lights, promoting particular interests by a mixture of sociability and commerce.

Thus, whereas government printing of historical documents tended to over-supply, societies could be quite specific in their print orders. At one extreme lay the Roxburghe Club, a group of bibliophiles dedicated to produce copies of rare printed tracts and other early mainly English literature for each other: founded on the occasion of the Roxburghe sale in 1812, in 1839 its membership was increased to forty.[72] The Bannatyne Club, founded in 1823 to promote the study of the history and literature of Scotland, was originally of just thirty-eight members, until in 1828 membership was increased to a hundred. The

---

70 *Ibid.*; Cantwell, *The Public Record Office*, p. 300; Gilburt, 'Remainders'.
71 For the following, see Hume, *Learned societies and printing clubs*; Steeves, *Learned societies and English literary scholarship*; Williams, *Book clubs & printing societies*.
72 Bigham, *The Roxburghe Club*; Barker, *The publications of the Roxburghe Club*.

very similar Maitland Club was founded at Glasgow in 1828, and there was a considerable overlap in membership.

While some of the productions of these societies were slight, there was much that was not. By 1847 they were considered important enough for a guide to their publications to be prepared by Abraham Hume, a Liverpool clergyman and antiquary. He distinguished between professional societies such as those for medicine, architects and engineers, and those of more general interest ('the Society for promoting the study of Gothic Architecture consists merely of the clergy') including the Royal Society among the more general. In 1864, Henry G. Bohn included a detailed bibliographical account in his appendix to Lowndes's *Bibliographer's manual*. He found about 230 publishing societies and other bodies, including some that were defunct and some, such as the Society of Antiquaries, who had long histories. A number were professional bodies, mainly in medicine and engineering. Most were amateur. Some published monographs, some texts, and some their proceedings or transactions. Bohn was thorough, and he cast his net widely, taking in the whole of the British Isles. Out of his total, over half had been founded in the 1830s and 1840s, and over 30 per cent had been founded in the 1840s: the introduction of the penny post in 1840 had had some effect, but it was not universally formative. The 1850s had seen about one-third fewer new publishing societies than had the 1830s.

Society publishing was distinctive, and it was substantial. In historical studies alone, the activities of such associations drew attention to the need for a programme to publish the national archive. The Surtees Society, founded in 1834 to print the records of early Northumbria, was followed by the Camden Society in 1838, with a more broadly English purpose. The Hakluyt Society, focussing on voyages and travels down to about 1700, followed in 1846.[73] Local history societies, usually organised according to counties, concentrated sometimes on publishing documents, and sometimes on secondary articles. Some concentrated on archaeological matters; some were as much concerned with natural history as with the past. Their collegial purposes were similar; the results were different in their emphasis. Beyond these were groups such as the Parker Society, founded in 1840 and devoted to printing documents of the English reformation, the parallel Wodrow Society (1841) addressing the Presbyterian church in Scotland, and the Harleian Society, founded in 1869 for the recording of genealogy. Later on, the Selden Society (1887)[74] concentrated on the publication of early English legal texts and the Henry

---

73 Nichols, *A descriptive catalogue of the first series of the Camden Society*; Bridges and Hair (eds.), *Compassing the vast globe of the earth.*
74 *A centenary guide to the publications of the Selden Society.*

Bradshaw Society (1890),[75] named after the learned Librarian of Cambridge University (d.1886), on early liturgies. Some lasted only a few years; others survive to this day. While the annual subscriptions of members helped to guarantee the cost of publications, they did not necessarily control ambitions. The Ossianic Society, founded at Dublin in 1853 for the publication and preservation of Irish manuscripts 'illustrative of the Fenian period', rapidly attracted a membership of 900, only to slump to 300 ten years after its inauguration. Yet Bohn reported that the society had seven books in preparation. Societies failed for many reasons. The Cymmrodorion, founded in London in 1751 to promote Welsh interests, was dissolved in 1787 after a steep decline in membership. With the revival of the Welsh language and other traditions in the second decade of the nineteenth century, epitomised in the great Carmarthen Eisteddfod in 1819, interest revived, the society was relaunched in 1820 and a series of *Transactions* was inaugurated. But this in turn faltered, and by 1855 it had disappeared. Interests among the London Welsh had changed, and the society was not revived again until the 1870s.[76]

Although there was no government interest in publishing literature, the development of literary societies offered much in parallel to major historical enterprises. They often grew more as a result of individual enthusiasm than the kindred interests that inspired and supported the more general historical societies. John Payne Collier, later tarred as a forger and an adulterator of archives, founded the Shakespeare Society in 1840 in order to produce modestly priced editions of Shakespeare's contemporaries.[77] The Early English Text Society, founded by F. J. Furnivall in 1864, was by far the most successful of the literary societies in the long term. Unstoppable in his enthusiasms, seemingly impervious to criticism and deeply irritating to people who could not appreciate his wide but often inadequate knowledge, Furnivall followed this with the Chaucer Society (1868), chiefly a vehicle for the publishing of his own edition of the poet: his edition was mostly superseded by that of W. W. Skeat in 1894–7. Furnivall went on to found the Ballad Society in 1868 and the New Shakspeare Society in 1873, and he shared in the formation of the Spenser Society in 1866. None lasted into the new century.[78] Not all societies were for ancient texts. All were susceptible to personal ambitions. The Shelley Society

75 Ward, *The publications of the Henry Bradshaw Society.*
76 Jenkins and Ramage, *A history of the Honorable Society of Cymmrodorion and of the Gwyneddigion and Cymreigyddion Societies.*
77 Freeman and Freeman, *John Payne Collier.*
78 *Frederick James Furnivall;* Benzie, *Dr. F. J. Furnivall.*

became the playground of Thomas Wise, and in its facsimile printing lay some of the seeds of the forgeries perpetrated by Buxton Forman and Wise.[79]

The Pâli Text Society (1882), the Irish Texts Society (1898), and the Malone Society (1907) for the publication of sixteenth- and early seventeenth-century English drama and related documents,[80] were among the many that found successful niches. The membership of the last, set at first at twenty-five members, was deliberately minute, as if such a coterie arrangement would add value by virtue of self-assessment. The same self-imposed restriction was followed by the Bibliographical Society (founded in 1892) for many years, until shortage of cash made an extension to the membership urgent.[81]

Club- and society-forming – and there were dozens more besides those just named – became a habit, whether for publishing or for social, religious, political or professional purposes: they were often mixtures of several, and had both clannish and more public aspects. For some, dinners were as important as meetings or publication programmes. In their very different ways, they offered alternatives and complements to other more demotic groupings. Their exclusivity was a strength, both in their own control of membership and in the required dedication of their members. In the case of publishing societies, the financial commitment was maintained by the promise of books to come. But, most importantly, they promoted the subjects to which they were allied, not just by encouraging and supporting minority interests but also by providing a means to enlarge public knowledge. They ventured where ordinary commercial publishers could not; and, especially in their commitment to the publishing of national history, they supplemented and eventually supplanted programmes that were directly supported by central government.

Societies were natural vehicles for learned journals. In the seventeenth century, the Royal Society established its reputation not so much through its meetings, which were attended by comparatively few people, as through the *Philosophical Transactions*, which won an international audience. Copies of the *Transactions* were distributed liberally as gifts and exchanges.[82] The Cambridge Philosophical Society (devoted to the study of the natural sciences and mathematics), founded in 1819, launched its own *Transactions* in 1821, the Royal Astronomical Society (founded 1820) launched its *Memoirs* in the following

79 Carter and Pollard, *An enquiry into the nature of certain nineteenth century pamphlets*; Barker and Collins, *A sequel to An enquiry*.
80 Wilson, 'The Malone Society: the first fifty years'.
81 Francis, 'The Bibliographical Society: a sketch of the first fifty years'; Roberts, 'The Bibliographical Society as a band of pioneers'.
82 Hall, *All scientists now*, pp. 151–2, 194.

year, and the Royal Asiatic Society (1823) its *Transactions* in 1824, before moving from a quarto to an octavo format in 1836 with its *Journal*. The changes in attitude to such journals were displayed in the gradual decision by the Linnean Society to publish its proceedings. Its quarto *Transactions*, with colour plates, had appeared since 1791. A journal of its proceedings was first proposed in 1822. In 1838, the Society began publication of abstracts; but it was not until after the Secretary of the Society and J. D. Hooker proposed more formal *Proceedings* in 1855 that there was a regular journal in which papers were published in full.[83]

Most societies welcomed new faces provided they were properly introduced. Much was done by correspondence, and distance allowed a measure of informality, but the purpose was to engage both intellectually and socially. In this, societies were unlike the democracy of commercial publishing, where social structures of reading depended on pricing, not on social address. Societies of like-minded interests could lead rapidly to sociability in research that in turn could look forward to more formal collaborations. The transactions published by societies were not just matters of record; they were, in effect, parts of discussions. Meetings bred paper in their own ways. The annual gatherings of the British Association (founded in 1831)[84] and of the Archaeological Institute (founded in 1843) produced volumes rather than periodicals, but the purpose was the same. Research communities were mixtures of the professional and the amateur, the clerical and the secular, the full-time and the casual.[85] Just as publishers tended to bring like-minded people together for scholarly or social purposes, so societies formed bonds as much through their publications as through their meetings. If Alexander Macmillan's open house 'tobacco parliaments' became among the most celebrated of regular literary occasions, other publishers had their own circles of like-minded friends and allies: Valpy suffered much ridicule in the 1830s for his commitment to one camp of classical scholars rather than another, and Murray built up a confraternity not just around Byron, but also, and with much more variety, round the *Quarterly Review*.[86]

Finally, and to return to questions raised at the beginning of this chapter, what of the trade in new books, and of the ways in which publishers,

83 Gage, *A history of the Linnean Society*, pp. 117–23.
84 Howarth, *The British Association*; Morrell and Thackray, *Gentlemen of science*.
85 See for example Levine, *The amateur and the professional*.
86 Graves, *Life and letters of Alexander Macmillan*; Macmillan, *Letters*; McKitterick, 'Publishing and perishing in the classics'; Paston, *At John Murray's*.

booksellers and readers were kept in touch with each other? Much more every-day, and affecting many more people, was the need to keep abreast of new publications. Information, as comprehensive as possible, was of increasing necessity in a world where communications were more rapid, and where the number of books published, and the number and variety of publishers, were all increasing. For the first decades of the century, the trade relied on Bent's *Monthly Literary Advertiser* (founded 1805) and on the longer-established vol-umes of the *London catalogue*. The *Publishers' Circular*, issued by Sampson Low, began in 1837, and was followed by the *Bookseller* in 1858. *Bent's* was incor-porated into the *Bookseller* in 1860. Besides these there were various annual or multi-annual cumulations, successors to the old *London catalogue*. When in 1864 Sampson Low published a cumulation for the years since 1835, and named it the *English catalogue*, it displaced these older titles. The *English catalogue* in turn amalgamated the fortnightly and monthly lists into annual ones and then into longer periods.

None of these was comprehensive, and hundreds of provincial publications passed unnoticed. In the mid-century, a few large publishers formalised their lists of new books into periodicals. With two new volumes of Macaulay's best-selling *History of England* soon to be published, Longman launched their *Notes on books* in 1855, providing brief paragraphs puffing the firm's new titles and giving details of how certain classes of readers could request free copies. In 1891 Macmillan published a chronological list, extending to over 700 pages, of the firm's publications since 1843.[87] Oxford University Press issued a com-prehensive general catalogue in 1916, a hardback volume of 566 pages.[88] For more ordinary stock catalogues, the innovative *Reference catalogue of current literature* proved an immediate success. It was the brainchild of Joseph Whit-taker, who copied the idea from New York. The method was simple: to bind up the catalogues of such publishers who sent in sufficient copies, and to provide an accompanying index that would, in effect, be a list of books in print; none of the older compilations had provided this. The first accumula-tion was published in 1874. A second, much enlarged, appeared the following year. By 1910 the collection of catalogues from 195 publishers occupied about 50 cm of shelf space and weighed almost 28 lb. The three volumes, includ-ing, for the first time a separate index volume, contained details of about 185,000 books.

87 [Foster], *A bibliographical catalogue of Macmillan and Co.'s publications.*
88 Barker, *Oxford University Press*, p. 55.

For customers, or readers, needs were more than this. The tradition of reviewing established by the *Edinburgh Review* (1802) and the *Quarterly Review* (1809) persisted even while audiences for books, and the structures of the book trade as a whole, were transformed. But it was a tradition increasingly ill-suited to a world grown accustomed to speed and ever wider choice. Though there were many imitators, the long review, as much an essay for which the books in question were little more than inspirations and the thinnest of raiment, did not dominate influential opinion as it had. The mood inclined rather towards the briefer notices in magazines such as the *Athenaeum* (1828–) or the *Saturday Review* (1855–). The late nineteenth-century development of new structures of authorship, including new professional opportunities to write in the dozens of new journals founded for middle-class readerships, brought not just changes in writing practices, changes in authorial incomes and changes in patterns of publishing, but also new needs for readers.

In an age of periodicals, it was natural that these needs should be met in fresh kinds of journals. The long-established *Publishers' Circular* did not prevent an aspiring new title in 1884 claiming that there was no weekly organ 'representing in a direct and adequate manner the interests of the publishing world':

> The inrush of American publications, the development of the discount system, the issue on a vast scale of cheap editions of new works, the remarkable growth of the book trade with the colonies, the decay of reviewing in the daily press, and the international agitation for securing literary rights in every country, are among some of the modern problems of publishing, which . . . find no adequate expression in print.[89]

'There is at present no Journal or periodical in England devoted to the literature of other countries', alleged the publisher Edward Arnold in 1891, as he sought to remedy matters with his sixpenny monthly *Literary list of American and French books*. The first number included notes on the new American copyright legislation, and the beginning of a summary list of standard American literature compiled by a member of the staff of Harvard University Library. The French section included, unusually for such surveys, a brief list of recent children's books. In the following year, Sweet & Maxwell launched a sixpenny monthly list of legal literature, *The law library*, and paid for most of the cost with advertising revenue. From the late 1880s, Longman included pictures in their seasonal catalogues, first line drawings and then half-tones, to woo buyers.

89 *The Publisher and Bookbuyers' Journal*, 15 November 1884, 'Our programme'.

Henry Frowde issued the first number of the *Periodical*, devoted to the work of Oxford University Press, in 1896, given away free and providing easily digested tit-bits relating to new books.

Besides the trades whose needs were met by the *Bookseller* and the *Publishers' Circular* were others concerned only partially with books. The growth of the trade in stationery – office, social or fancy – was doubly supportive of book publishing. Many books, especially of a cheaper kind, were sold alongside stationery goods. Secondly, the expansion in newspaper and periodical publishing in the last decades of the nineteenth century, and the increasingly blurred distinctions between publishers of books and publishers of popular magazines, epitomised in the firm of Harmsworth, extended concepts of the book. It was to meet needs of this part of the trade that specialist periodicals were founded, such as the *Stationer, Printer, and Fancy Trades' Register* (1859), *Stationery, Bookselling and Fancy Goods* (1881–) and the *Newsagent and Booksellers' Review* (1888–).

Here, as elsewhere, were markets of experiment. In 1889, Trübner launched the *Periodical press index*, 'a monthly record of leading subjects in current literature'. The first issue, of twenty-six pages, indexed about 160 different periodicals, and promised that in subsequent months this would be considerably extended, to include American, colonial and continental publications. It covered all subjects, and yearly summary volumes were promised. But it never displaced Poole's indexes. Book reviews, on the other hand, were both a more familiar and a more difficult area, more difficult partly because of the great numbers of new books demanding attention and partly because of the demand for brevity. In March 1892, Hutchinson & Co., a firm better known as the publisher of Mary Cowden Clarke's series on the girlhood of Shakespeare's heroines, launched the *Library Review*. This was edited by Kineton Parkes, of the Nicholson Institute in Leek, Staffordshire. It restricted itself severely to literature, but in its mingling of belletristic articles, notes on recent events in libraries and select lists of new books it offered a model. The first issue included reports on Shelley and Horsham, the Pillone books (turned down by the British Museum in 1875 but still in Britain), the recent decision by the Literary and Philosophical Society in Newcastle only to admit novels published five or more years previously, and the need for a society in London to emulate the Bibliographical Society founded in Edinburgh. The national range was unusual. The journal was priced at just sixpence thanks to advertising support from publishers including Macmillan, Swan Sonnenschein, Lippincott and the Clarendon Press, besides Mudie's Library and Chivers, the leading binders for public libraries.

The *Library Review* lasted until the following year, and in 1898 Hutchinson tried again, this time with the *Book Lover*. Printed on wretched paper, a mixture of literary gossip that served as the merest veneer mainly for advertising novels priced from 1s 6d to 6s, it too was designed for some of the most popular parts of the market. By then, Marie Corelli's *The mighty atom* (first published in 1896) and Olive Schreiner's *Story of an African farm* (1883) were said to have sold 91,000 copies each. More comprehensively, the *Bookman*, launched in 1891 and with an initial circulation of perhaps 10,000, catered to a market that was willing or able to spend a little more. In the end, the most successful of the new reviewing periodicals came not from the library community, but from the London newspaper trade itself. The first number of *Literature*, published by *The Times*, appeared on 23 October 1897 and was edited by H. D. Traill, satirist, political commentator and biographer most recently of Sir John Franklin. Priced at sixpence, it was far larger than any comparable predecessor, with a larger page size, thirty-two pages of editorial matter and as many again of advertisements. Publishers were eager and curious to participate. They sent books published long since to be included in the list of the week's books, and they had to be warned that editorial or reviewers' comments would bear no relation to whether or not the publisher concerned was an advertiser. Reviews were anonymous; and the editorial preamble (presumably by Traill) emphasised both the long tradition of weekly literary criticism, dated from the publication of the *Literary Gazette* in 1817, and the necessity of selectivity. More pregnantly, such criticism had moved not just from incidental activity to a profession, but to an industry. By definition, reviews had in effect become an extension of the book trades. 'No apology . . . can be needed for adding another to the list of journals which devote themselves, exclusively or principally, to the art and industry of literary criticism. Vastly as that industry has developed of late years, its progress has been not equalled merely, but outstripped, within the same period by the growth of literary production.' Rudyard Kipling contributed a poem to the first number, and Augustine Birrell an article 'Among my books'. Books reviewed included the new *Memoir* of Tennyson and Mrs Oliphant's history of Blackwood's publishing house. Opinions of recent novels were mixed. Stevenson's unfinished last novel *St Ives* would 'hardly take rank with his strongest work', and James's *What Maisie knew* was 'hardly a book to enhance his great reputation'.

In all these ways, and many more, the world was organised by print. There has been space here only for a selection. As has been often remarked, the railways with their timetables calculated to the last minute brought a new sense of time, and a new sense of urgency. Bradshaw's timetables epitomised a world where even days off were measured according to the clock rather than the sun or mealtimes. Printed information was one form of knowledge. It was a taskmaster that had to be accommodated, but that could also be exploited. The following chapter, by Aileen Fyfe, explores some of the further ways in which print brought new attitudes, and new possibilities.

16

The information revolution

AILEEN FYFE

Introduction

The Victorians knew they were living through a time of transformation in the provision of information. As one author put it in 1853, 'The age in which we live, is unprecedented for the cheapness and abundant supply of its literature.' 'Huge costly tomes' had been replaced by 'the small and low-priced volume which is accessible to all'.[1] Literary reviews in the 1850s were full of articles headed 'Cheap literature', 'New and cheap forms of literature' and 'Reading for the million'.[2] The nineteenth century was widely proclaimed as the era of the final perfection of the art of printing from movable types. Thanks to steam-powered printing machines, stereotyping, machine-made paper and machine-made bindings, the Victorians prided themselves on having made print available to the masses.

Anachronistic as it is, the immediate benefit of using the term 'information revolution' to describe these changes is that it directs our attention to facts, information and knowledge – or, prosaically, non-fiction. With so many book historians working in literature departments, it is hardly surprising that the impact of the new printing technologies and the growth of new reading audiences have been most extensively sketched out in the realm of literature, whether poetry, drama, novels or short stories. But it was almanacs, spelling books and dictionaries that were the bread-and-butter of publishing, and Simon Eliot's figures suggest that literature still accounted for only a fifth of all titles published by 1870.[3] This chapter, therefore, seeks to put factual publishing back on the map. It is a twin to David McKitterick's chapter on

---

1 Thomas Pearson (1853), *Infidelity: its aspects, causes and agencies; being the prize essay of the British Organization of the Evangelical Alliance* (1853), p. 478.
2 'Cheap literature', *British Quarterly Review* 29 (1859), pp. 313–45; 'New and cheap forms of popular literature', *Eclectic Review* 22 (1845), pp. 74–84; [Oliphant] 'Byways of literature'.
3 Eliot, '*Patterns and trends* and the NSTC', p. 73. (The 1870 cut-off date is determined by the NSTC data on which this survey was based.)

'Organised knowledge', but the emphasis here is on popular information rather than scholarly learning. This chapter will discuss the attempts to make scholarly information more widely available through new publishing formats, but it will also include a wide variety of other factual publications, from railway timetables to cricket statistics, and from government proceedings to company reports. There is a huge range of publications which could be included under the generous definition of 'information', and it is an ocean into which scholars have not yet dipped more than a toe. This chapter can therefore be little more than a preliminary sketch of the nineteenth-century 'information revolution'.

Nineteenth-century commentators did not write in terms of an information revolution, for they did not commonly use the term 'information' in the sense we now give it, of raw, unprocessed neutral data, somehow distinct from 'knowledge'. In the nineteenth century, 'knowledge' and 'information' carried different connotations, but they shaded into one another. 'Knowledge' did seem more prestigious, and was the term selected by the Society for Promoting Christian Knowledge (f.1698) and the Society for the Diffusion of Useful Knowledge (f.1826), while 'information' was more likely to be used for a restricted set of facts about a specific subject or a particular item of news. However, 'information' could be used to refer to all the facts which a 'well-informed' person needed to know, and was thus sometimes equivalent to 'knowledge'. In this chapter, when I use the term 'information', I mean something like 'facts', very broadly defined. There are at least three groups of publications which might fall under such a heading.

Firstly, newspapers carried information about new or planned legislation, the doings of eminent public figures, and reports of murders, divorces and forgeries. This sort of information – 'news' – was usually of only passing interest, and was very specific to times and places. In contrast, the knowledge contained in encyclopaedias – national histories, celebrated biographies, astronomy, mathematics, botany and philosophy – was regarded as more enduring and universal. This second category of 'general knowledge' also appeared in print in textbooks, and in numerous books written for both the scholarly and the general public. The third category is 'practical knowledge' – although not all nineteenth-century philosophers would have been willing to grant the superior-sounding label, 'knowledge', to compendia as varied as cookery books, self-help medical manuals, train timetables or etiquette books.

By the end of the century, the Victorians were as likely to equate cheap print with novels as with information, but it is striking that, at mid-century, cheap print typically did mean information. The steam-powered printing machine was seen as an information technology. In what follows, I will argue that, in contrast to the invention of printing in the fifteenth century, the importance of industrial printing was not in the creation of a new information product (though there are some examples of this), but in the transformed role and position of printed information in society. Although the machine-printed book or magazine did not look (much) different from its early-modern predecessor, its cheapness and rapid distribution ensured that its uses were dramatically extended, to more people, in more places.

Technology, however, is only one of the reasons why we should think about the nineteenth century from the perspective of an information revolution. The other half of the story is about the enthusiasm for collecting information in the first place. Historians have described an 'avalanche of numbers' after 1820, when voluntary organisations and governmental departments began collecting statistics about everything from crime and lunacy rates, to births and deaths, railway accidents, and conversions to Christianity.[4] Statistics are an important fourth category of information publishing. Whereas the first three categories were broadly familiar to earlier generations, printed statistics were a distinctly nineteenth-century innovation. Eighteenth-century data-collecting efforts had rarely been made public. In the nineteenth century, governmental 'Blue Books' and missionary society reports were full of statistics, and there were even dedicated statistical journals. Thus, the nineteenth-century information revolution is not simply about existing forms of information being disseminated more widely: it is also about a change in the nature of the information being put into print.

This chapter begins by discussing the rise of statistics and by asking why so much of that new information was then published. Government information activities will be a key part of this story, but charities and companies will also appear. Then, we turn to the new technologies of print production and distribution. These have been dealt with in detail elsewhere in this volume, so the discussion will be restricted to their impact on information provision. The chapter ends with a discussion of the mechanisms, techniques and technologies which were introduced to help people to cope with what would now be termed 'information overload'.

Information gathering

Local and central governments have been collecting information about their citizens since the early modern period, for purposes of taxation, conscription,

4 Hacking, *The taming of chance*, pp. 2–5.

justice and poor relief, and it is this state-related information that gives us the word 'statistics'.[5] But until the nineteenth century, little of this information was organised for subsequent retrieval or used to assist policy decisions, let alone made publicly available through the medium of print. The expansion of missionary activities, scientific investigation, exploration overseas and social investigation at home generated masses of new information. Some of it was left to moulder in official repositories, and much of it was analysed only simplistically. But one of the truly striking changes during the nineteenth century is that a huge amount of this information found its way into print.

The enthusiasm for gathering data was partly a result of the development of new techniques for analysing and using information, starting with the work of the Belgian astronomer Adolphe Quetelet, and culminating with Francis Galton and Karl Pearson, who made statistics into the advanced mathematical subject we know today.[6] Quetelet investigated human vital statistics, crime rates and suicide, and searched for links with place, age or time of year. His address at the 1833 meeting of the British Association for the Advancement of Science inspired the foundation of statistical societies across the United Kingdom, most famously the Manchester Statistical Society (1833) and the London (1834, later Royal) Statistical Society. His book *Sur l'homme et le développement de ses facultés, ou Essai de physique sociale* (1835) was also influential in generating interest in statistics; its first English translation (as *A treatise on man*) appeared in 1842 as one of the cheap People's Editions published by W. & R. Chambers.

The early statistical societies were interested in information which would have the power to promote change, and they undertook significant research into crime, poverty, disease, literacy rates and religious observation.[7] Since the members typically hoped to shock the relevant agencies into reforms, merely gathering information was not enough: it had to be made known. Newspaper reports of society meetings could fulfil this role, but the societies also worked with local printers. The Manchester society, for instance, published reports on the state of education in Manchester in 1834, and on the injuries incurred by railway labourers and employees in 1846. In 1853, it began to issue a regular series of *Transactions*, as the London society had done since 1838 (as the *Journal of the Statistical Society*).

---

5 For early modern information-gathering, see Higgs, *The information state in England*, ch. 3.
6 Hacking, *The taming of chance*; Porter, *The rise of statistical thinking, 1820–1900*; Stigler, *Statistics on the table*.
7 See, for instance, Daly, *The spirit of earnest inquiry*.

The enthusiasm for statistical information permeated other organisations, from charities to the civil service, as statisticians zealously sought to persuade everyone to collect as many statistics as possible. For instance, Bible and tract societies routinely published the numbers of their publications circulated, while missionary societies reported on the numbers of families visited, infidels converted and children sent to Sunday school. Thus, the Town Missionary and Scripture Readers Society reported that, in 1849, its agents had sold over 24,000 copies of the Scriptures and over 68,000 Religious Tract Society publications.[8] In 1889, the Religious Tract Society itself reported that it had circulated 25,840,900 tracts and 36,855,290 other publications in the previous year.[9] Such statistics were often little more than enumerations, but they demonstrated to members that subscriptions were well spent, and encouraged continuing support.

While some European countries quickly established central statistics bureaux (e.g. Prussia, in 1805), the collection of national statistics in Britain was notoriously fragmented. Efforts to create a central office routinely foundered on the question of which government department would have responsibility for it. Although the Treasury could see benefits in a statistics department under its own control, other departments were unhappy with the idea of greater oversight. As a result, in 1880, there were at least fourteen government departments issuing printed statistical reports of some kind. The War Office issued reports on the strength of the regular and reserve forces; the Admiralty published on the health of the navy; the Home Office published criminal statistics; the Board of Trade reported on everything from foreign trade to railway accidents and bankruptcy statistics; even the Lunacy Commissioners issued statistics.[10]

It was population data that became the most prominent example of central government information gathering in the nineteenth century, with the decennial census from 1801 and the civil registration of births, marriages and deaths from 1837. The census began as an attempt to assess British manpower in the midst of the wars with France, and was continued in part as an effort to answer the heated debate about whether the population in the 1820s was shrinking or growing. The censuses resulted in a set of published tables, organised chronologically, and known from 1851 onwards as the *Population tables*. Statisticians routinely pushed for the inclusion of more questions in the census, but were usually resisted by the General Register Office (which had been given charge of the census in 1841). The exceptional questions which were accepted included

8 Quoted in RTS Annual Report (1849), appendix III, section 8.
9 RTS Annual Report (1889), p. 2.
10 This discussion draws upon Agar, *Government machine*, ch. 3.

that on literacy in the Irish 1841 census, and those on education and religious observance in the 1851 census. By the end of the century, government departments stepped up the pressure for the census to be used to produce a more accurate picture of the British population, and they eventually succeeded in getting the reporting of occupational categories improved in 1891.[11]

The General Register Office (GRO) had been established by the Civil Registration Act of 1836 to coordinate the new system of civil registration, and is usually represented as the key statistical office in Victorian Britain, even though its statistical department never had more than nineteen staff during the century.[12] Civil registration was intended to relieve the penalties on those who were not members of the Church of England, and to provide all citizens with documentary proofs which would enable them to gain access to certain rights. A birth certificate, for instance, could demonstrate that a child was old enough to be sent to work, or that an adult was entitled to vote. With a parents' marriage certificate, it could be essential in securing an inheritance.

As well as preserving and organising registration certificates, the GRO published analyses of the nation's vital statistics in the *Annual Reports of the Registrar General for England and Wales* (from 1839; also reports from the Scottish and Irish registrars general) and their various *Supplements*, such as that on the cholera epidemic of 1866.[13] The first annual report had been under two hundred pages, but by mid-century, they were twice that size. The early reports had concentrated on actuarial data (i.e. life expectancy), but by the mid-1840s the medical interests of William Farr, the senior statistical officer, became apparent. It was Farr who insisted on the introduction of a 'cause of death' on death certificates, which he could then analyse to reveal the occupational hazards of certain industries and the urgent need to reduce the incidence of puerperal fever.

The reports of the registrar general exemplify one of the key themes behind the extensive publication of government information in the nineteenth century: the desire to make public the existing state of affairs, in order to encourage something to be done about it. This meshes with the style of most mid-Victorian reform legislation, such as that about public health, water supply and public library provision. The parliamentary acts typically enabled local authorities to take action, but did not force them to do so. Something else was needed to stimulate action, and that was where the publication of shocking statistics could come in.

11 Higgs, *The information state*, pp. 70–1.   12 *Ibid.*, p. 91.
13 Higgs, 'The annual report of the Registrar General, 1839–1920'.

In addition to the desire to stimulate local authorities to action, much government information was collected (and published) as part of the process of passing legislation. During the nineteenth century, numerous Royal Commissions and parliamentary Select Committees were set up to investigate issues which might be in need of reform. There were, for instance, Royal Commissions to investigate municipal corporations (1834), railways (1867), scientific instruction (1874), vaccination (1889) and secondary education (1895). Meanwhile, Select Committees were set up to recommend whether the newspaper tax should be repealed (1851) and to investigate censorship and licensing (1909). These investigations routinely involved gathering and recording large amounts of information, sometimes taken as oral testimony from witnesses and sometimes as written returns to enquiries. The resulting 'Blue Books' were huge publications incorporating both the report itself and the massive appendices of evidence. Not everyone welcomed such outpourings of information: in 1865, William Ewart complained in Parliament that 'It had rained blue-books', and pointedly commented that 'if you wanted to hide a question the best plan is to bury it in a blue-book'.[14]

The 'Blue Books' were monuments to the gathering and dissemination of information about Victorian moral and social concerns. They gave commentators access to a wealth of information that transcended what any worried clergyman or doctor could hope to amass on his own. Yet the 'Blue Books' themselves were only the beginning of the flood of information that they stimulated. A very few became best-sellers in their own right, but most were known to Victorian readers through newspaper reports and articles in the literary reviews. For instance, the press took a particular interest in the proceedings of the Select Committee on the Newspaper Stamp. The report was printed in *The Times* in July 1851, and extensively discussed in the *Examiner*, the *British Quarterly Review* and the *Westminster Review*.[15]

There seems no doubt that central government in the nineteenth century was gathering far more information than before, but Edward Higgs warns us that this was not yet the creation of a modern information state, using information on citizens for surveillance, security and social control. He points to the facts that so much government-collected information was made public, and that so little of it was collected in a manner that linked it to specific individuals. Census

---

14 Hansard 178 [1865]: 215, cited in Frankel, 'Blue books and the Victorian reader', p. 308. See also O'Neill, *British Parliamentary papers*.

15 *The Times* 26 July 1851, p. 5, col. D; 'The newspaper stamp', *Examiner* 2 August 1851, pp. 481–2; 'Newspapers and the stamp question', *British Quarterly Review* 15 (1852), pp. 135–62; Chapman, 'The commerce of literature'.

returns, for instance, were originally simple enumerations of the people in each parish. From 1841, returns were filed for each household, but the purpose was still to enable clerks to enumerate the population. The returns themselves were not always kept for future retrieval, and cannot be regarded as a database of information on individuals.[16] Similarly, taxation statistics were compiled to check the efficiency of the administrating system, and recorded the total amounts gathered in each geographical unit; they did not comprise records about individual tax-payers.

Central government did begin to collect information on individuals in the late nineteenth century, with the development of the criminal registers (attempted first in 1869, and again in 1900) and the establishment of security forces such as Special Branch (1887) and MI5 (1909), which kept records on Fenian suspects, aliens resident in Britain and the owners of wireless sets (lest they interfere with military communications). But it was not until the very end of our period that government began to collect information on all its citizens, with the introduction of the old age pension in 1908 and of national health and unemployment insurance in 1911.[17]

If the desire to impel change was one major factor behind the publication of so much information, the other appears to have been a growing desire for efficiency and standardisation in administration. By the 1850s, public appointments had ceased to be sinecures, and corruption was being stamped out. Meanwhile, a growing awareness of the difficulty of controlling distant agents – and of the desirability of standardising procedures across the United Kingdom and the colonial possessions – led to the production of large quantities of printed information and guidance.[18] And since standards, once set, had to be policed, there were increased expectations of reporting back to London. The Treasury had always been keen to encourage departments to make efficient use of resources, and the production of departmental reports on trade, industry, excise duties and emigration went some way towards this. Both the excise and the taxation statistics enabled central officers to check the activities of local agents. The use of statistics to inform future policy – rather than reporting upon an existing situation – would become significant only in the twentieth century, when it would stimulate the collection – but not necessarily publication – of huge amounts of information by central government. In the nineteenth century, however, the publication of these reports gave the public

---

16 Higgs, *The information state*, p. 72. It was only in the twentieth century, and particularly with electronic databases, that the census returns became so useful to family historians.
17 Higgs, *The information state*, pp. 95, 108–12.
18 Burroughs, 'Imperial institutions and the government of Empire'.

and their representatives in the media a degree of oversight of government activities. The publication of information about the processes of government was thus part of the process of making government more efficient and more accountable.

Despite the increasing emphasis on standardisation and efficiency – and thus the increase of bureaucracy – it is striking that the size of the civil service did not grow significantly during the nineteenth century: there were still only 100,000 civil servants in 1902.[19] But the service was reformed. The Northcote–Trevelyan report of 1854 recommended that appointments be based on merit, determined by a competitive examination system, and that there should be a distinction between specialist clerks and the more senior generalists.[20] These reforms took decades to be fully implemented, but they spawned a substantial print literature of their own. There were guides to help candidates through the entry process, such as *The complete practical guide to Her Majesty's Civil Service* (Blackwood, 1860), which contained details of entry requirements and the full past examination papers, and the intriguingly titled *Self-culture: a practical answer to the questions, What to learn?, How to learn?, When to learn?. . . for the Civil Service examinations* (Simpkin, Marshall, c.1859). The publishers of textbooks on specialist topics were also quick to see the potential of expanding their target audience to include would-be civil servants, as the sub-titles of their books often reveal. For instance, Williams & Norgate issued a *Handbook of Sanskrit literature . . . intended especially for candidates for the Indian Civil Service, and missionaries to India* (1866), while Blackie's *Manual of organic chemistry* (1879) addressed itself to 'colleges and schools, medical and civil service examinations'. Once successful, the new civil servant would have to master the official regulations, such as the *Manual of rules and regulations applicable to members of the Indian Civil Service* (published by authority in Calcutta, 2nd edn 1891).

Printed information enabled politicians and civil servants in London to set (and enforce) standards for the behaviour and activities of government agents throughout the United Kingdom and the formal Empire. Given the ongoing importance of local government, regular circulars and manuals were issued to educate and inform local officials. The Poor Law Commissioners issued a monthly *Official Circular of Public Documents and Information* (1840–51), containing statistical reports on pauperism, disease and workhouse expenditure, along with accounts of legal cases or new Acts of Parliament of relevance to Boards of Guardians, and letters recounting good practice in education, diet

19 Higgs, *The information state*, p. 133.   20 Agar, *Government machine*, ch. 2.

and management. The provision of such information helped weave local practices into a national system for the administration of the poor law. The *Manual for medical officers of health* (Knight, by authority, 1873) and the *Manual of public health: for the use of local authorities, medical officers of health and others* (Smith, Elder, 1874) played a similar role after the new Public Health Act of 1872.

But it was not just civil servants, administrators and local officials whose efficiency and uprightness needed to be observed. Until the late eighteenth century, publication of proceedings within the houses of parliament was a punishable offence; by the early nineteenth century, there had been several attempts to record parliamentary speeches, most notably by Thomas Curson Hansard from 1812. Hansard's importance as a permanent record was ultimately recognised by Parliament, which began to subsidise its publication in 1889, and took it over entirely in 1909. Before 1909, Hansard did not record every speech and every vote, but it was nevertheless an important resource for journalists and (at least in theory) the electorate to check upon the activities of their representatives. Important speeches and votes were made public far more quickly through the reports in the daily newspapers.

The use of printed information to encourage efficiency and enforce standards extended into the corporate world, where life was characterised by a growing amount of 'paperwork' (the word came in at the very end of the century). For instance, there was an increased emphasis on financial accounting procedures, on formal contracts rather than verbal agreements, and on reporting to shareholders, particularly after the introduction of limited liability companies. Business information expanded alongside government information.

This expansion is particularly clear with railway companies. Its most visible manifestation was in customer relations, including timetables, promotional leaflets, posters, timetables, and the printed tickets themselves. The contents of the John Johnson Collection in Oxford clearly demonstrate that such printed paraphernalia became ever more elaborate over the century, eventually including guidebooks, excursion flyers and dining-car menus.[21] But there was also a substantial amount of printed information involved in the actual business operations. Before a railway company even came into existence, its supporters usually produced a one-page prospectus and a list of subscribers; they commissioned surveys; they usually sent a printed circular to all parties whose property would be affected; and the granting of royal assent was typically the

---

21 See, for instance, the illustrations in Freeman, *Railways and the Victorian imagination* and in the 'Transport' appendix to Twyman, *Printing 1770–1970*, both of which draw upon the John Johnson Collection.

occasion for yet another printed circular to interested parties.[22] The amount of paperwork involved was nicely expressed by an image in the *Illustrated London News* showing railway speculators rushing to deposit their paperwork with the Board of Trade in November 1845.[23]

Once a railway company had been set up, two more types of internal paperwork were needed: for shareholder relations and for management. Shareholders had to be issued with share certificates, and subsequently with dividend certificates, voting papers for general meetings, and six-monthly reports from the directors. Meanwhile, standardised forms and printed memoranda were used to coordinate the activities of agents throughout a company's system. By the 1850s, most companies issued manuals of regulations to their employees, which were revised throughout the century: *Rules and regulations to be observed by engine-men & others employed on the East Lancashire Railway* (1846) and the *Code of signals and general instructions for the use of the superintendents, clerks, guards, police, porters, &c* (Great Western Railway, 1852). On top of this, reports had to be made to the Railway Inspectorate of the Board of Trade, which then published statistics on numbers of passengers carried, amount of freight carried, miles of track opened, and numbers of people injured or killed on the railways. Excerpts from these appeared in the newspapers, and Dionysius Lardner made good use of them in his *Railway economy* (1850).

In addition to the printed information produced by the railway companies themselves, substantial amounts of paper were generated by commercial firms targeting railway investors. In the days of the railway mania, periodicals proliferated: the *Railway Times* (1837) and *Railway Journal* (1839) were joined by at least fifteen weekly periodicals and one daily (the *Iron Times*) in the mid-1840s.[24] Most of these were short-lived, but they offered shareholders and potential investors the latest information on proposed railway schemes at home and abroad, along with reports on schemes already underway. Although other railway magazines were launched later in the century, the 1840s had been the heyday. Subsequent magazines started to cater to an audience of enthusiasts (e.g. *Railway Magazine*, 1897) rather than investors.

The mania for railway shares is often said to have made investing respectable: everyone from clergymen to spinsters owned railway shares. This meant that information about share prices came to be of interest to an audience far wider

---

22 See the contents of Railways Box 1, John Johnson Collection, Bodleian Library.
23 *Illustrated London News* 6 December 1845, reproduced in Freeman, *Railways and the Victorian imagination*, p. 97.
24 Simmons, *The Victorian railway*, pp. 243–4.

than merchants and businessmen. *The Times* carried a column on 'The Money-Market' throughout our period: it had begun in the mid-1820s as a relatively gossipy column discussing recent arrivals at the docks, but by mid-century the prices of commodities and shares (especially railway shares) were becoming increasingly noticeable. The prices of such commodities as tallow, tea and oil acquired their own column in 1839, and railway shares followed suit in 1850. Ten years later, the list of share prices ran to two columns, and included not just railways, but mining companies, joint-stock banks, telegraph companies and the London General Omnibus Company. Stock market information has remained a regular feature of the daily newspapers, even though the 1880s saw the rise of specialist periodicals for investors, including the *Financial News* (1884) and the *Financial Times* (1888, but not pink until 1893).

The broader Victorian trends involving the use of printed information were also reflected in the operations of charitable societies. Indeed, the officers of voluntary associations had long taken it for granted that one of their duties was to report to the subscribers on the year's activities, both to allay fears of mismanagement and to encourage future donations. For instance, the Religious Tract Society (whose foundation in 1799 had been announced via the *Evangelical Magazine*) kept its members informed through verbal reports at the annual meeting each May, which were widely reported in the religious periodical press. It also issued a printed annual report, which had swollen to two hundred pages plus photographs by 1900. The annual report devoted most of its descriptions to overseas tract and missionary activity, with only a few pages on the actual running of the charitable publishing house which funded those activities. A financial balance sheet had been included since at least the 1840s. In addition to these formal reports to members, the society also issued a monthly (later bimonthly) newsletter, called the *Christian Spectator* (1838; renamed *RTS Reporter*, 1857), to keep members informed, interested and engaged. It included advance notice of new publications, details of grants made, letters to the editor, and discussion of the past and future development of the society. Such publications helped to create a sense of community among the subscribers of all sorts of voluntary societies.

The twin desires to stimulate activity (whether among society members or intransigent local authorities) and for standardisation and efficiency (in government and in business) are important reasons behind the accumulation and publication of so much governmental, corporate and charitable information during the nineteenth century. To understand how so much of that information became so widely disseminated once it was printed, we need to return to the history of the book trade.

Information dissemination

As other chapters in this volume have shown, the processes of print production and distribution were transformed by mechanisation and steam power. For many in the first half of the century, steam-powered printing machines were the most visible sign of the changes. Both the *Penny Magazine* and *Chambers's Edinburgh Journal* entertained their readers with detailed descriptions of their own production processes, in which the new methods of mechanical paper-making, stereotyping and steam-printing took pride of place.[25] When we consider the publishers who were the first to make use of steam-powered printing and the associated technologies, we can see why the cheapening of print was explicitly equated with the wider accessibility of knowledge and information. Although there were exceptions (for instance, Walter Scott's later novels), the majority of steam-printed publications prior to the 1840s were broadly informational: newspapers, instructive penny magazines, instructive part-works, Bibles and tracts (many contemporaries regarded such religious publications as conveying the most important knowledge of all). Printing technologies were information technologies.

Newspaper printers were in the vanguard of those adopting the new technologies because the hefty investment needed to purchase steam-printing machinery could only be justified by printers who really needed the speed. The obvious candidates were those whose periodicals had both a rapid periodicity and a large circulation, which in practice meant the few national newspapers and one or two weekly magazines. Thus, from its earliest days, steam-powered printing was associated with the dissemination of news, from the reports of parliamentary and royal proceedings in *The Times*, to the literary, artistic, dramatic and scientific news in the *Literary Gazette*. Newspaper printers would continue to be at the forefront of technological innovations in the print trades throughout the nineteenth century, and beyond.

The next wave of printers and publishers to turn to the new technologies were also information publishers, but they focussed on general knowledge rather than news. For charitable organisations, such as the Society for the Diffusion of Useful Knowledge and the Religious Tract Society, and certain private firms with philanthropically motivated owners (such as W. & R. Chambers and Charles Knight), steam-powered printing seemed the best route towards large runs and cheap unit prices, and thus, ultimately, to popular education. Although these publishers had rather varied definitions of education, they all

25 The account in the *Penny Magazine* in 1833 was republished as Cohen (ed.), *Paper & printing*. See also 'Mechanism of *Chambers's Journal*', *Chambers's Edinburgh Journal* 6 June 1835, pp. 149–51.

shared the desire to reach new readers and the willingness to use new techniques to do so. That commitment to education ensured that they continued the trend of using the new technologies specifically to spread factual literature. They presented history, geography, the natural sciences and (in some cases) theology in the accessible format of penny magazines, part-works, and religious and secular tracts.

By the 1850s, however, the early link between new technologies and the provision of information was weakened. With the success of the *London Journal, Reynolds's Miscellany* and Routledge's Railway Library, it was clear that there were far larger sales (and hence profits) to be made from cheap fiction than from cheap education. From this point on, the transformation in informational publishing was obscured by the meteoric rise of popular fiction, and the debates about cheap print have tended to be less celebratory of its benefits to popular education, and more worried about the effects of so much low-quality cheap fiction. Nevertheless, informational publishing, with the rest of the book trade, did continue to grow throughout the later nineteenth century.

If we think in terms of the three older categories of information outlined at the start of this chapter, we will see that they were differently affected by the transformation of the book trade. Its time-critical nature and high demand meant that news was always in the vanguard of the information revolution. The combination of new printing technologies, faster distribution methods and increasing literacy rates enabled newspapers to reach vast audiences after the removal of the stamp duty in 1855. Rotary printing machines and mechanical composition processes brought about another revolution in the 1890s. Moreover, the introduction of the electric telegraph enabled editors to get news into print far more rapidly than had been possible when information could travel only as fast as the steamship or the railway. By the 1880s, news from India could reach London within a few hours, and be in print the next day. By 1914, all parts of the British dominions were in telegraphic communication with each other and with London.[26] Thus, not only the appearance, price and frequency of newspapers but their very contents were transformed by the information technologies of the nineteenth century.

General knowledge was less obviously affected, since scholarly treatises would only ever command a small audience. What the new technological capabilities did was to encourage publishers to create new formats for repackaging

26 Potter, *News and the British world.*

knowledge and thus making it available to new audiences. Although the steam-powered book or magazine was still recognisably a book or magazine, a range of new publishing formats and genres emerged, including the part-work and the cheap book series. The philanthropically motivated educational publishers of the 1830s were innovators with both of these formats, though such formats would ultimately be widely adopted by profit-seeking publishers in the second half of the century.

Part-issues were an obvious means for bringing expensive multi-volume reference works like encyclopaedias within the reach of more people.[27] New editions of the *Encyclopaedia Britannica* were issued in parts, and so too were the volumes of the *Oxford English dictionary*. These parts, however, were not particularly cheap. In the 1830s, Charles Knight (working with the Society for the Diffusion of Useful Knowledge) and W. & R. Chambers were both using steam-powered printing to produce weekly instructive magazines at just a penny or a penny halfpenny, and were proving that such low prices could find substantial numbers of purchasers. Both publishers used a variant of the penny magazine instalment to issue their encyclopaedic information products. Knight's *Penny cyclopaedia* (1833–43) aped a traditional encyclopaedia, and ran to twenty-seven volumes plus supplements.

Chambers did not produce a traditional encyclopaedia until *Chambers's encyclopaedia: a dictionary of universal knowledge for the people* (1860–8).[28] The firm's initial offering was far more radical in concept than Knight's. The first edition of *Information for the people* (1833–4, 1½d pamphlets) contained only forty-eight topics, and the later editions still covered only a hundred topics. As the preface to the second edition (1841–2) explained, only 'the most important branches' of knowledge were to be included, and all 'minutiae of biography and topography' and 'scientific technicalities' were ruthlessly omitted. The resulting work still contained all that was deemed necessary to make its reader 'a *well-informed man*', but was complete in two volumes and cost just 12s 6d in total; the first parts sold an average of 16,000 copies each within a year, and the work was to be revised and reissued three times before 1860.[29] Chambers continued to use the format of short instructive pamphlets (or secular tracts) issued in series until the mid-1850s, only abandoning it in the face of competition from the new generation of cheap books. Nevertheless, the firm continued to focus on educational products for ordinary people: its *Chambers's English dictionary*

27 On encyclopaedias, see Yeo, *Encyclopaedic visions*.
28 Cooney, 'A catalogue of *Chambers's Encyclopaedia* 1868'.
29 *Information for the people* 2nd edn, 2 vols. (1841–2) 1, p. iii. Editorial, *Chambers's Edinburgh Journal* 1 February 1834, p. 1.

(1872) was a single-volume everyday reference work, in contrast to the monumental *Oxford English dictionary* (begun in 1879 and published between 1884 and 1928).

Very cheap books often appeared in publishers' series, to enable them to benefit from shared marketing and reputation.[30] Non-fiction series had become common from the 1820s, but the early series, such as those from J. F. Dove and William Milner, had typically cost around five or six shillings and contained reprints of out-of-copyright works. During the 1830s and 1840s, the same publishers who experimented with steam-printed instructive periodicals and part-works also experimented with much cheaper book series, with the result that commentators by the 1850s noted the proliferation of 'popular treatises and essays without number, and on all subjects – geology, political economy, politics and whatnot'.[31]

W. & R. Chambers may have been the first to apply steam-printing to non-fiction books on a large scale, after the success of their steam-printed edition of George Combe's *Constitution of man* (1828, Chambers's edn 1835), which sold 40,000 copies at 1s 6d within a year.[32] Their People's Editions made a variety of non-copyright books (some foreign, some out-of-copyright) available for just 1s or 1s 6d for the whole book. The difficulty lay in producing original works as cheaply: as the SDUK had discovered with the Library of Entertaining Knowledge, paying a handsome author's fee for the copyright forced prices up to 2s 6d or more.[33] The solution was to find authors who would work for extremely modest fees, and by 1850 the Religious Tract Society, the Society for Promoting Christian Knowledge and W. & R. Chambers were all producing very cheap steam-printed volumes of general knowledge, written specially for their intended audiences.[34]

After 1850, philanthropic publishers no longer had a monopoly on cheap print. The proliferation of fiction-carrying penny periodicals in the late 1840s marked the end of the road for several of the older instructive periodicals (including those issued by the SDUK and the SPCK), and new cheap book series from publishers like George Routledge had a similar effect on the instructive book series. Routledge's Railway Library (1848) was not the first to issue entire novels in a single volume for just one shilling, but it was the longest-running and most famous series to do so, and it spawned numerous competitors, both fiction

30 Howsam, 'Sustained literary ventures'. See also Altick, 'From Aldine to Everyman'.
31 [David Masson] 'Present aspects and tendencies of literature', p. 166.
32 Van Wyhe, *Phrenology and the origins of Victorian scientific naturalism*, pp. 218–19.
33 On the SDUK, see Bennett, 'Revolutions in thought', and on the similarly ambitious but not-that-cheap Family Library series, see Bennett, 'John Murray's Family Library'.
34 Fyfe, *Science and salvation*.

and non-fiction.[35] The railway bookstalls – which were increasingly coming under the central control of W. H. Smith & Son[36] – provided an effective distribution system, something which had always eluded the philanthropic publishers, who were far better at producing cheap books than they were at selling them in the necessary large numbers. By 1855, many other commercial publishers had joined the railway literature phenomenon, and at least eleven series of cheap non-fiction appeared, the most important of which were John Murray's Reading for the Rail (1851), Longman's Travellers' Library (1851) and Routledge's own Popular Series (1850, later amalgamated into the Cheap Series, 1853).[37]

The phenomenon of cheap series specifically for railway travellers was to die away by the mid-1850s, but it left behind changed perceptions of cheap print. The railway series would demonstrate beyond a doubt that there was an enormous market for cheap print, and the bookstalls offered a mechanism for reaching that audience. With new-found confidence, publishers in the later nineteenth century could aim their cheap series at the general public.

Alexis Weedon has shown that, although the typical print-run in the 1850s was still only a thousand copies, the average print-run rose to over 3,000 copies – demonstrating that a small proportion of titles were being printed in significantly higher runs.[38] Railway novels were planned with a break-even point of 10,000 or more, and although non-fiction volumes were more likely to be aiming for about half that, even 5,000 copies was a significant circulation.[39] In late 1851, the volumes in Longman's series had print-runs of 5,000, though by 1854 only the most topical volumes were managing to sell that many within twelve months: Charles Brooks's *Russians of the South* (1854) and the Marquis de Custine's *Russia* (1854) both managed the feat, cashing in on events in the Crimea.[40] Routledge – who were rather more attuned to the economics of cheap publishing than Longman – typically printed their non-fiction volumes in batches of two or three thousand, and their typical volumes in the mid-1850s seem to have sold around five or six thousand copies within

35 Simms & McIntyre's Parlour Library had produced shilling novels earlier in 1848. On Routledge's series, see Topp, *Victorian yellowbacks and paperbacks* 1.

36 Wilson, *First with the news.*

37 For the fuss about railway literature, see in particular [Phillips] *The literature of the rail.*

38 *Victorian publishing*, p. 49.

39 The figure of 10,000 is apparent from Knight's comments, for instance Knight, *The case of the authors as regards the paper duty*, pp. 15–16.

40 The Traveller's Library printing and sales figures are in the Longman Archives, book F2.

the year.[41] However, the true potential of cheap books on railway bookstalls was demonstrated by the unusually successful titles: Routledge printed 25,000 copies of a *Life of Robert Peel* between July and November 1850, to cash in on the former Prime Minister's death;[42] likewise, Longman sold 32,800 copies of a biography of Wellington in the year of his death (though the firm had over-optimistically printed 64,000 copies).[43] One of Routledge's great successes was with chef Alexis Soyer's *Shilling cookery* (1854), which claimed to have reached its 185th thousand by 1858.[44]

Railway literature had also transformed readers' expectations of what cheap books should look like. In contrast to the worthy but plain and dull volumes produced by Knight, the Chambers brothers and the religious publishing societies, after 1850 a shilling could buy something new and up-to-date, bound in a striking, brightly coloured wrapper. Routledge's volumes were particularly notable in this regard. He had pioneered the 'yellowback' for his Railway Library and other series, and he continued to be innovative in his use of colour in later series.[45] His Books for the Country (which included John George Wood's successful series of natural history books, starting with *Common objects of the country*, 1857 (fig. 1.3)) came in striking three-colour printed boards for a shilling, or with colour illustrations and a cloth binding for 3s 6d. Routledge's enthusiasm for colour and illustration was given full rein in his prize and reward books of the later nineteenth century. Such books were a world away from what a few shillings would have bought in 1830.

As Leslie Howsam has pointed out, series continued to be a popular way of marketing cheap books throughout the late nineteenth century – especially for children's books and textbooks. Chambers's Educational Course (1835) had used the series concept as a way to structure the entire learning experience, expecting a student to progress from one volume to the next through the series. More commonly, publishers used a range of series to distinguish the books most suitable for different age-groups or classes of learners. The number of textbook series increased after the educational reforms of the 1870s.[46] Yet even as formal education became more widespread, the market of autodidacts that Chambers had once provided for continued to catch publishers' attention.

41 The Routledge publications book gives printing figures but not sales figures. The cheap series were frequently planned as five impressions, but often only had two or three. For an example, see Routledge Archives, Publication Book, vol. 1 (1850–8), folio 284 (for G. B. Earp's *What we did in Australia*, 1853, of which 6,000 copies were printed).
42 Routledge Archives, Publication Book, vol. 1 (1850–8), folio 12.
43 The Traveller's Library printing and sales figures are in the Longman Archives, book F2.
44 See entry for Soyer's book in Topp, *Victorian yellowbacks* 1.
45 Topp, *Victorian Yellowbacks* 1; Schmoller, 'The paperback revolution'.   46 See also chapter 9.

Perhaps the most influential of these later series was the Home University Library of Modern Knowledge, launched by Williams & Norgate in 1911, with a particular emphasis on the natural sciences.[47]

The series mentioned above all fall under my rubric of 'general knowledge', since their contents came from the traditional areas of scholarly knowledge: history, the sciences, philosophy, perhaps theology. They were innovative in their publishing format and price (and perhaps writing style), rather than their subject matter. But the later nineteenth century also saw a rise in a different style of information publication: my third category, of 'practical knowledge'. In an age of unprecedented geographical and social mobility, there was a vastly expanded range of things about which one might need to learn, which went far beyond any formal school curriculum. Publishers discovered lucrative markets for books advising readers on everything from using railways to writing formal letters, from keeping poultry to cooking them, and from collecting beetles to playing chess.

One indication of the range of such 'practical' guides can be gleaned from another of the mid-century Routledge series, the Useful Library (1854). In contrast to the scientific focus of the SDUK's Library of Useful Knowledge, Routledge's definition of 'useful' was more mundane. The series opened with *A new letter-writer for the use of gentlemen and ladies* (1854), and continued with books of hints on household management, domestic cookery, family health and legal matters. The volume on *Landlord and tenant* (1857) went through three printings, totalling 7,000 copies, by April 1858.[48] The titles clearly suggest an intended readership among the upwardly mobile, who found themselves needing to deal with things beyond the scope of their limited education.

Some publishers specialised in particular areas: for instance, Effingham Wilson's Legal Handy Books were launched in the late 1850s and were still selling at the end of the century. The original titles covered the laws of banking, bankruptcy, trustees and private trading partnerships. They were joined in the late 1880s by directly practical advice on *Income tax: how to get it refunded* (before 1887), *How to appeal against your rates* (1889) and *How to obtain a divorce* (1895). Their title-pages suggest a continuing demand for such advice: the volume on *Bills, cheques and notes* (c.1866) reached its 43rd thousand by 1876, while the *Income tax* volume reached its twentieth edition in 1907.

Publishers also provided advice and tips on a range of more pleasurable activities. In the 1830s, Robert Tyas had launched a series of sporting handbooks,

47 Glasgow, 'The origins of the Home University Library'.
48 Routledge Archives, Publication Book, vol. 2 (1855–8), folio 273.

covering angling (1838), cricket (1838) and chess (1839), before branching out into wine (1840). This sort of series blossomed in the second half of the century, a combination of the growing recognition of the youth market and of the enthusiasm for out-of-door activities. Routledge issued a series of Six-Penny Handbooks to swimming, skating, gymnastics and chess (1858). Competing series included Ward & Lock's Indispensable Handy Books (1861), and Frederick Warne's Country Library and Family Circle Books (1866) which introduced readers to the seashore, angling and ferns (the latter being the latest craze in the early 1860s).

Indeed, the growth of tourism in general and railway travel in particular inspired a whole new sort of practical literature. John Murray began issuing his continental Handbooks for Travellers in 1836, and launched a companion series of British county guides in 1851. The subsequent additions to Murray's series charted the increasing adventurousness of British travellers, with volumes on Syria and Palestine (1858), India (1859) and Russia (1865).[49] Although Murray's famous red cloth handbooks had become 'the badge of the British traveller' by the 1890s,[50] they never had the market to themselves. A. & C. Black of Edinburgh had preceded Murray into the domestic tourism market with the Picturesque Tourist guidebooks, beginning with Scotland in 1840 and the English Lakes in 1841. The Blacks were also quicker to recognise the purchasing power of less affluent tourists, issuing shilling editions of some of their guides from 1853 onwards. Meanwhile George Measom compiled illustrated and 'official' guidebooks to all the principal railway companies in Britain between 1852 and 1870.[51]

Given the newness of the railways, it is perhaps surprising that there seems to have been only one *Handy hints for railway travellers* (1862), and remarkably belated, at that.[52] However, the railways did spawn one of the most widely used factual works in Britain. Manchester engraver George Bradshaw issued his first compilation of *Railway time tables* for sixpence in 1839; in 1841, he began to issue a regular *Monthly railway guide*, also for sixpence. By 1847, Ralph Waldo Emerson could note that 'every man in England carries a little book in his pocket called "Bradshaws Guide"', a popularity which is corroborated by the surviving sales figures for the W. H. Smith railway bookstall at Rugby

---

49 Lister, *A bibliography of Murray's Handbooks for Travellers*.

50 Samuel Smiles, 1891, cited in Simmons, 'Introduction' to Murray, p. 27.

51 Bennett, 'The railway guidebooks of George Measom'; Martin, 'Sir George Samuel Measom'. See also chapter 13.

52 *The railway traveller's handy book of hints, suggestions, and advice: before the journey, on the journey and after the journey* [1862], repr. with introduction by J. Simmons (Bath, 1971).

in 1856.[53] By this time, *Bradshaw* had incorporated steamship routes, and was called *Bradshaw's railway and steam navigation guide of Great Britain and Ireland*. Despite the rise and fall of competitors (often marketing themselves as more 'intelligible'), *Bradshaw* survived into the twentieth century. From mid-century, the company issued an annual *Railway almanack* (which was also a 'Directory, Shareholder's Guide and Manual'), a *Continental railway guide* and a series of railway maps. The rapid growth of the railways was such that the *Almanack* expanded from 145 to 500 pages between 1848 and 1858, while other publishers found markets for travellers needing guidance on what could be seen from the carriage windows (fig. 16.1).

Almanacs are compilations of information with a long history, but by the nineteenth century their combination of calendrical information (including dates of law terms and full moons) and practical hints (when to sow seed and unlucky days) was seen as a remnant of the old days of superstition and astrology. Charles Knight claimed that one of the achievements of the SDUK had been to 'destroy... for ever, the astrological and indecent almanacs'.[54] The SDUK's alternative *British almanac* (1828–88) kept the calendar-format of the old almanacs, but marked dates and offered advice based on scientific knowledge rather than folk tales. The most famous of the new almanacs was *Whitaker's almanack*, launched in 1868 by Joseph Whitaker, publisher of the *Bookseller*; he is said to have sold 36,000 subscriptions in advance.[55] As almanacs became increasingly devoted to the provision of information, their calendar function was being taken over by printed diaries, such as those issued by John Letts from 1812. By the 1830s, when Thomas Letts took over and expanded his father's firm, there were more than twenty varieties of Letts diaries with printed dates for the coming year.[56] Such diaries sometimes also carried information, but the advance calendar was their primary function.

Almanacs and diaries were usually published for the coming year, but John Timbs's *Year-book of facts* (1838–73) did the reverse. Its retrospective look at the preceding year focussed (as its sub-title announced) on 'the most important discoveries and improvements of the past year in mechanics and the useful arts; natural philosophy; electricity; chemistry; zoology and botany; geology and mineralogy; meteorology and astronomy'.[57] Another variant of the form was

53 Emerson to Thoreau, 2 December 1847, quoted in Ashton, *142 Strand*, p. 35. Colclough, '"Purifying the sources of amusement and information"?', p. 44.
54 Knight, *The old printer and the modern press*, p. 242.
55 H. R. Tedder, 'Whitaker, Joseph (1820–1895)', rev. Joseph Coohill, *ODNB*.
56 Adrian Room, 'Letts, John (bap. 1772, d. 1851)', *ODNB*; and Anita McConnell, 'Letts, Thomas (1803–1873)', *ODNB*.
57 On Timbs, see J. R. MacDonald, 'Timbs, John (1801–1875)', rev. Nilanjana Banerji, *ODNB*.

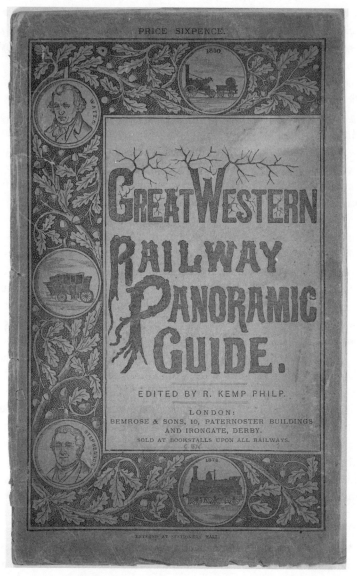

Fig. 16.1 *Great Western Railway panoramic guide* [1876]. This sixpenny guide was one of many such publications promoting railway travel and providing information about the main features on the routes: its origins lay in the road books of the eighteenth century. At this period the GWR, based at Paddington Station in London, covered not only the West Country but also as far north as Manchester and Liverpool, and it had connections to the Kent and Sussex ports. It did not yet control central Wales. The price, sixpence, was supported by copious advertising at each end of the book. (Private collection)

created by John Wisden, with his *Cricketers' almanack*, first published in 1864. By the 1880s, *Wisden* published the full scores and bowling summaries of the principal matches played in the previous year, as well as the rules of the game, the names of available umpires, and the deaths of eminent cricketers. Wisden himself had been a cricketer and then a sports equipment retailer, but he must have had a love of statistics: his almanac not only recorded the final scores of matches, but calculated the batting and bowling averages for each player and used these statistics to draw attention to particularly unusual achievements. *Wisden* clearly illustrates that the Victorian mania for statistics spread even to leisure activities.[58]

A final example of a typical nineteenth-century form of practical information is the directory, or biographical listing. There were trade and city directories in the eighteenth century, but they became nationalised and standardised in the hands of a few firms during the nineteenth century – most notably, with Frederick Kelly's series of *Post Office directories* (1845). The first telephone directory appeared for London in 1880. There were also specialised listings for particular social or professional groups. Several were continuations from an earlier period: the *Monthly army list* dated from the end of the eighteenth century; and John Debrett had issued the first edition of his *Peerage of England, Scotland, and Ireland* in 1803, followed by the *Baronetage of England* five years later. John Burke's competing *General and heraldic dictionary of the Peerage and Baronetage of the United Kingdom* first appeared in 1826, using an innovative alphabetical format (which Debrett adopted in 1840). Despite their competition, Debrett's and Burke's were long-lived; both were appearing in new editions annually by the second half of the nineteenth century, and Debrett was producing an illustrated edition by the 1860s. Among the other works produced by Burke (with his son Bernard), the most notable was the *Landed gentry* (first published 1833–5, as *History of the commoners of Great Britain*), which appealed to genealogical interests in a far wider segment of society.[59] *Who's who* began life in 1849 as a combined almanac and list of public officials, but it was to give a new twist to the genre of biographical directory in 1897, when A. & C. Black took it over and introduced *auto*-biographical entries. The monument of biographical information – though not of widely available information – was, of course, the *Dictionary of national biography*, begun by Leslie Stephen in 1882.

The later nineteenth century saw the emergence of directories for increasingly specialised social groups. The *Clergy list* (1841) and Crockford's *Clerical*

58 Eric Midwinter, 'Wisden, John (1826–1884)', *ODNB*.
59 Thomas Woodcock, 'Burke, John (1786–1848)', *ODNB*.

directory (1858) both served the Church of England, and eventually merged in 1917. Similar functions were performed by the *Congregational yearbook* (1846) and the *Manual of the Baptist denomination* (1845; from 1861, the *Baptist handbook*). The *Medical directory* (1871) had been known as the *London and provincial medical directory* since the 1847 merger of two separate medical directories. The various branches of the legal profession could consult the *Law list* (1816), the *Solicitors' diary, almanac and legal directory* (1844) and the *Index juridicus: the annual Scottish law list* (1848).

While we can see the growth of 'official information' as part of wider trends in the science of statistics, the organisation of government, and the management of businesses and charities, it seems more difficult – at first glance – to explain what underlay the enthusiasm for all sorts of curious and useful information that is revealed by the record of publications. Indeed, considering the range of informative publications – only some of which could be mentioned here – one is left with the impression that the Victorians quite simply grew to love statistics and compendia, and this spread to all walks of life. Charles Dickens had certainly noted such a phenomenon when he created the character of Mr Gradgrind and argued that a world of facts alone – with no room for creativity and the imagination – would be a dull place. Yet the sheer numbers of directories, almanacs and compilations suggest that many of Dickens's contemporaries actually revelled in facts.

Managing information

The cheapening of print was widely linked with the spread of knowledge, and thus the impact of the new technologies of production and distribution were welcomed by all supporters of popular education. But amidst the enthusiastic rhetoric, there were also concerns about the social impact, revolving around the sheer quantity of information being made available, and the effect of certain sorts of information upon those readers seen as being vulnerable. Until about 1850, the religious publishing societies and the secular philanthropic publishers had dominated cheap informative print, thus ensuring a certain degree of quality control. But once profit-seeking publishers entered the marketplace, quality often seemed to be forgotten. In 1848, the *People's Journal* remarked that there was too much temptation 'to introduce . . . ingredients merely to please the taste, without much inquiry as to their properties, or the effects they are likely to produce'.[60] Sloppy authorship was a particular worry, as the

---

60 Sinnett, 'What is popular literature?', pp. 7–8.

British Quarterly Review's complaint about anonymous historical compilations illustrates: the reviewer reckoned that most were nothing more than 'different dilutions of some fourth compilation, which again, in its turn, may be the third dilution of some substantial book'.[61] Were readers of such books really being instructed? Was a smattering of learning really better than ignorance? As in so many things, religious commentators were among the most outspoken. For instance, in 1853, the Rev. Thomas Pearson welcomed the press's role in banishing superstition and despotism (through spreading the Christian message), yet noted that 'it is unquestionably a powerful agency for evil also'.[62] Pearson realised that cheap print could circulate atheistic sentiments as efficiently as Christian truths, and he worried that vulnerable readers – the young, and the working classes – might be led astray.

An even bigger problem for proponents of popular education was the rise of cheap fiction: from the 1850s onwards, commentators routinely bemoaned the public's enthusiasm for fiction and disinclination for instructive reading. Charles Knight reported that, 'It is useless to urge an adult, whether male or female, to buy a solid book when an exciting one is longed for... If they want fiction, they will not look at science or history.'[63] According to Knight, the railway bookstall and its cheap fiction sounded the death-knell for cheap, worthy, informative publications such as those he himself had produced. As is so often the case, the pronouncement of death was premature, but Knight's remark illustrates familiar concerns about the literary tastes of the masses. With so much cheap print being available, it was easy to read for entertainment rather than instruction; and even those who sought instruction might be ill-served by the low quality of the works available to them.

But quality was just one part of the problem. Even if all informative books published could be trusted as reliable, their sheer quantity made it difficult for readers to keep up. Such fears were not new: French philosophers had attempted to organise the sum of all knowledge in the great Enlightenment *Encyclopédie*, while in Britain magazines such as the *Monthly Magazine* and *Monthly Review* provided lists of books to help those who struggled to keep abreast of each month's new publications.[64] The great quarterly reviews, from the *Edinburgh Review* (1802) onwards, enabled readers to keep up to date with the key arguments of new books without necessarily reading the books for themselves. Such techniques for coping with the growth of information

---

61 [Masson] 'Aspects of literature', p. 170. On these issues, see Fyfe, 'Expertise and Christianity'.
62 Pearson, *Infidelity*, p. 477.   63 Knight, *The old printer and the modern press*, p. 247.
64 On the ambitions of the *Encyclopédie*, see Darnton, 'Philosophers trim the tree of knowledge'; on the early literary reviews, see Butler, 'Culture's medium'.

became increasingly more sophisticated and specialised during the nineteenth century.

John Lubbock's famous list of one hundred recommended books (1886) held out the promise of simplifying things by identifying a set of 'good' or 'classic' books. His list contained a high proportion of non-fiction, though relatively little of it had been first published in the nineteenth century. Such lists, and the series of classics issued by publishers from Routledge to Dent, appealed to readers who did not know where to start. Those who were interested in the latest publications could turn to the reviews – now appearing not just quarterly, but in weekly magazines and in the daily papers. Yet by the end of the century there were so many review journals that it was barely feasible for one reader to keep up with them all (let alone the books that they summarised). Hence, the popularity of eclectic magazines like George Newnes's weekly *Tit-Bits* (1881) and W. H. Stead's monthly *Review of Reviews* (1890). Such magazines appealed to those readers who strove for universal coverage, offering them snippets and summaries of the contents of other periodicals.

Those with more specialised requirements could turn to the new scientific abstracts journals. John Churchill's *Half-Yearly Abstract of Medical Science* (1845, monthly from 1875) was one of the earliest. It was followed by the *Zoological Record* (1864), *Physics Abstracts* (1895, renamed *Science Abstracts*, 1897) and *Chemical Abstracts* (1900). Such journals summarised the latest articles in a wide range of British and foreign publications, offering the man of science a quick way to keep abreast of the international developments in a particular field.[65]

For those with more bibliophilic interests, Sampson Low compiled the first volume of the *English catalogue of books* in 1863, in the hope of producing a master list of all books published in Britain. It became an essential tool for those hunting for scarce or out-of-print books. Another tool beloved by historians arose from William Frederick Poole's work in the library of a debating society at Yale University, where he compiled a master index to all the periodicals received, as a finding aid.[66] It first appeared in print in New York in 1848 as *Index to the reviews and periodicals*, and was updated in 1852 as *An index to periodical literature*. Since most of the magazines Poole was indexing were British, British bibliophiles were quick to see the attractions of his work and it was imported by John Chapman, and later by Low.[67] In 1876, Poole was asked by the American Library Association to update his index, and the resulting *Poole's index to*

---

65 Manzer, *The Abstract Journal 1792–1920*.   66 Williamson, *William Frederick Poole*.
67 See advertisements in *Publishers' Circular* 1 September 1848, p. 287 (advert 855); and 1 May 1852, p. 174 (advert 437).

periodical literature (6 vols.) appeared between 1882 and 1908. The British edition was published by Kegan Paul. The efficient retrieval of information was a clear concern for librarians like Poole and his contemporary, Melvil Dewey, as they sought ways to organise, classify and catalogue their holdings to make it easier for both librarians and readers to find what they sought.

Civil servants and administrators were equally concerned that the vast amount of information being gathered by government departments should be organised for analysis and retrieval. The General Register Office, for instance, developed innovative systems of filing and indexing to enable access to its ever-increasing store of certificates. Most of the customers of the GRO reading room were lawyers' clerks tracking down property rights. The same was true of the Public Record Office, established in 1838 as a repository for court papers and other legal records. In 1852, the PRO also became the repository for state papers, and its staff developed the catalogues, indexes and finding aids which were essential to the late nineteenth-century generation of constitutional historians.

Most of the actual processing of information during the nineteenth century was done by hand. The Astronomer Royal's team of human 'calculators' at the Royal Observatory and the work of the Railway Clearing House are well-known examples of pencil and paper being used to process large batches of information.[68] Similarly, at the GRO, the census returns were analysed by a team of clerks going through return after return, and keeping a tally of the number of people in each category of interest. The practical limitations of this method made it impossible to carry out more sophisticated analyses. The situation was transformed with the introduction of mechanical (and, later, electronic) methods of information processing. Hermann Hollerith's mechanical tabulator for reading punch-cards had been used on the United States Census of 1890. The information on each census return was punched onto a card, and the stacks of cards were then fed through the tabulating machines. The machines could be set to enumerate particular categories and combinations of categories, and they worked far faster than human clerks. The result was the possibility of carrying out a whole new set of analyses on the census data.[69] The Hollerith tabulator was introduced for the British census of 1911. This is easily the most famous technological innovation in information processing of our period, though it is worth remembering that the hanging file, the paper clip,

---

68 On Greenwich, see Smith, 'A national observatory transformed' and Ashworth, 'John Herschel, George Airy, and the roaming eye of the state', p. 164. For the Railway Clearing House, see Campbell-Kelly, 'The Railway Clearing House and Victorian data processing'.
69 Agar, *Government machine*, pp. 147–59; Higgs, 'The statistical big bang of 1911'.

the treasury tag, carbon paper and the typewriter undoubtedly had far more impact on the day-to-day use of information in offices throughout Britain.

Conclusion

The term 'information revolution' usually refers to the increasing use of electronic computers in the 1960s and 1970s.[70] As with many non-political 'revolutions', the concept has its problems, among them the question of whether the transition to electronic storage and processing is in fact the most important development in the history of information. One could certainly argue for the invention of writing or printing, and once one starts looking at the long history of information, the idea of a single 'revolution' becomes difficult to sustain. There have certainly been occasional moments of rapid growth punctuating the gradual development of information: typically at the moments when new techniques fundamentally changed the nature of the information-containing product, as from oral culture to clay tablet, or from written word to printed word. But in such a scheme of things, the nineteenth century does not loom particularly large.[71]

Nevertheless, something significant happened to the type and quantity of information which was publicly available in the nineteenth century – and the emphasis should be on 'availability'. I would argue that the important change was in the social and cultural prominence of information. In contrast to earlier generations, the Victorians loved facts – albeit with what sometimes seems a naïve enthusiasm. From local charities to government officials to entrepreneurial publishers, many Victorians set out to gather facts – numerical or narrative – and, amazingly often, they made the results of their efforts public by committing them to print. The key reasons for this commitment to publishing (and not merely gathering) information seem to have been a desire to bring about reforms by demonstrating the moral need for change, and the desire for smoother, more efficient administrative procedures, coupled with a growing acknowledgement of the need for public accountability. The desire to make information public coincided with the ability to do so on a far grander scale than ever before – thanks to the new industrial technologies of print production and distribution – and thus resulted in a significant change in the sorts of information available to the general public, and in the proportion of the population thus engaged.

70 See 'information', meaning III.8 in the *Oxford English Dictionary*. See also Agar, *Government machine*, introduction.
71 Although see Headrick, *When information came of age*.

17

A place in the world

JOHN BARNES,

BILL BELL, RIMI B. CHATTERJEE,

WALLACE KIRSOP AND MICHAEL WINSHIP

While it has been customary to frame the history of the book in terms of the nation-state, the story of the British book trade between 1830 and 1914 is one of increased internationalisation, and no account of even the domestic trade – its structure and organisation, as well as its products and customers – would be complete without a serious consideration of the larger global implications of the period.

Although an overseas trade in books was nothing new – printers had learned to exploit effectively the transatlantic and continental markets throughout the eighteenth century – one of the distinguishing factors of the British book trade in the early part of this period is its role in the extension of a new kind of cultural empire. This was first manifest in a more concerted organisation of the greater British book market in the early years of the nineteenth century, transforming the way in which English, principally London, firms related to the home markets of Scotland and Ireland. With the steady growth of the nation's overseas interests, by the end of the century its book producers could boast a formidable distribution network constituting an international trade with global reach.

While it would be over-deterministic to attribute the rise of the international book trade to technological factors alone, there were a number of advances in the conquest of space and time that can be cited as having conspired to make this global reach possible, so that it can be argued that, without such technological innovations, the overseas impact of the British book trade would not to the same extent have been possible. Thanks to advances in the industrial manufacture of paper, printing and binding, by the mid-nineteenth century the British book trade was transformed from a cottage trade into a mass manufacturing industry. Improved communication networks also had an important role to play, serving to revolutionise the gathering of information and the distribution of print.

As John Chapman observed, by the 1850s the new integrated systems of rail, post and telegraph were having revolutionary implications for practices in the book trade.[1] Within a few decades, Britain and its dominions were coming to operate within the first modern information society, a process in which the nation's printers, publishers and authors were to play a central role.

From home market to empire

The home markets of Scotland, Wales and Ireland had been implicated in the English book trade well before the nineteenth century, most notably through bookselling and joint ventures that had linked booksellers and printers in Edinburgh, Dublin and elsewhere with their counterparts in London. Throughout the early years of the nineteenth century, however, increasingly well-organised and codified methods were to lead to agency arrangements that would facilitate greater cooperation in printing, advertising and bookselling. While the course of such arrangements had not always run smoothly, early in the century a set of more or less standard trade practices was in place. By and large, cooperative publishing arrangements worked to varying degrees in the interests of all parties involved. By the 1830s, there existed a complex network of agents in the book trade who acted as wholesalers and retailers within defined territory, and it was not unusual for Scottish agents to cover their native country, northern England and Ireland while London agents were responsible for southern England and Wales. It was also customary for agents to oversee the advertisement of stock in provincial newspapers as well as their own catalogues. These arrangements frequently led to joint publications, allowing investors to share financial risk and spread the responsibility for distribution.[2] Such arrangements were not without their risks: the notorious book trade 'crash' of 1825–6, caused by the insolvency of the London publisher Hurst, Robinson & Co., famously brought the financial downfall of the Edinburgh firm of Archibald Constable, until that time one of the major players in the Scottish book trade. By and large, though, reciprocal arrangements for printing, distribution and advertising worked to the advantage of most parties concerned, in a period when transport between capitals was often time-consuming and difficult.

---

1 Chapman, *Cheap books and how to get them*, p. 52.   2 See Alloway, 'Agencies and joint ventures'.

Although Ireland continued to retain a greater geographical and fiscal distance from the mainland book market, British publishers and booksellers were coming by mid-century to compete for the same expanding market, so that it became increasingly difficult to speak in terms of separate English, Scottish and Welsh book trades. Although printing and publishing continued to grow more or less throughout all major conurbations, a tendency towards increased centralisation began to be apparent, as London's place at the heart of Empire became increasingly powerful. Before long, a number of major Scottish firms had established their own agencies in the capital. Blackie opened a London office in 1837; Blackwood in 1840; Nelson in 1844; Chambers in 1860; and the cartographic publisher W. & A. K. Johnston in 1869.

Britain's export trade

Although London was to remain the principal producer of books for Britain and its dominions, this is not to suggest that it was the only significant player in a growing national and international market for books. Scotland's two major book-producing centres, Edinburgh and Glasgow, also became major producers in the nineteenth century, companies like Nelson (who in 1854 was the first British publishing company to open a United States office) and Collins becoming important suppliers of educational titles to the Empire. Throughout the nineteenth century, however, London remained the largest international producer of English-language titles, with New York, Boston and Edinburgh following far behind.

The growth in the home market found a correspondingly dramatic increase in the value of books for export, customs records showing a total of £35,841 in 1828 rising to £1,336,549 in 1898.

Despite a general increase of British sales throughout all parts of the nineteenth-century world, as Table 17.1 shows, there were, during these years, some dramatic regional variations, determined not only by local change but also by the shifting political and economic relationships of the respective regions to the imperial centre.

The United States appears to have been the most volatile of the overseas markets, the result presumably of its already postcolonial status. A number of other complicating factors were to make for its unpredictability as a consumer of British books, the most obvious of which was a severe slump during the Civil War of 1861–5. Throughout the previous decade, book sales to American customers had been relatively stable, making it by far the largest overseas market, with customs returns of £140,941 in 1860. Thereafter, a dramatic decline

Table 17.1 *Values of British book exports, 1828–98*
Declared value (£)

	Aus	USA	BEI	BNA	BP	Total
1828	3933	–	22,226	8178	1504	35,841
1838	14,278	–	33,038	9357	3409	60,082
1848	27,248	–	43,048	15,156	4633	90,086
1858	98,961	110,231	31,814	15,096	17,179	273,281
1868	148,413	184,670	58,698	64,139	21,160	684,243
1878	312,878	223,709	81,495	64,504	44,854	890,846
1888	396,571	369,877	136,220	79,052	59,768	1,245,959
1898	418,215	301,636	126,593	77,586	164,910	1,336,549

Source: Weedon, *Victorian publishing*, p. 39.

was registered in 1861 (£62,345), dropping even further in the following year (£50,386). After the war, the market for British books was to see an immediate recovery, rising again to £176,183, a figure outstripping all antebellum sales, followed by a general, though erratic, increase during the second half of the century.

Perhaps the most dramatically visible rise in Britain's overseas markets is detectable in the steep increase in Australasian sales throughout the century. Before the immigrant boom of the 1850s, book exports to Australia and New Zealand were relatively modest, but nevertheless continued to register healthy increases between 1828 (£3,933) and 1848 (£27,249). By 1853, exports had risen to £142,154 and, although inconsistent thereafter, they continued to show healthy returns. Australia and New Zealand eventually outstripped the USA to become the prime overseas destination for British books in 1875, a position they retained for the rest of the century.

The third most remunerative overseas market overall, the British East Indies, had been the most significant importer of British books in the early years of the century. But, as British foreign policy shifted towards its Australasian and North American interests, Indian book sales nevertheless continued to rise steadily, peaking in 1890 at £154,422, and dropping to around £120,000 in the final years of the century.

Although not so large in terms of sales, the Empire's other foreign interests were nevertheless to provide important destinations for British books. Both British North America and the British Protectorates in South Africa were to show gradual increases. The former was to leap with Confederation in 1867, thereafter levelling off, while the latter was to continue to rise well into the twentieth century.

Despite regional variations, and unevenness of development, it is nevertheless possible to detect a number of unifying trends in Britain's overseas markets during this period. Adapting Wallace Kirsop's description of phases in the development of the Australian book trade, it is possible to think about the transformation that a number of British colonies underwent during the course of the nineteenth century.[3]

1. The first phase is characterised by ad hoc arrangements with regard to the import and export of print. Those British settlers who could afford to brought their own personal libraries with them, or had books occasionally sent out from home. In the early years of settlement, the provision of reading matter, sometimes for free distribution, was provided by church and philanthropic agencies. Small-scale pockets of printing activity are sometimes visible in this early phase, with missionaries often among the first printers in a colonial settlement. Such book-work as existed was often basic, its products finding it hard to compete with better-produced imported printed matter.

2. The second phase is characterised by the establishment of rudimentary infrastructures for the supply of books and periodicals to remote communities, usually in the form of subscription libraries, the establishment of schools and churches, and the opening of local newspaper offices. In moderately sized settlements, small booksellers (often the local newspaper office) distributed books as they arrived by sea. In such a transitional period, the supply of books could often be unreliable and unpredictable, with small-scale colonial booksellers and their customers finding themselves at the mercy of their overseas suppliers. It is in this second phase that the notorious practice of 'dumping' was most common, London publishers emptying their warehouses of unsold stock for distribution in overseas markets hungry for printed matter. Over time, however, distribution networks strengthened, as did a realisation on the part of suppliers that the audience for print overseas represented an important and potentially lucrative market. This led first to the growth of a vigorous consignment trade, through which booksellers could request titles from London or Edinburgh, and later to more formal agency arrangements.

3. The third phase can be described as an organised response on the part of indigenous members of the book trade to arrangements largely determined by British publishers and booksellers. As immigrant printers began to establish

3 Kirsop, *Books for colonial readers*. Kirsop describes four phases, while I have integrated the last two categories, on the assumption that the British response to indigenous publishing practices was part of the same dynamic.

themselves, so there emerged a concerted effort to create national book trades of their own. In response to the move towards self-determination, and in order to stabilise and extend their overseas markets, British publishers would eventually enter into agency arrangements with overseas publishers and booksellers, who would distribute their titles for a percentage of the profits, some going on to establish agencies of their own in course of time.

Books for itinerant readers

As Richard Altick observed several decades ago, for an itinerant population 'popular books had to be portable, for an ever-increasing amount of reading was done in railway carriages and buses, and they had to be small enough to find room in the cramped households of the lower-middle and working classes, who were coming more and more to constitute the bulk of the reading audience. The day of the folio and quarto was over.'[4] As Britain became a more mobile society, so competition for the new resulting reading constituencies was to increase. By the middle of the nineteenth century a number of British publishers were coming to specialise in titles for readers on the move. The embodiment in print of this new geo-information order was *Bradshaw's monthly railway guide*, launched as *Bradshaw's railway time tables and assistant to railway travelling* in 1839. At one time reputed to have been the most consulted publication in Britain after the Bible, Bradshaw's timetable was for over a century the sine qua non for domestic rail passengers. In 1847 Bradshaw launched his highly successful *Continental railway guide*, which was published uninterrupted until the outbreak of the First World War and grew to over 1,000 pages. It finally ceased publication with the beginning of the Second World War in 1939.

One of the earliest, although financially unsuccessful, attempts to exploit the new captive audience for cheap and portable books was by John Murray, who repackaged as affordable reprints a number of his back titles as the first Railway Reading list. Similarly unsuccessful in economic terms though also highly innovative was Murray's Colonial and Home Library, launched in 1843 and retitled Home and Colonial in 1844, which effectively set the trend for the series conspicuously targeted at an international market. As ever, Murray was ahead of his time but the firm's back-list lacked appeal for a popular international audience. Others fared better, and one of the most successful imitators was Richard Bentley whose first Empire Library ran from 1878 to 1881, followed by an equally popular second series in the 1880s, its success

4 Altick, 'From Aldine to Everyman', p. 16.

resting mainly on its repackaging of Dickens in cheap editions. The most successful series of its kind was without doubt Macmillan's Colonial Library, begun in 1886, and issuing no fewer than 1,738 titles up to 1960.[5] If other firms were to eclipse John Murray's early experiments to capture readers on the move, one venture in which the firm was to corner the market for over three decades was the traveller's guidebook. Although the genre in its widest sense can be seen to have existed well before this period, by mid-century the guidebook had become almost wholly associated with Murray. Murray's first venture into the guidebook market was in 1836 with his *Handbook for travellers on the Continent*, but he was later to add more distant locations. *A Handbook to the East* was published in 1845; *India* was added in 1859, and *Japan* in 1881. Distributed widely abroad, Murray handbooks, with their familiar red covers, could be purchased by British tourists in bookshops in every major tourist destination. Murray's main competitor was Karl Baedeker of Leipzig, whose titles were also widely available throughout Europe. By the 1870s Baedeker had begun to overtake Murray as the leading supplier of English-language guidebooks, though they would face a temporary setback in the First World War when commercial links were severed with Germany. The beginnings of mass tourism can be said to have truly arrived with Thomas Cook, himself a printer and bookseller, who found novel ways to exploit the new rail network with excursions throughout the British Isles for an emerging popular market. In 1851 he arranged for 160,000 customers to visit the Great Exhibition, but he was soon expanding his horizons. In 1865 he organised tours to American Civil War sites, and by the end of the decade Cook's package tourists were invading the continent, as well as further-flung destinations, including Egypt and the Holy Land, by their thousands, carrying with them Cook's popular guidebooks.

One close relative to the guidebook, though aimed at a distinctly different class of reader, was the emigration manual, a genre that had begun to pro-liferate by the 1830s, initially offering advice to emigrants bound for North America. With descriptive titles like *The emigrant's guide to, and description of, the United States of America including several authentic and highly important letters, from English emigrants, now in America, to their friends in England* (Hull: Joseph Noble, 1830) and *The emigrant's introduction to an acquaintance with the British American colonies, and the present conditions and prospects of the colonists* (London: Parbury & Co., 1837), they offered advice on travel arrangements, climate, social conduct and topography, providing one of the most important and tangible points of

5 See Johanson, *A study of colonial editions in Australia*, p. 103.

contact between the old and new worlds for thousands of emigrant Britons. The increasing emphasis on Australasia as a prime destination for settlement from the 1850s onwards created an even greater demand for emigrant guides to Britain's colonies in the southern hemisphere. Among the most popular titles in the latter category were Sidney Smith's *The settler's new home, or, Whether to go, and whither?* (London: Kendrick, 1850) and John Hill Burton's *The emigrants' manual: Australia, New Zealand . . . and South Africa* (Edinburgh: W. & R. Chambers, 1851). Although many such publications were produced non-commercially by settlement agencies and religious organisations, the books that hundreds of thousands of emigrant readers took with them served to make this little-regarded genre one of the most remunerative areas of publishing in the nineteenth century.

Helpful as such publications were in the creation of imagined British communities across vast distances, more direct contributors to the business of international governance were also to emerge in this period, none more so than official publications whose contents reflected the imperial infrastructure in more explicit ways. The *India list* was, in many respects, the embodiment of empire in print. A directory of all military and civilian personnel stationed in India, it was produced from 1877 to 1906 by W. H. Allen, 'publishers to the India Office'. The imperial infrastructure also benefited greatly from the presence of a periodical press which met the need for up-to-date 'foreign intelligence'. Chief among these was *Blackwood's Edinburgh Magazine*, which began publication in 1817. In 1911, Joseph Conrad remarked that 'Maga' was to be found in every naval mess-room, while J. E. C. Bodley, himself a contributor, encountered it in all the South African clubs and magistrates' residences. A typical issue included a number of topical articles on foreign politics, imperial policy and the latest scientific expeditions. Perhaps no publications embodied the imperial communications network more appositely than Smith, Elder's *Overland Mail* and its counterpart *Homeward Mail*, one publishing home news for distribution overseas, the other overseas news for readers at home. The same firm published a *Monthly Circular*, reputed to be one of the first mail order catalogues, from which overseas customers could order everything from tinned food and fiction to camping equipment and theodolites.

Explorers and adventurers

One of the consequences of the opening up of the Middle East, Africa and South-East Asia was an increased desire for armchair adventures emphasising the exoticism of strange lands. By mid-century a number of publishers were directly implicated in the literature of exploration – the major players including Smith, Elder, Blackwood & Sons and John Murray – their involvement often extending far beyond the production of accounts themselves. In an age of the celebrity explorer, expensive expeditionary costs were in part sometimes met by authors' advances and it was in the prospect of a published work, at once the disseminator of new information as well as the maker of reputations, that many expeditions found their initial impetus.

The more lucrative exploration titles of the period included Franklin's *Narrative of a journey to the shores of the Polar Sea* (John Murray, 1823), Thomas Pringle's *African sketches* (Moxon, 1834), Austen Layard's *Nineveh and its remains* (John Murray, 1849), Alexander Armstrong's *A personal narrative of the discovery of the North-West Passage* (Hurst & Blackett, 1857), David Livingstone's *Missionary travels and researches in South Africa* (John Murray, 1857) and John Hanning Speke's *Journal of the discovery of the source of the Nile* (Blackwood, 1864). At the more popular end of the market, there was growing appetite for tales of espionage and derring-do, none more spectacular than Richard Burton's famous account of the hajj in *Al-Medina and Meccah* (Longman, 1855), which described his arrival in Mecca masquerading as a pilgrim. One of the most celebrated books of the era was Frederick Burnaby's *A ride to Khiva* (Cassell, Petter & Galpin, 1876), recounting the author's journey of espionage through Central Asia. By the mid-nineteenth century there had also developed a vogue for the travel accounts of intrepid women travellers, tailored to the interests of female readers, few more sensational than the travels of Isabella Bird, not least her account of adventures among the 'desperadoes' of Colorado. Somewhat tamer, though similarly popular, were Susanna Moodie's tale of Canadian life, *Roughing it in the bush* (Bentley, 1852), Elizabeth McMullin Muter's *Travels and adventures of an officer's wife in India, China, and New Zealand* (Hurst & Blackett, 1864), and Mrs Barker's *Station life in New Zealand*, the first book issued in the Macmillan Colonial Library, in 1886.

News of grand historical events overseas tended to spawn flurries of publishing activity, as authors and publishers responded to the latest causes célèbres. The loss of the Franklin Expedition in 1854 caught the public imagination, as did the Indian Uprising in 1857, and the Relief of Mafeking in 1900. If anything, this was a literary genre whose appeal increased in proportion to the decline of Britain's imperial domination. The tragic account of Robert Falcon Scott's last attempt on the south pole, published by Murray as *Scott's last expedition* in 1913, might be seen to herald the end of the golden age of heroic British colonial adventure.

Travel and exploration literature found a fictional counterpart in the colonial adventure novel, which enjoyed its greatest vogue between the 1880s and the First World War: narratives based on the desire to solve geographical mysteries, whose standard fare was lost tribes and new worlds. The adventure novel for children had continued to be popular, with *Robinson Crusoe* going into countless editions in the nineteenth century. The imperial ethos engendered periodical revivals of the Robinsonnade, of which Ballantyne's *Coral island* (1857) was the most popular. Intrepid stories such as Stevenson's *Treasure Island* (1883), Haggard's *King Solomon's mines* (1885), Kipling's *The man who would be king* (1888) and Conan Doyle's *The lost world* (1912) were the high points in a genre which had many lesser imitators.

The end of the nineteenth century saw increasing efforts to represent a declining empire in favourable terms. Thanks to the development of new photographic printing techniques, faraway lands were given more verisimilitude to British readers than ever before. In 1898, Newnes launched the *Wide World Magazine*, which, with its motto 'truth is stranger than fiction', fed the popular appetite for exotic adventure, arguably paving the way for pulp fiction like Edgar Rice Burroughs's *Tarzan of the apes* (1914).

Authors in the international marketplace

One consequence of the internationalisation of the English-language book trade was the emergence of a new kind of international celebrity author. But as Catherine Seville and Michael Winship demonstrate elsewhere in this volume, literary property and its piracy – particularly in a transatlantic context – remained a problem for writers and their publishers alike until its resolution in 1911.

The attitudes of writers towards the piracy of their works could sometimes be mixed. In 1876, Longfellow observed that, of his twenty-two British publishers to date, only four had acknowledged their debt to him. Yet he also saw that such editions could bring about an increase in readership that could help the sales of future works.[6] Kipling, on the other hand, spent many years pursuing payments for the reissues of the early works that had been published in India.[7]

Some authors were more skilled than others at overcoming such legal difficulties. Anthony Trollope, who knew how to maximise the returns on his

6 See Ghodes, 'Longfellow and his authorized British publishers'.
7 Richards, 'Kipling and pirates'.

literary property better than most, worked the international market with consummate skill. Typical in this regard were the complicated publishing arrangements for his *Australia and New Zealand*, which in 1873 alone was issued by Chapman & Hall in two volumes and by the German English-language publisher Tauchnitz in three volumes, serialised in the *Australasian* and issued in parts by George Robertson of Melbourne. In the following year it was issued in four parts by Chapman & Hall and was published in one volume as the 'first Australian edition' by Robertson.

Given its position at the centre of the imperial trade in books, London became an important destination for many of the English-speaking world's aspirant writers. Herman Melville had visited for the express purpose of negotiating terms with London publishers in 1849. The first British editions of Melville's novels, although set from proofs of the American editions, were often published beforehand, on the assumption that thereby a certain amount of protection was possible. Thus *Redburn* (1849), *White-jacket* (1850) and *Moby-Dick* (as *The whale*, 1851) were all published by the firm of Bentley several months in advance of their first American editions.

By the time that Henry James arrived in England in 1876, American copyright law protected the rights of American authors, while British copyright applied to resident writers only. Over the subsequent years, James established close business relations with two of the chief London publishing houses, Macmillan and Smith, Elder, the first of which had strong reciprocal arrangements with American publishers. James shrewdly saw to it, in the years before transatlantic copyright, that he came to legal arrangements with firms on both sides of the Atlantic. Consequently, the first editions of his novels were sometimes published in New York and Boston, thus allowing himself to keep a shrewd eye on his British interests.

While he was in Britain, Henry Lawson brokered the publication of the first edition of Miles Franklin's *My brilliant career*, which was published by Blackwood in 1901. The New Zealand writer Katherine Mansfield was to settle permanently in London in 1908, establishing a relationship with literati through her personal relationship with John Middleton Murry. The Indian poet Rabindranath Tagore visited in 1912 with several translations of his work which were subsequently championed by a number of his literary contacts in London, not least W. B. Yeats, who wrote an introduction to an edition of Tagore's *Gitanjali* (Chiswick Press, 1912).

Such informal arrangements were not unusual in the years before the rise of the international literary agent. Colonel Thomas Aspinwall, American consul general in London, had received fees to represent a number of American authors in London, including Washington Irving. Similar tasks were under-taken by the bookseller Obadiah Rich and the banker Russell Sturgis.[8] The rise of the professional literary agent, who brokered arrangements with pub-lishers in London and New York, was to alleviate the plight of many of the leading authors of the day.[9] The first and foremost of these was A. P. Watt, who had launched his career as a publicist as early as 1880, later founding the firm that became styled A. P. Watt & Son in 1892. Watt represented some of the leading authors of the day, including Arnold Bennett, G. K. Chesterton, Wilkie Collins, Marie Corelli, Arthur Conan Doyle, Rider Haggard, Bret Harte, Rudyard Kipling, W. Somerset Maugham, Olive Schreiner, H. G. Wells and W. B. Yeats. Watt's main competitor was J. B. Pinker, who established his literary agency in London in 1896, and soon counted among his clients Stephen Crane, Henry James, Henry Lawson, Joseph Conrad, Ford Madox Ford, John Galsworthy, George Gissing, George Bernard Shaw and Oscar Wilde.

Even after the Copyright Act of 1911, making the vagaries of the interna-tional literary market less precarious to negotiate, the intervention of agents, a commercial necessity of an earlier time, had become part of the everyday business of writers and publishers.

Worlds elsewhere

While this introduction has sought to account, in its broadest sense, for Britain's international book trade, we cannot forget that in most parts of the Empire indigenous book trades were in operation throughout this period to varying degrees. In speaking about the history of the book trade in the colonial world, it is all too easy to slip into assumptions about centre and periphery and the domination of third world cultures by the technically superior political power. While this model can be seen to work fairly unproblematically in the first phase of colonisation, a phase whose residual effects could nevertheless be long-lasting, the legacy of many aspects of colonialism are not necessar-ily coterminous with the original aims of imperialism. The establishment of missionary presses, despite the fact that equipment and labour were more often than not imported from Europe, was often to provide the first manifes-tation of and model for indigenous publishing practices. As Rimi Chatterjee observes below, such a publishing counter-frontier had been visible in Bengal,

---

8 See Barnes, review of Hepburn, *The author's empty purse.*   9 Hepburn, *The author's empty purse.*

for instance, from the beginning of the nineteenth-century, and was soon to develop into a press that came increasingly to serve local needs and interests.[10]

By the late nineteenth century, there had developed a powerful symbiotic relationship between new political formations and the printed word. The establishment of indigenous newspaper presses was a crucial agent in this process, reflecting the interests and aspirations of the various colonial peripheries. Even where the content of periodicals was loyalist in persuasion, the very fact that the local could now represent itself politically and culturally had the effect of creating an independence of political temper as well as a public sphere in which new kinds of self-definition could take root.

While new communicative models imposed on colonial societies by the coming of the printing press sometimes transformed an otherwise traditional way of life based on orality and vernacular languages, the arrival of print could also be an important factor in the move from regionalism to nationalism. Elizabeth E. McDonald has demonstrated how the standardisation of the Marathi language on the part of government and church agencies created a means by which indigenous literature would eventually come to flourish.[11] In a very literal sense, late nineteenth-century Bengali nationalism was fuelled by printing machines and type imported from Europe.

By the middle years of the century, considerable centres of English-language publishing were well established in major cities such as Toronto, Melbourne, Sydney, Calcutta and Madras.[12] Large-scale printing and publishing had arrived in the former colonies, with firms like Angus & Robertson of Sydney and Neilson of Montreal serving their own hinterlands, and even in some instances producing printed matter for export. One innovator was the Australian publisher George Robertson who, in 1857, opened a London office through which he could acquire stock for distribution throughout Australasia.

The final identifiable phase in the development of the colonial book trade, as described earlier, might therefore be described in terms of an increasingly *postcolonial* tendency, involving the establishment of widespread indigenous bookselling, and the displacement of British literary production by those of newly emerging nationalist publishing industries. By the early twentieth century, British publishers were coming to realise that, if they were to continue to hold on to their overseas trade, then new means would have to be found to penetrate markets in the developing world. Initially, William Collins's books were

---

10 Ghosh, 'An uncertain "Coming of the book" '.
11 McDonald, 'The modernizing of communication'. See also van Bijlert, 'Bengal's modernity and nationalism 1880–1910'.
12 Weedon, *Victorian publishing*, pp. 42–3.

distributed through Bright Brothers of Sydney; later on, the firm's Australian and New Zealand sales were handled by McGreadie, Thomas & Niven. In 1874, Collins opened its own warehouse in Sydney, adding a New Zealand branch in 1888. By the 1880s, other British firms with Australian branches included Macmillan, Cassell and Ward Lock. In Canada, where geographical and political distance was less of a problem, agencies took longer to establish themselves, with Macmillan arriving in 1905 and Cassell in 1907. By the beginning of the twentieth century Collins had appointed permanent representatives in South Africa 'to disseminate not only English books but readers and dictionaries in their own tongue among the Afrikaner population'.[13] Macmillan opened branches in Bombay (1901), Calcutta (1907) and Madras (1913), while Oxford University Press sent E. V. Rieu as their agent to Bombay in 1912 to investigate the possibility of providing educational books suited to local requirements.

While it is often said that trade had a tendency to 'follow the flag' in the nineteenth century, there is a sense in which the book trade not only can be seen to have exploited colonial infrastructures, but was a key agent in the consolidation and extension of them. If British authors and publishers may have gleaned a seemingly endless supply of copy from foreign lands, this was by no means a one-way relationship. The export of Anglophone printed texts to the remotest outposts of Empire served to bring colonial values more effectively to these same distant lands than any other medium.

Although some were slow to recognise it, in due course British publishers would have to learn to adjust their business practices to accommodate a vast overseas market for their products. If Britain's publishers had learned to exploit their commonwealth markets early on, the second half of the nineteenth century was to bring new challenges, with the rise of indigenous publishing industries centred on newly industrialised cities like Toronto, Sydney and Melbourne, and the additional competition presented by that other major producer of English-language books, the United States. Whatever the regional differences, the larger story of Britain's overseas book trade in this period can therefore be seen as one that begins with opportunism and exploitation and ends with competition and compromise.

BB

The United States

Between 1830 and 1914, the United States expanded substantially. The number of states increased from twenty-four to forty-eight, which now spanned the

---

13 Kier, *The house of Collins*, pp. 180, 182.

continent, and the nation grew in area from 1,788,006 to 3,022,387 square miles. Population expanded nearly eightfold, from just under 13 million to nearly 100 million (12,901,000 to 99,118,000), as it also became less rural. By 1920 over half of the population lived in towns or cities with at least 2,500 inhabitants; there had been three cities with a population of over one million since at least 1890.[14] Over the same period, the book trades in the United States grew into a substantial and thriving industry: the value of books and pamphlets published, which in 1830 had been estimated at $3.5 million, was reported to be nearly $67.3 million in 1914.[15] Publishing itself, just emerging from its infancy in 1830 and then chiefly consisting of small firms organised as proprietary partnerships, sometimes informal or family based, had also matured. By 1914 major trade publishing firms were privately held corporations and mainly based in only a few financial centres: chiefly New York, but also Boston, Philadelphia and Chicago. These firms were organised internally into departments that specialised in separate functions such as editorial, production, advertising and sales, and that were staffed by a professional managerial staff.

As in Britain, this was the period of industrialisation in the book trades in the United States, which soon became a leader in technological and industrial innovation. In 1817, George Clymer was forced to take his design for the Columbian Press to England, where it could be reliably manufactured and was soon to become the standard hand-press in use. The first practical papermaking machine, a Fourdrinier, was imported from England in 1827, but in the 1830s these and the cheaper cylinder machines were being produced domestically. The pivotal typecasting machine, the Smyth book-sewing machine, and both the Linotype and Monotype typesetting machines were invented and developed in the United States during the period. R. Hoe & Co. of New York became an international supplier of its large power-driven cylinder and rotary printing machines.

Industrialisation in the United States altered the processes of manufacture of books, the working lives of those who produced them, and their appearance. If the 'industrial' book shared many similarities between the United States and Great Britain, there were also marked differences. With less strong trade traditions, American book manufacturers seem to have endorsed new technological developments more readily than their British counterparts. The use of printing

---

14 *Historical statistics of the United States: colonial times to 1957*, pp. 7–13. For a fuller discussion of the matters discussed in this chapter, see my contributions to volumes 3 and 4 of Casper and others (eds.), *A history of the book in America* 3 (Chapel Hill, NC, 2007) and 4 (forthcoming).
15 Goodrich, *Recollections of a lifetime* 2, p. 380; *Fourteenth census of the United States, taken in the year 1920* (Washington, DC, 1928) 10, p. 578.

plates, both stereotype (a process developed in England early in the century) and electrotype, became nearly universal for all but the most ephemeral printing, and American printers believed that American plates were superior to British ones. Relief cuts and type could be cast in a single plate, and by the 1870s books that integrated image and text on a single page in attractive ways became far more common than in Britain. As the century closed, photochemical and photomechanical processes further reduced the cost of reproducing illustrations, and illustrated books and periodicals proliferated. Cloth-covered, case-bound publishers' bindings often carried distinctively American designs.

Industrialisation not only affected book manufacture, but also had major implications for distribution. Reaching the market, difficult in 1830, continued to be the major problem as the United States expanded and its population grew and diversified. In 1830 the chief means of moving goods to market in the United States was by water, either coastal or by river and canal; overland transportation remained difficult and expensive. During the nineteenth century, an extensive rail network was created – 166,703 miles of track were in operation by 1890.[16] Another key development was the emergence in the 1840s of express companies, firms that managed the delivery of small packages, chiefly by rail. This improved transportation system also served to improve the flow of information between publisher and customer and within the trade. The postal system, which came to depend upon the rail system, was used extensively to transmit orders, printed advertisements, trade lists and catalogues. The federal government subsidised the delivery of newspapers and periodicals through the mails, and specialised book trade periodicals, of which *Publishers' Weekly* became the most important, sprang up. Advertisements, notices and reviews of books appeared widely in other magazines and newspapers, and many major trade publishers also issued general-interest monthly magazines – the *Atlantic Monthly*, *Harper's New Monthly Magazine*, *Putnam's Monthly*, *Scribner's Monthly Magazine* – that served to promote their book publications. Finally, an efficient means for transferring credit from customer or distributor to publisher needed to be established. Specie and hard currency were scarce in 1830, and credit exchange depended upon commercial bills and notes (often disputed) and bank notes (regularly discounted or found to be counterfeit). In 1862 the federal government first issued the greenback, paper money that was backed as legal tender by the government but unsecured by specie, and in 1863 it authorised the charter of national banks that could issue paper money backed by federal bonds.

16 *Historical statistics of the United States: colonial times to 1957*, p. 427.

Within this environment, a distribution system for trade books emerged that chiefly relied upon retail bookstores that received stock from publishers or wholesalers at a discount large enough to cover shipping and overhead costs and to provide a reasonable profit. Large, urban bookstores often served as regional distributors, passing along popular titles in small numbers to general stores and other retailers, or served as agents in supplying the needs of local libraries and schools. Inexpensive, paper-covered books were widely available at newsagents, and, by the end of the period, many department stores, most notably R. H. Macy & Co. and John A. Wanamaker & Co., maintained large, thriving book departments. Outside cities and towns, however, most customers would find only a few books for sale tucked away on a single shelf amid the varied stock of a general or variety store.

The distribution of trade books by discount quickly replaced earlier practices of exchange (where two publishing firms bartered stock) and commission (where retail establishments acted as agents of the publisher, taking a commission on the sale price of any copy sold), but alternative means of distribution continued throughout the period. Most important were the book trade sales, which were Dutch auction sales of books, stationery and other book trade items, restricted to publishers, booksellers and members of the trade. Trade sales took place regularly at set times: spring and fall in New York, Philadelphia and Cincinnati, and every August in Boston. They were initiated with a Philadelphia sale in 1824 and continued into the early twentieth century, though their importance declined in the 1860s, and from 1879 they were held only in New York. As the trade sales declined, a number of large book wholesaling or jobbing firms emerged, and publishers and wholesalers increasingly depended on commercial travellers to reach retail bookstores. Earlier, some publishers had acted as agents for retailers at the trade sales and in gathering books from local publishers to make up an order, but these new jobbing firms specialised in supplying the retail trade, libraries and schools with a wide range of books at a reasonable discount. The first, the American News Company of New York, was organised in 1864, and in 1874 the New York firm that survives as Baker & Taylor was formed. Philadelphia's J. B. Lippincott & Co. and Chicago's A. C. McClurg & Co. also were major wholesalers, though both are usually remembered today as publishers.

Throughout the period, the import and export of books, both bound and in sheets, as well as printing plates and other trade material, to and from Britain and British possessions, chiefly Canada, remained a significant part of the American book trade. In the federal fiscal year ending in 1876, for example, the value of books and other printed material imported from the United Kingdom was $1,536,599 and from Canada $23,817, but the United States only exported $97,499 to the former compared with $481,148 to Canada.[17] Again, this substantial trade depended on new industrial developments: regular packet service, first sail then steam, and the transatlantic telegraph, supplementing the mails after 1866, provided a regular means of transportation and communication between publishing centres in Great Britain and the United States. It was not uncommon for British publishers to offer lots of their publications at the American trades sales, and independent auction sales of their works were also held from time to time. The transatlantic trade was facilitated by London firms that served as agents for American publishers and booksellers: those managed by Sampson Low and Nicolas Trübner were the most important, and Henry Stevens was instrumental in the trade in used and rare books. In addition, a number of American firms – examples are B. Westermann & Co. and F. W. Christern of New York – specialised in importing foreign books.

More important, however, was the international trade in texts rather than physical books, a business that also largely relied on the use of London-based agents, though by 1914 several publishing houses, both British and American, had established branch offices in London or New York. American publishers regularly undertook to arrange for the publication of works by their American authors in Britain, where they were generally protected by copyright if certain conditions were met – prior or simultaneous publication in Britain, deposit of copies, and after 1854 nominal residence in Britain or its dominions. The reverse was not the case: until 1891 legal copyright was denied to any author not a citizen or resident of the United States.[18] Both British and American authors felt that this situation disadvantaged them and cost them earnings, but in fact the situation was more complicated. Market imperatives meant that American publishers developed a set of conventions known as 'courtesy of the trade' that established a de facto copyright in the works of foreign authors.[19] Trade courtesy gave rights in a foreign work to the American publisher that first announced it as 'in press' and then gave that publisher rights in subsequent works by that author. Both claims were strengthened should the publisher also offer remuneration, and it was quite usual for British authors or their publishers

---

17 *Commerce and navigation of the United States for the fiscal year ended June 30, 1876*, 44th Cong., 2nd sess., House Executive Document 13, no. 46 (Washington, DC, 1877; serial set 1760), *passim*.
18 For international copyright see Barnes, *Authors, publishers, and politicians* and Nowell-Smith, *International copyright and the publisher*. See also chapter 5 above.
19 For this, see Jeffrey D. Groves, 'Courtesy of the trade', in Casper and others (eds.), *A history of the book in America* 3, pp. 139–48.

to receive a payment, either a flat fee or a royalty, from American publishers when their texts were published in American periodicals or as books.

Trade courtesy proved quite serviceable and was widely respected within the trade: for example, when Boston publishers Ticknor & Fields published the first American edition of Tennyson's *Poems* in 1842, they paid him $150 (equivalent to a royalty of 10 per cent) and until 1870 remained the sole American publisher of his works. Similarly, in 1855 the same firm wrote to Robert Browning that it was unable to add a new work by his wife, Elizabeth Barrett Browning, to its list, as the New York firm C. S. Francis & Co. had published her earlier volumes and had a prior claim.[20] The system was often strained, however, especially by popular authors like Charles Dickens, and began to collapse during the 1870s when a number of publishers of inexpensive 'library' series largely consisting of British works refused to honour it, and as authors' rights came to be understood to include a complex of serial, dramatic and translation rights. After years of debate, the 'Chace Act', a law that authorised the government to enter into treaty agreements to extend legal copyright protection to foreign works, was passed in 1891. Protectionist interests did succeed in including a requirement that foreign works be manufactured in the United States, and when a revised Copyright Code was passed in 1909 this infamous 'manufacturing clause' remained in force. The passage of an international copyright law signalled the maturation of the American publishing and book trades, however, and by 1914 it was poised to grow into the international force in publishing that it became during the twentieth century.

MW

Australia and New Zealand

In looking at the British book world of Australia and New Zealand between 1830 and the outbreak of the First World War, it is important to recognise – beyond the continuing preponderance of London and Glasgow – the different perspectives of writers and of readers and book-buyers. On the one hand there was the pressure to bring an exotic and imperial subject-matter to English-speaking audiences at large. On the other there was the demand for cheap and accessible books covering all the interests and needs of customers residing on the other side of the world and determined to overcome their perceived deprivation. The tensions between these two groups are an integral part of

20 Winship, *American literary publishing*, pp. 136, 138–9.

the ongoing story of publishing and bookselling in Britain's colonies and dominions in the South Seas.

New subjects and new voices

'A new heaven and a new earth!' exclaims the narrator of Henry Kingsley's novel *Geoffry Hamlyn* (1859), introducing the Australian setting to his readers. The British settlement of Australia (beginning with the penal colony in Sydney in 1788) and of New Zealand (following the Treaty of Waitangi in 1840) opened up new territory for the British book trade. Descriptions of this 'new heaven' and 'new earth', with its unique flora and fauna and indigenous peoples (Aborigines and Maoris), soon had a prominent place in the burgeoning literature of exploration and travel produced for the British market. By the end of the nineteenth century, the Australasian colonies (predominantly Australian) had become a source of new publications as well as a significant market for British books.

In 1830 Britain had not yet taken possession of New Zealand, but descriptive accounts of the coasts of both countries in eighteenth-century journals of sea-explorers, notably James Cook, were already in print. Personal narratives of the first convict settlement (Phillip, Tench, Collins) had catered to the public curiosity about 'Botany Bay', which had become a trope in British writing. Exploration of the Australian inland was underway, and the first journals of land-explorers were starting to appear in print: Oxley's *Journals of two expeditions into the interior of New South Wales* had been published by 1820, followed by those of Sturt (1833), Mitchell (1838), Grey (1841), Eyre (1845), Leichhardt (1847), Mitchell (1848) and Sturt (1849). The 'romance of exploration' continued to be a popular subject into the second half of the century, even when the emphasis in writing about the colonies had shifted from 'discovery' to 'social observation'.

The 'beauties and wonders of nature' in the new imperial possessions were recorded and illustrated in various forms of publication: scientific studies, systematically classifying and documenting the flora and fauna; illustrated 'albums' and 'sketch books'; and personal narratives of colonists, explorers and travellers. Botanical studies initiated by Joseph Banks, who had sailed with Cook and had conceived a plan for a series of Colonial Floras, included such major works as Joseph Hooker's *Flora Tasmaniae* (1859) and Baron von Mueller's *Flora of Australia* (1863–78). John Gould combined the roles of ornithologist and publisher, issuing books displaying the flora and fauna of Australia and New Guinea. His own lavish seven-volume *The birds of Australia* (1840–8), consisting of hand-coloured lithographs mainly the work of his wife, offered both scientific exactness and aesthetic pleasure. Books documenting the natural world benefited from the developments in lithography and wood-engraving, and then of photography, as did narratives of explorers and settlers, in which the text was accompanied by illustrations. The ways in which the flora, the fauna and the indigenous people were portrayed in illustrations powerfully influenced the conception that the British reading public formed of the Australasian colonies.

Following Darwin's *Origin of species* (1859), the indigenous people in both Australia and New Zealand were increasingly studied in the frame of evolutionary theory. Of the pioneering studies, *The native tribes of central Australia* by W. B. Spencer and F. J. Gillen (1899) exercised considerable influence on the development of anthropology in Australia. To the British reading public, however, Aborigines were simply a picturesque element, along with convicts and bushrangers, in the early versions of colonial experience. Charles Rowcroft's novel *Tales of the colonies* (1843), and Alexander Harris's semi-fictional 'memoir' *Settlers and convicts* (1849) were among the first successful attempts to exploit the interest in emigration by writers who had some first-hand knowledge of conditions in the colonies. With the gold rushes in mid-century, interest in Australia was intensified, and a further convention was added to stories of imperial adventure. In the later nineteenth century, Life in Our Colonies was a theme of countless books, both factual and fictional, and sometimes fictional masquerading as factual, issuing from London publishers.

There were no British publishers for poetry and plays from the colonies. There was, however, a continuing demand for memoirs of colonial experience and books of travel and description, including books about the social characteristics and emerging institutions of 'Greater Britain'. British public figures such as the politician Sir Charles Dilke, who visited in 1866–7, the novelist Anthony Trollope (1871–2) and the historian J. A. Froude (1885) wrote travel books in which they commented on colonial society from an imperial perspective.

Other visitors, less searching in their approach, provided the equivalent of a tourists' guide to the exotic and strange. 'Somehow it is assumed that people in the mother country continue to be interested only in the picturesque, the curious and the unusual in Australian life', complained an Australian commentator at the end of the century.[21] The tastes, expectations and preconceptions of readers became more and more an issue for publishers and booksellers as colonies became more independent and could no longer be considered merely as an extension of Britain.

21 Byrne, *Australian writers*, p. 19.

In the British market Anglo-Australian authors in London exploited imperial sentiment with anthologies such as *Oak-bough and wattle-blossom* (1888),
*Australian ballads and rhymes: poems inspired by life and scenery in Australia and
New Zealand during the first century of British colonization* (1888), *In Australian
wilds and other colonial sketches* (1889) and *By creek and gully: stories and sketches,
mostly of bush life, told in prose and rhyme by Australian writers in England* (1899).
London-based writers, especially those who had been born in Australia or had
lived there for a time, incorporated Australian material in popular romances
and adventure novels that found ready acceptance with British publishers and
public. They included two extremely prolific fiction writers, who began their
careers in Australia before moving to London. Fergus Hume set his pioneer
crime novel, *The mystery of a hansom cab*, in 'Marvellous Melbourne', where
he was living. Its success in Melbourne in 1886, and even greater success in
London the following year, led to the formation of the Hansom Cab Publishing Company, and a further 140 or so novels by Hume, none of which had
the phenomenal sales of his first. Manchester-born Nat Gould was working in
Australia as a journalist when he wrote a serial, *With the tide*, which became an
instant success on publication in London in 1891 as a book entitled *The double
event: a tale of the Melbourne Cup*. It was the first of his highly readable novels
with a sporting interest, many of which drew on his Australian experience.

The position of the writer in the colonies was complicated. Publication in
the colonies meant small circulation and lack of critical interest. The writer
who could not go to London had to rely upon the sympathetic discernment of
the distant publisher's reader and the book editor. Recognition of one's work
by English readers could transform one's reputation in the colonies. A striking
example is *Robbery Under Arms*, by 'Rolf Boldrewood', which was published
first as a serial in the *Sydney Mail* in 1882–3, then as a three-decker in London
in 1888, but did not attract much attention until published in Macmillan's
Colonial Library in 1889. Boldrewood's reputation in the colonies was made,
and he went on to have eighteen titles in the series, which began in 1886
and lasted until 1913. His fiction, unlike that of the nationalist writers, suited
the taste for romantic adventure and did not challenge established British
preconceptions about Australian life.

Even a major work by a colonial writer that had received local recognition
benefited from a London publisher. Marcus Clarke's novel of the transportation
system, *His natural life*, first appeared as a serial in the *Australian Journal* (1870–
2). It was then considerably abridged and revised for publication in a single
volume by the Melbourne publisher George Robertson in 1874. When Clarke
sought English publication Bentley originally asked for a 'happy ending', and

an editor revised the whole text for the three-volume publication in 1875. The subsequent reissues of the title included a cheap 1885 edition, jointly with Robertson, for circulation in the Australian colonies only. This sold in substantial quantities, and by the time that Macmillan took over Bentley in 1897 approximately 45,000 copies had been sold. Clarke's novel was eventually included in Macmillan's Colonial Library.

By the turn of the century, with the development of a local publishing industry, authors with a local perspective were being promoted. The Sydney publishers Angus & Robertson had had a remarkable success with books from Henry Lawson and A. B. Paterson, both of whom had already achieved national reputations in the pages of the influential Sydney weekly, the *Bulletin*. The newspaper itself undertook book publishing for a brief period, its greatest success being Steele Rudd's *On our selection*, a book which sold 22,000 copies in the four years after being published in 1899. These were straws in the wind; but, as Miles Franklin observed, 'some of the most acclaimed and admittedly "dinky-di" Australian works have had to leave Australia to find publishers'.[22] The most notable instances of this failure are two important prose works by women: her own novel, *My brilliant career*, which was published by Blackwood in 1901, and Baynton's short story collection, *Bush studies*, published by Duckworth in 1902, neither of which had found a publisher in Australia.

At the end of the period London still remained the literary centre for Australian and New Zealand writers, even for Henry Lawson, whose countrymen thought him the most Australian of all writers. He had gone to London in 1900, encouraged by approaches from Fisher Unwin, Blackwood and Methuen, who had been impressed by his first volume of short stories, *While the billy boils* (1896), published by Angus & Robertson. Although he had J. B. Pinker as his literary agent, a sympathetic publisher in William Blackwood, and the practical support and advice of Edward Garnett and E. V. Lucas, and although he received good reviews in London, Lawson's hopes of establishing himself on the English literary scene were not realised. His stories appeared in *Blackwood's Magazine*, and Blackwood published two collections: *The country I come from* (1901) and *Joe Wilson and his mates* (1902); but domestic and personal stress brought him to near-collapse, and he returned to Australia in 1902, while a third volume of his prose, *Children of the bush*, being published by Methuen, was still in the press. Two months before his departure Edward Garnett had hailed him in the *Academy* as 'one of the very few genuinely democratic writers

---

22 Franklin, *Joseph Furphy*, p. 3.

that the literature of "Greater Britain" can show'.[23] While the proposition that whatever succeeded 'at home' would succeed in the colonies remained generally true, what succeeded in the colonies did not necessarily succeed 'at home'. Some of Lawson's best work was first published in Britain, but it appealed less to the British reading public than that of his less original and less distinctive contemporaries.

Within what has been called the 'imperial cultural space',[24] there were often joint publishing arrangements; most writers aspired to get 'a London hearing', which could mean greater sales and reputation; the colonial public showed a preference for London publications; and colonial publishers and booksellers were reluctant to take risks with local writing. Despite the growth of local publishing, which saw the rapid success of the popular Bookstall paperback series ('Written by Australians for Australians') established in 1904, as well as an increasing production of quality hardbacks, in 1914 it remained true that more Australian titles were appearing from British publishing houses than from any other source. The taste of the metropolitan publishers generally reflected imperialist values, but there were exceptions, the most notable being Edward Garnett who, in his role as publisher's reader, encouraged Henry Lawson and other nationalist writers, recognising that 'wherever an English-speaking community settles and opens up new lands, it speedily speaks for itself as a Centre'.[25]

JB

The distribution of British books in Australia and New Zealand

Throughout the long nineteenth century that began in 1789 and ended in 1914 books produced in Great Britain had pride of place in Australian and New Zealand shops and libraries. Even after substantial political independence was achieved in 1901, the paradox was that readers still looked above all to English, Scottish and Irish suppliers. In this respect there was no break in continuity between convict days and federation.[26]

23 'An appreciation', *Academy and Literature* 8 March 1902; reprinted as 'Henry Lawson and the democracy' in Garnett, *Friday nights*, p. 186.
24 M. Lyons, 'Britain's largest export market', in Lyons and Arnold (eds.), *A history of the book in Australia 1891–1945*, p. 22.
25 E[dward] G[arnett], 'The Overseas Library': statement printed on front endpapers of volumes in the series, issued by T. Fisher Unwin from 1899.
26 The basis for the following summary account will be found in Borchardt and Kirsop (eds.), *The book in Australia*; Johanson, *A study of colonial editions*; Kirsop, *Books for colonial readers*; Kirsop and Webby (eds.), *A history of the book in Australia. 1. To 1890*; and Lyons and Arnold (eds.), *A history of the book in Australia. 2. 1891–1945*. In addition careful rereading was done of the Australian booksellers' advertising magazines for the years following the flowering of colonial editions in the 1880s.

For the greater part of the first half-century of European settlement in Australia after 1788, the provision of printed matter was essentially haphazard. Government presses in Sydney and Hobart supplied local administrative needs and issued newspapers whose primary purpose was official even if they made room for the rudimentary commercial activities of the colonies. The authorities and missionary societies imported books and pamphlets for the instruction and edification of the convict population and, to a lesser extent, of the Aborigines. Free settlers and military personnel relied on the personal libraries they brought with them and on private arrangements concluded with correspondents and booksellers in the British Isles. It was only during the period of consolidation that began in the 1820s that regular trade structures can be said to have emerged alongside the first institutions – mechanics' institutes, subscription libraries, secondary schools and learned societies – of a more mature civilisation. Much was to change between 1830 and 1914, including the decision by New Zealanders not to join the Australian federation in 1901, but in literary, intellectual and cultural matters one thing remained constant: the fact that the various British possessions in the South Seas never ceased to recognise that they were part of the global English-speaking community. For this reason alone book trade relations with London, Glasgow, Edinburgh and Dublin – even more than with New York, Philadelphia and Boston – have to be central in any study of Australasia before the First World War. Despite the nationalism of the Sydney *Bulletin* school of the 1880s and 1890s, reading horizons were always wider than purely local ones. It is therefore critical to learn how Britain reached markets that were at first many months and even at the last several weeks away from Paternoster Row.

During the penal and pastoral decades that preceded the gold rushes of the 1850s there were two ways in which the relatively isolated booksellers of the colonies received their supplies. The first involved direct links between houses in the British Isles and businesses established in Sydney, Hobart, Launceston, Melbourne and other centres, whereas the second was based on the regular export of speculative consignments – usually put together by London specialists in the remainder trade – for auction in ports scattered round Australia and New Zealand. Neither formula proved to be satisfactory in the long run for a public of growing size and sophistication.

The use of family connections continued a pattern illustrated in North America in the eighteenth century by the Rivingtons and others. Sydney's first effective bookseller, William McGarvie (1810–41), operating from the 'Australian Stationery Warehouse' as early as 1828, was clearly dependent on his Glasgow and Presbyterian antecedents in ways that would be echoed by other traders throughout the nineteenth century. However, the most obvious example of a carefully constructed network was the multi-faceted concern set up both in Sydney and in Van Diemen's Land by the Tegg family.[27] Two of Thomas Tegg's sons, James and Samuel Augustus, were active in Sydney, Hobart and Launceston between 1835 and 1847, providing a service not only for retail customers, but also as wholesaler-importers for other members of the trade, as can be inferred from the records left by the Walches, successors in the Hobart shop. Catalogues and newspaper advertisements suggest that the wares being offered covered a range of relatively cheap books suitable for the nursery, the schoolroom, household recreation, and common pursuits and professions. Subscriptions to periodicals and to novels published in parts were also available. On the other hand the scientific institutions and the more ambitious subscription libraries continued to direct their custom to London houses like Orger & Meryon particularly interested in the colonial trade.

The market for current fiction was largely confined to the commercial cir-culating libraries that began to appear in the 1820s and then developed during the 1830s and 1840s throughout the continent. Many of these establishments were almost as short-lived as their stock. In one case at least – the Australian Circulating Library in Sydney in 1832 – the books and the catalogue printed by J. Darling of Leadenhall Street were supplied direct from London. Later in the century three-deckers retired from Mudie's regularly surfaced in libraries on the other side of the world.

It is hard to escape the impression that a substantial part of what was for sale before the late 1850s came from the consignments sent by remainder merchants like Bohn and Edward Lumley. Typically a few cases of books, and perhaps of music and prints, would be packed in London and dispatched, sometimes with a hastily prepared catalogue, to an agent in an Australasian port. An auctioneer would be found and the public, both booksellers and private persons, would be invited to the ensuing sale. The content of the invoices was determined by exporters consulting their own notions of what was required in the colonies: cheap and practical books situated in the mainstream. Beyond this there was the convenience of getting rid of excess stocks. Apart from pulping, the con-signment trade is one of the often shadowy and imprecise measures of the miscalculations that lay behind the hyperbole of nineteenth-century Britain's best-sellers and large editions. There were exceptions, for example Lumley's recourse to antiquarian material alongside his remainders, but overall one is dealing with a downmarket phenomenon. Sales, too, were uncertain, because

27 Crittenden, *James Tegg*.

cargoes arrived in a way that often saw glut following dearth. This was particularly irritating for the new professional booksellers of Melbourne, Hobart and Sydney after the gold rushes. Their more fastidious customers expected better, so other methods of supply had to be found. Although consignments of the old speculative kind continued to arrive till the end of the century, their importance receded markedly. Bernard Quaritch, seeking to exploit a parvenu taste for rather showy modern books, burned his fingers badly in the Melbourne crash of 1892.[28] The future lay elsewhere.

It was quite fortuitous that the discovery of gold in New South Wales and Victoria coincided with Lord Campbell's determination of 1852 that opened an era of 'free trade in books' till the end of the century. What this achieved, however, was that booksellers based in Australasia, and first of all the Walches of Hobart and George Robertson of Melbourne,[29] could set up buying offices in London to facilitate their retail and wholesale operations in the South Seas. By obtaining good discounts for cash purchases, the Australians' 'home' managers made it possible for their principals to have most books sold, except in remote areas, at London retail prices. At the same time there was a quite spectacular increase in the colonial population, with the result that the newly organised market became within decades the most important external outlet for the British trade. Coping with the official export and import statistics, by weight and by value, is no easy matter over a long period in which definitions could change and fluctuations due to economic crises were endemic. As an internal memorandum of Richard Bentley & Son in 1885 had it: 'The reading season in Australia is the reverse of that in Europe and North America (and the sale of books varies considerably according to the export of wool).' In fact, this is only the beginning of the predictable complications of Britain's Australasian colonies, which cannot be reduced to some sort of uniformity that ignores significant ethnic, economic, social, cultural and religious differences.

While it is necessary to recognise that 'our Southern Colonies' were comparatively much less populous in the late nineteenth century than now, the 1885 figures given in the first number – September 1887 – of E. A. Petherick's *Colonial book circular and bibliographical record* illustrate the extent of importations from the British Isles. Australia and New Zealand had 3,401,699 inhabitants, of whom just over one million were in each of New South Wales and Victoria. Three cities had more than 100,000 inhabitants: Melbourne (345,380), Sydney (282,843) and Adelaide (127,013). Total book imports were valued at

28 On a similar venture to New Zealand, see Kirsop, 'Bernard Quaritch's Wellington consignment sale, 1893'.
29 Holroyd, *George Robertson of Melbourne*.

£1,437,807. This leaves out of account the consumption of local publications, including 'nearly 700 newspapers'. Petherick was concerned, of course, to play up the 'flourishing condition' of the trade to bolster his own advertising and exporting business, which collapsed in the 1890s depression.

As long as the good times lasted, and notably through the boom of the 1880s, there was a clear pattern of organisation of Australasian bookselling. The basis was laid in the 1850s with the London offices and their efficient procurement procedures. In the 1870s the Suez Canal, the completion of the cable link to the outside world and the progressive installation of universal education – itself a stimulus to a huge market for imports as well as for some local publications – were all part of the streamlining and expansion of the trade. Melbourne's primacy and the leadership of George Robertson & Co. were the outstanding features of the model provided by the great wholesaler-importers. A warehouse holding 54,000 separate titles in 1874, regular trade sales and catalogues as well as the circulation of masses of advertising material to retail customers (including a monthly magazine), commercial travellers covering both sides of the Tasman Sea alongside branches in other colonial capitals, these were all services offered by a thorough professional who had had his own shop in Dublin before reaching Melbourne in 1852. The size of Robertson's firm should not mask the fact that he had strong rivals and competitors even in Melbourne: Samuel Mullen, also Dublin-trained and proprietor of the continent's major circulating library,[30] and the maverick E. W. Cole of the Book Arcade, which may well have been the largest bookshop in the world by the end of the century.[31] In an earlier decade Henry Tolman Dwight had dominated the second-hand and antiquarian trade in Victoria's capital.[32] The different styles and emphases of these major figures indicate how much local book-buyers could expect from their booksellers. Books could be and were freely imported from Britain, from the United States of America (provided they were not piracies) and from continental Europe. Overwhelmingly it was the imported product that was sought, despite home-grown successes like *Cole's funny picture book*.

Detailed mapping of the extent of the sales of British titles has not really been undertaken. Discussing the arrangements Robertson made to issue from the 1860s cheap one-volume editions of works still available in London only in their three-volume form, Petherick notes that 'several thousand copies were sold' of Farrar's *Life of Christ*. Contending with the much smaller Tasmanian market

---

30 Kirsop, 'From Curry's to Collins Street'.
31 Turnley, *Cole of the Book Arcade* and Kirsop, 'Cole's Book Arcade'.
32 McLaren, *Henry Tolman Dwight*.

of the 1880s and 1890s – the island's population was 133,791 in 1885 – the Walches reported various highlights: an order on 23 July 1888 for five hundred copies of the cheap edition of *Robert Elsmere* by Mrs Humphry Ward, whose local connection was played up; 250 copies in June 1890 of the sixpenny edition of Bellamy's *Looking backward*. It was symptomatic both of the requirement for cheapness and of a growing patriotism that there was a 'Special Cheap Edition of Five Thousand issued for the Colonies' of Sir Julius Vogel's *Anno Domini 2000; or; woman's destiny.*

The question of the access of American piracies to the Australian market was hotly debated in the nineteenth century. Robertson in protectionist Victoria was a stout defender of British copyrights as far afield as New Zealand, but free-trading New South Wales was suspected of being quite lax. If the Imperial Copyright Act of 1842 cut off Australian 'reprints' like the *Pickwick papers* (Launceston: Dowling, 1838-9)[33] and *Charles O'Malley, the Irish dragoon* (Sydney: Baker, 1842-3)[34] in the longer term, later breaches in the form of illicit imports are much harder to document because of the disappearance of nineteenth-century Victorian customs records. What is clear is that in societies where book lending was done through modest mechanics' institutes rather than prosperous circulating libraries there was an insistent demand for cheap editions of recent literature.

The push to attract and provide for the widest possible public was an integral part of the crusade of Redmond Barry,[35] presiding genius of the Melbourne Public Library from its foundation in 1854 till his death in 1880, on behalf of libraries everywhere in the colony. Though his favourite creation was Australia's major collection until well into the twentieth century, it lent boxes of books to inland towns, large and small, which all shared in a book culture of a notably democratic temper from before 1850 onwards. Barry and his peers, men like Sir Charles Nicholson and Sir George Grey,[36] saw no contradiction in working for the public good while being discriminating collectors in traditional European fields for the benefit of institutions in Sydney, Cape Town and Auckland. The local antiquarian trade began to take shape in the first gold rush decade, with clear signs that the collection of Australiana would become a major interest. The career of David Scott Mitchell (1836-1907)[37] showed that a colonial – born, bred and of constant residence in Sydney – could become an internationally significant bibliophile and inspire emulators like Alexander

33 Craig, *The Van Diemen's Land edition of* The Pickwick Papers.
34 Kirsop, 'Baker's Juvenile Circulating Library'.   35 Galbally, *Redmond Barry*.
36 Kerr, *Amassing treasures for all times*.
37 Ellis, 'Truth and fiction: the bequest of David Scott Mitchell'.

Turnbull in New Zealand.[38] An annotated Melbourne auction catalogue of 1891 in the State Library of Victoria documents the advance in prices of many items of Australiana during these decades.

In the late 1880s, a generation after Murray's ultimately abortive Colonial and Home Library[39] and somewhat in advance of the collapse of the three-decker in 1894, Macmillan launched a major new special series aimed at readers outside Britain. The colonial edition, a formula taken up eventually by many firms, was to have a significant role in the Australasian market before 1914, although it did not supplant arrangements that allowed Robertson, Cole and others to badge British publications, for example those of Walter Scott of Tyneside, as their own. From 1888 Scott had his own representative, John Lothian, in Melbourne.[40] Above all, as was recognised in a sharp and perceptive editorial in *Walch's Literary Intelligencer and General Advertiser* in July 1886, Macmillan's initiative was an admission that the colonial customers mattered commercially. The public had access to cheaper books, and more quickly than under earlier arrangements, but the writers, with many Australian residents among them, had to be content with reduced royalties.

The discovery of Australian and New Zealand book-buyers lay behind the progressive return of agencies and branches of British firms to Sydney and Melbourne from the late 1870s onwards. By the time of the 1892 crash George Robertson & Co. no longer dominated distribution in the old way, a parallel to the decline of the wholesaler-importers in many other branches of business in the last two decades of the century. With the Net Book Agreement of 1899 and the retreat of free trade, Australasian distributors were to become subservient to the interests of British publishers, a state of affairs enshrined legislatively in the Commonwealth of Australia Copyright Act of 1912 and symbolised by the closure of *Walch's Literary Intelligencer* three years later.

WK

India

By 1800 printing in the European fashion with movable type had been known in India for two and a half centuries, but a printing industry of any description was yet to develop. Printing was generally used by missionaries and administrators, but was largely unknown to the common people. Post-1800 we see this rapidly change. Printing becomes an industry first in Bengal, then in rapid succession

---

38 McCormick, *Alexander Turnbull*.   39 Fraser, 'John Murray's Colonial and Home Library'.
40 Sayers, *The company of books*; Turner, *The Walter Scott Publishing Company*.

in Bombay, Madras and Sri Lanka (where the Dutch used it), then in the United Provinces, Punjab, Central Provinces, Hyderabad and beyond.

In Bombay by 1812 Fardunji Marzaban's press had printed the first Gujarati almanac.[41] A company report of 1832 stated that of the books and tracts printed at the Elphinstone Institute in Bombay, 234 were disposed of in Surat, of which nine were bought by village schoolmasters and the remainder distributed in the city. Books on arithmetic were the most likely to sell, but piles of books were mouldering in all warehouses because they were too expensive.[42] Ganpathi Krishnaji brought out the first Marathi periodical in Bombay, *Digdarshan*, in 1840, followed by Bhau Mahajan in 1843 with *Prabhakar*.[43]

The first Bengali book in Bengal, Nathaniel Brassey Halhed's *Grammar of the Bengali language*,[44] appeared in 1778, and was printed with Bengali types designed and produced by Charles Wilkins and Panchanan Karmakar, on a press in Hooghly.[45] Subsequently Charles Wilkins brought his types to Calcutta and reprinted the book at the Honourable Company's Press, begun by James Augustus Hickey in 1780. There was a rapid proliferating of English-language newspapers run by expatriates in Calcutta, and these printed all manner of news including scurrilous rumour, culminating in Governor General Richard Wellesley's restricting ordinance on the Indian newspaper press in 1799. This stayed materially in force till Charles Metcalf repealed it in 1835, but not before it had finished off Ram Mohan Roy's Persian newspaper *Mirat-ul-Akhbar* and James Silk Buckingham's *Calcutta Journal* in 1823. Ram Mohan Roy and five others presented a plea which they titled the 'Areopagitica of the Indian Press' to the Supreme Court. Having fought his case all the way to the Privy Council, Roy was forced to close; in the final issue he cited as forerunners both Milton and Hafiz.[46]

---

41 See for instance Kesavan, *History of printing and publishing in India*, pp. 14–30. Most of the early titles are no longer extant, the earliest surviving book, the *Compendio Spiritual da Vida Christi*, dating to 1561. See also Radha Prasad Gupta, 'Chhapakhana: Chin Theke Chinsurah (The printing press: from China to Chinsurah)', in Bandyopadhyay (ed.), *Dui shotoker Bangla mudron ō prōkashon*, pp. 18–19, and Priolkar, *The printing press in India*, pp. 2–6, 71–3. For the British background and its relationship to Indian printing to about 1800, see Ogborn, *Indian ink*.

42 Report of the 'Sudder Dewanny Adawlet', *Parliamentary Papers* 1832.ix, p. 288.

43 Veena Naregal, 'Vernacular culture and political formation in western India', in Chakravorty and Gupta (eds.), *Print areas*, p. 153.

44 The first printed Bengali in the world is probably in the *China Illustrata*, published in 1667 in Amsterdam, where, however, the Bengali text is printed from blocks and serves as an illustration. A handful of 'incunabula' containing Bengali appeared from various European presses till 1778, but none of them used movable type cast from matrices. Barun Kumar Mukhopadhyay, 'Bangla mudroner char jug' (The four ages of Bengali printing), in Bandyopadhyay (ed.), *Dui shotoker Bangla mudron ō prōkashon*, p. 89. Also see Kesavan, *History of printing and publishing in India*, p. 182.

45 Barun Kumar Mukhopadhyay, 'Bangla mudroner char jug', p. 90.

46 Sripantho (Nikhil Sarkar), 'Tolōwar bonam kolōm: prothom shotōborshō' (Sword vs. pen: the first hundred years), in Bandyopadhyay (ed.), *Dui shotoker Bangla mudron ō prōkashon*, pp. 130–5.

After Hickey's ejection the Company Press, now under Wilkins, produced Bengali translations of important Acts and a vocabulary of English and
'Bangalee', as well as Company notices, handbooks, publications of the Asiatic
Society (established 1784) and official reports. Many periodical presses such
as the *Calcutta Gazette* Press, *Chronicle* Press and *India Gazette* Press also produced books, a side business that became more significant once Wellesley's
crackdown limited the saleability of news.

The Baptist Mission Press had been putting out Bengali publications since
1800. While working for an indigo planter, William Carey had translated
the New Testament into Bengali. His plans to print it were scuttled by the
Company's antipathy to dissenting missionaries, which forced him to shift
to Srirampur, a Danish colony. There the new press, joined by Panchanan
Karmakar, began to produce Carey's Bible, a Bengali translation of *Pilgrim's
progress* (1802); Krittibas's *Ramayana* (a popular Bengali transcreation of the
original Sanskrit epic) and the first four parts of Kashiram's *Mahabharata* (1803),
as well as Bengali textbooks for the mission's schools.[47] Carey criticised the
textbooks used at Fort William College as too 'uniform and monotonous' to
interest young minds.[48] From 1817 the Baptist Mission Press regularly did jobs
for the Calcutta School Book Society (CSBS).[49] In 1818, the Baptists began
two Bengali periodicals, *Digdarshan* and *Samachar Darpan*, aimed at providing
useful information on science, current affairs, administration and history to
the youth.[50] In 1821 the CSBS bought 61,250 copies of *Digdarshan*.[51] In 1820,
the Baptist Mission Press set up the first captive paper mill in India to be powered by steam, after a labourer was accidentally killed in the treadmill where
relays of forty men were used to tread the raw material for paper making.[52]
Between 1800 and 1832 the Baptist Mission Press printed 212,000 volumes
in forty languages. In 1832 the CSBS published thirty-nine major titles and
a huge number of smaller textbooks in English and Indian languages.[53] The

---

The first Persian, Urdu and Hindi newspapers in India were produced in Calcutta between 1821
and 1822. Persian was then the language of the Bengali elite. Ram Mohan Roy was a prolific writer
in it but unfortunately most of his Persian works have been lost.

47 Shishir Kumar Das, 'Shahebder thakur' (The Englishman's idol), in Bandyopadhyay (ed.), *Dui
shotoker Bangla mudron ō prōkashon*, pp. 71–2. The title refers to the reaction of the natives of
Madnabati when Carey's press arrived: watching his rapturous reception of it they thought it was
his god!

48 *Ibid.*, p. 73.   49 Sripantho 'Tolōwar bonam kolōm', p. 135.

50 Das, 'Shahebder thakur', p. 74.

51 *Parliamentary Papers* 1831–2.ix, Appendix I, p. 449. The entire list is given here.

52 Priolkar, *The printing press in India*, pp. 69–70. It was a 12-horsepower engine by Thwaites &
Rothwell of Bolton, and drew crowds of Indians and Europeans alike.

53 *Parliamentary Papers* 1831–2.ix, Appendix I, p. 449. The entire list is given here.

CSBS was active in promoting illustration, very necessary for children's texts; from 1825, lithography became a popular way of producing pictures for sale as well as illustrating books.[54]

From the mid-1830s the CSBS's output declined, as it could no longer compete with commercial publishers. In 1885, Maurice Macmillan heard that the Calcutta School Book Society had gone bankrupt at the hands of an adventurer called Brown and was up for sale. Negotiations with the Bengal Department of Public Instruction fell through, but in 1910 Macmillan made another offer for the CSBS which was accepted. The CSBS was bought, renamed the Indian School Supply Depot and put under the management of M. Graham Brash. However, in the 1920s Brash quarrelled with Macmillan and left to go native in Lucknow and marry an Indian. In 1934 Brash started Allied Publishers, and in 1947 it was taken over by R. N. Sachdeva and turned into one of the biggest book wholesalers in India.

By 1807 the first totally native press in Calcutta, owned and operated by Babu Ram in Kidderpore, was printing Hindi and Sanskrit books for Fort William College, by which Babu Ram was said to have earned lakhs of rupees.[55] A decade later Gangakishor Bhattacharya was printing the first Bengali periodicals. Around 1815 the first printer (probably Biswanath Deb) set up shop under a banyan tree (Bat-tala) in the Shobhabazar area, laying the foundations of the popular Bat-tala Press. Little is known about the origins of the presses here, since the early Bat-tala books were printed in imitation of palm leaf manuscripts, in 'landscape' format on a long page, bound at the top margin and without copyright notice. It was legally required for periodicals to carry the name and address of the printer, but not books until 1867.[56] Most of the Bat-tala output was religious or cultic texts, often dealing with the Indian erotic sublime (with appropriate illustrations), some of which earned them the reputation of being pornographers. The truth was more complex, as the rigid English division between secular and sacred was unknown in India. The presses also printed Perso-Bengali texts such as *Gulebakaoli*, *Hatim Tai* and *Yusuf-Zuleikha*; almanacs and manuals; and pictures and texts lampooning the manners of westernised babus consumed by the educated lower middle class. Collections of obscene songs sung on wedding nights by women, called *basorghorer gan*, were also popular, and much of the Bat-tala readership comprised women, even women from upper-class households. Organisations like

54 Mukhopadhyay, 'Bangla mudroner char jug', p. 99.
55 *Ibid.*, p. 95, and Shaw, *Printing in Calcutta*.
56 Sukumar Sen, 'Bat-talar boi' (Bat-tala books), in Bandyopadhyay (ed.), *Dui shotoker Bangla mudron ō prōkashon*, p. 270.

the Brahmo Samaj, influenced by European disgust, campaigned to 'clean up' Bengali literature and life, and saw little to recommend in the Bat-tala books.[57]

The 1830s saw the spread of printing to north India. A feature of presses there was the widespread use of lithography, since many of the texts used the Perso-Arabic script for which the cutting of type that can match the sinuous beauty of calligraphy is a very difficult and expensive business. So the preferred method here was to have a skilled calligrapher write the script (laterally inverted, of course) on a litho stone, and print from there. Lucknow, Benares and Kanpur became centres of printing, barring a slight hiccup in Lucknow in 1849 when something in a history of the royal family angered the Nawab of Oudh, who banished printing and printers from the city for a few years.[58] The Newal Kishore Press was established in 1858 by the journalist Neval Kishore Bhargava and printed on the latest European presses. They were particularly noted for their Koran printing. In the second half of the nineteenth century, with the spread of British rule up the Ganges valley, the cantonment towns of Meerut, Allahabad, Agra and Bareilly acquired nascent printing industries, as well as some pilgrimage centres like Mathura and Gorakhpur. Missionaries also brought presses with them as they pushed north and west into the Punjab. The output of these presses included the kind of hybrid literature Bengal was producing, as well as Urdu *qissas*, *dastans* (tales and exploits) and *masnavis* (long poems). Calcutta proved to be a rich source for translatable literature and in the early twentieth century certain genres, like popular Bengali detective thrillers, acquired Urdu and Hindi cousins.

As the printing industry grew, the lack of adequate copyright legislation was felt more keenly, and after representations from various colonial authorities the Act of 10 & 11 Vict. c.95, 1847 was passed and ratified for each British colony and territory, including India.[59] But this law was to prove inadequate for India in a mere decade. In 1857 for one year there was a return to the policy of muzzling the press and again in 1878 with the Vernacular Press Act (repealed 1881). Copyright was updated in 1914 with the Indian Copyright Act (similar to the 1911 British Act with significant differences regarding translation). The Rowlatt Acts tried to impose censorship in 1919, with little success. Post-Independence, the 1955 Copyright Act (amended 1995) updated the 1914 Act.[60]

---

57 Ghosh, 'Cheap books, "bad" books'.   58 Orsini, 'Publishing in nineteenth century Benares'.
59 Nowell-Smith, *International copyright law*, p. 26. The Foreign Reprints Act of 1847 was a restating of the Copyright Act of 1842 (5 & 6 Vict., c.45).
60 For more on Indian copyright see Chatterjee, 'Pirates and philanthropists'. See also Bently, 'Copyright, translations, and relations'.

Akshay Kumar Datta, the first editor of the *Tattvabodhini Potrika* (begun 1843), the official organ of the Brahmo Samaj, was like Ram Mohan Roy a wealthy man who could publish his own books, a pattern very common in nineteenth-century Bengal. Several of his books were written 'in the shadow of' English texts. For instance, his *Bajhyobostur shohit manobprokritir shombondho bichar* was based on George Coombe's *The constitution of man*, and his *Bharotborsher upashok somproday* on Horace Hayman Wilson's *The religious sects of the Hindus*. But these were not exactly translations as he freely adapted, argued with and moulded his material, as many who came after were to do as well. Moreover he acted as an important conduit for the entry of European ideas into the Bengali public space.[61]

In 1852 Bengal's first bibliographer, the Rev. James Long, published a list of Bengali books which was to be the first of a series of increasingly detailed catalogues that endeavoured to keep track of a rapidly expanding body of works – an enterprise redoubled by the 1857 war. Long then ruffled feathers by facilitating the translation into English of Dinabandhu Mitra's anti-indigo play *Nil Darpan*, originally printed in 1860 in Dhaka by Ramchandra Bhowmik. The English version made its way to London, raising a clamour for reform of the indigo plantations, and Long was fined for libel in 1861 and jailed for a month. It is believed that Long's case led to the passing of Act no. 25 of 1867 governing the registration of Indian publications. This Act required a copy of every book printed within an administrative area to be deposited with the District Magistrate, and sent on to the Libraries of Record in the Presidencies. In return, copyright would be legally secured to the author and publisher, who had to be named. The Registers so generated, now held by the British Library, contain a wealth of information about Indian printing.

Ishwar Chandra Vidyasagar set up the Sanskrit Press and Depository (i.e. bookshop) with Madan Mohan Tarkalankar in 1847 with a loan of 600 rupees; his first titles were Bharat Chandra Ray's *Annadamangal* for which his copytext was a rare manuscript owned by the Krishnanagar *zamindars*, and the *Betal panchabingshati* (Twenty-five tales of a vampire). Madan Mohan Tarkalankar began in 1849 an illustrated series for children, *Shishu shiksha* (A child's lessons), the third number of which was Bidyasagar's *Bodhodoy* (Dawning comprehension, 1850). In 1855 came Bidyasagar's *Borno porichoy* (An introduction to the alphabet), the most famous Bengali primer ever. These books were designed to displace the ubiquitous *Shishubodhak*, *Ballobodh*, *Bornobodh* and other popular

61 Nirmalyo Acharya, 'Bangla godder dui shotabdi' (Two centuries of Bengali prose), in Bandyopadhyay (ed.), *Dui shotoker Bangla mudron ō prōkashon*, p. 230.

textbooks, often written by many hands, which were rag-bag compendia of folk tales, proverbs, rules for negating curses, *shlokas* from the *Arthashastra*, and other edifying fragments.[62] Bidyasagar undertook a much-needed reform of Bengali typography; he rationalised it into an alphabet of twelve vowels and forty consonants. He also grappled with the problem of 'joined letters' without success.[63] In 1857 the Sanskrit Press printed 84,200 copies of its books, against the CSBS's 32,000.[64] Unlike most of the reformers of the day, he had no personal wealth to subsidise his projects. The Sanskrit Press provided him with a platform from which he could launch his campaigns for widow remarriage and women's upliftment. Although the first autobiography in Bengali, *Amar jibon*, was by a woman, Rash Sundari Devi, women writers were not common till the last decades of the nineteenth century, though the spread of education meant women readers became more plentiful.

The 1850s saw a new kind of publishing – playscripts. These were not, in the main, intended to be acted. The earliest printed playscripts date from the 1820s, but they are barebones renditions of popular *jatras* such as *Vidyasundar* (originally an epic poem by Bharat Chandra Ray). The *jatra* incorporated music, recitation and dance, so could hardly be reduced to a text. This decade also saw a number of Bengali translations of classical Sanskrit plays. But in the 1850s playwrights began consciously to write in the European mode, with acts and scenes. In most cases, these plays were too stiff to be acted, but in the hands of men like Ramnarayan Tarkaratna they became vehicles for debate over widow remarriage, polygamy, the age of consent, women's education and so on, such that 'plays and novels' became the traditionalist formula for decadent modern literature.

Peary Chand Mitra's *Alaler Ghorer Dulal* (The spoilt child of a rich father, 1857) is often cited as one of the first stories in colloquial Bengali prose. Mitra had entered the world of print by co-publishing the journal *Mashik Potrika* (started 1854) with Radhanath Shikdar, and he had written a number of essay collections and a life of the educationist David Hare. *Hutom Pyanchar Noksha* (The barn owl's tale) by Kali Prasanna Sinha was published in 1862. It is a deliciously scandalous picture of the profligate society of the time, told in a world-weary tone at once scatological and sophisticated.

By 1860 a new generation of graduates from the universities was to be the powerhouse of an unprecedented public explosion of debate, thought and

---

62 Nikhil Sarkar, 'Adijuger patthopustak' (Early textbooks), in Bandyopadhyay (ed.), *Dui shotoker Bangla mudron ō prōkashon*, pp. 172–4.
63 Mukhopadhyay, 'Bangla mudroner char jug', p. 101; Ross, *The printed Bengali character*, pp. 129–30.
64 Nikhil Sarkar, 'Adijuger Pathhopustak', p. 167.

creativity, known as the Bengal Renaissance. For instance, the man who was single-handedly to establish the novel as a Bengali art form, Bankim Chandra Chattopadhyay, also edited *Banga Darshan* (started 1872), a journal through which he could comment on affairs as they happened and guide and admonish his community of followers. One of the contributors was the young Hara Prasad Shastri.

By the 1870s the spread of primary education in both English and the vernaculars had created a huge book market. The Bat-tala presses had added notebooks and 'keys' to their popular repertoire, as well as a little piracy of 'set' textbooks. Calcutta was the entrepôt for English books headed west to Lucknow, Allahabad, Delhi and the Punjab, north to Assam and the north-eastern states or south to Orissa and the Nizamate of Hyderabad, while Bombay served the western coast and east Africa, and Madras served the south including many princely states. Indian wholesalers kept a close eye on the British book market, getting all the latest publications including periodicals such as *Chambers's Journal* within eighteen months (reduced to six months after the opening of the Suez Canal in 1869). Coursebooks for government schools *c.*1852 included Shakespeare, Milton, Johnson, Bacon, Goldsmith, Gray, Addison and Pope, as well as histories of Greece, Horace Wilson's *Universal history*, Adam Smith's *Moral sentiments*, Abercrombie's *Intellectual powers* and William Whewell's *Moral philosophy*. Missionary schools tended to include more poetry and less history and natural philosophy, as well as little books from the London Tract and Book Society.[65] Thomas Nelson's Royal Readers were used in English schools in Bengal, but they were unpopular because they were very 'English', containing references to 'birds' nesting' and May fairs (some educationists preferred them for that reason). Peary Churn Sircar's Reading Books, originally published by Thacker & Spink of Calcutta (a branch of W. Thacker & Co.), were prepared to replace the Royal Readers and later taken over by Macmillan. Thacker was one of the best-known 'Anglo-Indian' booksellers in India; its headquarters was 2 Newgate Street, London. Another Anglo-Indian firm was A. H. Wheeler & Co., which had bookshops in most of the major railway stations in north India and was known as the 'W. H. Smith' of India. Wheeler was a collaboration set up in 1887 between Emile Moreau, T. K. Banerjee, two Englishmen and another Indian; since 1950 Banerjee's heirs have owned it. A. H. Wheeler now has 258 railway bookshops, but its exclusive right to serve the railway is gone. Higginbotham's Bookstore, established in 1844 in Madras, was another such important outlet for European books.

65 Vishwanathan, 'The ideology of literary education in British India 1813–1880'.

In 1875, the Sircar readers passed to Macmillan, forming the foundation of Macmillan's first series of textbooks for Indian schools. Sircar's Reading Books sold at least 3 million copies up to the 1930s and taught English to a whole generation of Bengalis. J. C. Nesfield's Anglo Oriental Readers (originally published by the Wesleyan Mission Press of Lucknow, taken over in 1891 by Macmillan) did for northern India what Sircar's Reading Books had done for Bengal. In 1874 Alexander Macmillan had published the Rev. Lal Behary Day's *Folktales of Bengal* and *Govinda Samanta* (later titled *Bengal peasant life*).[66]

Alexander Macmillan had close ties with Cambridge men who went out to teach in India, and his position as Publisher to the University of Oxford from 1863 to 1880 put him in touch with F. T. Palgrave. Palgrave's *Golden treasury* was first published in 1861, and though it first appeared in an edition for Indian schools in 1885, it was a popular textbook long before that. Macmillan also published Hall & Knight's *Algebra* and Hall & Stevens's *Geometry*, still used today. In 1886 Maurice Macmillan took over the Indian operation and began Macmillan's Colonial Library[67] and Macmillan's English Classics for Indian Universities, which included Scott, Shakespeare, Samuel Smiles, Bacon and Milton. Books were also commissioned from Indian educationists, including Ashutosh Mukhopadhyay and Gopal Krishna Gokhale. Macmillan began to issue textbooks in many Indian languages simultaneously: a European would produce an English manuscript, which was copied and sent out to an army of Indian translators. The English manuscript was usually not published: it was a template for the Indian-language textbooks. Macmillan also won an exclusive contract to print Bombay Presidency's vernacular textbooks from 1904 to 1926.

It was also in 1886 that Rudyard Kipling began to publish his work. He was then on the staff of the *Civil and Military Gazette*, a small Anglo-Indian newspaper based in Lahore, where Kipling's father was the principal of the Government Art College. Kipling printed *Departmental ditties* and the collection that later became *Plain tales from the hills* on the *Gazette*'s press. In 1887 he transferred to the *Pioneer* newspaper in Allahabad, where he produced six more collections of short stories. He left the *Pioneer*'s staff over a dispute and sailed to England in 1889. His works were widely read by the British in India and formed a staple of the club and cantonment libraries dotted over Britain's Indian possessions. The various Colonial Libraries (the first being Macmillan's,

---

66 Macmillan Archive, General Letterbook Series, British Library MS Add. 55396, fo. 637, Alexander Macmillan to Rev. Lal Behari Day, 15 December 1874.

67 For an account of colonial libraries in India, see Joshi, *In another country*, and Chatterjee, 'Far flung fiction'.

begun 1886, see above) published cheap fiction for this market, and in fact these books were treated as contraband in metropolitan Britain; this was to protect the higher prices of books in Britain. Sales of the Libraries were surprisingly good and were largely though not exclusively expatriate European.

Oxford University Press published many Indological titles in the nineteenth century, such as the Sacred Books of the East and the Rulers of India series. Friedrich Max Müller, Sir William Markby and Sir William Wilson Hunter showed a keen interest in OUP's India affairs. From 1906 onwards, commercial travellers were sent out every year to India, until in 1912 E.V. Rieu set up the Indian Branch in Bombay.[68] Their first Indian titles were Sarvepalli Radhakrishnan's *Essentials of psychology* and J. N. Farquhar's *The crown of Hinduism*. The new Branch weathered World War I and set up branch offices in Calcutta and Madras. Blackie was also active in India, especially Bombay, and published one blockbuster title, Wren & Martin's *Grammar*. P. C. Wren was later to write *Beau Geste*.

By the 1910s, subsequent to Lord Curzon's controversial criticism of Indian education, an overhaul was under way. Books such as the *Panchatantra* were now favoured over European texts for children in some centres. There was also a feeling that old cultures were in danger. In this context one has to see the publication of Dakshina Ranjan Mitra Majumdar's pathbreaking *Thakurmar Jhuli* (Grandma's tales) in 1901, with a foreword by Rabindranath Tagore. Tagore was never entirely satisfied with the commercial printing of his works, and part of his plan for a World University in Santiniketan, to which he assigned his copyrights, included a publications division. The Tagore family was also remarkable (like many Brahmin families) for producing pioneer women writers.

The printing and publishing house of Upendra Kishore Ray (Choudhury; his son dropped this from his surname), U. Ray & Sons, did for the twentieth century what the Sanskrit Press did for the nineteenth. Upendra Kishore began in 1913 the whimsical and innovative children's periodical *Sandesh*. He pioneered a new method of half-tone printing, but failed to gain recognition for it, having been anticipated by a printer in St Petersburg. Sukumar Ray's books of nonsense verse carried on the Ray legacy, and he became editor of *Sandesh* after his father's death in 1915, but tragically died at the age of 36 in 1923. The journal shut down shortly afterwards and was revived thirty years later by Satyajit Ray, whose contribution to literature and film is too well known to need recounting here.[69]

---

68 See Chatterjee, *Empires of the mind*.
69 Lila Majumdar, 'Chhotoder jonno boi' (Books for children), in Bandyopadhyay (ed.), *Dui shotoker Bangla mudron ō prōkashon*, pp. 244–6.

Statistics gathered by the various Departments of Public Instruction show that the numbers of children in primary education rose steeply in the early twentieth century, and new universities came up all over northern India.[70] There were small scholarly presses such as Shams ul Ulama Zakaullah of Delhi, who won a case in 1894 against Macmillan regarding the translation of mathematics textbooks.[71] There were presses such as S. K. Lahiri & Co., run by scions of aristocratic families (Lahiri's grandfather was Ramtanu Lahiri, an important Brahmin reformer). There were booksellers such as D. B. Taraporevala, who traded not only all over India's western coast but in east Africa as well. There were firms like Radhabai Atmaram Sagoon of Bombay, run by a woman. There were missionary presses, like the centuries-old SPCK at Vepery near Madras, the YMCA Press in Calcutta (established 1857) and the Basle Mission Press at Mangalore. There were presses which printed nationalist, revolutionary or seditious material, often underground outfits functioning in secret locations. There was a flourishing used-book market that was regularly cursed by British publishers for cutting into demand, and there was a notorious grey market where keys, epitomes, unauthorised translations, notebooks and crib books circulated. In 1914 India acquired a comprehensive copyright law which recognised the peculiarities of the Indian system, and the general political and national awakening after the First World War was to fuel further the growth of India's publishing industry.

RBC

---

70 See Chatterjee, 'How India took to the book'.   71 See Chatterjee, 'Pirates and philanthropists'.

18

Second-hand and old books

DAVID MCKITTERICK

The world of old books ranged from the waste paper of the dung heap to the wariness and snobberies of private collectors; and many more old books reached the former than reached the shelves of the latter. Here was one self-confessed bibliomaniac's view:

> When the *Hatton Library* was sold, Mr. Sheaf, of Ipswich in Suffolk, paid for as many books as loaded two waggons and a cart only 30*l*., and many of the MSS. were literally thrown to the dunghill . . .
>
> Nothing is much more to be regretted than such a gothic disregard to the interests of literature, unless it be the selfish and narrowminded principle of exclusion, which renders many valuable and interesting collections either inaccessible, or what is tantamount to it, only to be obtained through such cringing servility and teasing importunity as few men of real genius or talents can descend to practise.[1]

Ideally, the history of books is concerned as much with what has been thrown away as what has been kept, though since the former is difficult to evaluate emphasis naturally falls on the latter. Just how far one was from the other – and not only in 1831, when these words were written – is reflected in the choice here of the word 'gothic' to denote unregenerate ignorance. The appreciation of old books was a self-consciously modern occupation. It depended on knowledge of editions, of literary history and of rarity.

Most of this volume is concerned with new books, their manufacture, sale, reception and use.[2] Yet most books in circulation, to say nothing of those in libraries, were not new. The market in new books was always affected by those that were available second-hand. The large circulating libraries, led by Mudie's, relied for their reputations on being able to supply new titles immediately on publication, to whoever demanded them. As excitement fell away, so the many

---

1 Letter signed 'A Bibliomaniac', *Gentleman's Magazine* 100.1 (1831), p. 586.
2 But see also pp. 620–2.

extra copies that were initially needed could be sold off, either to other smaller libraries, or to individuals, or to booksellers. In the mid-1890s, for example, Mudie's were offering novels by R. M. Ballantyne, Besant and Rice, R. D. Blackmore, M. E. Braddon, James Grant, Mrs Henry Wood and others, all of whom were enjoying heavy demand in the new books market as well. Nor was it only fiction. The International Scientific Series and the series of English Men of Letters also figured among these bargains. The thousands of recent books available in this way, like the huge and well-organised trade in remainders and overstocks, make it difficult to link printing and publication figures to the real scale of purchasing demand for the most-read authors.

For every new book, there were many thousands of old ones in circulation, neither new nor current, from carefully preserved bibliophile copies to the rag-bags on market stalls, the penny boxes outside second-hand booksellers' shops, the assortments of old printed matter lurking amongst the detritus of junk shops, and the trash of the so-called 'hand-sellers', supplied from Ireland and large conurbations with odd or imperfect volumes.[3] The simple need of households to dispose of books meant that every town of any size had its second-hand shop; and these were organised on quite different principles from those selling new books. Where the latter had to attract custom by careful displays, the used-book trade could not afford such luxuries. Books spread from the packed shelves to floors, staircases and the darkest corners, they stayed in stock often for decades, and they tended always to increase in numbers. Overcrowding was even a virtue, since it might signify a large, and possibly rich, stock.[4] Books are not like most other commodities. Their useful lives can spread over generations, and they fall in and out of use. Their financial values fall and rise, and fall again. Though writing a little later, Arnold Bennett, in *Riceyman steps* (1923), eloquently portrayed the confused, overpowering and often dirty accumulations that characterised hundreds of the less prosperous second-hand shops by the early twentieth century. Ever since early in the nineteenth century it had been customary to laud technological progress in the printing trades, and to wonder at a world so well supplied with reading matter. The outfall was in the second-hand trade. The natural reluctance to discard what might have some value, whether residual or as an investment, meant that it was only with the waste-paper drives in the world wars of the twentieth century, and with the late twentieth-century escalation in property

---

3 'Felix Folio', *The hawkers and street dealers of the north of England manufacturing districts* (Manchester [1858?], pp. 78–80.
4 Brown and Brett, in *The London bookshop*, portray a trade still exhibiting many features of the pre-1914 world.

values that drove booksellers to close shops, followed by the development of Web-based sales, that this trade was irrevocably changed.

In this trade, whether books are referred to as antiquarian or merely second-hand, or described on a scale of rarity ranging from unique to the equivalent of waste paper, all have a value that depends on demand. But demand varies according to fashion, current events or debate, and the extent to which they can be met. Whatever the price level, it depends on customers' interest, and their willingness and ability to spend. The following pages are concerned with such questions as they apply to older printed books, and the ways in which such books impinged on new ones. They are not concerned with manuscripts medieval or modern. These have their own trajectories, which during this period include a developing and gradually better-informed taste for illuminated manuscripts, culminating in the work of (for example) M. R. James and Sydney Cockerell.[5] Nor are they concerned with collecting manuscripts. In this, the name of Sir Thomas Phillipps dominates the entire period. He was already established as a major force in 1830, and lionised by Dibdin in 1836, and his collection had been only partially dispersed by 1914. Others, such as the 4th Earl of Ashburnham, Robert Curzon, and the 25th and 26th Earls of Crawford, assembled collections of medieval manuscripts of international importance, and much of the last is now in Manchester.[6] By contrast, and as a reminder of the often divergent purposes of different collectors, John Ruskin is remembered more for his habit of cutting interesting initials out of his illuminated manuscripts than for the overall quality of his collection.

Though some booksellers had been distinguished in the trade even in the seventeenth century as dealing only in old books, in practice most dealt in both new and old; and many had a sideline as well, frequently in patent medicines but also in prints, stationery, coins and assortments of curiosities and 'antiquities'. Circulating libraries remained an essential adjunct to many bookselling businesses until the First World War and in some places until the 1950s or later still. The reign of Queen Victoria saw a large increase in the number of people able to make a living from second-hand bookselling. This was thanks partly to a growth in the numbers of those who were literate, and who sought cheap reading matter; but it was also due to increased supplies in the wake of the great rise in numbers of new books and new editions beginning in the last decades of the eighteenth century. In times of depression, the second-hand trade served as a means of discreetly raising money and also as a cheaper source

---

5 Munby, *Connoisseurs and medieval miniatures*; Pfaff, *Montague Rhodes James*; Blunt, *Cockerell*.
6 De Ricci, *English collectors of books & manuscripts*; Munby, *Phillipps studies*; Barker, *Portrait of an obsession*; Barker, *Bibliotheca Lindesiana*.

of reading. Industrial growth and prosperity encouraged the trade, though by no means all of it was on a large scale and much was little better than marginal. Of the seven second-hand book businesses in Bradford by the 1890s, two were in the covered market, while at the other extreme one had premises at three separate locations. Of ten firms in Newcastle-upon-Tyne at that time, five were in the market, and one dealt also in old china.

The increase in numbers of books in the latter part of the nineteenth century, and the increase in sales from long-established private libraries, fuelled the book trade. No bookseller in Britain rivalled Ludwig Rosenthal in Munich, who claimed in 1914 to have a stock of a million books, much of it consisting of early printing and medieval manuscripts.[7] Second-hand bookselling requires little capital to begin, and many of the shops – in Britain as in the rest of the world – were small, poorly stocked and poorly placed. Many did not last to a second generation of owner. Nonetheless, some of the firms that were to be key to the antiquarian trade in the twentieth century dated from between the 1880s and about 1910, including Commin in Bournemouth (1889), Sherratt & Hughes in Manchester (1898), Thorp in Guildford (1906) and Steedman in Newcastle-upon-Tyne (1907). In London, the story was the same.

Though many firms traded in both, distinctions between old and new bookselling became clearer during the nineteenth century. The first directory specifically of second-hand booksellers, rather than booksellers or the book trade in general, was published only in 1886 – not in London but in Nottingham. Instructively, it was intended as a link between collectors and the trade, not just for the trade's own internal relations. By the time it reached its fourth edition in 1894, now edited by James Clegg, printer in Rochdale, it was also a 'bibliophile's manual' and contained copious details of overseas booksellers as well as libraries, learned societies and suggested reading. It was in this world, international and institutional as well as private, embracing both education and recreation, that booksellers sought to place themselves, and to organise their own businesses collaboratively so as to make the most of the general trade in old as well as new books. The Antiquarian Booksellers' Association was founded only in 1906.[8] The bi-weekly *Book Finder*, established in 1890 to list books wanted or for sale, appeared in the same year as the longer-lived *Clique*, but differed from the latter in that it was available to both booksellers and bookbuyers. Advertising in its first issue was drawn from businesses from Scotland to Brighton, as well as from Canada, France and Germany. If this range proved somewhat over-optimistic, booksellers meanwhile showed themselves

7 Rosenthal (ed.), *Die Rosenthal*.   8 Mandelbrote (ed.), *Out of print and into profit*.

especially anxious to dispose of runs of periodicals: Thomas Wilson in Manchester offered the first seventy volumes of the *Quarterly Review* for four guineas, and the first sixty-one of the *Edinburgh* for 32s 6d. He was apparently cheap compared with Halewood in Preston, the first fifty-two volumes of the *Cornhill* costing £8 in Manchester, contrasting with thirty-eight volumes for £21 5s in Preston.

Besides bookshops, there were innumerable less formal ways of selling books, and particularly on stalls of all sizes, from semi-permanent structures to street barrows. They retained their clearly defined place in the commercial hierarchy even as the trade itself altered in the face of changes in supply and demand. In the mid-century, Henry Mayhew noted of those in London that

> There has been a change, and in some respects a considerable change, in the character or class of books sold at the street-stalls, within the last 40 or 50 years, as I have ascertained from the most experienced men in the trade. Now sermons, or rather the works of the old divines, are rarely seen at these stalls, or if seen, are rarely purchased. Black-letter editions are very unfrequent at street book-stalls, and it is twenty times more difficult, I am assured, for street-sellers to pick up anything really rare and curious, than it was in the early part of the century.
>
> One reason assigned for this change by an intelligent street-seller was, that black-letter or any ancient works were almost all purchased by the second-hand booksellers, who have shops and issue catalogues as they had a prompt sale for them whenever they could pick them up at book-auctions or elsewhere.[9]

Mayhew noted changes in the wares offered. Andrew Wynter, in an article first published in 1847, noted a more general development. If his description of the stall-keeper ('that sharp little face peeping out of a peep-hole between the books, like a spider watching for a heedless fly') was derogatory, contrasting the bookseller's boy deliberately with the 'presiding genius in ancient spectacles' of popular imagination, the days of stalls were clearly numbered, soon to be replaced by 'glaring plate-glass'.[10]

Meanwhile, stalls were to be found scattered across the capital city, though some localities were especially popular.[11] East of the City, Whitechapel Road and Shoreditch were well-known hunting grounds. South of the river, New Cut was favoured. But gradually much of this kind of trade gathered increasingly in Faringdon Road, above the Metropolitan Railway. Most of stallholders'

---

9 Mayhew, *London labour and the London poor* 1, p. 293; Mayhew's work was originally published in the *Morning Chronicle*, in 1849–50.

10 Wynter, 'A chapter on shop windows', repr. in his *Pictures of town & country life*.

11 Roberts, *The book-hunter in London*, pp. 149–67.

supplies came as large miscellaneous lots at auction, especially at Hodgson's and at Puttick & Simpson, though any general market was a potential source. The resulting wares were a mixture of treasures and tat. Though they sat at the outer edge of the trade, bookstalls could not be ignored – and collectors even as established as Macaulay and Gladstone were diligent purchasers at them. In the rest of the country the pattern of existence was very similar, and chance could bring the occasional triumph. In 1905, one of Gustave David's sacks of books bought in London and offered in Cambridge market included Edmond Halley's copy of the first edition of Newton's *Principia*, bought on the Faringdon Road for fourpence and sold unrecognised to the young John Maynard Keynes for just four shillings: Keynes himself seems never to have realised what he had bought.[12]

In 1830, the major London dealers in old books and manuscripts were headed by Thomas Thorpe in Bedford Street (he moved to larger and better premises in Piccadilly in 1836, and then to Covent Garden in 1849), Thomas Rodd in Great Newport Street at the foot of Long Acre, and the Quaker brothers John and Arthur Arch in the City.[13] Thomas and William Boone moved from Covent Garden to New Bond Street in 1830. Apart from the Boones, none of these firms lasted past the middle years of the century: Rodd, who had generally acted as agent for the British Museum at auction, died in 1849; Thorpe in 1851; John Arch at the age of 87 in 1853. William Boone retired in 1860. There was a clear distinction between generations. The career of C. J. Stewart, in King William Street, straddled the middle of the century: like some others in the trade he was also responsible for cataloguing major private libraries, in his case Hatfield House and that belonging to Frances Richardson Currer in Yorkshire. Joseph Lilly, whose stock at his death included at least four first folios of Shakespeare, and to whom the collector Henry Huth owed much of his library, died in 1870.[14] Henry George Bohn, whose 1841 'guinea catalogue' contained no fewer than 1,948 pages, who built up an unparalleled business in remainders, and who also founded in 1846 a successful library of reprints and of standard literature much of whose advantage lay in its uniform format, sold his second-hand stock at a series of auctions between 1868 and 1882: he died only in 1884.[15]

Of the new names, by far the most prominent was Bernhard (later Bernard) Quaritch, born in Saxony in 1819, who learned his trade in London with

12 This copy is now in King's College, Cambridge.
13 The following is based partly on Roberts, *The book-hunter in London*.
14 West, *The Shakespeare first folio: the history of the book* 1, pp. 32, 194.
15 Cordasco, *The Bohn libraries*; Lister, 'Henry George Bohn (1796–1884)'.

H. G. Bohn.[16] In 1847 he established himself on his own in Castle Street (at the southern end of what is now Charing Cross Road), until in 1860 he moved to 18 Piccadilly. Proud, immensely hard-working (he was no friend of the new-fangled bank holidays), professing a dislike of foreign countries with all the intensity of a convert, and with an encyclopaedic memory for new as well as old books, he expected as much loyalty from his customers as he liked to be thought to give to them. He was, in effect, the successor both of Rodd and of Stewart, who had acted for Cambridge University Library at auction and who retired in 1882. Long before then, Henry Bradshaw, the pioneering Cambridge librarian who transformed the collections of early printing in the University Library, had come to depend on Quaritch's skills.[17] With Quaritch's help, the Earls of Crawford built up the most ambitious private library in Britain, first in Lancashire and then at Balcarres, overlooking the Firth of Forth.[18] At auction, Quaritch bought aggressively. At the Sunderland sales in 1881–3 and at the Hamilton Palace Beckford sales in 1882–4 he spent over half the total achieved for the entire sales. This was only possible thanks to extended credit arrangements, but the auctioneers had little choice at a difficult financial period, and Quaritch was in effect supporting much of the trade. His campaign, which placed him unquestionably at the head of his profession in Britain, was no mere greed. In bidding energetically, and in believing that he could sell within a reasonable time to the new collectors who were being encouraged by colourful newspaper reports of these and other sales, he was also supporting a market where supply temporarily outstripped demand. The lessons of two generations earlier, when the market had also been over-supplied, had not been forgotten.

If Quaritch, who died in 1899, dominated, other new names were also prominent at the end of the century. F. S. Ellis, first established in 1860 in King Street, Covent Garden, and then in 1870 taking over Boone's old premises in New Bond Street, was Quaritch's nearest rival in the 1870s and early 1880s. Both firms courted the new American bibliophiles, taking stock with them on transatlantic visits: in 1890, the books taken over by Quaritch's son included the Syston Park copy of the 1459 Psalter (sold eventually to J. Pierpont Morgan), William Blake's watercolours illustrating Milton (now in San Marino), the Hamilton Palace tenth-century Gospels written in gold on purple (sold to Theodore Irwin of Oswego, who in turn sold them to Pierpont Morgan) and, not least, the original Spanish edition of the so-called Columbus letter, acquired by Quaritch in Paris only a few weeks earlier. The last did not

---

16 Barker, 'Bernard Quaritch'.
17 McKitterick, *Cambridge University Library*; Hunt, 'The view from Cambridge'.
18 Barker, *Bibliotheca Lindesiana*.

sell immediately, and it was finally bought by the Lenox Library in 1892.[19] In 1885 Ellis meanwhile sold his stock at auction and retired to Torquay, where he edited the Kelmscott Chaucer (1896) and in the same year was appointed one of William Morris's executors: he died in 1901. His nephew Gilbert Ellis (d.1902) went into partnership with R. V. Elvey, at the same address.[20] Among later arrivals, Uriah Maggs opened his first shop in Paddington in 1855, and in 1939 his descendants moved to Berkeley Square. The continuing drift to London's West End of the major second-hand booksellers was unmistakable, as book-collecting became fashionable but also as dealers sought out better or more spacious premises. The firm of Francis Edwards found large premises within five years of its founding, and remained in Marylebone High Street from 1860 onwards.

Others found it easier to afford premises between the West End and the city. Holywell Street, between St Mary le Strand and St Clement Danes, represented the opposite extreme, for many years a mixture of Grub Street, trade in old clothes and cheap bookselling.[21] Renowned as much as a survival of sixteenth-century London architecture as for its smutty books, with the adjoining Wych Street it was the base between the 1830s and the 1850s of the notorious radical publisher turned pornographer and cheap fiction publisher, William Dugdale (d.1868).[22] Holywell Street retained its reputation for the sale of smut even after it had been demolished. The change in emphasis to a slightly better class of bookselling began in the 1850s, and it became popularly known as Book-sellers' Row. By the 1860s it was home to a dozen such businesses, although as one observer noted some years later, a single owner might trade under several different styles at different addresses: the street never lost its reputation for unscrupulousness towards customers.[23] By the 1890s the names included Henry Hill, long established on the first corner, William Ridler, Mrs S. H. Lazarus and Joseph Poole (who subsequently moved to Charing Cross Road). The area was transformed with the widening of the Strand, when the decrepit buildings were demolished. Walford, David Nutt and Sotheran (whose family had been selling books in the eighteenth century in York) remained among the leading booksellers in the Strand itself during the 1890s, though Sotheran's principal shop, specially designed for antiquarian allure, was in Piccadilly.

19 Morris, 'Bernard Alfred Quaritch in America'; Quaritch and Kerney, *The Spanish Columbus letter*.
20 Smith and Benger, *The oldest London bookshop*.
21 Nead, in *Victorian Babylon*, pp. 161–89, emphasises the street's reputation in the first half of the century. See also [Burn] *The language of the walls* and, for a further view, see Roberts, *The Book-hunter in London*, pp. 227–31.
22 For Dugdale, see McCalman, *Radical underworld*, and *ODNB*.
23 Pratt, *Unknown London*, pp. 84–9.

Of the other traditional areas for bookselling, Holborn and the nearby streets remained a key until the end of our period. The old shops in Middle Row were demolished in 1867, but this scarcely affected trade. The Caxton Head Bookshop, founded in Birmingham in 1874, moved to the corner of Lower Turnstile at the end of the 1880s, and soon afterwards James Tregaskis married into the family. A little to the west was Walter T. Spencer, who specialised in the fast-developing market for modern first editions. Charing Cross Road, built as part of a programme of slum clearance in the 1880s, became a centre for second-hand bookselling within a decade. In 1886, Bertram Dobell moved from Haverstock Hill to take over the premises of Alfred Russell Smith, and eight years later he acquired a second shop on the opposite side of the road. Marrying a literary career to one in bookselling, Dobell (d.1914) identified the work of Thomas Traherne and was instrumental in the publication of James Thomson (author of *The city of dreadful night*), besides becoming one of the best sources for early-modern English literature in the capital.

The major auction houses were concentrated in London, and the major second-hand and antiquarian booksellers were mostly there as well. In the 1830s, most of the London auction trade in old books was shared between Robert Evans in Pall Mall, Sotheby & Son in Wellington Street, and Southgate in Fleet Street. Evans died in 1857, and the firm of Southgate closed in 1866. By the end of the century Sotheby's was dominant, but their rise was not always a steady one.[24] Though their rivals in the latter part of the century, Puttick & Simpson in Leicester Square and Hodgson's in Chancery Lane, tended to deal in lesser properties, both were capable of attracting important clients and both claimed a long history, since 1794 and 1807 respectively. When Dawson Turner's printed books were sold in stages, first in 1853 following his removal from Great Yarmouth to London and then most of the residue after his death, in 1859, the first sale was handled by Sotheby's, and the second by Puttick & Simpson. His celebrated collection of autographs, including several archives of national importance that were bought by the British Museum, was sold by the latter. As soon as whisper reached London that he was contemplating a sale, both Sotheby and Puttick courted him assiduously.[25] The landmark sale of the library of William Perkins in 1873 was handled at Hanworth Park by Gadsen, Ellis & Co.; and the much larger Sunderland sales in 1881–3, of books – not in the best of condition, but many of them nonetheless rare – from Blenheim Palace, were handled by Puttick & Simpson.

24 Herrmann, *Sotheby's*.   25 McKitterick, 'Dawson Turner and book collecting'.

Voraciously, London booksellers and auctioneers alike drew stock constantly in from other parts of the country. But a few businesses had capital enough to rival London, both in quantity and to some extent in quality. In Manchester, William Ford, who corresponded with many of the most prominent collectors of his day, had issued catalogues easily commensurate with the leading figures in the capital until his business contracted in the last years of his life, and he moved to Liverpool. He died in 1832. His real successor in Manchester was the firm of James and Joseph Thomson, whose catalogue of 1829 ran to about six hundred pages.[26] In the late 1830s and 1840s, difficult years for the trade in early books, two firms of London auctioneers, Southgate and Lewis, dealt with the stocks of booksellers from Lincoln, Manchester (the bankrupt stock of Bancks & Co., of Manchester, was spread over four sales in 1841–2), Lynn, Preston, Oxford, Liverpool and Cambridge, besides more from London. After the Cambridge bookseller Thomas Stevenson died, it required eight auctions in London to dispose of his stock between December 1845 and July 1847. More commonly, only the best books went to London. James Crossley, prominent alike in the early years of the Chetham Society and of Manchester Public Library, but also the greatest of all Manchester book collectors in the century, died in 1883. Sotheby's held two sales, in 1884–5, spread over sixteen days: there was a further local auction where the books took up most of seven days.[27]

In the nineteenth century the substantial private library became possible not just for the wealthy but also for thousands of people of middling income. By 1914 there were dozens of manuals offering guidance, whether to tyro collectors of early printing or to those who merely wished to possess a representative selection of the main figures of English literature and history. In their published reminiscences, collectors from Dibdin to William Carew Hazlitt had offered further assortments of advice. At every level of income, it was possible to build a library.

In 1830, a person wishing to study the bibliographical history of early English printing relied on work first published in the middle of the previous century. Joseph Ames's *Typographical antiquities* had originally appeared in 1749. Though in its revised form by Thomas Frognall Dibdin, published in 1810–19, it had been vastly extended so as to take account of the books unearthed by specialist book collectors from Richard Farmer (d.1797) to Dibdin's friend and patron Lord Spencer (d.1834), the information remained not only incomplete, but also difficult to follow in the order chosen by Ames, whose interest was

26 Slugg, *Reminiscences of Manchester fifty years ago*, p. 79.
27 Collins, ' "An eminent bibliophile and man of letters" ', pp. 150–1.

primarily in the history of printing, not of authors. By 1914, a similar person was faced with a shelf of reference books some of which have retained authority nearly a hundred years later. William Thomas Lowndes, William Blades, W. C. Hazlitt, Henry Bradshaw,[28] Edward Gordon Duff and others had not only established their subjects on new footings. In presenting a mixture of retrospective bibliography, typographical and other bibliographical analysis, and historical investigation, they had also brought to the attention of a much wider world the interest of old books as more than curiosities.

For much of the first half of the nineteenth century, by far the most influential figure in British book-collecting and bibliographical circles was Thomas Frognall Dibdin (1776–1847), whose immense authority as a bibliophile and bibliographer was founded on almost a quarter-century's collaboration with Lord Spencer.[29] In 1814 he produced a catalogue of the Spencer library, *Bibliotheca Spenceriana*, which thanks to its comprehensiveness was in the forefront of reference works on early printed books for a generation and more. It was followed by books including *The bibliographical decameron, or ten days pleasant discourse upon illuminated manuscripts, and subjects connected with early engraving, typography and bibliography* (1817), and by a *Bibliographical, antiquarian and picturesque tour in France and Germany* (1821). A self-conscious stylist, but unstoppable in the cause of old books, Dibdin was widely quoted. His leading part in the foundation in 1812 of the Roxburghe Club, a group of wealthy bibliophiles drawn from the aristocracy and commoners, added further to his status. But in the 1830s his view of the trade in older printed books was pessimistic. The dramatic successes of the Roxburghe sale had been due to a small group of enthusiasts, and over the next dozen years several large libraries were formed in its wake. Most of these proved short-lived, and their books were released back into the market at auction. In an account of visits to the principal London dealers in old books Dibdin now found a succession of booksellers apparently in despair. William Pickering, he reported, lamented that 'the Jenson and Froben-loving days are gone – never to return'. The taste for books on vellum had collapsed. The London bookseller Henry Bohn (1796–1884) was said to attribute the decline in interest to preoccupation with parliamentary reform. Thomas Thorpe, too, the most powerful bookseller of his generation, found that interest in incunabula had disappeared. With the death of major collectors such as John Dent, John North and others who had supported the

28 Needham, *The Bradshaw method*.
29 Lister, 'George John, 2nd Earl Spencer and his "librarian" '. For Dibdin's voluminous writings, see Windle and Pippin, *Thomas Frognall Dibdin*.

London market, booksellers were said to be staring at the future with long faces.[30]

Even if the situation was not quite so devastating, as Dibdin himself admitted when he reminded his readers of collectors such as the Duke of Devonshire and the Duke of Sussex, there was nonetheless a strong sense of change. The recent financial crisis in publishing, the collapse of Sir Walter Scott's fortunes, and the disappointing prices realised when the manuscripts of his novels were auctioned in 1831,[31] had their indirect effect on the mood of the trade in old books. The extraordinary price realised for the Valdarfer Boccaccio at the Roxburghe sale in 1812 had drawn attention to early printing, and helped to create a fashion for it; but that price had depended, as so often in the auction rooms, on two determined and wealthy bidders; it was not a reflection of the state of the market overall, nor could such a level be sustained. A copy of Livy, printed on vellum by Sweynheym and Pannartz in 1469, formerly belonging to the Benedictines in Milan, fetched £903 at the Edwards sale in 1815, but was bought at the Mark Masterman Sykes sale in 1824 for £472 10s and fell to only £262 10s at the John Dent sale in 1827. It was then bought by Thomas Grenville, who left it to the British Museum.

Dibdin's bibliographical books were expensive. The four volumes of his catalogue of the *Bibliotheca Spenceriana* cost eight guineas on ordinary paper, or sixteen on large; prices for his *Bibliographical decameron* were nine and fifteen guineas.[32] For those unable to afford such amounts, and for whom possession of early printed books was a dream at best, publishers paid increasing attention to providing books of reproductions, with accompanying texts of variable authority. Such books, often involving chromolithography on a large scale, could be costly to produce, and the first albums about the history of the book were mostly concerned with medieval manuscripts: Henry Shaw and Sir Frederic Madden's *Illuminated ornaments selected from manuscripts and early printed books from the sixth to the seventeenth centuries* (1830–3), J. O. Westwood's *Palaeographia sacra pictoria* (1843), and a pair of books by Henry Noel Humphreys, *The illuminated books of the middle ages* (1844–9) and *The origin and progress of the art of writing* (1853).[33] In 1867, Quaritch published Humphreys's *History of the art of printing*, initially in a limited edition, and then Sotheran followed this up with another highly illustrated album with little more than a smattering of text from the same hand, *Masterpieces of mediaeval*

30 "Mercurius Rusticus' [i.e. T. F. Dibdin], *Bibliophobia.*
31 [Dibdin] *Bibliophobia*, pp. 8–11. For details of prices and buyers at the Scott sale, see [Stirling-Maxwell] *The Scott exhibition MDCCCLXXI.*
32 Windle and Pippin, *Thomas Frognall Dibdin*, pp. 76, 100.   33 Beckwith, *Victorian bibliomania.*

printers and engravers, price either four guineas or coloured at five guineas. The fact that these books, and some others like them, were issued by some of the best-known West End antiquarian booksellers rather than by an ordinary publisher is itself not without interest, reflecting the kinds of books to which they and their customers aspired.

Though there had been various efforts, some printed and some in manuscript, at gathering the prices and values of old books, the lack of up-to-date guidance was by the 1880s a matter of inconvenience. A collector like William Carew Hazlitt could make a reasonable living by buying cheap, and selling on, in his case either to the wealthy collector Henry Huth (1815–78) or to the British Museum. But increasing numbers of collectors, and growing activity in the sale rooms, made some more systematic guidance essential. The prices in one of the most widely used of all reference books, Brunet's *Manuel du libraire et de l'amateur des livres* (1810; 5th edn 1860–5, supplement 1878–80) were out of date, and misleading. When in 1887 the publishers Elliot Stock launched *Book prices current*, both collectors and the trade were for the first time provided with records of recent sales, and thus with the means for comparisons and for measuring investments. Slater himself emphasised the importance of averages of prices recorded in the accumulating volumes, though inevitably attention focussed on the higher ones. Most country auctions remained uncharted, and they in particular were prey to dishonest and immoral trade practices that have persisted.[34]

Book collecting, and especially collecting old books, could both serve a moral purpose and provide an investment. Books became furnishings. The ornate cloth bindings of new books made the point at once, though the desire among some collectors of older books to enhance the appearance of their libraries was traceable long before Samuel Pepys had spent money on gilt-decorated spines in the late seventeenth century. The nineteenth-century bookbinding trade offered an ever-growing range of qualities of leather or pseudo-leather bindings, at prices to suit and with ever more emphasis on gilt decoration. Books were literally packaged. W. J. Loftie, antiquary, advocate for unrestored churches, and amateur, pleaded for art not just for the 'manifest prudence' of making collections, but also for its 'civilising effects of taste upon young persons, the pleasure of pursuing an object, and, generally, the economical value of art training both to the individual, the family, and the nation at

---

34 For one example of the 'ring' at work, whereby a group of booksellers agreed not to bid against each other during an auction sale, but to meet afterwards and to put up their purchases again among just themselves, see Freeman and Freeman, *Anatomy of an auction*. The practice, now illegal, has never been wholly suppressed.

large'.[35] In a book on art in the middle-class house, he opened his first chapter, on prudence, with a tale of how he had once found a rare black-letter Bible among a tinker's wares in Canterbury; then he continued at more length with an account of a person who had bought four small sixteenth-century books for four shillings, and sold them at auction for £400, which after expenses represented 'about two thousand per cent per annum'.[36] As with printed books, so with manuscripts, which he viewed as being second only to pictures in their value as ornament (others, he acknowledged, would prefer china). He drew attention to the relative cheapness of many Books of Hours, and after making somewhat obvious points about completeness (Missals should, for example, have a picture of the crucifixion, and Books of Hours should include a calendar), he returned to the importance of regarding collecting as an investment: 'Of manuscripts, too, it may safely be said that some of the most gaudy are the least valuable, and that the judicious buyer will prefer that which has an especially quaint treatment of a subject.'[37] Loftie found an audience, and booksellers were only too happy to meet the needs of a further market. Much more investigation is needed of the middle-class market for old books, a market whose values were reflected even in the collection formed by Samuel Sandars, much of which is now in Cambridge University Library. It was almost wholly thanks to his mentor, Henry Bradshaw, that Sandars rose above what might have been everyday, prosaic and ill-informed.[38]

But it was Loftie who was also responsible for the catalogue of one of the earliest public loan exhibitions of early printed books in London, held at the Royal Archaeological Institute in 1871. The location was important. Outside the British Museum and the South Kensington Museum, the study of old books had no natural home. It had no journal, learned or popular, devoted to it. The Library Association, founded in 1877, was to provide some hospitality, but there were many other calls on this new body as different groups sought to wield influence: the early annual conferences proved ready jousting-yards. In the early 1870s, published studies of old books were not just dominated by amateurs; the subject was almost entirely defined by them.

Just as the development and application of photography transformed the appearance of new books, so too it transformed the treatment of and attitudes to older ones. The discovery in the late 1850s of a method of applying a photographic image to a lithographic plate meant that it was for the first time possible to reprint manuscripts and printed books in accurate facsimile. Until

---

35 Loftie, *A plea for art in the house*, preface.   36 *Ibid.*, pp. 2–3.   37 *Ibid.*, p. 73.
38 McKitterick, *Cambridge University Library*, pp. 692–701.

that time, the customary method, both in Britain and in mainland Europe, was either type-facsimile or by tracing: in London, John Harris (1791–1873) traced hundreds of images for booksellers desirous of replacing missing leaves.[39] In England, a lead in the new process was taken by Colonel Sir Henry James, Director of the Ordnance Survey, who applied photography to map production and thus began the end of traditional engraving. The first widely published experiments in photolithography (or more precisely, because zinc plates rather than lithographic stones were used, photozincography[40]) were on subjects of national interest: Domesday book, selections of key documents in English and Scottish history, and the 1662 *Book of common prayer*. Gladstone's keen interest in the process helped to ensure adequate funding, though in fact some of these projects sold very well indeed. Facsimilists and publishers soon turned their attention to Shakespeare. The first photographic facsimiles of the 1603 and 1604 quartos of *Hamlet* were published in 1858–9, after copies belonging to the Duke of Devonshire. They were followed by a much more ambitious undertaking, when in 1861 William Ashbee and J. O. Halliwell-Phillipps began a programme to publish all the quarto plays not in photographic facsimile, but using the old technique of tracing. The first photographic facsimile of the first folio was published in parts in 1864–6, and when in 1876 Chatto & Windus published a cheap edition in reduced facsimile much play was made of the fact that modern technology brought within reach what had become unattainable to all but a tiny minority. At a time when the exceptional Burdett-Coutts copy had cost a record £716 at the sale of the library of George Daniel in 1864, some more general morals could be drawn about a work that had been 'for generations the almost exclusive property of wealthy collectors, and a sealed book to the generality of readers and students. By the aid of modern science it is now placed in a conveniently reduced form within reach of all.'[41]

High claims were made for the new photolithographic facsimiles. They were cheap, but they were not always as accurate representations of the originals as was alleged: the temptation to touch up and improve could be overwhelming. For some years there also continued to be a considerable market for type-facsimiles that existed alongside photography. In particular, attention was focussed on books that obtained exceptionally high prices at auction. First editions of *The pilgrim's progress*, Walton's *Compleat angler* and Goldsmith's *Vicar of*

39 Gaines, 'A forgotten artist'; Harris, 'The Ripoli *Decameron*, Guglielmo Libri and the "incomparable" Harris'.
40 James, *Photo-zincography*.
41 Halliwell-Phillipps, preface to the 1876 facsimile. See also West, *The Shakespeare first folio: the history of the book* 2, p. 153.

Wakefield were all reproduced in type-facsimile several years after the invention of photozincography. The first edition of Burns's poems (Kilmarnock, 1786), one of the most notorious rarities in the national literature, was printed in type-facsimile to mark the centenary of the original. In such ways, while book-sellers and collectors collaborated or competed in the auction rooms, another related culture became established for those having more ordinary incomes but yet persuaded of the need to own some of the canonical texts of literature in English.

Public acceptance of such books led to public expectations and needs. The Shelley Society (founded in 1885) published type-facsimiles of books that were otherwise all but unobtainable. It was this tradition that was exploited and extended by Harry Buxton Forman and Thomas James Wise, the one a respected editor of Keats and the other a book collector of formidable deter-mination, not in the least shy of importuning, misleading and misrepresenting authors whose works he collected. The forgeries now associated with Forman and Wise gulled many a collector; but Wise extended the deception to includ-ing a mass of dishonest information in the printed catalogues of his Ashley Library (1901 etc.) and in a succession of bibliographies of authors including Swinburne, Tennyson, the Brontës and George Borrow. On occasion he may have been the victim,[42] but the extent of the confusion sown by his own bib-liographical frauds – by no means confined to the celebrated forgeries linked with his name – has still not been fully established.[43]

Increasingly, wide appreciation of the appearance of early printed books as something more than the generic black-letter of popular imagination had its effect on taste more generally. Typefounders were called on to provide faces suitable to recreate an illusion of earlier books, not just the late seventeenth-century black-letter of Bunyan, but also the eighteenth-century roman of Gold-smith. In 1855 the founders V. and J. Figgins issued a type imitating one used by Caxton and it found some use in the general trade as well as in the type-facsimile of *Game of the chesse* published in that year. In the last decade of the century the Leadenhall Press made a virtue of typographical antiquarianism, with large-scale sellers such as the pocket-sized *London street cries* and historical works on Bartolozzi, on early children's books and on the horn book.[44]

---

42 See for example Foxon, 'The printing of *Lyrical ballads*, 1798'.
43 Of the extensive literature on the forgeries, see especially Carter and Pollard, *An enquiry*, and Barker and Collins, *A sequel to An enquiry*. For his thefts from the British Museum, and subsequent meddling with copies of seventeenth-century plays, see Foxon, *Thomas J. Wise and the pre-Restoration drama*.
44 Bury, 'A. W. Tuer and the Leadenhall Press'.

Besides this publishing activity, the growing interest in public exhibitions produced its own flowering in temporary and permanent displays of early printed books, whether to mark particular occasions or as a part of museum requirements. The Caxton exhibition in 1877 to mark the anniversary of the beginning of printing in England (only subsequently was this date found to be a year too late) presented to the public not just a collection of his works, and an ambitious mixture of equipment ancient and modern, but also hundreds of other examples of early printing from Britain and overseas.[45] The British Museum had a permanent exhibition of printed books only from 1857, when the King's Library was at last opened to the public.[46] In 1880 the Museum guide to the exhibition recorded that the last of the fourteen cases shared between the Grenville Library and the King's Library was devoted to examples of bookbindings. But among the others, the showcase on 'specimens of fine and sumptuous printing' also contained work by Pynson and Aldus Manutius together with more recent specimens of the work of Charles Whittingham in 1831 and the oriental printers Stephen Austin in 1855. In mingling the old and the new, the context for modern, or at least recent, achievement could hardly have been made more specific.

Looming over the shoulder of Dibdin had always stood the figure of William Caxton, the subject in the eighteenth century of studies by Conyers Middleton, Librarian of Cambridge University, John Lewis, antiquary of Margate, and Joseph Ames, on whom Dibdin based much of his own work.[47] To Edward Gibbon, as to many others, he had been the father of printing.[48] In the nineteenth century he took on fresh significances. Along with King Alfred, Shakespeare and Milton, he became a national hero. But only gradually so. In 1820 the Dean and Chapter of Westminster demanded £120 to allow a tablet to be erected in his memory in the Abbey; instead, a modest monument by Henry Westmacott was set up in St Margaret's Church, next door.[49] More positively, when in 1833 the Society for the Diffusion of Useful Knowledge published a volume of *Lives of eminent persons*, it opened with Galileo, Kepler, Newton and Mahomet, and closed with Michelangelo. Caxton stood between Lord Somers (credited with a leading role in establishing William and Mary on the throne) and Admiral Blake. For bibliophiles, Caxton's books had their values in cash

45 Bullen (ed.), *Caxton celebration, 1877*; Stevens, *The Bibles in the Caxton exhibition*; Myers, 'The Caxton celebration of 1877'.

46 Harris, *A history of the British Museum Library*, p. 197; [J.Winter Jones] *A guide to the printed books exhibited to the public in the Grenville Library and the King's Library* [1858].

47 Middleton, *A dissertation concerning the origin of printing in England*; Lewis *The life of mayster Wyllyam Caxton*; Ames, *Typographical antiquities*, rev. Herbert and Dibdin.

48 Gibbon, *English essays*, p. 537.   49 Bigham, *The Roxburghe Club*, p. 6.

and in rarity. For historians of the English language such as W. W. Skeat and James Murray they had quite different import. For social reformers, he was representative of the power of the press itself. No other figure from Britain's past commanded such a range of authority, and few became more familiar at least in name. Thanks to print, and thanks therefore to Caxton, knowledge was advanced and social reform was possible. 'The future history of the world may, indeed, disclose enough both of misery and of vice; but it cannot again present an universal blank, or be disgraced by another age of utter and cheerless ignorance.'[50] If it suited reformers to read history under their own clouds of ignorance, the message was nonetheless powerful to those who knew no better. Charles Knight hoped that printing would make wars more difficult, and he used his shilling biography of Caxton (1844) as yet another opportunity to pursue the cause of cheap books. The history of printing gave him confidence for the future. Printing was not, for him, the means to revolution. Rather, it offered the route to social contentment even amongst those possessing very little in the world – 'those who, for the most part, must necessarily remain in that station which requires great self-denial and great endurance; but which is capable of becoming not only a condition of comfort, but of enjoyment, through the exercise of these very virtues, in connexion with a desire for that improvement of the understanding which, to a large extent, is independent of rank and riches'.[51] In this spirit, Caxton's name was also borrowed by a Society formed to publish English chronicles and similar documents.

By contrast, Gutenberg seemed all but to have passed by unnoticed a generation earlier in Britain, when Thorvaldsen's statue had been unveiled in Mainz to the accompaniment of days of celebration in 1837, and when further statues had been erected in Strasburg and other cities. Haarlem erected its own statue of Laurens Coster, whom some loyally persisted in believing to be the inventor of printing, in 1856.[52] Charles Knight seems to have been one of the few Englishmen to consider it worthwhile to attend the Mainz celebrations in 1837 and to see the new statue,[53] while one of the few articles to appear during the anniversary year of 1840 in British journals was by a foreigner, G. C. F. Mohnike.[54] His focus was on Leipzig, centre of the German book trade.

Wherever you go, Gutenberg busts and Gutenberg pictures stare you in the face, and the papers are filled with advertisements alluding in some way or

---

50 *Lives of eminent persons* (1833), Life of Caxton, p. 32.   51 Knight, *William Caxton*, p. 239.
52 For Coster and Haarlem, see Hellinga-Querido and de Wolf, *Laurens Janszoon Coster*.
53 Knight, *William Caxton*, pp. 79–84.
54 [G. C. F. Mohnike] Review article, 'The Gutenberg jubilee in Germany'. For these celebrations see also Estermann *'O werthe Druckerkunst / Du Mutter alle Kunst'*.

other to the engrossing subject ... Catchpenny articles are manufactured, and tradesmen allure their customers by christening their wares after the hero of the day. Gutenberg pipes and Gutenberg sticks, Gutenberg caps and Gutenberg handkerchiefs, Gutenberg beer and Gutenberg schnaps attest of the popularity of the printer of Mayence.[55]

The celebrations not just in Leipzig, but also in Frankfurt, Berlin, Hamburg and elsewhere, became a nationalist rallying cry. If, in Britain, the history of the first thirty years of printing with movable types meant little to most people, there was still room for nationalism. Later on, Daniel Maclise painted Caxton at his press at Westminster showing his work to the King. The picture was acquired by John Forster, and was full of technical detail more appropriate to the nineteenth than the fifteenth century; it was published as a vast engraving in 1858.

If the nineteenth century was the age of the newspaper and periodical, a period when the new steam presses were able to manufacture unheard-of quantities of print in extraordinarily short times, when the telegraph and railways transformed newspaper publishing, when electricity made reading easier, drove machines and enabled rapid world-wide communication, and when print was as yet unchallenged by later media such as cinema or wireless, it was also a period that was concerned simultaneously with progress and with the past. Walter Bagehot had more than technological progress in mind when he wrote of progress in the physical sciences meaning that 'everything is made "an antiquity" '.[56] Past and present confronted each other not just in modernity, but in how modernity was to be explained, whether in Darwinian theories of evolution, in geology, in archaeology, in the search for the history of man, in arguments about social justice, or in the latest patents. Charles Knight, advocate and exploiter of the fastest printing machinery available, also wrote a life of William Caxton. William Blades, a leading printer in mid-Victorian London, wrote the first modern and authoritative account also of Caxton, drawing on his own knowledge of practical printing and typefounding: his first edition, in two volumes, later became a successful one-volume popular edition in octavo. Talbot Baines Reed, owner of one of the largest typefounders in late nineteenth-century London, wrote a detailed and deeply researched account of the history of typefounding in Britain. The link between past and present hardly needed to be drawn:

In this age of progress, when the fine arts are rapidly becoming trades, and the machine is on every side superseding that labour of head and hand which our

---

55 'The Gutenberg jubilee', p. 446.   56 Walter Bagehot, *Physics and politics* (1872), ch. 1.

fathers called Handicraft, we are in danger of losing sight of, or, at least, of undervaluing the genius of those who, with none of our mechanical advantages, established and made famous in our land those arts and handicrafts of which we are now the heritors.[57]

Gutenberg and Caxton were as much heroes, with all the mixture of fact and fantasy that this implied, as were King Alfred and Shakespeare. For the last quarter of the nineteenth century, Samuel Timmins of Birmingham devoted his time to writing a life of another hero, the eighteenth-century Birmingham printer John Baskerville: his work was eventually taken over by Robert Dent and was subsumed into what became the standard life, published in 1907.[58] While Baskerville never quite achieved the popular renown enjoyed by Gutenberg and Caxton, the efforts to establish him spoke of a more general perspective. Printing, and book production, were matters of vital interest, to be recounted and described alongside the wonders of modern communication and (in the case of paper manufacture) the wonders of nature. In a collection of stories of inventors published in 1860, the voluminous writer John Timbs set the theme of printing in one of his popular books after chapters on Archimedes and on the invention of the magnet. In less than a page he leapt from the fifteenth-century presses of Fust and Schoeffer to the machine press introduced at *The Times* in 1814.[59] Two years earlier, in 1858, at a lecture given to the Royal Institution, Henry Bradbury likewise linked the past to the future.[60]

If the quality of Caxton's presswork could not stand unstinted acclaim, at least his typefaces were worthy of resurrection for antiquarian printing and for special effects in advertising. By 1877, he had been corralled by the modern printing trade for quite different reasons. In America, his name was lent in 1861 to a jobbing platen press.[61] In London, the *Caxton Circular and Type Founder* had been published since 1875. With the exhibition and celebrations of the coming of printing to England in 1877 the superior importance of Caxton, the Englishman, over Gutenberg, the German, seemed confirmed in popular imagination. In stained glass windows designed by Henry Holiday for Trinity College, Cambridge in 1871 and ten years later for St Margaret's Westminster, Caxton took his place alongside early saints and the heroes of the English Reformation.

57 Reed, *A history of the old English letter foundries* (1887), preface.
58 Straus and Dent, *John Baskerville: a memoir* (1907).
59 Timbs, *Stories of inventors and discoverers in science and the useful arts* (1860), p. 18.
60 Bradbury, *Printing: its dawn, day and destiny* (1858).   61 Moran, *Printing presses*, p. 148.

There was, however, no library or museum devoted solely to the history of printing. When in 1895 the St Bride Printing Library was opened, it made available the collection on the history of printing formed by the late William Blades (d.1890), to which, thanks to a gift of £500 from J. Passmore Edwards, was added a collection of books on modern methods of book production. Even if, as was remarked in 1899 in its own printed catalogue, there seemed to be a 'singular lack of interest' in the subject of how books were made, the new library represented more than parochial self-advancement.[62]

In the book trade new and old, as in the fine arts, the customer was king. His needs had to be met, but he was also a victim waiting to be misled and relieved of his money. Fakes and forgeries were nothing new, but the dependence of increasingly ambitious education policies in museums on copies – casts of sculpture, electrotypes of coins, facsimiles of engravings and drawings – helped to change public attitudes. The boundaries between fakes and forgeries were confused, and facsimiles sat as sometimes uneasy representations of originals. In the South Kensington Museum, where casts had been a feature ever since its foundation, the large cast courts were built in the 1870s.[63] While many visitors were no doubt misled into thinking that they were facing originals rather than plaster or metal reproductions, there was nevertheless a clear frame of reference and authority that could be readily referred to if wished. In the world of printed books it was not always so. It was a short step from traced facsimiles, or photographed images used to make good incomplete copies of rare books, to wholesale reproduction intended to deceive on much greater scales. Here again, the boundaries were not clear, and were not just of scale. The temptation was strong for booksellers to pass off as complete copies that had been made up with facsimile pages. Ignorance was an easy plea, by booksellers or by auctioneers. On 4 July 1899 an imperfect copy of the Kilmarnock Burns was put up for auction by Sotheby's, after it had failed to sell previously, when it had been under-described. The resulting price, £96, was a fraction of what a perfect copy might have fetched: an exceptional copy sold in Edinburgh eighteen months previously had fetched £572 5s. In 1899 also, J. Pierpont Morgan bought from the London bookseller James Toovey a copy of the Shakespeare first folio in a binding bearing the arms of Robert Sidney of Penshurst. It seemed an attractive, even irresistible, provenance. Though suspicions were provoked, only a century later was the reality discovered: that the binding had been added in recent times from another book, in order to turn an expensive one into an irresistible one, and that the most probable

---

62 Saint Bride Foundation, *Catalogue*.   63 Burton, *Vision & accident*.

culprit was Toovey.[64] Such sharp practices were not unique to the period of this volume, and they did not die with the First World War.

Conventions as to the most desirable form in which to possess early books changed slowly. The old practice of washing copies, in order to remove stains and unsightly early annotations, remained acceptable at the end of the century, albeit usually less fiercely practised by then.[65] Booksellers and collectors alike rarely hesitated before making up a perfect copy out of two or more imperfect ones, and the London booksellers Pickering & Chatto were celebrated for their stock of books kept for such purposes. In amassing what was probably the largest collection of Bibles ever assembled by a private individual in Britain, Francis Fry exchanged leaves between copies and had lithographed facsimiles made to provide what could not otherwise be had, in order to make up as many perfect copies of the rarer editions as possible. Much of his collection went to the British and Foreign Bible Society, but the integrity of these made-up copies had been destroyed. With a craving for early printed books went a demand for a kind of perfection, or at least completeness – a desire strengthened by the demands of collectors who were exhorted never to be content with an imperfect book.

The trade in made-up copies was not restricted to old books. Condition could be crucial for modern books as well. Collectors of Dickens or Thackeray were exhorted not to bind up novels originally published in parts, but to ensure that they were preserved as they first appeared. The reasons offered for so doing were, again, almost wholly financial, and specialist guides for collectors of both these authors were published in the 1880s.[66] But whether the books were old or new, there was a wide measure of acceptance – much more than mere tolerance – in considering what was, and what was not, perfect. As J. H. Slater explained, in a much-read manual for collectors, the grounds were often more financial than bibliographical:

> Imperfect books are frequently what is called 'made up,' that is, completed from other copies, themselves imperfect in other respects. One complete book is worth more than two incomplete ones, and many desirable specimens, in the public libraries and elsewhere, are made up so well that it is frequently impossible to detect the hand of the renovator.
>
> So long as all the leaves of a made-up book are of the same measurement, there would not seem to be much objection to this practice, but there certainly

64 Warkentin and Hoare, 'Sophisticated Shakespeare'.
65 For washing methods, see for example John Hannett, *Bibliopegia*, pp. 176–81.
66 See for example Johnson, *Hints to collectors of original editions of the works of Charles Dickens*; Johnson, *Hints to collectors of original editions of the works of William Makepeace Thackeray*; *Dickens memento*, including hints to Dickens collectors by John F. Dexter.

is when the paper of the interpolated leaves is different from the rest, or smaller in size, which it will be if cut down by the binder. Great care must be taken to see that neither of these defects is present, especially when, from the value of a book offered for sale, it may have been worth anyone's while to perfect it.[67]

Such an attitude was by no means new: it can be found for several generations previously. But, as a consequence, the normal vocabulary of comparison could take on new meanings. When in 1902 Sidney Lee published a census of surviving copies of the Shakespeare first folio,[68] he divided them into four classes, beginning with those in 'good, unrestored condition'. But even these included copies where the order of leaves had been changed, leaves had been repaired or reinserted, and in one instance leaves had been inserted from another copy.

For most collectors, first editions were the principal, and in almost all cases the only, attraction. This had been true of *editiones principes* of classical texts at the beginning of the century, and it remained true of modern authors as the market for these developed from the 1870s onwards. Always with the exception of Shakespeare, of whom most wealthy collectors sought to possess all four folio editions (1623, 1632, 1663, 1685), there was little interest in following the bibliographical careers of authors and their reputations once their books had been first published.

The extraordinary fashion that seized on Fitzgerald's *Rubáiyát of Omar Khayyám*, making it one of the most printed books of the late nineteenth century, was in marked contrast to its first publication in 1859 and descent within a few months into Quaritch's outside penny-box.[69] The episode passed quickly into book-collecting lore. Meanwhile, the pioneering bibliographies of modern authors by T. J. Wise placed emphasis and value on first appearances. As for earlier authors, so for modern ones, first editions were crucial. By the new century, competition especially for Kipling's early work published in Lahore was fierce. It was not always well founded. The first edition of his *Schoolboy lyrics*, written when he was sixteen and privately published in Lahore in 1881, fetched £135 when it first appeared in the London auction houses in 1899. Success bred further copies, and the price dropped as seven more copies quickly appeared and fetched as little as £27. Publishers were quick to recognise that book collecting in some quarters was little better than investing, and produced large-paper editions or *éditions de luxe* to suit.

Most of all there was the Bible, whose social and imperial significance, quite apart from its religious status, ensured it a central place in bibliophily

67 Slater, *Book collecting*, p. 41.   68 Lee, *Shakespeare's comedies, histories, & tragedies*.
69 Freeman, 'Bernard Quaritch and "my Omar"'.

and in bibliographical studies, rivalled in the English-speaking world only by Shakespeare. The Gutenberg Bible (discussed further below), printed at Mainz in the early 1450s and commonly held to be the first printed book, stood at the head, as its price rose quickly in the last decades of the century. The first copy of it to cross the Atlantic was bought by Wiley & Putnam, bidding against Sir Thomas Phillipps at the John Wilks sale in 1847 for £500, and was sold by them to James Lenox of New York. The price seemed at the time over-excited, and indeed disturbed even the wealthy Lenox.[70] For collectors of English books, some books were much rarer.

The bibliography of the English Bible had been the subject of separate monographs and studies since the work of Joseph Ames in the eighteenth century. According to J. H. Slater, writing in 1892, collectors of Bibles customarily ended with the Vinegar Bible of 1717, though he might also have added the Baskerville Bible of 1763. Both were easy to find. But the earliest printed English translations were much rarer than the Gutenberg Bible, many of the surviving copies being only fragments. On 5 July 1905 (property of the late John Quicke) the second perfect copy then known of Tyndale's Pentateuch (1530), taller than the Grenville copy in the British Museum, was bought by Quaritch for £940. The King James version of 1611 enjoyed a position unequalled by any other translation, its status unaffected, and even enhanced, by the short-lived hysteria that greeted the Revised Version published in 1881–5. Oxford University Press published a reduced type-facsimile of the 1611 version in 1833 and a further facsimile for a more general market in 1911. F. H. Scrivener compiled a long and detailed introduction to a new edition for Cambridge University Press in 1873, and his study was then published separately. More generally, in 1911 A. W. Pollard brought together the crucial early records of the translation, publication and early use of the English Bible, after writing the bibliographical introduction to the anniversary Oxford University Press reduced-size facsimile of the King James version. The bibliographical work, and confused legacy, of Francis Fry have already been mentioned. When J. R. Dore wrote an account of the early versions of the English Bible he was by no means the first to call 1611 a pearl of great price. Above all in these studies stood T. H. Darlow and H. F. Moule's chronological survey in 1903 of editions of the English Bible in their catalogue of the library of the British and Foreign Bible Society, including an account of the 1,200 volumes assembled by Fry and bought for the Society for £6,000.[71] Most of this work had little to do with the

---

70 Munby, *Phillipps studies* 4, pp. 22–4.
71 Scrivener, *The authorized edition of the English Bible*; Dore, *Old Bibles*; Darlow and Moule, *Historical catalogue*; Pollard, *Records of the English Bible*.

book trade, but it was all seized on by booksellers as support in their search for price structures.

In many areas more generally, books that had hardly been noticed in the 1820s were keenly fought over sixty years later. Prices for some kinds of books rose rapidly in the mid-century as the new American libraries sought to build up their stocks, and to obtain the representative literature of the old world. Thomas Rodd, one of the leading London booksellers in the mid-century, reckoned that his stock of old English books rose 25 per cent in value within five years in the 1840s, entirely because of American demand.[72] Not all subjects rose this fast, and many dull books remained dull in the market. High spot prices told one story. Underneath them were thousands of other books. But the doldrums of the second quarter of the century were brought to an end mainly by this new and aggressively competitive market, where the statistics of library stocks – 'new light on our advancement as a people' – were monitored closely by Washington.[73] Increasing interest in old books in the United States led not only to advanced prices for the more obvious old books in the British market, but also to the rise of the concept of Americana, books either printed in or having some allusion to the Americas. In June 1888 a volume of twelve pamphlets from the Hardwicke collection at Wimpole, mostly relating to America, caused much comment when it was bought at auction by the bookseller Henry Stevens for £555. Stevens was for many years the principal instigator and leader in this trade. He came from Vermont, and much of his business lay in obtaining duplicates from major British libraries in exchange for new books published in the United States.[74]

This was just one market where tastes, needs and (therefore) prices changed. In the case of the most celebrated books, high prices were paid by a handful of American private collectors. George Brinley (d.1875), John Carter Brown (d.1874) and James Lenox (d.1880) spent much of their energies on collecting Americana. Their successors had wider opportunities, as major English libraries were dispersed in the 1880s and 1890s, and Brayton Ives, Robert Hoe and others worked with Quaritch to build their collections. Abbie Pope established her reputation as a collector when she secured the Osterley Park copy of Caxton's *Morte D'Arthur*. They in turn were succeeded by the banker J. Pierpont Morgan (who bought many of William Morris's books in 1902) and the railway magnate Henry E. Huntington (whose purchases included the

72 *Report from the Select Committee on Public Libraries* (1849), para. 1643.
73 Jewett, *Notices of public libraries in the United States of America*; Rhees, *Manual of public libraries*: the quotation is from the Introduction, p. v; *Public libraries in the United States of America*.
74 Parker, *Henry Stevens of Vermont*; McKitterick, *Cambridge University Library*, pp. 634–44.

Kemble plays, bought from the Duke of Devonshire in 1914, and the library of the Earl of Ellesmere in 1917). But the American market was influenced in much wider ways by institutional demand, fed in turn by nationalist impulses, a search to document historical roots, and inter-state rivalries. The creation of new university and state libraries in the United States, and editorial programmes for the publication of public and private archives, stoked demand for background printed literature. By 1914, Maggs were shipping to America every week, while Edmund Brooks in Minneapolis advertised for first editions of Browning, Keats, Meredith, Swinburne, Tennyson and others: he represented a taste for which the Buxton Forman–Wise forgeries of a few years earlier were ideally suited.

Meanwhile, for most parts of an ever more international market private individuals remained more influential than institutions. In the early decades of the century, a taste for classical texts had fed a demand for much more than the main (and always paramount) *editiones principes*. This taste was catered for by such surveys as Dibdin's *Introduction to the knowledge of rare and valuable editions of the Greek and Roman classics* (1802; 2nd edn 1804; 3rd edn 1808). But the market for many classical editions weakened noticeably by the mid-century, and demand strengthened for other kinds of books instead. Though the Heber sales of 1834–7, which brought an estimated 150,000 volumes back into the market,[75] were identified as contributing to a downturn in the prices of many kinds of books, the heyday of high prices had in fact already passed, and many of Heber's books were not in the best condition. The sales also released quantities of early English literature much of which passed into the hands of W. H. Miller's Britwell Library.[76] The taste for black-letter books – that is, books printed in the British Isles in black-letter types, mostly before the early years of the seventeenth century – can be traced back to before 1700; and such books featured prominently in the bibliophile world recorded by Dibdin. Though the term gradually dropped out of fashion, the taste for early English printing, and particularly for English literature, did not. Prices fetched by the Shakespeare first folio were watched keenly. In 1829, John Bohn offered an imperfect and poorly repaired copy, 'extremely rare', for seven guineas – the same price as a copy of Dibdin's revision of Ames's *Typographical antiquities.*[77] Copies were still plentiful in the early 1890s, when prices began well below £100: as always, price depended mainly on condition. But Henry Folger paid the equivalent of £900 for a copy in 1896, and in 1899 a fine copy reached

75 Hunt, 'The sale of Richard Heber's library'.   76 *The Britwell handlist.*
77 John Bohn, *A catalogue of an extensive collection of English books* (1829).

£1,700. By 1909, Francis Edwards were offering an only slightly imperfect copy of the First Folio for £2,700, the price determined partly by claiming an association of the copy with Handel.[78]

The Settled Estates legislation of the 1880s led to the release into the market of a more general supply of early books of a quality not seen for half a century, and in quantities not seen since the sales of Heber's library. The Osterley Park sale alone (1885), deriving from the collection of Bryan Fairfax, produced eleven books printed by Caxton, of which five had passed to J. Pierpont Morgan in New York by 1909. In 1897–8 the auction of the library of the Earl of Ashburnham produced twenty-seven, sixteen of which later came into the hands of Pierpont Morgan.[79] Between 1873 and 1911, six complete or substantially complete copies of the Gutenberg Bible passed through the London trade.[80] In 1873, the Perkins library produced two copies, on vellum and on paper, and the prices for both were remarkable. The vellum copy, sold for £3,400 and acquired by the Earl of Ashburnham, broke the record price for a printed book held since the sale of the Valdarfer Boccaccio at the Roxburghe sale in 1812. Quaritch paid £2,690 for the paper copy, more than five times the price fetched by the Wilks copy a quarter of a century previously. In a market for this book that was dominated by Quaritch and his customers, prices did not always rise. After the Thorold/Syston Park copy fetched £3,900 in 1884, neither the Crawford copy (1887) nor the Hopetoun copy (1889) even nudged this figure, the latter selling for just £2,000. Even the Streatfield copy on vellum was sold by Sotheran to J. Pierpont Morgan for just £2,750. But in the following year, the Perkins–Ashburnham copy on vellum fetched £4,000, bought by Quaritch and passed on to the manufacturer of printing presses in America, Robert Hoe. It was only in 1911, with Quaritch's successful bid of £5,800 for the Huth copy (formerly Perkins), and its passing to Pierpont Morgan, that the market for what was often billed as the first book printed with metal types began to assume its modern trajectory.[81] Apart from the prices realised, two features of these sales were notable. First, most owners were able to hold on to their copies only for quite short periods, a single generation, before they disposed of them. Second, the drift to American libraries and collectors was firmly established. Of the six copies, only the Hopetoun copy remains in England, given by A. W. Young to Cambridge University Library in 1933.

---

78 Francis Edwards, *Catalogue of old English literature* (1909). For further copies mentioned here, see West, *The Shakespeare first folio* 1, pp. 95–7.
79 De Ricci, *A census of Caxtons*.   80 Folter, 'The Gutenberg Bible in the antiquarian book trade'.
81 De Ricci, *Catalogue raisonné des premières impressions de Mayence*; Folter, 'The Gutenberg Bible in the antiquarian book trade'.

Demand for the Gutenberg Bible remained resolutely among private customers, but this was scarcely an ordinary book. The shift from private to
institutional influence in the British market for early printed books more generally was characterised not by the university library buying that became so
familiar a feature of the post-1945 world, but by the demands of the new public
libraries. For the larger municipal libraries, it became a declared policy to build
up collections of early books. At Wigan there was a special fund for the purpose, and many early books were given by James Ludovic Lindsay, later Earl of
Crawford and Balcarres.[82] At Birmingham and Manchester, as in many other
places, local impulses were influenced by awareness of London's dominance.
Bristol City Library dated from 1613, long before the Public Libraries Act of
1850; but it was only in 1855, and even then as a pioneer in such an approach,
that it began seriously to collect local literature. Its systematic attention to
the work of the poet Thomas Chatterton dated from about the same time.
Norwich Public Library instigated a local collection in 1880. Cardiff Public
Library, founded in 1862, was given a collection of sixty-seven incunabula by
a group of local well-wishers in 1902, six years after it had acquired a hundred
Welsh manuscripts from the estate of Sir Thomas Phillipps. Although interest
was often primarily in local printing and local authors, there was also a desire
to possess the obvious works of English literature.

The effect on modern book design of fashions for particular kinds of early
books was long-lasting. Between the mid-1860s and his death in 1896, William
Morris assembled a collection of early printed books, paying especial attention
to their visual features – illustration, type and lay-out. In this he was guided
partly by the scholar-bookseller F. S. Ellis and partly by Emery Walker, who
combined a knowledge of early printing with the skills of a modern manufacturer of book illustrations. Walker's ability to handle modern printing
methods, and Morris's instinct for handcrafts – whether in fabrics, wallpapers, furniture, manuscript illumination or printing – combined to spectacular
effect in the books printed at the Kelmscott Press.[83] Writing retrospectively
in 1895, Morris reflected on his purpose:

> I began printing books with the hope of producing some which would have a
> definite claim to beauty, while at the same time they should be easy to read and
> should not dazzle the eye, or trouble the intellect of the reader by eccentricity
> of form in the letters . . . As to the fifteenth-century books, I had noticed that

82 Like many other pubic libraries, Wigan disposed of much of its collection of early printed books
in the last quarter of the twentieth century.
83 Needham, Dunlap and Dreyfus, *William Morris and the art of the book*; Peterson, *A bibliography of the
Kelmscott Press*.

they were always beautiful by force of the mere typography, even without the added ornament, with which many of them are so lavishly supplied. And it was the essence of my undertaking to produce books which it would be a pleasure to look upon as pieces of printing and arrangement of type. Looking at my adventure from this point of view then, I found I had to consider chiefly the following things: the paper, the form of the type, the relative spacing of the letters, the words, and the lines; and lastly the position of the printed matter on the page.[84]

Of the three types designed by Morris for use at the press, Golden type (so called because he used it to print the *Golden legend*) was based on a type used by Jacobus Rubeus at Venice in 1476; Troy (used for the *Recuyell of the historyes of Troy*) was based on a study of the work of Peter Schoeffer at Mainz, Gunther Zainer at Augsburg and Anton Koberger at Nuremberg; and Chaucer type, used for his masterpiece the collected works of Chaucer completed in 1896, was a smaller cutting of Troy. All were cast for setting by hand.

The idea of type revivals was not new. Longman had used Caslon's type for antiquarian effect in the fictitious *Diary of Lady Willoughby* in 1844, and Thackeray had used it for a similar purpose in *Henry Esmond* (1852). In the 1840s and 1850s, the publisher William Pickering owed much of his reputation to his antiquarian taste in typography, that in turn was dependent on the printer Charles Whittingham at the Chiswick Press.[85] The typefounders Miller & Richard had issued an old face type based on the work of Caslon, and others made much play of 'neat Elsevir letter' alluding to the work of the Elzevier family, printed in the Netherlands in the late seventeenth century. The ideals of typographic individuality as a defining aspect of a private press were celebrated in the same antiquarian manner. Most famous were the types designed in 1898 for the Doves Press (based again on those used by Jacobus Rubeus, but now markedly closer to the original than Morris's interpretations[86]) cast under the supervision of Walker as joint owner of the press, and in the Ashendene Press's Subiaco type (1902),[87] based on that used by Sweynheym and Pannartz in what has for long been thought to be the first press in Italy. They were derived from a mixture of bibliographical investigation and bibliophily. Other owners of private presses imitated the connection, with mixed success.

---

84 William Morris, *Note . . . on his aims in founding the Kelmscott Press* (1896), repr. in Morris, *The ideal book*, p. 75
85 Warren, *The Charles Whittinghams*; Keynes, *William Pickering*; (Porter), *Catalogue of a William Pickering collection*.
86 Dreyfus, 'New light on the design of types for the Kelmscott and Doves Presses'; Dreyfus, 'The Kelmscott Press'.
87 *A descriptive bibliography of the books printed at the Ashendene Press, MDCCCXCV–MCMXXXV* (Chelsea, 1935).

Morris's influence spread well beyond the world of private presses. More importantly, in helping to develop Morris's and his own ideas, Walker had shown how photography could be applied to revivals of old type designs; and Morris himself had shown how, by closer spacing, and a careful balance between the weight of the type and the white space in which it sat, books could benefit from denser colour on a typographic page. Less than twenty years after Morris's death, some of these ideas were being applied to designs of type for machine composition, often most successfully in revivals of types cut originally in the fifteenth, sixteenth and seventeenth centuries. In 1912, the Monotype Corporation issued Imprint, a typeface designed for machine composition and derived from Caslon's Great Primer; and in 1913 it issued Plantin, a typeface based on types cut in the sixteenth century and used by Christophe Plantin in Antwerp.[88] These were to prove the beginning of a long list of revivals, in what after the First World War developed into a programme.

Morris, rightly, has received the lion's share of credit for putting in place the means to help change attitudes to the design of books. But for many people the prices of his books were of more immediate interest, as Kelmscott Press books rapidly became objects for investment. The books, awkward to handle and visually unfamiliar, scarcely needed for this purpose the advocacy of the respected commentator Temple Scott in *Book Prices Current*, as the price of Keats's poems (1894, 30s) climbed to £12 in just four years, and *The story of the glittering plain* (1891, £2 2s) reached £33 10s in eight. Most celebrated of all, the collected Chaucer (1896), published at £20, reached £36 10s in 1898, a year in which several collectors decided to realise their investments in this book. The price rose modestly, only to fall back in the first years of the twentieth century. Many important incunables cost less. For the book trade, the current price of the Kelmscott Chaucer was to become a weathervane indicating the health or otherwise of business.

But there were other historical strands to the revived interest in type design that was to bloom in the early twentieth century. In his authoritative *History of the old English letter foundries* (1887), Talbot Baines Reed, typefounder and contributor to the *Boy's Own Paper*,[89] laid out and elucidated the tradition. The influence on faces for machine setting of Caslon and of the typefaces used by Plantin have already been mentioned. The work of the eighteenth-century Birmingham printer and typefounder John Baskerville was brought back into public view when in 1909 the typefounders Stephenson Blake reissued Fry's Baskerville, dating from 1768. Two years earlier, Ralph Straus and Robert

88 Morison, *A tally of types*.   89 Morison, *Talbot Baines Reed*.

K. Dent had incorporated into their *Memoir* of Baskerville material that had been gathered over many years by a succession of enthusiasts, and in 1903 the Baskerville Club was founded at Cambridge by a group of committed bibliophiles. In Greek, both Selwyn Image and Robert Proctor adapted the face used in the Complutensian polyglot Bible (Alcalá, 1514–20) in designing Macmillan Greek and Otter respectively: the results were very different, but neither achieved a long-term commercial career.[90]

Links between ancient and modern were not confined to typography. In 1846, Charles Tuckett, a commercial bookbinder, isssued an album of colour lithographs of *Specimens of ancient and modern binding, selected chiefly from the library of the British Museum*. It was the first book of its kind in Britain, in what became a recognised genre.[91] Guglielmo Libri employed the same idea, linking it also to illuminated manuscripts and to more general questions respecting the history of manuscripts, when he included dozens of pictures of bindings in his *Monuments inédits ou peu connus*, published by the booksellers Dulau in 1862.[92] If the purpose of these two works was more antiquarian or bibliophilic than commendatory to modern binders, this was not always true subsequently. The educational and training aims of the South Kensington (later the Victoria and Albert) Museum were exemplified in the exhibition of early bookbindings there in 1862. Further exhibitions were held at Liverpool in 1882 and (with a catalogue including notes by E. Gordon Duff and Sarah Prideaux) at Nottingham in 1891.[93] In 1891 the Burlington Fine Arts Club hosted a major loan exhibition in London of historic bookbindings, and there was more than a hint of sympathy for Morris's attitudes to design in the remark by Sarah Prideaux in the introduction that 'as the mechanical aids to the art grew in number, taste declined'. Apart from decoration, the emphasis on this occasion was firmly on well-known provenances. In 1894, three years later, the antiquarian booksellers Tregaskis mounted an exhibition intended to show off the best of modern international designs in bindings.[94] All of the seventy-five exhibits were copies of the Kelmscott Presss edition of Morris's *King Florus and the fair Jehane* – 'one of the handsomest examples of typography of this century', in the words of the accompanying catalogue. Most of the very eclectic

---

90 Scholderer, *Greek printing types*; Bowman, *Greek printing types in Britain*.
91 Breslauer, *The uses of bookbinding literature*.
92 Maccioni Ruju and Mostert, *The life and times of Guglielmo Libri*, pp. 299–301.
93 Robinson (ed.), *Catalogue of the special exhibition of works of art*; [Newton] *Catalogue of a loan collection of ancient and modern bookbindings exhibited at the Liverpool Art Club*; *Catalogue of the special exhibition of art bookbindings*.
94 Burlington Fine Arts Club, *Exhibition of bookbindings*; Tidcombe and Middleton, *Tregaskis centenary exhibition*.

exhibits were of leather bindings, and many made some historical allusion. It was noticeable that there were few signs, from any country, of the most common modern covering materials, cloth and paper. 'It is only when the book, the impression, and the binding, are the productions of the same time, and of the same influences, that the art [of bookbinding] in its finest and most satisfactory condition is possible.'[95] Herbert Horne, biographer of Botticelli and one of the founders of the *Burlington Magazine*, wrote these words in the same year as the Tregaskis exhibition. But, outside the very limited world of private presses, private enthusiasm and private money, the interests of booksellers, book collectors, publishers, printers, ink-makers, paper-makers and bookbinders could rarely be reconciled. And on the whole, unlike printing, and despite the efforts of members of the arts and crafts circles who sought to introduce better structures and better materials, modern mass bookbinding owed very little to its predecessors.

In the hands of people like Henry Wheatley, antiquary, bibliographer and editor of Samuel Pepys, and Cyril Davenport of the British Museum, bookbinding was treated more as one of the fine arts than a craft.[96] The confusion of design with appearance, against which Ruskin, Morris and others in the arts and crafts movement laboured, was in this respect as damaging to historical understanding as it was to modern manufacture. This arts and crafts perception underpinned differences in the approach to the past adopted by Thomas Cobden-Sanderson, who applied an informed, albeit less extensive, knowledge of the past to his own, modern, skills as a bookbinder. W. H. J. Weale, who published his survey of early bindings in South Kensington in 1894-8, had no such skill.[97] Possessed of greater critical acumen than Davenport or Wheatley, he came to the question as an antiquary, but his approach was developed by Edward Gordon Duff. By the nature of their interests (which lay almost wholly in late medieval bindings) unencumbered by the demands of modern manufacture, these two began to set the study of the history of bookbinding on a new footing.[98]

The link between past practices and modern conditions – not in design but in materials and construction – was firmly made at the British Museum in 1900, when G. K. Fortescue, Keeper of Printed Books, reported that most of the books bound in leather between 1860 and 1890, and including even

95 Horne, *The binding of books*, p. 220. For Horne, see Sutton, 'Herbert Horne'.
96 Wheatley, *Remarkable bindings in the British Museum*. Some of Davenport's work in particular has been revised and criticised: see for example Nixon, *Five centuries of English bookbinding*, p. 60.
97 Weale, *Bookbindings and rubbings of bindings*; van Biervliet, *Leven en werk van W. H. James Weale*.
98 See further below, p. 671.

morocco, either had been rebound, or were awaiting repair.[99] It was damning for the national library; but the case was made for a much wider audience by Douglas Cockerell in the first of a series of manuals on 'artistic crafts' (later ones included metalwork, wood-carving and Edward Johnston's influential *Writing & illuminating, & lettering*) published in 1901. Cockerell was in charge of the bindery at W. H. Smith, and dealt with both old and new books. He wrote concisely, and he wrote firmly:

> That bindings are made, that fail to protect books, may be seen by visiting any large library, when it will be found that many bindings have their boards loose and the leather crumbling to dust. Nearly all librarians complain, that they have to be continually rebinding books, and this after not four hundred, but after only five or ten years.
>
> It is no exaggeration to say that ninety per cent. of the books bound in leather during the last thirty years will need rebinding during the next thirty. The immense expense involved must be a very serious drag on the usefulness of libraries; and as rebinding is always to some extent damaging to the leaves of a book, it is not only on account of the expense that the necessity for it is to be regretted.
>
> ... The materials are badly selected or prepared, and the method of binding is faulty. Another factor in the decay of bindings, both old and new, is the bad conditions under which they are often kept.[100]

His scathing remarks, directed at leather suppliers, fellow bookbinders and librarians, found a select audience, and suited the persisting anxieties about the longevity of modern paper. They also bore an important documentary point that Cockerell did not pursue, and which was only gradually to be recognised sufficiently to have an influence on repair and conservation practice. Frequent rebinding was not only expensive. It was also destructive of historical evidence.

In a world where the best books deserved the best bindings, there was a natural tendency to rebind older books, in morocco and with gilt decoration. In the eighteenth century, craftsmen such as Christopher Chapman (working extensively for the Earl of Oxford) and Roger Payne had catered for such needs; and Charles Lewis had a large business in the first decades of the nineteenth. In the mid-century much of this trade was in the hands of Francis Bedford, whose work was promoted especially by the London antiquarian bookseller Joseph Lilly. By the end of the century the more expensive parts of the London trade

---

99 Harris, *History of the British Museum Library*, p. 427.
100 Cockerell, *Bookbinding, and the care of books*, pp. 17–18.

in repairing early books were dominated by Rivière (whose business traced its history back to Bath in the 1820s) and Zaehnsdorf. For many, their names became synonymous with the highest qualities of this particular workmanship and binding.[101] But if such investment in the outside of a book acknowledged the value of what was within, it often came at the price of destroying much of that book's history. For books in early bindings, it was normal practice to discard any manuscript endpapers: the accumulations of Philip Bliss in Oxford testify both to this habit and to the lack of interest by owners.[102] For all kinds of books, names of earlier owners were of limited interest, and usually only if they were well known. Similarly, where early bindings were valued, association with named (and preferably distinguished) historical figures offered especial cachet.

Though Quaritch had already included substantial sections of historic book-bindings in a catalogue in 1883, prefacing the section on the subject with a brief history stretching from the ninth century to Francis Bedford in his own time, what seems to have been the earliest bookseller's catalogue princi-pally concerned with them appeared, again from Quaritch, in 1889.[103] Here too he noted the absence of a history of the subject, but this time he traced its modern development only from the fifteenth century. And this time he concluded not with Bedford, for whom he repeated his admiration, but with Cobden-Sanderson, 'an amateur binder, who has already produced some fine work in flat contradiction to the *précieuseté* of his theories'. In further sin-gling out Zaehnsdorf for praise, he added that amongst his employees was 'a young Frenchman named Hagué, an artist of consummate skill and taste, who ought rather to have lived in the late sixteenth than in the second half of the nineteenth century'. Hagué's pastiche bindings, derived from sixteenth-century ideas, not only deceived some of Quaritch's customers; they were also reminders of the strength of the antiquarian book trade's hold over some aspects of public taste.[104]

By the time of the Burlington exhibition, collectors and historians had available to them several collections of plates, more or less reliable in their attributions; but it was only with the work of Strickland Gibson at Oxford and George J. Gray at Cambridge that the study of early bindings came into its

---

101 Broomhead, *The Zaehnsdorfs*.
102 Ker, *Pastedowns in Oxford bindings*, pp. xiv–xvi. Most of Bliss's collection has recently been sold by Quaritch.
103 Quaritch, *A catalogue of fifteen hundred books remarkable for the beauty or age of their bindings*.
104 Foot, 'Double agent: M. Caulin and M. Hagué'; Foot, Blacker and Poole-Wilson, 'Collector, dealer and forger'.

own, both men showing how documentary investigation could contribute to more precise history.[105]

All this militated against less obviously distinguished appearances: the term 'divinity calf', much employed in some sections of the book trade, was disparaging both of the subject and of the duller style of binding. It also reflected the strictly circumscribed interest in copy-specific values. To the bibliophile, lineage was important; but as with social classes who could turn to the *Almanach de Gotha* or to Debrett, so too it was only a select group of older or more celebrated kinds of books that attracted such treatment. As we have seen, Caxton attracted serious bibliographical research in the eighteenth century. In the mid-nineteenth century the study of his work was transformed with William Blades's analysis, praised by Bradshaw as the 'first attempt to treat books as a naturalist treats his specimens': bibliophilic study caught up a generation later in Seymour de Ricci's *Census of Caxtons* (1909), which attempted to set out the ownership history of each known surviving copy. Bernard Quaritch's *Contributions towards a dictionary of English book-collectors* (1892–9) brought before the public many forgotten names, but it was still selective, even in what was known to Quaritch himself. It was only with the publication of the list of the thousands of English book auction catalogues in the British Museum published since 1676 (1915) that there was at last a survey that could claim to be indifferent as to status or fame. But all these several projects reflected attention to aspects of old books that had scarcely existed in the years after the Napoleonic wars.

When, therefore, the original Bodleian copy of the Shakespeare first folio reappeared in private hands in 1905, its recognition caused excitement for many reasons. The copy had been acquired by the library shortly after its publication in 1623, but had been discarded probably in the 1660s. It had lain in its plain original binding for almost three centuries, and benign neglect could now be shown to have served a double advantage. Not only had an unusual artefact been preserved. Because it had not been rebound, it was possible to ascertain its uniquely interesting history, and to show its connection with the library. As the report on the volume summarised:

> The Turbutt Shakespeare . . . will serve as a warning against the folly of having books re-bound merely because their bindings are old and shabby. Thirty years ago this very copy was taken to a large and first-rate English Library (not the Bodleian) with a view of finding out what might be best done for it. The advice

---

105 Gibson, *Early Oxford bindings*; Gray, *The earlier Cambridge stationers and bookbinders and the first Cambridge printer*.

given was that it should be re-bound in full morocco. Fortunately that advice was not followed; had it been, the Shakespeare would have emerged from the binder's hands beautiful perhaps in appearance, but all which could tell of its past history would have perished amid the rubbish and waste of a binder's workshop. To-day, it exhibits one of the very few Shakespeare bindings which show no traces whatever of the re-binder's or restorer's hand; the gashes where the iron staple was torn off are still there, with rough edges of broken leather, and the broken corners still hang limply, as when the injury was first inflicted.[106]

Strickland Gibson, who wrote these words, was among those most responsible for advocating, by demonstration, an approach to the repair of old books that sought to preserve evidence of all kinds.

In a century that witnessed so many new learned societies, it took an extraordinarily long time for the world of old books to organise itself sufficiently to bring professional and bibliophile interests together. The initiative came in Edinburgh, with the foundation of the Edinburgh Bibliographical Society in 1890. In London, the Bibliographical Society followed in 1892. At first, and despite the presence amongst its earliest members of experienced bibliographers and interpreters of early printing such as Talbot Baines Reed, R. Copley Christie and Francis Jenkinson, it was a society more often concerned to amalgamate knowledge than to re-examine its foundations. Some of Henry Bradshaw's influence was personified in Jenkinson, University Librarian at Cambridge from 1889. But Edward Gordon Duff, who failed to obtain employment at both the British Museum and the Bodleian Library, was of much wider influence than Jenkinson. His manual *Early printed books* (1893) was published by Kegan Paul in a series edited by A. W. Pollard of the British Museum that also included Falconer Madan of Oxford on books in manuscript, W. J. Hardy on bookplates and the designer and art historian Herbert P. Horne on bookbinding. Duff looked explicitly back to Bradshaw, dedicating his book to his memory and quoting extensively from Bradshaw's uncompleted article on typography intended for the *Encyclopaedia Britannica*. With Duff, the general public was told something of what Bradshaw had managed to communicate only to specialists. Like Robert Proctor (1868–1903) in the British Museum, he sought to arrange lists of fifteenth-century books in order of their printers rather than in alphabetical order by author or town. Bradshaw's work depended on this approach, though he brought to it an acute codicological sense as well. Duff looked also back to the other, English, tradition that had dominated

---

106 Strickland Gibson, in *The original Bodleian copy of the first folio of Shakespeare*, p. 13.

much of the century, before developing it further: 'The more popular, generally associated with the name of Dibdin, treats specimens of early printing merely as curiosities, valuable only according to their rarity or intrinsic worth, or for some individual peculiarity found in them.'[107] Following Bradshaw, and quoting him, Duff insisted on the importance of the individual copy, the 'habit of patiently watching a book, and listening while it tells you its own story'.

From 1893, Duff was employed briefly as librarian to Mrs Rylands, in Manchester, where he oversaw the publication of a three-volume catalogue of the whole collection, including the Spencer library that had been so lionised by Dibdin and which Mrs Rylands bought in 1892. Had Duff remained in this post, his interests might have been more circumscribed; and he might have proved less influential. But he resigned, and for the rest of his life depended on an insecure income from his books or from contributing to catalogue entries for bookselling firms including J. Pearson in Pall Mall Place, London. At the same time, partly inspired by Weale's catalogue of bindings in the Victoria and Albert Museum (1894–8), he was building up his own reference collection of early blind-stamped bindings that, when it came to auction in 1925, was immediately recognised as the most valuable and far-reaching survey of its kind to date. As so often in historical bibliography, a subject very far from defined even within the confines of its most influential group of advocates, the Bibliographical Society, some of the most influential figures were not in academe, but in libraries and in the book trade. Like E. P. Goldschmidt, who established himself as an independent bookseller only after the end of our period and was to buy heavily at the Duff auction sales, Duff was not least a bookseller. Goldschmidt benefited both from training with the Viennese firm of Gilhofer & Ranschburg and, in London, from the former Polish activist W. M. Woynicz, who escaped from Siberia to England in 1890 and brought a firmly continental outlook to the London trade. The extent to which British bookselling and bibliographical scholarship benefited from immigrants such as Quaritch, Woynicz (who anglicised his name to Voynich) and, later, the Dutch-Austrian Goldschmidt, has still to be properly explored.

Duff tried to see printing with the eyes of Bradshaw. Though his interests also encompassed bookbinding and the prosopography of the British book trade, he did not display Bradshaw's codicological acuity. He also had little interest in the application of printing history to textual bibliography. This changed with the advent of two young men who were impatient of much received practice, and who found an ally in the older and more experienced A. W. Pollard at the

107 Duff, *Early printed books*, p. 201.

British Museum. W. W. Greg and Ronald B. McKerrow were contemporaries at Trinity College, Cambridge, Greg from the family that owned *The Economist* and McKerrow from a family of engineers. Concentrating on English books printed before 1641 (and hence following the time-limit established by George Bullen's catalogue of early English books in the British Museum, published in 1884), they campaigned for a better understanding not just of the appearance of early books, but of how this was affected by their manufacture. When in 1914 McKerrow sought to assemble guidance on bibliographical evidence, he remarked the 'curious ignorance of the most elementary facts of the mechanical side of book-production during the Tudor and Jacobean period which is sometimes shown even by scholars in other respects well equipped'.[108] He encouraged potential editors to gain some experience in setting type and in printing on a wooden press (an experience not easily to be found); he set out systematically the main procedures of the British printing house in the sixteenth and seventeenth centuries; and he displayed the arrangements of pages on the full sheet of paper by which formats were to be established and described. Only by understanding the processes and sequences of manufacture could an editor expect to arrive at an understanding of how a printer had tackled an author's manuscript in the first place.

This reversal of emphasis, on manufacture rather than on the finished book, was not entirely new, and in any case it relied primarily on the artefactual evidence of what could be seen and handled. In some respects McKerrow was simply extending the work of Talbot Baines Reed on the history of printing types, of Henry Bradshaw on the codicology of the early printed book, and of Edward Gordon Duff on the history of the book trade. For printing itself he drew on Blades and on J. Southward's *Modern printing* (1898): he showed no sign of having seen the American T. L. de Vinne's edition of Moxon's *Mechanick exercises . . . applied to the art of printing* (London, 1683), published at New York in 1896 and a more authoritative means of understanding the early printing house than Southward's explicitly modern work.

In crucial respects, and despite their real achievements in returning *ad fontes*, Pollard, Greg and McKerrow sometimes depended too much for their understanding of early printed books on observation of modern practices. But in many others they revolutionised attitudes and methods of study. Their goals were the provision of reliably edited texts, and they added materially to what W. G. Clark and the other Cambridge editors had provided for Shakespeare in the 1860s, and William Aldis Wright had understood about the variations in

---

108 McKerrow, 'Notes on bibliographical evidence for literary students and editors', p. 217.

early printing, in his work on Francis Bacon. In reflecting on the first twenty-one years of the Bibliographical Society in 1913, Pollard concluded by drawing attention to the need to provide underpinning for the historian and for the student of literature, and to preserve the inheritance of old books. If this seems too subservient a role, it was one that also showed signs of dramatic extension in the work of the more readily argumentative and determinedly analytical W. W. Greg. Pollard, McKerrow and Greg, different in their characters and in their approaches, were born into a generation already partly provided with the means to look on older printed books with new eyes and new perspectives. In their turn they were to dominate editorial work until well after the Second World War. As part of this new scholarly approach to old books, they managed to carry much of the book trade with them in a web of connections that spread across the Atlantic Ocean and provided a distinctive Anglo-American approach to historical bibliography and editorial theory and practice.

19

A year of publishing: 1891

SIMON ELIOT AND RICHARD FREEBURY

Introduction

The year 1891 saw innovations which would have a distinct if modest impact on the subsequent century: the zip fastener was invented, and the Swiss Army knife was developed. More momentously, a man named Burroughs was granted a patent for an adding machine.

Death culled Herman Melville, Charles Stuart Parnell, Arthur Rimbaud, Walt Whitman. Sir Joseph Bazalgette, the great civil engineer who had sorted out many of London's sewerage problems, died on 15 March, and the painter Georges Seurat followed on 29th of the same month. On 7 April the American showman P. T. Barnum died at the age of 80 asking 'How were the receipts today at Madison Square Garden?'

The year 1891 saw a Factory and Workshops Act raise the minimum working age to 11, and an Assisted Education Act that abolished fees for elementary education. This was an act the results of which would have been watched closely by all those members of the publishing and printing trades, rightly convinced that they could make money out of the provision of textbooks and other school supplies.

The number of those employed in the 'Paper, Printing, Books, and Stationery' sector of the UK economy had more than doubled in the twenty years since 1871 and was now at 256,000.[1] This sector was serving a population of 37.7 million, the overwhelming majority of whom were literate to some degree or other. However, the market for printed texts in English was by 1891 much wider than the UK: there was the still-expanding British Empire; there was the USA and a significant audience for English books on the continent of Europe. Much of the trade was served by two journals – the *Publishers' Circular* established in 1837 and the *Bookseller* which was started in 1858 – whose

---

1 Eliot, *Some patterns and trends*, Table F6, p. 154.

collective reach and range meant that together they mapped most of the new and continuing features of book production in the UK in the late nineteenth century.

The *Circular* had been recording rises in annual title production through the late 1870s and 1880s; this had peaked in 1888 at 6,591 but had declined marginally in the period 1889–91.[2] Yet what preoccupied the editorials of the journal in 1891 was not quantity but quality or, rather, the implied decline in quality brought on by increases in production. In part the *Circular* ascribed this to the educational system in critical terms that would be familiar a century and more later: 'Worthless books are increasing because the School Board begins an education which it does not finish.'[3] In another editorial Henry James is quoted to reinforce the point: 'The case, therefore', he says, 'is one for recognising with dismay that we are paying a tremendous price for the diffusion of penmanship and opportunity, that the multiplication of endowments for chatter may be as fatal as an infectious disease.'[4] But, ever optimistic, the editor found a silver lining: 'While it remains true, as Mr. Murray pointed out, that there are at present more bad books in the hands of the public than at any previous period, it is likewise true that there are more good ones.'[5] And felt a pride in catering, with substantial success, to a popular market: 'It is the fashion in some quarters to decry the literature of to-day. It is said that in this unfortunate era we have no great writers and no great books. Possibly this is true. But in popular literature we do "very well indeed".'[6] The journals, rather like the publishers and booksellers they served, struggled to reconcile their cultural and commercial roles, and defended one position when they could not hold the other.

Major changes in the book trade

After several decades in which the idea of free trade had encouraged competition and easy access to goods and texts, in 1891 members of the British book trade made some progress in their attempts to protect their property and livelihoods. The House of Representatives of the United States had already passed a bill to allow foreign authors US copyright on condition that their work was printed and manufactured in the USA, the work was published in the USA no

---

2 *Ibid.*, Tables A9–10, p. 115.
3 *Publishers' Circular* (subsequently abbreviated *PC*. All references are to 1891 unless otherwise stated) (1), p. 271.
4 *PC* (1), p. 469.   5 *PC* (1), p. 271.   6 *PC* (1), p. 581.

later than in its home country, and the foreign authors' country offered American citizens similar protection.[7] However, as the *Publishers' Circular* noted, it was still far from certain that the bill would become law.[8] Congress had made several attempts to introduce such legislation since the 1830s but all had been successfully opposed by American book publishers or manufacturers who profited from reprinting British books which did not enjoy copyright. When amendments were introduced in the Senate it seemed likely that opponents of legislation would win again as time ran out for the bill to pass before the end of the 51st Congress.[9] However, the Act to amend Title Sixty, Chapter Three, of the Revised Statutes of the United States, relating to Copyright, which became known as the Chace Act after one of its original proposers, was passed on 4 March, the last possible day, 'unexpectedly', as the *Author*, the journal of the Society of Authors, commented.[10] It came into force on 1 July.

British authors had long looked forward to gaining the legal right to payment for their works in America. The publisher Edward Marston warned that only the most famous English authors would benefit, as fewer English works would be printed in the United States.[11] But the main concern of the *Author* was that authors should not sign their American rights away.[12] The literary agent A. P. Watt advertised his 'friendly business relations with all the leading Publishers, both in this country and in America', claiming he was 'in the best position to take advantage of the present state of affairs, and obtain in both countries the very best terms for Authors'.[13]

Reaction in the British book trade was, however, more guarded. The *Bookseller* saw the legislation largely as an American protectionist measure, protecting American publishers from rival reprinters, American authors from the competition for publication of freely available British works, and the American paper and print trades from foreign book producers. It feared that the American requirement for printing and manufacture in the United States would mean that British works would in future be manufactured in America to avoid the double cost of production in both countries. To avert this danger Sir Roper Lethbridge MP proposed a balancing measure to secure British copyright only to those authors whose works were printed in the United Kingdom, its colonies and dependencies, or signatories to the Berne Convention.[14] The London trade supported the measure.[15] But the *Bookseller* recognised that such

---

7 *Bookseller*, pp. 8–10 (subsequently abbreviated *BS*. All references are to 1891 unless otherwise stated).

8 *PC* (1), p. 63.   9 *PC* (1), pp. 122, 165, 168–9, 218.

10 *Author* (All references are to 1891 unless otherwise stated) (1), p. 282.   11 *PC* (1), p. 15.

12 *Author* (1), pp. 223, 232.   13 *Author* (1), p. 307.

14 *BS*, p. 8. On Lethbridge's views, see also *PC* (1), p. 15.   15 *BS*, p. 532.

a measure flew in the face of British support for free trade.[16] The President of the Board of Trade, Sir Michael Hicks-Beach, gave little encouragement to a deputation from the book trades.[17] Others, including Edward Marston, believed that most publishers would in any case find it more profitable to print twice than to transport sheets across the Atlantic.[18] The one-sidedness of the Act was widely regretted but there was no agreement on the need for counter-legislation. As an alternative, an advertisement in the *Bookseller* offered British printers 'a flourishing Business in the United States' which 'affords a good opportunity for a firm of English printers to take a branch in America, to do work in accordance with the new International Copyright law'.[19]

In practice, however, the immediate effect of the Act was to give British publishers, like authors, additional protection in America, particularly where they already had American branches or connections. Prior to the Act's coming into force, C. H. Sergel of Chicago published in the USA James Bryce's *The American commonwealth* (without the copyright material of American contributors), even though Macmillan had published the work in England and America.[20] After the Act Macmillan was able to obtain copyright for the whole of Bryce's third edition.[21] Some British publishers rearranged their schedules to meet the requirement for simultaneous publication. In May Sampson Low, Marston & Co. announced that they were delaying the publication of George Russell's *Biography of the Right Hon. W. E. Gladstone, M.P.* until 6 July 'to meet the requirements of the American Copyright Act'.[22] George Allen similarly delayed publication of W. G. Collingwood's edition of *The poems of John Ruskin*.[23] By the Christmas season the *Bookseller* was noting: 'The number of books which are to be published simultaneously on both sides of the Atlantic testifies to the effects wrought by the new American Copyright Act.'[24]

While it was not ideal, the American Copyright Act at least provided British authors and publishers with more assured protection, and reward, for their works in America than they had previously enjoyed under the system of 'early sheets' (where American publishers paid for the early receipt of English works) and 'the courtesy of the trade' (where other American publishers did not reprint works acknowledged informally to be the property of one publisher).

---

16 *BS*, p. 633.   17 *BS*, p. 717.
18 *BS*, p. 8. Dangers to the British print trade were likewise played down by Walter Besant in *Author* (1), p. 231 and Sir Frederick Pollock, *PC* (1), p. 351.
19 *BS*, p. 1104.   20 *PC* (1), 2 May 1891, p. 447.
21 Nowell-Smith, *International copyright law*, p. 71. The third edition was published in two volumes in 1893 and 1895 (*English catalogue 1890–1897*, p. 134).
22 *BS*, p. 480.   23 *PC* (1), p. 417; *BS*, pp. 753, 993.   24 *BS*, p. 943.

By 1891 booksellers were also enjoying a greater degree of protection for their livelihoods than they had enjoyed since Lord Campbell's committee ended the policy of fixed retail prices in 1852. After decades of booksellers' complaining about the difficulty of making a living, two separate initiatives were starting to gain acceptance. The London Booksellers' Society, founded in 1890, accepted the public's right to a discount but aimed to restrict it to threepence in a shilling. By 1891 it had gained the support of a large number of London booksellers, some provincial booksellers and some publishers. Routledge, Low and Warne cooperated by not supplying booksellers who they thought would not observe the threepence in the shilling rule. The Society, on the other hand, criticised Cassell for not enforcing the maximum discount.[25] Cassell responded that they had in fact closed the account to which the Society referred but that they would 'much prefer to see ... a total abolition of the system of discount'.[26]

Sir Frederick Macmillan's alternative plan, also revealed in 1890, was to issue selected books at 'net prices' on which the public would be allowed no discount. Macmillan led the way in issuing 'net books' in 1890. By April 1891 the *Bookseller* noted: 'A very considerable number of net price books have been issued within the past month.' It noted works published by Macmillan, Griffith & Farran, Philip & Son, T. Fisher Unwin and Longman.[27] Advertisements and notices in the *Bookseller* in 1891 reflect a wide range of publishers offering 'net books', including new publishers such as Edward Arnold, Heinemann, Methuen, Yardley & Hanscomb and Lawrence & Bullen, alongside established publishers such as George Bell, Blackie & Son, Cambridge University Press, Cassell & Co., Henry Frowde, Hutchinson & Co., Low, Marston & Co., John Murray, J. C. Nimmo, Nisbet, D. Nutt, Swan Sonnenschein, Sweet & Maxwell, Wells Gardner, Darton & Co., Whitaker & Co. and Williams & Norgate.[28] The *Bookseller* reflected some concern at the scope of the initiative. It thought that, while the application of the 'net' system was beneficial for more expensive books, a 'mistake' was made 'in applying the net system to popular books of low price' such as Arnold's 7s 6d *Light of the world*. It believed that there should still be a place for 'booksellers who deal in wholesale quantities' such as Stonehams.[29]

25 *BS*, p. 129.   26 *BS*, p. 232.   27 *BS*, p. 325.
28 E.g. Arnold, p. 478; Heinemann, p. 345; Methuen, p. 350; Yardley & Hanscomb, p. 102; Lawrence & Bullen, p. 1036; Bell, p. 757; Blackie, p. 862; Cambridge University Press, p. 1149; Cassell, p. 856; Frowde, p. 1019; Hutchinson, p. 1030; Low, Marston, p. 1044; Murray, p. 1053; Nimmo, p. 487; Nisbet, p. 650; Nutt, p. 789; Sonnenschein, p. 286; Sweet & Maxwell, p. 1122; Wells Gardner, Darton, p. 1021; Whitaker, p. 625; Williams & Norgate, p. 221.
29 *BS*, p. 325.

Both initiatives were also largely aimed at London booksellers. The London Booksellers' Society circulated a letter inviting provincial booksellers to become members.[30] Several members of the provincial trade were present for the Society's 1891 dinner.[31] The Council report said that it 'would be glad to see branch Societies established in all large towns, these being affiliated to the London Society'.[32] The Oxford Street bookseller David Stott tried to reassure provincial booksellers that membership would not require them to give 'more than twopence off, nor even to give that. If they can get the full price let them do it.'[33] But it was to be another four years before the Society became a national institution. Provincial booksellers also felt excluded from the new arrangements for 'net books' and resented the publishers' interference in their affairs. Green & Son of Beverley, for example, felt that 'country booksellers clearly have not been considered' in the 'netting' of journals such as the *English Illustrated Magazine*. They thought it would have been better if 'Macmillan had refrained from making so bold an innovation'.[34]

The latest attempt by authors to extend domestic copyright also, like so many previous attempts since the last major reform of 1842, failed to gain the agreement of all those affected. On 11 May 1891 the Copyright Amendment Bill, introduced in the House of Lords on 25 November 1890, was read a second time, but in return Lord Monkswell agreed not to proceed in the current session.[35] The bill had been prepared by the Society of Authors and included provisions to extend the term of copyright to the life of the author and thirty years after his death and to safeguard to authors the right to abridge and dramatise their own works.[36] The *Author* proclaimed that the bill was 'a very apt illustration of what may be done when authors combine'.[37] But the *Bookseller* warned that the bill reflected the concerns only of 'the small group of authors who have incorporated themselves into a society'.[38] The Stationers' Company, for example, was concerned about the inclusion in the bill of a proposal for a Copyright Registration Office to supersede Stationers' Hall as the depository for new books.[39] On 26 February 1891 it petitioned that the bill be referred to a select committee and that petitioners be heard against the

---

30 *BS*, p. 325.   31 *BS*, pp. 929–30.   32 *BS*, p. 927.   33 *BS*, p. 929.
34 *BS*, pp. 428–9. See also R. Pelton of Tunbridge Wells (*BS*, pp. 430–1) and Turner Brothers of Reading (*PC* (1), p. 559). *BS* itself (p. 325) did not see the sale of the *English Illustrated Magazine* net as a problem.
35 *Parliamentary Debates* (3rd series), 353 cc. 437–60.
36 Lely, *Copyright law reform*, pp. 10–16, 85–94; Bonham-Carter, *Authors by profession*, pp. 161–2.
37 *Author* (1), p. 311.   38 *BS* 1890, p. 1373.
39 Lely, *Copyright law reform*, pp. 14, 87. In fact, Stationers' Hall had lost its most important depository functions after the 1842 Copyright Act, see Eliot, ' "Mr. Greenhill, whom you cannot get rid of" '.

bill.[40] Like previous attempts at domestic copyright reform, this one failed for lack of a consensus among the different interested groups. The work on discounting, 'net books' and copyright, nevertheless, continued. The London Booksellers' Society expanded to become the Associated Booksellers of Britain and Northern Ireland in 1895. The following year the Publishers Association was founded. The booksellers', publishers' and authors' groups cooperated to agree the Net Book Agreement, which came into force on 1 January 1900, and contributed to the next major Copyright Act in 1911.[41]

The dynamics of the book trade

There were a number of significant deaths in the trade in 1891, including William Henry Smith of W. H. Smith, George Dean of Dean & Son, George Lock of Ward, Lock, Bowden & Co., and Edmund Sydney Williams of Williams & Norgate.[42] Adam W. Black retired from A. & C. Black.[43] If these businesses were to survive they needed to be prepared for such losses and able to hold their ground against new rivals. In 1891 established publishers, for example, faced competition from new entrants such as the revived Constable, and Lawrence & Bullen.[44] The establishment of the American company Osgood McIlvaine in London in 1891 was a sign of the international nature of the competition. This was also reflected in F. A. Brockhaus of Leipzig's new branch at 48 Old Bailey, and E. Lyon-Claesen of Brussels's new branch at 13 Paternoster Row.[45] Established authors were likewise competing against writers aiming at new markets, booksellers against general stores, department stores and other sellers of discount books, and circulating libraries against cheap booksellers and public libraries. After a slow start (133 adoptions up to 1886), over a hundred libraries were adopted between 1886 and 1891.[46]

In this competitive world individuals were advised to be businesslike. In January 1891 Walter Besant in the *Author* warned fellow-writers: 'Never forget that publishing is a business, like any other business, totally unconnected with philanthropy, charity or pure love of literature. You have to do with business men.' He encouraged authors to negotiate 'on business principles'.[47] In

---

40 *BS*, p. 428; *Parliamentary Debates* (3rd series), 350 c.1617.
41 Barnes, *Free trade in books*, pp. 144–6; Feather, *Publishing, piracy and politics*, pp. 195–204.
42 Smith, *BS*, pp. 925–6; Dean, *BS*, pp. 535–6; Lock, *BS*, pp. 836–7, (correction) p. 917; Williams, *BS*, p. 838.
43 *BS*, p. 531.
44 Constable, *BS*, p. 632; Lawrence & Bullen and Osgood McIlvaine, *BS*, p. 424; Mumby and Norrie, *Publishing and bookselling*, 5th edn, pp. 277–81.
45 *BS*, p. 1268; *BS*, p. 254.   46 Greenwood, *Public libraries*, p. 1.   47 *Author* (1), pp. 223, 224.

New Grub Street (published in 1891 but set in 1882) George Gissing contrasted Edward Reardon, 'the old type of unpractical artist', with Jasper Milvain, 'the literary man of 1882', who argued that 'literature nowadays is a trade'.[48] Contemporaries argued about the authenticity of Gissing's harsh picture of writers struggling to survive.[49] But, as Cross has shown, there were real-life counterparts to the characters portrayed.[50] A few established authors were well paid. George Meredith received £1,000 for a six-year lease of copyright on *One of our conquerors*.[51] Gissing himself, however, sold the copyright of *New Grub Street* to Smith, Elder & Co. for the very modest sum of £150.[52] And below that, others paid to have their work published, sometimes losing their money to fraudsters.[53] The *Author* warned writers not to pay for the production of their works or to send off manuscripts in response to dubious advertisements.[54]

Booksellers likewise were being told to be financially aware. 'Devonia', a correspondent to the *Bookseller*, wrote: 'From my study of bankruptcy cases I find that the majority of retail traders who fail have not any proper system of book-keeping. Consequently, they do not know what their working expenses are.'[55] A number of correspondents pointed to the impossibility for country booksellers of making a profit from books allowing for all their expenses and the discounts that they gave.[56] Some succeeded by adjusting their businesses. Edwin Shepherd and Arthur Lee Humphreys bought Hatchard's of Piccadilly in 1891 after it had been losing money publishing *Atalanta*, a girls' magazine.[57] They reprinted classics in the Royal Library series, expanded the second-hand department and continued Humphreys's previous line creating and organising private libraries.[58] Others chose to specialise. W. E. Goulden of Canterbury disposed of his new books so that he could devote his 'sole attention to the old print, second-hand books, and remainder trades'.[59] This was trade in which less money was tied up and you were frequently dealing in tried and tested goods.

Some in the trade sought to strengthen their financial positions by turning their businesses into limited companies. George Newnes, proprietor of *Tit-Bits* and the *Strand Magazine*, for example, offered shares to newsagents,

48 George Gissing, *New Grub Street*, ed. Bernard Bergonzi (Harmondsworth, 1968), p. 38.
49 For example, *Author* (2), pp. 15, 43–4; Keating, *The haunted study*, p. 31.
50 Cross, *The common writer*, pp. 223–40.   51 Bonham-Carter, *Authors by profession*, p. 155.
52 Nesta, 'Smith, Elder & Co. and the realities of New Grub Street', p. 214.
53 Keating, in *The haunted study*, p. 53, notes the Society of Authors' support for the prosecution of William James Morgan by a Mr Swindells.
54 *Author* (1), pp. 223, 226.   55 *BS*, p. 534.   56 *BS*, pp. 638–9, 719–20, 835–6.
57 *BS*, p. 324; Mumby and Norrie, *Publishing and bookselling*, pp. 282–3.
58 Laver, *Hatchard's of Piccadilly*, pp. 40–1.   59 *BS*, p. 836.

booksellers, advertisers and staff while he himself retained 250,000 of the 400,000 shares, became Permanent Governing Director and sought to retain 'absolute authority in his own hands, just as though it continued a private business of which he was the sole proprietor'.[60] After the death of Robert Farran, another publisher Griffith, Farran, Okeden & Welsh likewise converted to a private limited company, this time with the whole of the issued capital taken up by members of the business.[61] Conversion into a limited company in 1890 was not, however, enough to save the publisher Groombridge & Sons. The original partners, G. S. and H. Y. Groombridge, were unable to discharge the debts of the firm for which they remained liable and the company was wound up in 1891.[62] The copyrights, stock, plates, engravings and goodwill of the business were put up for sale. W. H. & L. Collingridge, who began publishing gardening magazines in 1884, bought the stock, copyright, engravings and stereotype plates of Shirley Hibberd's gardening books.[63]

Other businesses sought to exploit the international trade. In 1891 Heinemann & Balestier published the English Library on the continent as a rival to the older Tauchnitz series.[64] Gay & Bird joined in a new business importing American books, magazines and newspapers.[65] By 1891 many businesses had branches in various countries. The lithographers, colour and letterpress printers and embossers J. M. Kronheim had offices in London, Manchester, Dublin, Glasgow and Melbourne.[66] The Nops' Electrotype Agency had offices in London, Paris, New York, Melbourne, Ontario and Bombay.[67] Some of these businesses were also among those making the most of recent technology. Kronheim and Nops were among the few advertisers in the *Bookseller* to give a telegraphic address and four-digit telephone number as well as a mail address.[68] Also seeking international coverage, the Edison Mimeograph Company sought 'responsible agents... all over the world' for its 'perfect copying apparatus, invented by the great and only Edison', 'the only device by which quantities of copies may be obtained from one... original', 'invaluable to the Book Trade for circularising and issuing Lists'.[69]

---

60 *BS*, p. 636.

61 *BS*, p. 1128. So also the wholesale bookbinder E. Symmons & Sons (*BS*, p. 632) and the bookseller Olley of Belfast (*BS*, p. 833).

62 *BS*, p. 425. See also pp. 323, 423, 531.

63 *BS*, pp. 716, 1270; Mumby and Norrie, *Publishing and bookselling*, p. 276.

64 *BS*, p. 1272; *PC* (2), p. 667. Although *BS* regarded it as 'a very successful rival' to Tauchnitz it lost money and was wound up in 1893 (St John, *William Heinemann*, pp. 20–1).

65 *BS*, pp. 228, 1127.   66 *BS*, p. 101   67 *BS*, p. 86.

68 The other regular advertiser to do so was the bookbinders Leighton Son & Hodge (*BS*, p. 104).

69 *PC* (2), p. 469.

While individual businesses sought to strengthen their positions, competition also encouraged various forms of consolidation within businesses and within the trade. Kegan Paul, Trench, Trübner & Co. concentrated the three businesses comprising the company in a new building, Paternoster House, Charing Cross Road, 'specially erected to meet their requirements'.[70] Low, Marston & Co. purchased the whole of the home and export business of William Dawson & Sons, Cannon Street, including the newspaper, bookselling, advertising and stationery departments.[71] John Ogden & Co. Limited, printers of the *Bookseller*, amalgamated with James Smale & Co. Limited to form Ogden, Smale & Co. Limited.[72] Various manufacturers of bookbinders' cloth amalgamated to form the Winterbottom Book Cloth Company Limited under the supervision of three of the principal English manufacturers.[73] Not all amalgamations went so smoothly, however. The Hansard Printing Union had by 1891 incorporated a range of London printing, publishing, bookbinding and wholesale concerns as well as being the proprietor and publisher of Hansard Parliamentary Debates. It was wound up on 13 May after it was unable to pay its debts.[74] George Simpson, wholesale bookbinder of Paternoster Square, repurchased from the liquidators all the interest in his business acquired by the Union.[75]

Competition was also giving way to cooperation as participants in the book trade worked together to protect their collective interests. The London Booksellers' Society took up the booksellers' long-standing complaint against publishers who refused to replace imperfect books with good ones and instead kept booksellers' customers waiting while they corrected the imperfect book. It obtained the agreement of 'a great majority' of publishers to exchange a new copy for each imperfect book at once.[76] Country booksellers were less successful in ending what they saw as another injustice, the loading of periodicals with advertisements, for which the bookseller had to pay the carriage but for which he received no reward. Correspondents to the *Bookseller* made various suggestions that booksellers and customers should share the benefit of including the inserts or that booksellers should simply burn them. But no

---

70 *BS*, p. 632.   71 *BS*, p. 832.   72 *BS*, p. 128.   73 *BS*, p. 1269.   74 *BS*, p. 531.

75 *BS*, pp. 716, 803. In June *BS* also reported a rumour that Simpkin Marshall, Hamilton, Kent & Co. had arranged the purchase of wholesale businesses of the late Henry Vickers of 317 Strand and Edward Curtice, Catherine Street, which had been part of the Hansard Publishing Union. In August, p. 716, it reported that the company 'have just removed the business recently acquired by them from Catherine Street to larger and more convenient premises at 317 Strand'. Simpkin Marshall had previously amalgamated with Hamilton, Adams & Co. and Kent & Co. in 1889 (Mumby and Norrie, *Publishing and bookselling*, p. 284).

76 *BS*, pp. 129, 229, 927, 928.

solution was agreed.[77] A trade committee did, however, succeed in dissuading the railway companies from some proposed increases in the rates for the carriage of books and stationery.[78]

Employers and employees were also coming together formally or informally to negotiate reduced working hours. On a formal level, the London master bookbinders agreed to their journeymen's request for an eight-hour day, forty-eight-hour week, starting from 1 January 1892, with the same pay as for their current fifty-four hours, and additional rates for overtime.[79] Less formally, the booksellers' assistants, 'not a very demonstrative set of men' who 'do not form unions and proclaim strikes', were more quietly seeking a seven o'clock closing time from Monday to Friday and five o'clock on Saturday, claiming that, with a proper sense of Victorian priorities, they had 'no time either for self-improvement or enjoyment'. David Stott had already introduced the reduced hours at his Oxford Street bookshop without, he supposed, any loss of business. Jarrold & Sons of Norwich had decided to close their establishment on Thursday afternoons during the summer season. The firm had also encouraged the formation of a cricket and tennis club to which they had made 'a very handsome donation'.[80] Some booksellers at least were showing that being businesslike and financially aware was not altogether incompatible with philanthropy and a concern for employees' welfare.

New books and magazines

In 1891 a reviewer in the *Bookseller* highlighted the predictability of the three-volume novel *That affair*: 'There is nothing especially remarkable in Mrs. Cudlip's new novel. The sweet story of love is told for the thousandth time, and conducted through various vicissitudes to its happiest issue.' The next novel, *A bitter birthright*, by Dora Russell, was 'neither better nor worse than nine-tenths of contemporary literature of the kind'.[81] The *Publishers' Circular* acknowledged contemporary criticism 'that the age of great writers... is gone: that Scott, Thackeray, Dickens, George Eliot, have no successors; and in particular that the weekly and monthly publications of the time have no stories worth reading'. It responded, however, by pointing to works by Bret Harte in *Macmillan's Magazine*; Stevenson in *Scribner's*; Hardy in the *Graphic*;

---

77 *BS*, pp. 7, 428, 430–1, 534, 1129, 1271.   78 *BS*, p. 230.

79 *BS*, pp. 717, 832, 917. As a result most London bookbinders raised prices for cloth and leather binding by 7.5 per cent. It was expected that the price for magazine and pamphlet work would be greater (*BS*, p. 1268).

80 *BS*, pp. 230, 231, 325, 328–9, 426.   81 *BS*, p. 234.

Hall Caine in the *Illustrated London News*; Stanley J. Weyman in the *Cornhill*; and J. M. Barrie in *Good Words*.[82] While there was no one outstanding author or novel there was a variety of content suited to different tastes. Novels in 1891 ranged from the social utopianism in William Morris's *News from nowhere* and the historical romance of Conan Doyle's *The white company* to the reality of literary life in George Gissing's *New Grub Street* and the subject of anti-semitic persecution in Hall Caine's *The scapegoat*.[83]

As well as a variety of content, novels were increasingly reflecting a variety of values as authors and publishers challenged the self-censorship that their predecessors had exercised to meet the demands of circulating libraries and their middle-class readers.[84] Hardy's *Tess of the D'Urbervilles* was eventually published in book form in 1891 by Osgood, McIlvaine after Hardy rejected the changes demanded by the Tillotson newspaper syndicate and after Murray and Macmillan turned it down because of what their readers described as 'frequent and detailed reference to immoral situations' and things 'which might give offence'.[85] Oscar Wilde's *The picture of Dorian Gray* was published as a book by Ward & Lock in April 1891 following criticism of its serialisation the previous year. Its preface, first published in the *Fortnightly Review* in March 1891, reflected the challenging moral tone, including the comment that 'There is no such thing as a moral or an immoral book. Books are well written, or badly written. That is all.' As elsewhere in 1891, in *Lord Arthur Savile's crime* and his collection of critical works, *Intentions* (incorporating 'The decay of lying', 'Pen, pencil and poison', 'The critic as artist' and 'The truth of masks'), Wilde questioned the moral norms and the truthfulness of life and art. The *Bookseller*, rather bemused as to whether the work was 'a novel, or a philosophy, or a criticism', saw 'the whole story from beginning to end' as breathing 'an unwholesome hothouse atmosphere' while admitting 'its cleverness and artistic qualities are not to be denied'.[86]

Novels were also appearing in a variety of forms. Significant fiction continued to be produced at 31s 6d in three-volume form. This included *New Grub Street*, *Tess of the D'Urbervilles* and *The white company*, already mentioned, as well as George Meredith's *One of our conquerors*, J. M. Barrie's *The little minister* and Mary Elizabeth Braddon's *Gerard*.[87] But *The picture of Dorian Gray*, *News from nowhere*, Rudyard Kipling's *The light that failed* and H. Rider Haggard's *Eric*

82 *PC* (2), p. 276.   83 Morris, *BS*, p. 352; Doyle, *BS*, p. 1084; Gissing, *BS*, p. 385; Caine, *BS*, p. 968.
84 *The haunted study*, pp. 256–7.
85 *BS*, p. 1263 (November back cover); Keating, *The haunted study*, pp. 260–3.
86 *BS*, pp. 449, 528 (May back cover); Gagnier, *Idylls of the marketplace*, pp. 49–99.
87 Meredith, *BS*, p. 469; Barrie, *BS*, p. 1007; Braddon, *BS*, pp. 849, 908.

Brighteyes were among novels initially published in one volume.[88] Cassell used 'the passing of the American Copyright Act' as a pretext for 'a Series of entirely new and original novels' by 'leading Writers in England, on the Continent and in America' at 'a uniform price of 7s 6d . . . instead of in the usual Three-Volume form'.[89] The increasingly international market was contributing to making the peculiarly English three-volume form less attractive.[90]

The *Publishers' Circular* also pointed to the growing popularity of the short story, which it felt was more suited to people's busy lives. It 'can be got through . . . in an odd half-hour after dinner, or during a short railway journey'.[91] Magazines increasingly included short stories rather than lengthy novels. In September the *Bookseller* noted that the new volume of the *English Illustrated Magazine* was to drop its twelve-monthly story and replace it with shorter tales by Mrs Oliphant, Clark Russell, Bret Harte and other well-known writers.[92] In doing so it was following the lead of the new magazines.[93] The *Strand Magazine*, started in January, included series of short stories involving the same character, starting with Conan Doyle's Sherlock Holmes.[94] *Black and White*, started in February, announced that there would be 'no serial stories: but a complete short story . . . in each number'.[95] Cassell again responded to 'the growing desire for Short Stories which is so striking a feature in the public taste of today' with 'a Series of Original Works by popular English and American Authors', the Short Story Library, at five or six shillings.[96] Some publishers produced collections of short stories issued in different periodicals. These included Hardy's *A group of noble dames*, Kipling's *Life's handicap* and Wilde's *Lord Arthur Savile's crime & other stories*.[97]

Popular works were still being issued in three-volume form but the speed with which one-volume editions of three-volume novels were published continued to undermine the value of the form to the circulating libraries that required at least a year to cover the cost of their purchases. *New Grub Street*, for example, after being published by Smith, Elder in April at 31s 6d, was available at six shillings by October.[98] An article in *Lippincott's* saw the form as lingering 'by grace of Mudie. When the circulating library gives forth its long-delayed

---

88 Kipling, *BS*, p. 272; Haggard, *BS*, p. 479; Cross, *The common writer*, p. 207.
89 *BS*, pp. 856, 1004.
90 See *PC* (1), p. 15 on the threat of the Chace Act to the three-volume form and circulating library.
91 *PC* (2), p. 33.   92 *BS*, p. 834.
93 It was also following their lead in illustrating every article (*BS*, p. 834).
94 Ashley, *The age of the storytellers*, pp. 196–200.   95 Keating, *The haunted study*, p. 39.
96 *PC* (2), p. 351; *BS*, p. 856.
97 Hardy, *BS*, p. 527 (May back cover); Kipling, *BS*, pp. 839, 868; Wilde, *BS*, pp. 744, 827 (August back cover).
98 Eliot, 'The three-decker novel and its first cheap reprint'.

fiat, this cumbrous form will give way to American compactnesss.'[99] It was largely anticipating what happened in 1894 when the rival libraries of Smith and Mudie combined to end the three-volume novel.[100]

In non-fiction the *Publishers' Circular* noted that 1891 was a year 'of great activity in publishing monographs on distinguished persons'.[101] We have already noted George Russell's *Biography of the Right Hon. W. E. Gladstone, M.P.* Other biographies included Lord Rosebery's *Pitt*, Justin McCarthy's *Sir Robert Peel*, Randall Thomas Davidson's *The life of Archibald Campbell Tait, Archbishop of Canterbury*, Sir H. S. Cunningham's *Earl Canning*, William Stebbing's *Sir Walter Raleigh* and C. F. Holder's *Charles Darwin: his life and work*.[102] It was also a significant year for travel. Jerome K. Jerome's *The diary of a pilgrimage* told of his journey to Germany to see the passion play at Oberammergau.[103] More politically sensitive, the *Bookseller*'s notice of George Kennan's views of *Siberia and the exile system* was obliterated by the Russian censor in copies sent to its Russian readers.[104] It was, however, particularly the European intervention in Africa that produced a flood of works of exploration and travel. These included Major Casati's *Ten years in Equatoria*; *New light on dark Africa*, the journal of Dr Carl Peters; S. T. Pruen's *The Arab and the African*; T. H. Parke's *My personal experiences in equatorial Africa, as medical officer of the Emin Pasha Relief Expedition*; and F. R. Wingate's *Mahdiism and the Egyptian Sudan*.[105]

In other areas, there were some distinguished religious and historical works. Richard William Church's *History of the Oxford movement* was published the year after John Henry Newman died.[106] *The imperial history of England* continued the history started by David Hume to the current day.[107] Sir Edwin Arnold produced *The light of the world* on the life of Christ.[108] A new quarterly periodical, the *Economic Review*, began in February, published by the Oxford University Branch of the Christian Social Union. It was primarily intended 'for the study of duty in relation to social life', containing articles 'dealing with Economic Morals from the point of view of Christian teaching'.[109] Elsewhere, the interest in socialism reflected in Morris's *News from nowhere* was evident in the start of the *Clarion*, edited by Robert Blatchford, and *Labour Leader*, edited by Keir Hardie, and in Wilde's article 'The soul of man under

99 Frederic M. Bird, 'Brevity in fiction', *Lippincott's* 47 (April 1891), pp. 531–2.
100 Griest, *Mudie's circulating library and the Victorian novel*, pp. 171–5.   101 PC 1892(1), p. 7.
102 Pitt, *Christmas BS*, p. 43; Peel, *BS*, p. 439; Tait, *BS*, pp. 537, 590; Canning, *BS*, p. 1273; Raleigh, *BS*, p. 1272; Darwin, *BS*, p. 544.
103 *BS*, pp. 440, 472.   104 *BS*, p. 1273; censored, 1892, p. 5.
105 Casati, *PC* (1), p. 451; *BS*, pp. 224, 434; Pruen, *BS*, p. 545; Parke, *BS*, p. 1131; *Christmas BS*, p. 225; Wingate, *BS*, p. 1048.
106 *BS*, pp. 339, 377.   107 *BS*, pp. 725–30.   108 *BS*, p. 316.   109 *BS*, p. 128.

socialism'.[110] It was answered by *A plea for liberty: an argument against socialism and socialistic legislation*, produced by the Liberty and Property Defence League, which included chapters criticising state involvement in areas such as libraries, education and postal services.[111] In a different direction, an early article by H. G. Wells, 'Zoological retrogression', picked up on the degenerative theories of the period, questioning man's permanence or permanent ascendency.[112]

A. H. Miles produced the first of his ten-volume *The poets and the poetry of the century*[113] and Ellis and Elvey produced a new one-volume edition of *The poetical works of Dante Gabriel Rossetti*.[114] The man of letters Edmund Gosse translated Ibsen's *Hedda Gabler* and collected thoughts about some of the books in his private library in *Gossip in a library*.[115] John Churton Collins, who had been fiercely critical of Gosse's inaccurate scholarship when Gosse was Clark Lecturer at Cambridge, argued the appropriateness of literature as a university subject of study distinct from philology in *The study of English literature: a plea for its recognition and organisation at the universities*.[116]

Cheap series continued to be started. Warne's two-shilling Crown Library[117] and Routledge's sixpenny Caxton Novels[118] were among those started in 1891. But there were also printers and publishers interested in producing books of quality. The new publisher Lawrence & Bullen planned to publish mainly 'high-class books, of which limited editions only will be issued'.[119] Their Muses' Library was a five-shilling 'series of English poets well edited and well printed'.[120] The Leadenhall Press produced for its subscribers *London city*, which the *Bookseller* praised for its 'wealth of illustration and beauty of typography'.[121] Under the title of Chiswick Press editions C. Whittingham & Co. planned a series of select English classical works printed at hand-press, starting with a reprint of Fielding's *Journal of a voyage to Lisbon*.[122]

Of the new general magazines in 1891, George Newnes's *Strand Magazine*, started in January, was the most successful. Aimed at a more middle-class market than Newnes's earlier *Tit-Bits*, the *Strand* was a sixpenny monthly with 'stories and articles by the best British writers, and special translations from

---

110 Mutch, *English Socialist periodicals*, p. 1. Wilde's article was published in *Fortnightly Review* (1891), pp. 292–319.
111 *PC* (1), p. 126.
112 Published in *Gentleman's Magazine* 271 (1891), pp. 246–53. See also below, pp. 701–3.
113 *BS*, p. 266.   114 *BS*, p. 40.   115 *PC* (1), p. 103; (2), p. 694.
116 Charteris, in *The life and letters of Sir Edmund Gosse*, p. 194, sees parallels between Collins's attack on Gosse and Gosse's description of the attack on Camden by Ralph Brooke in his essay on Camden's *Britannia* in *Gossip in a library*. On the dispute generally see pp. 193–200; Thwaite, *Edmund Gosse*, pp. 276–97.
117 *BS*, p. 601.   118 *BS*, p. 1129.   119 *BS*, p. 424.   120 *BS*, p. 1036.   121 *BS*, pp. 532, 640.
122 *BS*, p. 1268.

the first foreign authors . . . illustrated by eminent artists'.[123] Undercutting the *Strand Magazine*, at threepence, the *Ludgate Monthly* started in May; 'An illustrated family magazine', it included contributions from Florence Marryat and Rudyard Kipling in its first number.[124] *Black and White*, a sixpenny newspaper which started in February, concentrated on art and literature and shared the contemporary interest in illustration and short stories.[125] The *Victorian Magazine*, another illustrated sixpenny monthly started in December, included serials by Mrs Oliphant and Sarah Doudney. This was incorporated in *Atalanta* the following year.[126] Some new periodicals did not last their first year. These included *Groombridge's Magazine* and the *Ladder*, 'A Review of Public Affairs, Literature, Science and Art'.[127] Among established magazines, *Murray's Magazine* was suspended after its December number. The *Bookseller* commented: 'Perhaps the literary flavour of its contents has been a trifle too delicate for the jaded appetite of the multitude.'[128]

Longer-term patterns and trends in the trade

However various and new the events of the year were, the trade in 1891 was defined as much by what it had done in the past and what it was continuing to do, as by the novelties of the year. For instance, the frequency with which the manufacturers of stationery items advertised reminds one of an aspect of the industry which, though frequently ignored, played an important role in both production and retail.[129] Few bookshops in 1891 exclusively sold books: printed books would be only one, and often not the most important, item of stock. Booksellers would frequently have made more profit from selling writing paper, envelopes, diaries, scrapbooks, stamp albums, personalised printed stationery and fancy goods than from books.[130] Most offices, though

---

123 Sullivan (ed.), *British literary magazines*, pp. 397–402; Jackson, *George Newnes*, pp. 87–118; Ashley, *The age of the storytellers*, pp. 196–208. In March 1950 it merged with *Men Only*.

124 *BS*, p. 432. This was taken over by *Black and White* in 1895 and merged with the *Universal Magazine* in 1901 (Ashley, *The age of the storytellers*, pp. 118–22).

125 *PC* (1), p. 143; Ashley, *The age of the storytellers*, p. 244. It merged with the *Sphere* in 1912.

126 *BS*, pp. 1130a, 1185; Ashley, *The age of the storytellers*, p. 243.

127 *Index to the periodical literature of the world (covering the year 1891)*, p. 32. On the *Ladder* see *BS*, pp. 6, 227.

128 *BS*, p. 1270.

129 In 1907 manuscript books were worth 4.7 per cent of the total net value of printing and related industries; in the same year printed books accounted for 5.3 per cent; see Eliot, *Patterns and trends*, p. 157.

130 For instance, on just one page of *BS* in 1891 there were advertisements for the following businesses: 'bookselling, stationery, library and fancy trade in west-end suburb'; 'bookselling, stationery, fancy, library and printing business in cathedral city'; 'bookselling, stationery, library and fancy trade in country town'; 'bookselling, library, stationery, etc in London thoroughfare', p. 1104.

typewriters and filing cabinets were beginning to have an impact, were still run using letter and ledger books, and this demand was steady and relatively easy to satisfy, not something that could be said, for instance, of the market for fiction. Paper manufacturers such as Spicers and John Dickinson & Co. advertised their wares frequently,[131] as did Bemrose and Cassell, whose calendars and diaries for 1892 were being promoted as early as 16 May 1891.[132] There was even a trade journal devoted to this specialism: the *Stationer, Printer and Fancy Trades Register* advertised monthly in the *Circular*.[133]

There seemed to be a journal for virtually every aspect of the book trade; this reflected a growing self-consciousness, allied to a recognition of the need to defend common interests collectively, that characterised the intellectual trades in the 1880s and 1890s. The process had started with the creation of the Society of Authors (SoA) in 1884. As we have seen, this was followed by the London Booksellers' Society in 1890,[134] which later became the Booksellers' Association. The year 1896 saw the formation of the Publishers Association. The *Circular* recorded the creation of the Museums Association in 1891,[135] and also of the less successful 'Retail Booksellers Co-operative Society', which called two poorly attended meetings before disappearing from the journal's pages.[136] This was but another expression of anxieties about bookselling that were being more effectively articulated by the debate on the Net Book Agreement (see above).

As befits the year that saw *New Grub Street* published, the trade journals offered many services to would-be authors: advertisements for such handbooks as Percy Russell's *The author's manual*, or *The art of authorship* compiled by George Bainton,[137] and *How to print and publish a book* issued at sixpence by Warren & Son, Winchester.[138] Editorial services were being touted, literary agents were promoting their services in the SoA's journal, the *Author*,[139] and modern technology offered support in terms of advertisements for typewriters and typing.[140]

---

131 *PC* (2), p. 287.   132 *PC* (1), pp. 492–3.   133 See, for instance, *PC* (1), p. 484.
134 *BS*, p. 916. On 1 October 1891 Booksellers' held their second dinner attended by nearly a hundred members.
135 *PC* (1), p. 97.   136 *PC* (1), pp. 305–6.
137 14 February, *PC* (1), p. 161. Bainton was accused of gathering these reminiscences under false pretences. Russell was published by Digby & Long, see *PC* (2), p. 52.
138 Announced 24 January, *PC* (1), p. 90.
139 A. P. Watt advertised his services in the *Author* – the journal of the Society of Authors – and listed Walter Besant, Rider Haggard and Rudyard Kipling among his authors. *Author*, 16 March 1891, p. 307.
140 For example, *Author*, 15 January 1891, pp. 250, iv.

Technology was also evident in the provision of illustrations, in particular the use of electrotypes to provide large libraries of stock images. S. W. Partridge offered 45,000 images; the Religious Tract Society advertised the availability of 50,000 images that had first appeared in its publications;[141] while Nops' Electrotype Agency frequently advertised its 2 million engravings 'suitable for illustrating newspapers, books, circulars, magazines, pamphlets, children's papers'.[142] Perry, Gardner & Co.'s 'Cliché Department' (a title that explains the origins of the modern use of the word) offered 'electrotypes of thousands of original wood engravings'.[143] Simple standardised technology and low-cost warehousing had by 1891 created a reservoir of images, images that were cheap enough to flow into virtually every form of print on offer. This was evident in the trade journals themselves, quintessentially in the Christmas issue of the *Circular*, which was a celebration of the interplay of text and image, and in which books with coloured illustrations vied with children's pictorial annuals, comics and cheap classics for the attention of the present-buyer.[144]

Cheap books

Cheapness was a recurrent theme in 1891 as it had been in the 1880s and was to be in the 1900s. On 25 July an editorial in the *Circular* celebrated the extreme cheapness of good literature: 'Nearly all the old favourites can now be bought for a few pence. Anyone who cares to examine publishers' catalogues will probably be surprised to learn of the bargains that are offered to the public in classics, ancient and modern.'[145] You would not have to go to publishers' catalogues, for the trade journals presented plenty of evidence. Tauchnitz, specialising in editions in English to be sold in continental Europe, were by 1 August advertising their titles in the *Circular* at '2s per volume sewed 1s 6d' (despite a letter from Longman on 7 February objecting to the sale even of second-hand copies of Tauchnitz in the UK);[146] on 22 August Frederick Warne's Chandos Classics were priced similarly at 1s 6d to 2s 6d.[147] But by 1891 such series appeared relatively expensive. On 19 September Chapman & Hall were promoting the 'Sixpenny Copyright Edition of *David Copperfield*',[148] while John F. Shaw & Co.'s advertisement on 16 May listed '*Shaw's Shilling Juveniles, Shaw's Penny Series*'.[149] Sixpence had been the price at which tens if not hundreds of thousands of copies of novels had been sold from the late 1860s onwards, but by the 1890s it had become the standard price for a paperbound

141 *PC* (1), pp. 347, 603.   142 *BS*, p. 196.   143 *PC* (1), p. 315.
144 The 1891 Christmas issue (vol. 55 no. 1327 A, pp. i–viii, 1–304) was published at 2s 6d.
145 *PC* (2), p. 79.   146 *PC* (1), pp. 145–6.   147 *PC* (2), p. 201.   148 *PC* (2), p. 299.
149 *PC* (1), p. 499.

novel. Certainly the real mass market competition lay in prices under a shilling, and many publishers were now competing at threepence and at a penny. On 28 March the *Publishers' Circular* was advertising 'The Crystal Stories Monthly, one penny, beautifully illustrated' published by Richard Willoughby of Paternoster Row;[150] Cameron, Ferguson & Co.'s 'Prairie Series of Penny Novels... Splendid Coloured Covers' were tempting readers on 5 September. 'Horner's Penny Stories for the People' were frequently advertised throughout the year and often carried a list of titles with numbers of copies sold against each title. On 20 June there were eighty-one titles with sales varying from 100,000 to 300,000.

Very cheap books raised the problem of quality versus quantity in its acutest form. One can almost hear the relief of the *Circular*'s editor on 19 December when he commented: 'We have received from Messrs. Jarrold & Sons a number of "Penny Popular Stories," which seem to be excellently adapted for spreading the influence of healthy literature among the people.'[151]

In contradistinction to healthy literature, just occasionally the trade journals revealed details about publications which for most of the time flowed subterraneously beneath the trade's more respectable activities. On 11 July the *Circular* reported on the seizure of a large quantity of indecent books and prints whose prices ranged from £1 to £86.[152] On 12 September it carried an editorial concerned with pornography and censorship. Its attitude was predictable, as was its British suspicion of continental moral laxness:

> The liberty of the press is a glorious thing when it is used and not abused. But when liberty degenerates into licence, and licence results in revolting spectacles of moral pollution, such as are sometimes presented to the public on the Continent, then it is time for the State to interfere.[153]

Education

The Victorians' optimistic answer to the threat from corrupting literature was 'education', and at least one issue per year of the *Circular* had been devoted to educational texts since 1840.[154] In 1891 there were two, one published on 17 January, and the other on 15 August in time for the new academic year. The January education number saw extensive advertising from the major textbook publishers: OUP, CUP, Longman, Macmillan, Blackie, Murray, Sampson Low, and many others. Most of these were broad in range but some were very specific. CUP advertised 'books suitable for Cambridge, Oxford and London

---

150 *PC* (1), p. 337.   151 *PC* (2), p. 688.   152 *PC* (2), pp. 38–9.   153 *PC* (2), p. 275.
154 See Eliot and Sutherland, 'Introduction' to *The Publishers' Circular*, pp. 13–14.

Examinations' which remind us of the extent to which textbook publishing was by now being focussed through the lens of examination systems.[155]

Educational texts cropped up throughout the year in both major trade journals. For any publisher, a range of textbooks that would sell to secure markets – with repeat orders – in their thousands every year was investment well worth making, for they created an ideal back-list which helped both to define and to underwrite a publishing house. But it was not just textbooks: the expansion of schools and Sunday schools meant that there was now a large demand for school prize books, a market which the publishers of the *Circular* – Sampson Low, Marston & Co. – catered for to the extent of offering different sets of prize books for girls and for boys.[156] Sampson Low were also very quick to respond to any change in the legislation governing the education system. By 28 February they were advertising 'New Code 1890, Sampson Low Readers' which have been 'specially prepared to meet the Code requirements'.[157]

By 1891 the schoolbook market was large enough to support specialist publishers, such as John Marshall, 'school teacher, publisher, provider of educational materials', who was featured in the *Circular*'s long-running feature 'Booksellers of today' on 17 January.[158]

But in the 1890s it was not just a schoolbook market. With the expansion of universities, university colleges and extension courses, and with the emergence of text-intensive new subjects (such as English), the university book market was becoming a significant one. In the *Circular* on 11 April W. B. Clive & Co. of 13 Booksellers Row, Strand offered a 'Tutorial Series, which includes over 200 works specially adapted for London University Examination'.[159] In the *Bookseller* on 10 October Murray's University Extension Manuals were being advertised 'to bring the higher education within reach of attainment by students of sufficient intellectual endowment, but whose scholastic training has been curtailed by circumstance'.[160]

Self-help and self-education were also catered for. On 16 May the *Circular* was advertising Simpkin, Marshall, Hamilton, Kent & Co. Ltd's Everbody's Series which, in order to help its promotion, 'May be obtained with show cases'. Among the titles were *Everybody's book of indoor games*, *Everybody's pocket lawyer* and *Everybody's book of proverbs*.[161] There were few areas in which self-improvement was not offered: throughout much of 1891 Sampson Low were advertising a guide to housewives on the subject of *Salads and sandwiches* by T. Herbert 'in boards 6d'.[162]

---

155 *PC* (1), p. 41.   156 See *PC* (2), pp. 70, 72.   157 *PC* (1), p. 230.   158 *PC* (1), pp. 60–2.
159 *PC* (1), p. 369.   160 *BS*, p. 1052.   161 *PC* (1), p. 533.   162 For example, *PC* (1), p. 675.

Technical and vocational skills training was not ignored. On 10 October the *Circular* advertised Sampson Low's Nursing Record Series of Text Books and Manuals.[163] On 11 April Crosby Lockwood & Sons of 7 Stationers' Hall Court were promoting a wide range of specialist training manual and 'how-to' books including *The colliery manager's handbook*, *The prospector's handbook*, *Safe railway working*, *Auctioneers: their duties and liabilities*, *The modern flour confectioner*. A more innocent world could also offer *Asbestos: its properties, occurrence, and uses*, while titles such as *Dynamo construction* and *Electric light fitting* remind us of the growing importance of domestic electricity to readers and others as it gradually replaced gas lighting, though not without complaints such as Marian Yule's in *New Grub Street*.[164] 'But then flashed forth the sputtering whiteness of the electric light, and its ceaseless hum was henceforth a new source of headache.'[165] Miss Yule would certainly not have appreciated Mrs J. E. H. Gordon's *Decorative electricity* published by Sampson Low at twelve shillings in April.[166]

In 1891 electricity was also having an impact on manufacturing and on the sale of books: the *Bimingham Daily Gazette* announced that it was employing the first rotary newspaper press powered by electricity in the country,[167] while D. Burchell Friend's new bookshop in Brighton included 'amongst other improvements, the adoption of the electric light'.[168]

Seasonal publishing

The nineteenth-century book trade witnessed the growth not only of valuable genre markets such as educational texts, but also of specific seasonal markets. In the *Circular* the summer holiday reading season was kicked off in its 'Export Number' of 23 May in which Smith, Elder advertised its list of 'Books for Seaside and Holiday Reading'.[169] The 13 June issue saw a flurry of holiday reading advertisements: 'Mr Murray's Handbooks', Sampson Low's 'Books for Travellers and Tourists' and W. H. Smith offering greatly reduced prices on 'A Selection of Books of Sport, Travel, etc.'[170] The following week Ward, Lock & Co. were offering their 'Illustrated Guide Books' and Nelson their 'new Chromo views and Guide books'.[171] By 27 June Henry & Co. were promoting the third edition of Zangwill's *The bachelors' club* as 'the book of the holiday season'.[172] On 11 July Bentley advertised not only their famous (if now seriously over-priced) '6s Favourite Novels' but also 'books for seaside and country', while J. W. Arrowsmith's Bristol Library's advertisement specifically addressed

---

163 *PC* (2), p. 420.   164 *PC* (1), p. 371.   165 Gissing, *New Grub Street*, ed. Bergonzi, p. 138.
166 *PC* (1), p. 396.   167 Clair, *A history of printing in Britain*, p. 273.   168 *BS*, p. 426.
169 *PC* (1), p. 545.   170 *PC* (1), pp. 625, 627, 629.   171 *PC* (1), pp. 649, 653.
172 *PC* (1), p. 675.

itself 'To Holiday Trippers – Special'.[173] We are reminded that this was the age of H. G. Wells's bicycling heroes: the 4 July issue of the *Circular* carries advertisements for 'Gall & Inglis' Cycling and Tourists' maps' and 'Iliffe & Son's "Books for Tourists" including *Cyclists' route book* (fifth thousand)'.[174]

The *Publishers' Circular* was no mere passive carrier of holiday reading promotions. On 4 July it printed an editorial on the necessity of holidays and thus of guidebooks: 'Steam, electricity and Mr. Thomas Cook have revolutionised the national tastes and habits, and travelling is a necessity of the age. In this era of high pressure a general breakdown would be the result if we were denied the annual visit to the Continent or the Scottish Highlands, the English Lakes or the seaside.'[175] And on the 25th of that month it followed this up with a discussion on 'Holiday reading': 'The Englishman may or may not be a lover of books at home, but he seldom leaves for a holiday without making some sort of provision for the mind, and part of every well-ordered travelling kit is devoted to literature.'[176]

However, busy though it was in terms of promotion, the summer holiday season was completely eclipsed by the Christmas market for books. With the invention of the modern Christmas in the early Victorian period, printers and publishers had found a new and profitable selling season which, by the 1840s, was larger than the traditional spring season. By the 1890s the Christmas market saw something close to double the number of titles produced in spring, the largest production now being in October and November so as to give plenty of time for present-buying. For decades the *Circular* had been issuing a separate Christmas Number in early December. In 1891 it cost 2s 6d, was issued on 4 December and charged substantial advertising rates.[177] It displayed the wares and services of at least 183 advertisers (some taking out multiple advertisements). The editorial core of the Christmas Number consisted of an alphabetical review of 'Gift Books of the Season' which was copiously illustrated from the books. Indeed, illustration was a predominant feature of this issue, with virtually every page displaying one or more illustrations, some of them being full-page. Children's books and annuals featured strongly, but the coverage was broad and most markets for books and related goods were catered for.

With appropriate amplitude and philanthropic tone, the *Circular*'s editor reviewed the recurrent triumph of planning and production represented by the issue:

---

173 *PC* (2), pp. 50, 53.   174 *PC* (2), pp. 4, 19.   175 *PC* (2), p. 5.   176 *PC* (2), p. 79.
177 £2 2s od half page, £4 4s od whole page; see *PC* (2), p. 473.

What the world, what England in particular, would be without his Christmas literature would be hard to imagine. Happily the supply is steady and ample. All through the spring and early summer innumerable busy pens are at work and in due season the stream of gift books begins to flow. It flew this year with as full a flood as ever.[178]

But he also had a very topical observation to make:

One thing more we must notice before closing this brief preliminary discourse, and that is that many of the books reviewed in the following pages bear the significant words 'Copyright in the United States.' This is a change from former years, that ought to make gladder the hearts of all who are concerned or connected with literature, and it will certainly make a still closer bond of union between the two great branches of the English speaking race.[179]

The publishing of information

Behind this rhetoric, which many authors and literary agents as well as publishers and booksellers used, was the reality of an international market for English texts of all sorts in which regularised copyright agreements (from Berne as well as with Washington) and speedy communications (in terms of steamships and the telegraph, and by 1891 the telephone) helped to create. This market demanded not merely novels and sentimental Christmas tales, but information as well as entertainments of all sorts. The importance of the common language and transatlantic cooperation is well illustrated by an advertisement from George Bell on 4 February for a 'fresh revision and further enlargement' of *Webster's international dictionary*. This had taken ten years and more than £60,000 to prepare.[180]

Information publishing, which took many forms including dictionaries, encyclopaedias, bibliographies, catalogues, handbooks, indexes, directories, almanacs and many other compilations, had been a striking feature of nineteenth-century publishing, and 1891 was no exception. There were the great multi-volume projects such as the *New English dictionary* (later to become the *Oxford English dictionary*) which had been issued in large paperbound parts called fascicles since January 1884. On 7 March OUP were advertising 'Vol. I. A. and B. Imperial 4to half-morocco' at £2 12s 6d, but also 'Part IV Section II. C–CASS (beginning of Vol. II.)' at five shillings, and promising 'Vol. III (E, F, and G) Part I' as being 'in the press'. On 4 July 1891 the *Bookseller* recorded

---

178 *PC* Christmas issue 1891, p. v.   179 *PC* Christmas issue 1891, p. vi   180 *BS*, pp. 129, 161.

the publication of 'Vol. III, Part 1, E–Every'.[181] This cumulative process was to continue until the project was completed in 1928.

Not quite as long in production but equally magisterial was the *Dictionary of national biography*, finally to be taken over by OUP but launched and published by Smith, Elder; 1891 saw volumes 25–28 published.[182] Given the rate of production, it is not surprising that the page of the *Bookseller* recording the publication of the twenty-seventh volume also carried the news that the first editor of the *DNB*, Leslie Stephen, had resigned because of ill health.

Many other publishing firms were engaged in information publishing. There was *Cassell's dictionary of the English language* in preparation which was to include scientific words, Americanisms, provincialisms and archaic words.[183] On 4 February the fourth volume of *The century dictionary* was issued by T. Fisher Unwin, with its fifth volume being announced on 6 June.[184] The *Bookseller* recorded Warne's publication of *Nuttall's standard pronouncing dictionary of the English language* on 6 May, and *Bryce's thumb English dictionary* – 15,000 words contained in 772 pages resulting in a book 2 × 2 inches and 3/4 inch thick – was published by David Bryce & Son, Glasgow at 1s 3d in June,[185] while the *New French dictionary* was announced on 7 August.[186] *A dictionary of classical antiquities* was noted on 6 June, and the *Dictionary of political economy* in quarterly parts from Macmillan was reviewed by the *Bookseller* on 7 August.[187] Dictionaries were also published in parts: on 4 April the *Circular* was advertising *Muret's encyclopaedic English–German dictionary*, the first number of which was available at 1s 6d.[188]

Volume 7 of *Chambers's encyclopedia* was noticed on 4 July.[189] On 24 January Sampson Low advertised the *Bibliotheca polytechnica*, 'a directory of technical literature', which had been first issued annually in 1889.[190] Directories flourished: a *Manchester diocesan directory* and a *Medical directory* published in January, a *Matriculation directory* in February, a *Director's directory* published in March, a *London directory* in November and most appropriately, given the volume of paper required by such productions, a *Paper mills directory* published at the beginning of the year and at the end (for 1892).[191]

Maps and atlases were produced in profusion at prices ranging from a shilling to twenty-one shillings and beyond by a host of publishers, including Charterhouse, Labberton, George Bell, Houlston, Cassell, Bacon, and Nelson who produced 'The Royal Wall Maps' of the British Isles and John Bartholomew's

181 *PC* (1), p. 238; *BS*, p. 641; advert 7 August, p. 714.   182 *BS*, pp. 34, 93, 325, 385, 637, 918.
183 *BS*, 4 February, p. 129.   184 *BS*, pp. 134, 499, 598.   185 See *PC* (1), p. 685; (2), p. 163.
186 *BS*, p. 719.   187 *BS*, pp. 538, 718.   188 *PC* (1), p. 347.   189 *BS*, p. 634.
190 *PC* (1), p. 105.   191 *English catalogue* 1891, p. 31.

School hand atlas at 2s 6d.[192] There was George Philip & Son with school atlases at 1s–1s 6d and a *Sixpenny unique atlas* 'Containing Seventy Maps and Ten Diagrams'.[193] Macmillan were also publishing John Bartholomew: on this occasion *The Library reference atlas of the world* available as one volume at £2 12s 6d and in eight monthly parts.[194] Cassell also exploited the part-issue system and advertised on 24 March part 1 of *The universal atlas* at one shilling, the whole to be completed in twenty-eight parts.[195]

Rather like a successful textbook, an extensively used, annually revised reference book offered a reliable source of income to a publisher and a stability to the back-list. Such publications as *Bradshaw's railway guides*, *Wisden* and *Whitaker's Almanack* could help sustain their publishers over decades and sometimes over centuries. The English class system was not only an invaluable source of comedy and tragedy on the stage and in novels; it also generated a highly profitable publishing line. There was, of course, Debrett's *Peerage, baronetage, knightage and companionage*, but also the now less well-known *Dod's peerage, baronetage and knightage*. Chatto & Windus made something of a specialism of this trade. On 7 March in the *Circular* their advertisement announced *Walford's Windsor peerage, baronetage and knightage* at 12s 6d, *Walford's county families of the United Kingdom 1891* at 50s, and Herbert Fry's *Royal guide to the London charities* which was 'published annually' at 1s 6d.[196] The relentlessly annual nature, and the huge size, of some forms of information publishing was made clear: on 26 December, Chatto announced *Walford's county families* for 1892; this, the thirty-second edition, came in at 1,300 pages.[197]

Textual self-consciousness

There was a form of information publishing recorded by the trade journals that could be regarded as highly self-referential. This was the effort to impose some form of bibliographical control on the promiscuous and fecund publishing industry on which the journals reported.

The obvious and most immediate example was the *Publishers' Circular*'s decision to move from fortnightly to weekly publication, and to increase its format from octavo to quarto at the same time. This occurred on 10 January 1891, the editor announcing that this move will 'renew its youthful vigour, thus appealing to a wider constituency than heretofore'. The company that produced the *Circular* was at the same time reconstructed, with two directors resigning – one, Mr Rivington, to devote 'his capital and his energies to the business of

192 *English catalogue* 1891, p. 6; *PC* (1), p. 395.   193 *PC* (1), p. 56.   194 *PC* (1), pp. 25, 287.
195 *PC* (1), p. 320.   196 *PC* (1), p. 233.   197 *PC* (2), p. 707.

electric lighting'.[198] Sampson Low, Marston & Co. were also responsible for the annual compilation of titles published, *The English catalogue of books*, whose 1890 edition was first advertised on 14 March 1891.[199] These annual lists were later compiled into longer runs: on 18 July work on *English catalogue of 1881–1889* was announced with a telling note attached: 'Publishers are requested to send particulars of any volumes belonging to **Series** which they have published during 1881–89, for insertion in the Appendix.'[200] The publication of books in series, and the frequent reissuing of reprints in new series, was a distinct and growingly important marketing tool in the later nineteenth century.

The *Circular* had published a long-running series of interviews with members of the book trade, and by 11 July it was advertising a list of these articles as *Booksellers and publishers of to-day* available from the *Circular* office.[201] Another series of articles indicated that the *Circular* was thinking historically as well as bibliographically: during 1891 it ran 'The keepsake annuals of sixty years ago' over a number of months, exploring that extraordinary literary fashion of the 1820s and 1830s that provided publishers with handsome profits in North America, in the UK and in Europe from France to Russia.[202]

The *Circular* also carried extensive notices and advertisements of other publishers' bibliographical publications. On 5 September Griffith Farran Okeden & Welsh advertised *De fidiculis bibliographia*, 'being the basis of a bibliography of the violin and all other Instruments played with a bow in ancient and modern times'.[203] In December Thomas B. Smart produced a complete bibliography of Matthew Arnold in a limited edition; while in September Macmillan had produced a remarkable bibliographical catalogue of all the books published by the firm between 1843 and 1889.[204]

On 17 January Elliot Stock advertised volume III of *Book prices current* covering 1888–9, and also its journal, the *Book-Worm*, 'a treasury of old-time literature'.[205] Indeed, it was a year of magazines that tried to record and evaluate publications and the processes that brought them about. In January *Literary Opinion – Readers' Miscellany and Book Trade Review*, a 'new illustrated series monthly 2d', was launched.[206]

A more specialist journal was announced in January: the *Printing World*. This was also a significant year for printing with the establishment of William Morris's Kelmscott Press and its first outcome, *The story of the glittering plain*,

198 *PC* (1), p. 13.   199 *PC* (1), p. 268.   200 *PC* (2), p. 52.   201 *PC* (2), p. 31.
202 As an example see *PC* (1), p. 680.   203 *PC* (2), p. 247.   204 *BS*, pp. 1270, 833–4.
205 *PC* (1), p. 86.   206 *PC* (1), p. 3.

emerging in April 1891, while Elliot Stock published William Blades's *Penta-teuch of printing*.[207]

In literature, a new periodical, *World Literature*, reflected the increasing seriousness attached to its study. The mouthpiece of the Reading Guild, it was designed for 'the study of the best books available for the English, or for any other people, in their own tongue'.[208] In October the *Bookseller* noticed the establishment of Robertson Nicoll's *Bookman*; a later advertise-ment for it claimed that 10,000 copies had been sold. Nicoll's justification for yet another literary review was interesting if condescending: 'There are a good many people who like to know what is going on in the world of letters. They neither buy books nor read them; but still they like to be in touch with the literary gossip of the hour, in order to put a flavour into their dinner-table small-talk.'[209] Literacy has frequently brought with it various forms of social anxiety. In the 1840s and 1850s magazines aimed at the newly literate, aspiring working and lower-middle classes frequently published replies guiding inse-cure readers in the matter of what should be read and how one should read it. If anything, as literacy rates moved ever closer to 100 per cent, and English Literature became a respectable subject in school and university curricula, the need for guidance and reassurance became greater. Books as well as magazines offering advice and guidance proliferated. The publisher Swan Sonnenschein had issued his own *A guide to the choice of books for students* in 1887; in 1891 a second edition emerged updating the list to 1890 and this won an approving editorial in the *Circular* for 21 March.[210] On 6 June the *Circular* carried an advertisement for *A guide to the choice of books for students and general readers* by Arthur Acland MP, published by Edward Stanford.[211] Following hard on the heels of Stanford's offering was OUP's venture into the field, *A guide book to books* edited by Sargant and Wishaw, announced on 20 June at 5s in cloth and 3s 6d in paper. The books listed were 'carefully selected by a number of specialists' who included the bishop of Peterborough, Professor Max Müller, Sir Frederick Pollock, Mr George Saintsbury and Professor J. J. Thomson.[212] By combining such handbooks with 'Lubbock's One Hundred Best Books' and other reassuring series of similar sort, the Leonard Basts of this world might hope to feel intellectually secure and socially safe. As a *Circular* editorial of 27 June put it: 'With such an appreciation of books, and the blessings of International Copyright, the world ought to do very well.'[213]

---

207 *BS*, p. 1274.   208 *BS*, p. 924.   209 *BS*, pp. 917, 1025.   210 *PC* (1), p. 301.
211 *PC* (1), p. 602.   212 *PC* (1), p. 654.   213 *PC* (1), p. 677.

Present and past

This self-reflecting turn of mind was not devoted exclusively to current textual demands and anxieties. The 1890s were in the middle of an archaeological renaissance, particularly in terms of Egyptology. The discovery of the Fayum as a major source of Greco-Roman papyri in the later 1870s, the buying trips for the British Museum conducted by Wallis Budge from the 1880s, and Flinders Petrie's excavations from 1883 – which, among other things, threw up the remarkable funerary portraits from Hawara – had led to an increasing flow of ancient texts and images from the classical and pre-classical world into western Europe.[214] What was progressively revealed to the readers of the 1890s was a complex interplay of ancient societies (Egyptian, Greek, Roman) expressed in a diverse and extensive textual culture. As the 1890s progressed, the work of Grenfell and Hunt on the rubbish heaps of Oxyrhynchus revealed a textual culture so dense that most of what had been recently discovered had been thrown away by its users: the surviving rubbish implying the richness of what had been kept but had not survived over the subsequent millennia.

One of Budge's greatest finds, the hitherto assumed-lost text of Aristotle's *The constitution of Athens*, was first identified by Frederic Kenyon in 1890. Its publication in 1891 was a great event. In a breathless editorial on 23 January the *Circular* announced the discovery and mused on the disconcertingly important role chance had played in the process.[215] In a further comment later in the issue it was anticipated that this unique object would, courtesy of modern technology, be multiplied: 'photographic fac-similes will be spread over the whole of the civilised world'.[216] In fact readers would have to wait for another six months before publication took place, and by that time modern publishing competitiveness as well as technology was in evidence. As well as the Kenyon translation published by Bell at 4s 6d (large-paper edition 10s 6d) in the week of 18 July, there was another translation by E. Poste published by Macmillan at 3s 6d announced on the same day. By 25 July a third translation by T. J. Dymes, published by Seeley at 2s 6d, was on the market.[217]

Other ancient texts were published in 1891, such as Helen B. Harris, *The newly recovered Apology of Aristides* (a second-century Christian apologist). This text had been rediscovered in the Convent of St Catharine in Sinai in 1889 and was published by Hodder in early December at 2s 6d.[218] Petrie published the results of the 'research undertaken by the Palestine Exploration Fund' in *Tell*

---

214 Budge had also sent back clay tablet texts from Tell el Amarna and texts of the *Book of the Dead*; see Deuel, *Testaments of time*, pp. 120–1.
215 *PC* (1), p. 95.   216 *PC* (1), p. 98.   217 *English catalogue* 1891, p. 5.   218 *PC* (2), p. 647.

El Hesy (Lachish) in February at 10s 6d.[219] The great populariser of archaeology and supporter of the Egypt Exploration Fund (which was to support Grenfell and Hunt's work), Amelia B. Edwards, published her *Pharaohs, fellahs, and explorers* with Osgood in November at eighteen shillings.[220]

It seemed that in 1891, described as the '*annus mirabilis* of papyrology',[221] the great imperial textual culture of late Victorian Britain was rediscovering the lost imperial textual cultures of the ancient Mediterranean and the Near East. It is perhaps significant that the same links were being forged in the plot of a particularly successful novel first published in book form in 1891. *The wonderful adventures of Phra the Phoenician* by Edwin Lester Arnold had been serialised in the *Illustrated London News* in 1890. On 17 January 1891 Chatto & Windus announced its publication as a three-volume novel at the usual price of 31s 6d.[222] So successful was it that it went into a second three-volume edition, the latter being announced on 7 February within twenty days of the first edition.[223] *Phra* continued to feature in Chatto's monthly front-page advertisements in the *Circular* in March and April. By 2 May *Phra* in a single-volume version in Chatto's Piccadilly Novels series at 3s 6d was being advertised – with the teasing 'shortly' attached.[224] The cheap reprint emerged finally around 30 May, just four and a half months after the first edition, and at one-ninth of its price.[225]

The adventures were wonderful indeed: Phra sails to Britain with a British princess at the time of the Claudian invasion of Britain. He is executed by a druid but is resurrected a number of times – as a Roman centurion, a thane in King Harold's army, an English knight under Edward III – and lives his final incarnation in the Elizabethan period, during which a mad inventor reveals to him a machine that is clearly the forerunner of the steam engine. It is partly a history book (significantly its book publication was first announced in the *Circular*'s Education issue), partly science fiction, and is altogether tiresomely mystical. Phra moves from one culture to the next observing them flourish and fall. In a crude way it is reminiscent of H. G Wells's *The time machine* (1895). It certainly caught the mood of the time and proved a runaway best-seller.

The book is haunted by time and the decaying artefacts, particularly texts, that it leaves along its path. Phra records his adventures in 'a great volume' and, at the end of the novel, he muses 'Some other hand shall find that leaf, and me a dusty, ancient remnant. Some other hand shall turn these pages than those I

---

219 *PC* (1), p. 200.　220 *PC* (2), p. 537.　221 Deuel, *Testaments of time*, p. 113.
222 *PC* (1), p. 69.　223 *PC* (1), p. 137.　224 *PC* (1), p. 441; also on 16 May, p. 489.
225 *PC* (1), p. 589. The novel was to be variously reprinted in the 1890s and then was recast in 1910 as no. 178 in Newnes Sixpenny Copyright Novels. Chatto reprinted the novel for the last time in 1936.

meant them for.'[226] This sense of the remote past being partially recapturable through decayed fragments frames the novel for, on its very first page, we have:

> I was, in the very distance of the beginning, a citizen of that ancient city whose dominion once stretched from the blue waters of the Aegean round to and beyond the broad stream of the Nile herself. Your antiquities were then my household gods, your myths were my beliefs; those facts and fancies on the very fringe of records about which you marvel were the commonplace things of my commencement. Yes! And those dusty relics of humanity that you take with unholy zeal from the silent chambers of sarcophagi and pyramids . . . and the fair damsels who tripped our sunny streets when Sidon existed and Tyre was not a matter of speculation . . . [227]

Empires past and passing, leaving only fragmentary texts and dusty relics; the parallels between empires past and present were difficult to avoid. After all, it was to be only another five years before Kipling was to write 'Recessional':

> Far-called, our navies melt away;
> On dune and headland sinks the fire:
> Lo, all our pomp of yesterday
> Is one with Nineveh and Tyre!

226 Edwin Lester Arnold, *The wonderful adventures of Phra the Phoenician* (London: Chatto & Windus, 1892), p. 346.
227 *Ibid.*, p. 1.

20

Following up *The reading nation*

WILLIAM ST CLAIR

In offering personal ideas on how the 'history of the book' might be developed in the future, I do not aim to survey the field or to suggest a comprehensive plan, but to set out possible ways forward which others can follow if they choose. I mainly offer examples from the long – until 1914–18 – nineteenth century in Britain, concentrating on literary texts, with some examples taken from two unpublished archival sources.[1] I draw on the follow-up to my study of reading in the early nineteenth century Anglophone world, *The reading nation in the Romantic period* (2004) that has been the subject of many reviews, seminars, interrogations, blogs and personal communications.[2] Scholarly interest has

---

1 Gall & Inglis, publishers in Edinburgh and London, impression book, private collection; and file copies of books published by Frederick Warne & Co., London and New York, on deposit at Reading University.

2 The substantial published reviews and articles that I know of are (alphabetically): Ricardo Miguel Alfonso, *Atlantis, revista de la Asociación Espanola de Estudios Anglo-Norteamericanos* (2005); David Allan, *Scottish Historical Review* 85(2) (2006); Maureen Bell, *Journal of the Printing Historical Society* 9 (spring 2006); Henry Berry, *Midwest Book Review* (September 2004); Christoph Bode, *Anglistik* (summer 2007); Uwe Böker, *IASLonline* (2005); Asa Briggs, *Times Higher Education Supplement* 24 June 2006; Mary Ellen Brown, *Journal of Folklore Research* (2006); Marie-Françoise Cachin, *Histoire et civilisation du livre* (2006); Peter Cochran, *Byron Journal* 32(2) (2006); Stephen Colclough, *SHARP News* 14(4) (2005); Richard Cronin, *Modern Language Review* 101 (July 2006); Gary Dyer, *Wordsworth Circle* (2004); Hon. Lord Eassie, *Legal Information Management* (2005); Andrew Elfenbein, *Victorian Studies* (spring 2005); Doucet Devin Fischer, *Keats-Shelley Journal* (2006); Michael Foot, *Tribune* (August 2004); Ian Gilmour, *London Review of Books* 20 January 2005; Noah Heringman, *Studies in English Literature 1500–1900* 45(4) (2005); Leslie Howsam, *Papers of the Bibliographical Society of America* 100(1) (2006); Robert D. Hume, *Philological Quarterly* 83 (summer 2004 – printed autumn 2006); H. J. Jackson, *Times Literary Supplement* 23 July 2004; Robin Jarvis, British Association for Romantic Studies (BARS) *Bulletin and Review* 28 (October 2005); Christine Kenyon Jones, *Romanticism* 12(2) (2006); Nigel Leask, *History Workshop Journal* 61 (2006); The Little Professor [anon.], *Things Victorian and Academic*, online, 5 August 2005; Tom Lockwood, *British Journal for Eighteenth-Century Studies* 28(2) (2005); Michelle Levy, *Huntington Library Quarterly* 69 (September 2006); Deidre Lynch, *Journal of British Studies* 45(1) (2006); Robert Mankin, *Cercles, Revue Pluridisciplinaire du Monde Anglophone* (2006); Robert J. Mayhew, *Journal of Historical Geography* (2005); Robert Morrison, *Essays in Criticism* 55 (2005); Robert L. Patten, 'Matters of material interest', *Victorian Literature and Culture* 35(1) (2007); Seamus Perry, *Keats-Shelley Review* 19 (2005); Diego Saglia, *Nineteenth-Century Literature* 60(2) (2005); Susanne Schmid, *Anglia, Tübingen-Zeitschrift für Englische Philologie* 2006 (Heft 2); Peter Washington, *Literary Review* (December 2004); Jack Gumpert Wasserman, *Byron Journal* 32(2) (2006). Although errors have been identified, so far no scholar has

---

focussed both on the findings for that period and on how the approach might be developed, added to, and modified for potential use in addressing other research questions; for example, how far it would be applicable in other reading nations.[3] There has been much interest too in how my emerging models of the links between texts, books, prices, access, timing of access, readerships and consequences – 'the political economy of reading' – may be applicable to current public policy issues, notably those relating to intellectual property.[4] The follow-up, that is ongoing, although focussed on that one book, has therefore enabled a wide debate to occur about the traditions, limitations, aims and opportunities of 'book history' as a whole.

Widen our ambitions?

My first suggestion is that book historians should be more ambitious. The 'history of the book' – a term adapted from the French *histoire du livre* – is, in my view, unnecessarily limiting, appearing to centre on the 'book' as material artefact, rather than seeing paper imprinted with verbal or visual symbols as the material carrier of potentially readable texts.

Much book history is concerned with the producer interest (authors, publishers, book manufacturers), with less attention to the consumer interest (purchasers and readers). It is rare, for example, to find much analysis of the consequences of decisions taken by book producers for prices, production or readerships, or for the effects of these decisions on the national culture more widely, except in the most general terms. Indeed the titles of such works, variations on 'history of the British book trade', often disavow any ambition to discuss the consumer interest.[5] Works written in this tradition, which pays

offered alternative data of the kind that would be needed to invalidate the data or the results. One area that needs to be investigated further is the extent to which there was some competitive reprinting of the old ballads in the seventeenth century, although, if so, it had stopped by 1710. I have a large amount of additional data that could not be included in the book for reasons of space or in order to maintain representative quality, and more has been collected subsequently by myself or others. Although the discovery of occasional exceptions would not disprove the main findings – industries often tolerate an unruly periphery if their main business is not put at risk – all the information to which I at present have access tends to confirm the patterns identified in the book, with only small amendments and modifications needed. A few authors have decided not to engage with the findings or the methodology, although they deal in part with subjects discussed in *The reading nation*, and mention the book in passing, viz. Sher, *The Enlightenment and the book*; Franta, *Romanticism and the rise of the mass public*, p. 98 (who appears to argue that the perception that authors had of their reading audiences was more important than the actuality known to their publishers); Raven, *The business of books*.

3 'the seeds of a hundred doctoral theses' (Jarvis, BARS *Bulletin and Review* 28 (October 2005).

4 For example a passage about the effects of perpetual intellectual property was quoted in an appeal to the United States Supreme Court in the Grokster case, 2004.

5 The tradition includes Plant, *The English book trade* 3rd edn; Feather, *A history of British publishing*; and Raven, *The business of books*.

disproportionate attention to dominant firms, have sometimes adopted condescending and disdainful attitudes picked up from sources on which they are overdependent.[6]

Producer-interest book history draws on, and participates in, the traditions of business histories of individual publishing companies, often commissioned to mark an anniversary, that tell of the founding of the firm, offer thumbnail biographical sketches of family members and managers, engravings and photographs of buildings, extracts from correspondence with authors, and anecdotes. Although book-publishing is primarily and essentially a commercial activity, such business histories only occasionally offer commercial information, and, when they do, never enough to enable any serious economic analysis to be undertaken.[7] In cases where the archives of the firm have been lost and all we have is the business history, they are frustratingly inadequate.[8]

As with the parade-of-author literary histories, with which book history often shares a celebratory tone of occasionally interrupted national progress, the past has normally been presented as a series of events, arranged round the contribution of individuals regarded as autonomous agents, especially when they were innovators. This approach is at its most successful when, like literary history, it is concerned with the first and early publication of new titles of works subsequently regarded as of great literary or scientific value, and when it includes consolidated factual quantified information and presents it in a form easily comprehensible to the reader.[9] The tradition, with few exceptions, has hitherto paid little attention to the many authors whose books, whatever our present-day opinion of them, were in their time highly praised and much

---

6 For example Sutherland, in *Victorian novelists and publishers*, p. 66, decided not to consider less expensive books sold at railway stations: 'These volumes are beneath our notice here, concentrating as we are on work of some literary quality.' Raven scarcely mentions the huge sector of the industry, including pirate publishers that existed alongside the mainstream firms in the early nineteenth century and brought important modern texts to huge readerships.

7 Examples for publishing firms in the long nineteenth century include *Archibald Constable and his literary correspondents* (1873); *William Blackwood and his sons* (1897/8); Septimus Rivington, *The publishing family of Rivington* (1919); George Paston, *At John Murray's* (1932); Charles Morgan, *The house of Macmillan* (1944); David Keir, *The house of Collins* (1952); Arthur Waugh, *A hundred years of publishing, being the story of Chapman and Hall Ltd* (1930); F. A. Mumby, *The house of Routledge 1834–1934* (1934); Hugh R. Dent, *The house of Dent, 1888–1938* (1938); Arthur King and A. F. Stuart, *The house of Warne: one hundred years of publishing* (1965); Jenifer Glynn, *Prince of publishers: a biography of the great Victorian publisher George Smith* (1986); Rosemary Ashton, *142 Strand: a radical address in Victorian London* (2006).

8 For example Nowell-Smith, *The house of Cassell*.

9 An outstanding example is Patten, *Charles Dickens and his publishers*. Finkelstein, in *The house of Blackwood*, usefully tabulates the titles, initial prices, print-runs, sales and profits of the commercially most successful publications of the firm from 1860 to 1910, the same information for the works of Margaret Oliphant, 1860–97, and sales, including American sales, of *Blackwood's Magazine*, 1856–1915. Zachs, in *The First John Murray*, usefully lists the publications of the firm, including titles in which the firm took an equity share, with print-runs and prices.

demanded, and may have been influential. Silas K. Hocking, for example, a novelist at the turn of the nineteenth century, whose books received numerous favourable reviews, sold more than a million copies in his lifetime.[10] And, again following the tradition of parade-of-canonical-authors literary history, book historians have only recently taken an interest in the fact that most reading that occurred in the past was not of newly published texts but of reprints of texts first written or compiled in the past, sometimes the remote past.[11]

A complex literary and cultural system

My approach has been to conceive of texts, books, reading and consequences not only as a chronological parade of book producers (and others) but as a complex literary system, within a wider cultural system, into which the writing, subsequent publication and reading of texts were interventions that had consequences. In adopting this approach, I was following a lead set by others long ago. To an extent, it was because bibliographers and book historians questioned the assumptions of parade-of-great-author literary history (and histories of science that told only of men of genius and their discoveries) that they described the roles of publishers, printers, booksellers, reviewers, librarians, distributors and other intermediaries between authors and readers. However, that perception has only rarely been carried through to the methodologies employed. Despite the claims that, in 'book history', a new field of academic study has been established, much of what is published in, for example, the recently founded journal *Book History* is little different from what was appearing in the *Library* a century or more ago when the main tradition was descriptive bibliography.

I detect a reluctance to consider approaches that have successfully applied in the study of other large and complex systems, both natural and human, a fear of quantification, indeed a fear of scientific method generally. Despite the fact that some of the clearest thinkers, including Robert Escarpit, D. F. McKenzie and Wolfgang Iser, called for a 'sociology' and an 'anthropology' of literature,

---

10 The claim, along with numerous quotations from favourable reviews, is printed in catalogues of Warne's lists, for example in *Dick's fairy, a tale of the streets* (no date, c.1900). The claim is largely confirmed by the archival record. That title, one of over thirty, sold 10,000 copies in 1883, then about 25,000 to 1895. For the popularity of Nat Gould, another mass-seller, see Waller, *Writers, readers, and reputations*.

11 Examples from *The reading nation* of the effects of taking account of the reading of reprints of older texts include the entrenchment of eighteenth-century rural, 'old canon', religious literature, into schoolbooks and into notions of essential Englishness far into the urban industrialised age; and the effects on mentalities of the surge in reading of the Romantic period writers when their works came out of copyright in the later nineteenth century.

I detect a lingering, though seldom explicitly admitted, aversion to enlisting the help of the social sciences, occasionally coupled with the suggestion that to do so is somehow improper.[12] Book history, which to an extent was invented to confront the ahistorical, conventionalised, and often condescending and exclusionary views of the literary past that centred on authors and texts, has also been slow to learn from other disciplines that should be amongst its closest allies. Scholars who could speak authoritatively about the rhetorical effects of the lay-out of a title-page, the aesthetics of fonts and ornaments, and the design structure of a Victorian three-decker novel, sometimes appear unwilling, when they present information for their own readers, to depart from the false security of the narrative prose sentence, even if their sentences are little more than lists of names.[13] Financial information especially resists being turned into narrative prose.[14] This form of writing not only makes for heavy reading but, as a literary means of conveying meanings to readers, makes it harder for them to appreciate the dynamic interactive nature of the system being described.

If a piece of printed matter is conceived of not only as a manufactured material object, a 'book', but as a carrier of a potentially readable text, then we can extend our questions further on the history of reading, the construction of knowledge, the diffusion of ideas and the competition for allegiance of minds.[15] Relocating the main site of the creation of meaning from the author's writing of a text to the reader's encounter with the material book does not undermine, in any way, notions of literary, aesthetic or scientific value, nor reduce the value of studying texts in other ways.[16] Studies of books and readers done in accordance with rigorous methodologies, overtly presented, need not lapse into simplistic errors such as equating weight of production with extent of influence, nor do they exclude discovering that some readers or groups of readers were disproportionately influential, although, for the Victorian period, even with the general layering of readerships, it is not simple to identify

---

12 For example Sher, in *The Enlightenment and the book*, p. 29, appears to posit 'history' as excluding economic analysis and to misunderstand that the effects of the changing intellectual property regime on prices, production and reading is a replicable finding from the data, and does not depend even indirectly on postmodern theory, of which he mistakenly suggests that reader-response theory is an 'offshoot'. Briggs, author of a forthcoming business history of Longman, who dislikes systems thinking, appears to suggest that readers should read the appendices as if they were a continuation of the linear narrative – 'More patience is needed if the reader moves on to the appendices.'
13 Many examples of prose lists in Sher, *The Enlightenment and the book*.
14 For example, Shillingsburg, *Pegasus in harness*, a highly illuminating work in many respects, sets out information about costs, print-runs, prices, sales and receipts as prose narrative, e.g. pp. 97–8.
15 To avoid overloading the text I use 'book' to include journals, newspapers and printed illustrations.
16 A worry noted by, for example, Alfonso, *Atlantis*.

avant-gardes except among the higher socio-economic groups.[17] What book history could do, avoiding such pitfalls, is make a huge, and otherwise unobtainable, contribution to the history of mentalities – by which I mean the beliefs, feelings, values and dispositions to act in certain ways that are prevalent in a society at a particular historical and cultural conjuncture, including not only states of mind that are explicitly acknowledged but others that are unarticulated or regarded as fixed or natural. And it could bring in, as an integral part of the total system, the readers outside the elites that have been academically ghettoised, as 'folklore' or 'popular culture'. The astonishingly illuminating results that were obtained by taking a single, previously little regarded, text all the way from the rhetoric of how it presented itself to readers, through its material forms, to its reception by readers, the discussions and disputes it generated, and the resultant effects on the mentalities of Victorian society, have been shown by James Secord's study of *Vestiges of the natural history of creation*.[18]

If extended in this way, the prize that awaits book history is a big one. Widened and renamed, it has the opportunity to shake off the lingering, sometimes justified, suspicion that it consists of antiquarians collecting scattered atomistic bibliographical information for its own sake, or that it merely provides an ancillary service to other disciplines that deal with larger questions. It could become a cooperative enterprise that, by accumulating – and theorising – hard empirical information about the material carriers of knowledge and ideas, leads towards an ever deeper and more truthful understanding of how it has come about that societies (and groups within societies) came to think the way they did, why they acted as they did as a result, and how change occurred.[19] It could contribute directly to some of the most vital questions in the study

17 The worry that quantification may exclude the contribution of influential minorities, voiced for example by Michelle Levy, appears to be part of a general fear about social science approaches as somehow dehumanising the contribution of individuals. The risk of an alternative approach, adopted for example by Rose in *The intellectual life of the British working classes*, is that by relying mainly on anecdotal information about the reading of a self-selected sample of unusual citizens, it produces a reassuring narrative about another elite, while still leaving the majority of readers (and non-readers) disenfranchised.

18 Secord, *Victorian sensation*. The making available of the nineteenth-century archives of the publishing firm of John Murray at the National Library of Scotland should enable other studies of the history of the diffusion of scientific knowledge to be undertaken, adding to what is already available in, for example, *The correspondence of Charles Darwin 7* (Cambridge, 1991).

19 As Mayhew commented of the implications for his own branch of the history of science, 'Clearly, if we want to recover the geographical culture of past ages as opposed to which texts we retrospectively value as geographers, we will be sent to the grammars and gazetteers which have too long been dismissed as dinosaurs just as assuredly as St Clair sends students of romantic literature to Bloomfield rather than Blake. The idea may sound rather offputting to some, but the result will be a better grounded form of intellectual history, towards which endeavour St Clair's book serves as both a powerful manifesto and an important exemplification.'

of the humanities.[20] To develop a political economy of knowledge – to begin to do for ideas what Adam Smith did for goods and services – would be an enterprise in the best traditions of the European Enlightenment.

Economics of the printed book industry, macro and micro

Although in the follow-up to *The reading nation* there has been some doubt whether it is fruitful to investigate the whole process of cultural formation (from the minds of authors through the materiality of print to the minds of readers) as a single system, there has been, with only a handful of exceptions, no reluctance to accept the inquiry's findings about the direct usefulness of analysing the historic printed book industry as an economic system.[21] An analysis of the historic book industry seen this way sets out to retrieve the changing governing structures within which books were produced in the form that they were and not in others, including state textual controls, the legal framework, intellectual property regime, fiscal conditions, tariff and non-tariff barriers restricting exports and imports of texts and books, technological, customary and commercial restraints and opportunities, and business practices. It compiles economic data on the actual economic behaviour of the industry, quantified wherever possible – preferring, in accordance with the norms of economics as a discipline, hard data of this kind to statements by producers about what they claim, or believe, they are doing. It attempts to ensure the representative quality of the data when they are incomplete – as they normally are – by targeted sampling and by actively identifying and offsetting gaps.

Its approach is determined by the research questions it is addressing, not by the information that happens to be available. Having gathered the requisite data, it seeks patterns, generates provisional findings, interrogates, experiments, attempts to replicate, and offers others the opportunity to interrogate and replicate. It escapes the readerly suspicion that attaches to studies that proceed only by proposition and example that the narrative may not take sufficient

---

20 Washington doubts whether it is worthwhile even to address the question I pose, 'how did the reading of books lead to change?', calling it 'impossible grandeur'. But innumerable writings on history, literature, philosophy, science and other subjects that have followed the parade tradition have made, and continue to make, claims of this kind as a matter of routine.

21 It has been said, for example, that 'the reading nation' that I retrieved was principally the book-owning nation, or the access-to-books nation, and that the gap in our knowledge of what happened to mental processes in the reading event itself – the transfer from symbols on paper to mind – was not adequately filled. Although I fully accept the general validity of the comment, I know of no studies about which the same could not be said, except possibly in the case of live individual readers encountering an individual text in controlled experimental conditions.

account of other examples that are not offered. If we are to write histories of the material book, let alone histories of reading or of the consequences of the consumption of cultural production, then, in my view, given the sheer complexity, numbers of agents, and extent and variety of transactions, we cannot hope adequately to analyse the history of books except as the material component of a complex literary/cultural system that stretches from the writing of the texts to the reading of the books and back.

As far as the British printed book industry is concerned, it should have caused no surprise that, inquired into in that way, it yielded at once to methods of economic analysis that have been successfully applied to many industries, including pharmaceuticals and information technology, with which it shares economic characteristics. One striking conclusion has been the extent to which simple, well-understood and empirically well-tested economic models, such as price and quantity, monopoly and competition, not only are observable as having operated in the economic behaviour of the historic printed book industry – so giving the models themselves added confirmation – but have been able to account for the behaviour of the industry, and therefore also the patterns of readerly access to particular texts, during all the centuries when print was the paramount medium. My study of the Anglophone world in a particular historical period has shown that the tendency of monopolistic industries to pay most attention to the topmost tranches of the market, to move slowly down the demand curve, to ration supply to the market in order to protect the market value of their properties, to neglect large constituencies of the market altogether or to supply them with obsolete and often shoddy goods, can be observed in the monopolies and cartels operated by the printed book industry through the institutions of private intellectual property. Basic economic analysis has, therefore, helped to explain how the reading nation came to be divided into overlapping layers of readers, differentiated not only by income, by socio-economic class and by educational attainment, but by the degree of obsolescence of the print to which each layer had access.[22] There is already enough information to confirm that many of the same general findings emerge in the Victorian book industry.

---

22 By which I mean the time that has passed since a text was first written or made available in print. Readers have often been able to draw contemporary, maybe even universal, meanings from texts that are not contemporary, sometimes from unpromising material, and there are innumerable examples of men, women and young people successfully surmounting the obstacles to access to knowledge and education brought about by high prices. But, for an understanding of the political economy of reading, we should beware of putting too much weight on anecdotal evidence whose representative quality is uncertain.

Although for non-Anglophone jurisdictions the data so far available are inadequate, it seems from what is already available that the microeconomics as well as the macroeconomics of text copying by movable type was also much the same from the late fifteenth to the early nineteenth centuries. This is evidenced by, for example, the similar range within which print-runs per edition were manufactured in every jurisdiction in the Europeanised reading world for which we have information, a phenomenon readily explained by a microeconomic analysis of cost, price and risk within the technological opportunities available. During the long eighteenth century, for example, although the British economy tripled, the population doubled, and incomes per head rose steadily if slowly, most book editions were in the range 500 to 3,000 copies with some readily explainable outliers such as privately printed pamphlets at one end and semi-compulsory religious texts and almanacs (on which all economic activity depended) at the other.[23] Everywhere we look, we see simple demand curves that relate production with price, price with access and timing of access, and readerships layered both by socio-economic constituency and by the degree of obsolescence of the print to which each layer had access. There is every reason to believe that, with appropriate modification, we would find similar results if the economic analysis of *The reading nation* were to be applied to the book industries operating in other jurisdictions in the European tradition, including piracy and offshore publication.

Without a knowledge of which constituencies of readers had access to which texts at which times, all attempts to relate the reading of texts to the effects of reading are bound to be inadequate. And the starting point for answering such questions is to retrieve information about the production and prices of books. Such information does not, by itself, take us to sales, sales to reading, or to multiplier effects, to imports and exports, second-hand markets, losses, reception or to cultural formation. For these parts of the system we need other methodologies, new and old, but retrieving information on production and prices is, I would say, the indispensable precondition without which more refined questions cannot be reliably pursued.

---

23 That the printed book industry fully appreciated the shape of the (rising) marginal unit cost curve – and the resulting (falling) marginal unit profit – and that it was not just applying internalised industry experience is evidenced not only by the hard data of its economic behaviour but by occasional records of explicit calculations of ranges of alternatives to which the calculation of the shape of the curve was crucial. Tables of unit costs for the printed illustration sector of the industry are set out, for example, in *A manual of lithography; or, Memoir on the lithographical experiments made in Paris, at the Royal School of the Roads and Bridges* (trans. from the French of Colonel Antoine Raucourt) by C. Hullmandel (London 1821).

Intellectual property

In order to understand the economic relationships between prices, production and timing of access, we need to retrieve the intellectual property regime within which book publishing occurred. Economic behaviour turns out to have been highly sensitive to changes, both large, for example from perpetual intellectual property to a short and then a long copyright, and small, for example the dates at which certain texts became available cheaply as a result of falling out of private monopoly ownership.[24] As with other aspects of book history, the emphasis in histories of copyright law has been on the producer interest and on the arguments deployed by producers.[25] Studies of the nineteenth-century Anglo-American dispute about copyright, have, for example, concentrated on the interests of publishers and authors, with little attention to the immense benefits that accrued to the United States from having quick and cheap access to modern knowledge from Europe.[26] And we cannot retrieve an understanding of how intellectual property operated in practice solely from studying the law.[27] In 1812, 102 years after perpetual copyright had been prohibited by law, the publisher John Murray was still requiring authors to sign contracts that transferred 'the entire and perpetual Copy right'.[28] Many forms of intellectual property were not even set out in documents – their existence has to be inferred from observed economic behaviour. And alongside the formal discourses of legal theory, there has coexisted a long history of conceptualisations of what is now called 'intellectual property' that were also directly influential on decisions, books, prices and access. Indeed, when regarded as a business practice – a state-guaranteed monopoly right to copy and sell a text – the present discourse of 'property and piracy' emerges as only the most recent of a long series of other metaphors that have been employed since the late fifteenth century. In the Anglophone world, its origin can be precisely dated to the last years of the seventeenth century and the formalisation of the transatlantic slave

---

24 Examples from *The reading nation* are quoted in a summarising chapter, William St Clair, 'Publishing, authorship, and reading', in Richard Maxwell and Katie Trumpener (eds.), *Cambridge companion to fiction in the Romantic period* (Cambridge, 2008).

25 For example, Sherman and Bently, *The making of modern intellectual property law*, and Deazley, *On the origin of the right to copy, charting the movement of copyright law in eighteenth century Britain (1696–1775)* (Oxford, 2004).

26 Beginning with Barnes, *Authors, publishers and politicians*. The full account of the dispute by Seville, in *The internationalisation of copyright law* (Cambridge 2006), shows how the producer interest of publishers and authors, and occasionally printers, was able to dominate the argument on both sides of the Atlantic, and how they not only put pressures on governments but found imaginative ways of condemning low book prices as harmful. Compare *The reading nation*, pp. 382–93.

27 Many examples of extra-statutory and illegal intellectual property practice are noted in *The reading nation*.

28 *The letters of John Murray to Lord Byron*, ed. Andrew Nicholson (2007), p. 6.

trade into chartered companies.[29] If book history is to advance, we need an easily accessible guide to the changing historical intellectual property regime as it was actually operated, and of its close associate, state textual controls, in a form that would enable a scholar quickly to discover the limitations and other conditions within which any particular book, including a reprinted book, was produced, priced and distributed.

Mapping the past worlds of print

The putting online of the catalogues of libraries and databases, such as the *English short title catalogue (ESTC)* that goes up to 1800, has greatly enlarged and speeded up the opportunities and possibilities for research, interrogation, and replicability of results that would have been impossibly time-consuming even a few years ago. However the ready availability of lists of titles in *ESTC* and library and union catalogues has also fostered an illusion of completeness. It has long been known that the survival rate of books and print from the early centuries is incomplete, perhaps badly incomplete. D. F. McKenzie's observation that the size of the English printing industry, as measured by the physical capital (presses) and personnel employed (apprentices and printers), scarcely changed between the mid sixteenth and late seventeenth century can only be squared with the sharp rise in surviving titles over the same period by postulating either that a high proportion of the industry was maintained in unemployment or that more output occurred than has survived, or some combination.[30] Since, until the early eighteenth century, the English state attempted to control the texts that were permitted to circulate within its jurisdiction not only by an array of direct textual controls but also by limiting the capacity of the industry, measured not by titles but by numbers of printed sheets, it is unlikely that a high proportion of capacity was kept in idleness or in reserve. It has been known too, at least since the 1870s, that the Stationers' Company Register included only a proportion of titles of which copies survive.[31] But the register also includes many titles, particularly of ballads, that have not survived and whose former existence is not noted in *ESTC*. My finding that large numbers of abridged 'ballad versions' of biblical stories were officially permitted until a sudden stop around 1600 depended upon taking account of these lost, but

---

29 William St Clair, 'Metaphors of intellectual property', forthcoming.
30 In *Cambridge history of the book in Britain* 4, pp. 17–18, 556–63.
31 The first volume of E. Arber, *A transcript of the Registers of the Company of Stationers of London 1554–1640* was published in 1875.

registered, pieces of printed literature.[32] And it is not only in the early centuries of print that our lists of titles are inadequate. For the eighteenth century, the survival rate of books known to have been produced, for example by being listed in advertisements, looks good for expensive books, patchy for some genres such as novels, and extremely poor for cheaper print.[33] Titles of books that survive to the present day provide a poor indicator of what was produced.

And even if we were to be only interested in production measured by titles without taking account of print-runs, resorting to *ESTC* is liable to produce bogus statistics, even for titles, even for trends. The rising curves are not usually adjusted for population or market size. If we take the population of England as say 3 million in 1550 and 5.5 million in 1650, a rise in absolute terms over that century may be a fall in adjusted terms. By 1800 the English-speaking market may have been over 12 million. Nor are the curves adjusted for changes in the price of books or changes in the general price levels in the economy. Nor do the curves take account of the vast amount of print known to have been produced but no longer surviving and therefore excluded from *ESTC*. Without wishing to prejudge the answer to a properly designed research project, it is possible that there was more reading in the years before 1600 relative to the size of the population and economy, and that reading penetrated farther down the socio-economic scale, than at any time before the late eighteenth/early nineteenth century. At the very least, a proper study would, by flattening the falsely progressive – whiggish – curves, offer a more truthful view of the past, and it might cause a major rethink about how knowledge was constituted and how cultural change occurred.

As for the Victorian age, our maps of what was available to be read are also incomplete, and therefore potentially biased and misleading, as the Victorians knew. In 1858 the novelist Wilkie Collins talked about the unknown reading public, 3 million 'right out of the pale of literary civilization'.[34] From the Gall & Inglis archives, which are themselves a small, randomly surviving, sample, it emerges that a vast amount of cheap books never made it into libraries and therefore into lists of titles (see table 20.1).

The price range continues with books at ninepence, one shilling, one shilling and sixpence, two shillings, two shillings and sixpence, three shillings, three shillings and sixpence and five shillings, after which price they merge with print

---

32 See *The reading nation*, pp. 74–5 and 495–6. For statistics of the American trade, cf. Hugh Amory, 'The New England book trade, 1713-1790', in Hugh Amory and David D. Hall (eds.), *A history of the book in America. 1. The colonial book in the Atlantic world* (Cambridge, 2000), pp. 314–46, including tables 9.1 and 9.2, and his 'A note on statistics', *ibid*., pp. 504–18.

33 Especially the two Dicey catalogues. Discussed in *The reading nation*, p. 340.

34 *The reading nation*, p. 355.

Table 20.1 *Gall & Inglis, publishers in Edinburgh and London: examples of production of cheap books*

Farthing books [0.25 of an old penny, 0.08 of an old pound]	
1851–80	about 93,000
Halfpenny books [0.5 of an old penny]	
1852–80	about 89,000
Three farthing books [0.75 of an old penny]	
1859–74	about 8,000
Penny books	
1853–85	about 131,000
Another penny series	about 50,000
Three halfpenny books	
1860–86	about 8,000
Twopenny books	
1854–80	about 84,000
Threepenny books	
1853–84	about 85,000
Another threepenny series, 16 titles	
1890–8	about 4,000–6,000 each
Fourpenny books	
1856–1901	about 122,000
Sixpenny books [14 titles]	
1855–75	about 290,000

produced for groups with higher incomes for which information is much fuller. The survival rate of cheaper print is very poor, and the extent of production could not have been guessed without some deliberate attempt to offset the incompleteness of lists, for example by searching for lost titles in booksellers' advertisements and by formally building ranges of estimates based on what is deducible from similar sources (see table 20.2).

The huge late Victorian paperback industry, of which the survival rate is tiny, scarcely features in lists and author bibliographies (see table 20.3).[35]

If, as I conjecture, the firm referred to in table 20.3 is Routledge, then there were 800 paperback titles and the stereotype plates from which copies were made were all melted for armaments in 1914. Warne had 150 volumes in their competing series, also all sent for armaments, all the unsold stocks of books being donated to hospitals for soldiers. These actions, taken with the melting of innumerable other plates, brought about a severe, and irreversible, external shock to the whole material base of books and reading for adults and children.[36]

35 See, for example, the many items noted by Topp, *Victorian yellowbacks and paperbacks.*
36 *The reading nation*, pp. 430–2.

Table 20.2 *Gall & Inglis, works of James Gall*

Instant Salvation by the instant acceptance of a Mediator and Surety
1866–1904, 16 impressions in English, 5 in Dutch
English   94,000
Dutch   9,000
Immediate Salvation for the Chief of Sinners: or, a practical guide for anxious inquirers. [Being an abridgment of 'Instant Salvation,']
1866–1906, 23 impressions in English, 2 in Gaelic
English   217,000
Gaelic   5,000
Favourite authors
Sold in 20 parts, 1876–95, initial impression normally about 1,000, but parts were frequently reprinted. For example no. 9 had 19 impressions totalling about 36,000 copies. Not a single part from total production of over 200,000 copies is known to have survived.

Table 20.3 *Late Victorian sixpenny [0.5 shilling] paperback editions, one firm unnamed only, annually**

Lytton's novels	80,000
Scott's novels	30,000
Marryat's novels	60,000
Robinson Crusoe	40,000 (18 months)

* Russell, *The author's manual* (1891, 8th edn 1895), p. 210. Whelpdale, a character in George Gissing's *New Grub Street* whose business is advising authors, and who quickly becomes rich, wrote an *Author's guide* (Oxford World Classics, ed. John Goode, 1993), pp. 216, 457.

Estimating output from movable type and stereotype

In the age of exclusively movable type, when edition sizes were confined within much the same band, it would be possible, if we were satisfied that we had reasonably complete information about the number of newly printed titles and editions produced, to make usable estimates of the likely range of total production, wide though that range might have to be. And from format, other bibliographical signs and the prices at which the books were sold, where retrievable, much can be deduced about likely readerships.

During the guild period, roughly until the abandonment of effective price controls during the seventeenth century, the book industry was thought of – and regulated – primarily as a manufacturing industry, that is as an industry selling printed paper. In the guild system, prices of manufactured goods were controlled both formally and – in the case of books formally and legally – in accordance with a general understanding that they should reflect manufacturing costs plus a reasonable profit margin. The guild system as it applied to books was, in economic terms, therefore very different in this respect from the period that follows (the 'high monopoly period') which was essentially a tolerated commercial monopoly in which producers could charge whatever price they chose, and in accordance with what they judged the market could bear. As emerges from my inquiry, producers' economic behaviour was as one would expect from such a monopoly. It was also, in economic terms, essentially different from the period after 1774 when a range of older texts were produced to be sold in conditions of economic competition, another area for which the economic analysis has been done and which fits what one would have expected.

The question is, do we have enough archival information for the guild period to enable the economics to be reconstructed? The reasonably complete records of the Stationers' Company's production of almanacs, ABCs, psalters, primers and other semi-official routine print that survive for the latter half of the seventeenth century have been investigated, most recently by John Barnard.[37] These records, although confined to a particular class of print, may, when put with other surviving information, reveal relationships between cost, production and price that have wider applicability. A carefully designed arithmetical study – essentially quadratic equations – might yield models (or rules of thumb used in that period) that would enable us to recover the economics of the guild period and estimate print-runs with confidence. That would be a huge prize that, if attained, might transform our understanding both of the industry and of access and reading patterns.

In the age of stereotype that began in Britain in the 1820s, the microeconomics of text copying are very different from those of the age of exclusively

---

37 Barnard, 'The survival and loss rates of psalms, ABCs, psalters and primers from the stationers' stock, 1660–1700', *The Library* 6th ser. 21 (1999), pp.148–50, and 'The stationers' stock 1663/4 to 1705/6: psalms, psalters, primers and ABCs', *The Library* 6th ser. 21 (1999), pp. 369–75.

movable type that preceded it.[38] And the problems of assessing production, if we do not have archival sources, are severe.[39] In the nineteenth century a high proportion of print was undated – perhaps deliberately so in many cases in order to offset readerly resistance to perceived obsolescence. For many types of print, reliance on titles as a rough surrogate for output or reading can be so misleading as to be worthless. Some examples follow.

The long life of stereotypes

The poetical works of Lord Byron

Frederick Warne's editions in the Lansdowne Poets and Chandos Classics series, 1868–1908: fifty impressions taken, ranging from 24,000 to 250 copies per impression. These plates produced a total of over 170,000 copies, plus an unknown further number before the plates were melted in 1937. In terms of 'titles' or 'editions' as judged by changing title-pages, this vast output over forty years would count as two, given the same equivalence with two privately financed pamphlets or books of verse typically printed in editions of 500 and circulating in even smaller numbers.

The poetical works of Lord Byron (but actually a self-censored selection)

Gall and Inglis's editions in various binding styles, 1857–94: forty-four impressions ranging from 5,267 to 310 copies per impression (including the 'over-copies' of 30 per 1,000, that are not always included in the archival record or the accounts). These plates, that were added to in 1860, the year in which *Childe Harold's pilgrimage, Canto the fourth* came out of copyright (forty-two years from first publication in 1818), produced over 80,000 copies. In terms of 'titles' this vast output counts as three.

On the eve of the First World War, the works of Byron were available at five shillings or less from seventeen different British publishers.[40]

If, in the absence of archival information, we cannot easily estimate the print-runs of impressions, the problem of estimating total output is even greater. Cumulative output from one set of plates can range from the low thousands

---

38 Discussed in *The reading nation*, pp. 179–84, 416–18.
39 Occasional figures quoted in printed sources may be abnormal. According to G. H. P. J. B. P. [Putnam], the authors of *Authors and publishers, a manual of suggestions for beginners in literature* (7th edn 1897), p. 38, who were in a good position to know, the 10,000 copies quoted by Walter Besant as the typical sales of a six-shilling novel, was 'decidedly exceptional'.
40 *Literary yearbook for 1912*, ed. Basil Stewart, p. xv.

to many tens of thousands, and plates themselves could be duplicated. One possible solution, added to what is determinable about the date of manufacture of a particular volume by binding style, inserted advertisements and other bibliographical signs, is to assess the degree of wear on the manufacturing plates and therefore the extent of usage, both absolute and comparative, of particular printed books and groups of books. Many late Victorian books are printed from plates that are so worn and damaged that the text as printed on the paper is almost unreadable. Modern imaging techniques, that can assess comparative blurring, may be able to provide part of the solution, although expensive if applied on a large scale.

Serials, periodicals and newspapers

In responses to *The reading nation in the Romantic period*, it has been correctly commented that I mainly confined my inquiry to books, with little attention to periodicals and newspapers, with the implied question whether the results would have been different if I had given them more attention. In fact the book contains more consolidated information about absolute and relative circulations of periodicals and newspapers in the Romantic period than had ever previously been assembled. And, fortunately for the inquirer into the reading of that period, periodicals such as the *Edinburgh Review* and *Quarterly Review* had many of the characteristics of expensive books, and the newspapers, mostly also expensive, were mainly filled with day-to-day news. Although we do not have the information to enable the judgement to be proved, I remain of the view that adding more about the reading of periodicals and newspapers in the Romantic period would be unlikely to require my main findings to be drastically revised.

For the Victorian period, by contrast, the problem of how to retrieve an understanding of periodicals and newspapers, of their relationship with books, and of the effect of their being read, is of an altogether different order of magnitude. By 1855 national output from the paper and printing industry had grown strongly since the Romantic period but it was still only 6.5 per cent of what it was to become by 1913.[41] In 1889, there were estimated to be around 650 periodicals and 500 newspapers in London alone.[42] By 1901 Mitchell's

---

41 C. H. Feinstein, *National income, expenditure and output of the United Kingdom 1855–1965* (Cambridge, 1972), T114. The sector as measured produced other goods besides books and newspapers, but the growth for them is likely to have been at least as strong.
42 Estimate by Russell, *The author's manual*, p. 3. He reckoned 2,400 for the whole country.

Newspaper press directory notes nearly 5,000 titles.[43] And they offered a vast range of information, comment and literature, far beyond anything available in the Romantic period. Although there have been many studies of Victorian periodicals and newspapers, so far they have largely consisted of dips into this or that, picking up points of particular interest to the scholar concerned, for example the extent that women participated. But, useful though these may be, it is difficult to see how, if we are interested in readers and consequences and not just in texts, such selective – often unquantified – approaches deal fairly with the sheer amount and variety of materials and the vast number of acts of reading. And that is before we have factored in free elementary education and public libraries, or considered formally the extent to which knowledge available to elites trickled down in the Victorian period, an effect that is likely to have been patchy at best. With periodicals and newspapers, as with books, if we do not try to discover who read what, and when, how can we assess consequences?

Prices, incomes and access

Although writings on book history frequently record scattered pieces of financial information, a price charged here, a payment made there, the figures often hang uninterpreted, like words from a past language no longer commonly known, as indeed they are. The only way, I would say, to relieve the reader of legitimate puzzlement – is that a big number or a small number? – is to place financial information into the context of comparable information of the time. Since the prices of most books published by the London industry are readily available in the annual trade publications, only a few more examples need be given here, chosen to show how some Victorian texts were typically tranched down the demand curve (see table 20.4).

Table 20.4 *Some typical Victorian book prices, shillings*

Normal price of a three-volume novel, new	31.5
Reprinted later in one volume	6
1847, Chapman & Hall's 'cheap' editions	3.5
Yellowbacks	2.5–1
Late nineteenth century, paperback editions of out-of-copyright novels	0.5
Cheapest subscription to Mudie's Library, 1911, one not-new book, exchangeable weekly for 3 months	3.5

43 Quoted by Eliot 'The business of Victorian publishing', p. 48.

As far as the meaning of book prices is concerned, translating nominal historic money values into present-day nominal values is highly misleading, almost always overestimating the opportunities for access.[44] The relevant comparator is not the changing purchasing power of money – a conjecture of little value when the goods and services that money could buy were radically different from what they have since become. A preferable approach is to compare prices with the economic situation of potential purchasers, including incomes, wealth, distribution of income and wealth, expectations, disposable income, and time and opportunities available for reading.

In the Victorian period, the society from which book readers were drawn was stratified not only by income, and extent of leisure time, but by lack of upward mobility. Entry to the professions and to many clerical and manual occupations was, for example, much constrained by the upfront costs of education and training, including apprenticeships, which only certain families and individuals could afford – with the result that entry to middle-class occupations was normally only open to those who had access to savings or credit from family or friends. The differential between the highest paid and the norm was wide and the differential within professions, for example the high salaries given to newspaper leader writers – who were believed to have power over opinion – was different from what might have been guessed.[45] The upper and upper-middle socio-economic groups of the landed, political, ecclesiastical, professional (including army and navy officers) and commercial classes were to a large extent hereditary, with many members living on investment incomes with ample leisure. Since few women from this socio-economic group were in paid occupations, the time they had available for reading was also often plentiful.

For those without advantages who were obliged to earn their living by working, pay levels were reasonably steady in nominal terms but rising in purchasing power terms. As a measure against which the wide range of book prices may be judged, table 20.5 notes a few employments of the late Victorian period, many in the newspaper, periodical and book industries, from whose members many of those at the lower socio-economic boundaries of the reading nation were drawn. I include ladies and gentlemen dependent on 'literary work', the subject of some famous Victorian novels.[46] And few men or women in employment

---

44 As suggested, for example, for the eighteenth century by Sher, *The Enlightenment and the book*.
45 See table 20.5.
46 Especially W. M. Thackeray's *Pendennis*, Lytton's *My novel* and George Gissing's *New Grub Street*, but there were many others. The 1911 Mudie's Catalogue lists thirty-six fiction titles in its classification 'London, Journalistic and Literary'.

Table 20.5 *Illustrative pay rates in late Victorian Britain,[a] mostly London, shillings, weekly except where stated: 20 shillings [s] in a pound [£]*

Book industry

Novelists

Tit-Bits estimate, including those starting off	£20 to £1,000 a novel
Russell's estimate, a middle-class novel 'at all saleable'	£100 to £500
'a good writer can produce at least two fictions in a year'[b]	
Novelettes, each	21, 42, 63 up to 210 'when very good'

Other workers in the book industry

Starting pay for a trainee in a publishing firm, six-day week.[c]	5
Proof readers	42 to 84
Women proof readers	30 to 35
Indexers	

'Publishers give a good deal of work to ladies patient enough to compile indexes … [and] a good deal of arranging literary matter for compilation that publishers are willing to give out to ladies.'

'Compilation is a more important branch of the literary profession than is usually supposed. At the British Museum in London, there are a number of ladies and gentlemen employed by publishers in the preparation of biographies and other works.'

Typing	n/a but some prices charged
per 1,000 words	1
carbon copies	0.25
over 10,000 words	0.8
Miss Fowler 'highest testimonials for deciphering illegible Manuscripts'[d]	
Pay may have been around half the rates	
Printers, mainly men, after apprenticeship[e]	36 to 60
until 1866, 8 to 8 every working day	
after 1872, 54 hours a week, piecework rates adjusted to preserve minimum of 36[f]	
Engravers	30 to 40
Press men and machine men	20 to 35
Bookbinding, folding, collating, sewing, covering, laying on gold, piece work folding 100 sheets	0.12
'much of the work of the leading publishers is taken home by women, who are often assisted by members of their families'	n/a

Newspapers and periodicals

Editor	£500 to £2,000 a year
Leader writer	£500 to £1,500 a year
Sub-editor	100 to 320
London newspaper reporters	60 to 120

(*cont.*)

Table 20.5 *(cont.)*

Junior newspaper reporters	15 to 20
Articles on topical subjects, often condensed from longer works	40 to 60
Arthur Conan Doyle's earnings, 1870s, 1880s, when he began, writing occasional stories	£10 to £15 a year, average of £4 a story
For his first Sherlock Holmes short novel[g]	£30
'The fiction weekly papers are almost entirely written by women'	
Writers on piece rates	12.5 per 1,000 words
Press cutting from newspapers, hours 9 to 7	7 to 16
Other occupations, mainly women	
Governesses	

'It is fortunate that the demand for governesses increases, in some measure, with the supply. The creation of a wealthy middle class has opened up a field of magnitude ... First qualifications are ... a really excellent education, English, French, some German, arithmetic, writing, drawing, music, singing, and if possible Latin.'

	£50 to £100 a year, all found, exceptionally £150
Other governesses	£30 to £50 a year
Plan tracing in architects' offices	20 to 40
Artificial flower making, hours 9 to 8	20 to 30
Barmaids	7 to 14
Feather making, 'pleasant and easy work', 10 hours a day	3.5 to 20
Other occupations, mainly men	
Metropolitan policemen	24 rising to 30
Bank clerks	20 to 30 rising by incremental seniority to 5 times these amounts[h]
Army schoolmasters, all found	4 to 7 a day
Army clerks, all found	2.5 rising to 4 a day
Brick-making (amongst the highest paid manual labour occupations, piecework)	
moulders	27
sorters and loaders	25
barrowmen	18 to 21

[a] Extracted, for mainstream middle-class occupations, from Russell, *The authors's manual*, and for others from *A thousand ways to earn a living* (Tit-Bits Office, c.1888), a guide to careers.
[b] Russell, *The author's manual*, p. 212.
[c] *The house of Warne*, p. 10.
[d] *Literary yearbook for 1912*, p. xv.
[e] Some printing shops employed women.
[f] Gould, *The letter-press printer* [after 1881], p. 169.
[g] Doyle, *Memoirs and adventures*, p. 72.
[h] Women were also increasingly employed in clerical work, notably in shops and hospitals, usually at less pay than men.

had much time at their own disposal for reading. Some commentators have queried whether figures for incomes of groups can adequately capture the wide variety of spending patterns, some individuals choosing, for example, to skimp on other expenditures in order to be able to buy books.[47] The point is a valid one, and other – complementary – approaches such as the Reading Experience Database, if structured to try to ensure representative quality, may be able to refine our information, although they are unlikely to alter the main relationships between prices, incomes and access. We may also be able to reconstruct horizons of expectations, that is harder to do for the Victorian period than for earlier times when reading was less universal.[48] My aim in table 20.5 is not to reconstruct typical readers but to set out the range of limitations on groups of citizens becoming readers.

From author to reader and back

There is much excellent writing on how, in the nineteenth century, many aspects of national life – although not as many as in France – were discussed in the form of fiction. Few then doubted the power of reading, particularly the reading of fiction, not only to diffuse information but to shape mentalities. As Percy Russell, author of a guide to authors, wrote in 1891, 'I would earnestly ask all who take up the pen of the story-teller to recognise the great responsibility which rests upon them as makers, in some sense, of human character through the novels they write.'[49] We know too an increasing amount about the power that the commercial renting sector exercised over the nature of the fictional texts that were made available to the upper income groups.[50] The owner of Mudie's, the largest and dominant circulating library, which operated nation-wide in a highly monopolised market, read some novels personally before deciding whether to make a bulk purchase, and if his decision, or that of his managers, was negative, an author could find that his book remained uncirculated, little read, and unlikely to be reprinted at a less expensive price for a wider readership, and that his authorial career and future commercial prospects were severely set back.

The correspondence of Victorian novelists – mostly only recently published or used in literary biographies – enables us to appreciate how merciless that

---

47 Notably Robert Hume who notes some contemporaneous sources I did not use.
48 For example, Pettitt, *Patent inventions*, p. 96, reveals the attempts of the men and women of the Victorian age, who, as my work shows, were steeped in childhood in the rural religious 'old canon' culture of the pre-Enlightenment pre-industrial age, to 'write machines into the narrative of nature'.
49 Russell, *The author's manual*, p. 278.
50 Beginning with Griest, *Mudie's Circulating Library*, and Sutherland, *Victorian novelists and publishers*.

mechanism could be. In 1859, for example, George Meredith, writing in a letter about his early novel *The Ordeal of Richard Feverel*, reported that it had 'offended Mudie and the British Matron. He will not, or haply, dare not put me in his advertised catalogue. Because of the immoralities I depict! O canting Age! . . . Meanwhile I am tabooed from all decent drawing room tables.' Mudie's had subscribed for three hundred copies and then withdrawn upon 'urgent remonstrances of several respectable families', who objected to it 'as dangerous and wicked and damnable'.[51] Who exactly complained, if the alleged reports were not just invented as an excuse for caution, is not recorded, nor whether they were private individuals or organised groups, but they exercised their power even if they remained anonymous and silent, or did not exist. It was only after authors became well known, and commercially successful, that they could assert an increasing degree of independence.[52]

Since the first edition of a newly published novel in three volumes often consisted of only 1,000 copies selling retail at 31s 6d, those whose reactions Mudie feared, and attempted to forestall, were, at most, a thin slice at the top of the socio-economic scale, a minority of a minority, a self-selecting group who used their social position or ecclesiastical office to intervene to patrol the limits of what texts should be made available to their fellow countrymen and women. Those tens of thousands of readers who bought or rented the books after they had been tranched down the demand curve had market power to buy or decline to buy. But they had no direct way of influencing the textual content of what was made available at the top of the supply chain and which reached them long after the time of writing.[53] They were not in the loop. Attempts to equate the mentalities of Victorian readers with the ideologies revealed by the texts they read, 'Victorian values', are methodologically insecure if they do not take account of the fact that most readers did not participate in these mechanisms.

The feedback may have operated in similar ways at other times. For the Romantic period, the letters of John Murray to Byron, read alongside Byron's to Murray, show similar processes at work – removing or amending passages that might provoke a handful of activists was part of the role of Murray's in-house readers. But, as with Victorian fiction, it was mainly in the case of the first publication of a text that the activists were feared. In one of his

---

51 George Meredith, *Letters*, ed. C. K. Cline (Oxford, 1970) 1, p. 39.
52 Examples of authors evading or resisting Mudie, notably George Moore, in Simon Eliot, 'The business of Victorian publishing'.
53 A few Victorian demand curves noted as tables from information in the Warne archives in *The reading nation*, pp. 523–4, 713, 717–18.

many arguments with Byron – who resisted attempts to change his texts and eventually broke with Murray in frustration – Murray, a timid man, unilaterally removed a passage that he feared might bring down complaints from royalists, but simultaneously volunteered to reinstate it in the second edition.[54] Even earlier, the reinstatement of the politically highly sensitive 'deposition' scene in the 1608 reprint of Shakespeare's *King Richard the Second*, after at least two editions in 1597–8 from which it had been omitted, has not been satisfactorily explained, except as possible evidence that the monarchy was then less afraid of discussions of legitimacy and rebellion.

In the nineteenth-century fiction sector, besides Mudie's, there were many other intermediaries with a professional role in the feedback loop. On the production side, they included fellow authors, authors of books of advice to authors, suppliers of training courses for authors, literary agents who specialised in the problems of new authors, agents who acted for established authors in negotiations, valuers who estimated how much a proposed work might fetch, and publishers and their employees – in particular, the busy publisher's reader who 'has a drawerful or more at a time, perhaps even a load enough to make a donkey stagger', and normally came to his judgement by a quick perusal of the first chapter.[55] And then, after a manuscript was accepted for publication, the feedback agents included internal editors, designers who chose format, length, illustrations and binding styles, managers who decided how the company should position itself in the market, how it should be recognisable as a distinctive brand, and how the books should be classed in catalogues and described in advertisements. On the way back from the consumption side, the formal feedbacking agents included reviewers, the trade press, such as the *Publishers' Circular*, agents for overseas publishers and publications, institutional book-buyers, librarians, authors of books of advice to readers on what and how to read, advice to librarians on what to buy, teachers in universities, schools, and religious and military organisations, and eventually readers, all linked by correspondence and word of mouth comment in both directions. These agents, who were all active participants in 'the history of the book', assumed an increasingly influential role in the nineteenth century as it became harder for book-buyers and readers to find their way through the mass of available print on offer. And there is every reason to believe that the feedback mechanism will be found to have been operating, in one way or another, across the whole field of Victorian print, including periodicals and newspapers.

54 *The letters of John Murray to Lord Byron*, ed. Andrew Nicholson (2007), p. 202.
55 Russell, *The author's manual*, p. 208.

The Victorian feedback was not a communications circuit.[56] It was rather that the participants devoted professional efforts in trying to imagine the reactions of other participants, in some cases to influence the texts to keep them within imagined safety limits, and in other cases to influence access, reading and reception. At its heart lay a struggle between two opposed views: should literature be regarded as a means by which writers offered – and readers sought to obtain – an ever fuller and more truthful view of the complexity of the human world? Or was it an instrument of cultural governance by which elites within elites could influence the beliefs, knowledge and behaviour of others by presenting them with role models and mythic stories? Although a number of fiction writers, including some who are now most admired, successfully struggled against the power of the feedback, and readers might themselves offset what they perceived as disguised propaganda in a text by reading against the grain, the general tendency of the mechanism was to encourage stability, and therefore obsolescence, in the cultural system, a process encouraged by the material durability of plates.

And although in Victorian times the attention of the informal censors some-times appears to be mainly concentrated on the regulation of love, sexuality and marriage customs, the traditional domain of the novel, the feedback helped to slow the pace of cultural change across a broad range of knowledge and ideas. Russell's guide to aspiring writers, for example, in calling for the regulation of the press in the interests of 'family morality', and noting that he had persuaded Prime Minister Gladstone to back him, picks out for special censure writings that give credibility to Darwinism.[57] 'The religious novel', he advises aspiring authors, 'has not been written out as yet, and it offers a wide field for those who could meet and defeat the agnostic and the evolutionist each on his own grounds.'[58]

Alongside the adult fiction sector, another sector, of similar size, supplied fiction for children. Most cohorts of adults who later read sophisticated Vic-torian literature had had their mentalities – and horizons of expectations – influenced by reading Victorian children's literature. In this sector, since chil-dren were supposed to be confused by ambiguity, we can see the operation of the mechanism even more starkly. If the intended reader was allegedly the child, the purchaser was almost always an adult, and the presumed views of groups of actively intervening adults were given overriding priority. Just as the producers of novels for adults were under pressure to make their products

---

56 Discussed in *The reading nation*, pp. 443–9.   57 Russell, *The author's manual*, p. 85.
58 Russell, *The author's manual*, p. 195.

conform with the anticipated attitudes of the buying managers of the commercial circulating libraries, so the eyes of the producers of children's literature were on institutional buyers, especially school boards, individual schools, the Church of England Sunday School Institute, the Sunday School Union, the Wesleyan Methodist Sunday School Union, the Band of Hope, the Scottish Temperance Union and others who bought books to give to children as prizes, and also societies such as 'Pleasant Sunday Afternoons for Men', and paternalistic libraries for industrial workers such as railway institutes.[59] As with adult fiction, the feedback was mainly from other participants in the feedback responding to their fears about the imagined reactions of small groups of potential interventionists.

From memoranda written by the internal editors at Warne, a firm that published books for both children and adults, we can see the attitudes they applied in their professional role.[60] The opinions these employees offered were not their personal opinions – one editor describes a book as 'almost insufferable' while approving it.[61] However, the more they internalised the presumed attitudes of imagined hostile censors, the fewer risks they ran and the more commercially successful the firm was likely to be within its chosen market. What the Warne internal editors wanted to see was 'a good book, dealing pleasantly with pleasant people, cheerily written'.[62] It should contain moral lessons, either overt or thinly disguised. *Gilbert's shadow*, by the Hon. Mrs Greene, was reckoned to be 'a good book for a prize, its object being to show how a little thing may lead to a falsehood and farther on to worse mistakes and greater misery. The story is interesting and not too thickly overlaid with moralising!' However Greene's grasp of other matters was regarded as weak – she confused Africa and India and her attempt to describe a game of cricket had to be rewritten in-house.

Books for children were divided sharply into those for boys and those for girls, reflecting an ideology of essential gender difference as well as a sharp division of roles endorsed by the official English religion. Charlotte M. Yonge, author of many books for women and girls, for example, saw herself as 'a sort of instrument for popularising church views'.[63] The gender division extended right through the feedback, being found for example in the catalogues of what books were available to be bought or rented. The books for both sexes were

---

59 Many surviving copies have labels of institutional buyers.
60 Among the examples I have seen, all are written by two hands, unidentified, and undated.
61 Hon. Mrs Greene, *The schoolboy baronet*, of which 14,500 copies were produced between 1869 and 1892.
62 Mary C. Rowsell, *The boys of Fairmead* (1898).
63 Quoted by Rowbotham, *Good girls make good wives*, p. 6.

unashamedly nationalist. Children and adults were expected to read about what Laura Valentine called 'the divine light which has shone on our race'.[64] As principal editor at Warne from c.1865 to 1899, prolific in-house writer, anthologist, compiler, writer of prefaces, editor of the Chandos Classics series, and strict guardian of the textual limits permitted in the firm's lists, Laura Jewry Valentine (1814–99), 'Aunt Louisa', 'Aunt Friendly', was amongst the most influential figures in the Victorian book industry. Daughter of an admiral, she had lived in India and had been married to an English clergyman, and was herself an embodiment of the military–ecclesiastical complex that promoted the overseas empire in Victorian times.[65]

Seven to seventeen, or Veronica Gordon by M. M. Bell pleased the editor: 'This story of the building up of a girl's character principally in the religious vein, makes a nice, quiet book, readable and lady like that many women would think highly of.' As for stories for boys, many tell of brave little gentlemen bravely facing challenges at school or at home that would confront them later in the navy, the army, India or the colonies – a count would probably show 'brave' among the commonest words in literature for boys. But, at whatever cost to plausibility, care always had to be taken to avoid offending the imagined educational and ecclesiastical institutions, and the imagined activists that breathed down their necks. James Skipp Borlase's *Daring deeds and tales of adventure and peril* was discontinued because, according to the internal editor's judgement, 'Tales about criminals – bushrangers, and others. Not suitable for a prize book as it would provoke protest if so used.' *Hunting for gold, adventures in Klondyke* by Hume Nisbet, author of forty novels and many other works, was described by an editor as 'a splendid but rather roughly written yarn on a subject of interest to many. Though worth reading and keeping in print, I have a doubt as to whether the people who buy reward books will think as well of it as the boys who receive it, for gambling incidents are prominent and are too much interwoven in the plot to be dispensed with.' The editor went through Nisbet's text, that Warne had taken over from another publisher, to make the style more genteel. Where the Scottish/Australian author wrote 'the moon came out beautiful', his text was amended to 'came out in glory'. A 'smashing girl' became merely 'charming'.[66]

---

64 Preface to [Laura Valentine, ed.] *Dawn to daylight, or gleams from the poets of twelve centuries* (no date [1874]).

65 Apart from what can be deduced from the Warne books that she wrote, contributed to, or endorsed, and a few mentions in King and Stuart, *The house of Warne*, the only source I know is a paragraph in *Notes and Queries* series 11, vol. 12 (1915), pp. 266–7.

66 Amended copy, Warne archives.

With many titles, the Warne editors were engaged in a Dutch auction in unexceptionability – and therefore in implausibility – always trying to outbid rival firms who were under the same pressures.[67] The 1911 Mudie's classified catalogue of 'Boys, Juvenile Fiction', for example, lists five competing titles under 'Klondyke, Gold Fields'.[68] One of them, *Off to Klondyke* by Gordon Stables (no date [1898]), makes emigration to the gold fields of the Canadian far north appear attractive, romantic and lucrative. The boy hero is 'a truly manly and handsome English boy', 'no rarity in this dear country of ours . . . boys who when they grow up to be men, fight our battles among the wild and far-off hills of India, or in the African jungles, and perform deeds of valour which make the blood tingle within our veins, as we read of them at our quiet fireside in England'. The dangers of Dawson City, 'the alluring dance, the drinking-bar, and the gambling-table', are mentioned only once. One of the miners promises to become teetotal 'and kept his word', and is told 'you mustn't say "bloomin'," it's a bad word, except when applied to flowers'.[69]

Valentine and her team at Warne led as well as followed her imagined constituency. In her version of the old children's rhyme 'Sing a song of sixpence', by changing the traditional blackbird into a thieving jackdaw, and adding a few lines, Valentine was able simultaneously to celebrate the socially most elevated member of the medical profession and to commend capital punishment for assault. 'The maid was in the garden, / Hanging out the clothes; / By came a jackdaw, / And snapt off her nose. / They sent for the King's doctor, / who sewed it on again, / He sewed it on so neatly, / the seam was never seen; / And the jackdaw for his naughtiness / deservedly was slain.'[70] Valentine may have been the first publisher of books for children to put cats and dogs in dinner jackets, simultaneously hiding their sexual potential and upholding upper-class dress codes.

Decade after decade the Warne metal stereotypes turned out cultural stereotypes allegedly offered to children and young people for them to admire and imitate. With every title newly accepted – or rejected – for publication, every re-impression and every turn of the feedback mechanism, the Warne lists reinforced the presumed opinions of the imagined interventionists that they feared, and the plausibility gap widened. It is no surprise that the firm turned down Arthur Conan Doyle's first Sherlock Holmes story, *A study in scarlet*: it

---

67 The firm kept copies of books published by Seeley, a rival firm that specialised in religious books for children.

68 P. 927.

69 *Off to Klondyke* by Gordon Stables, a surgeon in the Royal Navy (no date [1898]) published by James Nisbet & Co., pp. 3, 210, 215.

70 *Aunt Louisa's keepsake* (1860s and later).

begins with Dr Watson, an Indian army doctor, describing being wounded in Afghanistan, catching an eastern illness, being invalided out, and gravitating 'to London, that great cesspool into which all the loungers and idlers of the Empire are irresistibly drained'. If Laura Valentine or one of her readers had got further in reading the offered manuscript, they would found that Dr Watson's fortunes only took a turn for the better when he ran into a friend at the Criterion bar. Warne was among the publishers who, Conan Doyle recalled in his *Memoirs*, 'sniffed and turned away'.[71]

The world of Warne, with its hierarchies, was expected to be permanent. *True to the watchword*, a story about the 1688–9 siege of Londonderry, was hailed by an internal editor as 'never likely to go out of date'. *The babes in the basket*, an editor advised, 'has become a sort of nursery classic. It deals with the bravery and fidelity of an old Negress nurse, who saves the lives of her two infant charges, and after years of toil and care in their behalf has the joy of restoring them to their parents who are supposed to have been murdered during the rising of Negro slaves on their plantation. I see no reason why this story should not be continuously reprinted.'

In Beatrice Marshall's *Nancy's nephew; or, Mike's first campaign* the children wear sailor suits, have their own ponies, live in big houses with 'noble' tiger-skins on the floor, are taught not to laugh at their German governesses, and worry that there may not be enough countries for the British to explore. Their prayers – 'dear Jesus who died on the cross for Jack and Sprat and me, who wants us to be good boys and grow up good men, and then go to live in heaven . . .' – are answered or an explanation offered that the death of a child is all for the best. The book was regarded, with barely concealed contempt, by the internal editor as

> A prettily told story of an orphan boy named Mike and his aunt Nancy, who is very slightly his senior. His mother had died through nursing Mike through an attack of scarlet fever, and his father regards Mike as the cause of his lonely life. The father goes for a protracted yachting cruise and leaves Mike to the care of his maternal grandparents and his mostly juvenile aunts and uncles. The story is chiefly concerned with his doings among them, and his efforts to conquer his resentment of his father's aversion to him. After two years his father returns with a new bride, a handsome animated doll, and there seems little prospect of any better relations between father and son; but events bring about an understanding between them. The story is more suitable for girls than boys; but contains nothing that is likely to render it out of date. Though the

71 *Memories and adventures* (1924), p. 74.

general appearance of the plates is good and clean there are a number of little points in which repair or correction is needed . . .

By single word changes to the plates, the internal editor made the text even more unexceptionable than it had been hitherto. When Mike says of his young stepmother, he is lucky 'to have another mother like you', the editor changes 'another' to the less threatening 'a'. Where, in the existing text, Mike is recommended 'sometimes' to 'talk things out', the 'sometimes' – that may imply that he has an option – is removed. When Mike says 'What a shame it is that every body shouldn't be taught about God', and declares that when he is a man and rich, he will found a school to teach 'all the poor, dirty boys I can find', the word 'all' is removed. Upper-middle-class bourgeois morality encouraged philanthropy but not as an open-ended charge on the purse.

Texts written decades before could be given a contemporary veneer by changing the binding styles and illustrations of the re-impressions from the plates. Title-pages rarely included a date. Texts that went factually out of date could be altered provided that it was economical to amend the plates. At the beginning of the twentieth century, plates were altered to take account of the death of Queen Victoria. There came a time when *Brave Bobby, Peter and his pony*, that referred to whale oil as the main form of household lighting, was reluctantly removed from the lists, although it included the typical and unexceptionable advice offered to a poor shrimp boy: 'If you always try to be useful, and honest, and kind to others, as you do now, you will grow up a happy man, and be our joy and comfort.' A story about boy sailors that referred to training establishments that had closed could not be easily updated, but a replacement story could be commissioned which the editors believed would in its turn 'help to man the Navy'. The editors understood that they had market power to push certain texts in order to squeeze the last drop of output from their plates. As was noted of *The lost heir, or Truth and falsehood*, 'this story is . . . hardly in accordance with modern juvenile tastes; but as the plates appear to be not much worn, it might be advisable to wear them out. From the moral point of view there is nothing against the book.'[72]

Developing provisional theoretical frameworks

Besides continuing to develop our understanding of the economics of the book industry, the future opens up possibilities of developing more explicit

---

72 For the economics of working stereotypes, 'plant', until it wore out see *The reading nation*, pp. 414–15, here given documentary evidence that it was an explicitly pursued policy.

provisional models of the wider literary system within which the book industry operated, of which I have suggested three, author-led, reader-led, and commercial and political. These already enable us to make reliable general statements in some cases even where archival information is thin. Empirical studies of, for example, the operation of the feedback can help to enlarge, refine and improve the usability of such models. Also needed, as I have already suggested, is another methodology drawn from the success of disciplines that study other complex human systems, a formal means of taking account of the counterfactual, against which all statements of causation or influence are questionable and risk appearing teleological. One solution for a reasonably fixed comparator that I favour, and have attempted to build for the Romantic period, is to build a statement of the mainstream official ideology as it existed at any historical conjuncture.[73]

What should be our priorities?

Book history can proceed successfully across a wide front, as it has done hitherto. Studies of authors, or firms, of the publication, reading and possible impact of particular texts or groups of texts, and many other studies, all contribute to the advance of knowledge. But the book industry is not like other industries, such as coal, where the product is much the same. Books can be regarded as commodities, and general output statistics found, for example, in government statistics can help us understand the changing fortunes of the industry as a whole. But, for those who may wish to follow the move to questions about reading and the effects of reading, we need information about texts, and texts are individual. For this approach to be advanced, the first priority is to obtain and make available the basic information about the production and prices of individual named books, including reprints, abridgements and other derivatives of texts, and their prices. Only in that way can we develop a fuller understanding of the vital role of books as the material carriers of ideas.

The two main priorities I suggest in addition to those mentioned earlier in this chapter are straightforward and easily feasible within our existing knowledge.

First, develop a short simple guide for scholars and students that would enable them quickly to understand the material component of the literary

---

73 My choice of the sermons of Hugh Blair, and other texts, as statements of the mainstream ideology of the Romantic period against which comparisons can be made was challenged by Kenyon Jones but, as far as I know, no alternative way of dealing with the problem of the implicit counterfactual in the notion of influence has been suggested.

system from author to reader and back, and offer practical advice on how to read and use archival sources.[74]

Second, institute a national project, with many hands contributing from many centres, to develop a Record of Historic Book Production and Prices (HBPP). The age of print gave us a few excellent full printed transcriptions of publishing, and especially printing, archives.[75] But in the age of the internet, there is little to be gained by putting raw publishing archives online, unless that is accompanied by a collating of the information drawn from them, a project of higher priority.[76] One task would be to include in *ESTC* – or develop alongside it – titles known to have existed but which are now lost. But the main work would be to put alongside our lists of titles whatever information can be found about print-runs and prices. That is the essential precondition for studies of which constituencies could have read which texts in what numbers and when. We should avoid the temptation to pile on information, just because it is there, for example about paper and printing costs, and other matters that can be added later by those with a particular interest. The information should be compiled in a form that not only enables the record to be searched, but designed, with professional help, to be interrogable to yield general patterns and explanations, taking account of gaps. Although ambitious in scope such a project is limited by the fact that the number of surviving archives before, say 1918, is itself limited, and it could be accomplished within a few years.[77] Nor does it require much skilled or expensive labour.

The Victorians, with the technology available to them, produced, with amazing speed, lists and catalogues of titles of books known to have survived, information which transformed understanding of many historical questions, and which we still use every day. It would be in the same confident tradition if our generation were to add to that achievement with the help of the new technologies that we have. Or put the other way, if the book history profession does not improve the factual empirical basis of its subject of study, as it now has the opportunity to do, its potential contribution to helping to address wider questions will remain unfulfilled.

---

74 We already have lists of surviving publishing, printing and bookselling archives.
75 Notably McKenzie and Ross, *A ledger of Charles Ackers*; Maslen and Lancaster (eds.), *The Bowyer ledgers*; Kaser (ed.), *The cost book of Carey and Lea*; Tryon and Charvat (eds.), *The cost books of Ticknor and Fields*.
76 The microfilm photographic reproductions of certain publishers' archives have not been much used.
77 A *Guide to archives of 19th c. British publishers* by Alexis Weedon is available online. Other lists, including those of printers, for earlier periods are noted in bibliographies.

Bibliography

All books are published in London unless otherwise indicated. For further contemporary literature, attention is drawn to Joanne Shattock (ed.), *The Cambridge bibliography of English literature*, 3rd edn. 4. *1800–1900* (Cambridge, 1999).

Abbey, J. R. *Scenery of Great Britain and Ireland in aquatint and lithography 1770–1860* (1952)
   Travel in aquatint and lithography 1770–1860, 2 vols. (1956–7)
Ackland, Joseph 'Elementary education and the decay of literature', *Nineteenth Century* 35 (1894), pp. 412–33
Act, An, for securing to authors in certain cases the benefit of international copyright (1838) 1 & 2 Vict. c.59
Act, An, for the general regulation of the Customs (1842) 5 & 6 Vict. c.47
Act, An, to amend the law relating to international copyright (1844) 7 & 8 Vict. c.12
Act, An, to regulate the trade of British possessions abroad (1845) 8 & 9 Vict. c.93
Act, An, to amend the law relating to the protection in the colonies of works entitled to copyright in the United Kingdom (1847) 10 & 11 Vict. c.95
Act, An, to enable Her Majesty to carry into effect a connection with France on the subject of copyright, to extend and explain the international copyright acts, and to explain the acts relating to copyright in engravings (1852) 15 & 16 Vict. c.12
Acton, J. D. 'Nationality', *Home and Foreign Review* 1 (1862), pp. 1–25, repr. in his *The history of freedom and other essays*, ed. J. N. Figgis and R. V. Laurence (1907), pp. 270–300
Adams, J. R. R. *The printed word and the common man: popular culture in Ulster, 1700–1900* (Belfast, 1987)
Adey, Lionel *Class and idol in the English hymn* (Vancouver, 1988)
Adler, Michael H. *The writing machine: a history of the typewriter* (1973)
Advice to authors, inexperienced writers, and possessors of manuscripts, on the efficient publication of books (Saunders and Otley [c.1850])
Agar, Jon *Government machine: a revolutionary history of the computer* (Cambridge, MA, 2003)
Akenson, Donald H. *The Irish education experiment: the National System of education in the nineteenth century* (1970)
Alderson, Brian *Hans Christian Andersen and his eventyr in England, some notes and observations* (Wormley, 1982)
   'Just-so pictures: illustrated versions of *Just-so stories for children*', *Children's Literature* 20 (1992), pp. 147–54

'Novelty books and movables: questions of terminology', *Children's Books History Society Newsletter* 61 (1998), pp. 14–22

'Some notes on James Burns as a publisher of children's books', *Bulletin of the John Rylands University Library* 76 (1994), pp. 103–26

Alderson, Brian and Felix de Marez Oyens *Be merry and wise: the origins of children's book publishing in England, 1650–1850* (2006)

Allen, D. *The naturalist in Britain: a social history* (1976)

'Tastes and crazes', in N. Jardine *et al.* (eds.), *Cultures of natural history* (Cambridge, 1996), pp. 394–407

The Victorian fern craze: a history of pteridomania (1969)

[Allen, Grant] 'The trade of author', *Fortnightly Review* 51 (1889), pp. 261–74

Allen, John Naule 'Railway reading, with a few hints to travellers', *Ainsworth's Magazine* 24 (1853), pp. 483–7; repr. in Andrew King and John Plunkett (eds.), *Victorian print media: a reader* (Oxford, 2005)

Allen, W. O. B. and Edmund MacClure *Two hundred years: the history of the Society for Promoting Christian Knowledge, 1698–1898* (1898)

Allnutt, W. H. 'Printers and printing in the provincial towns of England and Wales', in Henry R. Tedder and Ernest C. Thomas (eds.), *Transactions and proceedings of the first annual meeting of the Library Association of the United Kingdom . . . 1878* (1879), pp. 101–3

Alloway, Ross 'Agencies and joint ventures', in B. Bell (ed.), *The Edinburgh history of the book in Scotland. 3. Ambition and industry, 1800–1880* (Edinburgh, 2007), pp. 385–95

Altholz, Josef *Anatomy of a controversy: the debate over Essays and reviews, 1860–1864* (Aldershot, 1994)

The religious press in Britain, 1760–1900 (New York, 1988)

'The Vatican decrees controversy, 1874–5', *Catholic Historical Review* 57 (1972), pp. 593–605

Altick, Richard D. *The English common reader: a social history of the mass reading public, 1800–1900* (Chicago, 1957)

'English publishing in 1852', in his *Writers, readers, and occasions: selected essays on Victorian literature and life* (Columbus, OH, 1989), pp. 141–230

'From Aldine to Everyman: cheap reprint series of the English classics, 1830–1906', *Studies in Bibliography* 11 (1958), pp. 3–24; repr. in his *Writers, readers, and occasions* (Columbus, OH, 1989)

'Nineteenth-century English best-sellers: a further list', *Studies in Bibliography* 22 (1969), pp. 197–206

'Nineteenth-century English best-sellers: a third list', *Studies in Bibliography* 39 (1986), pp. 235–41

The presence of the present (Columbus, OH, 1991)

'The sociology of authorship', *Bulletin of the New York Public Library* 56 (1962), pp. 389–404; repr. in his *Writers, readers, and occasions* (Columbus, OH, 1989)

Writers, readers, and occasions: selected essays on Victorian literature and life (Columbus, OH, 1989)

American, The, catalogue of books: or, English guide to American literature (1856)

Ames, Joseph *Typographical antiquities* (1749), rev. William Herbert and T. F. Dibdin, 4 vols. (1810–19)

Amory, Hugh and David D. Hall (eds.) *A history of the book in America*. 1. *The colonial book in the Atlantic world* (Cambridge, 2000)

Analytical, An, catalogue of Mr. Chapman's publications (London, 1852)

Anderson, Benedict *Imagined communities: reflections on the origins and spread of nationalism*, rev. edn (1991)

Anderson, Patricia *The printed image and the transformation of popular culture 1790-1860* (Oxford, 1991)

Anderson, Patricia and Jonathan Rose (eds.) *British literary publishing houses, 1881-1965* (Detroit, 1991)

Anderson, R. D. *Education and opportunity in Victorian Scotland* (Oxford, 1983)

'Education and the state in nineteenth-century Scotland', *Economic History Review* 2nd ser. 36 (1983), pp. 518-34

Andrews, Alexander *The history of British journalism*, 2 vols. (1859)

Andrews, J. H. *A paper landscape: the Ordnance Survey in nineteenth-century Ireland*, 2nd edn (Dublin, 2002)

Andrews, Martin 'Hare & Co., commercial wood-engravers: Jabez Hare, founder of the firm, and his letters 1846 to 1847', *JPHS* 24 (1995), pp. 53-106

Anesko, Michael *'Friction with the market': Henry James and the profession of authorship* (Oxford, 1986)

Anglo, Sydney *Images of Tudor kingship* (1992)

Anstruther, G. E. and P. E. Hallet *The Catholic Truth Society: the first fifty years* (1934)

Anstruther, Ian *Oscar Browning: a biography* (1983)

Arbour, Keith *Canvassing books, sample books, and subscription publishers' ephemera, 1833-1951, in the collection of Michael Zinman* (Ardsley, NY, 1996)

Archer, William *English dramatists of today* (1882)

Archives of the Royal Literary Fund: 1790-1918 (London: World Microfilms, 1984)

Armstrong, C. and C. de Zegher (eds.) *Ocean flowers: impressions from nature* (Princeton, NJ, 2004)

Arnold, Matthew 'Copyright', *Fortnightly Review* n.s. 27 (1880), pp. 319-34

Letters, ed. C. Y. Lang, 6 vols. (Charlottesville, VA, 1996-2001)

Ashley, Mike *The age of storytellers: British popular fiction magazines, 1880-1950* (2006)

Ashton, J. *Chapbooks of the eighteenth century* (1882)

Ashton, Rosemary 'Doubting clerics: from James Anthony Froude to *Robert Elsmere* via George Eliot', in David Jasper and T. R. Wright (eds.), *The critical spirit and the will to believe: essays in nineteenth century literature and religion* (1989)

George Eliot: a life (1997)

Little Germany: exile and asylum in Victorian England (Oxford, 1986)

142 Strand: a radical address in Victorian London (2006)

Ashworth, W. J. 'John Herschel, George Airy, and the roaming eye of the state', *History of Science* 36 (1998), pp. 151-78

Astore, W. *Observing God: Thomas Dick, evangelicalism, and popular science in Victorian Britain and America* (Aldershot, 2001)

Attar, Dena *A bibliography of household books published in Britain, 1800-1914* (1987)

Attenborough, John *A living memory: Hodder and Stoughton publishers 1868-1975* (1975)

Auerbach, Jeffrey A. *The Great Exhibition of 1851: a nation on display* (New Haven, CT, 1999)

Auerbach, Nina and U. C. Knoepflmacher (eds.) *Forbidden journeys: fairy tales and fantasies by Victorian women writers* (Chicago, 1992)

Avery, Gillian *Behold the child: American children and their books 1621–1922* (1994)

Axon, William E. A. 'The largest book in the world', in *Companion to the [British] almanac* (1872), pp. 105–23

Ayerst, David *Guardian: biography of a newspaper* (1971)

Babbage, Charles *Reflections on the decline of science in England, and on some of its causes* (1830)

Badia, Janet and Jennifer Phegley (eds.) *Reading women: literary figures and cultural icons from the Victorian age to the present* (Toronto, 2005)

Bagehot, Walter *Physics and politics* (1872: 1887 edn)

Baggs, Chris 'How well read was my valley? Reading, popular fiction, and the miners of South Wales, 1875–1939', *Book History* 4 (2001), pp. 277–301

Bailey, Peter 'The politics and poetics of modern British leisure: a late twentieth-century review', *Rethinking History* 3 (1999), pp. 131–75

Baker, Joseph Ellis *The novel and the Oxford movement* (Princeton, NJ, 1932)

Ball, Douglas *Victorian publishers' bindings* (1985)

Bamford, T. W. *The rise of the public schools* (1967)

Bandyopadhyay, Chittaranjan (ed.) *Dui shotoker Bangla mudron ō prōkashon* (Two centuries of Bengali printing and publishing) (Calcutta, 1981)

Barber, Giles 'Galignani and the publication of English books in France from 1800 to 1852' *The Library* 5th ser. 16 (1961), pp. 267–86

Barbier, Frédéric and Catherine Bertho-Lavenir *Histoire des médias: de Diderot à Internet* (Paris, 1996)

Barker, Hannah *Newspapers, politics and English society 1695–1855* (2000)

Barker, Nicolas 'Bernard Quaritch', *The Book Collector* special number for the 150th anniversary of Bernard Quaritch (1977), pp. 3–34

    Bibliotheca Lindesiana (Roxburghe Club, 1977)

    Oxford University Press and the spread of learning (Oxford, 1978)

    Portrait of an obsession: the life of Sir Thomas Phillipps (1967)

    The publications of the Roxburghe Club, 1814–1962 (Roxburghe Club, 1964)

Barker, Nicolas and John Collins, *A sequel to An enquiry into the nature of certain nineteenth century pamphlets* (1983)

Barnard, John 'The stationers' stock 1663/4 to 1705/6: psalms, psalters, primers and ABCs', *The Library* 6th ser. 21 (1999), pp. 369–75

    'The survival and loss rates of psalms, ABCs, psalters and primers from the stationers' stock, 1660–1700', *The Library* 6th ser. 21 (1999), pp. 148–50

Barnes, James J. *Authors, publishers and politicians: the quest for an Anglo-American copyright agreement, 1815–1854* (1974)

    Free trade in books (Oxford, 1964)

    'Galignani and the publication of English books in France: a postscript', *The Library* 5th ser. 25 (1970), pp. 294–313

    Review of Hepburn, *The author's empty purse*, *American Historical Review* 74 (1969), pp. 1281–2

Barnes, John (ed.) *The writer in Australia: a collection of literary documents 1856–1964* (Melbourne, 1969)

Barnicoat, John *A concise history of posters* (1972)

Barrett, Daniel 'Play publication, readers, and the "decline" of Victorian drama', *Book History* 2 (1999), pp. 173–87

Barrow-Green, J. '"The advantage of proceeding from an author of some scientific reputation": Isaac Todhunter and his mathematics textbooks', in J. Smith and C. Stray (eds.), *Teaching and learning in nineteenth-century Cambridge* (Woodbridge, 2001), pp. 176–203

Bartle, G. J. 'The teaching manuals and lesson books of the British and Foreign School Society', *History of Education Society Bulletin* 46 (1990), pp. 22–33

Barton, R. 'Just before Nature: the purpose of science and the purpose of popularization in some English popular science journals of the 1860s', *Annals of Science* 55 (1998), pp. 1–33
  '"Men of science": language, identity and professionalization in the mid-Victorian scientific community', *History of Science* 41 (2003), pp. 73–119

Bartram, Alan *Futurist typography and the liberated text* (2005)
  Lettering in architecture (1975)
  Street name lettering in the British Isles (1978)

Bartrip, P. W. J. *Mirror of medicine: a history of the British Medical Journal* (Oxford, 1990)

Barty-King, Hugh *Her Majesty's Stationery Office: the story of the first 200 years, 1786–1986* (1986)

Batalden, Stephen, Kathleen Cann and John Dean (eds.) *Sowing the word: the cultural impact of the British and Foreign Bible Society, 1804–2004* (Sheffield, 2004)

Bayly, C. A. *The birth of the modern world, 1780–1914: global connections and comparisons* (Oxford, 2004)
  Empire and information: intelligence gathering and social communication in India, 1780–1870 (Cambridge, 1996)

Bayly, Susan 'The evolution of colonial cultures: nineteenth-century Asia', in Andrew Porter (ed.), *The Oxford history of the British Empire. 3. The nineteenth century* (Oxford, 1999), pp. 447–69

Beare, Geoffrey *The illustrations of W. Heath Robinson* (1983) and supplement (1994)

Beavan, Iain 'Bookselling', in B. Bell (ed.), *The Edinburgh history of the book in Scotland. 3. Ambition and Industry, 1800–1880* (Edinburgh, 2007), pp. 123–40
  '"What constitutes the crime which it is your pleasure to punish so mercilessly?": Scottish booksellers' societies in the nineteenth century', in Peter Isaac and Barry McKay (eds.), *The moving market: continuity and change in the book trade* (New Castle, DE, 2001), pp. 71–82
  'Working in the margins: some aspects of the late nineteenth-century book and magazine trade in northeast Scotland', *Bibliotheck* 15 (1988), pp. 76–95

Bebbington, David *Evangelicalism in modern Britain: a history from the 1730s to the 1980s* (1989)
  'Henry Drummond, evangelicalism and science', *Records of the Scottish History Society* 28 (1998), pp. 129–48

Beckwith, Alice H. *Victorian bibliomania: the illuminated book in 19th-century Britain* (Providence, RI, 1987)

Beckwith, F. *The Leeds Library, 1768–1968* (Leeds, 1968)

Beeching, Wilfred A. *Century of the typewriter* (1974)

Beer, G. *Darwin's plots: evolutionary narrative in Darwin, George Eliot and nineteenth-century fiction* (1983)
  Open fields: science in cultural encounter (Oxford, 1996)

Beetham, Margaret *A magazine of her own? Domesticity and desire in the woman's magazine, 1800–1914* (1996)

Bell, Bill (ed.), *The Edinburgh history of the book in Scotland. 3. Ambition and industry, 1800–1880* (Edinburgh, 2007)

'From Parnassus to Grub Street', in Elizabeth James (ed.), *Macmillan: a publishing tradition* (Basingstoke, 2002), pp. 52–69

'"Pioneers of literature" – the commercial traveller in the early nineteenth century', in Peter Isaac and Barry McKay (eds.), *The reach of print* (New Castle, DE, 1998), pp. 121–34

Bell, Duncan *The idea of Greater Britain: empire and the future of world order, 1860–1900* (Princeton, NJ, 2007)

Bell, Florence *At the works: a study of a manufacturing town* [1911]

Bennett, Arnold *Books and persons* (1917)

Letters to J. B. Pinker, ed. James Hepburn (Oxford, 1966)

The truth about an author (1903; 3rd edn 1914)

Bennett, J. D. 'The railway guidebooks of George Measom', *BackTrack* 15 (2001), pp. 379–81

Bennett, Scott 'John Murray's Family Library and the cheapening of books in early nineteenth-century Britain', *Studies in Bibliography* 29 (1976), pp. 139–66

'Revolutions in thought: serial publication and the mass market for reading', in J. Shattock and M. Wolff (eds.), *The Victorian periodical press: samplings and soundings* (Leicester, 1982), pp. 225–57

Bentham, Jeremy *An essay on political tactics* (1816), in *Works*, ed. John Bowring, 11 vols. (Edinburgh, 1843) 2, pp. 301–73

Bently, Lionel 'Copyright, translations, and relations between Britain and India in the nineteenth and early twentieth centuries', *Chicago-Kent Law Review*, 82 (2007), pp. 1181–1242.

Benzie, William *Dr. F. J. Furnivall: Victorian scholar adventurer* (Norman, OK, 1983)

Berg, M. *The machinery question and the making of political economy, 1815–1848* (Cambridge, 1980)

Berger, Stefan and others (eds.) *Writing national histories: western Europe since 1800* (1999)

Berman, Morris *Social change and scientific organization: the Royal Institution, 1799–1844* (1978)

Berry, W. Turner and H. Edmund Poole *Annals of printing: a chronological encyclopaedia from the earliest times to 1950* (1966)

Bertrum, James *Some memories of books, authors, and events* (1893)

Besant, Annie *Annie Besant: an autobiography* (1893)

Besant, Walter *Fifty years ago* (1888)

'The first Society of British Authors, 1843', *Contemporary Review* 56 (1889), pp. 10–27, repr. in his *Essays and historiettes* (1903), pp. 271–307

'Literature as a career', *Forum* (August 1892), pp. 693–708

The pen and the book (1899)

Bevington, Merle Mowbray *The Saturday Review: 1855–1868: representative educated opinion in Victorian England* (New York, 1941)

Bewick, Thomas *My life*, ed. and with an introduction by Iain Bain (1981)

Biervliet, Lori van *Leven en werk van W. H. James Weale, een Engelskunsthistoricus in Vlaanderen in de 19de eeuw* (Brussels, 1991)

Biesalski, Ernst-Peter *Die Mechanisierung der deutschen Buchbinderei, 1850–1900* (Frankfurt am Main, 1991), repr. from *Archiv für Geschichte des Buchwesens* 36 (1991)

Bigham, Clive *The Roxburghe Club: its history and its members, 1812–1927* (Roxburghe Club, 1928)

Billington, Louis 'The religious periodical and newspaper press, 1770–1870', in Michael Harris and Alan Lee (eds.), *The press in English society from the seventeenth to nineteenth centuries* (1986), pp. 113–32

Binfield, Clyde 'Hymns and an orthodox dissenter: in commemoration of Bernard Lord Manning, 1892–1941', *Journal of the United Reformed Church History Society* (1992), pp. 86–109

Birrell, Augustine *Essays about men, women and books* (1894)

Bishop, A. S. *The rise of a central authority for English education* (Cambridge, 1971)

Black, M. H. *Cambridge University Press: 1584–1984* (Cambridge, 1984)

Blackie, Agnes A. C. *Blackie and Son, 1809–1959* (1959)

Blamires, David 'Social satire in English Struwwelpeter parodies', *Princeton University Library Chronicle* 62 (2000), pp. 45–58

Bland, David *A history of book illustration* (1958)

Bluhm, Lothar *Die Brüder Grimm und der Beginn der deutschen Philologie: eine Studie zu Kommunikation und Wissenschaftsbildung im frühen 19. Jahrhundert* (Hildesheim, 1997)

Blunt, Wilfrid *The art of botanical illustration* (1950; new edn with W. T. Stearn, Woodbridge, 1994)

   Cockerell (1964)

Boardman, Kay and Shirley Jones (eds.) *Popular Victorian women writers* (Manchester, 2004)

Boas, G. *Lays of learning* (1926)

Bonham-Carter, Victor *Authors by profession. 1. From the introduction of printing until the Copyright Act 1911* (1978)

Bonython, Elizabeth and Anthony Burton, *The great exhibitor: the life and work of Henry Cole* (2003)

Booth, William *In darkest England and the way out* (1890)

Borchardt, D. H. and W. Kirsop (eds.) *The book in Australia: essays towards a cultural and social history* (Melbourne, 1988)

Borrow, George *The Bible in Spain* (1843)

Borsay, Peter *A history of leisure* (Basingstoke, 2006)

Bostetter, Mary 'The journalism of Thomas Wakley', in Joel H. Wiener (ed.), *Innovators and preachers: the role of the editor in Victorian England* (Westport, CT, 1985), pp. 275–92

Bourne, H. R. Fox *English newspapers: chapters in the history of journalism*, 2 vols. (1887)

Bowen, Desmond *The Protestant crusade in Ireland, 1800–70: a study of Protestant–Catholic relations between the Act of Union and disestablishment* (Montreal, 1978)

Bowen, H.V. *The business of empire: the East India Company and imperial Britain, 1756–1833* (Cambridge, 2006)

Bowler, P. 'Experts and publishers: writing popular science in early twentieth-century Britain, writing popular history of science now', *British Journal for the History of Science* 39 (2006), pp. 159–87

Bowman, Anne *The common things of everyday life: a book of home wisdom for mothers and daughters* (1857)

Bowman, John H. *Greek printing types in Britain from the eighteenth to the early twentieth century* (Thessaloniki, 1998)

Boyce, G., J. Curran and P. Wingate (eds.) *Newspaper history from the seventeenth century to the present day* (1978)

Bradbury, Henry *Printing: its dawn, day and destiny* (1858)

Bradley, Ian *Abide with me: the world of Victorian hymns* (1997)

'Vaughan Williams's "Chamber of horrors": changing attitudes to Victorian hymns', in Alan Luff (ed.), *Strengthen for service: 100 years of the English hymnal, 1906-2006* (Norwich, 2005), pp. 231-44

Brake, L. *Print in transition, 1850-1910* (Basingstoke, 2001)

Brake, Laurel *Subjugated knowledges: journalism, gender and literature in the nineteenth century* (New York, 1994)

Brant, Clare *Eighteenth-century letters and British culture* (2006)

Brantlinger, Patrick *The reading lesson: the threat of mass literacy in nineteenth-century British fiction* (Bloomington, IN, 1998)

Brayley, E. W. *Catalogue of the library of the Russell Institution* (1849)

Breslauer, B. H. *The uses of bookbinding literature* (New York, 1986)

[Brewster, D.] 'Decline of science in England', *Quarterly Review* 43 (1830), pp. 305-42

Bridges, R. C. and P. E. H. Hair (eds.) *Compassing the vast globe of the earth: studies in the history of the Hakluyt Society, 1846-1996* (1996)

Briggs, Asa *The age of improvement, 1783-1867* (1959)

(ed.) *Essays in the history of publishing, in celebration of the 250th anniversary of the house of Longman, 1724-1974* (1974)

Victorian things (1988)

'The view from Badminton', in Asa Briggs (ed.), *Essays in the history of publishing in celebration of the 250th anniversary of the house of Longman, 1724-1974* (1974), pp. 189-218

Briggs, Asa and Peter Burke, *A social history of the media: from Gutenberg to the Internet* (Cambridge, 2002)

Briggs, Julia, 'A liberating imagination: Hans Christian Andersen in England', *Marvels & Tales* 20 (2006), pp. 179-82

Briggs, Julia and Dennis Butts, 'The emergence of form (1850-90)', in Peter Hunt (ed.), *Children's literature: an illustrated history* (Oxford, 1995), pp. 130-66

Bright, Charles *The story of the Atlantic cable* (1903)

Brindle, Patrick 'Past histories: history and the elementary school classroom in early twentieth century England', PhD thesis, University of Cambridge (1998)

Brock, C. 'The public worth of Mary Somerville', *British Journal for the History of Science* 39 (2006), pp. 255-72

Brock, M. G. and M. C. Curthoys (eds.), *The history of the University of Oxford. 6. Nineteenth-century Oxford*, part 1 (Oxford, 1997)

Brock, Peter 'A Polish "proscrit" in Jersey', *Bulletin of the Société Jersiaise* 16 (1953-4), pp. 179-94

Brock, W. H. 'Brewster as scientific journalist', in A. Morison-Low and J. R. R. Christie (eds.), *'Martyr of Science': Sir David Brewster, 1781-1863: proceedings of a bicentennial symposium* (Edinburgh, 1984), pp. 37-42

'The development of commercial science journals in Victorian Britain', in A. J. Meadows (ed.), *Development of science publishing in Europe* (Amsterdam, 1980), pp. 95-122

The Fontana history of chemistry (1992)

'The lamp of learning: Richard Taylor and the textbook', *Paradigm* 2.4 (2001), pp. 2–5

'Science periodicals', in J. D. Vann and R. T. VanArsdel (eds.), *Victorian periodicals and Victorian society* (Toronto, 1994), pp. 81–96

Brock, W. H. and A. J. Meadows *The lamp of learning: two centuries of publishing at Taylor & Francis*, rev. edn (1998)

Broks, Peter *Media science before the Great War* (Basingstoke, 1996)

Brooks, Jeffrey *When Russia learned to read* (Princeton, NJ, 1985)

Broomhead, Frank *The book illustrations of Orlando Jewitt* (1995)

The Zaehnsdorfs (1842–1947): craft bookbinders (1986)

Brougham, Henry 'Taxes on knowledge', *Edinburgh Review* 62 (1835), pp. 126–32

Brown, Andrew 'Martineau's hymn books', *Transactions of the Unitarian Historical Society* 22 (2002), pp. 393–408

Brown, Callum *Religion and society in Scotland since 1707* (Edinburgh, 1997)

'The Sunday School movement in Scotland, 1780–1914', *Records of the Scottish Church History Society* 21 (1983), pp. 3–26

Brown, Lucy *Victorian news and newspapers* (Oxford, 1985)

Brown, Richard and Stanley Brett *The London bookshop*, 2 vols. (1971–7)

Brown, Richard D. *Knowledge is power: the diffusion of knowledge in early America, 1700–1865* (New York, 1989)

The strength of a people: the idea of an informed citizenry in America, 1650–1870 (Chapel Hill, NC, 1996)

Brown, Stewart J. *The national churches of England, Ireland, and Scotland, 1801–1846* (Oxford, 2001)

Browne, J. *Charles Darwin: the power of place* (2002)

Brundage, Anthony *The people's historian: John Richard Green and the writing of history in Victorian England* (Westport, CT, 1994)

Buchanan-Brown, John *Early Victorian illustrated books: Britain, France and Germany 1820–1860* (2005)

Bullen, George (ed.) *Caxton celebration, 1877: catalogue of the loan collection . . . connected with the art of printing, South Kensington* (1877)

Bunbury, F. (ed.) *Memorials of Sir C. J. F. Bunbury, Bart* 9 vols. (Mildenhall, 1890–3)

Bunsen, Henry de *The bookhawker: his work and his day: being a paper read at the Conference of the Church of England Bookhawking Union, held at Derby, 21 September, 1859* (1859)

Burch, R. M. *Colour printing and colour printers* (1910)

Burlington Fine Arts Club *Exhibition of bookbindings* (1891)

[Burn, James Dawson] *The language of the walls* (Manchester, 1855)

Burnett, John *Plenty and want: a social history of food in England from 1815 to the present day*, 3rd edn (1989)

Burroughs, Peter 'Defence and imperial disunity', in Andrew Porter (ed.), *The Oxford history of the British Empire. 3. The nineteenth century* (Oxford, 1999), pp. 320–45

'Imperial institutions and the government of empire', in Andrew Porter (ed.), *The Oxford history of the British Empire. 3. The nineteenth century* (Oxford, 1999), pp. 170–97

Burstein, Miriam Elizabeth 'Reviving the reformation: Victorian women writers and the Protestant historical novel', *Women's Writing* 12 (2005), pp. 73–84

Burton, Anthony *Vision & accident: the story of the Victoria and Albert Museum* (1999)

Bury, J. P. T. 'A. W. Tuer and the Leadenhall Press', *Book Collector* 36 (1987), pp. 225–43

Bury, Stephen (ed.) *Breaking the rules: the printed face of the European avant garde, 1900–1937* (2007)

Bushaway, Bob ' "Things said or sung a thousand times"; customary society and oral culture in rural England, 1700–1900', in Adam Fox and Daniel Woolf (eds.), *The spoken word: oral culture in Britain, 1500–1850* (Manchester, 2002), pp. 256–83

Butler, Marilyn 'Culture's medium: the role of the review', in Stuart Curran (ed.), *The Cambridge companion to British romanticism* (Cambridge, 1993), pp. 120–47

Butts, Dennis 'The beginnings of Victorianism (c. 1820–1850)', in Peter Hunt (ed.), *Children's literature: an illustrated history* (Oxford, 1995), pp. 77–100

Butts, Dennis and Pat Garrett (eds.) *From* The dairyman's daughter *to* Worrals of the WAAF: *the Religious Tract Society, Lutterworth Press, and children's literature* (Cambridge, 2006)

Buzard, John *The beaten track: European tourism, literature and the ways to culture, 1800–1918* (Oxford, 1993)

Byrne, D. *Australian writers* (1896)

Cambridge, The, history of libraries in Britain and Ireland 3 vols. (Cambridge, 2006), vol. 2, *1640–1850*, ed. Giles Mandelbrote and K. A. Manley; vol. 3, *1850–2000*, ed. Alistair Black and Peter Hoare

Campbell, F. B. F. 'A plea for annual lists of state-papers and annual reviews of state-papers, as being essential preliminaries to state-paper catalogues', *The Library* 4 (1893), pp. 175–83

Campbell-Kelly, Martin 'The Railway Clearing House and Victorian data processing', in L. Bud-Frierman (ed.), *Information acumen* (1994), pp. 51–74

Cannon, S. F. *Science in culture: the early Victorian period* (New York, 1978)

Canton, William *A history of the British and Foreign Bible Society*, 5 vols. (1904–10)

Cantor, G. and S. Shuttleworth (eds.) *Science serialized: representations of the sciences in nineteenth-century periodicals* (Cambridge, MA, 2004)

Cantor, G. and others *Science in the nineteenth-century periodical* (Cambridge, 2004)

Cantwell, John D. *The Public Record Office, 1838–1958* (1991)

Carlisle, Nicholas *Concise description of the endowed schools in England and Wales* (1818; repr. Bristol, 2004)

Caroe, Gwendy *The Royal Institution: an informal history* (1985)

Carpenter, Mary Wilson *Imperial Bibles, domestic bodies: women, sexuality, and religion in the Victorian market* (Athens, OH, 2003)

Carr-Saunders, A. M. and P. A. Wilson *The professions* (Oxford, 1933)

Carter, Dee 'The golden thread: some early tract writers', in Dennis Butts and Pat Garrett (eds.), *From* The dairyman's daughter *to* Worrals of the WAAF: *the Religious Tract Society, Lutterworth Press, and children's literature* (Cambridge, 2006), pp. 49–64

Carter, Harry *Orlando Jewitt* (Oxford, 1962)

'Thomas Routledge and the introduction of esparto in papermaking', *Seventh International Congress of Paper Historians* (1967), pp. 201–10

Wolvercote Mill: a study in paper-making at Oxford (Oxford, 1957)

Carter, John and Graham Pollard *An enquiry into the nature of certain nineteenth century pamphlets* (1934; rev. edn 1983)

Carter, John and John Sparrow *A. E. Housman, a bibliography* (Godalming, 1982)

Casper, Scott E. and others (eds.) *A history of the book in America. 3. The industrial book, 1840–1880* (Chapel Hill, NC, 2007)

Cass, E. and M. Garratt (eds.) *Printing and the book in Manchester, 1700–1850* (Manchester, 2001)

Catalogue of the British section of the International Exhibition of the Book Industry & Graphic Arts (Leipzig, 1914)

Catalogue of the special exhibition of art bookbindings (Nottingham Castle Museum and Art Gallery, 1891)

Catalogue, A, of the Bradshaw collection of Irish books in the University Library, Cambridge, 3 vols. (Cambridge, 1916)

Cavallo, Guglielmo and Roger Chartier (eds.) *A history of reading in the west* (Amherst, MA, 1999)

Centenary, A, guide to the publications of the Selden Society (1987)

Centenary, The, volume of Charles Griffin and Company Ltd, publishers, 1820–1920 (1920)

Chambers, William *Memoir of Robert Chambers, with autobiographical reminiscences of William Chambers* (Edinburgh, 1872)

    Memoirs of William and Robert Chambers (1893)

    Story of a long and busy life (Edinburgh, 1882)

Chancellor, Valerie E. *History for their masters: opinion in the English history textbook 1800–1914* (Bath, 1970)

Chaplin, A. H. *GK: 150 years of the general catalogue of printed books in the British Museum* (1987)

Chapman, John W. *Cheap books, and how to get them: being a reprint, from the Westminster Review for April 1852 of the article on 'The commerce of literature'* (1852)

    'The commerce of literature', *Westminster Review*, n.s. 1 (1852), pp. 511–54

[Chapman, R. W.] *Some account of the Oxford University Press 1468–1921* (Oxford, 1922)

Chapman, Ronald *Father Faber* (1961)

Charles, Mrs Rundle *Our seven homes: autobiographical reminiscences* (Cambridge, 1896)

Charteris, Evan *The life and letters of Sir Edmund Gosse* (1931)

Chartier, Roger 'Labourers and voyagers: from the text to the reader', *Diacritics* 22 (1992), pp. 46–91; repr. in David Finkelstein and Alistair McCleery (eds.), *The book history reader* (2002), pp. 47–58

    The order of books (Cambridge, 1994)

Chatterjee, Rimi B. *Empires of the mind: a history of the Oxford University Press in India under the Raj* (New Delhi, 2006)

    'Far flung fiction: colonial libraries and the British Raj', *Jadavpur University Essays and Studies* 17 (2007)

    'How India took to the book: British publishers at work under the Raj', in Jacques Michon and Jean-Yves Mollier (eds.), *Les mutations du livre et de l'édition dans le monde du XVIIIe siècle à l'an 2000* (Quebec, 2001), pp. 100–21

    'Pirates and philanthropists: British publishers and copyright in India, 1880–1935', in Abhijit Gupta and Swapan Chakravorty (eds.), *Movable types: book history in India 2* (Delhi, forthcoming)

[Chatto, W. A. and] J. Jackson *A treatise on wood engraving, historical and practical* (1839)

'Cheap literature', *British Quarterly Review* 29 (1859), pp. 313–45

Chick, Arthur *Towards today's book: progress in 19th century Britain* (1997)

Chilcott, T. J. *A publisher and his circle* (1972)

Chivers, Cedric *The paper of lending library books, with some remarks on their bindings* (1909)

Cipolla, Carlo M. *Literacy and development in the west* (Harmondsworth, 1969)

Clair, Colin *A history of printing in Britain* (1965)

Clare, John *John Clare by himself*, ed. Eric Robinson and David Powell (Ashington and Manchester, 1996)

Clark, Peter *British clubs and societies, 1580–1800: the origins of an associational world* (Oxford, 2000)

Clegg, James (ed.) *The international directory of booksellers* (1914)

Clery, E. J., C. Franklin and P. Garside (eds.) *Authorship, commerce and the public* (Basingstoke, 2002)

Cliff, P. B. *The rise and development of the Sunday school movement in England 1780–1980* (Redhill, 1986)

Cochrane, J. G. *Catalogue of the London Library* (1847)

Cockerell, Douglas *Bookbinding, and the care of books* (1901)

Coffey, J. 'Democracy and popular religion: Moody and Sankey's mission to Britain, 1873–5', in Eugenio Biagini (ed.), *Citizenship and community: liberals, radicals and collective identities in the British Isles, 1865–1931* (Cambridge, 1996), pp. 93–119

Cohen, Colin (ed.) *Paper & printing; the new technology of the 1830s: taken from the Monthly Supplement of the Penny Magazine of the Society for the Diffusion of Useful Knowledge, August to December 1833* (Oxford, 1982)

Cohen, Morton N. and Anita Gandolfo (eds.) *Lewis Carroll and the house of Macmillan* (Cambridge, 1987)

Cohen, Morton N. and Edward Wakeling (eds.), *Lewis Carroll & his illustrators: collaborations and correspondence, 1865–1898* (2003)

Colclough, Stephen '"A grey goose quill and an album": the manuscript book and text transmission', in Robin Myers, Michael Harris and Giles Mandelbrote (eds.), *Owners, annotators and the signs of reading* (2005), pp. 153–74

'J. Sheridan le Fanu and the "Select Library of Fiction"', *Publishing History* 60 (2006), pp. 5–19

'"Purifying the sources of amusement and information"? The railway bookstalls of W. H. Smith & Son, 1855–60', *Publishing History* 56 (2004), pp. 27–51

'The railways', in B. Bell (ed.), *The Edinburgh history of the book in Scotland. 3. Ambition and industry, 1800–1880* (Edinburgh, 2007), pp. 141–52.

Cole, Richard Cargill *Irish booksellers and English writers, 1740–1800* (1986)

Coleman, D. C. *The British paper industry, 1495–1860: a study in industrial growth* (Oxford, 1958)

Coleridge, Christabel *Charlotte Mary Yonge: her life and letters* (1903)

Coleridge, H. J. *Life of Lady Georgiana Fullerton, from the French of Mrs. Augustus Craven* (1888)

Colles, W. M. *Literature and the Pension List* (Society of Authors, 1889)

Collet, Collet Dobson *History of the taxes on knowledge*, 2 vols. (1899)

Colley, Linda *Britons: forging the nation, 1707–1837*, 2nd edn (1994)

Collin, Dorothy W. 'Edward Garnett, publisher's reader, and Samuel Rutherford Crockett, writer of books', *Publishing History* 30 (1991), pp. 89–121

Collingwood, Cuthbert *The Catholic Truth Society* (1955)

Collini, S. *Public moralists: political thought and intellectual life in Britain* (Oxford, 1991)

Collins, Steve ' "An eminent bibliophile and man of letters": James Crossley of Manchester', in E. Cass and M. Garratt (eds.) *Printing and the book in Manchester, 1700–1850* (Manchester, 2001), pp. 137–52

Collins, Tony *Rugby's great split: class, culture and the origins of rugby league football* (1998)

Collins, Wilkie 'The unknown public', *Household Words* 18, 439 (27 August 1858), p. 217

Comerford, R.V. 'Ireland 1850–1870', in W. E. Vaughan. (eds.), *Ireland under the Union*. 1. *1801–1870* (Oxford, 1989)

Comparato, Frank E. *Books for the millions: a history of the men whose methods and machines packaged the printed word* (Harrisburg, PA, 1971)

Constable, Thomas *Archibald Constable and his literary correspondents*, 3 vols. (1873)

Cooney, Sondra Miley 'A catalogue of *Chambers's Encyclopaedia* 1868', *Bibliotheck* 24 (1999), pp. 17–110

'Publishers for the people: W. & R. Chambers – the early years, 1832–50', unpublished PhD thesis, Ohio State University (1970)

Cooper, James Fenimore *Letters and journals*, ed. James Franklin Beard, 6 vols. (Cambridge, MA, 1960–8)

Cooper, Jane *Mrs Molesworth* (Crowborough, 2002)

Cooper, Victoria *The house of Novello: practice and policy of a Victorian music publisher, 1829–1866* (Aldershot, 2003)

Cooper-Richet, Diana and Emily Borgeaud *Galignani* (Paris, 1999)

Cooter, R. and S. Pumfrey 'Separate spheres and public places: reflections on the history of science popularization and science in popular culture', *History of Science* 32 (1994), pp. 237–67

Cope, Dawn and Peter *Postcards from the nursery: the illustrators of children's books and postcards 1900–1950* (2000)

Cordasco, Francesco *The Bohn libraries: a history and a checklist* (New York, 1951)

Corfield, Penelope J. *Power and the professions in Britain, 1700–1850* (1995)

Cormack, Michael J. *The Stirling Tract Enterprise and the Drummonds* (Stirling, 1984)

Cosgrove, Richard A. 'Victorian legal periodicals', *Victorian Periodicals Newsletter* 8 (1975), pp. 21–5

Coutts, Henry T. and Geo. A. Stephen, *Manual of library bookbinding, factual and historical* (1911)

Cowan, R. M. *The newspaper in Scotland: a study of its first expansion, 1815–1860* (Glasgow, 1946)

Cox, Harold and J. E. Chandler *The house of Longman: a record of their bicentenary celebrations* (1925)

Cox, Jeffrey *The English churches in a secular society: Lambeth, 1870–1930* (Oxford, 1982)

Cragoe, M. *Culture, politics and national identity in Wales, 1832–1886* (Oxford, 2004)

Craig, C. *The Van Diemen's Land edition of* The Pickwick Papers (Hobart, 1973)

[Craik, G. L.] *The pursuit of knowledge under difficulties*, 2 vols. (1830)

Creighton, Louise *Life and letters of Mandell Creighton*, 2 vols. (1904)

Memoir of a Victorian woman: reflections of Louise Creighton, 1850–1936, ed. J. T. Covert (Bloomington, IN, 1994)

Crittenden, V. *James Tegg: early Sydney publisher and printer* (Canberra, 2000)

Cross, Nigel *The common writer: life in nineteenth-century Grub Street* (Cambridge, 1985) (ed.) *The Royal Literary Fund, 1790–1918: an introduction to the Fund's history and archives, with an index of applicants* (London: World Microfilms, 1984)

Crouzet, François *De la supériorité de l'Angleterre sur la France* (Paris, 1985), trans. as *Britain ascendant: comparative studies in Franco-British economic history* (Cambridge, 1985)

Crowe, Joseph *Reminiscences of thirty-five years of my life* (1895)

Crowley, Tony *Wars of words: the politics of language in Ireland, 1537–2004* (Oxford, 2005)

Crowther, M. A. *Church embattled: religious controversy in mid-Victorian England* (Newton Abbot, 1970)

Crumb, Lawrence 'Publishing the Oxford Movement: Francis Rivington's letters to Newman', *Publishing History* 28 (1990), pp. 5–53

Cullen, L. M. *Eason & Son: a history* (Dublin, 1989)

Cunningham, Hugh *The invention of childhood* (2006)

Curthoys, M. C. 'The careers of Oxford men', in M. G. Brock and M. C. Curthoys (eds.), *The history of the University of Oxford. 6. Nineteenth-century Oxford part 1* (Oxford, 1997), pp. 477–510

Curtis, Gerard *Visual words: art and the material book in Victorian England* (Aldershot, 2002)

Curtis, L. P. *Apes and angels: the Irishman in Victorian caricature* (Newton Abbot, 1971)

Curwen, Henry *A history of booksellers: the old and the new* (1874)

Cutt, Margaret Nancy *Ministering angels: a study of nineteenth-century evangelical writing for children* (Wormley, 1979)

Mrs Sherwood and her books for children (Oxford, 1974)

Dagnall, H. *The taxation of paper in Great Britain, 1643–1861: a history and documentation* (Edgware, 1998)

'The taxes on knowledge: excise duty on paper', *The Library* 6th ser. 20 (1998), pp. 347–63

Dahl, F. *A bibliography of English corantos and periodical newsbooks, 1620–1642* (1952)

Daiches, D. 'Presenting Shakespeare', in A. Briggs (ed.), *Essays in the history of publishing* (1974), pp. 61–112

Daly, Mary E. *The spirit of earnest inquiry: the Statistical and Social Inquiry Society of Ireland, 1847–1997* (Dublin, 1997)

[Dalziel, G. and E.] *The brothers Dalziel: a record of fifty years' work in conjunction with many of the most distinguished artists of the period, 1840–1890* (1901)

Darley, Lionel *Bookbinding then and now: a survey of the first hundred and seventy-eight years of James Burn and Company* (1959)

Darlow, T. H. *William Robertson Nicoll: life and letters* (1925)

Darlow, T. H. and H. F. Moule *Historical catalogue of the printed editions of holy scripture in the library of the British and Foreign Bible Society*, 2 vols. in 4 (1903–11)

Darnton, Robert *The forbidden best-sellers of pre-Revolutionary France* (1995)

The great cat massacre and other episodes in French cultural history (New York, 1985)

The literary underground of the old régime (Cambridge, MA, 1982)

'What is the history of books', in D. Finkelstein and A. McCleery (eds.), *The book history reader* (2002), pp. 9–26

Darton, F. J. Harvey *Children's books in England: five centuries of social life*, 3rd edn, rev. Brian Alderson (1999)

Darwin, Charles *Correspondence*, ed. Frederick Burckhardt *et al.*, vols. 1– (Cambridge, 1985–)

Daunton, Martin (ed.) *The Cambridge urban history of Britain. 3. 1840–1950* (Cambridge, 2000)

(ed.) *The organisation of knowledge in Victorian Britain* (Oxford, 2005)

Royal Mail (1985)

Trusting Leviathan: the politics of taxation in Britain, 1799–1914 (Cambridge, 2001)

Dauphin, Cécile 'Letter-writing manuals in the nineteenth century', in Roger Chartier, Alain Boureau and Cécile Dauphin, *Correspondence: models of letter-writing from the middle ages to the nineteenth century* (Cambridge, 1997), pp. 112–57, originally published as part of *La correspondance* (Paris, 1991)

Davies, Gareth Alban 'The Welsh book in Patagonia', in Philip Henry Jones and Eiluned Rees (eds.), *A nation and its books: a history of the book in Wales* (Aberystwyth, 1998), pp. 265–76

Davies, W. J. Frank *Teaching reading in early England* (1973)

Davin, Anna *Growing up poor: home, school and street in London 1870–1914* (1996)

Davis, Norma A. *A lark ascends: Florence Kate Upton artist and illustrator* (Metuchen, NJ, 1992)

Davis, R. W. and Richard Helmstadter (eds.) *Religion and irreligion in Victorian society* (1992)

Dawson, G. *Darwin, literature and Victorian respectability* (Cambridge, 2007)

'Day, A, at a bookbinder's' [Westley and Clark, City of London], *Penny Magazine* 24 September 1842 Supplement

'Day, A, at a leather-factory' [Neckinger Mills, Bermondsey], *Penny Magazine* 28 May 1842 Supplement

'Day, A, at the London free libraries', *All the Year Round* 35 (1892), pp. 305–9

Day, Kenneth (ed.) *Book typography, 1815–1965, in Europe and the United States of America* (1966)

de Brún, Pádraig and Máire Herbert *Catalogue of Irish manuscripts in Cambridge libraries* (Cambridge, 1986)

de Ricci, S. *Catalogue raisonné des premières impressions de Mayence* (Mainz, 1911)

A census of Caxtons (Bibliographical Society, 1909)

English collectors of books & manuscripts (1530–1930) and their marks of ownership (Cambridge, 1930)

Dean, Dennis 'John W. Parker', in Patricia Anderson and Jonathan Rose (eds.), *British literary publishing houses, 1820–1880* (Detroit, 1991), pp. 233–6

Deazley, Ronan *On the origin of the right to copy: charting the movement of copyright law in eighteenth-century Britain (1696–1775)* (Oxford, 2004)

Dempster, John A. H. *The T. and T. Clark story: a Victorian publisher and the new theology* (Edinburgh, 1992)

'Thomas Nelson and Sons in the late nineteenth century: a study in motivation: part I', *Publishing History* 13 (1983), pp. 41–87

'Thomas Nelson and Sons in the late nineteenth century: a study in motivation: part II', *Publishing History* 14 (1984), pp. 5–63

Dennis, Barbara *Charlotte Yonge (1823–1901): novelist of the Oxford movement: a literature of Victorian culture and society* (Lampeter, 1992)

Dent, Hugh R. *The house of Dent, 1888–1938* (1938)

Dent, J. M. *Memoirs* (1928)

Descriptive, A, bibliography of the books printed at the Ashendene Press, MDCCCXCV–MCMXXXV (Chelsea, 1935)

Desideri, L. (ed.) *Il Vieusseux: storia di un gabinetto di lettura, 1819–2000* (Florence, 2001)

Desmond, A. 'Artisan resistance and evolution in Britain, 1819–1848', *Osiris* 2nd ser. 3 (1987), pp. 77–110

'Redefining the X axis: "professionals", "amateurs", and the making of mid-Victorian biology – a progress report', *Journal of the History of Biology* 34 (2001), pp. 3–50

Desmond, Ray *Great natural history books and their creators* (2003)

The India Museum, 1801–1879 (1982)

Deuel, Leo *Testaments of time* (1966)

[Dibdin, T. F.] *Bibliophobia: remarks on the present languid and depressed state of literature and the book trade* (1832)

Dick, Thomas *On the improvement of society by the diffusion of knowledge* (1833)

Dickens, Charles 'Bill-sticking', in *Selected journalism 1850–1870*, ed. David Pascoe (1997), pp. 283–93

Dickens's journalism: the amusements of the people and other papers, 1834–51, ed. Michel Slater (1996)

Letters, ed. Madeline House, Graham Storey and Kathleen Tillotson, 12 vols. (Oxford, 1965–2002)

Speeches, ed. K. J. Fielding (Oxford, 1960)

Dickens memento (1885)

Dicks, Guy *The John Dicks Press* (New York, 2004)

Dickson, Lovat *H. G. Wells* (1969)

Digby, Anne and Peter Searby, *Children, school and society in nineteenth-century England* (1981)

Dilke, Charles W. *Greater Britain: a record of travel in English-speaking countries during 1866–7*, 2 vols. (1868; 8th edn 1885)

Disraeli, Benjamin *Sybil, or the two nations* (1845)

Dodgson, C. L. *Lewis Carroll's diaries*, ed. Edward Wakeling, 8 vols. (Luton, 1992–8)

Doherty, Gillian M. *The Irish Ordnance Survey: history, culture and memory* (Dublin, 2004)

Donaldson, William *Popular literature in Victorian Scotland: language, fiction, and the press* (Aberdeen, 1986)

Dore, J. R. *Old Bibles: an account of the early versions of the English Bible*, 2nd edn (1888)

[Dorrington, William] 'Incidents of my life', *London, Provincial, and Colonial Press News* October 1886, p. 18

Dorson, Richard M. *The British folklorists: a history* (Chicago, 1968)

Doyle, Arthur Conan *Memoirs and adventures* (1924)

Drain, Susan 'An "incomprehensible innovation": the application of copyright law to hymn publishing in the Church of England', *Publishing History* 15 (1984), pp. 65–90

The Anglican church in nineteenth century Britain: hymns ancient and modern, 1860–1875 (Lampeter, 1989)

Dreyfus, John 'Emery Walker's 1888 lecture on "letterpress printing": a reconstruction and a reconsideration', *Craft History* 1 (1988), pp. 115–30

'The Kelmscott Press', in Linda Parry (ed.), *William Morris* (1996), pp. 310–41

'New light on the design of types for the Kelmscott and Doves Presses', *The Library* 5th ser. 29 (1974), pp. 36–41

Driver, Elizabeth *A bibliography of cookery books published in Britain, 1875–1914* (1989)

Drotner, Kirstin *English children and their magazines 1751–1948* (New Haven, CT, 1988)

Duff, Mrs Adrian Grant (ed.) *The life-work of Lord Avebury (Sir John Lubbock)* (1924)

Duff, E. Gordon *Early printed books* (1893)

Duffy, Patrick *The skilled compositor, 1850–1914: an aristocrat among working men* (Aldershot, 2000)

Duman, Daniel *The judicial bench in England, 1727–1875* (1982)

Dunning, Eric and Kenneth Sheard *Barbarians, gentlemen and players* (New York, 1979)

Durbach, Nadja *Bodily matters: the anti-vaccination movement in England, 1853–1907* (Durham, NC, 2005)

Durbridge, Nicholas 'Beatrix Potter's side shows', *Beatrix Potter Studies* 10 (2002), pp. 85–95

Dyos, H. J. and Michael Wolff (eds.) *The Victorian city: images and realities*, 2 vols. (1973)

Easley, Alexis *First person anonymous: women writers and Victorian print media, 1830–70* (Aldershot, 2004)

Eaton, Andrew J. 'The American movement for international copyright, 1837–60', *Library Quarterly* 15 (1945), pp. 95–122

Eddy, John and Deryck Schreuder (eds.) *The rise of colonial nationalism: Australia, New Zealand, Canada and South Africa first assert their nationalities, 1880–1914* (1988)

Edwards, Owen Dudley and Patricia J. Storey, 'The Irish press in Victorian Britain', in Roger Swift and Sheridan Gilley (eds.), *The Irish in the Victorian city* (1985), pp. 158–66

Edwards, P. D. *Dickens's young men: George Augustus Sala, Edmund Yates and the world of Victorian journalism* (Aldershot, 1997)

Eggert, Paul and Elizabeth Webby (eds.) *Books & empire: textual production, distribution and consumption in colonial and postcolonial countries. Bulletin of the Bibliographical Society of Australia and New Zealand* Special issue 28 (2004)

Egoff, Sheila A. *Children's periodicals of the nineteenth century* (1951)

Ehrlich, Cyril *The piano: a history* (Oxford, 1976; rev. edn 1990)

Eidson, John Olin *Tennyson in America* (Athens, GA, 1943)

Eliot, George *Letters*, ed. Gordon S. Haight, 9 vols. (New Haven, CT, 1954–78)

Eliot, Simon 'Bookselling by the backdoor', in Robin Myers and Michael Harris (eds.), *A genius for letters* (Winchester, 1995), pp. 145–66

'The business of Victorian publishing', in Deirdre David (ed.), *The Cambridge companion to the Victorian novel* (Cambridge, 2000), pp. 37–60

'Circulating libraries in the Victorian age and after', in Alistair Black and Peter Hoare (eds.), *The Cambridge history of libraries in Britain and Ireland* 3 (Cambridge, 2006), pp. 125–46

'"Mr. Greenhill, whom you cannot get rid of": copyright, legal deposit and the Stationers' Company in the 19th century', in Robin Myers, Michael Harris and Giles Mandelbrote (eds.), *Libraries and the book trade* (Winchester, 2000), pp. 51–84

'*Patterns and trends* and the NSTC: some initial observations', *Publishing History* 42 (1997), pp. 79–104 and 43 (1998), pp. 71–112

Some patterns and trends in British publishing, 1800–1919 (1994)

'Some trends in British book production', in John O. Jordan and Robert L. Patten (eds.), *Literature in the marketplace* (Cambridge, 1989), pp. 19–43

'The three-decker novel and its first cheap reprint 1862–94', *The Library* 6th ser. 7 (1985), pp. 37–53

'"To You in your vast business": some features of the quantitative history of Macmillan 1843–91', in E. James (ed.), *Macmillan: a publishing tradition* (Basingstoke, 2002), pp. 11–51

'What price poetry?' *PBSA* 100 (2006), pp. 425–45

Eliot, Simon, Andrew Nash and Ian Willison (eds.) *Literary cultures and the material book* (2007)

Eliot, Simon and John Sutherland 'Introduction' to *The Publishers' Circular 1837–1900: guide to the microfiche edition* (Cambridge, 1988)

Ellegård, A. H. *The readership of the periodical press in mid-Victorian Britain* (1957)

Ellis, A. *Educating our masters* (Aldershot, 1985)

Ellis, Alec *History of children's reading and literature* (Oxford, 1968)
  Books in Victorian elementary schools (1971)

Ellis, E. 'Truth and fiction: the bequest of David Scott Mitchell', *Journal of the Royal Australian Historical Society* 92 (2006), pp. 81–100

Ellis, Ieuan 'Dean Farrar and the quest for the historical Jesus', *Theology* 89 (1986), pp. 108–15
  Seven against Christ: a study of 'Essays and reviews' (Leiden, 1980)

Ellis, Sarah Stickney *The mothers of England* (1843)

Engel, A. J. *From clergyman to don: the rise of the academic profession in nineteenth-century Oxford* (Oxford, 1983)

Engel, Eliot 'The heir of the Oxford Movement: Charlotte Yonge's *Heir of Redclyffe*', *Etudes Anglaises* 33 (1980), pp. 132–41

Entwistle, Dorothy 'Counteracting the street culture: book prizes in English Sunday schools at the turn of the century', *History of Education Society Bulletin* 55 (1995), pp. 26–34
  'Embossed gilt and moral tales: reward books in English Sunday schools', *Journal of Popular Culture* 28 (1994), pp. 81–96
  'Sunday-school book prizes for children: rewards and socialization', *Studies in Church History* 31 (1994), pp. 405–16

Erickson, Lee *The economy of literary form: English literature and the industrialization of publishing, 1800–1850* (Baltimore, MD, 1996)

Escott, T. S. H. *Social transformations of the Victorian age* (1897)

Estermann, Monika *'O werthe Druckerkunst/ Du Mutter alle Kunst': Gutenbergfeiern im Laufe der Jahrhunderte* (Mainz, 1999)

Evans, Edmund *Reminiscences*, ed. Ruari McLean (Oxford, 1967)

Evans, Eric 'Englishness and Britishness: national identities, c.1790–c.1870', in Alexander Grant and Keith J. Stringer (eds.), *Uniting the kingdom? The making of British history* (1995), pp. 223–43

Evans, Joan *The endless web: John Dickinson & Co. Ltd, 1804–1954* (1955)

Ewing, J. A. *The university training of engineers: an introductory lecture, delivered January 20, 1891* (Cambridge, 1891)

Exman, Eugene *The house of Harper: one hundred and fifty years of publishing* (New York, 1967)

Fairman, Tony 'Words in English record office documents of the early 1800s', in M. Kytö, M. Rydén and E. Smitterberg (eds.), *Nineteenth century English: stability and change* (Cambridge, 2006), pp. 56–88

Faithfull, Emily *Three visits to America* (Edinburgh, 1884)

Farrar, Reginald *The life of Frederic William Farrar, sometime dean of Canterbury* (1904)

Farrer, T. H. 'The principle of copyright', *Fortnightly Review* 24 (1878), pp. 836–51

Fawkes, Richard *Dion Boucicault: a biography* (1979)

Faxon, Frederick W. *Literary annuals and gift books: a bibliography, 1823–1903*; repr. with supplementary essays by Eleanore Jamieson and Iain Bain (1973)

Feather, John *A history of British publishing* (1988)
  'John Walter and the Logographic Press', *Publishing History* 1 (1977), pp. 92–134
  Publishing, piracy and politics: an historical study of copyright in Britain (1994)

Feinstein, C. H. *National income, expenditure and output of the United Kingdom 1855–1965* (Cambridge, 1972)

Feldman, David *Englishmen and Jews: social relations and political culture, 1840–1914* (New Haven, CT, 1994)

'The importance of being English: Jewish immigration and the decay of liberal England', in David Feldman and Gareth Stedman Jones (eds.), *Metropolis London: histories and representations since 1800* (1989), pp. 56–84

'Felix Folio', *The hawkers and street dealers of the north of England manufacturing districts* (Manchester [1858?])

Feltes, N. N. *Literary capital and the late Victorian novel* (Madison, WI, 1993)

Modes of production of Victorian novels (Chicago, 1986)

Ferguson, F. S. 'English books before 1640', in *The Bibliographical Society: studies in retrospect* (1945), pp. 42–75

Festing, Sally *Gertrude Jekyll* (1993)

Fichte, J. G. *Reden an die deutsche Nation* (Berlin, 1808)

Fieldhouse, Ken and Jan Woudstra *The regeneration of public parks* (2000)

Fielding, Penny *Writing and orality: nationality, culture and nineteenth-century Scottish* (Oxford, 1996)

Fildes, Paul 'Phototransfer of drawings in wood-block engraving', *JPHS* 5 (1969), pp. 87–97

Findlater, Richard (ed.) *Author! Author!* (1984)

Finkelstein, David *The house of Blackwood: author–publisher relations in the Victorian era* (Philadelphia, 2002)

(ed.) *Print culture and the Blackwood tradition, 1805–1930* (Toronto, 2006)

'"The secret": British publishers and Mudie's struggle for survival, 1861–64', *Publishing History* 34 (1993), pp. 21–50

Finkelstein, David and Alistair McCleery (eds.) *The book history reader* (2002)

Finnegan, Ruth *Literacy and orality: studies in the technology of communication* (Oxford, 1988)

First, The, hundred and fifty years of John Wiley and Sons, Incorporated, 1807–1957 (New York, 1957)

Fisher, W. E. G. 'Paper: India paper', *Encyclopaedia Britannica*, 11th edn (1910)

Fison, Margaret *Colportage: its history and relation to home and foreign evangelisation* (1859)

Fitch, J. G. 'The Chautauqua reading circle', *Nineteenth Century* 24 (1888), pp. 487–500

Flanders, Judith *Consuming passions: leisure and pleasure in Victorian Britain* (2006)

Fleming, Patricia Lockhart, Gilles Gallichan and Yvan Lamonde (eds.), *History of the book in Canada*, 3 vols. (Toronto, 2004–7)

Flint, Kate *The woman reader, 1837–1914* (Oxford, 1993)

Flint, Weston *Statistics of public libraries in the United States and Canada* (Washington, DC, 1893)

Folkard, H. T. *Wigan Free Public Library: its rise and progress* (Wigan, 1901)

Folter, R. 'The Gutenberg Bible in the antiquarian book trade', in Martin Davies (ed.), *Incunabula: studies in fifteenth-century printed books presented to Lotte Hellinga* (1999), pp. 271–351

Foot, Mirjam M. 'Double agent: M. Caulin and M. Hagué', *The Book Collector* special number for the 150th anniversary of Bernard Quaritch (1997), pp. 136–50

Foot, Mirjam M., Carmen Blacker and Nicholas Poole-Wilson, 'Collector, dealer and forger: a fragment of nineteenth-century binding history', in M. M. Foot (ed.), *Eloquent witnesses: bookbindings and their history* (2004), pp. 264–81

Forby, Robert *The vocabulary of East Anglia*, 2 vols. (1830)

(Foster, James) *A bibliographical catalogue of Macmillan and Co.'s publications from 1843 to 1889* (1891)

Fourth estate, The: or the moral influence of the press. By a student at law (1839)

Fox, Celina *Graphic journalism in England during the 1830s and 1840s* (New York, 1988)

Foxon, D. F. 'The printing of *Lyrical ballads,* 1798', *The Library* 5th ser. 9 (1954), pp. 221–41

Thomas J. Wise and the pre-Restoration drama: a study in theft and sophistication (1959)

Fraenkel, Josef *The Jewish press in Great Britain, 1823–1963* (1963)

France, Peter and Kenneth Haynes (eds.) *The Oxford history of English literature in translation.* 4. *1790–1900* (Oxford, 2006)

Francis, F. C. 'The Bibliographical Society: a sketch of the first fifty years', in *The Bibliographical Society, 1892–1942: studies in retrospect* (1945), pp. 1–22

Francis, J. C. *Notes by the way: with memoirs of Joseph Knight and Joseph Woodfall Ebsworth* (1909)

Frankel, Oz, 'Blue books and the Victorian reader', *Victorian Studies* 46 (2004), pp. 308–18

States of inquiry: social investigations and print culture in nineteenth-century Britain and the United States (Baltimore, MD, 2006)

Franklin, Miles (in association with Kate Baker) *Joseph Furphy: the legend of a man and his book* (Sydney, 1944)

Franta, Andrew *Romanticism and the rise of the mass public* (Cambridge, 2007)

Fraser, Angus 'John Murray's Colonial and Home Library', *PBSA* 91 (1997), pp. 339–408

Fraser, W. Hamish *The coming of the mass market, 1850–1914* (1981)

Fredeman, William E. 'Emily Faithfull and the Victoria Press', *The Library* 5th ser. 29 (1974), pp. 139–64

Frederick James Furnivall: a volume of personal record (Oxford, 1911)

Freeman, Arthur, 'Bernard Quaritch and "my Omar": the struggle for Fitzgerald's Rubáiyát', *The Book Collector* special number for the 150th anniversary of Bernard Quaritch (1997), pp. 60–75

Freeman, Arthur and Janet Ing Freeman *Anatomy of an auction: rare books at Ruxley Lodge, 1919* (1990)

John Payne Collier: scholarship and forgery in the nineteenth century 2 vols. (New Haven, CT, 2004)

Freeman, Michael J. *Railways and the Victorian imagination* (New Haven, CT, 1999)

Freeman, R. B. *British natural history books, 1495–1900: a handlist* (Folkestone, 1980)

Freeman, R. B. and D. Wertheimer *Philip Henry Gosse: a bibliography* (Folkestone, 1980)

Friederichs, Hulda *The life of Sir George Newnes, Bart* (1911)

Fripp, C. B. 'Report of an inquiry into the condition of the working classes of the city of Bristol', *Journal of the Statistical Society* 2 (1839), pp. 368–75

Fritzsche, Peter *Reading Berlin, 1900* (Cambridge, MA, 1996)

Froude, J. A. 'The Copyright Commission', *Edinburgh Review* 148 (1878), pp. 295–343

Furet, François and Jacques Ozouf, *Reading and writing: literacy in France from Calvin to Jules Ferry* (Cambridge, 1982)

Fyfe, Aileen 'Commerce and philanthropy: the Religious Tract Society and the business of publishing', *Journal of Victorian Culture* 9 (2004), pp. 164–88

'Conscientious workmen or booksellers' hacks? The professional identities of science writers in the mid-nineteenth century', *Isis* 96 (2005), pp. 192–223

'Expertise and Christianity: high standards versus the free market in popular publishing', in David M. Knight and Matthew D. Eddy (eds.), *Science and beliefs: from natural philosophy to natural science, 1700–1900* (Aldershot, 2005), pp. 113–26

'Industrialised conversion: the Religious Tract Society and popular science publishing in Victorian Britain', PhD thesis, University of Cambridge (2000)

'Periodicals and book series: complementary aspects of a publisher's mission', in Louise Henson *et al.* (eds.), *Culture and science in the nineteenth-century media* (Aldershot, 2004), pp. 71–82

Science and salvation: evangelical popular science publishing in Victorian England (Chicago, 2004)

Fyfe, Aileen and B. Lightman (eds.) *Science in the marketplace: nineteenth-century sites and experiences* (Chicago, 2007)

Gaehtgens, T. W. and N. Hochner (eds.) *L'image du roi, de François I à Louis XIV* (Paris, 2006)

Gage, A. T. *A history of the Linnean Society of London* (1938)

Gage, John *Colour and culture: practice and meaning from antiquity to abstraction* (1993)

Gagnier, Regenia *Idylls of the marketplace: Oscar Wilde and the Victorian public* (Aldershot, 1987)

Gaines, Barry 'A forgotten artist: John Harris and the Rylands copy of Caxton's edition of Malory', *Bulletin of the John Rylands Library* 52 (1969), pp. 115–28

Galbally, A. *Redmond Barry: an Anglo-Irish Australian* (Melbourne, 1995)

Gamble, Charles W. *Modern illustration processes* (1938)

Gange, David 'Religion and science in late nineteenth-century British Egyptology', *Historical Journal* 49 (2006), pp. 1083–1103

Gardiner, Leslie *Bartholomew, 150 years* (Edinburgh, 1976)

The making of John Menzies (Edinburgh, 1983)

Gardner, Philip *The lost elementary schools of Victorian England* (1985)

Garnett, Edward *Friday nights* (1922)

Garnett, Jane 'Evangelicalism and business in mid-Victorian Britain', in John Wolffe (ed.), *Evangelical faith and public zeal* (1995), pp. 59–80

Garvey, Ellen Gruber 'Scissorizing and scrapbooks: nineteenth-century reading, remaking, and recirculating', in Lisa Gitelman and Geoffrey B. Pingree (eds.), *New media, 1740–1915* (Cambridge, MA, 2003), pp. 207–27

Gascoigne, Bamber 'The earliest English chromolithographs', *JPHS* 17 (1982/3), pp. 62–71

Milestones in colour printing 1470–1859 (Cambridge, 1997)

Gash, Norman *Reaction and reconstruction in English politics 1832–52* (Oxford, 1965)

Gaskell, Elizabeth *Further letters of Mrs Gaskell*, ed. John Chapple and Alan Shelston (Manchester, 2000)

Wives and daughters (1866)

Gaskell, Philip *A new introduction to bibliography* (Oxford, 1972)

Gasson, Andrew *Wilkie Collins: an illustrated guide* (Oxford, 1998)

Gates, B. T. *Kindred nature: Victorian and Edwardian women embrace the living world* (Chicago, 1998)

Gattie, W. M. 'What English people read', *Fortnightly Review* 52 (1889), pp. 307–21

Gattrell, Vic *City of laughter: sex and satire in eighteenth-century London* (2006)

Geison, G. *Michael Foster and the Cambridge school of physiology* (Princeton, NJ, 1978)

General report of the Commissioners appointed to visit the universities and colleges of Scotland (1830). Parliamentary papers 1831.xii

George, M. Dorothy *Hogarth to Cruikshank: social change in graphic satire* (1967)

Gerber, David A. *Authors of their lives: the personal correspondence of immigrants to North America in the nineteenth century* (New York, 2006)

Gernsheim, Helmut *Incunabula of British photographic literature* (1984)

The rise of photography, 1850–1880: the age of collodion (The History of Photography 2) (1988)

Gerrard, Teresa 'New methods in the history of reading: "Answers to correspondents" in the *Family Herald*, 1860–1900', *Publishing History* 43 (1998), pp. 52–69

Gettmann, R. A. *A Victorian publisher: a study of the Bentley papers* (Cambridge, 1960)

Ghodes, Clarence *American literature in nineteenth century England* (Carbondale, IL, 1944)

'Longfellow and his authorized British publishers', *PMLA* 55 (1940), pp. 1165–79

Ghosh, Anindita 'Cheap books, "bad" books: contesting print cultures in colonial Bengal', in Abhijit Gupta and Swapan Chakravorty (eds.), *Print areas: book history in India* (Delhi, 2004), pp. 169–96

'An uncertain "Coming of the Book"', *Book History* 6 (2003), pp. 23–55

Gibbon, Edward *English essays*, ed. Patricia B. Craddock (Oxford, 1972)

Giberne, Agnes *A lady of England: the life and letters of Charlotte Maria Tucker* (1895)

Gibson, Strickland *Early Oxford bindings* (1903)

Gilburt, Joseph 'Remainders', *The Library* 4 (1893), pp. 324–8

Gilley, Sheridan 'John Keble and the Victorian churching of Romanticism', in J. R. Watson (ed.), *An infinite variety: essays in Romanticism* (Edinburgh, 1983)

Gilson, David *A bibliography of Jane Austen* (Oxford, 1982)

Gitelman, Lisa and Geoffrey B. Pingree (eds.) *New media, 1740–1915* (Cambridge, MA, 2003)

Glasgow, E. 'The origins of the Home University Library', *Library Review* 50 (2001), pp. 95–9

Gleadle, Katherine 'Charlotte Elizabeth Tonna and the mobilisation of Tory women in early Victorian England', *Historical Journal* 50 (2007), pp. 97–117

Glover, T. R. *Evangelical Nonconformists and higher criticism in the nineteenth century* (1954)

Glynn, Jenifer *Prince of publishers: a biography of the great Victorian publisher George Smith* (1986)

Godfroid, François *Aspects inconnus et méconnus de la contrefaçon en Belgique* (Brussels, 1998)

Goldman, Lawrence *Science, reform, and politics in Victorian Britain: the Social Science Association, 1857–1886* (Cambridge, 2002)

Goldman, Paul *Beyond decoration: the illustrations of John Everett Millais* (2005)

John Everett Millais, illustrator and narrator (Birmingham, 2004)

Victorian illustrated books, 1850–1870: the heyday of wood-engraving (1994)

Victorian illustration: the Pre-Raphaelite, the idyllic school and the high Victorians (Aldershot, 1996; rev. edn Aldershot, 2004)

Goldstrom, J. M. *The social content of education 1808–1870: a study of the working class school reader in England and Ireland* (Totowa, NJ, 1972)

Gooday, G. *The morals of measurement: accuracy, irony, and trust in late Victorian electrical practice* (Cambridge, 2004)

'"Nature" in the laboratory: domestication and discipline with the microscope in Victorian life and science', *British Journal for the History of Science* 24 (1991), pp. 307–41

Goodman, D. C. 'Wollaston, William Hyde', in C. Gillispie. (ed.), *Dictionary of scientific biography* (1970)

Goodrich, Samuel G. *Recollections of a lifetime*, 2 vols. (New York, 1857)

Gosse, Edmund *Gossip in a library* (1891)

Gould, Frederick J. *The pioneers of Johnson's Court: a history of the Rationalist Press Association from 1899 onwards* (1935)

Gould, Joseph *The letter-press printer* (1876 and later editions)

Graff, Harvey J. *The legacies of literacy* (Bloomington, IN, 1987)

(ed.) *Literacy and social development in the west* (Cambridge, 1981)

Grant, Alexander and Keith J. Stringer (eds.) *Uniting the kingdom? The making of British history* (1995)

[Grant, James], 'Authorship as a profession', *London Saturday Journal* 9 January 1841

Grant, James *Joseph Jenkins: leaves from the life of a literary man* (1843)

The metropolitan weekly and provincial press: third and concluding volume of the history of the newspaper press [1872]

The newspaper press: its origin, progress and present position, 2 vols. (1871)

Grant, Joy *Harold Monro & the Poetry Bookshop* (1967)

'Graphic, The, and the Post Office', *Graphic* 21 July 1883, p. 58

Graves, Charles L. *Life and letters of Alexander Macmillan* (1910)

Graves, N. J. M. D. *Meiklejohn, prolific textbook author* (Reading, 2008)

Gray, Donald 'The birth and background of the *English hymnal*', in Alan Luff (ed.), *Strengthen for service: 100 years of the* English hymnal, *1906–2006* (Norwich, 2005), pp. 1–30

Gray, George J. *The earlier Cambridge stationers and bookbinders and the first Cambridge printer* (1904)

Gray, Nicolete *Lettering on buildings* (1960)

Gray, Valerie *Charles Knight: educator, publisher, writer* (Aldershot, 2006)

Green, Roger Lancelyn *Andrew Lang* (Leicester, 1946)

Green, S. C. *The story of the Religious Tract Society for one hundred years* (1899)

Green, S. J. D. *Religion in the age of decline: organisation and experience in industrial Yorkshire, 1870–1920* (Cambridge, 1996)

Greenhalgh, Paul *Ephemeral vistas: the expositions universelles, great exhibitions and world's fairs, 1851–1939* (Manchester, 1988)

Greenwood, Thomas *Museums and art galleries* (1888)

Public libraries: a history of the movement and a manual for the organization and management of rate-supported libraries, 4th edn (1891)

Greenwood's library year book (1897)

Gregory, E. David *Victorian songhunters: the recovery and editing of English vernacular ballads and folk lyrics, 1820–1883* (Lanham, MD, 2006)

Gretton, J. R. *Baedeker's English guidebooks: a checklist of English-language editions, 1861–1939* (Dereham, 1994)

Griest, Guinevere L. *Mudie's circulating library and the Victorian novel* (Newton Abbot, 1970)

Grievances, The, between authors and publishers (Society of Authors, 1887)

Grobel, Monica 'The Society for the Diffusion of Useful Knowledge 1826–46', 4 vols. MA thesis, University of London (1933)

Groser, W. H. *A hundred years' work for the children: the centenary record of the Sunday School Union* (1903)

Gross, John *The rise and fall of the man of letters* (1969; Harmondsworth, 1991)

Growoll, A. *The profession of bookselling* (1893)

Gunn, Simon 'The ministry, the middle class and the "civilizing mission" in Manchester, 1850–80', *Social History* 21 (1996), pp. 22–36

Gupta, Abhijit and Swapan Chakravorty (eds.) *Print areas: book history in India* (Delhi, 2004)

Gustafson, Sandra *Eloquence is power: oratory and performance in early America* (Chapel Hill, NC, 2000)

Guttman, Allen *From ritual to record: the nature of modern sports* (New York, 1978)

Guy, Josephine M. and Ian Small, *Oscar Wilde's profession: writing and the culture industry in the late nineteenth century* (Oxford, 2000)

Hack, Daniel 'Literary paupers and professional authors: the Guild of Literature and Art', *Studies in English Literature, 1500–1900* 39 (1999), pp. 691–713

Hacking, Ian *The taming of chance* (Cambridge, 1990)

Hackleman, Charles W. *Commercial engraving and printing: a manual of practical instruction and reference covering commercial illustrating and printing by all the processes* (Indianapolis, 1921; 2nd edn 1924)

Hagen, June Steffensen *Tennyson and his publishers* (1979)

Haining, G. P. *The penny dreadful* (1975)

Hall, C. Newman *Newman Hall: an autobiography* (1898)

Hall, Catherine, Keith McClelland and Jane Rendall, *Defining the Victorian nation: class, race, gender and the British Reform Act of 1867* (Cambridge, 2000)

Hall, Mary Boas *All scientists now: the Royal Society in the nineteenth century* (Cambridge, 1984)

Hall, N. John *Trollope: a biography* (Oxford, 1993)

Hamber, Anthony J. *'A higher branch of the art': photographing the fine arts in England, 1839–1880* (Amsterdam, 1996)

Hammond, Mary *Reading, publishing and the formation of literary taste in England 1880–1914* (Aldershot, 2006)

Hancock, Claire *'Capitale du plaisir*: the remaking of imperial Paris', in Felix Driver and David Gilbert (eds.), *Imperial cities: landscape, display and identity* (Manchester, 1999)

Hannett, John *Bibliopegia; or, bookbinding*, 2nd edn (1836)

Hansard, T. C. *Typographia: an historical sketch of the origin and progress of the art of printing* (1825)

Hardie, Martin *English coloured books* (1906)

Harer, Pamela K. 'Dumpy Books for Children', *Antiquarian Book Monthly Review* 22.251 (1995), pp. 20–4

Harper, Charles G. *A practical handbook of drawing for modern methods of reproduction*, 2nd edn (1901)

Harris, Elizabeth M. 'Experimental graphic processes in England 1800–1859, part 1', *JPHS* 4 (1968), pp. 74–86

'Experimental graphic processes in England 1800–1859, part 3', *JPHS* 6 (1970), pp. 53–65

Harris, Michael and Alan Lee (eds.) *The press in English society from the seventeenth to nineteenth centuries* (Cranbury, NJ, 1996)

Harris, Neil 'The Ripoli *Decameron*, Guglielmo Libri and the "incomparable" Harris', in Denis V. Reidy (ed.), *The Italian book, 1465–1800: studies presented to Dennis E. Rhodes on his 70th birthday* (1993), pp. 323–33

Harris, P. R. *A history of the British Museum Library, 1753–1973* (1998)

Hart, Horace *Charles Earl Stanhope and the Oxford University Press* repr. with notes by James Mosley (1966)

Harte, Negley *The University of London 1836–1986* (1986)

Hartley, Jenny '*Little Dorrit* in real time: the embedded text', *Publishing History* 52 (2002), pp. 5–18

Haslam, J. H. *The press and the people* (1906)

Havens, Earle *Commonplace books: a history of manuscripts and printed books from antiquity to the twentieth century* (New Haven, CT, 2001)

Haywood, Ian *The revolution in popular literature: print, politics and the people, 1790–1860* (Cambridge, 2004)

Headrick, Daniel R. *The invisible weapon: telecommunications and international politics, 1851–1945* (New York, 1991)

   When information came of age: technologies of knowledge in the age of reason and revolution, 1700–1850 (Oxford, 2001)

Heathorn, Stephen *For home, country and race: constructing gender, class, and Englishness in the elementary school, 1880–1914* (Toronto, 2000)

Heimann, Mary *Catholic devotion in Victorian England* (Oxford, 1996)

Heinemann, William 'The middleman as viewed by a publisher', *Athenaeum* 11 November 1893, p. 663

Hellinga-Querido, Lotte and Clemens de Wolf, *Laurens Janszoon Coster was zijn naam* (Haarlem, 1988)

Helmstadter, Richard 'The Reverend Andrew Reed (1787–1862): evangelical pastor as entrepreneur', in R. W. Davis and Richard Helmstadter (eds.), *Religion and irreligion in Victorian society* (1992), pp. 7–28

Hempton, David *Methodism: empire of the spirit* (2005)

Hempton, David and Myrtle Hill *Evangelical Protestantism in Ulster Society, 1740–1890* (1992)

Henkin, David M. *City reading: written words and public spaces in antebellum New York* (New York, 1998)

   The postal age: the emergence of modern communications in nineteenth-century America (Chicago, 2006)

Henson, Louise and others (eds.) *Culture and science in nineteenth-century media* (Aldershot, 2004)

Hentschel, K. *Mapping the spectrum: techniques of visual representation in research and teaching* (Oxford, 2002)

Hepburn, James *The author's empty purse and the rise of the literary agent* (Oxford, 1968)

Herrmann, Frank *Sotheby's: portrait of an auction house* (1980)

Herschel, J. F. W. 'Address delivered to the subscribers to the Windsor and Eton Public Library, 29 January 1833', in *The importance of literature to men of business* (1852), pp. 31–48

Hewish, John *Rooms near Chancery Lane: the Patent Office under the Commissioners, 1852–1883* (2000)

Hewitt, Gordon *Let the people read: a short history of the United Society for Christian Literature* (1949)

Higgs, Edward 'The annual report of the Registrar General, 1839–1920: a textual history', in Eileen Magnello and Anne Hardy (eds.), *The road to medical statistics* (Amsterdam, 2002), pp. 55–76

   The information state in England: the central collection of information on citizens since 1500 (Basingstoke, 2004)

'The statistical big bang of 1911: ideology, technological innovation and the production of medical statistics', *Social History of Medicine* 9 (1996), pp. 409–26

Hiley, Nicholas ' "Can you find me something nasty?" Circulating libraries and literary censorship in Britain from the 1890s to the 1910s', in R. Myers and M. Harris (eds.), *Censorship and the control of print in England and France, 1600–1910* (Winchester, 1992)

Hill, Draper *Mr. Gillray the caricaturist: a biography* (1965)

[Hill, M. D.] 'The Post Office', *Fraser's Magazine* 66 (1862), pp. 319–36

Hilliard, Christopher 'Modernism and the common writer', *Historical Journal* 48 (2005), pp. 769–87

Hilton, Boyd *The age of atonement* (Oxford, 1997)

Corn, cash, commerce: the economic policies of the Tory governments, 1815–1830 (Oxford, 1977)

A mad, bad, and dangerous people? (New Oxford History of England) (Oxford, 2006)

Hinchliff, Peter *John William Colenso: Bishop of Natal* (1964)

Hindley, Charles *Curiosities of cheap literature* (1871)

The life and times of James Catnach (late of Seven Dials) (1878)

Hinds, James Pitcairn *Bibliotheca Jacksoniana: catalogue* (Kendal, 1909)

Hinks, John and Catherine Armstrong (eds.) *Worlds of print: diversity in the book trade* (2006)

Hinrichsen, Alex *Baedeker's Reisehandbücher, 1832–1944* (Holzminden, 1981)

Historical register of the University of Oxford (Oxford, 1900)

Historical statistics of the United States: colonial times to 1957 (Washington, DC, 1960)

History, The, of The Times: the twentieth century test, 1884–1912 (1947)

Hitchman, Francis 'Penny fiction', *Quarterly Review* 171 (1890), pp. 150–71

Hoberman, Ruth ' "A thought in the huge bald forehead": depictions of women in the British Museum reading room, 1857–1929', in Janet Badia and Jennifer Phegley (eds.), *Reading women* (Toronto, 2006), pp. 168–91

Hobhouse, Hermione *The Crystal Palace and the Great Exhibition: art, science and productive industry. A history of the Royal Commission for the Exhibition of 1851* (2002)

Hocking, Silas *My book of memory* (1923)

Hodgson, W. B. 'Exaggerated estimates of reading and writing', *Transactions of the National Association for the Promotion of Social Sciences* (1867), p. 398

Hodson's Booksellers, publishers and stationers directory 1855: a facsimile, ed. Graham Pollard (Oxford, 1972)

Hogarth, Paul *Arthur Boyd Houghton* (1981)

Hoggart, Richard *The uses of literacy* (Harmondsworth, 1958)

Hollis, Patricia *The pauper press: a study in working-class radicalism of the 1830s* (Oxford, 1970)

Holloway, Merlyn *Steel engravings in nineteenth century British topographical books* (1977)

Holmes, C. J. *Self & partners (mostly self)* (1936)

Holmes, Janice 'Irish evangelicals and the British evangelical community, 1820s–1870s', in James H. Murphy (ed.), *Evangelicals and Catholics in nineteenth-century Ireland* (Dublin, 2005)

Holroyd, J. *George Robertson of Melbourne, 1825–1898, pioneer bookseller & publisher* (Melbourne, 1968)

Holt, Richard *Sport and the British* (Oxford, 1989)

Holyoake, G. J. *Sixty years of an agitator's life*, 2 vols. (1892)

Honey, J. R. De S. *Tom Brown's universe* (1977)

Hoppen, K. Theodore *The mid-Victorian generation, 1846–1886* (New Oxford History of England) (Oxford, 1998)

Horne, Herbert *The binding of books: an essay in the history of gold-tooled bindings* (1894)

Horowitz, Helen Liefkowitz *Rereading sex: battles over sexual knowledge and suppression in nineteenth-century America* (New York, 2002)

Houghton, Walter E. 'Periodical literature and the articulate classes', in Joanne Shattock and Michael Wolff (eds.), *The Victorian periodical press: samplings and soundings* (Toronto, 1982), pp. 17–19

Houghton, Walter E., Esther Rhoads Houghton and Jean Slingerland *The Wellesley index to Victorian periodicals, 1824–1900*, 5 vols. (Toronto, 1966–89)

House of Commons Select Committee on Printing, *Report. Parliamentary papers* 1854-5.xi

'How we get our newspapers', *All the Year Round*, 25 December 1875, pp. 305–9

'How we get our newspapers', *Chambers's Journal* 9 December 1865, pp. 669–74

Howarth, O. J. R. *The British Association for the Advancement of Science: a retrospect 1831–1921* (1922)

Howe, Ellic *Newspaper printing in the nineteenth century* (1943)

Howsam, Leslie 'The Bible Society and the book trade', in Stephen Batalden, Kathleen Cann and John Dean (eds.), *Sowing the word: the cultural impact of the British and Foreign Bible Society, 1804–2004* (Sheffield, 2004), pp. 24–37

　　Cheap bibles: nineteenth-century publishing and the British and Foreign Bible Society (Cambridge, 1991)

　　'An experiment with science for the nineteenth-century book trade: the International Scientific Series', *British Journal for the History of Science* 33 (2000), pp. 187–207

　　Kegan Paul: a Victorian imprint: publishers, books and cultural history (1998)

　　'Sustained literary ventures: the series in Victorian book publishing', *Publishing History* 31 (1992), pp. 5–26

Howsam, L., C. Stray, A. Jenkins, J. A. Secord and A. Vaninskaya 'What the Victorians learned: perspectives on nineteenth-century schoolbooks', *Journal of Victorian Culture* 12 (2007), pp. 262–85

Hudson, Graham 'Artistic printing: a re-evaluation', *JPHS* n.s. 9 (2006), pp. 31–63

Hughes, Kathryn *The short life and long times of Mrs Beeton* (2005)

Hughes, L. K. and M. Lund *The Victorian serial* (Charlottesville, VA, 1991)

Hume, Abraham *Learned societies and printing clubs of the United Kingdom* (1847; enlarged edn 1853)

Hunnisett, Basil *Engraved on steel: the history of picture production using steel plates* (Aldershot, 1998)

　　Steel-engraved book illustration in England (1980)

Hunt, Arnold, 'The sale of Richard Heber's library', in Robin Myers, Michael Harris and Giles Mandelbrote (eds.), *Under the hammer: book auctions since the seventeenth century* (2001), pp. 143–71

　　'The view from Cambridge: Henry Bradshaw & Bernard Quaritch', *The Book Collector* special number for the 150th anniversary of Bernard Quaritch (1977), pp. 94–107

Hunt, F. Knight *The fourth estate: contributions towards a history of newspapers, and of the liberty of the press*, 2 vols. (1850)

Hunt, Julia and Frederick Hunt *Peeps into Nisterland* (Blacon, Cheshire, 2005)

Hunt, William *Then and now; or, Fifty years of newspaper work* (Hull, 1887)

Huss, Richard E. *The development of printers' mechanical typesetting methods, 1822–1925* (Charlottesville, VA, 1973)

Hutchins, Michael (ed.) *Yours pictorially: illustrated letters of Randolph Caldecott* (1976)

Hutchinson, H. G. (eds.) *Cricket* (1903)

Hüther, Andreas 'A transnational nation-building process: philologists and universities in nineteenth-century Ireland and Germany', in Leon Litvack and Colin Graham (eds.), *Ireland and Europe in the nineteenth century* (Dublin, 2006)

Hutt, Allen *The changing newspaper: typographic trends in Britain and America, 1622–1972* (1973)

[Hutton, Richard Holt], 'Puseyite novels', *Prospective Review* 6 (1850), pp. 512–34

Hyde, Ralph *Printed maps of Victorian London, 1851–1900* (Folkestone, 1975)

Hyman, A. *Charles Babbage: pioneer of the computer* (Oxford, 1984)

Imholtz, A. A., Jr. 'Liddell and Scott: the predecessors, the 19th-century editions and the American contributions', in C. A. Stray (ed.), *Oxford classics: teaching and learning 1800–2000* (2007)

Immel, Andrea, 'James Pettit Andrews's "Books" (1790): the first critical survey of English children's literature', *Children's Literature* 28 (2000), pp. 147–63

In the High Court of Justice, Queen's Bench Division, June 18th, 1877; The Queen v. Charles Bradlaugh and Annie Besant [1877]

Irvine, William and Park Honan, *The book, the ring, and the poet* (1974)

Irving, Washington *Letters*, ed. Ralph M. Aderman, Herbert L. Kleinfield and Jenifer S. Banks, 4 vols. (Boston, 1978–82)

Isaac, Peter and Barry McKay (eds.) *The moving market: continuity and change in the book trade* (New Castle, DE, 2001)

(eds.), *The reach of print: making, selling and using books* (Winchester, 1998)

Jackson, H. J. *Marginalia: readers writing in books* (New Haven, CT, 2001)

Jackson, John and W. A. Chatto *A treatise on wood engraving, historical and practical*, 2nd edn (1861)

Jackson, Kate *George Newnes and the new journalism in Britain, 1880–1910: culture and profit* (Aldershot, 2001)

Jackson, Mason *The pictorial press: its origin and progress* (1885)

Jäger, Georg and others (eds.) *Geschichte des deutschen Buchhandels im 19. und 20. Jahrhundert.* 1. *Das Kaiserreich, 1870–1918*, 3 vols. (Frankfurt am Main, 2001–7)

James, Elizabeth *The Victoria & Albert Museum: a bibliography and exhibition chronology, 1852–1996* (1998)

James, Elizabeth (ed.) *Macmillan: a publishing tradition* (Basingstoke, 2002)

James, Elizabeth and Helen R. Smith *Penny dreadfuls and boys' adventures: the Barry Ono collection of Victorian popular literature in the British Library* (1998)

James, F. A. J. L. 'Books on the natural sciences in the nineteenth century', in A. Hunter (ed.), *Thornton and Tully's scientific books, libraries, and collectors* (Aldershot, 2000), pp. 258–71

James, G. P. R. 'Some observations on the book trade, as connected with literature in England', *Journal of the Statistical Society of London* 6 (1843), pp. 50–60

James, Sir Henry *Photo-zincography* (Southampton, 1860)

James, Louis *Fiction for the working man, 1830–1850* (Oxford, 1963; Harmondsworth, 1974)
Print and the people, 1819–1951 (1976; Harmondsworth, 1978)

Jamieson, Eleanore *English embossed bindings, 1825–1850* (Cambridge, 1972)

Javal, Emile 'L'évolution de la typographie considérée dans ses rapports avec l'hygiène de la vue', *Revue Scientifique* 27 (1881), pp. 802–13

Physiologie de la lecture et de l'écriture (Paris, 1905), repr. with introduction by François Richaudeau (Paris, 1978)

Jay, Elisabeth 'Oliphant, Margaret Oliphant Wilson (1828–1897)' *ODNB*

The religion of the heart: Anglican Evangelicalism and the nineteenth-century novel (Oxford, 1979)

Jefferson, George 'The children's library', *Private Library* 5th ser. 2 (1999), pp. 5–14

Jekyll, Gertrude *The unknown Gertrude Jekyll*, ed. Martin Wood (2006)

Jenkins, A. 'Geometry', in L. Howsam *et al.*, 'What the Victorians learned', *Journal of Victorian Culture* 12 (2007), pp. 267–72

Jenkins, Geraint H. (ed.) *Language and community in the nineteenth century* (Cardiff, 1998)

(ed.) *The Welsh language and its social domains 1801–1911* (Cardiff, 2000)

Jenkins, R. T. and Helen M. Ramage *A history of the Honorable Society of Cymmrodorion and of the Gwyneddigion and Cymreigyddion Societies (1751–1951)* (1951)

Jeremy, David J. (ed.) *Business and religion in Britain* (Aldershot, 1988)

'Important questions about business and religion in modern Britain', in David J. Jeremy (ed.), *Business and religion in Britain* (Aldershot, 1988), pp. 1–26

Jewett, C. C. *Notices of public libraries in the United States of America* (Appendix to the 4th report of the Board of Regents of the Smithsonian Institution) (Washington, DC, 1851)

Johanningsmeier, Charles *Fiction and the American literary marketplace: the role of newspaper syndicates in America, 1860–1900* (Cambridge, 1997)

Johanson, G. *A study of colonial editions in Australia, 1843–1972* (Wellington, 2000)

John Johnson collection (The), catalogue of an exhibition (Oxford: Bodleian Library, 1971)

Johns, A. *The nature of the book: print and knowledge in the making* (Chicago, 1998)

Johns, B. G. 'The literature of the streets', *Edinburgh Review* 165 (1887), pp. 40–65

Johnson, C. P. *Hints to collectors of original editions of the works of Charles Dickens* (1885)

Hints to collectors of original editions of the works of William Makepeace Thackeray (1885)

Johnson, Henry *An introduction to logography* (1783)

Johnson, R. ' "Really useful knowledge": radical education and working-class culture, 1790–1848', in J. Clarke, C. Critcher and R. Johnson (eds.), *Working-class culture: studies in history and theory* (1979), pp. 73–102

Jones, Aled 'Constructing the readership in 19th-century Wales', in Robin Myers and Michael Harris (eds.), *Serials and their readers* (1993), pp. 145–62

'The Welsh language and journalism', in Geraint H. Jenkins (ed.), *The Welsh language and its social domains 1801–1911* (Cardiff, 2000), pp. 379–403

Jones, H. Kay *Butterworths: history of a publishing house* (1980)

[Jones, J. Winter] *A guide to the printed books exhibited to the public in the Grenville Library and the King's Library* [1858]

Jones, K. and K. Williamson 'The birth of the schoolroom', *Ideology and Consciousness* 6 (1979), pp. 73–8

Jones, Philip Henry 'A golden age reappraised: Welsh-language publishing in the nineteenth century', in Peter Isaac and Barry McKay (eds.), *Images & texts: their production and distribution in the 18th and 19th centuries* (Winchester, 1997), pp. 121–41

'Printing and publishing in the Welsh language, 1800–1914', in Geraint H. Jenkins (ed.), *The Welsh language and its social domains 1801–1911* (Cardiff, 2000), pp. 314–47

Jones, Philip Henry and Eiluned Rees (eds.) *A nation and its books: a history of the book in Wales* (Aberystwyth, 1998)

Jones, R. Tudur 'Nonconformity and the Welsh language in the nineteenth century', in Geraint H. Jenkins (ed.), *The Welsh language and its social domains 1801–1911* (Cardiff, 2000), pp. 239–63

Jones, W. *The jubilee memorial of the Religious Tract Society* (1850)

Jordan, John O. and Robert L. Patten (eds.) *Literature in the marketplace* (Cambridge, 1995)

Joshi, Priya *In another country: colonialism, culture, and the English novel in India* (New York, 2002)

Joyce, Patrick *Visions of the people: industrial England and the question of class, 1848–1914* (Cambridge, 1991)

JPHS Journal of the Printing Historical Society

Jupp, James (ed.) *The Australian people* (Cambridge, 2001)

Kahan, Basil *Ottmar Mergenthaler, the man and his machine* (New Castle, DE, 2000)

Kainen, Jacob 'The development of the halftone screen', from the *Smithsonian Report* for 1851, pp. 409–25 (Washington, DC, 1952)

Kapp, Friedrich and Johann Goldfriedrich, *Geschichte des deutschen Buchhandels*, 4 vols. (Leipzig, 1886–1913)

Karr, M. Seton 'The proud story of Blackie and Son', *Books* (1959), p. 213

Kaser, David (ed.) *The cost book of Carey and Lea* (Philadelphia, 1963)

Kearney, Hugh *The British Isles: a history of four nations*, 2nd edn (Cambridge, 2006)

Keating, Peter *The haunted study: a social history of the English novel 1875–1914* (1989)

Keir, David *The house of Collins: the story of a Scottish family of publishers from 1789 to the present day* (1952)

Kelly, Thomas *A history of public libraries in Great Britain 1845–1965* (1973)

Kent, Charles *Charles Dickens as a reader* (1872)

Kent, Christopher 'Higher journalism and the mid-Victorian clerisy', *Victorian Studies* 13 (1969), pp. 181–98

Kent, John *Hold the fort: studies in Victorian revivalism* (1978)

Kerr, Donald J. *Amassing treasures for all times: Sir George Grey, colonial bookman and collector* (Dunedin, 2006)

Kesavan, B. S. *History of printing and publishing in India: a story of cultural awakening* (New Delhi, 1985)

Keynes, Geoffrey *William Pickering, publisher* (1924)

Keynes, J. M. 'The society's jubilee, 1890–1940', *Economic Journal* 50 (1940), pp. 401–9

Kiger, Robert (ed.) *Kate Greenaway: catalogue of an exhibition* (Hunt Institute for Botanical Documentation, Pittsburgh, 1980)

Kinane, Vincent *A brief history of printing and publishing in Ireland* (Dublin, 2002)

Kinealy, Christine 'At home with the Empire: the example of Ireland', in Catherine Hall and Sonya D. Rose (eds.), *At home with the Empire: metropolitan culture and the imperial world* (Cambridge, 2006), pp. 77–100

King, Andrew and John Plunkett (eds.) *Victorian print media: a reader* (Oxford, 2005)

King, Arthur and A. F. Stuart *The house of Warne: one hundred years of publishing* (1965)

Kirchberger, Ulrike *Aspekte deutsch-britischer Expansion: die Ueberseeinteressen der deutschen Migranten in Grossbritannien in der Mitte des 19. Jahrhunderts* (Stuttgart, 1999)

Kirsop, W. 'Baker's Juvenile Circulating Library in Sydney in the 1840s', in B. McKay, J. Hinks and M. Bell (eds.), *Light on the book trade: essays in honour of Peter Isaac* (New Castle, DE, 2004), pp. 130–40

'Bernard Quaritch's Wellington consignment sale, 1893', *The Turnbull Library Record* 14 (1981), pp. 13–22

Books for colonial readers: the nineteenth-century Australian experience (Melbourne, 1995)

'Cole's Book Arcade: Marvellous Melbourne's "Palace of Intellect"', in J. Hinks and C. Armstrong (eds.), *Worlds of print: diversity in the book trade* (New Castle, DE, 2006), pp. 31–40

'From Curry's to Collins Street, or how a Dubliner became the "Melbourne Mudie"', in P. Isaac and B. McKay (eds.), *The moving market: continuity and change in the book trade* (New Castle, DE, 2001), pp. 83–92

Kirsop, W. and E. Webby (eds.) *A history of the book in Australia. 1. To 1890: establishing a colonial print culture* (St Lucia, forthcoming)

Kitton, Frederic G. *Dickens and his illustrators* (1899)

Klingberg, Göte *Denna lilla gris går till torget och andra brittiska toy books i Sverige 1869–1879* (Stockholm, 1987)

Knight, Charles *The case of the authors as regards the paper duty* (1851)

    Knowledge is power: a view of the productive forces of modern society, and the results of labour, capital and skill (1855; new edn 1866)

    London, 6 vols. (1841–4)

    The old printer and the modern press (1854)

    Once upon a time, 2nd edn (1859)

    Passages of a working life, 3 vols. (1864–5)

    William Caxton, the first English printer (1844)

Knight, David M. *Natural science books in English, 1600–1900* (1972; 1989)

Knoepflmacher, U. C. '*Aunt Judy's Magazine* and the uses of collaboration', *Princeton University Library Chronicle* 67 (2005), pp. 146–55

Knowles, David *Great historical enterprises* (1962)

Koops, Matthias *Historical account of the substances which have been used to describe events . . . from the earliest date to the invention of paper* (1800; 2nd edn 1801)

Koss, Stephen *The rise and fall of the political press in Britain. 1. The nineteenth century* (1981)

Kramer, Sidney *A history of Stone & Kimball and Herbert S. Stone & Co.* (Chicago, 1940)

Kraus, Joe W. *Messrs Copeland & Day, 69 Cornhill, Boston, 1893–1899* (Philadelphia, 1979)

Krummel, D. W. and Stanley Sadie (eds.) *Music printing and publishing* (1980; 1990)

Krupp, Andrea 'Bookcloth in England and America, 1823–50', *PBSA* 100 (2006), pp. 25–87

Kuhn, T. S. *The structure of scientific revolutions*, 2nd edn (Chicago, 1970)

Kumar, Krishan *The making of English national identity* (Cambridge, 2003)

Laidlaw, Zoë *Colonial connections, 1815–45: patronage, the information revolution and colonial government* (Manchester, 2005)

Lamb, Horace *A treatise on the mathematical theory of the motion of fluids* (Cambridge, 1879)

Lampard, Eric E. 'The urbanizing world', in H. J. Dyos and Michael Wolff (eds.), *The Victorian city: images and realities*, 2 vols. (1973), 1, pp. 3–57

Landon, Richard 'A man under fire', in *Vizetelly & Compan(ies)* (Toronto, 2003), pp. 108–22

Langley, Leanne 'A descriptive catalogue of English periodicals containing music literature, 1665–1845', in 'The English musical journal in the early nineteenth century', unpublished PhD dissertation, University of North Carolina at Chapel Hill, NC (1983)

'Musical press', in Iain McCalman (ed.), *An Oxford companion to the Romantic age: British culture, 1776–1832* (Oxford, 1999)

Laqueur, Thomas *Religion and respectability: Sunday schools and working class culture 1780–1850* (1977)

Larkin, Emmet 'The devotional revolution in Ireland, 1850–75', *American Historical Review* 77 (1972), pp. 625–52

Larsen, Timothy *Crisis of doubt: honest faith in nineteenth-century England* (Oxford, 2006)

Friends of religious equality: nonconformist politics in mid-Victorian England (Woodbridge, 1999)

'Joseph Barker and popular Biblical criticism in the nineteenth century', *Bulletin of the John Rylands University Library of Manchester* 82 (2000), pp. 115–34

Larwood, Jacob and John Camden Hotten, *The history of signboards from the earliest times to the present day* (1866)

Latham, H. O. *On the action of examinations considered as a means of selection* (Cambridge, 1877)

Laurie, J. S. *Laurie's graduated series of reading lesson books* (1866)

Laver, James *Hatchard's of Piccadilly 1797–1947: one hundred and fifty years of bookselling* (1947)

Law, Graham ' "Nothing but a newspaper": serializing fiction in the press in the 1840s', in L. Brake and Julie F. Codell (eds.), *Encounters in the Victorian press: editors, authors, readers* (Basingstoke, 2004), pp. 229–49

Serializing fiction in the Victorian press (Basingstoke, 2000)

Lawler, T. B. *Seventy years of textbook publishing: a history of Ginn and Co. 1867–1937* (1938)

Layard, George Somes *A great 'Punch' editor: Shirley Brooks of Punch, his life, letters, and diaries* (New York, 1907)

Layton, D. 'Reading science: images of science in some nineteenth century reading lesson books', *Paradigm* 10 (1993), pp. 1–13

Le Quesne, L. P. 'Medicine', in F. M. L. Thompson (ed.), *The University of London and the world of learning, 1836–1986* (1990), pp. 125–45

Leary, Patrick '*Fraser's Magazine* and the literary life, 1830–1847', *Victorian Periodicals Review* 27 (1994), pp. 105–26

Leathlean, Howard 'H.N.H.: the work of Henry Noel Humphreys', PhD thesis, University of Reading (1989)

Leavis, Q. D. *Fiction and the reading public* (1932)

Leclaire, Lucien *A general analytical bibliography of the regional novelists of the British Isles, 1800–1950* (Paris, 1954)

Le roman régionaliste dans les Iles Britanniques (Paris, 1954)

Lee, Alan J. *The origins of the popular press in England, 1855–1914* (1976)

Lee, Sidney *Shakespeare's comedies, histories, & tragedies . . . A census of extant copies* (Oxford, 1902)

Leerssen, Joep *De bronnen van het vaderland: taal, literatuur en de afbakening van Nederland, 1806–1890* (Nijmegen, 2006)

LeFanu, W. R. *British periodicals of medicine, 1640–1899* (Oxford, 1984), a revision of articles in the *Bulletin of the Institute of the History of Medicine* 5 (1937)

Legg, Marie-Louise *Newspapers and nationalism: the Irish provincial press, 1850–1892* (Dublin, 1999)

Legros, L. A. and J. C. Grant *Typographical printing surfaces: the technology and mechanism of their production* (1916)

Leigh, Samuel *Leigh's new picture of London* (1819)

Leighton, Douglas 'Canvas and bookcloth: an essay on beginnings', *The Library* 5th ser. 3 (1949), pp. 39–49

Lely, J. M. *Copyright law reform: an exposition of Lord Monkswell's copyright bill now before Parliament* (1891)

Lennox, William Pitt *Celebrities I have known, with episodes political, social, and theatrical*, 2 vols. (1877)

Levine, Philippa *The amateur and the professional: antiquarians, historians and archaeologists in Victorian England, 1838–1886* (Cambridge, 1986)

[Lewes, George Henry] 'The condition of authors in England, Germany, and France', *Fraser's Magazine* 35 (1847), pp. 285–95

Lewis, Donald M. *Lighten their darkness: the evangelical mission to working-class London, 1828–1860* (1986)

Lewis, John *The life of mayster Wyllyam Caxton* (1737)

Lewis, John *Printed ephemera: the changing uses of type and letterforms in English and American printing* (Ipswich, 1962)

Liddington, Jill *Female fortune: land, gender and authority – the Anne Lister diaries and other writings, 1833–36* (1998)

Liddle, Dallas 'Salesmen, sportsmen, mentors: anonymity and mid-Victorian theories of journalism', *Victorian Studies* 41 (1997), pp. 31–68

Liddon, H. P. *Life of Edward Bouverie Pusey, D.D.*, 4 vols. (1894)

Life, The, of Florence L. Barclay (1921)

Lightman, B. (ed.) *Dictionary of nineteenth-century British scientists*, 4 vols. (Bristol, 2004)
   Victorian popularizers of science: designing nature for new audiences (Chicago, 2007)

Linder, Leslie *A history of the writings of Beatrix Potter* (1987)

Lindley, Kenneth *The woodblock engravers* (Newton Abbot, 1970)

List of some newspapers and other publications in Great Britain set by the Linotype Company machine (1901)

Lister, Anthony 'George John, 2nd Earl Spencer and his "librarian," Thomas Frognall Dibdin', in Robin Myers and Michael Harris (eds.), *Bibliophily* (Cambridge, 1986), pp. 90–120
   'Henry George Bohn (1796–1884)', *Antiquarian Book Monthly Review* February 1988, pp. 54–61

Lister, W. B. C. *A bibliography of Murray's Handbooks for travellers, and biographies of authors, editors, revisers and principal contributors* (Dereham, 1993)

Literary Yearbook, ed. Basil Stewart (1912)

Liveing, Edward *Adventure in publishing: the house of Ward Lock, 1854–1954* (1954)

Lives of eminent persons (1833)

Lloyd, Christopher and Simon Thurley *Henry VIII: images of a Tudor King* (1990)

Lockwood, Allison *Passionate pilgrims: the American traveler in Great Britain, 1800–1914* (New York, 1981)

Loeber, Rolf and Magda Loeber *A guide to Irish fiction, 1650–1900* (Dublin, 2006)

Loftie, W. J. *A plea for art in the house* (1876)

Lohrli, Anne *Household Words: a Weekly Journal 1850–59 conducted by Charles Dickens* (Toronto, 1973)

London and provincial medical directory (1864)

Lord, Peter *The visual culture of Wales*, 3 vols. (Cardiff, 1998–2003)

Loudon, Irvine *Medical care and the general practitioner, 1750–1850* (Oxford, 1986)

Low, W. *A classified catalogue of school, college, classical, training, and general educational works in use in Great Britain, etc.* (1871)

Lowerson, John *Sport and the English middle class* (Manchester, 1993)

Lowther-Clarke, W. K. *A hundred years of* Hymns ancient and modern (1960)

Lubbock, Sir John *The pleasures of life* (1887)

The use of life (1894)

[Lucas, E.V.] *Sir Algernon Methuen, Baronet: a memoir* (1925)

Luddy, Maria *Women and philanthropy in nineteenth-century Ireland* (Cambridge, 1995)

Ludlow, J. M. and L. Jones *The progress of the working class 1832–1867* (1867)

Lund, Michael *Reading Thackeray* (Detroit, 1988)

Lyons, Sir Henry *The Royal Society, 1660–1940: a history of its administration under its charters* (Cambridge, 1944)

Lyons, Martyn 'New readers in the nineteenth century: women, children, workers', in Guglielmo Cavallo and Roger Chartier (eds.), *A history of reading in the west* (Amherst, MA, 1999), pp. 313–44

Lyons, Martyn and John Arnold (eds.) *A history of the book in Australia. 2. 1891–1945: a national culture in a colonised market* (St Lucia, 2001)

Lytton, Edward Bulwer *England and the English* (1833)

MacAlister, J. Y. W. 'The durability of modern book papers', *The Library* 1st ser. 10 (1898), pp. 295–304

Maccioni Ruju, P. Alessandra and Marco Mostert *The life and times of Guglielmo Libri (1802–1869)* (Hilversum, 1995)

M'Cleod, W. *A first reading book for the use of families and schools* (1848)

M'Culloch, J. M. *A first reading book for the use of schools* (Edinburgh, 1837)

Macdonald, F. 'The Bible Societies in Scotland', in David F. Wright (ed.), *The Bible in Scottish life and literature* (Edinburgh, 1984), pp. 24–40

MacDonald, J. R. *Women in the printing trades: a sociological study* (1904)

MacHaffie, B. Z. ' "Monument facts and higher critical fancies": archaeology and the popularisation of Old Testament criticism in nineteenth-century Britain', *Church History* 50 (1981), pp. 316–28

'Old Testament criticism and the education of Victorian children', in Stewart J. Brown and Gerald Newlands (eds.), *Scottish Christianity in the modern world: in honour of A. C. Cheyne* (Edinburgh, 2000), pp. 91–118

Mackenzie, John M. 'Empires of travel: British guide books and cultural imperialism in the nineteenth and twentieth centuries', in J. K. Walton (ed.), *Histories of tourism: representation and conflict* (Clevedon, 2005)

Maclean, Virginia *A short-title catalogue of household and cookery books published in the English tongue, 1701–1800* (1981)

Macleod, Donald *Memoir of Norman Macleod, D.D.*, 2 vols. (1876)

MacLeod, Roy M. 'Evolutionism, internationalism and commercial enterprise in science: the International Scientific Series 1871–1910', in A. J. Meadows (ed.), *Development of science publishing in Europe* (Amsterdam, 1980), pp. 63–93

(ed.) *Government and expertise: specialists, administrators and professionals, 1860–1919* (Cambridge, 1988)

'Whigs and savants: reflections on the reform movement in the Royal Society, 1830–48', in I. Inkster and J. Morrell (eds.), *Metropolis and province: science in British culture, 1780–1850* (1983), pp. 55–90

Macmillan, Alexander *Letters*, ed. George A. Macmillan (1908)

Macmillan, Sir Frederick *The net book agreement 1899 and the book war 1906–1908* (1924)

Madan, F. 'What to aim at in local bibliography', *Library Chronicle* 4 (1887), pp. 144–8

Magee, Gary Bryan *Productivity and performance in the paper industry: labour, capital, and technology in Britain and America, 1860–1914* (Cambridge, 1997)

Maidment, Brian E. *Reading popular prints 1790–1870*, 2nd edn (Manchester, 2001)

Maison, Margaret *Search your soul, Eustace: a survey of the religious novel in the Victorian age* (1961)

'"Thine, only thine!" Women hymn writers in Britain, 1760–1835', in Gail Malmgreen (ed.), *Religion in the lives of English women, 1760–1930* (1986), pp. 11–40

Malavieille, Sophie *Reliures et cartonnages d'éditeur en France au XIXe siècle (1815–1865)* (Paris, 1985)

Mallett, Phillip *Rudyard Kipling: a literary life* (Basingstoke, 2003)

Manchester Statistical Society 'Report on the condition of the working class in the town of Kingston-upon-Hull', *Journal of the Statistical Society* 5 (1842), pp. 212–21

'Report on the state of education among the working classes in the parish of West Bromwich', *Journal of the Statistical Society* 2 (1839), pp. 375–7

Mandelbrote, Giles (ed.) *Out of print and into profit: a history of the rare and secondhand book trade in Britain in the twentieth century* (2006)

Mandelbrote, Giles and K. A. Manley (eds.) *The Cambridge history of libraries in Britain and Ireland* 2 (Cambridge, 2006)

Mandler, Peter *The English national character: the history of an idea from Edmund Burke to Tony Blair* (New Haven, CT, 2006)

'Hall, Samuel Carter (1800–1889)', *ODNB*

'"Race" and "nation" in Victorian thought', in S. Collini, R. Whatmore and B. Young (eds.), *History, religion and culture: British intellectual history, 1750–1950* (Cambridge, 2000), pp. 224–44

Manguel, Alberto *A history of reading* (1997)

Manley, K. A. 'Engines of literature: libraries in an era of expansion and transition', in Giles Mandelbrote and K. A. Manley (eds.), *The Cambridge history of libraries in Britain and Ireland* 2 (Cambridge, 2006), pp. 509–28

Manual for the system of primary instruction, pursued in the model schools of the B.F.S.S. (1831)

Manzer, Bruce M. (1977) *The Abstract Journal 1792–1920: origin, development and diffusion* (Metuchen, NJ, 1977)

Marcham, A. J. 'The Revised Code of Education 1862: reinterpretations and misinterpretations', *History of Education* 10 (1981), pp. 87–90

Marinetti, F. T. *Zang Tumb Tumb* (Milan, 1914)

Marks, Sylvia Kasey *Writing for the rising generation: British fiction for young people 1672–1839* (ELS Monographs 89) (Victoria, 2003)

Marsh, Joss *Word crimes: blasphemy, culture, and literature in nineteenth-century England* (Chicago, 1998)

Marston, Edward *After work: fragments from the workshop of an old publisher* (1904)

Martin, G. H. 'Sir George Samuel Measom (1818–1901) and his railway guides', in A. K. B. Evans and J. V. Gough (eds.), *The impact of the railway on society in Britain: essays in honour of Jack Simmons* (Aldershot, 2003)

Martin, Henri-Jean, Roger Chartier and others (eds.) *Histoire de l'édition française. 3. Le temps des éditeurs, du romantisme à la belle époque* (Paris, 1985) and *4. Le livre concurrencé, 1900–1950* (Paris, 1986)

Martin, J. E. 'Statistics of an agricultural parish in Bedfordshire', *Journal of the Statistical Society* 6 (1843), pp. 255–6

Martin, R. H. *Evangelicals united: ecumenical stirrings in pre-Victorian Britain, 1795–1830* (Metuchen, NJ, 1983)

Martineau, Harriet *Autobiography*, ed. Maria Weston Chapman, 3 vols. (1877)

Masaki, Tomoko *A history of Victorian popular picture books: the firm of Routledge 1852–1893* 2 vols. (Tokyo, 2006)

Maslen, Keith and John Lancaster (eds.) *The Bowyer ledgers* (1991)

Mason, Tony *Association football and English society, 1863–1915* (Brighton, 1980)

Masson, David *British novelists and their styles* (Boston, MA, 1859)

[Masson, David] 'Present aspects and tendencies of literature' *British Quarterly Review* 21 (1855), pp. 157–81

Matthews, M. *Teaching to read, historically considered* (Chicago, 1966)

Matthews, Samantha 'Psychological Crystal Palace? Late Victorian confession albums', *Book History* 3 (2000), pp. 125–54

Maurer, Oscar, Jr. 'Anonymity vs. signature in Victorian reviewing', *Studies in English* 27 (1948), pp. 1–27

Maxwell, R. *The mysteries of Paris and London* (Charlottesville, VA, 1992)

(ed.) *The Victorian illustrated book* (Charlottesville, VA, 2002)

May, J. Lewis *John Lane and the nineties* (1936)

May, Philip 'W. H. Smith's & Sons', *The Ludgate Monthly* May 1891, pp. 160–9

Mayhew, Henry *London labour and the London poor* (1861); 4 vols., ed. J. D. Rosenberg (New York, 1968); selected by Victor Neuberg (1985)

Maynard, F. W. *Descriptive notice of the drawings and publications of the Arundel Society* (1869)

Mayo, R. D. *The English novel in the magazines, 1714–1815* (Evanston, IL, 1962)

May's British & Irish Press Guide (1883)

Mays, K. J. 'The disease of reading and Victorian periodicals', in J. O. Jordan and R. L. Patten (eds.), *Literature in the marketplace* (Cambridge, 1995), pp. 165–94

McAleer, J. *Popular reading and publishing in Britain 1914–1950* (Oxford, 1992)

McCalman, Iain *Radical underworld: prophets, revolutionaries and pornographers in London, 1795–1840* (Oxford, 1993)

McCormack, W. J. 'Le Fanu, (Joseph Thomas) Sheridan (1814–1873)', *ODNB*

McCormick, E. H. *Alexander Turnbull: his life, his circle, his collections* (Wellington, 1974)

McCrimmon, Barbara *Power, politics, and print: the publication of the British Museum catalogue* (Hamden, CT, 1981)

McDonald, Elizabeth E. 'The modernizing of communication: vernacular publishing in nine-teenth century Maharashtra', *Asian Survey* 8 (1968), pp. 589–606

McDowell, R. *Trinity College Dublin, 1592–1952: an academic history* (Cambridge, 1982)

McKay, B., J. Hinks and M. Bell (eds.) *Light on the book trade: essays in honour of Peter Isaac* (New Castle, DE, 2004)

McKenzie, D. F. and J. C. Ross (eds.) *A ledger of Charles Ackers* (Oxford, 1968)

McKerrow, Ronald B. 'Notes on bibliographical evidence for literary students and editors', *Transactions of the Bibliographical Society* 12 (1911–13), pp. 211–318

McKitterick, David *Cambridge University Library. a history: the eighteenth and nineteenth centuries* (Cambridge, 1986)

'Dawson Turner and book collecting', in Nigel Goodman (ed.), *Dawson Turner: a Norfolk antiquary and his remarkable family* (Chichester, 2007), pp. 67–110

A history of Cambridge University Press 3 vols. (Cambridge, 1992–2004)

'Libraries, knowledge and public identity', in Martin Daunton (ed.), *The organisation of knowledge in Victorian Britain* (Oxford, 2005), pp. 287–312

'Publishing and perishing in the classics: E. H. Barker and the early nineteenth-century book trade', in C. A. Stray (ed.), *Classical books: scholarship and publishing 1800–2000* (2007), pp. 7–34

McLaren, I. F. *Henry Tolman Dwight: bookseller and publisher* (Parkville, Vic., 1989)

McLean, Ruari *Joseph Cundall, a Victorian publisher: notes on his life and a check-list of his books* (Pinner, 1970)

Victorian book design and colour printing, 2nd edn (1972)

Victorian publishers' book-bindings in cloth and leather (1974)

Victorian publishers' book-bindings in paper (1983)

McLelland, V. A. 'The Protestant Alliance and Roman Catholic schools, 1872–74', *Victorian Studies* 8 (1964), pp. 173–82

McNeely, Ian F. *The emancipation of writing: German civil society in the making, 1790s–1820s* (Berkeley, CA, 2003)

Meadows, A. J. (ed.) *Development of science publishing in Europe* (Amsterdam, 1980)

Meek, Margaret 'Literacy: redescribing reading', in K. Kimberley, M. Meek and J. Miller, *New readings: contributions to an understanding of literacy* (1993)

Meiklejohn, J. M. D. *Life and letters of William Ballantyne Hodgson, L.L.D.: late professor of economic science in the University of Edinburgh* (Edinburgh, 1883)

Memoranda on international and colonial copyright (1872)

Menzies, The, Group (Edinburgh, 1965)

Meredith, George *Letters*, ed. C. K. Cline, 3 vols. (Oxford, 1970)

[Merle, Gibbons] 'Provincial newspaper press', *Westminster Review* 12 (1830), pp. 69–103

Mermin, Dorothy *Godiva's ride: women of letters in England, 1830–1880* (Bloomington, IN, 1993)

Merriam, H. G. *Edward Moxon: publisher of poets* (New York, 1939)

Meynell, G. G. *The two Sydenham Societies: a history and bibliography* (Acrise, Kent, 1985)

Michael, Ian *Early textbooks of English* (Reading, 1993)

'The hyperactive production of English grammars in the nineteenth century: a speculative bibliography', *Publishing History* 41 (1997), pp. 24–61

The teaching of English (Cambridge, 1987)

Middleton, Bernard C. *A history of English craft bookbinding technique*, 2nd edn (1978)

Middleton, Conyers *A dissertation concerning the origin of printing in England* (Cambridge, 1735)

Miller, D. P. *Discovering water: James Watt, Henry Cavendish and the nineteenth-century 'water controversy'* (Aldershot, 2004)

Millgate, Jane *Scott's last edition: a study in publishing history* (Edinburgh, 1987)

Millgate, Michael 'Thomas Hardy and the house of Macmillan', in Elizabeth James (ed.), *Macmillan: a publishing tradition* (Basingstoke, 2002), pp. 70–82

Mitchell, B. R. *British historical statistics* (Cambridge, 1988)

Mitchell, C. Ainsworth *Inks: their composition and manufacture* (1937)

Mitchell, Charles *The newspaper press directory* (1846 etc.)

Mitchell, Rosemary 'Crosland, Camilla Dufour (1812–1895)', *ODNB*

Mitchell, Sally *Frances Power Cobbe: Victorian feminist, journalist, reformer* (Charlottesville, VA, 2004)

[Mohnike, G. C. F.] Review article, 'The Gutenberg jubilee in Germany', *Foreign Quarterly Review* 25 (1840), pp. 446–57

[Moll, G.] *On the alleged decline of science in England, by a foreigner* (1831)

Mollier, Jean-Yves *Louis Hachette* (Paris, 1999)

Moore, James 'The crisis of faith: reformation versus revolution', in Gerald Parsons (ed.), *Religion in Victorian Britain. 2. Controversies* (Manchester, 1998), pp. 225–34

   'Theodicy and society: the crisis of the intelligentsia', in R. J. Helmstadter and B. V. Lightman (eds.), *Victorian faith in crisis: essays on continuity and change in nineteenth-century religious belief* (1990), pp. 153–86

Moran, James *The composition of reading matter: a history from case to computer* (1961)

   Printing presses: history and development from the fifteenth century to modern times (1973)

Morgan, Charles *The house of Macmillan, 1843–1943* (1943)

Morgan, David *Protestants & pictures: religion, visual culture, and the age of American mass production* (New York, 1999)

Morgan, George E. *A veteran in revival: R. C. Morgan, his life and times* (1909)

[Morison, Stanley] *Printing The Times since 1785* (1953)

Morison, Stanley *Talbot Baines Reed: author, bibliographer, typefounder* (Cambridge, 1960)

   A tally of types, ed. Brooke Crutchley (Cambridge, 1973)

[Morley, John] 'Anonymous journalism', *Fortnightly Review* 8 (1867), pp. 287–92

Morley, John *The life of William Ewart Gladstone*, 3 vols. (1903)

Morrell, J. B. and A. Thackray *Gentlemen of science: early years of the British Association for the Advancement of Science* (Oxford, 1981)

Morris, Ellen K. and Edward S. Levin *The art of publishers' bookbindings, 1815–1915* (Los Angeles, 2000)

Morris, Leslie 'Bernard Alfred Quaritch in America', *The Book Collector* special number for the 150th anniversary of Bernard Quaritch (1977), pp. 180–97

Morris, William *The ideal book: essays and lectures on the arts of the book*, ed. William S. Peterson (Berkeley, 1982)

Morton, Peter *'The busiest man in England': Grant Allen and the writing trade, 1875–1914* (Basingstoke, 2005)

Morus, I. 'Currents from the underworld: electricity and the technology of display in early Victorian England', *Isis* 84 (1993), pp. 50–69

Muir, Percy *Victorian illustrated books* (1971)

Mullins, E. L. C. *Texts and calendars: an analytical guide to serial publications* (1958)

Mulvey, Christopher *Anglo-American landscapes: a study of nineteenth-century Anglo-American travel literature* (Cambridge, 1983)

Mumby, F. A. *The house of Routledge 1834–1934* (1934)

Publishing and bookselling (1930)

Mumby, F. A., and Ian Norrie *Publishing and bookselling*, 5th edn (1974)

Mumm, S. D. 'Writing for their lives: women applicants to the Royal Literary Fund, 1840–1880', *Publishing History* 27 (1990), pp. 27–47

Munby, A. N. L. *Connoisseurs and medieval miniatures* (Oxford, 1972)

Phillipps studies, 5 vols. (Cambridge, 1951–60)

Munro, Jane and Linda Goddard (eds.) *Literary circles: artist, author, word and image in Britain 1800 1920* (Cambridge. Fitzwilliam Museum, 2006)

Munson, James *The nonconformists: in search of a lost culture* (1991)

Murphy, Andrew *Shakespeare in print* (Cambridge, 2003)

Murphy, James H. (ed.) *Evangelicals and Catholics in nineteenth-century Ireland* (Dublin, 2005)

Murray, John *Practical remarks on modern paper, with an introductory account of its former substitutes; also observations on . . . the restoration of illegible manuscripts* (Edinburgh, 1829)

Murray, John *Letters of John Murray to Lord Byron*, ed. Andrew Nicholson (2007)

Murray, John 'History of British publishing', in *Catalogue of the British section of the International Exhibition of the Book Industry & Graphic Arts* (Leipzig, 1914)

Mutch, Deborah *English Socialist periodicals 1880–1900: a reference source* (Aldershot, 2005)

Myers, Robin 'The Caxton celebration of 1877: a landmark in bibliophily', in Robin Myers and Michael Harris (eds.), *Bibliophily* (Cambridge, 1986), pp. 138–63

Myers, Robin and Michael Harris (eds.) *A genius for letters* (Winchester, 1995)

(eds.) *Serials and their readers* (Winchester, 1993)

Myers, Robin, Michael Harris and Giles Mandelbrote (eds.) *Libraries and the book trade* (Winchester, 2000)

Naregal, Veena 'Vernacular culture and political formation in western India', in Abhijit Gupta and Swapan Chakravorty (eds.), *Print areas: book history in India* (Delhi, 2004), pp. 139–68

Nash, Andrew 'Life in Gissing's New Grub Street: David Christie Murray and the practice of authorship, 1880–1900', *Publishing History* 51 (2002), pp. 23–61

Nead, Lynda *Victorian Babylon: people, streets and images in nineteenth-century London* (New Haven, CT, 2000)

Needham, Paul *The Bradshaw method* (Chapel Hill, NC, 1988)

Needham, Paul, Joseph Dunlap and John Dreyfus *William Morris and the art of the book* (New York, 1976)

Nelson, C. and M. Seccombe *Periodical publications, 1641–1700: a survey with illustrations* (1986)

Nelson, James G. *The early nineties: a view from the Bodley Head* (Cambridge, MA, 1971)

Elkin Mathews: publisher to Yeats, Joyce, Pound (Madison, 1989)

Nesta, Frederick 'Smith, Elder & Co. and the realities of New Grub Street', in J. Hinks and C. Armstrong (eds.), *Worlds of print: diversity in the book trade* (2006), pp. 207–19

Neuburg, Victor E. *Popular literature: a history and guide* (Harmondsworth, 1977)

'New and cheap forms of popular literature', *Eclectic Review* 22 (1845), pp. 74–84

Newbolt, Peter *G. A. Henty, 1832–1902: a bibliographical study of his British editions* (Aldershot, 1996)

[Newmarch, William] 'Mechanics institutions', *Westminster Review* 41 (1844), pp. 416–45, repr. in Andrew King and John Plunkett (eds.), *Victorian print media: a reader* (Oxford, 2005), pp. 240–5

Newspaper Press Directory (1846–1916)

[Newton, J.] *Catalogue of a loan collection of ancient and modern bookbindings exhibited at the Liverpool Art Club* (Liverpool, 1882)

Nichols, John Gough *A descriptive catalogue of the first series of the Camden Society* 2nd edn (1872)

Nicholson, Alexander *Memoirs of Adam Black* (Edinburgh, 1885)

Nicoll, William Robertson *'Ian Maclaren': life of the Rev. John Watson, D.D.* (1908)

Nixon, H. M. *Five centuries of English bookbinding* (1978)

Nora, Pierre (ed.) *Les lieux de mémoire* 7 vols. (Paris, 1984–92), 3 vols. (Paris, 1997)

Nord, David Paul 'Free grace, free books, free riders: the economics of religious publishing in early nineteenth-century America', *Proceedings of the American Antiquarian Society* 106 (1996), pp. 214–72

Norman, Edward *The English Catholic Church in the nineteenth century* (Oxford, 1984)

[North, J. D.] *Adam and Charles Black, 1807–1957: some chapters in the history of a publishing house* (1957)

North, John S. (ed.) *The Waterloo directory of English newspapers and periodicals 1800–1900*, 7 vols. (Waterloo, Ont., 1997)

Nowell-Smith, Simon *The house of Cassell, 1848–1958* (1958)

International copyright law and the publisher in the reign of Queen Victoria (Oxford, 1968)

O Ciosain, Niall *Print and popular culture in Ireland, 1750–1850* (Basingstoke, 1997)

Ó Murchú, Máirtín 'Language and society in nineteenth-century Ireland', in Geraint H. Jenkins (ed.), *Language and community in the nineteenth century* (Cardiff, 1998), pp. 341–68

O'Connor, R. *The Earth on show: fossils and the poetics of popular science, 1802–1856* (Chicago, 2007)

O'Dea, William T. *The social history of lighting* (1958)

O'Neil, Robert *Cardinal Herbert Vaughan: Archbishop of Westminster, Bishop of Salford, founder of the Mill Hill Missionaries* (Tunbridge Wells, 1995)

O'Neill, Thomas P. *British Parliamentary papers: a monograph on blue books* (Shannon, 1968)

ODNB Oxford dictionary of national biography

Ogborn, Miles *Indian ink: script and print in the making of the English East India Company* (Chicago, 2007)

Ogle, John J. *The free library: its history and present condition* (1897)

Oldcastle, John *Journals and journalism* (1880)

[Oliphant, Margaret] 'Byways of literature: reading for the million', *Blackwood's Magazine* 84 (1858), pp. 200–16

Oliphant, Margaret *William Blackwood and his Sons* 2 vols. (1897–8)

One hundred years of type making, 1897–1997. Monotype Recorder new ser. 10 (1997)

Onslow, Barbara *Women of the press in nineteenth-century Britain* (Basingstoke, 2000)

Original, The, Bodleian copy of the first folio of Shakespeare (the Turbutt Shakespeare) (Oxford, 1905)

Orsini, Francesca 'Pandits, printers and others: publishing in nineteenth century Benares', in Abhijit Gupta and Swapan Chakravorty (eds.), *Print areas: book history in India* (Delhi, 2004), pp. 103–38

'Our modern mercury', *Once a Week*, 2 February 1861, pp. 161–3

Ousby, Ian *The Englishman's England: taste, travel and the rise of tourism* (Cambridge, 1990)

Oxford, Arnold W. *English cookery books to the year 1850* (Oxford, 1913)

Oxford University Commission *Report and evidence. Parliamentary papers* 1852.xxii

Oxford University Press *General catalogue* (November 1916)

P[utnam], G. H. and J. B. P[utnam] *Authors and publishers: a manual of suggestions for beginners in literature*, 7th edn (1897)

Padwick, E. W. *A bibliography of cricket* 1 (1984)

Pals, Daniel L. *The Victorian 'lives' of Jesus* (San Antonio, TX, 1982)

Pang, A. 'Victorian observing practices, printing technology and representations of the solar corona', *Journal for the History of Astronomy* 25 (1994), pp. 249–74 and 26 (1995), pp. 63–75

'Papers and porcelains: two recent gift collections', www.folger.edu/public/exhibit/PapersPorc/papers.htm

Parent-Lardeur, F. *Les cabinets de lecture: la lecture publique à Paris sous la Restauration* (Paris, 1982)

   Lire à Paris: les cabinets de lecture à Paris au temps de Balzac, 1815–1830 (Paris, 1999)

Parinet, Elisabeth *Une histoire de l'édition à l'époque contemporaine (xixe–xxe siècle)* (Paris, 2004)

Parish, Charles *History of the Birmingham Library* (1966)

[Parker, John W.] 'The makers, sellers, and buyers of books', *Fraser's Magazine* 45 (1852), pp. 711–24

Parker, Wyman W. *Henry Stevens of Vermont* (Amsterdam, 1963)

Paroissien, D. *The companion to Oliver Twist* (Edinburgh, 1992)

Parry, Ann 'George Newnes Limited', in Patricia Anderson and Jonathan Rose (eds.), *British literary publishing houses, 1881–1965* (Detroit, 1991), pp. 226–32

Parry, J. P. 'Nonconformity, clericalism and "Englishness": the United Kingdom', in Christopher Clark and Wolfram Kaiser (eds.), *Culture wars: secular–Catholic conflict in nineteenth-century Europe* (Cambridge, 2003), pp. 152–81

Parry, Jonathan *The politics of patriotism: English liberalism, national identity and Europe, 1830–1886* (Cambridge, 2006)

Parry, Linda (ed.) *William Morris* (1996)

Parsons, Gerald 'Biblical criticism in Victorian Britain: from controversy to acceptance?' in Gerald Parsons (ed.), *Religion in Victorian Britain. 2. Controversies* (Manchester, 1988)

Partridge, R. C. Barrington *The history of the legal deposit of books* (1938)

Paston, George *At John Murray's: records of a literary circle, 1843–1892* (1932)

Patten, Robert L. *Charles Dickens and his publishers* (Oxford, 1978)

   'The fight at the top of the tree: *Vanity Fair* versus *Dombey and Son*', *Studies in English Literature* 10 (1970), pp. 759–73

   George Cruikshank's life, times, and art 2 vols. (1992–6)

Patten, Robert L. and Patrick Leary 'Evans, Frederick Mullett (1803–1870)' *ODNB*

Payn, James *Gleams of memory* (1894)

Paz, D. G. *Popular anti-Catholicism in mid-Victorian England* (Stanford, CA, 1982)

PBSA Papers of the Bibliographical Society of America

Pearce, Susan (ed.) *Visions of antiquity: the Society of Antiquaries of London, 1707–2007* (2007)

Pearson, Thomas *Infidelity: its aspects, causes and agencies; being the prize essay of the British Organization of the Evangelical Alliance* (1853)

Peckham, M. 'Dr. Lardner's *Cabinet Cyclopaedia*', *PBSA* 45 (1951), pp. 37–58

Pedersen, Susan 'Hannah More meets Simple Simon: tracts, chapbooks, and popular culture in late eighteenth-century England', *Journal of British Studies* 25 (1986), pp. 84–113

Pedersen, Viggo Hjørnager *Ugly ducklings? Studies in the English translations of Hans Christian Andersen's tales and stories* (Odense, 2004)

Peltz, Lucy 'Facing the text: the amateur and commercial histories of extra-illustration', in R. Myers and M. Harris (eds.), *Owners, annotators and the signs of reading* (New Castle, DE, 2005), pp. 91–135

Pemble, John *The Mediterranean passion: Victorians and Edwardians in the south* (Oxford, 1988)

Perils, The, of authorship: an enquiry into the difficulties of literature [1840?]

Perkin, Harold *The rise of professional society: England since 1880* (Cambridge, 1989)

Peters, Lisa 'Distributing Wrexham's newspapers, 1850–1900' (forthcoming)

Peterson, William S. *A bibliography of the Kelmscott Press* (Oxford, 1984)

   'The type designs of William Morris', *JPHS* 19–20 (1985–7), pp. 5–61

   Victorian heretic: Mrs Humphry Ward's Robert Elsmere (Leicester, 1976)

Petrucci, Armando *Public lettering: script, power, and culture* (Chicago, 1986)

Pettitt, Clare *Patent inventions: intellectual property and the Victorian novel* (Oxford, 2004)

Pfaff, R. W. *Montague Rhodes James* (1980)

[Phillips, Samuel] *The literature of the rail* (1851)

Photography & the printed page in the nineteenth century (Oxford: Bodleian Library, 2000)

Pickstone, J. 'Museological science? The place of the analytical/comparative in nineteenth-century science, technology and medicine', *History of Science* 32 (1994), pp. 111–38

Pickwoad, Nicholas 'Onward and downward: how binders coped with the printing press before 1800', in R. Myers and M. Harris (eds.), *A millennium of the book: production, design and illustration in manuscript and print (900–1900)* (Winchester, 1994), pp. 61–106

Pigot & Co.'s National commercial directory. Various editions

Pitman, Henry *Hints on teaching and lecturing on phonography*, 2nd edn (1885)

Plant, Marjorie *The English book trade*, 3rd edn (1973)

Plunkett, John *Queen Victoria, first media monarch* (Oxford, 2003)

PMLA Publications of the Modern Language Association of America

Pocock, J. G. A. *The discovery of islands: essays in British history* (Cambridge, 2005)

Polkinghorn, Bette 'Jane Marcet and Harriet Martineau: motive, market experience, and reception of their works popularizing classical political economy', in M. A. Dimand, R. W. Dimand and E. L. Forget (eds.), *Women of value: feminist essays on the history of women in economics* (Aldershot, 1995), pp. 71–81

Pollard, A. W. *Records of the English Bible: the documents relating to the translation and publication of the Bible in English, 1525–1611* (1911)

Pollard, M. *Dublin's trade in books, 1550–1800* (Oxford, 1989)

Pollock, Frederick 'Our jubilee', *Law Quarterly Review* 51 (1935), pp. 5–10

Porter, Andrew (ed.) *The Oxford history of the British Empire. 3. The nineteenth century* (Oxford, 1999)

Porter, Bernard *The absent-minded imperialists: empire, society, and culture in Britain* (Oxford, 2004)

   The refugee question in mid-Victorian politics (Cambridge, 1979)

Porter, G. R. *The progress of the nation*, new edn, rev. F. W. Hirst (1912)

Porter, Mrs Gerald *Annals of a publishing house: John Blackwood* (Edinburgh, 1898)

(Porter, John) *Catalogue of a William Pickering collection* (privately printed, 2004)

Porter, Roy *Health for sale: quackery in England, 1660–1850* (Manchester, 1989)

Porter, Roy and Lesley Hall *The facts of life: the creation of sexual knowledge in Britain, 1650–1950* (New Haven, CT, 1995)

Porter, Theodore M. *The rise of statistical thinking, 1820–1900* (Princeton, NJ, 1986)

Potter, Esther 'The development of publishers' bookbinding in the nineteenth century'. *JPHS* 28 (1999), pp. 71–93

'The London bookbinding trade: from craft to industry', *The Library* 6th ser. 15 (1993), pp. 259–80

Potter, Simon J. *News and the British world: the emergence of an imperial press system 1876–1922* (Oxford, 2003)

Pound, Reginald *The Strand Magazine, 1891–1950* (1966)

Powell, Michael and Terry Wyke 'Penny capitalism in the Manchester book trade: the case of James Weatherley', in Peter Isaac and Barry McKay (eds.), *The reach of print: making, selling and using books* (Winchester, 1998), pp. 135–56

Pratt, A. T. Camden *Unknown London: its romance and tragedy* [1897]

Preston, William C. 'Messrs W. H. Smith and Son's bookstalls and library', *Good Words* 36 (1895), pp. 474–8

Price, D. *Little science, big science* (New York, 1963)

Price, J. H. 'Publication in parts: a background to the concept, efficacy and taxonomic complexity', *Archives of Natural History* 10 (1982), pp. 443–59

Price, Leah 'Reading matter', *PMLA* 121 (2006), pp. 9–16

Priolkar, A. K. *The printing press in India: its beginnings and early development* (Bombay, 1958)

Pritchard, Brian 'The musical festival and the choral society in England in the 18th and 19th centuries: a social history', unpublished PhD dissertation, University of Birmingham (1968)

Prochaska, F. 'Body and soul: Bible nurses and the poor in Victorian London', *Historical Research* 60 (1987), pp. 336–48

Public libraries in the United States of America: their history, condition and management (Washington, DC, 1876)

Publishers' Circular and Booksellers' Record, London, 1837–

Purvis, June *Hard lessons: the lives and education of working-class women in nineteenth-century England* (Cambridge, 1989)

Quaritch, Bernard *A catalogue of fifteen hundred books remarkable for the beauty or age of their bindings* (1889)

Quaritch, Bernard and Michael Kerney *The Spanish Columbus letter*, ed. Anthony Payne (2006)

Question, The, of unreciprocated foreign copyright in Great Britain (1851)

Raahman, Kate Sealey 'Russian revolutionaries in London, 1853–70: Alexander Herzen and the Free Russian Press', in Barry Taylor (ed.), *Foreign-language printing in London, 1500–1900* (2002), pp. 227–40

Ramalingam, C. 'The mathematician and the compositor', unpublished MPhil essay, University of Cambridge (2002)

Ransome, Arthur *Autobiography*, ed. Rupert Hart-Davis (1976)

Raucourt, Antoine *A Manual of lithography; or, Memoir on the lithographical experiments made in Paris, at the Royal School of the Roads and Bridges*, trans. C. Hullmandel, 2nd edn (1821)

Raven, James *The business of books: booksellers and the English book trade 1450–1850* (New Haven, CT, 2007)

Raven, James, Helen Small and Naomi Tadmor (eds.) *The practice and representation of reading in England* (Cambridge, 1996)

Ray, Gordon N. *Illustrators and the book in England from 1790 to 1914* (New York, 1976)

Reach, Angus B. 'The coffee houses of London', *New Parley Library* 1 (13 July 1844), 293–4, repr. in Andrew King and John Plunkett (eds.), *Victorian print media: a reader* (Oxford, 2005), pp. 246–9

Read, Donald *The power of news: the history of Reuters, 1849–1989* (Oxford, 1992)

Reade, Charles 'The rights and wrongs of authors', *Pall Mall Gazette*, July and September 1875

Reader, W. J. *Professional men: the rise of the professional classes in nineteenth-century England* (1966)

Redding, Cyrus *Fifty years' recollections, literary and personal, with observations on men and things*, 3 vols. (1858)

Reed, Talbot Baines *A history of the old English letter foundries* (1887)

'Old and new fashions in typography', *Journal of the Society of Arts* 18 August 1890, pp. 527–36

Reid, Forrest *Illustrators of the eighteen sixties: an illustrated survey of the work of 58 British artists* (1928)

Reilly, Catherine W. *Late Victorian poetry, 1880–1899: an annotated bibliography* (1994)

Renan, Ernest *Qu'est-ce qu'une nation? Conférence faite en Sorbonne, le 1 mars 1882* (Paris, 1882)

Report from the Select Committee on Public Libraries (1849), *Parliamentary papers* 1849.xvii

Report of Her Majesty's Commissioners appointed to inquire into the state, discipline, studies, and revenues of the University and colleges of Cambridge (1852), *Parliamentary papers* 1852–3.xliv

Reports of the Commissioners of Inquiry into the State of Education in Wales 3 parts. *Parliamentary papers* 1847.xxvii

Reynolds, Siân *Britannica's typesetters: women compositors in Edwardian Edinburgh* (Edinburgh, 1989)

Rhees, William J. *Manual of public libraries, institutions, and societies in the United States and British provinces of North America* (Philadelphia, 1859)

Rhodes, Barbara J. and William Wells Streeter, *Before photocopying: the art and history of mechanical copying, 1780–1930* (New Castle, DE, 1999)

Rhys, Ernest *Everyman remembers* (1931)

Richards, David Alan 'Kipling and pirates', *PBSA* 96 (2002), pp. 59–109

Richards, Grant *Author hunting* (1934)

Richards, Thomas *The commodity culture of Victorian England: advertising and spectacle, 1851–1914* (Stanford, CA, 1990)

Rickard, Suzanne, ' "A gifted author": Hesba Stretton and the Religious Tract Society', in Dennis Butts and Pat Garrett (eds.), *From* The dairyman's daughter *to* Worrals of the WAAF: *the Religious Tract Society, Lutterworth Press, and children's literature* (Cambridge, 2006), pp. 104–15

Rickards, Maurice *The encyclopedia of ephemera: a guide to the fragmentary documents of everyday life*, ed. and completed by Michael Twyman (2000)

Riddell, Mrs. J. H. 'Literature as a profession', *The Illustrated Review* 2 (1874), p. 7

Riesen, Richard Allen *Criticism and faith in late Victorian Scotland: A. B. Davidson, William Robertson Smith and George Adam Smith* (Lanham, MD, 1965)

Rink, John 'The profession of music', in Jim Samson (ed.), *The Cambridge history of nineteenth-century music* (Cambridge, 2002), pp. 55–86

Ritchie, G. S. *The Admiralty chart: British naval hydrography in the nineteenth century* new edn (Edinburgh, 1995)

Rivers, Isabel 'The first evangelical tract society', *Historical Journal* 50 (2007), pp. 1–22

Rivington, Septimus *The publishing family of Rivington* (1919)

Roach, John *Public examinations in England, 1850–1900* (Cambridge, 1971)

Roberts, R. J. 'The Bibliographical Society as a band of pioneers', in R. Myers and M. Harris (eds.), *Pioneers in bibliography* (Winchester, 1988), pp. 86–100

Roberts, Robert *The classic slum* (Harmondsworth, 1973)

Roberts, W. 'Lloyd's penny bloods', *Book-Collectors' Quarterly* 17 (1935), pp. 1–16

Roberts, William *The book-hunter in London* (1895)

Robinson, Howard *Britain's Post Office* (Oxford, 1953)

Robinson, J. (ed.) *Catalogue of the special exhibition of works of art of the mediaeval, renaissance and more recent periods, on loan at the South Kensington Museum, June 1862* (1863)

Rogers, Joseph W. 'The rise of American edition binding', in H. Lehmann-Haupt (ed.), *Bookbinding in America: three essays* (Portland, ME, 1941), pp. 131–85b.

Roldán Vera, Eugenia *The British book trade and Spanish American independence: education and knowledge transmission in transcontinental perspectives* (Aldershot, 2003)

Romance, The, of the Amalgamated Press (1925)

Rose, Jonathan 'How historians study reader response: or, what did Jo think of *Bleak House?*' in John O. Jordan and Robert L. Patten (eds.), *Literature in the marketplace* (Cambridge, 1995), pp. 195–212

The intellectual life of the British working classes (New Haven, CT, 2001)

Rose, R. N. *The Field, 1853–1953* (1953)

Rosenberg, Sheila 'The financing of radical opinion: John Chapman and the *Westminster Review*', in J. Shattock and M. Wolff (eds.), *The Victorian periodical press: samplings and soundings* (Leicester, 1982), pp. 167–93

'The "wicked Westminster": John Chapman, his contributors and promises fulfilled', *Victorian Periodicals Review* 33 (2000), pp. 225–46

Rosenthal, Bernard (ed.) *Die Rosenthal: der Aufstieg einer jüdischen Antiquarsfamilie zu Weltruhm* (Vienna, 2002)

Rosman, Doreen M. *Evangelicals and culture* (1984)

Ross, Fiona G. E. *The printed Bengali character and its evolution* (Richmond, 1999)

Rothblatt, Sheldon *The revolution of the dons: Cambridge and society in Victorian England* (1968)

Rothermel, H. 'Images of the sun: Warren De La Rue, George Biddell Airy and celestial photography', *British Journal for the History of Science* 26 (1993), pp. 137–70

Routley, Erik 'That dreadful red book (*Hymns ancient and modern*, 1904)', *Bulletin of the Hymn Society* 13 (1974)

Rowbotham, Judith *Good girls make good wives* (1989)

Royal Society of London, *Catalogue of scientific papers (1800–1900)* 19 vols. (1867–1925)

Royle, Edward *Radicals, secularists and republicans: popular freethought in Britain, 1866–1915* (Manchester, 1980)

Royle, J. Forbes *The fibrous plants of India fitted for cordage, clothing and paper* (1855)

Rudwick, M. 'Historical origins of the Geological Society's Journal', in M. J. Le Bas (ed.), *Milestones in geology* (1995), pp. 5–8

Rühle, Reiner *Böse Kinder: kommentierte Bibliographie von Struwwelpetriaden und Max-und-Moritziaden* (Osnabrück, 1999)

Russell, Dave *Looking north: northern England and the national imagination* (Manchester, 2004)

Russell, Percy *The author's manual* (1891, 8th edn 1895)

Ryan, Kara M. 'The siege of O'Connell: Charlotte Elizabeth Tonna's historical novels of Ireland', in James H. Murphy (ed.), *Evangelicals and Catholics in nineteenth-century Ireland* (Dublin, 2005), pp. 73–84

Sadleir, Michael *The evolution of publishers' binding styles, 1770–1900* (1930)

    XIX century fiction: a bibliographical record, 2 vols. (Cambridge, 1951)

    'Yellow-backs', in *New paths in book collecting*, ed. John Carter (London: Constable, 1934), pp. 127–61

Saint Bride Foundation, *Catalogue of the technical reference library of works on printing and the allied arts* (1919)

Sala, George Augustus *Letters to Edmund Yates*, ed. Judy McKenzie (Brisbane, 1953)

Salway, Lance *A peculiar gift* (Harmondsworth, 1976)

Sampson, Henry *A history of advertising from the earliest times* (1874)

Samson, Jim (ed.) *The Cambridge history of nineteenth-century music* (Cambridge, 2001)

Sanders, Moshe *Jewish books in Whitechapel: a bibliography of Narodiczky's press* (1991)

Sanders, Valerie ' "All sufficient to one another?" Charlotte Yonge and the family chronicle', in Kay Boardman and Shirley Jones (eds.), *Popular Victorian women writers* (Manchester, 2004), pp. 90–110

    (ed.) *Records of girlhood: an anthology of nineteenth-century women's childhoods* (Aldershot, 2000)

Sanderson, Michael *The universities and British industry, 1850–1970* (1972)

Sauer, Walter 'A classic is born: the "childhood" of "Struwwelpeter"' PBSA 97 (2003), pp. 215–63

Saunders, J. W. *The profession of English letters* (1964)

Saville, John *1848: the British state and the Chartist movement* (Cambridge, 1987)

Sayers, S. *The company of books: a short history of the Lothian book companies 1888–1988* (Melbourne, 1988)

Schäffer, J. C. *Versuche und Muster ohne alle Lumpen oder doch mit einem geringen zu Satze derselben Papier zu machen* 6 vols. (Ratisbon [Regensburg], 1765–71)

Schaffer, S. 'Late Victorian metrology and its instrumentation: a manufactory of ohms', in R. Bud and S. E. Cozzens (eds.), *Invisible connections: instruments, institutions, and science* (Bellingham, 1992), pp. 23–56

    'The nebular hypothesis and the science of progress', in J. R. Moore (ed.), *History, humanity and evolution* (Cambridge, 1989), pp. 131–64

    'On astronomical drawing', in C. A. Jones and P. Galison (eds.), *Picturing science, producing art* (New York, 1998), pp. 441–74

Schmoller, Hans 'The paperback revolution', in Asa Briggs (ed.), *Essays in the history of publishing, in celebration of the 250th anniversary of the House of Longman, 1724–1974* (1974), pp. 283–318

Schofield, Roger 'Dimensions of illiteracy in England 1750–1850', in Harvey J. Graff (ed.), *Literacy and social development in the west* (Cambridge, 1981), pp. 201–13

Scholderer, Victor *Greek printing types, 1465–1927* (1927)

'School-books and eyesight: report of the committee' (Chairman G. A. Auden), *Report of the 82nd meeting of the British Association for the Advancement of Science, Dundee*, 1912 (1913), pp. 295–318

Schwyzer, Philip *Literature, nationalism and memory in early modern England and Wales* (Cambridge, 2004)

Scott, Clement and Cecil Howard, *The life and reminiscences of E. L. Blanchard*, 2 vols. (1891)

Scott, John, 'The literature of the nursery', *London Magazine* 2 (1820), pp. 477–83

Scott, Patrick 'The business of belief: the emergence of "religious" publishing', in Derek Baker (ed.), *Sanctity and secularity: the church and the world* (Oxford, 1973), pp. 213–24

    'Richard Cope Morgan, religious periodicals, and the Pontifex factor', *Victorian Periodicals Newsletter* 16 (1972), pp. 1–14

Scott, Rosemary 'Pious verse in the mid-Victorian market place: facts and figures', *Publishing History* 33 (1993), pp. 37–58

Scott, Sir Walter *The Letters of Sir Walter Scott 1826–1828*, ed. H. J. C. Grierson (1936)

Scrivener, F. H. A. *The authorized edition of the English Bible (1611), its subsequent reprints and modern representatives* (Cambridge, 1884)

Seaborne, Malcolm 'E. R. Robson and the board schools of London', in T. G. Cook (ed.), *Local studies and the history of education* (1972), pp. 63–82

Searle, G. R. *A new England? Peace and war, 1886–1918* (New Oxford History of England) (Oxford, 2004)

Secord, A. 'Botany on a plate: pleasure and the power of pictures in promoting early nineteenth-century scientific knowledge', *Isis* 93 (2002), pp. 28–57

    'Science in the pub: artisan botanists in early nineteenth-century Lancashire', *History of Science* 32 (1994), pp. 269–315

Secord, James A. 'General introduction', in M. Somerville, *Collected works* 9 vols. (Bristol, 2004), 1, pp. xv–xxxix

    'How scientific conversation became shop talk', in A. Fyfe and B. Lightman (eds.), *Science in the marketplace: nineteenth-century sites and experiences* (Chicago, 2007), pp. 23–59

    'Science', in L. Howsam *et al.*, 'What the Victorians learned', *Journal of Victorian Culture* 12 (2007), pp. 272–6

    Victorian sensation: the extraordinary publication, reception, and secret authorship of Vestiges of the natural history of creation (Chicago, 2000)

Seeley, F. W. *The production of a Baxter colour print* (New Baxter Society, 2000)

Seeley, J.R. *The expansion of England* (1883)

    Introduction to political science (1896)

Seville, Catherine 'Edward Bulwer Lytton dreams of copyright: "It might make me a rich man"', in Francis O'Gorman (ed.), *Victorian literature and finance* (Oxford, 2007), pp. 55–72

    The internationalisation of copyright law: books, buccaneers and the black flag in the nineteenth century (Cambridge, 2006)

    Literary copyright reform in early Victorian England (Cambridge, 1999)

Sewell, Eleanor M. (ed.) *The autobiography of Elizabeth M. Sewell* (1907)

Seymour, T. *A guide to collecting Everyman's Library* (Bloomington, IN, 2005)

Seymour, W. A. (ed.) *A history of the Ordnance Survey* (Folkestone, 1980)

[Shand, Alexander Innes], 'Contemporary literature: 1. Journalists', *Blackwood's Magazine* 124 (1878), pp. 641–62

Shattock, Joanne (ed.) *The Cambridge bibliography of English literature*, 3rd edn 4 (Cambridge, 1999)

'The problem of parentage: the *North British Review* and the Free Church of Scotland', in J. Shattock and Michael Wolff (eds.), *The Victorian periodical press: samplings and soundings* (Leicester, 1982), pp. 145–66

Shattock, Joanne and Michael Wolff (eds.) *The Victorian periodical press: samplings and soundings* (Leicester, 1982)

Shaw, David 'French émigrés in the London book trade to 1850', in R. Myers, M. Harris and G. Mandelbrote (eds.), *The London book trade: topographies of print in the metropolis from the sixteenth century* (2003), pp. 127–43

'French-language publishing in London to 1900', in Barry Taylor (ed.), *Foreign-language printing in London, 1500–1900* (2002), pp. 101–22

Shaw, George T. *History of the Athenaeum, Liverpool, 1798–1898* (Liverpool, 1898)

Shaw, Graham *Printing in Calcutta to 1800: a description and checklist of printing in late 18th century Calcutta* (1981)

Shaylor, Joseph 'Reprints and their readers', *Cornhill Magazine* 18 (1905), pp. 538–45

Shea, Victor and William Whitla (eds.) *Essays and reviews: the 1860 text and its reading* (Charlottesville, VA, 2000)

Shearman, Montague *Athletics and football* (1887)

Sheets-Pyenson, S. 'From the North to Red Lion Court: the creation and early years of the *Annals of Natural History*', *Archives of Natural History* 10 (1981), pp. 221–49

'A measure of success: the publication of natural history journals in early Victorian Britain', *Publishing History* 9 (1981), pp. 21–36

'Popular science periodicals in Paris and London: the emergence of a low scientific culture, 1820–1875', *Annals of Science* 42 (1985), pp. 549–72

Shepard, Leslie *The history of street literature* (Newton Abbot, 1973)

Sher, Richard B. *The Enlightenment and the book* (Chicago, 2006)

Sherman, Brad and Lionel Bently *The making of modern intellectual property law* (Cambridge, 1999)

Shillingsburg, Peter *Pegasus in harness: Victorian publishing and W. M. Thackeray* (Charlottesville, VA, 1992)

Shore, Emily *Journal of Emily Shore: revised and expanded digital edition*, ed. Barbara Timm Gates (Charlottesville, VA, 2006)

Shteir, Ann B. *Cultivating women, cultivating science: Flora's daughters and botany in England, 1760 to 1860* (Baltimore, MD, 1996)

Silver, Rollo 'Efficiency improved: the genesis of the web press in America', *Proceedings of the American Antiquarian Society* n.s. 80 (1970), pp. 325–50

Simmons, Jack 'Introduction' to John Murray and William Brockeden, *Murray's Handbook for travellers in Switzerland, 1838* (Leicester, 1970)

'Introduction' to *The railway traveller's handy book of hints, suggestions, and advice: before the journey, on the journey and after the journey, 1862* (Bath, 1971)

The Victorian railway (1991)

Simon, Herbert *Song and words: a history of the Curwen Press* (1973)

Singleton, Frank *Tillotsons, 1850–1950: centenary of a family business* (Bolton, 1950)

Sinnett, Mrs Percy 'What is popular literature?' *The People's Journal* 5 (1848), pp. 7–8

Sixpenny wonderfuls (1985)

Skeat, Walter W. and J. H. Nodal (eds.) *A bibliographical list of the works . . . illustrative of the various dialects of English* (English Dialect Society, 1873–7)

Skelton-Foord, Christopher 'Economics, expertise, enterprise . . . British circulating libraries 1780–1830', in E. J. Clery, C. Franklin and P. Garside (eds.), *Authorship, commerce and the public: scenes of writing, 1750–1850* (Basingstoke, 2002), pp. 136–52

Sketchley, R. E. D. *English book illustration of today* (1903)

Skidelsky, Robert *John Maynard Keynes*, 3 vols. (1983–2000)

Skinner, S. A. 'Mozley, Thomas (1806–1893)', *ODNB*

Skinner, Simon *Tractarians and the 'Condition of England'* (Oxford, 2004)

Slater, J. H. *Book collecting: a guide for amateurs* (1892)

Slater, Michael *Douglas Jerrold, 1803–1857* (2002)

Slugg, J. T. *Reminiscences of Manchester fifty years ago* (Manchester, 1881)

Small, Helen 'A pulse of 124: Charles Dickens and a pathology of the mid-Victorian reading public', in James Raven *et al.* (eds.), *The practice and representation of reading in England* (Cambridge, 1996), pp. 263–90

Smelser, Neil J. *Social paralysis and social change: British working class education in the nineteenth century* (Berkeley, CA, 1991)

Smiles, Samuel *A publisher and his friends: memoir and correspondence of the late John Murray*, 2 vols. (1891)

Smith, Charles Manby *Curiosities of London life* (1853)

The little world of London (1857)

'Press of the Seven Dials', in *The little world of London* (1857)

The working man's way in the world (1853), introd. Ellic Howe (1967)

Smith, David *Victorian maps of the British Isles* (1985)

Smith, George and Frank Benger *The oldest London bookshop: a history of two hundred years* (1928)

Smith, Mark *Religion in industrial society: Oldham and Saddleworth, 1740–1865* (Oxford, 1994)

Smith, Robert W. 'A national observatory transformed: Greenwich in the nineteenth century', *Journal for the History of Astronomy* 22 (1991), pp. 5–20

'Smiths' Express Newspaper Office', *Leisure Hour* 18 October 1860, pp. 664–7

Snell, Keith D. M. 'The Sunday-School movement in England and Wales: child labour, denominational control and working-class culture', *Past & Present* 164 (1999), pp. 122–68

[Soane, George] *A hand-book of taste in book-binding*, new edn (E. Churton [c.1855])

Southey, Robert *Southey's common-place book*, 4 vols. (1849–50)

Southward, John *Practical printing: a handbook of the art of typography*, 6th edn by George Joyner [1911]

Spedding, James *Publishers and authors* (1867)

Spencer, Herbert *An autobiography* (New York, 1904)

Spicer, A. Dykes *The paper trade: a descriptive and historical survey of the paper trade from the commencement of the nineteenth century* (1907)

Spielmann, M. H. *The history of 'Punch'* (1895)

Sponza, L. *Italian immigrants in nineteenth-century Britain: realities and images* (Leicester, 1988)

Sprigge, S. S. *The life and times of Thomas Wakley* (1897)
  The methods of publishing (Society of Authors, 1890)
Spufford, Margaret *Small books and pleasant histories* (1981)
Srebrenik, Patricia Thomas *Alexander Strahan: Victorian publisher* (Ann Arbor, MI, 1986)
St Clair, William 'The political economy of reading', *The John Coffin Memorial Lecture in the History of the Book*, School of Advanced Study, University of London (2005)
  'Publishing, authorship, and reading', in Richard Maxwell and Katie Trumpener (eds.), *Cambridge companion to fiction in the Romantic period* (Cambridge, forthcoming)
  'Read the world', *Times Literary Supplement* 6 April 2007, p. 24
  The reading nation in the Romantic period (Cambridge, 2004)
St John, John *William Heinemann: a century of publishing 1890–1990* (1990)
Staff, Frank *The picture postcard and its origins* (1966)
Steeves, H. R. *Learned societies and English literary scholarship* (New York, 1913)
Stephen, George A. *Commercial bookbinding* (1910)
  Die moderne Grossbuchbinderei adapted for the German-speaking market by Hermann Scheibe (Vienna and Leipzig, 1910)
Stephens, John Russell *The profession of the playwright: British theatre, 1800–1900* (Cambridge, 1992)
Stephens, W. B. *Education, literacy and society, 1830–1870: the geography of diversity in provincial England* (Manchester, 1987)
Stetz, Margaret D. and Mark Samuels Lasner *England in the 1890s: literary publishing at the Bodley Head* (Washington, DC, 1990)
Stevens, E. T. and C. Hole *The grade lesson books in six standards* (1871)
Stevens, Henry *The Bibles in the Caxton exhibition, MDCCCLXXVII* (1878)
Stevenson, Laura ' "A vogue for small books": *The tale of Peter Rabbit* and its contemporary competitors', *Beatrix Potter Studies* 10 (2003), pp. 11–27
Stigler, Stephen M. *Statistics on the table: the history of statistical concepts and methods* (Cambridge, MA, 1999)
Stimpson, Felicity ' "Reading in circles": the National Home Reading Union 1889–1900', *Publishing History* 52 (2002), pp. 19–82
[Stirling-Maxwell, Sir William (ed.)] *The Scott exhibition MDCCCLXXI. Catalogue of the exhibition held at Edinburgh* (Edinburgh, 1872)
Stocqueler, J. H. *The memoirs of a journalist* (Bombay and London, 1873)
Stoddard, Roger *Marks in books* (Cambridge, MA, 1985)
Stoker, David A. (ed.) *Studies in the provincial book trade of England, Scotland and Wales before 1900* (Aberystwyth, 1990)
Story, The, of 'The Scotsman': a chapter in the annals of British journalism (Edinburgh, 1886)
Straus, Ralph and Robert K. Dent, *John Baskerville: a memoir* (1907)
Stray, C. A. 'A cellarful of ghosts? The library of the Educational Division of the South Kensington Museum', *Paradigm* 3 (1990), pp. 13–15
  Grinders and grammars: a Victorian controversy (Reading, 1992)
  (ed.) *Oxford classics: teaching and learning, 1800–2000* (2007)
  'Paper wraps stone: the beginnings of educational lithography', *JPHS* n.s. 9 (2006), pp. 13–29
  'Paradigms of social order: the politics of Latin grammar in 19th-century England', *Bulletin of the Henry Sweet Society* 13 (1989), pp. 13–24

'Sir William Smith and his dictionaries: a study in scarlet and black', in C. A. Stray (ed.), *Classical books: scholarship and publishing 1800-2000* (2007), pp. 35-54

Strong, Roy *The cult of Elizabeth: Elizabethan portraits and pageantry* (1977)

Student's, The, guide to the University of Cambridge (Cambridge, 1862)

Studio, The: a bibliography. The first fifty years, 1893-1943, introd. Bryan Holme (1978)

Successful, The, bookseller (1906)

Sullivan, Alvin (ed.) *British literary magazines: the Victorian and Edwardian age, 1837-1913* (Westport, CT, 1984)

Summerfield, Geoffrey 'The making of The home treasury', *Children's Literature* 8 (1980), pp. 35-52

Summers, Montague *A gothic bibliography* (1940)

Sutcliffe, Peter *The Oxford University Press: an informal history* (Oxford, 1978)

Sutherland, Gillian 'Education', in *Cambridge social history of Britain 1750-1950* 3, ed. F. M. L. Thompson (Cambridge, 1990), pp. 119-69

'Examinations and the construction of professional identity: a case study of England 1800-1950', *Assessment in Education* 8 (2001), pp. 51-64

Faith, duty and the power of mind: the Cloughs and their circle 1820-1960 (Cambridge, 2006)

Policy-making in elementary education 1870-1895 (Oxford, 1973)

Sutherland, John 'The British book trade and the crash of 1826', *The Library* 6th ser. 9 (1987), pp. 148-61

'*Cornhill*'s sales and payments: the first decade', *Victorian Periodicals Review* 19 (1986), pp. 106-8

The Longman (Stanford) companion to Victorian fiction (Harlow and Stanford, 1988)

Mrs Humphry Ward: eminent Victorian, pre-eminent Edwardian (Oxford, 1990)

Victorian fiction: writers, publishers, readers (Basingstoke, 1995, 2nd edn 2006)

Victorian novelists and publishers (1976)

Sutton, Denys 'Herbert Horne, a pioneer historian of early Italian art' [and] 'Letters from Herbert Horne to Roger Fry', *Apollo* August 1985, pp. 130-59

Swinnerton, Frank *Background with chorus* (1956)

Symon J. D. *The press and its story* (1914)

Symons, Michael *A history of cooks and cooking* (Urbana, IL, 2000)

Szreter, Simon *Fertility, class and gender in Britain, 1860-1940* (Cambridge, 1996)

Talbot, Henry Fox *The pencil of nature* facsimile, introd. Larry J. Schaaf (New York, 1989)

Tamke, Susan S. *Make a joyful noise unto the Lord: hymns as a reflection of Victorian social attitudes* (Athens, OH, 1978)

Tanner, J. R. (ed.) *Historical register of the University of Cambridge to the year 1910* (Cambridge, 1917)

Tanselle, G. Thomas 'The bibliographical description of patterns', *Studies in Bibliography* 23 (1970), pp. 71-102, repr. in his *Selected studies in bibliography* (Charlottesville, VA, 1979), pp. 171-202

'Dust-jackets, dealers, and documentation', *Studies in Bibliography* 56 (2003-4), pp. 45-140

Taylor, Barry (ed.) *Foreign-language printing in London, 1500-1900* (2002)

Taylor, John Russell *The art nouveau book in Britain* (1966; Edinburgh, 1979)

Taylor, M. A. *Hugh Miller: stonemason, geologist, writer* (Edinburgh, 2007)

Teitelbaum, Michael S. *The British fertility decline: demographic transition in the crucible of the industrial revolution* (Princeton, NJ, 1984)

Temperley, Nicholas (ed.) *The Romantic age, 1800–1914* (The Athlone History of Music in Britain) (1981)

Tennyson, Alfred *Poems*, ed. Christopher Ricks, 2nd edn, 3 vols. (1987)

Tennyson, G. B. *Victorian devotional poetry: the Tractarian mode* (Cambridge, MA, 1981)

Thackray, J. C. 'R. I. Murchison's *Geology of Russia* (1845)', *Journal of the Society for the Bibliography of Natural History* 9 (1979), pp. 421–33

'R. I. Murchison's *Siluria* (1854 and later)', *Archives of Natural History* 10 (1981), pp. 37–43

'R. I. Murchison's *Silurian system* (1839)', *Journal of the Society for the Bibliography of Natural History* 8 (1978), pp. 61–73

Thomas, Jane ' "Forging the literary tastes of the middle and higher classes": Elgin's circulating libraries and their proprietors, 1789–1870', in John Hinks and Catherine Armstrong (eds.), *Worlds of print: diversity in the book trade* (2006), pp. 91–111

Thompson, F. M. L. (ed.) *The University of London and the world of learning, 1836–1986* (1990)

Thompson, W. B. and J. D. Ridge *Catalogue of the national collection of Greek and Latin school text-books* 2 pts (University of Leeds Institute of Education, 1970–4)

Thomson, Robert S. 'The development of the broadside ballad trade and its influence upon the transmission of English folksong', unpublished PhD thesis, University of Cambridge (1974)

Thorne, Susan *Congregational missions and the making of an imperial culture in nineteenth-century England* (Stanford, CA, 1999)

Thorpe, James *English illustration: the nineties* (1935)

Thrall, Miriam M. H. *Rebellious Fraser's* (New York, 1934)

Thring, G. H. 'The Copyright Bill 1911', *Fortnightly Review* 89 (1911), pp. 901–10

Thwaite, Ann *Edmund Gosse: a literary landscape 1849–1928* (1984)

Tidcombe, Marianne *The Doves Press* (2002)

Tidcombe, Marianne and Bernard Middleton, *Tregaskis centenary exhibition: a catalogue of the Tregaskis centenary exhibition, 1994, together with a facsimile of the Tregaskis exhibition catalogue of 1894* (1994)

Tilleard, James 'On elementary school books', *Transactions of the National Association for the Promotion of Social Sciences* (1859), pp. 387–96

Tillmanns, Martin *Bridge Hall Mills: three centuries of paper & cellulose film manufacture* (Bury, 1978)

Tillotson, Kathleen *Novels of the eighteen-forties* (Oxford, 1961)

Timbs, John *Stories of inventors and discoverers in science and the useful arts* (1860)

Times, The, printing number, repr. from *The Times*, 10 September 1912 (1912)

Timperley, C. H. *Encyclopaedia of literary and typographical anecdote* (1842)

Tinsley, William *Random recollections of an old publisher*, 2 vols. (1900)

Todd, R. B. (ed.) *Dictionary of British classicists* (Bristol, 2004)

Todd, William B. and Ann Bowden *Sir Walter Scott: a bibliographical history, 1796–1832* (New Castle, DE, 1998).

Tauchnitz international editions in English 1841–1955: a bibliographical history (New York, 1988)

Tolles, Winton *Tom Taylor and the Victorian drama* (New York, 1940)

Tomlinson, William and Richard Masters *Bookcloth, 1823–1980* (Stockport, 1996)

Tooley, R. V. *English books with coloured plates 1790 to 1860* (1954)

Toon, Peter *Evangelical theology, 1833–1856: a response to Tractarianism* (1979)

Topham, Jonathan R. 'John Limbird, Thomas Byerley, and the production of cheap periodicals in the 1820s', *Book History* 8 (2005), pp. 75–106

    'Publishing "popular science" in early nineteenth-century Britain', in A. Fyfe and B. Lightman (eds.), *Science in the marketplace: nineteenth-century sites and experiences* (Chicago, 2007)

    'Science and popular education in the 1830s: the role of the *Bridgewater Treatises*', *British Journal for the History of Science* 25 (1992), pp. 397–430

    'Scientific publishing and the reading of science in early nineteenth-century Britain: an historiographical survey and guide to sources', *Studies in History and Philosophy of Science* 31A (2000), pp. 559–612

    'A textbook revolution', in M. Frasca-Spada and N. Jardine (eds.), *Books and the sciences in history* (Cambridge, 2000), pp. 317–37

Topp, Chester W. *Victorian yellowbacks & paperbacks, 1849–1905* 9 vols. (Denver, CO, 1993–2007)

Traice, W. J. *Handbook of mechanics' institutions* (1856)

Trevelyan, G. M. *The seven years of William IV: a reign cartooned by John Doyle* (1952)

Tritton, Paul *The lost voice of Queen Victoria: the search for the first royal recording* (1991)

Trollope, Anthony *Letters*, ed. Bradford Allen Booth (Oxford, 1951)

Tropp, Asher *The school teachers: the growth of the teaching profession in England and Wales from 1800 to the present day* (1957)

Tryon, Warren S. and William Charvat (eds.) *The cost books of Ticknor and Fields and their predecessors 1832–1858* (New York, 1949)

Tucker, J. *Nature exposed: photography as eyewitness in Victorian science* (Baltimore, MD, 2005)

Tufte, Edward R. *Envisioning information* (Cheshire, CT, 1990)

Turn, The, of the century, 1885–1910: art nouveau – Jugendstil books (Cambridge, MA: Houghton Library, 1970)

Turner, E. S. *Boys will be boys* (1948)

    The shocking history of advertising, rev. edn (Harmondsworth, 1965)

Turner, Frank M. *John Henry Newman: the challenge to evangelical religion* (London, 2002)

    'The religious and the secular in Victorian Britain', in his *Contesting cultural authority: essays in Victorian intellectual life* (Cambridge, 1993), pp. 3–37

Turner, John R. 'Books for prizes', in David A. Stoker (ed.), *Studies in the provincial book trade of England, Scotland and Wales before 1900* (Aberystwyth, 1990), pp. 1–12

    'The Camelot series, Everyman's Library, and Ernest Rhys', *Publishing History* 31 (1992), pp. 27–46

    The Walter Scott Publishing Company: a bibliography (Pittsburgh, 1997)

Turner, Michael 'Tillotson's fiction bureau: agreements with authors', in *Studies in the book trade in honour of Graham Pollard* (Oxford, 1975), pp. 351–78

Turnley, C. *Cole of the Book Arcade: a pictorial biography of E. W. Cole* (Hawthorn, Victoria, 1974)

Twyman, Michael 'Articulating graphic language', in M. E. Wrolstad and D. F. Fisher (eds.), *Toward a new understanding of literacy* (New York, 1986), pp. 188–251

    Early lithographed books (1990)

    'The emergence of the graphic book in the 19th century', in R. Myers and M. Harris (eds.), *A millennium of the book* (Winchester, 1995), pp. 135–80

Lithography 1800–1850: the techniques of drawing on stone in England and France and their application in works of topography (Oxford, 1970)

Printing 1770–1970: an illustrated history of its development and uses in England (1970; repr. 1998)

'The tinted lithograph', *JPHS* 1 (1965), pp. 39–56

Tylecote, M. P. *The mechanics' institutes of Lancashire and Yorkshire before 1851* (Manchester, 1957)

'Unknown, The, public', *Household Words* 18 (August 1858), pp. 217–22

Urry, John *The tourist gaze: leisure and travel in contemporary societies* (1990)

Vamplew, Wray *The turf: a social and economic history of horse racing* (1976)

van Bijlert, Victor A. 'Bengal's modernity and nationalism 1880–1910', IIAS Newsletter Online, no. 21 www.iias.nl/iiasn/21/theme/21T9.html

van Wyhe, John *Phrenology and the origins of Victorian scientific naturalism* (Aldershot, 2004)

Vann, J. D. and R. T. VanArsdel (eds.) *Victorian periodicals and Victorian society* (Toronto, 1994)

Vaughan, John *The English guide book, c. 1780–1870: an illustrated history* (Newton Abbot, 1974)

Vegetable substances: materials of manufactures (1833)

Vicinus, Martha *The industrial muse* (1974)

Vinay, Valdo *Evangelici italiani esuli a Londra durante il Risorgimento* (Turin, 1961)

Vincent, David *Bread, knowledge, and freedom: a study of nineteenth-century working class autobiography* (1981)

'Dickens's reading public', in John Bowen and Robert L. Patten (eds.), *Palgrave advances in Charles Dickens studies* (2006), pp. 176–97

Literacy and popular culture: England 1750–1914 (Cambridge, 1989)

'Literacy literacy', in H. J. Graff, A. Mackinnon, B. Sandin and I. Winchester (eds.), *Understanding literacy in its historical contexts: looking backward and looking forward – past approaches and work in progress, Interchange* (Calgary) 34, nos. 2 & 3 (2003), pp. 341–57

'Reading made strange: context and method in becoming literate in eighteenth and nineteenth-century England', in Ian Grosvenor, Martin Lawn and Kate Rousmaniere (eds.), *Silences and images: the social history of the classroom* (New York, 1999), pp. 180–5

The rise of mass literacy: reading and writing in modern Europe (Cambridge, 2000)

Vincent, E. R. *Gabriele Rossetti in England* (Oxford, 1936)

Vincent, William *Seen from the railway platform* (1919)

Vinogradoff, Paul 'Oxford and Cambridge through foreign spectacles', *Fortnightly Review* n.s. 37 (1885), pp. 862–8

Vishwanathan, Gauri 'The ideology of literary education in British India 1813–1880', unpublished PhD thesis, University of Columbia (1985)

Vizetelly, E. A. *With Zola in England* (1899)

Wagner, Leopold *How To publish* (1898)

Wakeman, Geoffrey *Victorian book illustration: the technical revolution* (1973)

Wakeman, Geoffrey and Gavin D. R. Bridson *A guide to nineteenth century colour printers* (Loughborough, 1975)

Walford, Cornelius 'A new general catalogue of English literature', in *Transactions and proceedings of the conference of librarians held in London, October 1877* (1878), pp. 101–3

Wallace, A. R. *The wonderful century: its successes and its failures*, 4th edn (1901)

Waller, Philip *Writers, readers and reputations: literary life in Britain, 1870–1918* (Oxford, 2006)

Wallis, L. W. 'Legros and Grant: the typographical connection', *JPHS* 28 (1999), pp. 5–39

Wallis, Philip *At the sign of the Ship, 1724–1974* (1974)

Walters, Huw 'The Welsh language and the periodical press', in Geraint H. Jenkins (ed.), *The Welsh language and its social domains* (Cardiff, 2000), pp. 349–78

Walton, John K. 'Towns and consumerism', in Martin Daunton (ed.), *The Cambridge urban history of Britain. 3. 1840–1950* (Cambridge, 2000), pp. 715–44

Walton, Susan 'Charlotte M. Yonge and the "historic harem" of Edward Augustus Freeman', *Journal of Victorian Culture* 11 (2006), pp. 226–55

Ward, Anthony *The publications of the Henry Bradshaw Society* (Rome, 1992)

Ward, J. P. ' "Came from yon fountain": Wordsworth's influence on Victorian education', *Victorian Studies* 29 (1986), pp. 406–36

Warkentin, Germaine and Peter Hoare, 'Sophisticated Shakespeare: James Toovey and the Morgan Library's "Sidney" First Folio', *PBSA* 100 (2006), pp. 313–56

Warren, Arthur *The Charles Whittinghams: printers* (New York, 1896)

Warren, Lynne ' "Women in conference": reading the correspondence columns in *Woman*, 1890–1910', in Laurel Brake and others (eds.), *Nineteenth-century media and the construction of identities* (Basingstoke, 2000)

Warwick, A. *Masters of theory: Cambridge and the rise of mathematical physics* (Chicago, 2003)

Watson, A. E. T. *A sporting and dramatic career* (1918)

Watson, J. R. *The English hymn: a critical and historical study* (Oxford, 1997)

Watson, R. S. *The history of the Literary and Philosophical Society of Newcastle-upon-Tyne (1793–1896)* (1897)

Watson, William Henry *The history of the Sunday School Union* (1853)

Watts, Cedric *Joseph Conrad: a literary life* (Basingstoke, 1989)

Watts, Michael R. *The dissenters. 2. The expansion of evangelical nonconformity* (Oxford, 1995)

Waugh, Arthur *A hundred years of publishing, being the story of Chapman & Hall, Ltd* (1930)

Weale, W. H. J. *Bookbindings and rubbings of bindings in the National Art Library, South Kensington Museum*, 2 vols. (1894–8)

Webb, R. K. *The British working class reader, 1790–1848: literacy and social tension* (1955)
'Working-class readers in early Victorian England', *English Historical Review* 65 (1950), pp. 333–51

[Webster, Thomas] Review of patents, *Quarterly Review* 105 (1859), pp. 136–55

Weedon, Alexis *Guide to archives of 19th c. British publishers* online at http://victorianresearch. org/pubarc.html
Victorian publishing: the economics of book production for a mass market, 1836–1916 (Aldershot, 2003)

Weedon, Alexis and Michael Bott *British book trade archives, 1830–1939* (Bristol, 1996)

Weintraub, Stanley *The London Yankees: portraits of American writers and artists in England, 1894–1914* (New York, 1979)

Weld, C. R. 'On the condition of the working classes in the Inner Ward of St. George's Parish, Hanover Square', *Journal of the Statistical Society* 6 (1843), p. 20

Wells, H. G. *Experiment in autobiography*, 2 vols. (1934)

West, Anthony James *The Shakespeare first folio: the history of the book*, 2 vols. (Oxford, 2001–3)

West, G. Derek *Guide to 'Lillywhite's Cricketers' Companion'* (Oxford, 1995)

Whalley, Joyce Irene and Tessa Rose Chester *A history of children's book illustration* (1988)

Wheatley, H. *Remarkable bindings in the British Museum selected for their beauty or historic interest* (1889)

Wheeler, Michael *The old enemies: Catholic and Protestant in nineteenth-century English culture* (Cambridge, 2006)

Whitaker's almanack (1869–)

White, Colin *The world of the nursery* (New York, 1984)

White, Gleeson *English illustration: 'the sixties': 1855–70* (1897)

White, Mus *From the mundane to the magical: photographically illustrated children's books 1854–1945* (Los Angeles, 1999)

White, P. 'Cross-cultural encounters: the co-production of science and literature in mid-Victorian periodicals', in R. Luckhurst and J. McDonagh (eds.), *Transactions and encounters: science and culture in the nineteenth century* (Manchester, 2002), pp. 75–95

  Thomas Huxley: making the 'man of science' (Cambridge, 2003)

White, Robert *Autobiographical notes* (Newcastle, 1966)

Whitton, Blair and Margaret Whitton *Collector's guide to Raphael Tuck & Sons: paper dolls, paper toys, children's books* (Cumberland, MD, 1991)

Wicks, Margaret C.W. *The Italian exiles in London, 1816–1848* (1937)

Wiener, Joel H. *A descriptive finding list of unstamped British periodicals, 1830–1836* (1970)

  (ed.) *Innovators and preachers: the role of the editor in Victorian England* (Westport, CT, 1985)

  The war of the unstamped: the movement to repeal the British newspaper tax, 1830–1836 (Ithaca, NY, 1969)

Wigley, John *The rise and fall of the Victorian Sunday* (Manchester, 1980)

Wiles, R. M. *Serial publication in England before 1750* (Cambridge, 1957)

Wilkes, Joanne 'Jewsbury, Geraldine Endsor (1812–1880)', *ODNB*

Wilkinson, W. T. *Photo-engraving, photo-litho, collotype and photogravure* (1892 and later editions)

William Milner of Halifax (bookseller's catalogue) (York: Ken Spelman, n.d.)

Williams, Bill *The making of Manchester Jewry, 1740–1875* (Manchester, 1976)

Williams, Harold *Book clubs & printing societies of Great Britain and Ireland* (1929)

Williams, Raymond *Culture and society, 1780–1950* (Harmondsworth, 1961)

  'The press and popular culture: an historical perspective', in G. Boyce, J. Curran and P. Wingate (eds.), *Newspaper history from the seventeenth century to the present day* (1978), pp. 41–50

Williamson, W. L. *William Frederick Poole and the modern library movement* (New York, 1963)

Wilson, Charles *First with the news: the history of W. H. Smith, 1792–1972* (1985)

Wilson, F. P. 'The Malone Society: the first fifty years, 1906–56', *Malone Society Collections* 4 (1956), pp. 1–16

Wilson, Fred J. F. and Douglas Grey *A practical treatise upon modern printing machinery and letterpress printing* (1888)

Wilson, John *The literature of photography* (privately published, n.d.)

Wilson, William and Robert Rainy *Memoirs of Robert Smith Candlish, D.D.* (Edinburgh, 1880)

Windle, John and Karma Pippin, *Thomas Frognall Dibdin, 1776–1847: a bibliography* (New Castle, DE, 1999)

Winship, Michael *American literary publishing in the mid-nineteenth century: the business of Ticknor and Fields* (Cambridge, 1995)

'In the four quarters of the globe, who reads an American book?' in Simon Eliot, Andrew Nash and Ian Willison (eds.), *Literary cultures and the material book* (2007), pp. 367–78

Withers, Charles W. J. *Gaelic Scotland, 1698–1981: the geographical history of a language* (Edinburgh, 1984)

Gaelic Scotland: the transformation of a culture region (1988)

Geography, science and national identity: Scotland since 1520 (Cambridge, 2001)

Urban highlanders: highland–lowland migration and urban Gaelic culture, 1700–1900 (East Linton, 1998)

Wolff, Robert Lee *Gains and losses: novels of faith and doubt in Victorian England* (1974)

Wolffe, John *The Protestant crusade in Great Britain, 1829–1860* (Oxford, 1991)

Wood, Butler 'Three special features of free library work – open shelves, women readers, and juvenile departments', *The Library* 4 (1892), pp. 105–14

Wood, Paul 'Otley and the Wharefedale printing machine', *Matrix* 4 (1985), pp. 13–23

Woods, Robert *The demography of Victorian England and Wales* (Cambridge, 2000)

'The population of Britain in the nineteenth century', in Michael Anderson (ed.), *British population history from the Black Death to the present day* (Cambridge, 1996), pp. 281–358

Woodward, H. B. *The history of the Geological Society of London* (1908)

Wordsworth, William *The letters of William and Dorothy Wordsworth*, ed. Alan G. Hill, 2nd edn, 8 vols. (Oxford, 1967–93)

Wormell, Deborah *Sir John Seeley and the uses of history* (Cambridge, 1980)

Worth, George *Macmillan's Magazine, 1859–1907: 'No flippancy or abuse allowed'* (Aldershot, 2003)

'Margaret Oliphant and Macmillan's Magazine', in Elizabeth James (ed.), *Macmillan: a publishing tradition* (Basingstoke, 2002), pp. 83–101

Wright, David F. (ed.) *The Bible in Scottish life and literature* (Edinburgh, 1984)

Wright, Elizabeth *The life of Joseph Wright*, 2 vols. (Oxford, 1932)

Wroot, H. E. 'A pioneer of cheap literature: William Milner of Halifax', *The Bookman* March 1897, pp. 169–75

Wynter, Andrew 'A chapter on shop windows', *Ainsworth's Magazine* 12 (1847), pp. 391–6, repr. in his *Pictures of town & country life* (1855)

Our social bees, or pictures of town and country life (1861)

Subtle brains and lissom fingers (1863)

Yeo, R. *Defining science: William Whewell, natural knowledge, and public debate in early Victorian Britain* (Cambridge, 1993)

Encyclopaedic visions: scientific dictionaries and Enlightenment culture (Cambridge, 2001)

Yonge, Charlotte Mary 'Children's literature of the last century', *Macmillan's Magazine* 20 (1869), pp. 229–37, 302–10

What books to lend and what to give [1887]

Zachs, William *The first John Murray* (1998)

Zon, Bennett *Music and metaphor in nineteenth-century British musicology* (Aldershot, 2000)

Index